SHOWCASE PRESENTS

LEGION of SUPER-HEROES

VOLUME ONE

Dan DiDio Senior VP-Executive Editor

Whitney Ellsworth, Mort Weisinger Editors-original series

Peter Hamboussi Editor-collected edition

Robbin Brosterman Senior Art Director

Paul Levitz President & Publisher

Georg Brewer VP-Design & DC Direct Creative

Richard Bruning Senior VP-Creative Director

Patrick Caldon Executive VP-Finance & Operations

Chris Caramalis VP-Finance

John Cunningham VP-Marketing

Terri Cunningham VP-Managing Editor

Alison Gill VP-Manufacturing

Hank Kanalz VP-General Manager, WildStorm

Jim Lee Editorial Director-WildStorm

Paula Lowitt Senior VP-Business & Legal Affairs

MaryEllen McLaughlin VP-Advertising & Custom Publishing

John Nee VP-Business Development

Gregory Noveck Senior VP-Creative Affairs

Sue Pohja VP-Book Trade Sales

Cheryl Rubin Senior VP-Brand Management

Jeff Trojan VP-Business Development, DC Direct

Bob Wayne VP-Sales

Cover illustration by Curt Swan and Stan Kaye.
Front cover colored by Alex Sinclair.

SHOWCASE PRESENTS: LEGION OF SUPER-HEROES VOL. ONE

Published by DC Comics. Cover and compilation
copyright © 2007 DC Comics. All Rights Reserved.

Originally published in single magazine form ADVENTURE COMICS 247, 267, 282, 290,
293, 300-328, ACTION COMICS 267, 276, 287, 289, SUPERBOY 86, 89, 98, 117,
SUPERMAN 147, SUPERMAN ANNUAL 4, SUPERMAN'S PAL, JIMMY OLSEN 72, 76
Copyright © 1958-1964 DC Comics. All Rights Reserved. All characters, their distinctive
likenesses and related elements featured in this publication are trademarks of DC Comics.

The stories, characters and incidents featured in this publication are entirely fictional.
DC Comics does not read or accept unsolicited submissions of ideas, stories or artwork.

DC Comics, 1700 Broadway, New York, NY 10019
A Warner Bros. Entertainment Company
Printed in Canada. First Printing.
ISBN: 1-4012-1382-0
ISBN 13: 978-1-4012-1382-4

TABLE OF CONTENTS

UNTIL THE 1970S IT WAS NOT COMMON PRACTICE IN THE COMIC BOOK INDUSTRY TO CREDIT ALL STORIES. IN THE PREPARATION OF THIS COLLECTION WE HAVE USED OUR BEST EFFORTS TO REVIEW ANY SURVIVING RECORDS AND CONSULT ANY AVAILABLE DATABASES AND KNOWLEDGEABLE PARTIES. WE REGRET THE INNATE LIMITATIONS OF THIS PROCESS AND ANY MISSING OR MISASSIGNED ATTRIBUTIONS THAT MAY OCCUR. ANY ADDITIONAL INFORMATION ON CREDITS SHOULD BE DIRECTED TO: EDITOR, COLLECTED EDITIONS, C/O DC COMICS.

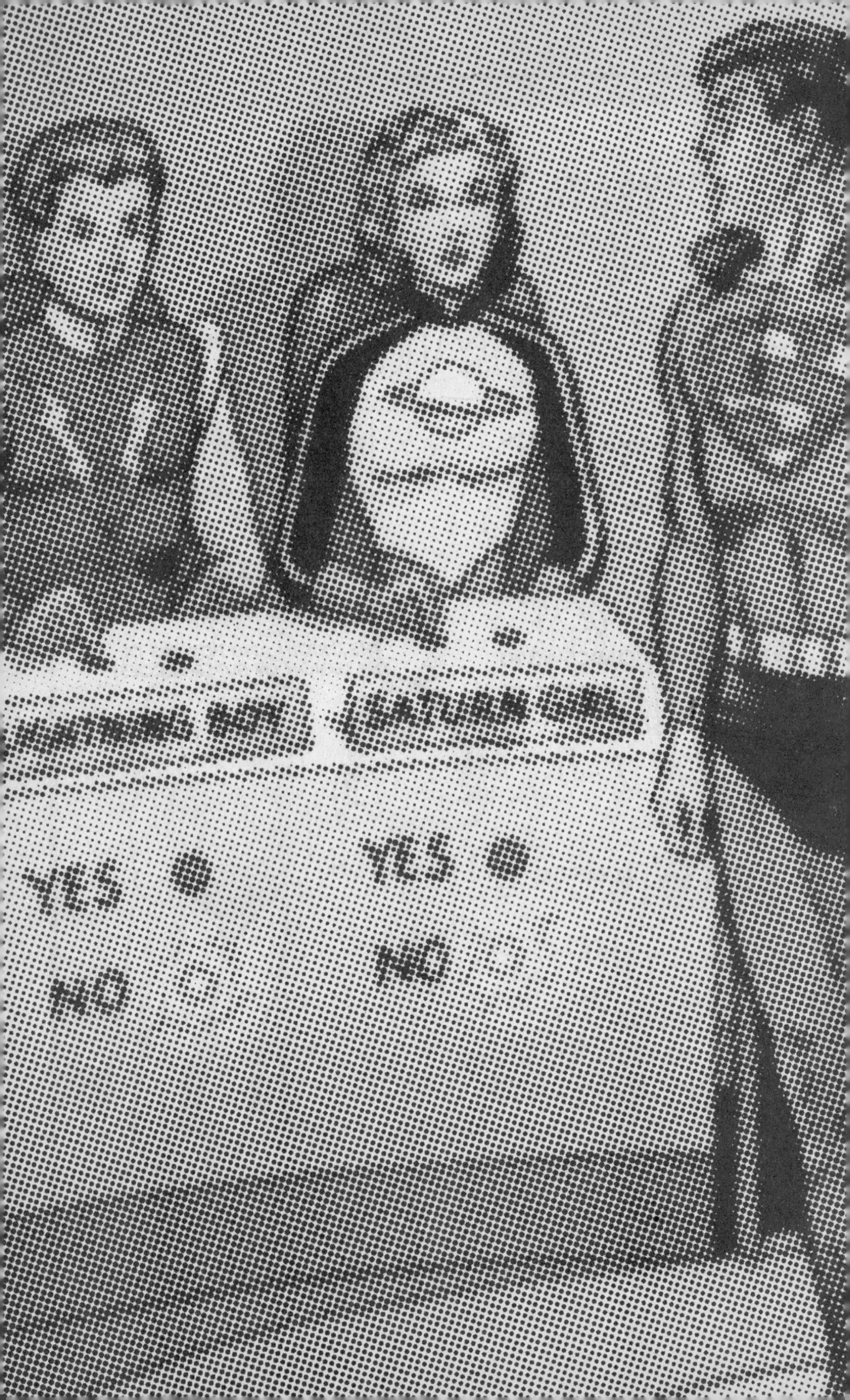
YES
NO
YES
NO

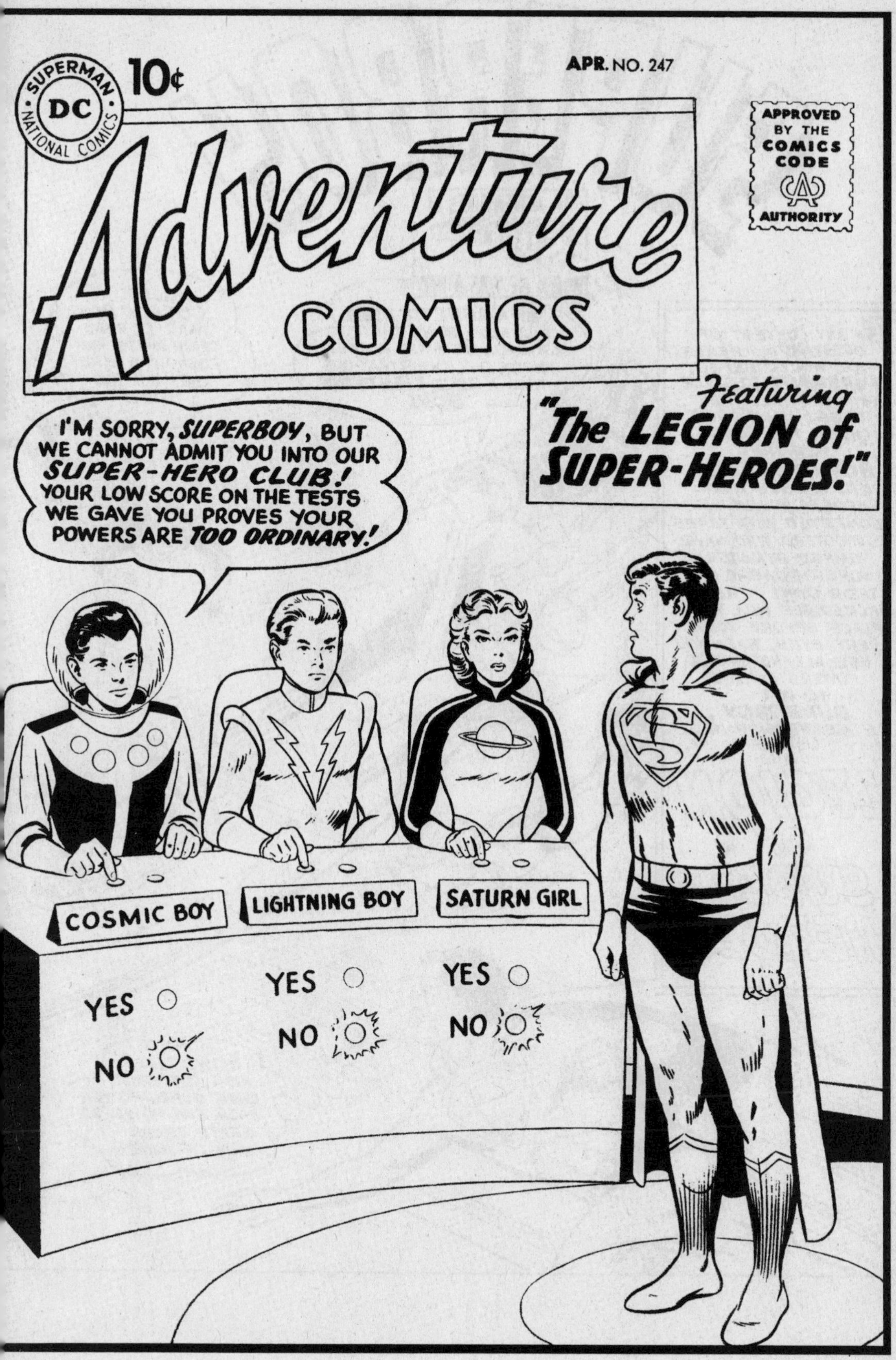
SUPERMAN DC NATIONAL COMICS
10¢
APR. NO. 247
APPROVED BY THE COMICS CODE AUTHORITY
Adventure COMICS
Featuring "The LEGION of SUPER-HEROES!"
I'M SORRY, SUPERBOY, BUT WE CANNOT ADMIT YOU INTO OUR SUPER-HERO CLUB! YOUR LOW SCORE ON THE TESTS WE GAVE YOU PROVES YOUR POWERS ARE TOO ORDINARY!
COSMIC BOY
LIGHTNING BOY
SATURN GIRL
YES
NO
YES
NO
YES
NO

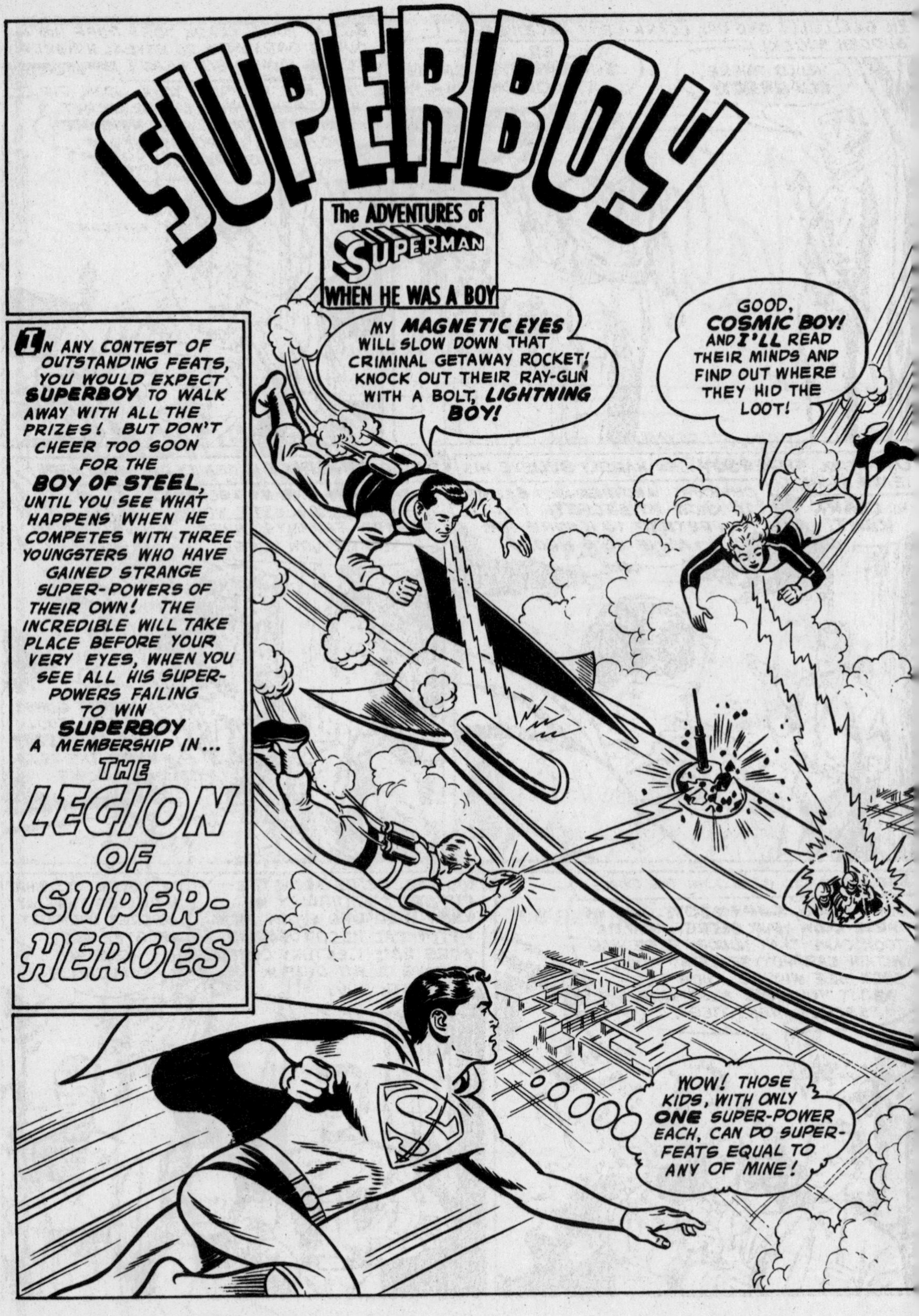
SUPERBOY
The ADVENTURES of SUPERMAN WHEN HE WAS A BOY
1 IN ANY CONTEST OF OUTSTANDING FEATS, YOU WOULD EXPECT SUPERBOY TO WALK AWAY WITH ALL THE PRIZES! BUT DON'T CHEER TOO SOON FOR THE BOY OF STEEL, UNTIL YOU SEE WHAT HAPPENS WHEN HE COMPETES WITH THREE YOUNGSTERS WHO HAVE GAINED STRANGE SUPER-POWERS OF THEIR OWN! THE INCREDIBLE WILL TAKE PLACE BEFORE YOUR VERY EYES, WHEN YOU SEE ALL HIS SUPER-POWERS FAILING TO WIN SUPERBOY A MEMBERSHIP IN...
THE LEGION OF SUPER-HEROES
MY MAGNETIC EYES WILL SLOW DOWN THAT CRIMINAL GETAWAY ROCKET! KNOCK OUT THEIR RAY-GUN WITH A BOLT, LIGHTNING BOY!
GOOD, COSMIC BOY! AND I'LL READ THEIR MINDS AND FIND OUT WHERE THEY HID THE LOOT!
WOW! THOSE KIDS, WITH ONLY ONE SUPER-POWER EACH, CAN DO SUPER-FEATS EQUAL TO ANY OF MINE!

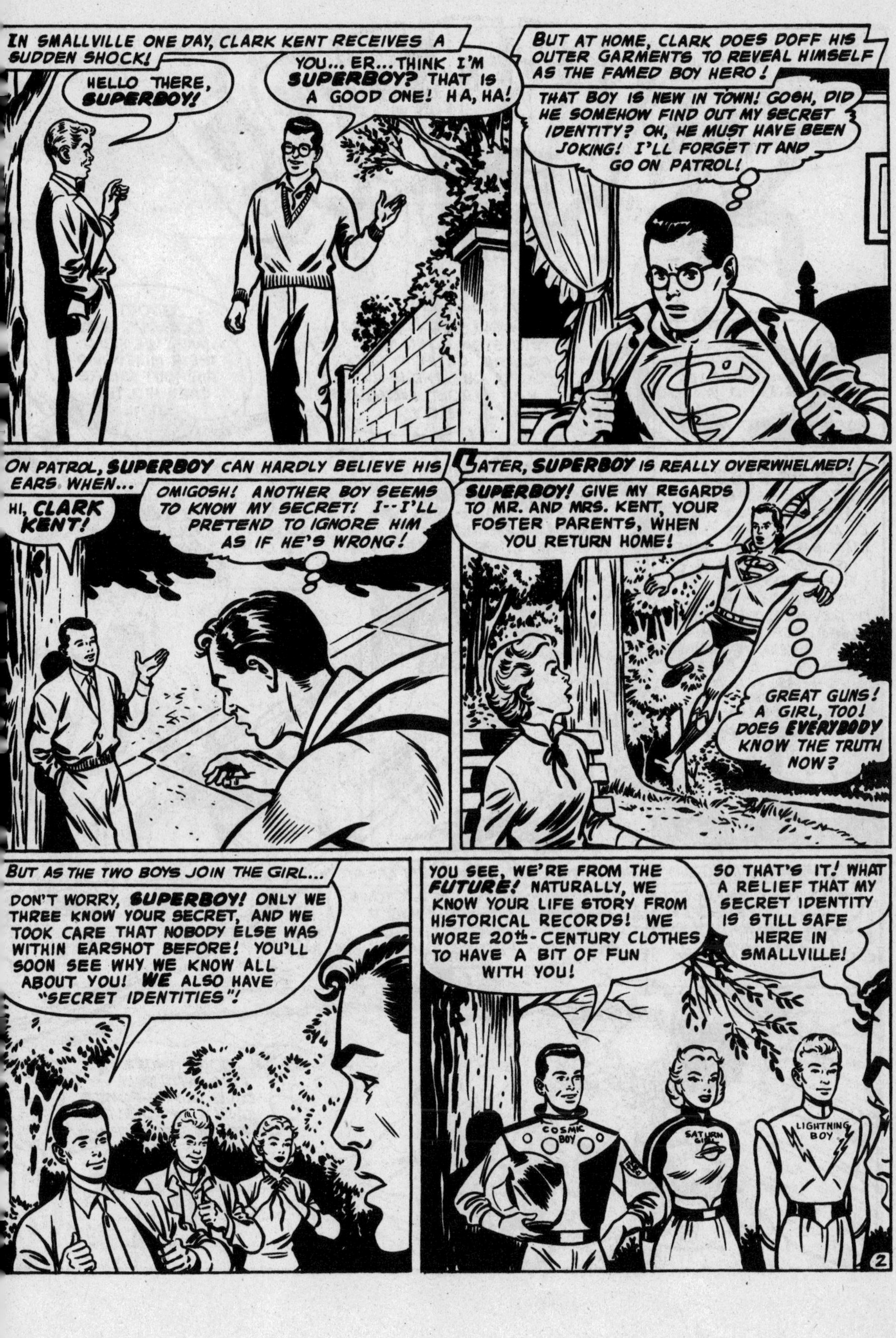
IN SMALLVILLE ONE DAY, CLARK KENT RECEIVES A SUDDEN SHOCK!
HELLO THERE, SUPERBOY!
YOU... ER... THINK I'M SUPERBOY? THAT IS A GOOD ONE! HA, HA!
BUT AT HOME, CLARK DOES DOFF HIS OUTER GARMENTS TO REVEAL HIMSELF AS THE FAMED BOY HERO!
THAT BOY IS NEW IN TOWN! GOSH, DID HE SOMEHOW FIND OUT MY SECRET IDENTITY? OH, HE MUST HAVE BEEN JOKING! I'LL FORGET IT AND GO ON PATROL!
ON PATROL, SUPERBOY CAN HARDLY BELIEVE HIS EARS WHEN...
HI, CLARK KENT!
OMIGOSH! ANOTHER BOY SEEMS TO KNOW MY SECRET! I--I'LL PRETEND TO IGNORE HIM AS IF HE'S WRONG!
LATER, SUPERBOY IS REALLY OVERWHELMED!
SUPERBOY! GIVE MY REGARDS TO MR. AND MRS. KENT, YOUR FOSTER PARENTS, WHEN YOU RETURN HOME!
GREAT GUNS! A GIRL, TOO! DOES EVERYBODY KNOW THE TRUTH NOW?
BUT AS THE TWO BOYS JOIN THE GIRL...
DON'T WORRY, SUPERBOY! ONLY WE THREE KNOW YOUR SECRET, AND WE TOOK CARE THAT NOBODY ELSE WAS WITHIN EARSHOT BEFORE! YOU'LL SOON SEE WHY WE KNOW ALL ABOUT YOU! WE ALSO HAVE "SECRET IDENTITIES"!
YOU SEE, WE'RE FROM THE FUTURE! NATURALLY, WE KNOW YOUR LIFE STORY FROM HISTORICAL RECORDS! WE WORE 20th-CENTURY CLOTHES TO HAVE A BIT OF FUN WITH YOU!
SO THAT'S IT! WHAT A RELIEF THAT MY SECRET IDENTITY IS STILL SAFE HERE IN SMALLVILLE!
COSMIC BOY
SATURN GIRL
LIGHTNING BOY
2

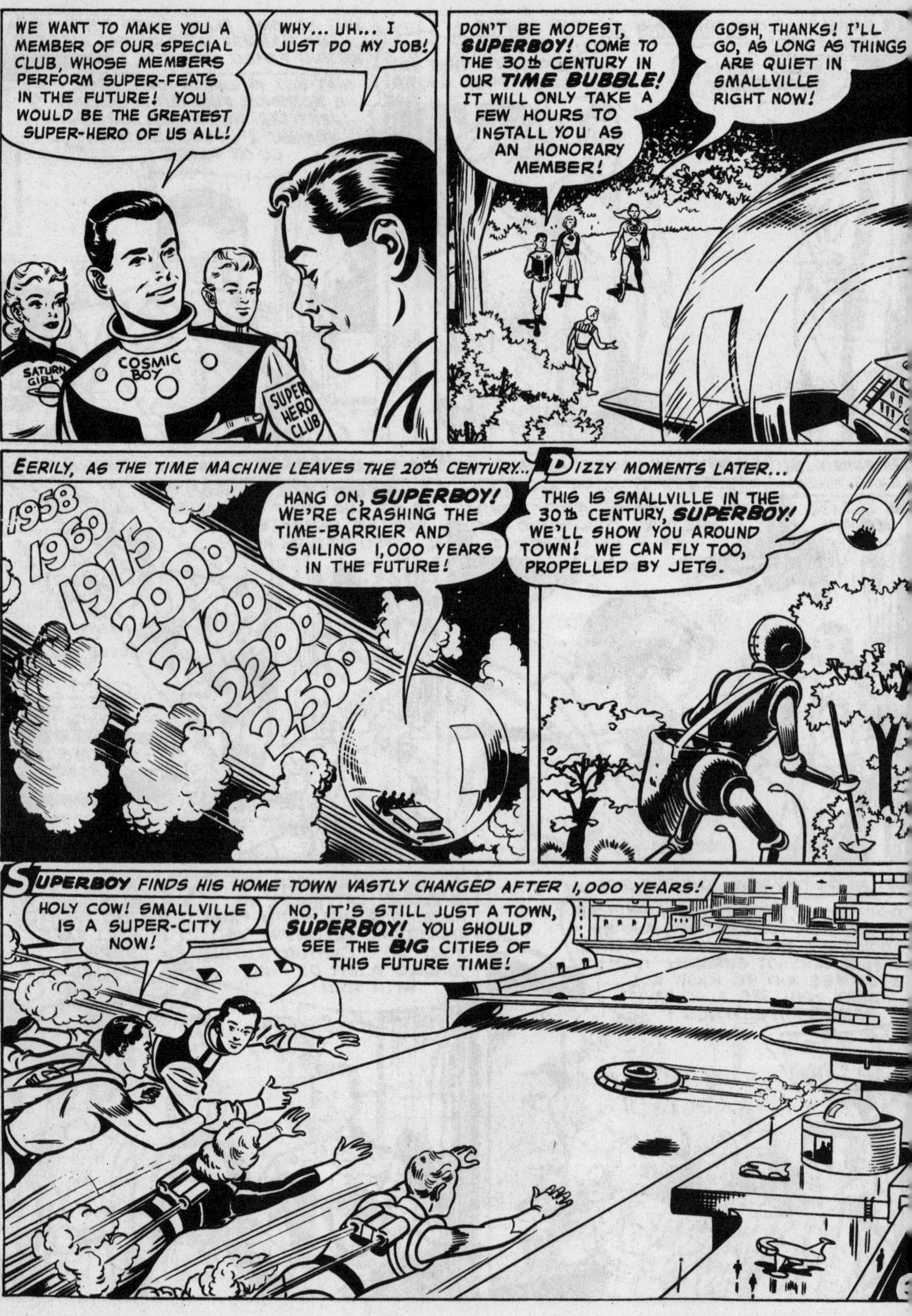
WE WANT TO MAKE YOU A MEMBER OF OUR SPECIAL CLUB, WHOSE MEMBERS PERFORM SUPER-FEATS IN THE FUTURE! YOU WOULD BE THE GREATEST SUPER-HERO OF US ALL!
WHY... UH... I JUST DO MY JOB!
SATURN GIRL
COSMIC BOY
SUPER HERO CLUB
DON'T BE MODEST, SUPERBOY! COME TO THE 30th CENTURY IN OUR TIME BUBBLE! IT WILL ONLY TAKE A FEW HOURS TO INSTALL YOU AS AN HONORARY MEMBER!
GOSH, THANKS! I'LL GO, AS LONG AS THINGS ARE QUIET IN SMALLVILLE RIGHT NOW!
EERILY, AS THE TIME MACHINE LEAVES THE 20th CENTURY...
1958 1960 1975 2000 2100 2200 2500
HANG ON, SUPERBOY! WE'RE CRASHING THE TIME-BARRIER AND SAILING 1,000 YEARS IN THE FUTURE!
DIZZY MOMENTS LATER...
THIS IS SMALLVILLE IN THE 30th CENTURY, SUPERBOY! WE'LL SHOW YOU AROUND TOWN! WE CAN FLY TOO, PROPELLED BY JETS.
SUPERBOY FINDS HIS HOME TOWN VASTLY CHANGED AFTER 1,000 YEARS!
HOLY COW! SMALLVILLE IS A SUPER-CITY NOW!
NO, IT'S STILL JUST A TOWN, SUPERBOY! YOU SHOULD SEE THE BIG CITIES OF THIS FUTURE TIME!

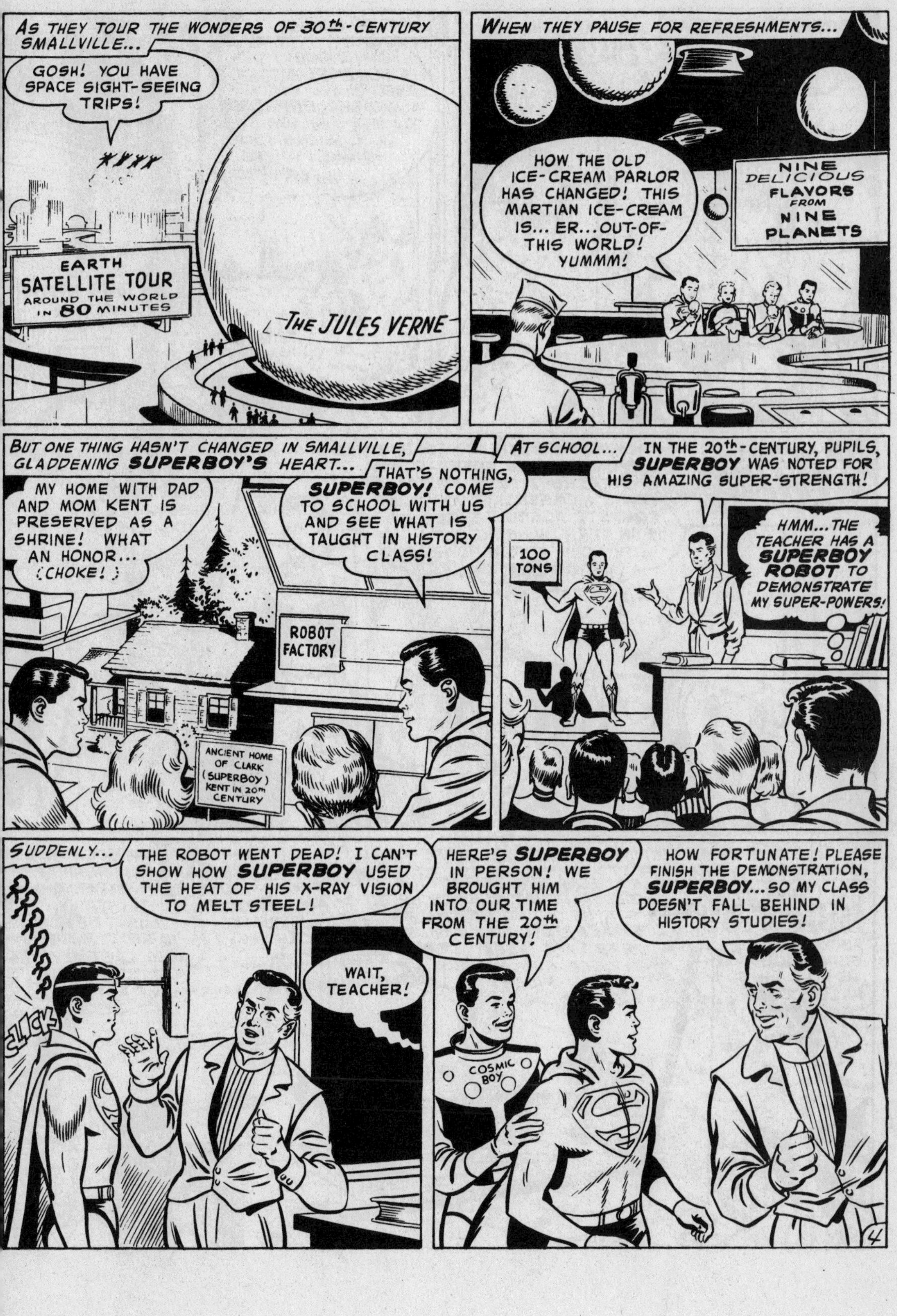
AS THEY TOUR THE WONDERS OF 30th-CENTURY SMALLVILLE...
GOSH! YOU HAVE SPACE SIGHT-SEEING TRIPS!
EARTH SATELLITE TOUR AROUND THE WORLD IN 80 MINUTES
THE JULES VERNE
WHEN THEY PAUSE FOR REFRESHMENTS...
HOW THE OLD ICE-CREAM PARLOR HAS CHANGED! THIS MARTIAN ICE-CREAM IS... ER...OUT-OF-THIS WORLD! YUMMM!
NINE DELICIOUS FLAVORS FROM NINE PLANETS
BUT ONE THING HASN'T CHANGED IN SMALLVILLE, GLADDENING SUPERBOY'S HEART...
MY HOME WITH DAD AND MOM KENT IS PRESERVED AS A SHRINE! WHAT AN HONOR... (CHOKE!)
THAT'S NOTHING, SUPERBOY! COME TO SCHOOL WITH US AND SEE WHAT IS TAUGHT IN HISTORY CLASS!
ROBOT FACTORY
ANCIENT HOME OF CLARK (SUPERBOY) KENT IN 20TH CENTURY
AT SCHOOL...
IN THE 20th-CENTURY, PUPILS, SUPERBOY WAS NOTED FOR HIS AMAZING SUPER-STRENGTH!
100 TONS
HMM...THE TEACHER HAS A SUPERBOY ROBOT TO DEMONSTRATE MY SUPER-POWERS!
SUDDENLY...
RRRRRRR
CLICK
THE ROBOT WENT DEAD! I CAN'T SHOW HOW SUPERBOY USED THE HEAT OF HIS X-RAY VISION TO MELT STEEL!
WAIT, TEACHER!
HERE'S SUPERBOY IN PERSON! WE BROUGHT HIM INTO OUR TIME FROM THE 20th CENTURY!
COSMIC BOY
HOW FORTUNATE! PLEASE FINISH THE DEMONSTRATION, SUPERBOY...SO MY CLASS DOESN'T FALL BEHIND IN HISTORY STUDIES!
4

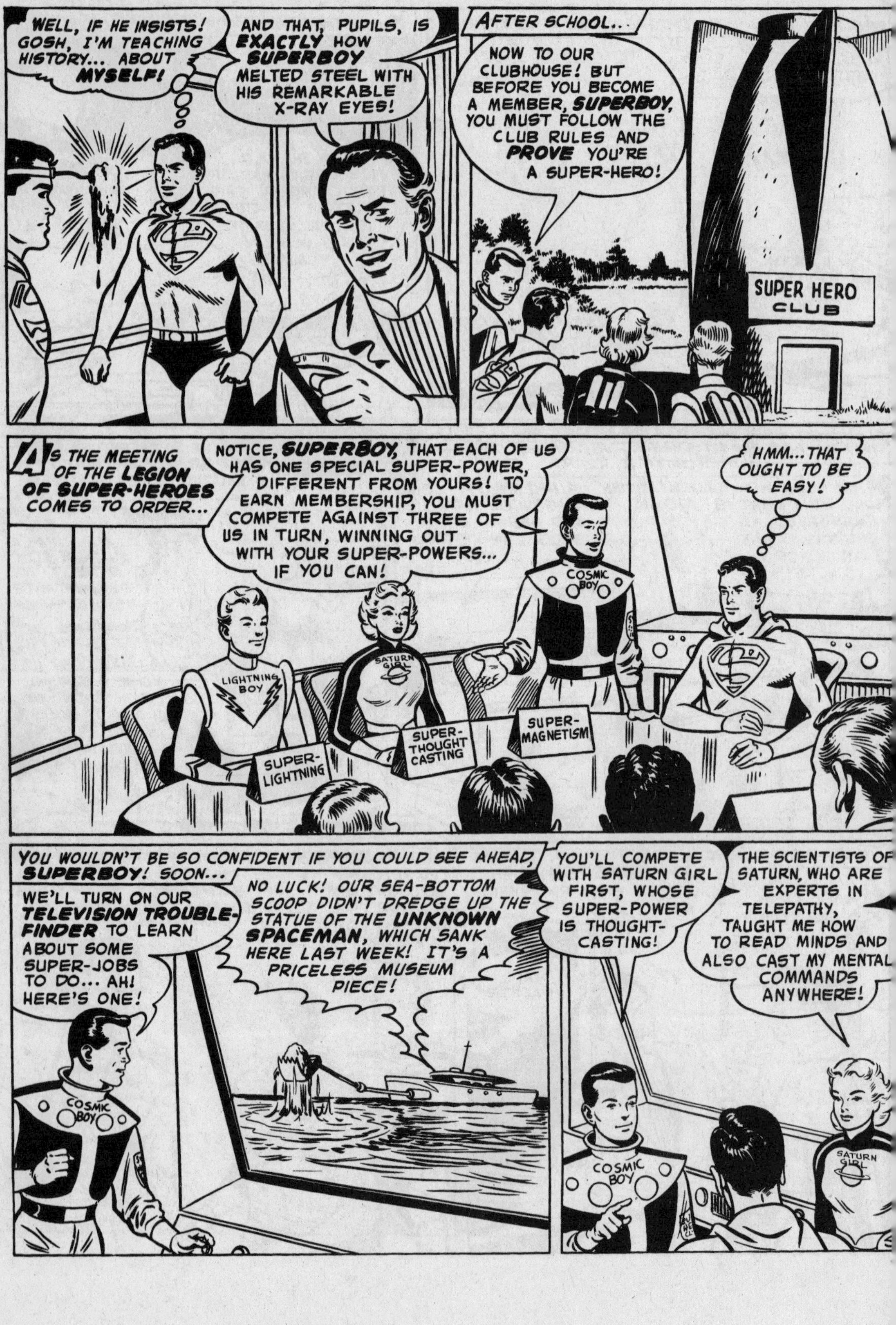
WELL, IF HE INSISTS! GOSH, I'M TEACHING HISTORY... ABOUT MYSELF!
AND THAT, PUPILS, IS EXACTLY HOW SUPERBOY MELTED STEEL WITH HIS REMARKABLE X-RAY EYES!
AFTER SCHOOL...
NOW TO OUR CLUBHOUSE! BUT BEFORE YOU BECOME A MEMBER, SUPERBOY, YOU MUST FOLLOW THE CLUB RULES AND PROVE YOU'RE A SUPER-HERO!
SUPER HERO CLUB
AS THE MEETING OF THE LEGION OF SUPER-HEROES COMES TO ORDER...
NOTICE, SUPERBOY, THAT EACH OF US HAS ONE SPECIAL SUPER-POWER, DIFFERENT FROM YOURS! TO EARN MEMBERSHIP, YOU MUST COMPETE AGAINST THREE OF US IN TURN, WINNING OUT WITH YOUR SUPER-POWERS... IF YOU CAN!
HMM... THAT OUGHT TO BE EASY!
COSMIC BOY
SATURN GIRL
LIGHTNING BOY
SUPER-LIGHTNING
SUPER-THOUGHT CASTING
SUPER-MAGNETISM
YOU WOULDN'T BE SO CONFIDENT IF YOU COULD SEE AHEAD, SUPERBOY! SOON...
WE'LL TURN ON OUR TELEVISION TROUBLE-FINDER TO LEARN ABOUT SOME SUPER-JOBS TO DO... AH! HERE'S ONE!
NO LUCK! OUR SEA-BOTTOM SCOOP DIDN'T DREDGE UP THE STATUE OF THE UNKNOWN SPACEMAN, WHICH SANK HERE LAST WEEK! IT'S A PRICELESS MUSEUM PIECE!
COSMIC BOY
YOU'LL COMPETE WITH SATURN GIRL FIRST, WHOSE SUPER-POWER IS THOUGHT-CASTING!
THE SCIENTISTS OF SATURN, WHO ARE EXPERTS IN TELEPATHY, TAUGHT ME HOW TO READ MINDS AND ALSO CAST MY MENTAL COMMANDS ANYWHERE!
COSMIC BOY
SATURN GIRL

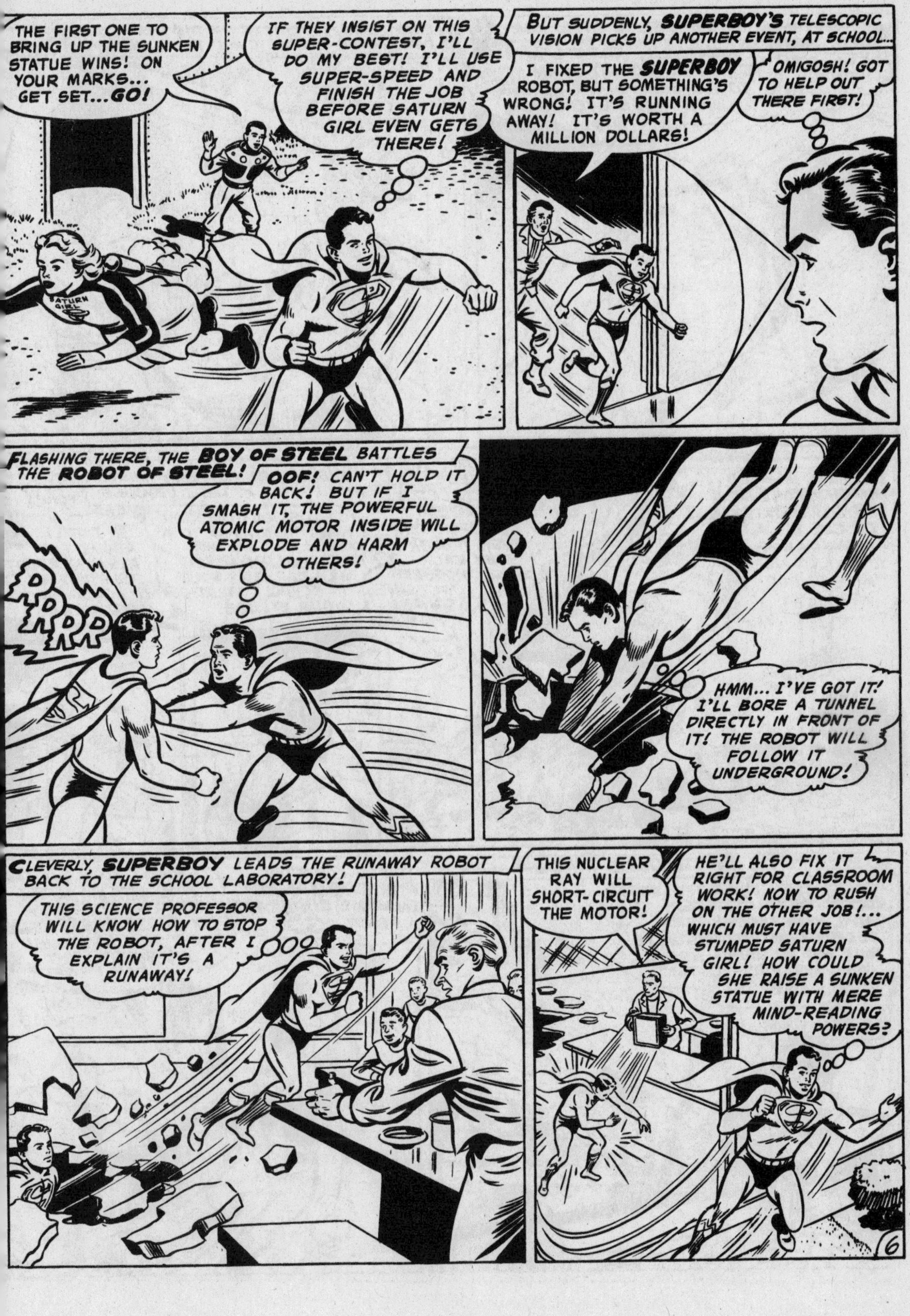
THE FIRST ONE TO BRING UP THE SUNKEN STATUE WINS! ON YOUR MARKS... GET SET...GO!
IF THEY INSIST ON THIS SUPER-CONTEST, I'LL DO MY BEST! I'LL USE SUPER-SPEED AND FINISH THE JOB BEFORE SATURN GIRL EVEN GETS THERE!
SATURN GIRL
BUT SUDDENLY, SUPERBOY'S TELESCOPIC VISION PICKS UP ANOTHER EVENT, AT SCHOOL...
I FIXED THE SUPERBOY ROBOT, BUT SOMETHING'S WRONG! IT'S RUNNING AWAY! IT'S WORTH A MILLION DOLLARS!
OMIGOSH! GOT TO HELP OUT THERE FIRST!
FLASHING THERE, THE BOY OF STEEL BATTLES THE ROBOT OF STEEL!
OOF! CAN'T HOLD IT BACK! BUT IF I SMASH IT, THE POWERFUL ATOMIC MOTOR INSIDE WILL EXPLODE AND HARM OTHERS!
RRRRR
HMM... I'VE GOT IT! I'LL BORE A TUNNEL DIRECTLY IN FRONT OF IT! THE ROBOT WILL FOLLOW IT UNDERGROUND!
CLEVERLY, SUPERBOY LEADS THE RUNAWAY ROBOT BACK TO THE SCHOOL LABORATORY!
THIS SCIENCE PROFESSOR WILL KNOW HOW TO STOP THE ROBOT, AFTER I EXPLAIN IT'S A RUNAWAY!
THIS NUCLEAR RAY WILL SHORT-CIRCUIT THE MOTOR!
HE'LL ALSO FIX IT RIGHT FOR CLASSROOM WORK! NOW TO RUSH ON THE OTHER JOB!... WHICH MUST HAVE STUMPED SATURN GIRL! HOW COULD SHE RAISE A SUNKEN STATUE WITH MERE MIND-READING POWERS?
6

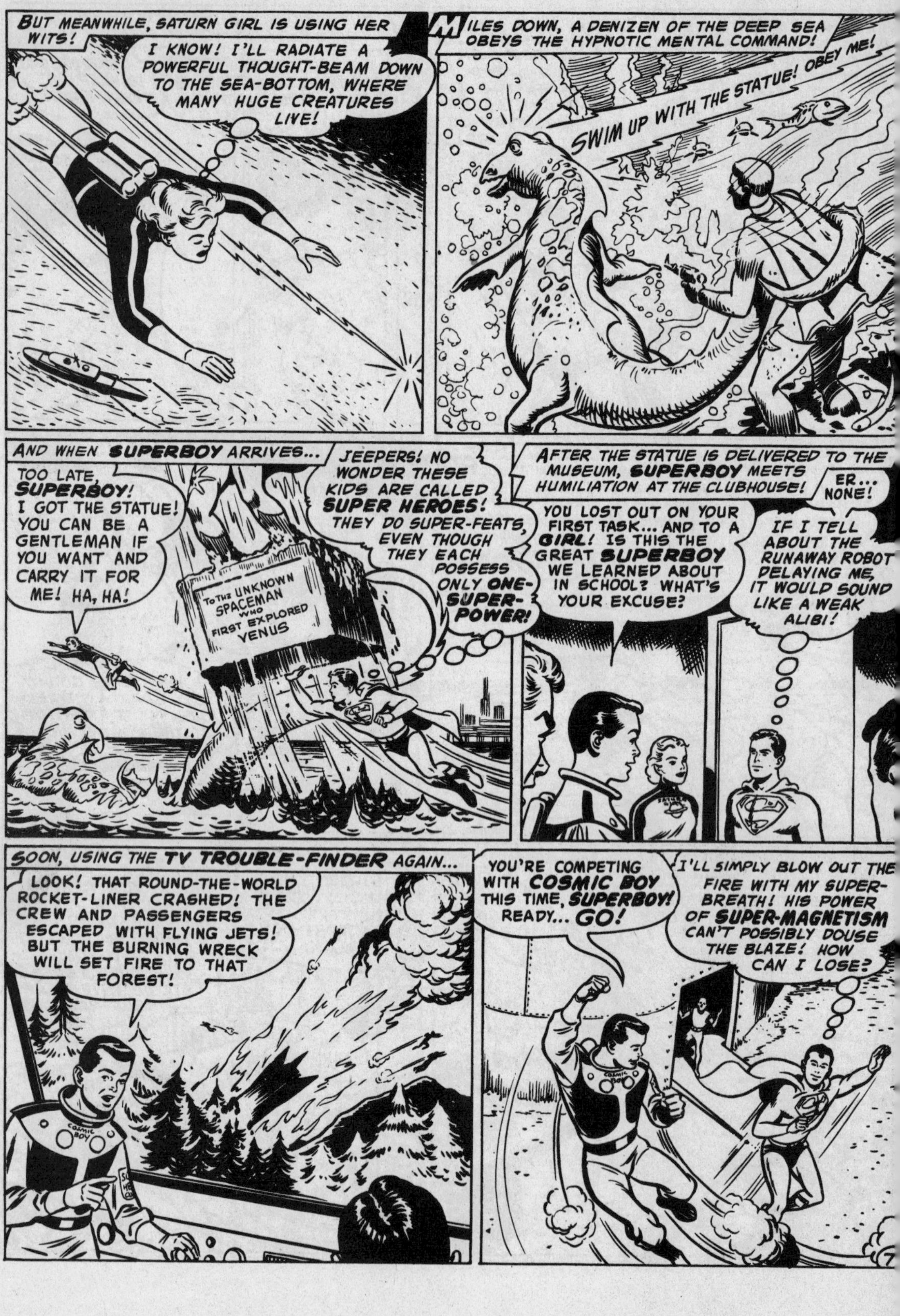
BUT MEANWHILE, SATURN GIRL IS USING HER WITS!
I KNOW! I'LL RADIATE A POWERFUL THOUGHT-BEAM DOWN TO THE SEA-BOTTOM, WHERE MANY HUGE CREATURES LIVE!
MILES DOWN, A DENIZEN OF THE DEEP SEA OBEYS THE HYPNOTIC MENTAL COMMAND!
SWIM UP WITH THE STATUE! OBEY ME!
AND WHEN SUPERBOY ARRIVES...
TOO LATE, SUPERBOY! I GOT THE STATUE! YOU CAN BE A GENTLEMAN IF YOU WANT AND CARRY IT FOR ME! HA, HA!
JEEPERS! NO WONDER THESE KIDS ARE CALLED SUPER HEROES! THEY DO SUPER-FEATS, EVEN THOUGH THEY EACH POSSESS ONLY ONE-SUPER-POWER!
To THE UNKNOWN SPACEMAN WHO FIRST EXPLORED VENUS
AFTER THE STATUE IS DELIVERED TO THE MUSEUM, SUPERBOY MEETS HUMILIATION AT THE CLUBHOUSE!
YOU LOST OUT ON YOUR FIRST TASK... AND TO A GIRL! IS THIS THE GREAT SUPERBOY WE LEARNED ABOUT IN SCHOOL? WHAT'S YOUR EXCUSE?
ER... NONE!
IF I TELL ABOUT THE RUNAWAY ROBOT DELAYING ME, IT WOULD SOUND LIKE A WEAK ALIBI!
SOON, USING THE TV TROUBLE-FINDER AGAIN...
LOOK! THAT ROUND-THE-WORLD ROCKET-LINER CRASHED! THE CREW AND PASSENGERS ESCAPED WITH FLYING JETS! BUT THE BURNING WRECK WILL SET FIRE TO THAT FOREST!
YOU'RE COMPETING WITH COSMIC BOY THIS TIME, SUPERBOY! READY... GO!
I'LL SIMPLY BLOW OUT THE FIRE WITH MY SUPER-BREATH! HIS POWER OF SUPER-MAGNETISM CAN'T POSSIBLY DOUSE THE BLAZE! HOW CAN I LOSE?
7

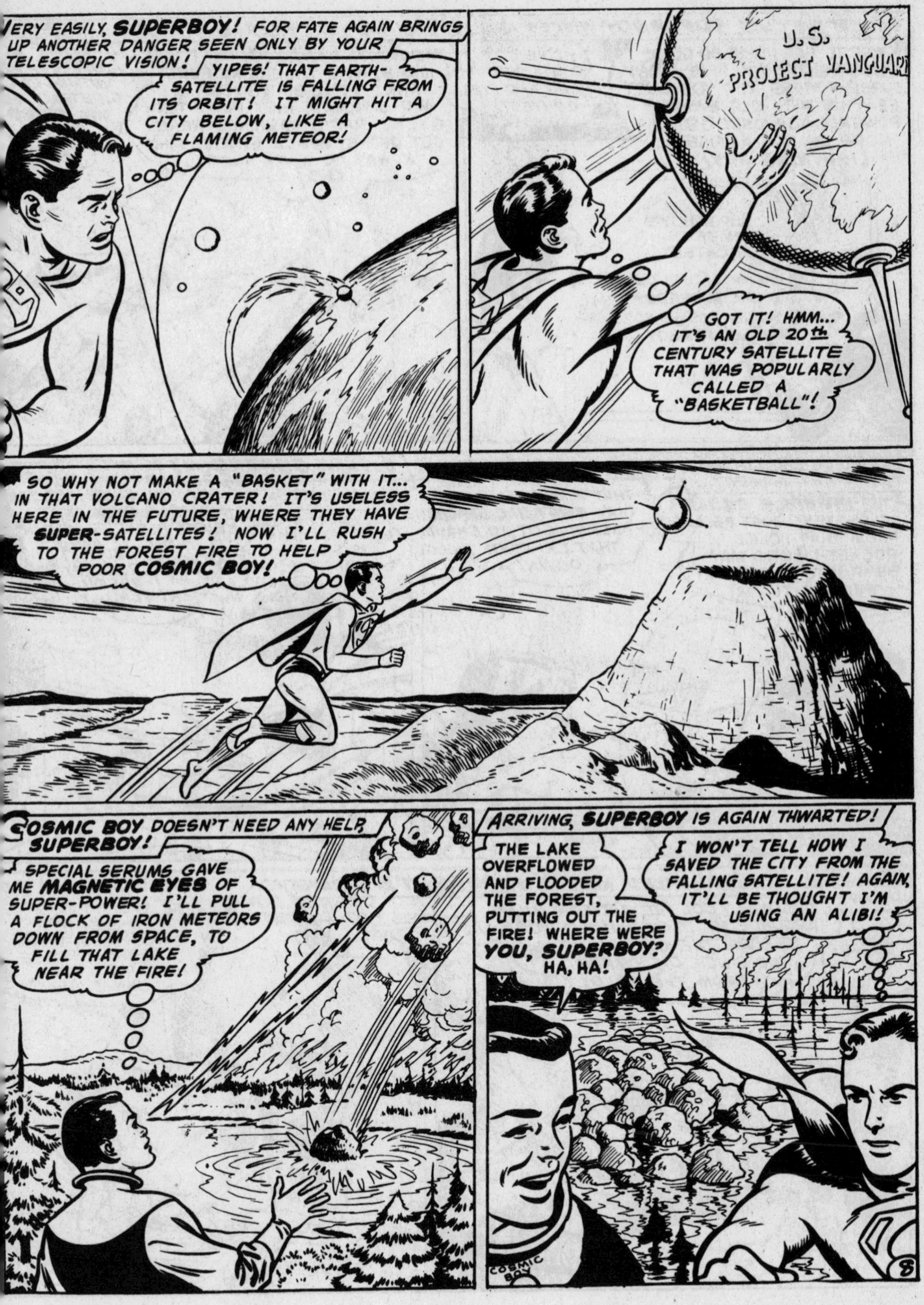
VERY EASILY, SUPERBOY! FOR FATE AGAIN BRINGS UP ANOTHER DANGER SEEN ONLY BY YOUR TELESCOPIC VISION!
YIPES! THAT EARTH-SATELLITE IS FALLING FROM ITS ORBIT! IT MIGHT HIT A CITY BELOW, LIKE A FLAMING METEOR!
U.S. PROJECT VANGUARD
GOT IT! HMM... IT'S AN OLD 20th CENTURY SATELLITE THAT WAS POPULARLY CALLED A "BASKETBALL"!
SO WHY NOT MAKE A "BASKET" WITH IT... IN THAT VOLCANO CRATER! IT'S USELESS HERE IN THE FUTURE, WHERE THEY HAVE SUPER-SATELLITES! NOW I'LL RUSH TO THE FOREST FIRE TO HELP POOR COSMIC BOY!
COSMIC BOY DOESN'T NEED ANY HELP, SUPERBOY!
SPECIAL SERUMS GAVE ME MAGNETIC EYES OF SUPER-POWER! I'LL PULL A FLOCK OF IRON METEORS DOWN FROM SPACE, TO FILL THAT LAKE NEAR THE FIRE!
ARRIVING, SUPERBOY IS AGAIN THWARTED!
THE LAKE OVERFLOWED AND FLOODED THE FOREST, PUTTING OUT THE FIRE! WHERE WERE YOU, SUPERBOY? HA, HA!
I WON'T TELL HOW I SAVED THE CITY FROM THE FALLING SATELLITE! AGAIN, IT'LL BE THOUGHT I'M USING AN ALIBI!
COSMIC BOY
8

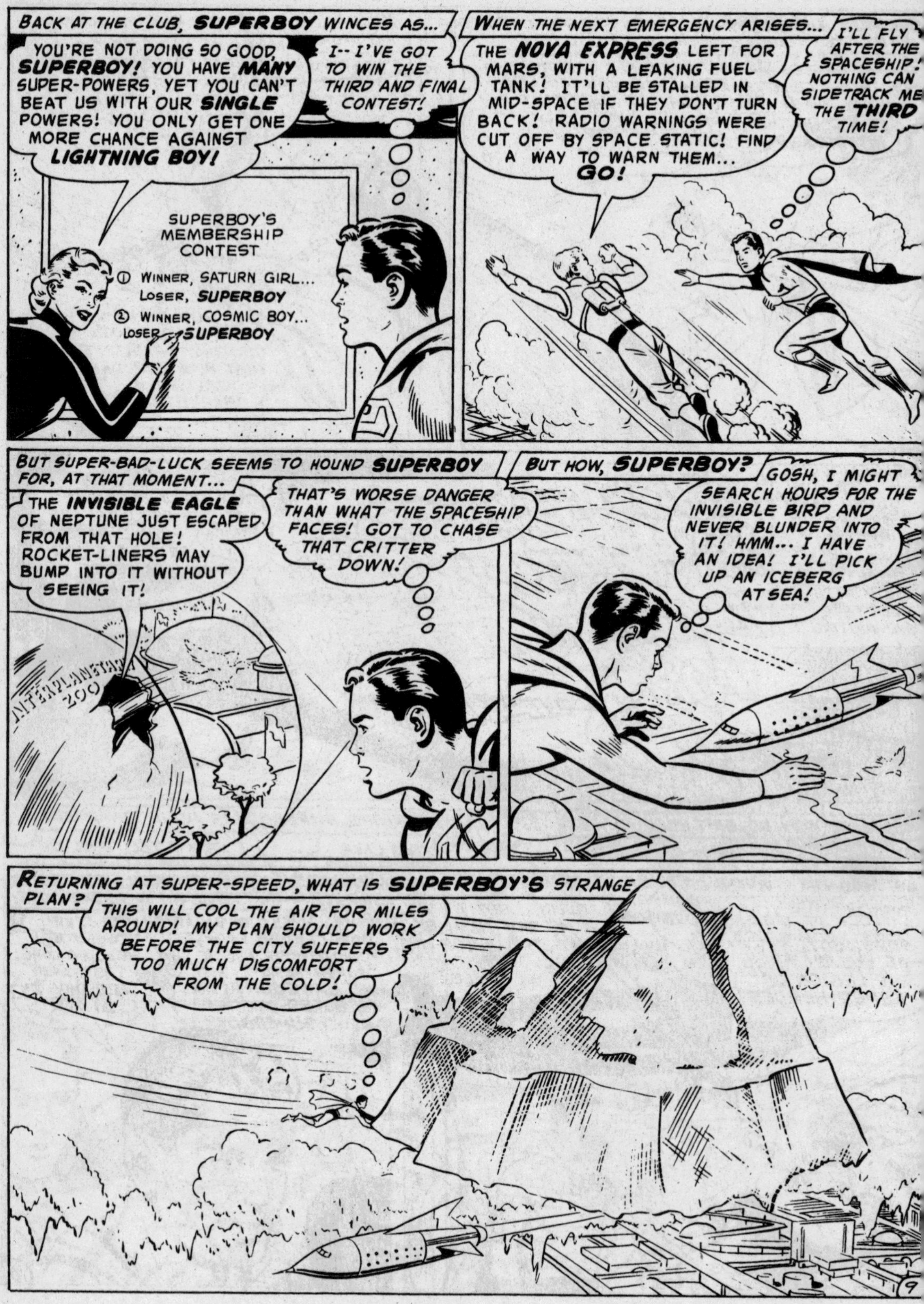
BACK AT THE CLUB, SUPERBOY WINCES AS...
YOU'RE NOT DOING SO GOOD, SUPERBOY! YOU HAVE MANY SUPER-POWERS, YET YOU CAN'T BEAT US WITH OUR SINGLE POWERS! YOU ONLY GET ONE MORE CHANCE AGAINST LIGHTNING BOY!
I-- I'VE GOT TO WIN THE THIRD AND FINAL CONTEST!
SUPERBOY'S MEMBERSHIP CONTEST
① WINNER, SATURN GIRL... LOSER, SUPERBOY
② WINNER, COSMIC BOY... LOSER SUPERBOY
WHEN THE NEXT EMERGENCY ARISES...
THE NOVA EXPRESS LEFT FOR MARS, WITH A LEAKING FUEL TANK! IT'LL BE STALLED IN MID-SPACE IF THEY DON'T TURN BACK! RADIO WARNINGS WERE CUT OFF BY SPACE STATIC! FIND A WAY TO WARN THEM... GO!
I'LL FLY AFTER THE SPACESHIP! NOTHING CAN SIDETRACK ME THE THIRD TIME!
BUT SUPER-BAD-LUCK SEEMS TO HOUND SUPERBOY FOR, AT THAT MOMENT...
THE INVISIBLE EAGLE OF NEPTUNE JUST ESCAPED FROM THAT HOLE! ROCKET-LINERS MAY BUMP INTO IT WITHOUT SEEING IT!
THAT'S WORSE DANGER THAN WHAT THE SPACESHIP FACES! GOT TO CHASE THAT CRITTER DOWN!
INTERPLANETARY ZOO
BUT HOW, SUPERBOY?
GOSH, I MIGHT SEARCH HOURS FOR THE INVISIBLE BIRD AND NEVER BLUNDER INTO IT! HMM... I HAVE AN IDEA! I'LL PICK UP AN ICEBERG AT SEA!
RETURNING AT SUPER-SPEED, WHAT IS SUPERBOY'S STRANGE PLAN?
THIS WILL COOL THE AIR FOR MILES AROUND! MY PLAN SHOULD WORK BEFORE THE CITY SUFFERS TOO MUCH DISCOMFORT FROM THE COLD!
9

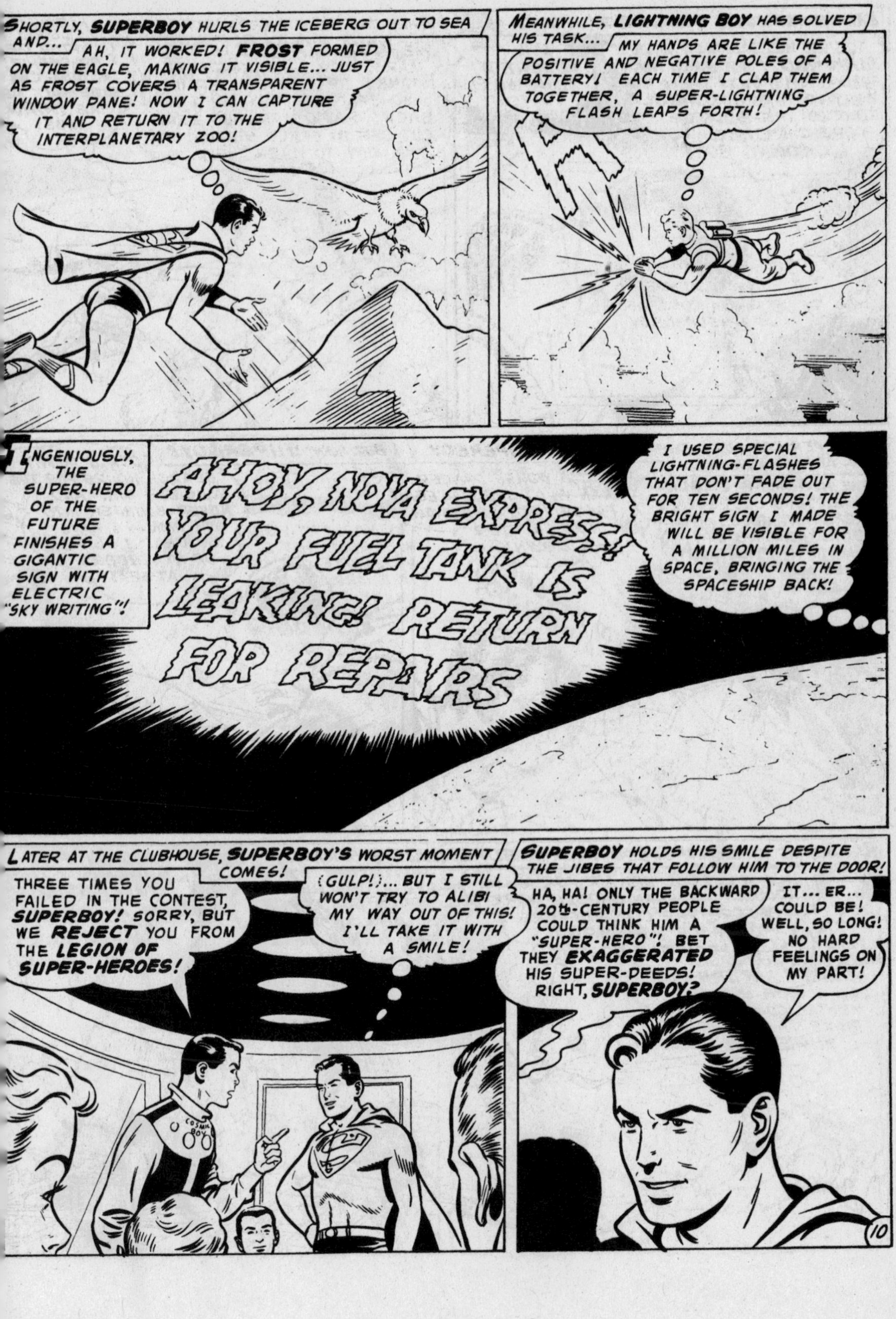
SHORTLY, SUPERBOY HURLS THE ICEBERG OUT TO SEA AND...
AH, IT WORKED! FROST FORMED ON THE EAGLE, MAKING IT VISIBLE... JUST AS FROST COVERS A TRANSPARENT WINDOW PANE! NOW I CAN CAPTURE IT AND RETURN IT TO THE INTERPLANETARY ZOO!
MEANWHILE, LIGHTNING BOY HAS SOLVED HIS TASK...
MY HANDS ARE LIKE THE POSITIVE AND NEGATIVE POLES OF A BATTERY! EACH TIME I CLAP THEM TOGETHER, A SUPER-LIGHTNING FLASH LEAPS FORTH!
INGENIOUSLY, THE SUPER-HERO OF THE FUTURE FINISHES A GIGANTIC SIGN WITH ELECTRIC "SKY WRITING"!
AHOY, NOVA EXPRESS! YOUR FUEL TANK IS LEAKING! RETURN FOR REPAIRS
I USED SPECIAL LIGHTNING-FLASHES THAT DON'T FADE OUT FOR TEN SECONDS! THE BRIGHT SIGN I MADE WILL BE VISIBLE FOR A MILLION MILES IN SPACE, BRINGING THE SPACESHIP BACK!
LATER AT THE CLUBHOUSE, SUPERBOY'S WORST MOMENT COMES!
THREE TIMES YOU FAILED IN THE CONTEST, SUPERBOY! SORRY, BUT WE REJECT YOU FROM THE LEGION OF SUPER-HEROES!
(GULP!)... BUT I STILL WON'T TRY TO ALIBI MY WAY OUT OF THIS! I'LL TAKE IT WITH A SMILE!
COSMIC BOY
SUPERBOY HOLDS HIS SMILE DESPITE THE JIBES THAT FOLLOW HIM TO THE DOOR!
HA, HA! ONLY THE BACKWARD 20th-CENTURY PEOPLE COULD THINK HIM A "SUPER-HERO"! BET THEY EXAGGERATED HIS SUPER-DEEDS! RIGHT, SUPERBOY?
IT... ER... COULD BE! WELL, SO LONG! NO HARD FEELINGS ON MY PART!
10

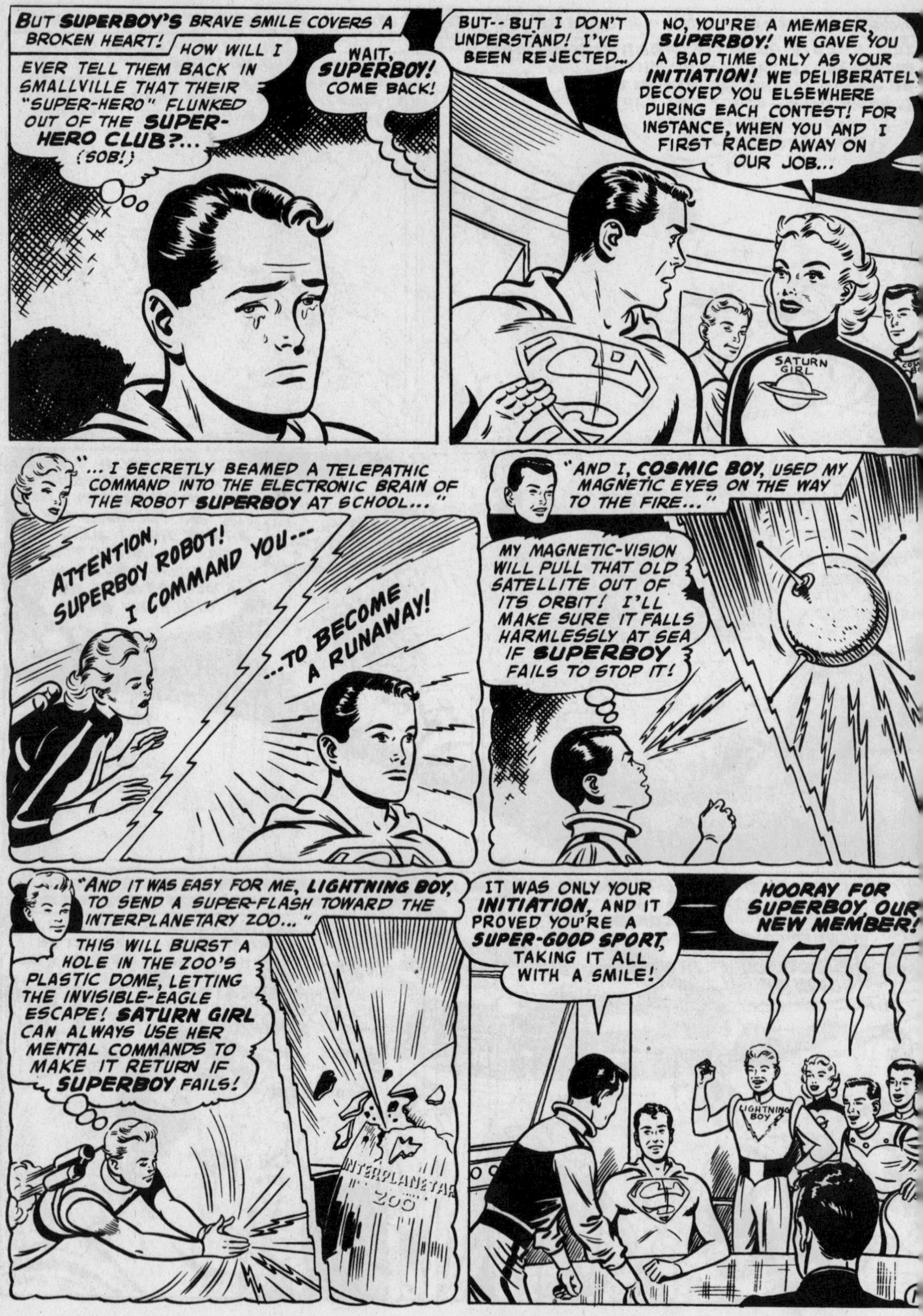
BUT SUPERBOY'S BRAVE SMILE COVERS A BROKEN HEART!
HOW WILL I EVER TELL THEM BACK IN SMALLVILLE THAT THEIR "SUPER-HERO" FLUNKED OUT OF THE SUPER-HERO CLUB?... (SOB!)
WAIT, SUPERBOY! COME BACK!
BUT-- BUT I DON'T UNDERSTAND! I'VE BEEN REJECTED...
NO, YOU'RE A MEMBER, SUPERBOY! WE GAVE YOU A BAD TIME ONLY AS YOUR INITIATION! WE DELIBERATELY DECOYED YOU ELSEWHERE DURING EACH CONTEST! FOR INSTANCE, WHEN YOU AND I FIRST RACED AWAY ON OUR JOB...
SATURN GIRL
"... I SECRETLY BEAMED A TELEPATHIC COMMAND INTO THE ELECTRONIC BRAIN OF THE ROBOT SUPERBOY AT SCHOOL..."
ATTENTION, SUPERBOY ROBOT! I COMMAND YOU---
...TO BECOME A RUNAWAY!
"AND I, COSMIC BOY, USED MY MAGNETIC EYES ON THE WAY TO THE FIRE..."
MY MAGNETIC-VISION WILL PULL THAT OLD SATELLITE OUT OF ITS ORBIT! I'LL MAKE SURE IT FALLS HARMLESSLY AT SEA IF SUPERBOY FAILS TO STOP IT!
"AND IT WAS EASY FOR ME, LIGHTNING BOY, TO SEND A SUPER-FLASH TOWARD THE INTERPLANETARY ZOO..."
THIS WILL BURST A HOLE IN THE ZOO'S PLASTIC DOME, LETTING THE INVISIBLE-EAGLE ESCAPE! SATURN GIRL CAN ALWAYS USE HER MENTAL COMMANDS TO MAKE IT RETURN IF SUPERBOY FAILS!
ZOO
IT WAS ONLY YOUR INITIATION, AND IT PROVED YOU'RE A SUPER-GOOD SPORT, TAKING IT ALL WITH A SMILE!
HOORAY FOR SUPERBOY, OUR NEW MEMBER!
LIGHTNING BOY

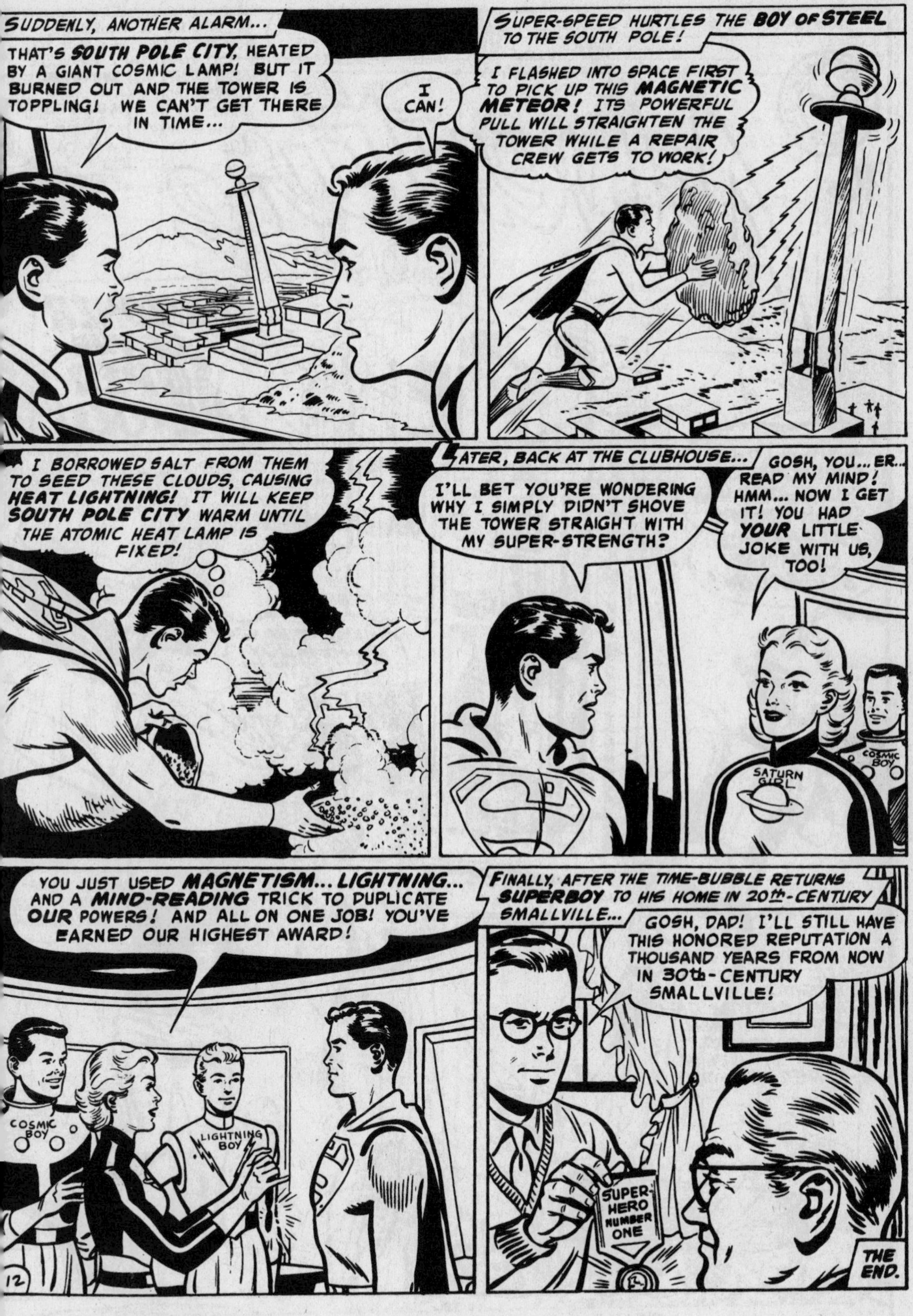
SUDDENLY, ANOTHER ALARM...
THAT'S SOUTH POLE CITY, HEATED BY A GIANT COSMIC LAMP! BUT IT BURNED OUT AND THE TOWER IS TOPPLING! WE CAN'T GET THERE IN TIME...
I CAN!
SUPER-SPEED HURTLES THE BOY OF STEEL TO THE SOUTH POLE!
I FLASHED INTO SPACE FIRST TO PICK UP THIS MAGNETIC METEOR! ITS POWERFUL PULL WILL STRAIGHTEN THE TOWER WHILE A REPAIR CREW GETS TO WORK!
I BORROWED SALT FROM THEM TO SEED THESE CLOUDS, CAUSING HEAT LIGHTNING! IT WILL KEEP SOUTH POLE CITY WARM UNTIL THE ATOMIC HEAT LAMP IS FIXED!
LATER, BACK AT THE CLUBHOUSE...
I'LL BET YOU'RE WONDERING WHY I SIMPLY DIDN'T SHOVE THE TOWER STRAIGHT WITH MY SUPER-STRENGTH?
GOSH, YOU... ER... READ MY MIND! HMM... NOW I GET IT! YOU HAD YOUR LITTLE JOKE WITH US, TOO!
SATURN GIRL
COSMIC BOY
YOU JUST USED MAGNETISM... LIGHTNING... AND A MIND-READING TRICK TO DUPLICATE OUR POWERS! AND ALL ON ONE JOB! YOU'VE EARNED OUR HIGHEST AWARD!
COSMIC BOY
LIGHTNING BOY
12
FINALLY, AFTER THE TIME-BUBBLE RETURNS SUPERBOY TO HIS HOME IN 20th-CENTURY SMALLVILLE...
GOSH, DAD! I'LL STILL HAVE THIS HONORED REPUTATION A THOUSAND YEARS FROM NOW IN 30th-CENTURY SMALLVILLE!
SUPER HERO NUMBER ONE
THE END.

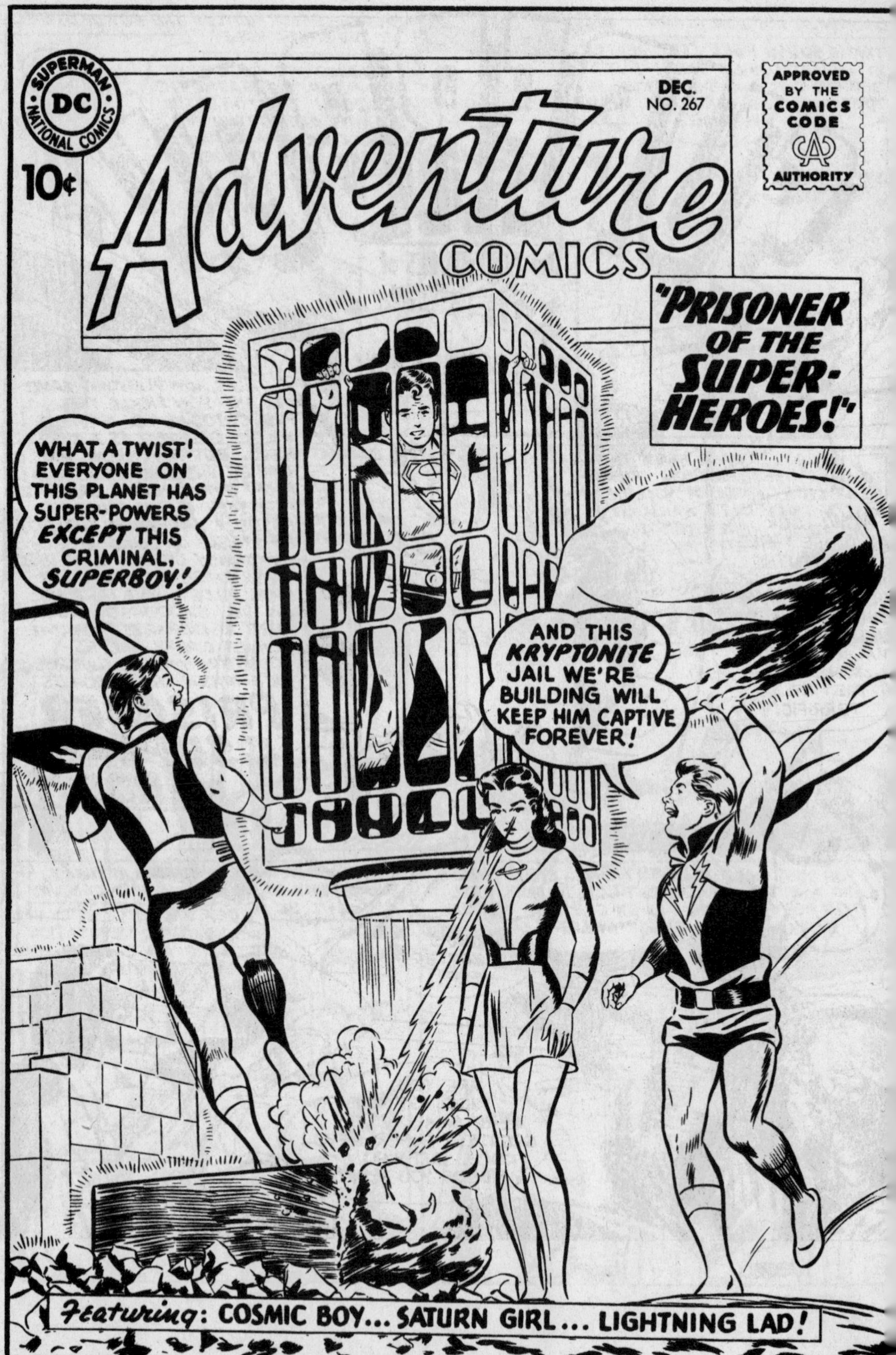
SUPERMAN DC NATIONAL COMICS
10¢
Adventure COMICS
DEC. NO. 267
APPROVED BY THE COMICS CODE AUTHORITY
"PRISONER OF THE SUPER-HEROES!"
WHAT A TWIST! EVERYONE ON THIS PLANET HAS SUPER-POWERS EXCEPT THIS CRIMINAL, SUPERBOY!
AND THIS KRYPTONITE JAIL WE'RE BUILDING WILL KEEP HIM CAPTIVE FOREVER!
Featuring: COSMIC BOY... SATURN GIRL... LIGHTNING LAD!

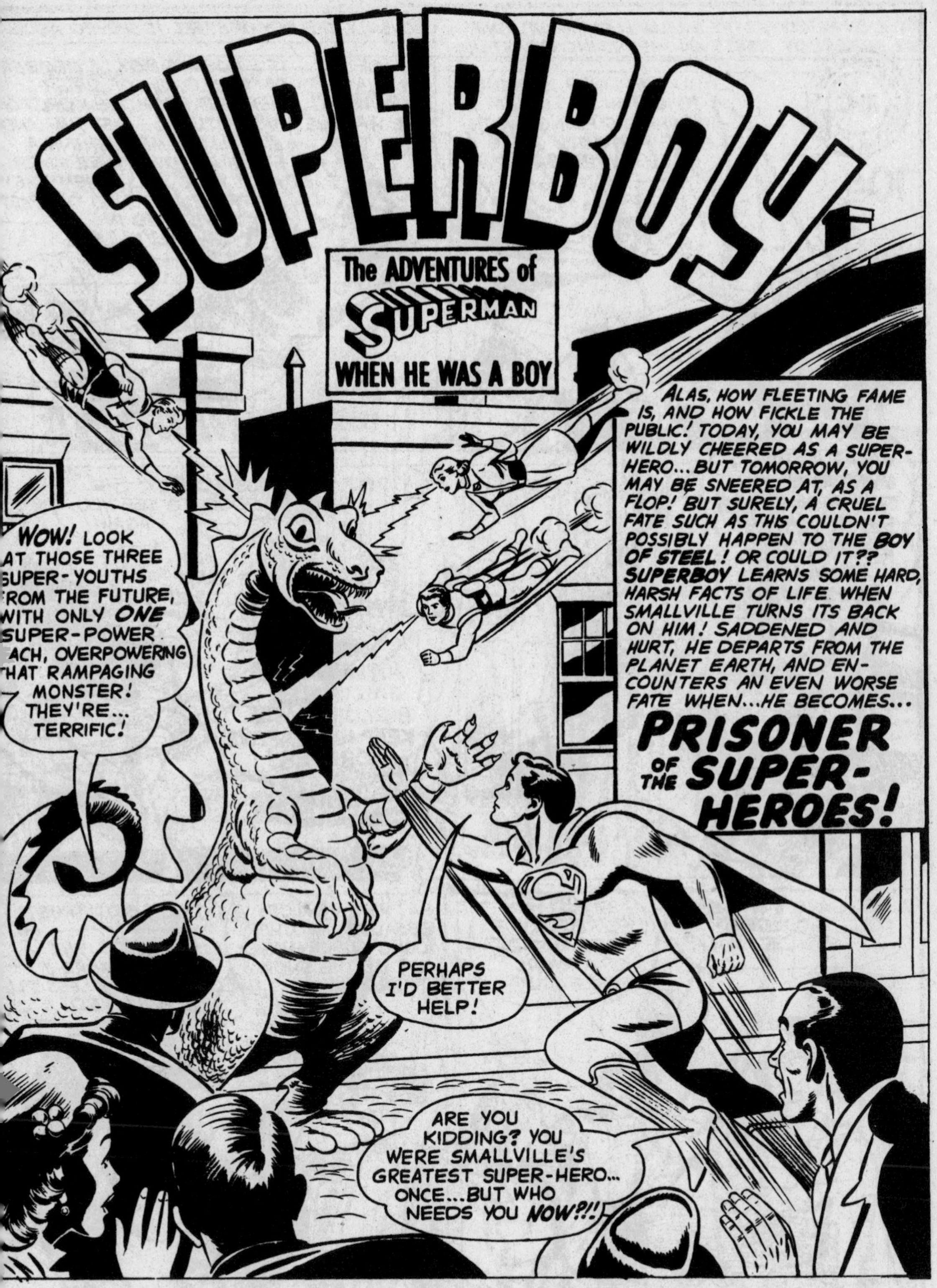
SUPERBOY
The ADVENTURES of SUPERMAN WHEN HE WAS A BOY
ALAS, HOW FLEETING FAME IS, AND HOW FICKLE THE PUBLIC! TODAY, YOU MAY BE WILDLY CHEERED AS A SUPER-HERO... BUT TOMORROW, YOU MAY BE SNEERED AT, AS A FLOP! BUT SURELY, A CRUEL FATE SUCH AS THIS COULDN'T POSSIBLY HAPPEN TO THE BOY OF STEEL! OR COULD IT?? SUPERBOY LEARNS SOME HARD, HARSH FACTS OF LIFE WHEN SMALLVILLE TURNS ITS BACK ON HIM! SADDENED AND HURT, HE DEPARTS FROM THE PLANET EARTH, AND ENCOUNTERS AN EVEN WORSE FATE WHEN...HE BECOMES...
PRISONER OF THE SUPER-HEROES!
WOW! LOOK AT THOSE THREE SUPER-YOUTHS FROM THE FUTURE, WITH ONLY ONE SUPER-POWER EACH, OVERPOWERING THAT RAMPAGING MONSTER! THEY'RE... TERRIFIC!
PERHAPS I'D BETTER HELP!
ARE YOU KIDDING? YOU WERE SMALLVILLE'S GREATEST SUPER-HERO... ONCE...BUT WHO NEEDS YOU NOW?!!

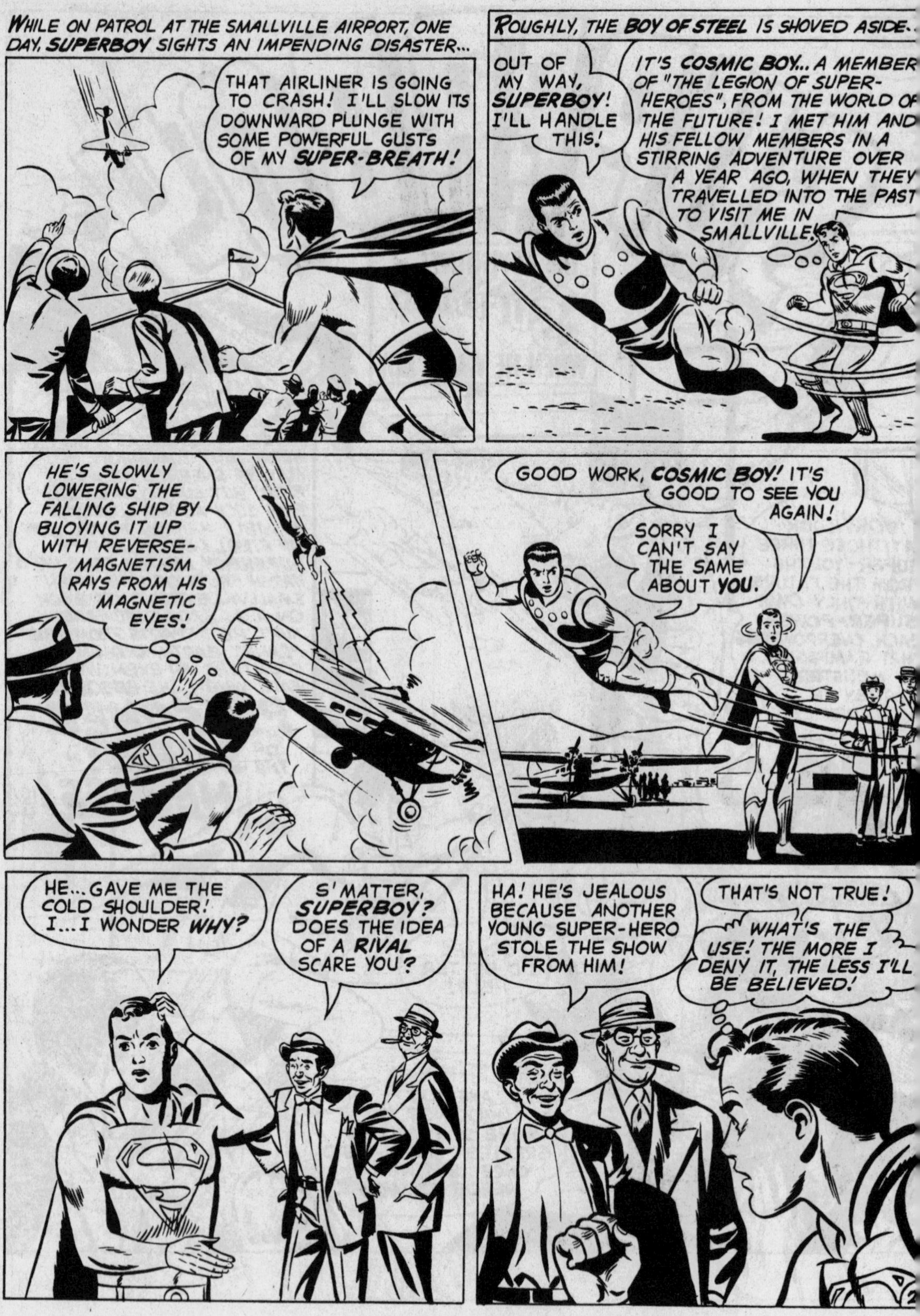
WHILE ON PATROL AT THE SMALLVILLE AIRPORT, ONE DAY, SUPERBOY SIGHTS AN IMPENDING DISASTER...
THAT AIRLINER IS GOING TO CRASH! I'LL SLOW ITS DOWNWARD PLUNGE WITH SOME POWERFUL GUSTS OF MY SUPER-BREATH!
ROUGHLY, THE BOY OF STEEL IS SHOVED ASIDE...
OUT OF MY WAY, SUPERBOY! I'LL HANDLE THIS!
IT'S COSMIC BOY... A MEMBER OF "THE LEGION OF SUPER-HEROES", FROM THE WORLD OF THE FUTURE! I MET HIM AND HIS FELLOW MEMBERS IN A STIRRING ADVENTURE OVER A YEAR AGO, WHEN THEY TRAVELLED INTO THE PAST TO VISIT ME IN SMALLVILLE!
HE'S SLOWLY LOWERING THE FALLING SHIP BY BUOYING IT UP WITH REVERSE-MAGNETISM RAYS FROM HIS MAGNETIC EYES!
GOOD WORK, COSMIC BOY! IT'S GOOD TO SEE YOU AGAIN!
SORRY I CAN'T SAY THE SAME ABOUT YOU.
HE... GAVE ME THE COLD SHOULDER! I... I WONDER WHY?
S'MATTER, SUPERBOY? DOES THE IDEA OF A RIVAL SCARE YOU?
HA! HE'S JEALOUS BECAUSE ANOTHER YOUNG SUPER-HERO STOLE THE SHOW FROM HIM!
THAT'S NOT TRUE!
WHAT'S THE USE! THE MORE I DENY IT, THE LESS I'LL BE BELIEVED!

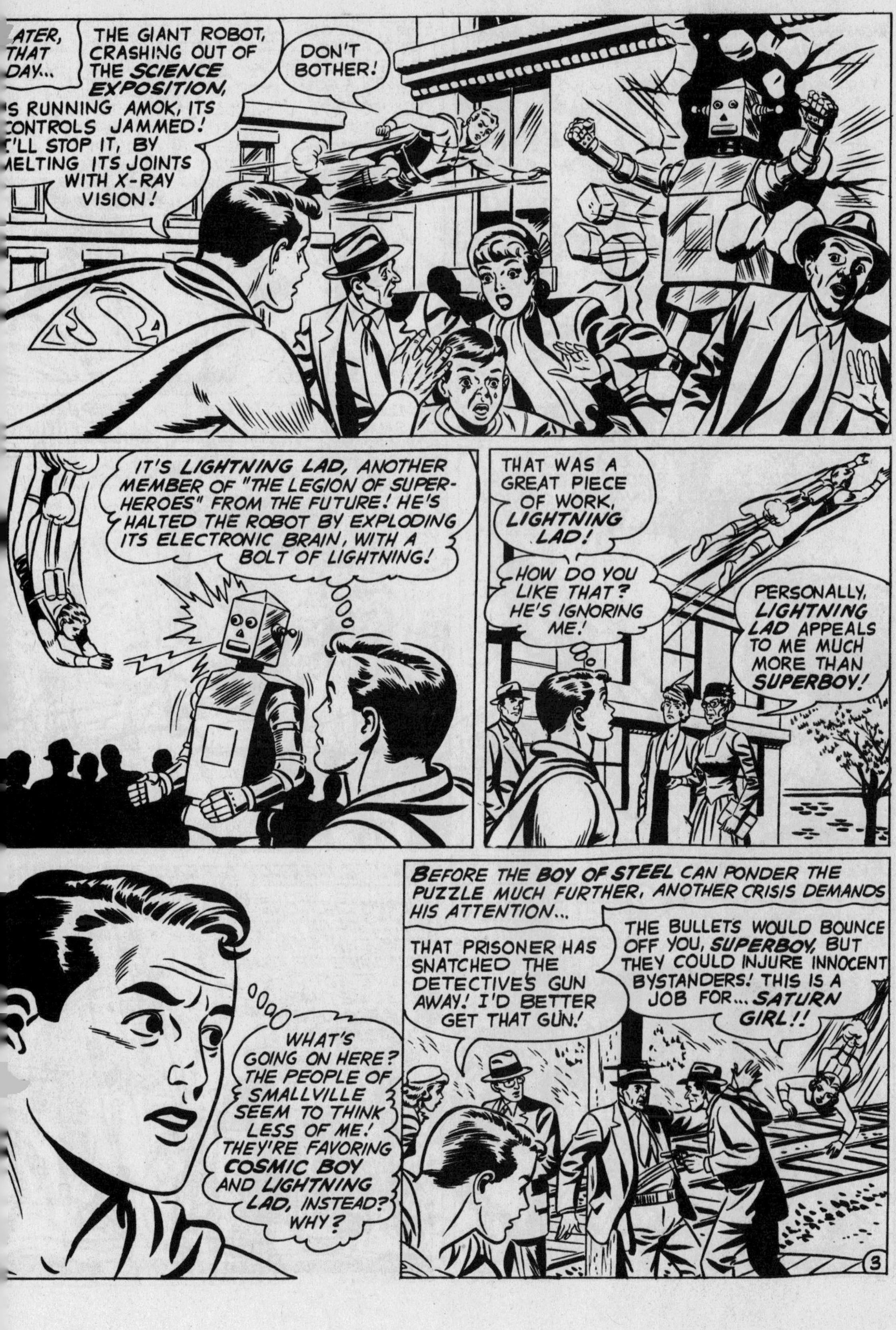
ATER, THAT DAY...
THE GIANT ROBOT, CRASHING OUT OF THE SCIENCE EXPOSITION, S RUNNING AMOK, ITS CONTROLS JAMMED! 'LL STOP IT, BY MELTING ITS JOINTS WITH X-RAY VISION!
DON'T BOTHER!
IT'S LIGHTNING LAD, ANOTHER MEMBER OF "THE LEGION OF SUPER-HEROES" FROM THE FUTURE! HE'S HALTED THE ROBOT BY EXPLODING ITS ELECTRONIC BRAIN, WITH A BOLT OF LIGHTNING!
THAT WAS A GREAT PIECE OF WORK, LIGHTNING LAD!
HOW DO YOU LIKE THAT? HE'S IGNORING ME!
PERSONALLY, LIGHTNING LAD APPEALS TO ME MUCH MORE THAN SUPERBOY!
WHAT'S GOING ON HERE? THE PEOPLE OF SMALLVILLE SEEM TO THINK LESS OF ME! THEY'RE FAVORING COSMIC BOY AND LIGHTNING LAD, INSTEAD? WHY?
BEFORE THE BOY OF STEEL CAN PONDER THE PUZZLE MUCH FURTHER, ANOTHER CRISIS DEMANDS HIS ATTENTION...
THAT PRISONER HAS SNATCHED THE DETECTIVE'S GUN AWAY! I'D BETTER GET THAT GUN!
THE BULLETS WOULD BOUNCE OFF YOU, SUPERBOY, BUT THEY COULD INJURE INNOCENT BYSTANDERS! THIS IS A JOB FOR... SATURN GIRL!!
3

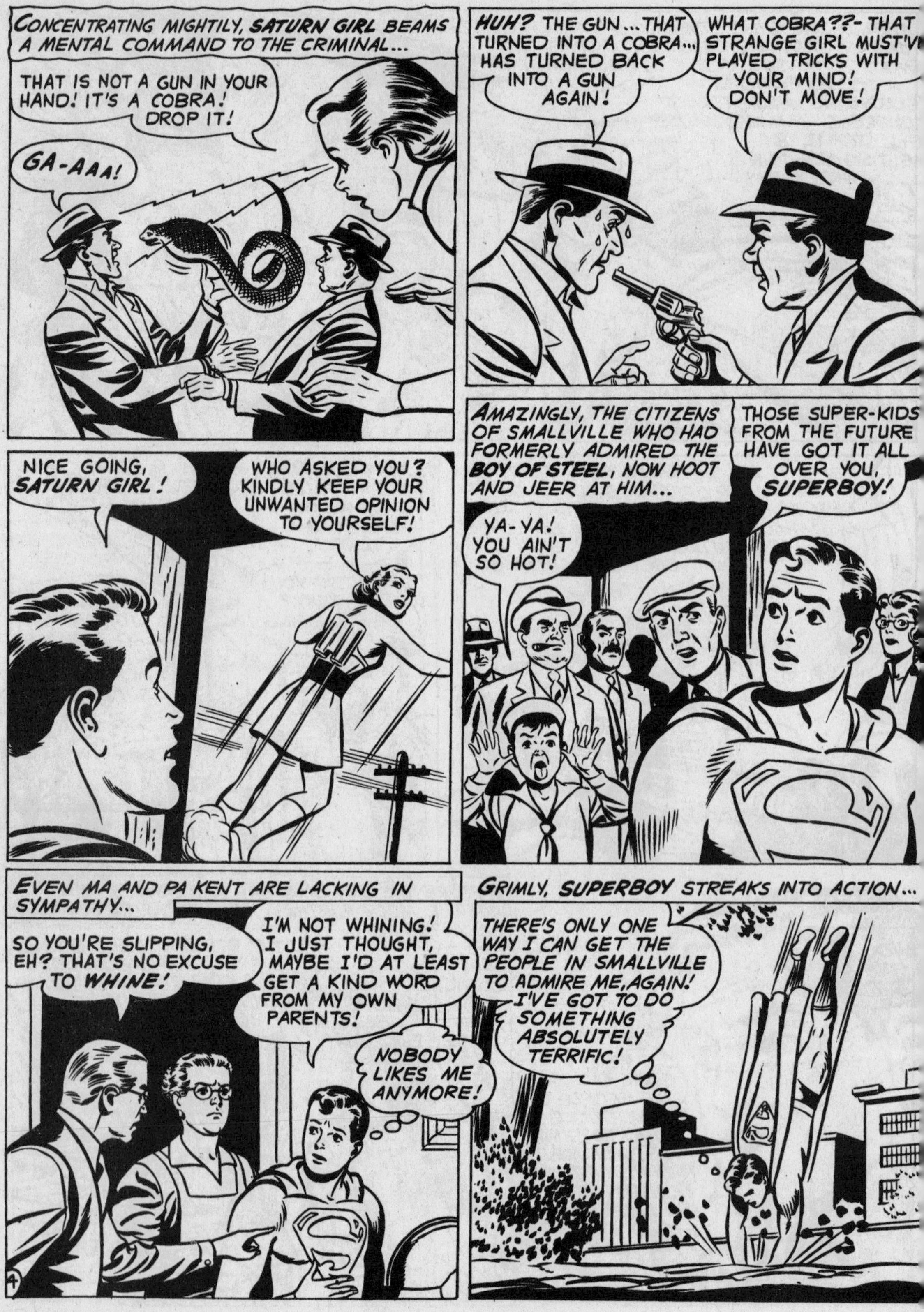
CONCENTRATING MIGHTILY, SATURN GIRL BEAMS A MENTAL COMMAND TO THE CRIMINAL...
THAT IS NOT A GUN IN YOUR HAND! IT'S A COBRA! DROP IT!
GA-AAA!
HUH? THE GUN... THAT TURNED INTO A COBRA... HAS TURNED BACK INTO A GUN AGAIN!
WHAT COBRA??- THAT STRANGE GIRL MUST'VE PLAYED TRICKS WITH YOUR MIND! DON'T MOVE!
NICE GOING, SATURN GIRL!
WHO ASKED YOU? KINDLY KEEP YOUR UNWANTED OPINION TO YOURSELF!
AMAZINGLY, THE CITIZENS OF SMALLVILLE WHO HAD FORMERLY ADMIRED THE BOY OF STEEL, NOW HOOT AND JEER AT HIM...
THOSE SUPER-KIDS FROM THE FUTURE HAVE GOT IT ALL OVER YOU, SUPERBOY!
YA-YA! YOU AIN'T SO HOT!
EVEN MA AND PA KENT ARE LACKING IN SYMPATHY...
SO YOU'RE SLIPPING, EH? THAT'S NO EXCUSE TO WHINE!
I'M NOT WHINING! I JUST THOUGHT, MAYBE I'D AT LEAST GET A KIND WORD FROM MY OWN PARENTS!
NOBODY LIKES ME ANYMORE!
4
GRIMLY, SUPERBOY STREAKS INTO ACTION...
THERE'S ONLY ONE WAY I CAN GET THE PEOPLE IN SMALLVILLE TO ADMIRE ME, AGAIN! I'VE GOT TO DO SOMETHING ABSOLUTELY TERRIFIC!

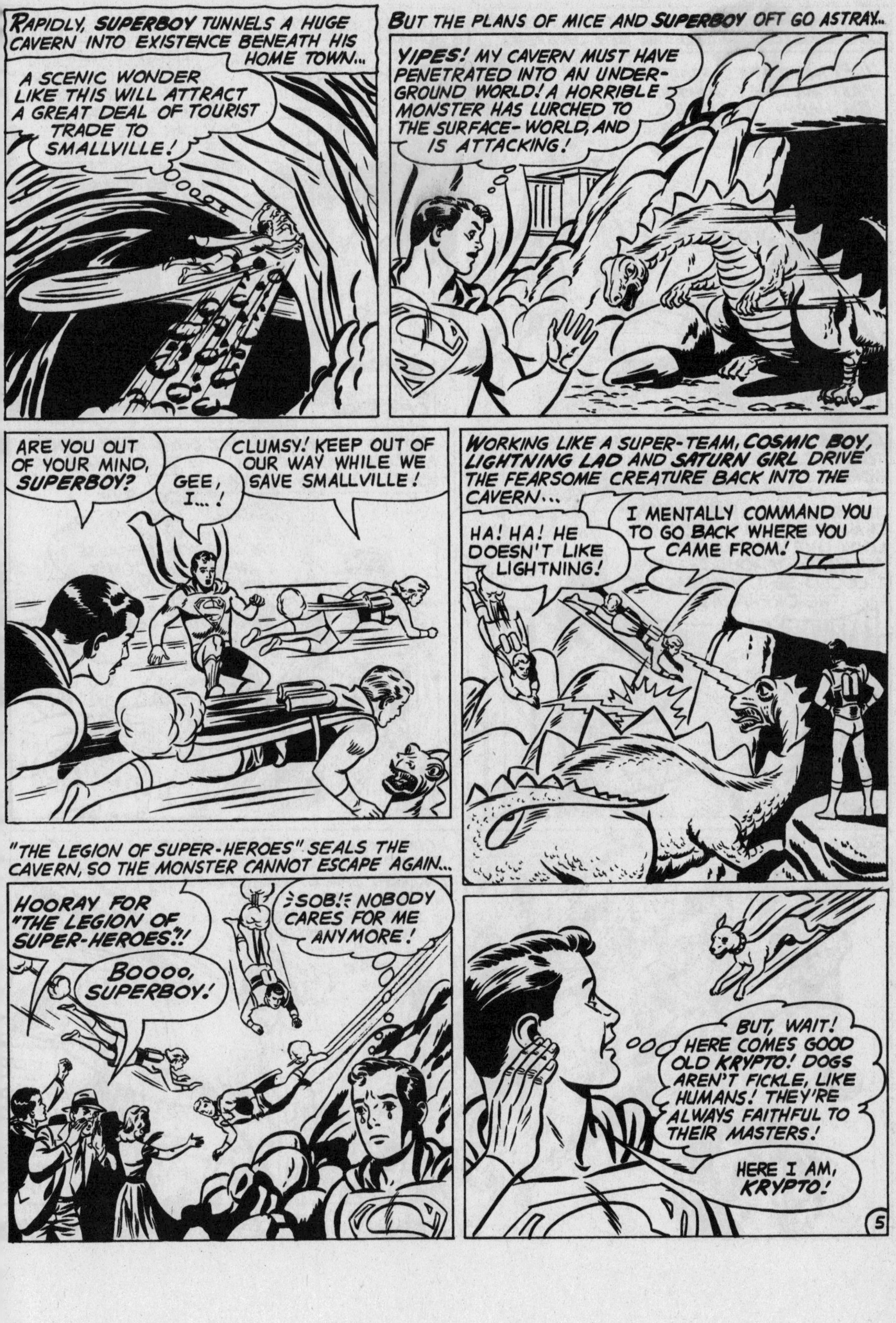
RAPIDLY, SUPERBOY TUNNELS A HUGE CAVERN INTO EXISTENCE BENEATH HIS HOME TOWN...
A SCENIC WONDER LIKE THIS WILL ATTRACT A GREAT DEAL OF TOURIST TRADE TO SMALLVILLE!
BUT THE PLANS OF MICE AND SUPERBOY OFT GO ASTRAY...
YIPES! MY CAVERN MUST HAVE PENETRATED INTO AN UNDER-GROUND WORLD! A HORRIBLE MONSTER HAS LURCHED TO THE SURFACE-WORLD, AND IS ATTACKING!
ARE YOU OUT OF YOUR MIND, SUPERBOY?
GEE, I... !
CLUMSY! KEEP OUT OF OUR WAY WHILE WE SAVE SMALLVILLE!
WORKING LIKE A SUPER-TEAM, COSMIC BOY, LIGHTNING LAD AND SATURN GIRL DRIVE THE FEARSOME CREATURE BACK INTO THE CAVERN...
HA! HA! HE DOESN'T LIKE LIGHTNING!
I MENTALLY COMMAND YOU TO GO BACK WHERE YOU CAME FROM!
"THE LEGION OF SUPER-HEROES" SEALS THE CAVERN, SO THE MONSTER CANNOT ESCAPE AGAIN...
HOORAY FOR "THE LEGION OF SUPER-HEROES"!
BOOOO, SUPERBOY!
SOB! NOBODY CARES FOR ME ANYMORE!
BUT, WAIT! HERE COMES GOOD OLD KRYPTO! DOGS AREN'T FICKLE, LIKE HUMANS! THEY'RE ALWAYS FAITHFUL TO THEIR MASTERS!
HERE I AM, KRYPTO!
5

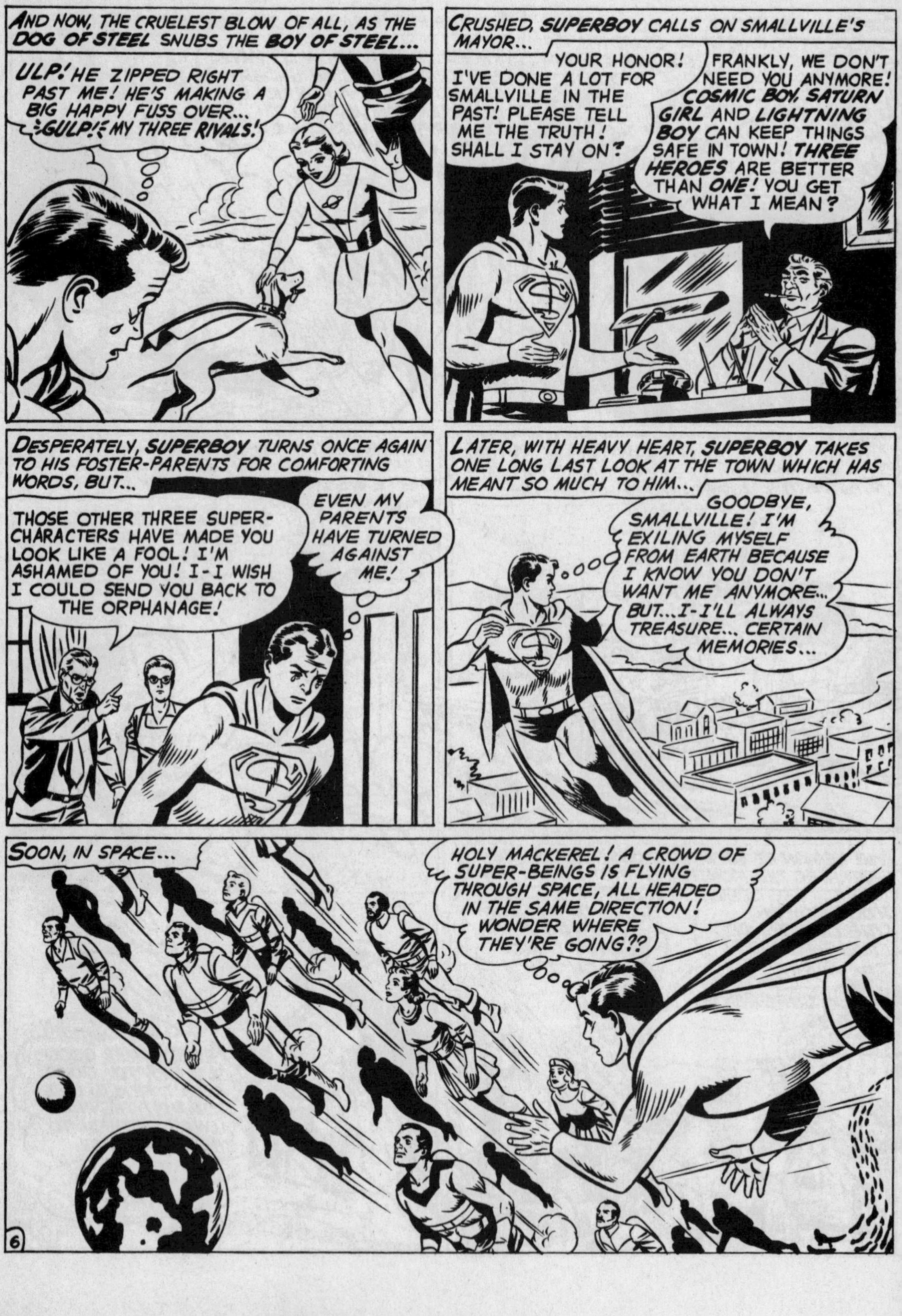
AND NOW, THE CRUELEST BLOW OF ALL, AS THE DOG OF STEEL SNUBS THE BOY OF STEEL...
ULP! HE ZIPPED RIGHT PAST ME! HE'S MAKING A BIG HAPPY FUSS OVER... GULP! MY THREE RIVALS!
CRUSHED, SUPERBOY CALLS ON SMALLVILLE'S MAYOR...
YOUR HONOR! I'VE DONE A LOT FOR SMALLVILLE IN THE PAST! PLEASE TELL ME THE TRUTH! SHALL I STAY ON?
FRANKLY, WE DON'T NEED YOU ANYMORE! COSMIC BOY, SATURN GIRL AND LIGHTNING BOY CAN KEEP THINGS SAFE IN TOWN! THREE HEROES ARE BETTER THAN ONE! YOU GET WHAT I MEAN?
DESPERATELY, SUPERBOY TURNS ONCE AGAIN TO HIS FOSTER-PARENTS FOR COMFORTING WORDS, BUT...
THOSE OTHER THREE SUPER-CHARACTERS HAVE MADE YOU LOOK LIKE A FOOL! I'M ASHAMED OF YOU! I-I WISH I COULD SEND YOU BACK TO THE ORPHANAGE!
EVEN MY PARENTS HAVE TURNED AGAINST ME!
LATER, WITH HEAVY HEART, SUPERBOY TAKES ONE LONG LAST LOOK AT THE TOWN WHICH HAS MEANT SO MUCH TO HIM...
GOODBYE, SMALLVILLE! I'M EXILING MYSELF FROM EARTH BECAUSE I KNOW YOU DON'T WANT ME ANYMORE... BUT...I-I'LL ALWAYS TREASURE... CERTAIN MEMORIES...
SOON, IN SPACE...
HOLY MACKEREL! A CROWD OF SUPER-BEINGS IS FLYING THROUGH SPACE, ALL HEADED IN THE SAME DIRECTION! WONDER WHERE THEY'RE GOING??
6

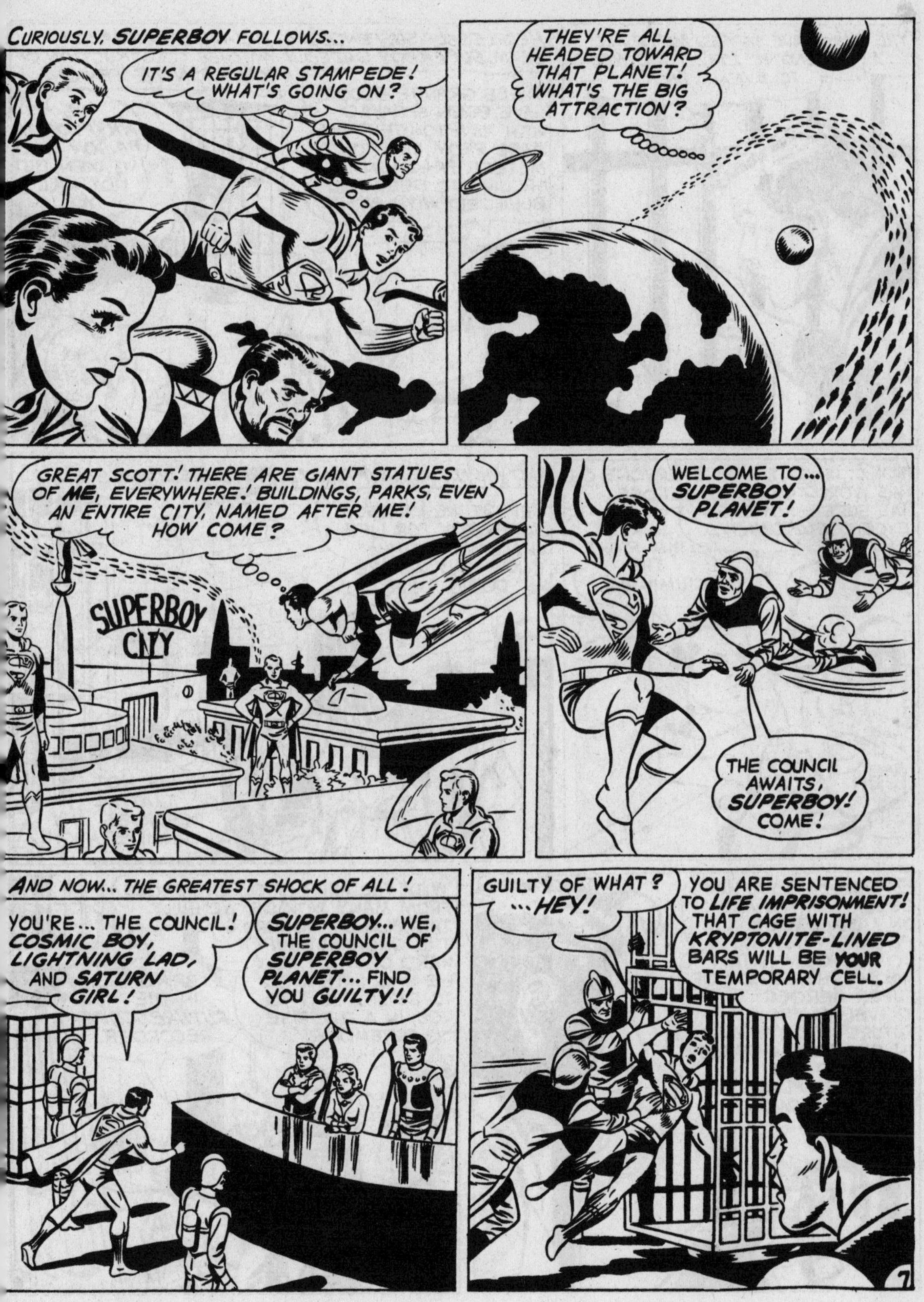
CURIOUSLY, SUPERBOY FOLLOWS...
IT'S A REGULAR STAMPEDE! WHAT'S GOING ON?
THEY'RE ALL HEADED TOWARD THAT PLANET! WHAT'S THE BIG ATTRACTION?
GREAT SCOTT! THERE ARE GIANT STATUES OF ME, EVERYWHERE! BUILDINGS, PARKS, EVEN AN ENTIRE CITY, NAMED AFTER ME! HOW COME?
SUPERBOY CITY
WELCOME TO... SUPERBOY PLANET!
THE COUNCIL AWAITS, SUPERBOY! COME!
AND NOW... THE GREATEST SHOCK OF ALL!
YOU'RE ... THE COUNCIL! COSMIC BOY, LIGHTNING LAD, AND SATURN GIRL!
SUPERBOY... WE, THE COUNCIL OF SUPERBOY PLANET... FIND YOU GUILTY!!
GUILTY OF WHAT? ...HEY!
YOU ARE SENTENCED TO LIFE IMPRISONMENT! THAT CAGE WITH KRYPTONITE-LINED BARS WILL BE YOUR TEMPORARY CELL.
7

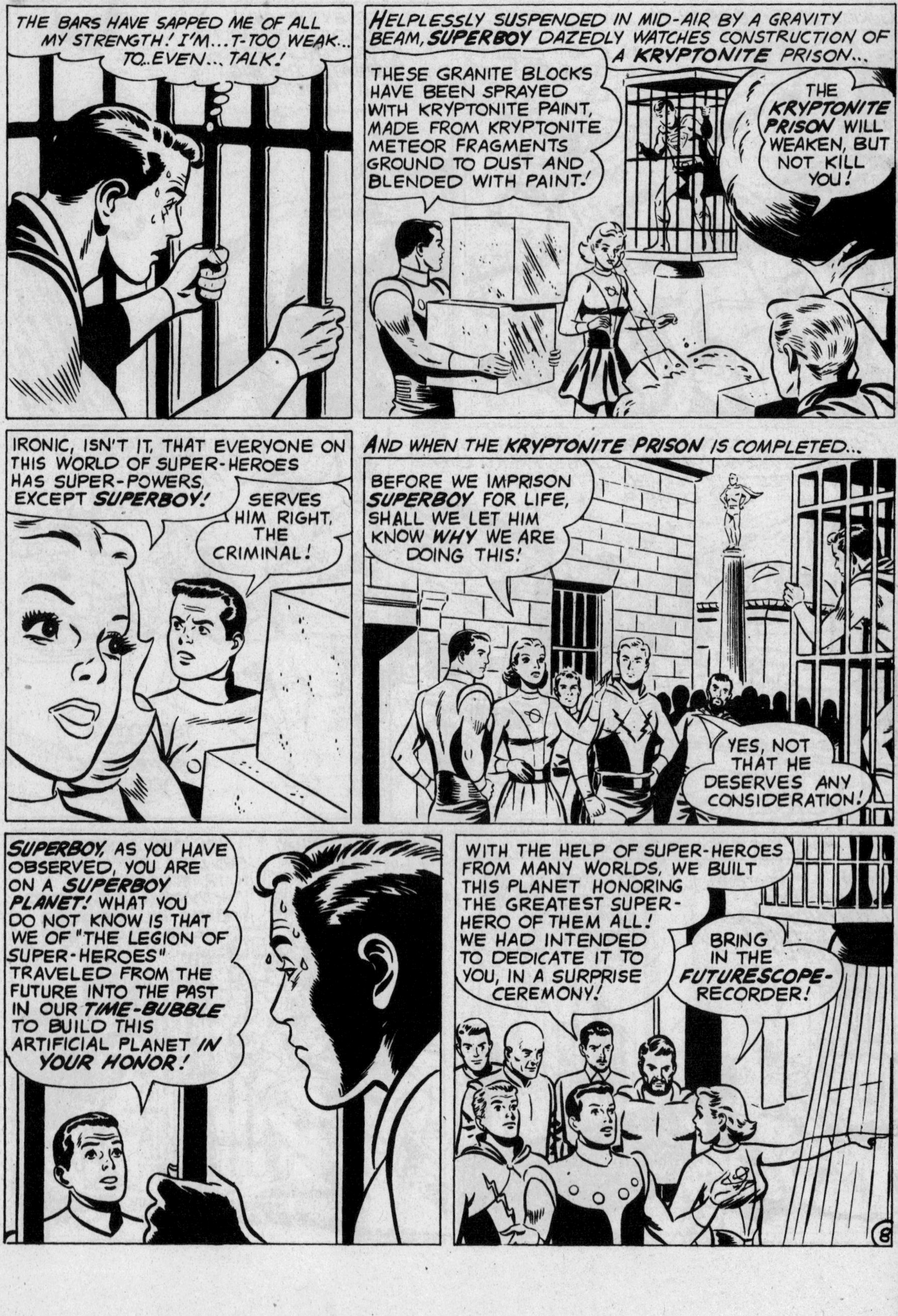
THE BARS HAVE SAPPED ME OF ALL MY STRENGTH! I'M...T-TOO WEAK... TO..EVEN...TALK!
HELPLESSLY SUSPENDED IN MID-AIR BY A GRAVITY BEAM, SUPERBOY DAZEDLY WATCHES CONSTRUCTION OF A KRYPTONITE PRISON...
THESE GRANITE BLOCKS HAVE BEEN SPRAYED WITH KRYPTONITE PAINT, MADE FROM KRYPTONITE METEOR FRAGMENTS GROUND TO DUST AND BLENDED WITH PAINT!
THE KRYPTONITE PRISON WILL WEAKEN, BUT NOT KILL YOU!
IRONIC, ISN'T IT, THAT EVERYONE ON THIS WORLD OF SUPER-HEROES HAS SUPER-POWERS, EXCEPT SUPERBOY!
SERVES HIM RIGHT, THE CRIMINAL!
AND WHEN THE KRYPTONITE PRISON IS COMPLETED...
BEFORE WE IMPRISON SUPERBOY FOR LIFE, SHALL WE LET HIM KNOW WHY WE ARE DOING THIS!
YES, NOT THAT HE DESERVES ANY CONSIDERATION!
SUPERBOY, AS YOU HAVE OBSERVED, YOU ARE ON A SUPERBOY PLANET! WHAT YOU DO NOT KNOW IS THAT WE OF "THE LEGION OF SUPER-HEROES" TRAVELED FROM THE FUTURE INTO THE PAST IN OUR TIME-BUBBLE TO BUILD THIS ARTIFICIAL PLANET IN YOUR HONOR!
WITH THE HELP OF SUPER-HEROES FROM MANY WORLDS, WE BUILT THIS PLANET HONORING THE GREATEST SUPER-HERO OF THEM ALL! WE HAD INTENDED TO DEDICATE IT TO YOU, IN A SURPRISE CEREMONY!
BRING IN THE FUTURESCOPE-RECORDER!
8

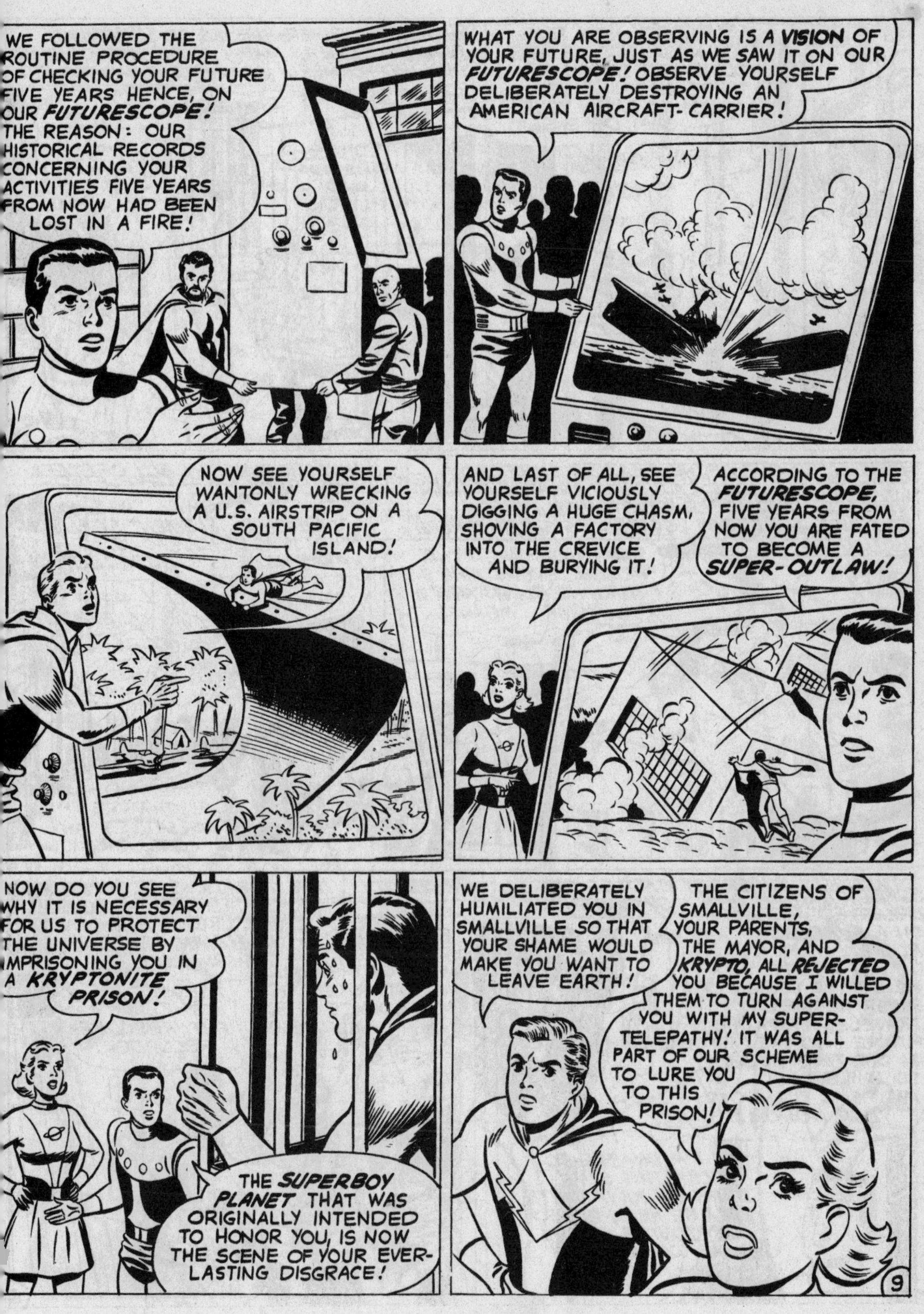
WE FOLLOWED THE ROUTINE PROCEDURE OF CHECKING YOUR FUTURE FIVE YEARS HENCE, ON OUR FUTURESCOPE! THE REASON: OUR HISTORICAL RECORDS CONCERNING YOUR ACTIVITIES FIVE YEARS FROM NOW HAD BEEN LOST IN A FIRE!
WHAT YOU ARE OBSERVING IS A VISION OF YOUR FUTURE, JUST AS WE SAW IT ON OUR FUTURESCOPE! OBSERVE YOURSELF DELIBERATELY DESTROYING AN AMERICAN AIRCRAFT-CARRIER!
NOW SEE YOURSELF WANTONLY WRECKING A U.S. AIRSTRIP ON A SOUTH PACIFIC ISLAND!
AND LAST OF ALL, SEE YOURSELF VICIOUSLY DIGGING A HUGE CHASM, SHOVING A FACTORY INTO THE CREVICE AND BURYING IT!
ACCORDING TO THE FUTURESCOPE, FIVE YEARS FROM NOW YOU ARE FATED TO BECOME A SUPER-OUTLAW!
NOW DO YOU SEE WHY IT IS NECESSARY FOR US TO PROTECT THE UNIVERSE BY IMPRISONING YOU IN A KRYPTONITE PRISON!
THE SUPERBOY PLANET THAT WAS ORIGINALLY INTENDED TO HONOR YOU, IS NOW THE SCENE OF YOUR EVER-LASTING DISGRACE!
WE DELIBERATELY HUMILIATED YOU IN SMALLVILLE SO THAT YOUR SHAME WOULD MAKE YOU WANT TO LEAVE EARTH!
THE CITIZENS OF SMALLVILLE, YOUR PARENTS, THE MAYOR, AND KRYPTO, ALL REJECTED YOU BECAUSE I WILLED THEM TO TURN AGAINST YOU WITH MY SUPER-TELEPATHY! IT WAS ALL PART OF OUR SCHEME TO LURE YOU TO THIS PRISON!
9

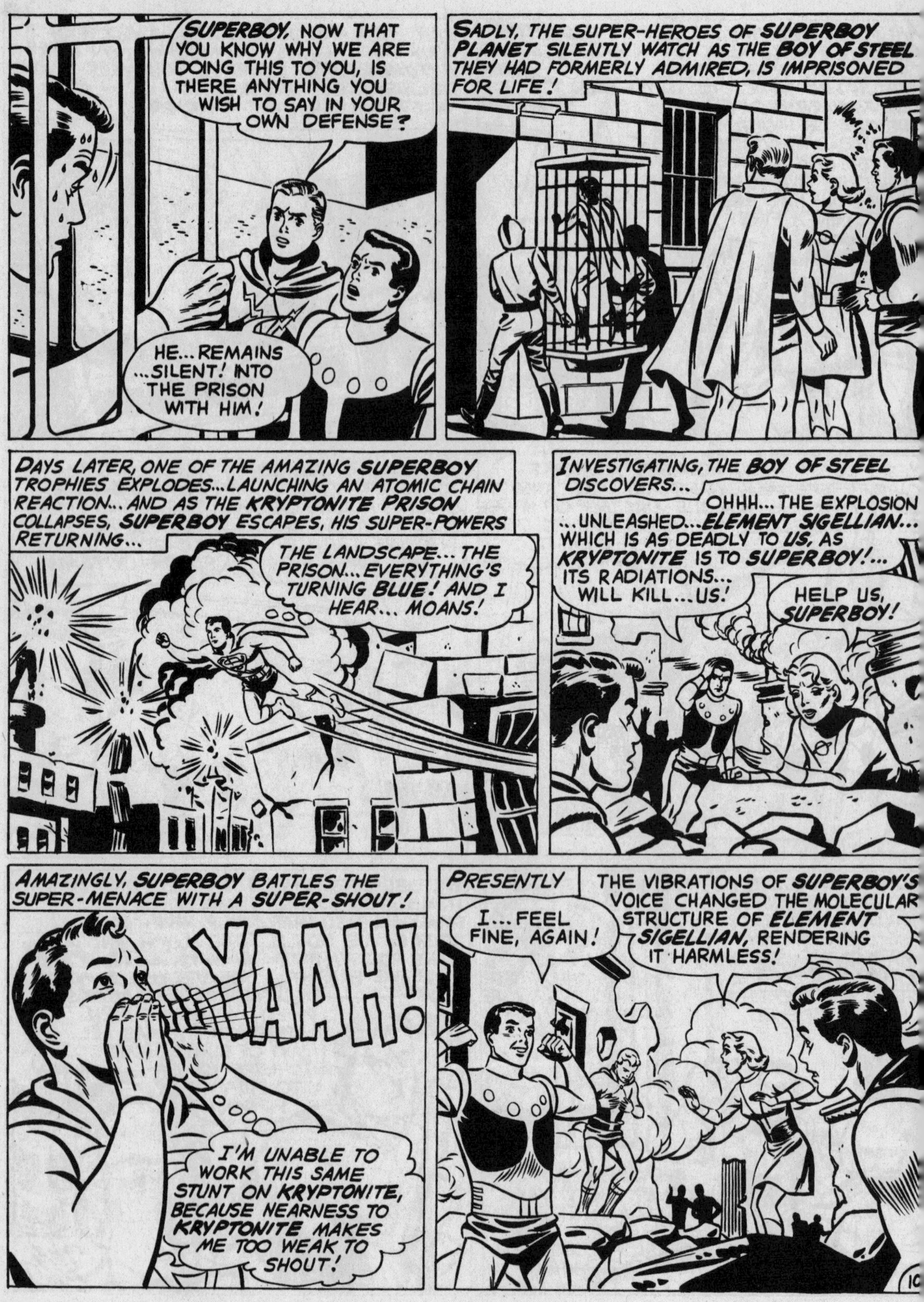
SUPERBOY, NOW THAT YOU KNOW WHY WE ARE DOING THIS TO YOU, IS THERE ANYTHING YOU WISH TO SAY IN YOUR OWN DEFENSE?
HE... REMAINS ...SILENT! INTO THE PRISON WITH HIM!
SADLY, THE SUPER-HEROES OF SUPERBOY PLANET SILENTLY WATCH AS THE BOY OF STEEL THEY HAD FORMERLY ADMIRED, IS IMPRISONED FOR LIFE!
DAYS LATER, ONE OF THE AMAZING SUPERBOY TROPHIES EXPLODES...LAUNCHING AN ATOMIC CHAIN REACTION... AND AS THE KRYPTONITE PRISON COLLAPSES, SUPERBOY ESCAPES, HIS SUPER-POWERS RETURNING...
THE LANDSCAPE... THE PRISON... EVERYTHING'S TURNING BLUE! AND I HEAR... MOANS!
INVESTIGATING, THE BOY OF STEEL DISCOVERS...
OHHH... THE EXPLOSION ...UNLEASHED...ELEMENT SIGELLIAN... WHICH IS AS DEADLY TO US, AS KRYPTONITE IS TO SUPERBOY!... ITS RADIATIONS... WILL KILL... US!
HELP US, SUPERBOY!
AMAZINGLY, SUPERBOY BATTLES THE SUPER-MENACE WITH A SUPER-SHOUT!
YAAH!
I'M UNABLE TO WORK THIS SAME STUNT ON KRYPTONITE, BECAUSE NEARNESS TO KRYPTONITE MAKES ME TOO WEAK TO SHOUT!
PRESENTLY
I... FEEL FINE, AGAIN!
THE VIBRATIONS OF SUPERBOY'S VOICE CHANGED THE MOLECULAR STRUCTURE OF ELEMENT SIGELLIAN, RENDERING IT HARMLESS!
10

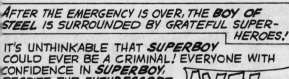

AFTER THE EMERGENCY IS OVER, THE *BOY OF STEEL* IS SURROUNDED BY GRATEFUL SUPER-HEROES!

IT'S UNTHINKABLE THAT *SUPERBOY* COULD EVER BE A CRIMINAL! EVERYONE WITH CONFIDENCE IN *SUPERBOY*, DESPITE THE *FUTURESCOPE*, SAY "AYE"! ... AYE!

AYE!

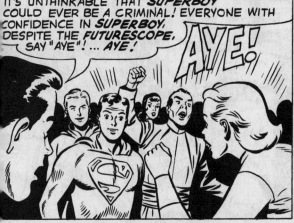

I HAVE MENTALLY PICKED UP A PUZZLING RADIO MESSAGE FROM EARTH! IT SAYS..." THE PRESIDENT OF THE UNITED STATES RELEASES *SUPERBOY* FROM HIS SECURITY OATH"!

THEN I AM FREE TO SPEAK, *NOW!*

YES, I DESTROYED AN *EMPTY* AIRCRAFT-CARRIER, THE *DESERTED* AIR-STRIP, AND THE *EMPTY* FACTORY IN A ONE-DAY MOP-UP SPREE... BUT ONLY BECAUSE THE PRESIDENT TOLD ME TO ERASE ALL TRACES OF A POISON GAS TOO HORRIBLE EVER TO BE USED! YOUR *FUTURESCOPE* PICKED UP THE SCENES AS THEY OCCURRED IN THE *PRESENT*, NOT THE *FUTURE!*

BY GOLLY... THERE IS A FLAW! THE MACHINE DID NOT WORK PROPERLY!

BUT WHY DID YOU DESTROY THOSE PARTICULAR THINGS?

THE FACTORY *MANUFACTURED* THE GAS... IT WAS *TRANSPORTED* FROM THE AIR-STRIP... TO THE WARSHIP! THE PRESIDENT WANTED EVERY TRACE OF THE GAS WIPED OUT, TO FOIL FOREIGN SPIES!

HAPPY THAT *SUPERBOY* HAS BEEN CLEARED, SEVERAL OF THE SUPER-HEROES QUICKLY SPEED TO EARTH AND BACK, ON A SPECIAL MISSION...

MA AND PA KENT! AND *KRYPTO!* GOSH, I'M GLAD YOU WEREN'T REALLY PEEVED AT ME!

SMALLVILLE KNOWS THE TRUTH NOW AND EVERYONE WANTS YOU BACK!

BUT BEFORE *SUPERBOY* RETURNS TO EARTH, THE VERY UNIVERSE ROCKS AS THE SUPER-HEROES OF *SUPERBOY* PLANET LOUDLY CHORUS...

THREE CHEERS FOR SUPERBOY!

The End.

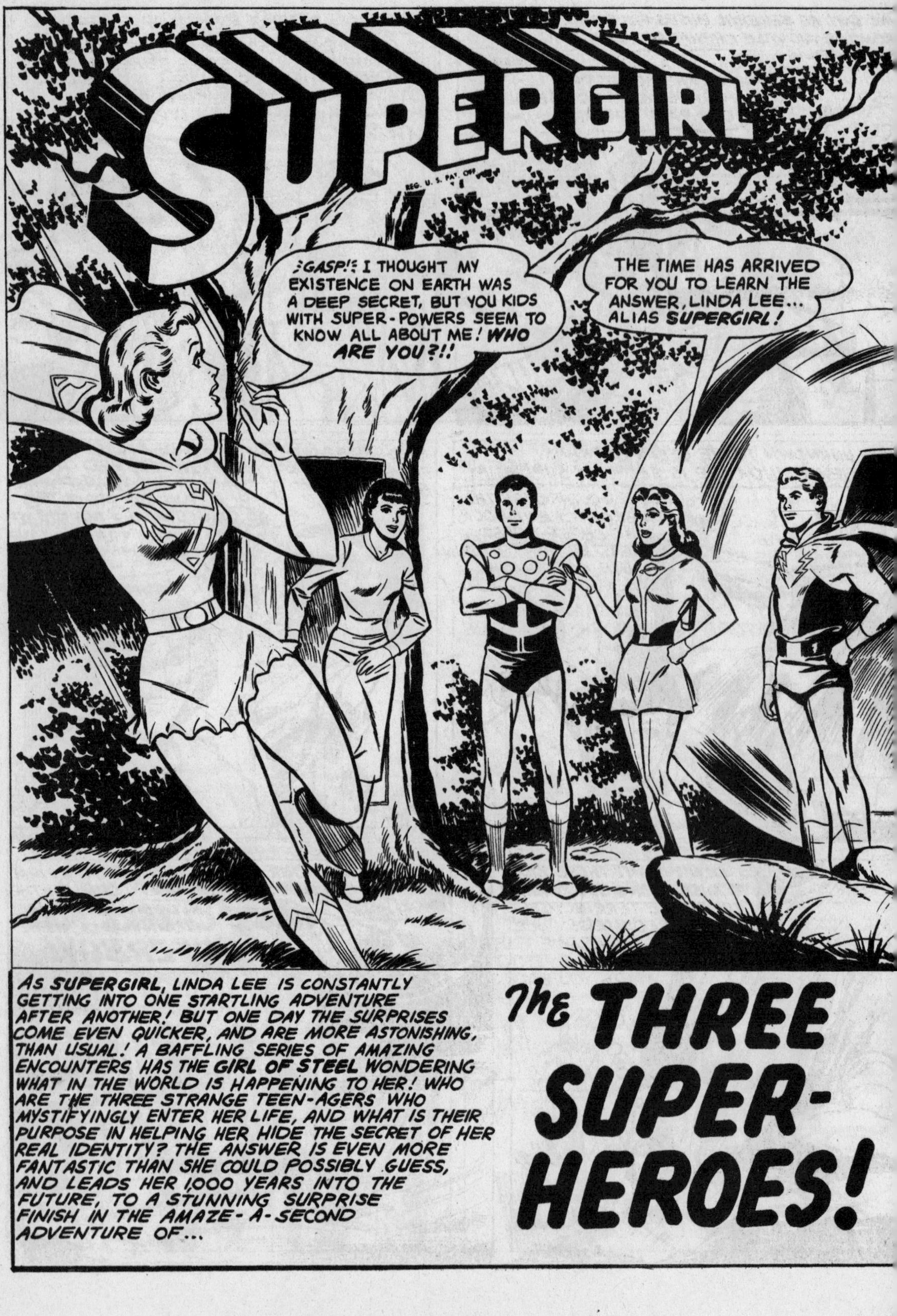
SUPERGIRL
REG. U. S. PAT. OFF.
GASP! I THOUGHT MY EXISTENCE ON EARTH WAS A DEEP SECRET, BUT YOU KIDS WITH SUPER-POWERS SEEM TO KNOW ALL ABOUT ME! WHO ARE YOU?!!
THE TIME HAS ARRIVED FOR YOU TO LEARN THE ANSWER, LINDA LEE... ALIAS SUPERGIRL!
AS SUPERGIRL, LINDA LEE IS CONSTANTLY GETTING INTO ONE STARTLING ADVENTURE AFTER ANOTHER! BUT ONE DAY THE SURPRISES COME EVEN QUICKER, AND ARE MORE ASTONISHING, THAN USUAL! A BAFFLING SERIES OF AMAZING ENCOUNTERS HAS THE GIRL OF STEEL WONDERING WHAT IN THE WORLD IS HAPPENING TO HER! WHO ARE THE THREE STRANGE TEEN-AGERS WHO MYSTIFYINGLY ENTER HER LIFE, AND WHAT IS THEIR PURPOSE IN HELPING HER HIDE THE SECRET OF HER REAL IDENTITY? THE ANSWER IS EVEN MORE FANTASTIC THAN SHE COULD POSSIBLY GUESS, AND LEADS HER 1,000 YEARS INTO THE FUTURE, TO A STUNNING SURPRISE FINISH IN THE AMAZE-A-SECOND ADVENTURE OF...
THE THREE SUPER-HEROES!

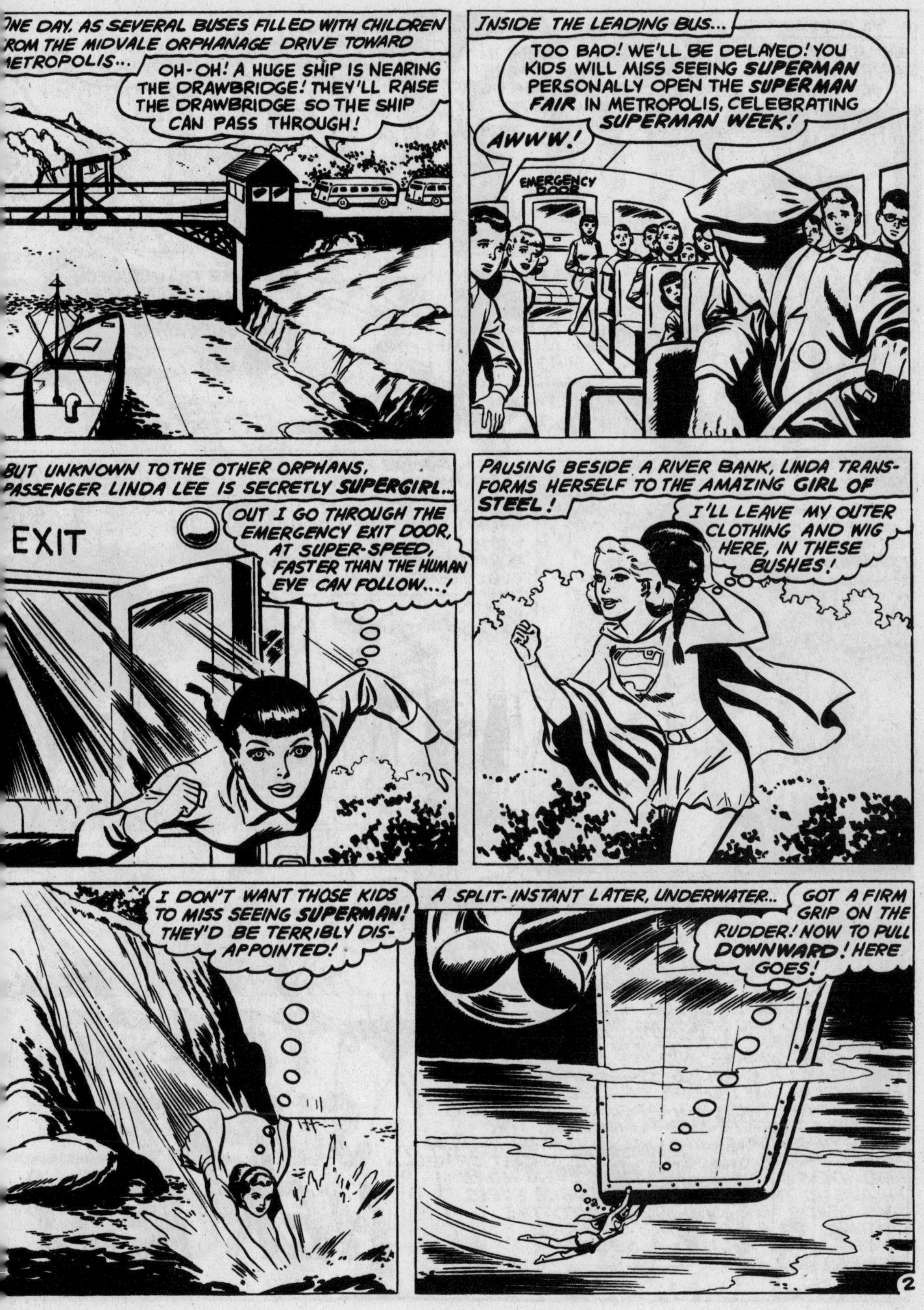
ONE DAY, AS SEVERAL BUSES FILLED WITH CHILDREN FROM THE MIDVALE ORPHANAGE DRIVE TOWARD METROPOLIS...
OH-OH! A HUGE SHIP IS NEARING THE DRAWBRIDGE! THEY'LL RAISE THE DRAWBRIDGE SO THE SHIP CAN PASS THROUGH!
INSIDE THE LEADING BUS...
TOO BAD! WE'LL BE DELAYED! YOU KIDS WILL MISS SEEING SUPERMAN PERSONALLY OPEN THE SUPERMAN FAIR IN METROPOLIS, CELEBRATING SUPERMAN WEEK!
AWWW!
EMERGENCY DOOR
BUT UNKNOWN TO THE OTHER ORPHANS, PASSENGER LINDA LEE IS SECRETLY SUPERGIRL...
EXIT
OUT I GO THROUGH THE EMERGENCY EXIT DOOR, AT SUPER-SPEED, FASTER THAN THE HUMAN EYE CAN FOLLOW...!
PAUSING BESIDE A RIVER BANK, LINDA TRANSFORMS HERSELF TO THE AMAZING GIRL OF STEEL!
I'LL LEAVE MY OUTER CLOTHING AND WIG HERE, IN THESE BUSHES!
I DON'T WANT THOSE KIDS TO MISS SEEING SUPERMAN! THEY'D BE TERRIBLY DISAPPOINTED!
A SPLIT-INSTANT LATER, UNDERWATER...
GOT A FIRM GRIP ON THE RUDDER! NOW TO PULL DOWNWARD! HERE GOES!
2

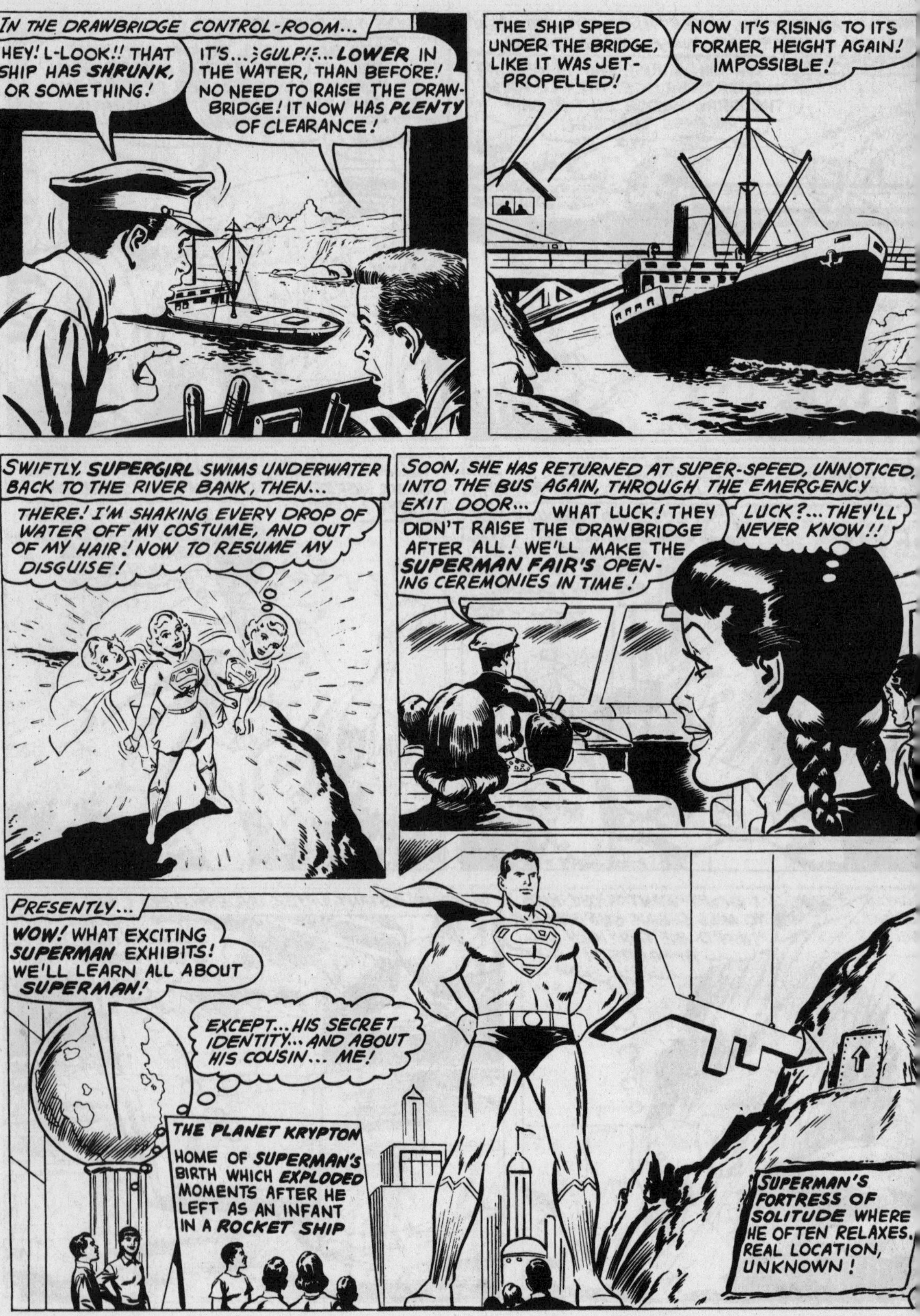
IN THE DRAWBRIDGE CONTROL-ROOM...
HEY! L-LOOK!! THAT SHIP HAS SHRUNK, OR SOMETHING!
IT'S... GULP!... LOWER IN THE WATER, THAN BEFORE! NO NEED TO RAISE THE DRAWBRIDGE! IT NOW HAS PLENTY OF CLEARANCE!
THE SHIP SPED UNDER THE BRIDGE, LIKE IT WAS JET-PROPELLED!
NOW IT'S RISING TO ITS FORMER HEIGHT AGAIN! IMPOSSIBLE!
SWIFTLY, SUPERGIRL SWIMS UNDERWATER BACK TO THE RIVER BANK, THEN...
THERE! I'M SHAKING EVERY DROP OF WATER OFF MY COSTUME, AND OUT OF MY HAIR! NOW TO RESUME MY DISGUISE!
SOON, SHE HAS RETURNED AT SUPER-SPEED, UNNOTICED, INTO THE BUS AGAIN, THROUGH THE EMERGENCY EXIT DOOR...
WHAT LUCK! THEY DIDN'T RAISE THE DRAWBRIDGE AFTER ALL! WE'LL MAKE THE SUPERMAN FAIR'S OPENING CEREMONIES IN TIME!
LUCK?... THEY'LL NEVER KNOW!!
PRESENTLY...
WOW! WHAT EXCITING SUPERMAN EXHIBITS! WE'LL LEARN ALL ABOUT SUPERMAN!
EXCEPT... HIS SECRET IDENTITY... AND ABOUT HIS COUSIN... ME!
THE PLANET KRYPTON
HOME OF SUPERMAN'S BIRTH WHICH EXPLODED MOMENTS AFTER HE LEFT AS AN INFANT IN A ROCKET SHIP
SUPERMAN'S FORTRESS OF SOLITUDE WHERE HE OFTEN RELAXES. REAL LOCATION, UNKNOWN!

THANKS TO *SUPERGIRL'S* DRAWBRIDGE FEAT, THE ORPHANS ARE IN TIME TO SEE MIGHTY *SUPERMAN* STAGE AN AMAZING EXHIBITION...

BILLIONS OF VOLTS ARE PASSING THROUGH MY BODY... ENOUGH TO DESTROY AN ORDINARY LIVING THING!

HOLY COW! CAN *HE* TAKE IT! WHEW!

OFF FLIES *SUPERMAN* AT THE CONCLUSION OF THE AMAZING DEMONSTRATION...

SO LONG, EVERYONE! AND THANKS AGAIN FOR HONORING ME WITH THIS *FAIR!*

HE'S WINKING AT ME! WE HAVE A *SUPER-SECRET,* ALL OUR OWN!

BUT AFTER THE *MAN OF STEEL* STREAKS OFF...

THE CONTROLS OF THIS CYCLOTRON ARE JAMMED, AND THE VOLTAGE IS INCREASING DANGEROUSLY!

UH-OH! I'VE GOT TO GO INTO ACTION AS *SUPERGIRL* TO SAVE LIVES, EVEN IF IT BETRAYS MY SECRET IDENTITY!

GROAN!... I PROMISED *SUPERMAN* NEVER TO REVEAL I AM *SUPERGIRL,* SO I CAN BE HIS SECRET WEAPON IN A REAL EMERGENCY! YET I CAN'T STAND BY AND PERMIT PEOPLE TO GET KILLED!

BUT SUDDENLY A HANDSOME YOUTH WHISPERS TO LINDA...

LET ME HANDLE THIS, *SUPERGIRL!*

??!... ELECTRIC BOLTS ARE FLASHING FROM HIS HANDS, DESTROYING THE FUSE BOX! THE DANGEROUS ELECTRICITY DISPLAY HAS STOPPED!

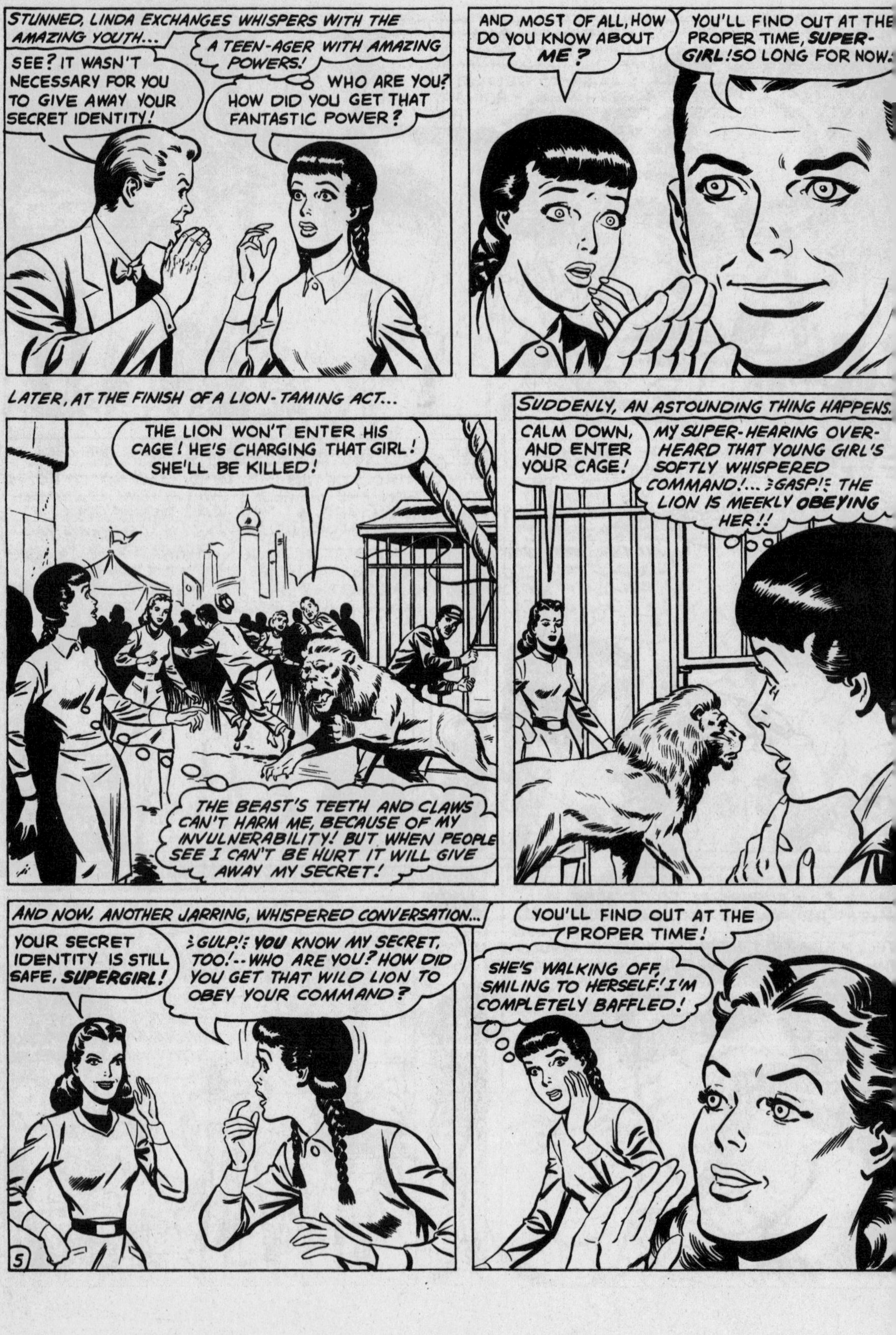
STUNNED, LINDA EXCHANGES WHISPERS WITH THE AMAZING YOUTH...
SEE? IT WASN'T NECESSARY FOR YOU TO GIVE AWAY YOUR SECRET IDENTITY!
A TEEN-AGER WITH AMAZING POWERS!
WHO ARE YOU? HOW DID YOU GET THAT FANTASTIC POWER?
AND MOST OF ALL, HOW DO YOU KNOW ABOUT ME?
YOU'LL FIND OUT AT THE PROPER TIME, SUPER-GIRL! SO LONG FOR NOW.
LATER, AT THE FINISH OF A LION-TAMING ACT...
THE LION WON'T ENTER HIS CAGE! HE'S CHARGING THAT GIRL! SHE'LL BE KILLED!
THE BEAST'S TEETH AND CLAWS CAN'T HARM ME, BECAUSE OF MY INVULNERABILITY! BUT WHEN PEOPLE SEE I CAN'T BE HURT IT WILL GIVE AWAY MY SECRET!
SUDDENLY, AN ASTOUNDING THING HAPPENS.
CALM DOWN, AND ENTER YOUR CAGE!
MY SUPER-HEARING OVER-HEARD THAT YOUNG GIRL'S SOFTLY WHISPERED COMMAND!... ;GASP!; THE LION IS MEEKLY OBEYING HER!!
AND NOW, ANOTHER JARRING, WHISPERED CONVERSATION...
YOUR SECRET IDENTITY IS STILL SAFE, SUPERGIRL!
;GULP!; YOU KNOW MY SECRET, TOO!--WHO ARE YOU? HOW DID YOU GET THAT WILD LION TO OBEY YOUR COMMAND?
YOU'LL FIND OUT AT THE PROPER TIME!
SHE'S WALKING OFF, SMILING TO HERSELF! I'M COMPLETELY BAFFLED!
5

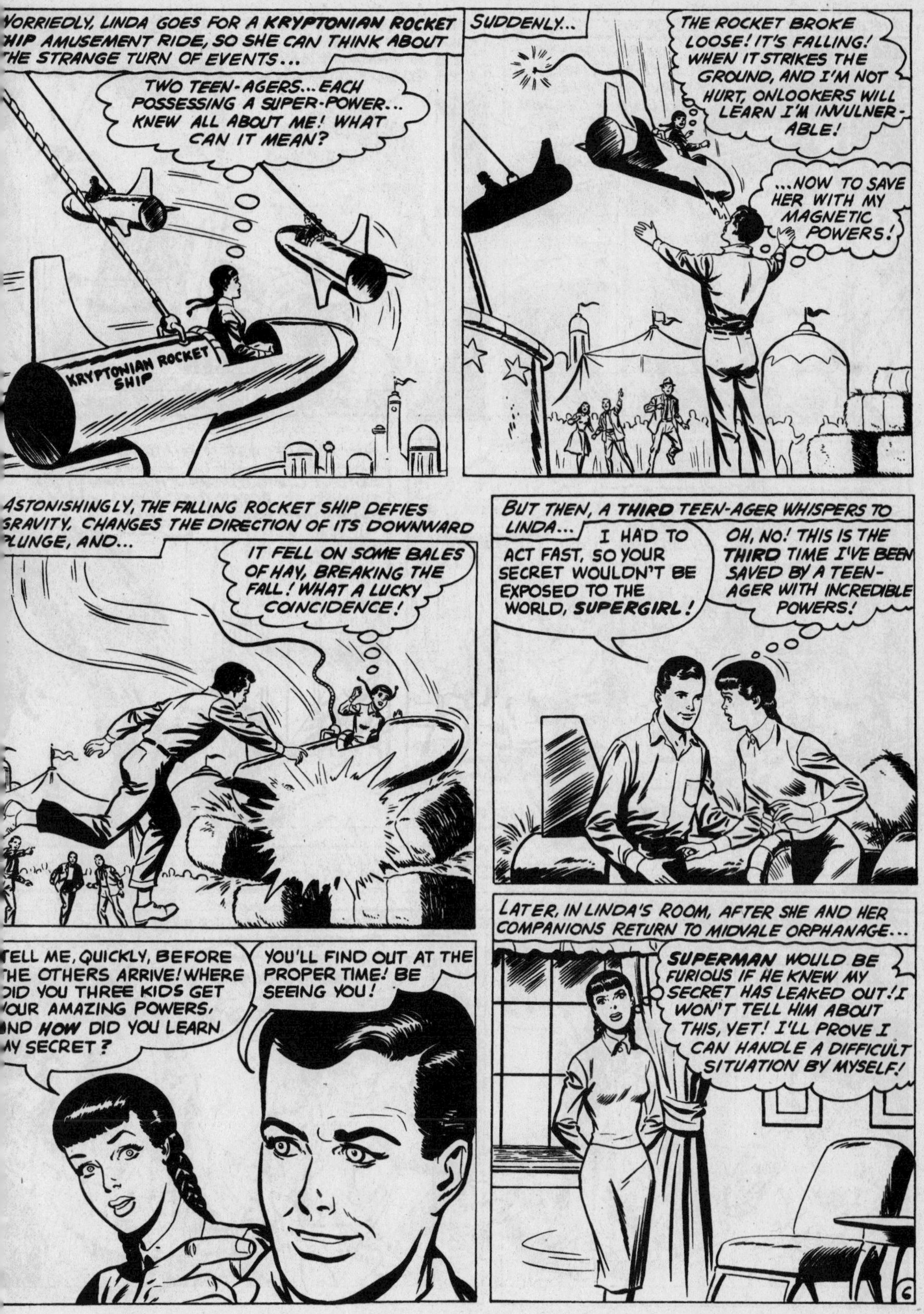
WORRIEDLY, LINDA GOES FOR A KRYPTONIAN ROCKET SHIP AMUSEMENT RIDE, SO SHE CAN THINK ABOUT THE STRANGE TURN OF EVENTS...
TWO TEEN-AGERS...EACH POSSESSING A SUPER-POWER... KNEW ALL ABOUT ME! WHAT CAN IT MEAN?
KRYPTONIAN ROCKET SHIP
SUDDENLY...
THE ROCKET BROKE LOOSE! IT'S FALLING! WHEN IT STRIKES THE GROUND, AND I'M NOT HURT, ONLOOKERS WILL LEARN I'M INVULNERABLE!
...NOW TO SAVE HER WITH MY MAGNETIC POWERS!
ASTONISHINGLY, THE FALLING ROCKET SHIP DEFIES GRAVITY, CHANGES THE DIRECTION OF ITS DOWNWARD PLUNGE, AND...
IT FELL ON SOME BALES OF HAY, BREAKING THE FALL! WHAT A LUCKY COINCIDENCE!
BUT THEN, A THIRD TEEN-AGER WHISPERS TO LINDA...
I HAD TO ACT FAST, SO YOUR SECRET WOULDN'T BE EXPOSED TO THE WORLD, SUPERGIRL!
OH, NO! THIS IS THE THIRD TIME I'VE BEEN SAVED BY A TEEN-AGER WITH INCREDIBLE POWERS!
TELL ME, QUICKLY, BEFORE THE OTHERS ARRIVE! WHERE DID YOU THREE KIDS GET YOUR AMAZING POWERS, AND HOW DID YOU LEARN MY SECRET?
YOU'LL FIND OUT AT THE PROPER TIME! BE SEEING YOU!
LATER, IN LINDA'S ROOM, AFTER SHE AND HER COMPANIONS RETURN TO MIDVALE ORPHANAGE...
SUPERMAN WOULD BE FURIOUS IF HE KNEW MY SECRET HAS LEAKED OUT! I WON'T TELL HIM ABOUT THIS, YET! I'LL PROVE I CAN HANDLE A DIFFICULT SITUATION BY MYSELF!
6

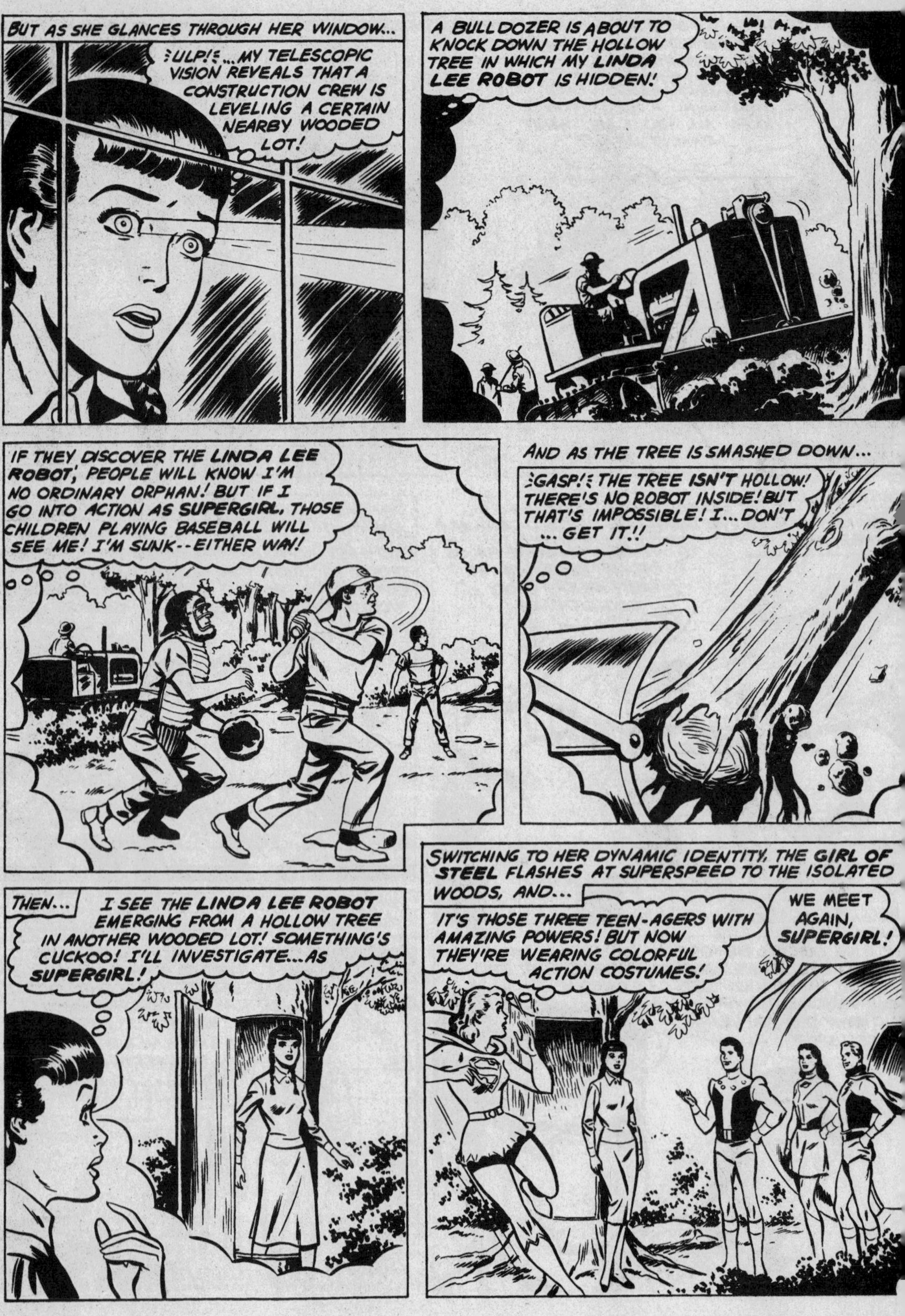
BUT AS SHE GLANCES THROUGH HER WINDOW...
ULP!...MY TELESCOPIC VISION REVEALS THAT A CONSTRUCTION CREW IS LEVELING A CERTAIN NEARBY WOODED LOT!
A BULLDOZER IS ABOUT TO KNOCK DOWN THE HOLLOW TREE IN WHICH MY LINDA LEE ROBOT IS HIDDEN!
IF THEY DISCOVER THE LINDA LEE ROBOT, PEOPLE WILL KNOW I'M NO ORDINARY ORPHAN! BUT IF I GO INTO ACTION AS SUPERGIRL, THOSE CHILDREN PLAYING BASEBALL WILL SEE ME! I'M SUNK--EITHER WAY!
AND AS THE TREE IS SMASHED DOWN...
GASP! THE TREE ISN'T HOLLOW! THERE'S NO ROBOT INSIDE! BUT THAT'S IMPOSSIBLE! I...DON'T ...GET IT!!
THEN...
I SEE THE LINDA LEE ROBOT EMERGING FROM A HOLLOW TREE IN ANOTHER WOODED LOT! SOMETHING'S CUCKOO! I'LL INVESTIGATE...AS SUPERGIRL!
SWITCHING TO HER DYNAMIC IDENTITY, THE GIRL OF STEEL FLASHES AT SUPERSPEED TO THE ISOLATED WOODS, AND...
IT'S THOSE THREE TEEN-AGERS WITH AMAZING POWERS! BUT NOW THEY'RE WEARING COLORFUL ACTION COSTUMES!
WE MEET AGAIN, SUPERGIRL!

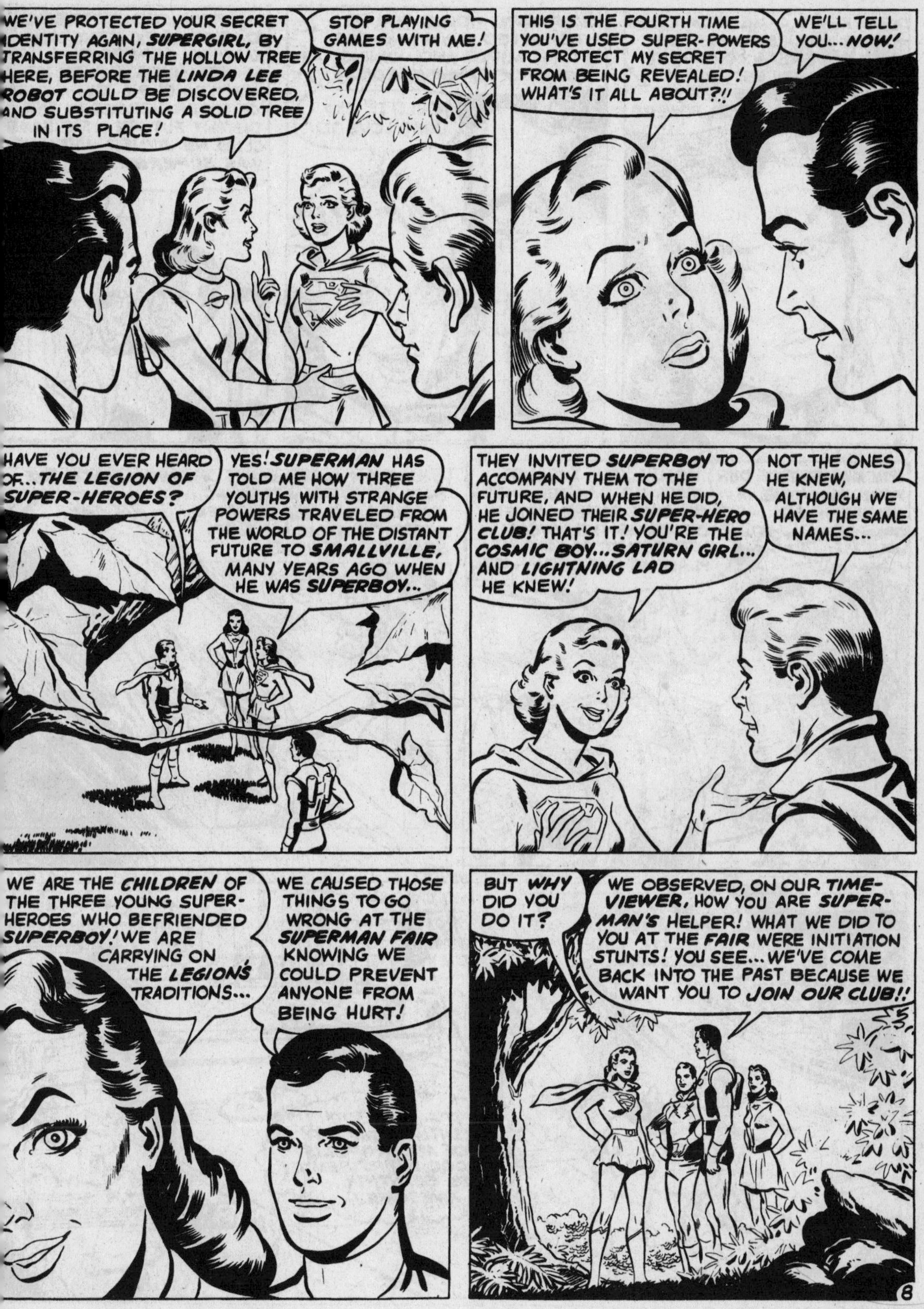
WE'VE PROTECTED YOUR SECRET IDENTITY AGAIN, SUPERGIRL, BY TRANSFERRING THE HOLLOW TREE HERE, BEFORE THE LINDA LEE ROBOT COULD BE DISCOVERED, AND SUBSTITUTING A SOLID TREE IN ITS PLACE!
STOP PLAYING GAMES WITH ME!
THIS IS THE FOURTH TIME YOU'VE USED SUPER-POWERS TO PROTECT MY SECRET FROM BEING REVEALED! WHAT'S IT ALL ABOUT?!!
WE'LL TELL YOU... NOW!
HAVE YOU EVER HEARD OF... THE LEGION OF SUPER-HEROES?
YES! SUPERMAN HAS TOLD ME HOW THREE YOUTHS WITH STRANGE POWERS TRAVELED FROM THE WORLD OF THE DISTANT FUTURE TO SMALLVILLE, MANY YEARS AGO WHEN HE WAS SUPERBOY...
THEY INVITED SUPERBOY TO ACCOMPANY THEM TO THE FUTURE, AND WHEN HE DID, HE JOINED THEIR SUPER-HERO CLUB! THAT'S IT! YOU'RE THE COSMIC BOY... SATURN GIRL... AND LIGHTNING LAD HE KNEW!
NOT THE ONES HE KNEW, ALTHOUGH WE HAVE THE SAME NAMES...
WE ARE THE CHILDREN OF THE THREE YOUNG SUPER-HEROES WHO BEFRIENDED SUPERBOY! WE ARE CARRYING ON THE LEGION'S TRADITIONS...
WE CAUSED THOSE THINGS TO GO WRONG AT THE SUPERMAN FAIR KNOWING WE COULD PREVENT ANYONE FROM BEING HURT!
BUT WHY DID YOU DO IT?
WE OBSERVED, ON OUR TIME-VIEWER, HOW YOU ARE SUPERMAN'S HELPER! WHAT WE DID TO YOU AT THE FAIR WERE INITIATION STUNTS! YOU SEE... WE'VE COME BACK INTO THE PAST BECAUSE WE WANT YOU TO JOIN OUR CLUB!!
8

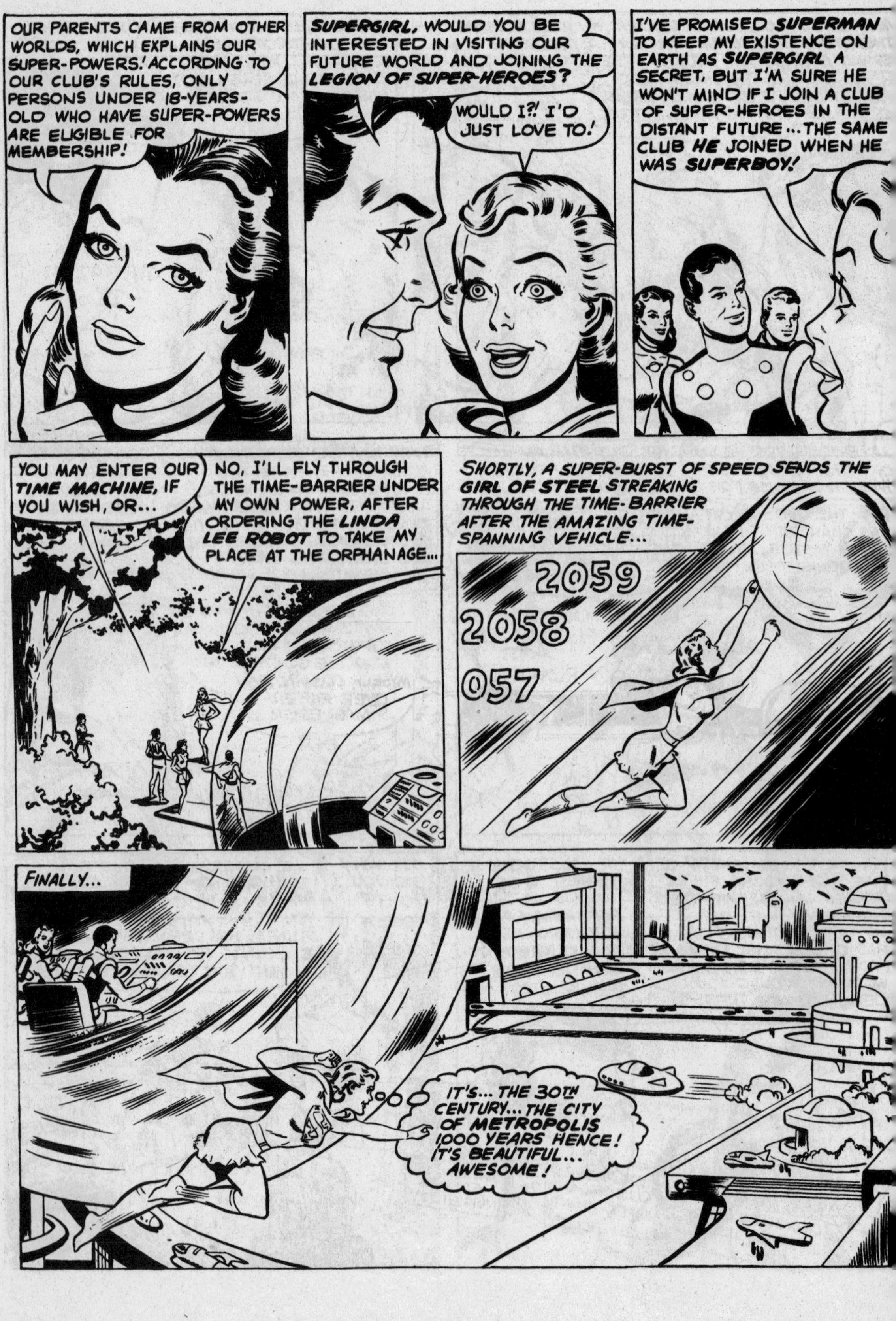
OUR PARENTS CAME FROM OTHER WORLDS, WHICH EXPLAINS OUR SUPER-POWERS! ACCORDING TO OUR CLUB'S RULES, ONLY PERSONS UNDER 18-YEARS-OLD WHO HAVE SUPER-POWERS ARE ELIGIBLE FOR MEMBERSHIP!
SUPERGIRL, WOULD YOU BE INTERESTED IN VISITING OUR FUTURE WORLD AND JOINING THE LEGION OF SUPER-HEROES?
WOULD I?! I'D JUST LOVE TO!
I'VE PROMISED SUPERMAN TO KEEP MY EXISTENCE ON EARTH AS SUPERGIRL A SECRET, BUT I'M SURE HE WON'T MIND IF I JOIN A CLUB OF SUPER-HEROES IN THE DISTANT FUTURE... THE SAME CLUB HE JOINED WHEN HE WAS SUPERBOY!
YOU MAY ENTER OUR TIME MACHINE, IF YOU WISH, OR...
NO, I'LL FLY THROUGH THE TIME-BARRIER UNDER MY OWN POWER, AFTER ORDERING THE LINDA LEE ROBOT TO TAKE MY PLACE AT THE ORPHANAGE...
SHORTLY, A SUPER-BURST OF SPEED SENDS THE GIRL OF STEEL STREAKING THROUGH THE TIME-BARRIER AFTER THE AMAZING TIME-SPANNING VEHICLE...
2059
2058
057
FINALLY...
IT'S... THE 30TH CENTURY... THE CITY OF METROPOLIS 1000 YEARS HENCE! IT'S BEAUTIFUL... AWESOME!

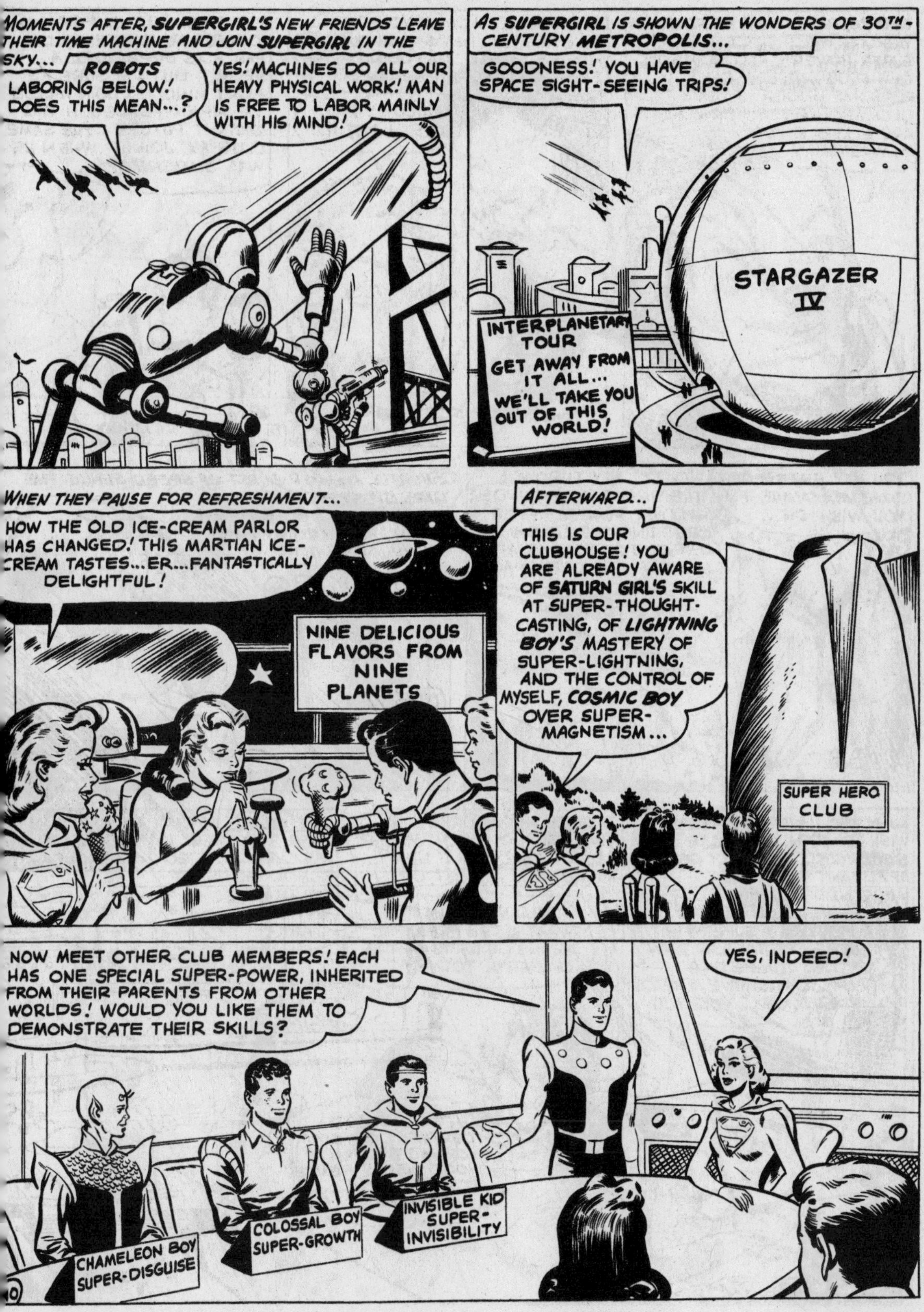
MOMENTS AFTER, SUPERGIRL'S NEW FRIENDS LEAVE THEIR TIME MACHINE AND JOIN SUPERGIRL IN THE SKY...
ROBOTS LABORING BELOW! DOES THIS MEAN...?
YES! MACHINES DO ALL OUR HEAVY PHYSICAL WORK! MAN IS FREE TO LABOR MAINLY WITH HIS MIND!
AS SUPERGIRL IS SHOWN THE WONDERS OF 30TH-CENTURY METROPOLIS...
GOODNESS! YOU HAVE SPACE SIGHT-SEEING TRIPS!
STARGAZER IV
INTERPLANETARY TOUR
GET AWAY FROM IT ALL... WE'LL TAKE YOU OUT OF THIS WORLD!
WHEN THEY PAUSE FOR REFRESHMENT...
HOW THE OLD ICE-CREAM PARLOR HAS CHANGED! THIS MARTIAN ICE-CREAM TASTES...ER...FANTASTICALLY DELIGHTFUL!
NINE DELICIOUS FLAVORS FROM NINE PLANETS
AFTERWARD...
THIS IS OUR CLUBHOUSE! YOU ARE ALREADY AWARE OF SATURN GIRL'S SKILL AT SUPER-THOUGHT-CASTING, OF LIGHTNING BOY'S MASTERY OF SUPER-LIGHTNING, AND THE CONTROL OF MYSELF, COSMIC BOY OVER SUPER-MAGNETISM...
SUPER HERO CLUB
NOW MEET OTHER CLUB MEMBERS! EACH HAS ONE SPECIAL SUPER-POWER, INHERITED FROM THEIR PARENTS FROM OTHER WORLDS! WOULD YOU LIKE THEM TO DEMONSTRATE THEIR SKILLS?
YES, INDEED!
CHAMELEON BOY SUPER-DISGUISE
COLOSSAL BOY SUPER-GROWTH
INVISIBLE KID SUPER-INVISIBILITY

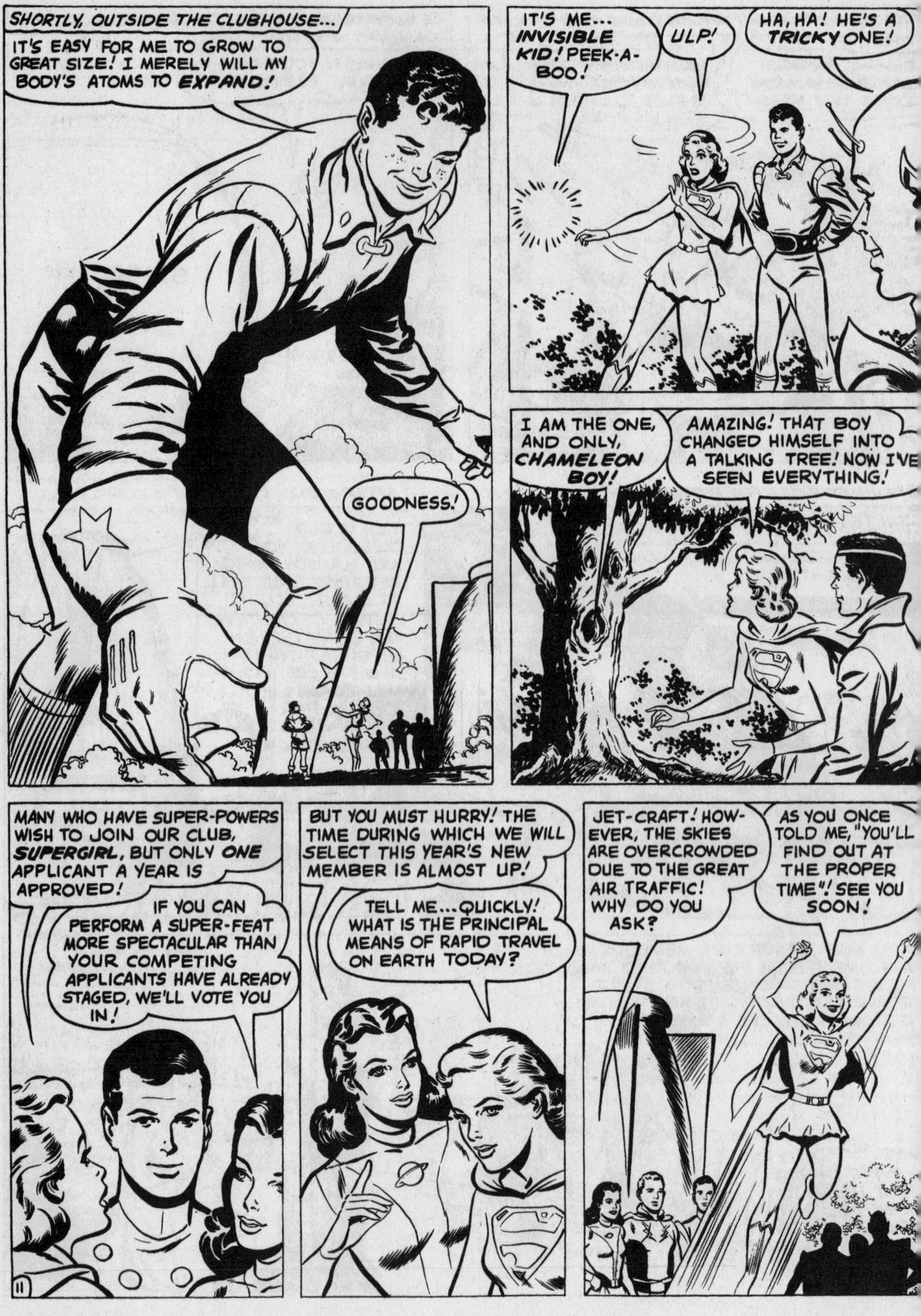
SHORTLY, OUTSIDE THE CLUBHOUSE...
IT'S EASY FOR ME TO GROW TO GREAT SIZE! I MERELY WILL MY BODY'S ATOMS TO EXPAND!
GOODNESS!
IT'S ME... INVISIBLE KID! PEEK-A-BOO!
ULP!
HA, HA! HE'S A TRICKY ONE!
I AM THE ONE, AND ONLY, CHAMELEON BOY!
AMAZING! THAT BOY CHANGED HIMSELF INTO A TALKING TREE! NOW I'VE SEEN EVERYTHING!
MANY WHO HAVE SUPER-POWERS WISH TO JOIN OUR CLUB, SUPERGIRL, BUT ONLY ONE APPLICANT A YEAR IS APPROVED!
IF YOU CAN PERFORM A SUPER-FEAT MORE SPECTACULAR THAN YOUR COMPETING APPLICANTS HAVE ALREADY STAGED, WE'LL VOTE YOU IN!
11
BUT YOU MUST HURRY! THE TIME DURING WHICH WE WILL SELECT THIS YEAR'S NEW MEMBER IS ALMOST UP!
TELL ME...QUICKLY! WHAT IS THE PRINCIPAL MEANS OF RAPID TRAVEL ON EARTH TODAY?
JET-CRAFT! HOW-EVER, THE SKIES ARE OVERCROWDED DUE TO THE GREAT AIR TRAFFIC! WHY DO YOU ASK?
AS YOU ONCE TOLD ME, "YOU'LL FIND OUT AT THE PROPER TIME"! SEE YOU SOON!

...INTO ACTION STREAKS THE MIGHTIEST MAID OF ALL TIME...

SHE'S DIGGING DOWN INTO THE GROUND!

I'LL BET SHE'S UP TO SOMETHING *SUPER-TERRIFIC!*

THROUGH THE EARTH BURROWS *SUPERGIRL*...

AS I DIG, I'LL LINE THE WALLS WITH ROCKS THAT ARE FUSED TOGETHER WITH THE SUPER-FRICTION CAUSED BY MY HANDS MOVING SUPER-SWIFTLY!

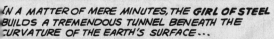

IN A MATTER OF MERE MINUTES, THE *GIRL OF STEEL* BUILDS A TREMENDOUS TUNNEL BENEATH THE CURVATURE OF THE EARTH'S SURFACE...

I WAS CAREFUL NOT TO DIG TOO DEEP, SO THAT I DIDN'T ENCOUNTER ANY MOLTEN, SUPER-HOT AREAS!

WHEN THE ASTOUNDING PROJECT IS COMPLETED, AND SHE REJOINS THE SUPER-HEROES...

NOW SOME OF THE PLANET'S HEAVY TRAFFIC CAN BE DIVERTED INTO THE SHORT-CUT, TRANS-EARTH TUNNEL I BUILT! AM I ACCEPTED INTO THE *LEGION* NOW?

NO! WE HAVE CHOSEN *SOMEONE ELSE* BECAUSE YOU ARE *OVER* OUR CLUB'S 18-YEAR-OLD AGE LIMIT!

YOU MUST BE JOKING! I'M ONLY FIFTEEN YEARS OLD! I...OH-OH! M-MY REFLECTION ON THE WALL OF THAT GLASS BUILDING I...!

SOMETHING HAS MYSTERIOUSLY AGED YOU FROM A *SUPER-GIRL* INTO...A *SUPERWOMAN!*

12

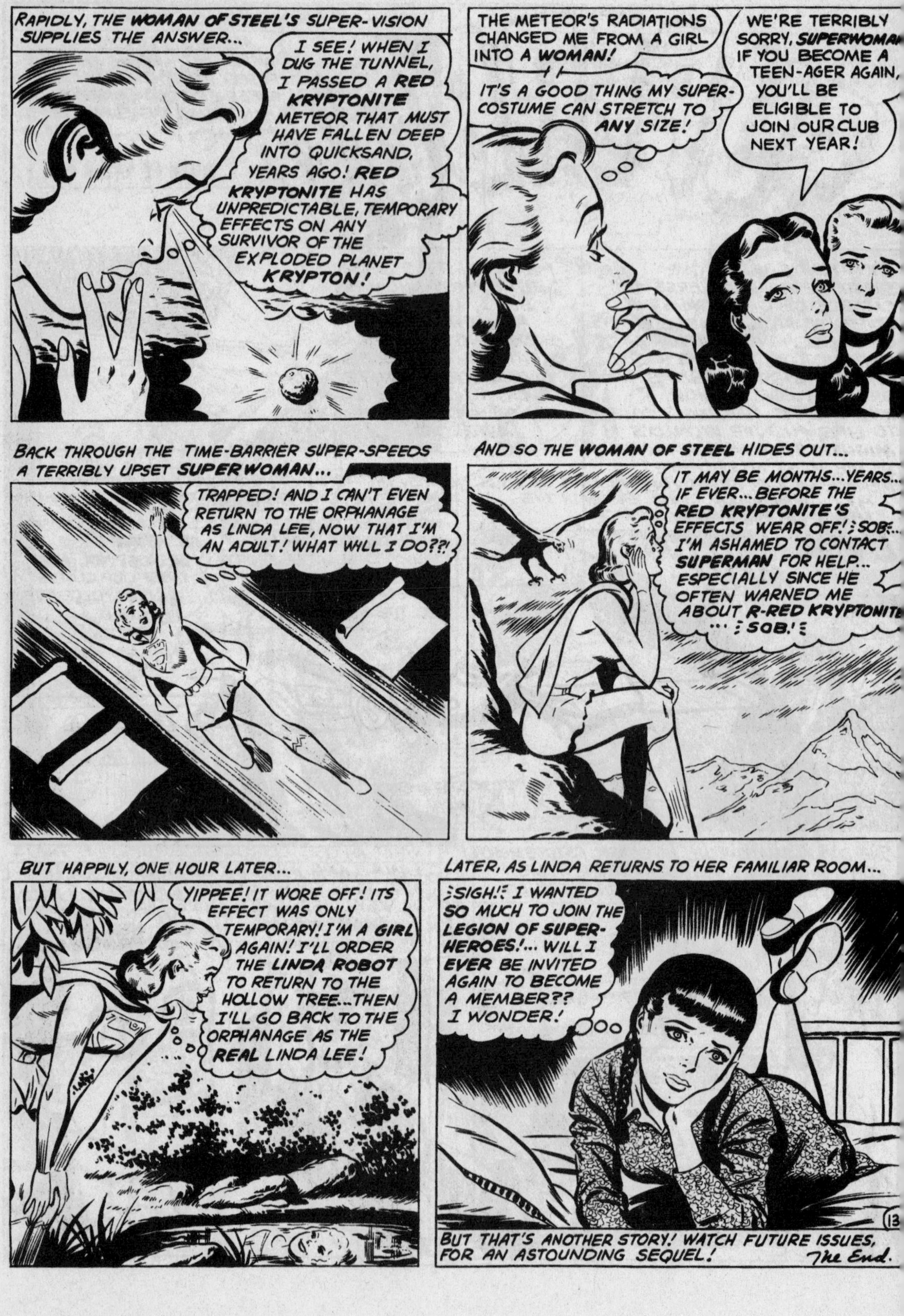
RAPIDLY, THE WOMAN OF STEEL'S SUPER-VISION SUPPLIES THE ANSWER...
I SEE! WHEN I DUG THE TUNNEL, I PASSED A RED KRYPTONITE METEOR THAT MUST HAVE FALLEN DEEP INTO QUICKSAND, YEARS AGO! RED KRYPTONITE HAS UNPREDICTABLE, TEMPORARY EFFECTS ON ANY SURVIVOR OF THE EXPLODED PLANET KRYPTON!
THE METEOR'S RADIATIONS CHANGED ME FROM A GIRL INTO A WOMAN!
IT'S A GOOD THING MY SUPER-COSTUME CAN STRETCH TO ANY SIZE!
WE'RE TERRIBLY SORRY, SUPERWOMA... IF YOU BECOME A TEEN-AGER AGAIN, YOU'LL BE ELIGIBLE TO JOIN OUR CLUB NEXT YEAR!
BACK THROUGH THE TIME-BARRIER SUPER-SPEEDS A TERRIBLY UPSET SUPERWOMAN...
TRAPPED! AND I CAN'T EVEN RETURN TO THE ORPHANAGE AS LINDA LEE, NOW THAT I'M AN ADULT! WHAT WILL I DO??!
AND SO THE WOMAN OF STEEL HIDES OUT...
IT MAY BE MONTHS...YEARS... IF EVER...BEFORE THE RED KRYPTONITE'S EFFECTS WEAR OFF! :SOB:... I'M ASHAMED TO CONTACT SUPERMAN FOR HELP... ESPECIALLY SINCE HE OFTEN WARNED ME ABOUT R-RED KRYPTONITE ... :SOB!:
BUT HAPPILY, ONE HOUR LATER...
YIPPEE! IT WORE OFF! ITS EFFECT WAS ONLY TEMPORARY! I'M A GIRL AGAIN! I'LL ORDER THE LINDA ROBOT TO RETURN TO THE HOLLOW TREE...THEN I'LL GO BACK TO THE ORPHANAGE AS THE REAL LINDA LEE!
LATER, AS LINDA RETURNS TO HER FAMILIAR ROOM...
:SIGH!: I WANTED SO MUCH TO JOIN THE LEGION OF SUPER-HEROES!... WILL I EVER BE INVITED AGAIN TO BECOME A MEMBER?? I WONDER!
13
BUT THAT'S ANOTHER STORY! WATCH FUTURE ISSUES, FOR AN ASTOUNDING SEQUEL!
The End.

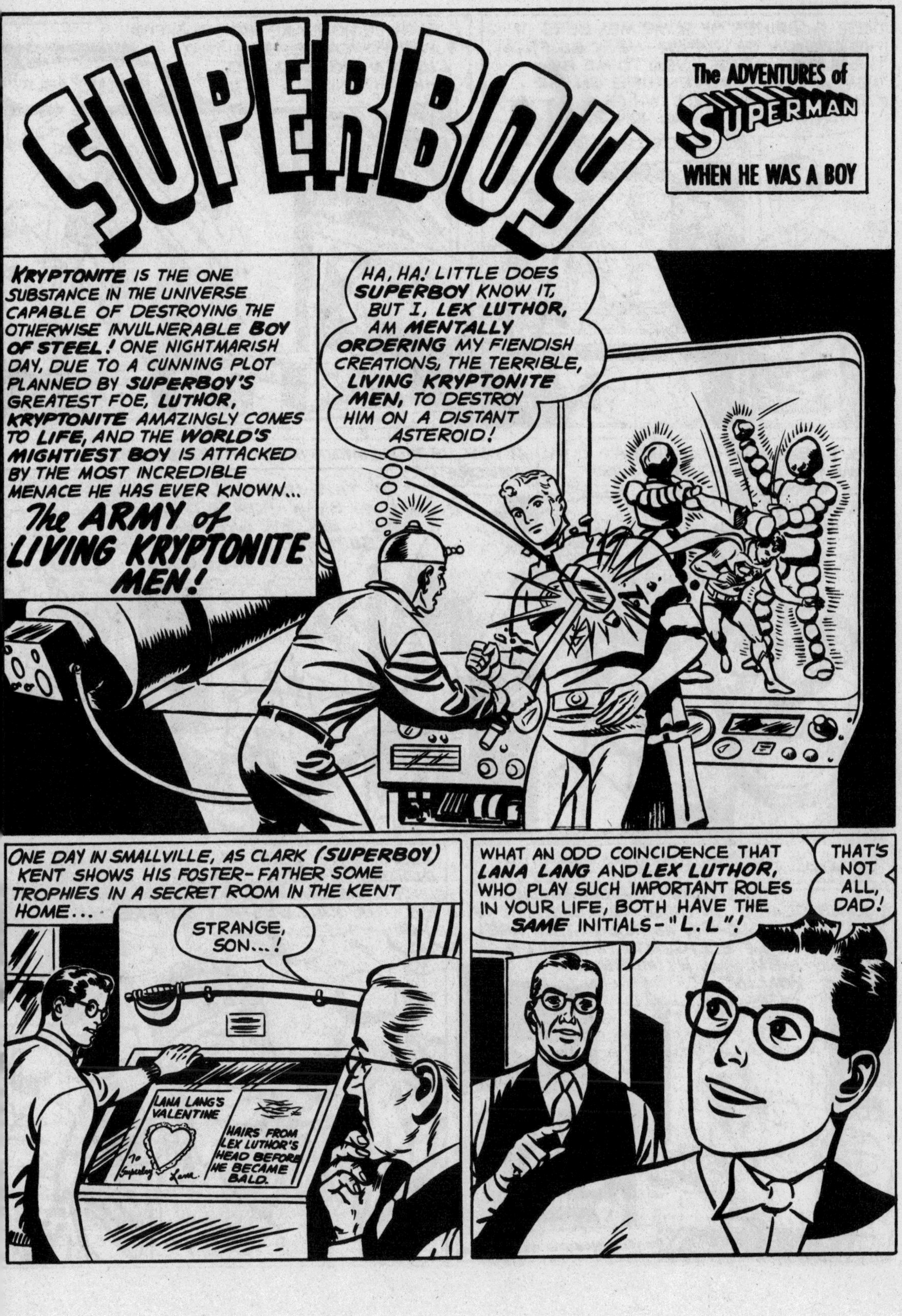
SUPERBOY
The ADVENTURES of SUPERMAN WHEN HE WAS A BOY
KRYPTONITE IS THE ONE SUBSTANCE IN THE UNIVERSE CAPABLE OF DESTROYING THE OTHERWISE INVULNERABLE BOY OF STEEL! ONE NIGHTMARISH DAY, DUE TO A CUNNING PLOT PLANNED BY SUPERBOY'S GREATEST FOE, LUTHOR, KRYPTONITE AMAZINGLY COMES TO LIFE, AND THE WORLD'S MIGHTIEST BOY IS ATTACKED BY THE MOST INCREDIBLE MENACE HE HAS EVER KNOWN...
The ARMY of LIVING KRYPTONITE MEN!
HA, HA! LITTLE DOES SUPERBOY KNOW IT, BUT I, LEX LUTHOR, AM MENTALLY ORDERING MY FIENDISH CREATIONS, THE TERRIBLE, LIVING KRYPTONITE MEN, TO DESTROY HIM ON A DISTANT ASTEROID!
ONE DAY IN SMALLVILLE, AS CLARK (SUPERBOY) KENT SHOWS HIS FOSTER-FATHER SOME TROPHIES IN A SECRET ROOM IN THE KENT HOME...
STRANGE, SON...!
LANA LANG'S VALENTINE
HAIRS FROM LEX LUTHOR'S HEAD BEFORE HE BECAME BALD.
WHAT AN ODD COINCIDENCE THAT LANA LANG AND LEX LUTHOR, WHO PLAY SUCH IMPORTANT ROLES IN YOUR LIFE, BOTH HAVE THE SAME INITIALS-"L.L"!
THAT'S NOT ALL, DAD!

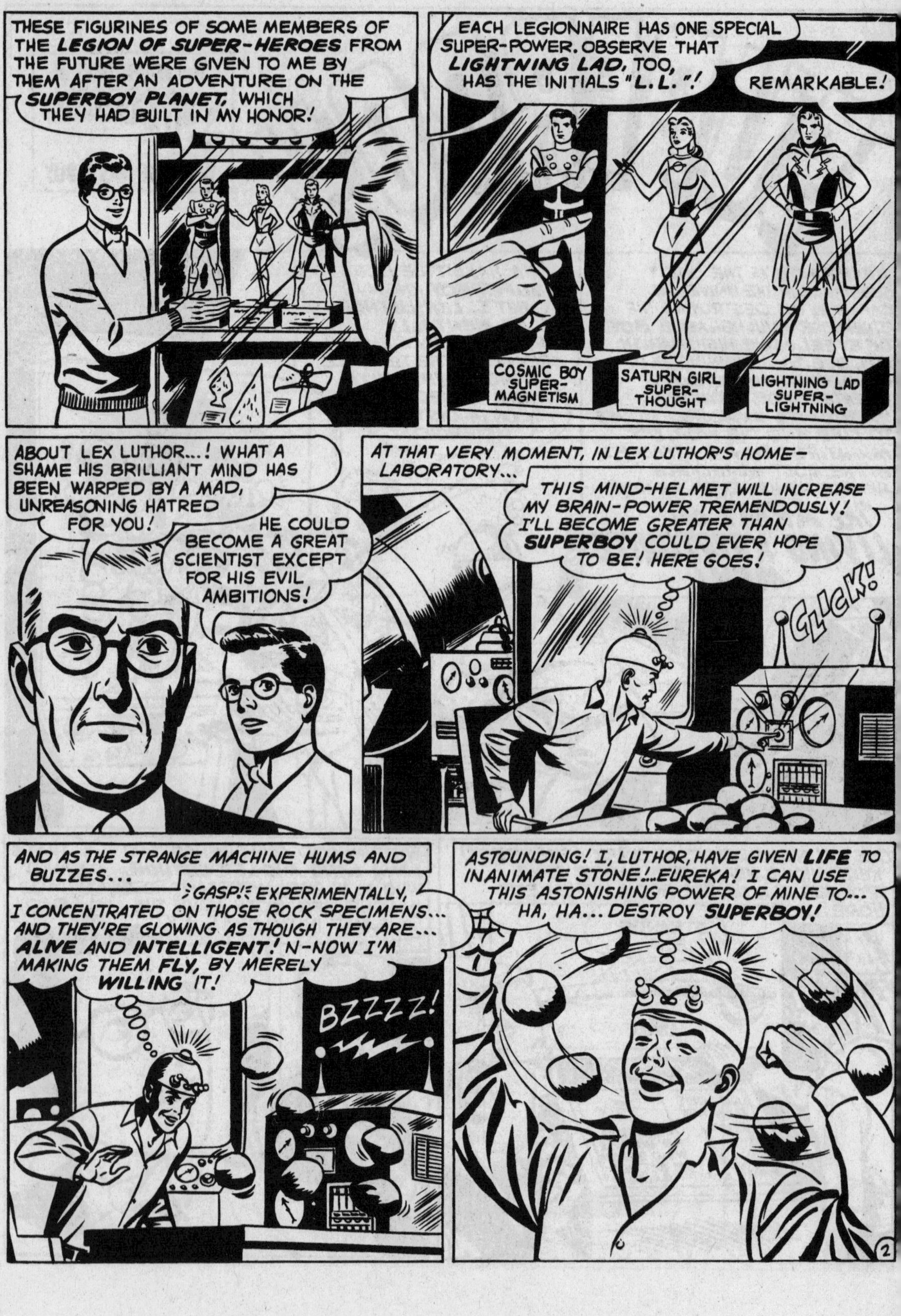
THESE FIGURINES OF SOME MEMBERS OF THE LEGION OF SUPER-HEROES FROM THE FUTURE WERE GIVEN TO ME BY THEM AFTER AN ADVENTURE ON THE SUPERBOY PLANET, WHICH THEY HAD BUILT IN MY HONOR!
EACH LEGIONNAIRE HAS ONE SPECIAL SUPER-POWER. OBSERVE THAT LIGHTNING LAD, TOO, HAS THE INITIALS "L. L."!
REMARKABLE!
COSMIC BOY SUPER-MAGNETISM
SATURN GIRL SUPER-THOUGHT
LIGHTNING LAD SUPER-LIGHTNING
ABOUT LEX LUTHOR...! WHAT A SHAME HIS BRILLIANT MIND HAS BEEN WARPED BY A MAD, UNREASONING HATRED FOR YOU!
HE COULD BECOME A GREAT SCIENTIST EXCEPT FOR HIS EVIL AMBITIONS!
AT THAT VERY MOMENT, IN LEX LUTHOR'S HOME-LABORATORY...
THIS MIND-HELMET WILL INCREASE MY BRAIN-POWER TREMENDOUSLY! I'LL BECOME GREATER THAN SUPERBOY COULD EVER HOPE TO BE! HERE GOES!
CLICK!
AND AS THE STRANGE MACHINE HUMS AND BUZZES...
GASP! EXPERIMENTALLY, I CONCENTRATED ON THOSE ROCK SPECIMENS... AND THEY'RE GLOWING AS THOUGH THEY ARE... ALIVE AND INTELLIGENT! N-NOW I'M MAKING THEM FLY, BY MERELY WILLING IT!
BZZZZ!
ASTOUNDING! I, LUTHOR, HAVE GIVEN LIFE TO INANIMATE STONE!...EUREKA! I CAN USE THIS ASTONISHING POWER OF MINE TO... HA, HA... DESTROY SUPERBOY!
2

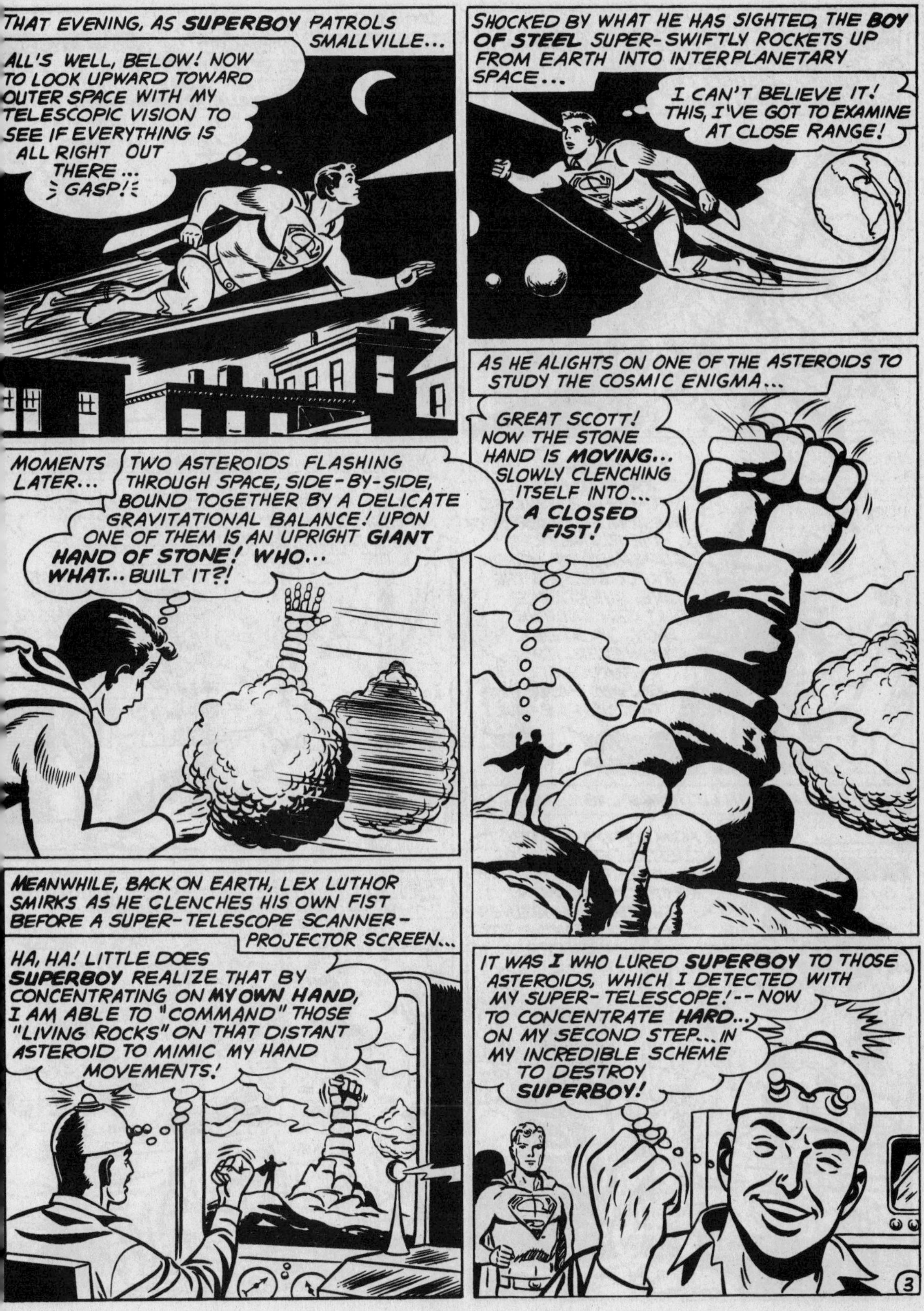
THAT EVENING, AS SUPERBOY PATROLS SMALLVILLE...
ALL'S WELL, BELOW! NOW TO LOOK UPWARD TOWARD OUTER SPACE WITH MY TELESCOPIC VISION TO SEE IF EVERYTHING IS ALL RIGHT OUT THERE... GASP!
SHOCKED BY WHAT HE HAS SIGHTED, THE BOY OF STEEL SUPER-SWIFTLY ROCKETS UP FROM EARTH INTO INTERPLANETARY SPACE...
I CAN'T BELIEVE IT! THIS, I'VE GOT TO EXAMINE AT CLOSE RANGE!
MOMENTS LATER...
TWO ASTEROIDS FLASHING THROUGH SPACE, SIDE-BY-SIDE, BOUND TOGETHER BY A DELICATE GRAVITATIONAL BALANCE! UPON ONE OF THEM IS AN UPRIGHT GIANT HAND OF STONE! WHO... WHAT... BUILT IT?!
AS HE ALIGHTS ON ONE OF THE ASTEROIDS TO STUDY THE COSMIC ENIGMA...
GREAT SCOTT! NOW THE STONE HAND IS MOVING... SLOWLY CLENCHING ITSELF INTO... A CLOSED FIST!
MEANWHILE, BACK ON EARTH, LEX LUTHOR SMIRKS AS HE CLENCHES HIS OWN FIST BEFORE A SUPER-TELESCOPE SCANNER-PROJECTOR SCREEN...
HA, HA! LITTLE DOES SUPERBOY REALIZE THAT BY CONCENTRATING ON MY OWN HAND, I AM ABLE TO "COMMAND" THOSE "LIVING ROCKS" ON THAT DISTANT ASTEROID TO MIMIC MY HAND MOVEMENTS!
IT WAS I WHO LURED SUPERBOY TO THOSE ASTEROIDS, WHICH I DETECTED WITH MY SUPER-TELESCOPE!--NOW TO CONCENTRATE HARD... ON MY SECOND STEP... IN MY INCREDIBLE SCHEME TO DESTROY SUPERBOY!
3

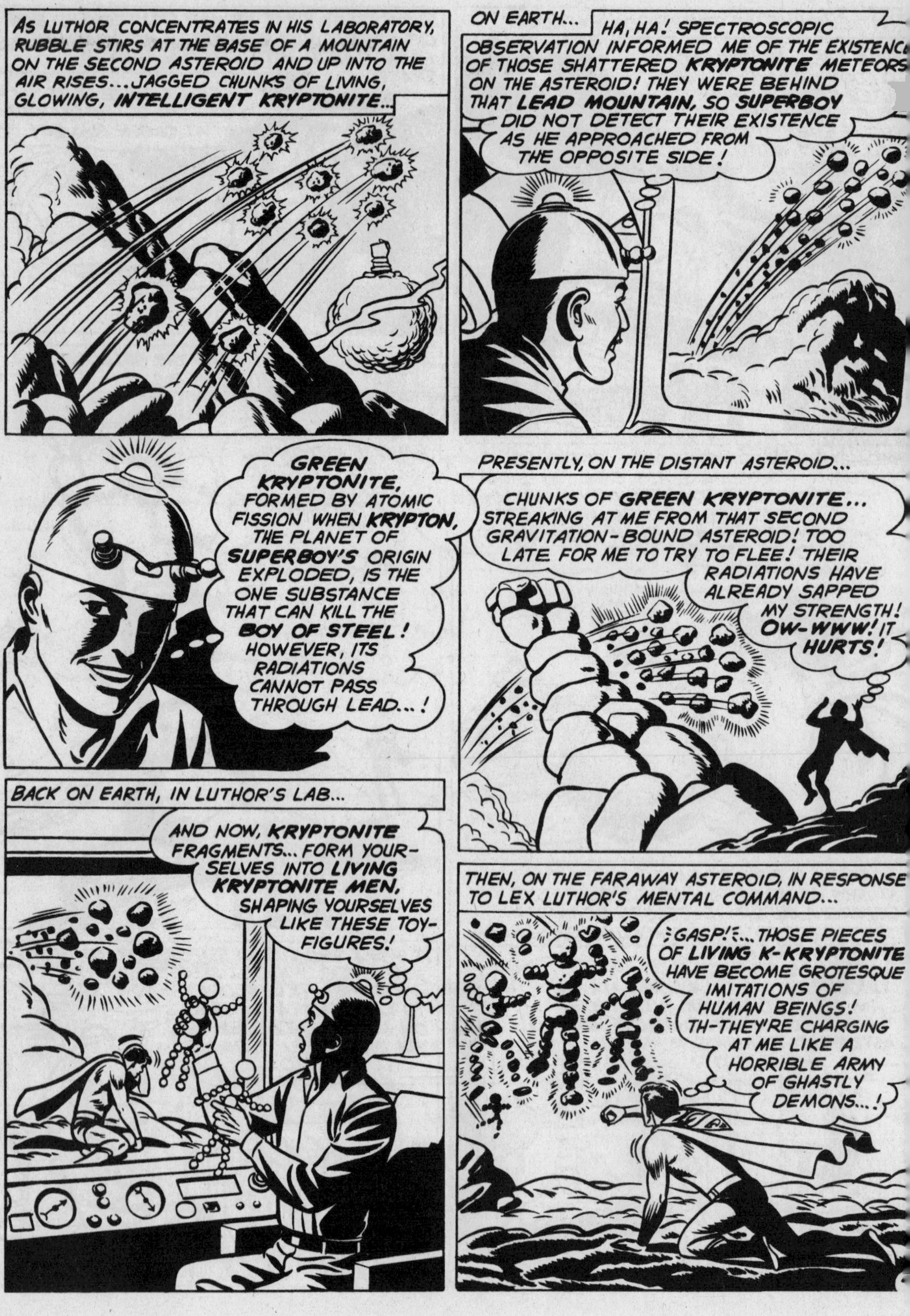
AS LUTHOR CONCENTRATES IN HIS LABORATORY, RUBBLE STIRS AT THE BASE OF A MOUNTAIN ON THE SECOND ASTEROID AND UP INTO THE AIR RISES...JAGGED CHUNKS OF LIVING, GLOWING, INTELLIGENT KRYPTONITE...
ON EARTH...
HA, HA! SPECTROSCOPIC OBSERVATION INFORMED ME OF THE EXISTENC OF THOSE SHATTERED KRYPTONITE METEORS ON THE ASTEROID! THEY WERE BEHIND THAT LEAD MOUNTAIN, SO SUPERBOY DID NOT DETECT THEIR EXISTENCE AS HE APPROACHED FROM THE OPPOSITE SIDE!
GREEN KRYPTONITE, FORMED BY ATOMIC FISSION WHEN KRYPTON, THE PLANET OF SUPERBOY'S ORIGIN EXPLODED, IS THE ONE SUBSTANCE THAT CAN KILL THE BOY OF STEEL! HOWEVER, ITS RADIATIONS CANNOT PASS THROUGH LEAD...!
PRESENTLY, ON THE DISTANT ASTEROID...
CHUNKS OF GREEN KRYPTONITE... STREAKING AT ME FROM THAT SECOND GRAVITATION-BOUND ASTEROID! TOO LATE FOR ME TO TRY TO FLEE! THEIR RADIATIONS HAVE ALREADY SAPPED MY STRENGTH! OW-WWW! IT HURTS!
BACK ON EARTH, IN LUTHOR'S LAB...
AND NOW, KRYPTONITE FRAGMENTS... FORM YOURSELVES INTO LIVING KRYPTONITE MEN, SHAPING YOURSELVES LIKE THESE TOY-FIGURES!
THEN, ON THE FARAWAY ASTEROID, IN RESPONSE TO LEX LUTHOR'S MENTAL COMMAND...
GASP!...THOSE PIECES OF LIVING K-KRYPTONITE HAVE BECOME GROTESQUE IMITATIONS OF HUMAN BEINGS! TH-THEY'RE CHARGING AT ME LIKE A HORRIBLE ARMY OF GHASTLY DEMONS...!

N *LUTHOR'S* LABORATORY, ON EARTH...

DON'T LET HIM CRAWL OFF! KEEP WEAKENING HIM! LIKE THIS! AND THIS!!! AND *THIS*!!!

MEANWHILE, ON THE ASTEROID.

CAN'T M-MOVE! THEY'RE PINNING ME DOWN! OHH-HHH... I-I'M T-TURNING **GREEN**! *GASP!* KRYPTONITE BLOOD-POISONING IS...SETTING IN!

MEANWHILE, IN SMALLVILLE, LANA LANG STEALTHILY ENTERS LUTHOR'S LABORATORY...

WONDER WHAT AMAZING EXPERIMENT LEX LUTHOR IS WORKING ON NOW! DRAT THIS CURIOSITY OF MINE! I'VE JUST GOT TO FIND OUT!

SOON, IN AN APPARATUS-JAMMED POWER-ROOM...

HMMM. I WONDER WHAT WOULD HAPPEN IF I WERE TO PULL THAT LEVER??

D-LEVER

UNKNOWN TO LANA, PULLING DOWN THE "D-LEVER" WOULD DESTROY LUTHOR'S MIND-MACHINE AND PUFF OUT OF EXISTENCE ALL OBJECTS MENTALLY ANIMATED BY THE YOUNG ARCH-VILLAIN!

BUILT THIS "D-LEVER" AS A PRECAUTIONARY MEASURE, JUST IN CASE I EVER HAVE TO DESTROY THIS INVENTION TO PREVENT THE LAW FROM USING IT AS INCRIMINATING EVIDENCE AGAINST ME!

D-LEVER

BUT NOT KNOWING THIS, NOR AWARE OF **SUPERBOY'S** DESPERATE PERIL, LANA TIMIDLY HESITATES...

SHOULD I, OR SHOULDN'T I??

D-LEVER

YOU DON'T KNOW IT, LANA, BUT IF YOU PULL THAT LEVER YOU SAVE **SUPERBOY**...

⑤

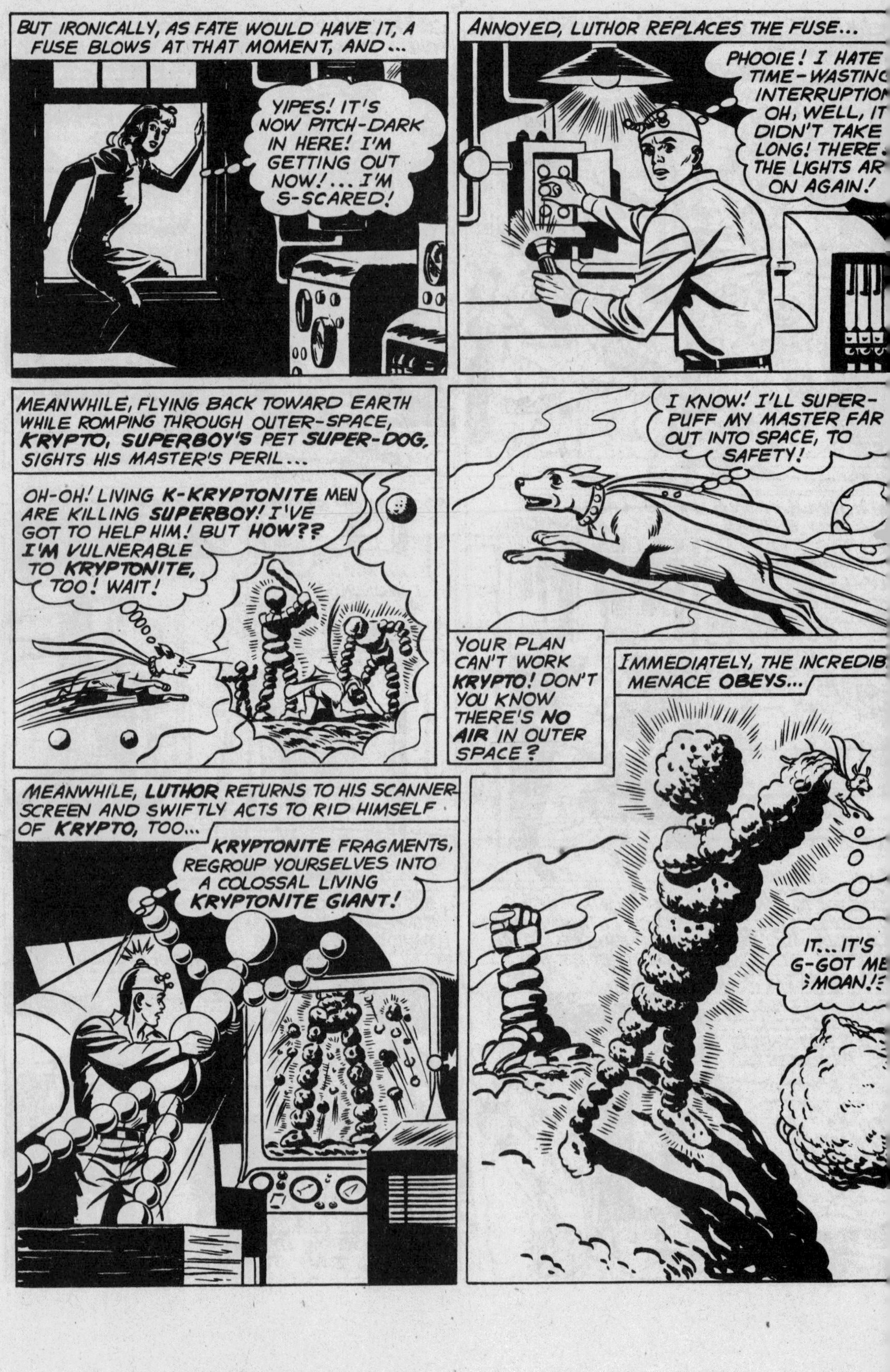
BUT IRONICALLY, AS FATE WOULD HAVE IT, A FUSE BLOWS AT THAT MOMENT, AND...
YIPES! IT'S NOW PITCH-DARK IN HERE! I'M GETTING OUT NOW!... I'M S-SCARED!
ANNOYED, LUTHOR REPLACES THE FUSE...
PHOOIE! I HATE TIME-WASTING INTERRUPTION OH, WELL, IT DIDN'T TAKE LONG! THERE THE LIGHTS AR ON AGAIN!
MEANWHILE, FLYING BACK TOWARD EARTH WHILE ROMPING THROUGH OUTER-SPACE, KRYPTO, SUPERBOY'S PET SUPER-DOG, SIGHTS HIS MASTER'S PERIL...
OH-OH! LIVING K-KRYPTONITE MEN ARE KILLING SUPERBOY! I'VE GOT TO HELP HIM! BUT HOW?? I'M VULNERABLE TO KRYPTONITE, TOO! WAIT!
I KNOW! I'LL SUPER-PUFF MY MASTER FAR OUT INTO SPACE, TO SAFETY!
YOUR PLAN CAN'T WORK KRYPTO! DON'T YOU KNOW THERE'S NO AIR IN OUTER SPACE?
IMMEDIATELY, THE INCREDIB MENACE OBEYS...
MEANWHILE, LUTHOR RETURNS TO HIS SCANNER SCREEN AND SWIFTLY ACTS TO RID HIMSELF OF KRYPTO, TOO...
KRYPTONITE FRAGMENTS, REGROUP YOURSELVES INTO A COLOSSAL LIVING KRYPTONITE GIANT!
IT... IT'S G-GOT ME MOAN!

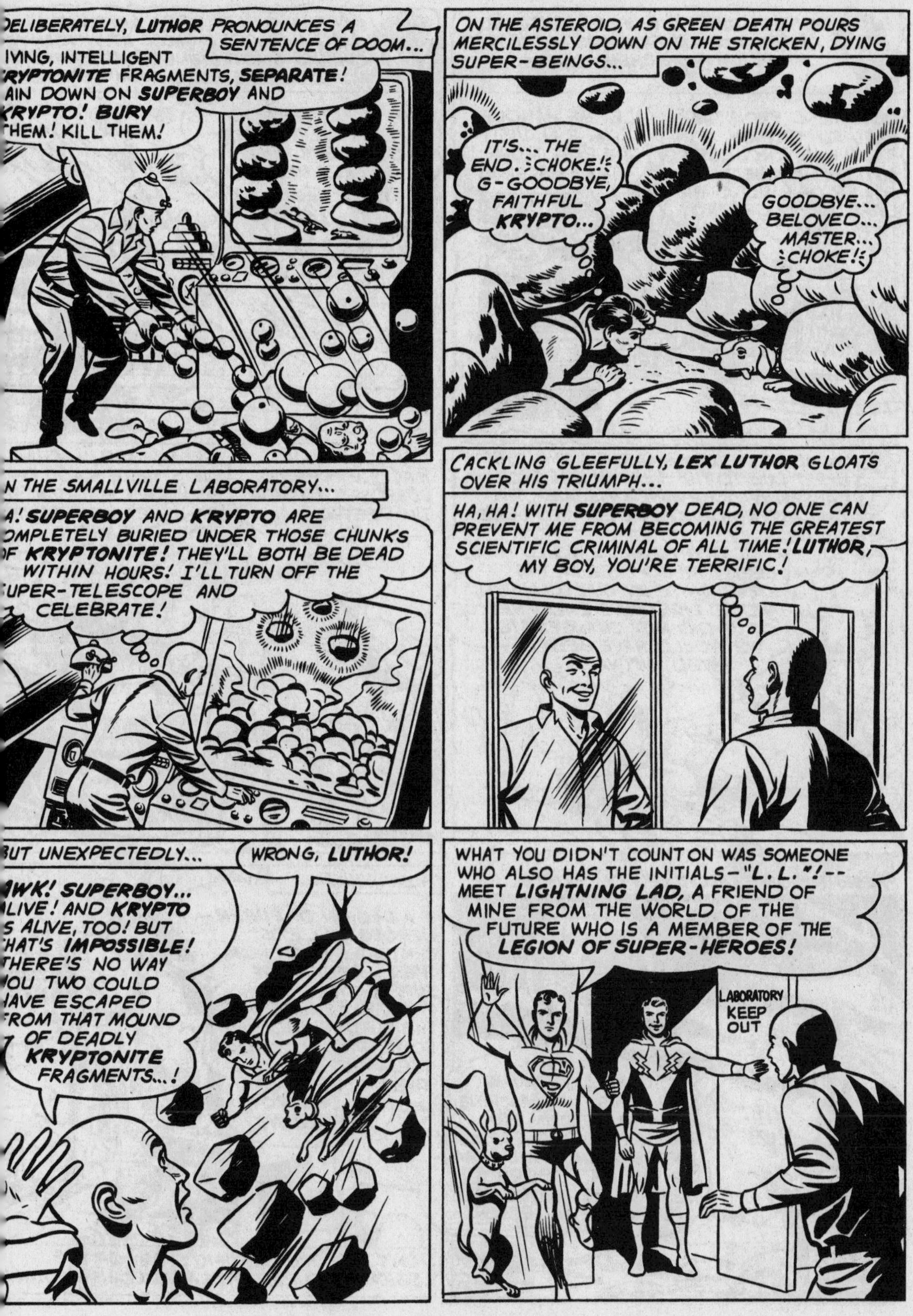
DELIBERATELY, LUTHOR PRONOUNCES A SENTENCE OF DOOM...
IVING, INTELLIGENT KRYPTONITE FRAGMENTS, SEPARATE! AIN DOWN ON SUPERBOY AND KRYPTO! BURY THEM! KILL THEM!
ON THE ASTEROID, AS GREEN DEATH POURS MERCILESSLY DOWN ON THE STRICKEN, DYING SUPER-BEINGS...
IT'S... THE END. CHOKE! G-GOODBYE, FAITHFUL KRYPTO...
GOODBYE... BELOVED... MASTER... CHOKE!
N THE SMALLVILLE LABORATORY...
A! SUPERBOY AND KRYPTO ARE OMPLETELY BURIED UNDER THOSE CHUNKS OF KRYPTONITE! THEY'LL BOTH BE DEAD WITHIN HOURS! I'LL TURN OFF THE UPER-TELESCOPE AND CELEBRATE!
CACKLING GLEEFULLY, LEX LUTHOR GLOATS OVER HIS TRIUMPH...
HA, HA! WITH SUPERBOY DEAD, NO ONE CAN PREVENT ME FROM BECOMING THE GREATEST SCIENTIFIC CRIMINAL OF ALL TIME! LUTHOR, MY BOY, YOU'RE TERRIFIC!
BUT UNEXPECTEDLY...
WRONG, LUTHOR!
AWK! SUPERBOY... ALIVE! AND KRYPTO S ALIVE, TOO! BUT THAT'S IMPOSSIBLE! THERE'S NO WAY YOU TWO COULD HAVE ESCAPED FROM THAT MOUND OF DEADLY KRYPTONITE FRAGMENTS...!
WHAT YOU DIDN'T COUNT ON WAS SOMEONE WHO ALSO HAS THE INITIALS—"L. L."!—MEET LIGHTNING LAD, A FRIEND OF MINE FROM THE WORLD OF THE FUTURE WHO IS A MEMBER OF THE LEGION OF SUPER-HEROES!
LABORATORY KEEP OUT

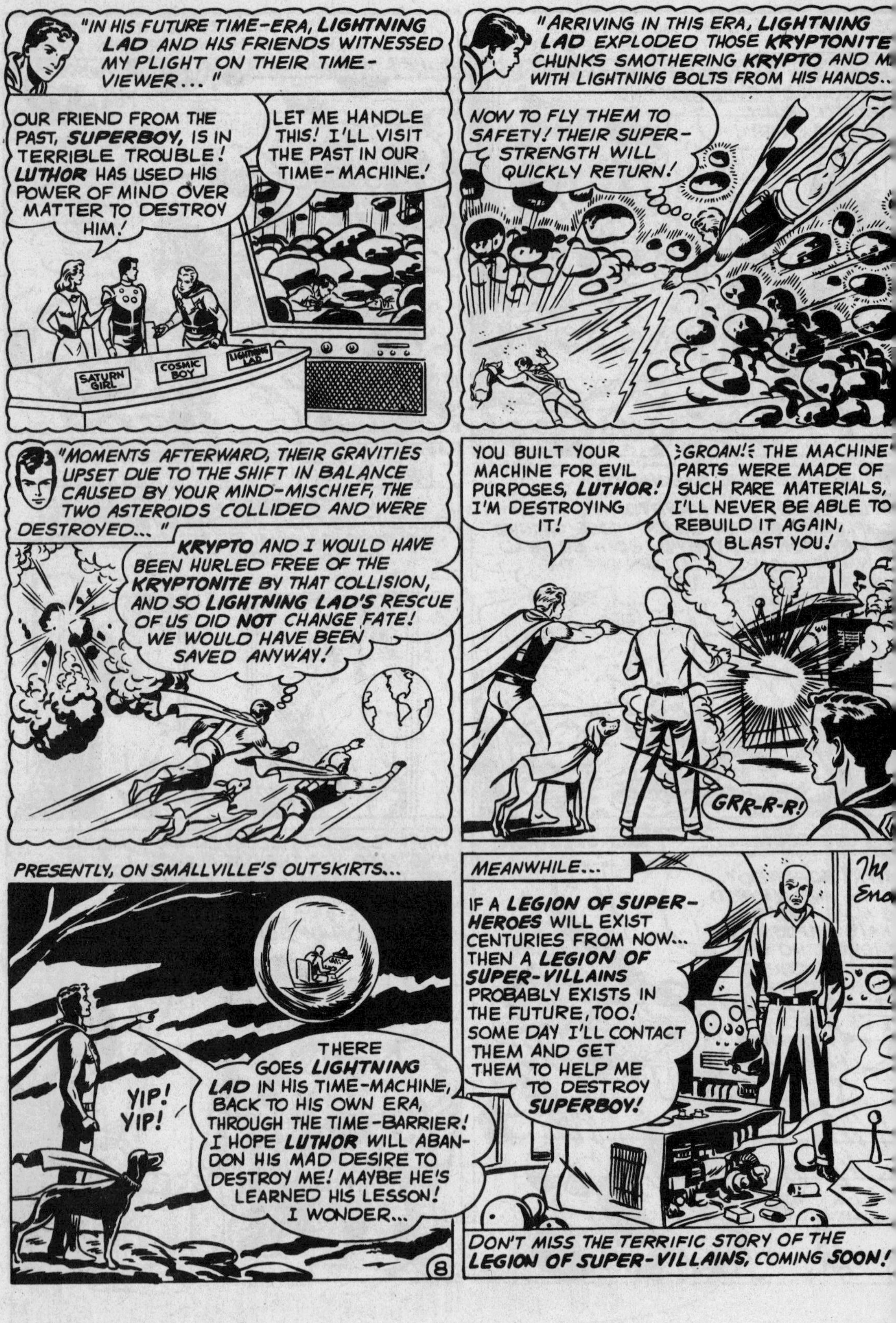
"IN HIS FUTURE TIME-ERA, LIGHTNING LAD AND HIS FRIENDS WITNESSED MY PLIGHT ON THEIR TIME-VIEWER..."
OUR FRIEND FROM THE PAST, SUPERBOY, IS IN TERRIBLE TROUBLE! LUTHOR HAS USED HIS POWER OF MIND OVER MATTER TO DESTROY HIM!
LET ME HANDLE THIS! I'LL VISIT THE PAST IN OUR TIME-MACHINE!
SATURN GIRL
COSMIC BOY
LIGHTNING LAD
"ARRIVING IN THIS ERA, LIGHTNING LAD EXPLODED THOSE KRYPTONITE CHUNKS SMOTHERING KRYPTO AND M WITH LIGHTNING BOLTS FROM HIS HANDS..
NOW TO FLY THEM TO SAFETY! THEIR SUPER-STRENGTH WILL QUICKLY RETURN!
"MOMENTS AFTERWARD, THEIR GRAVITIES UPSET DUE TO THE SHIFT IN BALANCE CAUSED BY YOUR MIND-MISCHIEF, THE TWO ASTEROIDS COLLIDED AND WERE DESTROYED..."
KRYPTO AND I WOULD HAVE BEEN HURLED FREE OF THE KRYPTONITE BY THAT COLLISION, AND SO LIGHTNING LAD'S RESCUE OF US DID NOT CHANGE FATE! WE WOULD HAVE BEEN SAVED ANYWAY!
YOU BUILT YOUR MACHINE FOR EVIL PURPOSES, LUTHOR! I'M DESTROYING IT!
GROAN! THE MACHINE' PARTS WERE MADE OF SUCH RARE MATERIALS, I'LL NEVER BE ABLE TO REBUILD IT AGAIN, BLAST YOU!
GRR-R-R!
PRESENTLY, ON SMALLVILLE'S OUTSKIRTS...
THERE GOES LIGHTNING LAD IN HIS TIME-MACHINE, BACK TO HIS OWN ERA, THROUGH THE TIME-BARRIER! I HOPE LUTHOR WILL ABANDON HIS MAD DESIRE TO DESTROY ME! MAYBE HE'S LEARNED HIS LESSON! I WONDER...
YIP! YIP!
8
MEANWHILE...
IF A LEGION OF SUPER-HEROES WILL EXIST CENTURIES FROM NOW... THEN A LEGION OF SUPER-VILLAINS PROBABLY EXISTS IN THE FUTURE, TOO! SOME DAY I'LL CONTACT THEM AND GET THEM TO HELP ME TO DESTROY SUPERBOY!
DON'T MISS THE TERRIFIC STORY OF THE LEGION OF SUPER-VILLAINS, COMING SOON!

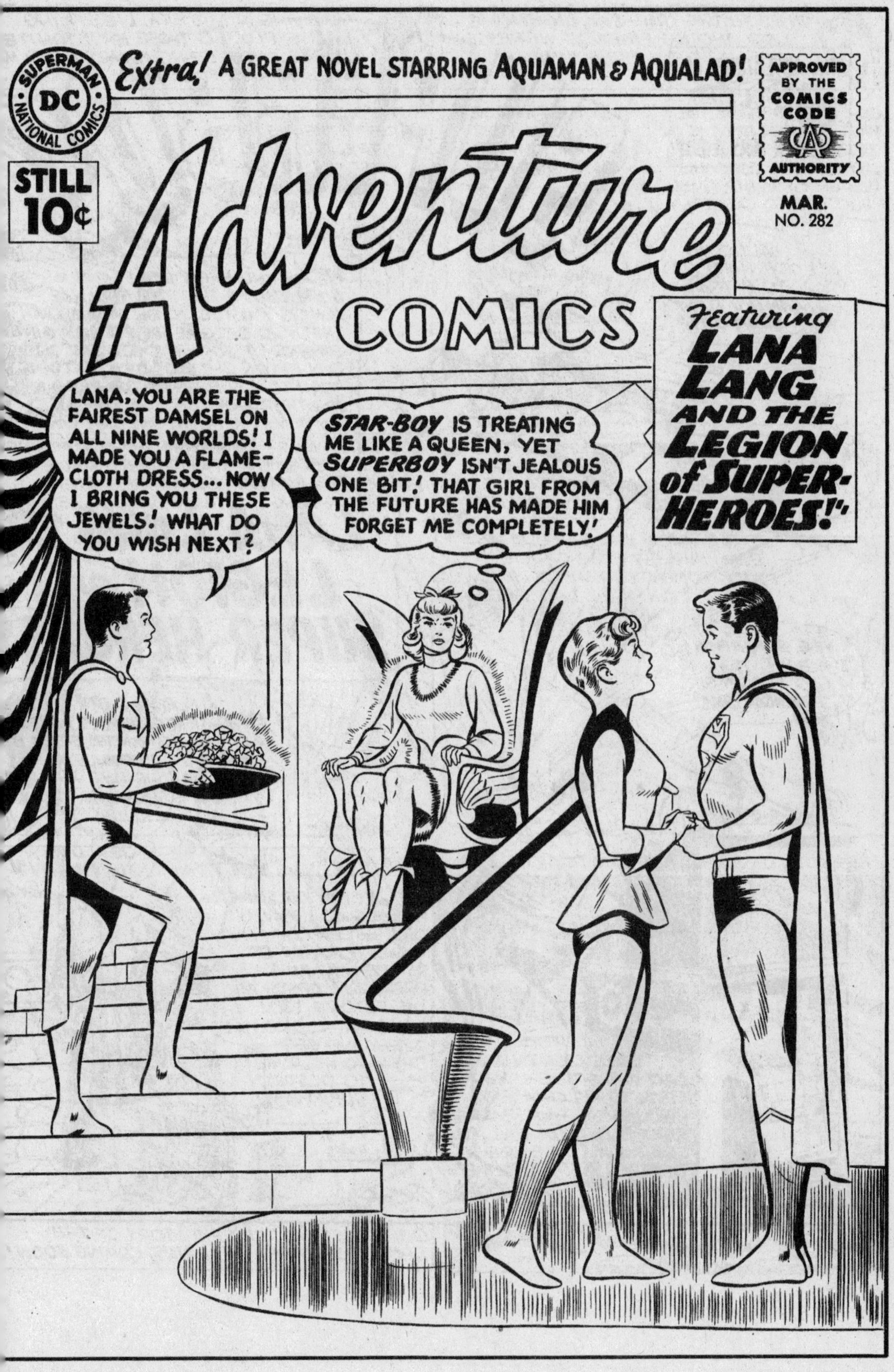
SUPERMAN DC NATIONAL COMICS
Extra! A GREAT NOVEL STARRING AQUAMAN & AQUALAD!
APPROVED BY THE COMICS CODE AUTHORITY
STILL 10¢
Adventure COMICS
MAR. NO. 282
Featuring LANA LANG AND THE LEGION of SUPER-HEROES!"
LANA, YOU ARE THE FAIREST DAMSEL ON ALL NINE WORLDS! I MADE YOU A FLAME-CLOTH DRESS... NOW I BRING YOU THESE JEWELS! WHAT DO YOU WISH NEXT?
STAR-BOY IS TREATING ME LIKE A QUEEN, YET SUPERBOY ISN'T JEALOUS ONE BIT! THAT GIRL FROM THE FUTURE HAS MADE HIM FORGET ME COMPLETELY!

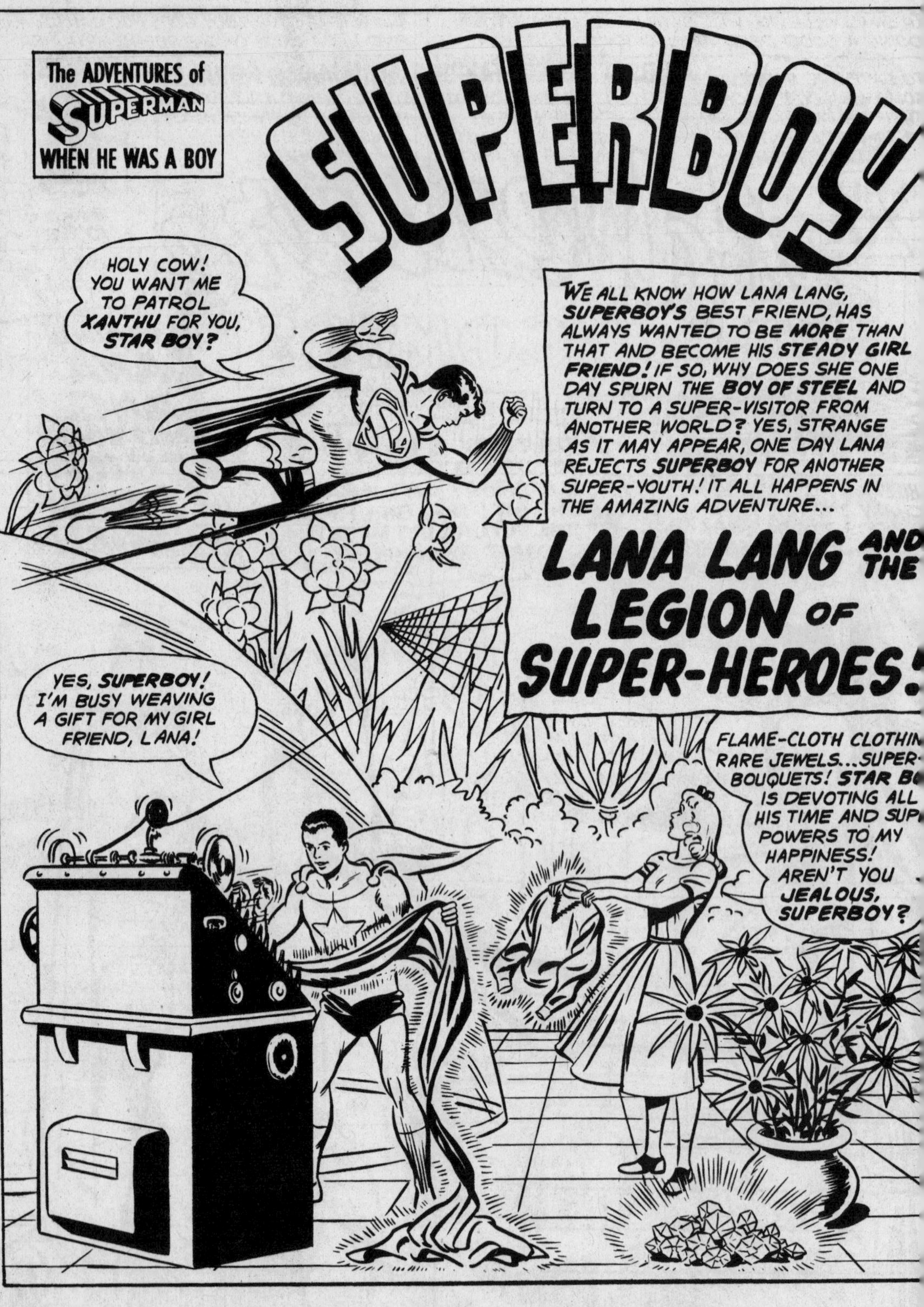

The ADVENTURES of SUPERMAN WHEN HE WAS A BOY
SUPERBOY
HOLY COW! YOU WANT ME TO PATROL XANTHU FOR YOU, STAR BOY?
WE ALL KNOW HOW LANA LANG, SUPERBOY'S BEST FRIEND, HAS ALWAYS WANTED TO BE MORE THAN THAT AND BECOME HIS STEADY GIRL FRIEND! IF SO, WHY DOES SHE ONE DAY SPURN THE BOY OF STEEL AND TURN TO A SUPER-VISITOR FROM ANOTHER WORLD? YES, STRANGE AS IT MAY APPEAR, ONE DAY LANA REJECTS SUPERBOY FOR ANOTHER SUPER-YOUTH! IT ALL HAPPENS IN THE AMAZING ADVENTURE...
LANA LANG AND THE LEGION OF SUPER-HEROES!
YES, SUPERBOY! I'M BUSY WEAVING A GIFT FOR MY GIRL FRIEND, LANA!
FLAME-CLOTH CLOTHIN RARE JEWELS...SUPER- BOUQUETS! STAR B IS DEVOTING ALL HIS TIME AND SUP POWERS TO MY HAPPINESS! AREN'T YOU JEALOUS, SUPERBOY?

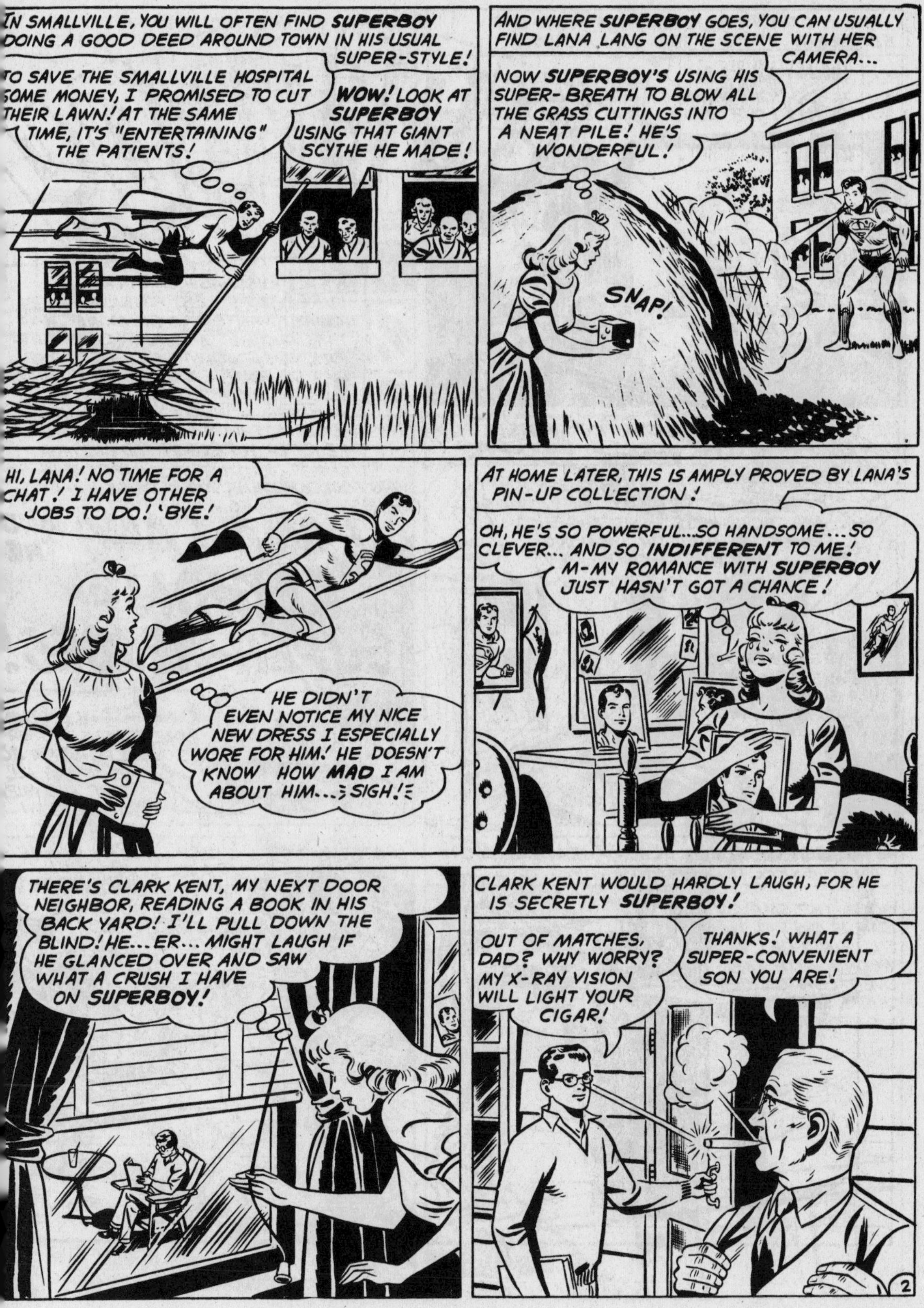
IN SMALLVILLE, YOU WILL OFTEN FIND SUPERBOY DOING A GOOD DEED AROUND TOWN IN HIS USUAL SUPER-STYLE!
TO SAVE THE SMALLVILLE HOSPITAL SOME MONEY, I PROMISED TO CUT THEIR LAWN! AT THE SAME TIME, IT'S "ENTERTAINING" THE PATIENTS!
WOW! LOOK AT SUPERBOY USING THAT GIANT SCYTHE HE MADE!
AND WHERE SUPERBOY GOES, YOU CAN USUALLY FIND LANA LANG ON THE SCENE WITH HER CAMERA...
NOW SUPERBOY'S USING HIS SUPER-BREATH TO BLOW ALL THE GRASS CUTTINGS INTO A NEAT PILE! HE'S WONDERFUL!
SNAP!
HI, LANA! NO TIME FOR A CHAT! I HAVE OTHER JOBS TO DO! 'BYE!
HE DIDN'T EVEN NOTICE MY NICE NEW DRESS I ESPECIALLY WORE FOR HIM! HE DOESN'T KNOW HOW MAD I AM ABOUT HIM... SIGH!
AT HOME LATER, THIS IS AMPLY PROVED BY LANA'S PIN-UP COLLECTION!
OH, HE'S SO POWERFUL...SO HANDSOME...SO CLEVER... AND SO INDIFFERENT TO ME! M-MY ROMANCE WITH SUPERBOY JUST HASN'T GOT A CHANCE!
THERE'S CLARK KENT, MY NEXT DOOR NEIGHBOR, READING A BOOK IN HIS BACK YARD! I'LL PULL DOWN THE BLIND! HE...ER... MIGHT LAUGH IF HE GLANCED OVER AND SAW WHAT A CRUSH I HAVE ON SUPERBOY!
CLARK KENT WOULD HARDLY LAUGH, FOR HE IS SECRETLY SUPERBOY!
OUT OF MATCHES, DAD? WHY WORRY? MY X-RAY VISION WILL LIGHT YOUR CIGAR!
THANKS! WHAT A SUPER-CONVENIENT SON YOU ARE!
2

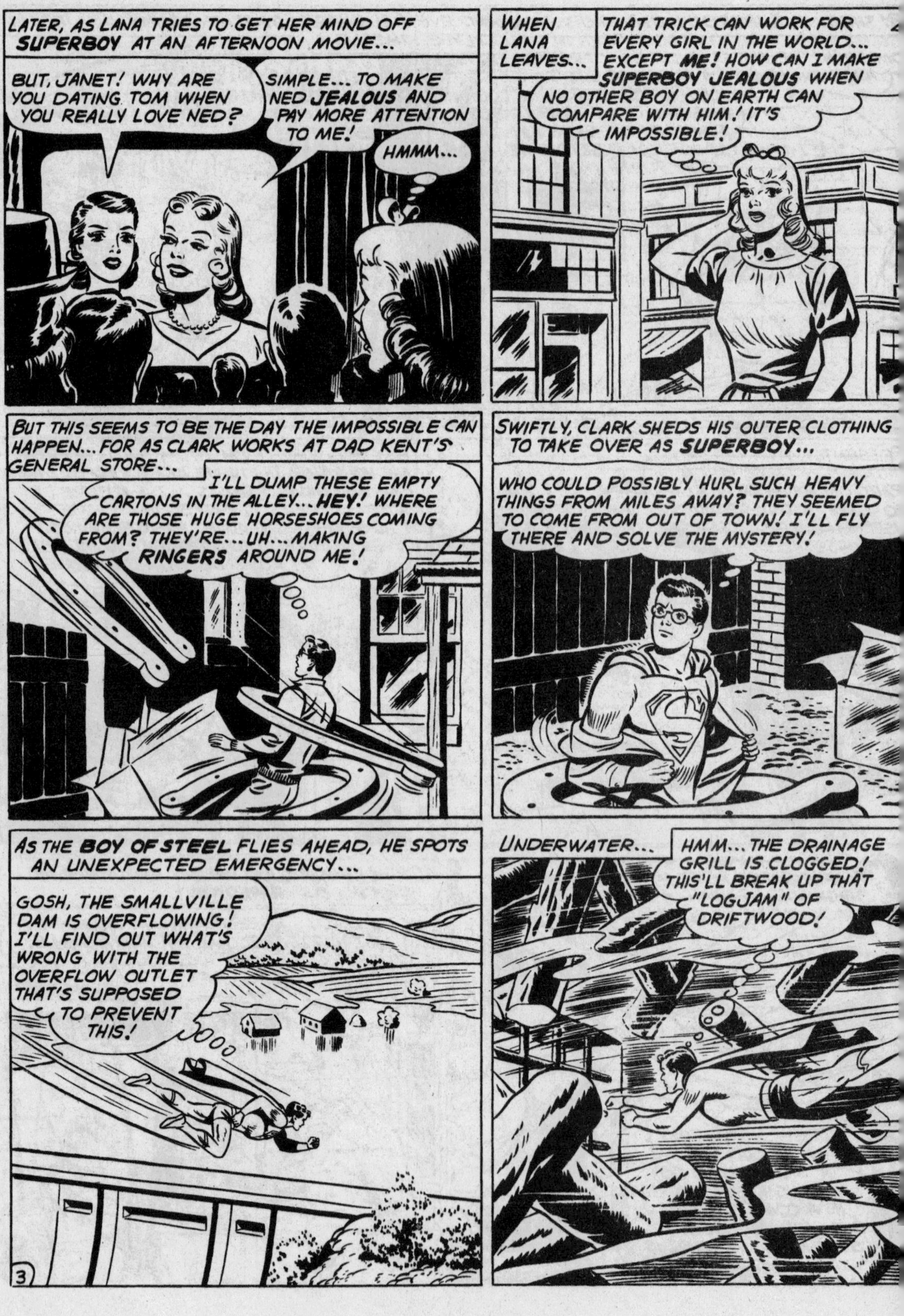
LATER, AS LANA TRIES TO GET HER MIND OFF SUPERBOY AT AN AFTERNOON MOVIE...
BUT, JANET! WHY ARE YOU DATING TOM WHEN YOU REALLY LOVE NED?
SIMPLE... TO MAKE NED JEALOUS AND PAY MORE ATTENTION TO ME!
HMMM...
WHEN LANA LEAVES...
THAT TRICK CAN WORK FOR EVERY GIRL IN THE WORLD... EXCEPT ME! HOW CAN I MAKE SUPERBOY JEALOUS WHEN NO OTHER BOY ON EARTH CAN COMPARE WITH HIM! IT'S IMPOSSIBLE!
BUT THIS SEEMS TO BE THE DAY THE IMPOSSIBLE CAN HAPPEN... FOR AS CLARK WORKS AT DAD KENT'S GENERAL STORE...
I'LL DUMP THESE EMPTY CARTONS IN THE ALLEY... HEY! WHERE ARE THOSE HUGE HORSESHOES COMING FROM? THEY'RE... UH... MAKING RINGERS AROUND ME!
SWIFTLY, CLARK SHEDS HIS OUTER CLOTHING TO TAKE OVER AS SUPERBOY...
WHO COULD POSSIBLY HURL SUCH HEAVY THINGS FROM MILES AWAY? THEY SEEMED TO COME FROM OUT OF TOWN! I'LL FLY THERE AND SOLVE THE MYSTERY!
AS THE BOY OF STEEL FLIES AHEAD, HE SPOTS AN UNEXPECTED EMERGENCY...
GOSH, THE SMALLVILLE DAM IS OVERFLOWING! I'LL FIND OUT WHAT'S WRONG WITH THE OVERFLOW OUTLET THAT'S SUPPOSED TO PREVENT THIS!
3
UNDERWATER...
HMM... THE DRAINAGE GRILL IS CLOGGED! THIS'LL BREAK UP THAT "LOGJAM" OF DRIFTWOOD!

BY THE TIME **SUPERBOY** ZOOMS UP...

OMIGOSH! THE WATER SUDDENLY FROZE AROUND ME INTO A BLOCK OF SOLID ICE! I WONDER... WAS THIS TRICK DONE TO ME BY THE SAME UNKNOWN PERSON WHO FLUNG THOSE HORSESHOES?

AND EVEN AS **SUPERBOY** FLIES AGAINST A CLIFF TO FREE HIMSELF...

...SUPERBOY MEET ME AT CALVIN'S CAVE

HOLY COW! NOW HUGE LETTERS OF BAKED CLAY ARE SAILING HERE, SPELLING OUT A MESSAGE BEFORE THEY SMASH AGAINST THE CLIFF!

PRESENTLY, AT THAT SPOT...

PARDON MY STUNTS, **SUPERBOY**! TO "LURE" YOU HERE QUICKLY, I USED MY SUPER-STRENGTH FOR THE HORSESHOES, MY SUPER-COOLING BREATH TO FREEZE WATER, AND MY INFRA-RED VISION TO BAKE CLAY LETTERS!

BUT WH-WHO ARE YOU? HOW CAN YOU HAVE SUPER-POWERS LIKE ME?

I'M **THOM KALLOR** FROM THE PLANET **XANTHU**, WHICH EXISTS IN THE FUTURE! I ARRIVED IN MY TIME-SHIP! WE ALSO HAVE SPACESHIPS ON MY WORLD AND ONE DAY...

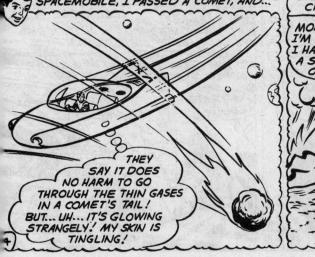

"...WHILE TAKING A SPIN IN THE FAMILY SPACEMOBILE, I PASSED A COMET, AND..."

THEY SAY IT DOES NO HARM TO GO THROUGH THE THIN GASES IN A COMET'S TAIL! BUT... UH... IT'S GLOWING STRANGELY! MY SKIN IS TINGLING!

"DRIVING HOME, ENGINE FAILURE MADE ME CRASH, BUT AMAZINGLY...

MOM! DAD! I'M NOT HURT! I HAVEN'T GOT A SCRATCH ON ME!

GREAT STARS! HOW DID YOU BECOME INVULNERABLE, SON? AND YOU CAN FLY, TOO!

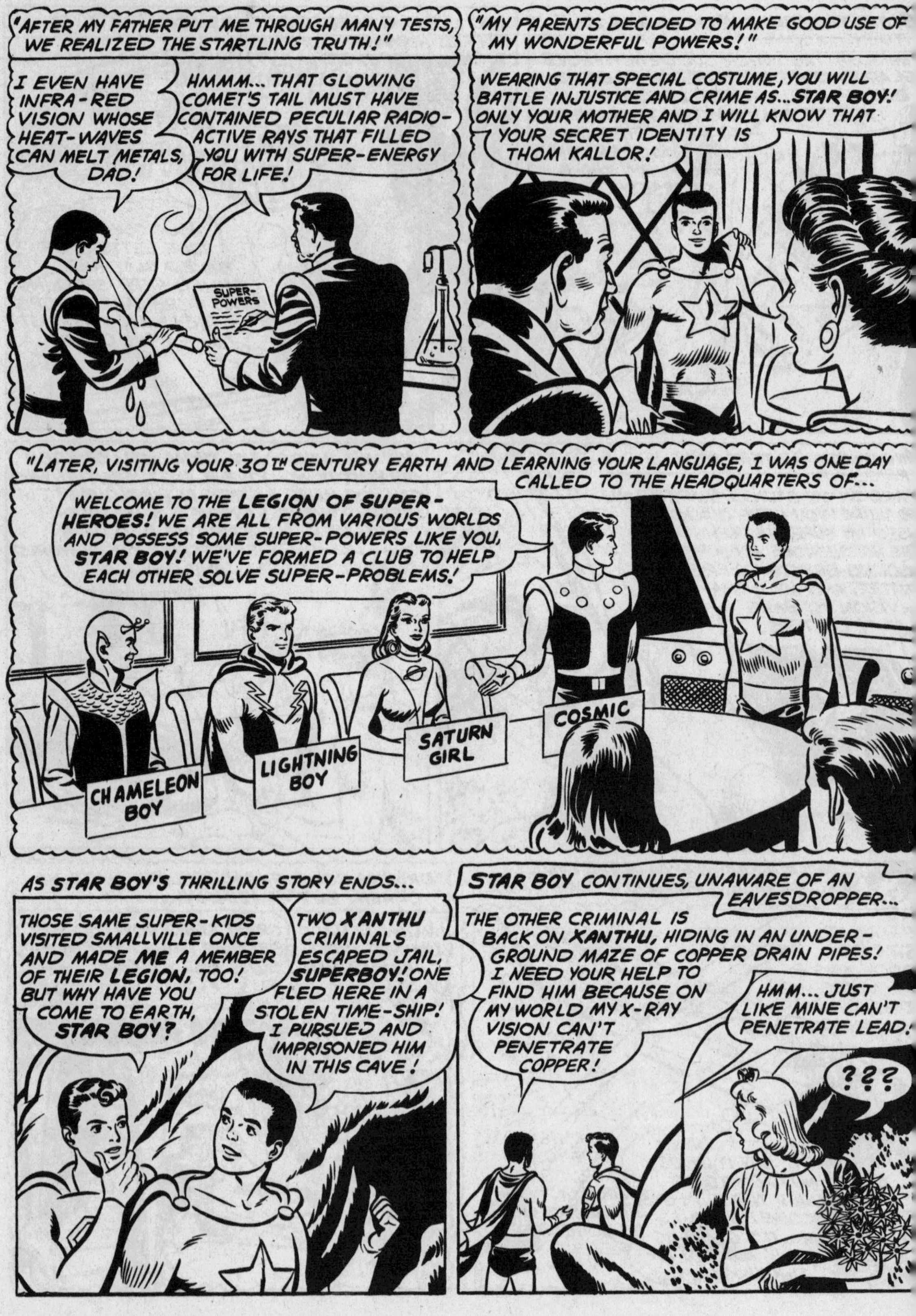
"AFTER MY FATHER PUT ME THROUGH MANY TESTS, WE REALIZED THE STARTLING TRUTH!"
I EVEN HAVE INFRA-RED VISION WHOSE HEAT-WAVES CAN MELT METALS, DAD!
HMMM... THAT GLOWING COMET'S TAIL MUST HAVE CONTAINED PECULIAR RADIO-ACTIVE RAYS THAT FILLED YOU WITH SUPER-ENERGY FOR LIFE!
SUPER-POWERS
"MY PARENTS DECIDED TO MAKE GOOD USE OF MY WONDERFUL POWERS!"
WEARING THAT SPECIAL COSTUME, YOU WILL BATTLE INJUSTICE AND CRIME AS...STAR BOY! ONLY YOUR MOTHER AND I WILL KNOW THAT YOUR SECRET IDENTITY IS THOM KALLOR!
"LATER, VISITING YOUR 30TH CENTURY EARTH AND LEARNING YOUR LANGUAGE, I WAS ONE DAY CALLED TO THE HEADQUARTERS OF...
WELCOME TO THE LEGION OF SUPER-HEROES! WE ARE ALL FROM VARIOUS WORLDS AND POSSESS SOME SUPER-POWERS LIKE YOU, STAR BOY! WE'VE FORMED A CLUB TO HELP EACH OTHER SOLVE SUPER-PROBLEMS!
CHAMELEON BOY
LIGHTNING BOY
SATURN GIRL
COSMIC
AS STAR BOY'S THRILLING STORY ENDS...
THOSE SAME SUPER-KIDS VISITED SMALLVILLE ONCE AND MADE ME A MEMBER OF THEIR LEGION, TOO! BUT WHY HAVE YOU COME TO EARTH, STAR BOY?
TWO XANTHU CRIMINALS ESCAPED JAIL, SUPERBOY! ONE FLED HERE IN A STOLEN TIME-SHIP! I PURSUED AND IMPRISONED HIM IN THIS CAVE!
STAR BOY CONTINUES, UNAWARE OF AN EAVESDROPPER...
THE OTHER CRIMINAL IS BACK ON XANTHU, HIDING IN AN UNDER-GROUND MAZE OF COPPER DRAIN PIPES! I NEED YOUR HELP TO FIND HIM BECAUSE ON MY WORLD MY X-RAY VISION CAN'T PENETRATE COPPER!
HMM... JUST LIKE MINE CAN'T PENETRATE LEAD!
???

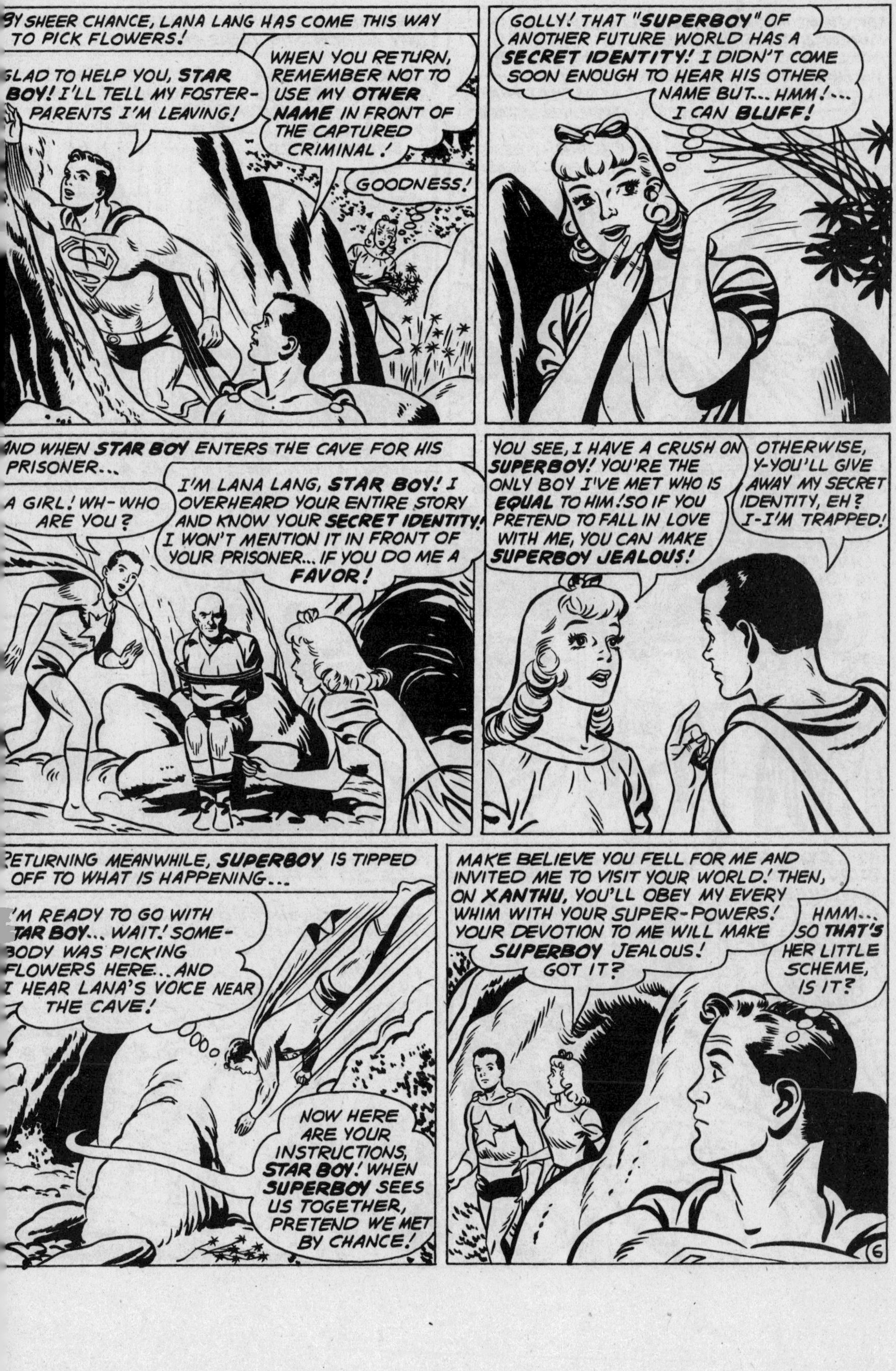
BY SHEER CHANCE, LANA LANG HAS COME THIS WAY TO PICK FLOWERS!
GLAD TO HELP YOU, STAR BOY! I'LL TELL MY FOSTER-PARENTS I'M LEAVING!
WHEN YOU RETURN, REMEMBER NOT TO USE MY OTHER NAME IN FRONT OF THE CAPTURED CRIMINAL!
GOODNESS!
GOLLY! THAT "SUPERBOY" OF ANOTHER FUTURE WORLD HAS A SECRET IDENTITY! I DIDN'T COME SOON ENOUGH TO HEAR HIS OTHER NAME BUT... HMM!... I CAN BLUFF!
AND WHEN STAR BOY ENTERS THE CAVE FOR HIS PRISONER...
A GIRL! WH-WHO ARE YOU?
I'M LANA LANG, STAR BOY! I OVERHEARD YOUR ENTIRE STORY AND KNOW YOUR SECRET IDENTITY! I WON'T MENTION IT IN FRONT OF YOUR PRISONER... IF YOU DO ME A FAVOR!
YOU SEE, I HAVE A CRUSH ON SUPERBOY! YOU'RE THE ONLY BOY I'VE MET WHO IS EQUAL TO HIM! SO IF YOU PRETEND TO FALL IN LOVE WITH ME, YOU CAN MAKE SUPERBOY JEALOUS!
OTHERWISE, Y-YOU'LL GIVE AWAY MY SECRET IDENTITY, EH? I-I'M TRAPPED!
RETURNING MEANWHILE, SUPERBOY IS TIPPED OFF TO WHAT IS HAPPENING...
I'M READY TO GO WITH STAR BOY... WAIT! SOMEBODY WAS PICKING FLOWERS HERE... AND I HEAR LANA'S VOICE NEAR THE CAVE!
NOW HERE ARE YOUR INSTRUCTIONS, STAR BOY! WHEN SUPERBOY SEES US TOGETHER, PRETEND WE MET BY CHANCE!
MAKE BELIEVE YOU FELL FOR ME AND INVITED ME TO VISIT YOUR WORLD! THEN, ON XANTHU, YOU'LL OBEY MY EVERY WHIM WITH YOUR SUPER-POWERS! YOUR DEVOTION TO ME WILL MAKE SUPERBOY JEALOUS! GOT IT?
HMM... SO THAT'S HER LITTLE SCHEME, IS IT?
6

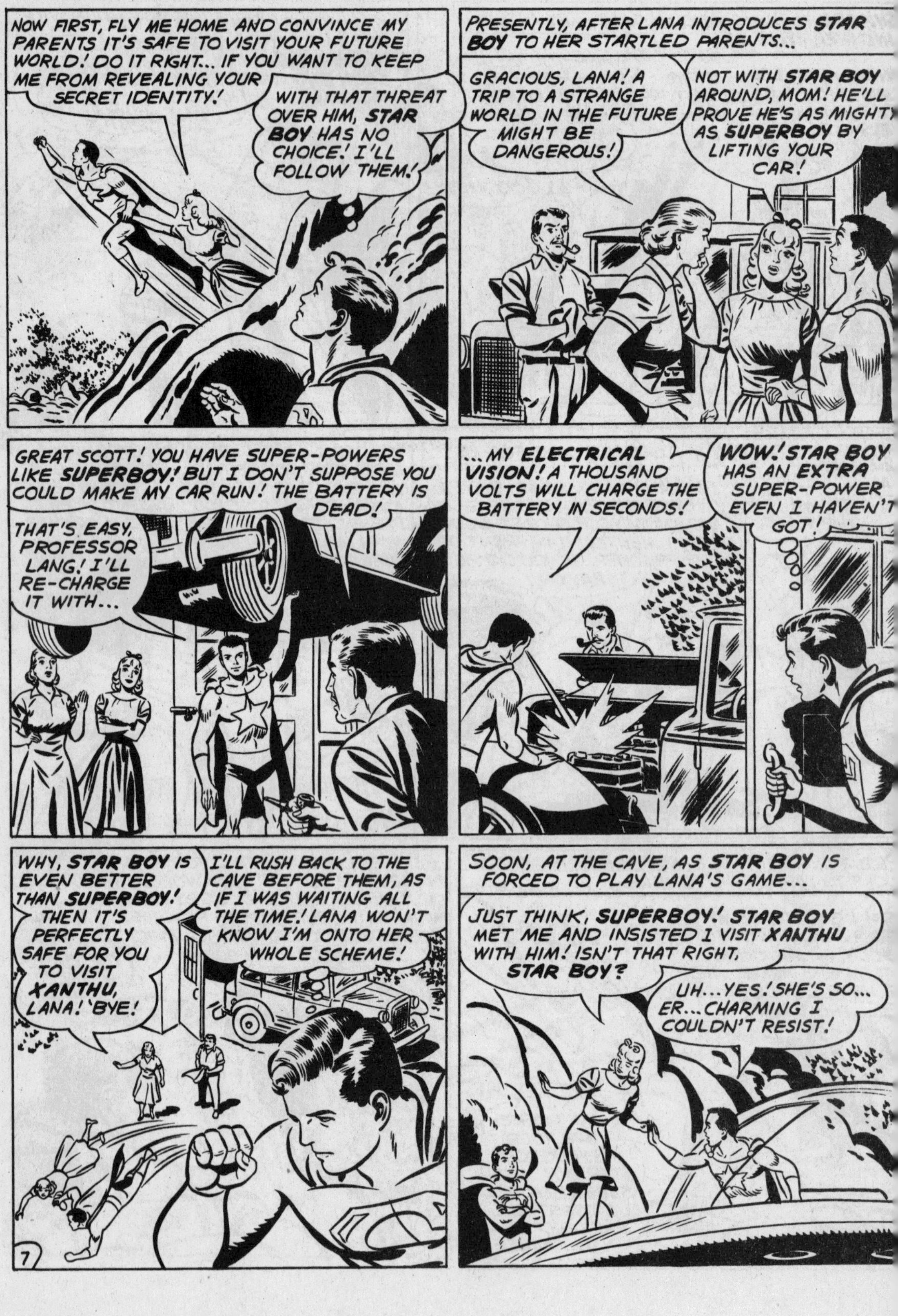
NOW FIRST, FLY ME HOME AND CONVINCE MY PARENTS IT'S SAFE TO VISIT YOUR FUTURE WORLD! DO IT RIGHT... IF YOU WANT TO KEEP ME FROM REVEALING YOUR SECRET IDENTITY!
WITH THAT THREAT OVER HIM, STAR BOY HAS NO CHOICE! I'LL FOLLOW THEM!
PRESENTLY, AFTER LANA INTRODUCES STAR BOY TO HER STARTLED PARENTS...
GRACIOUS, LANA! A TRIP TO A STRANGE WORLD IN THE FUTURE MIGHT BE DANGEROUS!
NOT WITH STAR BOY AROUND, MOM! HE'LL PROVE HE'S AS MIGHTY AS SUPERBOY BY LIFTING YOUR CAR!
GREAT SCOTT! YOU HAVE SUPER-POWERS LIKE SUPERBOY! BUT I DON'T SUPPOSE YOU COULD MAKE MY CAR RUN! THE BATTERY IS DEAD!
THAT'S EASY, PROFESSOR LANG! I'LL RE-CHARGE IT WITH...
...MY ELECTRICAL VISION! A THOUSAND VOLTS WILL CHARGE THE BATTERY IN SECONDS!
WOW! STAR BOY HAS AN EXTRA SUPER-POWER EVEN I HAVEN'T GOT!
WHY, STAR BOY IS EVEN BETTER THAN SUPERBOY! THEN IT'S PERFECTLY SAFE FOR YOU TO VISIT XANTHU, LANA! 'BYE!
I'LL RUSH BACK TO THE CAVE BEFORE THEM, AS IF I WAS WAITING ALL THE TIME! LANA WON'T KNOW I'M ONTO HER WHOLE SCHEME!
7
SOON, AT THE CAVE, AS STAR BOY IS FORCED TO PLAY LANA'S GAME...
JUST THINK, SUPERBOY! STAR BOY MET ME AND INSISTED I VISIT XANTHU WITH HIM! ISN'T THAT RIGHT, STAR BOY?
UH...YES! SHE'S SO... ER...CHARMING I COULDN'T RESIST!

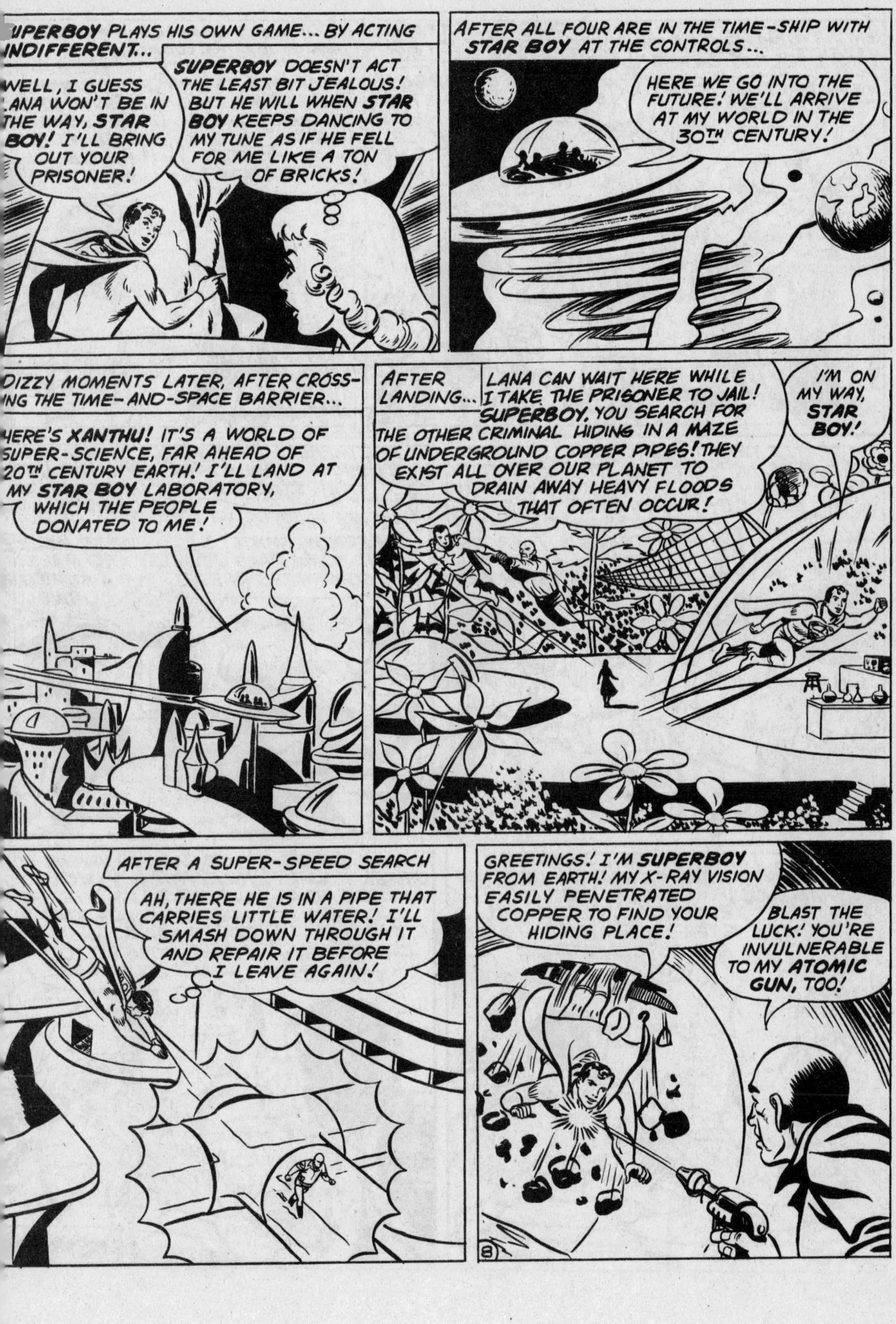
SUPERBOY PLAYS HIS OWN GAME... BY ACTING INDIFFERENT...
WELL, I GUESS LANA WON'T BE IN THE WAY, STAR BOY! I'LL BRING OUT YOUR PRISONER!
SUPERBOY DOESN'T ACT THE LEAST BIT JEALOUS! BUT HE WILL WHEN STAR BOY KEEPS DANCING TO MY TUNE AS IF HE FELL FOR ME LIKE A TON OF BRICKS!
AFTER ALL FOUR ARE IN THE TIME-SHIP WITH STAR BOY AT THE CONTROLS...
HERE WE GO INTO THE FUTURE! WE'LL ARRIVE AT MY WORLD IN THE 30TH CENTURY!
DIZZY MOMENTS LATER, AFTER CROSSING THE TIME-AND-SPACE BARRIER...
HERE'S XANTHU! IT'S A WORLD OF SUPER-SCIENCE, FAR AHEAD OF 20TH CENTURY EARTH! I'LL LAND AT MY STAR BOY LABORATORY, WHICH THE PEOPLE DONATED TO ME!
AFTER LANDING...
LANA CAN WAIT HERE WHILE I TAKE THE PRISONER TO JAIL! SUPERBOY, YOU SEARCH FOR THE OTHER CRIMINAL HIDING IN A MAZE OF UNDERGROUND COPPER PIPES! THEY EXIST ALL OVER OUR PLANET TO DRAIN AWAY HEAVY FLOODS THAT OFTEN OCCUR!
I'M ON MY WAY, STAR BOY!
AFTER A SUPER-SPEED SEARCH
AH, THERE HE IS IN A PIPE THAT CARRIES LITTLE WATER! I'LL SMASH DOWN THROUGH IT AND REPAIR IT BEFORE I LEAVE AGAIN!
GREETINGS! I'M SUPERBOY FROM EARTH! MY X-RAY VISION EASILY PENETRATED COPPER TO FIND YOUR HIDING PLACE!
BLAST THE LUCK! YOU'RE INVULNERABLE TO MY ATOMIC GUN, TOO!
8

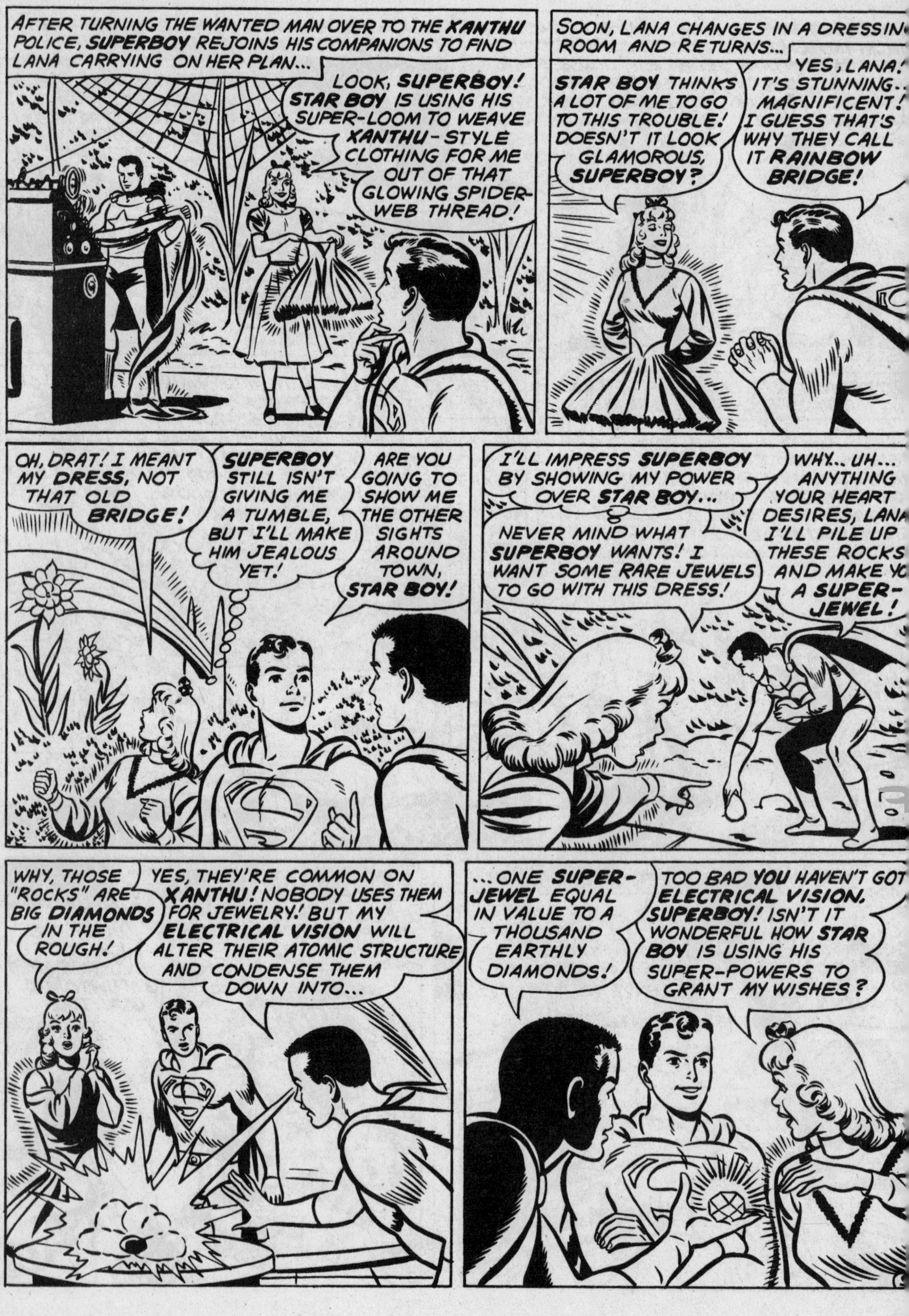

AFTER TURNING THE WANTED MAN OVER TO THE XANTHU POLICE, SUPERBOY REJOINS HIS COMPANIONS TO FIND LANA CARRYING ON HER PLAN...
LOOK, SUPERBOY! STAR BOY IS USING HIS SUPER-LOOM TO WEAVE XANTHU-STYLE CLOTHING FOR ME OUT OF THAT GLOWING SPIDER-WEB THREAD!
SOON, LANA CHANGES IN A DRESSIN ROOM AND RETURNS...
STAR BOY THINKS A LOT OF ME TO GO TO THIS TROUBLE! DOESN'T IT LOOK GLAMOROUS, SUPERBOY?
YES, LANA! IT'S STUNNING... MAGNIFICENT! I GUESS THAT'S WHY THEY CALL IT RAINBOW BRIDGE!
OH, DRAT! I MEANT MY DRESS, NOT THAT OLD BRIDGE!
SUPERBOY STILL ISN'T GIVING ME A TUMBLE, BUT I'LL MAKE HIM JEALOUS YET!
ARE YOU GOING TO SHOW ME THE OTHER SIGHTS AROUND TOWN, STAR BOY!
I'LL IMPRESS SUPERBOY BY SHOWING MY POWER OVER STAR BOY...
NEVER MIND WHAT SUPERBOY WANTS! I WANT SOME RARE JEWELS TO GO WITH THIS DRESS!
WHY... UH... ANYTHING YOUR HEART DESIRES, LANA I'LL PILE UP THESE ROCKS AND MAKE YO A SUPER-JEWEL!
WHY, THOSE "ROCKS" ARE BIG DIAMONDS IN THE ROUGH!
YES, THEY'RE COMMON ON XANTHU! NOBODY USES THEM FOR JEWELRY! BUT MY ELECTRICAL VISION WILL ALTER THEIR ATOMIC STRUCTURE AND CONDENSE THEM DOWN INTO...
...ONE SUPER-JEWEL EQUAL IN VALUE TO A THOUSAND EARTHLY DIAMONDS!
TOO BAD YOU HAVEN'T GOT ELECTRICAL VISION, SUPERBOY! ISN'T IT WONDERFUL HOW STAR BOY IS USING HIS SUPER-POWERS TO GRANT MY WISHES?

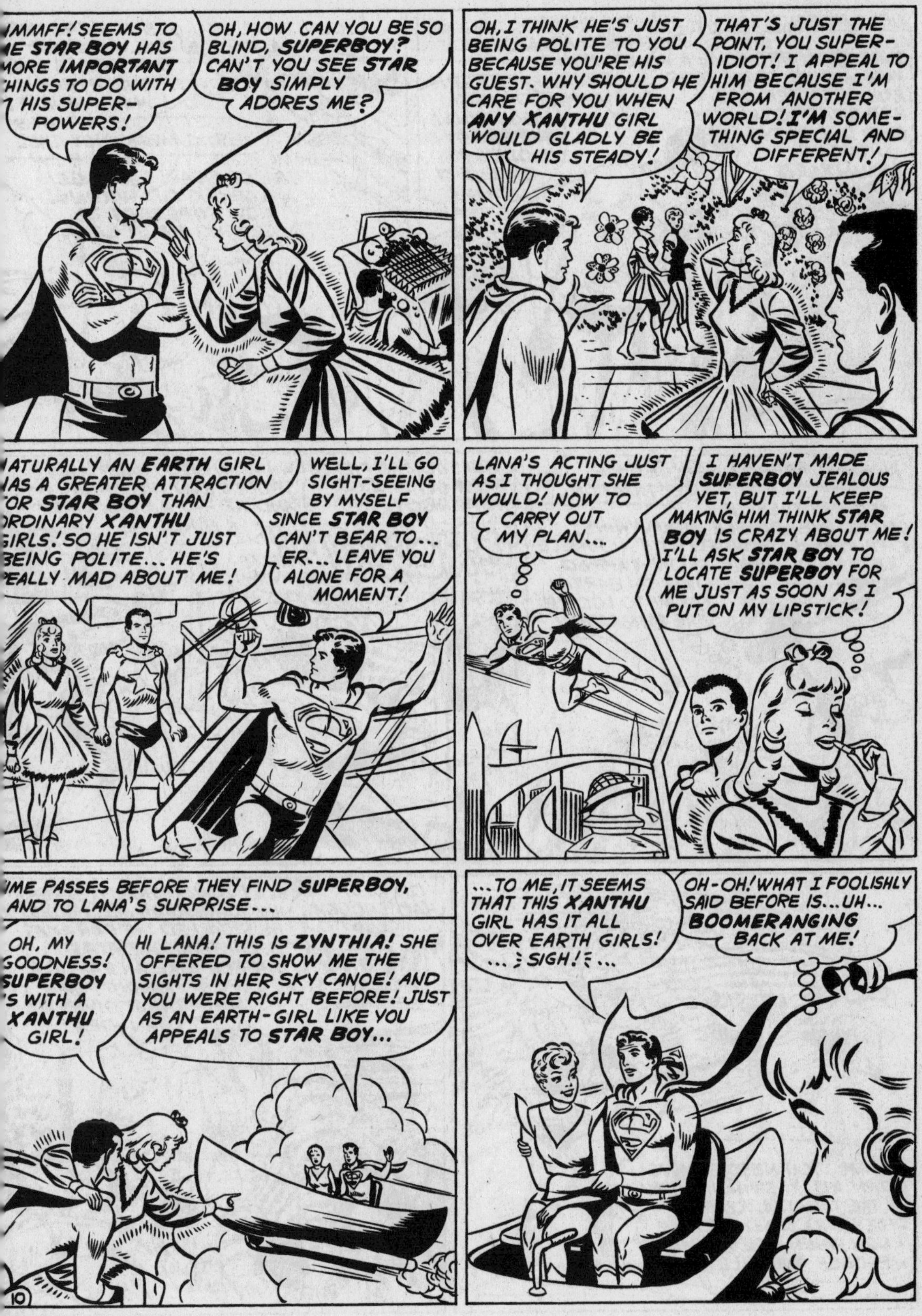
MMFF! SEEMS TO ME STAR BOY HAS MORE IMPORTANT THINGS TO DO WITH HIS SUPER-POWERS!
OH, HOW CAN YOU BE SO BLIND, SUPERBOY? CAN'T YOU SEE STAR BOY SIMPLY ADORES ME?
OH, I THINK HE'S JUST BEING POLITE TO YOU BECAUSE YOU'RE HIS GUEST. WHY SHOULD HE CARE FOR YOU WHEN ANY XANTHU GIRL WOULD GLADLY BE HIS STEADY!
THAT'S JUST THE POINT, YOU SUPER-IDIOT! I APPEAL TO HIM BECAUSE I'M FROM ANOTHER WORLD! I'M SOMETHING SPECIAL AND DIFFERENT!
NATURALLY AN EARTH GIRL HAS A GREATER ATTRACTION FOR STAR BOY THAN ORDINARY XANTHU GIRLS! SO HE ISN'T JUST BEING POLITE... HE'S REALLY MAD ABOUT ME!
WELL, I'LL GO SIGHT-SEEING BY MYSELF SINCE STAR BOY CAN'T BEAR TO... ER... LEAVE YOU ALONE FOR A MOMENT!
LANA'S ACTING JUST AS I THOUGHT SHE WOULD! NOW TO CARRY OUT MY PLAN....
I HAVEN'T MADE SUPERBOY JEALOUS YET, BUT I'LL KEEP MAKING HIM THINK STAR BOY IS CRAZY ABOUT ME! I'LL ASK STAR BOY TO LOCATE SUPERBOY FOR ME JUST AS SOON AS I PUT ON MY LIPSTICK!
TIME PASSES BEFORE THEY FIND SUPERBOY, AND TO LANA'S SURPRISE...
OH, MY GOODNESS! SUPERBOY IS WITH A XANTHU GIRL!
HI LANA! THIS IS ZYNTHIA! SHE OFFERED TO SHOW ME THE SIGHTS IN HER SKY CANOE! AND YOU WERE RIGHT BEFORE! JUST AS AN EARTH-GIRL LIKE YOU APPEALS TO STAR BOY...
10
...TO ME, IT SEEMS THAT THIS XANTHU GIRL HAS IT ALL OVER EARTH GIRLS! ... SIGH! ...
OH-OH! WHAT I FOOLISHLY SAID BEFORE IS...UH... BOOMERANGING BACK AT ME!

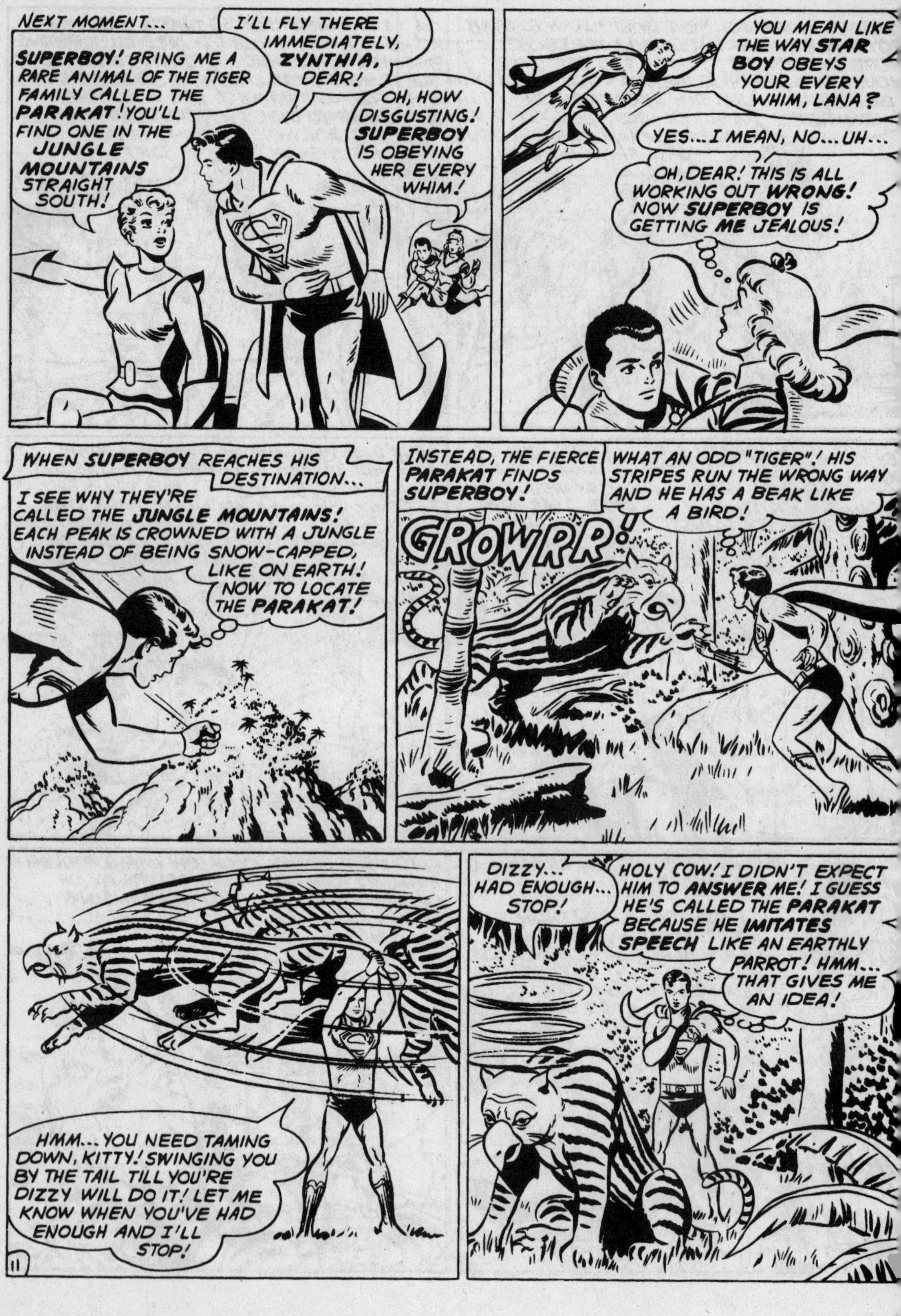
NEXT MOMENT...
SUPERBOY! BRING ME A RARE ANIMAL OF THE TIGER FAMILY CALLED THE PARAKAT! YOU'LL FIND ONE IN THE JUNGLE MOUNTAINS STRAIGHT SOUTH!
I'LL FLY THERE IMMEDIATELY, ZYNTHIA, DEAR!
OH, HOW DISGUSTING! SUPERBOY IS OBEYING HER EVERY WHIM!
YOU MEAN LIKE THE WAY STAR BOY OBEYS YOUR EVERY WHIM, LANA?
YES... I MEAN, NO... UH...
OH, DEAR! THIS IS ALL WORKING OUT WRONG! NOW SUPERBOY IS GETTING ME JEALOUS!
WHEN SUPERBOY REACHES HIS DESTINATION...
I SEE WHY THEY'RE CALLED THE JUNGLE MOUNTAINS! EACH PEAK IS CROWNED WITH A JUNGLE INSTEAD OF BEING SNOW-CAPPED, LIKE ON EARTH! NOW TO LOCATE THE PARAKAT!
INSTEAD, THE FIERCE PARAKAT FINDS SUPERBOY!
GROWRR!
WHAT AN ODD "TIGER"! HIS STRIPES RUN THE WRONG WAY AND HE HAS A BEAK LIKE A BIRD!
HMM... YOU NEED TAMING DOWN, KITTY! SWINGING YOU BY THE TAIL TILL YOU'RE DIZZY WILL DO IT! LET ME KNOW WHEN YOU'VE HAD ENOUGH AND I'LL STOP!
11
DIZZY... HAD ENOUGH... STOP!
HOLY COW! I DIDN'T EXPECT HIM TO ANSWER ME! I GUESS HE'S CALLED THE PARAKAT BECAUSE HE IMITATES SPEECH LIKE AN EARTHLY PARROT! HMM... THAT GIVES ME AN IDEA!

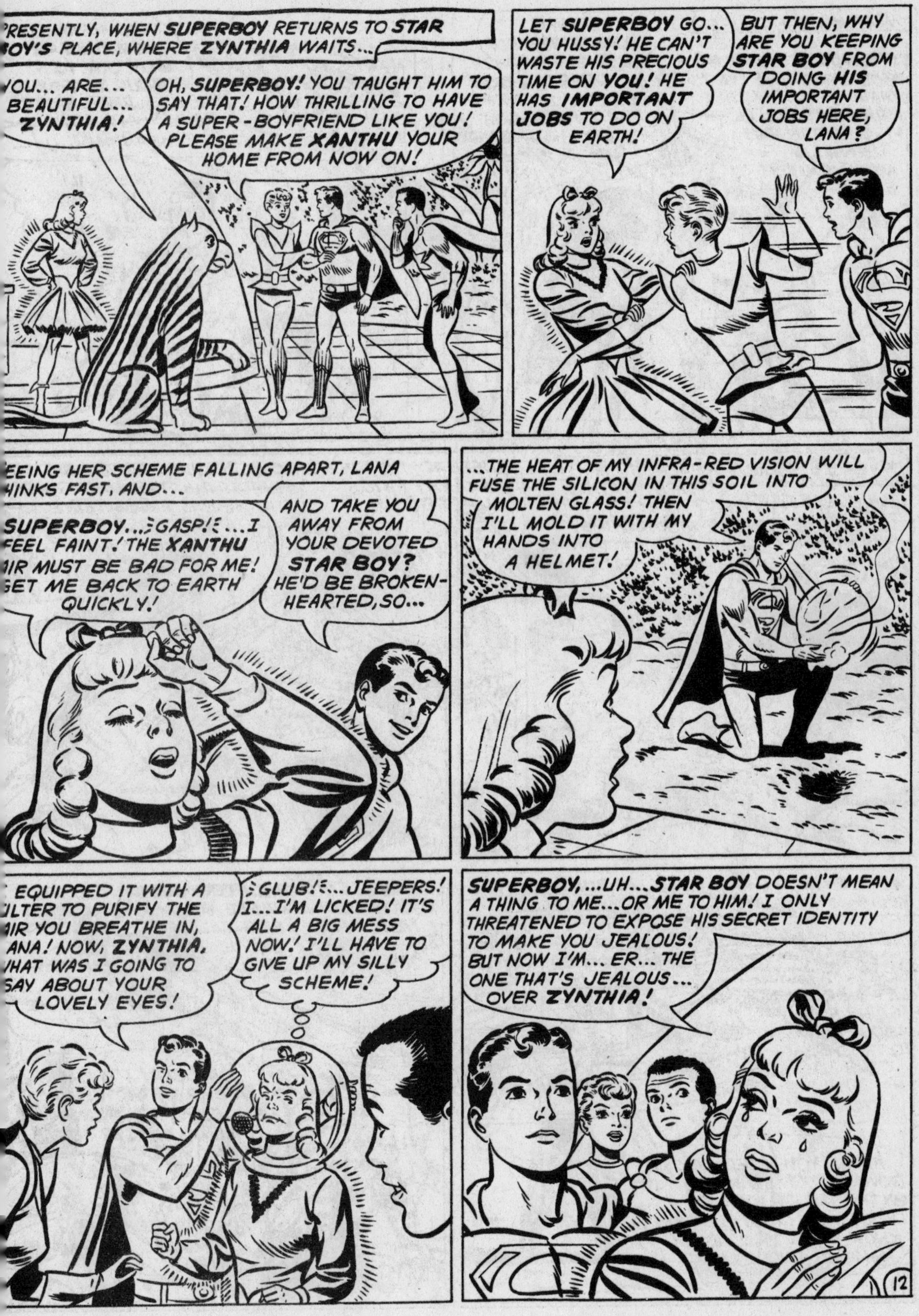
PRESENTLY, WHEN SUPERBOY RETURNS TO STAR BOY'S PLACE, WHERE ZYNTHIA WAITS...
YOU... ARE... BEAUTIFUL... ZYNTHIA!
OH, SUPERBOY! YOU TAUGHT HIM TO SAY THAT! HOW THRILLING TO HAVE A SUPER-BOYFRIEND LIKE YOU! PLEASE MAKE XANTHU YOUR HOME FROM NOW ON!
LET SUPERBOY GO... YOU HUSSY! HE CAN'T WASTE HIS PRECIOUS TIME ON YOU! HE HAS IMPORTANT JOBS TO DO ON EARTH!
BUT THEN, WHY ARE YOU KEEPING STAR BOY FROM DOING HIS IMPORTANT JOBS HERE, LANA?
SEEING HER SCHEME FALLING APART, LANA THINKS FAST, AND...
SUPERBOY... GASP! ...I FEEL FAINT! THE XANTHU AIR MUST BE BAD FOR ME! GET ME BACK TO EARTH QUICKLY!
AND TAKE YOU AWAY FROM YOUR DEVOTED STAR BOY? HE'D BE BROKEN-HEARTED, SO...
...THE HEAT OF MY INFRA-RED VISION WILL FUSE THE SILICON IN THIS SOIL INTO MOLTEN GLASS! THEN I'LL MOLD IT WITH MY HANDS INTO A HELMET!
I EQUIPPED IT WITH A FILTER TO PURIFY THE AIR YOU BREATHE IN, LANA! NOW, ZYNTHIA, WHAT WAS I GOING TO SAY ABOUT YOUR LOVELY EYES!
GLUB! ...JEEPERS! I... I'M LICKED! IT'S ALL A BIG MESS NOW! I'LL HAVE TO GIVE UP MY SILLY SCHEME!
SUPERBOY, ...UH... STAR BOY DOESN'T MEAN A THING TO ME... OR ME TO HIM! I ONLY THREATENED TO EXPOSE HIS SECRET IDENTITY TO MAKE YOU JEALOUS! BUT NOW I'M... ER... THE ONE THAT'S JEALOUS... OVER ZYNTHIA!
12

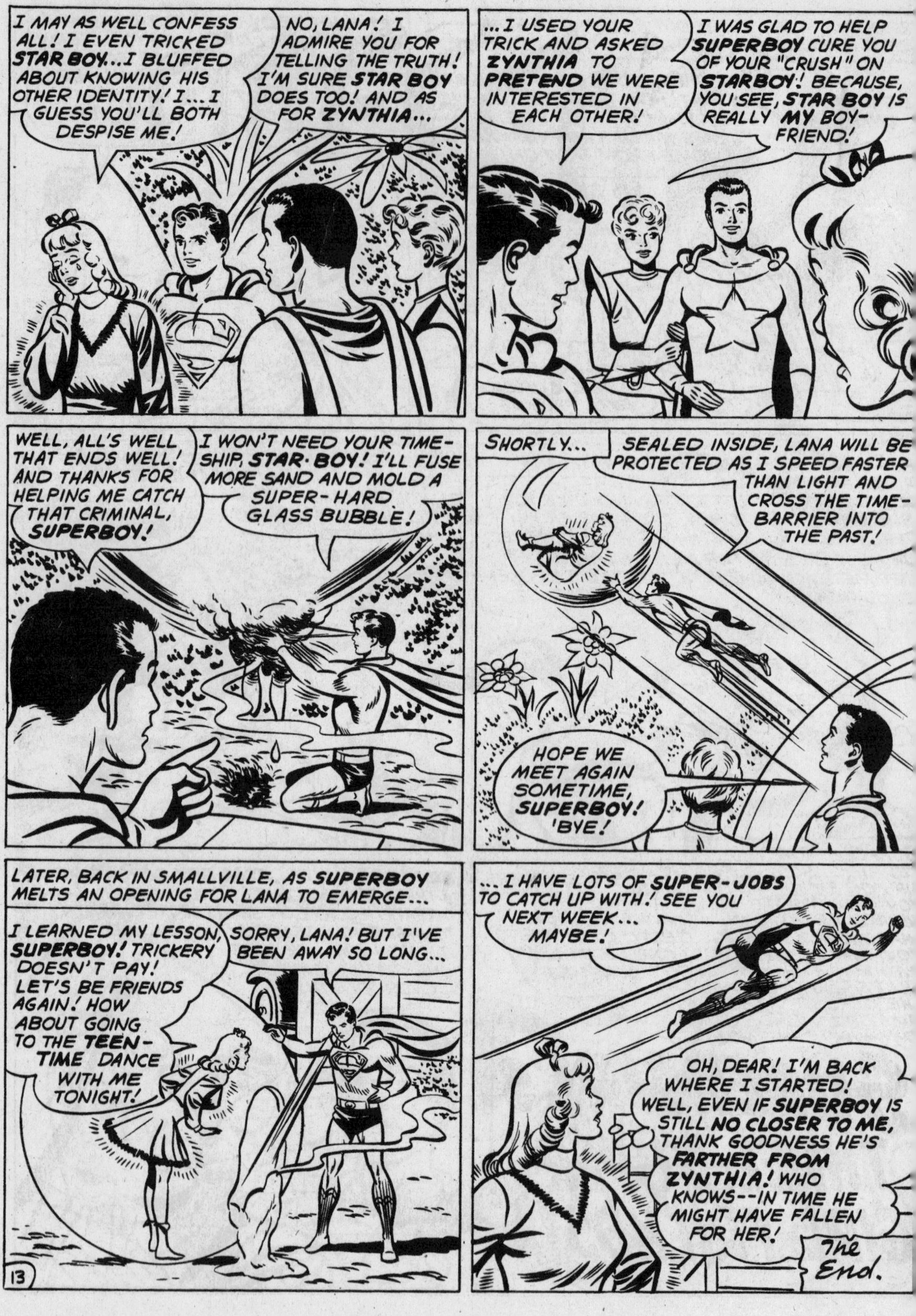
I MAY AS WELL CONFESS ALL! I EVEN TRICKED STAR BOY...I BLUFFED ABOUT KNOWING HIS OTHER IDENTITY! I...I GUESS YOU'LL BOTH DESPISE ME!
NO, LANA! I ADMIRE YOU FOR TELLING THE TRUTH! I'M SURE STAR BOY DOES TOO! AND AS FOR ZYNTHIA...
...I USED YOUR TRICK AND ASKED ZYNTHIA TO PRETEND WE WERE INTERESTED IN EACH OTHER!
I WAS GLAD TO HELP SUPERBOY CURE YOU OF YOUR "CRUSH" ON STARBOY! BECAUSE, YOU SEE, STAR BOY IS REALLY MY BOY-FRIEND!
WELL, ALL'S WELL THAT ENDS WELL! AND THANKS FOR HELPING ME CATCH THAT CRIMINAL, SUPERBOY!
I WON'T NEED YOUR TIME-SHIP, STAR BOY! I'LL FUSE MORE SAND AND MOLD A SUPER-HARD GLASS BUBBLE!
SHORTLY...
SEALED INSIDE, LANA WILL BE PROTECTED AS I SPEED FASTER THAN LIGHT AND CROSS THE TIME-BARRIER INTO THE PAST!
HOPE WE MEET AGAIN SOMETIME, SUPERBOY! 'BYE!
LATER, BACK IN SMALLVILLE, AS SUPERBOY MELTS AN OPENING FOR LANA TO EMERGE...
I LEARNED MY LESSON, SUPERBOY! TRICKERY DOESN'T PAY! LET'S BE FRIENDS AGAIN! HOW ABOUT GOING TO THE TEEN-TIME DANCE WITH ME TONIGHT!
SORRY, LANA! BUT I'VE BEEN AWAY SO LONG...
13
...I HAVE LOTS OF SUPER-JOBS TO CATCH UP WITH! SEE YOU NEXT WEEK... MAYBE!
OH, DEAR! I'M BACK WHERE I STARTED! WELL, EVEN IF SUPERBOY IS STILL NO CLOSER TO ME, THANK GOODNESS HE'S FARTHER FROM ZYNTHIA! WHO KNOWS--IN TIME HE MIGHT HAVE FALLEN FOR HER!
The End.

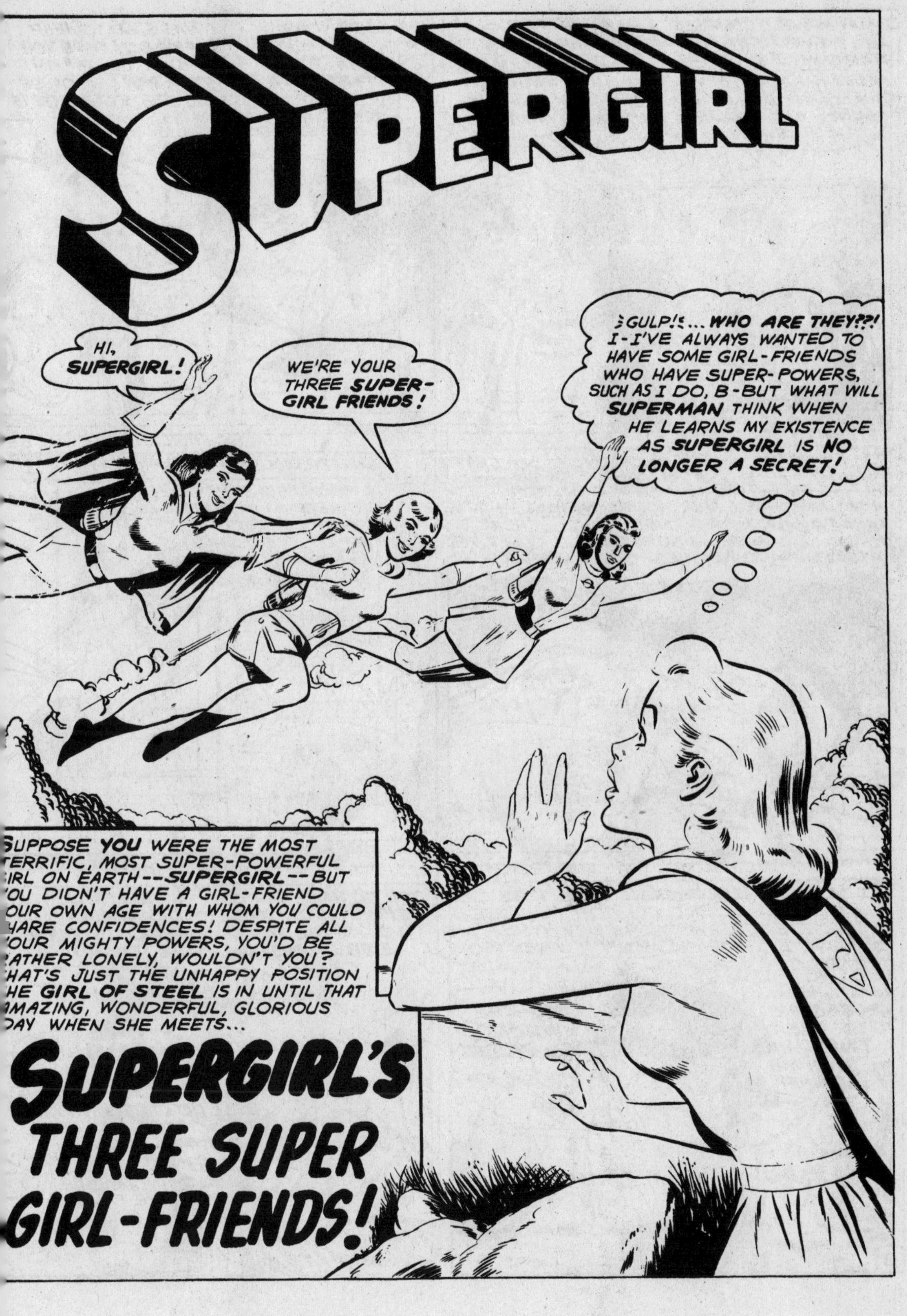
SUPERGIRL
HI, SUPERGIRL!
WE'RE YOUR THREE SUPER-GIRL FRIENDS!
GULP! ... WHO ARE THEY?? I-I'VE ALWAYS WANTED TO HAVE SOME GIRL-FRIENDS WHO HAVE SUPER-POWERS, SUCH AS I DO, B-BUT WHAT WILL SUPERMAN THINK WHEN HE LEARNS MY EXISTENCE AS SUPERGIRL IS NO LONGER A SECRET!
SUPPOSE YOU WERE THE MOST TERRIFIC, MOST SUPER-POWERFUL IRL ON EARTH--SUPERGIRL--BUT OU DIDN'T HAVE A GIRL-FRIEND OUR OWN AGE WITH WHOM YOU COULD HARE CONFIDENCES! DESPITE ALL OUR MIGHTY POWERS, YOU'D BE ATHER LONELY, WOULDN'T YOU? HAT'S JUST THE UNHAPPY POSITION HE GIRL OF STEEL IS IN UNTIL THAT MAZING, WONDERFUL, GLORIOUS DAY WHEN SHE MEETS...
SUPERGIRL'S THREE SUPER GIRL-FRIENDS!

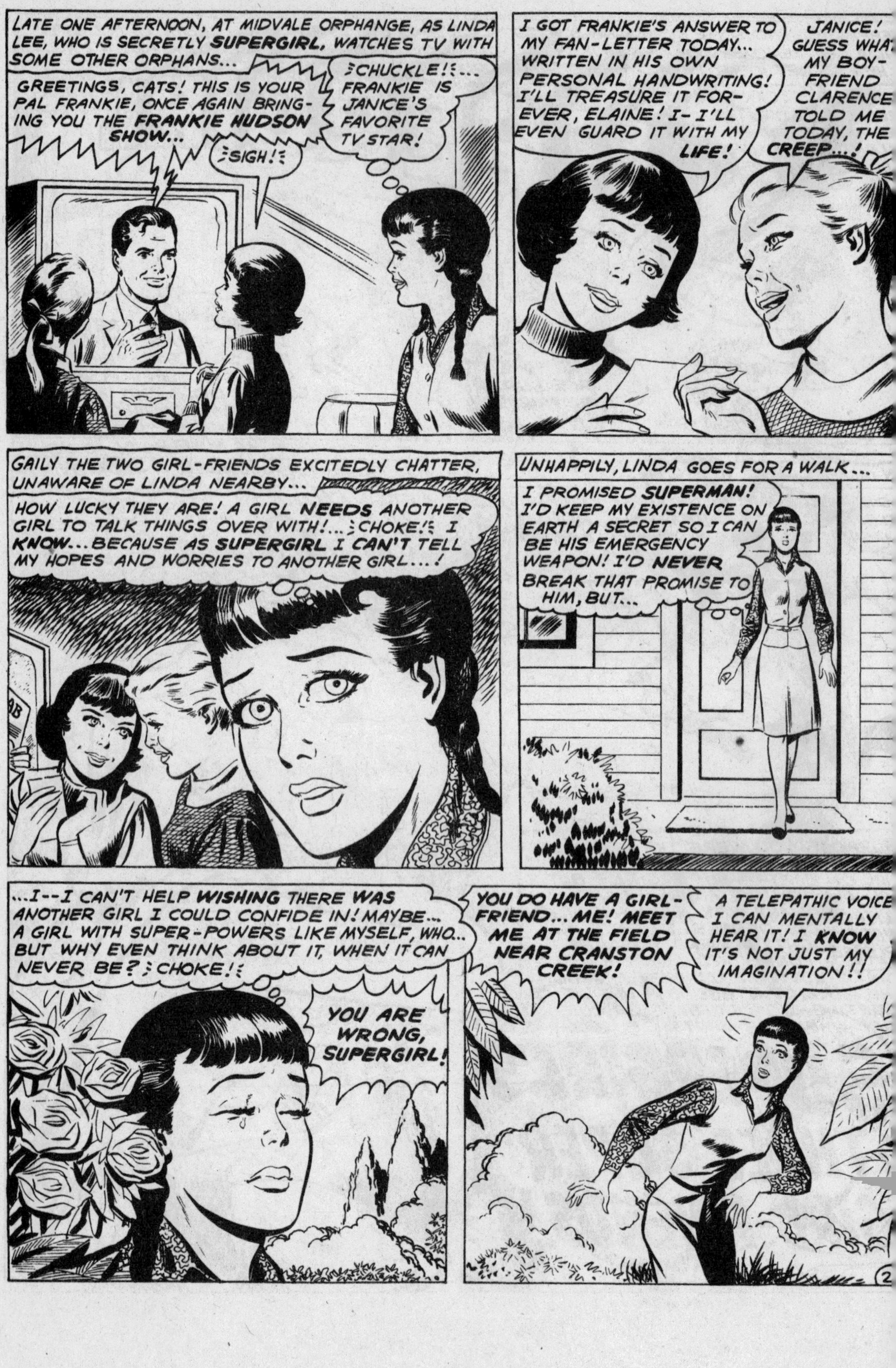
LATE ONE AFTERNOON, AT MIDVALE ORPHANGE, AS LINDA LEE, WHO IS SECRETLY SUPERGIRL, WATCHES TV WITH SOME OTHER ORPHANS...
GREETINGS, CATS! THIS IS YOUR PAL FRANKIE, ONCE AGAIN BRINGING YOU THE FRANKIE HUDSON SHOW...
SIGH!
CHUCKLE!... FRANKIE IS JANICE'S FAVORITE TV STAR!
I GOT FRANKIE'S ANSWER TO MY FAN-LETTER TODAY... WRITTEN IN HIS OWN PERSONAL HANDWRITING! I'LL TREASURE IT FOREVER, ELAINE! I- I'LL EVEN GUARD IT WITH MY LIFE!
JANICE! GUESS WHAT MY BOY-FRIEND CLARENCE TOLD ME TODAY, THE CREEP...!
GAILY THE TWO GIRL-FRIENDS EXCITEDLY CHATTER, UNAWARE OF LINDA NEARBY...
HOW LUCKY THEY ARE! A GIRL NEEDS ANOTHER GIRL TO TALK THINGS OVER WITH!... CHOKE! I KNOW... BECAUSE AS SUPERGIRL I CAN'T TELL MY HOPES AND WORRIES TO ANOTHER GIRL...!
UNHAPPILY, LINDA GOES FOR A WALK...
I PROMISED SUPERMAN! I'D KEEP MY EXISTENCE ON EARTH A SECRET SO I CAN BE HIS EMERGENCY WEAPON! I'D NEVER BREAK THAT PROMISE TO HIM, BUT...
...I--I CAN'T HELP WISHING THERE WAS ANOTHER GIRL I COULD CONFIDE IN! MAYBE... A GIRL WITH SUPER-POWERS LIKE MYSELF, WHO.. BUT WHY EVEN THINK ABOUT IT, WHEN IT CAN NEVER BE? CHOKE!
YOU ARE WRONG, SUPERGIRL!
YOU DO HAVE A GIRL-FRIEND... ME! MEET ME AT THE FIELD NEAR CRANSTON CREEK!
A TELEPATHIC VOICE! I CAN MENTALLY HEAR IT! I KNOW IT'S NOT JUST MY IMAGINATION!!
2

STEPPING BEHIND SOME SCREENING BUSHES, LINDA LEE REMOVES HER WIG, SWIFTLY CHANGING TO HER SECRET IDENTITY OF DYNAMIC *SUPERGIRL!*

I WONDER...! CAN THAT VOICE BELONG TO *LORI*, THE MERMAID FROM ATLANTIS? SHE HAS TELEPATHIC POWERS! I'LL SOON KNOW!

EN ROUTE TO CRANSTON CREEK, AS THE *GIRL OF STEEL* PASSES A HOLLOW TREE IN A WOODS...

TAKE OVER FOR ME AT THE ORPHANGE, LINDA ROBOT, WHILE I'M GONE! COVER MY ABSENCE!

I SHALL, MISTRESS!

AN INSTANT LATER, AT HER DESTINATION...

I DON'T SEE ANYONE! WAS THAT TELEPATHIC VOICE ONLY IN MY IMAGINATION, AFTER ALL?

DEFINITELY NOT!... LOOK BEHIND YOU!

AND AS *SUPERGIRL* OBEYS...

A GIRL IN A *MASK!* MY X-RAY VISION CAN'T PENETRATE THE MASK! IT MUST BE MADE OF *LEAD!*

WHO ARE YOU?

I AM YOUR *SUPER GIRL-FRIEND!* WE HAVE MET BEFORE! CAN YOU GUESS MY IDENTITY, BEFORE I REMOVE THE SCREENING LEAD-MASK?

I HAVEN'T THE SLIGHTEST IDEA WHO YOU ARE! PLEASE TELL ME!

FIRST, TURN AND LOOK BEHIND YOU, AGAIN!

SWIFTLY, THE *GIRL OF STEEL* WHIRLS ABOUT...

≤GASP!≥ WHO ARE *YOU?!!*

I AM YOUR SECOND *SUPER GIRL-FRIEND!* AND NOW, LOOK BEHIND YOU ONCE MORE FOR *ANOTHER* ASTOUNDING SURPRISE!

③

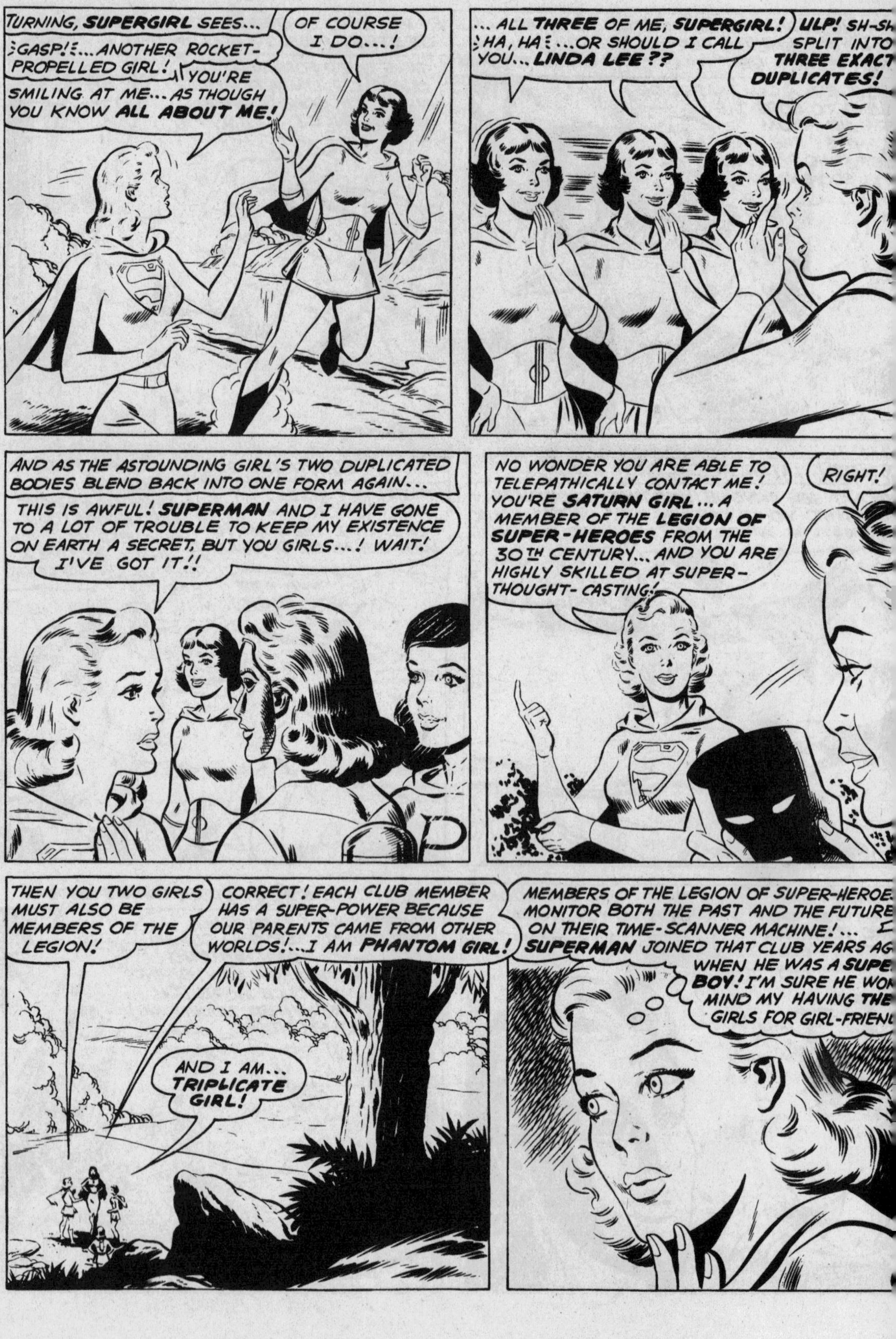
TURNING, SUPERGIRL SEES...
:GASP!:...ANOTHER ROCKET-PROPELLED GIRL! YOU'RE SMILING AT ME...AS THOUGH YOU KNOW ALL ABOUT ME!
OF COURSE I DO...!
...ALL THREE OF ME, SUPERGIRL! HA, HA:...OR SHOULD I CALL YOU...LINDA LEE??
ULP! SH-SH SPLIT INTO THREE EXACT DUPLICATES!
AND AS THE ASTOUNDING GIRL'S TWO DUPLICATED BODIES BLEND BACK INTO ONE FORM AGAIN...
THIS IS AWFUL! SUPERMAN AND I HAVE GONE TO A LOT OF TROUBLE TO KEEP MY EXISTENCE ON EARTH A SECRET, BUT YOU GIRLS...! WAIT! I'VE GOT IT!!
NO WONDER YOU ARE ABLE TO TELEPATHICALLY CONTACT ME! YOU'RE SATURN GIRL...A MEMBER OF THE LEGION OF SUPER-HEROES FROM THE 30TH CENTURY...AND YOU ARE HIGHLY SKILLED AT SUPER-THOUGHT-CASTING!
RIGHT!
THEN YOU TWO GIRLS MUST ALSO BE MEMBERS OF THE LEGION!
CORRECT! EACH CLUB MEMBER HAS A SUPER-POWER BECAUSE OUR PARENTS CAME FROM OTHER WORLDS!...I AM PHANTOM GIRL!
AND I AM... TRIPLICATE GIRL!
MEMBERS OF THE LEGION OF SUPER-HEROE MONITOR BOTH THE PAST AND THE FUTURE ON THEIR TIME-SCANNER MACHINE!... SUPERMAN JOINED THAT CLUB YEARS AG WHEN HE WAS A SUPE BOY! I'M SURE HE WO MIND MY HAVING THE GIRLS FOR GIRL-FRIEN

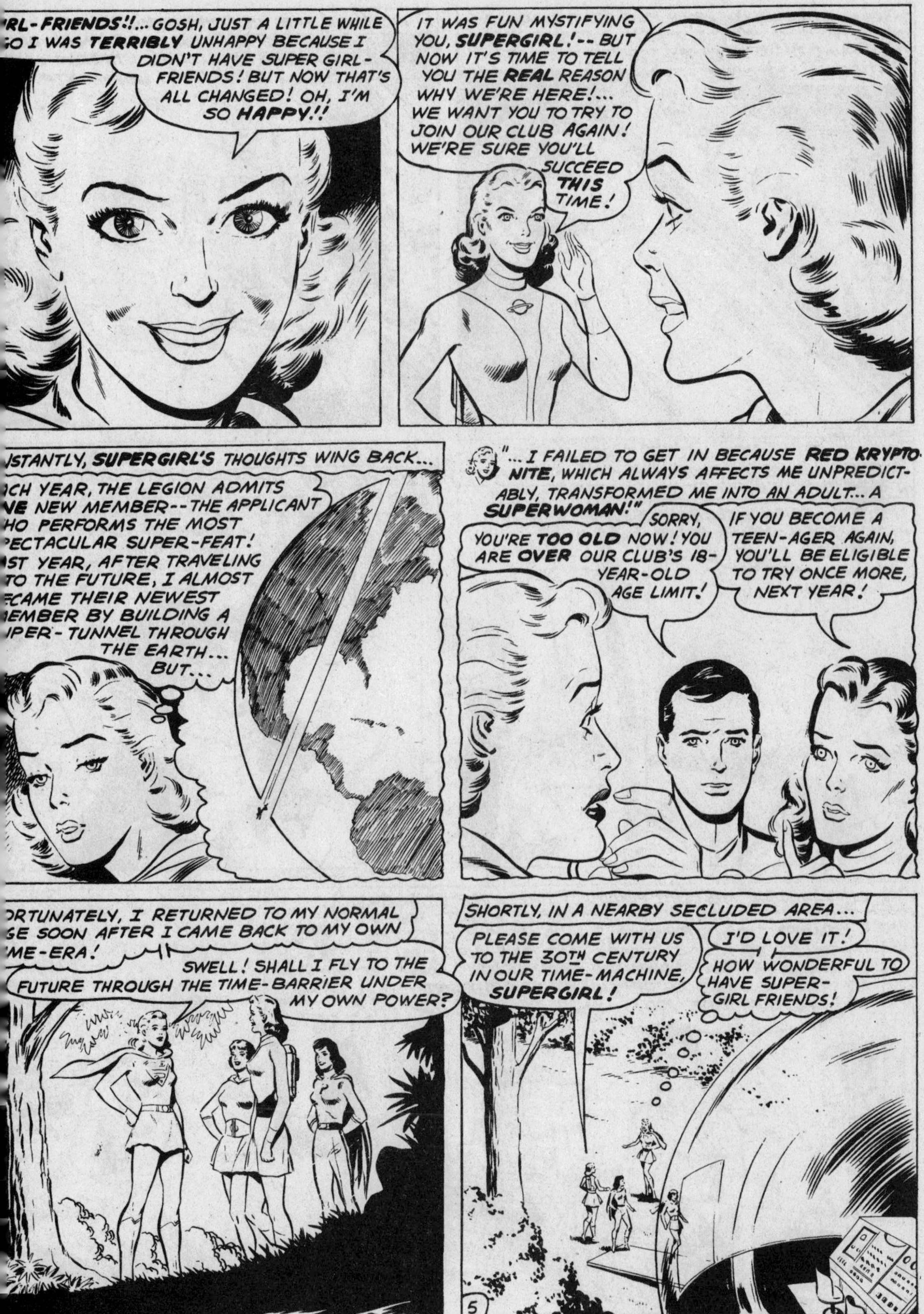
RL-FRIENDS!!... GOSH, JUST A LITTLE WHILE GO I WAS TERRIBLY UNHAPPY BECAUSE I DIDN'T HAVE SUPER GIRL-FRIENDS! BUT NOW THAT'S ALL CHANGED! OH, I'M SO HAPPY!!
IT WAS FUN MYSTIFYING YOU, SUPERGIRL!-- BUT NOW IT'S TIME TO TELL YOU THE REAL REASON WHY WE'RE HERE!... WE WANT YOU TO TRY TO JOIN OUR CLUB AGAIN! WE'RE SURE YOU'LL SUCCEED THIS TIME!
ISTANTLY, SUPERGIRL'S THOUGHTS WING BACK...
ACH YEAR, THE LEGION ADMITS NE NEW MEMBER--THE APPLICANT HO PERFORMS THE MOST PECTACULAR SUPER-FEAT! ST YEAR, AFTER TRAVELING TO THE FUTURE, I ALMOST ECAME THEIR NEWEST EMBER BY BUILDING A UPER-TUNNEL THROUGH THE EARTH... BUT...
"...I FAILED TO GET IN BECAUSE RED KRYPTONITE, WHICH ALWAYS AFFECTS ME UNPREDICTABLY, TRANSFORMED ME INTO AN ADULT... A SUPERWOMAN!"
SORRY, YOU'RE TOO OLD NOW! YOU ARE OVER OUR CLUB'S 18-YEAR-OLD AGE LIMIT!
IF YOU BECOME A TEEN-AGER AGAIN, YOU'LL BE ELIGIBLE TO TRY ONCE MORE, NEXT YEAR!
ORTUNATELY, I RETURNED TO MY NORMAL GE SOON AFTER I CAME BACK TO MY OWN ME-ERA!
SWELL! SHALL I FLY TO THE FUTURE THROUGH THE TIME-BARRIER UNDER MY OWN POWER?
SHORTLY, IN A NEARBY SECLUDED AREA...
PLEASE COME WITH US TO THE 30TH CENTURY IN OUR TIME-MACHINE, SUPERGIRL!
I'D LOVE IT!
HOW WONDERFUL TO HAVE SUPER-GIRL FRIENDS!
5

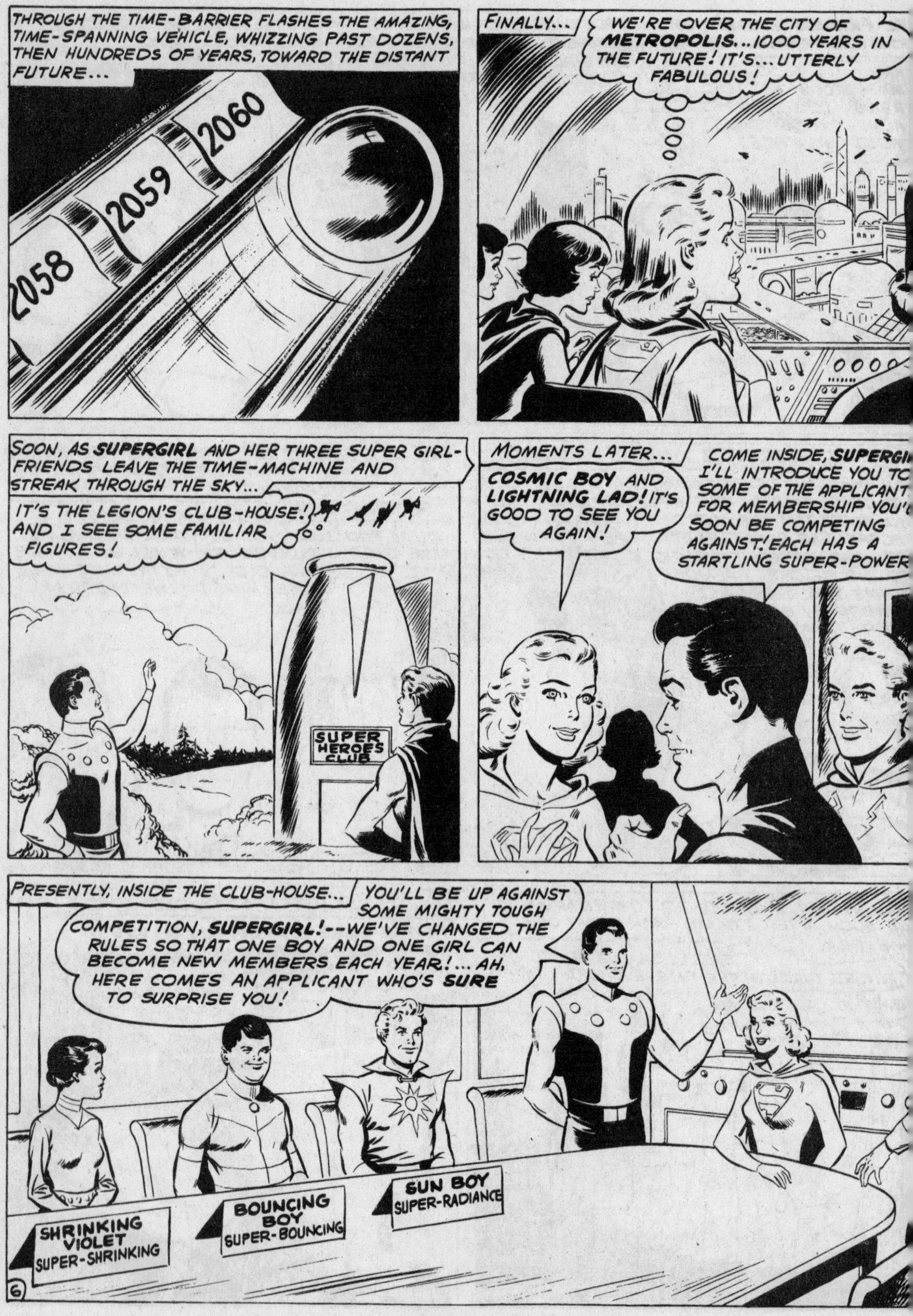
THROUGH THE TIME-BARRIER FLASHES THE AMAZING, TIME-SPANNING VEHICLE, WHIZZING PAST DOZENS, THEN HUNDREDS OF YEARS, TOWARD THE DISTANT FUTURE...
2058
2059
2060
FINALLY...
WE'RE OVER THE CITY OF METROPOLIS...1000 YEARS IN THE FUTURE! IT'S...UTTERLY FABULOUS!
SOON, AS SUPERGIRL AND HER THREE SUPER GIRL-FRIENDS LEAVE THE TIME-MACHINE AND STREAK THROUGH THE SKY...
IT'S THE LEGION'S CLUB-HOUSE! AND I SEE SOME FAMILIAR FIGURES!
SUPER HEROES CLUB
MOMENTS LATER...
COSMIC BOY AND LIGHTNING LAD! IT'S GOOD TO SEE YOU AGAIN!
COME INSIDE, SUPERGI I'LL INTRODUCE YOU TO SOME OF THE APPLICANT FOR MEMBERSHIP YOU' SOON BE COMPETING AGAINST! EACH HAS A STARTLING SUPER-POWER
PRESENTLY, INSIDE THE CLUB-HOUSE...
YOU'LL BE UP AGAINST SOME MIGHTY TOUGH COMPETITION, SUPERGIRL!--WE'VE CHANGED THE RULES SO THAT ONE BOY AND ONE GIRL CAN BECOME NEW MEMBERS EACH YEAR!... AH, HERE COMES AN APPLICANT WHO'S SURE TO SURPRISE YOU!
SHRINKING VIOLET SUPER-SHRINKING
BOUNCING BOY SUPER-BOUNCING
SUN BOY SUPER-RADIANCE
6

AS A HANDSOME, GREEN-SKINNED YOUTH APPROACHES THE CLUB TABLE...

HM-MM. I'VE NEVER MET HIM, OR MY PHOTOGRAPHIC MIND WOULD RECALL IT! BUT THERE'S SOMETHING ALMOST *HAUNTINGLY* FAMILIAR ABOUT HIS *FACE!*

SEATING HIMSELF, THE YOUTH PUTS HIS IDENTIFYING PLACARD ON THE TABLE...

OH, NO! IT ISN'T POSSIBLE! *NOW* I KNOW WHO HE RESEMBLES!

I AM *BRAINIAC 5,* SUPERGIRL....THE GREAT- GREAT-GREAT-GREAT- GRANDSON OF THE SPACE VILLAIN WHO WAS *SUPERMAN'S* FOULEST FOE!

BRAINIAC 5

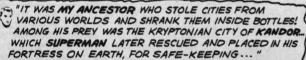

"IT WAS *MY ANCESTOR* WHO STOLE CITIES FROM VARIOUS WORLDS AND SHRANK THEM INSIDE BOTTLES! AMONG HIS PREY WAS THE KRYPTONIAN CITY OF *KANDOR...* WHICH *SUPERMAN* LATER RESCUED AND PLACED IN HIS FORTRESS ON EARTH, FOR SAFE-KEEPING..."

A FINE PRIZE, EH, KOKO? HA, HA!

I KNOW YOU WERE *SUPER- MAN'S* GREAT EMERGENCY WEAPON, CENTURIES AGO, *SUPERGIRL!* I UNDERSTAND YOUR LOATHING FOR THE FIEND WHO WAS MY ANCESTOR! BUT PLEASE... PLEASE...DON'T HATE *ME...!*

IS HE ONLY PRETENDING REMORSE?

I, TOO, DESPISE HIS CRIMES! FOR MANY CENTURIES MY ANCESTORS HAVE SOUGHT TO ATONE FOR HIS EVIL DEEDS! WE ARE *GLAD* HE DIED WHILE BATTLING *SUPERMAN!*

WHAT?!... TELL ME ABOUT IT!

SUPER HEROES CLUB

"THE END OF MY VILLAINOUS GREAT-GREAT-GREAT- GREAT-GRANDFATHER BEGAN WHEN *BRAINIAC* PREPARED TO SNEAK-ATTACK EARTH..."

HA, HA, HA! LIVE AND LEARN, EH, KOKO?

"INSIDE THE FLYING SAUCER..."

I WAS A FOOL MERELY TO STEAL CITIES! FROM NOW ON, I STEAL **WORLDS!** THE HYPER-FORCES IN MY RAY WILL REDUCE EARTH TO MINIATURE SIZE AND TRANSPORT IT INSIDE THIS BOTTLE!... EH?... WHAT'S **THAT** ON THE TELESCOPIC-SCREEN?!!

FORCE-SHIELD CONTROLS

OFF

ON

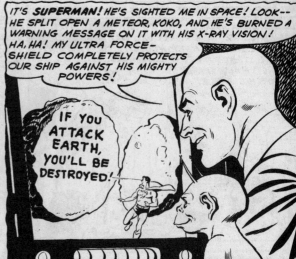

IT'S **SUPERMAN!** HE'S SIGHTED ME IN SPACE! LOOK-- HE SPLIT OPEN A METEOR, KOKO, AND HE'S BURNED A WARNING MESSAGE ON IT WITH HIS X-RAY VISION! HA, HA! MY ULTRA FORCE-SHIELD COMPLETELY PROTECTS OUR SHIP AGAINST HIS MIGHTY POWERS!

IF YOU ATTACK EARTH, YOU'LL BE DESTROYED!

"DISREGARDING THE WARNING, **BRAINIAC** TRIED TO SHRINK EARTH...BUT **SUPERMAN** TURNED THE FLYING-SAUCER SO ITS RAY MISSED EARTH...THEN HE SUPER-SWIFTLY FLUNG THE SAUCER INTO THE PATH OF ITS OWN RAY...!"

THE SHIP IS RAPIDLY **DWINDLING** DOWN... DOWN... DOWN...

THEN IT POPPED OUT OF EXISTENCE... REDUCED IN SIZE TO **NOTHINGNESS!**

BUT HOW WAS THAT POSSIBLE, WHEN **BRAINIAC'S** SHIP WAS PROTECTED BY ITS **ULTRA FORCE-SHIELD!**

IS BRAINIAC 5 LYING TO ME, FOR SOME REASON!

"**SUPERMAN'S** X-RAY VISION HAD OBSERVED...

BRAINIAC'S PET IS ACCIDENTALLY LEANING AGAINST A SWITCH WHICH HAS TURNED OFF THE SPACE-SHIP'S ULTRA FORCE-SHIELD! IF I HURL THE SHIP INTO THE REDUCING RAY **SWIFTLY** ENOUGH, THE SHIP WILL VANISH BEFORE **BRAINIAC** CAN LET GO OF THE REDUCING-RAY CONTROL-DEVICE!

CONTROLS

OFF

AS **BRAINIAC 5** COMPLETES HIS STORY, THE APPLICANTS FOR MEMBERSHIP DISPLAY THEIR SUPER-FEATS OUTSIDE THE CLUB-HOUSE...

NOW YOU KNOW WHY I'M CALLED **BOUNCING BOY!**

PEOPLE SAY I'M QUITE **BRIGHT!** THAT'S WHY I'M CALLED **SUN BOY!**

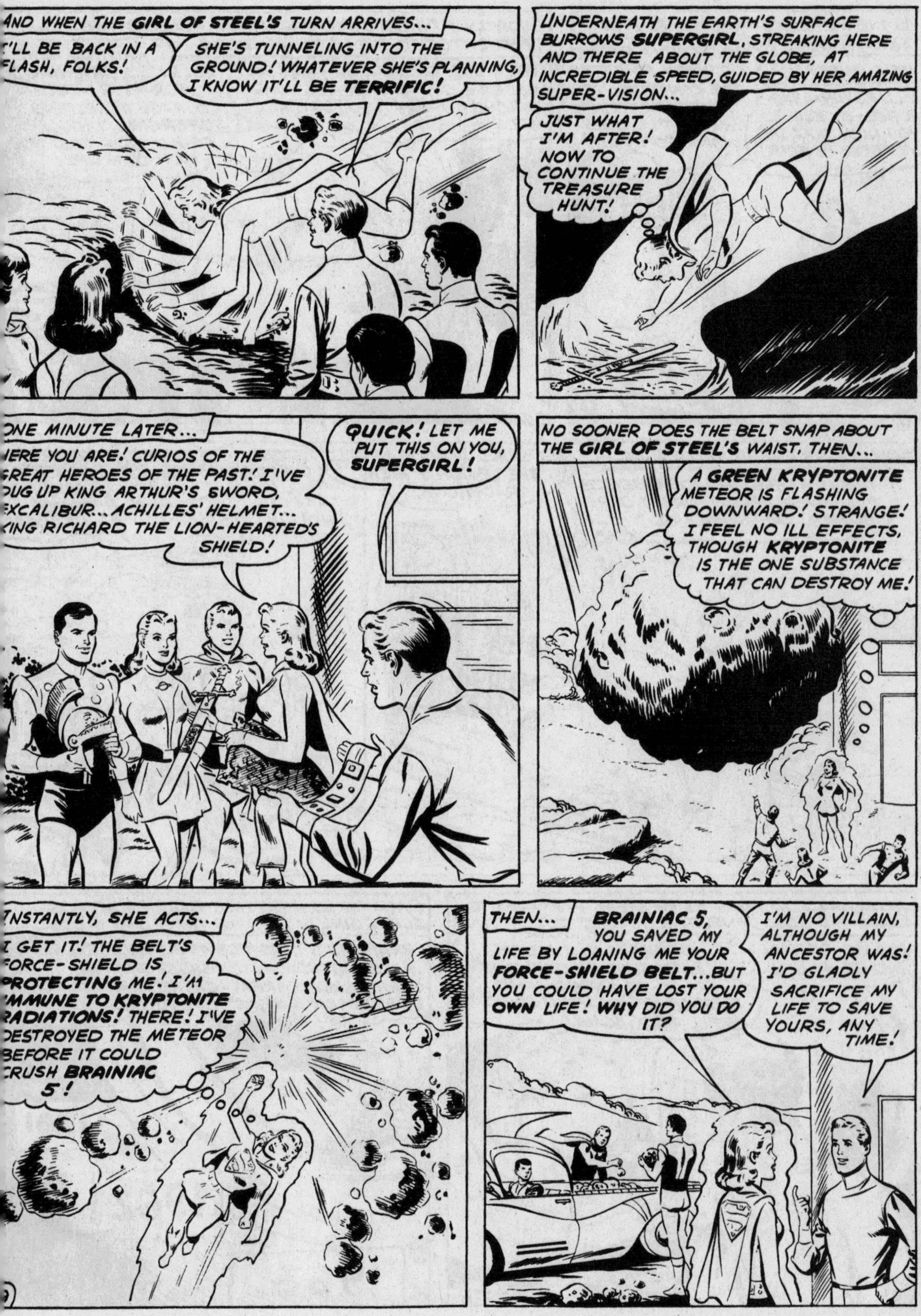
AND WHEN THE GIRL OF STEEL'S TURN ARRIVES...
I'LL BE BACK IN A FLASH, FOLKS!
SHE'S TUNNELING INTO THE GROUND! WHATEVER SHE'S PLANNING, I KNOW IT'LL BE TERRIFIC!
UNDERNEATH THE EARTH'S SURFACE BURROWS SUPERGIRL, STREAKING HERE AND THERE ABOUT THE GLOBE, AT INCREDIBLE SPEED, GUIDED BY HER AMAZING SUPER-VISION...
JUST WHAT I'M AFTER! NOW TO CONTINUE THE TREASURE HUNT!
ONE MINUTE LATER...
HERE YOU ARE! CURIOS OF THE GREAT HEROES OF THE PAST! I'VE DUG UP KING ARTHUR'S SWORD, EXCALIBUR... ACHILLES' HELMET... KING RICHARD THE LION-HEARTED'S SHIELD!
QUICK! LET ME PUT THIS ON YOU, SUPERGIRL!
NO SOONER DOES THE BELT SNAP ABOUT THE GIRL OF STEEL'S WAIST, THEN...
A GREEN KRYPTONITE METEOR IS FLASHING DOWNWARD! STRANGE! I FEEL NO ILL EFFECTS, THOUGH KRYPTONITE IS THE ONE SUBSTANCE THAT CAN DESTROY ME!
INSTANTLY, SHE ACTS...
I GET IT! THE BELT'S FORCE-SHIELD IS PROTECTING ME! I'M IMMUNE TO KRYPTONITE RADIATIONS! THERE! I'VE DESTROYED THE METEOR BEFORE IT COULD CRUSH BRAINIAC 5!
THEN...
BRAINIAC 5, YOU SAVED MY LIFE BY LOANING ME YOUR FORCE-SHIELD BELT...BUT YOU COULD HAVE LOST YOUR OWN LIFE! WHY DID YOU DO IT?
I'M NO VILLAIN, ALTHOUGH MY ANCESTOR WAS! I'D GLADLY SACRIFICE MY LIFE TO SAVE YOURS, ANY TIME!

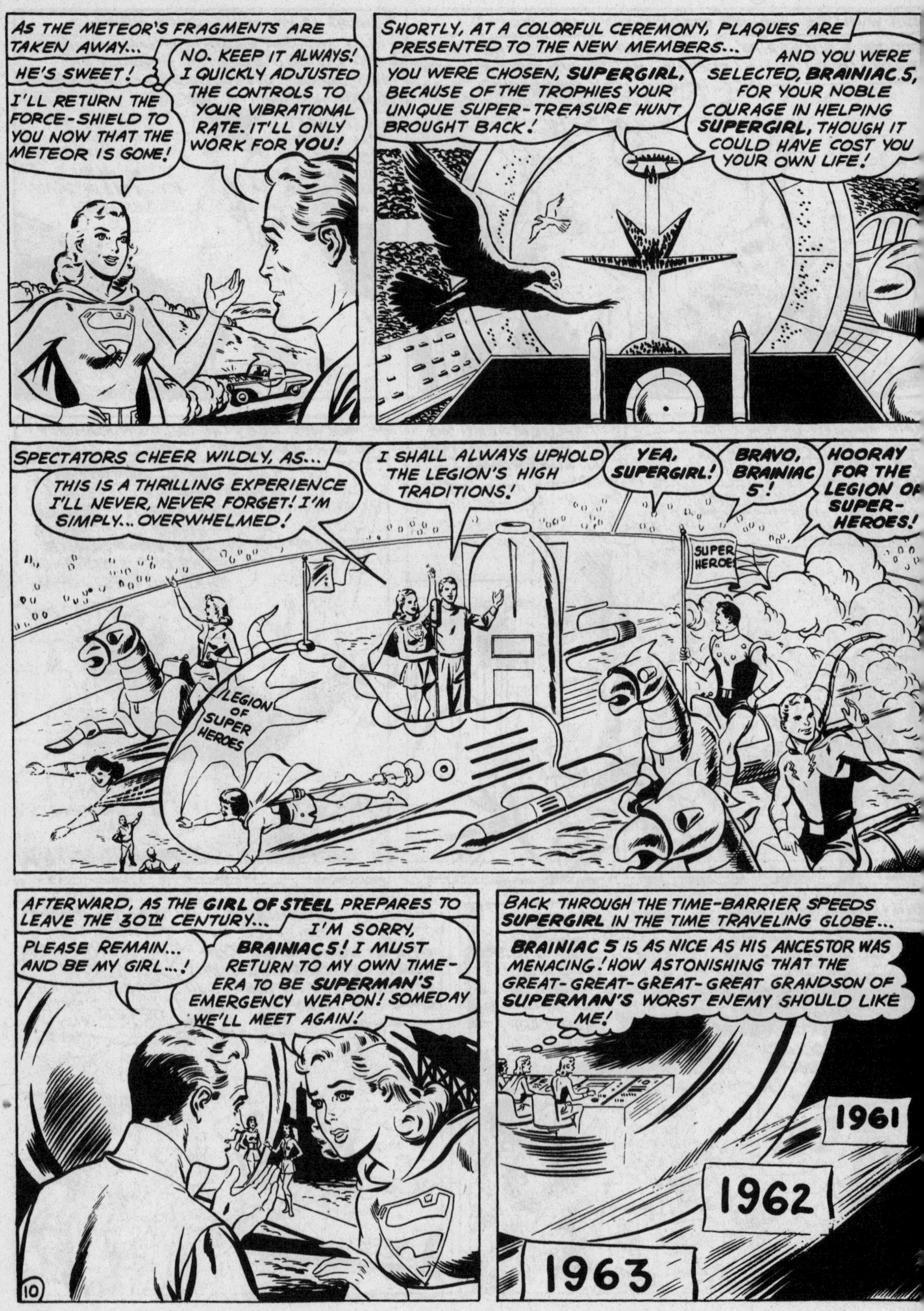
AS THE METEOR'S FRAGMENTS ARE TAKEN AWAY...
HE'S SWEET!
I'LL RETURN THE FORCE-SHIELD TO YOU NOW THAT THE METEOR IS GONE!
NO. KEEP IT ALWAYS! I QUICKLY ADJUSTED THE CONTROLS TO YOUR VIBRATIONAL RATE. IT'LL ONLY WORK FOR YOU!
SHORTLY, AT A COLORFUL CEREMONY, PLAQUES ARE PRESENTED TO THE NEW MEMBERS...
YOU WERE CHOSEN, SUPERGIRL, BECAUSE OF THE TROPHIES YOUR UNIQUE SUPER-TREASURE HUNT BROUGHT BACK!
AND YOU WERE SELECTED, BRAINIAC 5, FOR YOUR NOBLE COURAGE IN HELPING SUPERGIRL, THOUGH IT COULD HAVE COST YOU YOUR OWN LIFE!
SPECTATORS CHEER WILDLY, AS...
THIS IS A THRILLING EXPERIENCE I'LL NEVER, NEVER FORGET! I'M SIMPLY... OVERWHELMED!
I SHALL ALWAYS UPHOLD THE LEGION'S HIGH TRADITIONS!
YEA, SUPERGIRL!
BRAVO, BRAINIAC 5!
HOORAY FOR THE LEGION OF SUPER-HEROES!
SUPER HEROES
LEGION OF SUPER HEROES
AFTERWARD, AS THE GIRL OF STEEL PREPARES TO LEAVE THE 30TH CENTURY...
PLEASE REMAIN... AND BE MY GIRL...!
I'M SORRY, BRAINIAC 5! I MUST RETURN TO MY OWN TIME-ERA TO BE SUPERMAN'S EMERGENCY WEAPON! SOMEDAY WE'LL MEET AGAIN!
10
BACK THROUGH THE TIME-BARRIER SPEEDS SUPERGIRL IN THE TIME TRAVELING GLOBE...
BRAINIAC 5 IS AS NICE AS HIS ANCESTOR WAS MENACING! HOW ASTONISHING THAT THE GREAT-GREAT-GREAT-GREAT GRANDSON OF SUPERMAN'S WORST ENEMY SHOULD LIKE ME!
1961
1962
1963

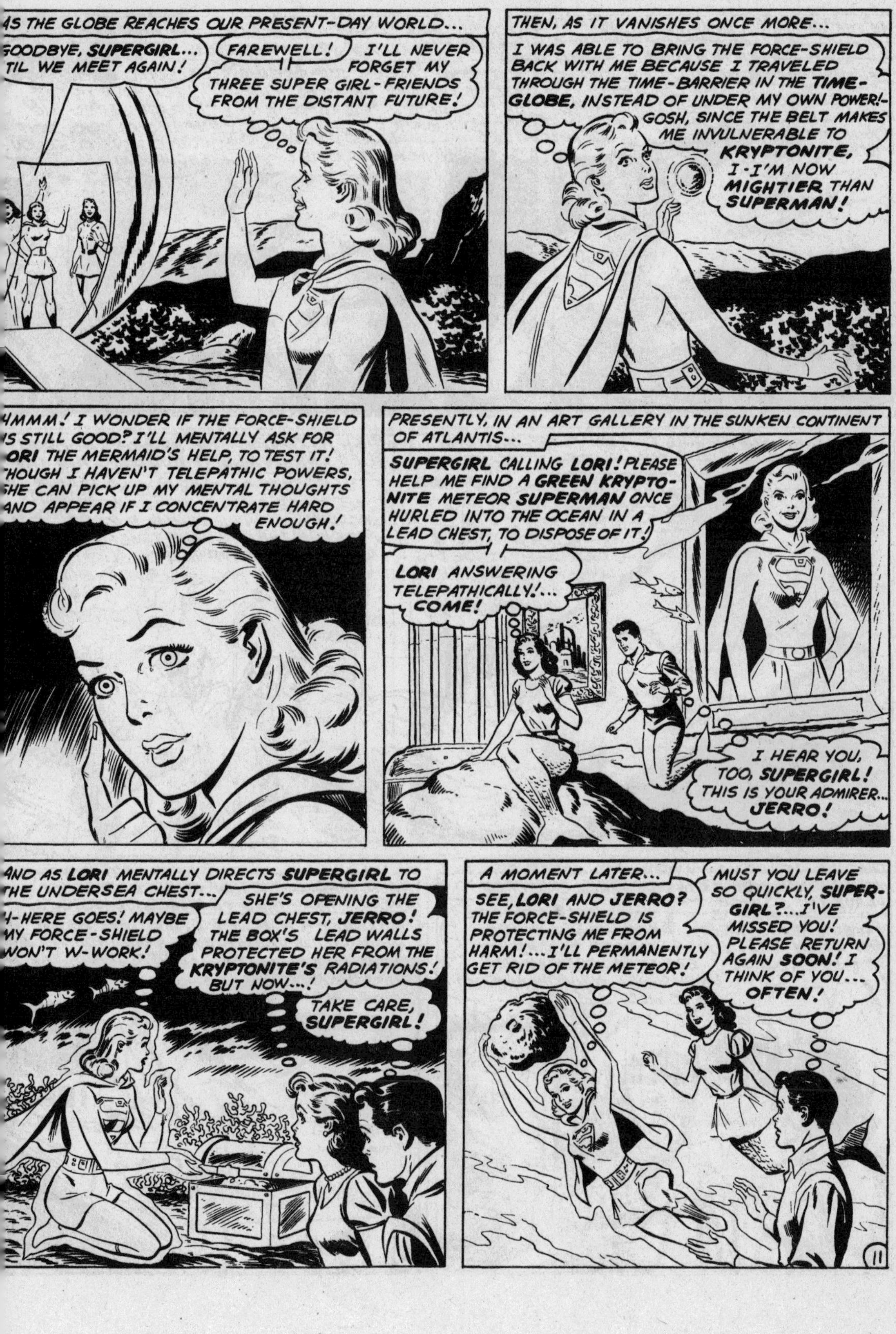
AS THE GLOBE REACHES OUR PRESENT-DAY WORLD...
GOODBYE, SUPERGIRL... TIL WE MEET AGAIN!
FAREWELL!
I'LL NEVER FORGET MY THREE SUPER GIRL-FRIENDS FROM THE DISTANT FUTURE!
THEN, AS IT VANISHES ONCE MORE...
I WAS ABLE TO BRING THE FORCE-SHIELD BACK WITH ME BECAUSE I TRAVELED THROUGH THE TIME-BARRIER IN THE TIME-GLOBE, INSTEAD OF UNDER MY OWN POWER!- GOSH, SINCE THE BELT MAKES ME INVULNERABLE TO KRYPTONITE, I-I'M NOW MIGHTIER THAN SUPERMAN!
HMMM! I WONDER IF THE FORCE-SHIELD IS STILL GOOD? I'LL MENTALLY ASK FOR LORI THE MERMAID'S HELP, TO TEST IT! THOUGH I HAVEN'T TELEPATHIC POWERS, SHE CAN PICK UP MY MENTAL THOUGHTS AND APPEAR IF I CONCENTRATE HARD ENOUGH!
PRESENTLY, IN AN ART GALLERY IN THE SUNKEN CONTINENT OF ATLANTIS...
SUPERGIRL CALLING LORI! PLEASE HELP ME FIND A GREEN KRYPTONITE METEOR SUPERMAN ONCE HURLED INTO THE OCEAN IN A LEAD CHEST, TO DISPOSE OF IT!
LORI ANSWERING TELEPATHICALLY!... COME!
I HEAR YOU, TOO, SUPERGIRL! THIS IS YOUR ADMIRER... JERRO!
AND AS LORI MENTALLY DIRECTS SUPERGIRL TO THE UNDERSEA CHEST...
H-HERE GOES! MAYBE MY FORCE-SHIELD WON'T W-WORK!
SHE'S OPENING THE LEAD CHEST, JERRO! THE BOX'S LEAD WALLS PROTECTED HER FROM THE KRYPTONITE'S RADIATIONS! BUT NOW...!
TAKE CARE, SUPERGIRL!
A MOMENT LATER...
SEE, LORI AND JERRO? THE FORCE-SHIELD IS PROTECTING ME FROM HARM!... I'LL PERMANENTLY GET RID OF THE METEOR!
MUST YOU LEAVE SO QUICKLY, SUPERGIRL?... I'VE MISSED YOU! PLEASE RETURN AGAIN SOON! I THINK OF YOU... OFTEN!
11

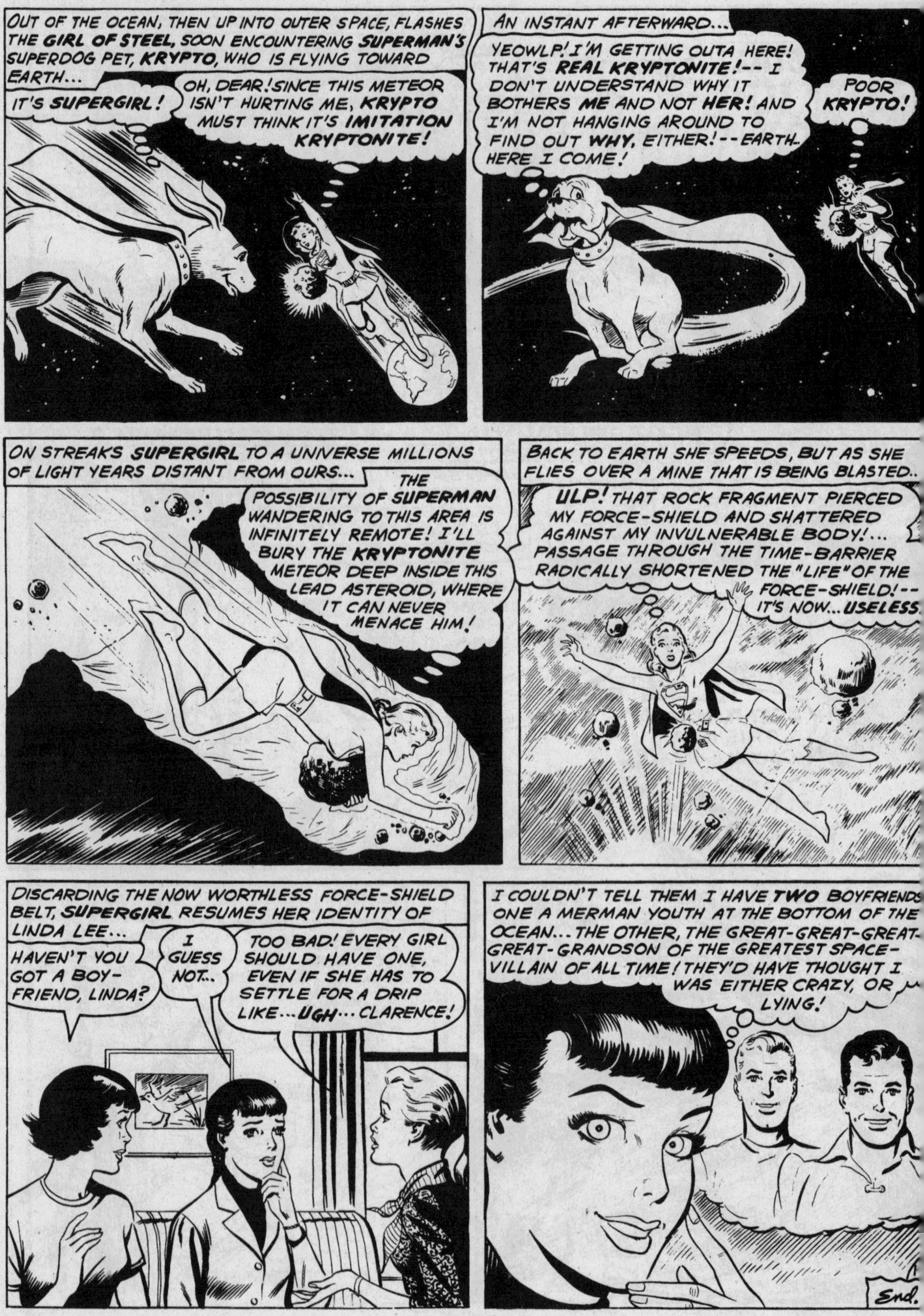
OUT OF THE OCEAN, THEN UP INTO OUTER SPACE, FLASHES THE GIRL OF STEEL, SOON ENCOUNTERING SUPERMAN'S SUPERDOG PET, KRYPTO, WHO IS FLYING TOWARD EARTH...
IT'S SUPERGIRL!
OH, DEAR! SINCE THIS METEOR ISN'T HURTING ME, KRYPTO MUST THINK IT'S IMITATION KRYPTONITE!
AN INSTANT AFTERWARD...
YEOWLP! I'M GETTING OUTA HERE! THAT'S REAL KRYPTONITE!-- I DON'T UNDERSTAND WHY IT BOTHERS ME AND NOT HER! AND I'M NOT HANGING AROUND TO FIND OUT WHY, EITHER!--EARTH, HERE I COME!
POOR KRYPTO!
ON STREAKS SUPERGIRL TO A UNIVERSE MILLIONS OF LIGHT YEARS DISTANT FROM OURS...
THE POSSIBILITY OF SUPERMAN WANDERING TO THIS AREA IS INFINITELY REMOTE! I'LL BURY THE KRYPTONITE METEOR DEEP INSIDE THIS LEAD ASTEROID, WHERE IT CAN NEVER MENACE HIM!
BACK TO EARTH SHE SPEEDS, BUT AS SHE FLIES OVER A MINE THAT IS BEING BLASTED...
ULP! THAT ROCK FRAGMENT PIERCED MY FORCE-SHIELD AND SHATTERED AGAINST MY INVULNERABLE BODY!... PASSAGE THROUGH THE TIME-BARRIER RADICALLY SHORTENED THE "LIFE" OF THE FORCE-SHIELD!-- IT'S NOW... USELESS
DISCARDING THE NOW WORTHLESS FORCE-SHIELD BELT, SUPERGIRL RESUMES HER IDENTITY OF LINDA LEE...
HAVEN'T YOU GOT A BOY-FRIEND, LINDA?
I GUESS NOT...
TOO BAD! EVERY GIRL SHOULD HAVE ONE, EVEN IF SHE HAS TO SETTLE FOR A DRIP LIKE...UGH...CLARENCE!
I COULDN'T TELL THEM I HAVE TWO BOYFRIENDS ONE A MERMAN YOUTH AT THE BOTTOM OF THE OCEAN... THE OTHER, THE GREAT-GREAT-GREAT-GREAT-GRANDSON OF THE GREATEST SPACE-VILLAIN OF ALL TIME! THEY'D HAVE THOUGHT I WAS EITHER CRAZY, OR LYING!
End.

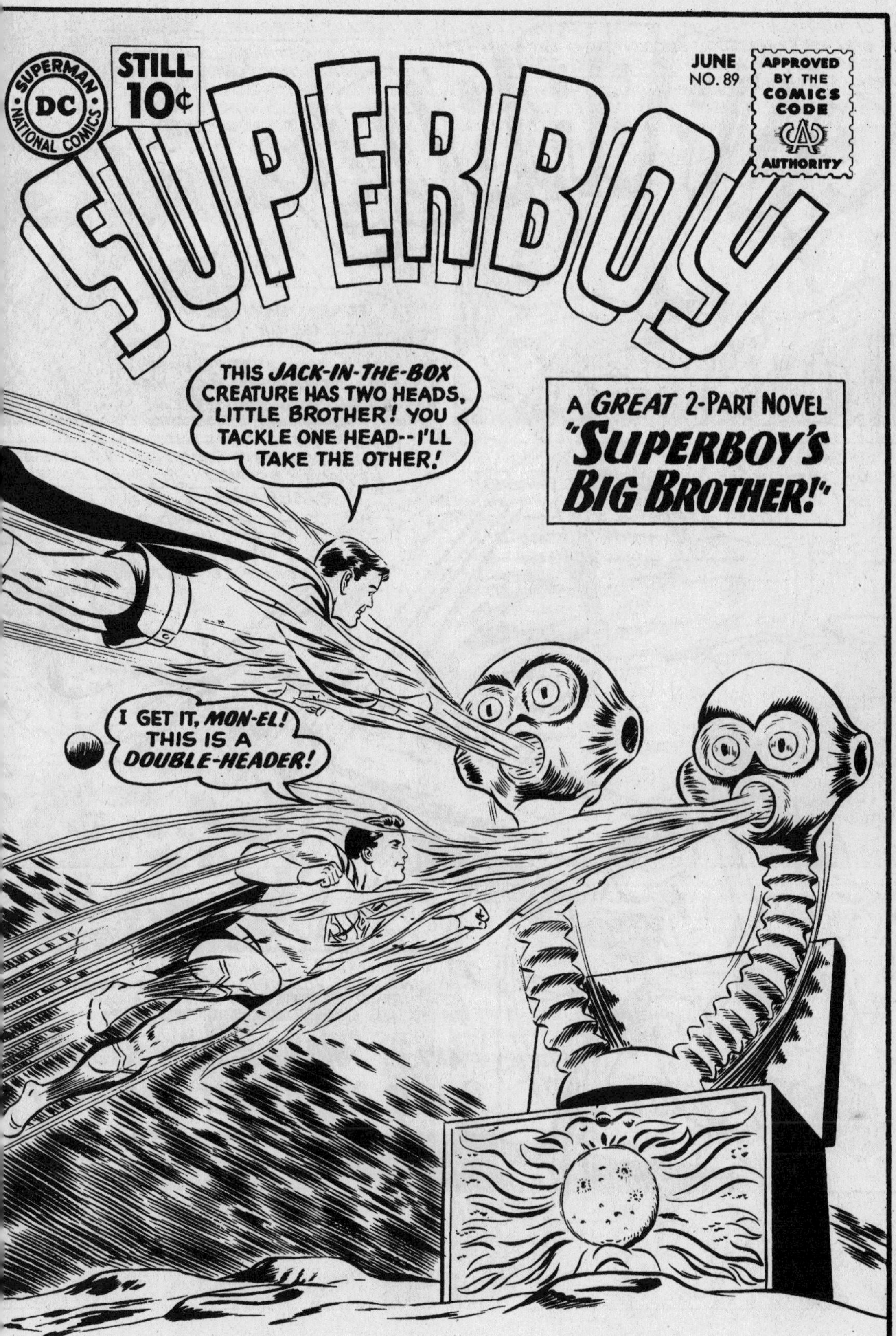
SUPERMAN DC NATIONAL COMICS
STILL 10¢
SUPERBOY
JUNE NO. 89
APPROVED BY THE COMICS CODE AUTHORITY
THIS JACK-IN-THE-BOX CREATURE HAS TWO HEADS, LITTLE BROTHER! YOU TACKLE ONE HEAD--I'LL TAKE THE OTHER!
A GREAT 2-PART NOVEL "SUPERBOY'S BIG BROTHER!"
I GET IT, MON-EL! THIS IS A DOUBLE-HEADER!

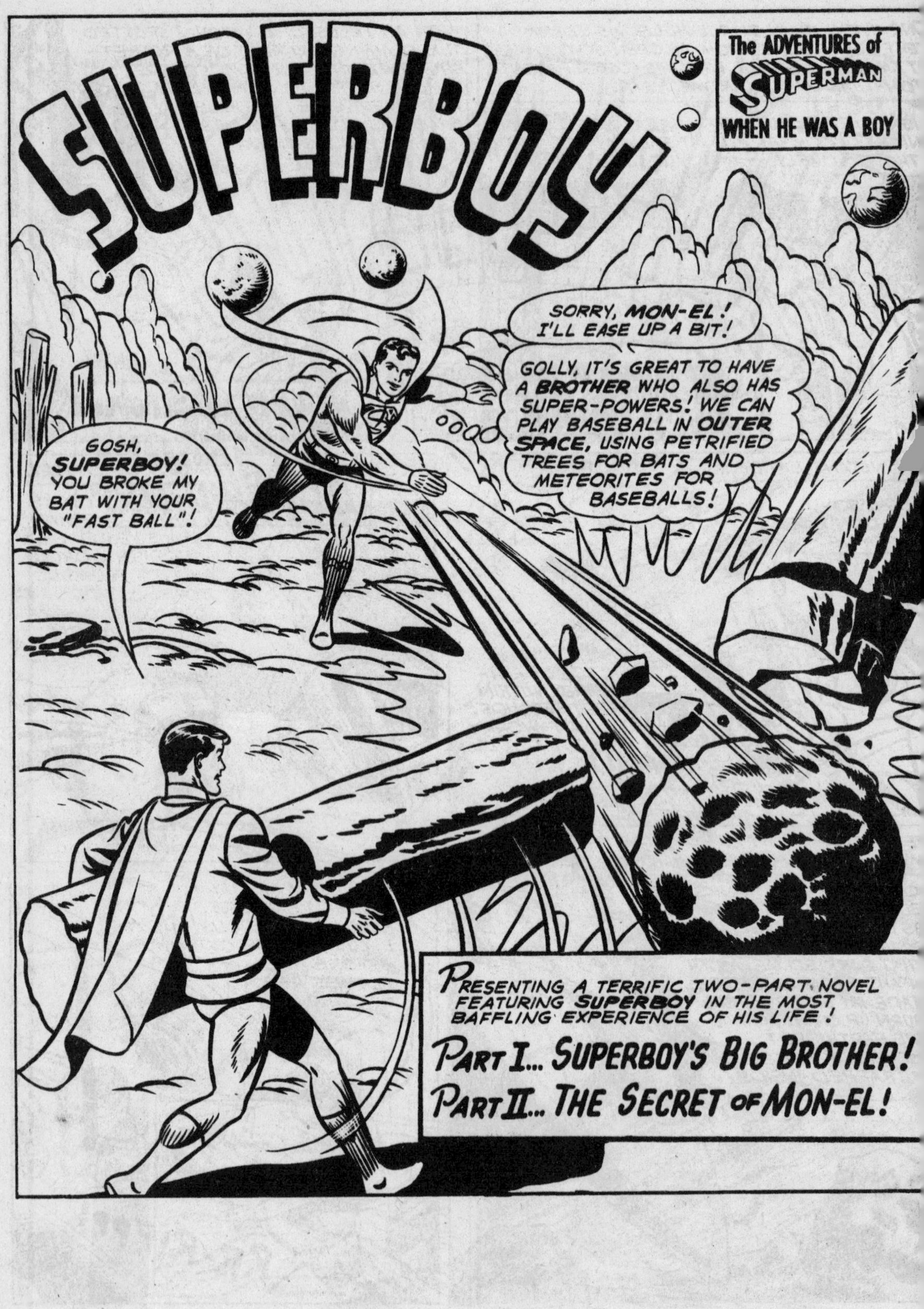
SUPERBOY
The ADVENTURES of SUPERMAN WHEN HE WAS A BOY
GOSH, SUPERBOY! YOU BROKE MY BAT WITH YOUR "FAST BALL"!
SORRY, MON-EL! I'LL EASE UP A BIT!
GOLLY, IT'S GREAT TO HAVE A BROTHER WHO ALSO HAS SUPER-POWERS! WE CAN PLAY BASEBALL IN OUTER SPACE, USING PETRIFIED TREES FOR BATS AND METEORITES FOR BASEBALLS!
PRESENTING A TERRIFIC TWO-PART NOVEL FEATURING SUPERBOY IN THE MOST BAFFLING EXPERIENCE OF HIS LIFE!
PART I... SUPERBOY'S BIG BROTHER!
PART II... THE SECRET OF MON-EL!

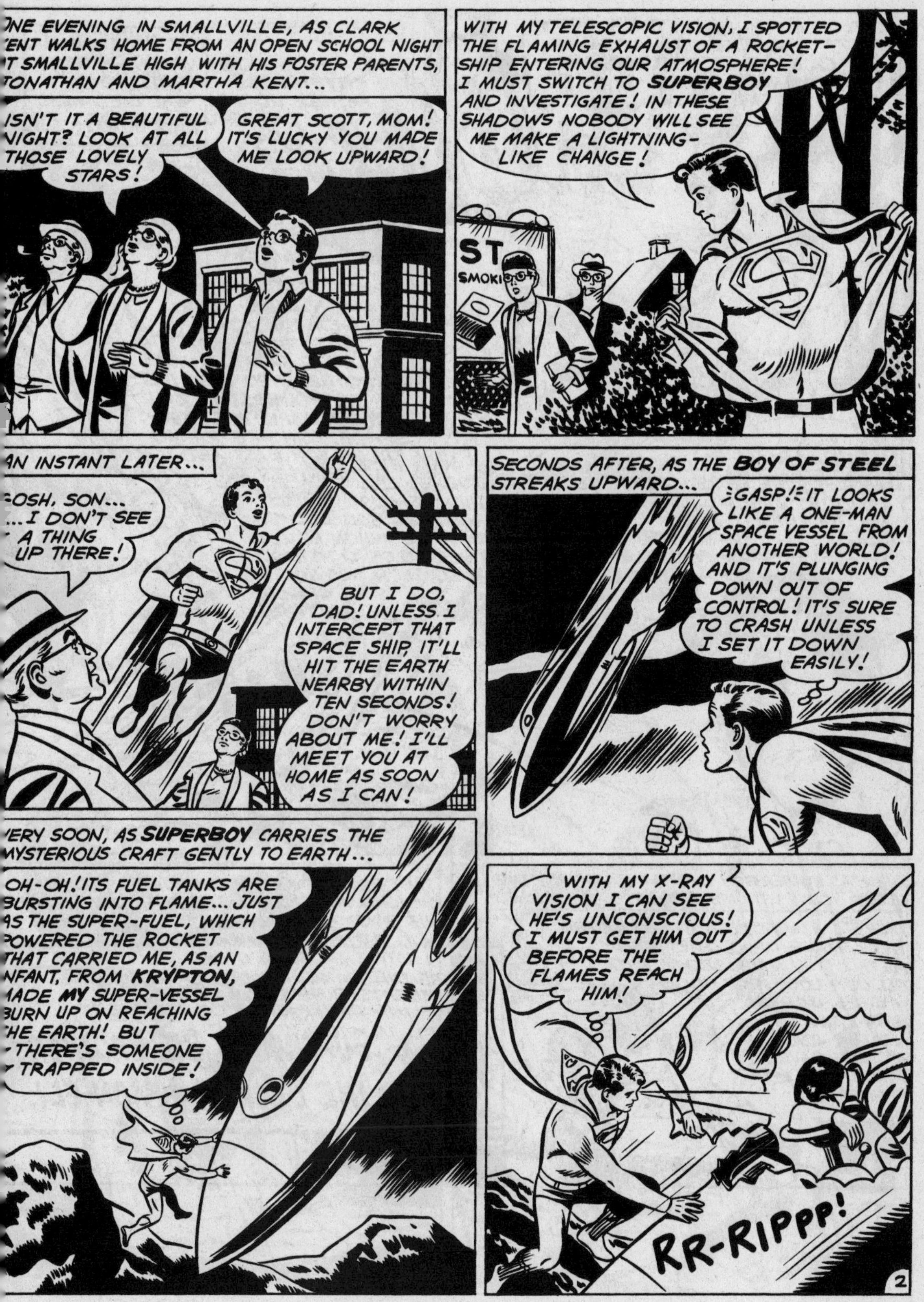
NE EVENING IN SMALLVILLE, AS CLARK ENT WALKS HOME FROM AN OPEN SCHOOL NIGHT T SMALLVILLE HIGH WITH HIS FOSTER PARENTS, ONATHAN AND MARTHA KENT...
ISN'T IT A BEAUTIFUL NIGHT? LOOK AT ALL THOSE LOVELY STARS!
GREAT SCOTT, MOM! IT'S LUCKY YOU MADE ME LOOK UPWARD!
WITH MY TELESCOPIC VISION, I SPOTTED THE FLAMING EXHAUST OF A ROCKET-SHIP ENTERING OUR ATMOSPHERE! I MUST SWITCH TO SUPERBOY AND INVESTIGATE! IN THESE SHADOWS NOBODY WILL SEE ME MAKE A LIGHTNING-LIKE CHANGE!
ST
SMOKI
AN INSTANT LATER...
OSH, SON... ...I DON'T SEE A THING UP THERE!
BUT I DO, DAD! UNLESS I INTERCEPT THAT SPACE SHIP, IT'LL HIT THE EARTH NEARBY WITHIN TEN SECONDS! DON'T WORRY ABOUT ME! I'LL MEET YOU AT HOME AS SOON AS I CAN!
SECONDS AFTER, AS THE BOY OF STEEL STREAKS UPWARD...
GASP! IT LOOKS LIKE A ONE-MAN SPACE VESSEL FROM ANOTHER WORLD! AND IT'S PLUNGING DOWN OUT OF CONTROL! IT'S SURE TO CRASH UNLESS I SET IT DOWN EASILY!
ERY SOON, AS SUPERBOY CARRIES THE MYSTERIOUS CRAFT GENTLY TO EARTH...
OH-OH! ITS FUEL TANKS ARE BURSTING INTO FLAME... JUST AS THE SUPER-FUEL, WHICH POWERED THE ROCKET THAT CARRIED ME, AS AN NFANT, FROM KRYPTON, MADE MY SUPER-VESSEL BURN UP ON REACHING HE EARTH! BUT THERE'S SOMEONE TRAPPED INSIDE!
WITH MY X-RAY VISION I CAN SEE HE'S UNCONSCIOUS! I MUST GET HIM OUT BEFORE THE FLAMES REACH HIM!
RR-RIPPP!
2

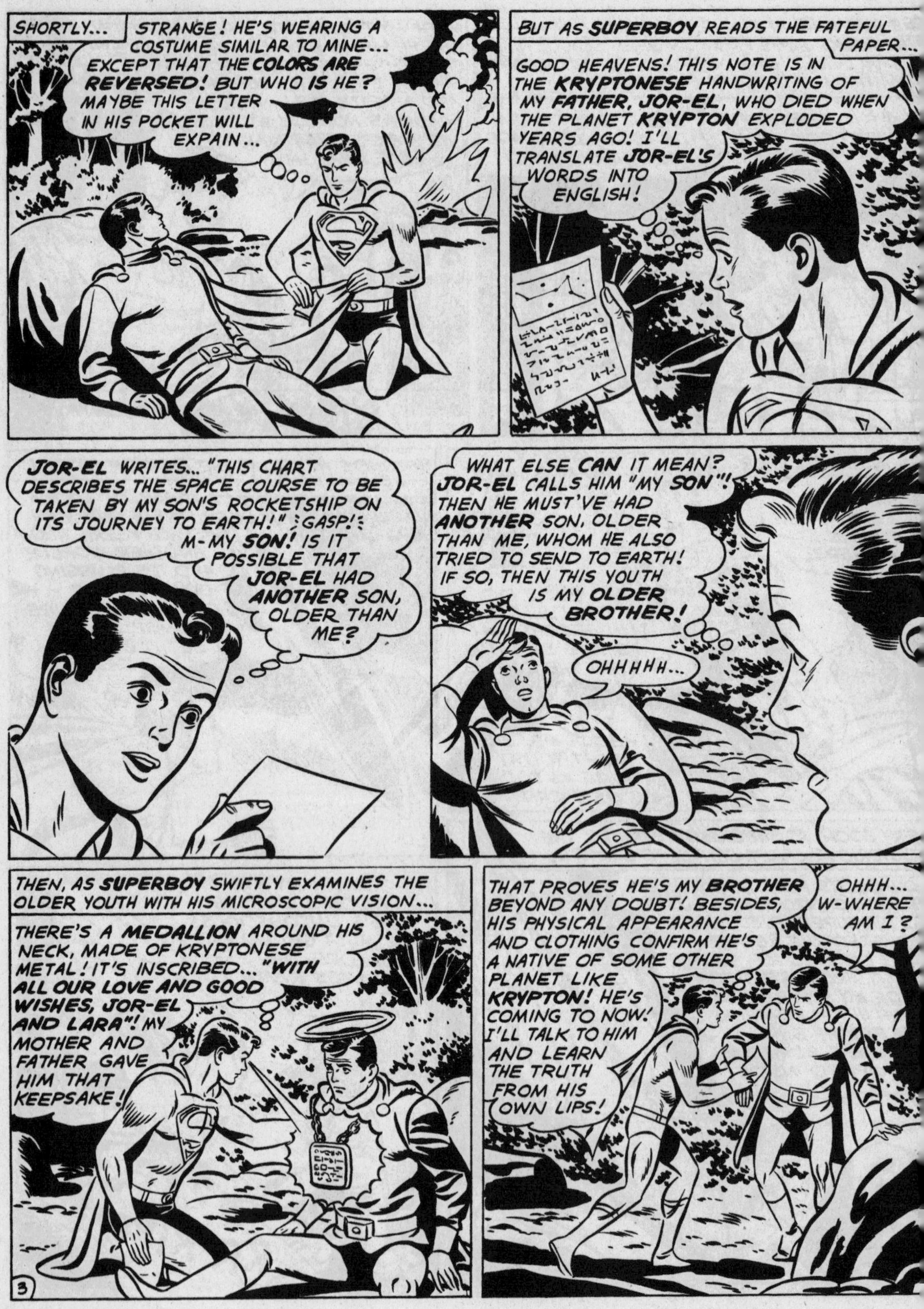
SHORTLY...
STRANGE! HE'S WEARING A COSTUME SIMILAR TO MINE... EXCEPT THAT THE COLORS ARE REVERSED! BUT WHO IS HE? MAYBE THIS LETTER IN HIS POCKET WILL EXPAIN...
BUT AS SUPERBOY READS THE FATEFUL PAPER...
GOOD HEAVENS! THIS NOTE IS IN THE KRYPTONESE HANDWRITING OF MY FATHER, JOR-EL, WHO DIED WHEN THE PLANET KRYPTON EXPLODED YEARS AGO! I'LL TRANSLATE JOR-EL'S WORDS INTO ENGLISH!
JOR-EL WRITES... "THIS CHART DESCRIBES THE SPACE COURSE TO BE TAKEN BY MY SON'S ROCKETSHIP ON ITS JOURNEY TO EARTH!" GASP! M-MY SON! IS IT POSSIBLE THAT JOR-EL HAD ANOTHER SON, OLDER THAN ME?
WHAT ELSE CAN IT MEAN? JOR-EL CALLS HIM "MY SON"! THEN HE MUST'VE HAD ANOTHER SON, OLDER THAN ME, WHOM HE ALSO TRIED TO SEND TO EARTH! IF SO, THEN THIS YOUTH IS MY OLDER BROTHER!
OHHHHH...
THEN, AS SUPERBOY SWIFTLY EXAMINES THE OLDER YOUTH WITH HIS MICROSCOPIC VISION...
THERE'S A MEDALLION AROUND HIS NECK, MADE OF KRYPTONESE METAL! IT'S INSCRIBED... "WITH ALL OUR LOVE AND GOOD WISHES, JOR-EL AND LARA"! MY MOTHER AND FATHER GAVE HIM THAT KEEPSAKE!
3
THAT PROVES HE'S MY BROTHER BEYOND ANY DOUBT! BESIDES, HIS PHYSICAL APPEARANCE AND CLOTHING CONFIRM HE'S A NATIVE OF SOME OTHER PLANET LIKE KRYPTON! HE'S COMING TO NOW! I'LL TALK TO HIM AND LEARN THE TRUTH FROM HIS OWN LIPS!
OHHH... W-WHERE AM I?

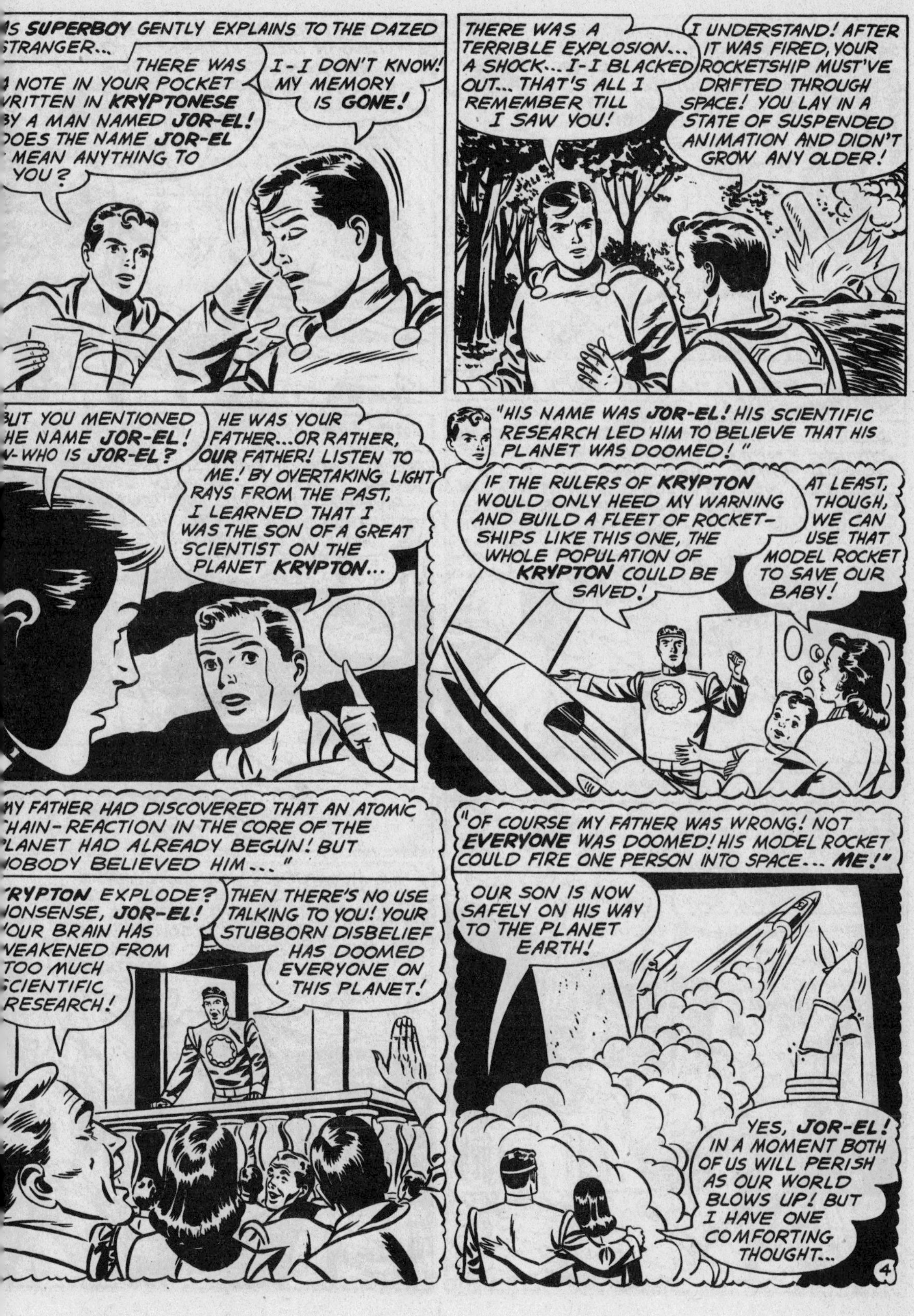
S SUPERBOY GENTLY EXPLAINS TO THE DAZED STRANGER...
THERE WAS A NOTE IN YOUR POCKET WRITTEN IN KRYPTONESE BY A MAN NAMED JOR-EL! DOES THE NAME JOR-EL MEAN ANYTHING TO YOU?
I-I DON'T KNOW! MY MEMORY IS GONE!
THERE WAS A TERRIBLE EXPLOSION... A SHOCK... I-I BLACKED OUT... THAT'S ALL I REMEMBER TILL I SAW YOU!
I UNDERSTAND! AFTER IT WAS FIRED, YOUR ROCKETSHIP MUST'VE DRIFTED THROUGH SPACE! YOU LAY IN A STATE OF SUSPENDED ANIMATION AND DIDN'T GROW ANY OLDER!
UT YOU MENTIONED HE NAME JOR-EL! -WHO IS JOR-EL?
HE WAS YOUR FATHER...OR RATHER, OUR FATHER! LISTEN TO ME! BY OVERTAKING LIGHT RAYS FROM THE PAST, I LEARNED THAT I WAS THE SON OF A GREAT SCIENTIST ON THE PLANET KRYPTON...
"HIS NAME WAS JOR-EL! HIS SCIENTIFIC RESEARCH LED HIM TO BELIEVE THAT HIS PLANET WAS DOOMED!"
IF THE RULERS OF KRYPTON WOULD ONLY HEED MY WARNING AND BUILD A FLEET OF ROCKET-SHIPS LIKE THIS ONE, THE WHOLE POPULATION OF KRYPTON COULD BE SAVED!
AT LEAST, THOUGH, WE CAN USE THAT MODEL ROCKET TO SAVE OUR BABY!
MY FATHER HAD DISCOVERED THAT AN ATOMIC CHAIN-REACTION IN THE CORE OF THE PLANET HAD ALREADY BEGUN! BUT NOBODY BELIEVED HIM..."
KRYPTON EXPLODE? NONSENSE, JOR-EL! YOUR BRAIN HAS WEAKENED FROM TOO MUCH SCIENTIFIC RESEARCH!
THEN THERE'S NO USE TALKING TO YOU! YOUR STUBBORN DISBELIEF HAS DOOMED EVERYONE ON THIS PLANET!
"OF COURSE MY FATHER WAS WRONG! NOT EVERYONE WAS DOOMED! HIS MODEL ROCKET COULD FIRE ONE PERSON INTO SPACE... ME!"
OUR SON IS NOW SAFELY ON HIS WAY TO THE PLANET EARTH!
YES, JOR-EL! IN A MOMENT BOTH OF US WILL PERISH AS OUR WORLD BLOWS UP! BUT I HAVE ONE COMFORTING THOUGHT...
4

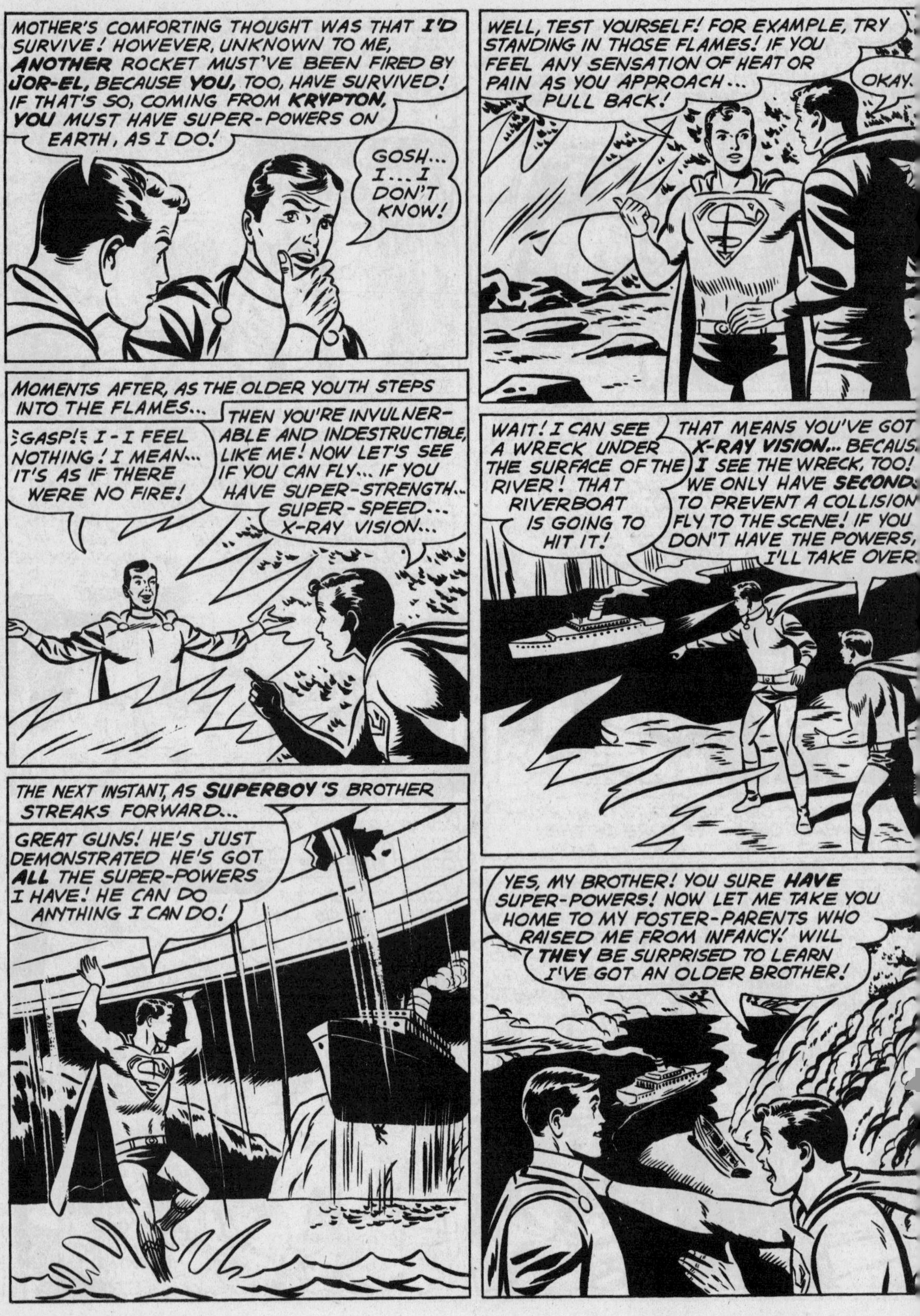
MOTHER'S COMFORTING THOUGHT WAS THAT I'D SURVIVE! HOWEVER, UNKNOWN TO ME, ANOTHER ROCKET MUST'VE BEEN FIRED BY JOR-EL, BECAUSE YOU, TOO, HAVE SURVIVED! IF THAT'S SO, COMING FROM KRYPTON, YOU MUST HAVE SUPER-POWERS ON EARTH, AS I DO!
GOSH... I...I DON'T KNOW!
WELL, TEST YOURSELF! FOR EXAMPLE, TRY STANDING IN THOSE FLAMES! IF YOU FEEL ANY SENSATION OF HEAT OR PAIN AS YOU APPROACH... PULL BACK!
OKAY.
MOMENTS AFTER, AS THE OLDER YOUTH STEPS INTO THE FLAMES...
GASP! I-I FEEL NOTHING! I MEAN... IT'S AS IF THERE WERE NO FIRE!
THEN YOU'RE INVULNERABLE AND INDESTRUCTIBLE, LIKE ME! NOW LET'S SEE IF YOU CAN FLY... IF YOU HAVE SUPER-STRENGTH... SUPER-SPEED... X-RAY VISION...
WAIT! I CAN SEE A WRECK UNDER THE SURFACE OF THE RIVER! THAT RIVERBOAT IS GOING TO HIT IT!
THAT MEANS YOU'VE GOT X-RAY VISION... BECAUS I SEE THE WRECK, TOO! WE ONLY HAVE SECOND TO PREVENT A COLLISION FLY TO THE SCENE! IF YOU DON'T HAVE THE POWERS, I'LL TAKE OVER
THE NEXT INSTANT, AS SUPERBOY'S BROTHER STREAKS FORWARD...
GREAT GUNS! HE'S JUST DEMONSTRATED HE'S GOT ALL THE SUPER-POWERS I HAVE! HE CAN DO ANYTHING I CAN DO!
YES, MY BROTHER! YOU SURE HAVE SUPER-POWERS! NOW LET ME TAKE YOU HOME TO MY FOSTER-PARENTS WHO RAISED ME FROM INFANCY! WILL THEY BE SURPRISED TO LEARN I'VE GOT AN OLDER BROTHER!

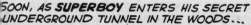

SOON, AS **SUPERBOY** ENTERS HIS SECRET UNDERGROUND TUNNEL IN THE WOODS...

I USE THIS TUNNEL TO COME AND GO FROM MY HOUSE UNOBSERVED! THUS, NOBODY KNOWS THAT **SUPERBOY** IS CLARK KENT. YOU SEE, IN REAL LIFE, I AM KNOWN AS CLARK KENT, SON OF JONATHAN AND MARTHA KENT...

MOMENTS AFTER, IN A HIDDEN ROOM IN THE KENT CELLAR...

I RECENTLY ADDED THIS ROOM! THESE PICTURES ARE OF OUR PARENTS... **JOR-EL**, OUR FATHER, AND LARA, OUR MOTHER!

BUT HOW CAN THEY BE SO **YOUNG**? I'M AT LEAST 18! AND YOUR ROCKET-SHIP... YOU CALLED IT A **MODEL-SHIP**! IF THAT IS SO, WHAT SHIP DID I USE?

JOR-EL

LARA

MAP OF KRYPTON

I'VE BEEN THINKING ABOUT THAT... AND I'LL OFFER A THEORY TO EXPLAIN IT! FIRST, ABOUT YOUR AGE! **KRYPTON** MUST'VE BEEN A PLANET WHOSE ATMOSPHERE SPEEDS UP THE LIFE-PROCESSES! THERE YOU AGED MORE RAPIDLY THAN YOU WOULD HAVE ON EARTH!

I LEFT **KRYPTON** WHEN I WAS A BABY SO I ESCAPED THE FAST-AGING PROCESS! THAT'S WHY YOU LOOK SO MUCH OLDER THAN ME! NOW AS FOR **YOUR** ROCKET-SHIP... I THINK THAT JOR-EL SENT YOU INTO SPACE **FIRST** BECAUSE YOU WERE HIS OLDEST SON! THEN, FEARING YOUR SHIP WAS DEFECTIVE...

...**JOR-EL** DECIDED TO WORK ON A NEW TYPE. MINE WAS THE MODEL SHIP OF THE NEW TYPE! BUT WHAT'S THE DIFFERENCE? YOU'RE HERE AND NOW I HAVE A REAL BROTHER, MY OWN FLESH AND BLOOD! I CAN'T WAIT TO INTRODUCE YOU TO MOM AND DAD! COME ON! THEY'RE UPSTAIRS...

MINUTES LATER, IN THE KENT LIVING ROOM...

DAD WENT TO THE STORE TO UNLOAD A SHIPMENT AND MEET A SALESMAN WITH WHOM HE HAD AN APPOINTMENT! GOODNESS... WILL DAD BE SHOCKED AT THIS NEWS!

I'LL RUN DOWN TO THE STORE AND TELL HIM MYSELF! MEANWHILE, YOU TWO GET ACQUAINTED!

6

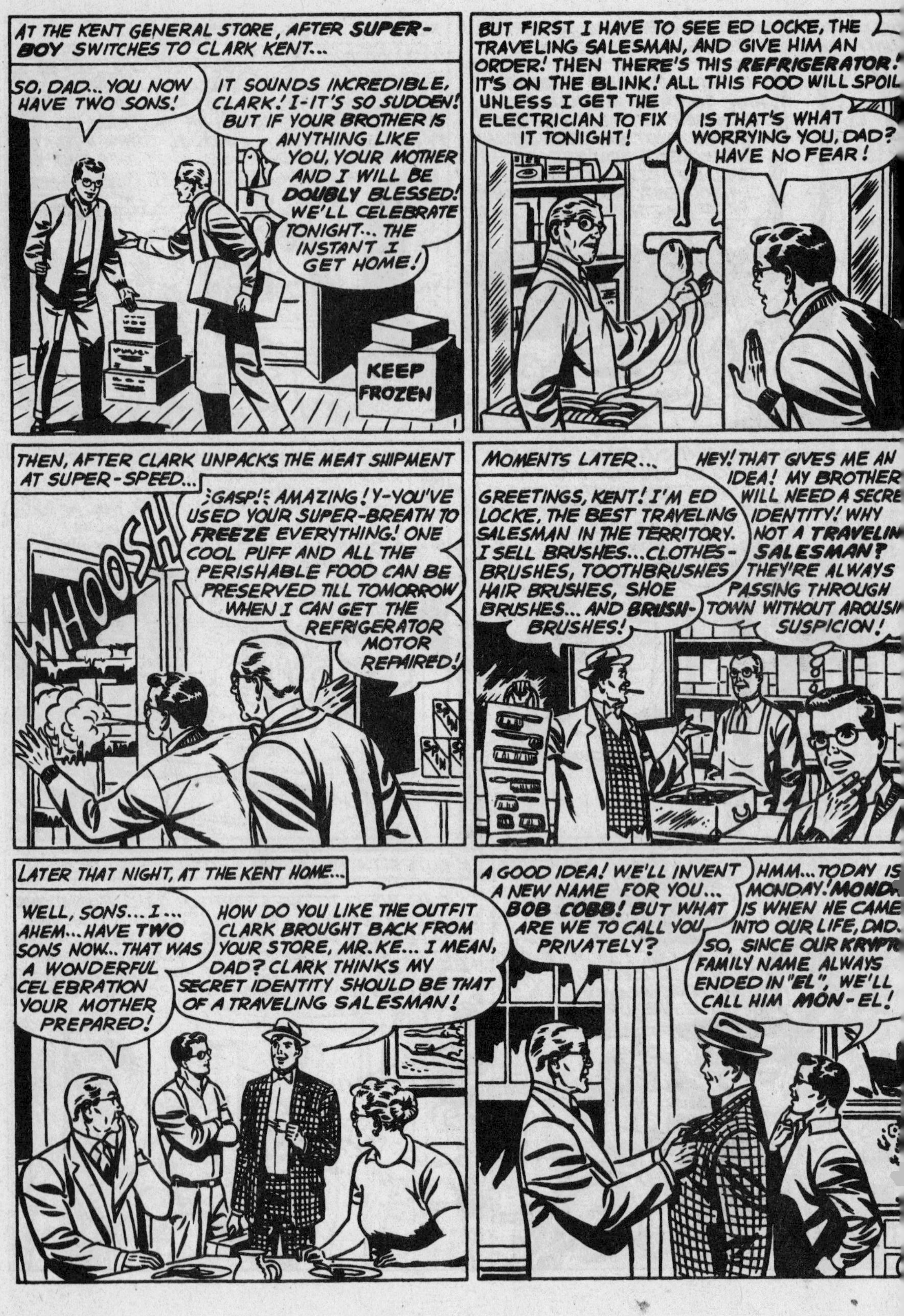
AT THE KENT GENERAL STORE, AFTER SUPER-BOY SWITCHES TO CLARK KENT...
SO, DAD... YOU NOW HAVE TWO SONS!
IT SOUNDS INCREDIBLE, CLARK! I-IT'S SO SUDDEN! BUT IF YOUR BROTHER IS ANYTHING LIKE YOU, YOUR MOTHER AND I WILL BE DOUBLY BLESSED! WE'LL CELEBRATE TONIGHT... THE INSTANT I GET HOME!
KEEP FROZEN
BUT FIRST I HAVE TO SEE ED LOCKE, THE TRAVELING SALESMAN, AND GIVE HIM AN ORDER! THEN THERE'S THIS REFRIGERATOR! IT'S ON THE BLINK! ALL THIS FOOD WILL SPOIL UNLESS I GET THE ELECTRICIAN TO FIX IT TONIGHT!
IS THAT'S WHAT WORRYING YOU, DAD? HAVE NO FEAR!
THEN, AFTER CLARK UNPACKS THE MEAT SHIPMENT AT SUPER-SPEED...
WHOOSH
GASP! AMAZING! Y-YOU'VE USED YOUR SUPER-BREATH TO FREEZE EVERYTHING! ONE COOL PUFF AND ALL THE PERISHABLE FOOD CAN BE PRESERVED TILL TOMORROW WHEN I CAN GET THE REFRIGERATOR MOTOR REPAIRED!
MOMENTS LATER...
GREETINGS, KENT! I'M ED LOCKE, THE BEST TRAVELING SALESMAN IN THE TERRITORY. I SELL BRUSHES... CLOTHES-BRUSHES, TOOTHBRUSHES HAIR BRUSHES, SHOE BRUSHES... AND BRUSH-BRUSHES!
HEY! THAT GIVES ME AN IDEA! MY BROTHER WILL NEED A SECRE IDENTITY! WHY NOT A TRAVELIN SALESMAN? THEY'RE ALWAYS PASSING THROUGH TOWN WITHOUT AROUSI SUSPICION!
LATER THAT NIGHT, AT THE KENT HOME...
WELL, SONS... I... AHEM... HAVE TWO SONS NOW... THAT WAS A WONDERFUL CELEBRATION YOUR MOTHER PREPARED!
HOW DO YOU LIKE THE OUTFIT CLARK BROUGHT BACK FROM YOUR STORE, MR. KE... I MEAN, DAD? CLARK THINKS MY SECRET IDENTITY SHOULD BE THAT OF A TRAVELING SALESMAN!
A GOOD IDEA! WE'LL INVENT A NEW NAME FOR YOU... BOB COBB! BUT WHAT ARE WE TO CALL YOU PRIVATELY?
HMM... TODAY IS MONDAY! MOND IS WHEN HE CAME INTO OUR LIFE, DAD. SO, SINCE OUR KRYPT FAMILY NAME ALWAYS ENDED IN "EL", WE'LL CALL HIM MON-EL!

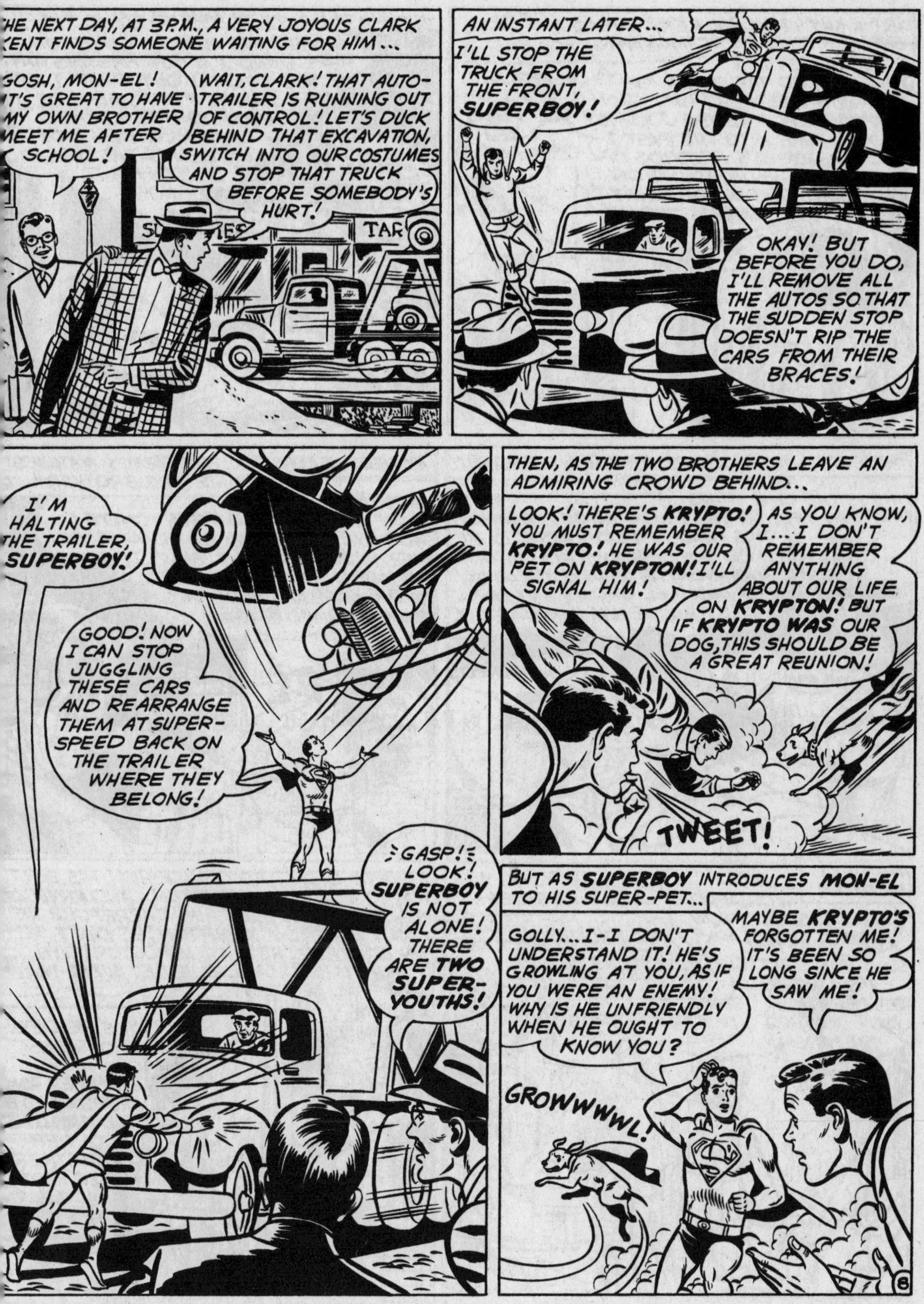
THE NEXT DAY, AT 3 P.M., A VERY JOYOUS CLARK KENT FINDS SOMEONE WAITING FOR HIM...
GOSH, MON-EL! IT'S GREAT TO HAVE MY OWN BROTHER MEET ME AFTER SCHOOL!
WAIT, CLARK! THAT AUTO-TRAILER IS RUNNING OUT OF CONTROL! LET'S DUCK BEHIND THAT EXCAVATION, SWITCH INTO OUR COSTUMES AND STOP THAT TRUCK BEFORE SOMEBODY'S HURT!
AN INSTANT LATER...
I'LL STOP THE TRUCK FROM THE FRONT, SUPERBOY!
OKAY! BUT BEFORE YOU DO, I'LL REMOVE ALL THE AUTOS SO THAT THE SUDDEN STOP DOESN'T RIP THE CARS FROM THEIR BRACES!
I'M HALTING THE TRAILER, SUPERBOY!
GOOD! NOW I CAN STOP JUGGLING THESE CARS AND REARRANGE THEM AT SUPER-SPEED BACK ON THE TRAILER WHERE THEY BELONG!
GASP! LOOK! SUPERBOY IS NOT ALONE! THERE ARE TWO SUPER-YOUTHS!
THEN, AS THE TWO BROTHERS LEAVE AN ADMIRING CROWD BEHIND...
LOOK! THERE'S KRYPTO! YOU MUST REMEMBER KRYPTO! HE WAS OUR PET ON KRYPTON! I'LL SIGNAL HIM!
AS YOU KNOW, I... I DON'T REMEMBER ANYTHING ABOUT OUR LIFE ON KRYPTON! BUT IF KRYPTO WAS OUR DOG, THIS SHOULD BE A GREAT REUNION!
TWEET!
BUT AS SUPERBOY INTRODUCES MON-EL TO HIS SUPER-PET...
GOLLY... I-I DON'T UNDERSTAND IT! HE'S GROWLING AT YOU, AS IF YOU WERE AN ENEMY! WHY IS HE UNFRIENDLY WHEN HE OUGHT TO KNOW YOU?
MAYBE KRYPTO'S FORGOTTEN ME! IT'S BEEN SO LONG SINCE HE SAW ME!
GROWWWWL!
8

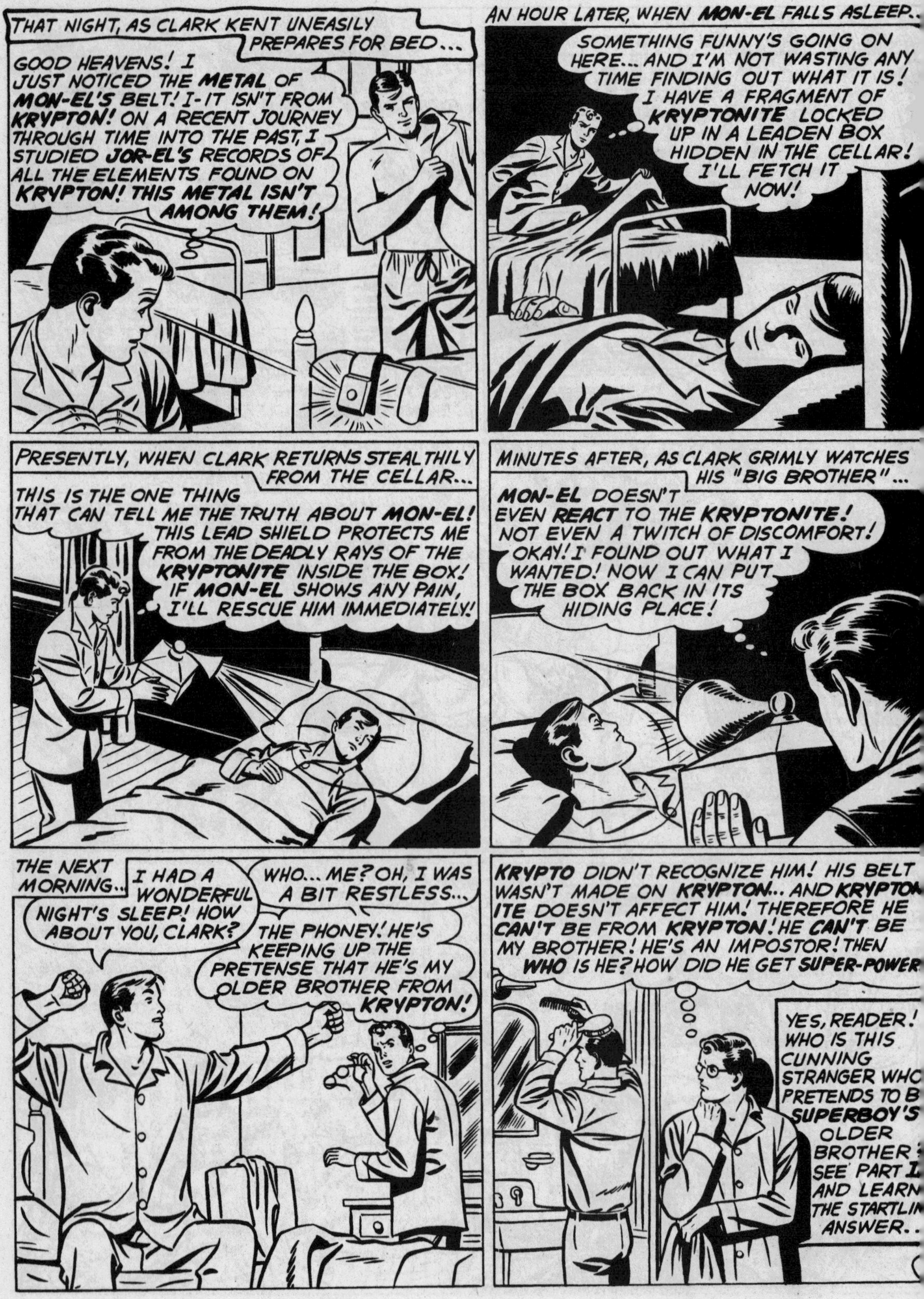
THAT NIGHT, AS CLARK KENT UNEASILY PREPARES FOR BED...
GOOD HEAVENS! I JUST NOTICED THE METAL OF MON-EL'S BELT! I-IT ISN'T FROM KRYPTON! ON A RECENT JOURNEY THROUGH TIME INTO THE PAST, I STUDIED JOR-EL'S RECORDS OF ALL THE ELEMENTS FOUND ON KRYPTON! THIS METAL ISN'T AMONG THEM!
AN HOUR LATER, WHEN MON-EL FALLS ASLEEP...
SOMETHING FUNNY'S GOING ON HERE... AND I'M NOT WASTING ANY TIME FINDING OUT WHAT IT IS! I HAVE A FRAGMENT OF KRYPTONITE LOCKED UP IN A LEADEN BOX HIDDEN IN THE CELLAR! I'LL FETCH IT NOW!
PRESENTLY, WHEN CLARK RETURNS STEALTHILY FROM THE CELLAR...
THIS IS THE ONE THING THAT CAN TELL ME THE TRUTH ABOUT MON-EL! THIS LEAD SHIELD PROTECTS ME FROM THE DEADLY RAYS OF THE KRYPTONITE INSIDE THE BOX! IF MON-EL SHOWS ANY PAIN, I'LL RESCUE HIM IMMEDIATELY!
MINUTES AFTER, AS CLARK GRIMLY WATCHES HIS "BIG BROTHER"...
MON-EL DOESN'T EVEN REACT TO THE KRYPTONITE! NOT EVEN A TWITCH OF DISCOMFORT! OKAY! I FOUND OUT WHAT I WANTED! NOW I CAN PUT THE BOX BACK IN ITS HIDING PLACE!
THE NEXT MORNING...
I HAD A WONDERFUL NIGHT'S SLEEP! HOW ABOUT YOU, CLARK?
WHO... ME? OH, I WAS A BIT RESTLESS...
THE PHONEY! HE'S KEEPING UP THE PRETENSE THAT HE'S MY OLDER BROTHER FROM KRYPTON!
KRYPTO DIDN'T RECOGNIZE HIM! HIS BELT WASN'T MADE ON KRYPTON... AND KRYPTONITE DOESN'T AFFECT HIM! THEREFORE HE CAN'T BE FROM KRYPTON! HE CAN'T BE MY BROTHER! HE'S AN IMPOSTOR! THEN WHO IS HE? HOW DID HE GET SUPER-POWER
YES, READER! WHO IS THIS CUNNING STRANGER WHO PRETENDS TO B SUPERBOY'S OLDER BROTHER? SEE PART II AND LEARN THE STARTLIN ANSWER...

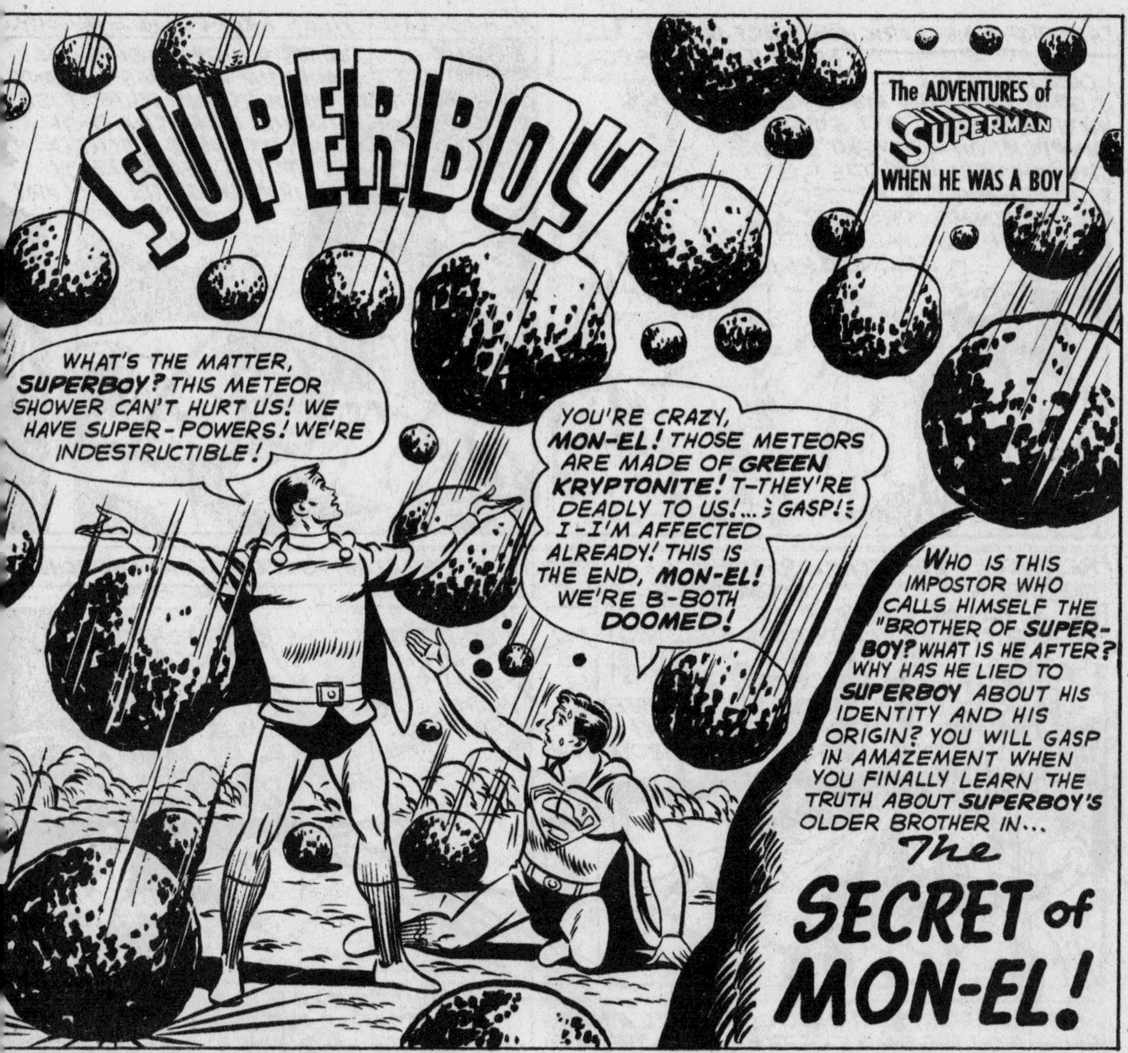
SUPERBOY
The ADVENTURES of SUPERMAN WHEN HE WAS A BOY
WHAT'S THE MATTER, SUPERBOY? THIS METEOR SHOWER CAN'T HURT US! WE HAVE SUPER-POWERS! WE'RE INDESTRUCTIBLE!
YOU'RE CRAZY, MON-EL! THOSE METEORS ARE MADE OF GREEN KRYPTONITE! T-THEY'RE DEADLY TO US!... GASP! I-I'M AFFECTED ALREADY! THIS IS THE END, MON-EL! WE'RE B-BOTH DOOMED!
WHO IS THIS IMPOSTOR WHO CALLS HIMSELF THE "BROTHER OF SUPERBOY? WHAT IS HE AFTER? WHY HAS HE LIED TO SUPERBOY ABOUT HIS IDENTITY AND HIS ORIGIN? YOU WILL GASP IN AMAZEMENT WHEN YOU FINALLY LEARN THE TRUTH ABOUT SUPERBOY'S OLDER BROTHER IN...
The SECRET of MON-EL!

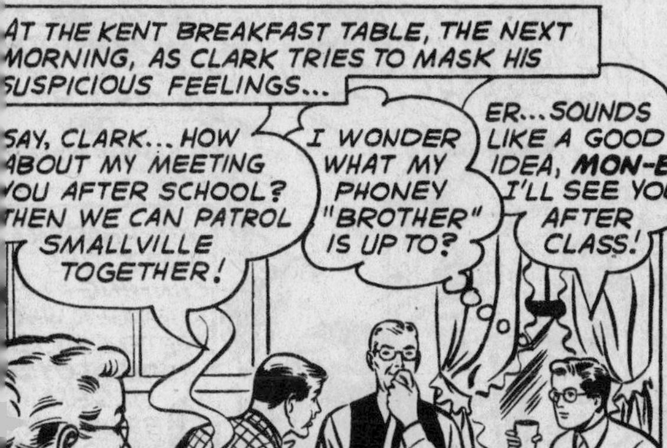
AT THE KENT BREAKFAST TABLE, THE NEXT MORNING, AS CLARK TRIES TO MASK HIS SUSPICIOUS FEELINGS...
SAY, CLARK... HOW ABOUT MY MEETING YOU AFTER SCHOOL? THEN WE CAN PATROL SMALLVILLE TOGETHER!
I WONDER WHAT MY PHONEY "BROTHER" IS UP TO?
ER... SOUNDS LIKE A GOOD IDEA, MON-EL! I'LL SEE YOU AFTER CLASS!

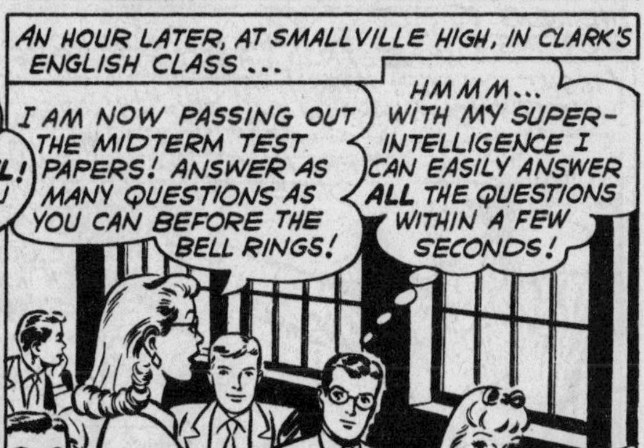
AN HOUR LATER, AT SMALLVILLE HIGH, IN CLARK'S ENGLISH CLASS...
I AM NOW PASSING OUT THE MIDTERM TEST PAPERS! ANSWER AS MANY QUESTIONS AS YOU CAN BEFORE THE BELL RINGS!
HMMM... WITH MY SUPER-INTELLIGENCE I CAN EASILY ANSWER ALL THE QUESTIONS WITHIN A FEW SECONDS!

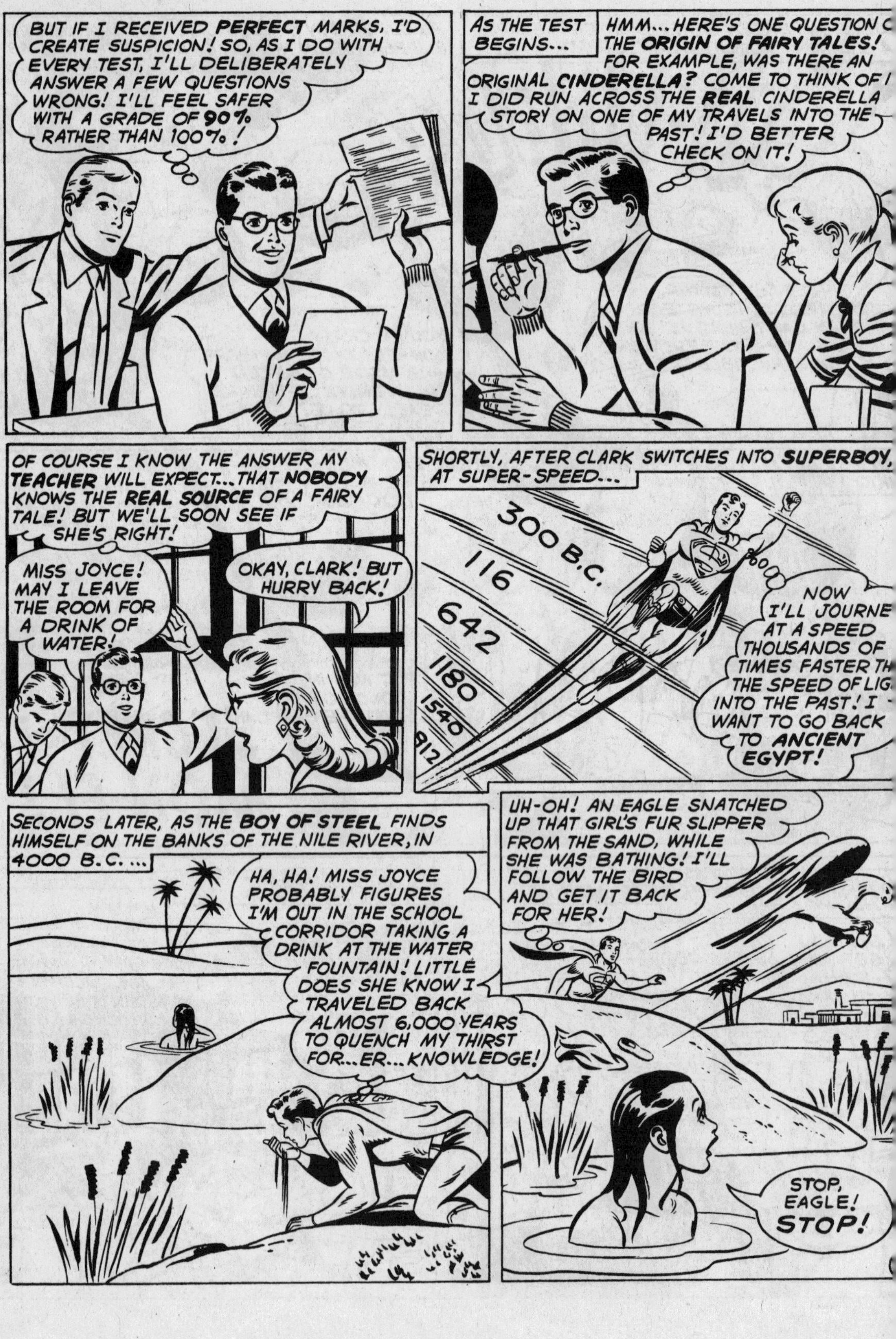
BUT IF I RECEIVED PERFECT MARKS, I'D CREATE SUSPICION! SO, AS I DO WITH EVERY TEST, I'LL DELIBERATELY ANSWER A FEW QUESTIONS WRONG! I'LL FEEL SAFER WITH A GRADE OF 90% RATHER THAN 100%!
AS THE TEST BEGINS...
HMM...HERE'S ONE QUESTION THE ORIGIN OF FAIRY TALES! FOR EXAMPLE, WAS THERE AN ORIGINAL CINDERELLA? COME TO THINK OF I DID RUN ACROSS THE REAL CINDERELLA STORY ON ONE OF MY TRAVELS INTO THE PAST! I'D BETTER CHECK ON IT!
OF COURSE I KNOW THE ANSWER MY TEACHER WILL EXPECT...THAT NOBODY KNOWS THE REAL SOURCE OF A FAIRY TALE! BUT WE'LL SOON SEE IF SHE'S RIGHT!
MISS JOYCE! MAY I LEAVE THE ROOM FOR A DRINK OF WATER?
OKAY, CLARK! BUT HURRY BACK!
SHORTLY, AFTER CLARK SWITCHES INTO SUPERBOY, AT SUPER-SPEED...
300 B.C.
116
642
1180
1540
1812
NOW I'LL JOURNE AT A SPEED THOUSANDS OF TIMES FASTER TH THE SPEED OF LIG INTO THE PAST! I WANT TO GO BACK TO ANCIENT EGYPT!
SECONDS LATER, AS THE BOY OF STEEL FINDS HIMSELF ON THE BANKS OF THE NILE RIVER, IN 4000 B.C. ...
HA, HA! MISS JOYCE PROBABLY FIGURES I'M OUT IN THE SCHOOL CORRIDOR TAKING A DRINK AT THE WATER FOUNTAIN! LITTLE DOES SHE KNOW I TRAVELED BACK ALMOST 6,000 YEARS TO QUENCH MY THIRST FOR...ER...KNOWLEDGE!
UH-OH! AN EAGLE SNATCHED UP THAT GIRL'S FUR SLIPPER FROM THE SAND, WHILE SHE WAS BATHING! I'LL FOLLOW THE BIRD AND GET IT BACK FOR HER!
STOP, EAGLE! STOP!

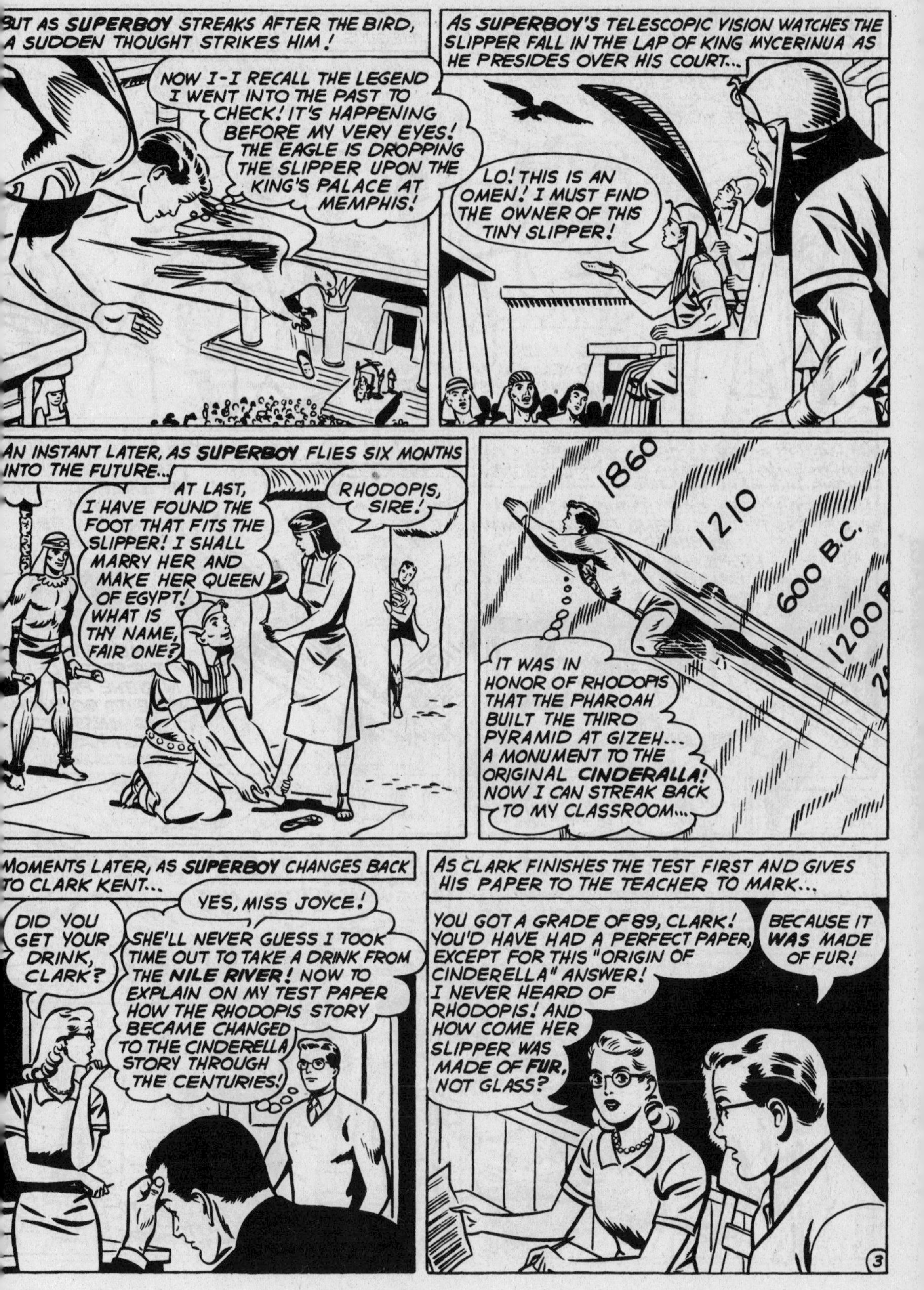
BUT AS SUPERBOY STREAKS AFTER THE BIRD, A SUDDEN THOUGHT STRIKES HIM!
NOW I-I RECALL THE LEGEND I WENT INTO THE PAST TO CHECK! IT'S HAPPENING BEFORE MY VERY EYES! THE EAGLE IS DROPPING THE SLIPPER UPON THE KING'S PALACE AT MEMPHIS!
AS SUPERBOY'S TELESCOPIC VISION WATCHES THE SLIPPER FALL IN THE LAP OF KING MYCERINUA AS HE PRESIDES OVER HIS COURT...
LO! THIS IS AN OMEN! I MUST FIND THE OWNER OF THIS TINY SLIPPER!
AN INSTANT LATER, AS SUPERBOY FLIES SIX MONTHS INTO THE FUTURE...
AT LAST, I HAVE FOUND THE FOOT THAT FITS THE SLIPPER! I SHALL MARRY HER AND MAKE HER QUEEN OF EGYPT! WHAT IS THY NAME, FAIR ONE?
RHODOPIS, SIRE!
1860
1210
600 B.C.
IT WAS IN HONOR OF RHODOPIS THAT THE PHAROAH BUILT THE THIRD PYRAMID AT GIZEH... A MONUMENT TO THE ORIGINAL CINDERALLA! NOW I CAN STREAK BACK TO MY CLASSROOM...
MOMENTS LATER, AS SUPERBOY CHANGES BACK TO CLARK KENT...
DID YOU GET YOUR DRINK, CLARK?
YES, MISS JOYCE!
SHE'LL NEVER GUESS I TOOK TIME OUT TO TAKE A DRINK FROM THE NILE RIVER! NOW TO EXPLAIN ON MY TEST PAPER HOW THE RHODOPIS STORY BECAME CHANGED TO THE CINDERELLA STORY THROUGH THE CENTURIES!
AS CLARK FINISHES THE TEST FIRST AND GIVES HIS PAPER TO THE TEACHER TO MARK...
YOU GOT A GRADE OF 89, CLARK! YOU'D HAVE HAD A PERFECT PAPER, EXCEPT FOR THIS "ORIGIN OF CINDERELLA" ANSWER! I NEVER HEARD OF RHODOPIS! AND HOW COME HER SLIPPER WAS MADE OF FUR, NOT GLASS?
BECAUSE IT WAS MADE OF FUR!
3

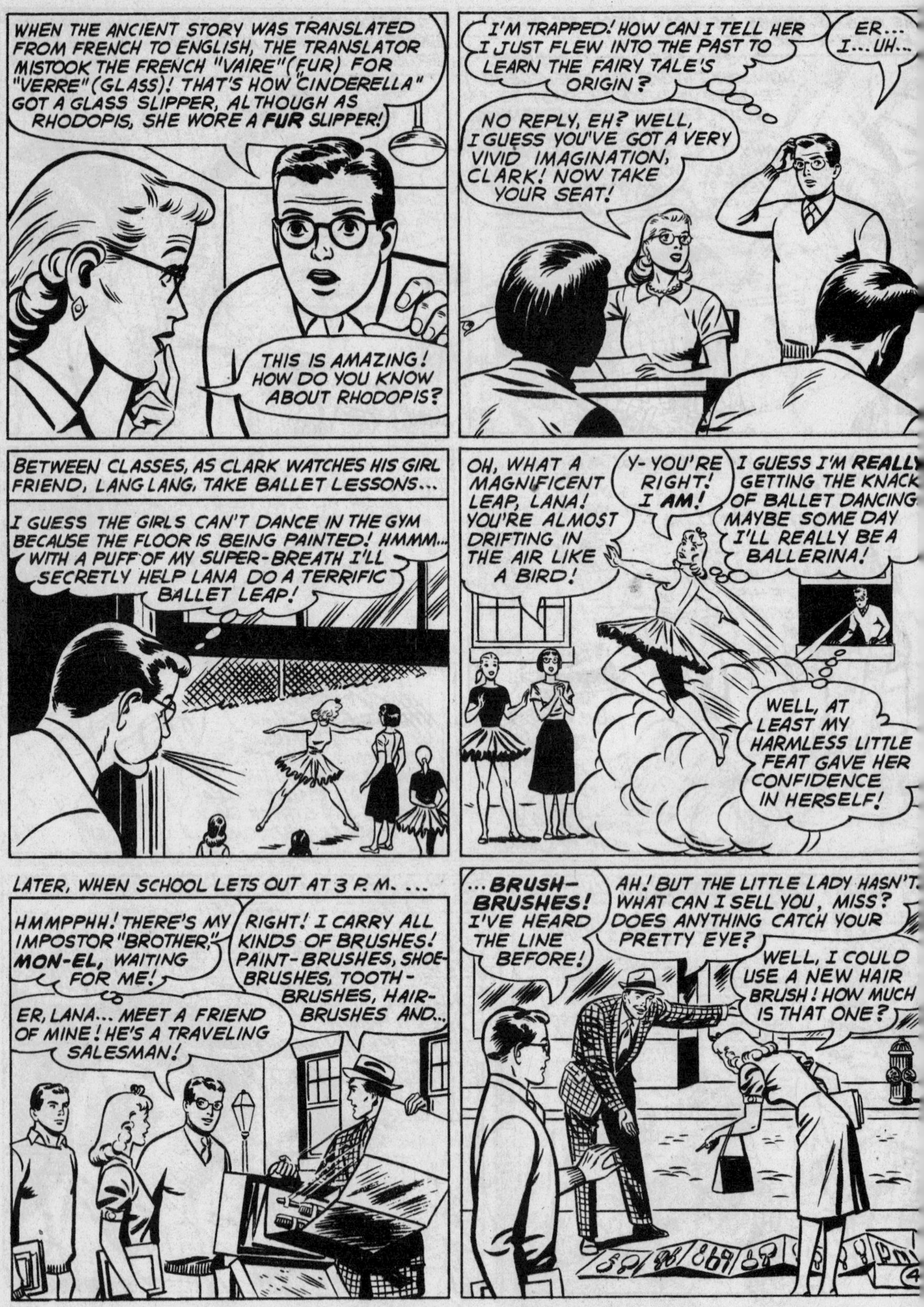
WHEN THE ANCIENT STORY WAS TRANSLATED FROM FRENCH TO ENGLISH, THE TRANSLATOR MISTOOK THE FRENCH "VAIRE" (FUR) FOR "VERRE" (GLASS)! THAT'S HOW "CINDERELLA" GOT A GLASS SLIPPER, ALTHOUGH AS RHODOPIS, SHE WORE A FUR SLIPPER!
THIS IS AMAZING! HOW DO YOU KNOW ABOUT RHODOPIS?
I'M TRAPPED! HOW CAN I TELL HER I JUST FLEW INTO THE PAST TO LEARN THE FAIRY TALE'S ORIGIN?
ER... I...UH...
NO REPLY, EH? WELL, I GUESS YOU'VE GOT A VERY VIVID IMAGINATION, CLARK! NOW TAKE YOUR SEAT!
BETWEEN CLASSES, AS CLARK WATCHES HIS GIRL FRIEND, LANG LANG, TAKE BALLET LESSONS...
I GUESS THE GIRLS CAN'T DANCE IN THE GYM BECAUSE THE FLOOR IS BEING PAINTED! HMMM... WITH A PUFF OF MY SUPER-BREATH I'LL SECRETLY HELP LANA DO A TERRIFIC BALLET LEAP!
OH, WHAT A MAGNIFICENT LEAP, LANA! YOU'RE ALMOST DRIFTING IN THE AIR LIKE A BIRD!
Y- YOU'RE RIGHT! I AM!
I GUESS I'M REALLY GETTING THE KNACK OF BALLET DANCING. MAYBE SOME DAY I'LL REALLY BE A BALLERINA!
WELL, AT LEAST MY HARMLESS LITTLE FEAT GAVE HER CONFIDENCE IN HERSELF!
LATER, WHEN SCHOOL LETS OUT AT 3 P. M. ...
HMMPPHH! THERE'S MY IMPOSTOR "BROTHER," MON-EL, WAITING FOR ME!
ER, LANA... MEET A FRIEND OF MINE! HE'S A TRAVELING SALESMAN!
RIGHT! I CARRY ALL KINDS OF BRUSHES! PAINT-BRUSHES, SHOE-BRUSHES, TOOTH-BRUSHES, HAIR-BRUSHES AND...
...BRUSH-BRUSHES! I'VE HEARD THE LINE BEFORE!
AH! BUT THE LITTLE LADY HASN'T. WHAT CAN I SELL YOU, MISS? DOES ANYTHING CATCH YOUR PRETTY EYE?
WELL, I COULD USE A NEW HAIR BRUSH! HOW MUCH IS THAT ONE?
4

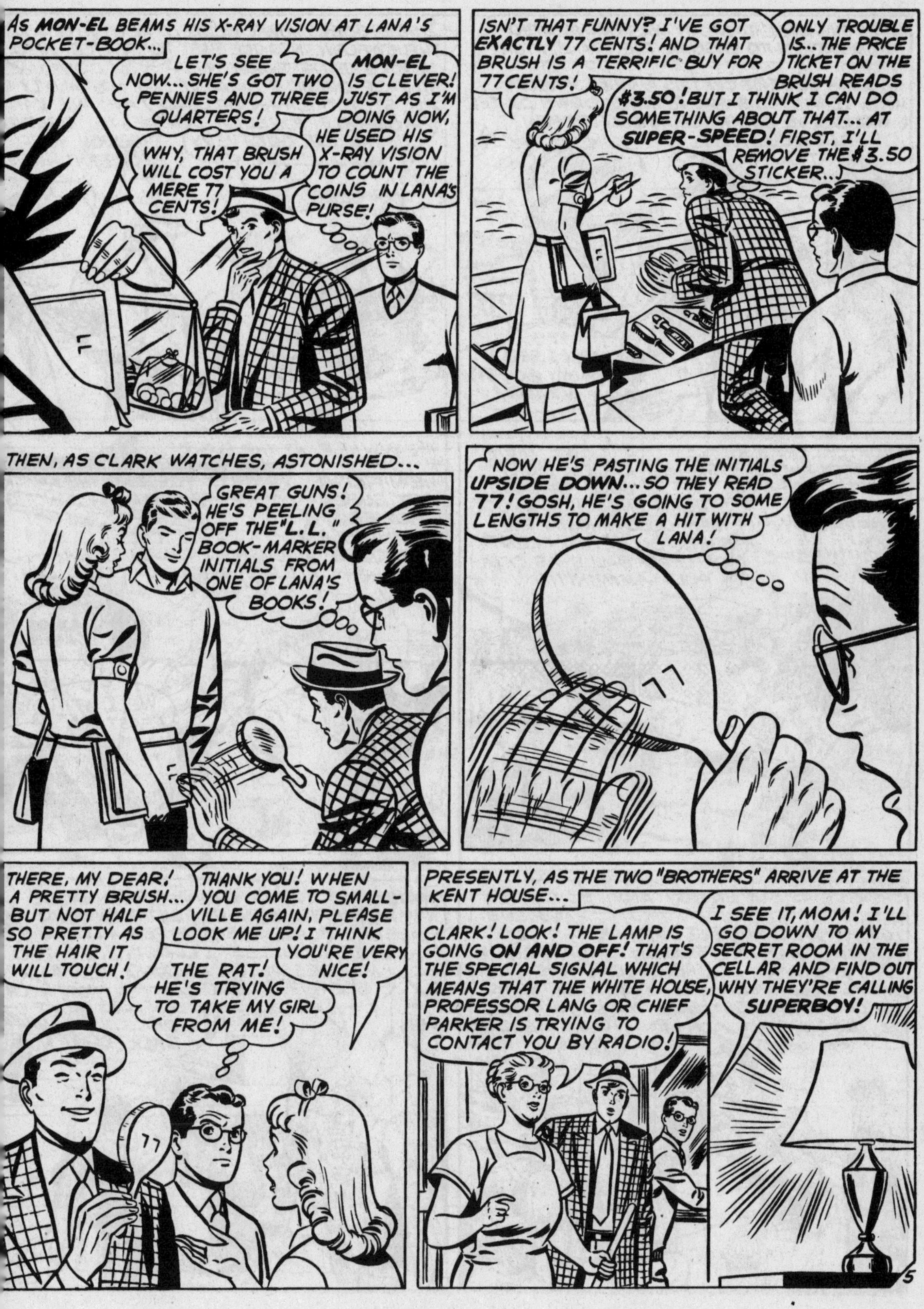
AS MON-EL BEAMS HIS X-RAY VISION AT LANA'S POCKET-BOOK...
LET'S SEE NOW... SHE'S GOT TWO PENNIES AND THREE QUARTERS!
WHY, THAT BRUSH WILL COST YOU A MERE 77 CENTS!
MON-EL IS CLEVER! JUST AS I'M DOING NOW, HE USED HIS X-RAY VISION TO COUNT THE COINS IN LANA'S PURSE!
ISN'T THAT FUNNY? I'VE GOT EXACTLY 77 CENTS! AND THAT BRUSH IS A TERRIFIC BUY FOR 77 CENTS!
ONLY TROUBLE IS... THE PRICE TICKET ON THE BRUSH READS $3.50! BUT I THINK I CAN DO SOMETHING ABOUT THAT... AT SUPER-SPEED! FIRST, I'LL REMOVE THE $3.50 STICKER...
THEN, AS CLARK WATCHES, ASTONISHED...
GREAT GUNS! HE'S PEELING OFF THE "L.L." BOOK-MARKER INITIALS FROM ONE OF LANA'S BOOKS!
NOW HE'S PASTING THE INITIALS UPSIDE DOWN... SO THEY READ 77! GOSH, HE'S GOING TO SOME LENGTHS TO MAKE A HIT WITH LANA!
THERE, MY DEAR! A PRETTY BRUSH... BUT NOT HALF SO PRETTY AS THE HAIR IT WILL TOUCH!
THANK YOU! WHEN YOU COME TO SMALL-VILLE AGAIN, PLEASE LOOK ME UP! I THINK YOU'RE VERY NICE!
THE RAT! HE'S TRYING TO TAKE MY GIRL FROM ME!
PRESENTLY, AS THE TWO "BROTHERS" ARRIVE AT THE KENT HOUSE...
CLARK! LOOK! THE LAMP IS GOING ON AND OFF! THAT'S THE SPECIAL SIGNAL WHICH MEANS THAT THE WHITE HOUSE, PROFESSOR LANG OR CHIEF PARKER IS TRYING TO CONTACT YOU BY RADIO!
I SEE IT, MOM! I'LL GO DOWN TO MY SECRET ROOM IN THE CELLAR AND FIND OUT WHY THEY'RE CALLING SUPERBOY!
5

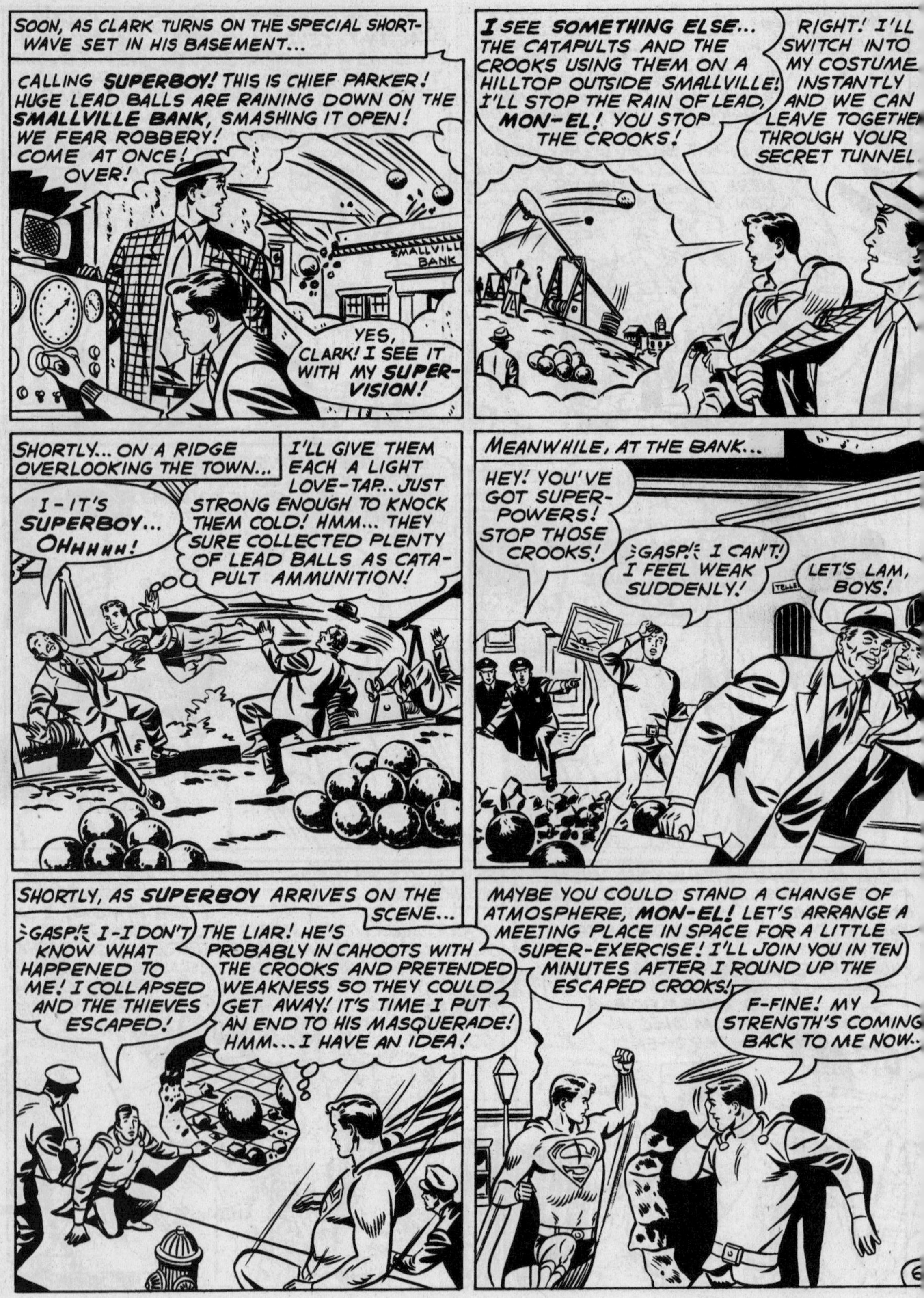
SOON, AS CLARK TURNS ON THE SPECIAL SHORT-WAVE SET IN HIS BASEMENT...
CALLING SUPERBOY! THIS IS CHIEF PARKER! HUGE LEAD BALLS ARE RAINING DOWN ON THE SMALLVILLE BANK, SMASHING IT OPEN! WE FEAR ROBBERY! COME AT ONCE! OVER!
SMALLVILLE BANK
YES, CLARK! I SEE IT WITH MY SUPER-VISION!
I SEE SOMETHING ELSE... THE CATAPULTS AND THE CROOKS USING THEM ON A HILLTOP OUTSIDE SMALLVILLE! I'LL STOP THE RAIN OF LEAD, MON-EL! YOU STOP THE CROOKS!
RIGHT! I'LL SWITCH INTO MY COSTUME INSTANTLY AND WE CAN LEAVE TOGETHER THROUGH YOUR SECRET TUNNEL
SHORTLY... ON A RIDGE OVERLOOKING THE TOWN...
I'LL GIVE THEM EACH A LIGHT LOVE-TAP.. JUST STRONG ENOUGH TO KNOCK THEM COLD! HMM... THEY SURE COLLECTED PLENTY OF LEAD BALLS AS CATAPULT AMMUNITION!
I-IT'S SUPERBOY... OHHHHH!
MEANWHILE, AT THE BANK...
HEY! YOU'VE GOT SUPER-POWERS! STOP THOSE CROOKS!
GASP! I CAN'T! I FEEL WEAK SUDDENLY!
LET'S LAM, BOYS!
SHORTLY, AS SUPERBOY ARRIVES ON THE SCENE...
GASP! I-I DON'T KNOW WHAT HAPPENED TO ME! I COLLAPSED AND THE THIEVES ESCAPED!
THE LIAR! HE'S PROBABLY IN CAHOOTS WITH THE CROOKS AND PRETENDED WEAKNESS SO THEY COULD GET AWAY! IT'S TIME I PUT AN END TO HIS MASQUERADE! HMM... I HAVE AN IDEA!
MAYBE YOU COULD STAND A CHANGE OF ATMOSPHERE, MON-EL! LET'S ARRANGE A MEETING PLACE IN SPACE FOR A LITTLE SUPER-EXERCISE! I'LL JOIN YOU IN TEN MINUTES AFTER I ROUND UP THE ESCAPED CROOKS!
F-FINE! MY STRENGTH'S COMING BACK TO ME NOW...

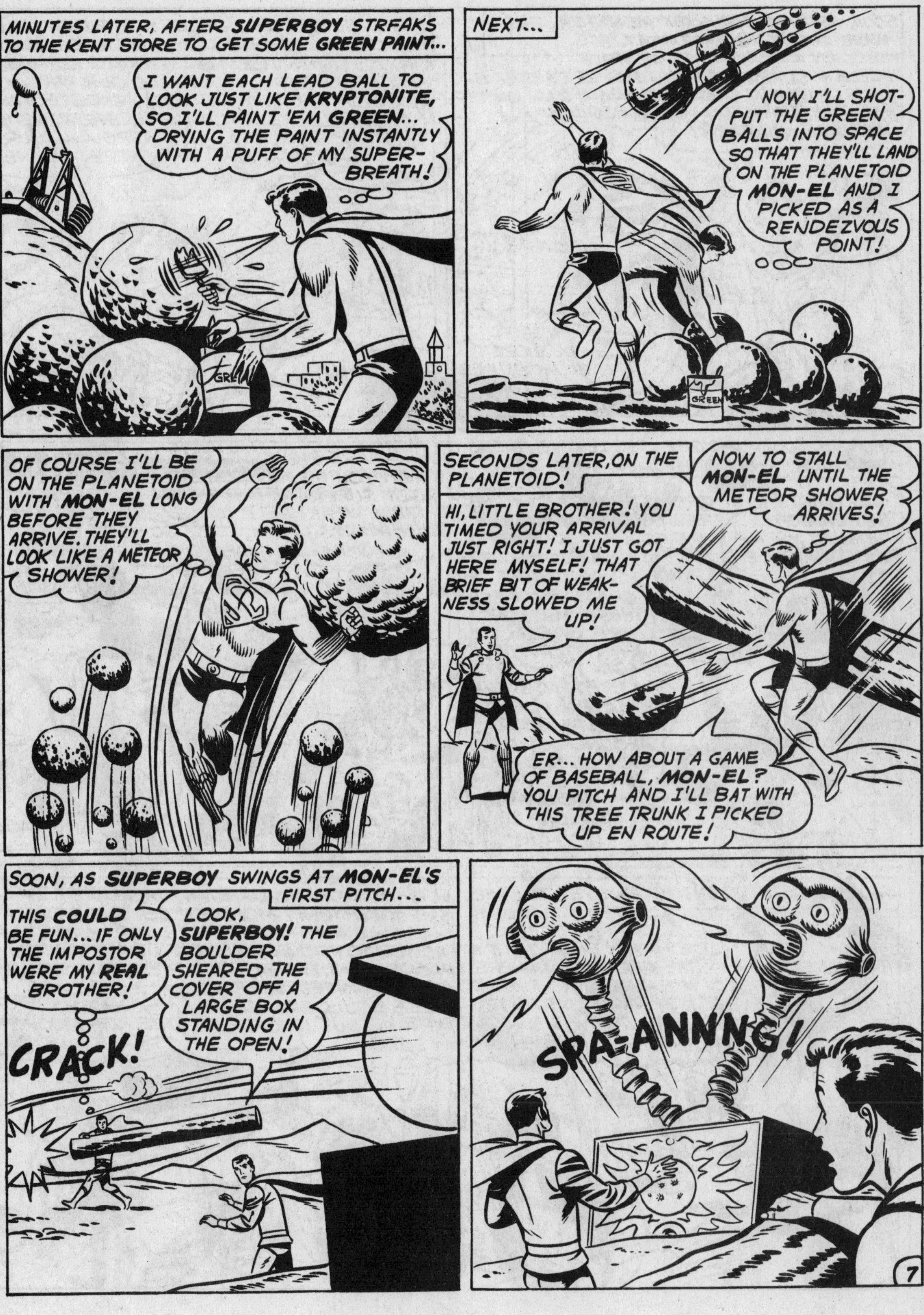
MINUTES LATER, AFTER SUPERBOY STRFAKS TO THE KENT STORE TO GET SOME GREEN PAINT...
I WANT EACH LEAD BALL TO LOOK JUST LIKE KRYPTONITE, SO I'LL PAINT 'EM GREEN... DRYING THE PAINT INSTANTLY WITH A PUFF OF MY SUPER-BREATH!
GRE
NEXT...
NOW I'LL SHOT-PUT THE GREEN BALLS INTO SPACE SO THAT THEY'LL LAND ON THE PLANETOID MON-EL AND I PICKED AS A RENDEZVOUS POINT!
GREEN
OF COURSE I'LL BE ON THE PLANETOID WITH MON-EL LONG BEFORE THEY ARRIVE. THEY'LL LOOK LIKE A METEOR SHOWER!
SECONDS LATER, ON THE PLANETOID!
NOW TO STALL MON-EL UNTIL THE METEOR SHOWER ARRIVES!
HI, LITTLE BROTHER! YOU TIMED YOUR ARRIVAL JUST RIGHT! I JUST GOT HERE MYSELF! THAT BRIEF BIT OF WEAKNESS SLOWED ME UP!
ER... HOW ABOUT A GAME OF BASEBALL, MON-EL? YOU PITCH AND I'LL BAT WITH THIS TREE TRUNK I PICKED UP EN ROUTE!
SOON, AS SUPERBOY SWINGS AT MON-EL'S FIRST PITCH...
THIS COULD BE FUN... IF ONLY THE IMPOSTOR WERE MY REAL BROTHER!
LOOK, SUPERBOY! THE BOULDER SHEARED THE COVER OFF A LARGE BOX STANDING IN THE OPEN!
CRACK!
SPA-ANNNG!
7

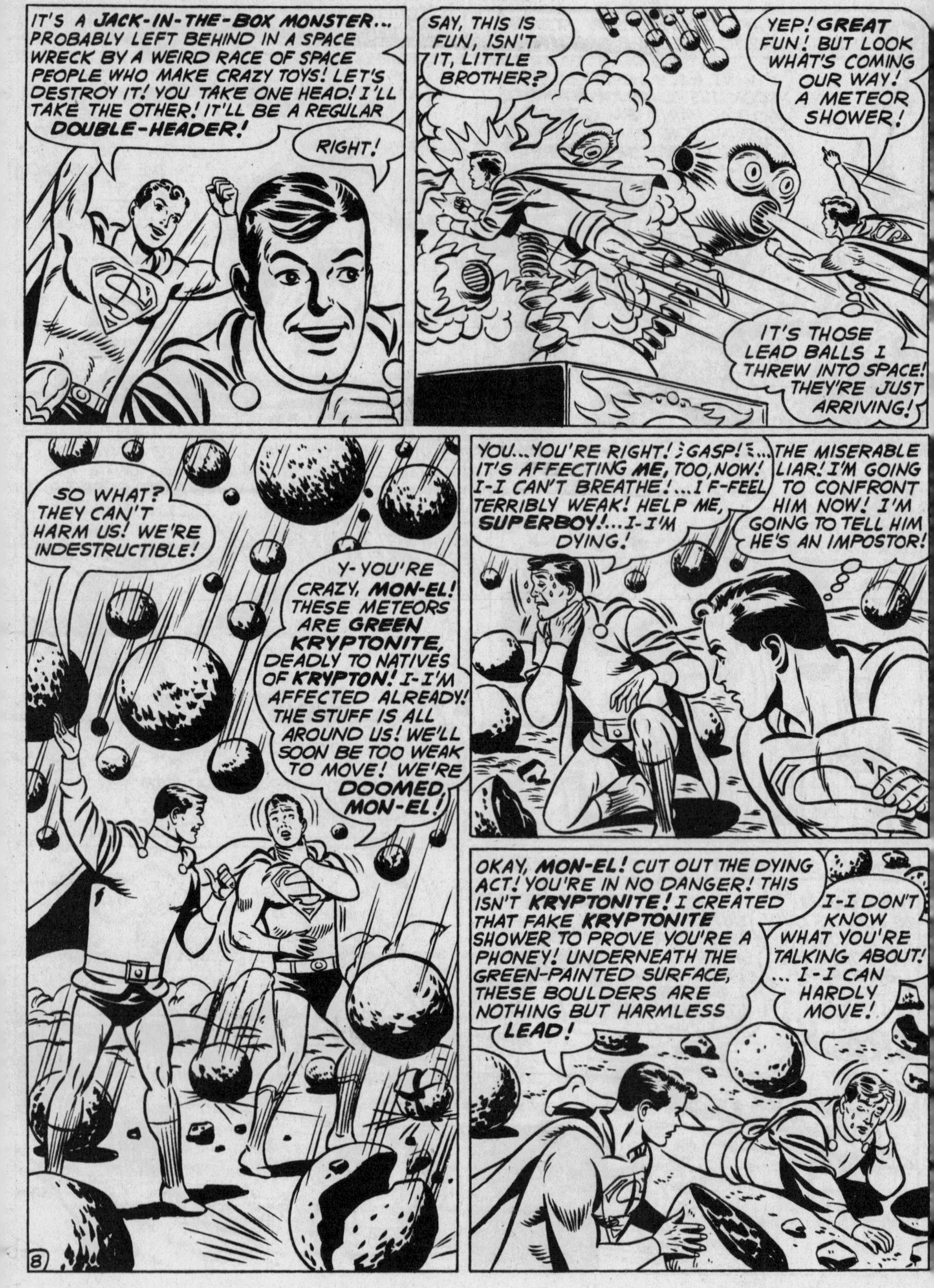
IT'S A JACK-IN-THE-BOX MONSTER... PROBABLY LEFT BEHIND IN A SPACE WRECK BY A WEIRD RACE OF SPACE PEOPLE WHO MAKE CRAZY TOYS! LET'S DESTROY IT! YOU TAKE ONE HEAD! I'LL TAKE THE OTHER! IT'LL BE A REGULAR DOUBLE-HEADER!
RIGHT!
SAY, THIS IS FUN, ISN'T IT, LITTLE BROTHER?
YEP! GREAT FUN! BUT LOOK WHAT'S COMING OUR WAY! A METEOR SHOWER!
IT'S THOSE LEAD BALLS I THREW INTO SPACE! THEY'RE JUST ARRIVING!
SO WHAT? THEY CAN'T HARM US! WE'RE INDESTRUCTIBLE!
Y-YOU'RE CRAZY, MON-EL! THESE METEORS ARE GREEN KRYPTONITE, DEADLY TO NATIVES OF KRYPTON! I-I'M AFFECTED ALREADY! THE STUFF IS ALL AROUND US! WE'LL SOON BE TOO WEAK TO MOVE! WE'RE DOOMED, MON-EL!
8
YOU...YOU'RE RIGHT! GASP! ...IT'S AFFECTING ME, TOO, NOW! I-I CAN'T BREATHE! ...I F-FEEL TERRIBLY WEAK! HELP ME, SUPERBOY! ...I-I'M DYING!
THE MISERABLE LIAR! I'M GOING TO CONFRONT HIM NOW! I'M GOING TO TELL HIM HE'S AN IMPOSTOR!
OKAY, MON-EL! CUT OUT THE DYING ACT! YOU'RE IN NO DANGER! THIS ISN'T KRYPTONITE! I CREATED THAT FAKE KRYPTONITE SHOWER TO PROVE YOU'RE A PHONEY! UNDERNEATH THE GREEN-PAINTED SURFACE, THESE BOULDERS ARE NOTHING BUT HARMLESS LEAD!
I-I DON'T KNOW WHAT YOU'RE TALKING ABOUT! ... I-I CAN HARDLY MOVE!

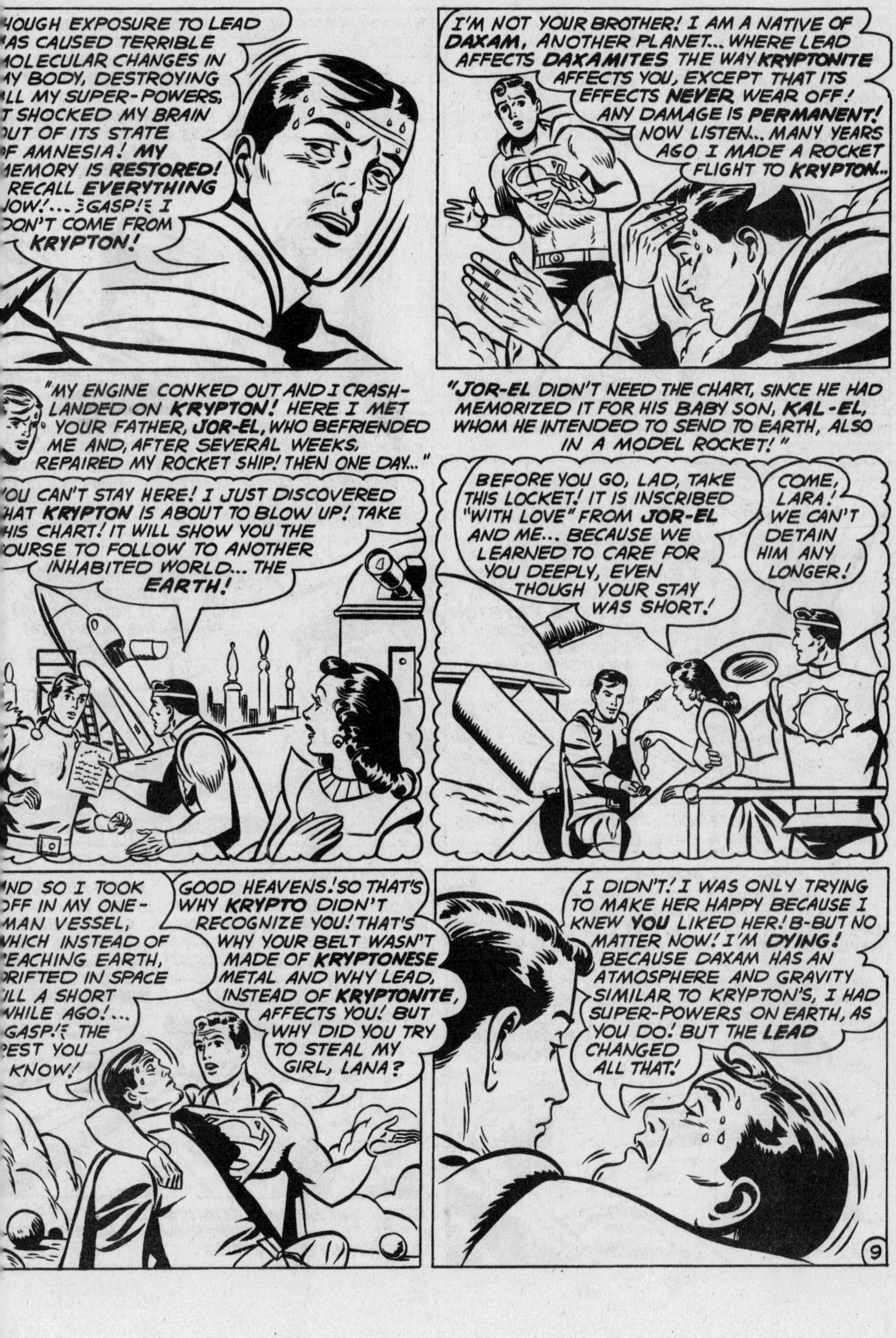
HOUGH EXPOSURE TO LEAD HAS CAUSED TERRIBLE MOLECULAR CHANGES IN MY BODY, DESTROYING ALL MY SUPER-POWERS, IT SHOCKED MY BRAIN OUT OF ITS STATE OF AMNESIA! MY MEMORY IS RESTORED! I RECALL EVERYTHING NOW!... GASP! I DON'T COME FROM KRYPTON!
I'M NOT YOUR BROTHER! I AM A NATIVE OF DAXAM, ANOTHER PLANET... WHERE LEAD AFFECTS DAXAMITES THE WAY KRYPTONITE AFFECTS YOU, EXCEPT THAT ITS EFFECTS NEVER WEAR OFF! ANY DAMAGE IS PERMANENT! NOW LISTEN... MANY YEARS AGO I MADE A ROCKET FLIGHT TO KRYPTON...
"MY ENGINE CONKED OUT AND I CRASH-LANDED ON KRYPTON! HERE I MET YOUR FATHER, JOR-EL, WHO BEFRIENDED ME AND, AFTER SEVERAL WEEKS, REPAIRED MY ROCKET SHIP! THEN ONE DAY..."
YOU CAN'T STAY HERE! I JUST DISCOVERED THAT KRYPTON IS ABOUT TO BLOW UP! TAKE THIS CHART! IT WILL SHOW YOU THE COURSE TO FOLLOW TO ANOTHER INHABITED WORLD... THE EARTH!
"JOR-EL DIDN'T NEED THE CHART, SINCE HE HAD MEMORIZED IT FOR HIS BABY SON, KAL-EL, WHOM HE INTENDED TO SEND TO EARTH, ALSO IN A MODEL ROCKET!"
BEFORE YOU GO, LAD, TAKE THIS LOCKET! IT IS INSCRIBED "WITH LOVE" FROM JOR-EL AND ME... BECAUSE WE LEARNED TO CARE FOR YOU DEEPLY, EVEN THOUGH YOUR STAY WAS SHORT!
COME, LARA! WE CAN'T DETAIN HIM ANY LONGER!
AND SO I TOOK OFF IN MY ONE-MAN VESSEL, WHICH INSTEAD OF REACHING EARTH, DRIFTED IN SPACE TILL A SHORT WHILE AGO!... GASP! THE REST YOU KNOW!
GOOD HEAVENS! SO THAT'S WHY KRYPTO DIDN'T RECOGNIZE YOU! THAT'S WHY YOUR BELT WASN'T MADE OF KRYPTONESE METAL AND WHY LEAD, INSTEAD OF KRYPTONITE, AFFECTS YOU! BUT WHY DID YOU TRY TO STEAL MY GIRL, LANA?
I DIDN'T! I WAS ONLY TRYING TO MAKE HER HAPPY BECAUSE I KNEW YOU LIKED HER! B-BUT NO MATTER NOW! I'M DYING! BECAUSE DAXAM HAS AN ATMOSPHERE AND GRAVITY SIMILAR TO KRYPTON'S, I HAD SUPER-POWERS ON EARTH, AS YOU DO! BUT THE LEAD CHANGED ALL THAT!
9

THIS IS ALL MY FAULT! BECAUSE I THOUGHT YOU WERE MY ENEMY, I PLAYED A FATAL TRICK ON YOU! BUT I'LL FLY YOU AWAY FROM HERE! THE EFFECTS OF THE LEAD WILL SOON WEAR OFF!

NO! IT'S NOT LIKE KRYPTONITE! ONCE EXPOSED TO LEAD, A DAXAMITE IS DOOMED! I'LL DIE WHEREVER YOU TAKE ME!

SUDDENLY, AS SUPERBOY GETS A DESPERATE IDEA.

IF YOU REMAIN IN THE REAL WORLD, YOU'LL DIE! BUT I CAN TRANSPORT YOU TO ANOTHER DIMENSION WHERE YOU COULD AT LEAST LIVE TILL I DISCOVER A CURE FOR THIS DEADLY MOLECULA EFFECT LEAD HAS ON YOU! WILL YOU GO THERE?

YES—ONLY H-HURRY I-I CAN' LAST LONG

SHORTLY, AS SUPERBOY STREAKS TO EARTH AND DIVES INTO THE ATLANTIC OCEAN...

HERE'S WHERE I RECENTLY THREW A SEALED BOX CONTAINING SOME TERRIBLE WEAPONS USED ON KRYPTON BEFORE IT EXPLODED! ONE WEAPON WAS A PUNISHMENT RAY, USED TO EXILE KRYPTON CRIMINALS! ACCORDING TO A DESCRIPTION OF THE WEAPONS WHICH I FOUND IN THIS BOX...

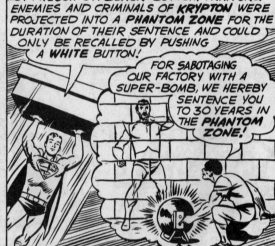

...BY PRESSING A BLACK BUTTON, TRAITORS, ENEMIES AND CRIMINALS OF KRYPTON WERE PROJECTED INTO A PHANTOM ZONE FOR THE DURATION OF THEIR SENTENCE AND COULD ONLY BE RECALLED BY PUSHING A WHITE BUTTON!

FOR SABOTAGING OUR FACTORY WITH A SUPER-BOMB, WE HEREBY SENTENCE YOU TO 30 YEARS IN THE PHANTOM ZONE!

SOON, ON THE ASTEROID, AS SUPERBOY PLACES THE LEAD BOX AT A SAFE DISTANCE...

I MUST WARN YOU, MON-EL! THERE ARE DANGEROUS VILLAINS AT LARGE IN THE PHANTOM ZONE! LIFE MAY BE HARD...BUT AT LEAST YOU'LL BE ALIVE! AND I PROMISE YOU, IN THE FUTURE I'LL FIND A CURE FOR THE DEADLY EFFECTS OF THE LEAD...AND RETURN YOU TO THE REAL WORLD!

I'M NOT AFRAID, SUPERBOY! SEND M-ME TO THE PHANTOM ZONE!

10

AFTER SUPERBOY PRESSES THE BLACK BUTTON...

FAREWELL, BROTHER THAT YOU ALMOST WERE! DON'T FORGET ME! RESCUE ME SOME DAY FROM THIS INVISIBLE DIMENSION!

MON-EL, WHERE EVER YOU ARE.. REMEMBER.. I'LL FREE YOU SOME DAY WHEN I GROW UP TO B SUPERMAN! I SWEAR IT!

WATCH SUPERMAN COMICS FOR A 3-PART NOVEL FEATURING SUPERMAN'S RETURN TO THE PHANTOM ZONE!

The End.

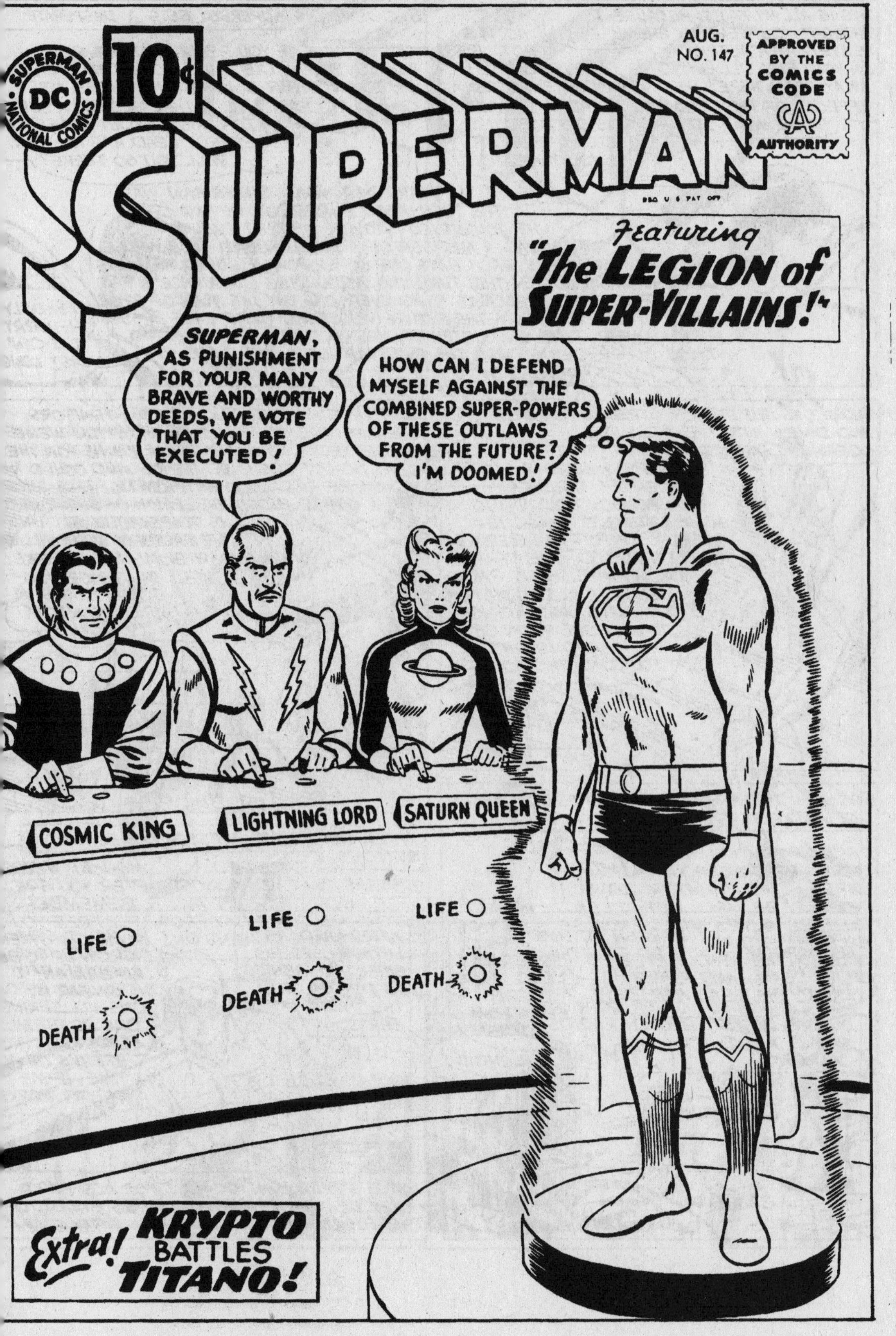
SUPERMAN DC NATIONAL COMICS
10¢
SUPERMAN
AUG. NO. 147
APPROVED BY THE COMICS CODE AUTHORITY
Featuring "The LEGION of SUPER-VILLAINS!"
SUPERMAN, AS PUNISHMENT FOR YOUR MANY BRAVE AND WORTHY DEEDS, WE VOTE THAT YOU BE EXECUTED!
HOW CAN I DEFEND MYSELF AGAINST THE COMBINED SUPER-POWERS OF THESE OUTLAWS FROM THE FUTURE? I'M DOOMED!
COSMIC KING
LIGHTNING LORD
SATURN QUEEN
LIFE
DEATH
LIFE
DEATH
LIFE
DEATH
Extra! KRYPTO BATTLES TITANO!

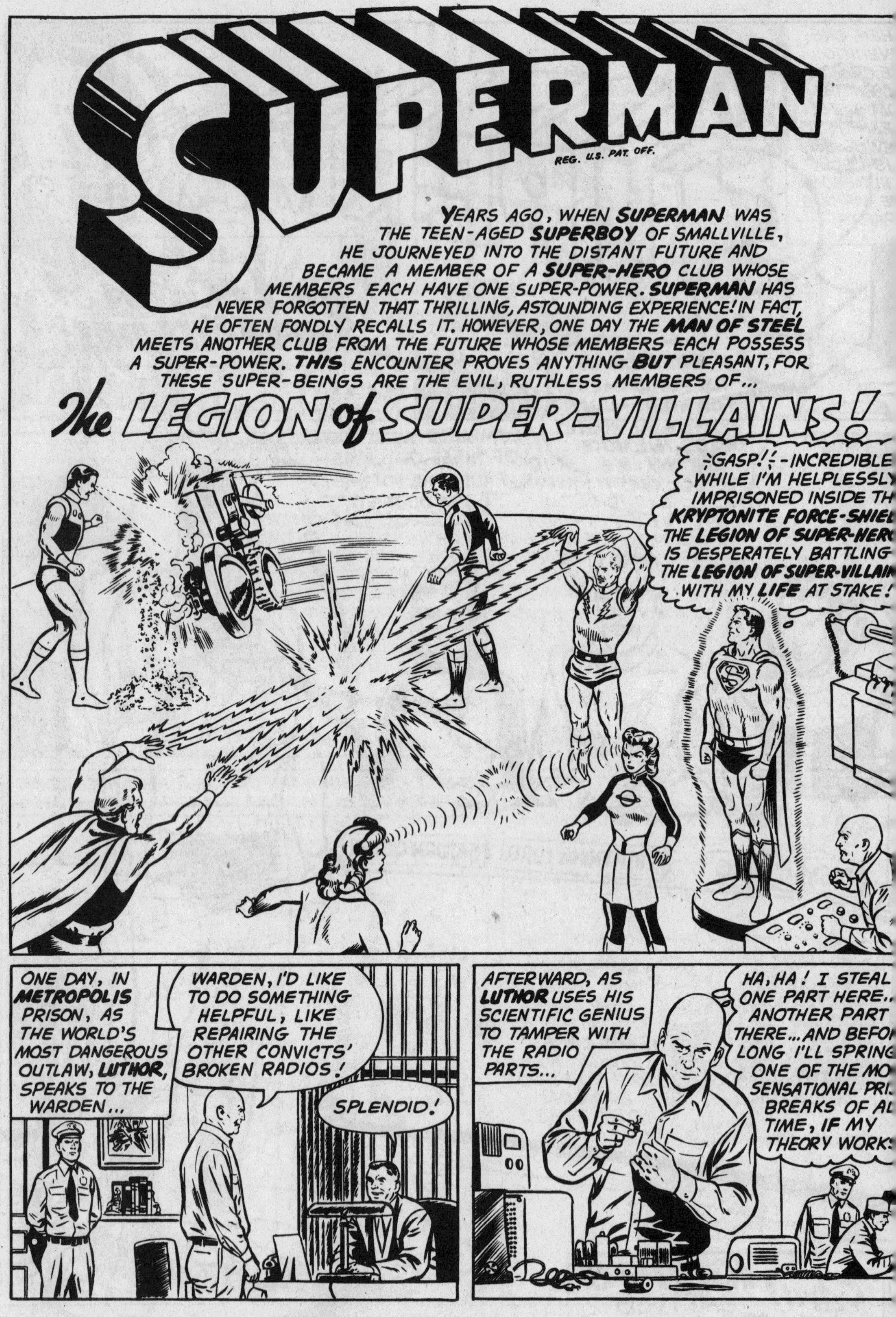
SUPERMAN
REG. U.S. PAT. OFF.
YEARS AGO, WHEN SUPERMAN WAS THE TEEN-AGED SUPERBOY OF SMALLVILLE, HE JOURNEYED INTO THE DISTANT FUTURE AND BECAME A MEMBER OF A SUPER-HERO CLUB WHOSE MEMBERS EACH HAVE ONE SUPER-POWER. SUPERMAN HAS NEVER FORGOTTEN THAT THRILLING, ASTOUNDING EXPERIENCE! IN FACT, HE OFTEN FONDLY RECALLS IT. HOWEVER, ONE DAY THE MAN OF STEEL MEETS ANOTHER CLUB FROM THE FUTURE WHOSE MEMBERS EACH POSSESS A SUPER-POWER. THIS ENCOUNTER PROVES ANYTHING BUT PLEASANT, FOR THESE SUPER-BEINGS ARE THE EVIL, RUTHLESS MEMBERS OF...
The LEGION of SUPER-VILLAINS!
-GASP!- -INCREDIBLE WHILE I'M HELPLESSL IMPRISONED INSIDE TH KRYPTONITE FORCE-SHIE THE LEGION OF SUPER-HER IS DESPERATELY BATTLING THE LEGION OF SUPER-VILLAI WITH MY LIFE AT STAKE!
ONE DAY, IN METROPOLIS PRISON, AS THE WORLD'S MOST DANGEROUS OUTLAW, LUTHOR, SPEAKS TO THE WARDEN...
WARDEN, I'D LIKE TO DO SOMETHING HELPFUL, LIKE REPAIRING THE OTHER CONVICTS' BROKEN RADIOS!
SPLENDID!
AFTERWARD, AS LUTHOR USES HIS SCIENTIFIC GENIUS TO TAMPER WITH THE RADIO PARTS...
HA, HA! I STEAL ONE PART HERE... ANOTHER PART THERE... AND BEFO LONG I'LL SPRIN ONE OF THE MO SENSATIONAL PRI BREAKS OF A TIME, IF MY THEORY WORK

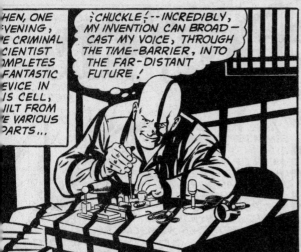

THEN, ONE EVENING, THE CRIMINAL SCIENTIST COMPLETES A FANTASTIC DEVICE IN HIS CELL, BUILT FROM THE VARIOUS PARTS...

¡CHUCKLE!--INCREDIBLY, MY INVENTION CAN BROAD-CAST MY VOICE, THROUGH THE TIME-BARRIER, INTO THE FAR-DISTANT FUTURE!

YEARS AGO, SUPERBOY... NOW GROWN INTO SUPERMAN... WAS SAVED FROM BEING DESTROYED BY ME, BY A MEMBER OF THE LEGION OF SUPER-HEROES FROM A FUTURE ERA!

I'VE LONG BELIEVED THAT IF A LEGION OF SUPER-HEROES EXISTS IN THE FUTURE, THEN A LEGION OF SUPER-VILLAINS PROBABLY EXISTS IN THE FUTURE TOO! IF THE HEROES COULD SAVE SUPERBOY, THE VILLAINS COULD SAVE ME!

FOR MANY HOURS, LUTHOR WHISPERS OVER AND OVER, INTO THE FANTASTIC DEVICE'S MICROPHONE...

CALLING THE FUTURE! ARCH-CRIMINAL LUTHOR FROM THE YEAR 1961 CALLING THE LEGION OF SUPER VILLAINS, IN THE FUTURE! AM IMPRISONED! NEED HELP! SAVE ME!

SUDDENLY, AT DAWN...

¡GASP!... THREE OBJECTS ARE MATERIALIZING ON THE FLOOR! THEY WEREN'T THERE A MOMENT AGO!... HAS MY APPEAL BEEN ANSWERED??

WE HEARD YOUR SUMMONS! USE THESE OBJECTS TO ESCAPE, LUTHOR! WE'LL JOIN YOU SOON IN YOUR OWN TIME!

QUICKLY, DONNING THE STRANGE BELT AND HELMET, LUTHOR FIRES THE WEIRD GUN AT THE CELL WALL...

EUREKA! THE WALL'S BURSTING OUTWARD!

SS-SSSST

BWANNNGG

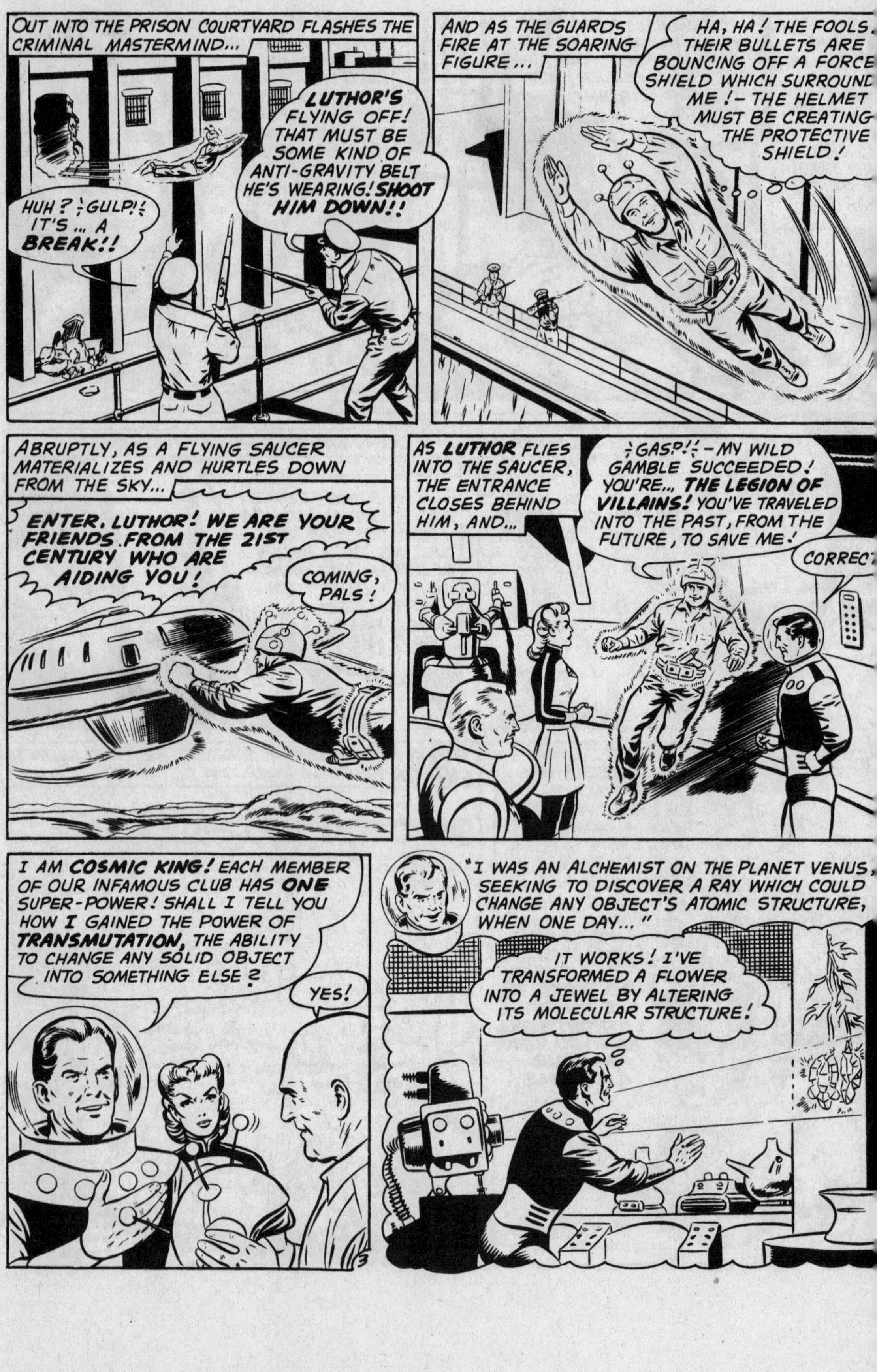
OUT INTO THE PRISON COURTYARD FLASHES THE CRIMINAL MASTERMIND...
LUTHOR'S FLYING OFF! THAT MUST BE SOME KIND OF ANTI-GRAVITY BELT HE'S WEARING! SHOOT HIM DOWN!!
HUH? -GULP!- IT'S... A BREAK!!
AND AS THE GUARDS FIRE AT THE SOARING FIGURE...
HA, HA! THE FOOLS. THEIR BULLETS ARE BOUNCING OFF A FORCE SHIELD WHICH SURROUND ME!- THE HELMET MUST BE CREATING THE PROTECTIVE SHIELD!
ABRUPTLY, AS A FLYING SAUCER MATERIALIZES AND HURTLES DOWN FROM THE SKY...
ENTER, LUTHOR! WE ARE YOUR FRIENDS FROM THE 21ST CENTURY WHO ARE AIDING YOU!
COMING, PALS!
AS LUTHOR FLIES INTO THE SAUCER, THE ENTRANCE CLOSES BEHIND HIM, AND...
-GASP!- -MY WILD GAMBLE SUCCEEDED! YOU'RE... THE LEGION OF VILLAINS! YOU'VE TRAVELED INTO THE PAST, FROM THE FUTURE, TO SAVE ME!
CORREC
I AM COSMIC KING! EACH MEMBER OF OUR INFAMOUS CLUB HAS ONE SUPER-POWER! SHALL I TELL YOU HOW I GAINED THE POWER OF TRANSMUTATION, THE ABILITY TO CHANGE ANY SOLID OBJECT INTO SOMETHING ELSE?
YES!
3
"I WAS AN ALCHEMIST ON THE PLANET VENUS, SEEKING TO DISCOVER A RAY WHICH COULD CHANGE ANY OBJECT'S ATOMIC STRUCTURE, WHEN ONE DAY..."
IT WORKS! I'VE TRANSFORMED A FLOWER INTO A JEWEL BY ALTERING ITS MOLECULAR STRUCTURE!

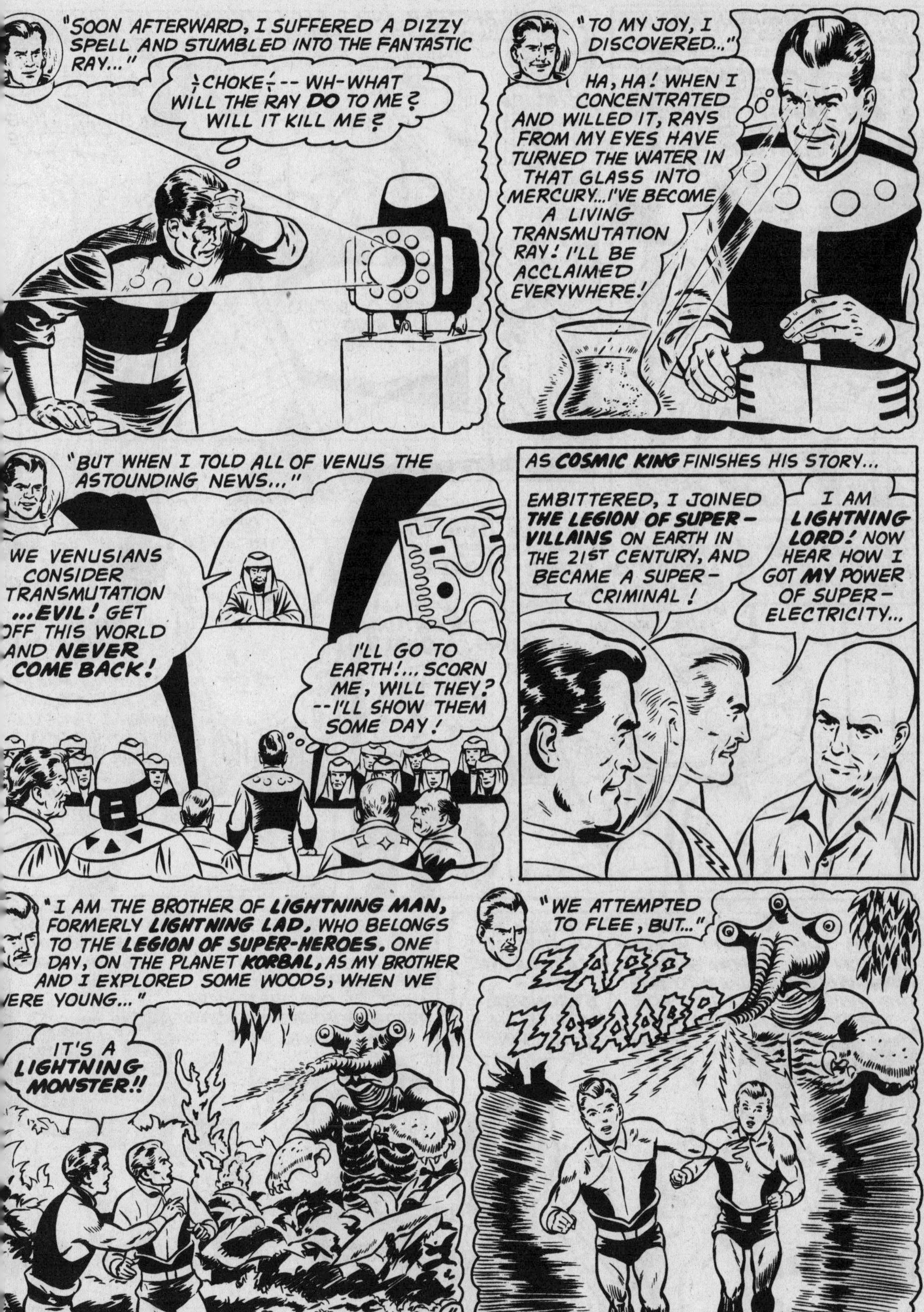
"SOON AFTERWARD, I SUFFERED A DIZZY SPELL AND STUMBLED INTO THE FANTASTIC RAY..."
÷CHOKE÷ -- WH-WHAT WILL THE RAY DO TO ME? WILL IT KILL ME?
"TO MY JOY, I DISCOVERED..."
HA, HA! WHEN I CONCENTRATED AND WILLED IT, RAYS FROM MY EYES HAVE TURNED THE WATER IN THAT GLASS INTO MERCURY...I'VE BECOME A LIVING TRANSMUTATION RAY! I'LL BE ACCLAIMED EVERYWHERE!
"BUT WHEN I TOLD ALL OF VENUS THE ASTOUNDING NEWS..."
WE VENUSIANS CONSIDER TRANSMUTATION ...EVIL! GET OFF THIS WORLD AND NEVER COME BACK!
I'LL GO TO EARTH!... SCORN ME, WILL THEY? --I'LL SHOW THEM SOME DAY!
AS COSMIC KING FINISHES HIS STORY...
EMBITTERED, I JOINED THE LEGION OF SUPER-VILLAINS ON EARTH IN THE 21ST CENTURY, AND BECAME A SUPER-CRIMINAL!
I AM LIGHTNING LORD! NOW HEAR HOW I GOT MY POWER OF SUPER-ELECTRICITY...
"I AM THE BROTHER OF LIGHTNING MAN, FORMERLY LIGHTNING LAD, WHO BELONGS TO THE LEGION OF SUPER-HEROES. ONE DAY, ON THE PLANET KORBAL, AS MY BROTHER AND I EXPLORED SOME WOODS, WHEN WE WERE YOUNG..."
IT'S A LIGHTNING MONSTER!!
4
"WE ATTEMPTED TO FLEE, BUT..."
ZAPP
ZAAAPP

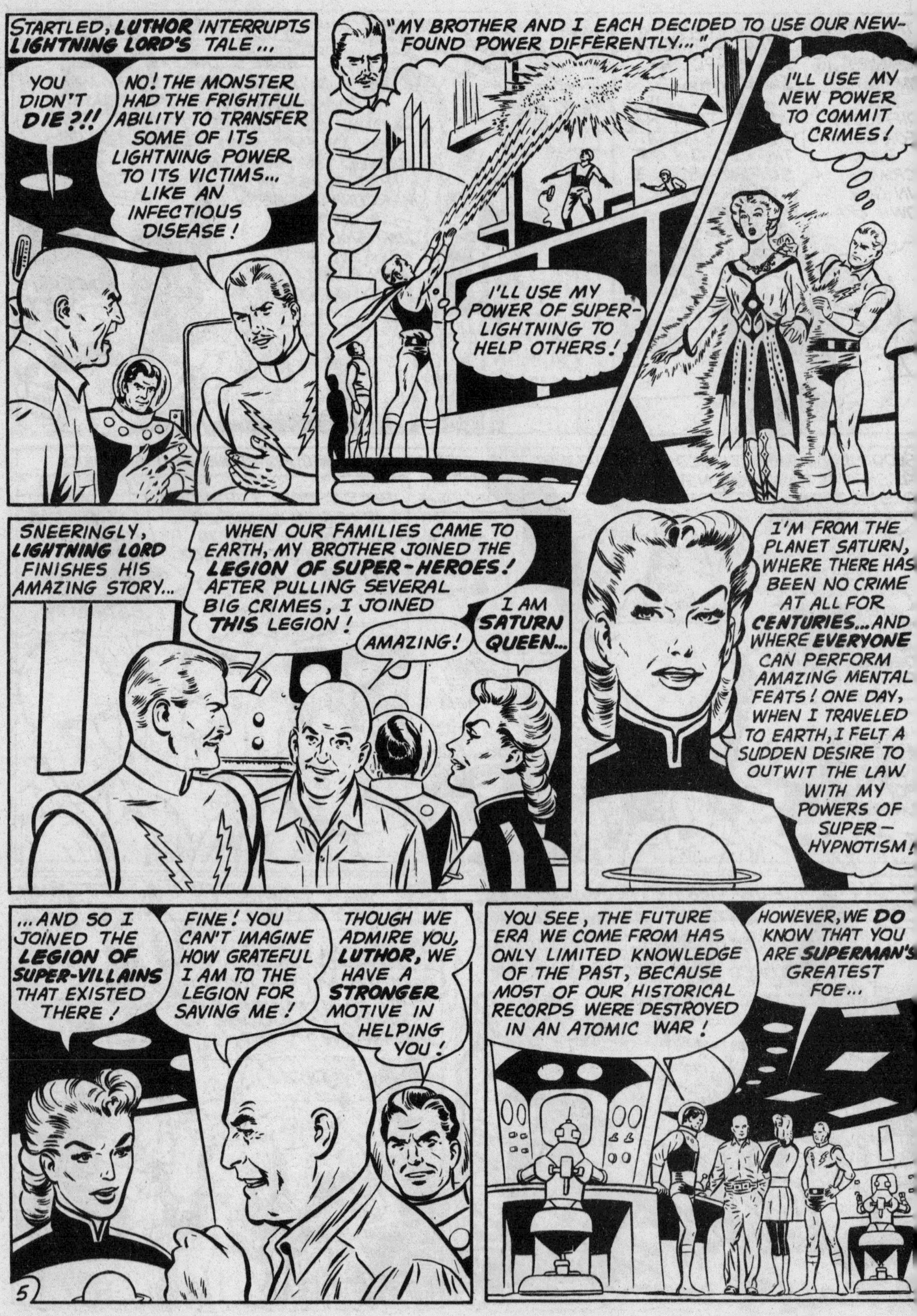
STARTLED, LUTHOR INTERRUPTS LIGHTNING LORD'S TALE...
YOU DIDN'T DIE?!!
NO! THE MONSTER HAD THE FRIGHTFUL ABILITY TO TRANSFER SOME OF ITS LIGHTNING POWER TO ITS VICTIMS... LIKE AN INFECTIOUS DISEASE!
"MY BROTHER AND I EACH DECIDED TO USE OUR NEW-FOUND POWER DIFFERENTLY..."
I'LL USE MY POWER OF SUPER-LIGHTNING TO HELP OTHERS!
I'LL USE MY NEW POWER TO COMMIT CRIMES!
SNEERINGLY, LIGHTNING LORD FINISHES HIS AMAZING STORY...
WHEN OUR FAMILIES CAME TO EARTH, MY BROTHER JOINED THE LEGION OF SUPER-HEROES! AFTER PULLING SEVERAL BIG CRIMES, I JOINED THIS LEGION!
AMAZING!
I AM SATURN QUEEN...
I'M FROM THE PLANET SATURN, WHERE THERE HAS BEEN NO CRIME AT ALL FOR CENTURIES...AND WHERE EVERYONE CAN PERFORM AMAZING MENTAL FEATS! ONE DAY, WHEN I TRAVELED TO EARTH, I FELT A SUDDEN DESIRE TO OUTWIT THE LAW WITH MY POWERS OF SUPER-HYPNOTISM!
...AND SO I JOINED THE LEGION OF SUPER-VILLAINS THAT EXISTED THERE!
FINE! YOU CAN'T IMAGINE HOW GRATEFUL I AM TO THE LEGION FOR SAVING ME!
THOUGH WE ADMIRE YOU, LUTHOR, WE HAVE A STRONGER MOTIVE IN HELPING YOU!
5
YOU SEE, THE FUTURE ERA WE COME FROM HAS ONLY LIMITED KNOWLEDGE OF THE PAST, BECAUSE MOST OF OUR HISTORICAL RECORDS WERE DESTROYED IN AN ATOMIC WAR!
HOWEVER, WE DO KNOW THAT YOU ARE SUPERMAN'S GREATEST FOE...

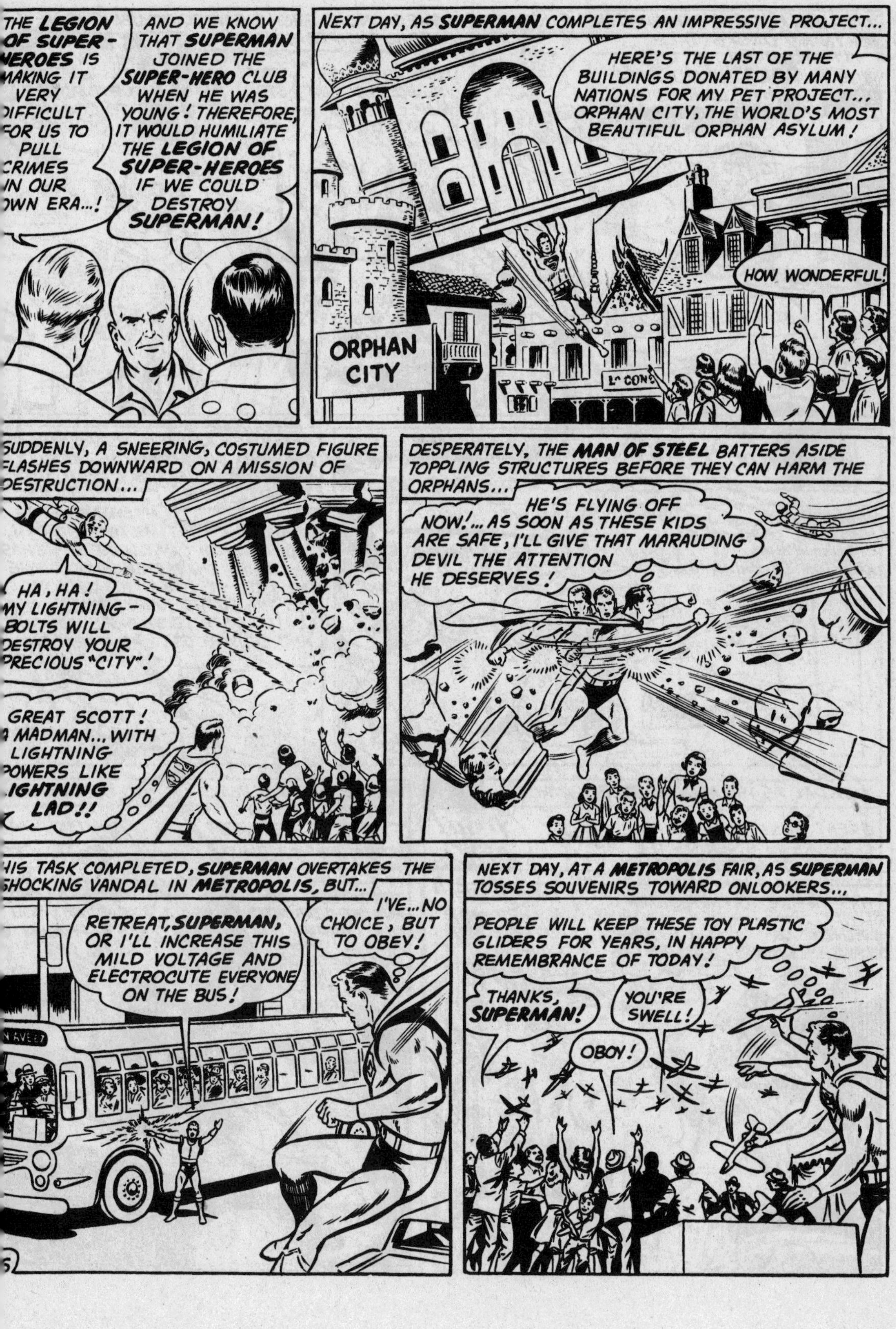
THE LEGION OF SUPER-HEROES IS MAKING IT VERY DIFFICULT FOR US TO PULL CRIMES IN OUR OWN ERA...!
AND WE KNOW THAT SUPERMAN JOINED THE SUPER-HERO CLUB WHEN HE WAS YOUNG! THEREFORE, IT WOULD HUMILIATE THE LEGION OF SUPER-HEROES IF WE COULD DESTROY SUPERMAN!
NEXT DAY, AS SUPERMAN COMPLETES AN IMPRESSIVE PROJECT...
HERE'S THE LAST OF THE BUILDINGS DONATED BY MANY NATIONS FOR MY PET PROJECT... ORPHAN CITY, THE WORLD'S MOST BEAUTIFUL ORPHAN ASYLUM!
HOW WONDERFUL!
ORPHAN CITY
SUDDENLY, A SNEERING, COSTUMED FIGURE FLASHES DOWNWARD ON A MISSION OF DESTRUCTION...
HA, HA! MY LIGHTNING-BOLTS WILL DESTROY YOUR PRECIOUS "CITY"!
GREAT SCOTT! A MADMAN... WITH LIGHTNING POWERS LIKE LIGHTNING LAD!!
DESPERATELY, THE MAN OF STEEL BATTERS ASIDE TOPPLING STRUCTURES BEFORE THEY CAN HARM THE ORPHANS...
HE'S FLYING OFF NOW!... AS SOON AS THESE KIDS ARE SAFE, I'LL GIVE THAT MARAUDING DEVIL THE ATTENTION HE DESERVES!
HIS TASK COMPLETED, SUPERMAN OVERTAKES THE SHOCKING VANDAL IN METROPOLIS, BUT...
RETREAT, SUPERMAN, OR I'LL INCREASE THIS MILD VOLTAGE AND ELECTROCUTE EVERYONE ON THE BUS!
I'VE... NO CHOICE, BUT TO OBEY!
NEXT DAY, AT A METROPOLIS FAIR, AS SUPERMAN TOSSES SOUVENIRS TOWARD ONLOOKERS...
PEOPLE WILL KEEP THESE TOY PLASTIC GLIDERS FOR YEARS, IN HAPPY REMEMBRANCE OF TODAY!
THANKS, SUPERMAN!
YOU'RE SWELL!
OBOY!

BUT SUDDENLY, A MACABRE INTERRUPTION, AS...

PLASTIC... TURN INTO *GOLD!!*

??!

GOLD!

GOLD??!

WOW!

IMMEDIATELY, THERE IS A WILD, GREEDY SCRAMBLE FOR THE UNEXPECTED RICHES...

PEOPLE WILL BE INJURED, IN THAT MAD, CLAWING CROWD!

STOP! STOP!

TRYING TO INTERFERE EH? I'LL FIX THAT! *SUPERMAN* STATUE, TURN INTO...

...KRYPTONITE!

SUPERMAN NEEDS HELP! COME ON!

OW-WWWW! *KRYPTONITE* RADIATIONS ...P-PAINING... W-WEAKENING ME! QUICK! SOMEONE... PLEASE PULL ME... TO SAFETY...

AFTER THE AMAZING FIGURE STREAKS OFF, AND *SUPERMAN* IS CARRIED A SAFE DISTANCE AWAY FROM THE *KRYPTONITE*...

MY STRENGTH'S RETURNING!--BUT MY TELE-SCOPIC VISION CAN'T LOCATE THE WEIRD CHARACTER WHO DID THIS!--I'LL ARRANGE FOR THE STATUE TO BE COATED WITH LEAD AND SUNK AT SEA!

NEXT DAY, AS THE *MAN OF STEEL* PATROLS...

GREAT GUNS! A MONSTROUS CREATURE IS STALKING THE STREETS OF *METROPOLIS!* IT'S SNATCHED UP LOIS LANE, WHO WAS TRYING TO PHOTOGRAPH IT!

YI-III! HELP, SUPERMAN ...HELP!!!

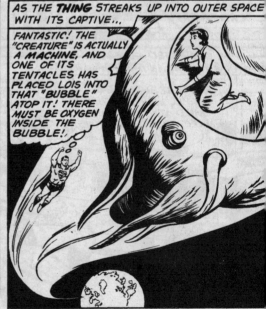

AS THE *THING* STREAKS UP INTO OUTER SPACE WITH ITS CAPTIVE...

FANTASTIC! THE "CREATURE" IS ACTUALLY A MACHINE, AND ONE OF ITS TENTACLES HAS PLACED LOIS INTO THAT "BUBBLE" ATOP IT! THERE MUST BE OXYGEN INSIDE THE BUBBLE!

7

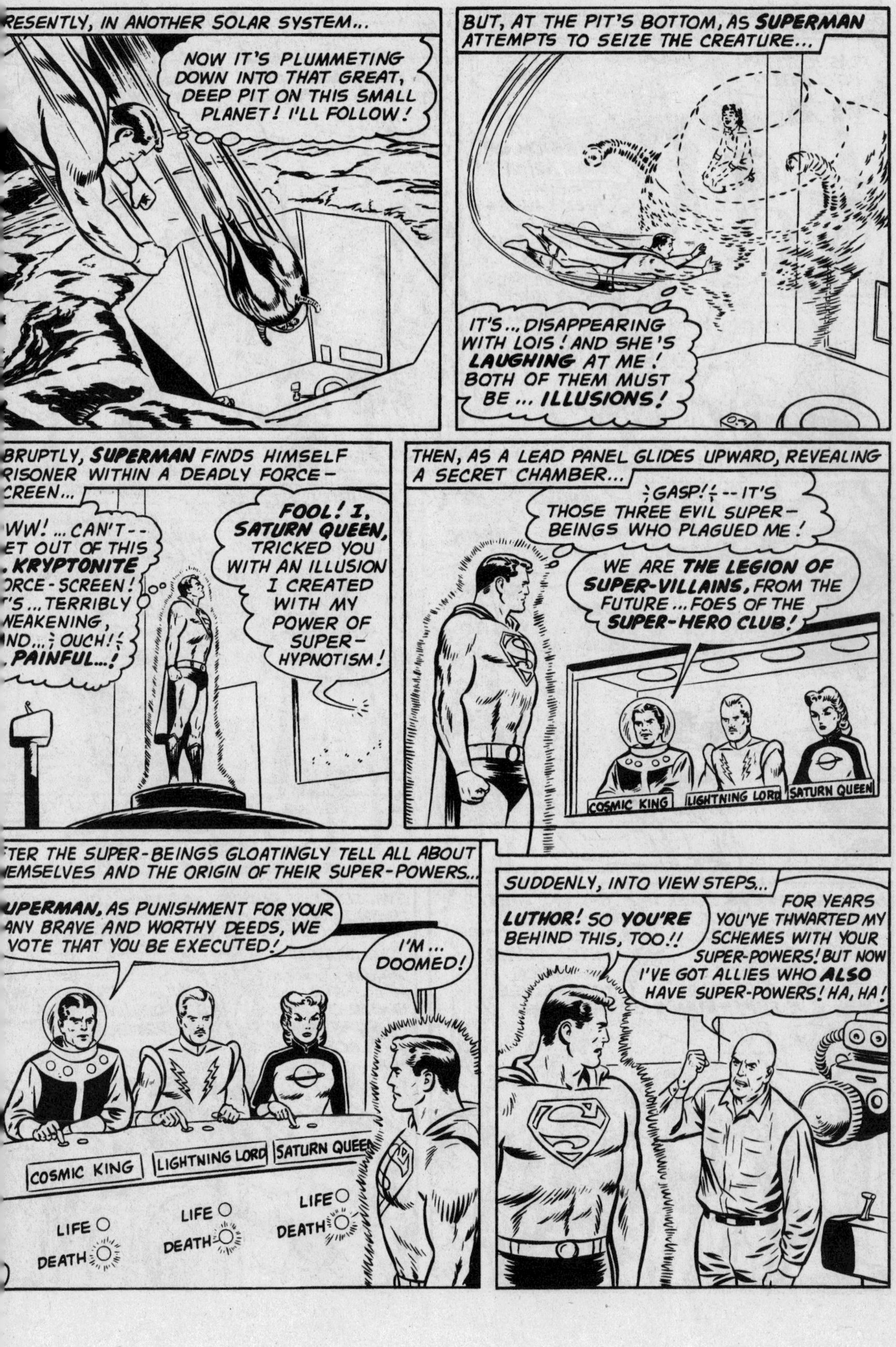
RESENTLY, IN ANOTHER SOLAR SYSTEM...
NOW IT'S PLUMMETING DOWN INTO THAT GREAT, DEEP PIT ON THIS SMALL PLANET! I'LL FOLLOW!
BUT, AT THE PIT'S BOTTOM, AS SUPERMAN ATTEMPTS TO SEIZE THE CREATURE...
IT'S... DISAPPEARING WITH LOIS! AND SHE'S LAUGHING AT ME! BOTH OF THEM MUST BE ... ILLUSIONS!
BRUPTLY, SUPERMAN FINDS HIMSELF RISONER WITHIN A DEADLY FORCE-CREEN...
WW! ... CAN'T-- ET OUT OF THIS KRYPTONITE ORCE-SCREEN! T'S ... TERRIBLY WEAKENING, ND... ¦OUCH!¦ PAINFUL...!
FOOL! I, SATURN QUEEN, TRICKED YOU WITH AN ILLUSION I CREATED WITH MY POWER OF SUPER-HYPNOTISM!
THEN, AS A LEAD PANEL GLIDES UPWARD, REVEALING A SECRET CHAMBER...
¦GASP!¦ -- IT'S THOSE THREE EVIL SUPER-BEINGS WHO PLAGUED ME!
WE ARE THE LEGION OF SUPER-VILLAINS, FROM THE FUTURE ... FOES OF THE SUPER-HERO CLUB!
COSMIC KING
LIGHTNING LORD
SATURN QUEEN
FTER THE SUPER-BEINGS GLOATINGLY TELL ALL ABOUT HEMSELVES AND THE ORIGIN OF THEIR SUPER-POWERS...
UPERMAN, AS PUNISHMENT FOR YOUR ANY BRAVE AND WORTHY DEEDS, WE VOTE THAT YOU BE EXECUTED!
I'M ... DOOMED!
COSMIC KING
LIGHTNING LORD
SATURN QUEE
LIFE
DEATH
LIFE
DEATH
LIFE
DEATH
SUDDENLY, INTO VIEW STEPS...
LUTHOR! SO YOU'RE BEHIND THIS, TOO!!
FOR YEARS YOU'VE THWARTED MY SCHEMES WITH YOUR SUPER-POWERS! BUT NOW I'VE GOT ALLIES WHO ALSO HAVE SUPER-POWERS! HA, HA!

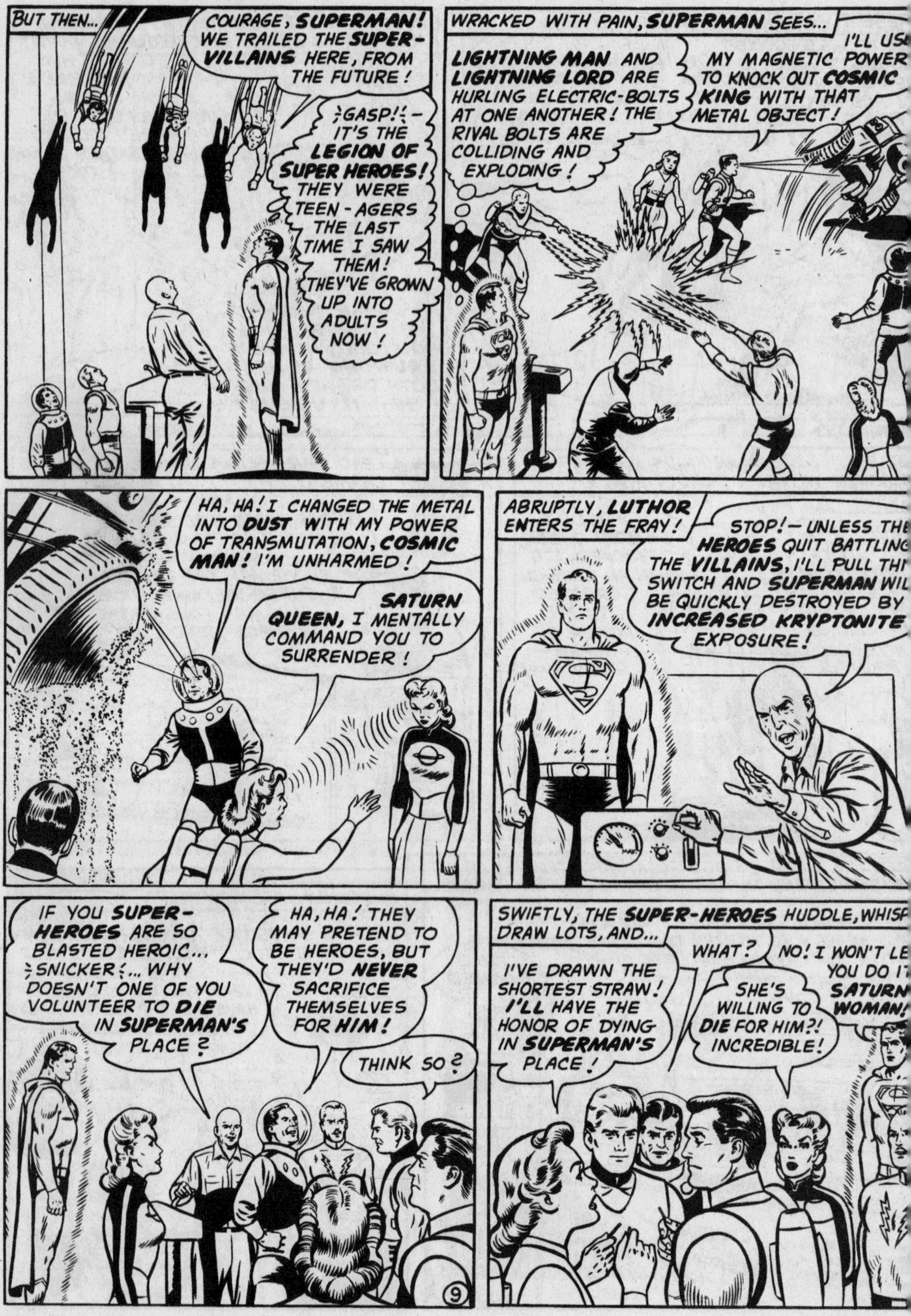
BUT THEN...
COURAGE, SUPERMAN! WE TRAILED THE SUPER-VILLAINS HERE, FROM THE FUTURE!
≷GASP!≶ -- IT'S THE LEGION OF SUPER HEROES! THEY WERE TEEN-AGERS THE LAST TIME I SAW THEM! THEY'VE GROWN UP INTO ADULTS NOW!
WRACKED WITH PAIN, SUPERMAN SEES...
LIGHTNING MAN AND LIGHTNING LORD ARE HURLING ELECTRIC-BOLTS AT ONE ANOTHER! THE RIVAL BOLTS ARE COLLIDING AND EXPLODING!
I'LL US MY MAGNETIC POWER TO KNOCK OUT COSMIC KING WITH THAT METAL OBJECT!
HA, HA! I CHANGED THE METAL INTO DUST WITH MY POWER OF TRANSMUTATION, COSMIC MAN! I'M UNHARMED!
SATURN QUEEN, I MENTALLY COMMAND YOU TO SURRENDER!
ABRUPTLY, LUTHOR ENTERS THE FRAY!
STOP! -- UNLESS THE HEROES QUIT BATTLING THE VILLAINS, I'LL PULL TH SWITCH AND SUPERMAN WIL BE QUICKLY DESTROYED BY INCREASED KRYPTONITE EXPOSURE!
IF YOU SUPER-HEROES ARE SO BLASTED HEROIC... ≷SNICKER≶... WHY DOESN'T ONE OF YOU VOLUNTEER TO DIE IN SUPERMAN'S PLACE?
HA, HA! THEY MAY PRETEND TO BE HEROES, BUT THEY'D NEVER SACRIFICE THEMSELVES FOR HIM!
THINK SO?
9
SWIFTLY, THE SUPER-HEROES HUDDLE, WHISP DRAW LOTS, AND...
I'VE DRAWN THE SHORTEST STRAW! I'LL HAVE THE HONOR OF DYING IN SUPERMAN'S PLACE!
WHAT?
SHE'S WILLING TO DIE FOR HIM?! INCREDIBLE!
NO! I WON'T LE YOU DO IT SATURN WOMAN!

...RRY, *SUPERMAN!* ...UT IF SHE'S FOOLISH ...NOUGH TO WANT TO ...E FOR YOU, SO BE ...! THIS DEATH ...RAY WILL ...ESTROY HER!

WAIT, *LUTHOR!* I ASK ONE FAVOR! RELEASE ME FOR A FEW MINUTES SO I CAN PERFORM ONE LAST SUPER-FEAT IN *SATURN WOMAN'S* HONOR!

RELEASE YOU? ARE YOU TRYING TO TRICK US?

I PROMISE NOT TO SAVE HER!

I KNOW HE'LL KEEP HIS WORD! I'LL FREE HIM FROM THE *KRYPTONITE* POWER-SCREEN! *SUPERMAN'S* PITIFUL SUPER-DEED WILL AMUSE US, BEFORE *SATURN WOMAN* DIES!

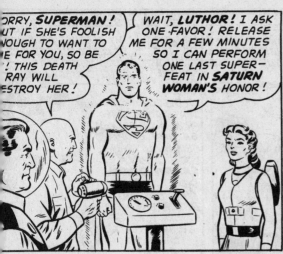

...N INSTANT LATER...

...O LONG, FOR ...OW, *SUPERMAN!* ...PLEASE DON'T ...REAK OUR ...HEARTS! ...HA, HA!

DESTINATION, SATURN!

REACHING THE PLANET SATURN, SUPERMAN CONSTRUCTS A GIANT SHOVEL, THEN...

THERE! I'VE SCOOPED UP MANY OF THE METEOR-FRAGMENTS THAT FORM SATURN'S RINGS! NOW TO FLY THE FRAGMENTS BACK TO THAT SMALL PLANETOID!

...MINUTES LATER...

I'VE MADE A RING ABOUT THIS PLANETOID WITH THE METEOR FRAGMENTS TAKEN FROM SATURN'S RINGS! UNLESS I'M VERY WRONG, *SATURN WOMAN* WON'T DIE NOW!

CAN YOU GUESS WHY?

SECONDS LATER, AS SUPERMAN RETURNS INTO THE PIT...

SEE, *SATURN WOMAN?* UP THERE ...A RING!

THANKS, *SUPERMAN!* IT REMINDS ME OF MY HOME WORLD, SATURN!

SENTIMENTAL DRIVEL!—YOU CHOSE TO DIE, *SATURN WOMAN,* SO I'LL OBLIGE YOU!

10

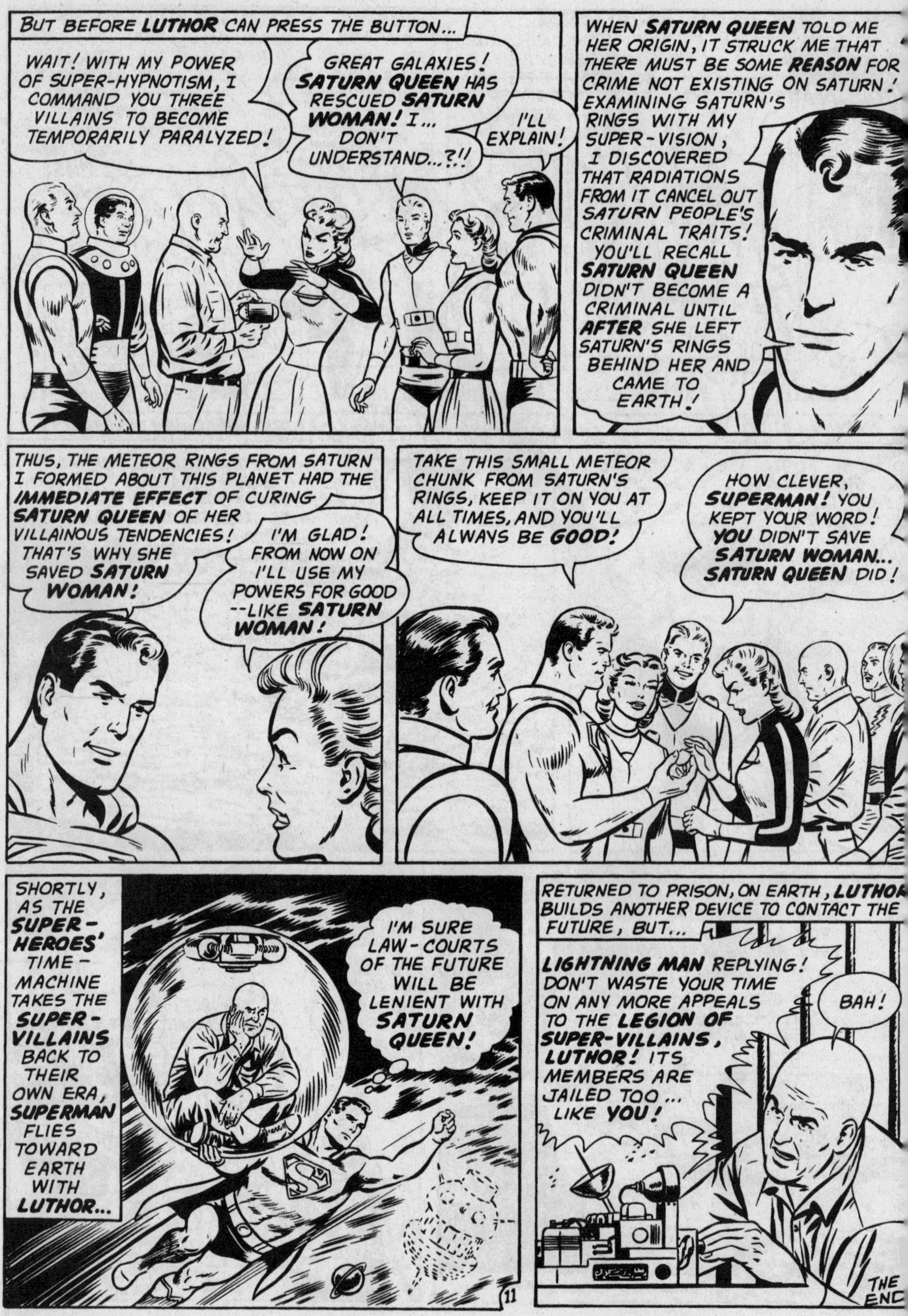
BUT BEFORE LUTHOR CAN PRESS THE BUTTON...
WAIT! WITH MY POWER OF SUPER-HYPNOTISM, I COMMAND YOU THREE VILLAINS TO BECOME TEMPORARILY PARALYZED!
GREAT GALAXIES! SATURN QUEEN HAS RESCUED SATURN WOMAN! I... DON'T UNDERSTAND...?!!
I'LL EXPLAIN!
WHEN SATURN QUEEN TOLD ME HER ORIGIN, IT STRUCK ME THAT THERE MUST BE SOME REASON FOR CRIME NOT EXISTING ON SATURN! EXAMINING SATURN'S RINGS WITH MY SUPER-VISION, I DISCOVERED THAT RADIATIONS FROM IT CANCEL OUT SATURN PEOPLE'S CRIMINAL TRAITS! YOU'LL RECALL SATURN QUEEN DIDN'T BECOME A CRIMINAL UNTIL AFTER SHE LEFT SATURN'S RINGS BEHIND HER AND CAME TO EARTH!
THUS, THE METEOR RINGS FROM SATURN I FORMED ABOUT THIS PLANET HAD THE IMMEDIATE EFFECT OF CURING SATURN QUEEN OF HER VILLAINOUS TENDENCIES! THAT'S WHY SHE SAVED SATURN WOMAN!
I'M GLAD! FROM NOW ON I'LL USE MY POWERS FOR GOOD --LIKE SATURN WOMAN!
TAKE THIS SMALL METEOR CHUNK FROM SATURN'S RINGS, KEEP IT ON YOU AT ALL TIMES, AND YOU'LL ALWAYS BE GOOD!
HOW CLEVER, SUPERMAN! YOU KEPT YOUR WORD! YOU DIDN'T SAVE SATURN WOMAN... SATURN QUEEN DID!
SHORTLY, AS THE SUPER-HEROES' TIME-MACHINE TAKES THE SUPER-VILLAINS BACK TO THEIR OWN ERA, SUPERMAN FLIES TOWARD EARTH WITH LUTHOR...
I'M SURE LAW-COURTS OF THE FUTURE WILL BE LENIENT WITH SATURN QUEEN!
11
RETURNED TO PRISON, ON EARTH, LUTHOR BUILDS ANOTHER DEVICE TO CONTACT THE FUTURE, BUT...
LIGHTNING MAN REPLYING! DON'T WASTE YOUR TIME ON ANY MORE APPEALS TO THE LEGION OF SUPER-VILLAINS, LUTHOR! ITS MEMBERS ARE JAILED TOO... LIKE YOU!
BAH!
THE END

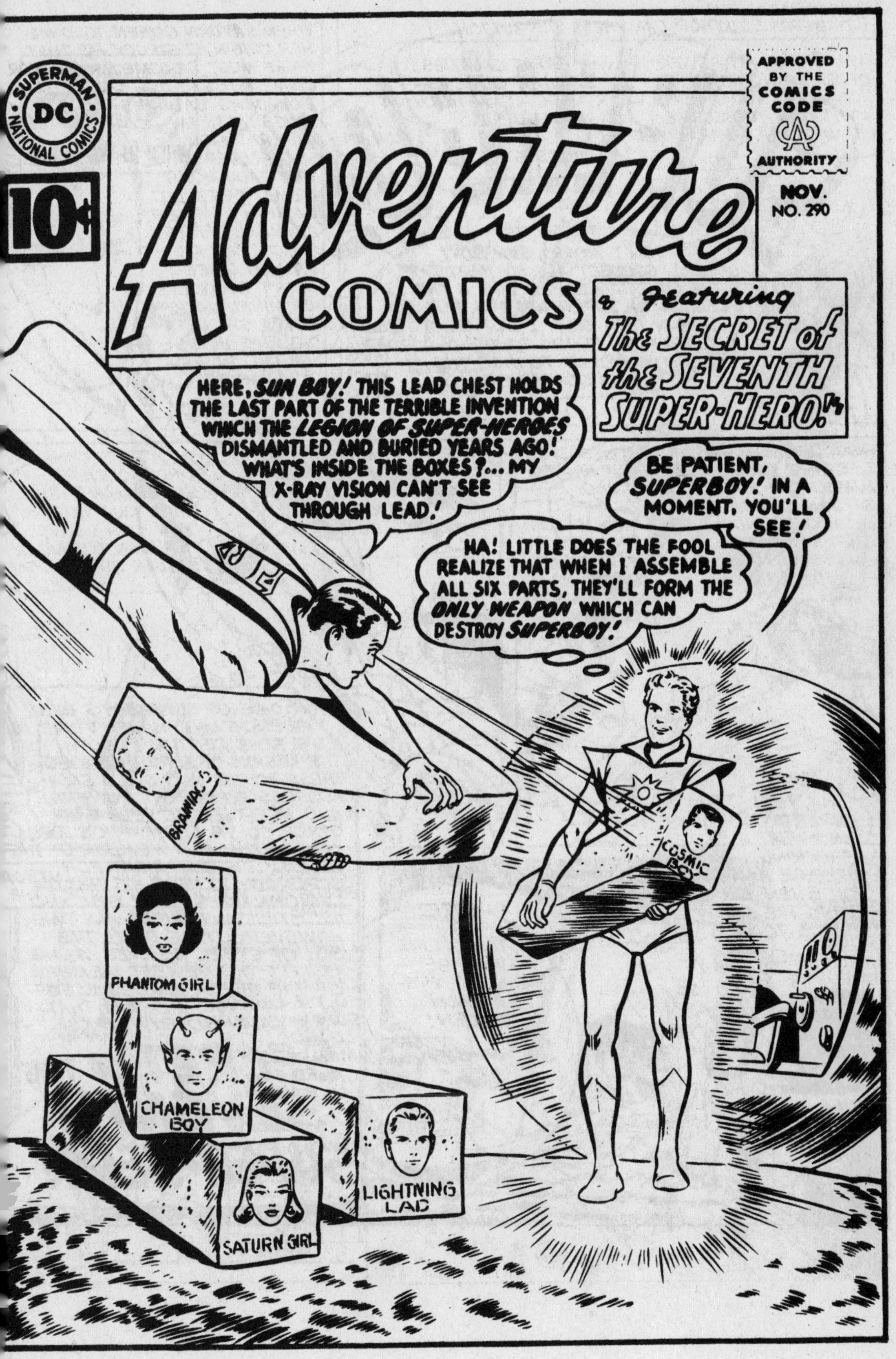
SUPERMAN DC NATIONAL COMICS
10¢
APPROVED BY THE COMICS CODE AUTHORITY
NOV. NO. 290
Adventure COMICS
Featuring The SECRET of the SEVENTH SUPER-HERO!
HERE, SUN BOY! THIS LEAD CHEST HOLDS THE LAST PART OF THE TERRIBLE INVENTION WHICH THE LEGION OF SUPER-HEROES DISMANTLED AND BURIED YEARS AGO! WHAT'S INSIDE THE BOXES?... MY X-RAY VISION CAN'T SEE THROUGH LEAD!
BE PATIENT, SUPERBOY! IN A MOMENT, YOU'LL SEE!
HA! LITTLE DOES THE FOOL REALIZE THAT WHEN I ASSEMBLE ALL SIX PARTS, THEY'LL FORM THE ONLY WEAPON WHICH CAN DESTROY SUPERBOY!
BRAINIAC 5
COSMIC BOY
PHANTOM GIRL
CHAMELEON BOY
LIGHTNING LAD
SATURN GIRL

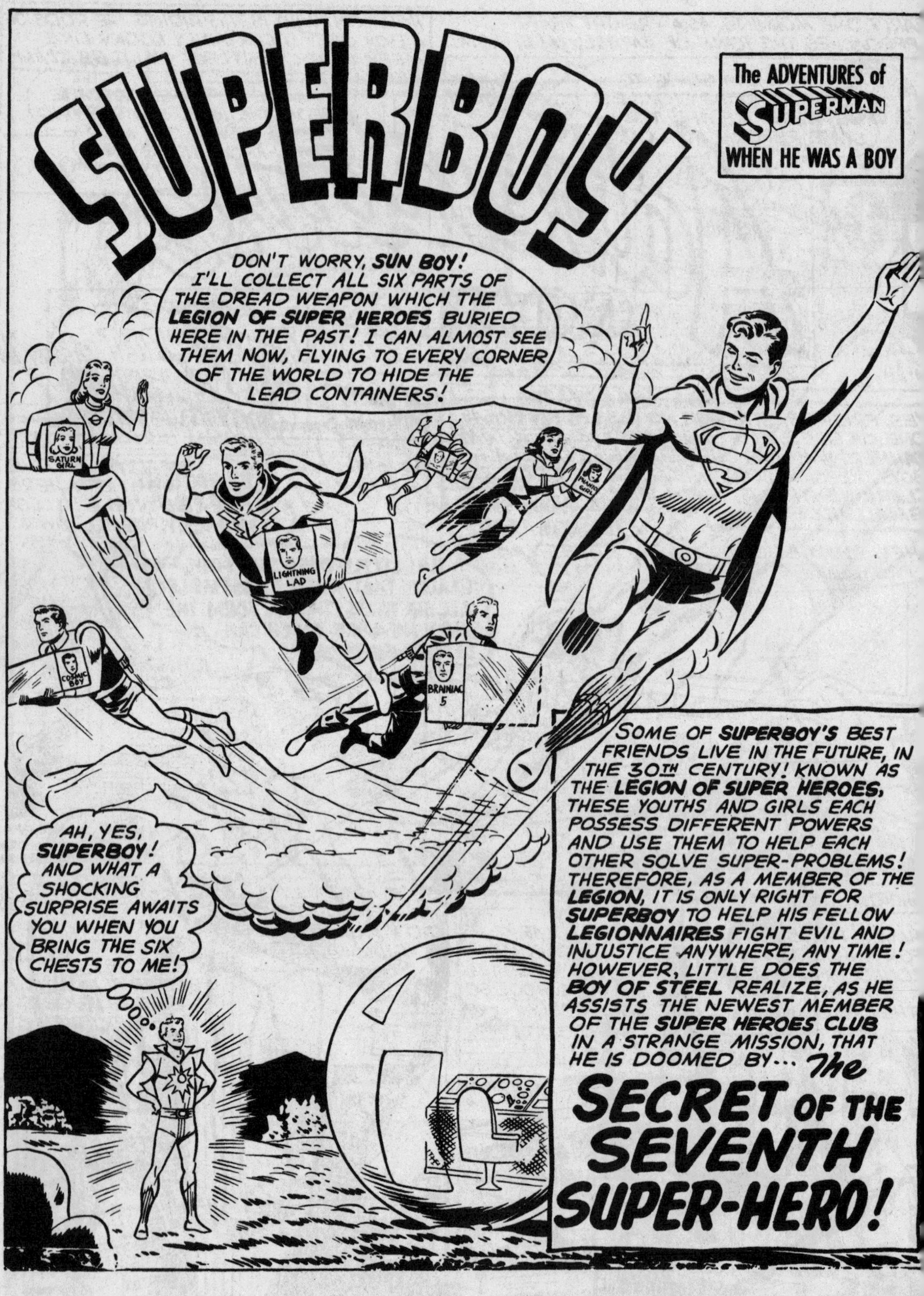
SUPERBOY
The ADVENTURES of SUPERMAN WHEN HE WAS A BOY
DON'T WORRY, SUN BOY! I'LL COLLECT ALL SIX PARTS OF THE DREAD WEAPON WHICH THE LEGION OF SUPER HEROES BURIED HERE IN THE PAST! I CAN ALMOST SEE THEM NOW, FLYING TO EVERY CORNER OF THE WORLD TO HIDE THE LEAD CONTAINERS!
SATURN GIRL
LIGHTNING LAD
COSMIC BOY
BRAINIAC 5
AH, YES, SUPERBOY! AND WHAT A SHOCKING SURPRISE AWAITS YOU WHEN YOU BRING THE SIX CHESTS TO ME!
SOME OF SUPERBOY'S BEST FRIENDS LIVE IN THE FUTURE, IN THE 30TH CENTURY! KNOWN AS THE LEGION OF SUPER HEROES, THESE YOUTHS AND GIRLS EACH POSSESS DIFFERENT POWERS AND USE THEM TO HELP EACH OTHER SOLVE SUPER-PROBLEMS! THEREFORE, AS A MEMBER OF THE LEGION, IT IS ONLY RIGHT FOR SUPERBOY TO HELP HIS FELLOW LEGIONNAIRES FIGHT EVIL AND INJUSTICE ANYWHERE, ANY TIME! HOWEVER, LITTLE DOES THE BOY OF STEEL REALIZE, AS HE ASSISTS THE NEWEST MEMBER OF THE SUPER HEROES CLUB IN A STRANGE MISSION, THAT HE IS DOOMED BY... The
SECRET OF THE SEVENTH SUPER-HERO!

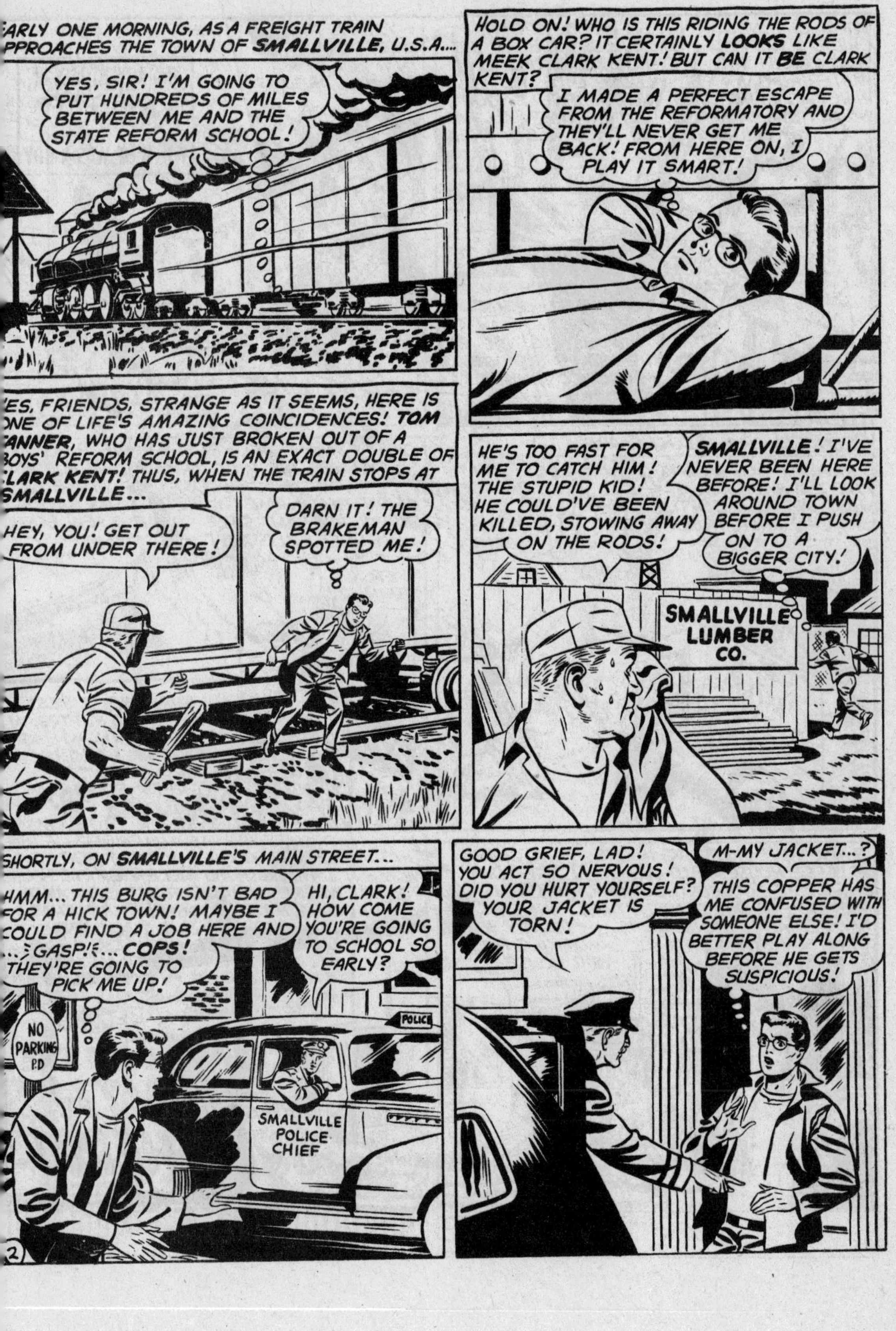
ARLY ONE MORNING, AS A FREIGHT TRAIN PPROACHES THE TOWN OF SMALLVILLE, U.S.A....
YES, SIR! I'M GOING TO PUT HUNDREDS OF MILES BETWEEN ME AND THE STATE REFORM SCHOOL!
HOLD ON! WHO IS THIS RIDING THE RODS OF A BOX CAR? IT CERTAINLY LOOKS LIKE MEEK CLARK KENT! BUT CAN IT BE CLARK KENT?
I MADE A PERFECT ESCAPE FROM THE REFORMATORY AND THEY'LL NEVER GET ME BACK! FROM HERE ON, I PLAY IT SMART!
ES, FRIENDS, STRANGE AS IT SEEMS, HERE IS NE OF LIFE'S AMAZING COINCIDENCES! TOM ANNER, WHO HAS JUST BROKEN OUT OF A OYS' REFORM SCHOOL, IS AN EXACT DOUBLE OF LARK KENT! THUS, WHEN THE TRAIN STOPS AT MALLVILLE...
HEY, YOU! GET OUT FROM UNDER THERE!
DARN IT! THE BRAKEMAN SPOTTED ME!
HE'S TOO FAST FOR ME TO CATCH HIM! THE STUPID KID! HE COULD'VE BEEN KILLED, STOWING AWAY ON THE RODS!
SMALLVILLE! I'VE NEVER BEEN HERE BEFORE! I'LL LOOK AROUND TOWN BEFORE I PUSH ON TO A BIGGER CITY!
SMALLVILLE LUMBER CO.
SHORTLY, ON SMALLVILLE'S MAIN STREET...
HMM... THIS BURG ISN'T BAD FOR A HICK TOWN! MAYBE I COULD FIND A JOB HERE AND ...GASP!...COPS! THEY'RE GOING TO PICK ME UP!
HI, CLARK! HOW COME YOU'RE GOING TO SCHOOL SO EARLY?
NO PARKING P.D
POLICE
SMALLVILLE POLICE CHIEF
2
GOOD GRIEF, LAD! YOU ACT SO NERVOUS! DID YOU HURT YOURSELF? YOUR JACKET IS TORN!
M-MY JACKET...?
THIS COPPER HAS ME CONFUSED WITH SOMEONE ELSE! I'D BETTER PLAY ALONG BEFORE HE GETS SUSPICIOUS!

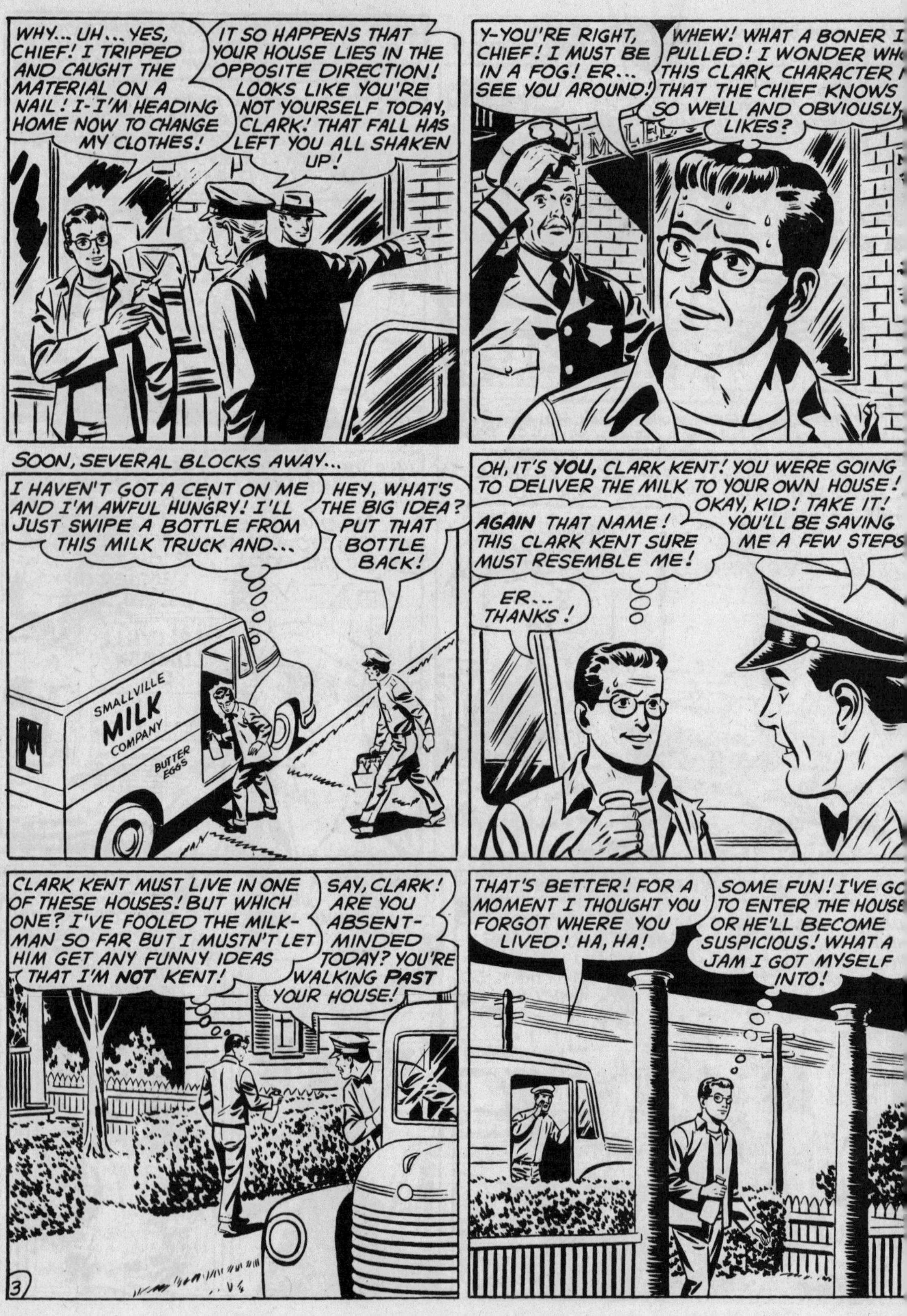
WHY... UH... YES, CHIEF! I TRIPPED AND CAUGHT THE MATERIAL ON A NAIL! I-I'M HEADING HOME NOW TO CHANGE MY CLOTHES!
IT SO HAPPENS THAT YOUR HOUSE LIES IN THE OPPOSITE DIRECTION! LOOKS LIKE YOU'RE NOT YOURSELF TODAY, CLARK! THAT FALL HAS LEFT YOU ALL SHAKEN UP!
Y-YOU'RE RIGHT, CHIEF! I MUST BE IN A FOG! ER... SEE YOU AROUND!
WHEW! WHAT A BONER I PULLED! I WONDER WHO THIS CLARK CHARACTER IS THAT THE CHIEF KNOWS SO WELL AND OBVIOUSLY LIKES?
SOON, SEVERAL BLOCKS AWAY...
I HAVEN'T GOT A CENT ON ME AND I'M AWFUL HUNGRY! I'LL JUST SWIPE A BOTTLE FROM THIS MILK TRUCK AND...
HEY, WHAT'S THE BIG IDEA? PUT THAT BOTTLE BACK!
SMALLVILLE MILK COMPANY
BUTTER EGGS
OH, IT'S YOU, CLARK KENT! YOU WERE GOING TO DELIVER THE MILK TO YOUR OWN HOUSE! OKAY, KID! TAKE IT! YOU'LL BE SAVING ME A FEW STEPS
AGAIN THAT NAME! THIS CLARK KENT SURE MUST RESEMBLE ME!
ER... THANKS!
CLARK KENT MUST LIVE IN ONE OF THESE HOUSES! BUT WHICH ONE? I'VE FOOLED THE MILK-MAN SO FAR BUT I MUSTN'T LET HIM GET ANY FUNNY IDEAS THAT I'M NOT KENT!
SAY, CLARK! ARE YOU ABSENT-MINDED TODAY? YOU'RE WALKING PAST YOUR HOUSE!
3
THAT'S BETTER! FOR A MOMENT I THOUGHT YOU FORGOT WHERE YOU LIVED! HA, HA!
SOME FUN! I'VE GOT TO ENTER THE HOUSE OR HE'LL BECOME SUSPICIOUS! WHAT A JAM I GOT MYSELF INTO!

...THAT MOMENT, IN CLARK KENT'S SECRET WORKSHOP...

SINCE I GOT UP EARLY THIS MORNING AND MOM HASN'T CALLED ME FOR BREAKFAST YET, I THINK I'LL PUT IN SOME WORK ON MY SCIENCE PROJECT ON MAGNETS!

I'LL LISTEN TO THE MORNING NEWS WHILE I PUTTER AROUND...

HERE'S A BULLETIN THAT JUST CAME IN! A STRANGE OBJECT HAS LANDED WITH A BLINDING ELECTRICAL FLASH IN A FIELD JUST WEST OF MAPLE GROVE!

AS CLARK'S SUPER-VISION INSTANTLY CHECKS THE SPOT...

THE STATE POLICE ARE RACING TO THE AREA NOW!

GOLLY! IT LOOKS LIKE THE TYPE OF MACHINE USED BY THE LEGION OF SUPER HEROES! HMM... I SEE WHERE I DON'T GO TO SCHOOL THIS MORNING!

NEXT MOMENT, AS CLARK OPENS THE SECRET CELLAR PANEL CONTAINING HIS ROBOTS...

AFTER I ACTIVATE THIS CLARK KENT ROBOT AND SEND HIM TO SCHOOL IN MY PLACE, I'LL SWITCH TO SUPERBOY AND... ⊰GASP!⊱...GOSH, THE ROBOT WON'T WORK! SOMETHING MUST'VE GONE WRONG WITH ITS MECHANISM!

SAME TROUBLE WITH ALL OF THEM! THAT BLINDING ELECTRICAL FLASH WHEN THE TIME BUBBLE LANDED MUST'VE SHORT-CIRCUITED THEIR SENSITIVE CONTROL SYSTEM! AFTER ALL, THESE ROBOTS AREN'T FOOLPROOF! THEY'RE STILL PRETTY EXPERIMENTAL! I'D BETTER MAKE A SWIFT CHANGE TO SUPERBOY!

AN INSTANT AFTER...

CAN'T TAKE TIME TO TELL MOM WHERE I'M GOING! I WANT TO BE ON THE SCENE BEFORE THE STATE TROOPERS ARRIVE!

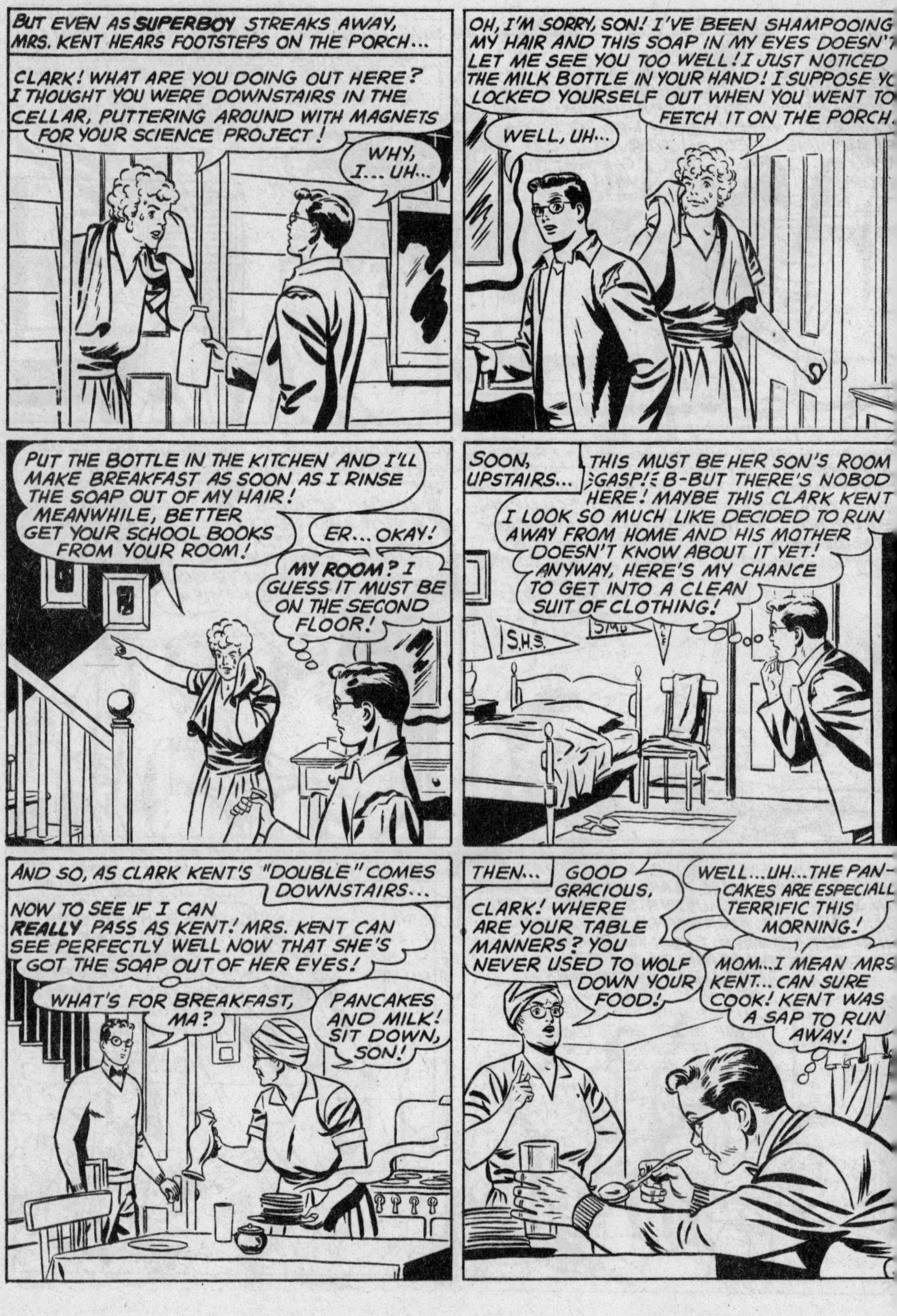
BUT EVEN AS SUPERBOY STREAKS AWAY, MRS. KENT HEARS FOOTSTEPS ON THE PORCH...
CLARK! WHAT ARE YOU DOING OUT HERE? I THOUGHT YOU WERE DOWNSTAIRS IN THE CELLAR, PUTTERING AROUND WITH MAGNETS FOR YOUR SCIENCE PROJECT!
WHY, I... UH...
OH, I'M SORRY, SON! I'VE BEEN SHAMPOOING MY HAIR AND THIS SOAP IN MY EYES DOESN' LET ME SEE YOU TOO WELL! I JUST NOTICED THE MILK BOTTLE IN YOUR HAND! I SUPPOSE YO LOCKED YOURSELF OUT WHEN YOU WENT TO FETCH IT ON THE PORCH.
WELL, UH...
PUT THE BOTTLE IN THE KITCHEN AND I'LL MAKE BREAKFAST AS SOON AS I RINSE THE SOAP OUT OF MY HAIR! MEANWHILE, BETTER GET YOUR SCHOOL BOOKS FROM YOUR ROOM!
ER... OKAY!
MY ROOM? I GUESS IT MUST BE ON THE SECOND FLOOR!
SOON, UPSTAIRS...
THIS MUST BE HER SON'S ROOM GASP! B-BUT THERE'S NOBOD HERE! MAYBE THIS CLARK KENT I LOOK SO MUCH LIKE DECIDED TO RUN AWAY FROM HOME AND HIS MOTHER DOESN'T KNOW ABOUT IT YET! ANYWAY, HERE'S MY CHANCE TO GET INTO A CLEAN SUIT OF CLOTHING!
S.H.S.
AND SO, AS CLARK KENT'S "DOUBLE" COMES DOWNSTAIRS...
NOW TO SEE IF I CAN REALLY PASS AS KENT! MRS. KENT CAN SEE PERFECTLY WELL NOW THAT SHE'S GOT THE SOAP OUT OF HER EYES!
WHAT'S FOR BREAKFAST, MA?
PANCAKES AND MILK! SIT DOWN, SON!
THEN...
GOOD GRACIOUS, CLARK! WHERE ARE YOUR TABLE MANNERS? YOU NEVER USED TO WOLF DOWN YOUR FOOD!
WELL...UH...THE PAN-CAKES ARE ESPECIALL TERRIFIC THIS MORNING!
MOM...I MEAN MRS KENT... CAN SURE COOK! KENT WAS A SAP TO RUN AWAY!

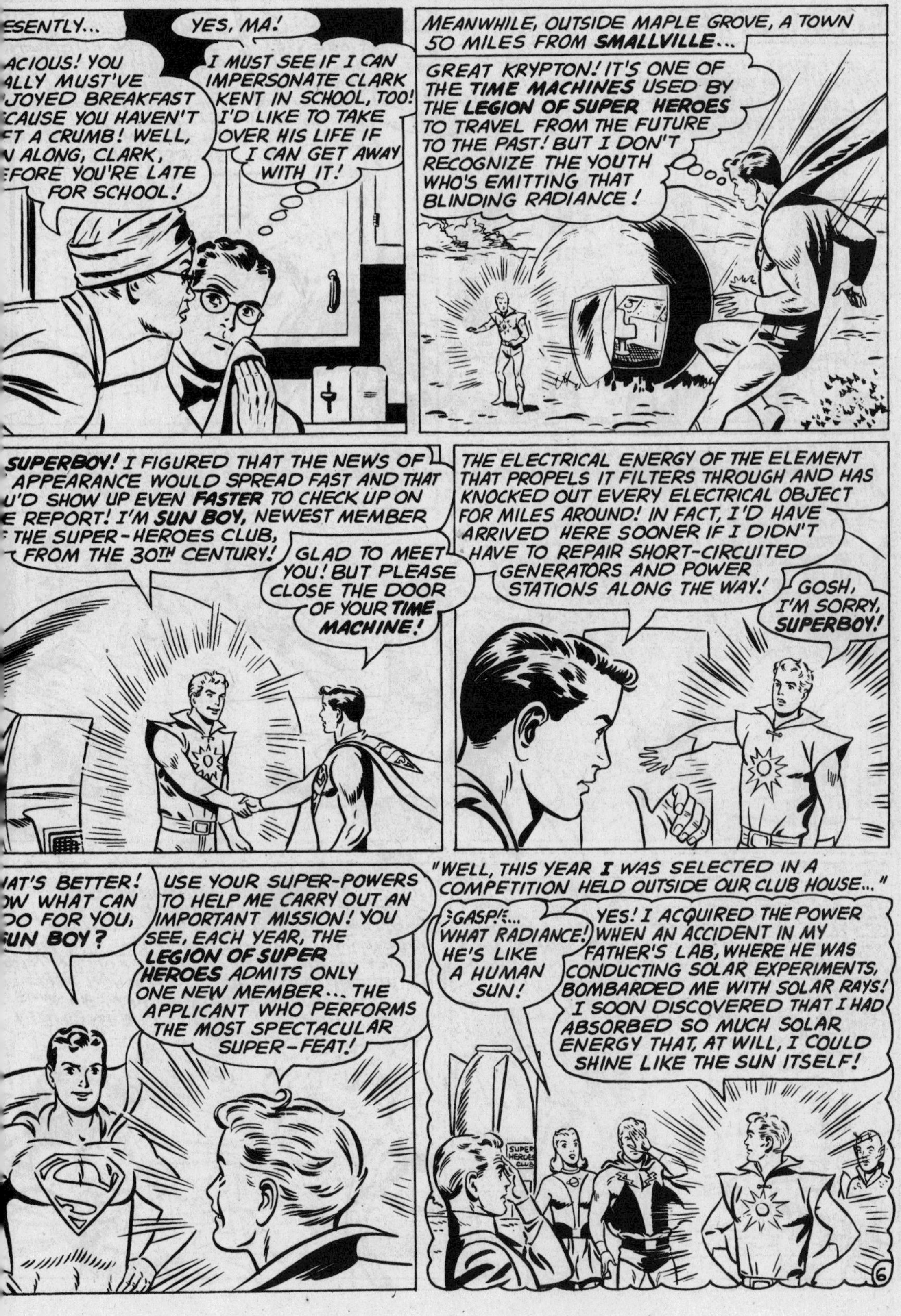
ESENTLY...
ACIOUS! YOU ALLY MUST'VE JOYED BREAKFAST CAUSE YOU HAVEN'T FT A CRUMB! WELL, N ALONG, CLARK, EFORE YOU'RE LATE FOR SCHOOL!
YES, MA!
I MUST SEE IF I CAN IMPERSONATE CLARK KENT IN SCHOOL, TOO! I'D LIKE TO TAKE OVER HIS LIFE IF I CAN GET AWAY WITH IT!
MEANWHILE, OUTSIDE MAPLE GROVE, A TOWN 50 MILES FROM SMALLVILLE...
GREAT KRYPTON! IT'S ONE OF THE TIME MACHINES USED BY THE LEGION OF SUPER HEROES TO TRAVEL FROM THE FUTURE TO THE PAST! BUT I DON'T RECOGNIZE THE YOUTH WHO'S EMITTING THAT BLINDING RADIANCE!
SUPERBOY! I FIGURED THAT THE NEWS OF APPEARANCE WOULD SPREAD FAST AND THAT U'D SHOW UP EVEN FASTER TO CHECK UP ON E REPORT! I'M SUN BOY, NEWEST MEMBER THE SUPER-HEROES CLUB, FROM THE 30TH CENTURY!
GLAD TO MEET YOU! BUT PLEASE CLOSE THE DOOR OF YOUR TIME MACHINE!
THE ELECTRICAL ENERGY OF THE ELEMENT THAT PROPELS IT FILTERS THROUGH AND HAS KNOCKED OUT EVERY ELECTRICAL OBJECT FOR MILES AROUND! IN FACT, I'D HAVE ARRIVED HERE SOONER IF I DIDN'T HAVE TO REPAIR SHORT-CIRCUITED GENERATORS AND POWER STATIONS ALONG THE WAY!
GOSH, I'M SORRY, SUPERBOY!
IAT'S BETTER! OW WHAT CAN DO FOR YOU, UN BOY?
USE YOUR SUPER-POWERS TO HELP ME CARRY OUT AN IMPORTANT MISSION! YOU SEE, EACH YEAR, THE LEGION OF SUPER HEROES ADMITS ONLY ONE NEW MEMBER... THE APPLICANT WHO PERFORMS THE MOST SPECTACULAR SUPER-FEAT!
"WELL, THIS YEAR I WAS SELECTED IN A COMPETITION HELD OUTSIDE OUR CLUB HOUSE..."
GASP!... WHAT RADIANCE! HE'S LIKE A HUMAN SUN!
YES! I ACQUIRED THE POWER WHEN AN ACCIDENT IN MY FATHER'S LAB, WHERE HE WAS CONDUCTING SOLAR EXPERIMENTS, BOMBARDED ME WITH SOLAR RAYS! I SOON DISCOVERED THAT I HAD ABSORBED SO MUCH SOLAR ENERGY THAT, AT WILL, I COULD SHINE LIKE THE SUN ITSELF!
SUPER HEROES CLUB
6

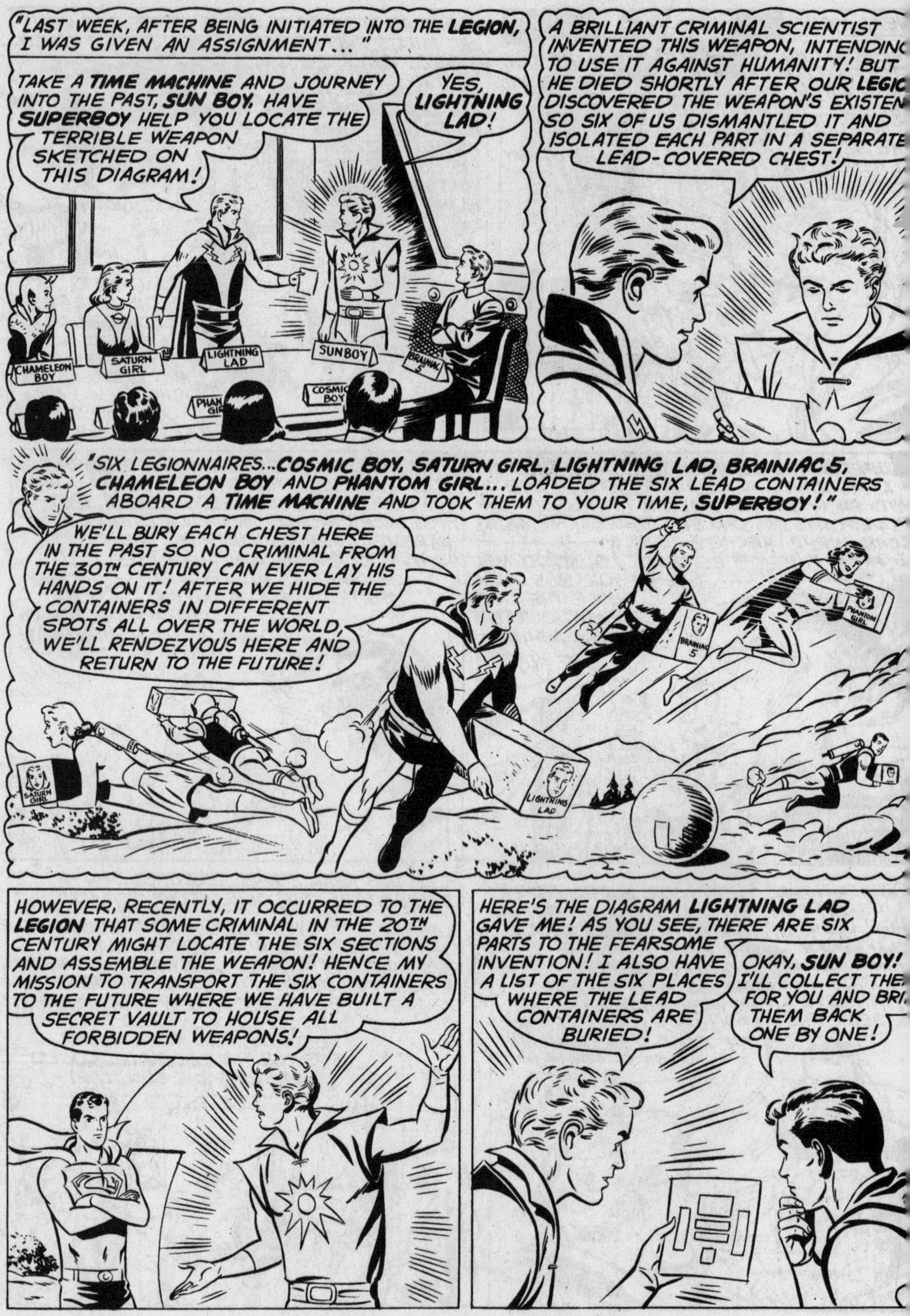
"LAST WEEK, AFTER BEING INITIATED INTO THE LEGION, I WAS GIVEN AN ASSIGNMENT..."
TAKE A TIME MACHINE AND JOURNEY INTO THE PAST, SUN BOY. HAVE SUPERBOY HELP YOU LOCATE THE TERRIBLE WEAPON SKETCHED ON THIS DIAGRAM!
YES, LIGHTNING LAD!
CHAMELEON BOY
SATURN GIRL
LIGHTNING LAD
SUNBOY
BRAINIAC 5
COSMIC BOY
A BRILLIANT CRIMINAL SCIENTIST INVENTED THIS WEAPON, INTENDIN TO USE IT AGAINST HUMANITY! BUT HE DIED SHORTLY AFTER OUR LEGIC DISCOVERED THE WEAPON'S EXISTEN SO SIX OF US DISMANTLED IT AND ISOLATED EACH PART IN A SEPARATE LEAD-COVERED CHEST!
"SIX LEGIONNAIRES...COSMIC BOY, SATURN GIRL, LIGHTNING LAD, BRAINIAC 5, CHAMELEON BOY AND PHANTOM GIRL... LOADED THE SIX LEAD CONTAINERS ABOARD A TIME MACHINE AND TOOK THEM TO YOUR TIME, SUPERBOY!"
WE'LL BURY EACH CHEST HERE IN THE PAST SO NO CRIMINAL FROM THE 30TH CENTURY CAN EVER LAY HIS HANDS ON IT! AFTER WE HIDE THE CONTAINERS IN DIFFERENT SPOTS ALL OVER THE WORLD, WE'LL RENDEZVOUS HERE AND RETURN TO THE FUTURE!
BRAINIAC 5
PHANTOM GIRL
SATURN GIRL
LIGHTNING LAD
HOWEVER, RECENTLY, IT OCCURRED TO THE LEGION THAT SOME CRIMINAL IN THE 20TH CENTURY MIGHT LOCATE THE SIX SECTIONS AND ASSEMBLE THE WEAPON! HENCE MY MISSION TO TRANSPORT THE SIX CONTAINERS TO THE FUTURE WHERE WE HAVE BUILT A SECRET VAULT TO HOUSE ALL FORBIDDEN WEAPONS!
HERE'S THE DIAGRAM LIGHTNING LAD GAVE ME! AS YOU SEE, THERE ARE SIX PARTS TO THE FEARSOME INVENTION! I ALSO HAVE A LIST OF THE SIX PLACES WHERE THE LEAD CONTAINERS ARE BURIED!
OKAY, SUN BOY! I'LL COLLECT THE FOR YOU AND BRI THEM BACK ONE BY ONE!

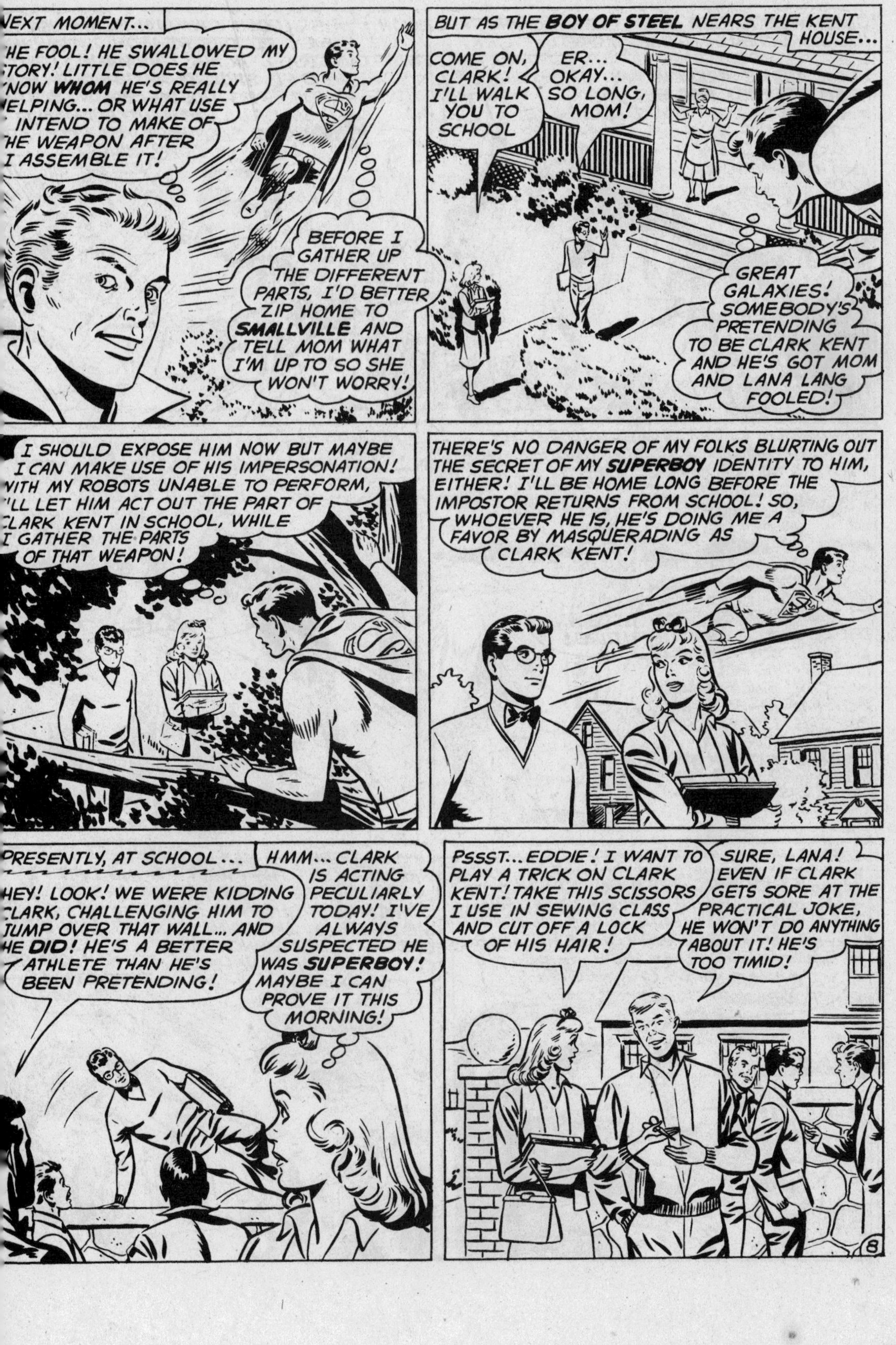
NEXT MOMENT...
HE FOOL! HE SWALLOWED MY TORY! LITTLE DOES HE NOW WHOM HE'S REALLY ELPING... OR WHAT USE INTEND TO MAKE OF HE WEAPON AFTER I ASSEMBLE IT!
BEFORE I GATHER UP THE DIFFERENT PARTS, I'D BETTER ZIP HOME TO SMALLVILLE AND TELL MOM WHAT I'M UP TO SO SHE WON'T WORRY!
BUT AS THE BOY OF STEEL NEARS THE KENT HOUSE...
COME ON, CLARK! I'LL WALK YOU TO SCHOOL
ER... OKAY... SO LONG, MOM!
GREAT GALAXIES! SOMEBODY'S PRETENDING TO BE CLARK KENT AND HE'S GOT MOM AND LANA LANG FOOLED!
I SHOULD EXPOSE HIM NOW BUT MAYBE I CAN MAKE USE OF HIS IMPERSONATION! WITH MY ROBOTS UNABLE TO PERFORM, 'LL LET HIM ACT OUT THE PART OF CLARK KENT IN SCHOOL, WHILE I GATHER THE PARTS OF THAT WEAPON!
THERE'S NO DANGER OF MY FOLKS BLURTING OUT THE SECRET OF MY SUPERBOY IDENTITY TO HIM, EITHER! I'LL BE HOME LONG BEFORE THE IMPOSTOR RETURNS FROM SCHOOL! SO, WHOEVER HE IS, HE'S DOING ME A FAVOR BY MASQUERADING AS CLARK KENT!
PRESENTLY, AT SCHOOL...
HEY! LOOK! WE WERE KIDDING CLARK, CHALLENGING HIM TO JUMP OVER THAT WALL... AND HE DID! HE'S A BETTER ATHLETE THAN HE'S BEEN PRETENDING!
HMM... CLARK IS ACTING PECULIARLY TODAY! I'VE ALWAYS SUSPECTED HE WAS SUPERBOY! MAYBE I CAN PROVE IT THIS MORNING!
PSSST... EDDIE! I WANT TO PLAY A TRICK ON CLARK KENT! TAKE THIS SCISSORS I USE IN SEWING CLASS AND CUT OFF A LOCK OF HIS HAIR!
SURE, LANA! EVEN IF CLARK GETS SORE AT THE PRACTICAL JOKE, HE WON'T DO ANYTHING ABOUT IT! HE'S TOO TIMID!
8

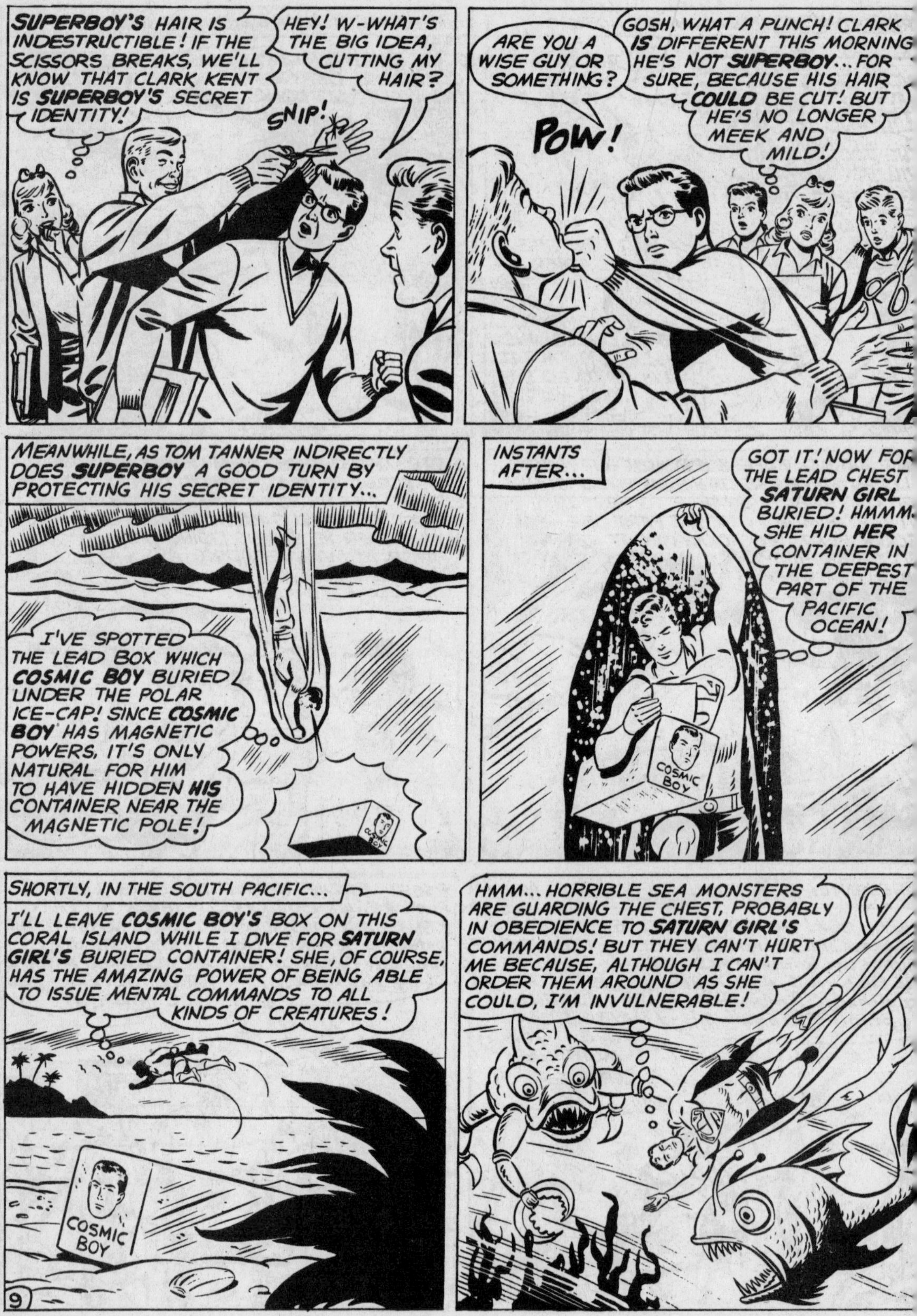
SUPERBOY'S HAIR IS INDESTRUCTIBLE! IF THE SCISSORS BREAKS, WE'LL KNOW THAT CLARK KENT IS SUPERBOY'S SECRET IDENTITY!
HEY! W-WHAT'S THE BIG IDEA, CUTTING MY HAIR?
SNIP!
ARE YOU A WISE GUY OR SOMETHING?
GOSH, WHAT A PUNCH! CLARK IS DIFFERENT THIS MORNING HE'S NOT SUPERBOY... FOR SURE, BECAUSE HIS HAIR COULD BE CUT! BUT HE'S NO LONGER MEEK AND MILD!
POW!
MEANWHILE, AS TOM TANNER INDIRECTLY DOES SUPERBOY A GOOD TURN BY PROTECTING HIS SECRET IDENTITY...
I'VE SPOTTED THE LEAD BOX WHICH COSMIC BOY BURIED UNDER THE POLAR ICE-CAP! SINCE COSMIC BOY HAS MAGNETIC POWERS, IT'S ONLY NATURAL FOR HIM TO HAVE HIDDEN HIS CONTAINER NEAR THE MAGNETIC POLE!
INSTANTS AFTER...
GOT IT! NOW FOR THE LEAD CHEST SATURN GIRL BURIED! HMMM. SHE HID HER CONTAINER IN THE DEEPEST PART OF THE PACIFIC OCEAN!
COSMIC BOY
SHORTLY, IN THE SOUTH PACIFIC...
I'LL LEAVE COSMIC BOY'S BOX ON THIS CORAL ISLAND WHILE I DIVE FOR SATURN GIRL'S BURIED CONTAINER! SHE, OF COURSE, HAS THE AMAZING POWER OF BEING ABLE TO ISSUE MENTAL COMMANDS TO ALL KINDS OF CREATURES!
COSMIC BOY
9
HMM... HORRIBLE SEA MONSTERS ARE GUARDING THE CHEST, PROBABLY IN OBEDIENCE TO SATURN GIRL'S COMMANDS! BUT THEY CAN'T HURT ME BECAUSE, ALTHOUGH I CAN'T ORDER THEM AROUND AS SHE COULD, I'M INVULNERABLE!

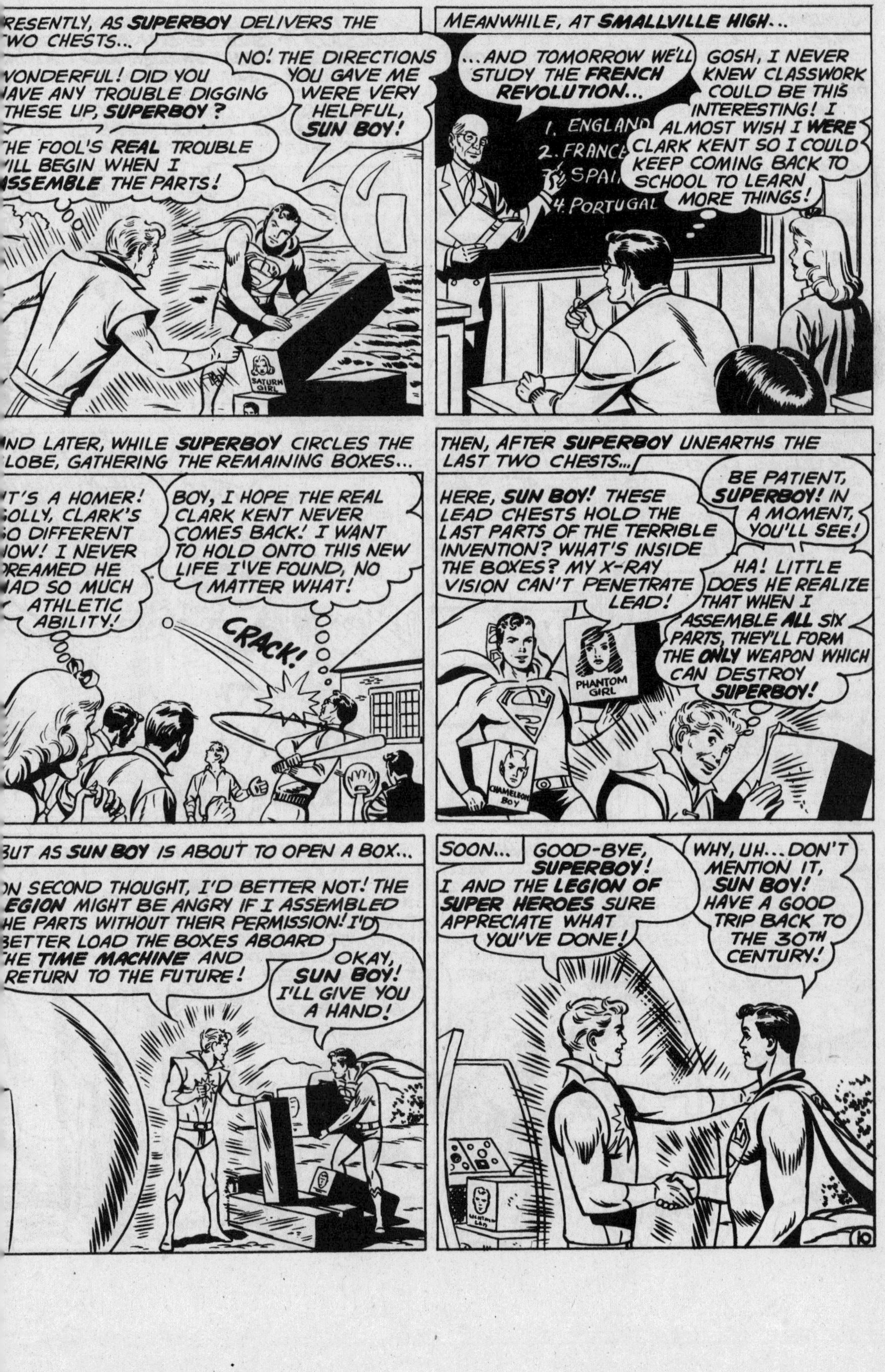
RESENTLY, AS SUPERBOY DELIVERS THE WO CHESTS...
VONDERFUL! DID YOU IAVE ANY TROUBLE DIGGING THESE UP, SUPERBOY?
NO! THE DIRECTIONS YOU GAVE ME WERE VERY HELPFUL, SUN BOY!
HE FOOL'S REAL TROUBLE VILL BEGIN WHEN I SSEMBLE THE PARTS!
SATURN GIRL
MEANWHILE, AT SMALLVILLE HIGH...
...AND TOMORROW WE'LL STUDY THE FRENCH REVOLUTION...
1. ENGLAND
2. FRANCE
3. SPAI
4. PORTUGAL
GOSH, I NEVER KNEW CLASSWORK COULD BE THIS INTERESTING! I ALMOST WISH I WERE CLARK KENT SO I COULD KEEP COMING BACK TO SCHOOL TO LEARN MORE THINGS!
ND LATER, WHILE SUPERBOY CIRCLES THE LOBE, GATHERING THE REMAINING BOXES...
T'S A HOMER! OLLY, CLARK'S O DIFFERENT OW! I NEVER REAMED HE AD SO MUCH ATHLETIC ABILITY!
BOY, I HOPE THE REAL CLARK KENT NEVER COMES BACK! I WANT TO HOLD ONTO THIS NEW LIFE I'VE FOUND, NO MATTER WHAT!
CRACK!
THEN, AFTER SUPERBOY UNEARTHS THE LAST TWO CHESTS...
HERE, SUN BOY! THESE LEAD CHESTS HOLD THE LAST PARTS OF THE TERRIBLE INVENTION? WHAT'S INSIDE THE BOXES? MY X-RAY VISION CAN'T PENETRATE LEAD!
BE PATIENT, SUPERBOY! IN A MOMENT, YOU'LL SEE!
HA! LITTLE DOES HE REALIZE THAT WHEN I ASSEMBLE ALL SIX PARTS, THEY'LL FORM THE ONLY WEAPON WHICH CAN DESTROY SUPERBOY!
PHANTOM GIRL
CHAMELEON BOY
BUT AS SUN BOY IS ABOUT TO OPEN A BOX...
ON SECOND THOUGHT, I'D BETTER NOT! THE EGION MIGHT BE ANGRY IF I ASSEMBLED HE PARTS WITHOUT THEIR PERMISSION! I'D BETTER LOAD THE BOXES ABOARD HE TIME MACHINE AND RETURN TO THE FUTURE!
OKAY, SUN BOY! I'LL GIVE YOU A HAND!
SOON...
GOOD-BYE, SUPERBOY! I AND THE LEGION OF SUPER HEROES SURE APPRECIATE WHAT YOU'VE DONE!
WHY, UH...DON'T MENTION IT, SUN BOY! HAVE A GOOD TRIP BACK TO THE 30TH CENTURY!
10

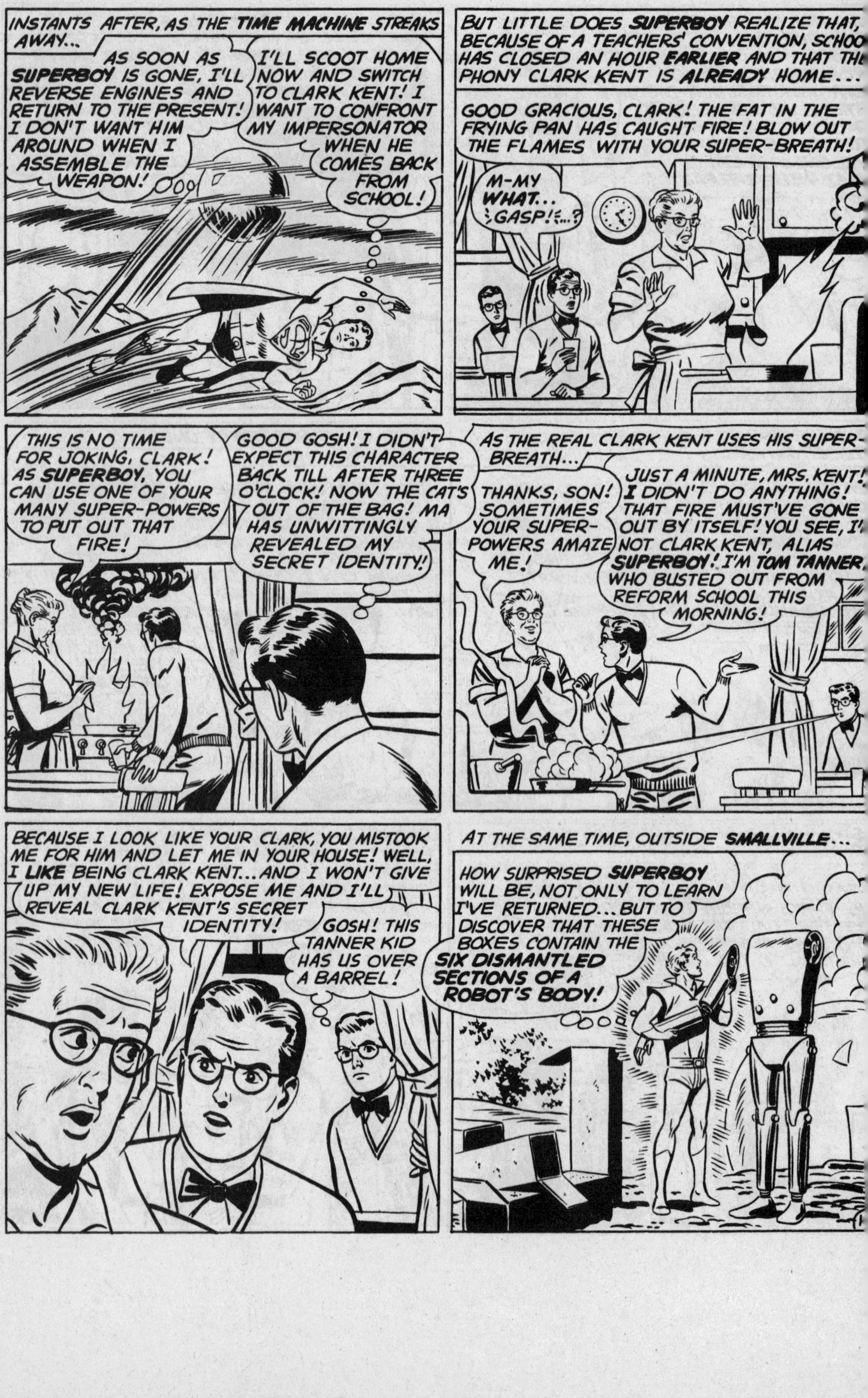
INSTANTS AFTER, AS THE TIME MACHINE STREAKS AWAY...
AS SOON AS SUPERBOY IS GONE, I'LL REVERSE ENGINES AND RETURN TO THE PRESENT! I DON'T WANT HIM AROUND WHEN I ASSEMBLE THE WEAPON!
I'LL SCOOT HOME NOW AND SWITCH TO CLARK KENT! I WANT TO CONFRONT MY IMPERSONATOR WHEN HE COMES BACK FROM SCHOOL!
BUT LITTLE DOES SUPERBOY REALIZE THAT, BECAUSE OF A TEACHERS' CONVENTION, SCHOO HAS CLOSED AN HOUR EARLIER AND THAT TH PHONY CLARK KENT IS ALREADY HOME...
GOOD GRACIOUS, CLARK! THE FAT IN THE FRYING PAN HAS CAUGHT FIRE! BLOW OUT THE FLAMES WITH YOUR SUPER-BREATH!
M-MY WHAT... GASP!...?
THIS IS NO TIME FOR JOKING, CLARK! AS SUPERBOY, YOU CAN USE ONE OF YOUR MANY SUPER-POWERS TO PUT OUT THAT FIRE!
GOOD GOSH! I DIDN'T EXPECT THIS CHARACTER BACK TILL AFTER THREE O'CLOCK! NOW THE CAT'S OUT OF THE BAG! MA HAS UNWITTINGLY REVEALED MY SECRET IDENTITY!
AS THE REAL CLARK KENT USES HIS SUPER-BREATH...
THANKS, SON! SOMETIMES YOUR SUPER-POWERS AMAZE ME!
JUST A MINUTE, MRS. KENT! I DIDN'T DO ANYTHING! THAT FIRE MUST'VE GONE OUT BY ITSELF! YOU SEE, I' NOT CLARK KENT, ALIAS SUPERBOY! I'M TOM TANNER, WHO BUSTED OUT FROM REFORM SCHOOL THIS MORNING!
BECAUSE I LOOK LIKE YOUR CLARK, YOU MISTOOK ME FOR HIM AND LET ME IN YOUR HOUSE! WELL, I LIKE BEING CLARK KENT... AND I WON'T GIVE UP MY NEW LIFE! EXPOSE ME AND I'LL REVEAL CLARK KENT'S SECRET IDENTITY!
GOSH! THIS TANNER KID HAS US OVER A BARREL!
AT THE SAME TIME, OUTSIDE SMALLVILLE...
HOW SURPRISED SUPERBOY WILL BE, NOT ONLY TO LEARN I'VE RETURNED... BUT TO DISCOVER THAT THESE BOXES CONTAIN THE SIX DISMANTLED SECTIONS OF A ROBOT'S BODY!

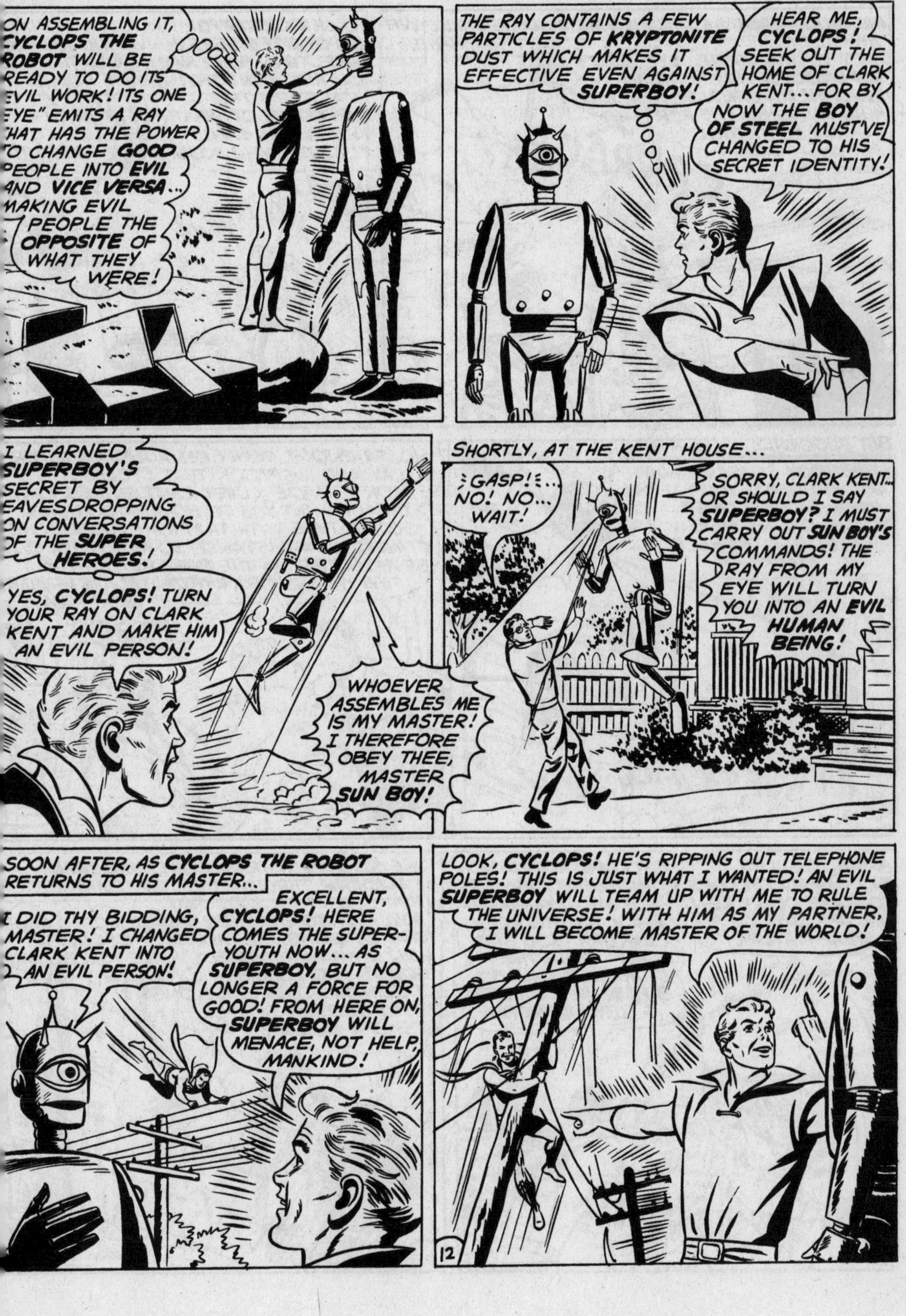
ON ASSEMBLING IT, CYCLOPS THE ROBOT WILL BE READY TO DO ITS EVIL WORK! ITS ONE "EYE" EMITS A RAY THAT HAS THE POWER TO CHANGE GOOD PEOPLE INTO EVIL AND VICE VERSA... MAKING EVIL PEOPLE THE OPPOSITE OF WHAT THEY WERE!
THE RAY CONTAINS A FEW PARTICLES OF KRYPTONITE DUST WHICH MAKES IT EFFECTIVE EVEN AGAINST SUPERBOY!
HEAR ME, CYCLOPS! SEEK OUT THE HOME OF CLARK KENT... FOR BY NOW THE BOY OF STEEL MUST'VE CHANGED TO HIS SECRET IDENTITY!
I LEARNED SUPERBOY'S SECRET BY EAVESDROPPING ON CONVERSATIONS OF THE SUPER HEROES!
YES, CYCLOPS! TURN YOUR RAY ON CLARK KENT AND MAKE HIM AN EVIL PERSON!
WHOEVER ASSEMBLES ME IS MY MASTER! I THEREFORE OBEY THEE, MASTER SUN BOY!
SHORTLY, AT THE KENT HOUSE...
GASP!... NO! NO... WAIT!
SORRY, CLARK KENT... OR SHOULD I SAY SUPERBOY? I MUST CARRY OUT SUN BOY'S COMMANDS! THE RAY FROM MY EYE WILL TURN YOU INTO AN EVIL HUMAN BEING!
SOON AFTER, AS CYCLOPS THE ROBOT RETURNS TO HIS MASTER...
I DID THY BIDDING, MASTER! I CHANGED CLARK KENT INTO AN EVIL PERSON!
EXCELLENT, CYCLOPS! HERE COMES THE SUPER-YOUTH NOW... AS SUPERBOY, BUT NO LONGER A FORCE FOR GOOD! FROM HERE ON, SUPERBOY WILL MENACE, NOT HELP, MANKIND!
LOOK, CYCLOPS! HE'S RIPPING OUT TELEPHONE POLES! THIS IS JUST WHAT I WANTED! AN EVIL SUPERBOY WILL TEAM UP WITH ME TO RULE THE UNIVERSE! WITH HIM AS MY PARTNER, I WILL BECOME MASTER OF THE WORLD!
12

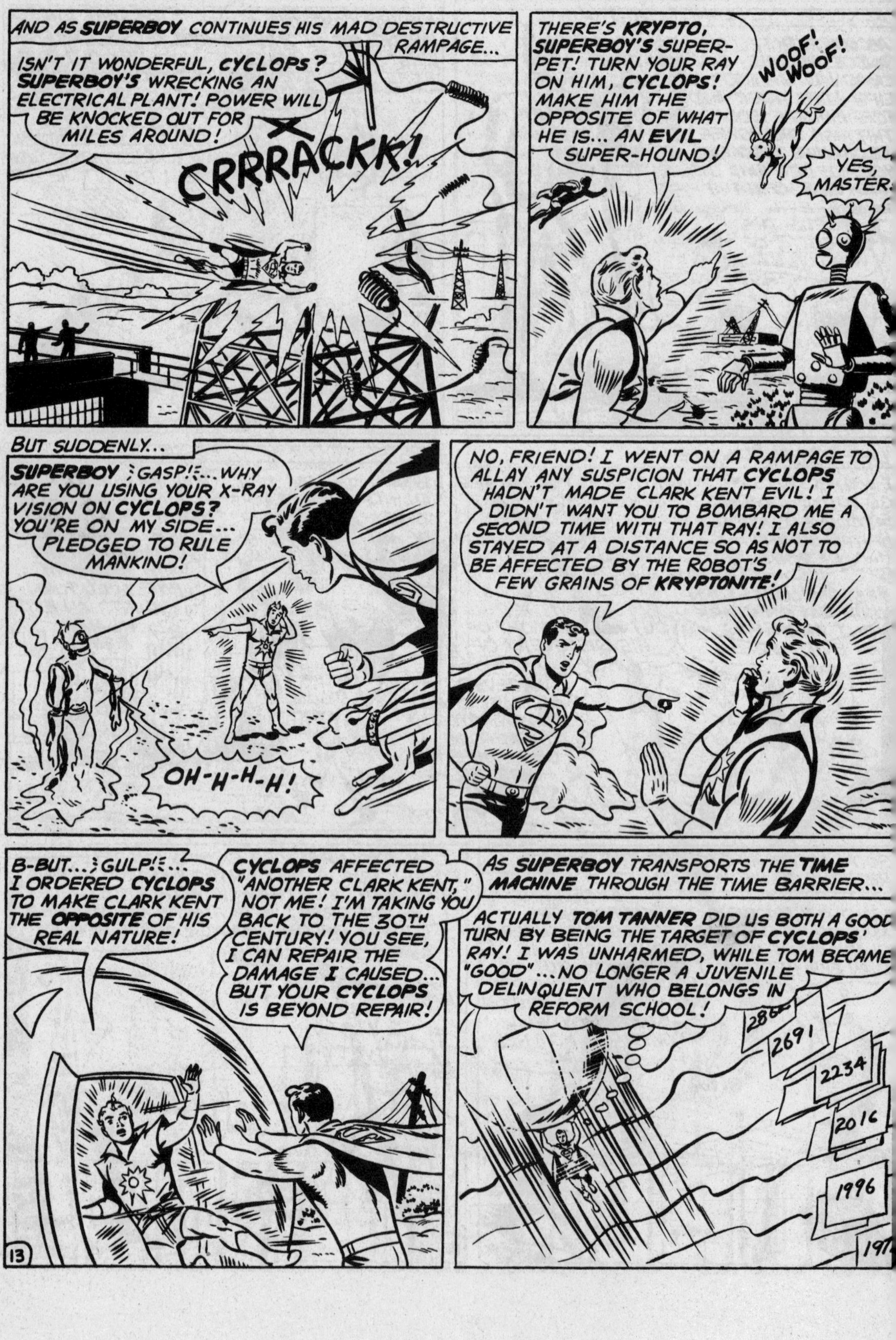
AND AS SUPERBOY CONTINUES HIS MAD DESTRUCTIVE RAMPAGE...
ISN'T IT WONDERFUL, CYCLOPS? SUPERBOY'S WRECKING AN ELECTRICAL PLANT! POWER WILL BE KNOCKED OUT FOR MILES AROUND!
CRRRACKK!
THERE'S KRYPTO, SUPERBOY'S SUPER-PET! TURN YOUR RAY ON HIM, CYCLOPS! MAKE HIM THE OPPOSITE OF WHAT HE IS... AN EVIL SUPER-HOUND!
WOOF! WOOF!
YES, MASTER.
BUT SUDDENLY...
SUPERBOY ;GASP!;...WHY ARE YOU USING YOUR X-RAY VISION ON CYCLOPS? YOU'RE ON MY SIDE... PLEDGED TO RULE MANKIND!
OH-H-H-H!
NO, FRIEND! I WENT ON A RAMPAGE TO ALLAY ANY SUSPICION THAT CYCLOPS HADN'T MADE CLARK KENT EVIL! I DIDN'T WANT YOU TO BOMBARD ME A SECOND TIME WITH THAT RAY! I ALSO STAYED AT A DISTANCE SO AS NOT TO BE AFFECTED BY THE ROBOT'S FEW GRAINS OF KRYPTONITE!
B-BUT... ;GULP!;... I ORDERED CYCLOPS TO MAKE CLARK KENT THE OPPOSITE OF HIS REAL NATURE!
CYCLOPS AFFECTED "ANOTHER CLARK KENT," NOT ME! I'M TAKING YOU BACK TO THE 30TH CENTURY! YOU SEE, I CAN REPAIR THE DAMAGE I CAUSED... BUT YOUR CYCLOPS IS BEYOND REPAIR!
13
AS SUPERBOY TRANSPORTS THE TIME MACHINE THROUGH THE TIME BARRIER...
ACTUALLY TOM TANNER DID US BOTH A GOOD TURN BY BEING THE TARGET OF CYCLOPS' RAY! I WAS UNHARMED, WHILE TOM BECAME "GOOD"... NO LONGER A JUVENILE DELINQUENT WHO BELONGS IN REFORM SCHOOL!
2691
2234
2016
1996

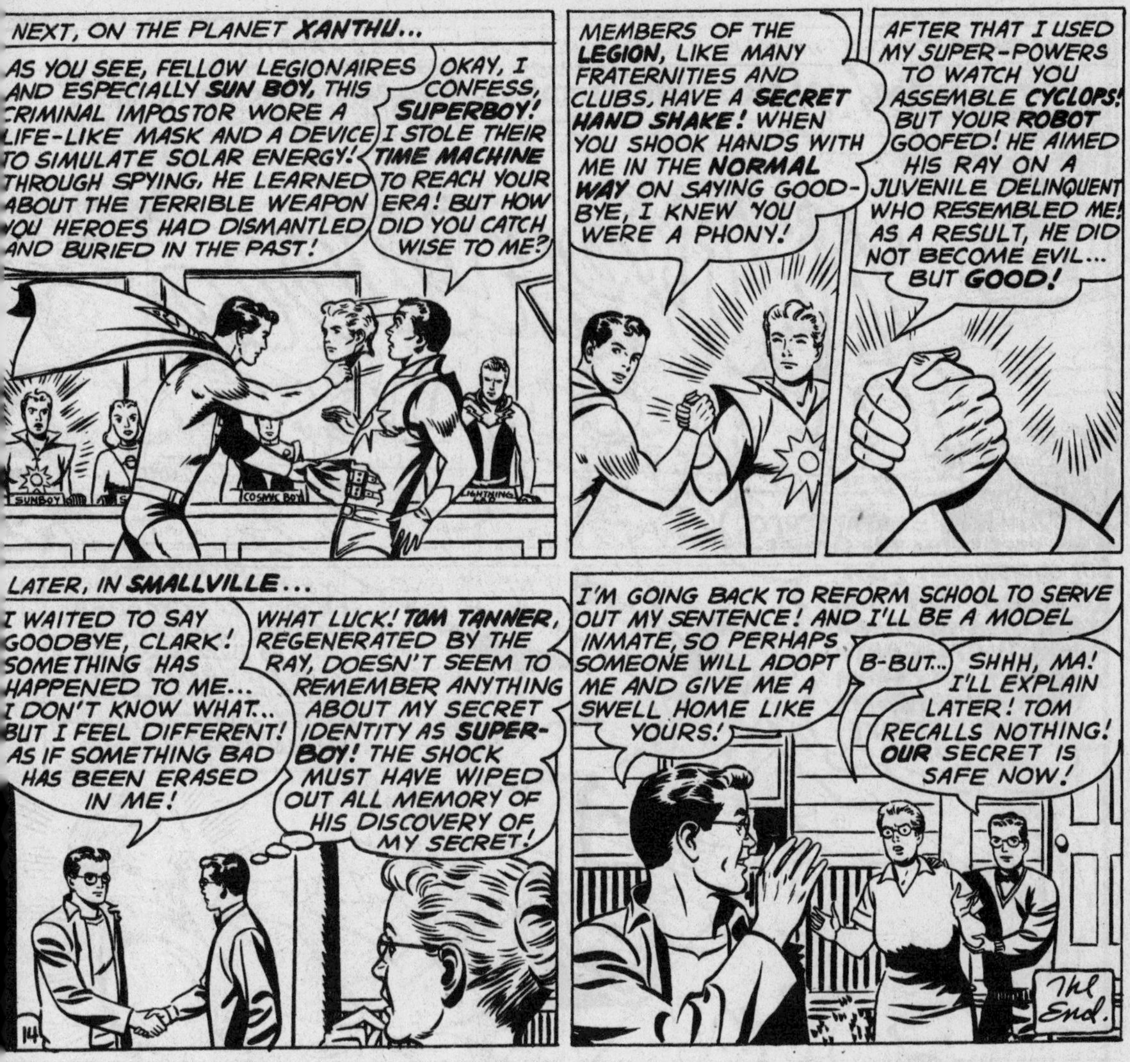
NEXT, ON THE PLANET XANTHU...
AS YOU SEE, FELLOW LEGIONAIRES AND ESPECIALLY SUN BOY, THIS CRIMINAL IMPOSTOR WORE A LIFE-LIKE MASK AND A DEVICE TO SIMULATE SOLAR ENERGY! THROUGH SPYING, HE LEARNED ABOUT THE TERRIBLE WEAPON YOU HEROES HAD DISMANTLED AND BURIED IN THE PAST!
OKAY, I CONFESS, SUPERBOY! I STOLE THEIR TIME MACHINE TO REACH YOUR ERA! BUT HOW DID YOU CATCH WISE TO ME?
SUNBOY
COSMIC BOY
LIGHTNING LAD
MEMBERS OF THE LEGION, LIKE MANY FRATERNITIES AND CLUBS, HAVE A SECRET HAND SHAKE! WHEN YOU SHOOK HANDS WITH ME IN THE NORMAL WAY ON SAYING GOOD-BYE, I KNEW YOU WERE A PHONY!
AFTER THAT I USED MY SUPER-POWERS TO WATCH YOU ASSEMBLE CYCLOPS! BUT YOUR ROBOT GOOFED! HE AIMED HIS RAY ON A JUVENILE DELINQUENT WHO RESEMBLED ME! AS A RESULT, HE DID NOT BECOME EVIL... BUT GOOD!
LATER, IN SMALLVILLE...
I WAITED TO SAY GOODBYE, CLARK! SOMETHING HAS HAPPENED TO ME... I DON'T KNOW WHAT... BUT I FEEL DIFFERENT! AS IF SOMETHING BAD HAS BEEN ERASED IN ME!
WHAT LUCK! TOM TANNER, REGENERATED BY THE RAY, DOESN'T SEEM TO REMEMBER ANYTHING ABOUT MY SECRET IDENTITY AS SUPER-BOY! THE SHOCK MUST HAVE WIPED OUT ALL MEMORY OF HIS DISCOVERY OF MY SECRET!
14
I'M GOING BACK TO REFORM SCHOOL TO SERVE OUT MY SENTENCE! AND I'LL BE A MODEL INMATE, SO PERHAPS SOMEONE WILL ADOPT ME AND GIVE ME A SWELL HOME LIKE YOURS!
B-BUT...
SHHH, MA! I'LL EXPLAIN LATER! TOM RECALLS NOTHING! OUR SECRET IS SAFE NOW!
The End.

LEGION of SUPER-HEROES

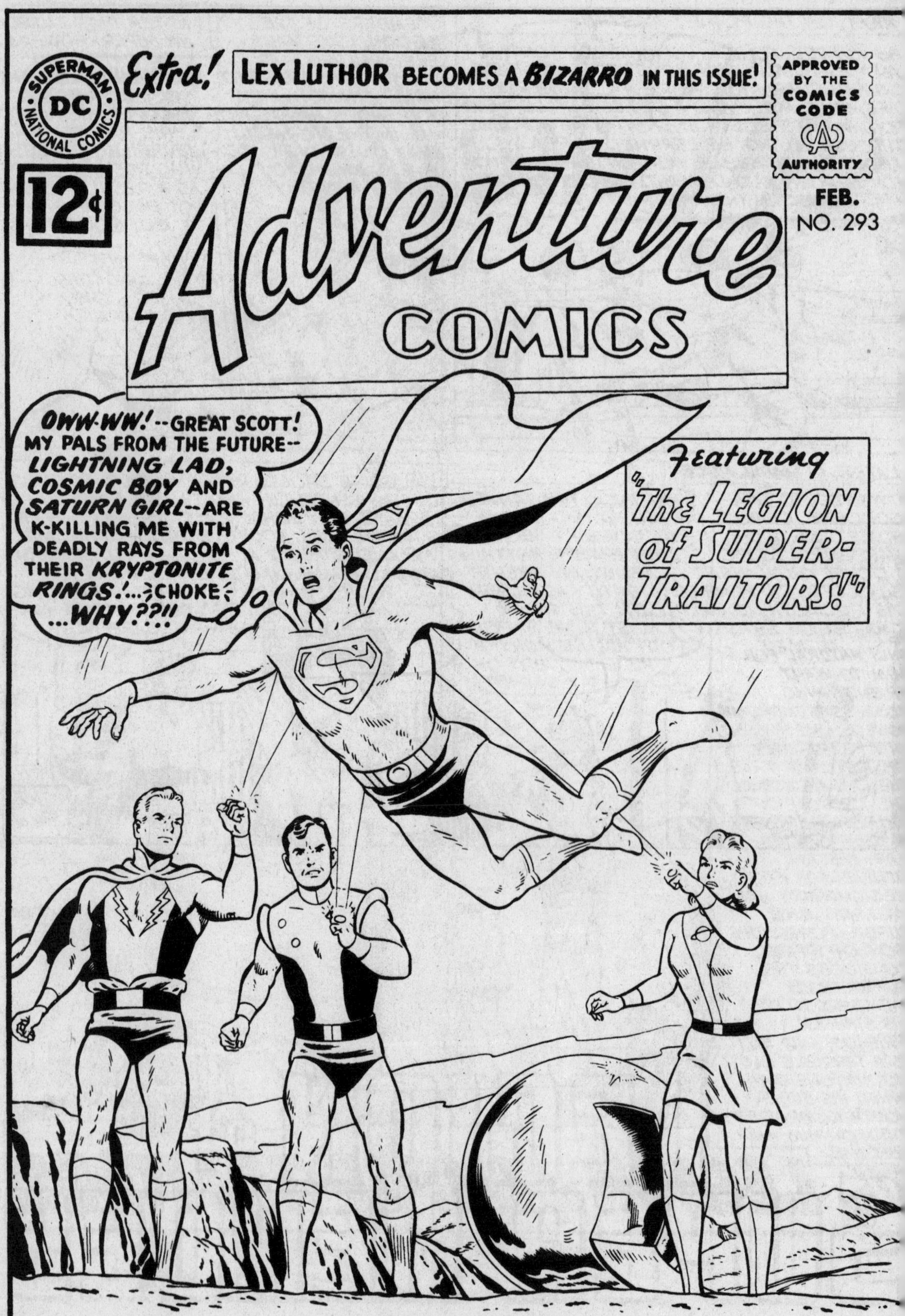
Extra! LEX LUTHOR BECOMES A BIZARRO IN THIS ISSUE!
SUPERMAN DC NATIONAL COMICS
APPROVED BY THE COMICS CODE AUTHORITY
12¢
Adventure COMICS
FEB. NO. 293
OWW-WW! --GREAT SCOTT! MY PALS FROM THE FUTURE-- LIGHTNING LAD, COSMIC BOY AND SATURN GIRL--ARE K-KILLING ME WITH DEADLY RAYS FROM THEIR KRYPTONITE RINGS!...CHOKE ...WHY??!!
Featuring "The LEGION of SUPER-TRAITORS!"

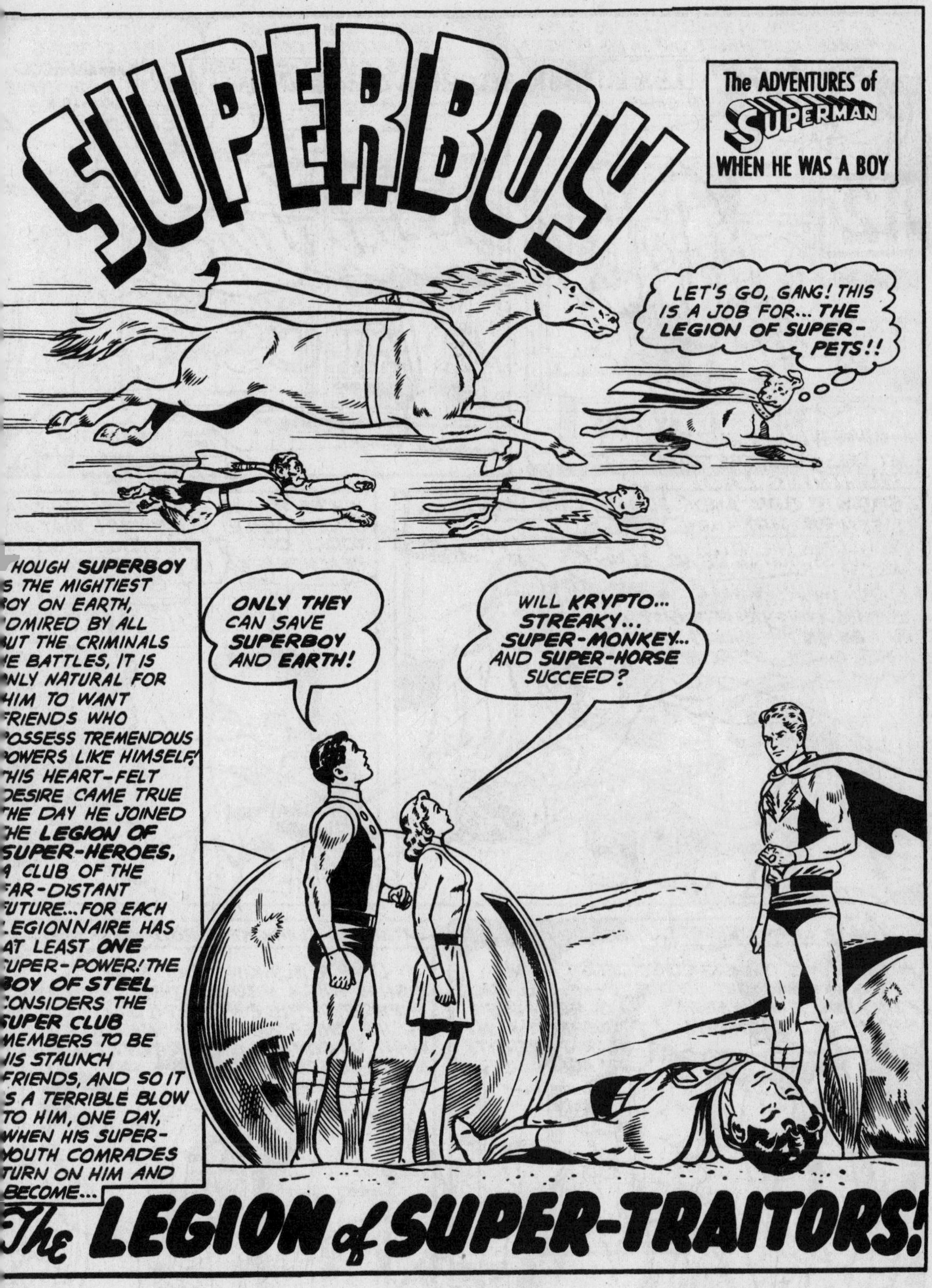
SUPERBOY
The ADVENTURES of SUPERMAN WHEN HE WAS A BOY
LET'S GO, GANG! THIS IS A JOB FOR... THE LEGION OF SUPER-PETS!!
HOUGH SUPERBOY S THE MIGHTIEST OY ON EARTH, DMIRED BY ALL UT THE CRIMINALS E BATTLES, IT IS NLY NATURAL FOR HIM TO WANT FRIENDS WHO OSSESS TREMENDOUS OWERS LIKE HIMSELF! THIS HEART-FELT DESIRE CAME TRUE THE DAY HE JOINED HE LEGION OF SUPER-HEROES, A CLUB OF THE AR-DISTANT UTURE...FOR EACH EGIONNAIRE HAS AT LEAST ONE UPER-POWER! THE OY OF STEEL ONSIDERS THE UPER CLUB MEMBERS TO BE IS STAUNCH FRIENDS, AND SO IT S A TERRIBLE BLOW TO HIM, ONE DAY, WHEN HIS SUPER-YOUTH COMRADES TURN ON HIM AND BECOME...
ONLY THEY CAN SAVE SUPERBOY AND EARTH!
WILL KRYPTO... STREAKY... SUPER-MONKEY... AND SUPER-HORSE SUCCEED?
The LEGION of SUPER-TRAITORS!

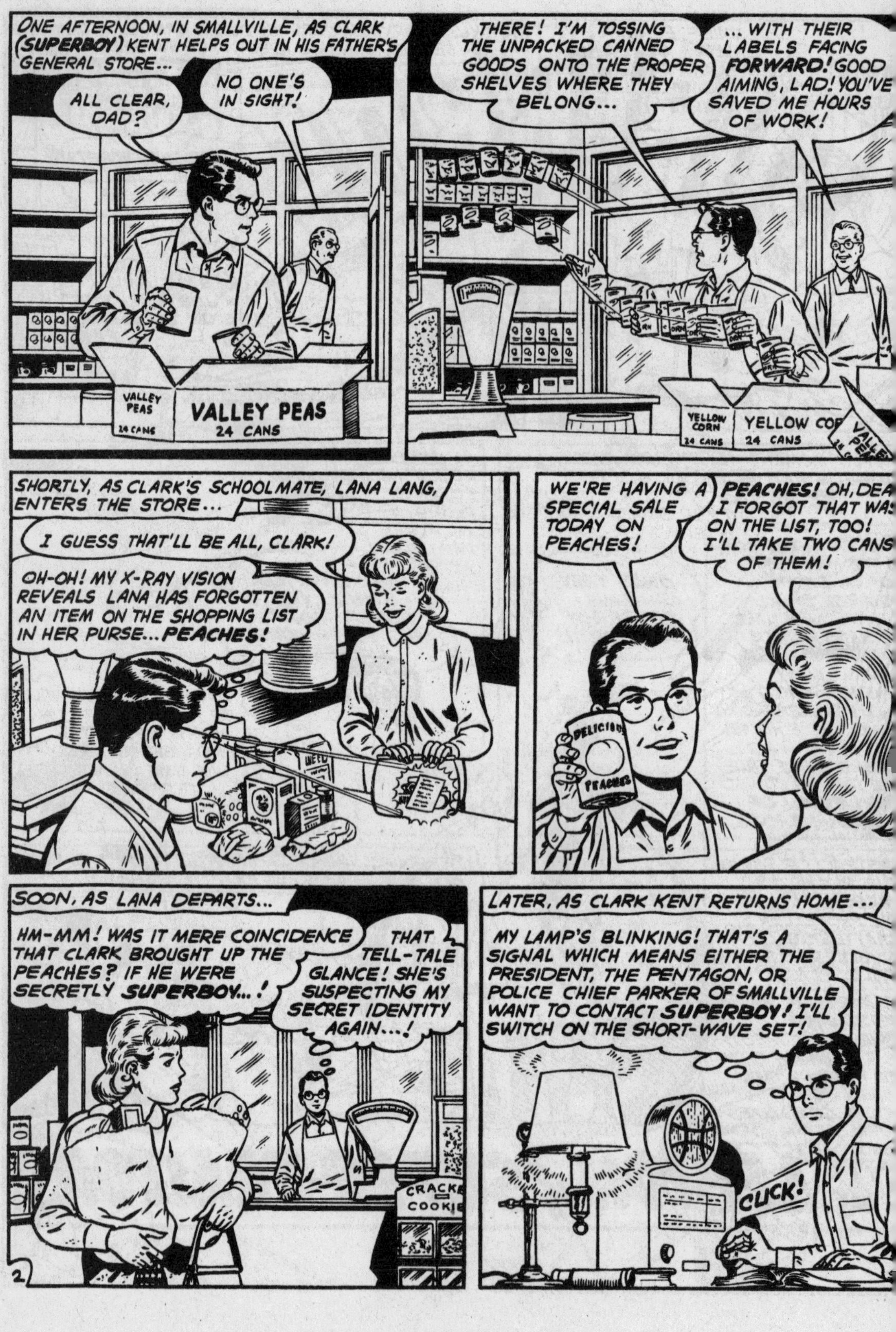
ONE AFTERNOON, IN SMALLVILLE, AS CLARK (SUPERBOY) KENT HELPS OUT IN HIS FATHER'S GENERAL STORE...
ALL CLEAR, DAD?
NO ONE'S IN SIGHT!
VALLEY PEAS 24 CANS
VALLEY PEAS 24 CANS
THERE! I'M TOSSING THE UNPACKED CANNED GOODS ONTO THE PROPER SHELVES WHERE THEY BELONG...
...WITH THEIR LABELS FACING FORWARD! GOOD AIMING, LAD! YOU'VE SAVED ME HOURS OF WORK!
YELLOW CORN 24 CANS
YELLOW COR 24 CANS
SHORTLY, AS CLARK'S SCHOOLMATE, LANA LANG, ENTERS THE STORE...
I GUESS THAT'LL BE ALL, CLARK!
OH-OH! MY X-RAY VISION REVEALS LANA HAS FORGOTTEN AN ITEM ON THE SHOPPING LIST IN HER PURSE...PEACHES!
WE'RE HAVING A SPECIAL SALE TODAY ON PEACHES!
DELICIOUS PEACHES
PEACHES! OH, DEA I FORGOT THAT WA ON THE LIST, TOO! I'LL TAKE TWO CANS OF THEM!
SOON, AS LANA DEPARTS...
HM-MM! WAS IT MERE COINCIDENCE THAT CLARK BROUGHT UP THE PEACHES? IF HE WERE SECRETLY SUPERBOY...!
THAT TELL-TALE GLANCE! SHE'S SUSPECTING MY SECRET IDENTITY AGAIN...!
CRACKE COOKIE
2
LATER, AS CLARK KENT RETURNS HOME...
MY LAMP'S BLINKING! THAT'S A SIGNAL WHICH MEANS EITHER THE PRESIDENT, THE PENTAGON, OR POLICE CHIEF PARKER OF SMALLVILLE WANT TO CONTACT SUPERBOY! I'LL SWITCH ON THE SHORT-WAVE SET!
CLICK!

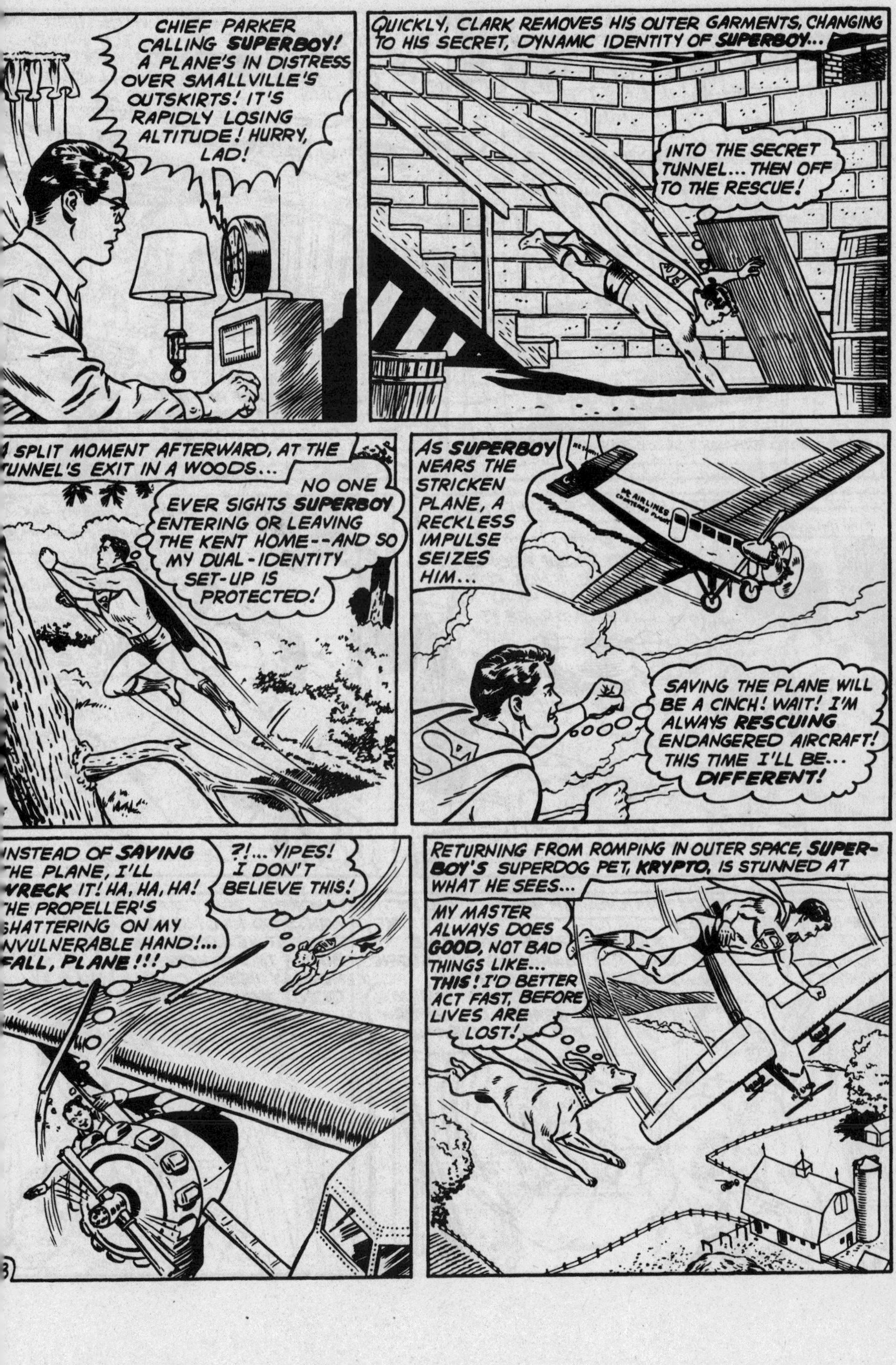
CHIEF PARKER CALLING SUPERBOY! A PLANE'S IN DISTRESS OVER SMALLVILLE'S OUTSKIRTS! IT'S RAPIDLY LOSING ALTITUDE! HURRY, LAD!
QUICKLY, CLARK REMOVES HIS OUTER GARMENTS, CHANGING TO HIS SECRET, DYNAMIC IDENTITY OF SUPERBOY...
INTO THE SECRET TUNNEL... THEN OFF TO THE RESCUE!
A SPLIT MOMENT AFTERWARD, AT THE TUNNEL'S EXIT IN A WOODS...
NO ONE EVER SIGHTS SUPERBOY ENTERING OR LEAVING THE KENT HOME--AND SO MY DUAL-IDENTITY SET-UP IS PROTECTED!
AS SUPERBOY NEARS THE STRICKEN PLANE, A RECKLESS IMPULSE SEIZES HIM...
SAVING THE PLANE WILL BE A CINCH! WAIT! I'M ALWAYS RESCUING ENDANGERED AIRCRAFT! THIS TIME I'LL BE... DIFFERENT!
INSTEAD OF SAVING THE PLANE, I'LL WRECK IT! HA, HA, HA! THE PROPELLER'S SHATTERING ON MY INVULNERABLE HAND!... FALL, PLANE!!!
?!... YIPES! I DON'T BELIEVE THIS!
RETURNING FROM ROMPING IN OUTER SPACE, SUPERBOY'S SUPERDOG PET, KRYPTO, IS STUNNED AT WHAT HE SEES...
MY MASTER ALWAYS DOES GOOD, NOT BAD THINGS LIKE... THIS! I'D BETTER ACT FAST, BEFORE LIVES ARE LOST!

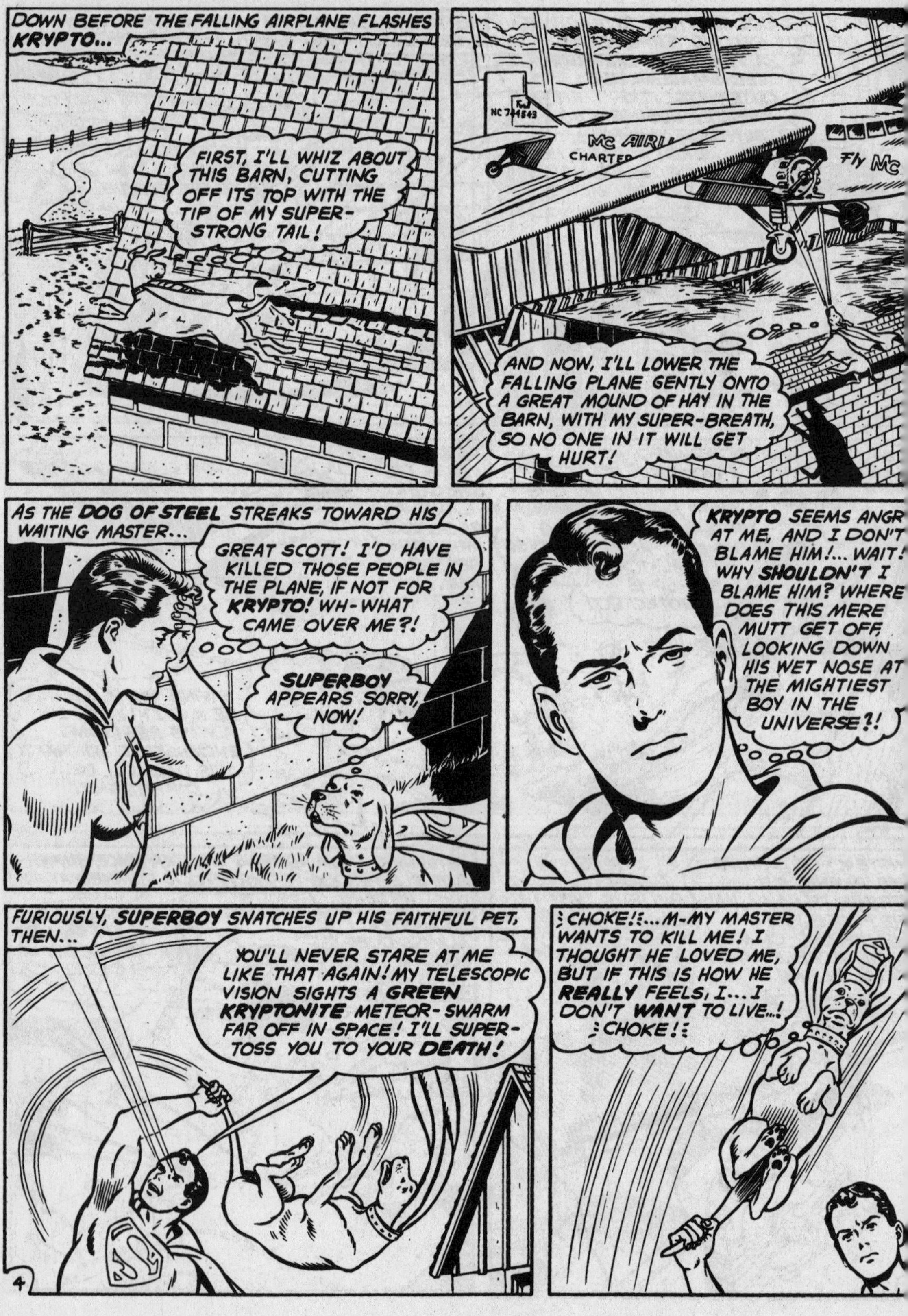

DOWN BEFORE THE FALLING AIRPLANE FLASHES KRYPTO...
FIRST, I'LL WHIZ ABOUT THIS BARN, CUTTING OFF ITS TOP WITH THE TIP OF MY SUPER-STRONG TAIL!
AND NOW, I'LL LOWER THE FALLING PLANE GENTLY ONTO A GREAT MOUND OF HAY IN THE BARN, WITH MY SUPER-BREATH, SO NO ONE IN IT WILL GET HURT!
AS THE DOG OF STEEL STREAKS TOWARD HIS WAITING MASTER...
GREAT SCOTT! I'D HAVE KILLED THOSE PEOPLE IN THE PLANE, IF NOT FOR KRYPTO! WH-WHAT CAME OVER ME?!
SUPERBOY APPEARS SORRY, NOW!
KRYPTO SEEMS ANGR AT ME, AND I DON'T BLAME HIM!... WAIT! WHY SHOULDN'T I BLAME HIM? WHERE DOES THIS MERE MUTT GET OFF, LOOKING DOWN HIS WET NOSE AT THE MIGHTIEST BOY IN THE UNIVERSE?!
FURIOUSLY, SUPERBOY SNATCHES UP HIS FAITHFUL PET, THEN...
YOU'LL NEVER STARE AT ME LIKE THAT AGAIN! MY TELESCOPIC VISION SIGHTS A GREEN KRYPTONITE METEOR-SWARM FAR OFF IN SPACE! I'LL SUPER-TOSS YOU TO YOUR DEATH!
CHOKE!... M-MY MASTER WANTS TO KILL ME! I THOUGHT HE LOVED ME, BUT IF THIS IS HOW HE REALLY FEELS, I... I DON'T WANT TO LIVE...! CHOKE!
4

...RUPTLY, THE **BOY OF STEEL'S** TERRIBLE *RAGE DEPARTS...

FORGIVE ME, **KRYPTO!** I DIDN'T MEAN THAT! I'M SORRY! I...DON'T KNOW **WHAT** POSSESSED ME...

I'M GLAD HE DOESN'T HATE ME ANY MORE!

*LATER, AS **SUPERBOY** RETURNS HOME, AND CONFIDES IN HIS PARENTS...*

FOLKS, I'M--SCARED! WHY'D I DO THOSE AWFUL THINGS? I WAS ALMOST A **MURDERER!** AND POOR **KRYPTO** WAS HEART-BROKEN...

:GASP!:

HOW TERRIBLE...!

...AFTER THEIR SON DROPS OFF TO SLEEP...

...DID **SUPERBOY** UNKNOWINGLY ENCOUNTER...ED KRYPTONITE, WHICH ...LWAYS AFFECTS HIM ...NPREDICTABLY?

MAYBE HE'S THE VICTIM OF SOME DELAYED REACTION CAUSED BY SOME UNKNOWN FORCE HE MET ON ANOTHER PLANET!

NEXT DAY, IN THE KENT HOME...

THE SIGNAL-LAMP IS NOW FLASHING A **CODE MESSAGE.** THAT CODE MEANS I'M TO CONTACT THE **LEGION OF SUPER-HEROES** FROM THE FUTURE, AT THE PLACE WE USUALLY MEET WHEN THEY VISIT THIS TIME-ERA!

...SWITCHING IDENTITIES, CLARK STREAKS OFF TO THE HEART OF THE GOBI DESERT...

HI, **SUPERBOY!** I SEE YOU GOT THE CODE MESSAGE I SENT OVER YOUR SIGNAL-LAMP, VIA MY MASTERY OF ELECTRICITY!

GOOD TO SEE YOU, **LIGHTNING LAD!** AND YOU, TOO, **COSMIC BOY** AND **SATURN GIRL!**

THEY TRAVELED HERE, THROUGH THE TIME-BARRIER, IN THEIR **TIME-CABINET!**...WHAT'S THAT STRANGE DEVICE THEY'VE SET UP, I WONDER??

5

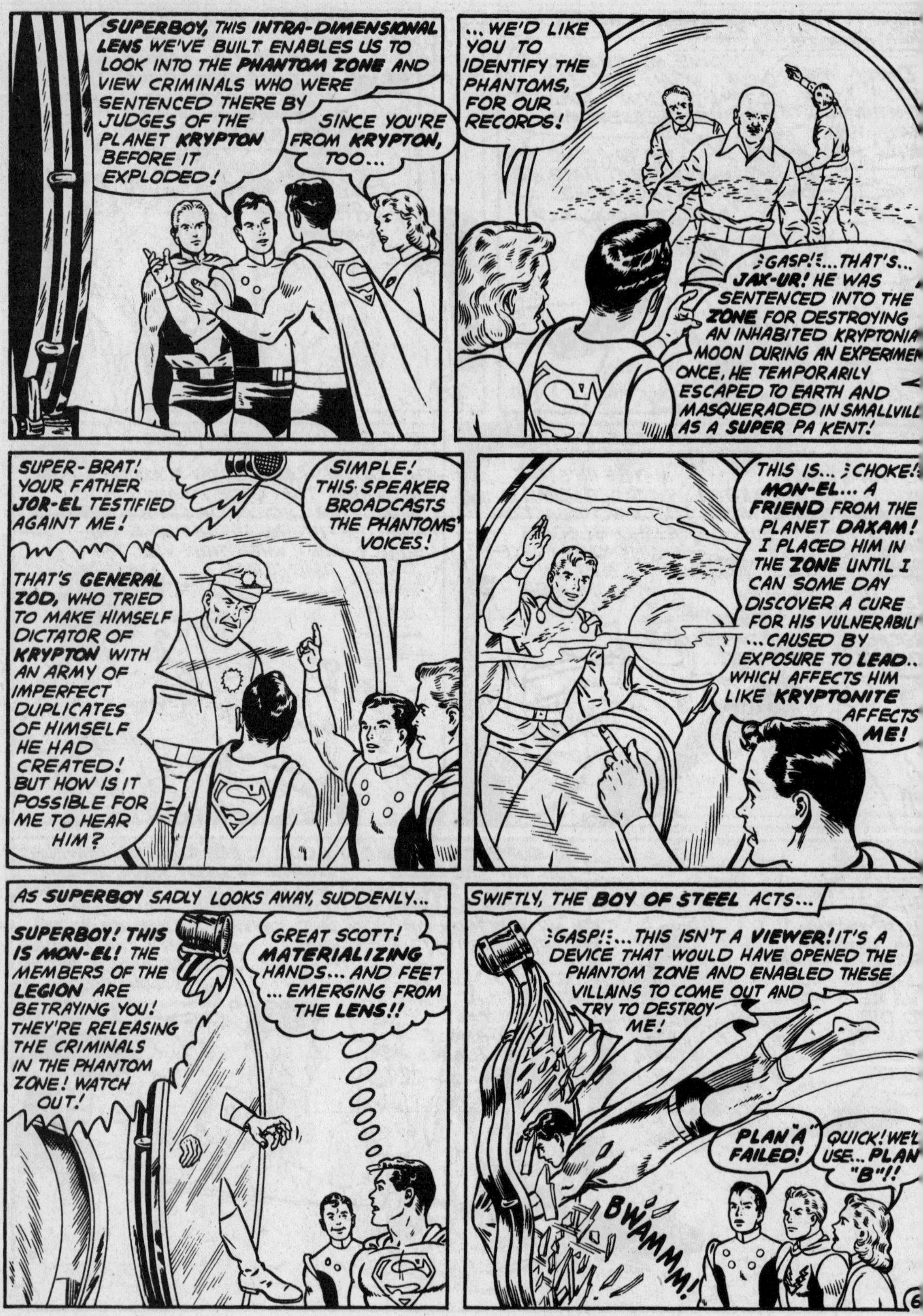
SUPERBOY, THIS INTRA-DIMENSIONAL LENS WE'VE BUILT ENABLES US TO LOOK INTO THE PHANTOM ZONE AND VIEW CRIMINALS WHO WERE SENTENCED THERE BY JUDGES OF THE PLANET KRYPTON BEFORE IT EXPLODED!
SINCE YOU'RE FROM KRYPTON, TOO...
...WE'D LIKE YOU TO IDENTIFY THE PHANTOMS, FOR OUR RECORDS!
GASP!...THAT'S... JAX-UR! HE WAS SENTENCED INTO THE ZONE FOR DESTROYING AN INHABITED KRYPTONIA MOON DURING AN EXPERIME ONCE, HE TEMPORARILY ESCAPED TO EARTH AND MASQUERADED IN SMALLVILL AS A SUPER PA KENT!
SUPER-BRAT! YOUR FATHER JOR-EL TESTIFIED AGAINT ME!
SIMPLE! THIS SPEAKER BROADCASTS THE PHANTOMS' VOICES!
THAT'S GENERAL ZOD, WHO TRIED TO MAKE HIMSELF DICTATOR OF KRYPTON WITH AN ARMY OF IMPERFECT DUPLICATES OF HIMSELF HE HAD CREATED! BUT HOW IS IT POSSIBLE FOR ME TO HEAR HIM?
THIS IS... CHOKE!... MON-EL... A FRIEND FROM THE PLANET DAXAM! I PLACED HIM IN THE ZONE UNTIL I CAN SOME DAY DISCOVER A CURE FOR HIS VULNERABILI ...CAUSED BY EXPOSURE TO LEAD... WHICH AFFECTS HIM LIKE KRYPTONITE AFFECTS ME!
AS SUPERBOY SADLY LOOKS AWAY, SUDDENLY...
SUPERBOY! THIS IS MON-EL! THE MEMBERS OF THE LEGION ARE BETRAYING YOU! THEY'RE RELEASING THE CRIMINALS IN THE PHANTOM ZONE! WATCH OUT!
GREAT SCOTT! MATERIALIZING HANDS... AND FEET ... EMERGING FROM THE LENS!!
SWIFTLY, THE BOY OF STEEL ACTS...
GASP!...THIS ISN'T A VIEWER! IT'S A DEVICE THAT WOULD HAVE OPENED THE PHANTOM ZONE AND ENABLED THESE VILLAINS TO COME OUT AND TRY TO DESTROY ME!
PLAN "A" FAILED!
QUICK! WE'L USE... PLAN "B"!!
BWAMMM!
6

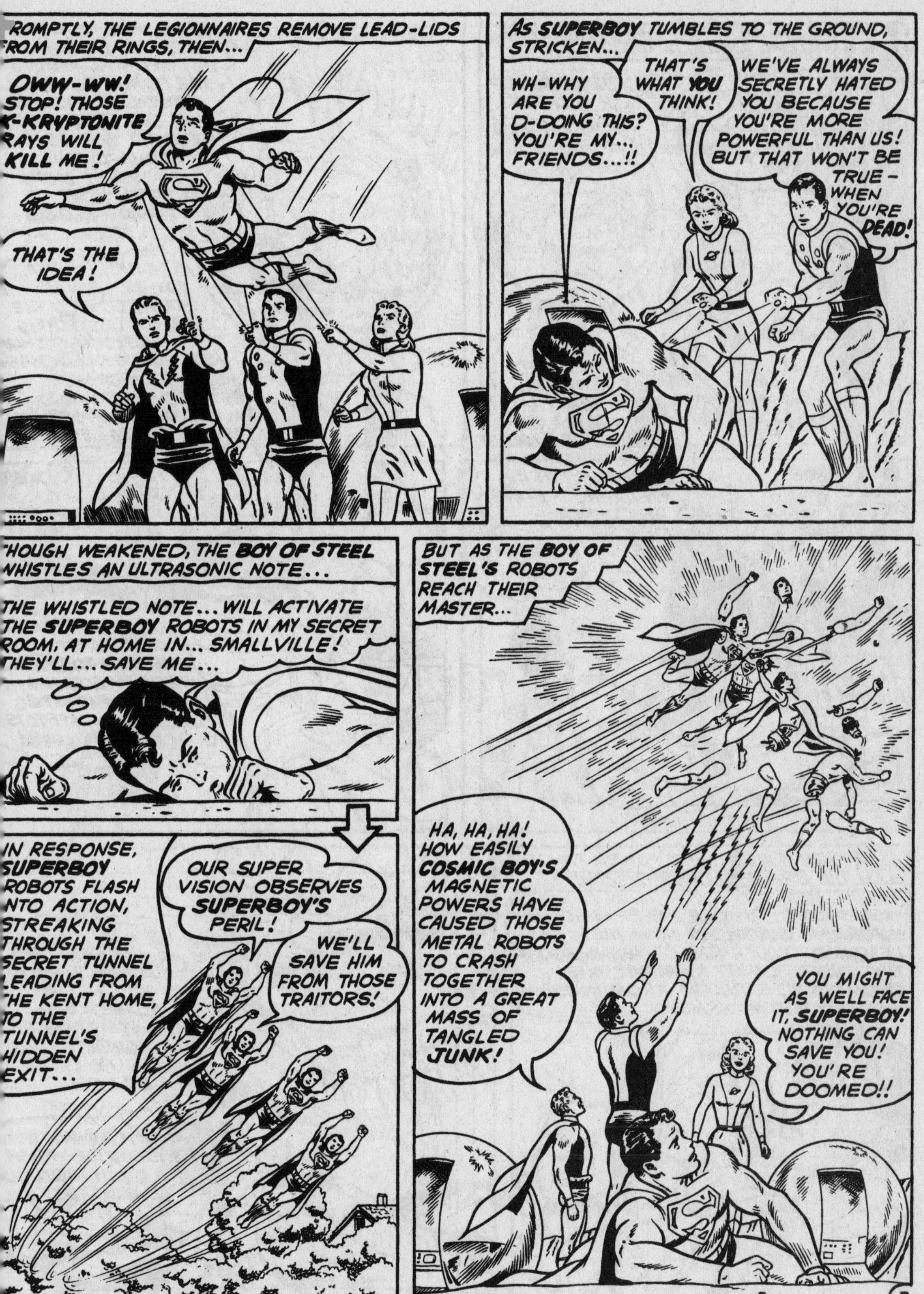
ROMPTLY, THE LEGIONNAIRES REMOVE LEAD-LIDS FROM THEIR RINGS, THEN...
OWW-WW! STOP! THOSE K-KRYPTONITE RAYS WILL KILL ME!
THAT'S THE IDEA!
AS SUPERBOY TUMBLES TO THE GROUND, STRICKEN...
WH-WHY ARE YOU D-DOING THIS? YOU'RE MY... FRIENDS...!!
THAT'S WHAT YOU THINK!
WE'VE ALWAYS SECRETLY HATED YOU BECAUSE YOU'RE MORE POWERFUL THAN US! BUT THAT WON'T BE TRUE-WHEN YOU'RE DEAD!
THOUGH WEAKENED, THE BOY OF STEEL WHISTLES AN ULTRASONIC NOTE...
THE WHISTLED NOTE... WILL ACTIVATE THE SUPERBOY ROBOTS IN MY SECRET ROOM, AT HOME IN... SMALLVILLE! THEY'LL... SAVE ME...
IN RESPONSE, SUPERBOY ROBOTS FLASH INTO ACTION, STREAKING THROUGH THE SECRET TUNNEL LEADING FROM THE KENT HOME, TO THE TUNNEL'S HIDDEN EXIT...
OUR SUPER VISION OBSERVES SUPERBOY'S PERIL!
WE'LL SAVE HIM FROM THOSE TRAITORS!
BUT AS THE BOY OF STEEL'S ROBOTS REACH THEIR MASTER...
HA, HA, HA! HOW EASILY COSMIC BOY'S MAGNETIC POWERS HAVE CAUSED THOSE METAL ROBOTS TO CRASH TOGETHER INTO A GREAT MASS OF TANGLED JUNK!
YOU MIGHT AS WELL FACE IT, SUPERBOY! NOTHING CAN SAVE YOU! YOU'RE DOOMED!!
7

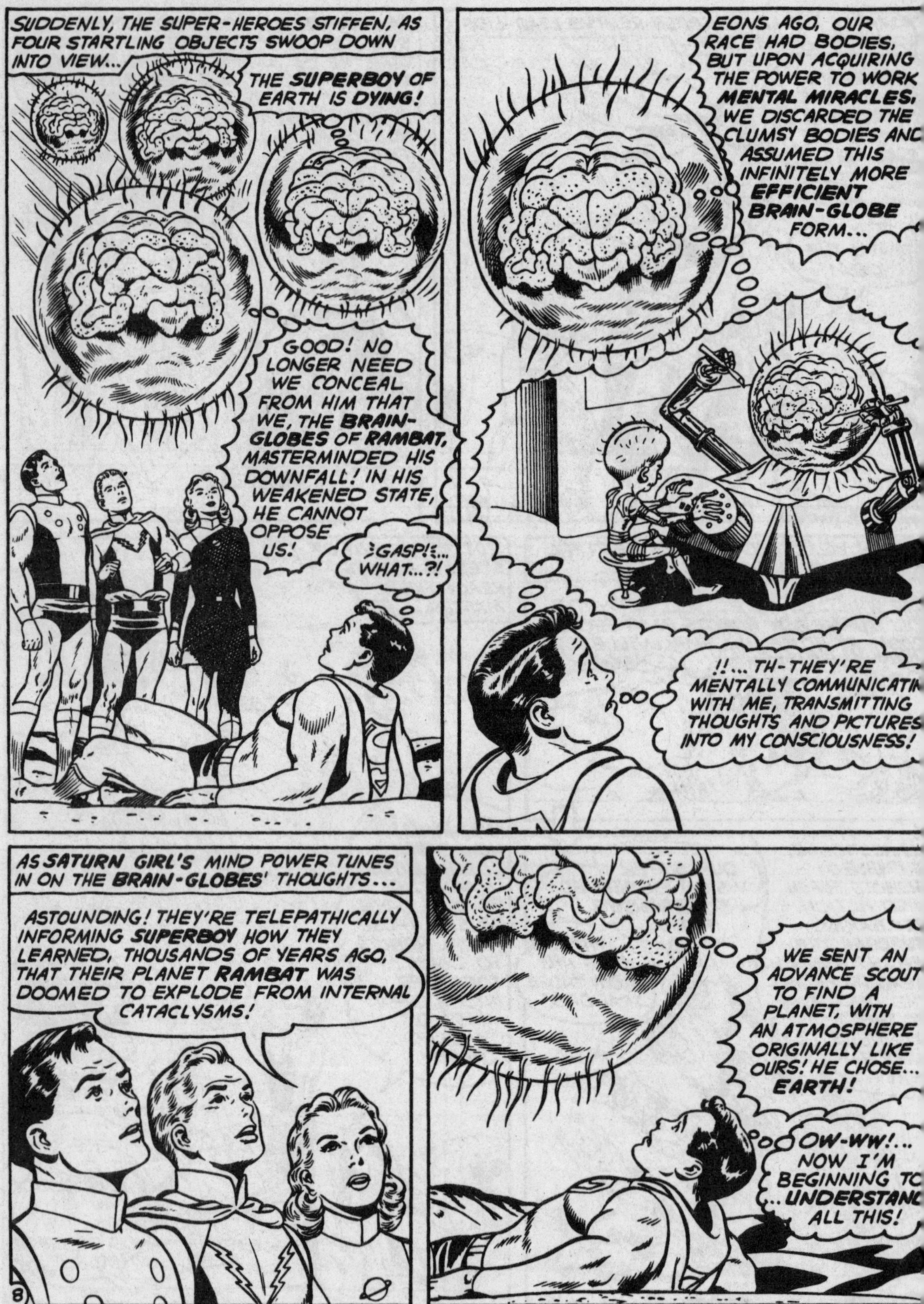
SUDDENLY, THE SUPER-HEROES STIFFEN, AS FOUR STARTLING OBJECTS SWOOP DOWN INTO VIEW...
THE SUPERBOY OF EARTH IS DYING!
GOOD! NO LONGER NEED WE CONCEAL FROM HIM THAT WE, THE BRAIN-GLOBES OF RAMBAT, MASTERMINDED HIS DOWNFALL! IN HIS WEAKENED STATE, HE CANNOT OPPOSE US!
GASP!... WHAT...?!
EONS AGO, OUR RACE HAD BODIES, BUT UPON ACQUIRING THE POWER TO WORK MENTAL MIRACLES, WE DISCARDED THE CLUMSY BODIES AND ASSUMED THIS INFINITELY MORE EFFICIENT BRAIN-GLOBE FORM...
!!... TH-THEY'RE MENTALLY COMMUNICATIN WITH ME, TRANSMITTING THOUGHTS AND PICTURES INTO MY CONSCIOUSNESS!
AS SATURN GIRL'S MIND POWER TUNES IN ON THE BRAIN-GLOBES' THOUGHTS...
ASTOUNDING! THEY'RE TELEPATHICALLY INFORMING SUPERBOY HOW THEY LEARNED, THOUSANDS OF YEARS AGO, THAT THEIR PLANET RAMBAT WAS DOOMED TO EXPLODE FROM INTERNAL CATACLYSMS!
8
WE SENT AN ADVANCE SCOUT TO FIND A PLANET, WITH AN ATMOSPHERE ORIGINALLY LIKE OURS! HE CHOSE... EARTH!
OW-WW!... NOW I'M BEGINNING TO ...UNDERSTAND ALL THIS!

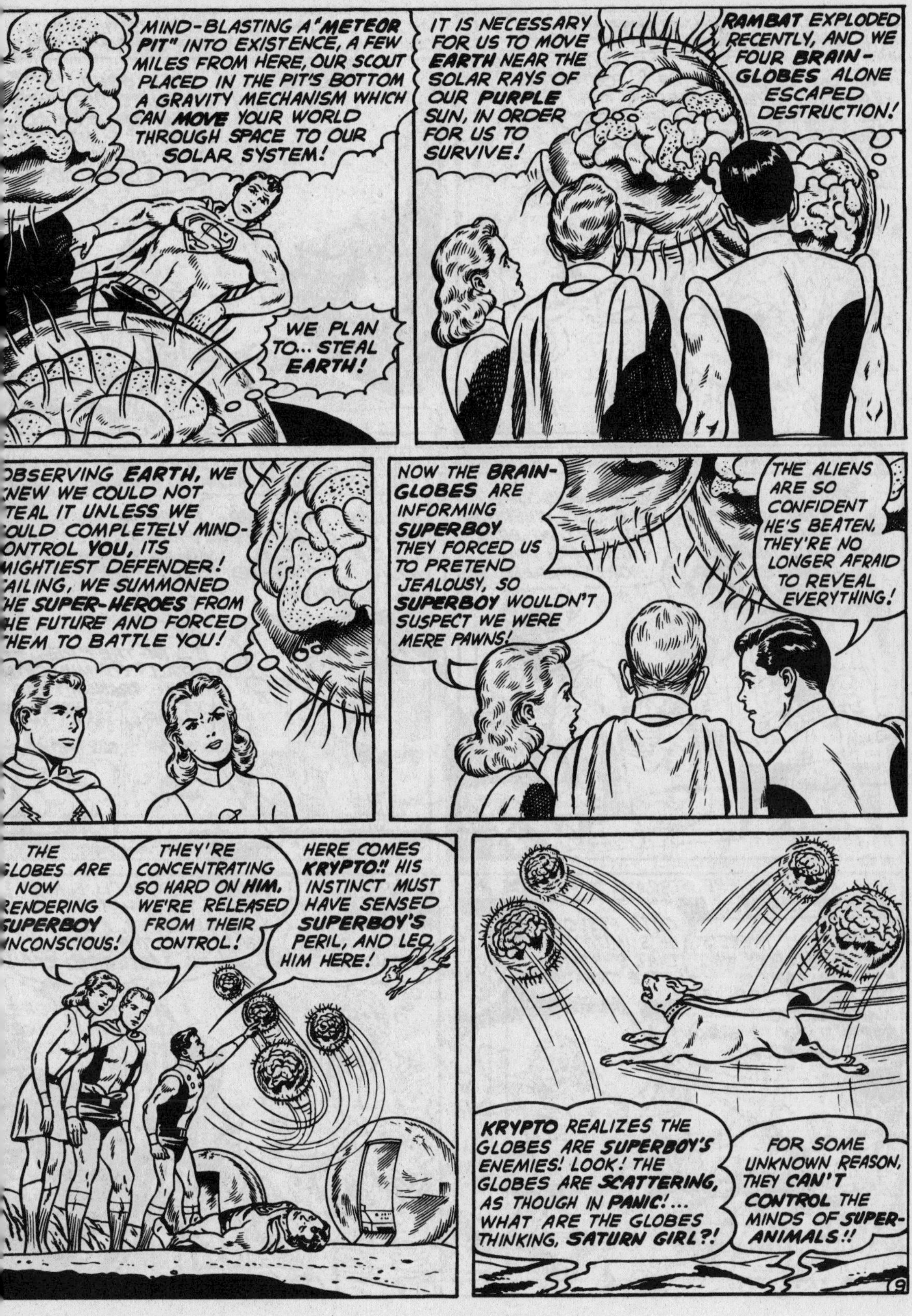
MIND-BLASTING A "METEOR PIT" INTO EXISTENCE, A FEW MILES FROM HERE, OUR SCOUT PLACED IN THE PIT'S BOTTOM A GRAVITY MECHANISM WHICH CAN MOVE YOUR WORLD THROUGH SPACE TO OUR SOLAR SYSTEM!
WE PLAN TO... STEAL EARTH!
IT IS NECESSARY FOR US TO MOVE EARTH NEAR THE SOLAR RAYS OF OUR PURPLE SUN, IN ORDER FOR US TO SURVIVE!
RAMBAT EXPLODED RECENTLY, AND WE FOUR BRAIN-GLOBES ALONE ESCAPED DESTRUCTION!
OBSERVING EARTH, WE KNEW WE COULD NOT STEAL IT UNLESS WE COULD COMPLETELY MIND-CONTROL YOU, ITS MIGHTIEST DEFENDER! FAILING, WE SUMMONED THE SUPER-HEROES FROM THE FUTURE AND FORCED THEM TO BATTLE YOU!
NOW THE BRAIN-GLOBES ARE INFORMING SUPERBOY THEY FORCED US TO PRETEND JEALOUSY, SO SUPERBOY WOULDN'T SUSPECT WE WERE MERE PAWNS!
THE ALIENS ARE SO CONFIDENT HE'S BEATEN, THEY'RE NO LONGER AFRAID TO REVEAL EVERYTHING!
THE GLOBES ARE NOW RENDERING SUPERBOY UNCONSCIOUS!
THEY'RE CONCENTRATING SO HARD ON HIM, WE'RE RELEASED FROM THEIR CONTROL!
HERE COMES KRYPTO!! HIS INSTINCT MUST HAVE SENSED SUPERBOY'S PERIL, AND LED HIM HERE!
KRYPTO REALIZES THE GLOBES ARE SUPERBOY'S ENEMIES! LOOK! THE GLOBES ARE SCATTERING, AS THOUGH IN PANIC!... WHAT ARE THE GLOBES THINKING, SATURN GIRL?!
FOR SOME UNKNOWN REASON, THEY CAN'T CONTROL THE MINDS OF SUPER-ANIMALS!!
9

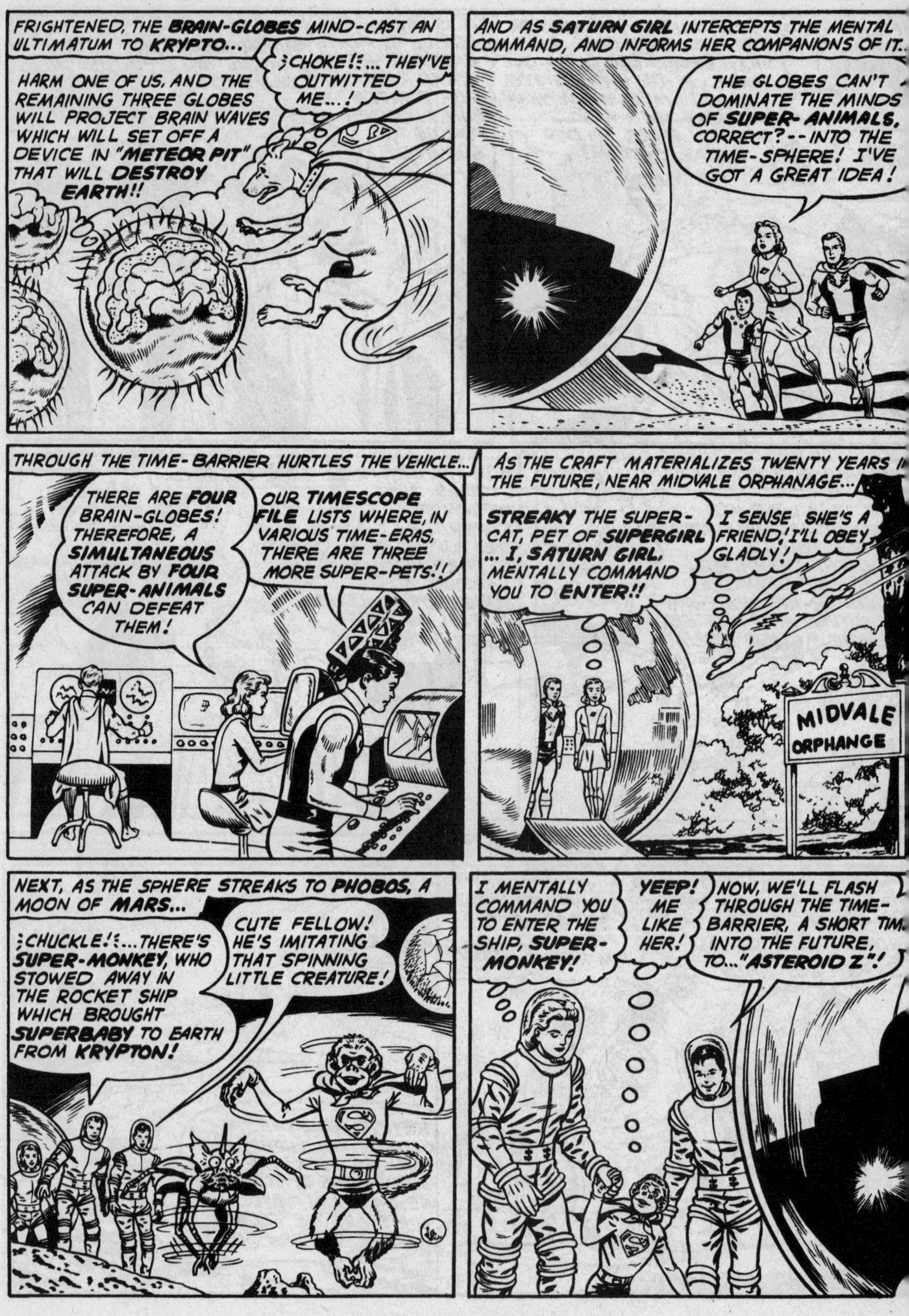
FRIGHTENED, THE BRAIN-GLOBES MIND-CAST AN ULTIMATUM TO KRYPTO...
;CHOKE!: ...THEY'VE OUTWITTED ME...!
HARM ONE OF US, AND THE REMAINING THREE GLOBES WILL PROJECT BRAIN WAVES WHICH WILL SET OFF A DEVICE IN "METEOR PIT" THAT WILL DESTROY EARTH!!
AND AS SATURN GIRL INTERCEPTS THE MENTAL COMMAND, AND INFORMS HER COMPANIONS OF IT...
THE GLOBES CAN'T DOMINATE THE MINDS OF SUPER-ANIMALS, CORRECT? --INTO THE TIME-SPHERE! I'VE GOT A GREAT IDEA!
THROUGH THE TIME-BARRIER HURTLES THE VEHICLE...
THERE ARE FOUR BRAIN-GLOBES! THEREFORE, A SIMULTANEOUS ATTACK BY FOUR SUPER-ANIMALS CAN DEFEAT THEM!
OUR TIMESCOPE FILE LISTS WHERE, IN VARIOUS TIME-ERAS, THERE ARE THREE MORE SUPER-PETS!!
AS THE CRAFT MATERIALIZES TWENTY YEARS IN THE FUTURE, NEAR MIDVALE ORPHANAGE...
STREAKY THE SUPER-CAT, PET OF SUPERGIRL ... I, SATURN GIRL, MENTALLY COMMAND YOU TO ENTER!!
I SENSE SHE'S A FRIEND, I'LL OBEY GLADLY!
MIDVALE ORPHANGE
NEXT, AS THE SPHERE STREAKS TO PHOBOS, A MOON OF MARS...
;CHUCKLE!: ...THERE'S SUPER-MONKEY, WHO STOWED AWAY IN THE ROCKET SHIP WHICH BROUGHT SUPERBABY TO EARTH FROM KRYPTON!
CUTE FELLOW! HE'S IMITATING THAT SPINNING LITTLE CREATURE!
I MENTALLY COMMAND YOU TO ENTER THE SHIP, SUPER-MONKEY!
YEEP! ME LIKE HER!
NOW, WE'LL FLASH THROUGH THE TIME-BARRIER, A SHORT TIME INTO THE FUTURE, TO..."ASTEROID Z"!

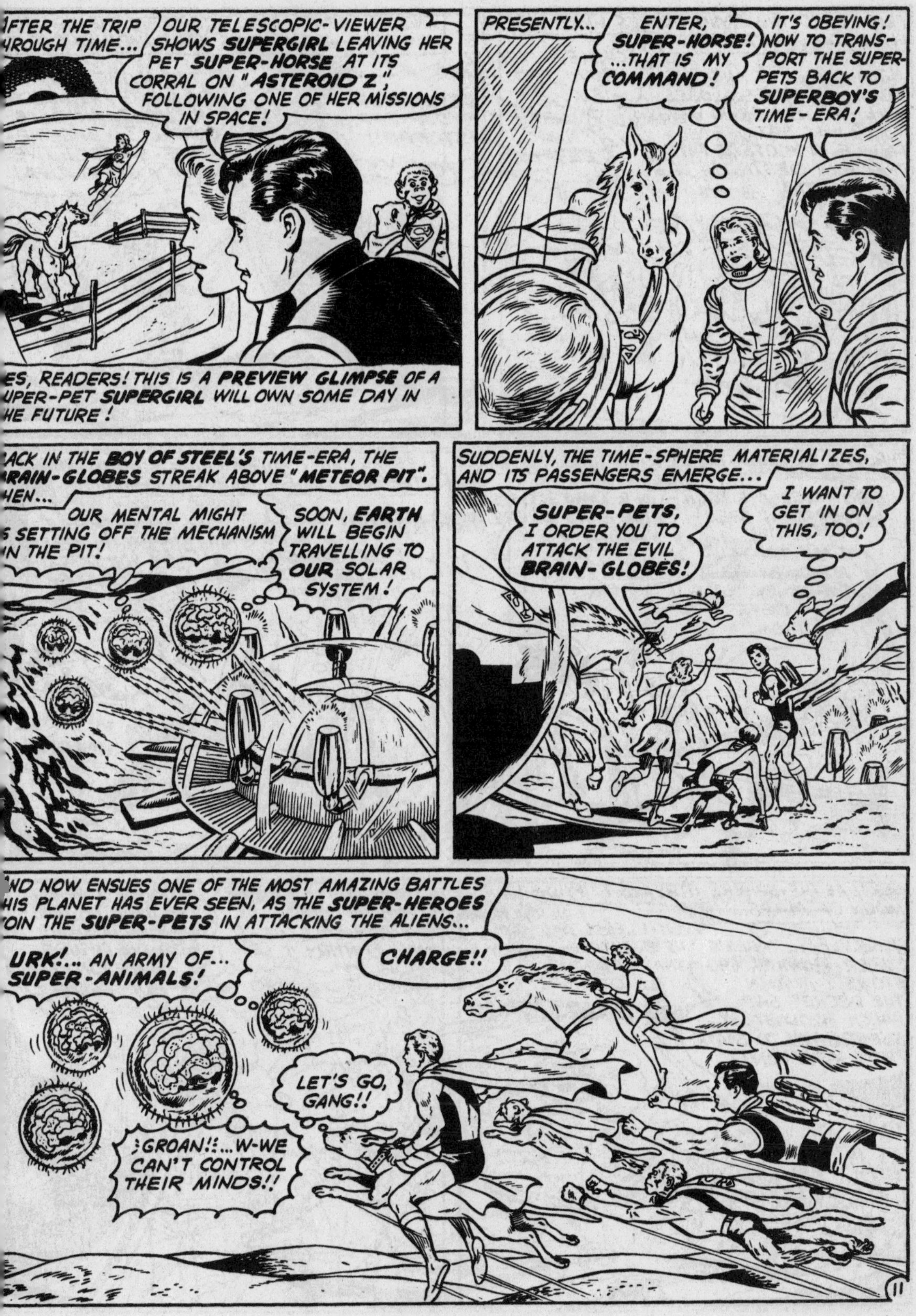
AFTER THE TRIP THROUGH TIME...
OUR TELESCOPIC-VIEWER SHOWS SUPERGIRL LEAVING HER PET SUPER-HORSE AT ITS CORRAL ON "ASTEROID Z", FOLLOWING ONE OF HER MISSIONS IN SPACE!
YES, READERS! THIS IS A PREVIEW GLIMPSE OF A SUPER-PET SUPERGIRL WILL OWN SOME DAY IN THE FUTURE!
PRESENTLY...
ENTER, SUPER-HORSE! ...THAT IS MY COMMAND!
IT'S OBEYING! NOW TO TRANSPORT THE SUPER-PETS BACK TO SUPERBOY'S TIME-ERA!
BACK IN THE BOY OF STEEL'S TIME-ERA, THE BRAIN-GLOBES STREAK ABOVE "METEOR PIT". THEN...
OUR MENTAL MIGHT IS SETTING OFF THE MECHANISM IN THE PIT!
SOON, EARTH WILL BEGIN TRAVELLING TO OUR SOLAR SYSTEM!
SUDDENLY, THE TIME-SPHERE MATERIALIZES, AND ITS PASSENGERS EMERGE...
SUPER-PETS, I ORDER YOU TO ATTACK THE EVIL BRAIN-GLOBES!
I WANT TO GET IN ON THIS, TOO!
AND NOW ENSUES ONE OF THE MOST AMAZING BATTLES THIS PLANET HAS EVER SEEN, AS THE SUPER-HEROES JOIN THE SUPER-PETS IN ATTACKING THE ALIENS...
URK!... AN ARMY OF... SUPER-ANIMALS!
CHARGE!!
LET'S GO, GANG!!
GROAN!!... W-WE CAN'T CONTROL THEIR MINDS!!
11

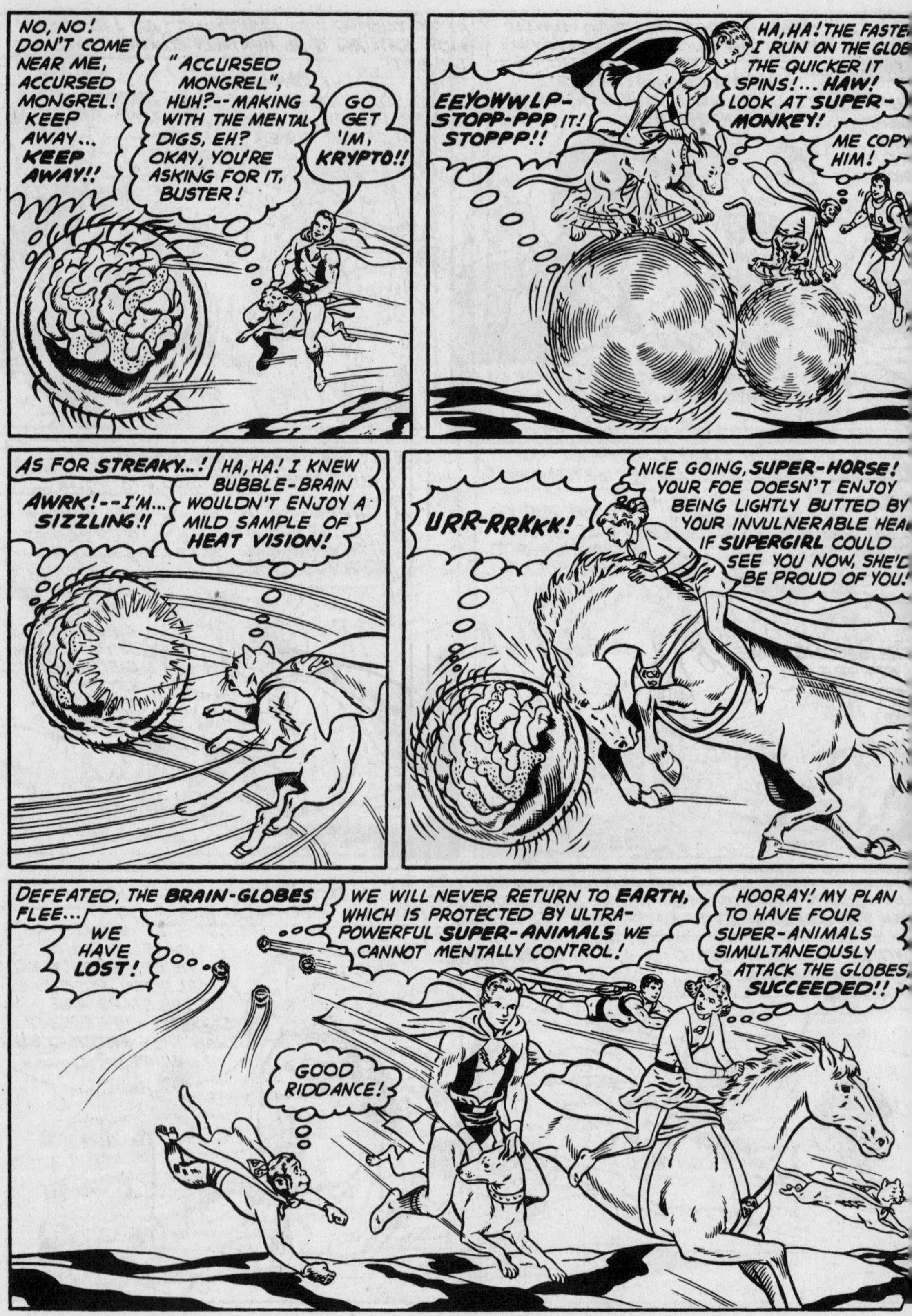
NO, NO! DON'T COME NEAR ME, ACCURSED MONGREL! KEEP AWAY... KEEP AWAY!!
"ACCURSED MONGREL", HUH?--MAKING WITH THE MENTAL DIGS, EH? OKAY, YOU'RE ASKING FOR IT, BUSTER!
GO GET 'IM, KRYPTO!!
EEYOWWLP-STOPP-PPP IT! STOPPP!!
HA, HA! THE FASTE I RUN ON THE GLOB THE QUICKER IT SPINS!... HAW! LOOK AT SUPER-MONKEY!
ME COPY HIM!
AS FOR STREAKY...!
AWRK!--I'M... SIZZLING!!
HA, HA! I KNEW BUBBLE-BRAIN WOULDN'T ENJOY A MILD SAMPLE OF HEAT VISION!
URR-RRKKK!
NICE GOING, SUPER-HORSE! YOUR FOE DOESN'T ENJOY BEING LIGHTLY BUTTED BY YOUR INVULNERABLE HEA IF SUPERGIRL COULD SEE YOU NOW, SHE'D BE PROUD OF YOU!
DEFEATED, THE BRAIN-GLOBES FLEE...
WE HAVE LOST!
WE WILL NEVER RETURN TO EARTH, WHICH IS PROTECTED BY ULTRA-POWERFUL SUPER-ANIMALS WE CANNOT MENTALLY CONTROL!
HOORAY! MY PLAN TO HAVE FOUR SUPER-ANIMALS SIMULTANEOUSLY ATTACK THE GLOBES, SUCCEEDED!!
GOOD RIDDANCE!

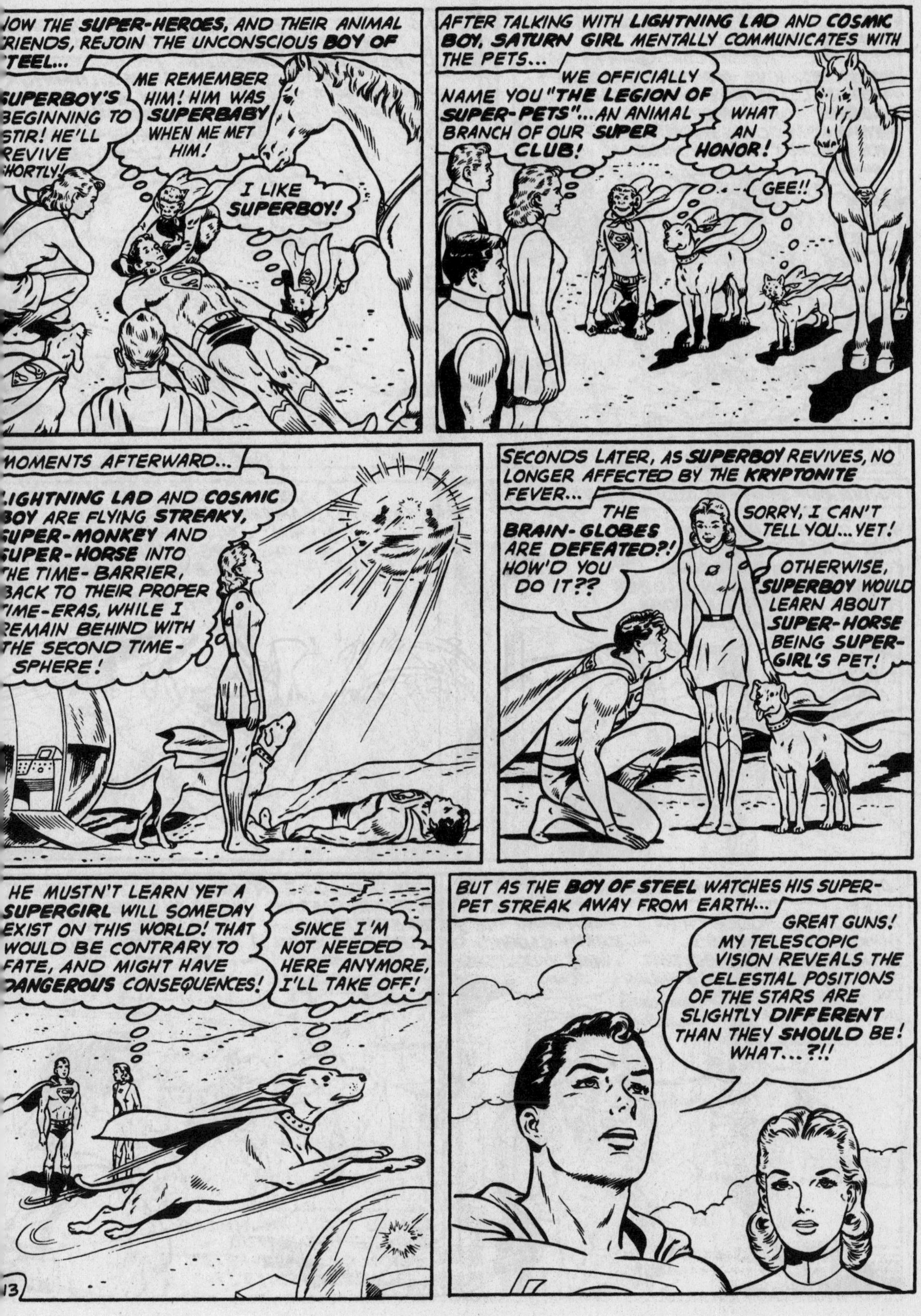
NOW THE SUPER-HEROES, AND THEIR ANIMAL FRIENDS, REJOIN THE UNCONSCIOUS BOY OF STEEL...
SUPERBOY'S BEGINNING TO STIR! HE'LL REVIVE SHORTLY!
ME REMEMBER HIM! HIM WAS SUPERBABY WHEN ME MET HIM!
I LIKE SUPERBOY!
AFTER TALKING WITH LIGHTNING LAD AND COSMIC BOY, SATURN GIRL MENTALLY COMMUNICATES WITH THE PETS...
WE OFFICIALLY NAME YOU "THE LEGION OF SUPER-PETS"...AN ANIMAL BRANCH OF OUR SUPER CLUB!
WHAT AN HONOR!
GEE!!
MOMENTS AFTERWARD...
LIGHTNING LAD AND COSMIC BOY ARE FLYING STREAKY, SUPER-MONKEY AND SUPER-HORSE INTO THE TIME-BARRIER, BACK TO THEIR PROPER TIME-ERAS, WHILE I REMAIN BEHIND WITH THE SECOND TIME-SPHERE!
SECONDS LATER, AS SUPERBOY REVIVES, NO LONGER AFFECTED BY THE KRYPTONITE FEVER...
THE BRAIN-GLOBES ARE DEFEATED?! HOW'D YOU DO IT??
SORRY, I CAN'T TELL YOU...YET!
OTHERWISE, SUPERBOY WOULD LEARN ABOUT SUPER-HORSE BEING SUPER-GIRL'S PET!
HE MUSTN'T LEARN YET A SUPERGIRL WILL SOMEDAY EXIST ON THIS WORLD! THAT WOULD BE CONTRARY TO FATE, AND MIGHT HAVE DANGEROUS CONSEQUENCES!
SINCE I'M NOT NEEDED HERE ANYMORE, I'LL TAKE OFF!
13
BUT AS THE BOY OF STEEL WATCHES HIS SUPER-PET STREAK AWAY FROM EARTH...
GREAT GUNS! MY TELESCOPIC VISION REVEALS THE CELESTIAL POSITIONS OF THE STARS ARE SLIGHTLY DIFFERENT THAN THEY SHOULD BE! WHAT...?!!

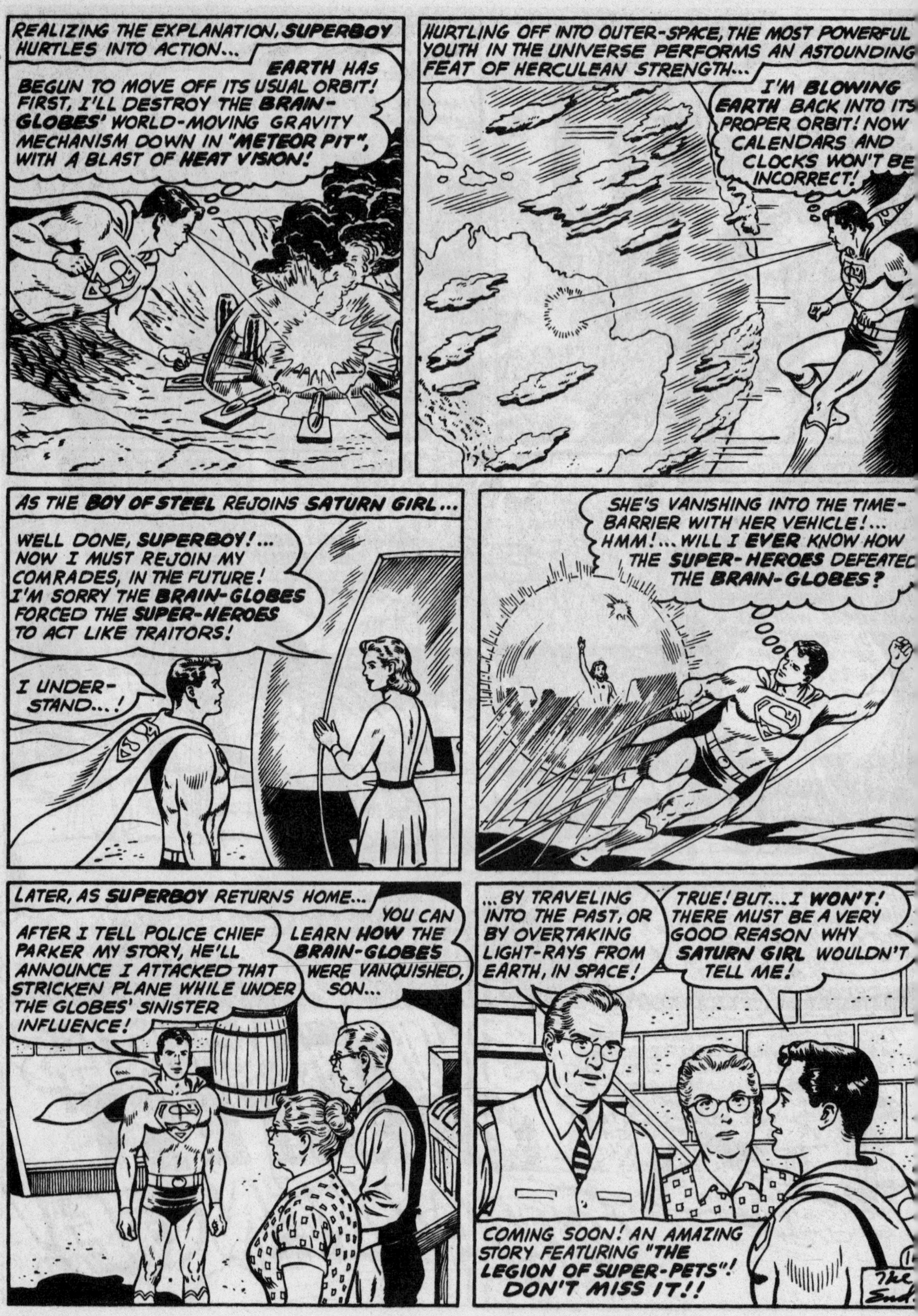
REALIZING THE EXPLANATION, SUPERBOY HURTLES INTO ACTION...
EARTH HAS BEGUN TO MOVE OFF ITS USUAL ORBIT! FIRST, I'LL DESTROY THE BRAIN-GLOBES' WORLD-MOVING GRAVITY MECHANISM DOWN IN "METEOR PIT", WITH A BLAST OF HEAT VISION!
HURTLING OFF INTO OUTER-SPACE, THE MOST POWERFUL YOUTH IN THE UNIVERSE PERFORMS AN ASTOUNDING FEAT OF HERCULEAN STRENGTH...
I'M BLOWING EARTH BACK INTO ITS PROPER ORBIT! NOW CALENDARS AND CLOCKS WON'T BE INCORRECT!
AS THE BOY OF STEEL REJOINS SATURN GIRL...
WELL DONE, SUPERBOY!... NOW I MUST REJOIN MY COMRADES, IN THE FUTURE! I'M SORRY THE BRAIN-GLOBES FORCED THE SUPER-HEROES TO ACT LIKE TRAITORS!
I UNDERSTAND...!
SHE'S VANISHING INTO THE TIME-BARRIER WITH HER VEHICLE!... HMM!... WILL I EVER KNOW HOW THE SUPER-HEROES DEFEATED THE BRAIN-GLOBES?
LATER, AS SUPERBOY RETURNS HOME...
AFTER I TELL POLICE CHIEF PARKER MY STORY, HE'LL ANNOUNCE I ATTACKED THAT STRICKEN PLANE WHILE UNDER THE GLOBES' SINISTER INFLUENCE!
YOU CAN LEARN HOW THE BRAIN-GLOBES WERE VANQUISHED, SON...
...BY TRAVELING INTO THE PAST, OR BY OVERTAKING LIGHT-RAYS FROM EARTH, IN SPACE!
TRUE! BUT...I WON'T! THERE MUST BE A VERY GOOD REASON WHY SATURN GIRL WOULDN'T TELL ME!
COMING SOON! AN AMAZING STORY FEATURING "THE LEGION OF SUPER-PETS"! DON'T MISS IT!!
The End

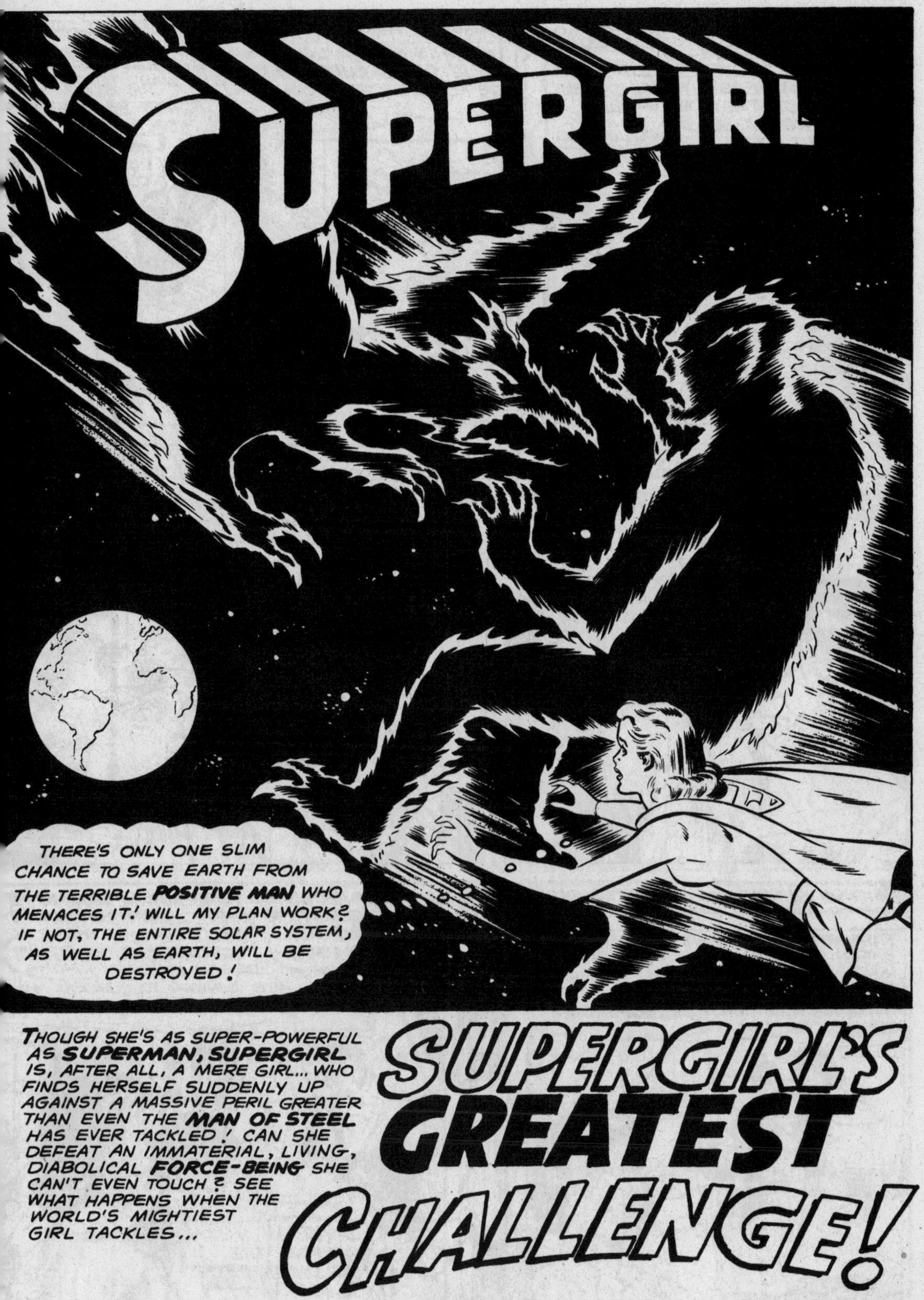
SUPERGIRL
THERE'S ONLY ONE SLIM CHANCE TO SAVE EARTH FROM THE TERRIBLE POSITIVE MAN WHO MENACES IT! WILL MY PLAN WORK? IF NOT, THE ENTIRE SOLAR SYSTEM, AS WELL AS EARTH, WILL BE DESTROYED!
THOUGH SHE'S AS SUPER-POWERFUL AS SUPERMAN, SUPERGIRL IS, AFTER ALL, A MERE GIRL... WHO FINDS HERSELF SUDDENLY UP AGAINST A MASSIVE PERIL GREATER THAN EVEN THE MAN OF STEEL HAS EVER TACKLED! CAN SHE DEFEAT AN IMMATERIAL, LIVING, DIABOLICAL FORCE-BEING SHE CAN'T EVEN TOUCH? SEE WHAT HAPPENS WHEN THE WORLD'S MIGHTIEST GIRL TACKLES...
SUPERGIRL'S GREATEST CHALLENGE!

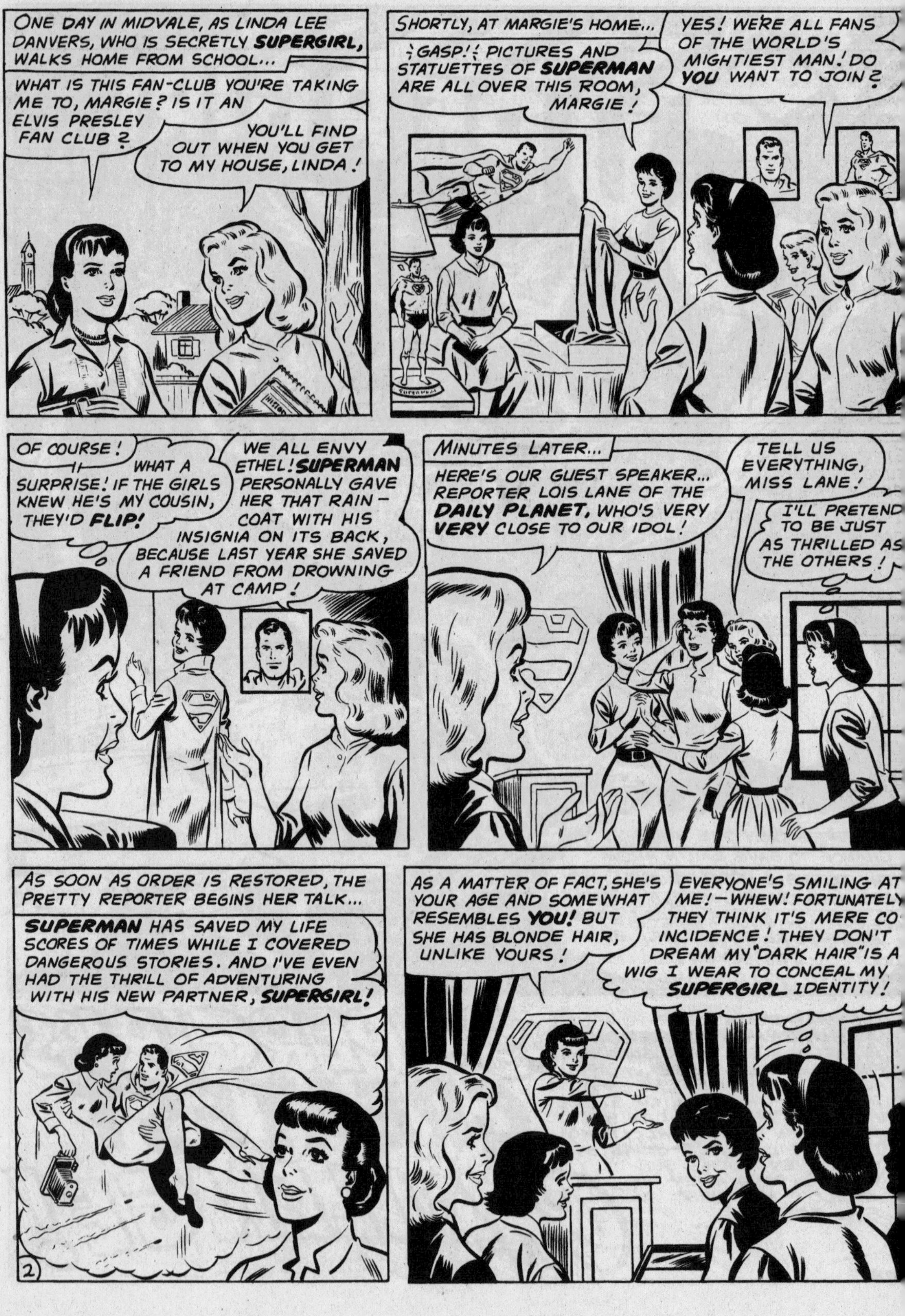
ONE DAY IN MIDVALE, AS LINDA LEE DANVERS, WHO IS SECRETLY SUPERGIRL, WALKS HOME FROM SCHOOL...
WHAT IS THIS FAN-CLUB YOU'RE TAKING ME TO, MARGIE? IS IT AN ELVIS PRESLEY FAN CLUB?
YOU'LL FIND OUT WHEN YOU GET TO MY HOUSE, LINDA!
SHORTLY, AT MARGIE'S HOME...
GASP! PICTURES AND STATUETTES OF SUPERMAN ARE ALL OVER THIS ROOM, MARGIE!
YES! WE'RE ALL FANS OF THE WORLD'S MIGHTIEST MAN! DO YOU WANT TO JOIN?
OF COURSE! WHAT A SURPRISE! IF THE GIRLS KNEW HE'S MY COUSIN, THEY'D FLIP!
WE ALL ENVY ETHEL! SUPERMAN PERSONALLY GAVE HER THAT RAIN-COAT WITH HIS INSIGNIA ON ITS BACK, BECAUSE LAST YEAR SHE SAVED A FRIEND FROM DROWNING AT CAMP!
MINUTES LATER...
HERE'S OUR GUEST SPEAKER... REPORTER LOIS LANE OF THE DAILY PLANET, WHO'S VERY VERY CLOSE TO OUR IDOL!
TELL US EVERYTHING, MISS LANE!
I'LL PRETEND TO BE JUST AS THRILLED AS THE OTHERS!
AS SOON AS ORDER IS RESTORED, THE PRETTY REPORTER BEGINS HER TALK...
SUPERMAN HAS SAVED MY LIFE SCORES OF TIMES WHILE I COVERED DANGEROUS STORIES. AND I'VE EVEN HAD THE THRILL OF ADVENTURING WITH HIS NEW PARTNER, SUPERGIRL!
2
AS A MATTER OF FACT, SHE'S YOUR AGE AND SOMEWHAT RESEMBLES YOU! BUT SHE HAS BLONDE HAIR, UNLIKE YOURS!
EVERYONE'S SMILING AT ME! —WHEW! FORTUNATELY THEY THINK IT'S MERE CO-INCIDENCE! THEY DON'T DREAM MY "DARK HAIR" IS A WIG I WEAR TO CONCEAL MY SUPERGIRL IDENTITY!

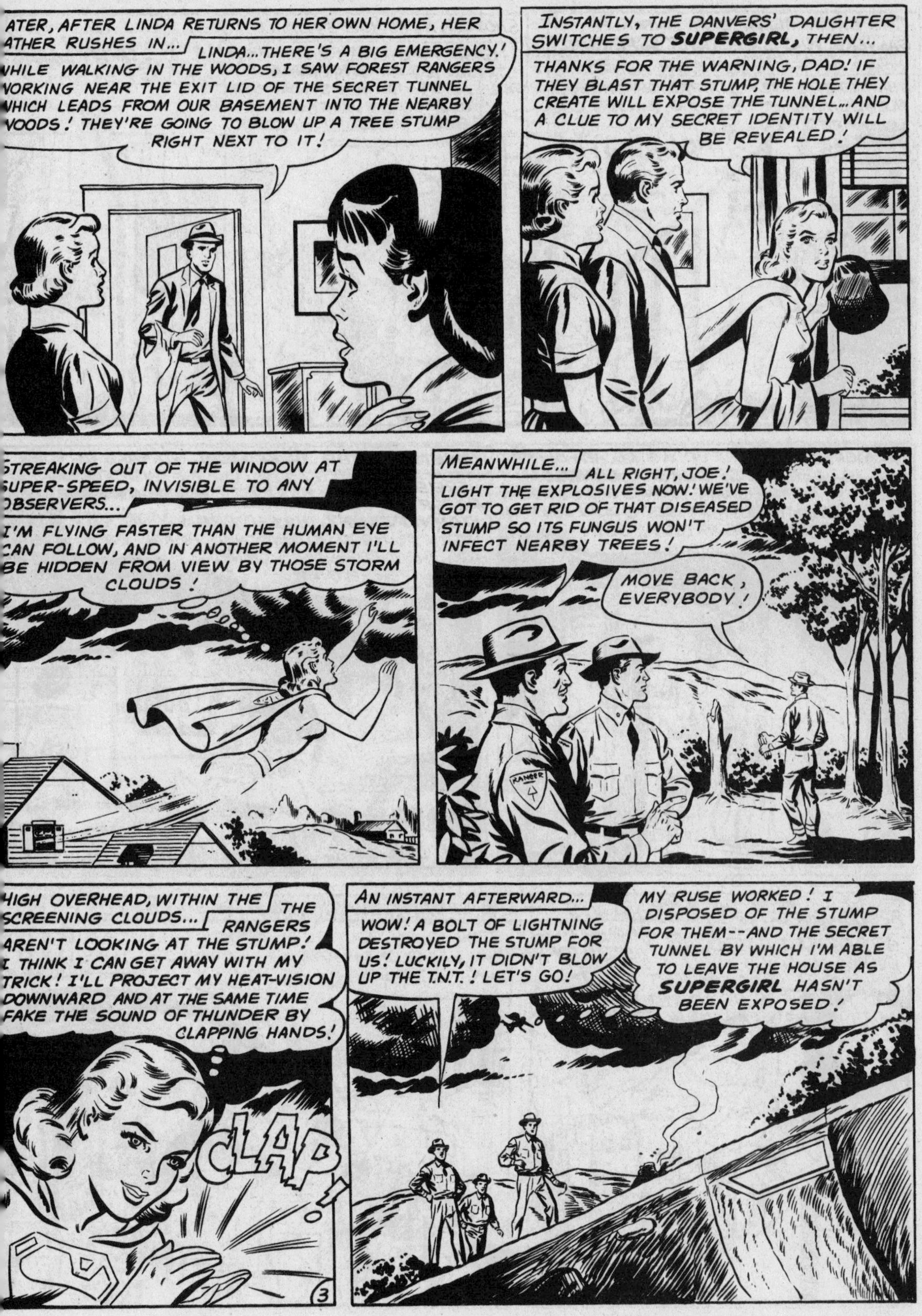
ATER, AFTER LINDA RETURNS TO HER OWN HOME, HER ATHER RUSHES IN...
LINDA... THERE'S A BIG EMERGENCY! WHILE WALKING IN THE WOODS, I SAW FOREST RANGERS WORKING NEAR THE EXIT LID OF THE SECRET TUNNEL WHICH LEADS FROM OUR BASEMENT INTO THE NEARBY WOODS! THEY'RE GOING TO BLOW UP A TREE STUMP RIGHT NEXT TO IT!
INSTANTLY, THE DANVERS' DAUGHTER SWITCHES TO SUPERGIRL, THEN...
THANKS FOR THE WARNING, DAD! IF THEY BLAST THAT STUMP, THE HOLE THEY CREATE WILL EXPOSE THE TUNNEL... AND A CLUE TO MY SECRET IDENTITY WILL BE REVEALED!
STREAKING OUT OF THE WINDOW AT SUPER-SPEED, INVISIBLE TO ANY OBSERVERS...
I'M FLYING FASTER THAN THE HUMAN EYE CAN FOLLOW, AND IN ANOTHER MOMENT I'LL BE HIDDEN FROM VIEW BY THOSE STORM CLOUDS!
MEANWHILE...
ALL RIGHT, JOE! LIGHT THE EXPLOSIVES NOW! WE'VE GOT TO GET RID OF THAT DISEASED STUMP SO ITS FUNGUS WON'T INFECT NEARBY TREES!
MOVE BACK, EVERYBODY!
RANGER
HIGH OVERHEAD, WITHIN THE SCREENING CLOUDS...
THE RANGERS AREN'T LOOKING AT THE STUMP! I THINK I CAN GET AWAY WITH MY TRICK! I'LL PROJECT MY HEAT-VISION DOWNWARD AND AT THE SAME TIME FAKE THE SOUND OF THUNDER BY CLAPPING HANDS!
CLAP!
3
AN INSTANT AFTERWARD...
WOW! A BOLT OF LIGHTNING DESTROYED THE STUMP FOR US! LUCKILY, IT DIDN'T BLOW UP THE T.N.T.! LET'S GO!
MY RUSE WORKED! I DISPOSED OF THE STUMP FOR THEM--AND THE SECRET TUNNEL BY WHICH I'M ABLE TO LEAVE THE HOUSE AS SUPERGIRL HASN'T BEEN EXPOSED!

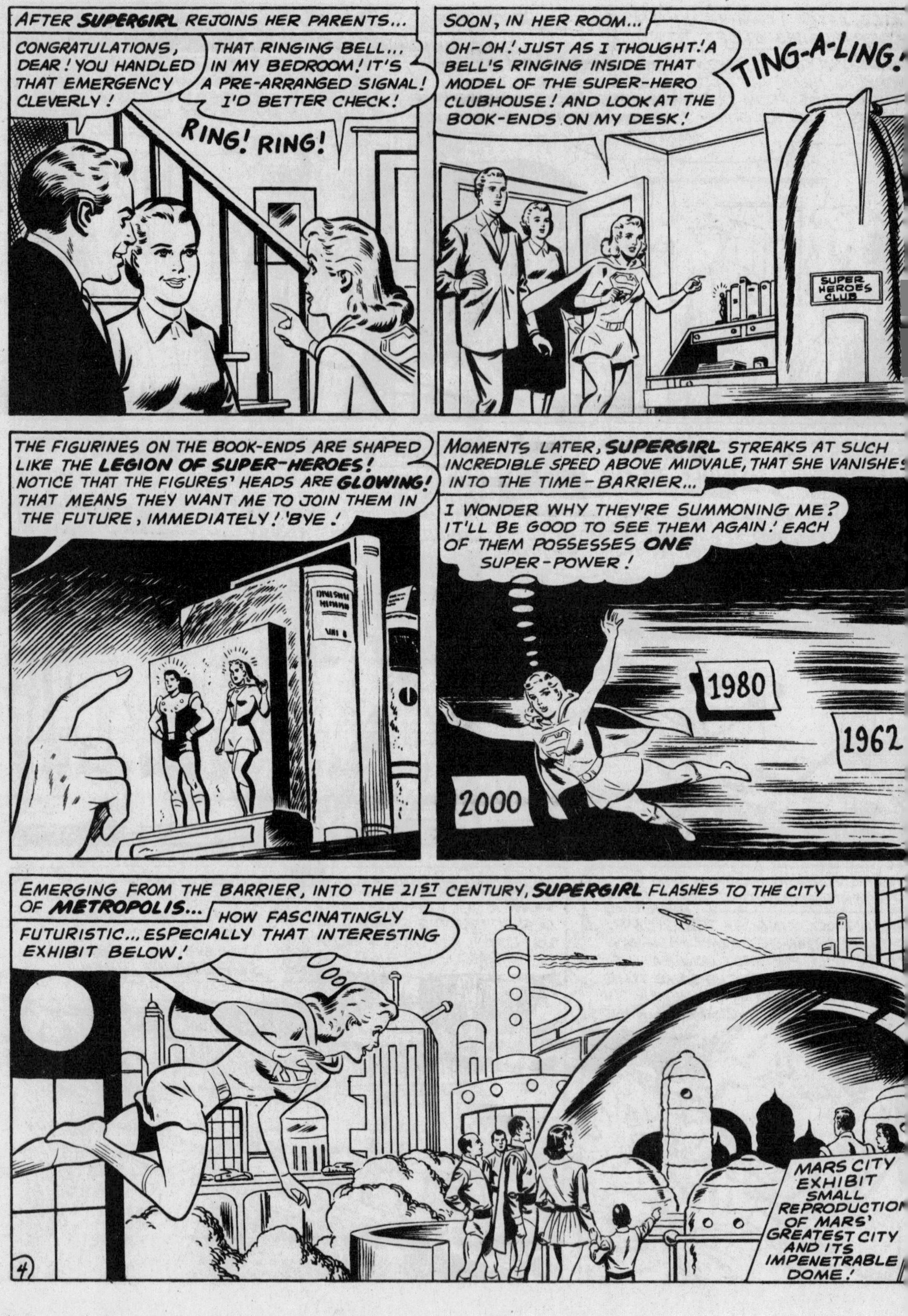
AFTER SUPERGIRL REJOINS HER PARENTS...
CONGRATULATIONS, DEAR! YOU HANDLED THAT EMERGENCY CLEVERLY!
THAT RINGING BELL... IN MY BEDROOM! IT'S A PRE-ARRANGED SIGNAL! I'D BETTER CHECK!
RING! RING!
SOON, IN HER ROOM...
OH-OH! JUST AS I THOUGHT! A BELL'S RINGING INSIDE THAT MODEL OF THE SUPER-HERO CLUBHOUSE! AND LOOK AT THE BOOK-ENDS ON MY DESK!
TING-A-LING!
SUPER HEROES CLUB
THE FIGURINES ON THE BOOK-ENDS ARE SHAPED LIKE THE LEGION OF SUPER-HEROES! NOTICE THAT THE FIGURES' HEADS ARE GLOWING! THAT MEANS THEY WANT ME TO JOIN THEM IN THE FUTURE, IMMEDIATELY! 'BYE!
MOMENTS LATER, SUPERGIRL STREAKS AT SUCH INCREDIBLE SPEED ABOVE MIDVALE, THAT SHE VANISHES INTO THE TIME-BARRIER...
I WONDER WHY THEY'RE SUMMONING ME? IT'LL BE GOOD TO SEE THEM AGAIN! EACH OF THEM POSSESSES ONE SUPER-POWER!
1980
1962
2000
EMERGING FROM THE BARRIER, INTO THE 21ST CENTURY, SUPERGIRL FLASHES TO THE CITY OF METROPOLIS...
HOW FASCINATINGLY FUTURISTIC... ESPECIALLY THAT INTERESTING EXHIBIT BELOW!
MARS CITY EXHIBIT SMALL REPRODUCTION OF MARS' GREATEST CITY AND ITS IMPENETRABLE DOME!
4

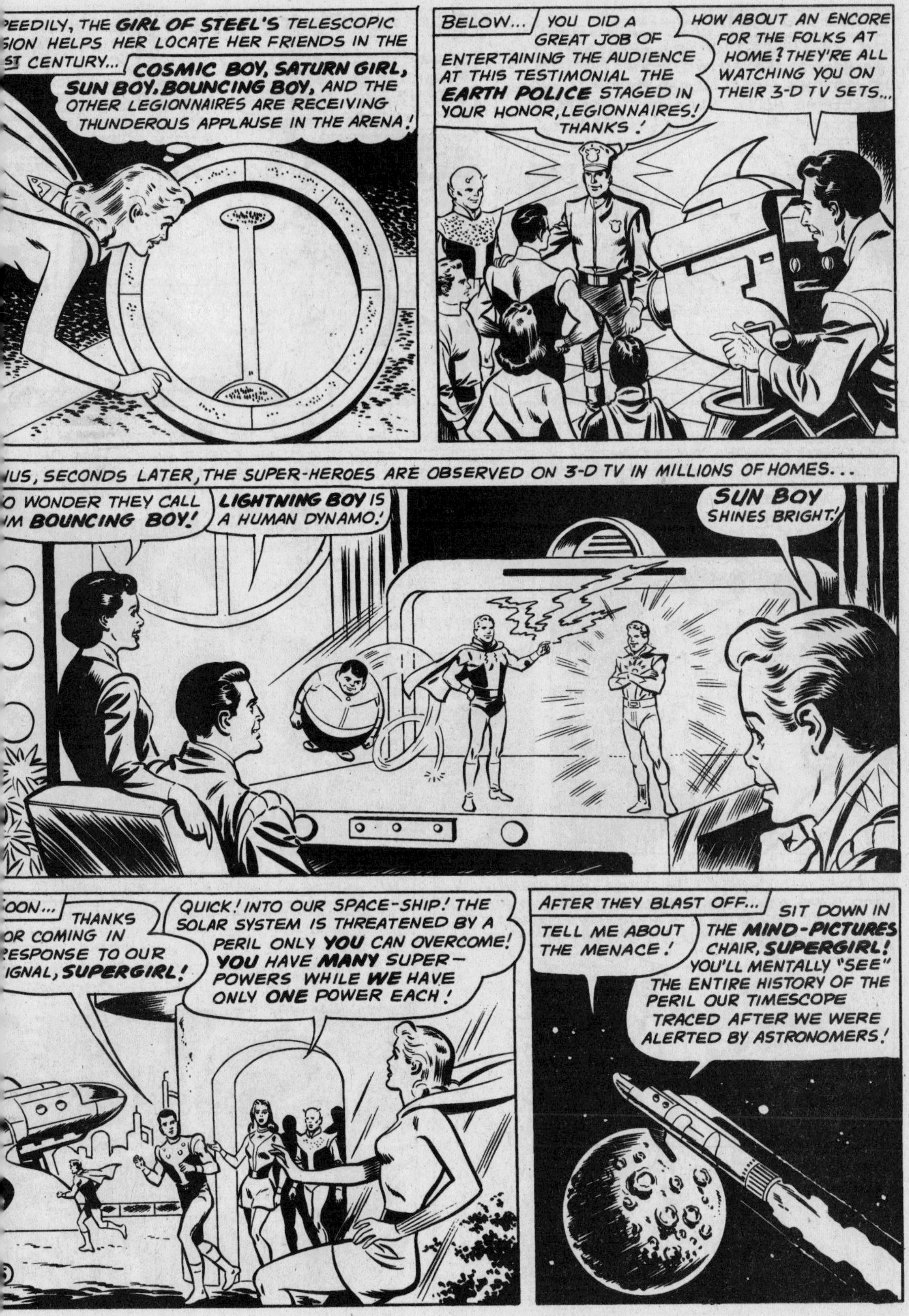
PEEDILY, THE GIRL OF STEEL'S TELESCOPIC SION HELPS HER LOCATE HER FRIENDS IN THE ST CENTURY...
COSMIC BOY, SATURN GIRL, SUN BOY, BOUNCING BOY, AND THE OTHER LEGIONNAIRES ARE RECEIVING THUNDEROUS APPLAUSE IN THE ARENA!
BELOW...
YOU DID A GREAT JOB OF ENTERTAINING THE AUDIENCE AT THIS TESTIMONIAL THE EARTH POLICE STAGED IN YOUR HONOR, LEGIONNAIRES!
THANKS!
HOW ABOUT AN ENCORE FOR THE FOLKS AT HOME? THEY'RE ALL WATCHING YOU ON THEIR 3-D TV SETS...
HUS, SECONDS LATER, THE SUPER-HEROES ARE OBSERVED ON 3-D TV IN MILLIONS OF HOMES...
O WONDER THEY CALL IM BOUNCING BOY!
LIGHTNING BOY IS A HUMAN DYNAMO!
SUN BOY SHINES BRIGHT!
OON...
THANKS OR COMING IN RESPONSE TO OUR IGNAL, SUPERGIRL!
QUICK! INTO OUR SPACE-SHIP! THE SOLAR SYSTEM IS THREATENED BY A PERIL ONLY YOU CAN OVERCOME! YOU HAVE MANY SUPER-POWERS WHILE WE HAVE ONLY ONE POWER EACH!
AFTER THEY BLAST OFF...
TELL ME ABOUT THE MENACE!
SIT DOWN IN THE MIND-PICTURES CHAIR, SUPERGIRL! YOU'LL MENTALLY "SEE" THE ENTIRE HISTORY OF THE PERIL OUR TIMESCOPE TRACED AFTER WE WERE ALERTED BY ASTRONOMERS!

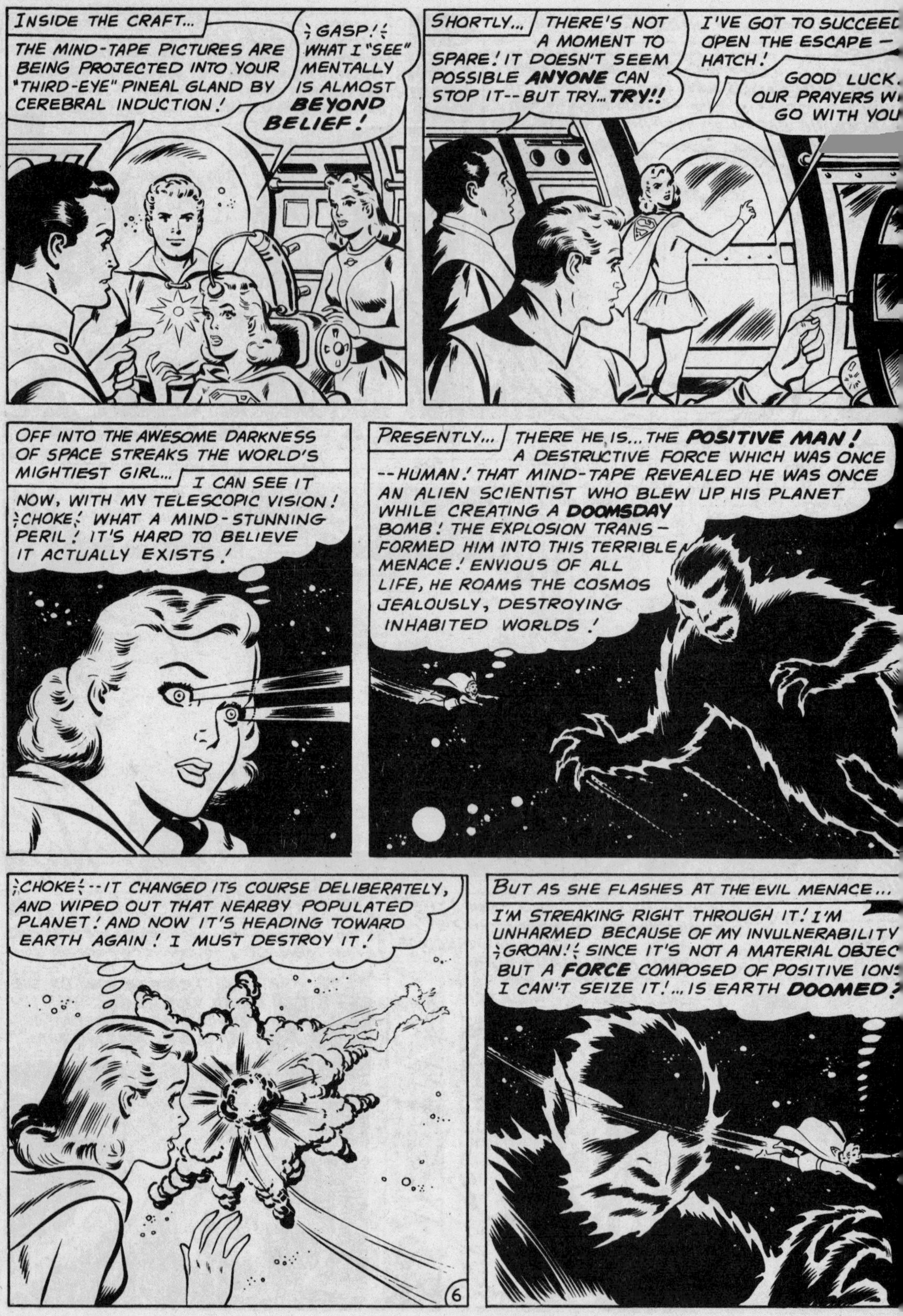
INSIDE THE CRAFT...
THE MIND-TAPE PICTURES ARE BEING PROJECTED INTO YOUR "THIRD-EYE" PINEAL GLAND BY CEREBRAL INDUCTION!
GASP! WHAT I "SEE" MENTALLY IS ALMOST BEYOND BELIEF!
SHORTLY...
THERE'S NOT A MOMENT TO SPARE! IT DOESN'T SEEM POSSIBLE ANYONE CAN STOP IT--BUT TRY...TRY!!
I'VE GOT TO SUCCEED OPEN THE ESCAPE-HATCH!
GOOD LUCK. OUR PRAYERS W GO WITH YOU
OFF INTO THE AWESOME DARKNESS OF SPACE STREAKS THE WORLD'S MIGHTIEST GIRL...
I CAN SEE IT NOW, WITH MY TELESCOPIC VISION! CHOKE! WHAT A MIND-STUNNING PERIL! IT'S HARD TO BELIEVE IT ACTUALLY EXISTS!
PRESENTLY...
THERE HE IS...THE POSITIVE MAN! A DESTRUCTIVE FORCE WHICH WAS ONCE --HUMAN! THAT MIND-TAPE REVEALED HE WAS ONCE AN ALIEN SCIENTIST WHO BLEW UP HIS PLANET WHILE CREATING A DOOMSDAY BOMB! THE EXPLOSION TRANS-FORMED HIM INTO THIS TERRIBLE MENACE! ENVIOUS OF ALL LIFE, HE ROAMS THE COSMOS JEALOUSLY, DESTROYING INHABITED WORLDS!
CHOKE--IT CHANGED ITS COURSE DELIBERATELY, AND WIPED OUT THAT NEARBY POPULATED PLANET! AND NOW IT'S HEADING TOWARD EARTH AGAIN! I MUST DESTROY IT!
6
BUT AS SHE FLASHES AT THE EVIL MENACE...
I'M STREAKING RIGHT THROUGH IT! I'M UNHARMED BECAUSE OF MY INVULNERABILITY GROAN! SINCE IT'S NOT A MATERIAL OBJEC BUT A FORCE COMPOSED OF POSITIVE IONS I CAN'T SEIZE IT!...IS EARTH DOOMED?

SECONDS AFTERWARD, INSIDE THE SPACESHIP...

SUPERGIRL'S FLYING OFF! SINCE SHE COULDN'T HARM THE POSITIVE MAN, HAS SHE GIVEN UP HOPE? IS SHE ABANDONING EARTH TO ITS FATE?

NOT SUPERGIRL! SHE'S NO QUITTER!

ACROSS BILLIONS OF MILES SPEEDS THE GIRL OF STEEL!

I RECALL THAT WHEN POSITIVE MAN WAS CREATED, THE SAME EXPLOSION ALSO AFFECTED A WILD ANIMAL BEING STUDIED FOR INTELLIGENCE BY SCIENTISTS, CONVERTING IT INTO A NEGATIVE CREATURE!

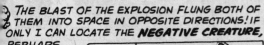

THE BLAST OF THE EXPLOSION FLUNG BOTH OF THEM INTO SPACE IN OPPOSITE DIRECTIONS! IF ONLY I CAN LOCATE THE NEGATIVE CREATURE, PERHAPS...

AFTER SUPERGIRL'S TELESCOPIC VISION LOCATES THE EERIE CREATURE...

COME AND GET ME, IF YOU CAN! — GOOD! YOU'RE FLYING AFTER ME! EXACTLY WHAT I WANT!!

BACK TOWARD OUR SOLAR SYSTEM STREAKS SUPERGIRL...

THE POSITIVE MAN IS GESTURING FRANTICALLY FOR THE NEGATIVE CREATURE TO STAY AWAY! TOO LATE! THEY'RE BEING DRAWN TOGETHER IRRESISTIBLY!

NEXT MOMENT...

HOORAY! THE TWO WERE DRAWN TOGETHER LIKE THE POSITIVE AND NEGATIVE POLES OF A MAGNET ATTRACTING EACH OTHER! AS A RESULT OF THIS FUSION, THEY'RE DISAPPEARING! THE CONTACT WAS SO TERRIFIC, THEY CANCELLED OUT EACH OTHER!!

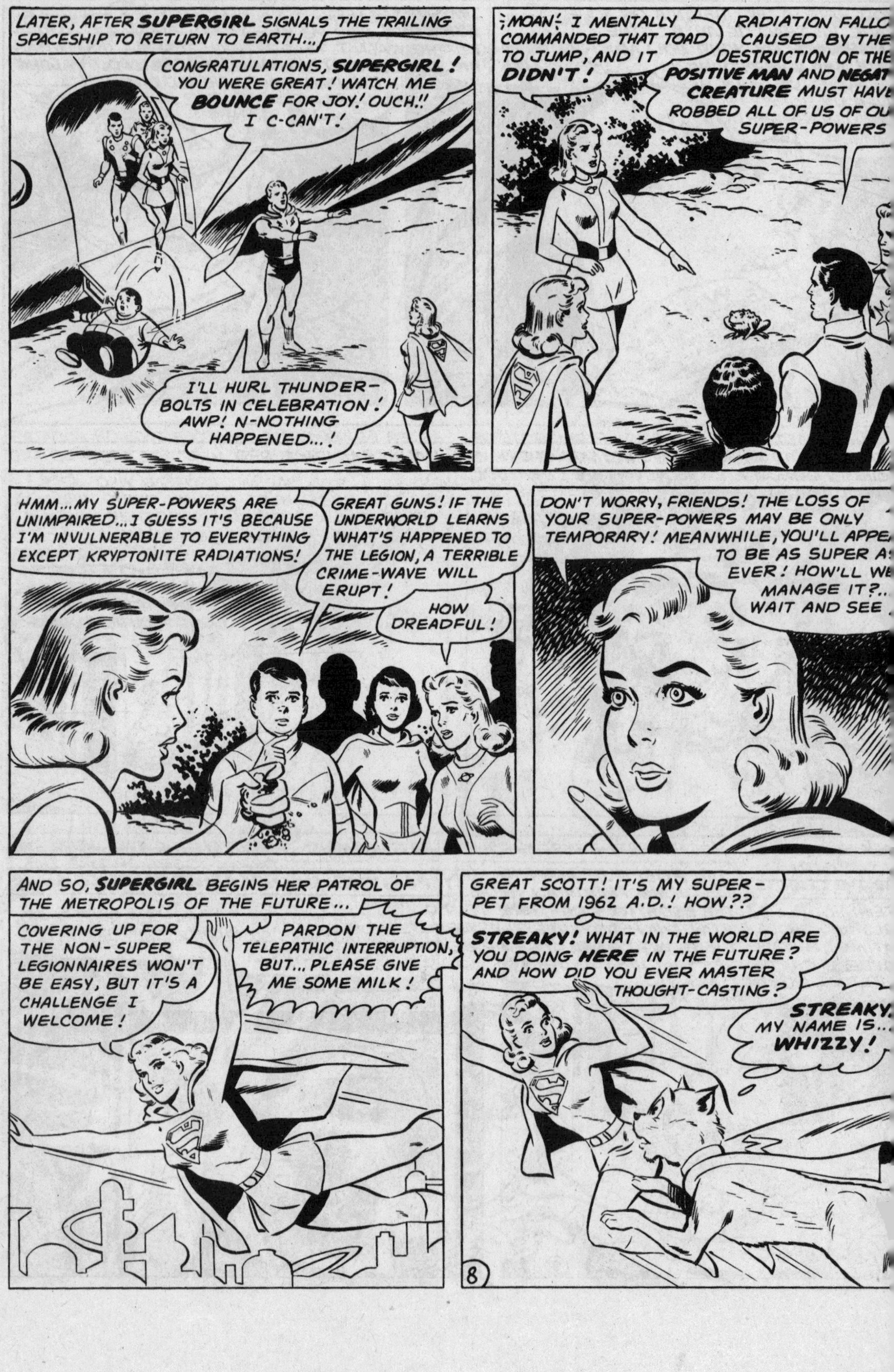
LATER, AFTER SUPERGIRL SIGNALS THE TRAILING SPACESHIP TO RETURN TO EARTH...
CONGRATULATIONS, SUPERGIRL! YOU WERE GREAT! WATCH ME BOUNCE FOR JOY! OUCH!! I C-CAN'T!
I'LL HURL THUNDER-BOLTS IN CELEBRATION! AWP! N-NOTHING HAPPENED...!
-MOAN- I MENTALLY COMMANDED THAT TOAD TO JUMP, AND IT DIDN'T!
RADIATION FALLO CAUSED BY THE DESTRUCTION OF THE POSITIVE MAN AND NEGAT CREATURE MUST HAVE ROBBED ALL OF US OF OU SUPER-POWERS
HMM... MY SUPER-POWERS ARE UNIMPAIRED... I GUESS IT'S BECAUSE I'M INVULNERABLE TO EVERYTHING EXCEPT KRYPTONITE RADIATIONS!
GREAT GUNS! IF THE UNDERWORLD LEARNS WHAT'S HAPPENED TO THE LEGION, A TERRIBLE CRIME-WAVE WILL ERUPT!
HOW DREADFUL!
DON'T WORRY, FRIENDS! THE LOSS OF YOUR SUPER-POWERS MAY BE ONLY TEMPORARY! MEANWHILE, YOU'LL APPE TO BE AS SUPER A EVER! HOW'LL WE MANAGE IT?... WAIT AND SEE
AND SO, SUPERGIRL BEGINS HER PATROL OF THE METROPOLIS OF THE FUTURE...
COVERING UP FOR THE NON-SUPER LEGIONNAIRES WON'T BE EASY, BUT IT'S A CHALLENGE I WELCOME!
PARDON THE TELEPATHIC INTERRUPTION, BUT... PLEASE GIVE ME SOME MILK!
GREAT SCOTT! IT'S MY SUPER-PET FROM 1962 A.D.! HOW??
STREAKY! WHAT IN THE WORLD ARE YOU DOING HERE IN THE FUTURE? AND HOW DID YOU EVER MASTER THOUGHT-CASTING?
STREAKY. MY NAME IS... WHIZZY!
8

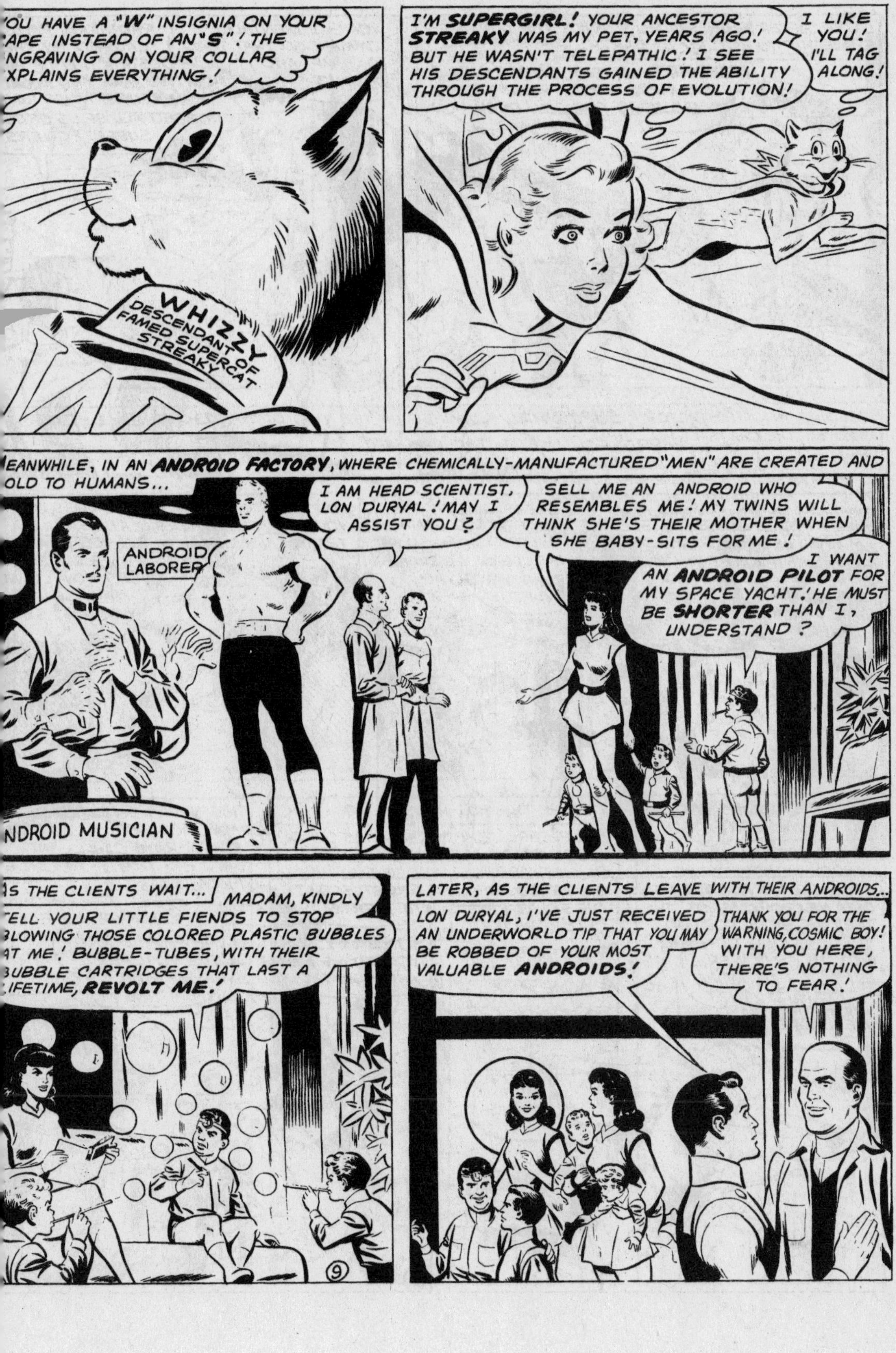
OU HAVE A "W" INSIGNIA ON YOUR APE INSTEAD OF AN "S"! THE NGRAVING ON YOUR COLLAR XPLAINS EVERYTHING!
WHIZZY DESCENDANT OF FAMED SUPERCAT STREAKY
I'M SUPERGIRL! YOUR ANCESTOR STREAKY WAS MY PET, YEARS AGO! BUT HE WASN'T TELEPATHIC! I SEE HIS DESCENDANTS GAINED THE ABILITY THROUGH THE PROCESS OF EVOLUTION!
I LIKE YOU! I'LL TAG ALONG!
EANWHILE, IN AN ANDROID FACTORY, WHERE CHEMICALLY-MANUFACTURED "MEN" ARE CREATED AND OLD TO HUMANS...
ANDROID LABORER
ANDROID MUSICIAN
I AM HEAD SCIENTIST, LON DURYAL! MAY I ASSIST YOU?
SELL ME AN ANDROID WHO RESEMBLES ME! MY TWINS WILL THINK SHE'S THEIR MOTHER WHEN SHE BABY-SITS FOR ME!
I WANT AN ANDROID PILOT FOR MY SPACE YACHT! HE MUST BE SHORTER THAN I, UNDERSTAND?
AS THE CLIENTS WAIT...
MADAM, KINDLY TELL YOUR LITTLE FIENDS TO STOP BLOWING THOSE COLORED PLASTIC BUBBLES AT ME! BUBBLE-TUBES, WITH THEIR BUBBLE CARTRIDGES THAT LAST A LIFETIME, REVOLT ME!
9
LATER, AS THE CLIENTS LEAVE WITH THEIR ANDROIDS...
LON DURYAL, I'VE JUST RECEIVED AN UNDERWORLD TIP THAT YOU MAY BE ROBBED OF YOUR MOST VALUABLE ANDROIDS!
THANK YOU FOR THE WARNING, COSMIC BOY! WITH YOU HERE, THERE'S NOTHING TO FEAR!

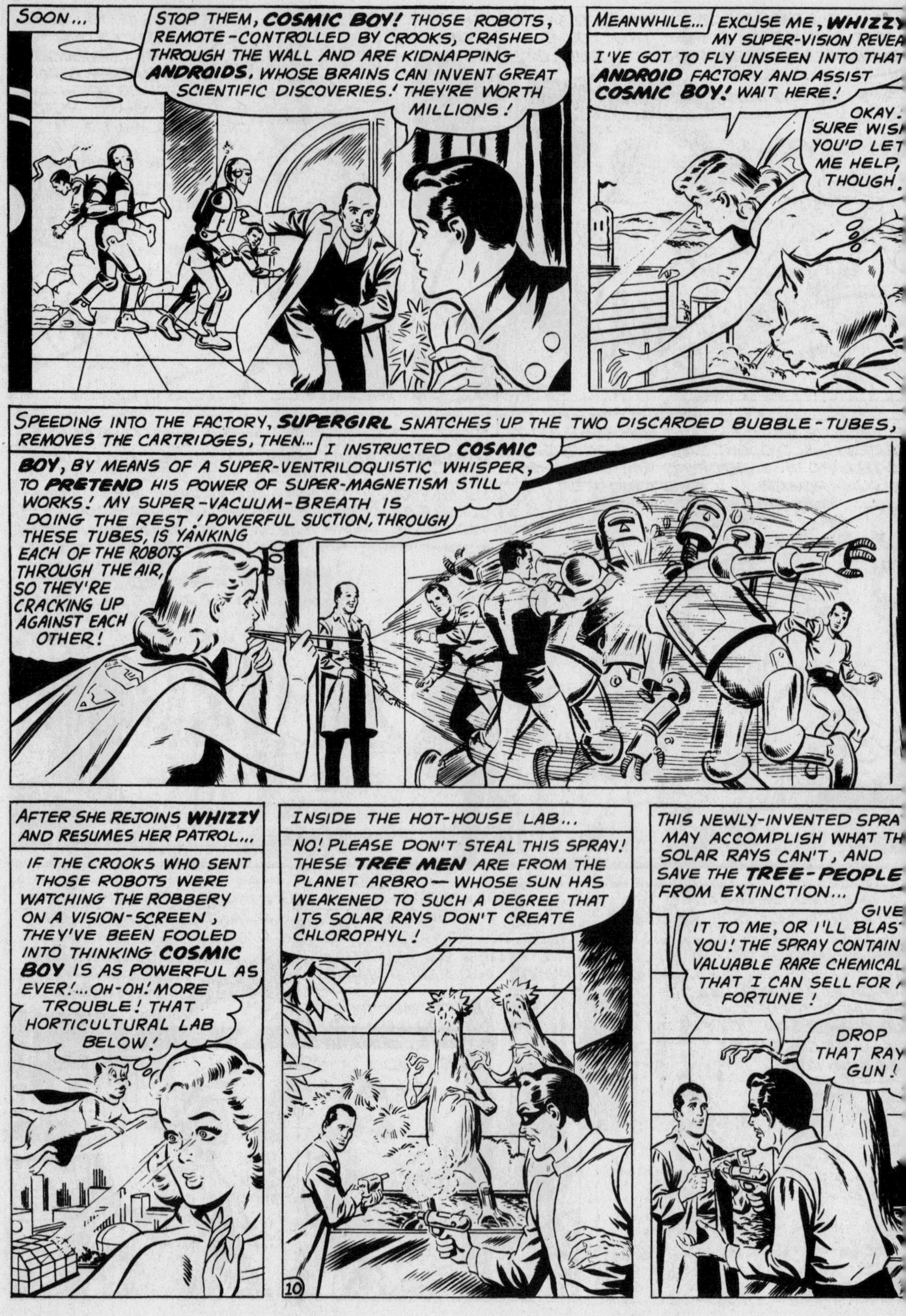
SOON...
STOP THEM, COSMIC BOY! THOSE ROBOTS, REMOTE-CONTROLLED BY CROOKS, CRASHED THROUGH THE WALL AND ARE KIDNAPPING ANDROIDS, WHOSE BRAINS CAN INVENT GREAT SCIENTIFIC DISCOVERIES! THEY'RE WORTH MILLIONS!
MEANWHILE...
EXCUSE ME, WHIZZY MY SUPER-VISION REVEA I'VE GOT TO FLY UNSEEN INTO THAT ANDROID FACTORY AND ASSIST COSMIC BOY! WAIT HERE!
OKAY. SURE WISH YOU'D LET ME HELP, THOUGH.
SPEEDING INTO THE FACTORY, SUPERGIRL SNATCHES UP THE TWO DISCARDED BUBBLE-TUBES, REMOVES THE CARTRIDGES, THEN...
I INSTRUCTED COSMIC BOY, BY MEANS OF A SUPER-VENTRILOQUISTIC WHISPER, TO PRETEND HIS POWER OF SUPER-MAGNETISM STILL WORKS! MY SUPER-VACUUM-BREATH IS DOING THE REST! POWERFUL SUCTION, THROUGH THESE TUBES, IS YANKING EACH OF THE ROBOTS THROUGH THE AIR, SO THEY'RE CRACKING UP AGAINST EACH OTHER!
AFTER SHE REJOINS WHIZZY AND RESUMES HER PATROL...
IF THE CROOKS WHO SENT THOSE ROBOTS WERE WATCHING THE ROBBERY ON A VISION-SCREEN, THEY'VE BEEN FOOLED INTO THINKING COSMIC BOY IS AS POWERFUL AS EVER!...OH-OH! MORE TROUBLE! THAT HORTICULTURAL LAB BELOW!
INSIDE THE HOT-HOUSE LAB...
NO! PLEASE DON'T STEAL THIS SPRAY! THESE TREE MEN ARE FROM THE PLANET ARBRO— WHOSE SUN HAS WEAKENED TO SUCH A DEGREE THAT ITS SOLAR RAYS DON'T CREATE CHLOROPHYL!
10
THIS NEWLY-INVENTED SPRA MAY ACCOMPLISH WHAT TH SOLAR RAYS CAN'T, AND SAVE THE TREE-PEOPLE FROM EXTINCTION...
GIVE IT TO ME, OR I'LL BLAS YOU! THE SPRAY CONTAIN VALUABLE RARE CHEMICAL THAT I CAN SELL FOR FORTUNE!
DROP THAT RAY GUN!

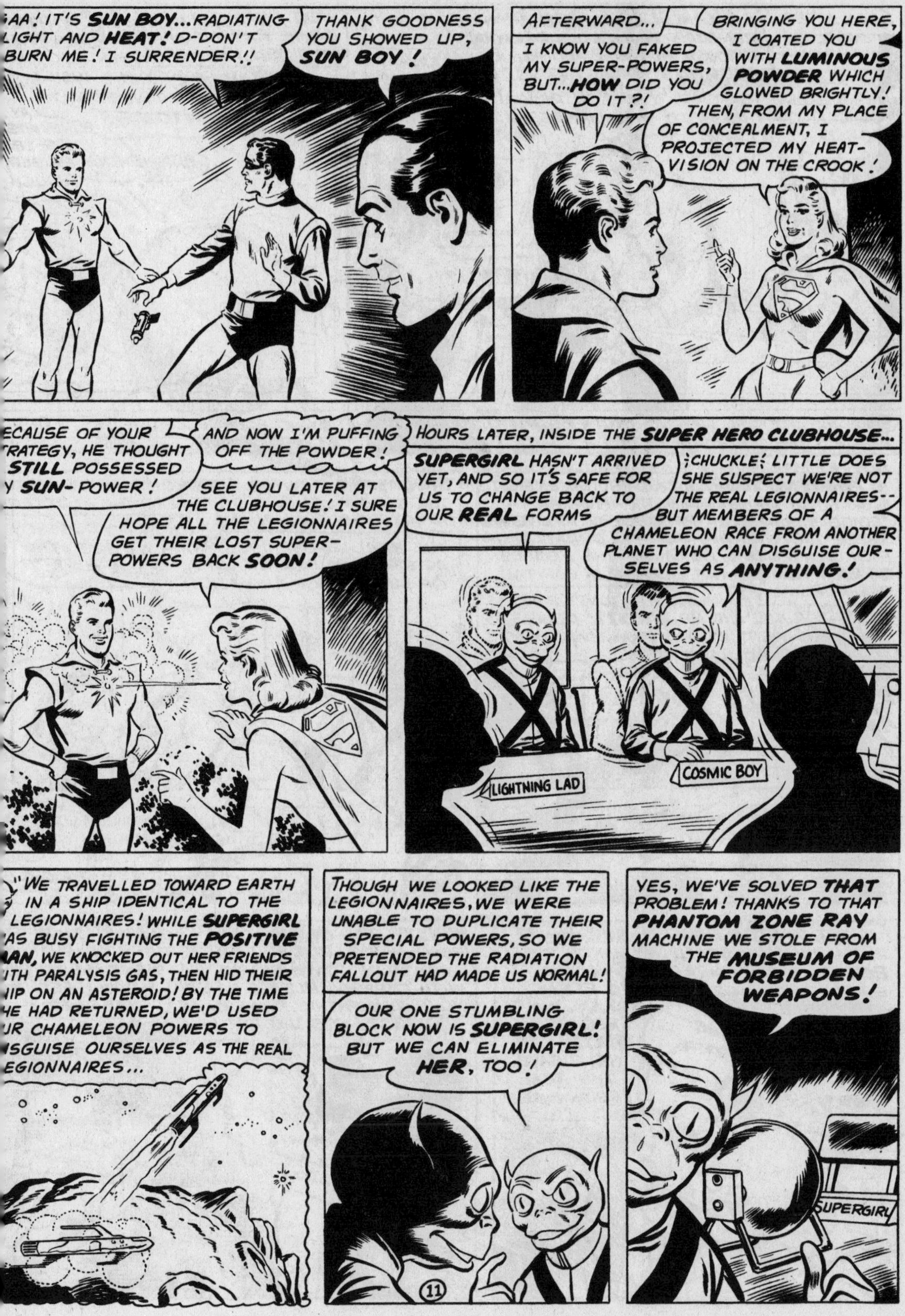
AA! IT'S SUN BOY... RADIATING LIGHT AND HEAT! D-DON'T BURN ME! I SURRENDER!!
THANK GOODNESS YOU SHOWED UP, SUN BOY!
AFTERWARD...
I KNOW YOU FAKED MY SUPER-POWERS, BUT... HOW DID YOU DO IT?!
BRINGING YOU HERE, I COATED YOU WITH LUMINOUS POWDER WHICH GLOWED BRIGHTLY! THEN, FROM MY PLACE OF CONCEALMENT, I PROJECTED MY HEAT-VISION ON THE CROOK!
ECAUSE OF YOUR TRATEGY, HE THOUGHT STILL POSSESSED Y SUN-POWER!
AND NOW I'M PUFFING OFF THE POWDER!
SEE YOU LATER AT THE CLUBHOUSE! I SURE HOPE ALL THE LEGIONNAIRES GET THEIR LOST SUPER-POWERS BACK SOON!
HOURS LATER, INSIDE THE SUPER HERO CLUBHOUSE...
SUPERGIRL HASN'T ARRIVED YET, AND SO IT'S SAFE FOR US TO CHANGE BACK TO OUR REAL FORMS
¡CHUCKLE¡ LITTLE DOES SHE SUSPECT WE'RE NOT THE REAL LEGIONNAIRES--BUT MEMBERS OF A CHAMELEON RACE FROM ANOTHER PLANET WHO CAN DISGUISE OURSELVES AS ANYTHING!
LIGHTNING LAD
COSMIC BOY
"WE TRAVELLED TOWARD EARTH IN A SHIP IDENTICAL TO THE LEGIONNAIRES! WHILE SUPERGIRL AS BUSY FIGHTING THE POSITIVE AN, WE KNOCKED OUT HER FRIENDS ITH PARALYSIS GAS, THEN HID THEIR IP ON AN ASTEROID! BY THE TIME HE HAD RETURNED, WE'D USED UR CHAMELEON POWERS TO SGUISE OURSELVES AS THE REAL EGIONNAIRES...
THOUGH WE LOOKED LIKE THE LEGIONNAIRES, WE WERE UNABLE TO DUPLICATE THEIR SPECIAL POWERS, SO WE PRETENDED THE RADIATION FALLOUT HAD MADE US NORMAL!
OUR ONE STUMBLING BLOCK NOW IS SUPERGIRL! BUT WE CAN ELIMINATE HER, TOO!
11
YES, WE'VE SOLVED THAT PROBLEM! THANKS TO THAT PHANTOM ZONE RAY MACHINE WE STOLE FROM THE MUSEUM OF FORBIDDEN WEAPONS!
SUPERGIRL

SOON AFTER THE **CHAMELEON-MEN** TRANSFORM THEMSELVES ONCE AGAIN INTO FAKE LEGIONNAIRES, **SUPERGIRL** ARRIVES AT THE MEETING...

SURPRISE, **SUPERGIRL!** WE'RE GOING TO SEND YOU OUT OF THIS WORLD!

THEY AREN'T JOKING!...MY MICROSCOPIC VISION REVEALS THEY'RE NOT IMPERSONATORS WEARING PLASTIC MASKS!

LIGHTNING LAD
COSM
SUPE

NEXT INSTANT, AS THE **PHANTOM ZONE RAY** MACHINE'S **BLACK BUTTON** IS PRESSED...

HA, HA, HA!

OH, NO! **WHIZZY** AND I HAVE BOTH BEEN CHANGED INTO **PHANTOMS!**

YIPES DARNED UNFRIENDLY OF THEM

SUPERGIRL

THE **PHANTOM ZONE**... A TWILIGHT DIMENSION INTO WHICH DANGEROUS KRYPTONIAN CRIMINALS HAD BEEN PROJECTED TO LIVE AS GHOST-LIKE WRAITHS FOR THE DURATION OF THEIR SENTENCES, BECAUSE THE PEOPLE OF **KRYPTON** DID NOT BELIEVE IN CAPITAL PUNISHMENT...

STRANGE... THE ZONE'S EMPTY EXCEPT FOR YOU AND ME, **WHIZZY!** I GUESS, AS THE YEARS WENT BY, THE PHANTOMS WHO WERE CONFINED HERE WERE RELEASED ONE BY ONE AS THEIR SENTENCES WERE COMPLETED!

THEN, AS THE PHANTOM **SUPERGIRL** RETURNS TO THE CLUBHOUSE AND DISCOVERS THE PLOTTERS' IDENTITIES AND PLANS...

NOW TO DESTROY THE REAL LEGIONNAIRES AFTER WE GO TO THE ASTEROID WHERE WE LEFT THEM IN A STATE OF SUSPENDED ANIMATION!

NO

I'VE GOT TO **STOP** THEM! B-BUT HOW?? IN MY PHANTOM STATE, MY HANDS PASS THROUGH SOLID OBJECTS-- AND I'M UNABLE TO SPEAK ALOUD!...WAIT... PERHAPS **WHIZZY** CAN HELP SAVE THE REAL LEGIONNAIRES!

(17)

WHIZZY... YOU CAN NOT ONLY READ MINDS, BUT YOU CAN MENTALLY COMMUNICATE WITH OTHERS! PLEASE USE YOUR TELEPATHIC POWERS AS I DIRECT! IT'S URGENT!

GLADLY! JUST THINK OF WHAT YOU WANT ME TO DO AND I'LL GET THE MESSAGE!

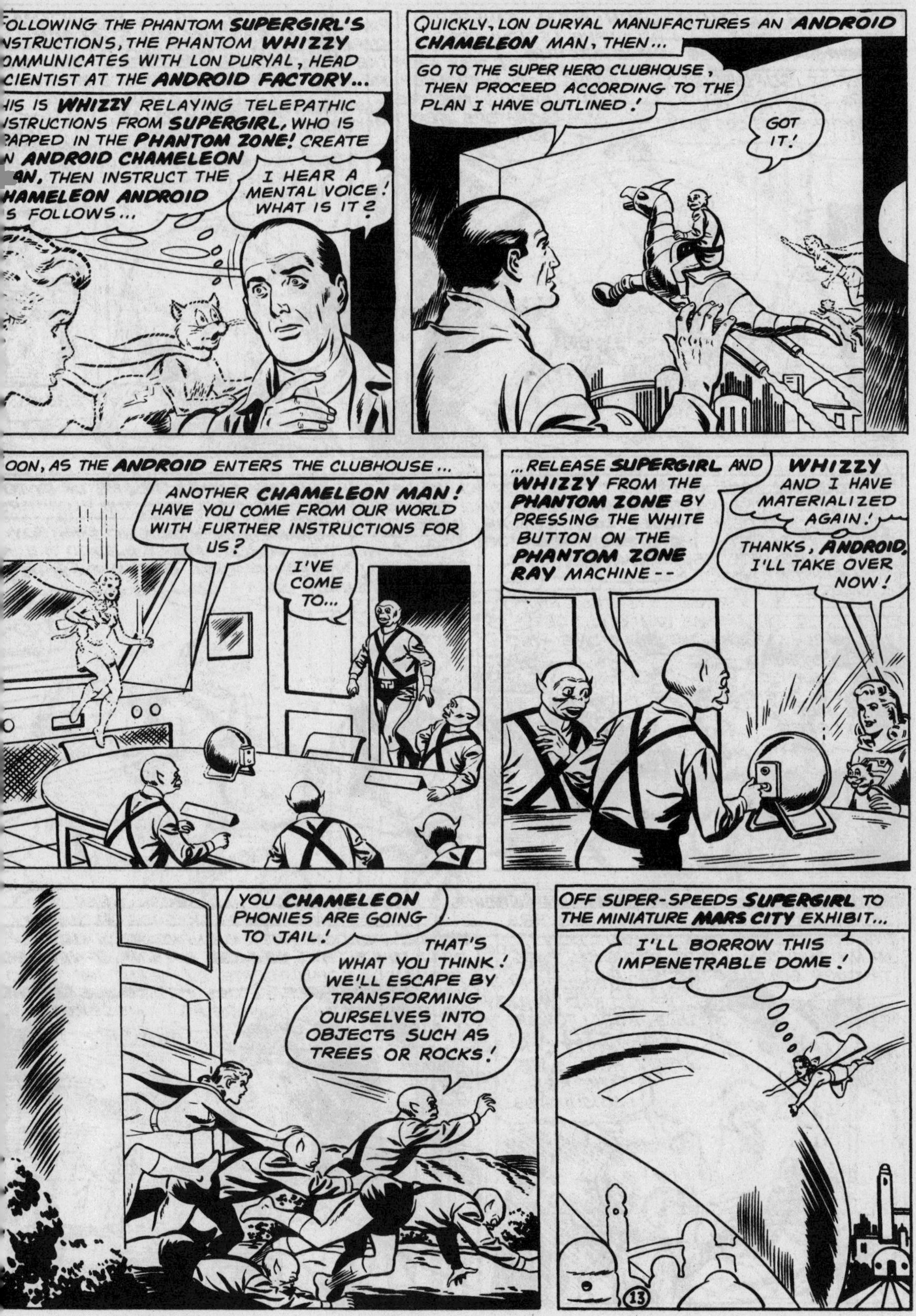
FOLLOWING THE PHANTOM SUPERGIRL'S INSTRUCTIONS, THE PHANTOM WHIZZY COMMUNICATES WITH LON DURYAL, HEAD SCIENTIST AT THE ANDROID FACTORY...
THIS IS WHIZZY RELAYING TELEPATHIC INSTRUCTIONS FROM SUPERGIRL, WHO IS TRAPPED IN THE PHANTOM ZONE! CREATE AN ANDROID CHAMELEON MAN, THEN INSTRUCT THE CHAMELEON ANDROID AS FOLLOWS...
I HEAR A MENTAL VOICE! WHAT IS IT?
QUICKLY, LON DURYAL MANUFACTURES AN ANDROID CHAMELEON MAN, THEN...
GO TO THE SUPER HERO CLUBHOUSE, THEN PROCEED ACCORDING TO THE PLAN I HAVE OUTLINED!
GOT IT!
SOON, AS THE ANDROID ENTERS THE CLUBHOUSE...
ANOTHER CHAMELEON MAN! HAVE YOU COME FROM OUR WORLD WITH FURTHER INSTRUCTIONS FOR US?
I'VE COME TO...
...RELEASE SUPERGIRL AND WHIZZY FROM THE PHANTOM ZONE BY PRESSING THE WHITE BUTTON ON THE PHANTOM ZONE RAY MACHINE--
WHIZZY AND I HAVE MATERIALIZED AGAIN!
THANKS, ANDROID, I'LL TAKE OVER NOW!
YOU CHAMELEON PHONIES ARE GOING TO JAIL!
THAT'S WHAT YOU THINK! WE'LL ESCAPE BY TRANSFORMING OURSELVES INTO OBJECTS SUCH AS TREES OR ROCKS!
OFF SUPER-SPEEDS SUPERGIRL TO THE MINIATURE MARS CITY EXHIBIT...
I'LL BORROW THIS IMPENETRABLE DOME!
13

AFTER *SUPERGIRL* RETURNS...

CHANGE INTO ANYTHING YOU WANT, NOW! YOU STILL WON'T BE ABLE TO ESCAPE FROM THIS DOME! NOW TO NOTIFY THE INTERPLANETARY POLICE TO TAKE YOU CHARACTERS INTO CUSTODY!

PRESENTLY, GUIDED BY HER SUPER-VISION *SUPERGIRL* LOCATES THE ASTEROID WHERE THE LEGIONNAIRES ARE IMPRISONED--AND REVIVES THEM WITH AN ANTIDOTE RAY...

SUPERGIRL! WH-WHAT HAPPENED T-TO US?

I'LL EXPLAIN EVERYTHING, *COSMIC BOY!*

LATER, AS THEY RETURN TO *METROPOLIS*...

WE OF THE FUTURE OWE YOU SO MUCH, *SUPERGIRL!* HOW CAN WE EVER THANK YOU?

SKIP IT! YOU'D DO THE SAME FOR MY TIME PERIOD! NOW I MUST RETURN! GOODBYE, EVERYBODY! YOU TOO, *WHIZZY!*

SO LONG, *SUPERGIRL!* I'LL NEVER FORGET YOU!

INTO THE TIME-BARRIER AND BACK TOWARD 1962 A.D. FLASHES THE *GIRL OF STEEL*

WHAT AN ADVENTURE THAT WAS! THE *CHAMELEON MEN* GANG SURE HAD ME FOOLED FOR A WHILE! I'D HAVE BEEN A GONER EXCEPT FOR *WHIZZY!*

2000

1968

1980

RETURNING TO THE PRESENT, *SUPERGIRL* SWITCHES TO HER IDENTITY AS LINDA LEE DANVERS...

IT'S GOOD TO BE BACK, *STREAKY!* I WONDER WHAT YOU'RE THINKING? HA, HA! IF YOU HAD *WHIZZY'S* TELEPATHIC POWERS YOU COULD *TELL* ME!

WHIZZY? WHO'S THAT!?

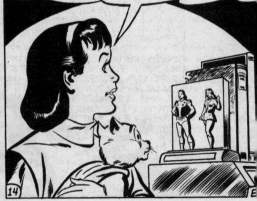

AND TO THINK IT ALL BEGAN WHEN THE HEADS ON THOSE BOOK-ENDS *GLOWED!* I WONDER WHEN I'LL NEXT BE SUMMONED TO VISIT THE *LEGION OF SUPER-HEROES*

14

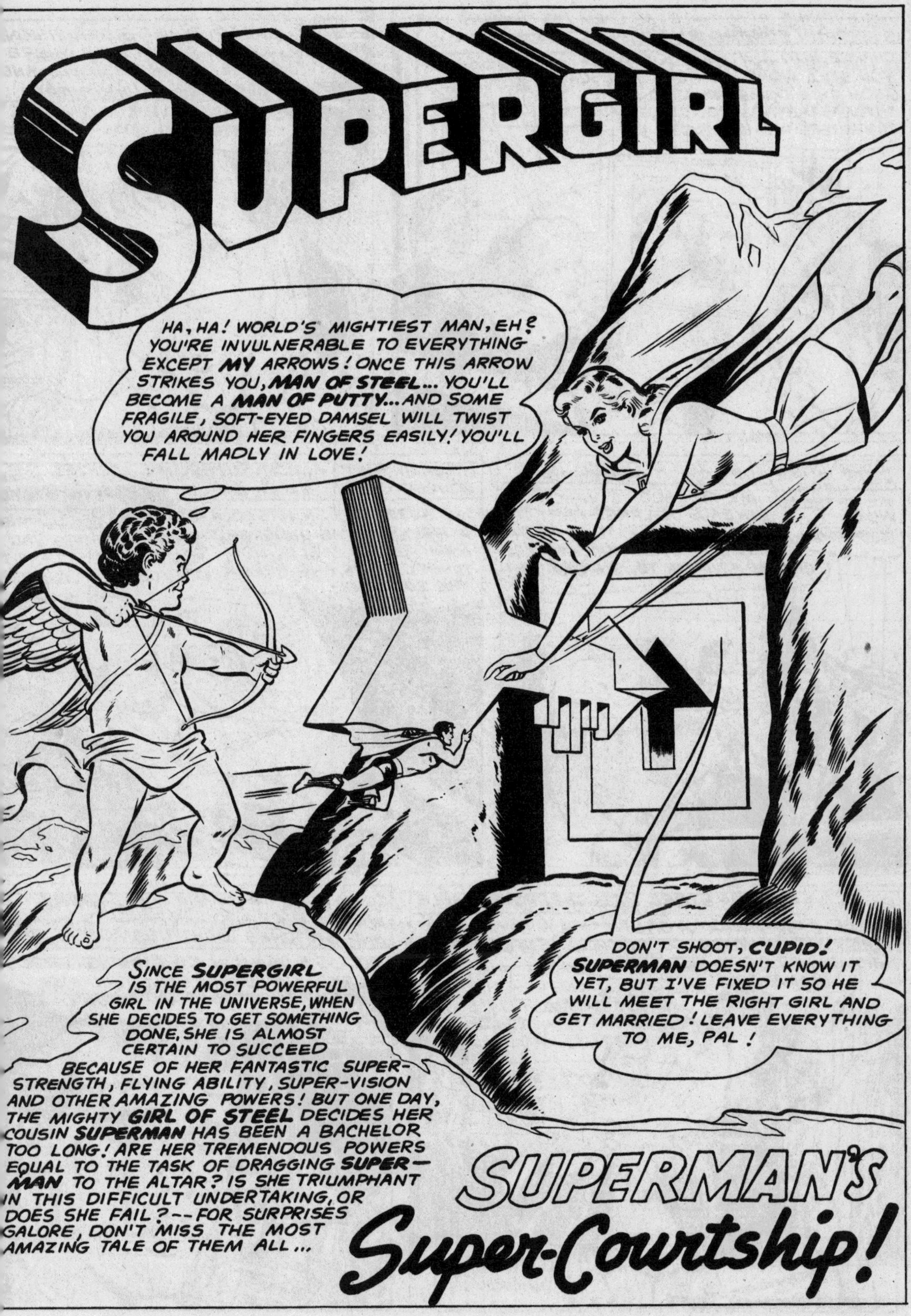
SUPERGIRL
HA, HA! WORLD'S MIGHTIEST MAN, EH? YOU'RE INVULNERABLE TO EVERYTHING EXCEPT MY ARROWS! ONCE THIS ARROW STRIKES YOU, MAN OF STEEL... YOU'LL BECOME A MAN OF PUTTY... AND SOME FRAGILE, SOFT-EYED DAMSEL WILL TWIST YOU AROUND HER FINGERS EASILY! YOU'LL FALL MADLY IN LOVE!
DON'T SHOOT, CUPID! SUPERMAN DOESN'T KNOW IT YET, BUT I'VE FIXED IT SO HE WILL MEET THE RIGHT GIRL AND GET MARRIED! LEAVE EVERYTHING TO ME, PAL!
SINCE SUPERGIRL IS THE MOST POWERFUL GIRL IN THE UNIVERSE, WHEN SHE DECIDES TO GET SOMETHING DONE, SHE IS ALMOST CERTAIN TO SUCCEED BECAUSE OF HER FANTASTIC SUPER-STRENGTH, FLYING ABILITY, SUPER-VISION AND OTHER AMAZING POWERS! BUT ONE DAY, THE MIGHTY GIRL OF STEEL DECIDES HER COUSIN SUPERMAN HAS BEEN A BACHELOR TOO LONG! ARE HER TREMENDOUS POWERS EQUAL TO THE TASK OF DRAGGING SUPERMAN TO THE ALTAR? IS SHE TRIUMPHANT IN THIS DIFFICULT UNDERTAKING, OR DOES SHE FAIL? -- FOR SURPRISES GALORE, DON'T MISS THE MOST AMAZING TALE OF THEM ALL...
SUPERMAN'S Super-Courtship!

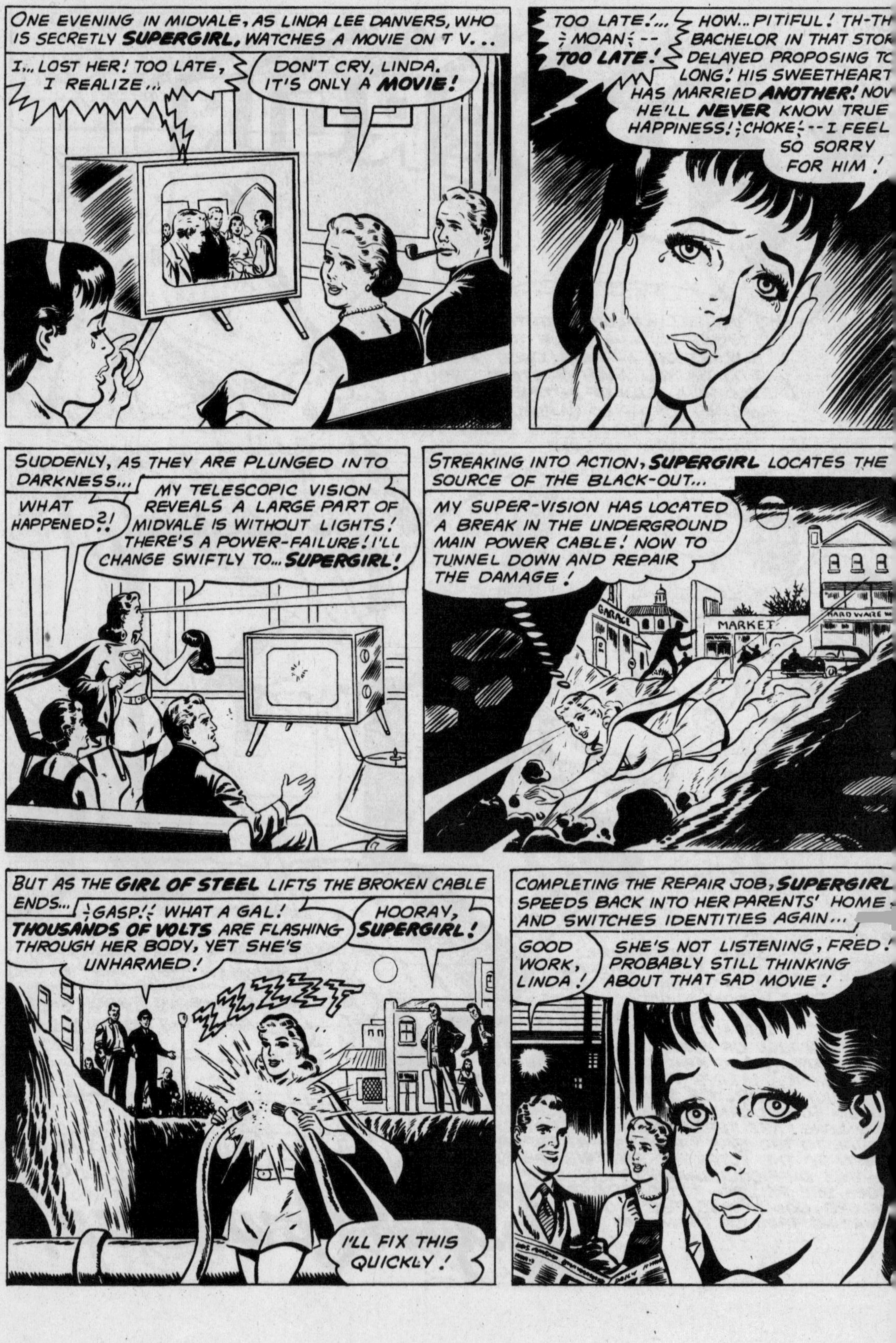
ONE EVENING IN MIDVALE, AS LINDA LEE DANVERS, WHO IS SECRETLY SUPERGIRL, WATCHES A MOVIE ON T V...
I... LOST HER! TOO LATE, I REALIZE...
DON'T CRY, LINDA. IT'S ONLY A MOVIE!
TOO LATE!... -MOAN- -- TOO LATE!
HOW... PITIFUL! TH-TH BACHELOR IN THAT STOR DELAYED PROPOSING TO LONG! HIS SWEETHEART HAS MARRIED ANOTHER! NOV HE'LL NEVER KNOW TRUE HAPPINESS! -CHOKE- --I FEEL SO SORRY FOR HIM!
SUDDENLY, AS THEY ARE PLUNGED INTO DARKNESS...
WHAT HAPPENED?!
MY TELESCOPIC VISION REVEALS A LARGE PART OF MIDVALE IS WITHOUT LIGHTS! THERE'S A POWER-FAILURE! I'LL CHANGE SWIFTLY TO... SUPERGIRL!
STREAKING INTO ACTION, SUPERGIRL LOCATES THE SOURCE OF THE BLACK-OUT...
MY SUPER-VISION HAS LOCATED A BREAK IN THE UNDERGROUND MAIN POWER CABLE! NOW TO TUNNEL DOWN AND REPAIR THE DAMAGE!
GARAGE
MARKET
HARDWARE
BUT AS THE GIRL OF STEEL LIFTS THE BROKEN CABLE ENDS...
-GASP!- WHAT A GAL! THOUSANDS OF VOLTS ARE FLASHING THROUGH HER BODY, YET SHE'S UNHARMED!
HOORAY, SUPERGIRL!
I'LL FIX THIS QUICKLY!
COMPLETING THE REPAIR JOB, SUPERGIRL SPEEDS BACK INTO HER PARENTS' HOME AND SWITCHES IDENTITIES AGAIN...
GOOD WORK, LINDA!
SHE'S NOT LISTENING, FRED! PROBABLY STILL THINKING ABOUT THAT SAD MOVIE!

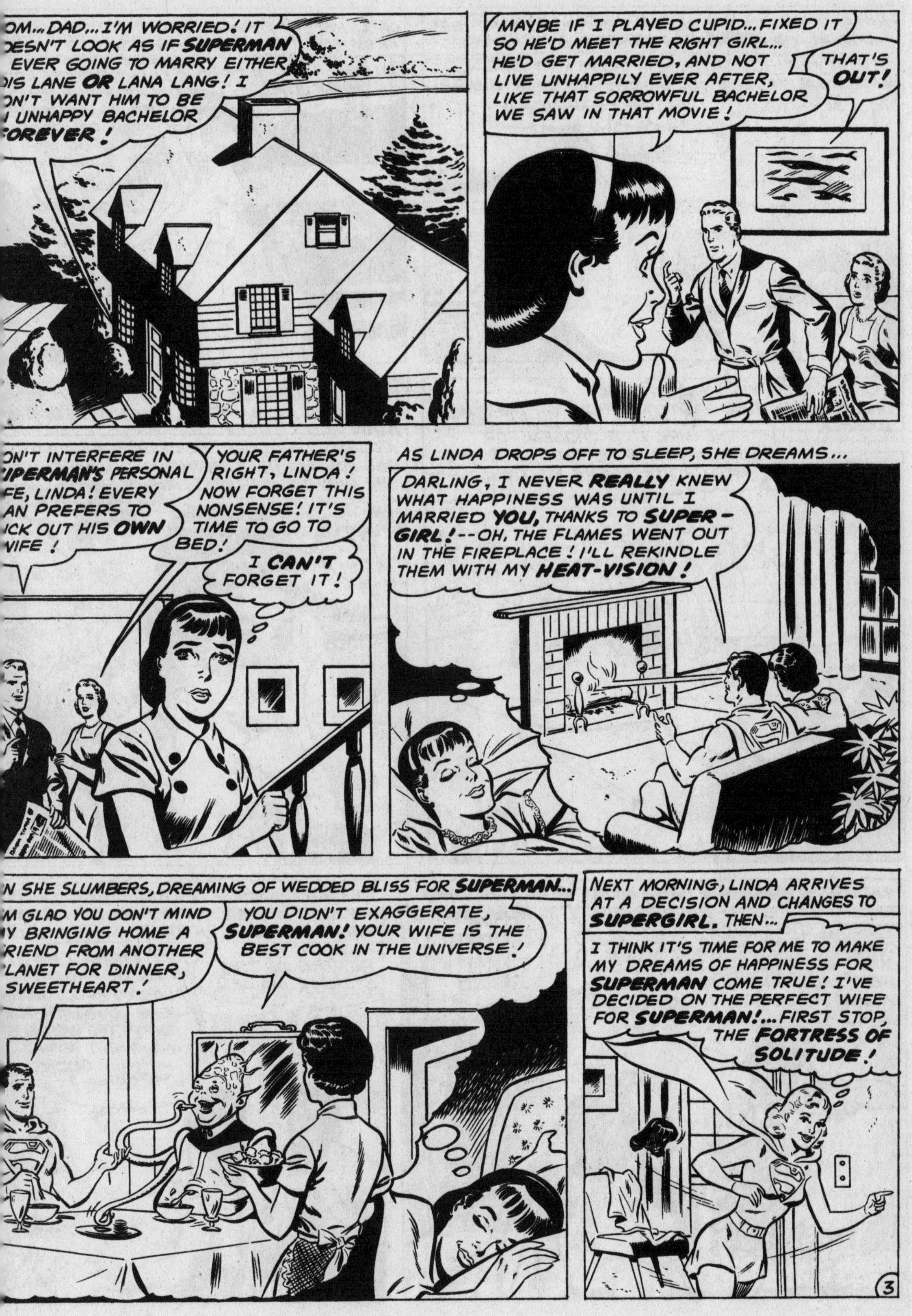
OM...DAD...I'M WORRIED! IT OESN'T LOOK AS IF SUPERMAN EVER GOING TO MARRY EITHER OIS LANE OR LANA LANG! I ON'T WANT HIM TO BE UNHAPPY BACHELOR OREVER!
MAYBE IF I PLAYED CUPID... FIXED IT SO HE'D MEET THE RIGHT GIRL... HE'D GET MARRIED, AND NOT LIVE UNHAPPILY EVER AFTER, LIKE THAT SORROWFUL BACHELOR WE SAW IN THAT MOVIE!
THAT'S OUT!
ON'T INTERFERE IN UPERMAN'S PERSONAL FE, LINDA! EVERY AN PREFERS TO ICK OUT HIS OWN WIFE!
YOUR FATHER'S RIGHT, LINDA! NOW FORGET THIS NONSENSE! IT'S TIME TO GO TO BED!
I CAN'T FORGET IT!
AS LINDA DROPS OFF TO SLEEP, SHE DREAMS...
DARLING, I NEVER REALLY KNEW WHAT HAPPINESS WAS UNTIL I MARRIED YOU, THANKS TO SUPER-GIRL!--OH, THE FLAMES WENT OUT IN THE FIREPLACE! I'LL REKINDLE THEM WITH MY HEAT-VISION!
N SHE SLUMBERS, DREAMING OF WEDDED BLISS FOR SUPERMAN...
M GLAD YOU DON'T MIND Y BRINGING HOME A RIEND FROM ANOTHER LANET FOR DINNER, SWEETHEART!
YOU DIDN'T EXAGGERATE, SUPERMAN! YOUR WIFE IS THE BEST COOK IN THE UNIVERSE!
NEXT MORNING, LINDA ARRIVES AT A DECISION AND CHANGES TO SUPERGIRL. THEN...
I THINK IT'S TIME FOR ME TO MAKE MY DREAMS OF HAPPINESS FOR SUPERMAN COME TRUE! I'VE DECIDED ON THE PERFECT WIFE FOR SUPERMAN!... FIRST STOP, THE FORTRESS OF SOLITUDE!
3

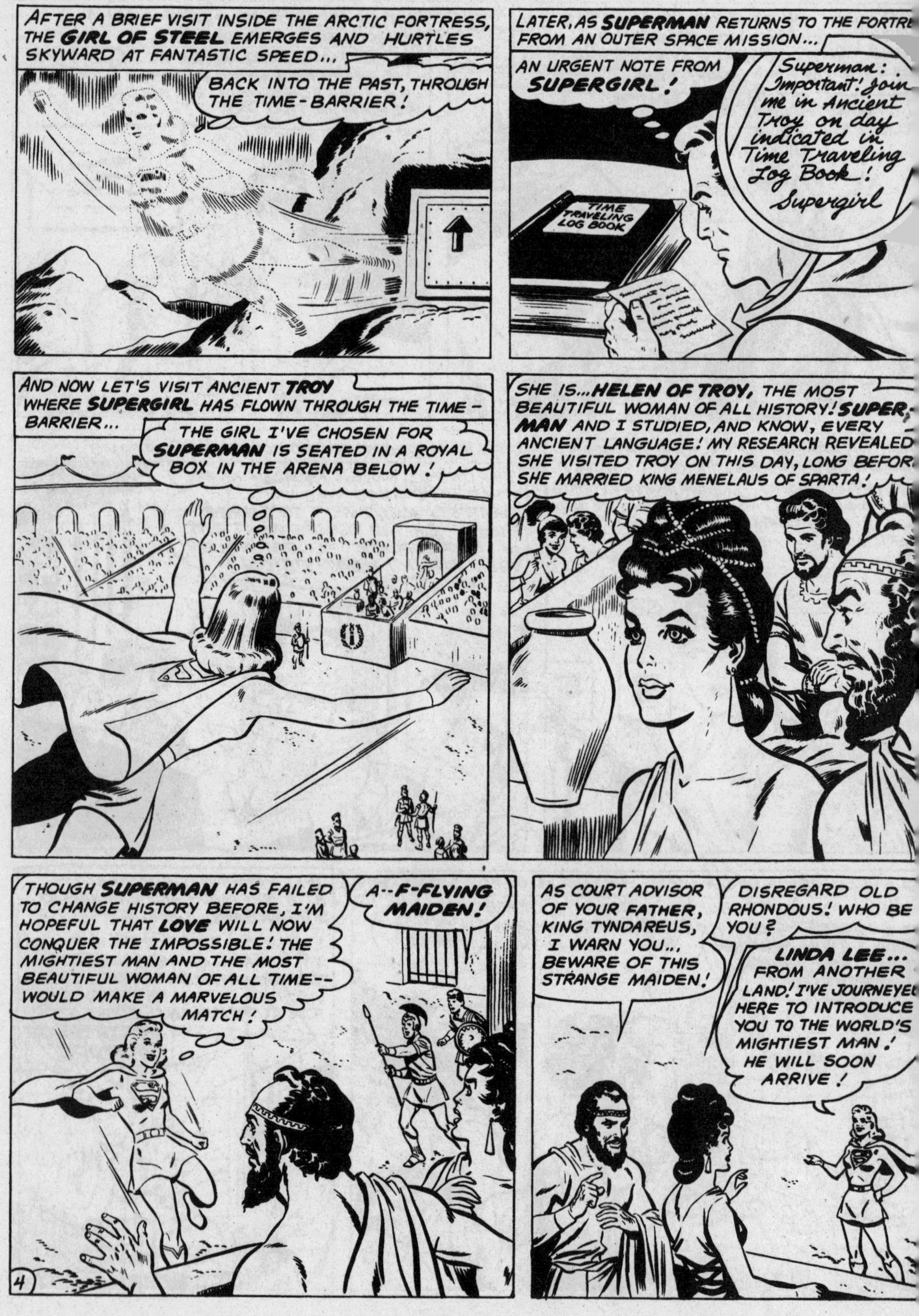
AFTER A BRIEF VISIT INSIDE THE ARCTIC FORTRESS, THE GIRL OF STEEL EMERGES AND HURTLES SKYWARD AT FANTASTIC SPEED...
BACK INTO THE PAST, THROUGH THE TIME-BARRIER!
LATER, AS SUPERMAN RETURNS TO THE FORTRE
FROM AN OUTER SPACE MISSION...
AN URGENT NOTE FROM SUPERGIRL!
Superman: Important! Join me in Ancient Troy on day indicated in Time Traveling Log Book! Supergirl
TIME TRAVELING LOG BOOK
AND NOW LET'S VISIT ANCIENT TROY WHERE SUPERGIRL HAS FLOWN THROUGH THE TIME-BARRIER...
THE GIRL I'VE CHOSEN FOR SUPERMAN IS SEATED IN A ROYAL BOX IN THE ARENA BELOW!
SHE IS...HELEN OF TROY, THE MOST BEAUTIFUL WOMAN OF ALL HISTORY! SUPERMAN AND I STUDIED, AND KNOW, EVERY ANCIENT LANGUAGE! MY RESEARCH REVEALED SHE VISITED TROY ON THIS DAY, LONG BEFOR SHE MARRIED KING MENELAUS OF SPARTA!
THOUGH SUPERMAN HAS FAILED TO CHANGE HISTORY BEFORE, I'M HOPEFUL THAT LOVE WILL NOW CONQUER THE IMPOSSIBLE! THE MIGHTIEST MAN AND THE MOST BEAUTIFUL WOMAN OF ALL TIME--WOULD MAKE A MARVELOUS MATCH!
A--F-FLYING MAIDEN!
4
AS COURT ADVISOR OF YOUR FATHER, KING TYNDAREUS, I WARN YOU... BEWARE OF THIS STRANGE MAIDEN!
DISREGARD OLD RHONDOUS! WHO BE YOU?
LINDA LEE... FROM ANOTHER LAND! I'VE JOURNEYE HERE TO INTRODUCE YOU TO THE WORLD'S MIGHTIEST MAN! HE WILL SOON ARRIVE!

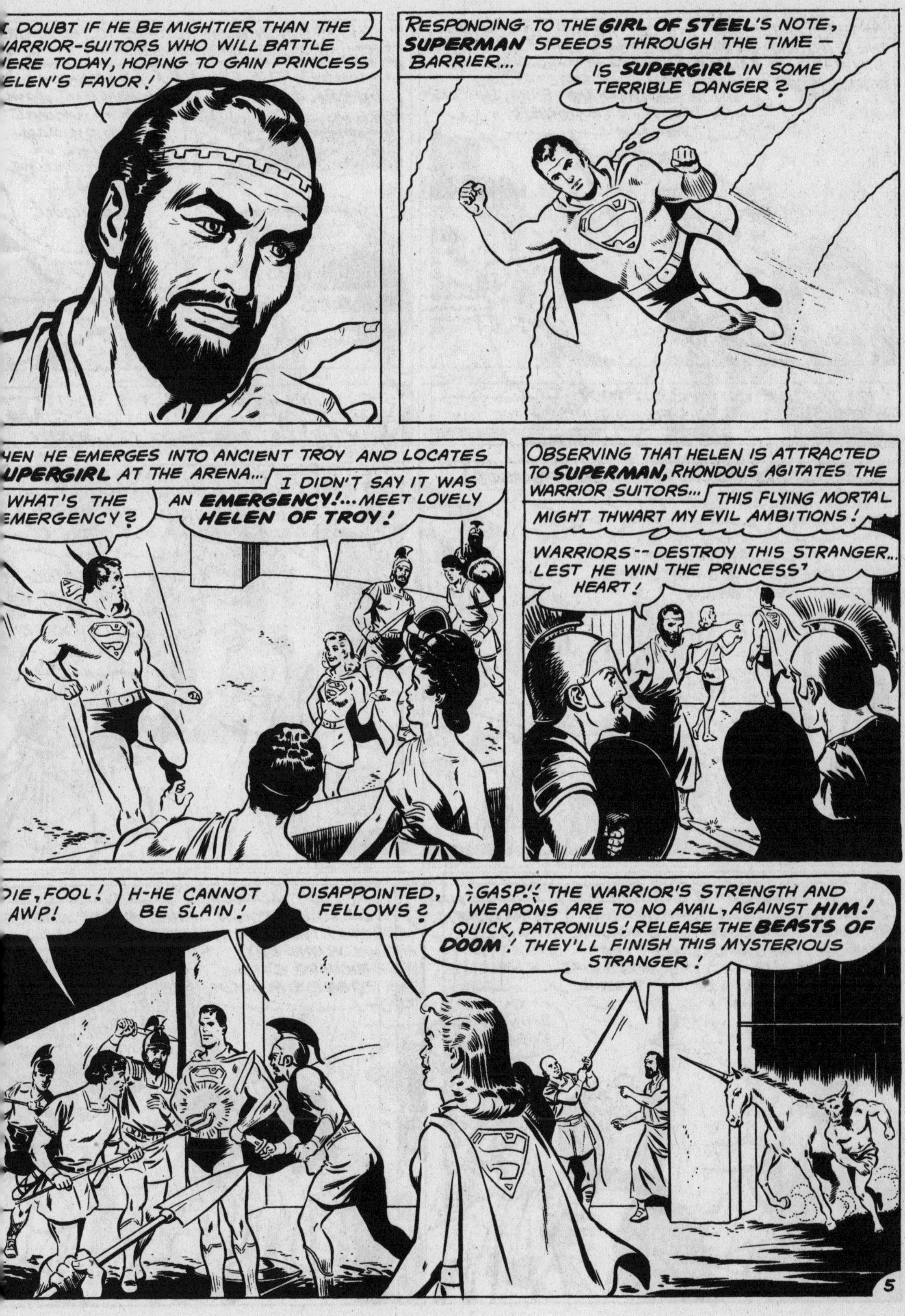
I DOUBT IF HE BE MIGHTIER THAN THE WARRIOR-SUITORS WHO WILL BATTLE HERE TODAY, HOPING TO GAIN PRINCESS HELEN'S FAVOR!
RESPONDING TO THE GIRL OF STEEL'S NOTE, SUPERMAN SPEEDS THROUGH THE TIME-BARRIER...
IS SUPERGIRL IN SOME TERRIBLE DANGER?
WHEN HE EMERGES INTO ANCIENT TROY AND LOCATES SUPERGIRL AT THE ARENA...
WHAT'S THE EMERGENCY?
I DIDN'T SAY IT WAS AN EMERGENCY!... MEET LOVELY HELEN OF TROY!
OBSERVING THAT HELEN IS ATTRACTED TO SUPERMAN, RHONDOUS AGITATES THE WARRIOR SUITORS...
THIS FLYING MORTAL MIGHT THWART MY EVIL AMBITIONS!
WARRIORS--DESTROY THIS STRANGER... LEST HE WIN THE PRINCESS' HEART!
DIE, FOOL! AWP!
H-HE CANNOT BE SLAIN!
DISAPPOINTED, FELLOWS?
GASP! THE WARRIOR'S STRENGTH AND WEAPONS ARE TO NO AVAIL, AGAINST HIM! QUICK, PATRONIUS! RELEASE THE BEASTS OF DOOM! THEY'LL FINISH THIS MYSTERIOUS STRANGER!
5

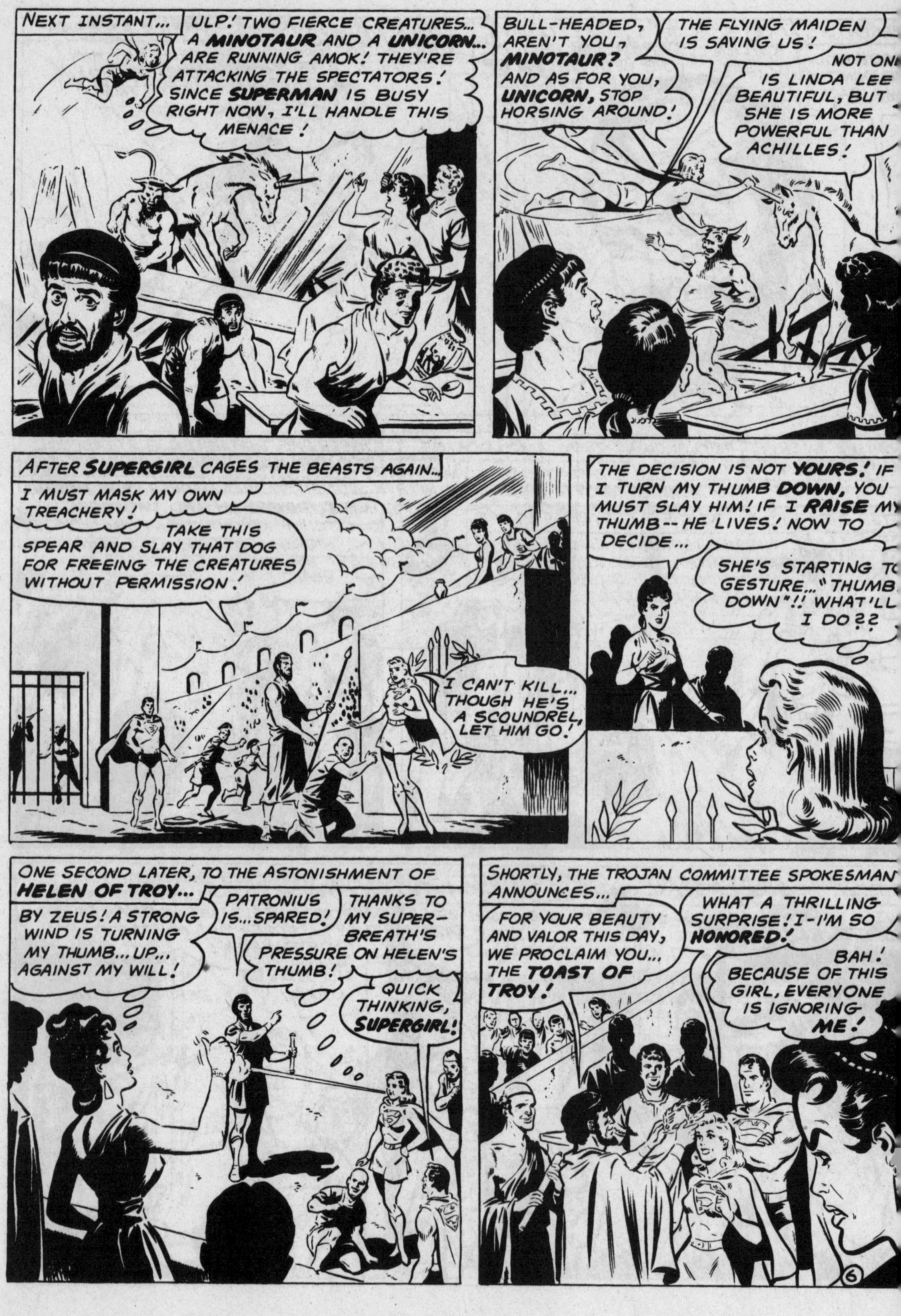
NEXT INSTANT...
ULP! TWO FIERCE CREATURES... A MINOTAUR AND A UNICORN... ARE RUNNING AMOK! THEY'RE ATTACKING THE SPECTATORS! SINCE SUPERMAN IS BUSY RIGHT NOW, I'LL HANDLE THIS MENACE!
BULL-HEADED, AREN'T YOU, MINOTAUR? AND AS FOR YOU, UNICORN, STOP HORSING AROUND!
THE FLYING MAIDEN IS SAVING US!
NOT ON IS LINDA LEE BEAUTIFUL, BUT SHE IS MORE POWERFUL THAN ACHILLES!
AFTER SUPERGIRL CAGES THE BEASTS AGAIN...
I MUST MASK MY OWN TREACHERY!
TAKE THIS SPEAR AND SLAY THAT DOG FOR FREEING THE CREATURES WITHOUT PERMISSION!
I CAN'T KILL... THOUGH HE'S A SCOUNDREL, LET HIM GO!
THE DECISION IS NOT YOURS! IF I TURN MY THUMB DOWN, YOU MUST SLAY HIM! IF I RAISE MY THUMB-- HE LIVES! NOW TO DECIDE...
SHE'S STARTING TO GESTURE..."THUMB DOWN"!! WHAT'LL I DO??
ONE SECOND LATER, TO THE ASTONISHMENT OF HELEN OF TROY...
BY ZEUS! A STRONG WIND IS TURNING MY THUMB... UP... AGAINST MY WILL!
PATRONIUS IS...SPARED!
THANKS TO MY SUPER-BREATH'S PRESSURE ON HELEN'S THUMB!
QUICK THINKING, SUPERGIRL!
SHORTLY, THE TROJAN COMMITTEE SPOKESMAN ANNOUNCES...
FOR YOUR BEAUTY AND VALOR THIS DAY, WE PROCLAIM YOU... THE TOAST OF TROY!
WHAT A THRILLING SURPRISE! I-I'M SO HONORED!
BAH! BECAUSE OF THIS GIRL, EVERYONE IS IGNORING ME!
6

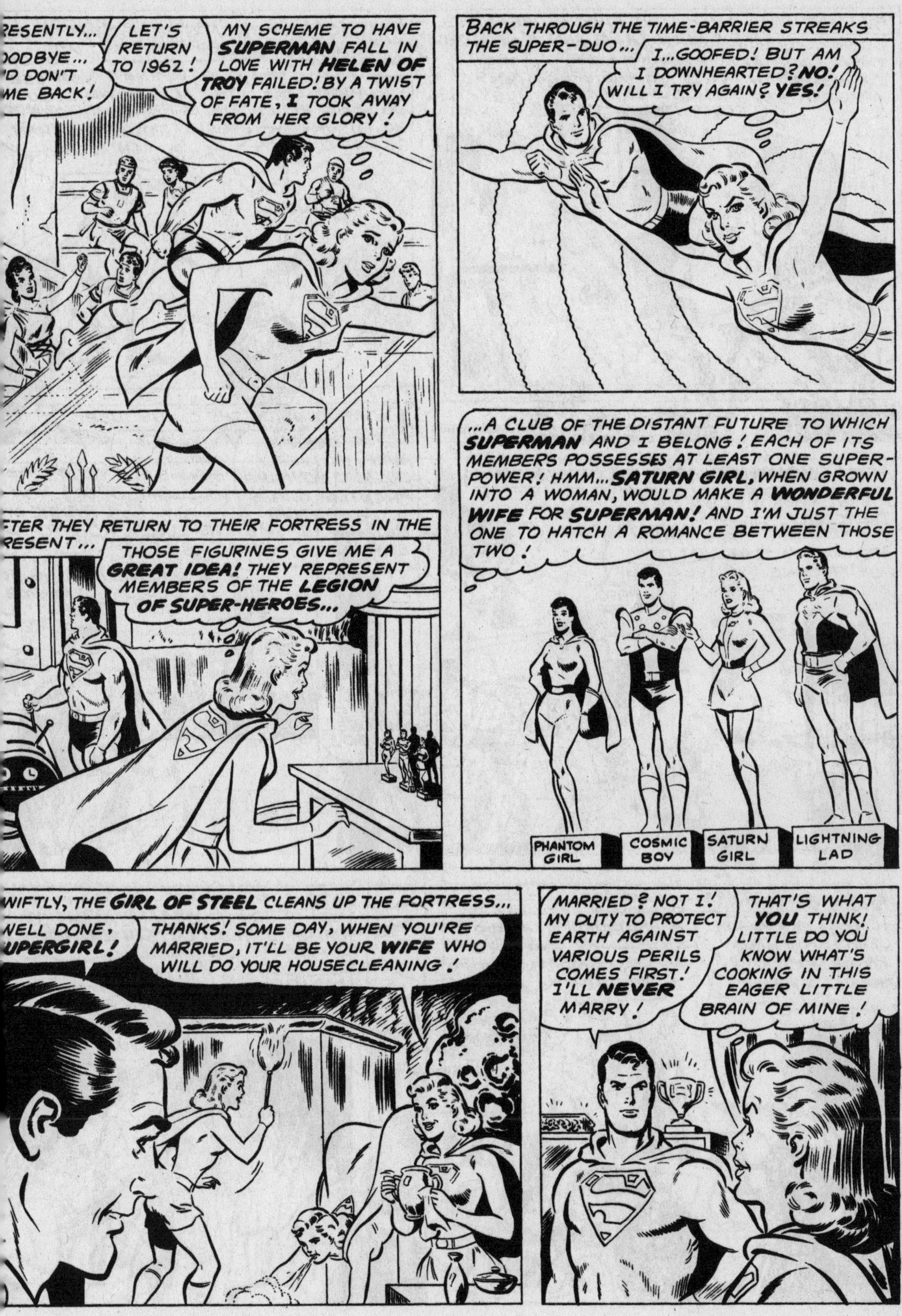
RESENTLY...
OODBYE... D DON'T ME BACK!
LET'S RETURN TO 1962!
MY SCHEME TO HAVE SUPERMAN FALL IN LOVE WITH HELEN OF TROY FAILED! BY A TWIST OF FATE, I TOOK AWAY FROM HER GLORY!
BACK THROUGH THE TIME-BARRIER STREAKS THE SUPER-DUO...
I...GOOFED! BUT AM I DOWNHEARTED? NO! WILL I TRY AGAIN? YES!
FTER THEY RETURN TO THEIR FORTRESS IN THE RESENT...
THOSE FIGURINES GIVE ME A GREAT IDEA! THEY REPRESENT MEMBERS OF THE LEGION OF SUPER-HEROES...
...A CLUB OF THE DISTANT FUTURE TO WHICH SUPERMAN AND I BELONG! EACH OF ITS MEMBERS POSSESSES AT LEAST ONE SUPER-POWER! HMM... SATURN GIRL, WHEN GROWN INTO A WOMAN, WOULD MAKE A WONDERFUL WIFE FOR SUPERMAN! AND I'M JUST THE ONE TO HATCH A ROMANCE BETWEEN THOSE TWO!
PHANTOM GIRL
COSMIC BOY
SATURN GIRL
LIGHTNING LAD
WIFTLY, THE GIRL OF STEEL CLEANS UP THE FORTRESS...
WELL DONE, UPERGIRL!
THANKS! SOME DAY, WHEN YOU'RE MARRIED, IT'LL BE YOUR WIFE WHO WILL DO YOUR HOUSECLEANING!
MARRIED? NOT I! MY DUTY TO PROTECT EARTH AGAINST VARIOUS PERILS COMES FIRST! I'LL NEVER MARRY!
THAT'S WHAT YOU THINK! LITTLE DO YOU KNOW WHAT'S COOKING IN THIS EAGER LITTLE BRAIN OF MINE!

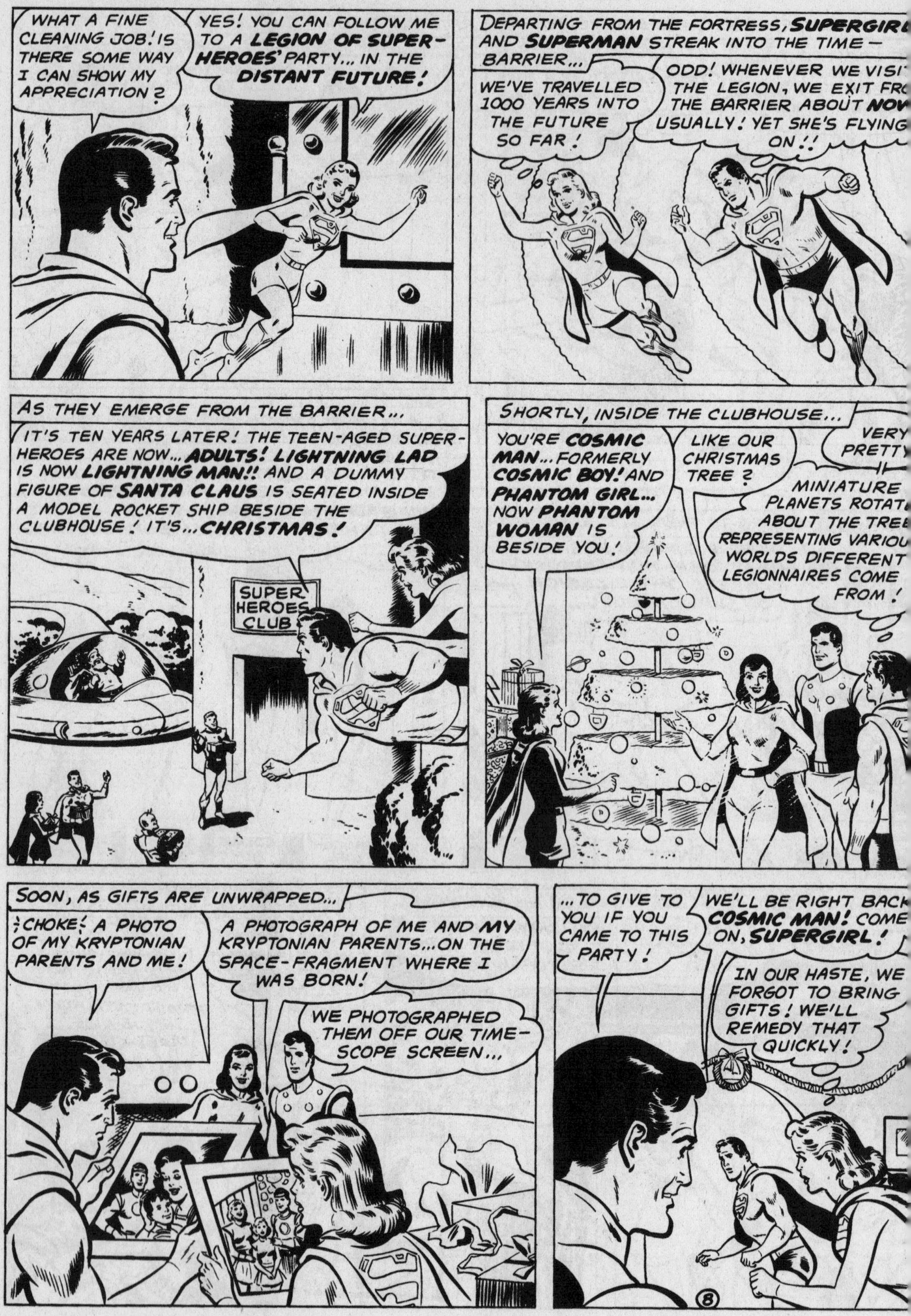
WHAT A FINE CLEANING JOB! IS THERE SOME WAY I CAN SHOW MY APPRECIATION?
YES! YOU CAN FOLLOW ME TO A **LEGION OF SUPER-HEROES'** PARTY... IN THE **DISTANT FUTURE!**
DEPARTING FROM THE FORTRESS, **SUPERGIRL** AND **SUPERMAN** STREAK INTO THE TIME-BARRIER...
WE'VE TRAVELLED 1000 YEARS INTO THE FUTURE SO FAR!
ODD! WHENEVER WE VISIT THE LEGION, WE EXIT FR THE BARRIER ABOUT **NOV** USUALLY! YET SHE'S FLYING ON!!
AS THEY EMERGE FROM THE BARRIER...
IT'S TEN YEARS LATER! THE TEEN-AGED SUPER-HEROES ARE NOW... **ADULTS! LIGHTNING LAD** IS NOW **LIGHTNING MAN!!** AND A DUMMY FIGURE OF **SANTA CLAUS** IS SEATED INSIDE A MODEL ROCKET SHIP BESIDE THE CLUBHOUSE! IT'S... **CHRISTMAS!**
SUPER HEROES CLUB
SHORTLY, INSIDE THE CLUBHOUSE...
YOU'RE **COSMIC MAN**... FORMERLY **COSMIC BOY!** AND **PHANTOM GIRL**... NOW **PHANTOM WOMAN** IS BESIDE YOU!
LIKE OUR CHRISTMAS TREE?
VERY PRETTY
MINIATURE PLANETS ROTAT ABOUT THE TREE REPRESENTING VARIOU WORLDS DIFFERENT LEGIONNAIRES COME FROM!
SOON, AS GIFTS ARE UNWRAPPED...
;CHOKE; A PHOTO OF MY KRYPTONIAN PARENTS AND ME!
A PHOTOGRAPH OF ME AND **MY** KRYPTONIAN PARENTS... ON THE SPACE-FRAGMENT WHERE I WAS BORN!
WE PHOTOGRAPHED THEM OFF OUR TIME-SCOPE SCREEN...
...TO GIVE TO YOU IF YOU CAME TO THIS PARTY!
WE'LL BE RIGHT BACK **COSMIC MAN!** COME ON, **SUPERGIRL!**
IN OUR HASTE, WE FORGOT TO BRING GIFTS! WE'LL REMEDY THAT QUICKLY!
8

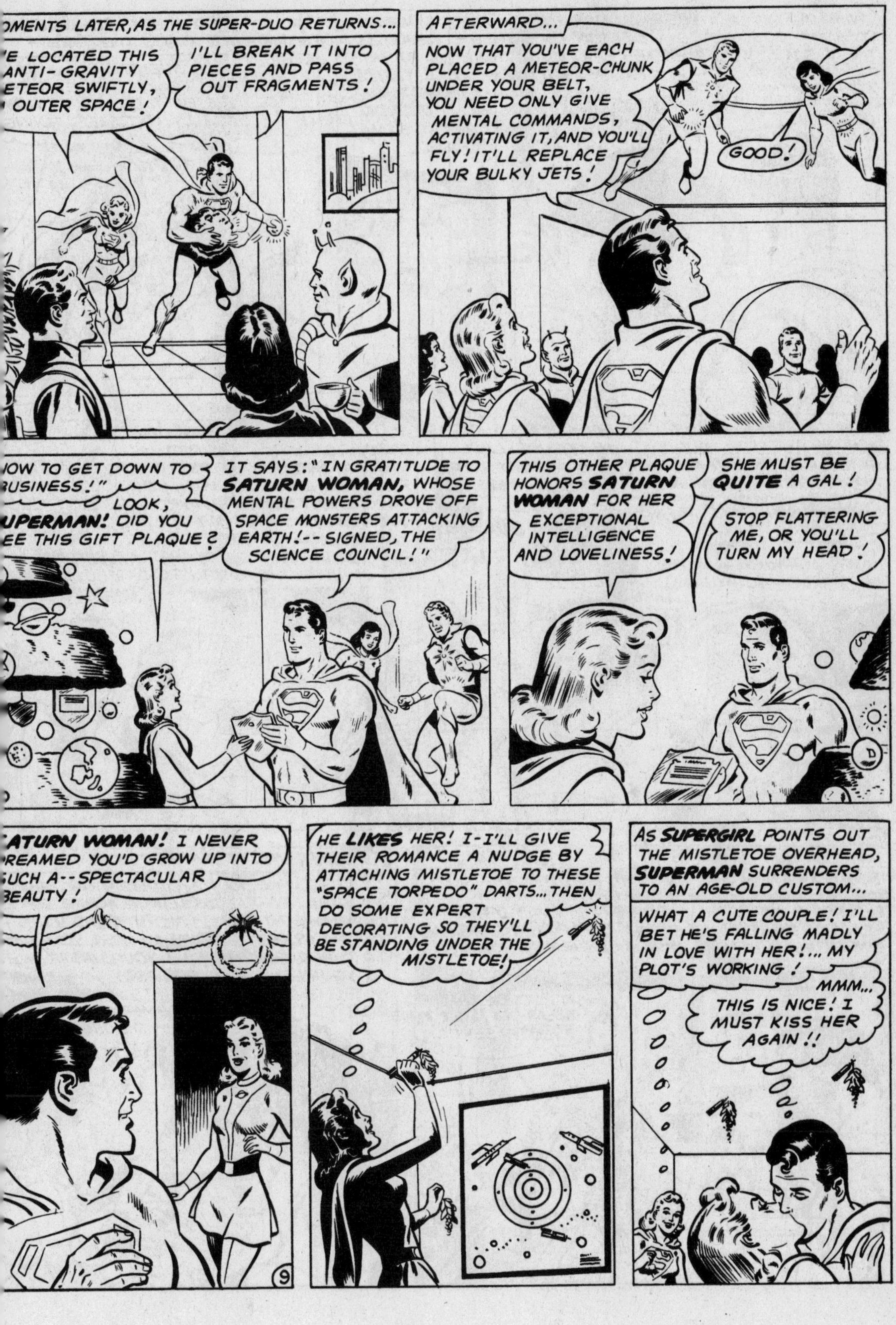
OMENTS LATER, AS THE SUPER-DUO RETURNS...
'E LOCATED THIS ANTI-GRAVITY ETEOR SWIFTLY, OUTER SPACE!
I'LL BREAK IT INTO PIECES AND PASS OUT FRAGMENTS!
AFTERWARD...
NOW THAT YOU'VE EACH PLACED A METEOR-CHUNK UNDER YOUR BELT, YOU NEED ONLY GIVE MENTAL COMMANDS, ACTIVATING IT, AND YOU'LL FLY! IT'LL REPLACE YOUR BULKY JETS!
GOOD!
IOW TO GET DOWN TO BUSINESS!" LOOK, UPERMAN! DID YOU EE THIS GIFT PLAQUE?
IT SAYS: "IN GRATITUDE TO SATURN WOMAN, WHOSE MENTAL POWERS DROVE OFF SPACE MONSTERS ATTACKING EARTH!-- SIGNED, THE SCIENCE COUNCIL!"
THIS OTHER PLAQUE HONORS SATURN WOMAN FOR HER EXCEPTIONAL INTELLIGENCE AND LOVELINESS!
SHE MUST BE QUITE A GAL!
STOP FLATTERING ME, OR YOU'LL TURN MY HEAD!
ATURN WOMAN! I NEVER REAMED YOU'D GROW UP INTO UCH A--SPECTACULAR BEAUTY!
9
HE LIKES HER! I-I'LL GIVE THEIR ROMANCE A NUDGE BY ATTACHING MISTLETOE TO THESE "SPACE TORPEDO" DARTS... THEN DO SOME EXPERT DECORATING SO THEY'LL BE STANDING UNDER THE MISTLETOE!
AS SUPERGIRL POINTS OUT THE MISTLETOE OVERHEAD, SUPERMAN SURRENDERS TO AN AGE-OLD CUSTOM...
WHAT A CUTE COUPLE! I'LL BET HE'S FALLING MADLY IN LOVE WITH HER!... MY PLOT'S WORKING!
MMM... THIS IS NICE! I MUST KISS HER AGAIN!!

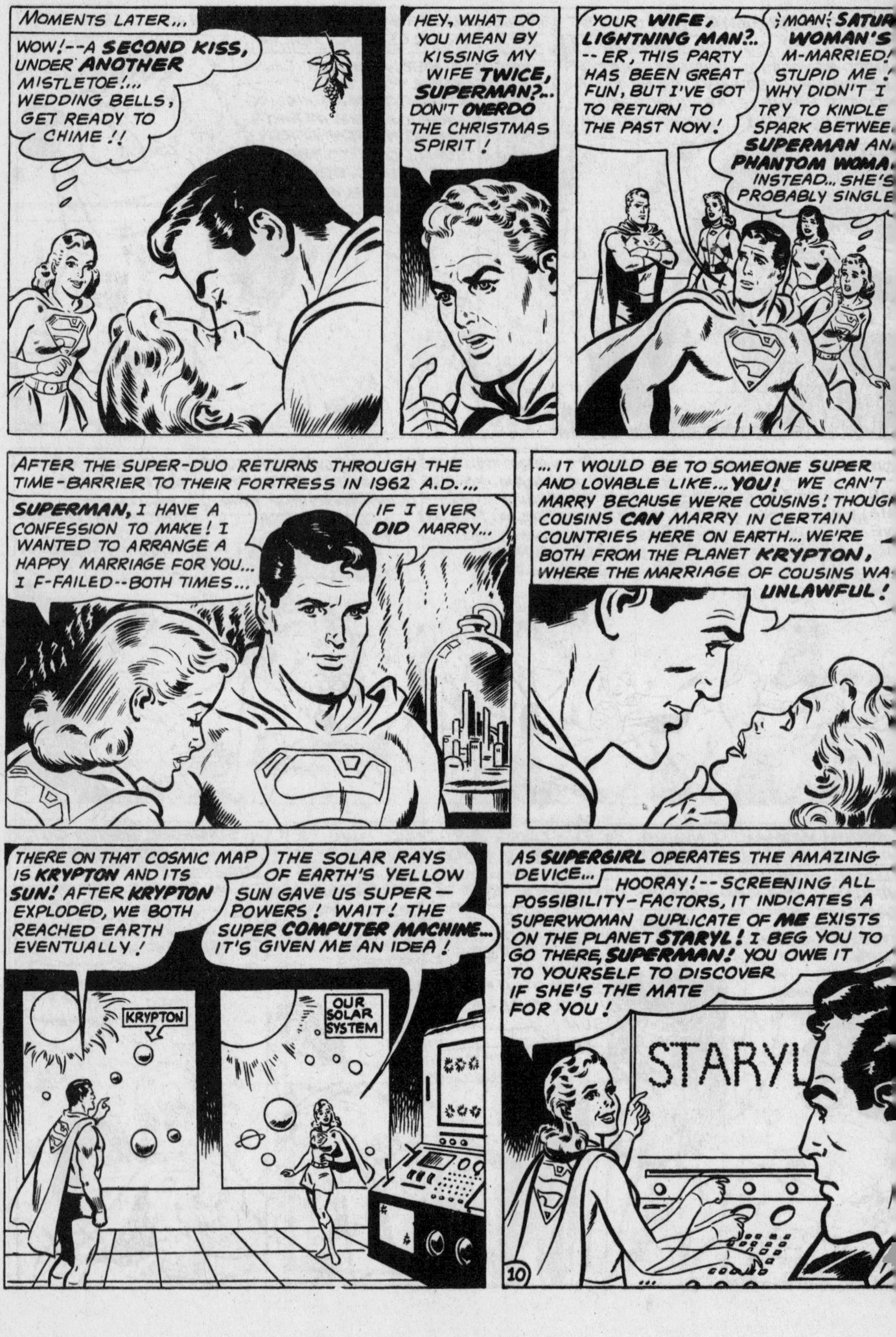

MOMENTS LATER...
WOW!--A SECOND KISS, UNDER ANOTHER MISTLETOE!... WEDDING BELLS, GET READY TO CHIME!!
HEY, WHAT DO YOU MEAN BY KISSING MY WIFE TWICE, SUPERMAN?... DON'T OVERDO THE CHRISTMAS SPIRIT!
YOUR WIFE, LIGHTNING MAN?.. -- ER, THIS PARTY HAS BEEN GREAT FUN, BUT I'VE GOT TO RETURN TO THE PAST NOW!
MOAN! SATUR WOMAN'S M-MARRIED! STUPID ME! WHY DIDN'T I TRY TO KINDLE SPARK BETWEE SUPERMAN AN PHANTOM WOMA INSTEAD... SHE'S PROBABLY SINGLE
AFTER THE SUPER-DUO RETURNS THROUGH THE TIME-BARRIER TO THEIR FORTRESS IN 1962 A.D....
SUPERMAN, I HAVE A CONFESSION TO MAKE! I WANTED TO ARRANGE A HAPPY MARRIAGE FOR YOU... I F-FAILED--BOTH TIMES...
IF I EVER DID MARRY...
... IT WOULD BE TO SOMEONE SUPER AND LOVABLE LIKE... YOU! WE CAN'T MARRY BECAUSE WE'RE COUSINS! THOUG COUSINS CAN MARRY IN CERTAIN COUNTRIES HERE ON EARTH... WE'RE BOTH FROM THE PLANET KRYPTON, WHERE THE MARRIAGE OF COUSINS WA UNLAWFUL!
THERE ON THAT COSMIC MAP IS KRYPTON AND ITS SUN! AFTER KRYPTON EXPLODED, WE BOTH REACHED EARTH EVENTUALLY!
THE SOLAR RAYS OF EARTH'S YELLOW SUN GAVE US SUPER-POWERS! WAIT! THE SUPER COMPUTER MACHINE... IT'S GIVEN ME AN IDEA!
KRYPTON
OUR SOLAR SYSTEM
AS SUPERGIRL OPERATES THE AMAZING DEVICE...
HOORAY!--SCREENING ALL POSSIBILITY-FACTORS, IT INDICATES A SUPERWOMAN DUPLICATE OF ME EXISTS ON THE PLANET STARYL! I BEG YOU TO GO THERE, SUPERMAN! YOU OWE IT TO YOURSELF TO DISCOVER IF SHE'S THE MATE FOR YOU!
STARYL
10

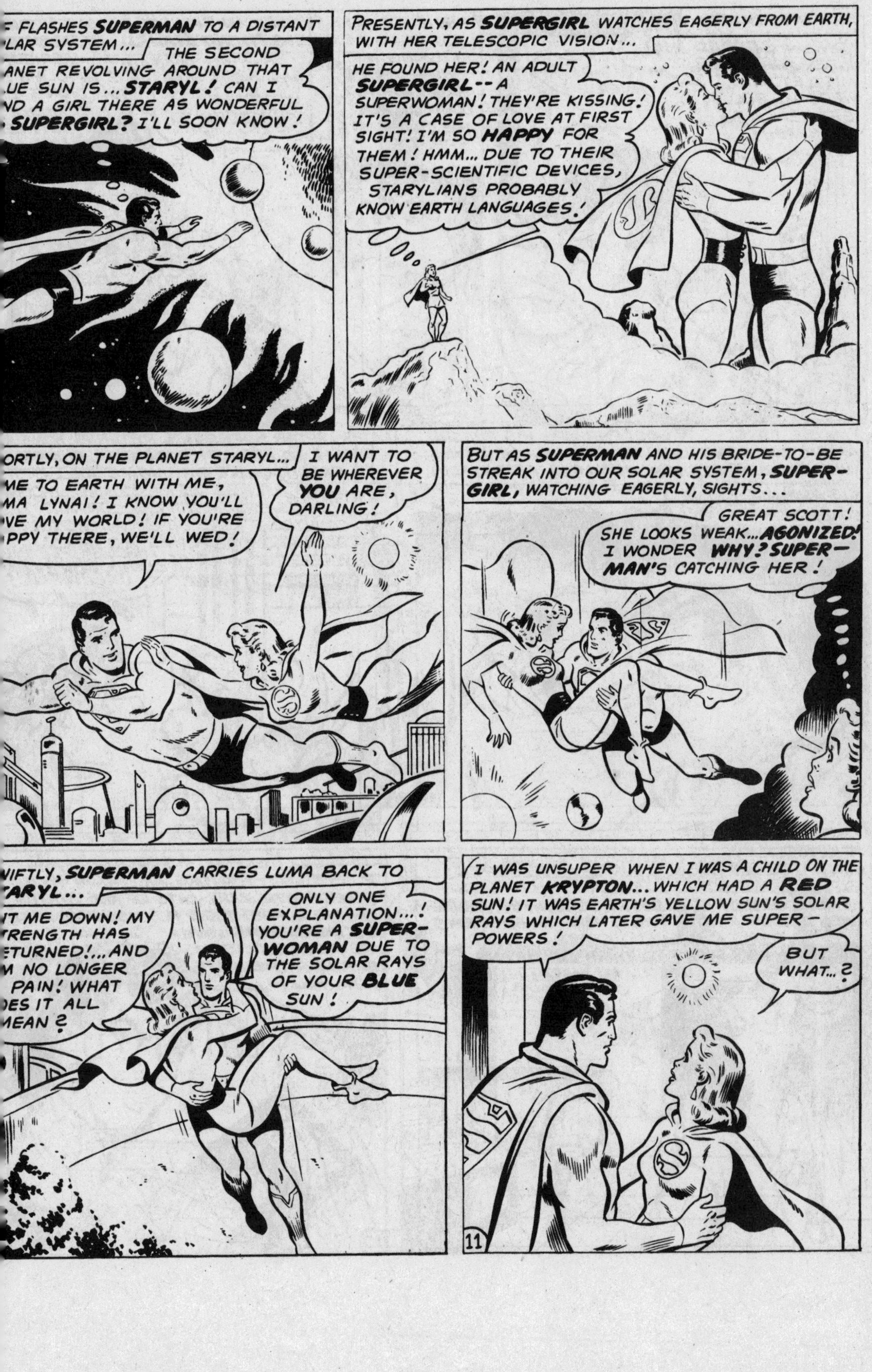
F FLASHES SUPERMAN TO A DISTANT
LAR SYSTEM...
THE SECOND
ANET REVOLVING AROUND THAT
UE SUN IS... STARYL! CAN I
D A GIRL THERE AS WONDERFUL
SUPERGIRL? I'LL SOON KNOW!
PRESENTLY, AS SUPERGIRL WATCHES EAGERLY FROM EARTH, WITH HER TELESCOPIC VISION...
HE FOUND HER! AN ADULT SUPERGIRL--A SUPERWOMAN! THEY'RE KISSING! IT'S A CASE OF LOVE AT FIRST SIGHT! I'M SO HAPPY FOR THEM! HMM... DUE TO THEIR SUPER-SCIENTIFIC DEVICES, STARYLIANS PROBABLY KNOW EARTH LANGUAGES!
ORTLY, ON THE PLANET STARYL...
ME TO EARTH WITH ME,
MA LYNAI! I KNOW YOU'LL
VE MY WORLD! IF YOU'RE
PPY THERE, WE'LL WED!
I WANT TO BE WHEREVER YOU ARE, DARLING!
BUT AS SUPERMAN AND HIS BRIDE-TO-BE STREAK INTO OUR SOLAR SYSTEM, SUPERGIRL, WATCHING EAGERLY, SIGHTS...
GREAT SCOTT! SHE LOOKS WEAK...AGONIZED! I WONDER WHY? SUPERMAN'S CATCHING HER!
WIFTLY, SUPERMAN CARRIES LUMA BACK TO
TARYL...
IT ME DOWN! MY
TRENGTH HAS
ETURNED!...AND
M NO LONGER
PAIN! WHAT
ES IT ALL
MEAN?
ONLY ONE EXPLANATION...! YOU'RE A SUPER-WOMAN DUE TO THE SOLAR RAYS OF YOUR BLUE SUN!
I WAS UNSUPER WHEN I WAS A CHILD ON THE PLANET KRYPTON...WHICH HAD A RED SUN! IT WAS EARTH'S YELLOW SUN'S SOLAR RAYS WHICH LATER GAVE ME SUPER-POWERS!
BUT WHAT...?
11

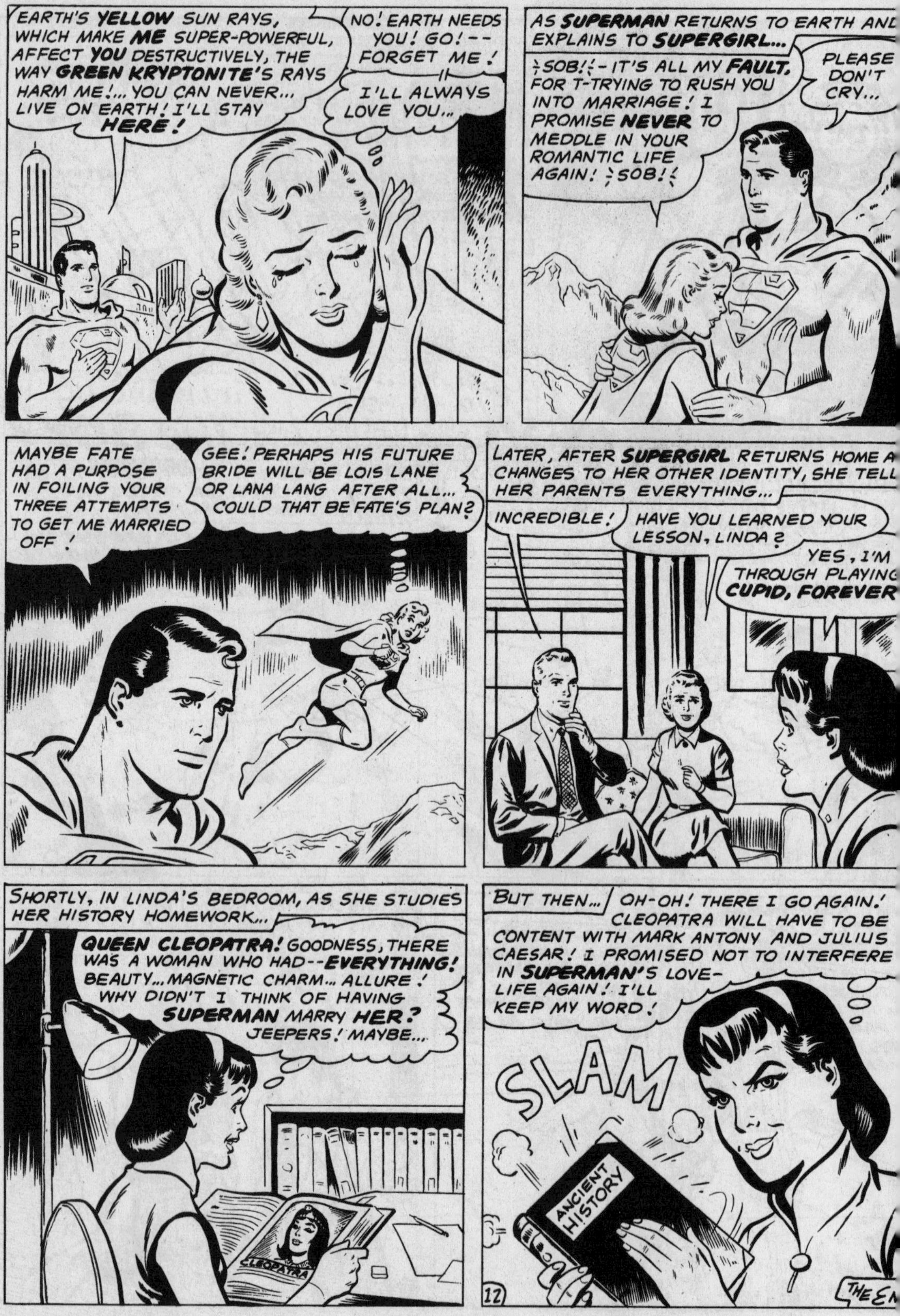
EARTH'S YELLOW SUN RAYS, WHICH MAKE ME SUPER-POWERFUL, AFFECT YOU DESTRUCTIVELY, THE WAY GREEN KRYPTONITE'S RAYS HARM ME!... YOU CAN NEVER... LIVE ON EARTH! I'LL STAY HERE!
NO! EARTH NEEDS YOU! GO! -- FORGET ME!
I'LL ALWAYS LOVE YOU...
AS SUPERMAN RETURNS TO EARTH AND EXPLAINS TO SUPERGIRL...
-SOB!- IT'S ALL MY FAULT. FOR T-TRYING TO RUSH YOU INTO MARRIAGE! I PROMISE NEVER TO MEDDLE IN YOUR ROMANTIC LIFE AGAIN! -SOB!-
PLEASE DON'T CRY...
MAYBE FATE HAD A PURPOSE IN FOILING YOUR THREE ATTEMPTS TO GET ME MARRIED OFF!
GEE! PERHAPS HIS FUTURE BRIDE WILL BE LOIS LANE OR LANA LANG AFTER ALL... COULD THAT BE FATE'S PLAN?
LATER, AFTER SUPERGIRL RETURNS HOME A CHANGES TO HER OTHER IDENTITY, SHE TELL HER PARENTS EVERYTHING...
INCREDIBLE!
HAVE YOU LEARNED YOUR LESSON, LINDA?
YES, I'M THROUGH PLAYING CUPID, FOREVER
SHORTLY, IN LINDA'S BEDROOM, AS SHE STUDIES HER HISTORY HOMEWORK...
QUEEN CLEOPATRA! GOODNESS, THERE WAS A WOMAN WHO HAD--EVERYTHING! BEAUTY... MAGNETIC CHARM... ALLURE! WHY DIDN'T I THINK OF HAVING SUPERMAN MARRY HER? JEEPERS! MAYBE...
CLEOPATRA
BUT THEN...
OH-OH! THERE I GO AGAIN! CLEOPATRA WILL HAVE TO BE CONTENT WITH MARK ANTONY AND JULIUS CAESAR! I PROMISED NOT TO INTERFERE IN SUPERMAN'S LOVE-LIFE AGAIN! I'LL KEEP MY WORD!
SLAM
ANCIENT HISTORY
12
THE EN

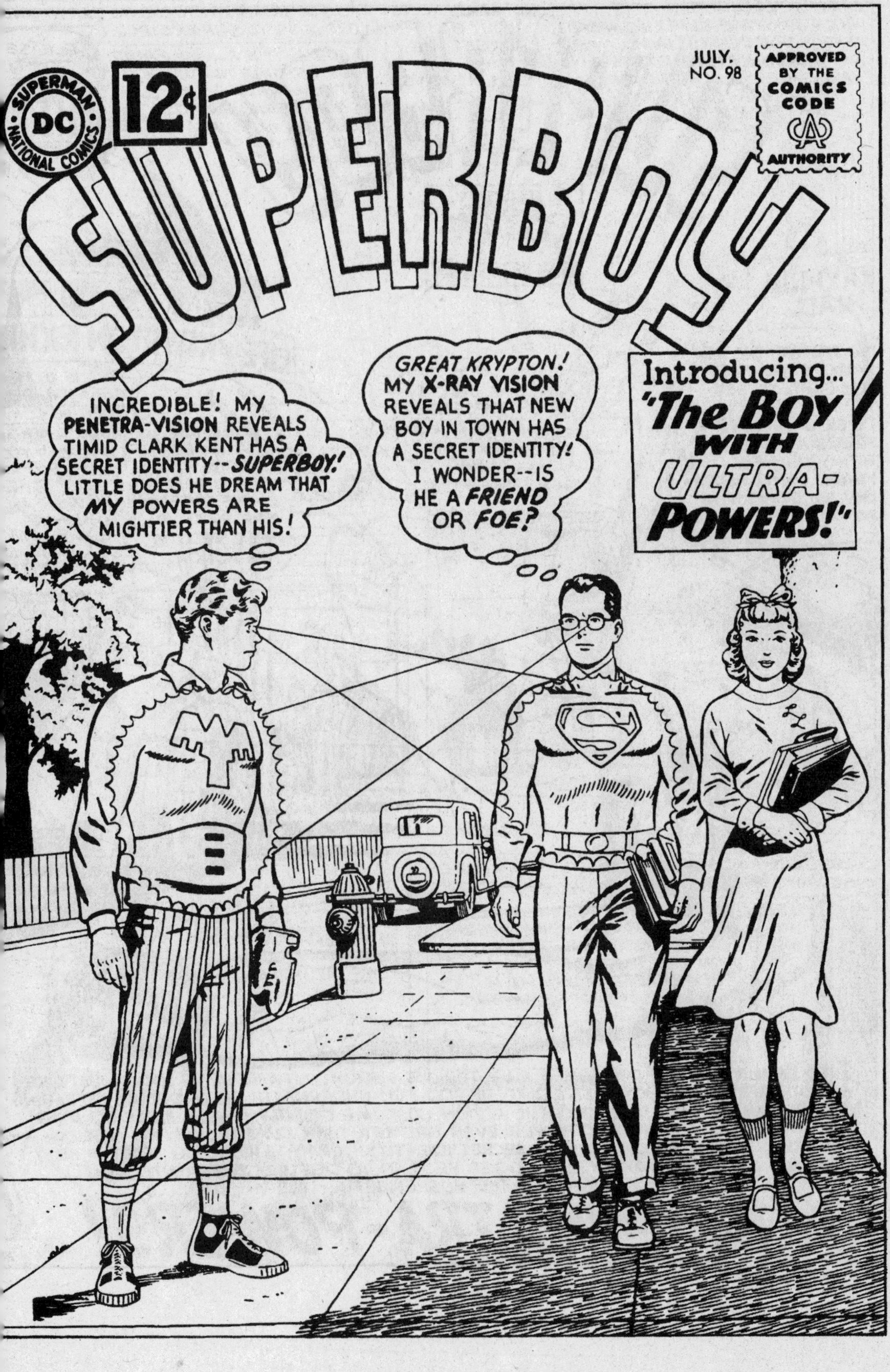
SUPERMAN DC NATIONAL COMICS
12¢
SUPERBOY
JULY. NO. 98
APPROVED BY THE COMICS CODE AUTHORITY
INCREDIBLE! MY PENETRA-VISION REVEALS TIMID CLARK KENT HAS A SECRET IDENTITY--SUPERBOY! LITTLE DOES HE DREAM THAT MY POWERS ARE MIGHTIER THAN HIS!
GREAT KRYPTON! MY X-RAY VISION REVEALS THAT NEW BOY IN TOWN HAS A SECRET IDENTITY! I WONDER--IS HE A FRIEND OR FOE?
Introducing... "The Boy with Ultra-Powers!"

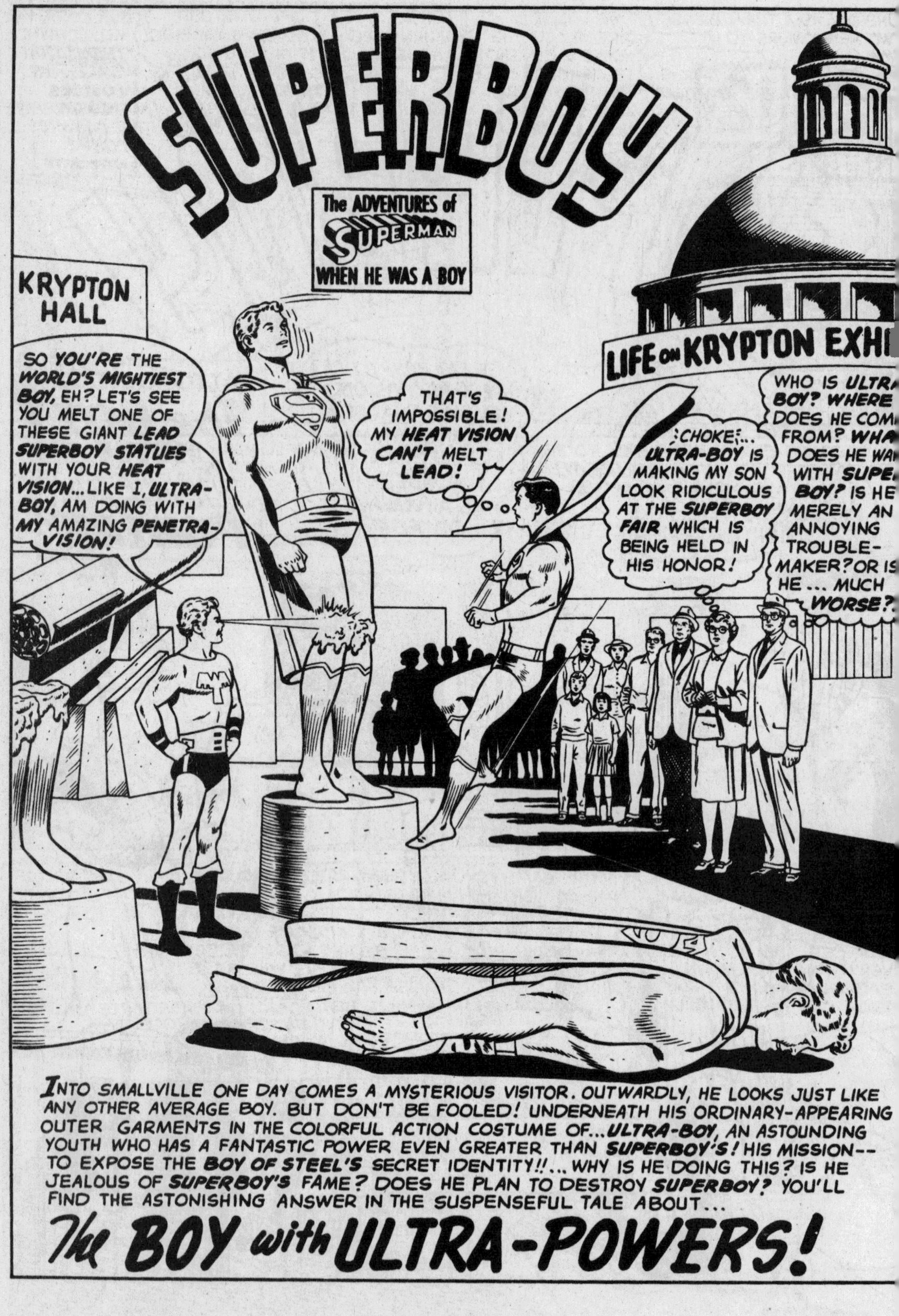
SUPERBOY
The ADVENTURES of SUPERMAN WHEN HE WAS A BOY
KRYPTON HALL
LIFE ON KRYPTON EXHI
SO YOU'RE THE WORLD'S MIGHTIEST BOY, EH? LET'S SEE YOU MELT ONE OF THESE GIANT LEAD SUPERBOY STATUES WITH YOUR HEAT VISION... LIKE I, ULTRA-BOY, AM DOING WITH MY AMAZING PENETRA-VISION!
THAT'S IMPOSSIBLE! MY HEAT VISION CAN'T MELT LEAD!
CHOKE... ULTRA-BOY IS MAKING MY SON LOOK RIDICULOUS AT THE SUPERBOY FAIR WHICH IS BEING HELD IN HIS HONOR!
INTO SMALLVILLE ONE DAY COMES A MYSTERIOUS VISITOR. OUTWARDLY, HE LOOKS JUST LIKE ANY OTHER AVERAGE BOY. BUT DON'T BE FOOLED! UNDERNEATH HIS ORDINARY-APPEARING OUTER GARMENTS IN THE COLORFUL ACTION COSTUME OF... ULTRA-BOY, AN ASTOUNDING YOUTH WHO HAS A FANTASTIC POWER EVEN GREATER THAN SUPERBOY'S! HIS MISSION-- TO EXPOSE THE BOY OF STEEL'S SECRET IDENTITY!!... WHY IS HE DOING THIS? IS HE JEALOUS OF SUPERBOY'S FAME? DOES HE PLAN TO DESTROY SUPERBOY? YOU'LL FIND THE ASTONISHING ANSWER IN THE SUSPENSEFUL TALE ABOUT...
The BOY with ULTRA-POWERS!

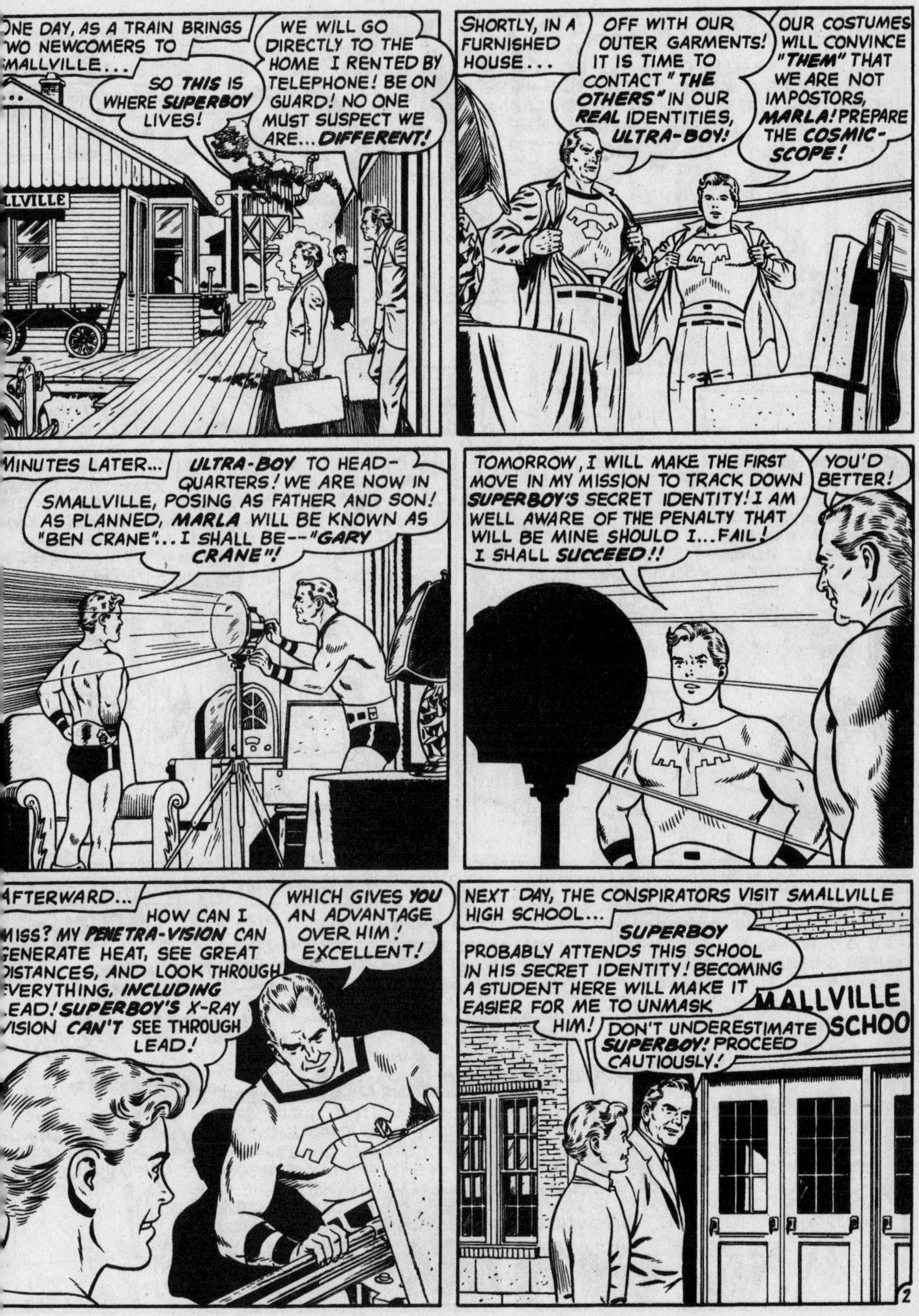
ONE DAY, AS A TRAIN BRINGS TWO NEWCOMERS TO SMALLVILLE...
SO THIS IS WHERE SUPERBOY LIVES!
WE WILL GO DIRECTLY TO THE HOME I RENTED BY TELEPHONE! BE ON GUARD! NO ONE MUST SUSPECT WE ARE... DIFFERENT!
SHORTLY, IN A FURNISHED HOUSE...
OFF WITH OUR OUTER GARMENTS! IT IS TIME TO CONTACT "THE OTHERS" IN OUR REAL IDENTITIES, ULTRA-BOY!
OUR COSTUMES WILL CONVINCE "THEM" THAT WE ARE NOT IMPOSTORS, MARLA! PREPARE THE COSMIC-SCOPE!
MINUTES LATER...
ULTRA-BOY TO HEAD-QUARTERS! WE ARE NOW IN SMALLVILLE, POSING AS FATHER AND SON! AS PLANNED, MARLA WILL BE KNOWN AS "BEN CRANE"... I SHALL BE--"GARY CRANE"!
TOMORROW, I WILL MAKE THE FIRST MOVE IN MY MISSION TO TRACK DOWN SUPERBOY'S SECRET IDENTITY! I AM WELL AWARE OF THE PENALTY THAT WILL BE MINE SHOULD I... FAIL! I SHALL SUCCEED!!
YOU'D BETTER!
AFTERWARD...
HOW CAN I MISS? MY PENETRA-VISION CAN GENERATE HEAT, SEE GREAT DISTANCES, AND LOOK THROUGH EVERYTHING, INCLUDING LEAD! SUPERBOY'S X-RAY VISION CAN'T SEE THROUGH LEAD!
WHICH GIVES YOU AN ADVANTAGE OVER HIM! EXCELLENT!
NEXT DAY, THE CONSPIRATORS VISIT SMALLVILLE HIGH SCHOOL...
SUPERBOY PROBABLY ATTENDS THIS SCHOOL IN HIS SECRET IDENTITY! BECOMING A STUDENT HERE WILL MAKE IT EASIER FOR ME TO UNMASK HIM!
DON'T UNDERESTIMATE SUPERBOY! PROCEED CAUTIOUSLY!
MALLVILLE SCHOO
2

SOON, IN THE PRINCIPAL'S OFFICE...

WELCOME TO SMALLVILLE! I'LL NEED YOUR SCHOLASTIC RECORD. WHAT CITY DO YOU COME FROM, GARY?

ER...A TOWN FAR AWAY. ALL THE SCHOLASTIC RECORDS WERE DESTROYED IN A TERRIBLE FIRE...

ASSISTING IN THE OFFICE IS PETE ROSS, WHO, UNKNOWN TO HIS FRIEND CLARK KENT, IS AWARE THAT CLARK IS SECRETLY *SUPERBOY.*

GARY CRANE SURE IS VAGUE ABOUT HIS BACKGROUND! HM-MM...

AFTER THE NEWCOMER REGISTERS...

I'M PETE ROSS. YOU'LL LIKE SMALLVILLE, GARY. IT'S NOT A VERY BIG CITY, BUT IT'S WORLD-FAMOUS BECAUSE *SUPERBOY* LIVES HERE.

I'LL START INVESTIGATING, IMMEDIATELY!

DO YOU KNOW *SUPERBOY'S* SECRET IDENTITY, PETE?

PRINCIPAL

ME? UH--ER--NO! OF COURSE NOT!

ULP! THAT QUESTION CAUGHT ME OFF-GUARD!

I GUESS IT WAS SILLY OF ME TO ASK!

HE LOOKS NERVOUS...SUSPICIOUS SO! I'LL EXAMINE HIS HEART WITH MY *PENETRA* VISION!

OH-OH! I CAN SEE HIS HEART BEATING MORE RAPIDLY! WHY SHOULD MY QUESTION EXCITE HIM, UNLESS... HE IS *SUPERBOY* SECRETLY! HE'S NOT WEARING A COSTUME UNDER HIS OUTER GARMENTS...POSSIBLY TO OUTWIT SOMEONE LIKE ME! CLEVER!!

3

WHEN SCHOOL IS OVER, GARY AND HIS "FATHER" TRAIL PETE...

THE ROSS BOY WORKS IN JONATHAN KENT'S GENERAL STORE AFTER SCHOOL. SO YOU THINK HE IS *SUPERBOY,* EH?

COME WITH ME BEHIND THE STORE! QUICK!

GENERAL STORE

JONATHAN KENT, PROPRIETOR

24 CANS CORN SYRUP

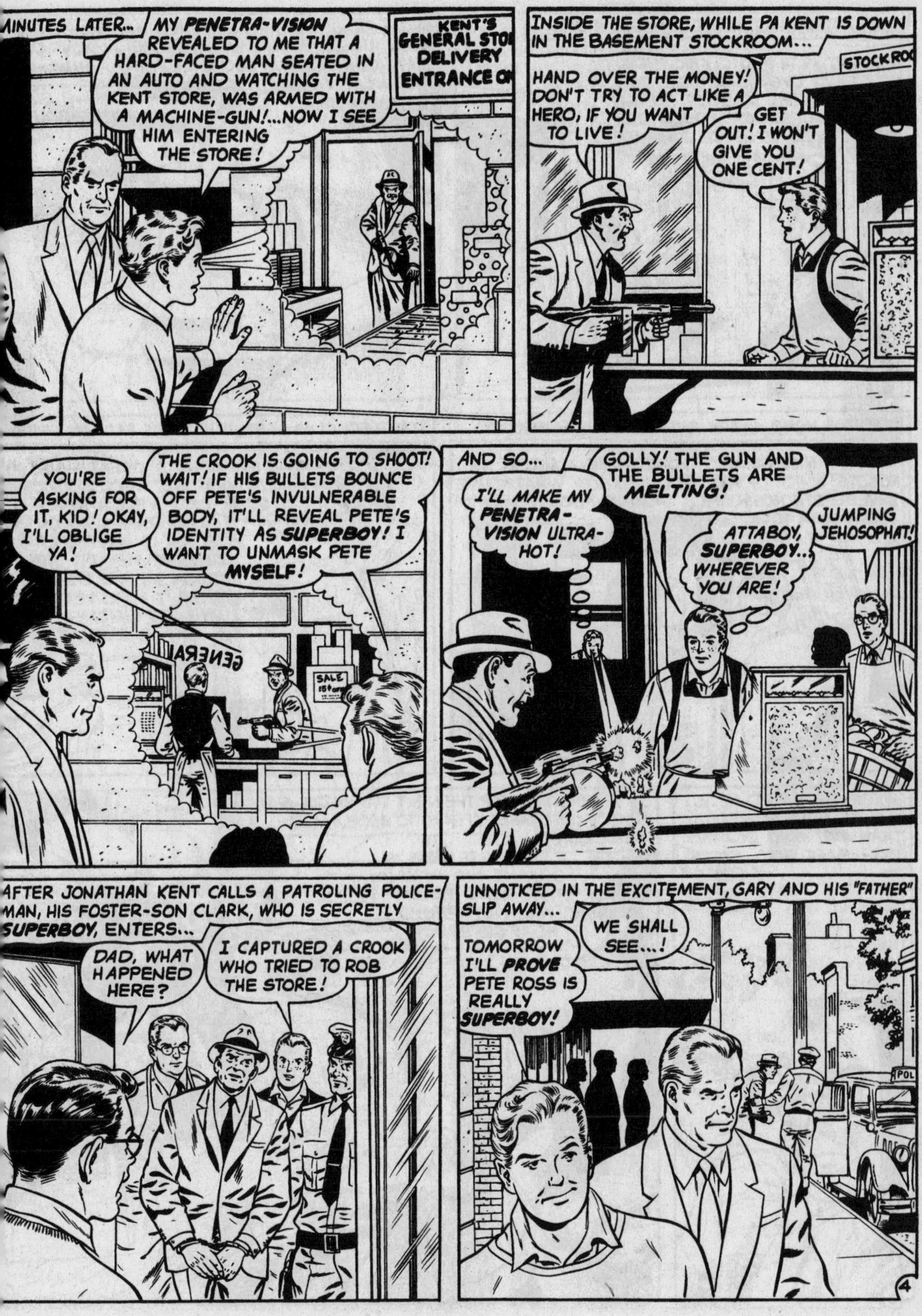
MINUTES LATER...
MY PENETRA-VISION REVEALED TO ME THAT A HARD-FACED MAN SEATED IN AN AUTO AND WATCHING THE KENT STORE, WAS ARMED WITH A MACHINE-GUN!...NOW I SEE HIM ENTERING THE STORE!
KENT'S GENERAL STO DELIVERY ENTRANCE O
INSIDE THE STORE, WHILE PA KENT IS DOWN IN THE BASEMENT STOCKROOM...
STOCKROO
HAND OVER THE MONEY! DON'T TRY TO ACT LIKE A HERO, IF YOU WANT TO LIVE!
GET OUT! I WON'T GIVE YOU ONE CENT!
YOU'RE ASKING FOR IT, KID! OKAY, I'LL OBLIGE YA!
THE CROOK IS GOING TO SHOOT! WAIT! IF HIS BULLETS BOUNCE OFF PETE'S INVULNERABLE BODY, IT'LL REVEAL PETE'S IDENTITY AS SUPERBOY! I WANT TO UNMASK PETE MYSELF!
SALE
AND SO...
I'LL MAKE MY PENETRA-VISION ULTRA-HOT!
GOLLY! THE GUN AND THE BULLETS ARE MELTING!
ATTABOY, SUPERBOY... WHEREVER YOU ARE!
JUMPING JEHOSOPHAT!
AFTER JONATHAN KENT CALLS A PATROLING POLICE-MAN, HIS FOSTER-SON CLARK, WHO IS SECRETLY SUPERBOY, ENTERS...
DAD, WHAT HAPPENED HERE?
I CAPTURED A CROOK WHO TRIED TO ROB THE STORE!
UNNOTICED IN THE EXCITEMENT, GARY AND HIS "FATHER" SLIP AWAY...
TOMORROW I'LL PROVE PETE ROSS IS REALLY SUPERBOY!
WE SHALL SEE...!
POL
4

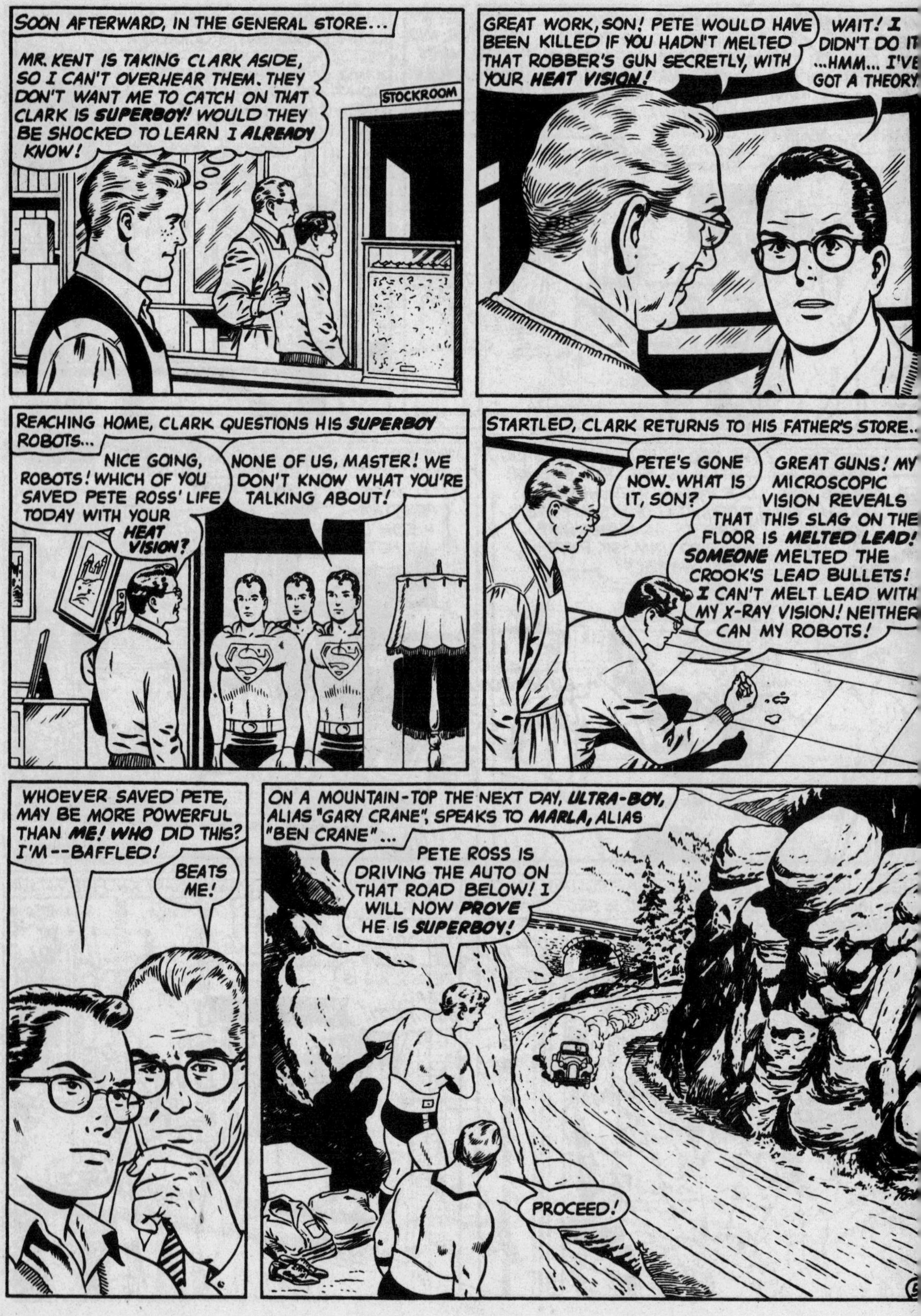
SOON AFTERWARD, IN THE GENERAL STORE...
MR. KENT IS TAKING CLARK ASIDE, SO I CAN'T OVERHEAR THEM. THEY DON'T WANT ME TO CATCH ON THAT CLARK IS SUPERBOY! WOULD THEY BE SHOCKED TO LEARN I ALREADY KNOW!
STOCKROOM
GREAT WORK, SON! PETE WOULD HAVE BEEN KILLED IF YOU HADN'T MELTED THAT ROBBER'S GUN SECRETLY, WITH YOUR HEAT VISION!
WAIT! I DIDN'T DO IT ...HMM... I'VE GOT A THEORY
REACHING HOME, CLARK QUESTIONS HIS SUPERBOY ROBOTS...
NICE GOING, ROBOTS! WHICH OF YOU SAVED PETE ROSS' LIFE TODAY WITH YOUR HEAT VISION?
NONE OF US, MASTER! WE DON'T KNOW WHAT YOU'RE TALKING ABOUT!
STARTLED, CLARK RETURNS TO HIS FATHER'S STORE...
PETE'S GONE NOW. WHAT IS IT, SON?
GREAT GUNS! MY MICROSCOPIC VISION REVEALS THAT THIS SLAG ON THE FLOOR IS MELTED LEAD! SOMEONE MELTED THE CROOK'S LEAD BULLETS! I CAN'T MELT LEAD WITH MY X-RAY VISION! NEITHER CAN MY ROBOTS!
WHOEVER SAVED PETE, MAY BE MORE POWERFUL THAN ME! WHO DID THIS? I'M--BAFFLED!
BEATS ME!
ON A MOUNTAIN-TOP THE NEXT DAY, ULTRA-BOY, ALIAS "GARY CRANE", SPEAKS TO MARLA, ALIAS "BEN CRANE"...
PETE ROSS IS DRIVING THE AUTO ON THAT ROAD BELOW! I WILL NOW PROVE HE IS SUPERBOY!
PROCEED!

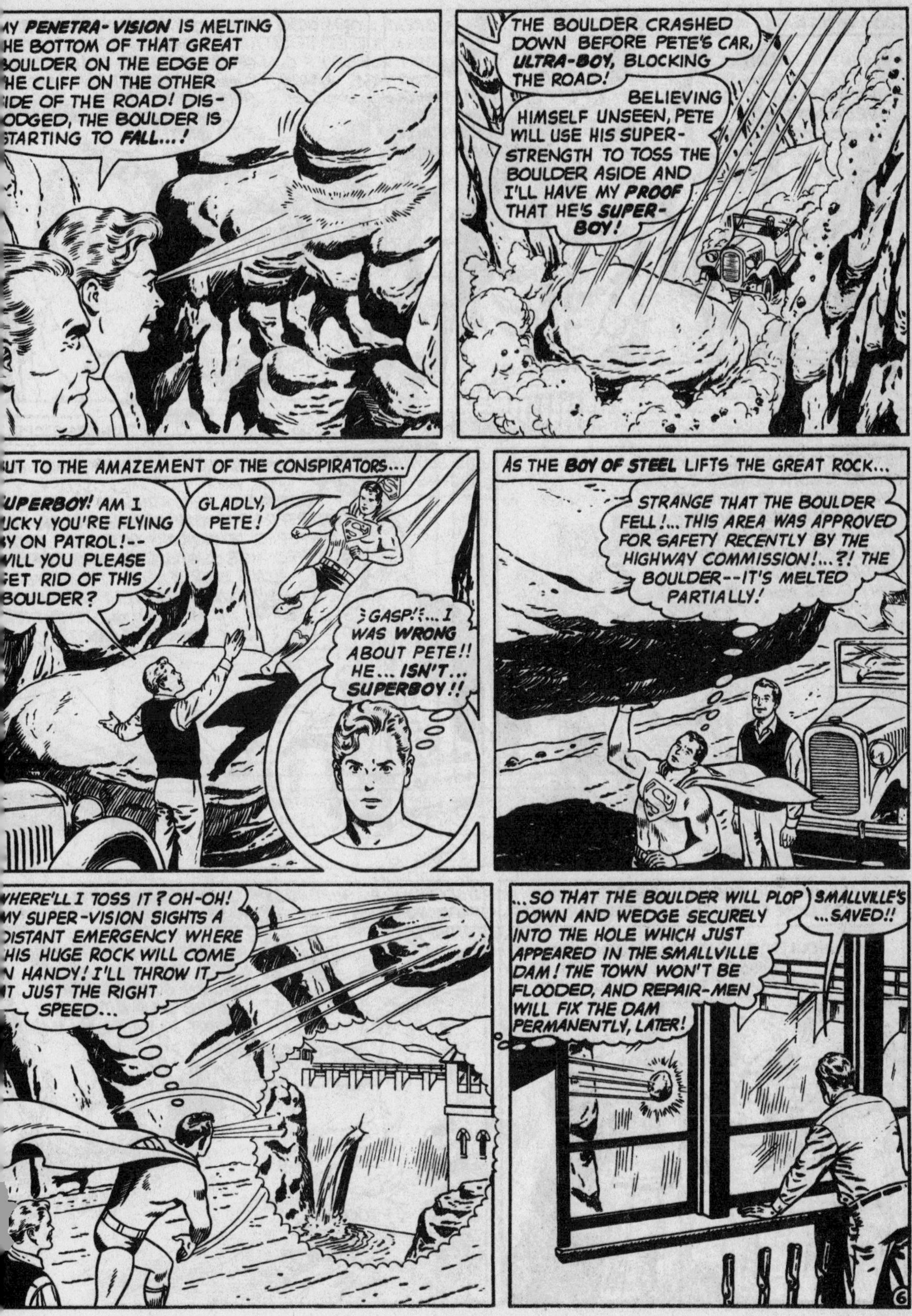
MY PENETRA-VISION IS MELTING THE BOTTOM OF THAT GREAT BOULDER ON THE EDGE OF THE CLIFF ON THE OTHER SIDE OF THE ROAD! DIS-LODGED, THE BOULDER IS STARTING TO FALL...!
THE BOULDER CRASHED DOWN BEFORE PETE'S CAR, ULTRA-BOY, BLOCKING THE ROAD!
BELIEVING HIMSELF UNSEEN, PETE WILL USE HIS SUPER-STRENGTH TO TOSS THE BOULDER ASIDE AND I'LL HAVE MY PROOF THAT HE'S SUPER-BOY!
BUT TO THE AMAZEMENT OF THE CONSPIRATORS...
SUPERBOY! AM I LUCKY YOU'RE FLYING BY ON PATROL!-- WILL YOU PLEASE GET RID OF THIS BOULDER?
GLADLY, PETE!
GASP!... I WAS WRONG ABOUT PETE!! HE... ISN'T... SUPERBOY!!
AS THE BOY OF STEEL LIFTS THE GREAT ROCK...
STRANGE THAT THE BOULDER FELL!... THIS AREA WAS APPROVED FOR SAFETY RECENTLY BY THE HIGHWAY COMMISSION!...?! THE BOULDER--IT'S MELTED PARTIALLY!
WHERE'LL I TOSS IT? OH-OH! MY SUPER-VISION SIGHTS A DISTANT EMERGENCY WHERE THIS HUGE ROCK WILL COME IN HANDY! I'LL THROW IT AT JUST THE RIGHT SPEED...
...SO THAT THE BOULDER WILL PLOP DOWN AND WEDGE SECURELY INTO THE HOLE WHICH JUST APPEARED IN THE SMALLVILLE DAM! THE TOWN WON'T BE FLOODED, AND REPAIR-MEN WILL FIX THE DAM PERMANENTLY, LATER!
SMALLVILLE'S ...SAVED!!
6

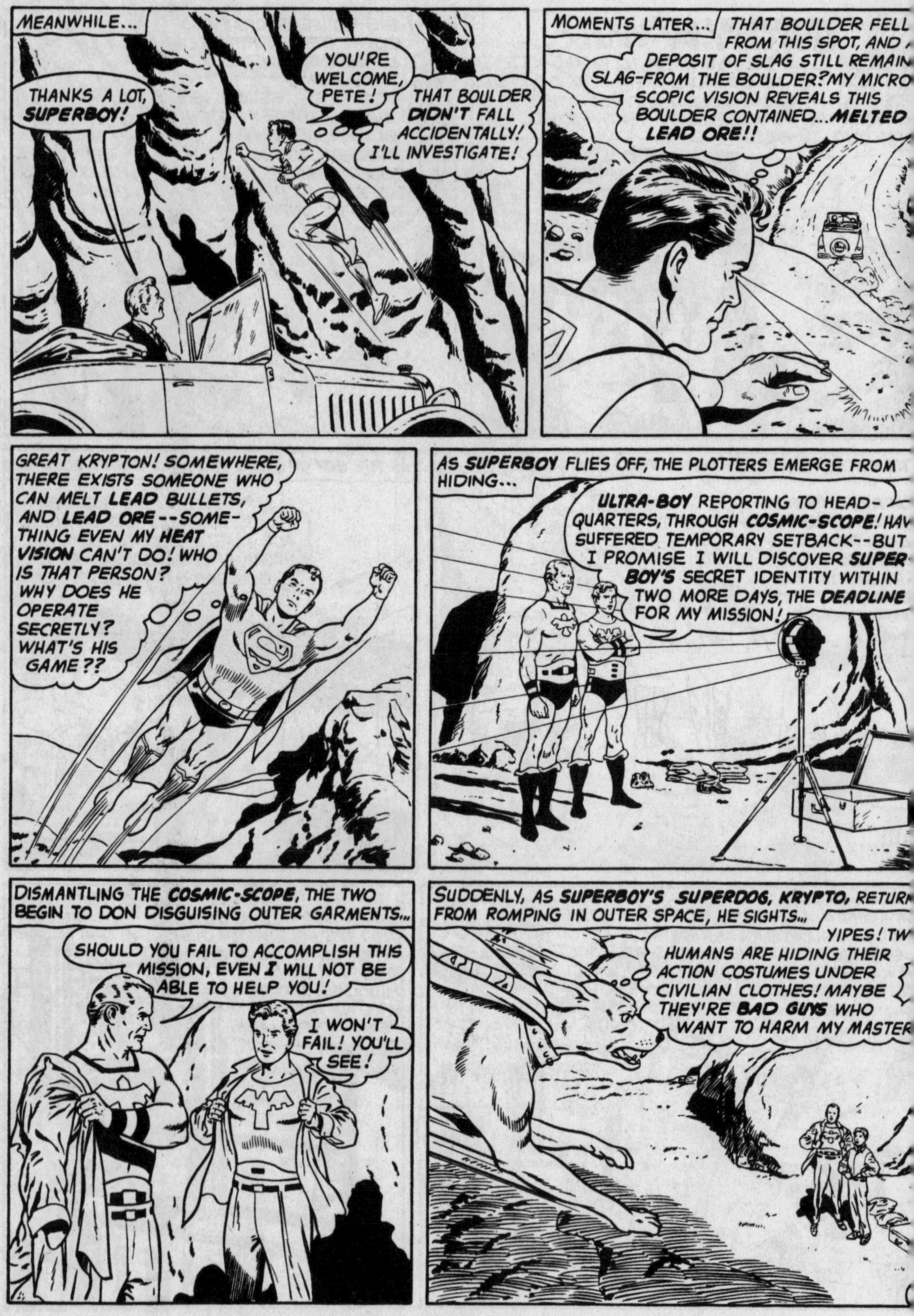
MEANWHILE...
THANKS A LOT, SUPERBOY!
YOU'RE WELCOME, PETE!
THAT BOULDER DIDN'T FALL ACCIDENTALLY! I'LL INVESTIGATE!
MOMENTS LATER...
THAT BOULDER FELL FROM THIS SPOT, AND DEPOSIT OF SLAG STILL REMAIN SLAG-FROM THE BOULDER? MY MICRO SCOPIC VISION REVEALS THIS BOULDER CONTAINED... MELTED LEAD ORE!!
GREAT KRYPTON! SOMEWHERE, THERE EXISTS SOMEONE WHO CAN MELT LEAD BULLETS, AND LEAD ORE--SOMETHING EVEN MY HEAT VISION CAN'T DO! WHO IS THAT PERSON? WHY DOES HE OPERATE SECRETLY? WHAT'S HIS GAME??
AS SUPERBOY FLIES OFF, THE PLOTTERS EMERGE FROM HIDING...
ULTRA-BOY REPORTING TO HEADQUARTERS, THROUGH COSMIC-SCOPE! HAV SUFFERED TEMPORARY SETBACK--BUT I PROMISE I WILL DISCOVER SUPERBOY'S SECRET IDENTITY WITHIN TWO MORE DAYS, THE DEADLINE FOR MY MISSION!
DISMANTLING THE COSMIC-SCOPE, THE TWO BEGIN TO DON DISGUISING OUTER GARMENTS...
SHOULD YOU FAIL TO ACCOMPLISH THIS MISSION, EVEN I WILL NOT BE ABLE TO HELP YOU!
I WON'T FAIL! YOU'LL SEE!
SUDDENLY, AS SUPERBOY'S SUPERDOG, KRYPTO, RETUR FROM ROMPING IN OUTER SPACE, HE SIGHTS...
YIPES! TW HUMANS ARE HIDING THEIR ACTION COSTUMES UNDER CIVILIAN CLOTHES! MAYBE THEY'RE BAD GUYS WHO WANT TO HARM MY MASTER

GROW-W-W-L!

I'LL FLY THEM TO SMALLVILLE, THEN RIP OFF THEIR OUTER GARMENTS AND EXPOSE THEIR COSTUMES UNDERNEATH TO EVERYBODY!

IT'S KRYPTO... SUPERBOY'S PET! IF HE SAW US SWITCH IDENTITIES...!

LEAVE HIM TO ME!

BUT THE NEXT MOMENT...

HA, HA, HA! I'M GIVING HIM A HOT FOOT WITH THE HEAT OF MY MIGHTY PENETRA-VISION! LOOK AT HIM FLEEING BACK TOWARD OUTER SPACE, HA, HA!

A-OOOWRRFFF!

AMAZING! THAT BOY'S HEAT VISION HURTS ME!!

THE FOLLOWING DAY, IN SMALLVILLE...

I'M RIGHT BACK WHERE I STARTED! HERE COMES CLARK KENT WITH LANA LANG, TWO STUDENTS I'VE SEEN AT SMALLVILLE HIGH!

CLARK'S A DRIP! LET'S HAVE SOME FUN!...PS-ST, PSS-ST!

DONALD MAC Photographe

HEY--!

HAW, HAW!

YOU LITTLE MONSTERS! STOP IT! THAT'S NOT FUNNY! YOU CAN HURT SOMEONE BADLY THAT WAY!

I'LL WHINE, SO LANA WILL THINK I'M A MEEK LAMB AND FORGET HER SUSPICION THAT I'M SECRETLY SUPERBOY!

LEAVE ME ALONE!

IT'S DISGUSTING! YOU'RE SO TIMID, THAT YOU'RE AFRAID OF KIDS HALF YOUR AGE! HERE... TAKE YOUR GLASSES! LUCKILY, THEY DIDN'T BREAK!

"DIDN'T BREAK"?!

THEY COULDN'T BREAK BECAUSE THE LENSES ARE MADE OF AN UNBREAKABLE MATERIAL TAKEN FROM THE ROCKET-SHIP THAT BROUGHT ME TO EARTH FROM KRYPTON AS A BABY!

BY THE THREE PURPLE MOONS OF RIMBOR...!

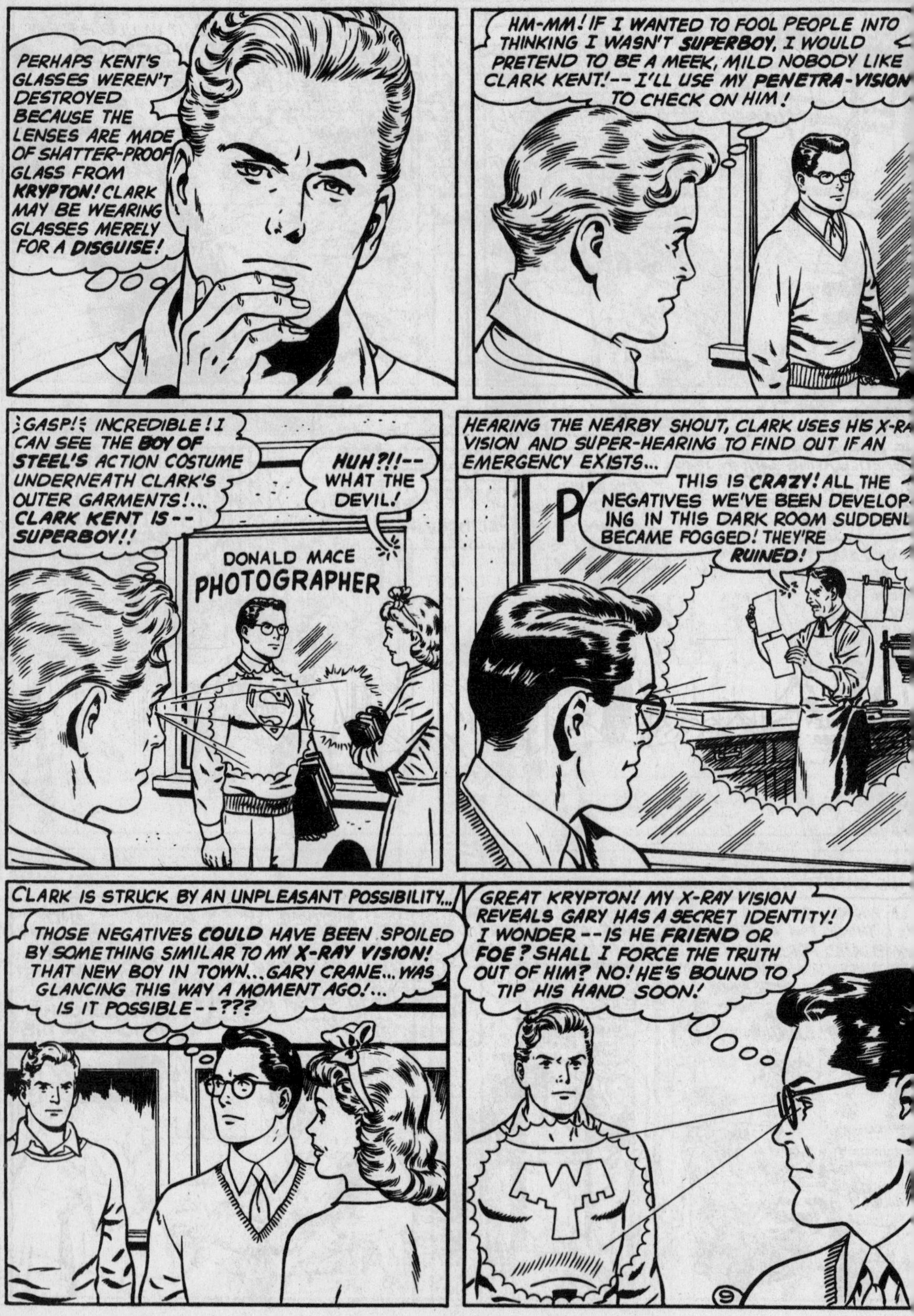
PERHAPS KENT'S GLASSES WEREN'T DESTROYED BECAUSE THE LENSES ARE MADE OF SHATTER-PROOF GLASS FROM KRYPTON! CLARK MAY BE WEARING GLASSES MERELY FOR A DISGUISE!
HM-MM! IF I WANTED TO FOOL PEOPLE INTO THINKING I WASN'T SUPERBOY, I WOULD PRETEND TO BE A MEEK, MILD NOBODY LIKE CLARK KENT!-- I'LL USE MY PENETRA-VISION TO CHECK ON HIM!
GASP! INCREDIBLE! I CAN SEE THE BOY OF STEEL'S ACTION COSTUME UNDERNEATH CLARK'S OUTER GARMENTS!... CLARK KENT IS-- SUPERBOY!!
HUH?!!-- WHAT THE DEVIL!
DONALD MACE PHOTOGRAPHER
HEARING THE NEARBY SHOUT, CLARK USES HIS X-RAY VISION AND SUPER-HEARING TO FIND OUT IF AN EMERGENCY EXISTS...
THIS IS CRAZY! ALL THE NEGATIVES WE'VE BEEN DEVELOPING IN THIS DARK ROOM SUDDENLY BECAME FOGGED! THEY'RE RUINED!
CLARK IS STRUCK BY AN UNPLEASANT POSSIBILITY...
THOSE NEGATIVES COULD HAVE BEEN SPOILED BY SOMETHING SIMILAR TO MY X-RAY VISION! THAT NEW BOY IN TOWN...GARY CRANE...WAS GLANCING THIS WAY A MOMENT AGO!... IS IT POSSIBLE--???
GREAT KRYPTON! MY X-RAY VISION REVEALS GARY HAS A SECRET IDENTITY! I WONDER--IS HE FRIEND OR FOE? SHALL I FORCE THE TRUTH OUT OF HIM? NO! HE'S BOUND TO TIP HIS HAND SOON!
9

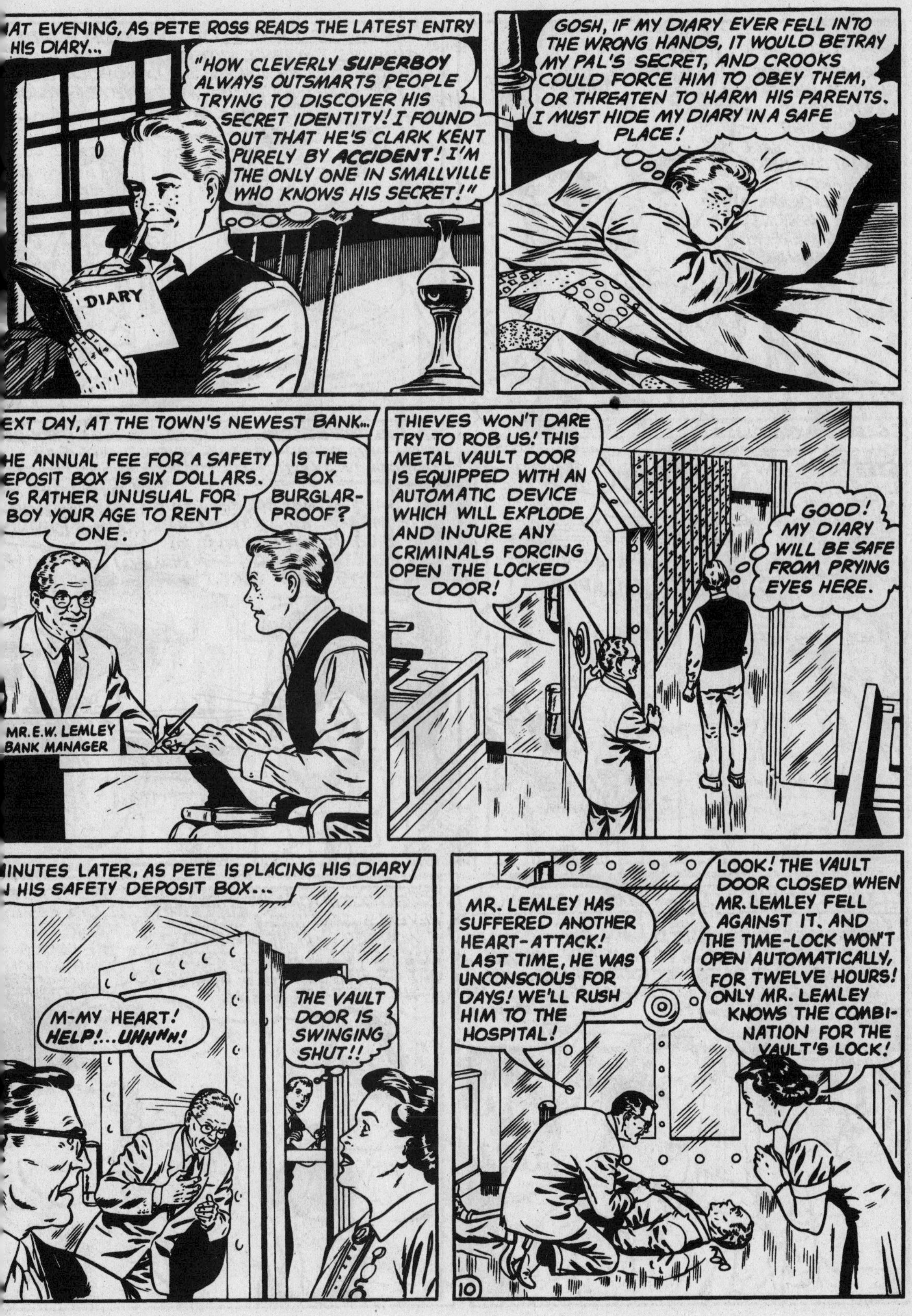
AT EVENING, AS PETE ROSS READS THE LATEST ENTRY HIS DIARY...
"HOW CLEVERLY SUPERBOY ALWAYS OUTSMARTS PEOPLE TRYING TO DISCOVER HIS SECRET IDENTITY! I FOUND OUT THAT HE'S CLARK KENT PURELY BY ACCIDENT! I'M THE ONLY ONE IN SMALLVILLE WHO KNOWS HIS SECRET!"
DIARY
GOSH, IF MY DIARY EVER FELL INTO THE WRONG HANDS, IT WOULD BETRAY MY PAL'S SECRET, AND CROOKS COULD FORCE HIM TO OBEY THEM, OR THREATEN TO HARM HIS PARENTS. I MUST HIDE MY DIARY IN A SAFE PLACE!
EXT DAY, AT THE TOWN'S NEWEST BANK...
HE ANNUAL FEE FOR A SAFETY EPOSIT BOX IS SIX DOLLARS. 'S RATHER UNUSUAL FOR BOY YOUR AGE TO RENT ONE.
IS THE BOX BURGLAR-PROOF?
MR. E.W. LEMLEY BANK MANAGER
THIEVES WON'T DARE TRY TO ROB US! THIS METAL VAULT DOOR IS EQUIPPED WITH AN AUTOMATIC DEVICE WHICH WILL EXPLODE AND INJURE ANY CRIMINALS FORCING OPEN THE LOCKED DOOR!
GOOD! MY DIARY WILL BE SAFE FROM PRYING EYES HERE.
INUTES LATER, AS PETE IS PLACING HIS DIARY N HIS SAFETY DEPOSIT BOX...
M-MY HEART! HELP!...UHHHH!
THE VAULT DOOR IS SWINGING SHUT!!
MR. LEMLEY HAS SUFFERED ANOTHER HEART-ATTACK! LAST TIME, HE WAS UNCONSCIOUS FOR DAYS! WE'LL RUSH HIM TO THE HOSPITAL!
LOOK! THE VAULT DOOR CLOSED WHEN MR. LEMLEY FELL AGAINST IT. AND THE TIME-LOCK WON'T OPEN AUTOMATICALLY, FOR TWELVE HOURS! ONLY MR. LEMLEY KNOWS THE COMBINATION FOR THE VAULT'S LOCK!
10

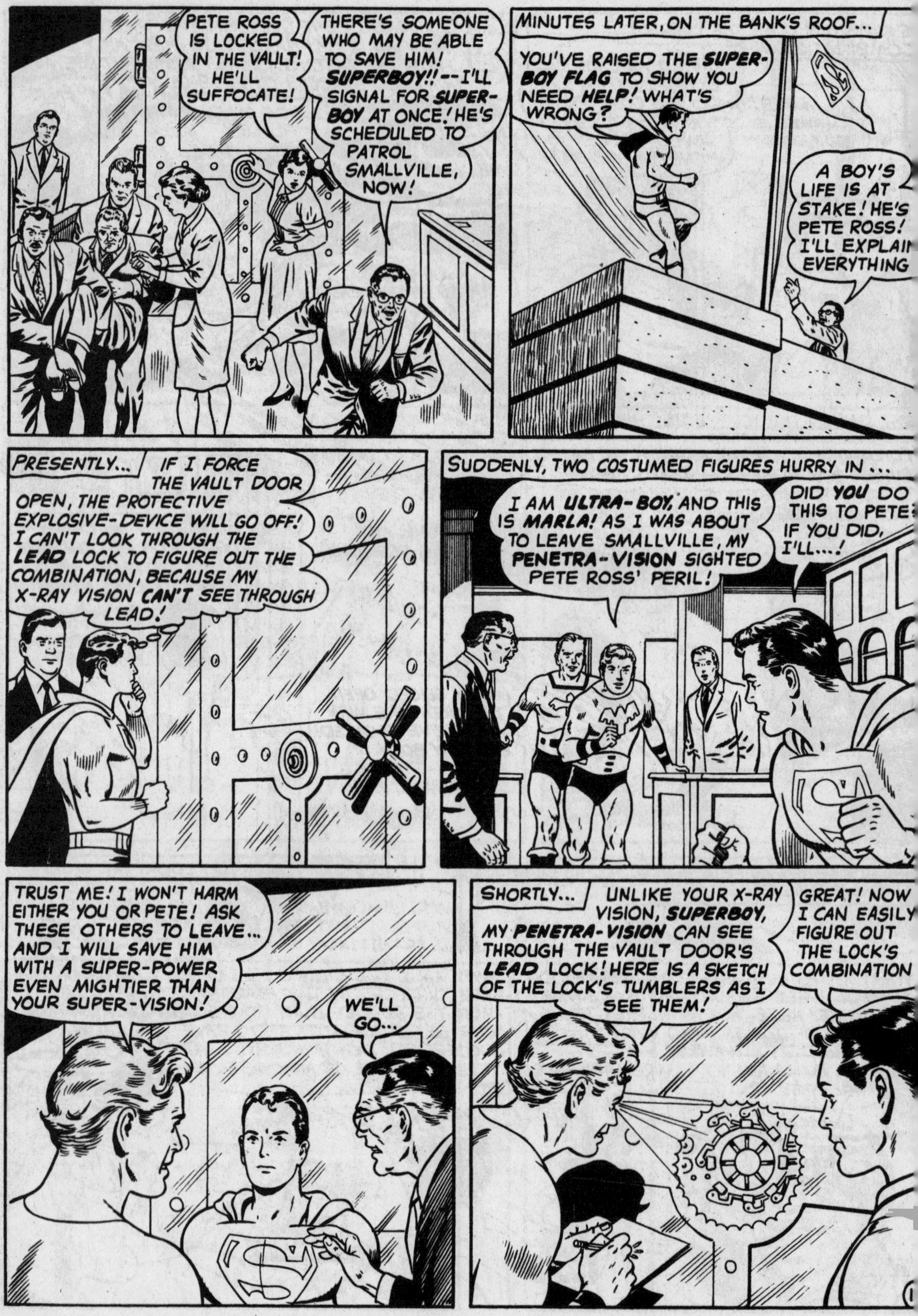
PETE ROSS IS LOCKED IN THE VAULT! HE'LL SUFFOCATE!
THERE'S SOMEONE WHO MAY BE ABLE TO SAVE HIM! SUPERBOY!!--I'LL SIGNAL FOR SUPERBOY AT ONCE! HE'S SCHEDULED TO PATROL SMALLVILLE, NOW!
MINUTES LATER, ON THE BANK'S ROOF...
YOU'VE RAISED THE SUPERBOY FLAG TO SHOW YOU NEED HELP! WHAT'S WRONG?
A BOY'S LIFE IS AT STAKE! HE'S PETE ROSS! I'LL EXPLAI EVERYTHING
PRESENTLY...
IF I FORCE THE VAULT DOOR OPEN, THE PROTECTIVE EXPLOSIVE-DEVICE WILL GO OFF! I CAN'T LOOK THROUGH THE LEAD LOCK TO FIGURE OUT THE COMBINATION, BECAUSE MY X-RAY VISION CAN'T SEE THROUGH LEAD!
SUDDENLY, TWO COSTUMED FIGURES HURRY IN ...
I AM ULTRA-BOY, AND THIS IS MARLA! AS I WAS ABOUT TO LEAVE SMALLVILLE, MY PENETRA-VISION SIGHTED PETE ROSS' PERIL!
DID YOU DO THIS TO PETE IF YOU DID, I'LL...!
TRUST ME! I WON'T HARM EITHER YOU OR PETE! ASK THESE OTHERS TO LEAVE... AND I WILL SAVE HIM WITH A SUPER-POWER EVEN MIGHTIER THAN YOUR SUPER-VISION!
WE'LL GO...
SHORTLY...
UNLIKE YOUR X-RAY VISION, SUPERBOY, MY PENETRA-VISION CAN SEE THROUGH THE VAULT DOOR'S LEAD LOCK! HERE IS A SKETCH OF THE LOCK'S TUMBLERS AS I SEE THEM!
GREAT! NOW I CAN EASILY FIGURE OUT THE LOCK'S COMBINATION

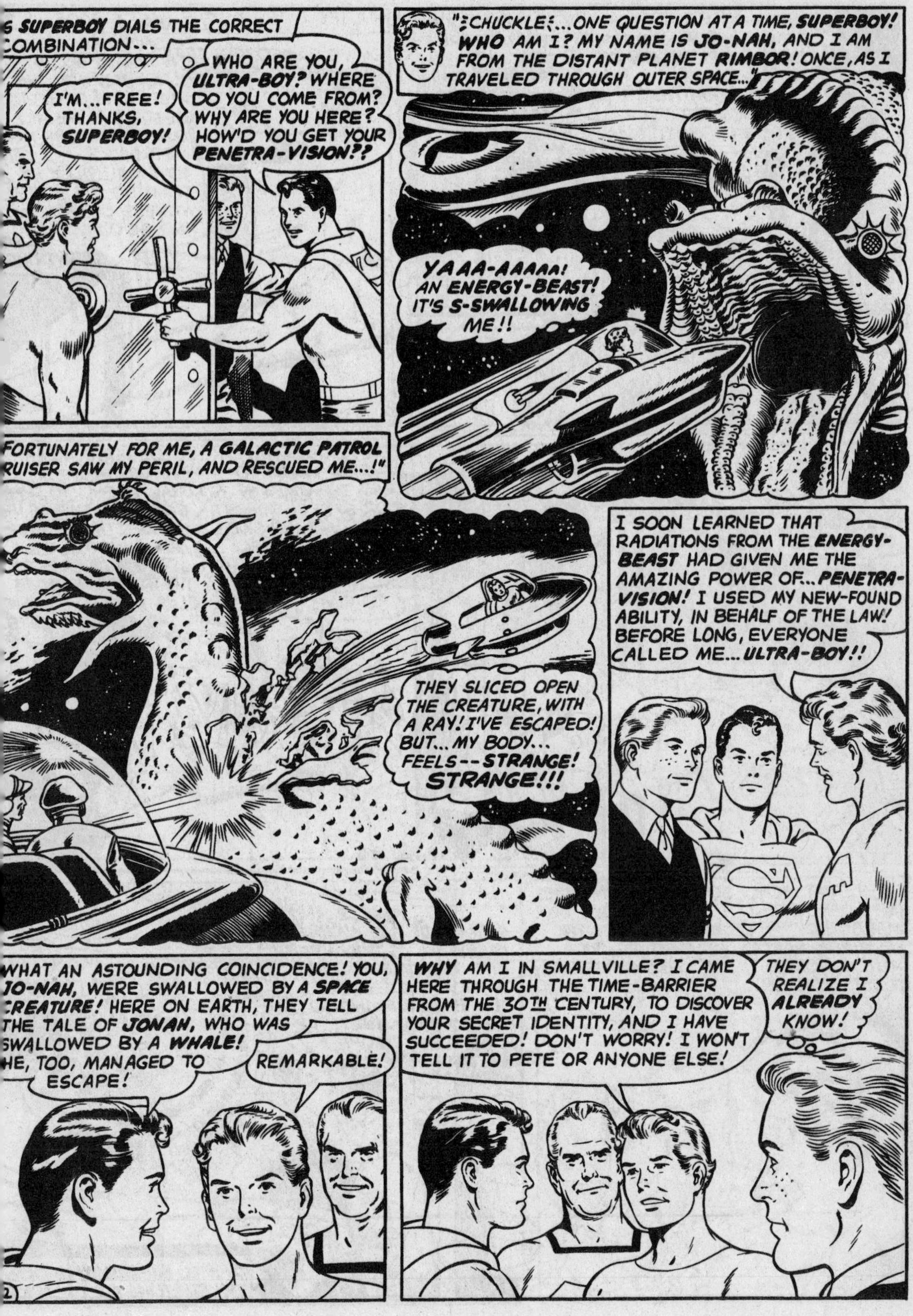
S SUPERBOY DIALS THE CORRECT COMBINATION...
I'M...FREE! THANKS, SUPERBOY!
WHO ARE YOU, ULTRA-BOY? WHERE DO YOU COME FROM? WHY ARE YOU HERE? HOW'D YOU GET YOUR PENETRA-VISION??
"CHUCKLE...ONE QUESTION AT A TIME, SUPERBOY! WHO AM I? MY NAME IS JO-NAH, AND I AM FROM THE DISTANT PLANET RIMBOR! ONCE, AS I TRAVELED THROUGH OUTER SPACE..."
YAAA-AAAAA! AN ENERGY-BEAST! IT'S S-SWALLOWING ME!!
FORTUNATELY FOR ME, A GALACTIC PATROL RUISER SAW MY PERIL, AND RESCUED ME...!"
THEY SLICED OPEN THE CREATURE, WITH A RAY! I'VE ESCAPED! BUT... MY BODY... FEELS--STRANGE! STRANGE!!!
I SOON LEARNED THAT RADIATIONS FROM THE ENERGY-BEAST HAD GIVEN ME THE AMAZING POWER OF...PENETRA-VISION! I USED MY NEW-FOUND ABILITY, IN BEHALF OF THE LAW! BEFORE LONG, EVERYONE CALLED ME...ULTRA-BOY!!
WHAT AN ASTOUNDING COINCIDENCE! YOU, JO-NAH, WERE SWALLOWED BY A SPACE CREATURE! HERE ON EARTH, THEY TELL THE TALE OF JONAH, WHO WAS SWALLOWED BY A WHALE! HE, TOO, MANAGED TO ESCAPE!
REMARKABLE!
WHY AM I IN SMALLVILLE? I CAME HERE THROUGH THE TIME-BARRIER FROM THE 30TH CENTURY, TO DISCOVER YOUR SECRET IDENTITY, AND I HAVE SUCCEEDED! DON'T WORRY! I WON'T TELL IT TO PETE OR ANYONE ELSE!
THEY DON'T REALIZE I ALREADY KNOW!

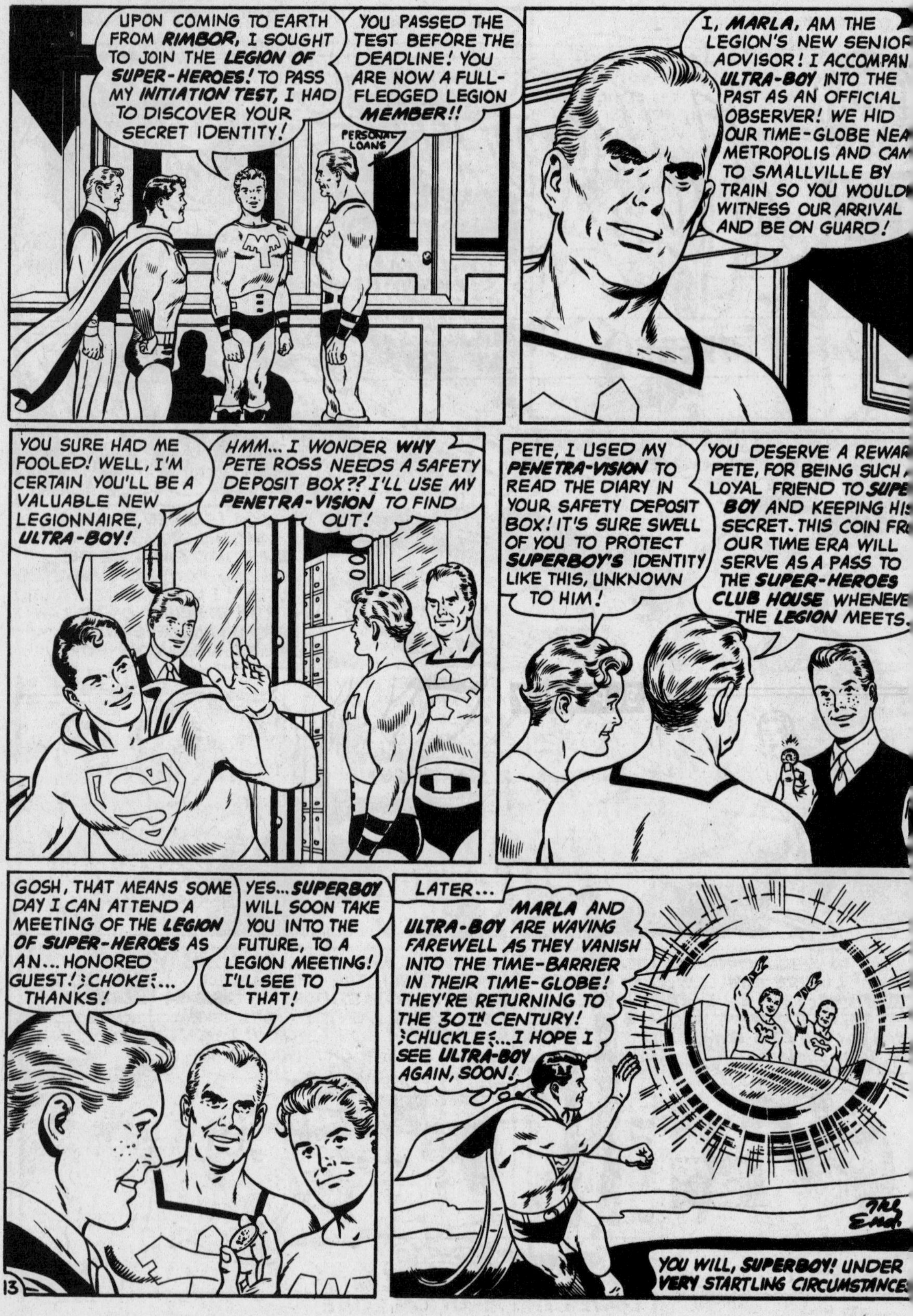
UPON COMING TO EARTH FROM RIMBOR, I SOUGHT TO JOIN THE LEGION OF SUPER-HEROES! TO PASS MY INITIATION TEST, I HAD TO DISCOVER YOUR SECRET IDENTITY!
YOU PASSED THE TEST BEFORE THE DEADLINE! YOU ARE NOW A FULL-FLEDGED LEGION MEMBER!!
PERSONAL LOANS
I, MARLA, AM THE LEGION'S NEW SENIOR ADVISOR! I ACCOMPAN ULTRA-BOY INTO THE PAST AS AN OFFICIAL OBSERVER! WE HID OUR TIME-GLOBE NEA METROPOLIS AND CAM TO SMALLVILLE BY TRAIN SO YOU WOULD WITNESS OUR ARRIVAL AND BE ON GUARD!
YOU SURE HAD ME FOOLED! WELL, I'M CERTAIN YOU'LL BE A VALUABLE NEW LEGIONNAIRE, ULTRA-BOY!
HMM... I WONDER WHY PETE ROSS NEEDS A SAFETY DEPOSIT BOX?? I'LL USE MY PENETRA-VISION TO FIND OUT!
PETE, I USED MY PENETRA-VISION TO READ THE DIARY IN YOUR SAFETY DEPOSIT BOX! IT'S SURE SWELL OF YOU TO PROTECT SUPERBOY'S IDENTITY LIKE THIS, UNKNOWN TO HIM!
YOU DESERVE A REWAR PETE, FOR BEING SUCH LOYAL FRIEND TO SUPE BOY AND KEEPING HIS SECRET. THIS COIN FR OUR TIME ERA WILL SERVE AS A PASS TO THE SUPER-HEROES CLUB HOUSE WHENEVE THE LEGION MEETS.
GOSH, THAT MEANS SOME DAY I CAN ATTEND A MEETING OF THE LEGION OF SUPER-HEROES AS AN... HONORED GUEST! CHOKE... THANKS!
YES... SUPERBOY WILL SOON TAKE YOU INTO THE FUTURE, TO A LEGION MEETING! I'LL SEE TO THAT!
13
LATER...
MARLA AND ULTRA-BOY ARE WAVING FAREWELL AS THEY VANISH INTO THE TIME-BARRIER IN THEIR TIME-GLOBE! THEY'RE RETURNING TO THE 30TH CENTURY!
CHUCKLE... I HOPE I SEE ULTRA-BOY AGAIN, SOON!
The End.
YOU WILL, SUPERBOY! UNDER VERY STARTLING CIRCUMSTANCE

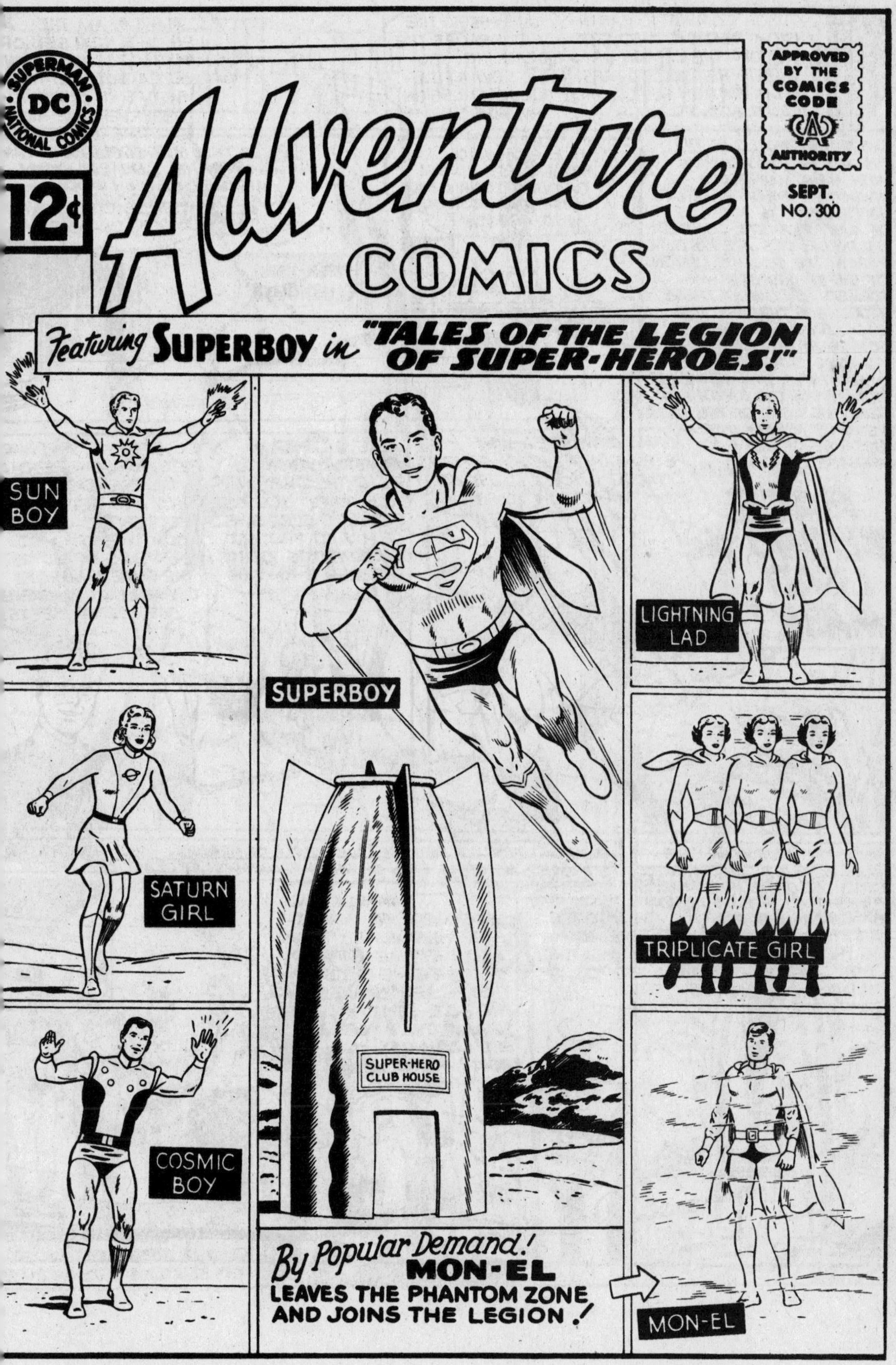
SUPERMAN DC NATIONAL COMICS
12¢
Adventure COMICS
APPROVED BY THE COMICS CODE AUTHORITY
SEPT. NO. 300
Featuring SUPERBOY in "TALES OF THE LEGION OF SUPER-HEROES!"
SUN BOY
SUPERBOY
LIGHTNING LAD
SATURN GIRL
TRIPLICATE GIRL
SUPER-HERO CLUB HOUSE
COSMIC BOY
By Popular Demand! MON-EL LEAVES THE PHANTOM ZONE AND JOINS THE LEGION!
MON-EL

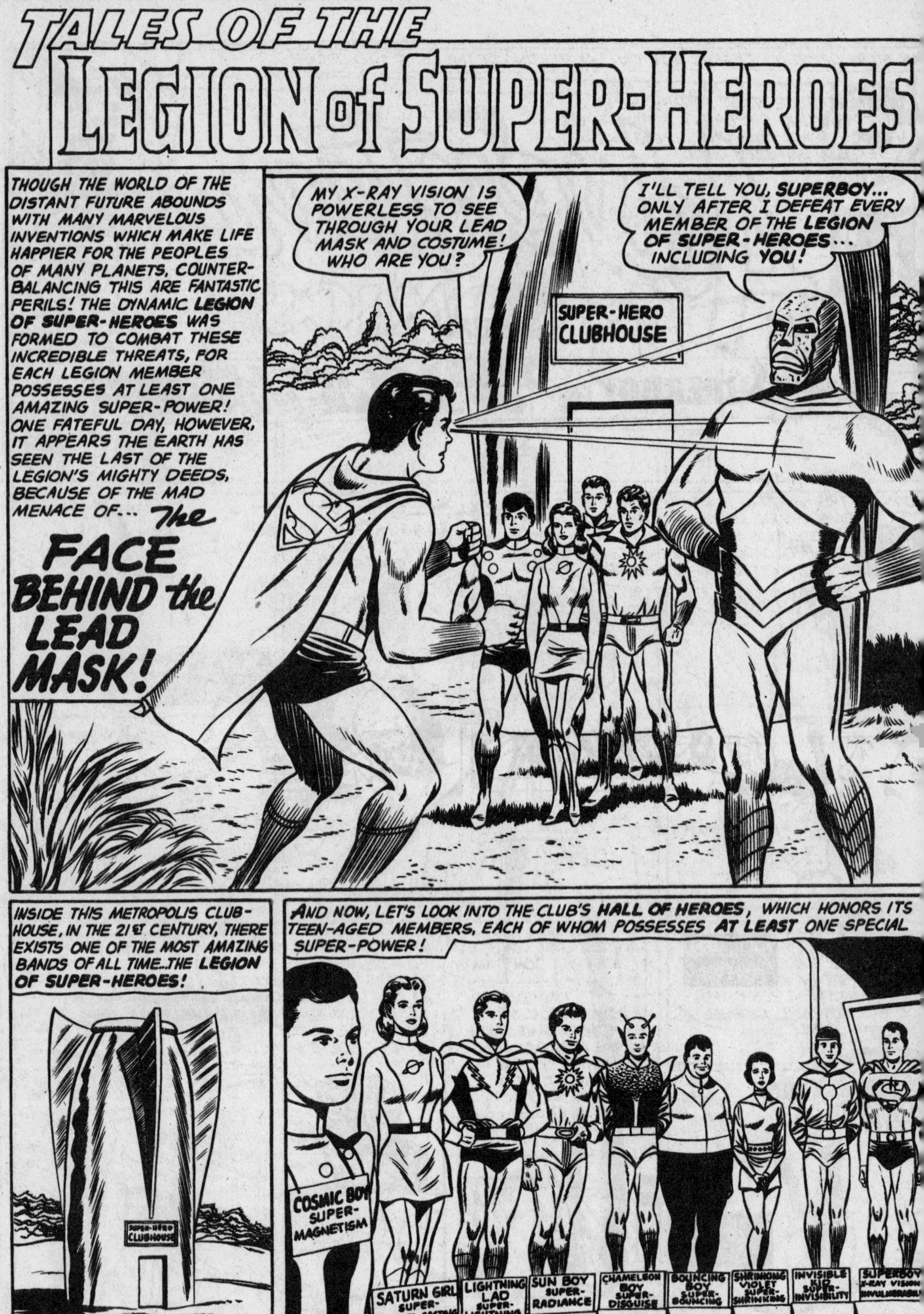
TALES OF THE
LEGION OF SUPER-HEROES
THOUGH THE WORLD OF THE DISTANT FUTURE ABOUNDS WITH MANY MARVELOUS INVENTIONS WHICH MAKE LIFE HAPPIER FOR THE PEOPLES OF MANY PLANETS, COUNTER-BALANCING THIS ARE FANTASTIC PERILS! THE DYNAMIC LEGION OF SUPER-HEROES WAS FORMED TO COMBAT THESE INCREDIBLE THREATS, FOR EACH LEGION MEMBER POSSESSES AT LEAST ONE AMAZING SUPER-POWER! ONE FATEFUL DAY, HOWEVER, IT APPEARS THE EARTH HAS SEEN THE LAST OF THE LEGION'S MIGHTY DEEDS, BECAUSE OF THE MAD MENACE OF... The
FACE BEHIND the LEAD MASK!
MY X-RAY VISION IS POWERLESS TO SEE THROUGH YOUR LEAD MASK AND COSTUME! WHO ARE YOU?
I'LL TELL YOU, SUPERBOY... ONLY AFTER I DEFEAT EVERY MEMBER OF THE LEGION OF SUPER-HEROES... INCLUDING YOU!
SUPER-HERO CLUBHOUSE
INSIDE THIS METROPOLIS CLUB-HOUSE, IN THE 21ST CENTURY, THERE EXISTS ONE OF THE MOST AMAZING BANDS OF ALL TIME...THE LEGION OF SUPER-HEROES!
SUPER-HERO CLUBHOUSE
AND NOW, LET'S LOOK INTO THE CLUB'S HALL OF HEROES, WHICH HONORS ITS TEEN-AGED MEMBERS, EACH OF WHOM POSSESSES AT LEAST ONE SPECIAL SUPER-POWER!
COSMIC BOY SUPER-MAGNETISM
SATURN GIRL SUPER-THOUGHT-CASTING
LIGHTNING LAD SUPER-LIGHTNING
SUN BOY SUPER-RADIANCE
CHAMELEON BOY SUPER-DISGUISE
BOUNCING BOY SUPER-BOUNCING
SHRINKING VIOLET SUPER-SHRINKING
INVISIBLE KID SUPER-INVISIBILITY
SUPERBOY X-RAY VISION

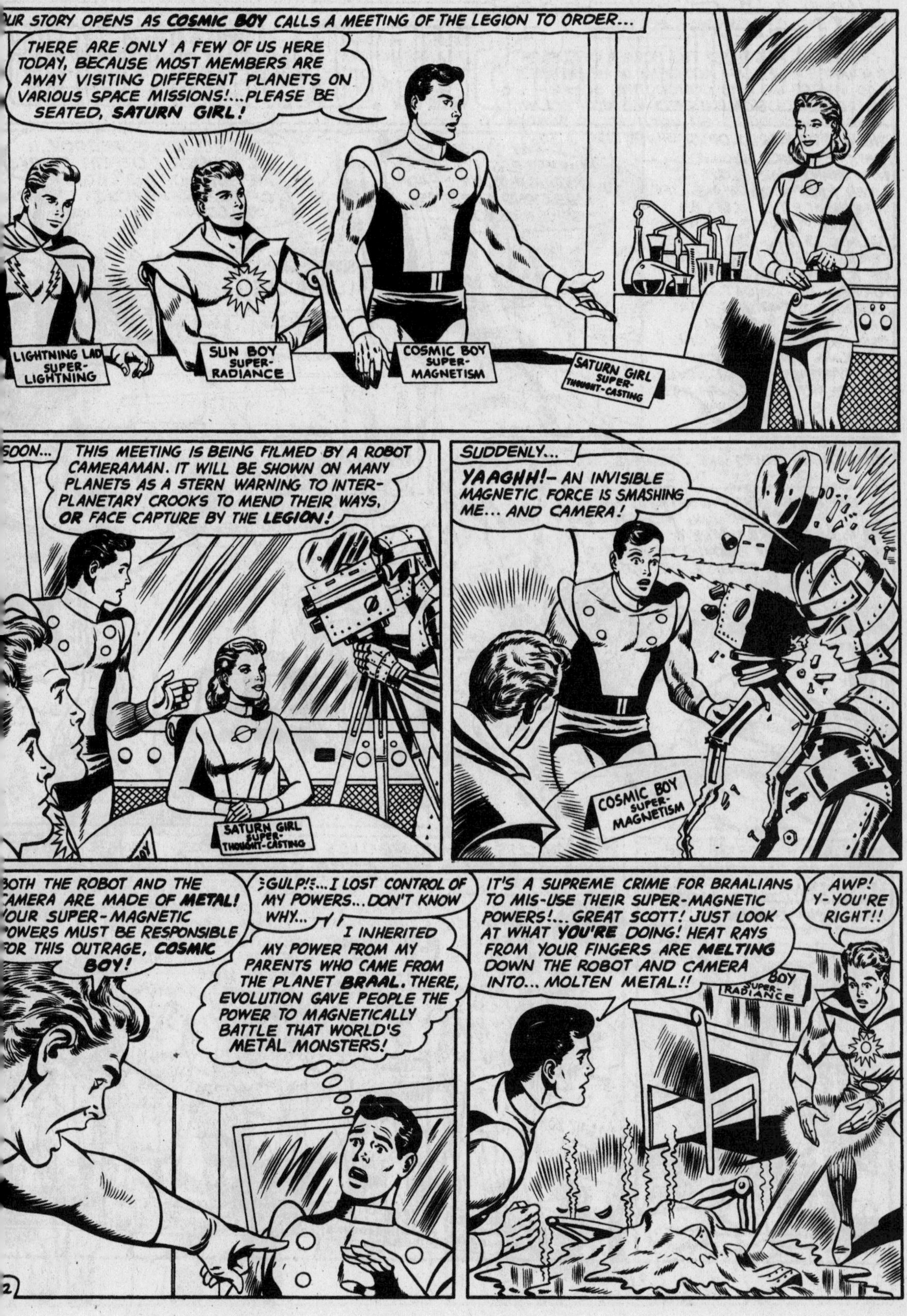
OUR STORY OPENS AS COSMIC BOY CALLS A MEETING OF THE LEGION TO ORDER...
THERE ARE ONLY A FEW OF US HERE TODAY, BECAUSE MOST MEMBERS ARE AWAY VISITING DIFFERENT PLANETS ON VARIOUS SPACE MISSIONS!...PLEASE BE SEATED, SATURN GIRL!
LIGHTNING LAD SUPER-LIGHTNING
SUN BOY SUPER-RADIANCE
COSMIC BOY SUPER-MAGNETISM
SATURN GIRL SUPER-THOUGHT-CASTING
SOON...
THIS MEETING IS BEING FILMED BY A ROBOT CAMERAMAN. IT WILL BE SHOWN ON MANY PLANETS AS A STERN WARNING TO INTER-PLANETARY CROOKS TO MEND THEIR WAYS, OR FACE CAPTURE BY THE LEGION!
SATURN GIRL SUPER-THOUGHT-CASTING
SUDDENLY...
YAAGHH!- AN INVISIBLE MAGNETIC FORCE IS SMASHING ME... AND CAMERA!
COSMIC BOY SUPER-MAGNETISM
BOTH THE ROBOT AND THE CAMERA ARE MADE OF METAL! YOUR SUPER-MAGNETIC POWERS MUST BE RESPONSIBLE FOR THIS OUTRAGE, COSMIC BOY!
GULP!...I LOST CONTROL OF MY POWERS...DON'T KNOW WHY...
I INHERITED MY POWER FROM MY PARENTS WHO CAME FROM THE PLANET BRAAL. THERE, EVOLUTION GAVE PEOPLE THE POWER TO MAGNETICALLY BATTLE THAT WORLD'S METAL MONSTERS!
IT'S A SUPREME CRIME FOR BRAALIANS TO MIS-USE THEIR SUPER-MAGNETIC POWERS!... GREAT SCOTT! JUST LOOK AT WHAT YOU'RE DOING! HEAT RAYS FROM YOUR FINGERS ARE MELTING DOWN THE ROBOT AND CAMERA INTO... MOLTEN METAL!!
AWP! Y-YOU'RE RIGHT!!
BOY SUPER-RADIANCE
2

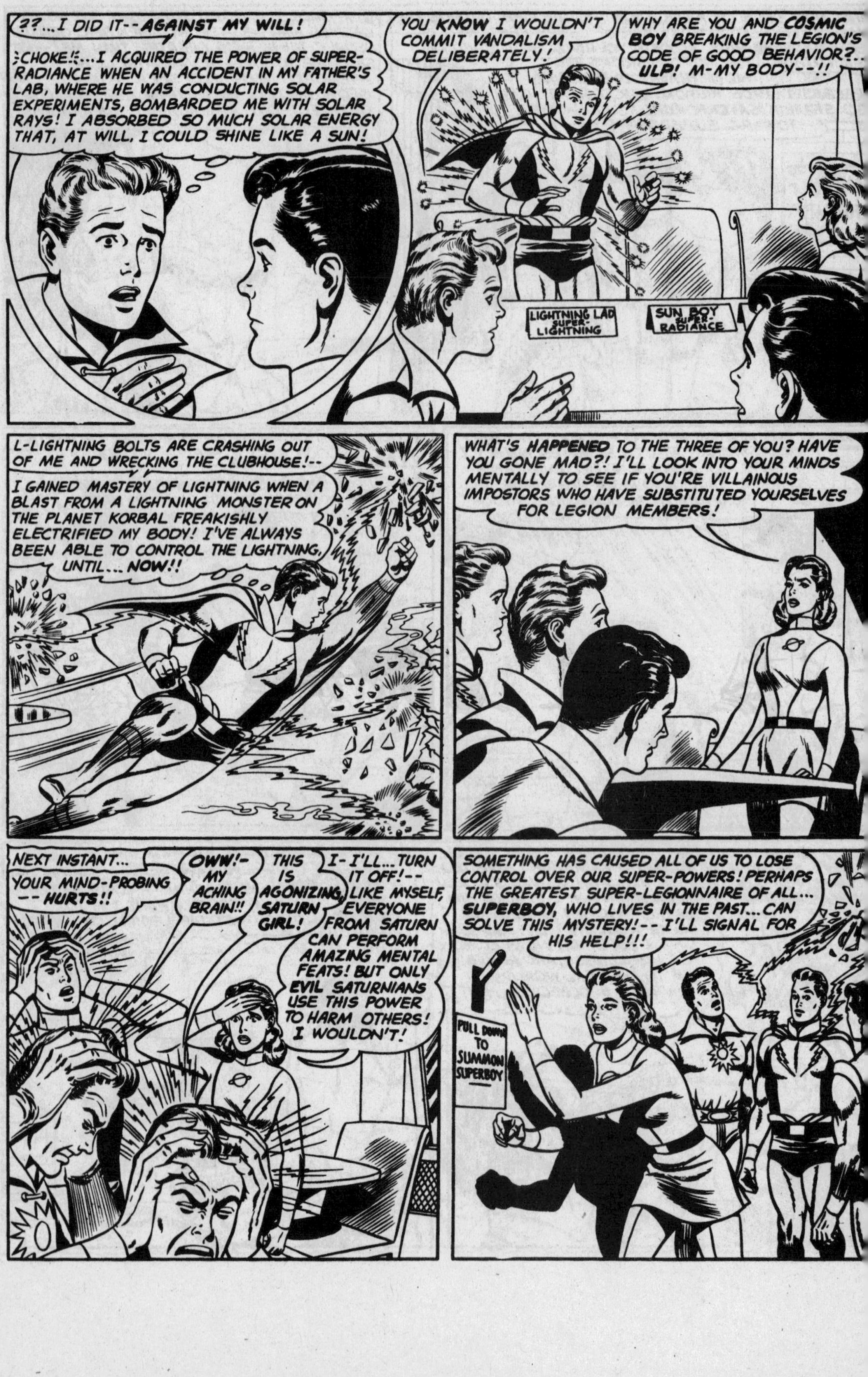
??...I DID IT--AGAINST MY WILL!
CHOKE!...I ACQUIRED THE POWER OF SUPER-RADIANCE WHEN AN ACCIDENT IN MY FATHER'S LAB, WHERE HE WAS CONDUCTING SOLAR EXPERIMENTS, BOMBARDED ME WITH SOLAR RAYS! I ABSORBED SO MUCH SOLAR ENERGY THAT, AT WILL, I COULD SHINE LIKE A SUN!
YOU KNOW I WOULDN'T COMMIT VANDALISM DELIBERATELY!
WHY ARE YOU AND COSMIC BOY BREAKING THE LEGION'S CODE OF GOOD BEHAVIOR?.. ULP! M-MY BODY--!!
LIGHTNING LAD SUPER-LIGHTNING
SUN BOY SUPER-RADIANCE
L-LIGHTNING BOLTS ARE CRASHING OUT OF ME AND WRECKING THE CLUBHOUSE!--
I GAINED MASTERY OF LIGHTNING WHEN A BLAST FROM A LIGHTNING MONSTER ON THE PLANET KORBAL FREAKISHLY ELECTRIFIED MY BODY! I'VE ALWAYS BEEN ABLE TO CONTROL THE LIGHTNING, UNTIL... NOW!!
WHAT'S HAPPENED TO THE THREE OF YOU? HAVE YOU GONE MAD?! I'LL LOOK INTO YOUR MINDS MENTALLY TO SEE IF YOU'RE VILLAINOUS IMPOSTORS WHO HAVE SUBSTITUTED YOURSELVES FOR LEGION MEMBERS!
NEXT INSTANT...
YOUR MIND-PROBING --HURTS!!
OWW!-MY ACHING BRAIN!!
THIS IS AGONIZING, SATURN GIRL!
I-I'LL...TURN IT OFF!-- LIKE MYSELF, EVERYONE FROM SATURN CAN PERFORM AMAZING MENTAL FEATS! BUT ONLY EVIL SATURNIANS USE THIS POWER TO HARM OTHERS! I WOULDN'T!
SOMETHING HAS CAUSED ALL OF US TO LOSE CONTROL OVER OUR SUPER-POWERS! PERHAPS THE GREATEST SUPER-LEGIONNAIRE OF ALL... SUPERBOY, WHO LIVES IN THE PAST...CAN SOLVE THIS MYSTERY!--I'LL SIGNAL FOR HIS HELP!!!
PULL DOWN TO SUMMON SUPERBOY

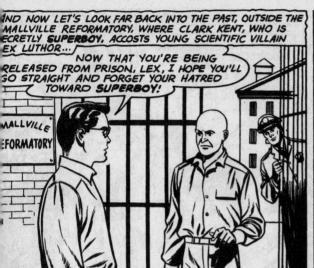

AND NOW LET'S LOOK FAR BACK INTO THE PAST, OUTSIDE THE MALLVILLE REFORMATORY, WHERE CLARK KENT, WHO IS SECRETLY *SUPERBOY*, ACCOSTS YOUNG SCIENTIFIC VILLAIN LEX LUTHOR...

NOW THAT YOU'RE BEING RELEASED FROM PRISON, LEX, I HOPE YOU'LL GO STRAIGHT AND FORGET YOUR HATRED TOWARD *SUPERBOY*!

BAH! ONCE I ADMIRED *SUPERBOY*, BUT NOW I DESPISE HIM! DESPITE MY SCIENTIFIC GENIUS, PEOPLE THINK *HE'S* GREATER THAN ME!--*HE* SENT ME TO JAIL! SOMEDAY I'LL BE AVENGED! WAIT AND SEE!... WHEN I GROW UP, IT'LL BE *LUTHOR*, THE WORLD'S GREATEST OUTLAW, AGAINST *SUPERMAN*!!

LATER, IN THE KENT HOME... HM-MM...TOO BAD LEX HATES ME SO! I WONDER IF I'LL EVER HAVE TO IMPRISON HIM INSIDE THE *PHANTOM ZONE*, THE TWILIGHT WORLD WHERE DANGEROUS KRYPTONIAN CRIMINALS WERE EXILED!

RECOLLECTION OF THE *PHANTOM ZONE* PROMPTS CLARK TO LOOK INTO A SPECIAL VIEWER...

THERE, IN THE ZONE, IS THE INVISIBLE FORM OF MY FRIEND *MON-EL*! HE CAME TO EARTH FROM THE PLANET *DAXAM*, ACQUIRING SUPER-POWERS LIKE MYSELF!

JUST AS KRYPTONITE CAN AFFECT ME, LEAD RADIATIONS AFFECTED MON-EL...ONLY HE WAS STRICKEN *PERMANENTLY*! I PLACED HIM IN THE TWILIGHT DIMENSION SO HE WOULDN'T DIE. SOME DAY I HOPE TO FIND A CURE FOR HIS ILLNESS, AND RETURN HIM TO THE REAL WORLD! I HAVEN'T SUCCEEDED...YET!

AS CLARK LOWERS THE VIEWER...

OH-OH! MY SIGNAL-LAMP IS NOW FLASHING A CODE MESSAGE! THAT CODE MEANS I'M TO CONTACT THE *LEGION OF SUPER-HEROES* IN THE FUTURE!

4.

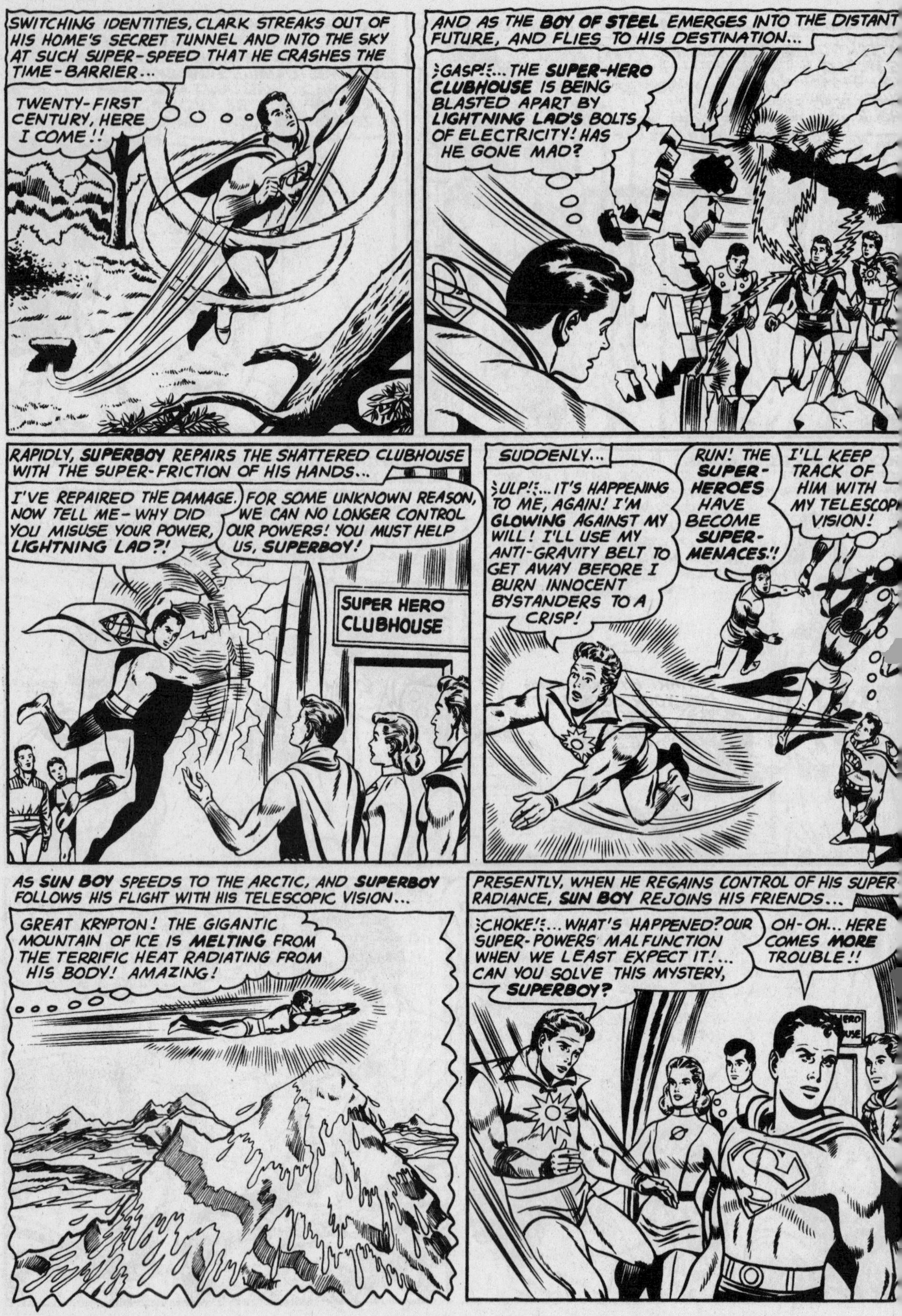
SWITCHING IDENTITIES, CLARK STREAKS OUT OF HIS HOME'S SECRET TUNNEL AND INTO THE SKY AT SUCH SUPER-SPEED THAT HE CRASHES THE TIME-BARRIER...
TWENTY-FIRST CENTURY, HERE I COME!!
AND AS THE BOY OF STEEL EMERGES INTO THE DISTANT FUTURE, AND FLIES TO HIS DESTINATION...
GASP!... THE SUPER-HERO CLUBHOUSE IS BEING BLASTED APART BY LIGHTNING LAD'S BOLTS OF ELECTRICITY! HAS HE GONE MAD?
RAPIDLY, SUPERBOY REPAIRS THE SHATTERED CLUBHOUSE WITH THE SUPER-FRICTION OF HIS HANDS...
I'VE REPAIRED THE DAMAGE. NOW TELL ME-WHY DID YOU MISUSE YOUR POWER, LIGHTNING LAD?!
FOR SOME UNKNOWN REASON, WE CAN NO LONGER CONTROL OUR POWERS! YOU MUST HELP US, SUPERBOY!
SUPER HERO CLUBHOUSE
SUDDENLY...
GULP!... IT'S HAPPENING TO ME, AGAIN! I'M GLOWING AGAINST MY WILL! I'LL USE MY ANTI-GRAVITY BELT TO GET AWAY BEFORE I BURN INNOCENT BYSTANDERS TO A CRISP!
RUN! THE SUPER-HEROES HAVE BECOME SUPER-MENACES!!
I'LL KEEP TRACK OF HIM WITH MY TELESCOP VISION!
AS SUN BOY SPEEDS TO THE ARCTIC, AND SUPERBOY FOLLOWS HIS FLIGHT WITH HIS TELESCOPIC VISION...
GREAT KRYPTON! THE GIGANTIC MOUNTAIN OF ICE IS MELTING FROM THE TERRIFIC HEAT RADIATING FROM HIS BODY! AMAZING!
PRESENTLY, WHEN HE REGAINS CONTROL OF HIS SUPER RADIANCE, SUN BOY REJOINS HIS FRIENDS...
CHOKE!... WHAT'S HAPPENED? OUR SUPER-POWERS MALFUNCTION WHEN WE LEAST EXPECT IT!... CAN YOU SOLVE THIS MYSTERY, SUPERBOY?
OH-OH... HERE COMES MORE TROUBLE!!

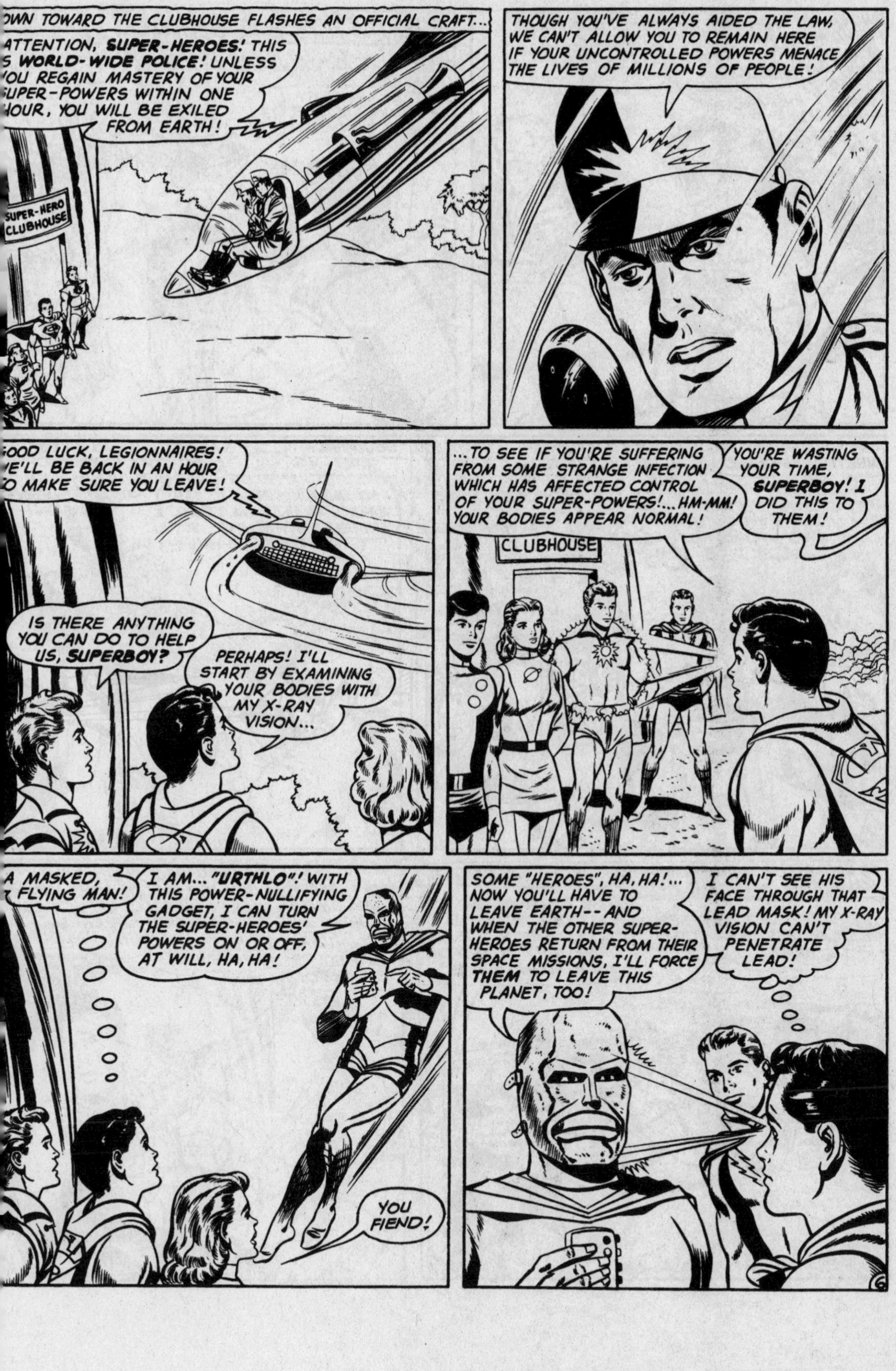
OWN TOWARD THE CLUBHOUSE FLASHES AN OFFICIAL CRAFT...
ATTENTION, SUPER-HEROES! THIS S WORLD-WIDE POLICE! UNLESS YOU REGAIN MASTERY OF YOUR SUPER-POWERS WITHIN ONE HOUR, YOU WILL BE EXILED FROM EARTH!
SUPER-HERO CLUBHOUSE
THOUGH YOU'VE ALWAYS AIDED THE LAW, WE CAN'T ALLOW YOU TO REMAIN HERE IF YOUR UNCONTROLLED POWERS MENACE THE LIVES OF MILLIONS OF PEOPLE!
GOOD LUCK, LEGIONNAIRES! WE'LL BE BACK IN AN HOUR TO MAKE SURE YOU LEAVE!
IS THERE ANYTHING YOU CAN DO TO HELP US, SUPERBOY?
PERHAPS! I'LL START BY EXAMINING YOUR BODIES WITH MY X-RAY VISION...
...TO SEE IF YOU'RE SUFFERING FROM SOME STRANGE INFECTION WHICH HAS AFFECTED CONTROL OF YOUR SUPER-POWERS!...HM-MM! YOUR BODIES APPEAR NORMAL!
YOU'RE WASTING YOUR TIME, SUPERBOY! I DID THIS TO THEM!
CLUBHOUSE
A MASKED, FLYING MAN!
I AM..."URTHLO"! WITH THIS POWER-NULLIFYING GADGET, I CAN TURN THE SUPER-HEROES' POWERS ON OR OFF, AT WILL, HA, HA!
YOU FIEND!
SOME "HEROES", HA, HA!... NOW YOU'LL HAVE TO LEAVE EARTH--AND WHEN THE OTHER SUPER-HEROES RETURN FROM THEIR SPACE MISSIONS, I'LL FORCE THEM TO LEAVE THIS PLANET, TOO!
I CAN'T SEE HIS FACE THROUGH THAT LEAD MASK! MY X-RAY VISION CAN'T PENETRATE LEAD!
6

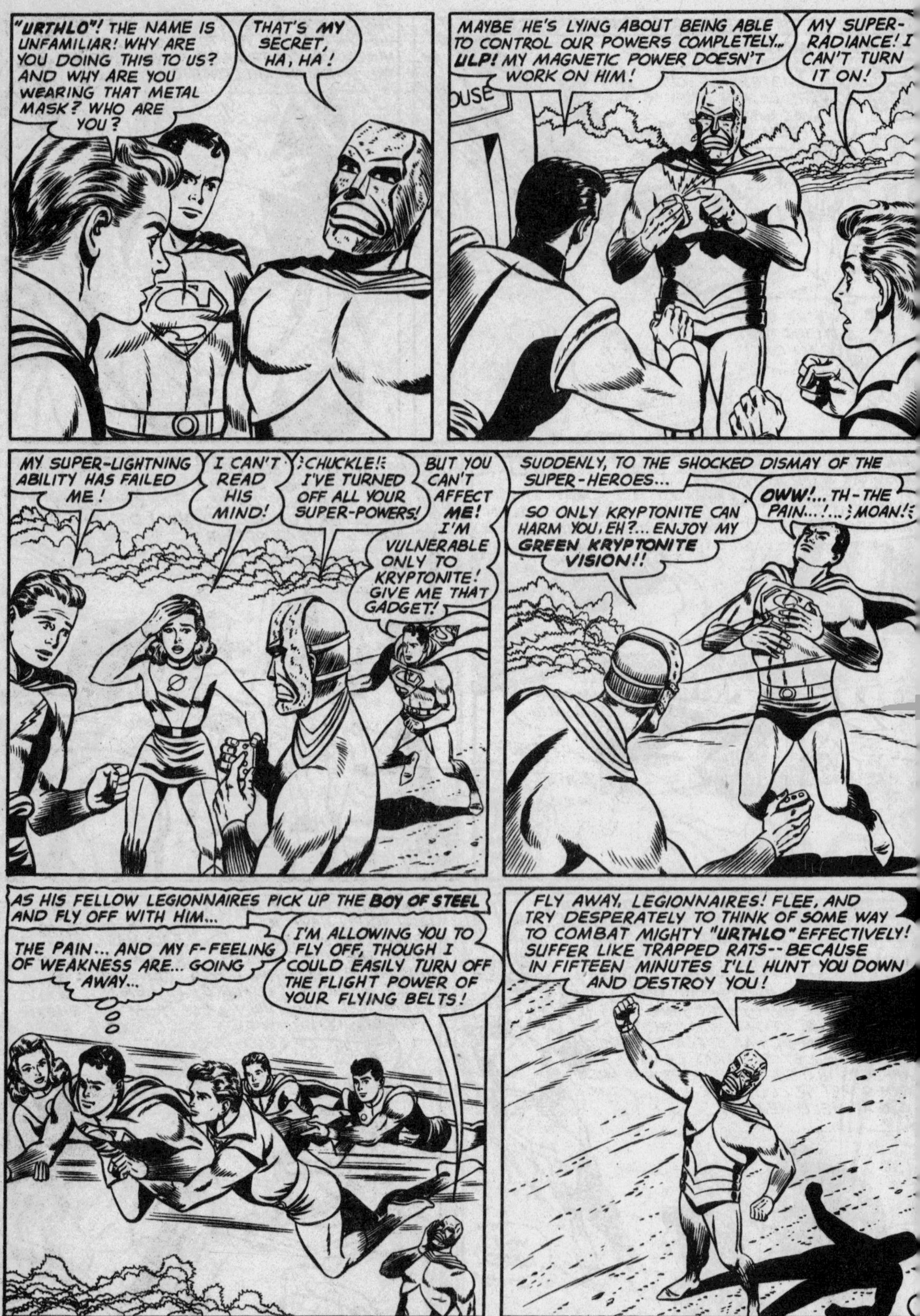
"URTHLO"! THE NAME IS UNFAMILIAR! WHY ARE YOU DOING THIS TO US? AND WHY ARE YOU WEARING THAT METAL MASK? WHO ARE YOU?
THAT'S MY SECRET, HA, HA!
MAYBE HE'S LYING ABOUT BEING ABLE TO CONTROL OUR POWERS COMPLETELY... ULP! MY MAGNETIC POWER DOESN'T WORK ON HIM!
MY SUPER-RADIANCE! I CAN'T TURN IT ON!
MY SUPER-LIGHTNING ABILITY HAS FAILED ME!
I CAN'T READ HIS MIND!
CHUCKLE! I'VE TURNED OFF ALL YOUR SUPER-POWERS!
BUT YOU CAN'T AFFECT ME! I'M VULNERABLE ONLY TO KRYPTONITE! GIVE ME THAT GADGET!
SUDDENLY, TO THE SHOCKED DISMAY OF THE SUPER-HEROES...
SO ONLY KRYPTONITE CAN HARM YOU, EH?... ENJOY MY GREEN KRYPTONITE VISION!!
OWW!... TH-THE PAIN...!... MOAN!
AS HIS FELLOW LEGIONNAIRES PICK UP THE BOY OF STEEL AND FLY OFF WITH HIM...
THE PAIN... AND MY F-FEELING OF WEAKNESS ARE... GOING AWAY...
I'M ALLOWING YOU TO FLY OFF, THOUGH I COULD EASILY TURN OFF THE FLIGHT POWER OF YOUR FLYING BELTS!
FLY AWAY, LEGIONNAIRES! FLEE, AND TRY DESPERATELY TO THINK OF SOME WAY TO COMBAT MIGHTY "URTHLO" EFFECTIVELY! SUFFER LIKE TRAPPED RATS--BECAUSE IN FIFTEEN MINUTES I'LL HUNT YOU DOWN AND DESTROY YOU!

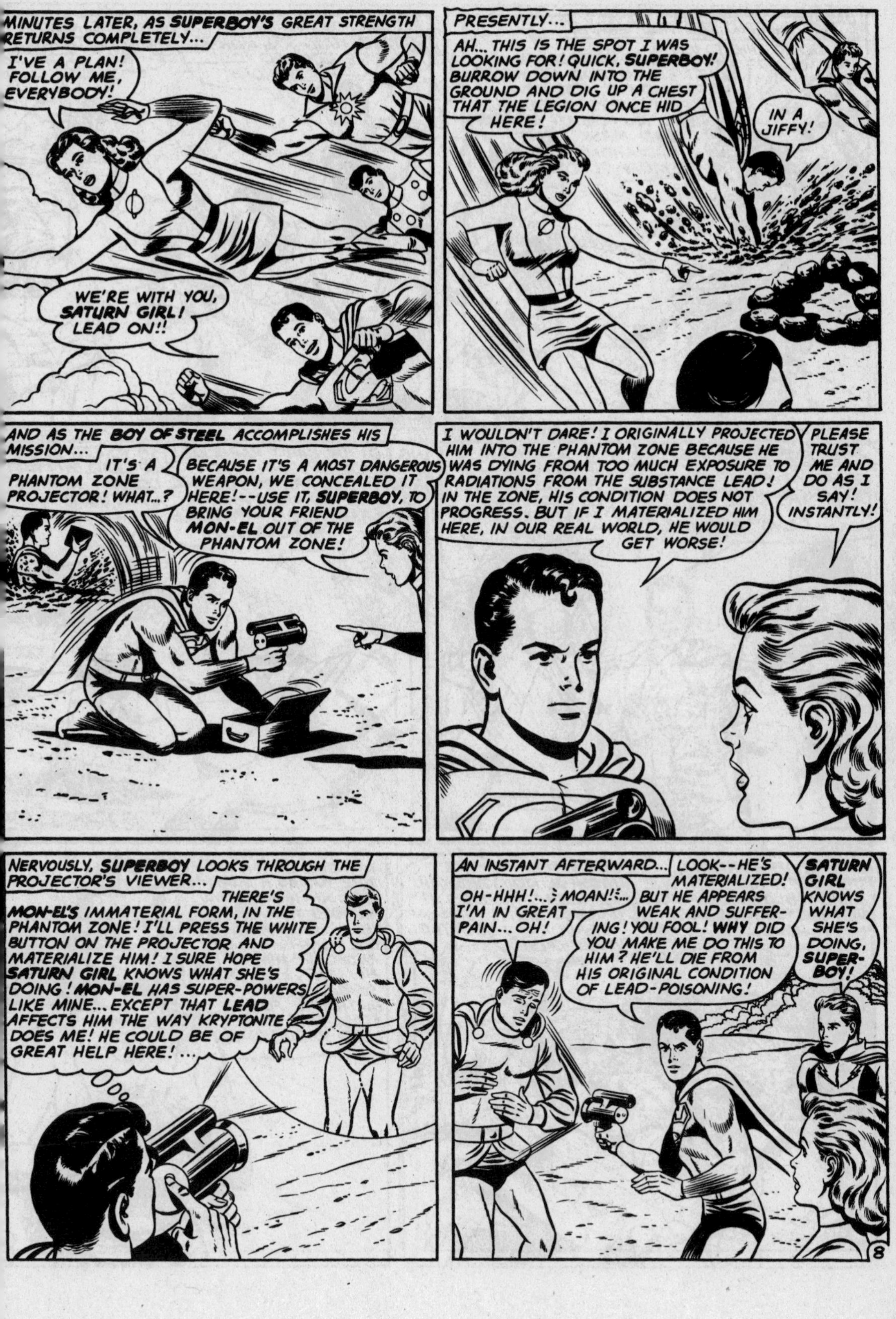
MINUTES LATER, AS SUPERBOY'S GREAT STRENGTH RETURNS COMPLETELY...
I'VE A PLAN! FOLLOW ME, EVERYBODY!
WE'RE WITH YOU, SATURN GIRL! LEAD ON!!
PRESENTLY...
AH... THIS IS THE SPOT I WAS LOOKING FOR! QUICK, SUPERBOY! BURROW DOWN INTO THE GROUND AND DIG UP A CHEST THAT THE LEGION ONCE HID HERE!
IN A JIFFY!
AND AS THE BOY OF STEEL ACCOMPLISHES HIS MISSION...
IT'S A PHANTOM ZONE PROJECTOR! WHAT...?
BECAUSE IT'S A MOST DANGEROUS WEAPON, WE CONCEALED IT HERE!--USE IT, SUPERBOY, TO BRING YOUR FRIEND MON-EL OUT OF THE PHANTOM ZONE!
I WOULDN'T DARE! I ORIGINALLY PROJECTED HIM INTO THE PHANTOM ZONE BECAUSE HE WAS DYING FROM TOO MUCH EXPOSURE TO RADIATIONS FROM THE SUBSTANCE LEAD! IN THE ZONE, HIS CONDITION DOES NOT PROGRESS. BUT IF I MATERIALIZED HIM HERE, IN OUR REAL WORLD, HE WOULD GET WORSE!
PLEASE TRUST ME AND DO AS I SAY! INSTANTLY!
NERVOUSLY, SUPERBOY LOOKS THROUGH THE PROJECTOR'S VIEWER...
THERE'S MON-EL'S IMMATERIAL FORM, IN THE PHANTOM ZONE! I'LL PRESS THE WHITE BUTTON ON THE PROJECTOR AND MATERIALIZE HIM! I SURE HOPE SATURN GIRL KNOWS WHAT SHE'S DOING! MON-EL HAS SUPER-POWERS LIKE MINE... EXCEPT THAT LEAD AFFECTS HIM THE WAY KRYPTONITE DOES ME! HE COULD BE OF GREAT HELP HERE! ...
AN INSTANT AFTERWARD...
OH-HHH!... MOAN!... I'M IN GREAT PAIN... OH!
LOOK--HE'S MATERIALIZED! BUT HE APPEARS WEAK AND SUFFERING! YOU FOOL! WHY DID YOU MAKE ME DO THIS TO HIM? HE'LL DIE FROM HIS ORIGINAL CONDITION OF LEAD-POISONING!
SATURN GIRL KNOWS WHAT SHE'S DOING, SUPERBOY!
8

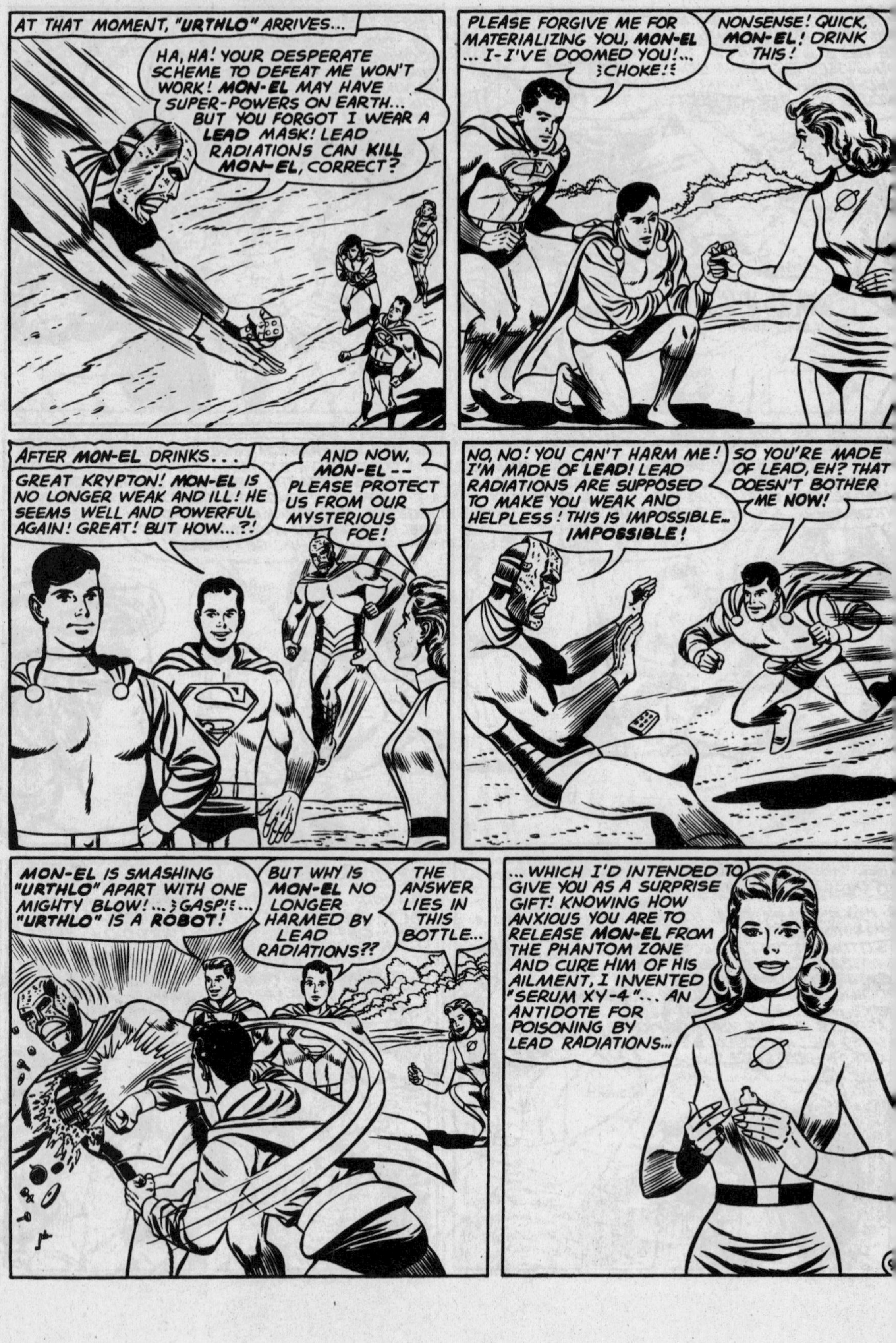
AT THAT MOMENT, "URTHLO" ARRIVES...
HA, HA! YOUR DESPERATE SCHEME TO DEFEAT ME WON'T WORK! MON-EL MAY HAVE SUPER-POWERS ON EARTH... BUT YOU FORGOT I WEAR A LEAD MASK! LEAD RADIATIONS CAN KILL MON-EL, CORRECT?
PLEASE FORGIVE ME FOR MATERIALIZING YOU, MON-EL ... I-I'VE DOOMED YOU!... CHOKE!
NONSENSE! QUICK, MON-EL! DRINK THIS!
AFTER MON-EL DRINKS...
GREAT KRYPTON! MON-EL IS NO LONGER WEAK AND ILL! HE SEEMS WELL AND POWERFUL AGAIN! GREAT! BUT HOW...?!
AND NOW, MON-EL -- PLEASE PROTECT US FROM OUR MYSTERIOUS FOE!
NO, NO! YOU CAN'T HARM ME! I'M MADE OF LEAD! LEAD RADIATIONS ARE SUPPOSED TO MAKE YOU WEAK AND HELPLESS! THIS IS IMPOSSIBLE... IMPOSSIBLE!
SO YOU'RE MADE OF LEAD, EH? THAT DOESN'T BOTHER ME NOW!
MON-EL IS SMASHING "URTHLO" APART WITH ONE MIGHTY BLOW!... GASP!... "URTHLO" IS A ROBOT!
BUT WHY IS MON-EL NO LONGER HARMED BY LEAD RADIATIONS??
THE ANSWER LIES IN THIS BOTTLE...
...WHICH I'D INTENDED TO GIVE YOU AS A SURPRISE GIFT! KNOWING HOW ANXIOUS YOU ARE TO RELEASE MON-EL FROM THE PHANTOM ZONE AND CURE HIM OF HIS AILMENT, I INVENTED "SERUM XY-4"... AN ANTIDOTE FOR POISONING BY LEAD RADIATIONS...

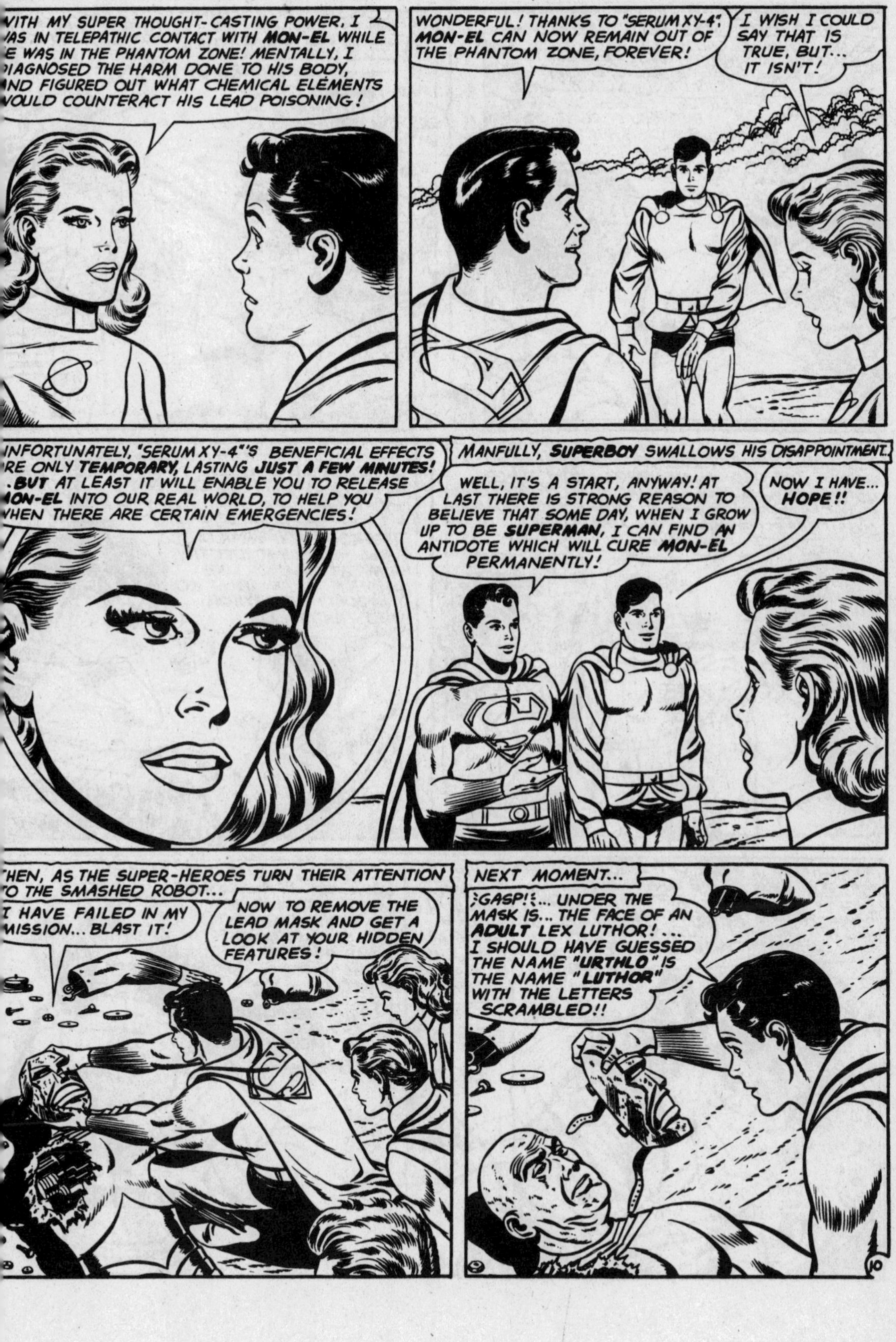
WITH MY SUPER THOUGHT-CASTING POWER, I WAS IN TELEPATHIC CONTACT WITH MON-EL WHILE HE WAS IN THE PHANTOM ZONE! MENTALLY, I DIAGNOSED THE HARM DONE TO HIS BODY, AND FIGURED OUT WHAT CHEMICAL ELEMENTS WOULD COUNTERACT HIS LEAD POISONING!
WONDERFUL! THANKS TO "SERUM XY-4", MON-EL CAN NOW REMAIN OUT OF THE PHANTOM ZONE, FOREVER!
I WISH I COULD SAY THAT IS TRUE, BUT... IT ISN'T!
UNFORTUNATELY, "SERUM XY-4"'S BENEFICIAL EFFECTS ARE ONLY TEMPORARY, LASTING JUST A FEW MINUTES! ..BUT AT LEAST IT WILL ENABLE YOU TO RELEASE MON-EL INTO OUR REAL WORLD, TO HELP YOU WHEN THERE ARE CERTAIN EMERGENCIES!
MANFULLY, SUPERBOY SWALLOWS HIS DISAPPOINTMENT..
WELL, IT'S A START, ANYWAY! AT LAST THERE IS STRONG REASON TO BELIEVE THAT SOME DAY, WHEN I GROW UP TO BE SUPERMAN, I CAN FIND AN ANTIDOTE WHICH WILL CURE MON-EL PERMANENTLY!
NOW I HAVE... HOPE!!
THEN, AS THE SUPER-HEROES TURN THEIR ATTENTION TO THE SMASHED ROBOT...
I HAVE FAILED IN MY MISSION... BLAST IT!
NOW TO REMOVE THE LEAD MASK AND GET A LOOK AT YOUR HIDDEN FEATURES!
NEXT MOMENT...
GASP!... UNDER THE MASK IS... THE FACE OF AN ADULT LEX LUTHOR! ... I SHOULD HAVE GUESSED THE NAME "URTHLO" IS THE NAME "LUTHOR" WITH THE LETTERS SCRAMBLED!!
10

IN A FEW MINUTES MY BROKEN MECHANISM WILL STOP FUNCTIONING! SOON "URTHLO" WILL BE NO MORE! BECAUSE YOU RECOGNIZE THE IMAGE IN WHICH I WAS CREATED, YOU MAY AS WELL KNOW THE REST!

"BACK IN SMALLVILLE, AFTER HE WAS RELEASED FROM PRISON, MY MASTER LEX LUTHOR CREATED ME IN HIS LABORATORY..."

SINCE THE LEGION OF SUPER-HEROES OF THE DISTANT FUTURE IS SO DEAR TO THE HEART OF MY ENEMY, SUPERBOY...

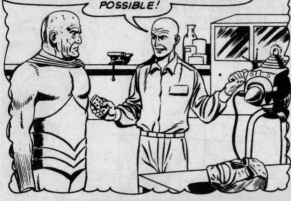

... I'LL TRANSPORT YOU INTO THE FUTURE WITH THIS TIME-RAY PROJECTOR! YOUR MISSION: TO CHANGE THE LEGION MEMBERS FROM SUPER-HEROES INTO SUPER-MENACES...SO THEY'LL BE FORCED TO LEAVE EARTH! THIS SUPER-POWERS NULLIFYING DEVICE WILL MAKE IT ALL POSSIBLE!

AS THE PERISHING ROBOT CONTINUES SPEAKING...

MY MASTER CONSTRUCTED ME OF LEAD, AND HAD ME DON A LEAD MASK, SO THAT IF I ENCOUNTERED YOU, SUPERBOY, YOU WOULDN'T GUESS MY SECRET IDENTITY! HE MADE ME LOOK LIKE HIMSELF AS AN ADULT SO IT WOULD BE LUTHOR WHO TRIUMPHED!!

MY CLOTHING IS MADE OF A SPECIAL MATERIAL THAT IS IMMUNE TO THE SUPER-HEROES' POWERS! HE GAVE ME KRYPTONITE VISION, TOO!--YOU'VE DEFEATED ME, BUT MY MASTER WILL YET CRUSH EVERY LAST ONE OF YOU!--AGH-HHHHHH...!

MOMENTS LATER...

THE ROBOT WITH THE ADULT LUTHOR FACE HAS "DIED"!...GREAT SCOTT! LOOK AT THESE HATE TAPES INSIDE HIS CHEST COMPARTMENT! NO WONDER THE AUTO-MATON LOATHED US!

HATE SUPERBOY

HATE LEGION OF SUPER-HEROES

HATE HATE HATE

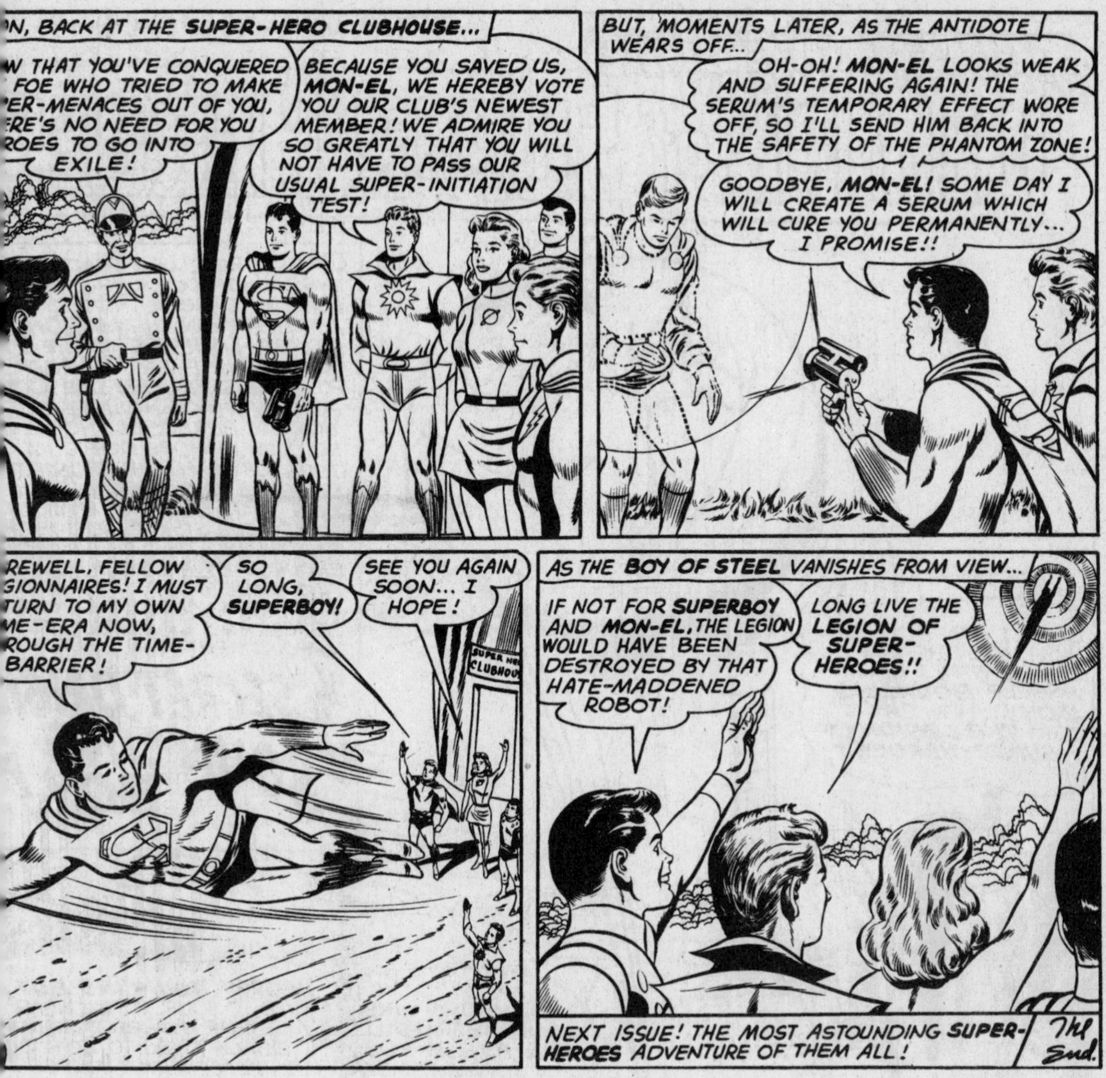
ON, BACK AT THE SUPER-HERO CLUBHOUSE...
W THAT YOU'VE CONQUERED FOE WHO TRIED TO MAKE ER-MENACES OUT OF YOU, RE'S NO NEED FOR YOU ROES TO GO INTO EXILE!
BECAUSE YOU SAVED US, MON-EL, WE HEREBY VOTE YOU OUR CLUB'S NEWEST MEMBER! WE ADMIRE YOU SO GREATLY THAT YOU WILL NOT HAVE TO PASS OUR USUAL SUPER-INITIATION TEST!
BUT, MOMENTS LATER, AS THE ANTIDOTE WEARS OFF...
OH-OH! MON-EL LOOKS WEAK AND SUFFERING AGAIN! THE SERUM'S TEMPORARY EFFECT WORE OFF, SO I'LL SEND HIM BACK INTO THE SAFETY OF THE PHANTOM ZONE!
GOODBYE, MON-EL! SOME DAY I WILL CREATE A SERUM WHICH WILL CURE YOU PERMANENTLY... I PROMISE!!
REWELL, FELLOW GIONNAIRES! I MUST TURN TO MY OWN ME-ERA NOW, ROUGH THE TIME-BARRIER!
SO LONG, SUPERBOY!
SEE YOU AGAIN SOON... I HOPE!
SUPER HE CLUBHOUS
AS THE BOY OF STEEL VANISHES FROM VIEW...
IF NOT FOR SUPERBOY AND MON-EL, THE LEGION WOULD HAVE BEEN DESTROYED BY THAT HATE-MADDENED ROBOT!
LONG LIVE THE LEGION OF SUPER-HEROES!!
NEXT ISSUE! THE MOST ASTOUNDING SUPER-HEROES ADVENTURE OF THEM ALL!

LEGION of SUPER-HEROES

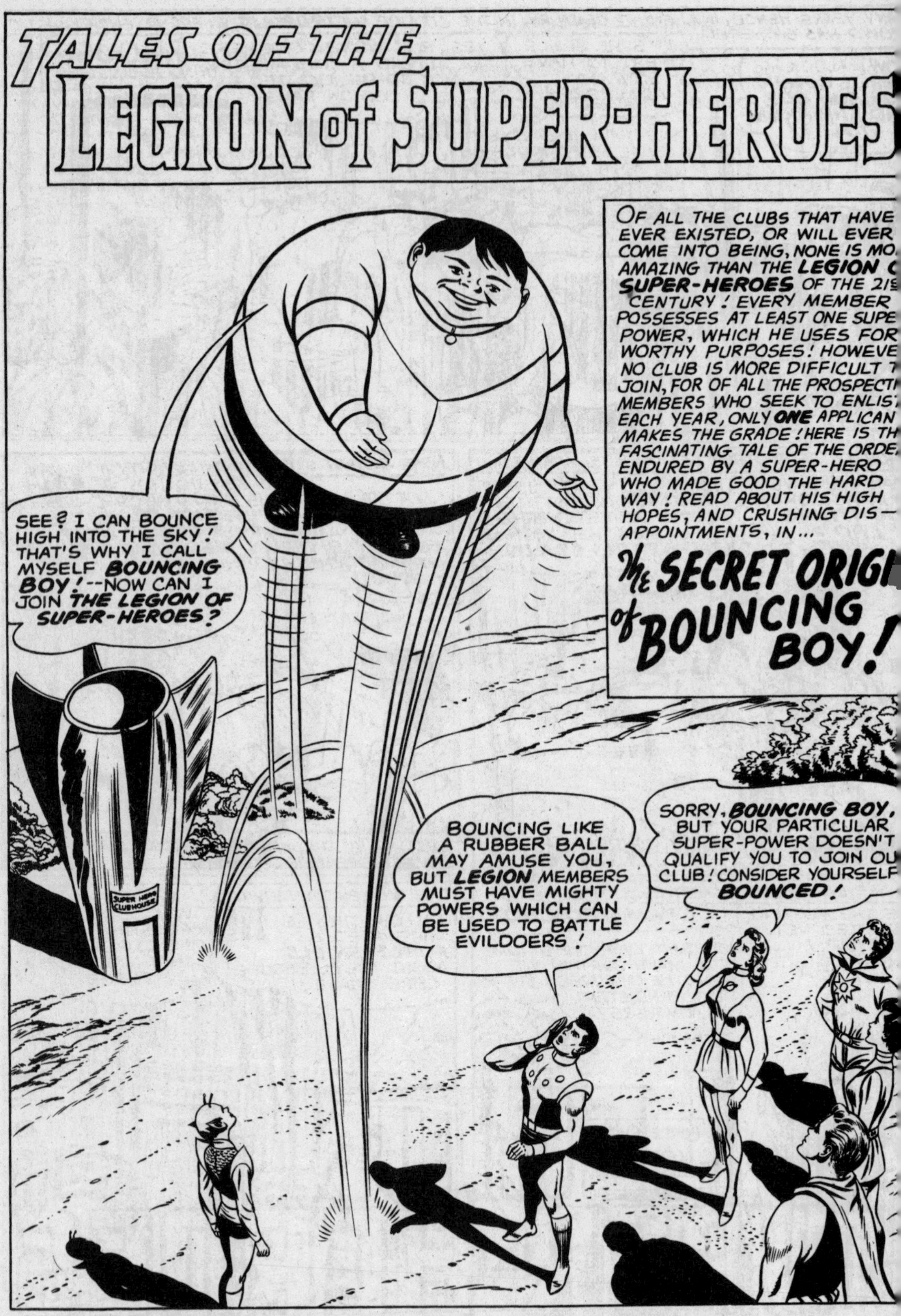
TALES OF THE
LEGION of SUPER-HEROES
OF ALL THE CLUBS THAT HAVE EVER EXISTED, OR WILL EVER COME INTO BEING, NONE IS MO AMAZING THAN THE LEGION SUPER-HEROES OF THE 21ST CENTURY! EVERY MEMBER POSSESSES AT LEAST ONE SUPE POWER, WHICH HE USES FOR WORTHY PURPOSES! HOWEVE NO CLUB IS MORE DIFFICULT T JOIN, FOR OF ALL THE PROSPECTI MEMBERS WHO SEEK TO ENLIS EACH YEAR, ONLY ONE APPLICAN MAKES THE GRADE! HERE IS TH FASCINATING TALE OF THE ORDE ENDURED BY A SUPER-HERO WHO MADE GOOD THE HARD WAY! READ ABOUT HIS HIGH HOPES, AND CRUSHING DIS-APPOINTMENTS, IN...
THE SECRET ORIGI of BOUNCING BOY!
SEE? I CAN BOUNCE HIGH INTO THE SKY! THAT'S WHY I CALL MYSELF BOUNCING BOY!--NOW CAN I JOIN THE LEGION OF SUPER-HEROES?
SUPER HERO CLUBHOUSE
BOUNCING LIKE A RUBBER BALL MAY AMUSE YOU, BUT LEGION MEMBERS MUST HAVE MIGHTY POWERS WHICH CAN BE USED TO BATTLE EVILDOERS!
SORRY, BOUNCING BOY, BUT YOUR PARTICULAR SUPER-POWER DOESN'T QUALIFY YOU TO JOIN OU CLUB! CONSIDER YOURSELF BOUNCED!

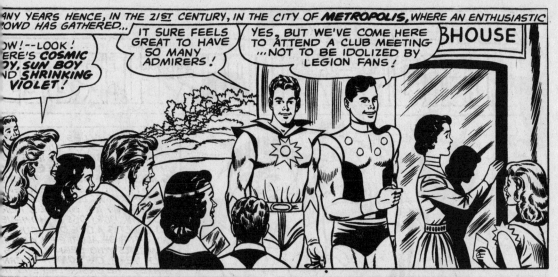

MANY YEARS HENCE, IN THE 21ST CENTURY, IN THE CITY OF **METROPOLIS**, WHERE AN ENTHUSIASTIC CROWD HAS GATHERED...

NOW!--LOOK! THERE'S **COSMIC BOY, SUN BOY** AND **SHRINKING VIOLET!**

IT SURE FEELS GREAT TO HAVE SO MANY ADMIRERS!

YES, BUT WE'VE COME HERE TO ATTEND A CLUB MEETING ...NOT TO BE IDOLIZED BY LEGION FANS!

BHOUSE

SHORTLY, AS ANOTHER LEGIONNAIRE ARRIVES...

CAN WE HAVE OUR AUTOGRAPH, **LIGHTNING LAD?**

-CHUCKLE-- OKAY! KINDLY HOLD YOUR SENSITIZED SCRIPTO-PLATES OVERHEAD, AND I'LL SIGN THEM WITH MY **DUPLI-WRITING STYLUS!**

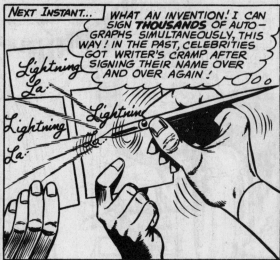

NEXT INSTANT...

WHAT AN INVENTION! I CAN SIGN **THOUSANDS** OF AUTO-GRAPHS SIMULTANEOUSLY, THIS WAY! IN THE PAST, CELEBRITIES GOT WRITER'S CRAMP AFTER SIGNING THEIR NAME OVER AND OVER AGAIN!

Lightning La.
Lightning
La.
Lightning
Lightning

IS THE LAST MEMBER ARRIVES...

IS THE MEETING STARTED YET, **SATURN GIRL?**

NOT YET, **CHAMELEON BOY!**

NOW THAT EVERYONE'S HERE, I'LL MAKE CERTAIN WE WON'T BE DISTURBED BY TOO PERSISTENT ADMIRERS!

FORCE-SHIELD ACTIVATOR

ONE MOMENT AFTERWARD...

OH-OH! THEY'VE ACTIVATED A **FORCE-SHIELD** ABOUT THE CLUBHOUSE! LET'S LEAVE!

WE MIGHT AS WELL SINCE IT'S **IMPOSSIBLE** FOR ANY-ONE TO PENETRATE THAT FIELD OF FORCE!

SUPER HERO CLUBHOUSE

2

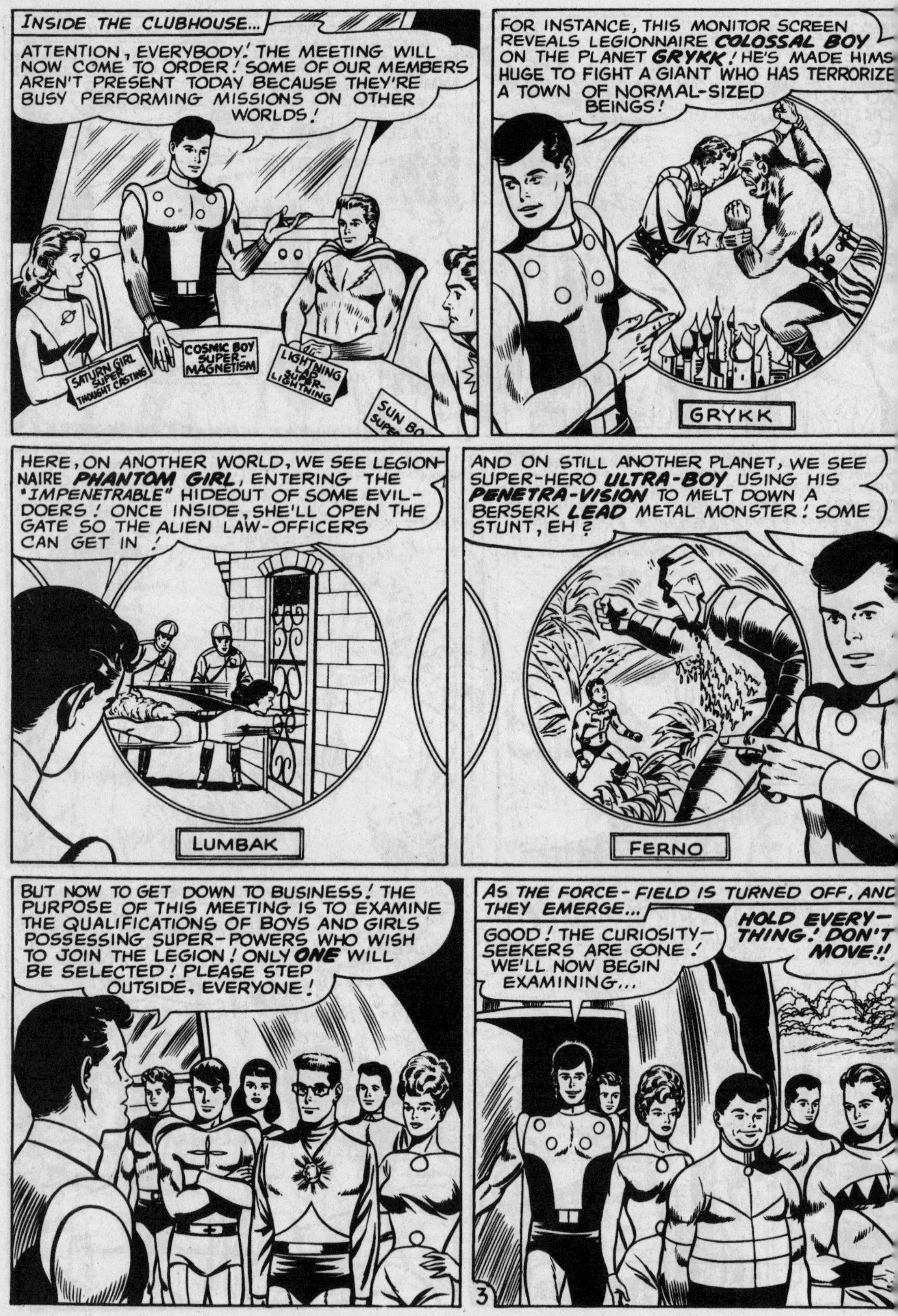
INSIDE THE CLUBHOUSE...
ATTENTION, EVERYBODY! THE MEETING WILL NOW COME TO ORDER! SOME OF OUR MEMBERS AREN'T PRESENT TODAY BECAUSE THEY'RE BUSY PERFORMING MISSIONS ON OTHER WORLDS!
SATURN GIRL SUPER THOUGHT CASTING
COSMIC BOY SUPER-MAGNETISM
LIGHTNING LAD SUPER-LIGHTNING
FOR INSTANCE, THIS MONITOR SCREEN REVEALS LEGIONNAIRE COLOSSAL BOY ON THE PLANET GRYKK! HE'S MADE HIMS HUGE TO FIGHT A GIANT WHO HAS TERRORIZE A TOWN OF NORMAL-SIZED BEINGS!
GRYKK
HERE, ON ANOTHER WORLD, WE SEE LEGIONNAIRE PHANTOM GIRL, ENTERING THE "IMPENETRABLE" HIDEOUT OF SOME EVIL-DOERS! ONCE INSIDE, SHE'LL OPEN THE GATE SO THE ALIEN LAW-OFFICERS CAN GET IN!
LUMBAK
AND ON STILL ANOTHER PLANET, WE SEE SUPER-HERO ULTRA-BOY USING HIS PENETRA-VISION TO MELT DOWN A BERSERK LEAD METAL MONSTER! SOME STUNT, EH?
FERNO
BUT NOW TO GET DOWN TO BUSINESS! THE PURPOSE OF THIS MEETING IS TO EXAMINE THE QUALIFICATIONS OF BOYS AND GIRLS POSSESSING SUPER-POWERS WHO WISH TO JOIN THE LEGION! ONLY ONE WILL BE SELECTED! PLEASE STEP OUTSIDE, EVERYONE!
AS THE FORCE-FIELD IS TURNED OFF, AND THEY EMERGE...
GOOD! THE CURIOSITY-SEEKERS ARE GONE! WE'LL NOW BEGIN EXAMINING...
HOLD EVERYTHING! DON'T MOVE!!
3

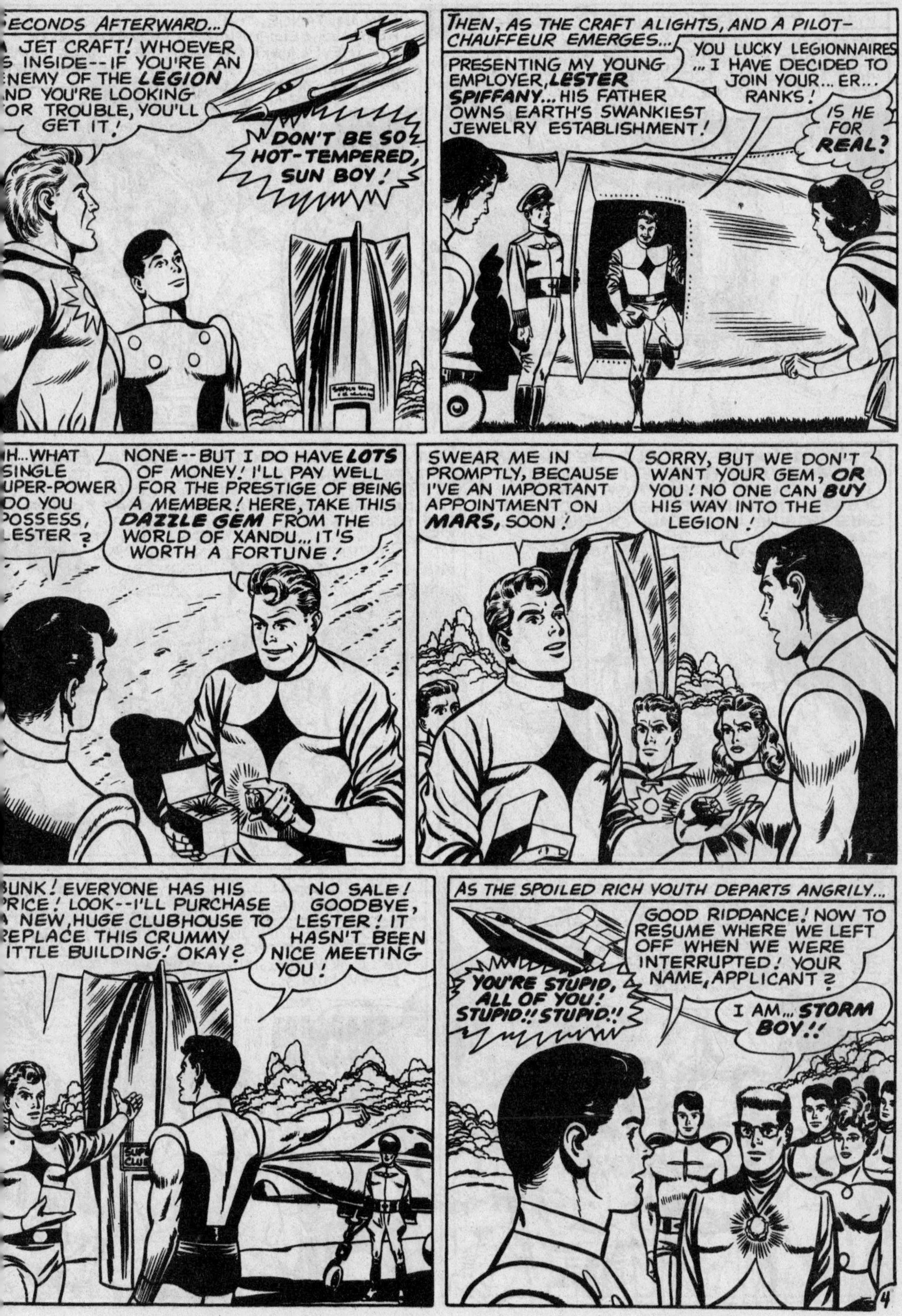
ECONDS AFTERWARD...
JET CRAFT! WHOEVER S INSIDE--IF YOU'RE AN NEMY OF THE LEGION ND YOU'RE LOOKING OR TROUBLE, YOU'LL GET IT!
DON'T BE SO HOT-TEMPERED, SUN BOY!
THEN, AS THE CRAFT ALIGHTS, AND A PILOT-CHAUFFEUR EMERGES...
PRESENTING MY YOUNG EMPLOYER, LESTER SPIFFANY... HIS FATHER OWNS EARTH'S SWANKIEST JEWELRY ESTABLISHMENT!
YOU LUCKY LEGIONNAIRES ... I HAVE DECIDED TO JOIN YOUR... ER... RANKS!
IS HE FOR REAL?
H...WHAT SINGLE UPER-POWER DO YOU POSSESS, LESTER ?
NONE--BUT I DO HAVE LOTS OF MONEY! I'LL PAY WELL FOR THE PRESTIGE OF BEING A MEMBER! HERE, TAKE THIS DAZZLE GEM FROM THE WORLD OF XANDU... IT'S WORTH A FORTUNE!
SWEAR ME IN PROMPTLY, BECAUSE I'VE AN IMPORTANT APPOINTMENT ON MARS, SOON!
SORRY, BUT WE DON'T WANT YOUR GEM, OR YOU! NO ONE CAN BUY HIS WAY INTO THE LEGION!
BUNK! EVERYONE HAS HIS PRICE! LOOK--I'LL PURCHASE A NEW, HUGE CLUBHOUSE TO REPLACE THIS CRUMMY ITTLE BUILDING! OKAY?
NO SALE! GOODBYE, LESTER! IT HASN'T BEEN NICE MEETING YOU!
AS THE SPOILED RICH YOUTH DEPARTS ANGRILY...
YOU'RE STUPID, ALL OF YOU! STUPID!! STUPID!!
GOOD RIDDANCE! NOW TO RESUME WHERE WE LEFT OFF WHEN WE WERE INTERRUPTED! YOUR NAME, APPLICANT ?
I AM... STORM BOY!!
4

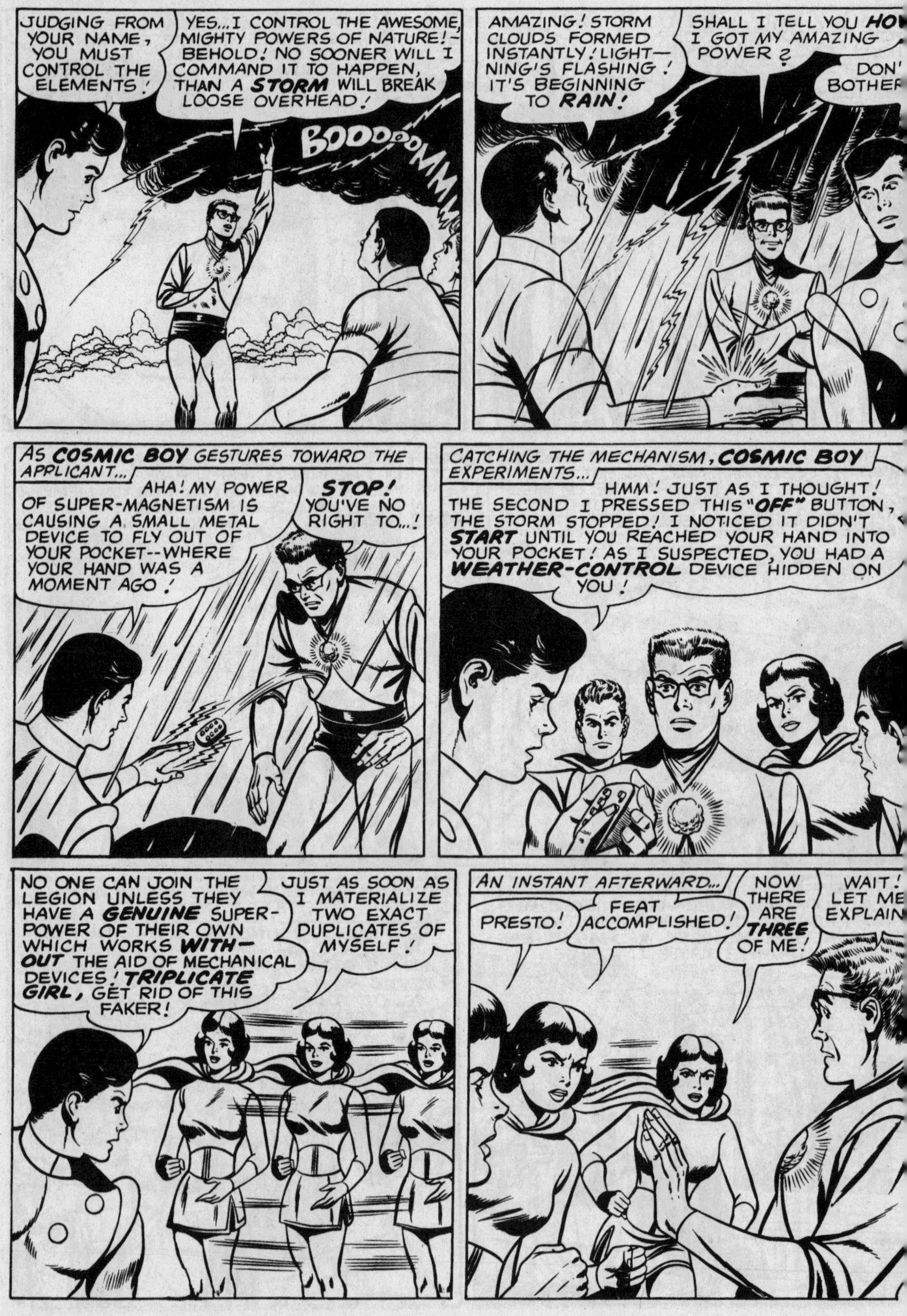
JUDGING FROM YOUR NAME, YOU MUST CONTROL THE ELEMENTS!
YES...I CONTROL THE AWESOME, MIGHTY POWERS OF NATURE!--BEHOLD! NO SOONER WILL I COMMAND IT TO HAPPEN, THAN A STORM WILL BREAK LOOSE OVERHEAD!
BOOOOOMM
AMAZING! STORM CLOUDS FORMED INSTANTLY! LIGHTNING'S FLASHING! IT'S BEGINNING TO RAIN!
SHALL I TELL YOU HO I GOT MY AMAZING POWER?
DON' BOTHER
AS COSMIC BOY GESTURES TOWARD THE APPLICANT...
AHA! MY POWER OF SUPER-MAGNETISM IS CAUSING A SMALL METAL DEVICE TO FLY OUT OF YOUR POCKET--WHERE YOUR HAND WAS A MOMENT AGO!
STOP! YOU'VE NO RIGHT TO...!
CATCHING THE MECHANISM, COSMIC BOY EXPERIMENTS...
HMM! JUST AS I THOUGHT! THE SECOND I PRESSED THIS "OFF" BUTTON, THE STORM STOPPED! I NOTICED IT DIDN'T START UNTIL YOU REACHED YOUR HAND INTO YOUR POCKET! AS I SUSPECTED, YOU HAD A WEATHER-CONTROL DEVICE HIDDEN ON YOU!
NO ONE CAN JOIN THE LEGION UNLESS THEY HAVE A GENUINE SUPER-POWER OF THEIR OWN WHICH WORKS WITHOUT THE AID OF MECHANICAL DEVICES! TRIPLICATE GIRL, GET RID OF THIS FAKER!
JUST AS SOON AS I MATERIALIZE TWO EXACT DUPLICATES OF MYSELF!
AN INSTANT AFTERWARD...
PRESTO!
FEAT ACCOMPLISHED!
NOW THERE ARE THREE OF ME!
WAIT! LET ME EXPLAIN

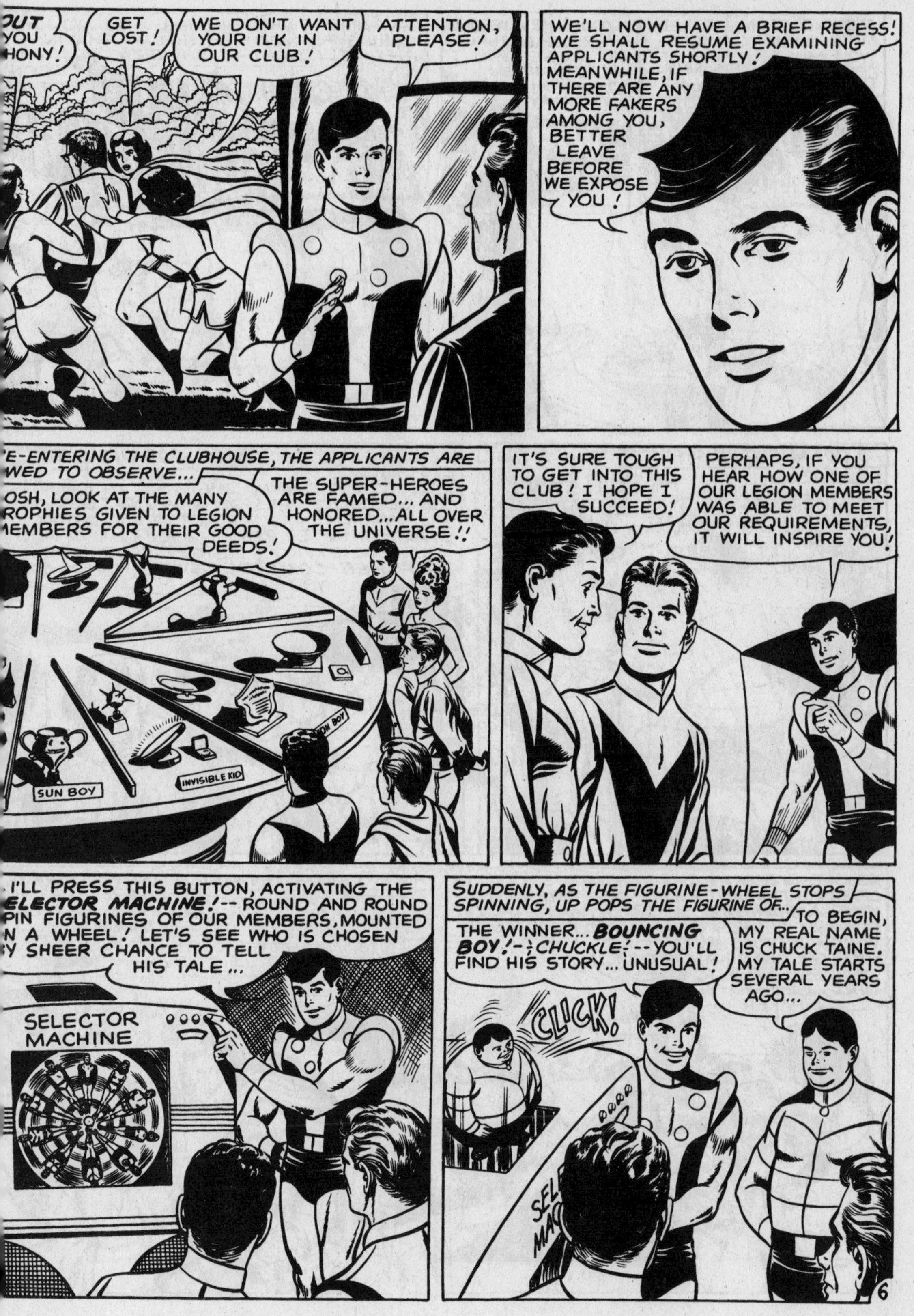
OUT YOU HONY!
GET LOST!
WE DON'T WANT YOUR ILK IN OUR CLUB!
ATTENTION, PLEASE!
WE'LL NOW HAVE A BRIEF RECESS! WE SHALL RESUME EXAMINING APPLICANTS SHORTLY! MEANWHILE, IF THERE ARE ANY MORE FAKERS AMONG YOU, BETTER LEAVE BEFORE WE EXPOSE YOU!
E-ENTERING THE CLUBHOUSE, THE APPLICANTS ARE WED TO OBSERVE...
OSH, LOOK AT THE MANY ROPHIES GIVEN TO LEGION EMBERS FOR THEIR GOOD DEEDS!
THE SUPER-HEROES ARE FAMED... AND HONORED... ALL OVER THE UNIVERSE!!
SUN BOY
INVISIBLE KID
ON BOY
IT'S SURE TOUGH TO GET INTO THIS CLUB! I HOPE I SUCCEED!
PERHAPS, IF YOU HEAR HOW ONE OF OUR LEGION MEMBERS WAS ABLE TO MEET OUR REQUIREMENTS, IT WILL INSPIRE YOU!
I'LL PRESS THIS BUTTON, ACTIVATING THE ELECTOR MACHINE!-- ROUND AND ROUND PIN FIGURINES OF OUR MEMBERS, MOUNTED N A WHEEL! LET'S SEE WHO IS CHOSEN Y SHEER CHANCE TO TELL HIS TALE...
SELECTOR MACHINE
SUDDENLY, AS THE FIGURINE-WHEEL STOPS SPINNING, UP POPS THE FIGURINE OF...
THE WINNER... BOUNCING BOY!-- CHUCKLE! --YOU'LL FIND HIS STORY... UNUSUAL!
TO BEGIN, MY REAL NAME IS CHUCK TAINE. MY TALE STARTS SEVERAL YEARS AGO...
CLICK!
6

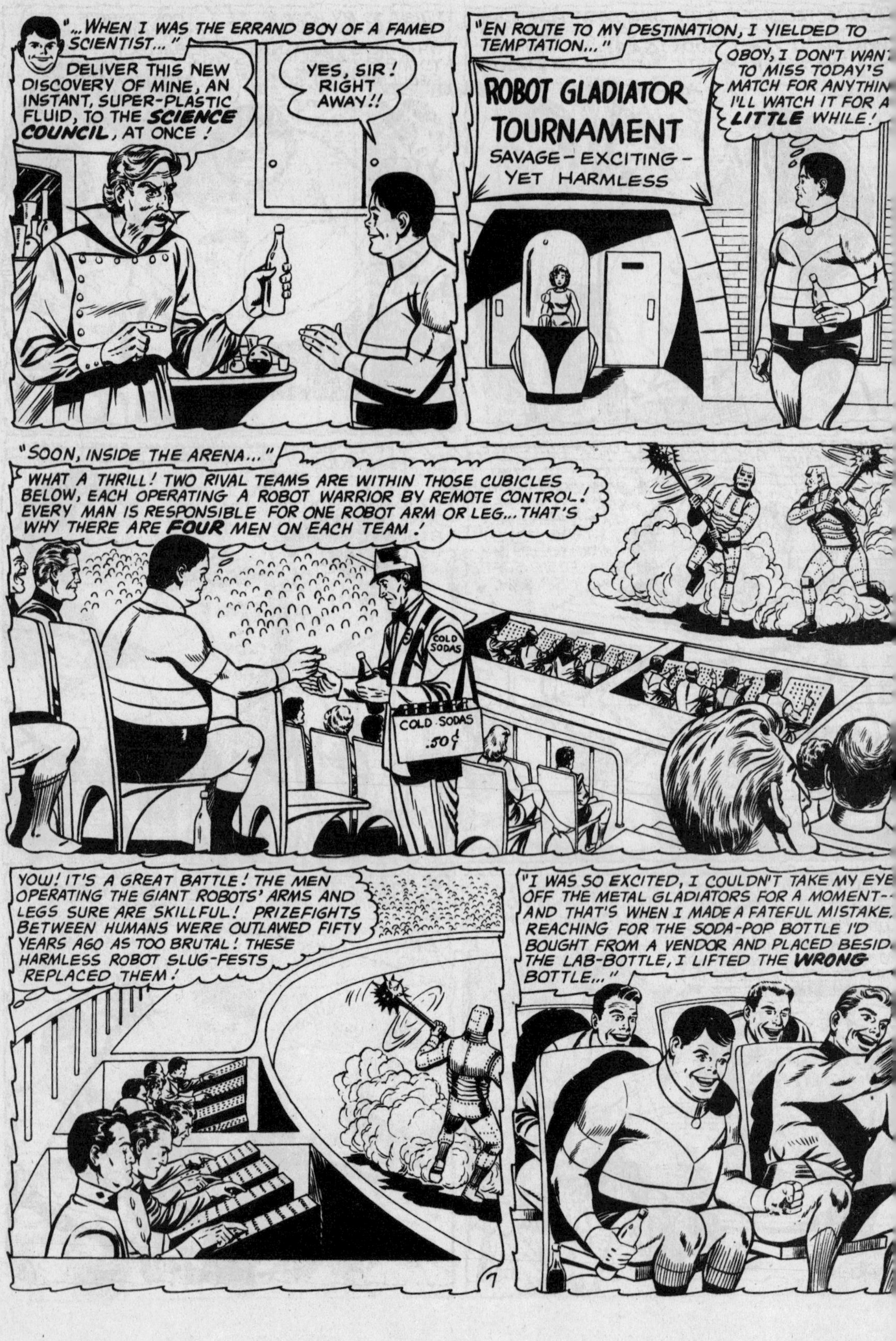
"...WHEN I WAS THE ERRAND BOY OF A FAMED SCIENTIST..."
DELIVER THIS NEW DISCOVERY OF MINE, AN INSTANT, SUPER-PLASTIC FLUID, TO THE SCIENCE COUNCIL, AT ONCE!
YES, SIR! RIGHT AWAY!!
"EN ROUTE TO MY DESTINATION, I YIELDED TO TEMPTATION..."
ROBOT GLADIATOR TOURNAMENT
SAVAGE - EXCITING - YET HARMLESS
OBOY, I DON'T WAN
TO MISS TODAY'S MATCH FOR ANYTHIN
I'LL WATCH IT FOR A LITTLE WHILE!
"SOON, INSIDE THE ARENA..."
WHAT A THRILL! TWO RIVAL TEAMS ARE WITHIN THOSE CUBICLES BELOW, EACH OPERATING A ROBOT WARRIOR BY REMOTE CONTROL! EVERY MAN IS RESPONSIBLE FOR ONE ROBOT ARM OR LEG...THAT'S WHY THERE ARE FOUR MEN ON EACH TEAM!
COLD SODAS
COLD SODAS .50¢
YOW! IT'S A GREAT BATTLE! THE MEN OPERATING THE GIANT ROBOTS' ARMS AND LEGS SURE ARE SKILLFUL! PRIZEFIGHTS BETWEEN HUMANS WERE OUTLAWED FIFTY YEARS AGO AS TOO BRUTAL! THESE HARMLESS ROBOT SLUG-FESTS REPLACED THEM!
"I WAS SO EXCITED, I COULDN'T TAKE MY EYE
OFF THE METAL GLADIATORS FOR A MOMENT--
AND THAT'S WHEN I MADE A FATEFUL MISTAKE
REACHING FOR THE SODA-POP BOTTLE I'D
BOUGHT FROM A VENDOR AND PLACED BESID
THE LAB-BOTTLE, I LIFTED THE WRONG
BOTTLE..."
7

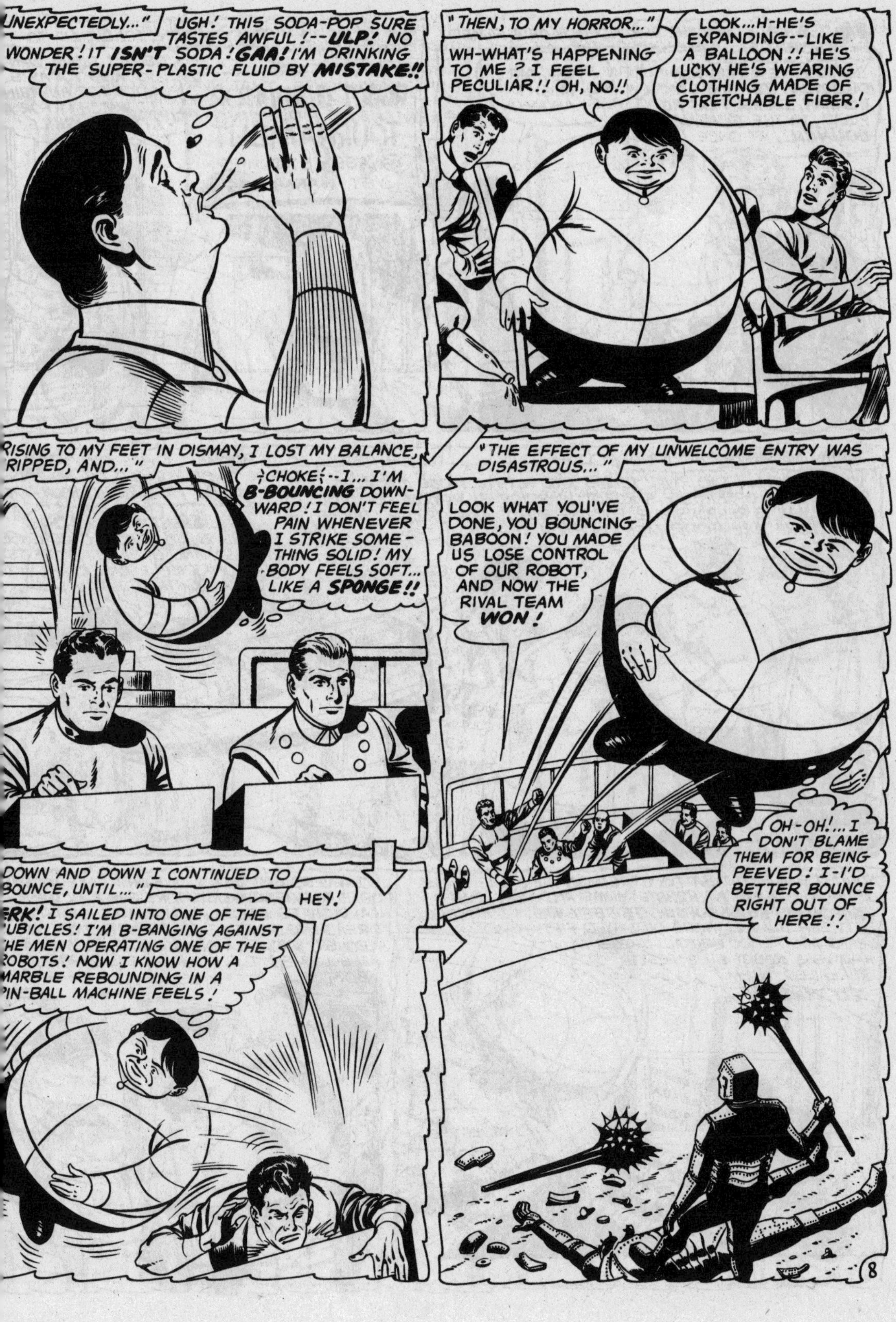
UNEXPECTEDLY..."
UGH! THIS SODA-POP SURE TASTES AWFUL!--ULP! NO WONDER! IT ISN'T SODA! GAA! I'M DRINKING THE SUPER-PLASTIC FLUID BY MISTAKE!!
"THEN, TO MY HORROR..."
WH-WHAT'S HAPPENING TO ME? I FEEL PECULIAR!! OH, NO!!
LOOK...H-HE'S EXPANDING--LIKE A BALLOON!! HE'S LUCKY HE'S WEARING CLOTHING MADE OF STRETCHABLE FIBER!
RISING TO MY FEET IN DISMAY, I LOST MY BALANCE, RIPPED, AND..."
¦CHOKE¦--I...I'M B-BOUNCING DOWNWARD! I DON'T FEEL PAIN WHENEVER I STRIKE SOMETHING SOLID! MY BODY FEELS SOFT... LIKE A SPONGE!!
DOWN AND DOWN I CONTINUED TO BOUNCE, UNTIL..."
ERK! I SAILED INTO ONE OF THE CUBICLES! I'M B-BANGING AGAINST THE MEN OPERATING ONE OF THE ROBOTS! NOW I KNOW HOW A MARBLE REBOUNDING IN A PIN-BALL MACHINE FEELS!
HEY!
"THE EFFECT OF MY UNWELCOME ENTRY WAS DISASTROUS..."
LOOK WHAT YOU'VE DONE, YOU BOUNCING BABOON! YOU MADE US LOSE CONTROL OF OUR ROBOT, AND NOW THE RIVAL TEAM WON!
OH-OH!...I DON'T BLAME THEM FOR BEING PEEVED! I-I'D BETTER BOUNCE RIGHT OUT OF HERE!!
8

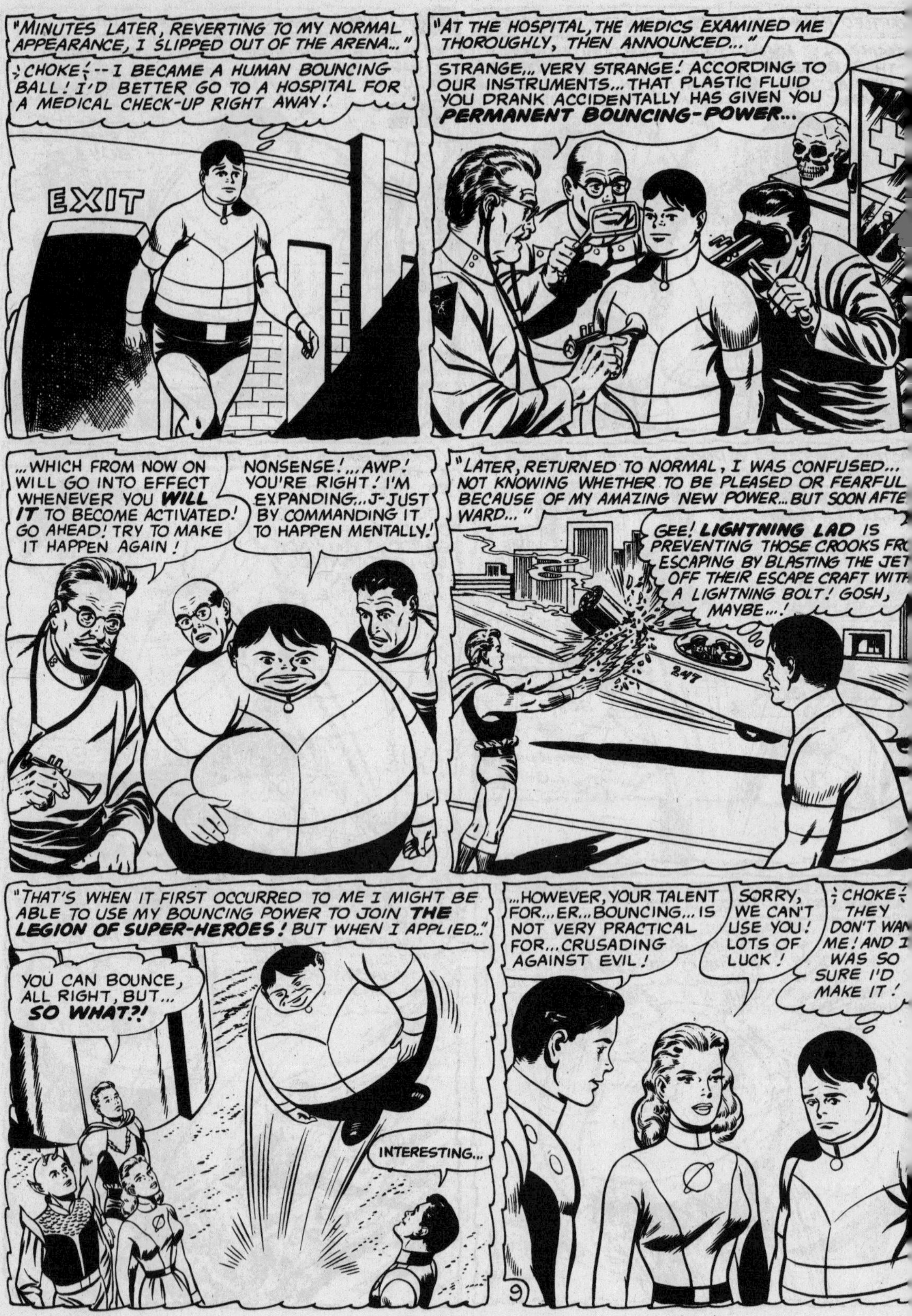
"MINUTES LATER, REVERTING TO MY NORMAL APPEARANCE, I SLIPPED OUT OF THE ARENA..."
-CHOKE- -- I BECAME A HUMAN BOUNCING BALL! I'D BETTER GO TO A HOSPITAL FOR A MEDICAL CHECK-UP RIGHT AWAY!
EXIT
"AT THE HOSPITAL, THE MEDICS EXAMINED ME THOROUGHLY, THEN ANNOUNCED..."
STRANGE... VERY STRANGE! ACCORDING TO OUR INSTRUMENTS... THAT PLASTIC FLUID YOU DRANK ACCIDENTALLY HAS GIVEN YOU **PERMANENT BOUNCING-POWER...**
...WHICH FROM NOW ON WILL GO INTO EFFECT WHENEVER YOU **WILL IT** TO BECOME ACTIVATED! GO AHEAD! TRY TO MAKE IT HAPPEN AGAIN!
NONSENSE!... AWP! YOU'RE RIGHT! I'M EXPANDING... J-JUST BY COMMANDING IT TO HAPPEN MENTALLY!
"LATER, RETURNED TO NORMAL, I WAS CONFUSED... NOT KNOWING WHETHER TO BE PLEASED OR FEARFUL BECAUSE OF MY AMAZING NEW POWER... BUT SOON AFTE WARD..."
GEE! **LIGHTNING LAD** IS PREVENTING THOSE CROOKS FRO ESCAPING BY BLASTING THE JET OFF THEIR ESCAPE CRAFT WITH A LIGHTNING BOLT! GOSH, MAYBE...!
247
"THAT'S WHEN IT FIRST OCCURRED TO ME I MIGHT BE ABLE TO USE MY BOUNCING POWER TO JOIN **THE LEGION OF SUPER-HEROES!** BUT WHEN I APPLIED..."
YOU CAN BOUNCE, ALL RIGHT, BUT... **SO WHAT?!**
INTERESTING...
...HOWEVER, YOUR TALENT FOR... ER... BOUNCING... IS NOT VERY PRACTICAL FOR... CRUSADING AGAINST EVIL!
SORRY, WE CAN'T USE YOU! LOTS OF LUCK!
-CHOKE- THEY DON'T WAN ME! AND I WAS SO SURE I'D MAKE IT!
9

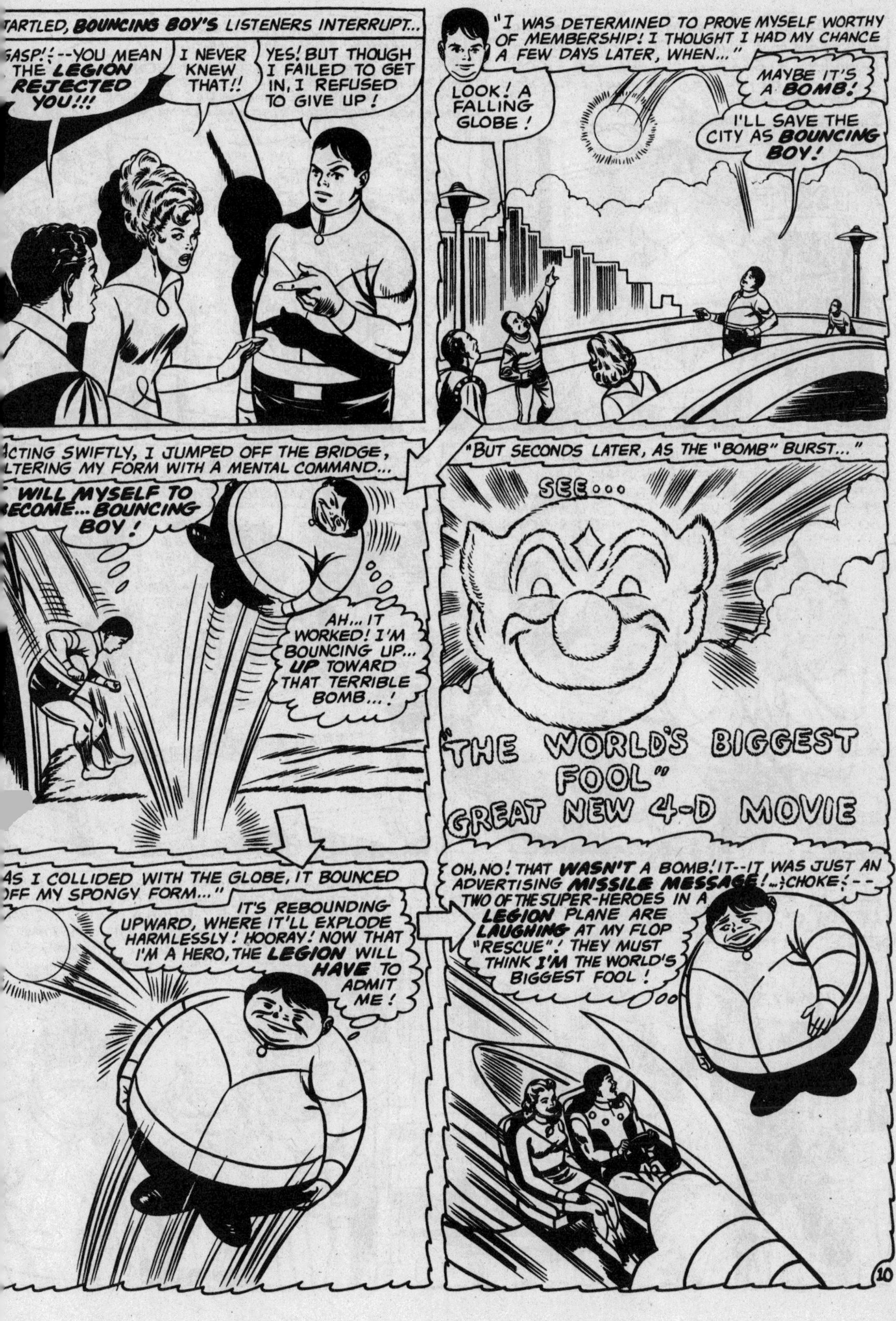
TARTLED, BOUNCING BOY'S LISTENERS INTERRUPT...
GASP! --YOU MEAN THE LEGION REJECTED YOU!!!
I NEVER KNEW THAT!!
YES! BUT THOUGH I FAILED TO GET IN, I REFUSED TO GIVE UP!
"I WAS DETERMINED TO PROVE MYSELF WORTHY OF MEMBERSHIP! I THOUGHT I HAD MY CHANCE A FEW DAYS LATER, WHEN..."
LOOK! A FALLING GLOBE!
MAYBE IT'S A BOMB!
I'LL SAVE THE CITY AS BOUNCING BOY!
ACTING SWIFTLY, I JUMPED OFF THE BRIDGE, ALTERING MY FORM WITH A MENTAL COMMAND...
I WILL MYSELF TO BECOME... BOUNCING BOY!
AH... IT WORKED! I'M BOUNCING UP... UP TOWARD THAT TERRIBLE BOMB...!
"BUT SECONDS LATER, AS THE "BOMB" BURST..."
SEE...
"THE WORLD'S BIGGEST FOOL" GREAT NEW 4-D MOVIE
"AS I COLLIDED WITH THE GLOBE, IT BOUNCED OFF MY SPONGY FORM..."
IT'S REBOUNDING UPWARD, WHERE IT'LL EXPLODE HARMLESSLY! HOORAY! NOW THAT I'M A HERO, THE LEGION WILL HAVE TO ADMIT ME!
OH, NO! THAT WASN'T A BOMB! IT--IT WAS JUST AN ADVERTISING MISSILE MESSAGE! ...CHOKE! -- TWO OF THE SUPER-HEROES IN A LEGION PLANE ARE LAUGHING AT MY FLOP "RESCUE"! THEY MUST THINK I'M THE WORLD'S BIGGEST FOOL!
10

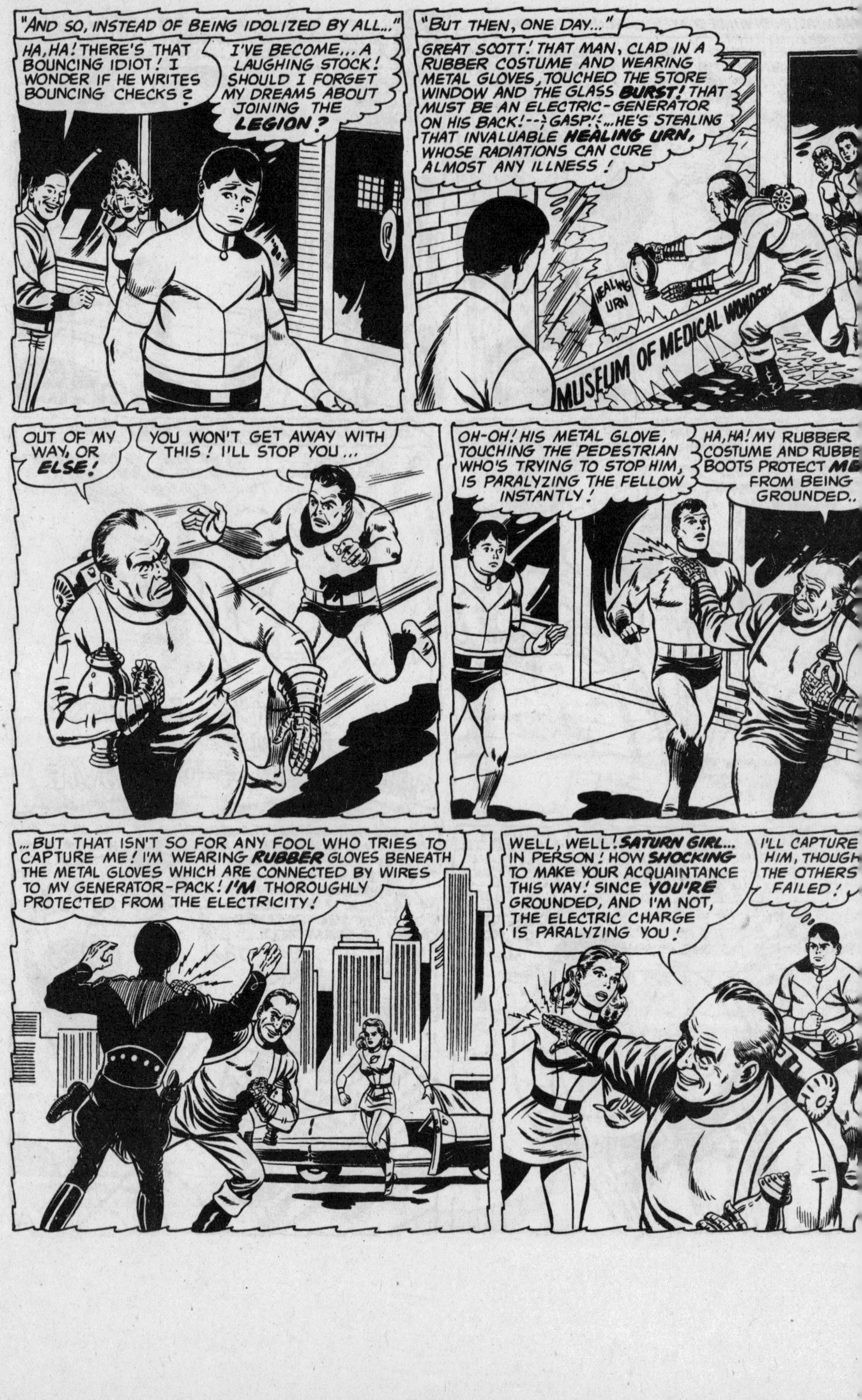
"AND SO, INSTEAD OF BEING IDOLIZED BY ALL..."
HA, HA! THERE'S THAT BOUNCING IDIOT! I WONDER IF HE WRITES BOUNCING CHECKS?
I'VE BECOME... A LAUGHING STOCK! SHOULD I FORGET MY DREAMS ABOUT JOINING THE LEGION?
"BUT THEN, ONE DAY..."
GREAT SCOTT! THAT MAN, CLAD IN A RUBBER COSTUME AND WEARING METAL GLOVES, TOUCHED THE STORE WINDOW AND THE GLASS BURST! THAT MUST BE AN ELECTRIC-GENERATOR ON HIS BACK!--GASP!... HE'S STEALING THAT INVALUABLE HEALING URN, WHOSE RADIATIONS CAN CURE ALMOST ANY ILLNESS!
HEALING URN
MUSEUM OF MEDICAL WONDERS
OUT OF MY WAY, OR ELSE!
YOU WON'T GET AWAY WITH THIS! I'LL STOP YOU...
OH-OH! HIS METAL GLOVE, TOUCHING THE PEDESTRIAN WHO'S TRYING TO STOP HIM, IS PARALYZING THE FELLOW INSTANTLY!
HA, HA! MY RUBBER COSTUME AND RUBBE BOOTS PROTECT ME FROM BEING GROUNDED..
...BUT THAT ISN'T SO FOR ANY FOOL WHO TRIES TO CAPTURE ME! I'M WEARING RUBBER GLOVES BENEATH THE METAL GLOVES WHICH ARE CONNECTED BY WIRES TO MY GENERATOR-PACK! I'M THOROUGHLY PROTECTED FROM THE ELECTRICITY!
WELL, WELL! SATURN GIRL... IN PERSON! HOW SHOCKING TO MAKE YOUR ACQUAINTANCE THIS WAY! SINCE YOU'RE GROUNDED, AND I'M NOT, THE ELECTRIC CHARGE IS PARALYZING YOU!
I'LL CAPTURE HIM, THOUGH THE OTHERS FAILED!

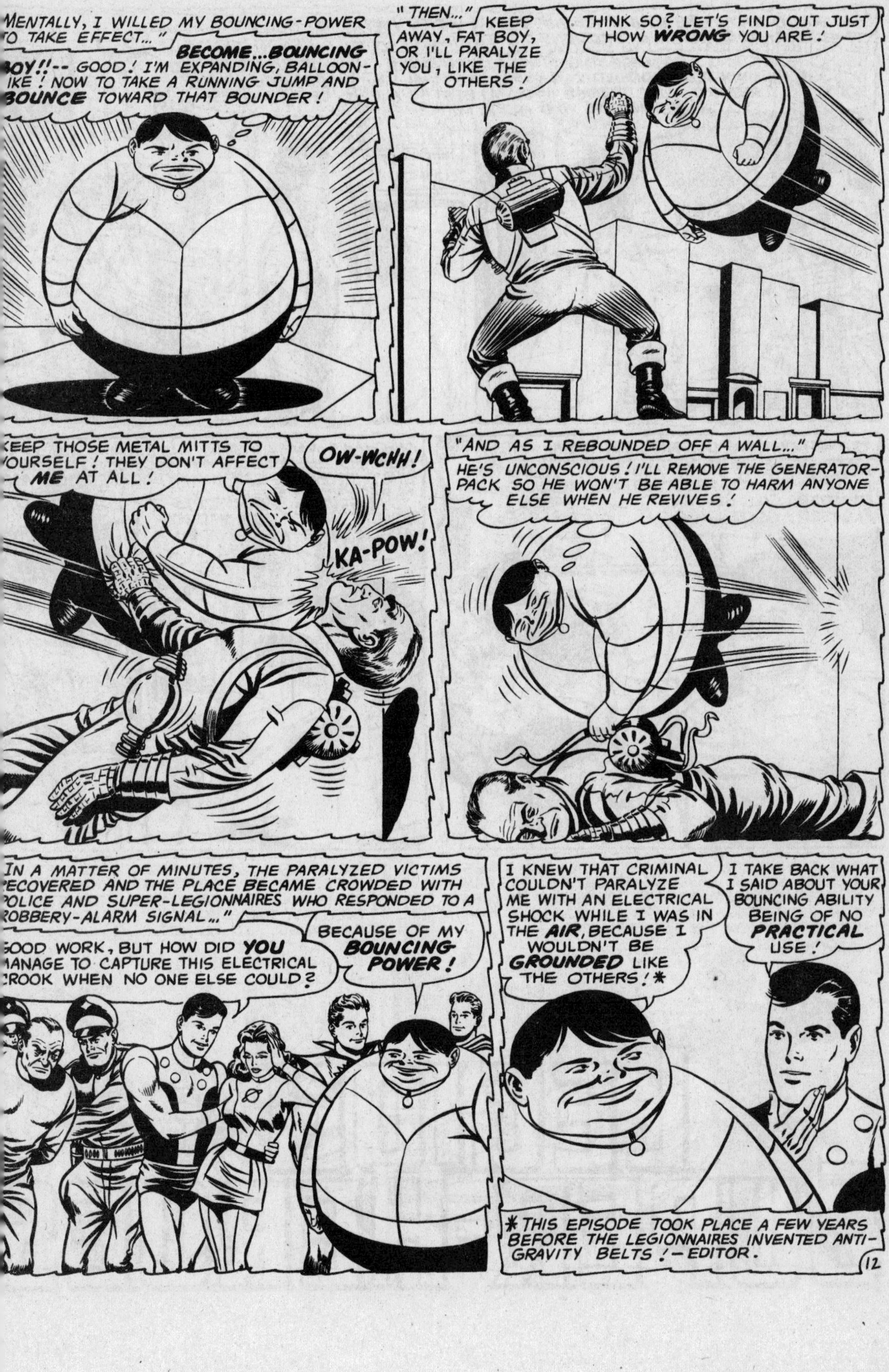
MENTALLY, I WILLED MY BOUNCING-POWER TO TAKE EFFECT..."
BECOME...BOUNCING BOY!!-- GOOD! I'M EXPANDING, BALLOON-LIKE! NOW TO TAKE A RUNNING JUMP AND BOUNCE TOWARD THAT BOUNDER!
"THEN..."
KEEP AWAY, FAT BOY, OR I'LL PARALYZE YOU, LIKE THE OTHERS!
THINK SO? LET'S FIND OUT JUST HOW WRONG YOU ARE!
KEEP THOSE METAL MITTS TO YOURSELF! THEY DON'T AFFECT ME AT ALL!
OW-WCHH!
KA-POW!
"AND AS I REBOUNDED OFF A WALL..."
HE'S UNCONSCIOUS! I'LL REMOVE THE GENERATOR-PACK SO HE WON'T BE ABLE TO HARM ANYONE ELSE WHEN HE REVIVES!
IN A MATTER OF MINUTES, THE PARALYZED VICTIMS RECOVERED AND THE PLACE BECAME CROWDED WITH POLICE AND SUPER-LEGIONNAIRES WHO RESPONDED TO A ROBBERY-ALARM SIGNAL..."
GOOD WORK, BUT HOW DID YOU MANAGE TO CAPTURE THIS ELECTRICAL CROOK WHEN NO ONE ELSE COULD?
BECAUSE OF MY BOUNCING-POWER!
I KNEW THAT CRIMINAL COULDN'T PARALYZE ME WITH AN ELECTRICAL SHOCK WHILE I WAS IN THE AIR, BECAUSE I WOULDN'T BE GROUNDED LIKE THE OTHERS! *
I TAKE BACK WHAT I SAID ABOUT YOUR BOUNCING ABILITY BEING OF NO PRACTICAL USE!
* THIS EPISODE TOOK PLACE A FEW YEARS BEFORE THE LEGIONNAIRES INVENTED ANTI-GRAVITY BELTS! — EDITOR.
12

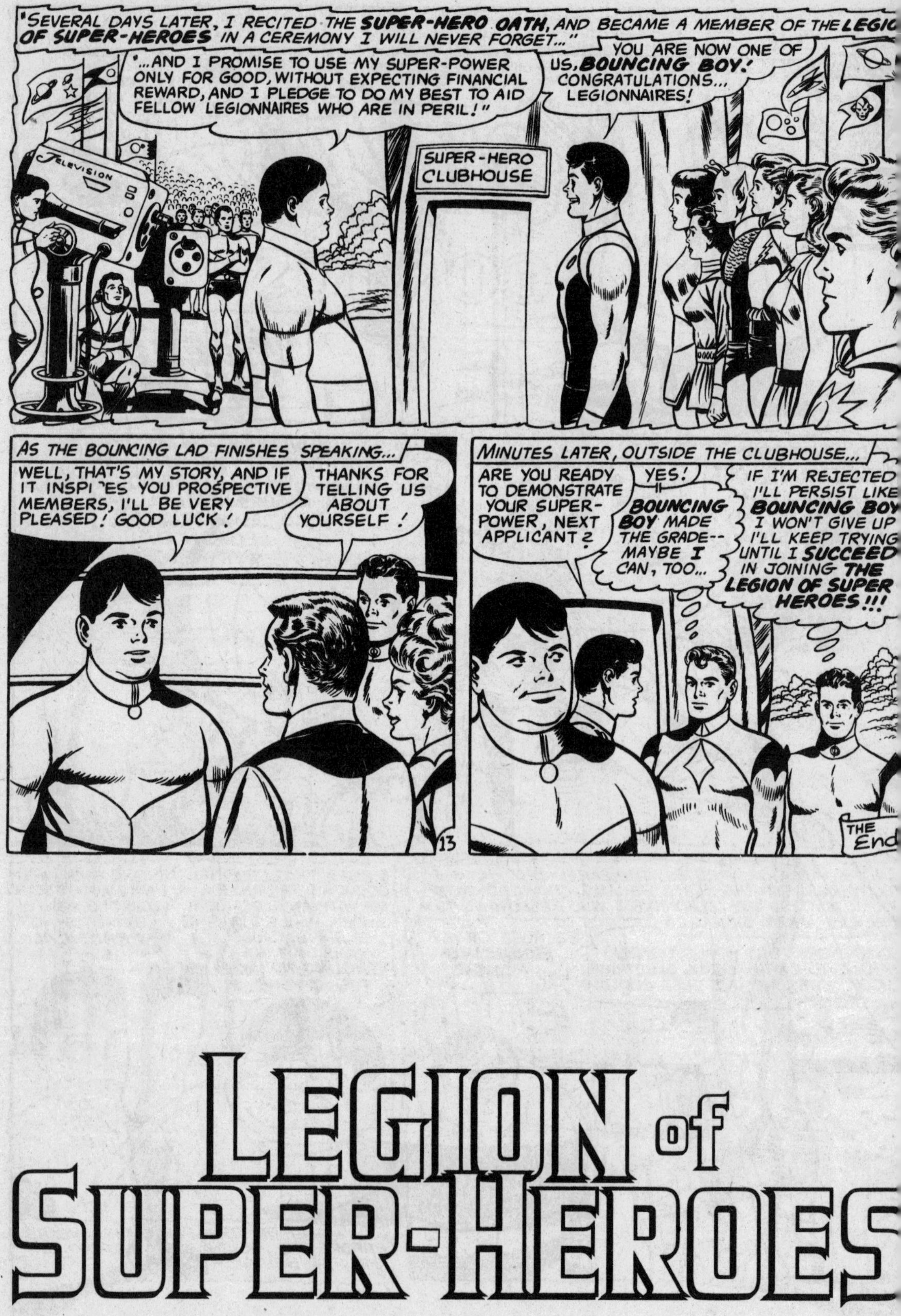
"SEVERAL DAYS LATER, I RECITED THE SUPER-HERO OATH, AND BECAME A MEMBER OF THE LEGION OF SUPER-HEROES IN A CEREMONY I WILL NEVER FORGET..."
"...AND I PROMISE TO USE MY SUPER-POWER ONLY FOR GOOD, WITHOUT EXPECTING FINANCIAL REWARD, AND I PLEDGE TO DO MY BEST TO AID FELLOW LEGIONNAIRES WHO ARE IN PERIL!"
YOU ARE NOW ONE OF US, BOUNCING BOY! CONGRATULATIONS... LEGIONNAIRES!
TELEVISION
SUPER-HERO CLUBHOUSE
AS THE BOUNCING LAD FINISHES SPEAKING...
WELL, THAT'S MY STORY, AND IF IT INSPIRES YOU PROSPECTIVE MEMBERS, I'LL BE VERY PLEASED! GOOD LUCK!
THANKS FOR TELLING US ABOUT YOURSELF!
13
MINUTES LATER, OUTSIDE THE CLUBHOUSE...
ARE YOU READY TO DEMONSTRATE YOUR SUPER-POWER, NEXT APPLICANT?
YES!
BOUNCING BOY MADE THE GRADE-- MAYBE I CAN, TOO...
IF I'M REJECTED I'LL PERSIST LIKE BOUNCING BOY I WON'T GIVE UP I'LL KEEP TRYING UNTIL I SUCCEED IN JOINING THE LEGION OF SUPER HEROES!!!
THE End

LEGION of SUPER-HEROES

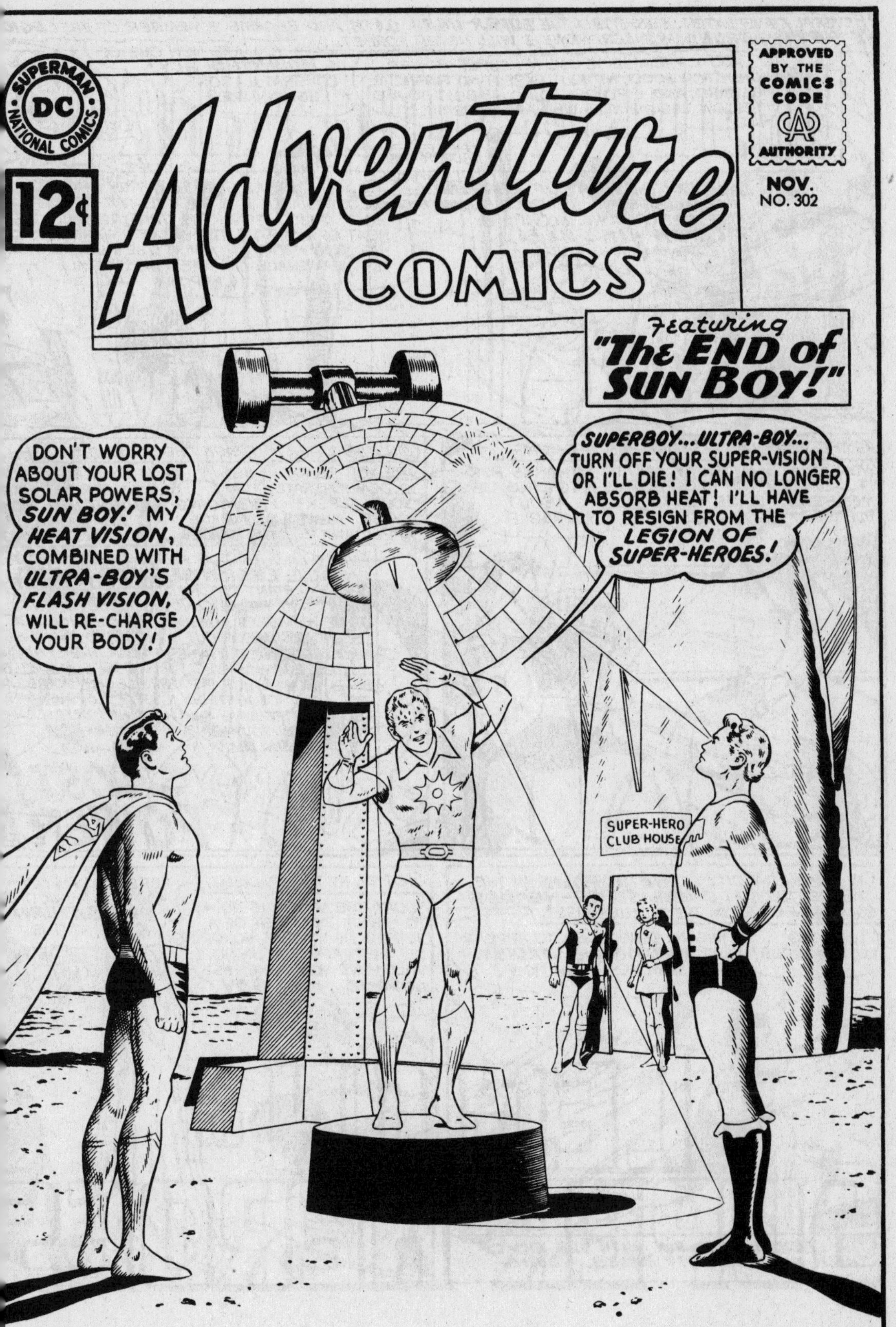
SUPERMAN DC NATIONAL COMICS
12¢
Adventure COMICS
APPROVED BY THE COMICS CODE AUTHORITY
NOV. NO. 302
Featuring "The END of SUN BOY!"
DON'T WORRY ABOUT YOUR LOST SOLAR POWERS, SUN BOY! MY HEAT VISION, COMBINED WITH ULTRA-BOY'S FLASH VISION, WILL RE-CHARGE YOUR BODY!
SUPERBOY...ULTRA-BOY... TURN OFF YOUR SUPER-VISION OR I'LL DIE! I CAN NO LONGER ABSORB HEAT! I'LL HAVE TO RESIGN FROM THE LEGION OF SUPER-HEROES!
SUPER-HERO CLUB HOUSE

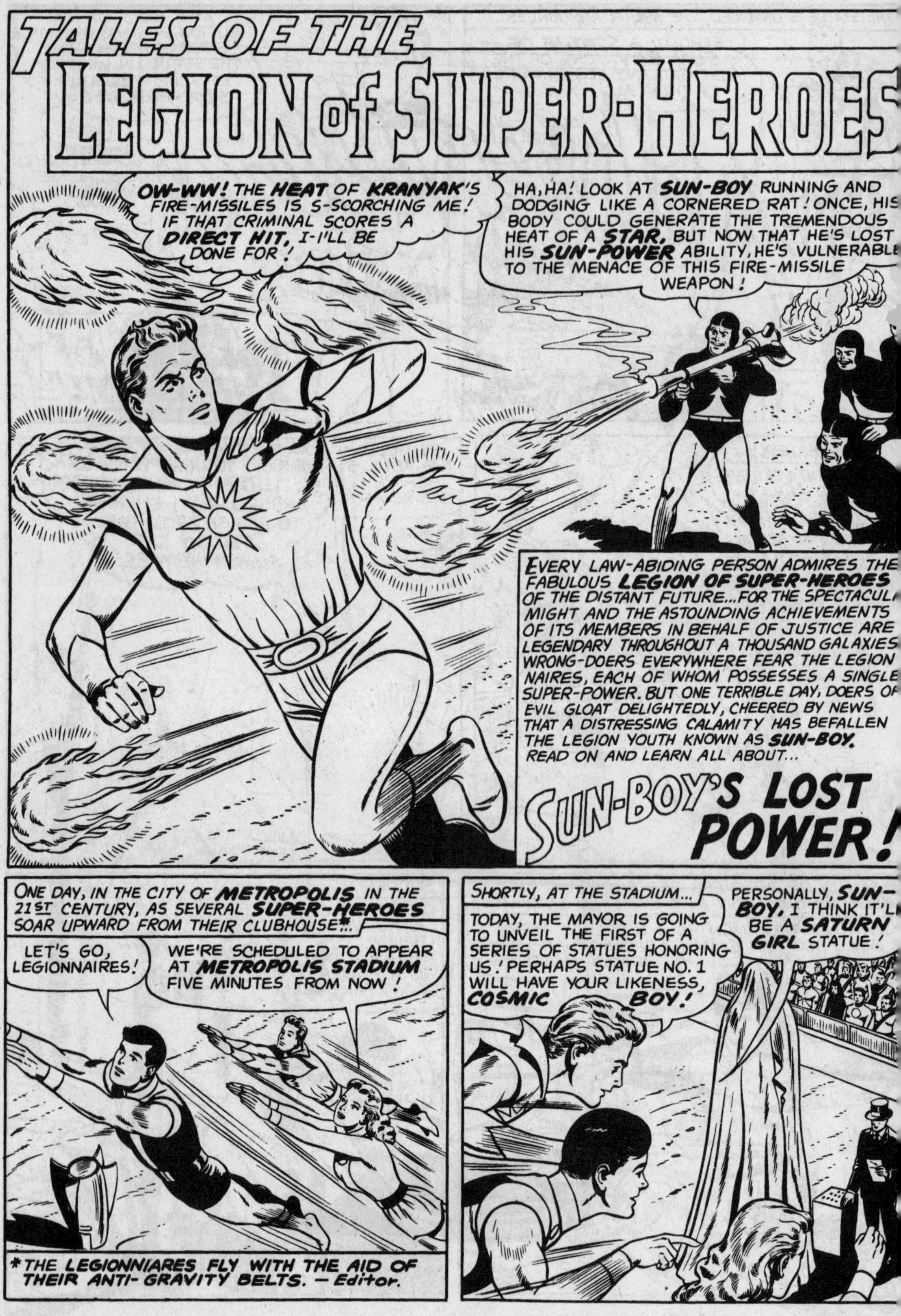
TALES OF THE
LEGION of SUPER-HEROES
OW-WW! THE HEAT OF KRANYAK'S FIRE-MISSILES IS S-SCORCHING ME! IF THAT CRIMINAL SCORES A DIRECT HIT, I-I'LL BE DONE FOR!
HA, HA! LOOK AT SUN-BOY RUNNING AND DODGING LIKE A CORNERED RAT! ONCE, HIS BODY COULD GENERATE THE TREMENDOUS HEAT OF A STAR, BUT NOW THAT HE'S LOST HIS SUN-POWER ABILITY, HE'S VULNERABLE TO THE MENACE OF THIS FIRE-MISSILE WEAPON!
EVERY LAW-ABIDING PERSON ADMIRES THE FABULOUS LEGION OF SUPER-HEROES OF THE DISTANT FUTURE...FOR THE SPECTACUL MIGHT AND THE ASTOUNDING ACHIEVEMENTS OF ITS MEMBERS IN BEHALF OF JUSTICE ARE LEGENDARY THROUGHOUT A THOUSAND GALAXIES WRONG-DOERS EVERYWHERE FEAR THE LEGION NAIRES, EACH OF WHOM POSSESSES A SINGLE SUPER-POWER. BUT ONE TERRIBLE DAY, DOERS OF EVIL GLOAT DELIGHTEDLY, CHEERED BY NEWS THAT A DISTRESSING CALAMITY HAS BEFALLEN THE LEGION YOUTH KNOWN AS SUN-BOY. READ ON AND LEARN ALL ABOUT...
SUN-BOY'S LOST POWER!
ONE DAY, IN THE CITY OF METROPOLIS IN THE 21ST CENTURY, AS SEVERAL SUPER-HEROES SOAR UPWARD FROM THEIR CLUBHOUSE*...
LET'S GO, LEGIONNAIRES!
WE'RE SCHEDULED TO APPEAR AT METROPOLIS STADIUM FIVE MINUTES FROM NOW!
*THE LEGIONNIARES FLY WITH THE AID OF THEIR ANTI-GRAVITY BELTS. —Editor.
SHORTLY, AT THE STADIUM...
TODAY, THE MAYOR IS GOING TO UNVEIL THE FIRST OF A SERIES OF STATUES HONORING US! PERHAPS STATUE NO. 1 WILL HAVE YOUR LIKENESS, COSMIC BOY!
PERSONALLY, SUN-BOY, I THINK IT'LL BE A SATURN GIRL STATUE!

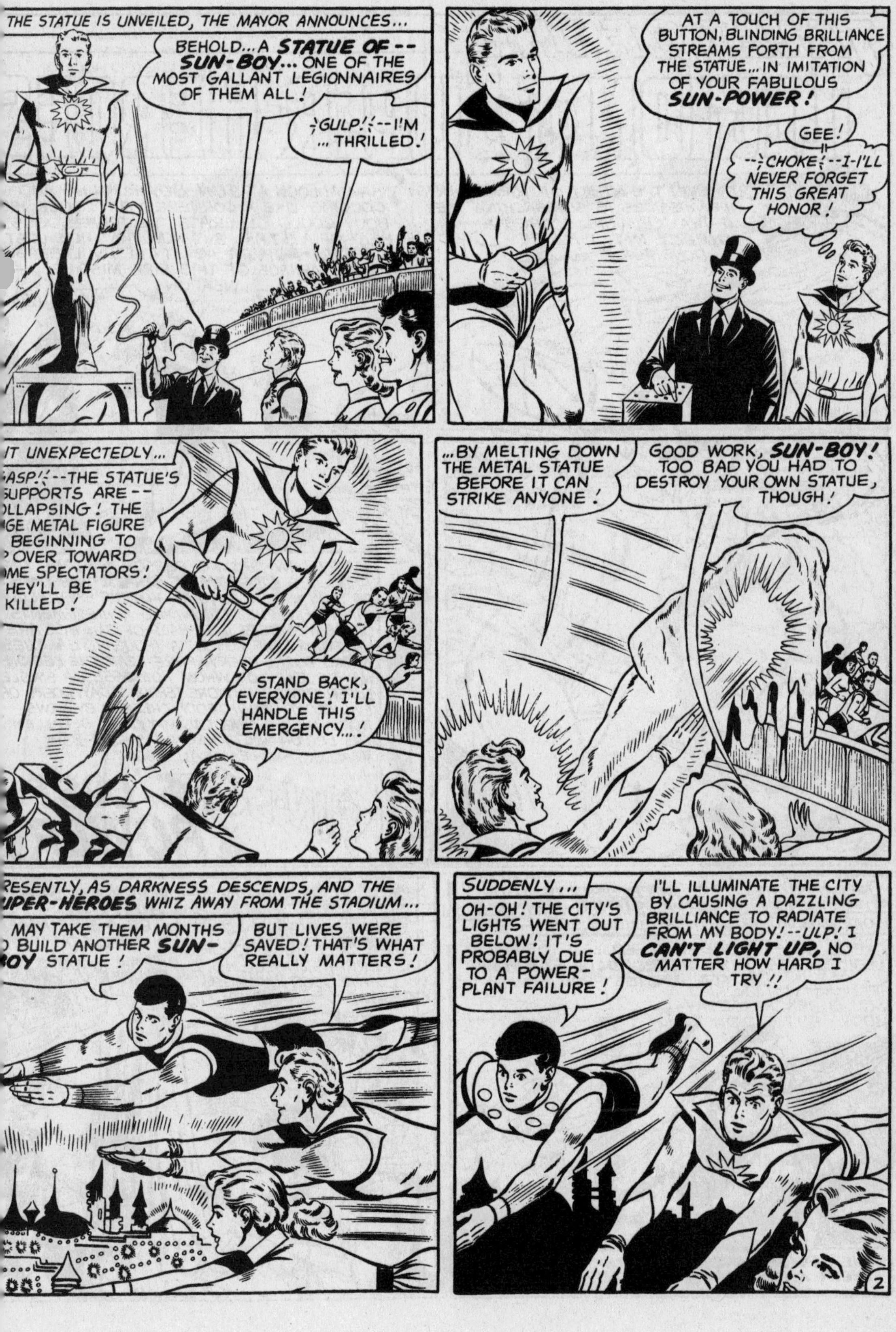
THE STATUE IS UNVEILED, THE MAYOR ANNOUNCES...
BEHOLD... A STATUE OF -- SUN-BOY... ONE OF THE MOST GALLANT LEGIONNAIRES OF THEM ALL!
GULP! --I'M ... THRILLED!
AT A TOUCH OF THIS BUTTON, BLINDING BRILLIANCE STREAMS FORTH FROM THE STATUE... IN IMITATION OF YOUR FABULOUS SUN-POWER!
GEE!
--CHOKE--I-I'LL NEVER FORGET THIS GREAT HONOR!
IT UNEXPECTEDLY...
ASP! --THE STATUE'S SUPPORTS ARE -- OLLAPSING! THE GE METAL FIGURE BEGINNING TO OVER TOWARD ME SPECTATORS! HEY'LL BE KILLED!
STAND BACK, EVERYONE! I'LL HANDLE THIS EMERGENCY...!
...BY MELTING DOWN THE METAL STATUE BEFORE IT CAN STRIKE ANYONE!
GOOD WORK, SUN-BOY! TOO BAD YOU HAD TO DESTROY YOUR OWN STATUE, THOUGH!
RESENTLY, AS DARKNESS DESCENDS, AND THE UPER-HEROES WHIZ AWAY FROM THE STADIUM...
MAY TAKE THEM MONTHS BUILD ANOTHER SUN-BOY STATUE!
BUT LIVES WERE SAVED! THAT'S WHAT REALLY MATTERS!
SUDDENLY...
OH-OH! THE CITY'S LIGHTS WENT OUT BELOW! IT'S PROBABLY DUE TO A POWER-PLANT FAILURE!
I'LL ILLUMINATE THE CITY BY CAUSING A DAZZLING BRILLIANCE TO RADIATE FROM MY BODY! --ULP! I CAN'T LIGHT UP, NO MATTER HOW HARD I TRY!!
2

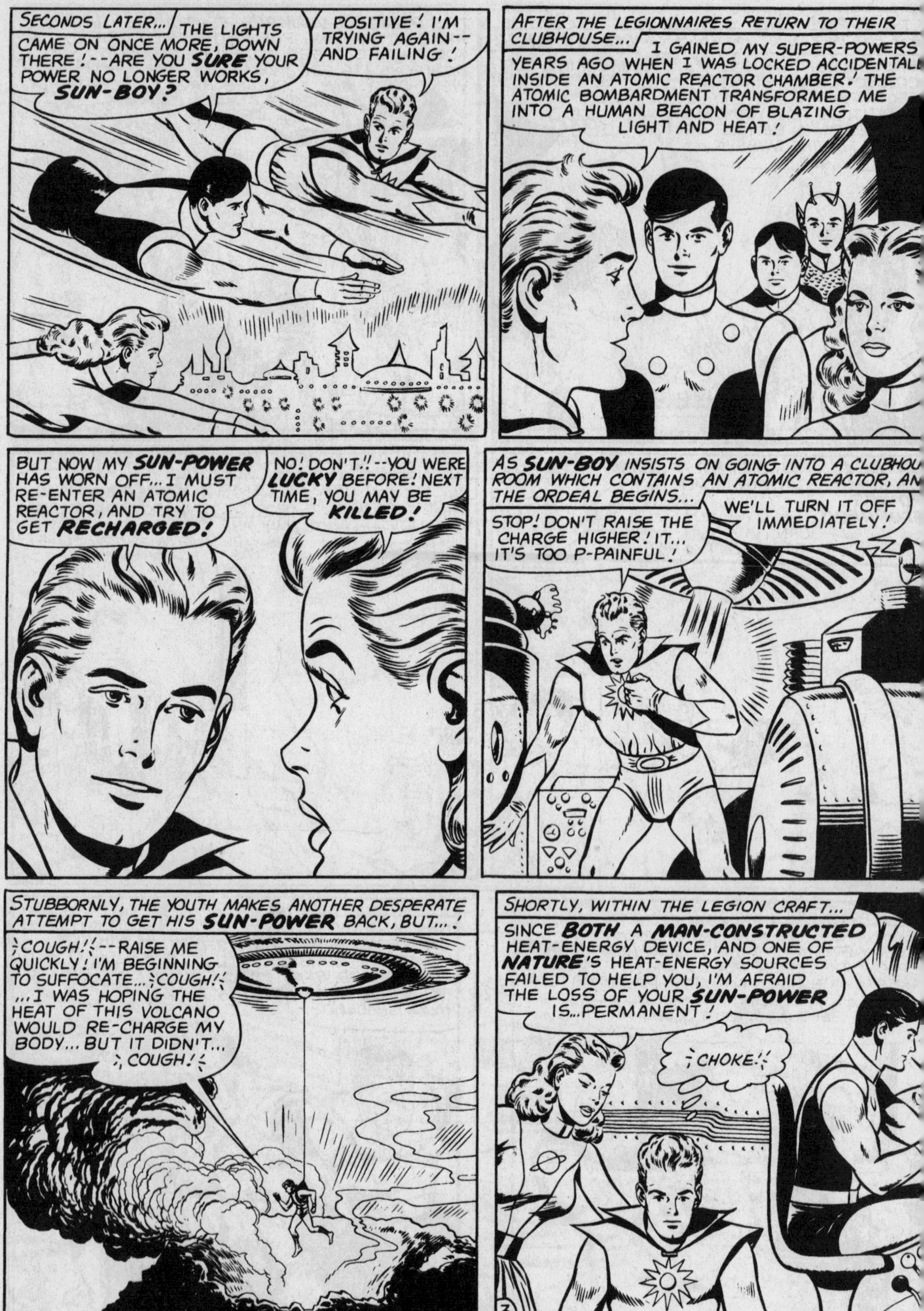
SECONDS LATER...
THE LIGHTS CAME ON ONCE MORE, DOWN THERE! --ARE YOU SURE YOUR POWER NO LONGER WORKS, SUN-BOY?
POSITIVE! I'M TRYING AGAIN-- AND FAILING!
AFTER THE LEGIONNAIRES RETURN TO THEIR CLUBHOUSE...
I GAINED MY SUPER-POWERS YEARS AGO WHEN I WAS LOCKED ACCIDENTALL INSIDE AN ATOMIC REACTOR CHAMBER! THE ATOMIC BOMBARDMENT TRANSFORMED ME INTO A HUMAN BEACON OF BLAZING LIGHT AND HEAT!
BUT NOW MY SUN-POWER HAS WORN OFF... I MUST RE-ENTER AN ATOMIC REACTOR, AND TRY TO GET RECHARGED!
NO! DON'T!! --YOU WERE LUCKY BEFORE! NEXT TIME, YOU MAY BE KILLED!
AS SUN-BOY INSISTS ON GOING INTO A CLUBHOU ROOM WHICH CONTAINS AN ATOMIC REACTOR, AN THE ORDEAL BEGINS...
STOP! DON'T RAISE THE CHARGE HIGHER! IT... IT'S TOO P-PAINFUL!
WE'LL TURN IT OFF IMMEDIATELY!
STUBBORNLY, THE YOUTH MAKES ANOTHER DESPERATE ATTEMPT TO GET HIS SUN-POWER BACK, BUT...!
COUGH! --RAISE ME QUICKLY! I'M BEGINNING TO SUFFOCATE... COUGH! ...I WAS HOPING THE HEAT OF THIS VOLCANO WOULD RE-CHARGE MY BODY... BUT IT DIDN'T... COUGH!
SHORTLY, WITHIN THE LEGION CRAFT...
SINCE BOTH A MAN-CONSTRUCTED HEAT-ENERGY DEVICE, AND ONE OF NATURE'S HEAT-ENERGY SOURCES FAILED TO HELP YOU, I'M AFRAID THE LOSS OF YOUR SUN-POWER IS...PERMANENT!
CHOKE!
3

THE **SUPER-HERO CLUBHOUSE** NEXT DAY, A [BE]ST ENTOMOLOGIST, PROFESSOR HARDING--PRESENTS...

[P]LEASE ACCEPT THIS GIFT... [A] COLLECTION OF STRANGE [IN]SECTS FROM OTHER PLANETS... [IN] GRATITUDE FOR YOUR MANY [GO]OD DEEDS IN BEHALF OF [SC]IENTISTS LIKE MYSELF!

SPEAKING FOR THE LEGION, I THANK YOU!

THIS **WINGED WAMPUS** IS MOST FASCINATING! WHILE ATTRACTING PREY WITH ITS COLORFUL FORM, IT RELEASES A DEADLY GAS THAT DESTROYS ITS FOE! DRAT! MY PIPE WENT OUT! MAY I PLEASE HAVE A LIGHT, SOMEONE?

CERTAINLY!

[S]UN-BOY! [OU]R SUN- [P]OWER [R]ETURNED!!

BUT ONLY FOR AN **INSTANT** ...WHEN I MOMEN- TARILY FORGOT I'D LOST THE POWER! I...I CAN'T MAKE IT WORK AGAIN!--BUT WHAT MADE IT FLARE BACK INTO EXISTENCE MOMENTARILY?

SOON AFTER THE LEGION'S GUEST LEAVES...

HELLO, FELLOW LEGIONNAIRES! I'VE JUST ARRIVED FROM OUT OF THE PAST!

SIT DOWN, **SUPERBOY!** YOU, TOO, **ULTRA-BOY, BOUNCING BOY** AND OTHER LATE-ARRIVALS! THE MEETING WILL NOW COME TO ORDER...

BOUNCING BOY

ULTRA BOY

COSMIC BOY

SHRINKING VIOLET

[M]INUTES LATER... FELLOW [LE]GIONNAIRES, THE PURPOSE OF TODAY'S [GA]THERING IS A SAD ONE!...**SUN-BOY** [H]AS LOST THE SUPER-POWER WHICH [M]AKES HIM ELIGIBLE FOR MEMBERSHIP! [W]ITHOUT IT, ACCORDING TO OUR RULES, [H]E CAN'T BELONG TO OUR CLUB...

WAIT...

COSMIC BOY

SUPERBOY

SATURN GIRL

WHILE IT'S TRUE THAT THE ATOMIC REACTOR, AND THE VOLCANO'S HEAT COULDN'T RESTORE MY **SUN-POWER** ...PERHAPS THE COMBINED MIGHT OF **SUPERBOY'S HEAT VISION** AND **ULTRA-BOY'S FLASH-VISION WOULD** SUCCEED!

I'M WILLING TO GIVE IT A TRY!

ME, TOO!

4

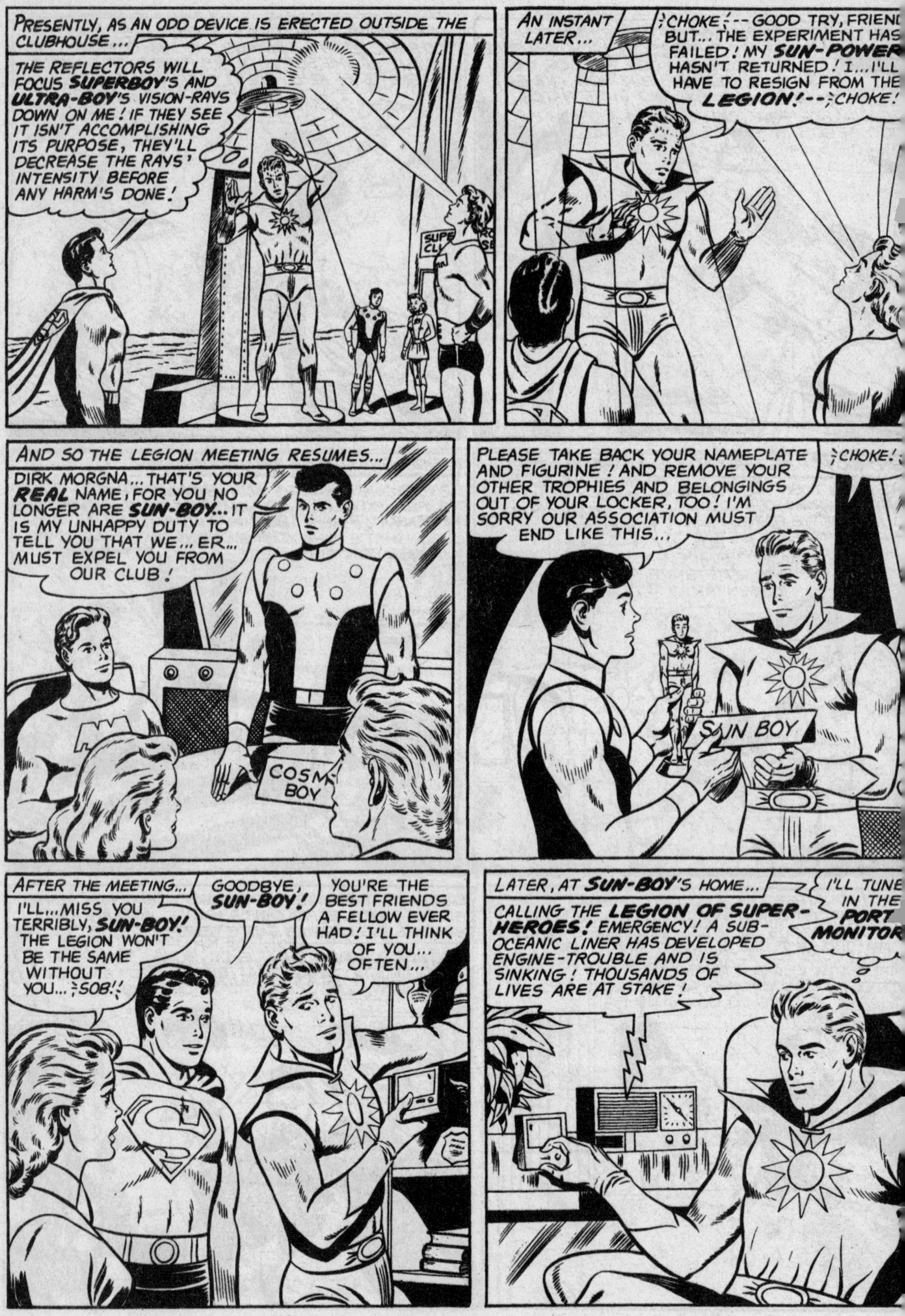
PRESENTLY, AS AN ODD DEVICE IS ERECTED OUTSIDE THE CLUBHOUSE...
THE REFLECTORS WILL FOCUS SUPERBOY'S AND ULTRA-BOY'S VISION-RAYS DOWN ON ME! IF THEY SEE IT ISN'T ACCOMPLISHING ITS PURPOSE, THEY'LL DECREASE THE RAYS' INTENSITY BEFORE ANY HARM'S DONE!
AN INSTANT LATER...
¡CHOKE¡ -- GOOD TRY, FRIEND BUT... THE EXPERIMENT HAS FAILED! MY SUN-POWER HASN'T RETURNED! I...I'LL HAVE TO RESIGN FROM THE LEGION! -- ¡CHOKE!
AND SO THE LEGION MEETING RESUMES...
DIRK MORGNA... THAT'S YOUR REAL NAME, FOR YOU NO LONGER ARE SUN-BOY... IT IS MY UNHAPPY DUTY TO TELL YOU THAT WE... ER... MUST EXPEL YOU FROM OUR CLUB!
COSM BOY
PLEASE TAKE BACK YOUR NAMEPLATE AND FIGURINE! AND REMOVE YOUR OTHER TROPHIES AND BELONGINGS OUT OF YOUR LOCKER, TOO! I'M SORRY OUR ASSOCIATION MUST END LIKE THIS...
¡CHOKE!
SUN BOY
AFTER THE MEETING...
I'LL... MISS YOU TERRIBLY, SUN-BOY! THE LEGION WON'T BE THE SAME WITHOUT YOU... ¡SOB!¡
GOODBYE, SUN-BOY!
YOU'RE THE BEST FRIENDS A FELLOW EVER HAD! I'LL THINK OF YOU... OFTEN...
LATER, AT SUN-BOY'S HOME...
CALLING THE LEGION OF SUPER-HEROES! EMERGENCY! A SUB-OCEANIC LINER HAS DEVELOPED ENGINE-TROUBLE AND IS SINKING! THOUSANDS OF LIVES ARE AT STAKE!
I'LL TUNE IN THE PORT MONITOR

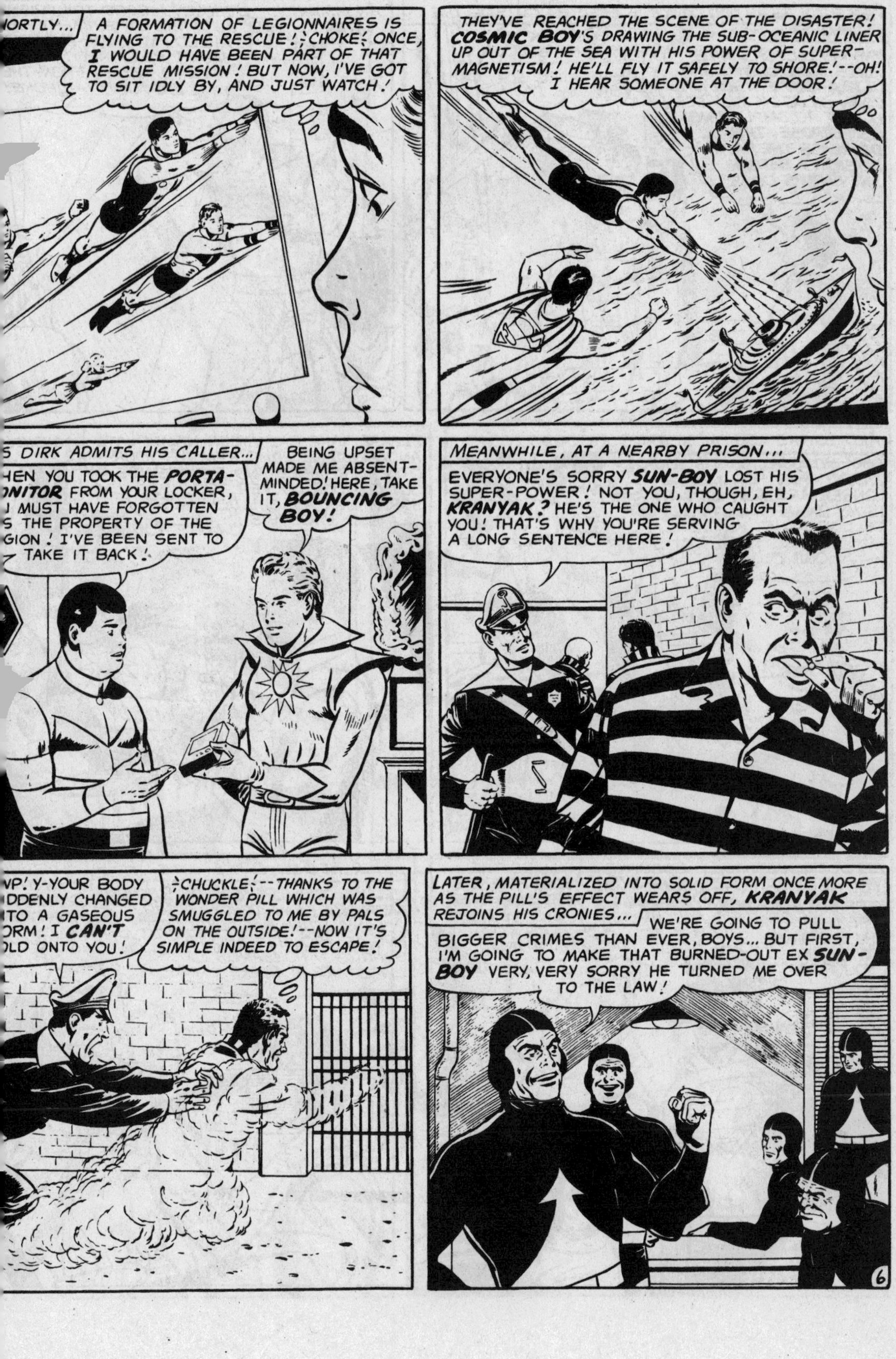

ORTLY...
A FORMATION OF LEGIONNAIRES IS FLYING TO THE RESCUE! -CHOKE- ONCE, I WOULD HAVE BEEN PART OF THAT RESCUE MISSION! BUT NOW, I'VE GOT TO SIT IDLY BY, AND JUST WATCH!
THEY'VE REACHED THE SCENE OF THE DISASTER! COSMIC BOY'S DRAWING THE SUB-OCEANIC LINER UP OUT OF THE SEA WITH HIS POWER OF SUPER-MAGNETISM! HE'LL FLY IT SAFELY TO SHORE!--OH! I HEAR SOMEONE AT THE DOOR!
S DIRK ADMITS HIS CALLER...
HEN YOU TOOK THE PORTA-ONITOR FROM YOUR LOCKER, MUST HAVE FORGOTTEN S THE PROPERTY OF THE GION! I'VE BEEN SENT TO TAKE IT BACK!
BEING UPSET MADE ME ABSENT-MINDED! HERE, TAKE IT, BOUNCING BOY!
MEANWHILE, AT A NEARBY PRISON...
EVERYONE'S SORRY SUN-BOY LOST HIS SUPER-POWER! NOT YOU, THOUGH, EH, KRANYAK? HE'S THE ONE WHO CAUGHT YOU! THAT'S WHY YOU'RE SERVING A LONG SENTENCE HERE!
NP! Y-YOUR BODY DDENLY CHANGED TO A GASEOUS ORM! I CAN'T OLD ONTO YOU!
-CHUCKLE- --THANKS TO THE WONDER PILL WHICH WAS SMUGGLED TO ME BY PALS ON THE OUTSIDE! --NOW IT'S SIMPLE INDEED TO ESCAPE!
LATER, MATERIALIZED INTO SOLID FORM ONCE MORE AS THE PILL'S EFFECT WEARS OFF, KRANYAK REJOINS HIS CRONIES...
WE'RE GOING TO PULL BIGGER CRIMES THAN EVER, BOYS... BUT FIRST, I'M GOING TO MAKE THAT BURNED-OUT EX SUN-BOY VERY, VERY SORRY HE TURNED ME OVER TO THE LAW!
6

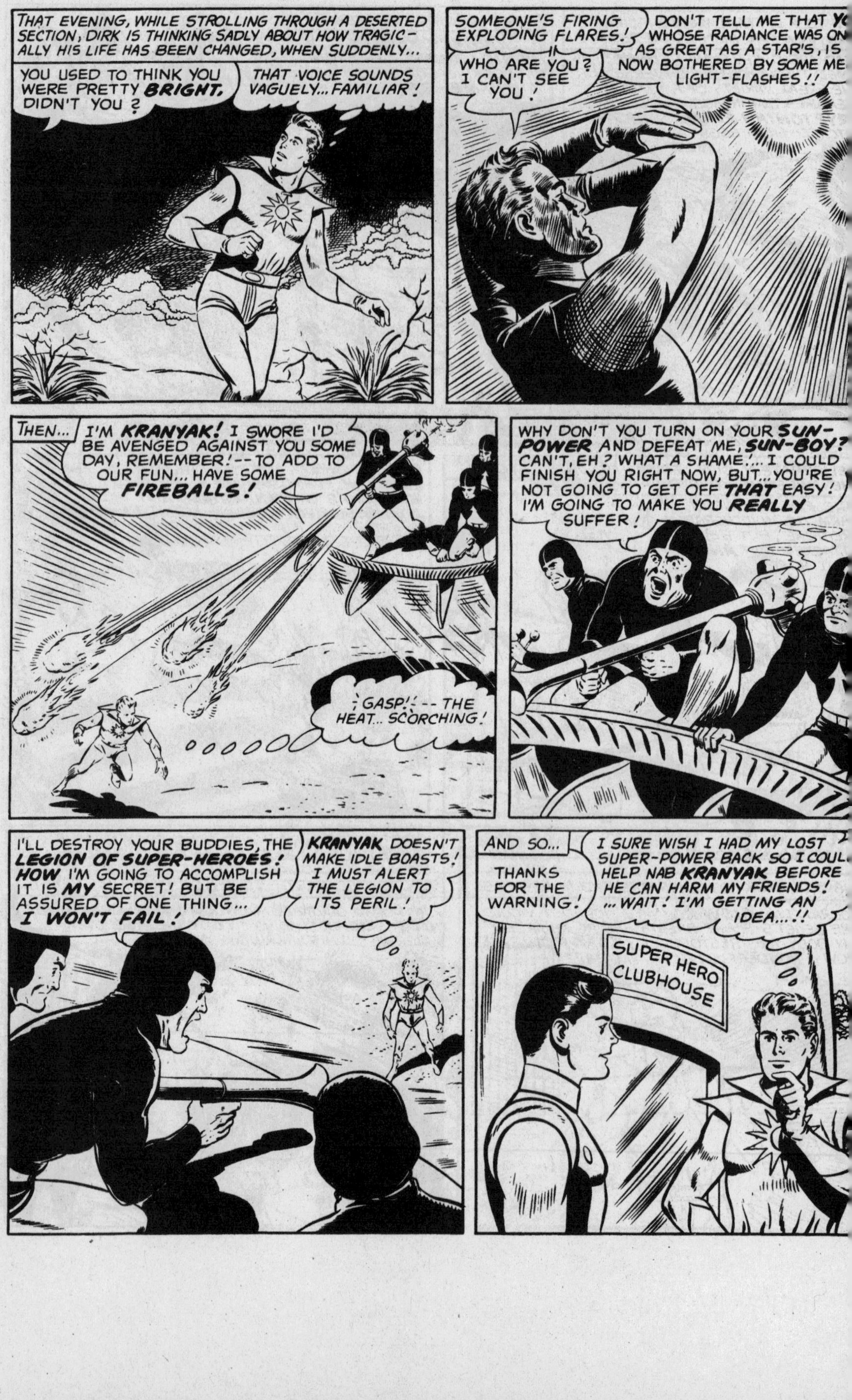
THAT EVENING, WHILE STROLLING THROUGH A DESERTED SECTION, DIRK IS THINKING SADLY ABOUT HOW TRAGICALLY HIS LIFE HAS BEEN CHANGED, WHEN SUDDENLY...
YOU USED TO THINK YOU WERE PRETTY **BRIGHT**, DIDN'T YOU?
THAT VOICE SOUNDS VAGUELY... FAMILIAR!
SOMEONE'S FIRING EXPLODING FLARES!
DON'T TELL ME THAT Y WHOSE RADIANCE WAS O AS GREAT AS A STAR'S, IS NOW BOTHERED BY SOME ME LIGHT-FLASHES!!
WHO ARE YOU? I CAN'T SEE YOU!
THEN...
I'M **KRANYAK!** I SWORE I'D BE AVENGED AGAINST YOU SOME DAY, REMEMBER!-- TO ADD TO OUR FUN... HAVE SOME **FIREBALLS!**
¡GASP!¡-- THE HEAT... SCORCHING!
WHY DON'T YOU TURN ON YOUR **SUN-POWER** AND DEFEAT ME, **SUN-BOY?** CAN'T, EH? WHAT A SHAME!... I COULD FINISH YOU RIGHT NOW, BUT... YOU'RE NOT GOING TO GET OFF **THAT** EASY! I'M GOING TO MAKE YOU **REALLY** SUFFER!
I'LL DESTROY YOUR BUDDIES, THE **LEGION OF SUPER-HEROES! HOW** I'M GOING TO ACCOMPLISH IT IS **MY** SECRET! BUT BE ASSURED OF ONE THING... **I WON'T FAIL!**
KRANYAK DOESN'T MAKE IDLE BOASTS! I MUST ALERT THE LEGION TO ITS PERIL!
AND SO...
THANKS FOR THE WARNING!
I SURE WISH I HAD MY LOST SUPER-POWER BACK SO I COUL HELP NAB **KRANYAK** BEFORE HE CAN HARM MY FRIENDS! ...WAIT! I'M GETTING AN IDEA...!!
SUPER HERO CLUBHOUSE

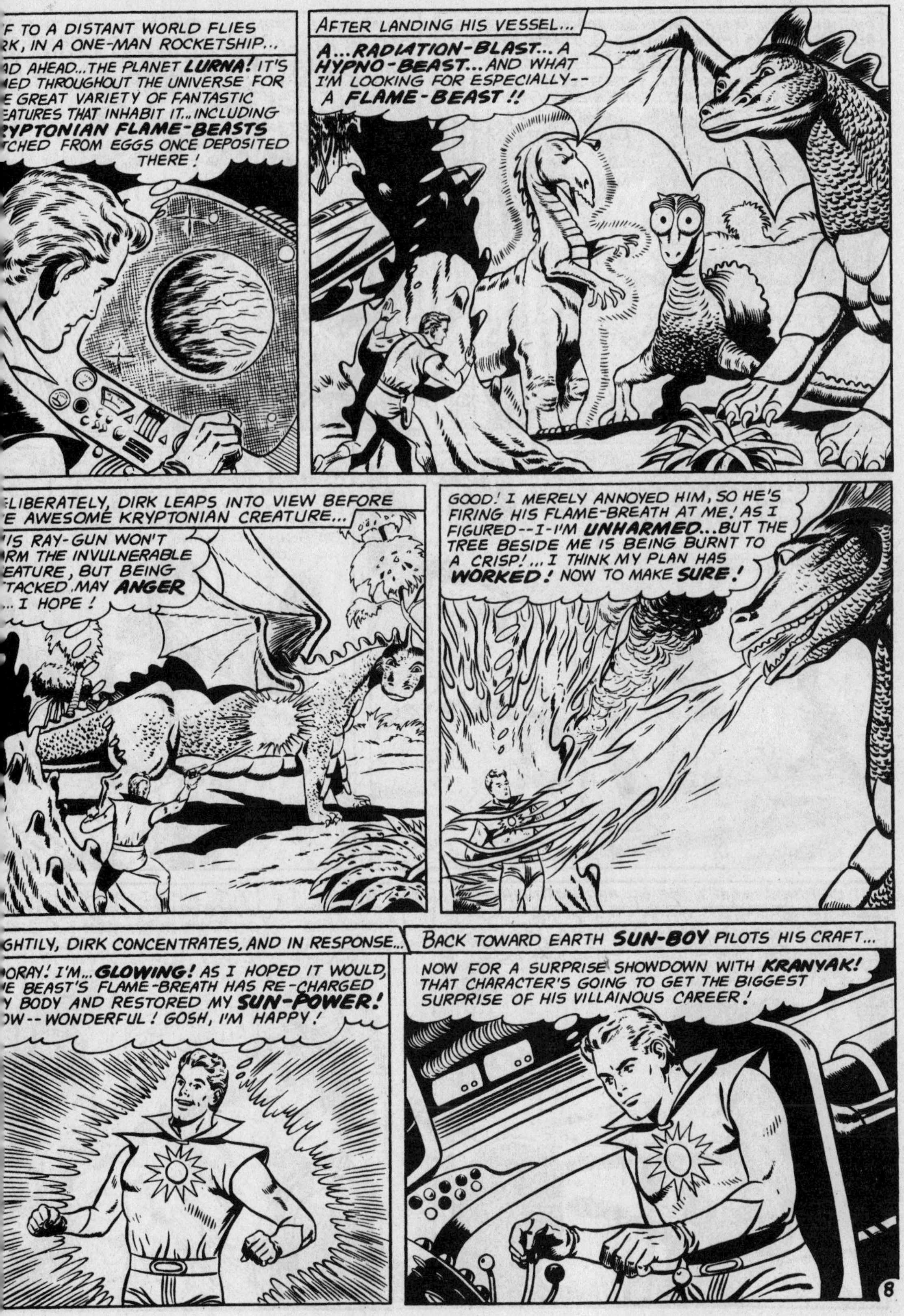
F TO A DISTANT WORLD FLIES
RK, IN A ONE-MAN ROCKETSHIP...
AD AHEAD...THE PLANET LURNA! IT'S
IED THROUGHOUT THE UNIVERSE FOR
E GREAT VARIETY OF FANTASTIC
EATURES THAT INHABIT IT...INCLUDING
RYPTONIAN FLAME-BEASTS
TCHED FROM EGGS ONCE DEPOSITED THERE!
AFTER LANDING HIS VESSEL...
A...RADIATION-BLAST...A HYPNO-BEAST...AND WHAT I'M LOOKING FOR ESPECIALLY-- A FLAME-BEAST!!
ELIBERATELY, DIRK LEAPS INTO VIEW BEFORE
E AWESOME KRYPTONIAN CREATURE...
IS RAY-GUN WON'T
RM THE INVULNERABLE
EATURE, BUT BEING
TACKED MAY ANGER
...I HOPE!
GOOD! I MERELY ANNOYED HIM, SO HE'S FIRING HIS FLAME-BREATH AT ME! AS I FIGURED--I-I'M UNHARMED...BUT THE TREE BESIDE ME IS BEING BURNT TO A CRISP!...I THINK MY PLAN HAS WORKED! NOW TO MAKE SURE!
GHTILY, DIRK CONCENTRATES, AND IN RESPONSE...
ORAY! I'M...GLOWING! AS I HOPED IT WOULD,
E BEAST'S FLAME-BREATH HAS RE-CHARGED
Y BODY AND RESTORED MY SUN-POWER!
OW--WONDERFUL! GOSH, I'M HAPPY!
BACK TOWARD EARTH SUN-BOY PILOTS HIS CRAFT...
NOW FOR A SURPRISE SHOWDOWN WITH KRANYAK! THAT CHARACTER'S GOING TO GET THE BIGGEST SURPRISE OF HIS VILLAINOUS CAREER!
8

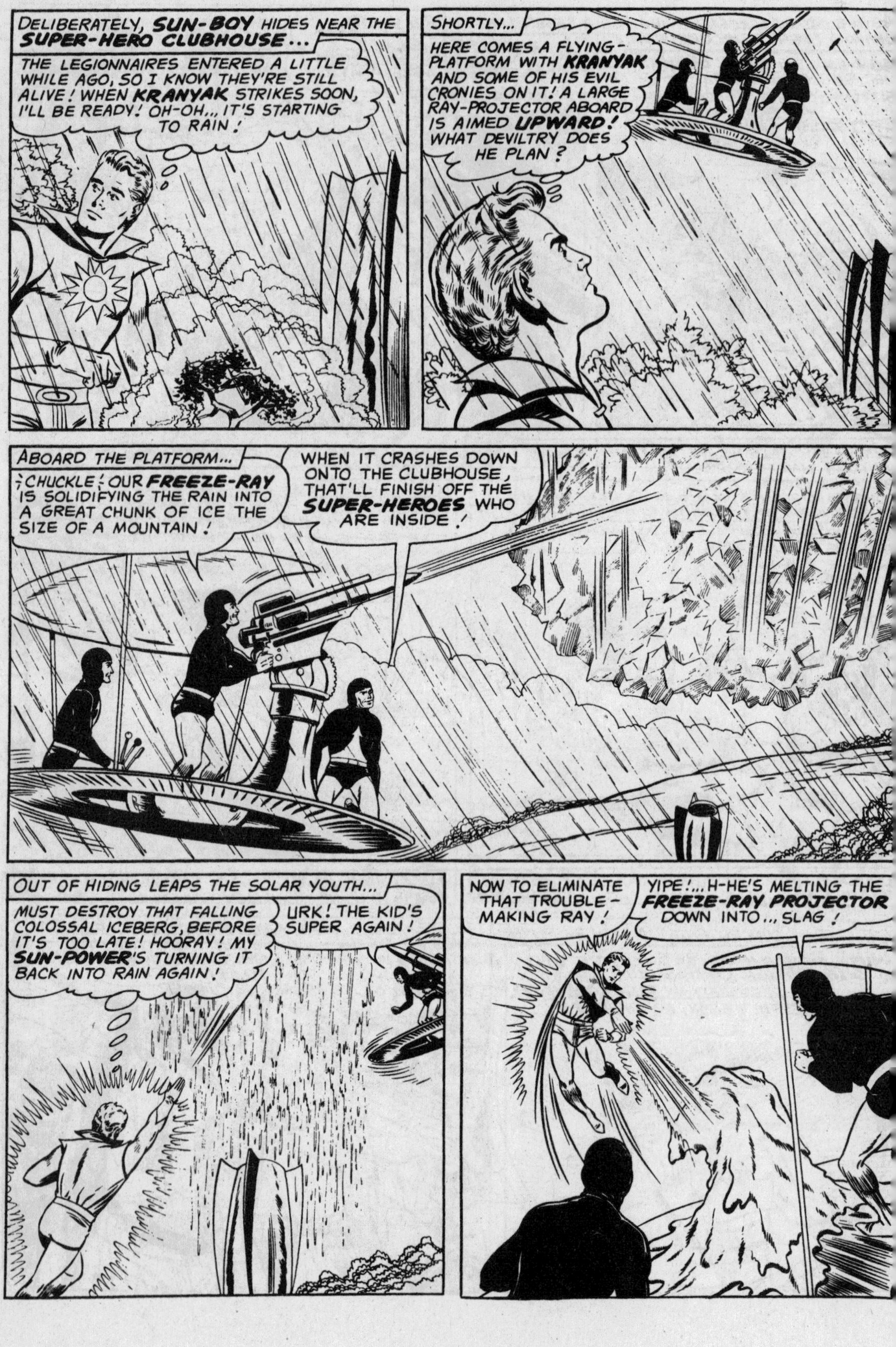
DELIBERATELY, SUN-BOY HIDES NEAR THE SUPER-HERO CLUBHOUSE...
THE LEGIONNAIRES ENTERED A LITTLE WHILE AGO, SO I KNOW THEY'RE STILL ALIVE! WHEN KRANYAK STRIKES SOON, I'LL BE READY! OH-OH... IT'S STARTING TO RAIN!
SHORTLY...
HERE COMES A FLYING-PLATFORM WITH KRANYAK AND SOME OF HIS EVIL CRONIES ON IT! A LARGE RAY-PROJECTOR ABOARD IS AIMED UPWARD! WHAT DEVILTRY DOES HE PLAN?
ABOARD THE PLATFORM...
;CHUCKLE; OUR FREEZE-RAY IS SOLIDIFYING THE RAIN INTO A GREAT CHUNK OF ICE THE SIZE OF A MOUNTAIN!
WHEN IT CRASHES DOWN ONTO THE CLUBHOUSE, THAT'LL FINISH OFF THE SUPER-HEROES WHO ARE INSIDE!
OUT OF HIDING LEAPS THE SOLAR YOUTH...
MUST DESTROY THAT FALLING COLOSSAL ICEBERG, BEFORE IT'S TOO LATE! HOORAY! MY SUN-POWER'S TURNING IT BACK INTO RAIN AGAIN!
URK! THE KID'S SUPER AGAIN!
NOW TO ELIMINATE THAT TROUBLE-MAKING RAY!
YIPE!... H-HE'S MELTING THE FREEZE-RAY PROJECTOR DOWN INTO... SLAG!

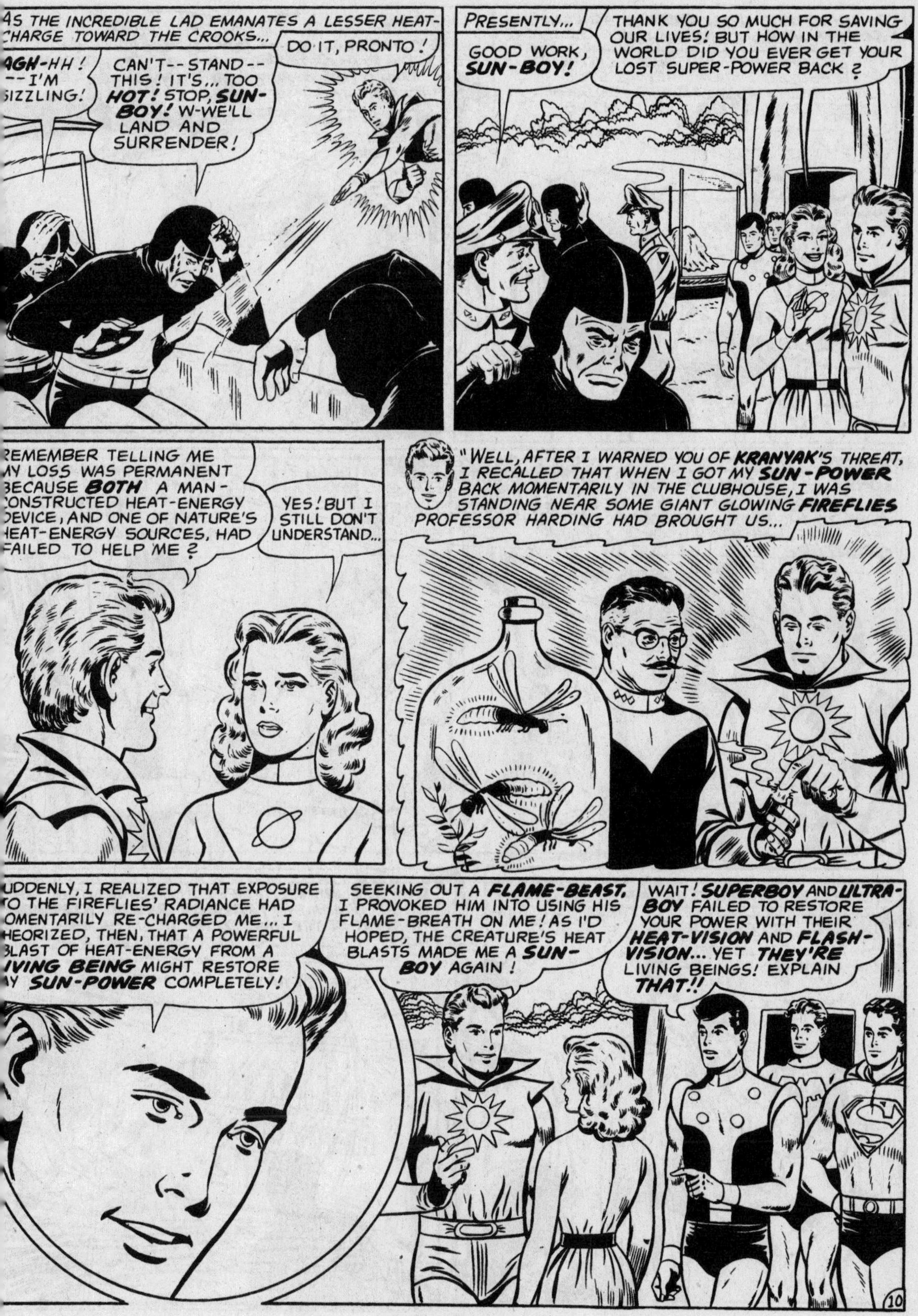
AS THE INCREDIBLE LAD EMANATES A LESSER HEAT-CHARGE TOWARD THE CROOKS...
AGH-HH! --I'M SIZZLING!
CAN'T--STAND--THIS! IT'S... TOO HOT! STOP, SUN-BOY! W-WE'LL LAND AND SURRENDER!
DO IT, PRONTO!
PRESENTLY...
GOOD WORK, SUN-BOY!
THANK YOU SO MUCH FOR SAVING OUR LIVES! BUT HOW IN THE WORLD DID YOU EVER GET YOUR LOST SUPER-POWER BACK?
REMEMBER TELLING ME MY LOSS WAS PERMANENT BECAUSE BOTH A MAN-CONSTRUCTED HEAT-ENERGY DEVICE, AND ONE OF NATURE'S HEAT-ENERGY SOURCES, HAD FAILED TO HELP ME?
YES! BUT I STILL DON'T UNDERSTAND...
"WELL, AFTER I WARNED YOU OF KRANYAK'S THREAT, I RECALLED THAT WHEN I GOT MY SUN-POWER BACK MOMENTARILY IN THE CLUBHOUSE, I WAS STANDING NEAR SOME GIANT GLOWING FIREFLIES PROFESSOR HARDING HAD BROUGHT US...
SUDDENLY, I REALIZED THAT EXPOSURE TO THE FIREFLIES' RADIANCE HAD MOMENTARILY RE-CHARGED ME... I THEORIZED, THEN, THAT A POWERFUL BLAST OF HEAT-ENERGY FROM A LIVING BEING MIGHT RESTORE MY SUN-POWER COMPLETELY!
SEEKING OUT A FLAME-BEAST, I PROVOKED HIM INTO USING HIS FLAME-BREATH ON ME! AS I'D HOPED, THE CREATURE'S HEAT BLASTS MADE ME A SUN-BOY AGAIN!
WAIT! SUPERBOY AND ULTRA-BOY FAILED TO RESTORE YOUR POWER WITH THEIR HEAT-VISION AND FLASH-VISION... YET THEY'RE LIVING BEINGS! EXPLAIN THAT!!
10

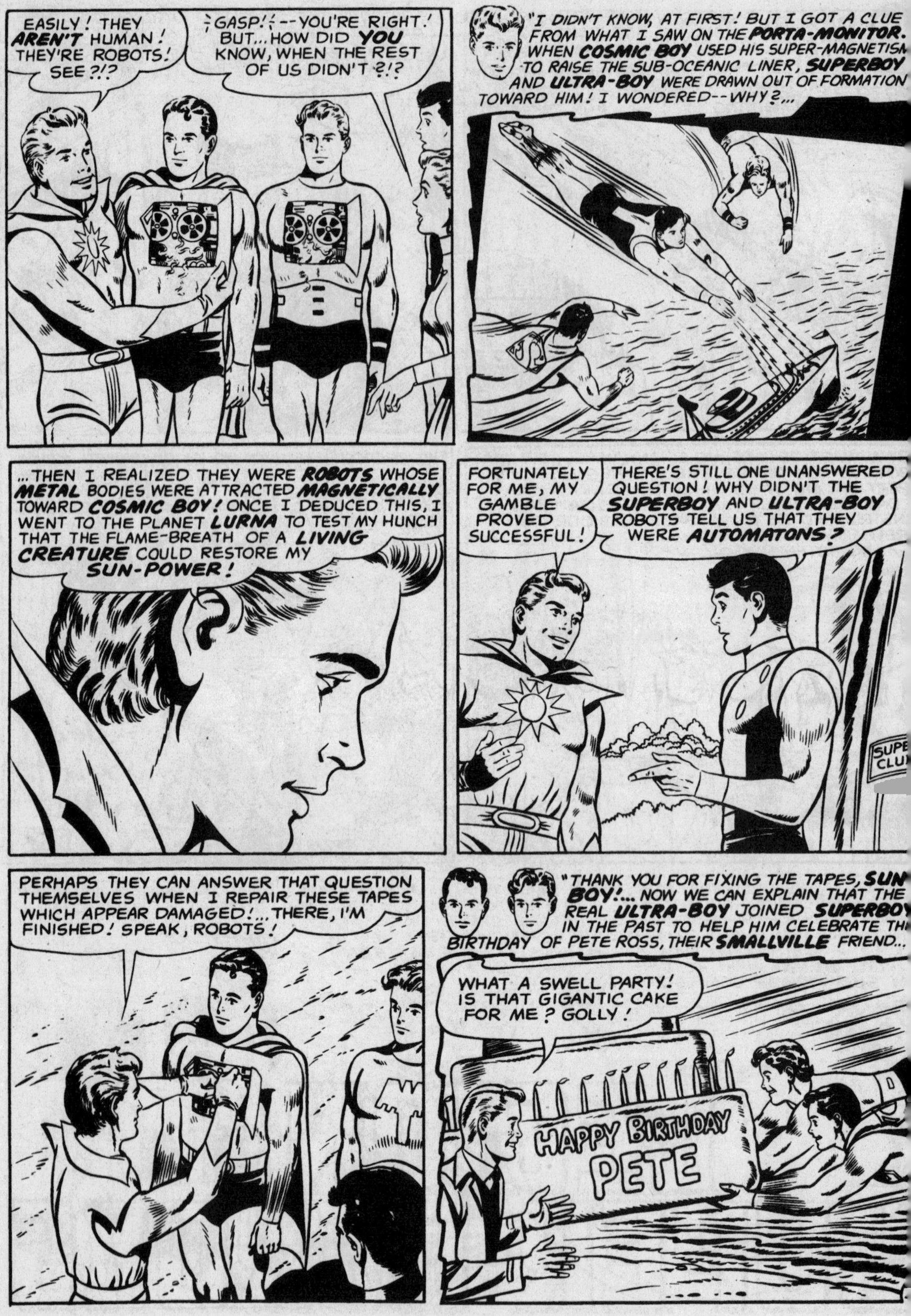
EASILY! THEY AREN'T HUMAN! THEY'RE ROBOTS! SEE?!?
¡GASP!¡ --YOU'RE RIGHT! BUT...HOW DID YOU KNOW, WHEN THE REST OF US DIDN'T?!?
"I DIDN'T KNOW, AT FIRST! BUT I GOT A CLUE FROM WHAT I SAW ON THE PORTA-MONITOR. WHEN COSMIC BOY USED HIS SUPER-MAGNETISM TO RAISE THE SUB-OCEANIC LINER, SUPERBOY AND ULTRA-BOY WERE DRAWN OUT OF FORMATION TOWARD HIM! I WONDERED--WHY?...
...THEN I REALIZED THEY WERE ROBOTS WHOSE METAL BODIES WERE ATTRACTED MAGNETICALLY TOWARD COSMIC BOY! ONCE I DEDUCED THIS, I WENT TO THE PLANET LURNA TO TEST MY HUNCH THAT THE FLAME-BREATH OF A LIVING CREATURE COULD RESTORE MY SUN-POWER!
FORTUNATELY FOR ME, MY GAMBLE PROVED SUCCESSFUL!
THERE'S STILL ONE UNANSWERED QUESTION! WHY DIDN'T THE SUPERBOY AND ULTRA-BOY ROBOTS TELL US THAT THEY WERE AUTOMATONS?
PERHAPS THEY CAN ANSWER THAT QUESTION THEMSELVES WHEN I REPAIR THESE TAPES WHICH APPEAR DAMAGED!... THERE, I'M FINISHED! SPEAK, ROBOTS!
"THANK YOU FOR FIXING THE TAPES, SUN BOY!... NOW WE CAN EXPLAIN THAT THE REAL ULTRA-BOY JOINED SUPERBOY IN THE PAST TO HELP HIM CELEBRATE THE BIRTHDAY OF PETE ROSS, THEIR SMALLVILLE FRIEND...
WHAT A SWELL PARTY! IS THAT GIGANTIC CAKE FOR ME? GOLLY!
HAPPY BIRTHDAY PETE

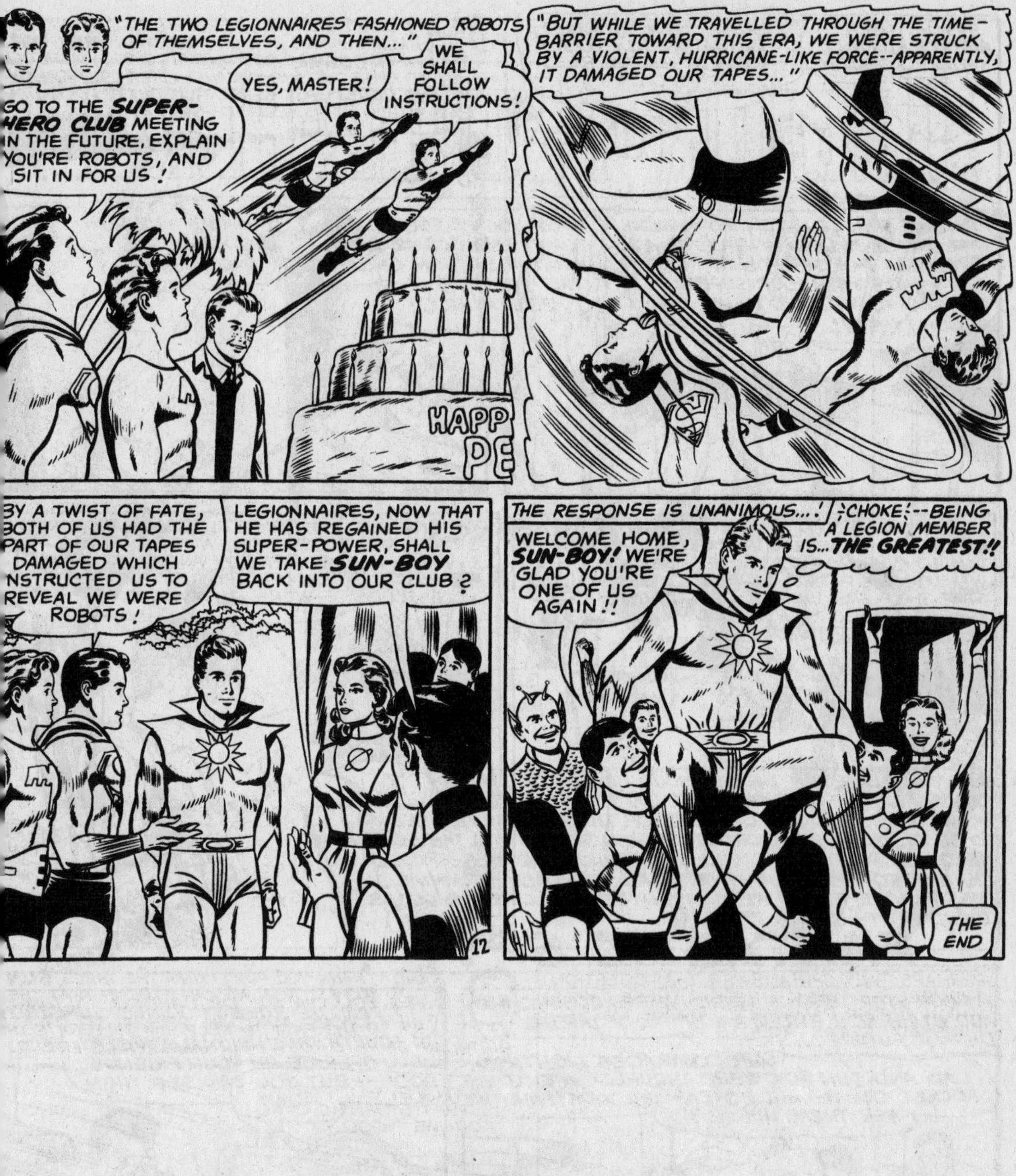
"THE TWO LEGIONNAIRES FASHIONED ROBOTS OF THEMSELVES, AND THEN..."
GO TO THE SUPER-HERO CLUB MEETING IN THE FUTURE, EXPLAIN YOU'RE ROBOTS, AND SIT IN FOR US!
YES, MASTER!
WE SHALL FOLLOW INSTRUCTIONS!
HAPP
PE
"BUT WHILE WE TRAVELLED THROUGH THE TIME-BARRIER TOWARD THIS ERA, WE WERE STRUCK BY A VIOLENT, HURRICANE-LIKE FORCE--APPARENTLY, IT DAMAGED OUR TAPES..."
BY A TWIST OF FATE, BOTH OF US HAD THE PART OF OUR TAPES DAMAGED WHICH INSTRUCTED US TO REVEAL WE WERE ROBOTS!
LEGIONNAIRES, NOW THAT HE HAS REGAINED HIS SUPER-POWER, SHALL WE TAKE SUN-BOY BACK INTO OUR CLUB?
12
THE RESPONSE IS UNANIMOUS...!
WELCOME HOME, SUN-BOY! WE'RE GLAD YOU'RE ONE OF US AGAIN!!
¡CHOKE!--BEING A LEGION MEMBER IS...THE GREATEST!!
THE END

LEGION of SUPER-HEROES

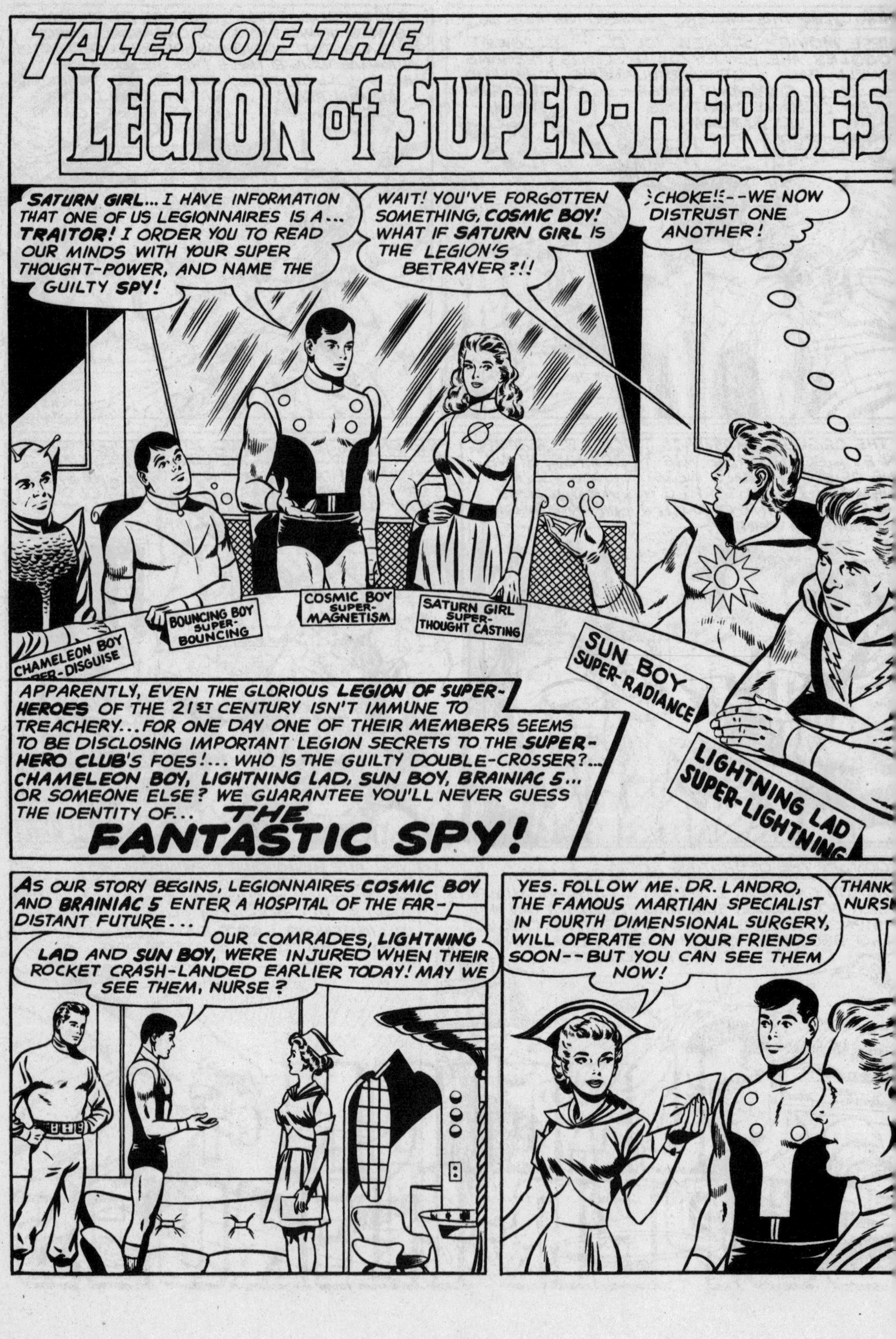
TALES OF THE
LEGION of SUPER-HEROES
SATURN GIRL... I HAVE INFORMATION THAT ONE OF US LEGIONNAIRES IS A... TRAITOR! I ORDER YOU TO READ OUR MINDS WITH YOUR SUPER THOUGHT-POWER, AND NAME THE GUILTY SPY!
WAIT! YOU'VE FORGOTTEN SOMETHING, COSMIC BOY! WHAT IF SATURN GIRL IS THE LEGION'S BETRAYER?!!
CHOKE!--WE NOW DISTRUST ONE ANOTHER!
CHAMELEON BOY
BOUNCING BOY SUPER-BOUNCING
COSMIC BOY SUPER-MAGNETISM
SATURN GIRL SUPER-THOUGHT CASTING
SUN BOY SUPER-RADIANCE
LIGHTNING LAD SUPER-LIGHTNING
APPARENTLY, EVEN THE GLORIOUS LEGION OF SUPER-HEROES OF THE 21ST CENTURY ISN'T IMMUNE TO TREACHERY... FOR ONE DAY ONE OF THEIR MEMBERS SEEMS TO BE DISCLOSING IMPORTANT LEGION SECRETS TO THE SUPER-HERO CLUB'S FOES!... WHO IS THE GUILTY DOUBLE-CROSSER?... CHAMELEON BOY, LIGHTNING LAD, SUN BOY, BRAINIAC 5... OR SOMEONE ELSE? WE GUARANTEE YOU'LL NEVER GUESS THE IDENTITY OF... THE FANTASTIC SPY!
AS OUR STORY BEGINS, LEGIONNAIRES COSMIC BOY AND BRAINIAC 5 ENTER A HOSPITAL OF THE FAR-DISTANT FUTURE...
OUR COMRADES, LIGHTNING LAD AND SUN BOY, WERE INJURED WHEN THEIR ROCKET CRASH-LANDED EARLIER TODAY! MAY WE SEE THEM, NURSE?
YES. FOLLOW ME. DR. LANDRO, THE FAMOUS MARTIAN SPECIALIST IN FOURTH DIMENSIONAL SURGERY, WILL OPERATE ON YOUR FRIENDS SOON--BUT YOU CAN SEE THEM NOW!
THANK
NURS

SHORTLY, AS THE CALLERS PRESENT GIFTS...

THESE **MOVIE-GOGGLES** ARE SWELL, PAL!

I KNEW YOU'D ENJOY THOSE SCENES OF YOURSELF USING YOUR **SUPER-LIGHTNING** POWER!

LOOK AT THE RING THROUGH THIS, **SUN BOY!**

SPUTTERING JETS! THE MAGNIFYING LENS REVEALS TINY LIVING ANIMALS INSIDE THE RING'S HOLLOW GEM, **BRAINIAC 5!**

THEY'RE DESCENDANTS OF CREATURES WHICH WERE REDUCED TO THIS MICROSCOPIC SIZE BY THE SHRINKING-RAY OF MY VILLAINOUS GREAT-GREAT-GREAT GRANDFATHER...

...THE ORIGINAL **BRAINIAC!** AN EVIL SCIENTIST, HE WAS ONE OF **SUPERMAN'S** WORST ENEMIES! I...I'M SORRY I'M THE DESCENDANT OF SUCH A WICKED MAN!

DON'T BE ASHAMED, **BRAINIAC 5!** WE KNOW YOU'RE AS **GOOD** AS HE WAS **BAD!**

PRESENTLY...

THIS IS DR. LANDRO!

I'M PROUD TO MEET YOU, LAD! I'M ONE OF THE LEGION'S GREATEST ADMIRERS! IN FACT, I'VE INSISTED ON OPERATING PERSONALLY ON YOUR FRIENDS, AND I REFUSE TO ACCEPT **ANY** PAYMENT!

SOON, IN THE OPERATING ROOM...

AS YOU CAN SEE, I OPERATE WITH INSTRUMENTS WHICH GO THROUGH SKIN AND FLESH VIA THE 4TH DIMENSION! NOTE HOW THIS **CURATIVE CAPSULE** ALSO BECOMES FOURTH-DIMENSIONAL UPON CONTACT WITH THE FORCEPS...

YOU ARE BEHOLDING A PAINLESS AND BLOODLESS OPERATION! AFTER PLACING THIS CAPSULE IN **SUN BOY'S** INJURED ANKLE, I'LL INSERT A SIMILAR CAPSULE IN **LIGHTNING LAD'S** DAMAGED KNEE!... THEY'LL BE CURED IN A FEW DAYS...!

2

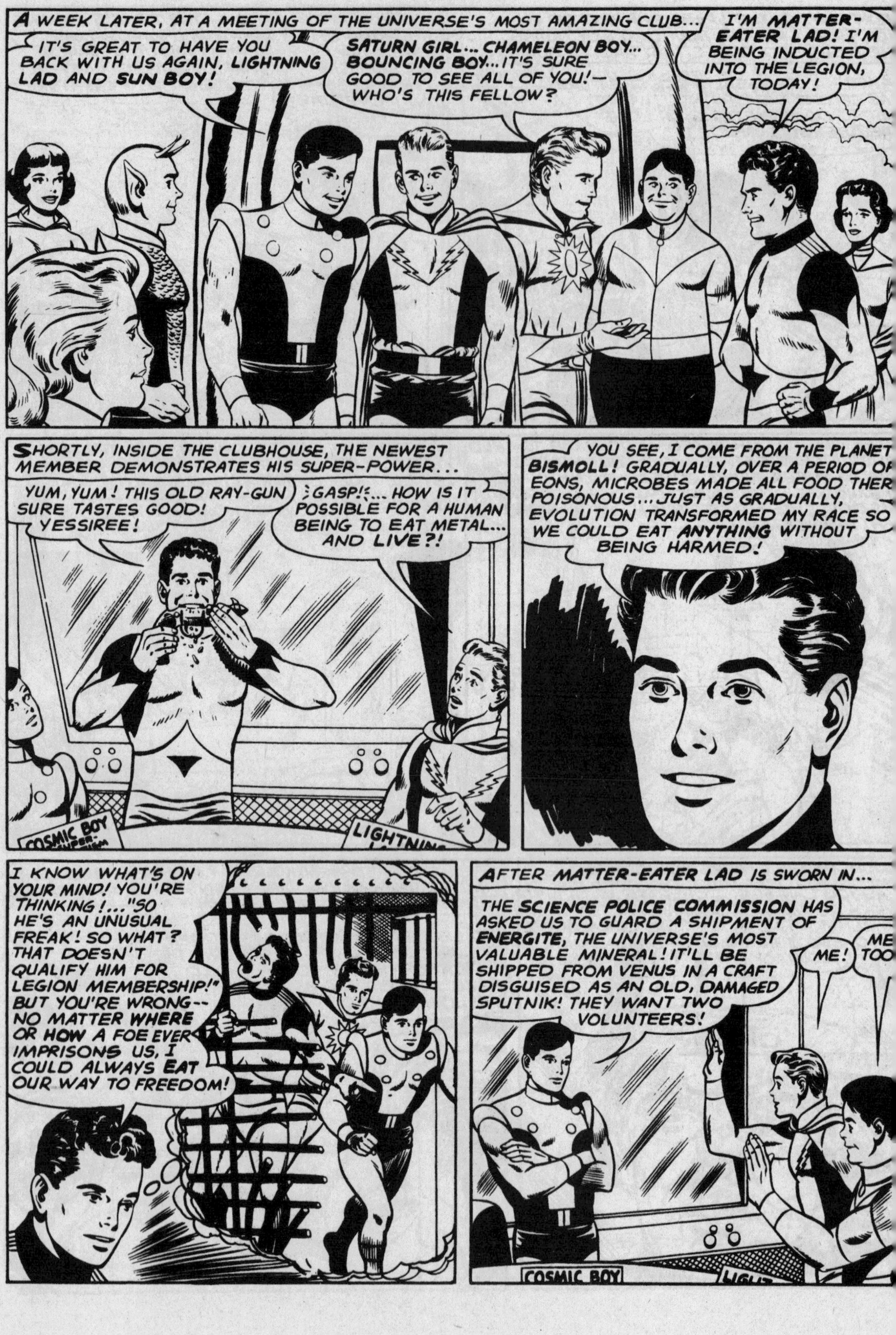
A WEEK LATER, AT A MEETING OF THE UNIVERSE'S MOST AMAZING CLUB...
IT'S GREAT TO HAVE YOU BACK WITH US AGAIN, LIGHTNING LAD AND SUN BOY!
SATURN GIRL... CHAMELEON BOY... BOUNCING BOY...IT'S SURE GOOD TO SEE ALL OF YOU!— WHO'S THIS FELLOW?
I'M MATTER-EATER LAD! I'M BEING INDUCTED INTO THE LEGION, TODAY!
SHORTLY, INSIDE THE CLUBHOUSE, THE NEWEST MEMBER DEMONSTRATES HIS SUPER-POWER...
YUM, YUM! THIS OLD RAY-GUN SURE TASTES GOOD! YESSIREE!
GASP!... HOW IS IT POSSIBLE FOR A HUMAN BEING TO EAT METAL... AND LIVE?!
COSMIC BOY
YOU SEE, I COME FROM THE PLANET BISMOLL! GRADUALLY, OVER A PERIOD OF EONS, MICROBES MADE ALL FOOD THERE POISONOUS... JUST AS GRADUALLY, EVOLUTION TRANSFORMED MY RACE SO WE COULD EAT ANYTHING WITHOUT BEING HARMED!
I KNOW WHAT'S ON YOUR MIND! YOU'RE THINKING!..."SO HE'S AN UNUSUAL FREAK! SO WHAT? THAT DOESN'T QUALIFY HIM FOR LEGION MEMBERSHIP!" BUT YOU'RE WRONG-- NO MATTER WHERE OR HOW A FOE EVER IMPRISONS US, I COULD ALWAYS EAT OUR WAY TO FREEDOM!
AFTER MATTER-EATER LAD IS SWORN IN...
THE SCIENCE POLICE COMMISSION HAS ASKED US TO GUARD A SHIPMENT OF ENERGITE, THE UNIVERSE'S MOST VALUABLE MINERAL! IT'LL BE SHIPPED FROM VENUS IN A CRAFT DISGUISED AS AN OLD, DAMAGED SPUTNIK! THEY WANT TWO VOLUNTEERS!
ME!
COSMIC BOY

NEXT DAY, AS THE SPACE SHIP PILOTED BY LIGHTNING LAD AND BOUNCING BOY NEARS THE DISGUISED CRAFT THEY ARE TO GUARD...

YAWP!- A COLOSSAL SPACE CREATURE HAS SEIZED THE "SPUTNIK"! WE'VE GOT TO DO SOMETHING, OR LOSE THE ENERGITE INSIDE IT!

AND NOW IT'S STREAKING OFF FASTER THAN OUR SHIP CAN TRAVEL! WE CAN'T OVERTAKE IT!

LOOK--THE THING'S LEAVING AN ATOMIC VAPOR TRAIL BEHIND IT! IT'S A SPACE SHIP DISGUISED CLEVERLY TO LOOK LIKE A CREATURE!!

ACCORDING TO OUR ASTRO-CALCULATOR, THE SPACE PIRATES ARE HEADING OUT OF OUR GALAXY TOWARD BISMOLL, THE PLANET THAT MATTER-EATER LAD CAME FROM! DO YOU THINK...?

I'D HATE TO TELL YOU WHAT I THINK!

BISMOLL

LATER THAT DAY, AT A MEETING OF THE SUPER HERO CLUB, THE LEGIONNAIRES ARE REBUKED BY THE CHIEF OF THE SCIENCE POLICE COMMISSION...

OUR SECRET PLAN WAS REVEALED ONLY TO YOU LEGIONNAIRES!

SPC CHIEF

WHICH MEANS... THERE'S A TRAITOR AMONG YOU! YOU MUST DISCOVER HIS IDENTITY... AND HAVE HIM ARRESTED! DO THIS WITHOUT DELAY!!

SPC CHIEF

RELUCTANT TO BELIEVE ONE OF THEIR NUMBER IS A TRAITOR, THE LEGIONNAIRES CHECK THEIR ANTI-SPYING INDICATOR...

NO SECRET MICROPHONE IS HIDDEN IN OUR CLUBHOUSE--IF IT WERE, THE INDICATOR-RAY'S COLOR WOULD HAVE TURNED FROM YELLOW TO RED!

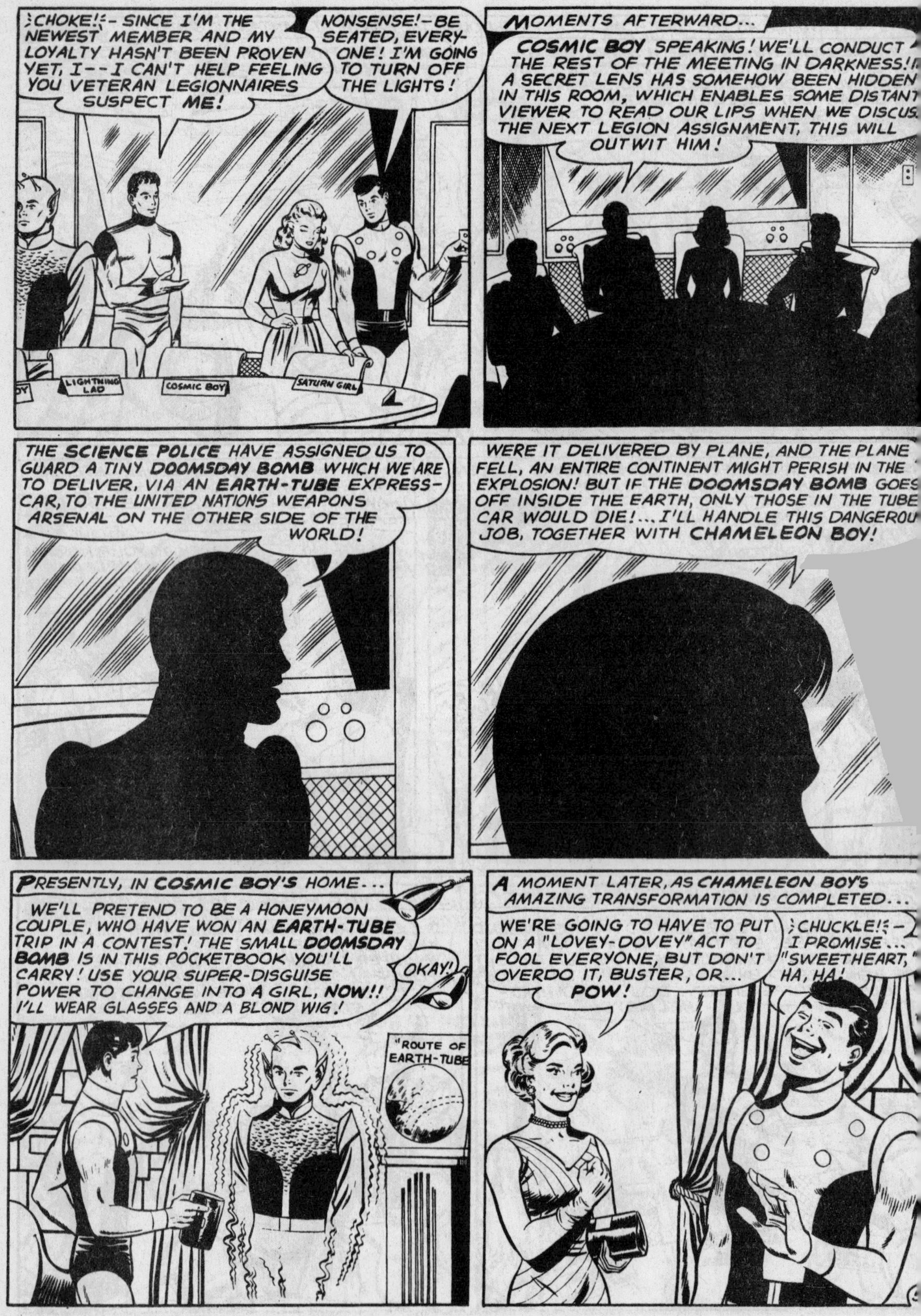

CHOKE! - SINCE I'M THE NEWEST MEMBER AND MY LOYALTY HASN'T BEEN PROVEN YET, I--I CAN'T HELP FEELING YOU VETERAN LEGIONNAIRES SUSPECT ME!
NONSENSE!-BE SEATED, EVERY-ONE! I'M GOING TO TURN OFF THE LIGHTS!
LIGHTNING LAD
COSMIC BOY
SATURN GIRL
MOMENTS AFTERWARD...
COSMIC BOY SPEAKING! WE'LL CONDUCT THE REST OF THE MEETING IN DARKNESS! A SECRET LENS HAS SOMEHOW BEEN HIDDEN IN THIS ROOM, WHICH ENABLES SOME DISTANT VIEWER TO READ OUR LIPS WHEN WE DISCUSS THE NEXT LEGION ASSIGNMENT. THIS WILL OUTWIT HIM!
THE SCIENCE POLICE HAVE ASSIGNED US TO GUARD A TINY DOOMSDAY BOMB WHICH WE ARE TO DELIVER, VIA AN EARTH-TUBE EXPRESS-CAR, TO THE UNITED NATIONS WEAPONS ARSENAL ON THE OTHER SIDE OF THE WORLD!
WERE IT DELIVERED BY PLANE, AND THE PLANE FELL, AN ENTIRE CONTINENT MIGHT PERISH IN THE EXPLOSION! BUT IF THE DOOMSDAY BOMB GOES OFF INSIDE THE EARTH, ONLY THOSE IN THE TUBE CAR WOULD DIE!... I'LL HANDLE THIS DANGEROUS JOB, TOGETHER WITH CHAMELEON BOY!
PRESENTLY, IN COSMIC BOY'S HOME...
WE'LL PRETEND TO BE A HONEYMOON COUPLE, WHO HAVE WON AN EARTH-TUBE TRIP IN A CONTEST! THE SMALL DOOMSDAY BOMB IS IN THIS POCKETBOOK YOU'LL CARRY! USE YOUR SUPER-DISGUISE POWER TO CHANGE INTO A GIRL, NOW!! I'LL WEAR GLASSES AND A BLOND WIG!
OKAY!
"ROUTE OF EARTH-TUBE
A MOMENT LATER, AS CHAMELEON BOY'S AMAZING TRANSFORMATION IS COMPLETED...
WE'RE GOING TO HAVE TO PUT ON A "LOVEY-DOVEY" ACT TO FOOL EVERYONE, BUT DON'T OVERDO IT, BUSTER, OR... POW!
CHUCKLE! - I PROMISE... "SWEETHEART," HA, HA!

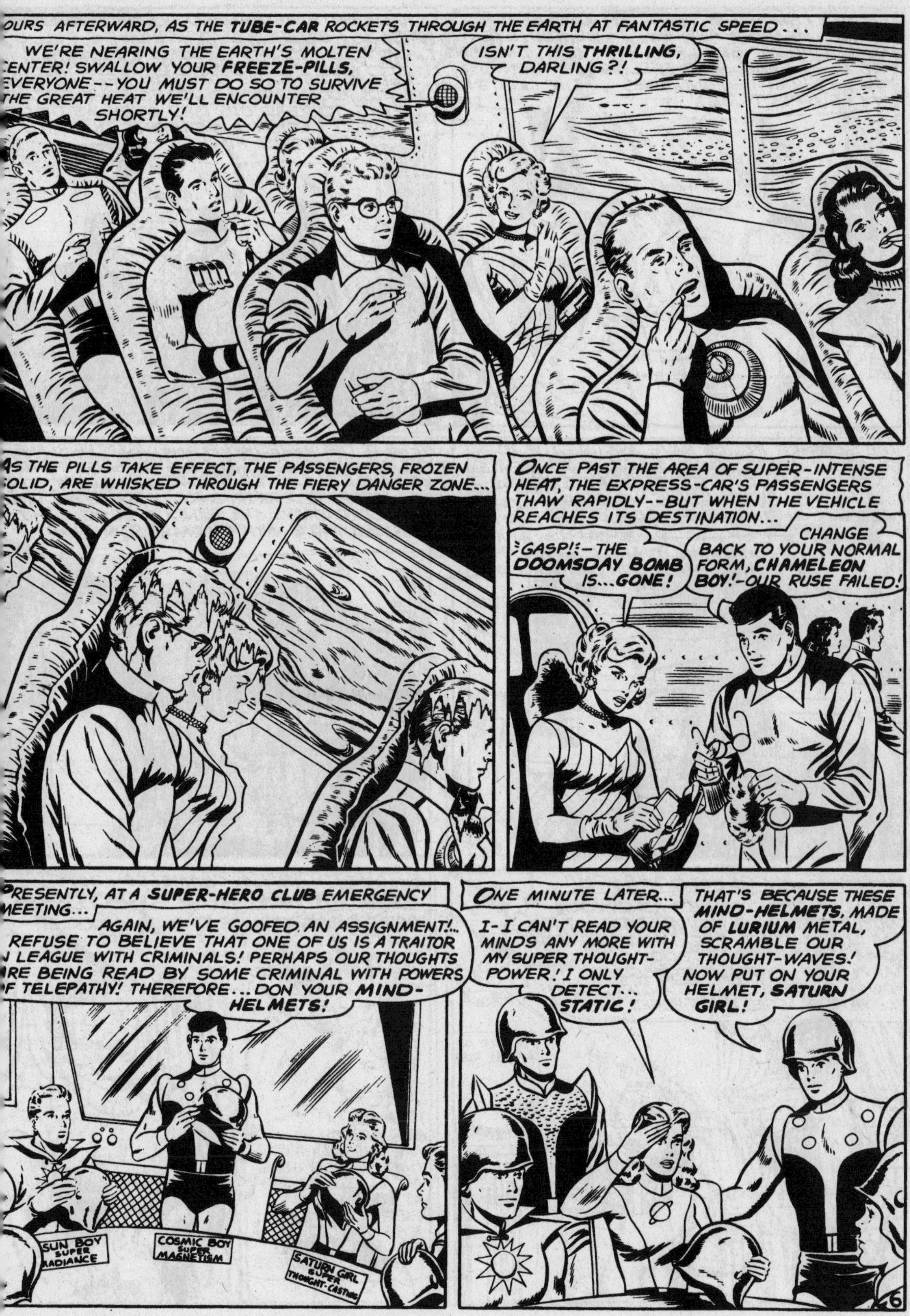
OURS AFTERWARD, AS THE TUBE-CAR ROCKETS THROUGH THE EARTH AT FANTASTIC SPEED...
WE'RE NEARING THE EARTH'S MOLTEN CENTER! SWALLOW YOUR FREEZE-PILLS, EVERYONE--YOU MUST DO SO TO SURVIVE THE GREAT HEAT WE'LL ENCOUNTER SHORTLY!
ISN'T THIS THRILLING, DARLING?!
AS THE PILLS TAKE EFFECT, THE PASSENGERS, FROZEN SOLID, ARE WHISKED THROUGH THE FIERY DANGER ZONE...
ONCE PAST THE AREA OF SUPER-INTENSE HEAT, THE EXPRESS-CAR'S PASSENGERS THAW RAPIDLY--BUT WHEN THE VEHICLE REACHES ITS DESTINATION...
GASP!--THE DOOMSDAY BOMB IS...GONE!
CHANGE BACK TO YOUR NORMAL FORM, CHAMELEON BOY!-OUR RUSE FAILED!
PRESENTLY, AT A SUPER-HERO CLUB EMERGENCY MEETING...
AGAIN, WE'VE GOOFED AN ASSIGNMENT!.. REFUSE TO BELIEVE THAT ONE OF US IS A TRAITOR N LEAGUE WITH CRIMINALS! PERHAPS OUR THOUGHTS RE BEING READ BY SOME CRIMINAL WITH POWERS F TELEPATHY! THEREFORE...DON YOUR MIND-HELMETS!
SUN BOY SUPER RADIANCE
COSMIC BOY SUPER MAGNETISM
SATURN GIRL SUPER THOUGHT-CASTING
ONE MINUTE LATER...
I-I CAN'T READ YOUR MINDS ANY MORE WITH MY SUPER THOUGHT-POWER! I ONLY DETECT... STATIC!
THAT'S BECAUSE THESE MIND-HELMETS, MADE OF LURIUM METAL, SCRAMBLE OUR THOUGHT-WAVES! NOW PUT ON YOUR HELMET, SATURN GIRL!
6

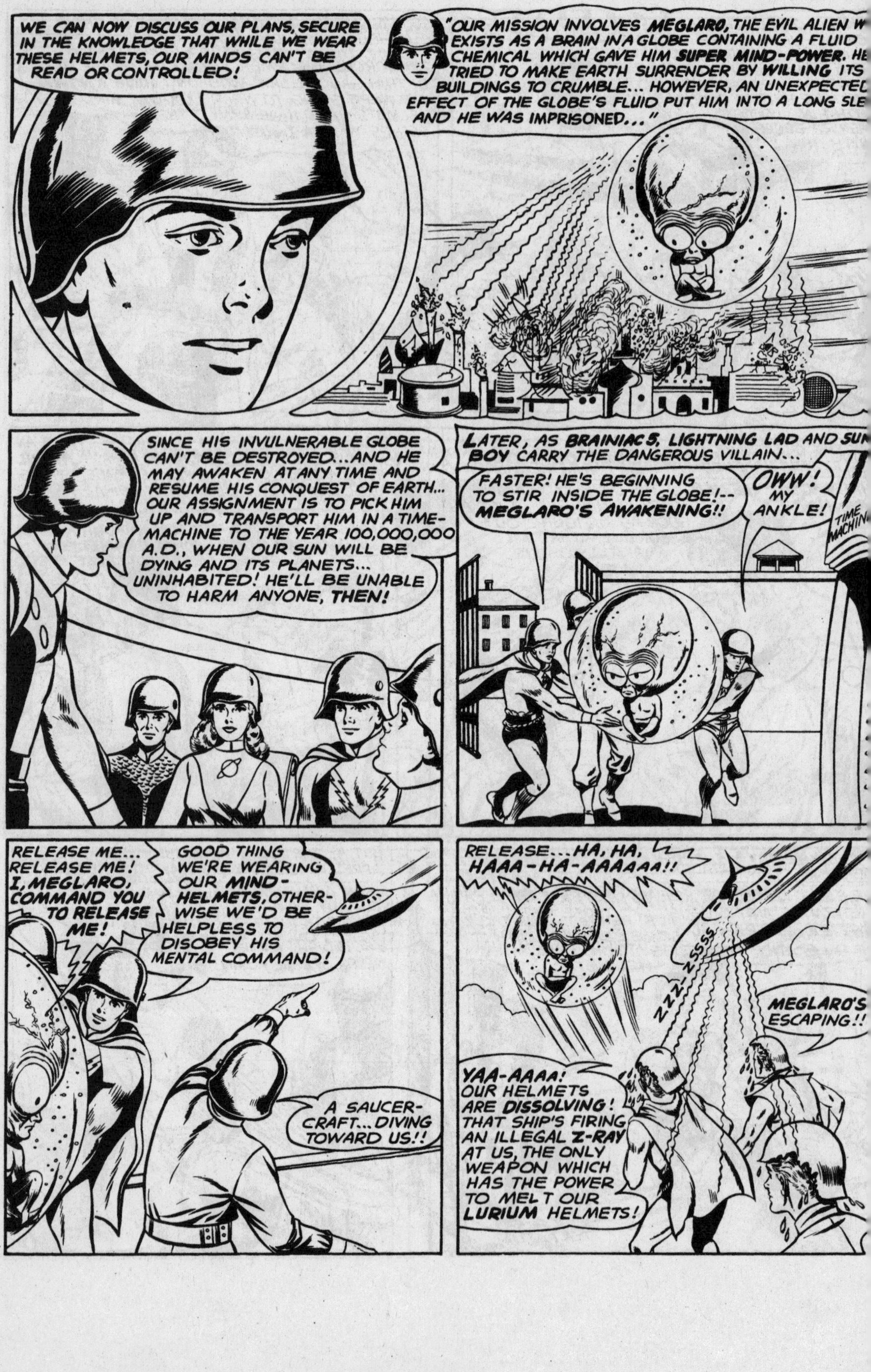
WE CAN NOW DISCUSS OUR PLANS, SECURE IN THE KNOWLEDGE THAT WHILE WE WEAR THESE HELMETS, OUR MINDS CAN'T BE READ OR CONTROLLED!
"OUR MISSION INVOLVES MEGLARO, THE EVIL ALIEN W EXISTS AS A BRAIN IN A GLOBE CONTAINING A FLUID CHEMICAL WHICH GAVE HIM SUPER MIND-POWER. HE TRIED TO MAKE EARTH SURRENDER BY WILLING ITS BUILDINGS TO CRUMBLE... HOWEVER, AN UNEXPECTED EFFECT OF THE GLOBE'S FLUID PUT HIM INTO A LONG SLE AND HE WAS IMPRISONED..."
SINCE HIS INVULNERABLE GLOBE CAN'T BE DESTROYED...AND HE MAY AWAKEN AT ANY TIME AND RESUME HIS CONQUEST OF EARTH... OUR ASSIGNMENT IS TO PICK HIM UP AND TRANSPORT HIM IN A TIME-MACHINE TO THE YEAR 100,000,000 A.D., WHEN OUR SUN WILL BE DYING AND ITS PLANETS... UNINHABITED! HE'LL BE UNABLE TO HARM ANYONE, THEN!
LATER, AS BRAINIAC 5, LIGHTNING LAD AND SUN BOY CARRY THE DANGEROUS VILLAIN...
FASTER! HE'S BEGINNING TO STIR INSIDE THE GLOBE!-- MEGLARO'S AWAKENING!!
OWW! MY ANKLE!
TIME MACHINE
RELEASE ME... RELEASE ME! I, MEGLARO, COMMAND YOU TO RELEASE ME!
GOOD THING WE'RE WEARING OUR MIND-HELMETS, OTHERWISE WE'D BE HELPLESS TO DISOBEY HIS MENTAL COMMAND!
A SAUCER-CRAFT... DIVING TOWARD US!!
RELEASE...HA, HA, HAAA-HA-AAAAAA!!
ZZZ-ZSSSS
MEGLARO'S ESCAPING!!
YAA-AAAA! OUR HELMETS ARE DISSOLVING! THAT SHIP'S FIRING AN ILLEGAL Z-RAY AT US, THE ONLY WEAPON WHICH HAS THE POWER TO MELT OUR LURIUM HELMETS!

CHOKE!--MEGLARO IS SOARING UP INTO THE SAUCER! ONLY CRIMINALS WOULD AID SUCH A CREATURE--PROBABLY WANTING TO JOIN FORCES WITH HIM! LOOK! THEY'RE ESCAPING WITH HIM!

AFTER ALL THE PRECAUTIONS WE TOOK, THERE CAN BE ONLY ONE ANSWER! ONE OF OUR LEGIONNAIRES HAS BETRAYED US AGAIN!

AS THE SUPER-HEROES ASSEMBLE AT THEIR CLUBHOUSE ONCE MORE... THERE'S DEFINITELY A TRAITOROUS INFORMER AMONG US, OR THE MEN IN THAT SAUCER-SHIP WOULDN'T HAVE KNOWN WE WERE GOING TO WEAR LURIUM MIND-HELMETS--AND HAVE ARMED THEM--SELVES WITH A Z-RAY!!

SATURN GIRL SUPER THOUGHT-CASTING

HAVE YOU DISCOVERED ANY-THING SUSPICIOUS BY EXAMINING US WITH THAT PROBE-VIEWER, BRAINIAC 5?

NO! BUT I'M SURE THE GUILT-DETECTOR WILL TELL US WHO THE DOUBLE-CROSSING LEGIONNAIRE IS, JUST AS SOON AS I FIGURE OUT A FORMULA THAT WILL WORK ON ALL OUR BODIES!

LET'S SEE...FW 21 OVER 17 W, MINUS 250 ROGOTS FOR THE DIFFERENCE IN EARTH'S GRAVITY...

PS-ST!--WHAT IF BRAINIAC 5 HAS TURNED RENEGADE, LIKE THE ORIGINAL BRAINIAC?

WHAT AN AWFUL THING TO SAY!

SOON, AS BRAINIAC 5 ADJUSTS THE METER'S CONTROLS, AND AIMS IT AT HIS COMRADES...

THE GUILT DETECTOR REVEALS THE TRAITOR AMONG US IS... MATTER-EATER LAD!

:GASP!:--MATTER-EATER LAD IS EATING THOSE METAL BARS BLOCKING THE ESCAPE CORRIDOR! STOP HIM!

BUT AS THE YOUTH WITH THE INCREDIBLE APPETITE CHOMPS HIS WAY TO FREEDOM...

YOUR LYING ACCUSATION IS UNTRUE! BUT I WON'T LET YOU GET ME! GOOD-BYE, LEGION! YOU'LL NEVER SEE ME AGAIN!!

8

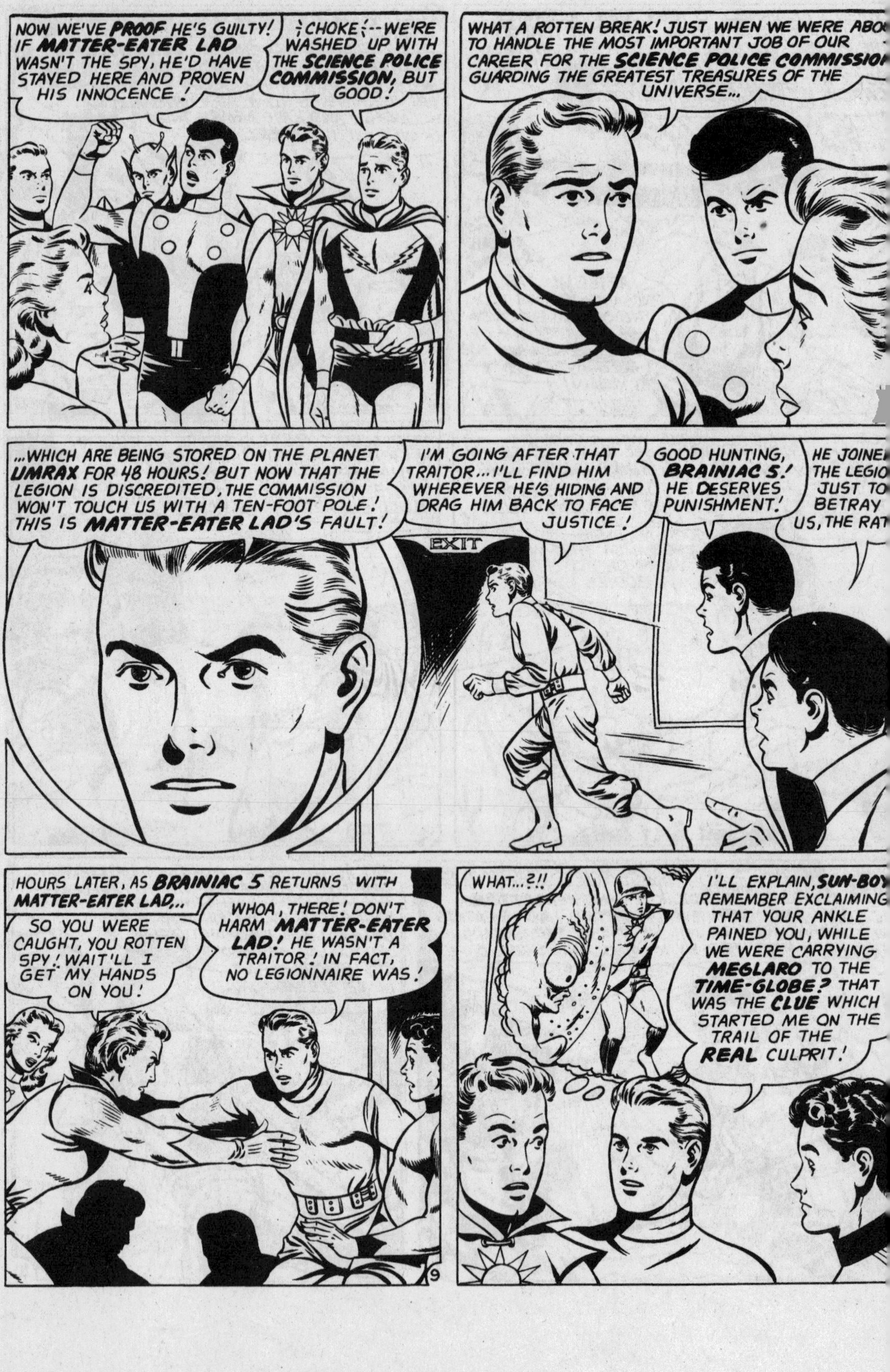
NOW WE'VE PROOF HE'S GUILTY! IF MATTER-EATER LAD WASN'T THE SPY, HE'D HAVE STAYED HERE AND PROVEN HIS INNOCENCE!
¡CHOKE¡--WE'RE WASHED UP WITH THE SCIENCE POLICE COMMISSION, BUT GOOD!
WHAT A ROTTEN BREAK! JUST WHEN WE WERE ABO TO HANDLE THE MOST IMPORTANT JOB OF OUR CAREER FOR THE SCIENCE POLICE COMMISSIO GUARDING THE GREATEST TREASURES OF THE UNIVERSE...
...WHICH ARE BEING STORED ON THE PLANET UMRAX FOR 48 HOURS! BUT NOW THAT THE LEGION IS DISCREDITED, THE COMMISSION WON'T TOUCH US WITH A TEN-FOOT POLE! THIS IS MATTER-EATER LAD'S FAULT!
I'M GOING AFTER THAT TRAITOR... I'LL FIND HIM WHEREVER HE'S HIDING AND DRAG HIM BACK TO FACE JUSTICE!
EXIT
GOOD HUNTING, BRAINIAC 5! HE DESERVES PUNISHMENT!
HE JOINE THE LEGIO JUST TO BETRAY US, THE RAT
HOURS LATER, AS BRAINIAC 5 RETURNS WITH MATTER-EATER LAD...
SO YOU WERE CAUGHT, YOU ROTTEN SPY! WAIT'LL I GET MY HANDS ON YOU!
WHOA, THERE! DON'T HARM MATTER-EATER LAD! HE WASN'T A TRAITOR! IN FACT, NO LEGIONNAIRE WAS!
9
WHAT...?!!
I'LL EXPLAIN, SUN-BOY REMEMBER EXCLAIMING THAT YOUR ANKLE PAINED YOU, WHILE WE WERE CARRYING MEGLARO TO THE TIME-GLOBE? THAT WAS THE CLUE WHICH STARTED ME ON THE TRAIL OF THE REAL CULPRIT!

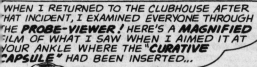

WHEN I RETURNED TO THE CLUBHOUSE AFTER THAT INCIDENT, I EXAMINED EVERYONE THROUGH THE *PROBE-VIEWER!* HERE'S A *MAGNIFIED* FILM OF WHAT I SAW WHEN I AIMED IT AT YOUR ANKLE WHERE THE *"CURATIVE CAPSULE"* HAD BEEN INSERTED...

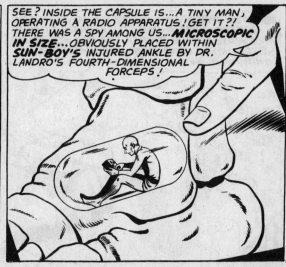

SEE? INSIDE THE CAPSULE IS...A TINY MAN, OPERATING A RADIO APPARATUS! GET IT?! THERE WAS A SPY AMONG US...*MICROSCOPIC IN SIZE*...OBVIOUSLY PLACED WITHIN *SUN-BOY'S* INJURED ANKLE BY DR. LANDRO'S *FOURTH-DIMENSIONAL FORCEPS!*

GET IT! DR. LANDRO WORKS WITH A GANG OF INTERPLANETARY CROOKS! WHEN WE WERE HURT IN THAT SPACESHIP ACCIDENT AND LET HIM OPERATE ON US, IT GAVE HIM THE OPPORTUNITY TO PLANT THE TINY SPY AND HIS RADIO APPARATUS INSIDE *SUN-BOY'S* BODY!

HE PLACED A *REAL* CURATIVE CAPSULE IN MY KNEE...AND PUT THE *FAKE* ONE, CONTAINING THE SPY, IN *SUN-BOY'S* ANKLE! THAT'S WHY I WAS CURED, BUT *SUN-BOY* STILL SUFFERS SOME PAIN!!

"CORRECT! AND AS TO *HOW* THE SPY BECAME SO TINY, MY GUESS IS THAT HE WAS A NORMAL-SIZED MAN UNTIL DR. LANDRO'S GANG REDUCED HIM, TOGETHER WITH A HUGE CAPSULE AND RADIO, TO MINIATURE SIZE...USING ONE OF THE SHRINKING-RAYS INVENTED BY MY EVIL ANCESTOR..."

NOW I SEE! HIDDEN INSIDE *SUN-BOY'S* ANKLE, THE TINY SPY MONITORED EVERYTHING WE SAID AT OUR CLUB MEETINGS, AND RADIOED THE INFORMATION TO HIS GANG!

EXACTLY.!!

10

"SO THAT'S WHY YOU SCRIBBLED A CERTAIN MESSAGE ON PAPER, FOR OUR BENEFIT, WHILE PRETENDING TO WRITE A FORMULA FOR YOUR SO-CALLED *GUILT-DETECTOR*, WHICH WE ALL *KNEW* WAS PHONY..."

Pretend to "escape" when I accuse you — you'll learn why later!!

YOU PLAYED ALONG WITH MY PLAN VERY NICELY, *MATTER-EATER LAD!*--WHY DID I FALSELY ACCUSE YOU?...BECAUSE I REALIZED THAT THE SPY IN *SUN-BOY'S* HEEL WOULD BE LISTENING TO EVERYTHING WE SAID, AND I WANTED HIM TO BELIEVE WE HADN'T LEARNED THE GANG'S CUNNING SCHEME...!

AFTER THAT, I PRETENDED TO LOSE MY TEMPER AND SPOKE "ANGRILY" OF THE LEGION LOSING OUT ON GUARDING A FABULOUS TREASURE ON THE PLANET *UMRAX*--A TREASURE WHICH *NEVER EXISTED!* IT WAS MERELY *BAIT* TO LURE THE GANG TO *UMRAX!*

NOW I'LL TURN ON THIS SPACE MONITOR, AND YOU'LL SEE HOW THEY SWALLOWED THE BAIT!

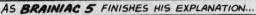

PLANET UMRAX

SUPERBOY... TYING DR. LANDR AND SOME SPACE PIRATES TO--GETHER... THE VILLAINS ARE UNCONSCIOUS!--:CHUCKLE;--I GET IT!! YOU SUMMONED *SUPERBOY* TO FLY TO OUR ERA THROUGH THE TIME-BARRIER, AND HELP OUT!

HA, HA! ONLY WE LEGIONNAIRES KNOW THAT THE PLANET *UMRAX* CONTAINS A GASEOUS ATMOSPHERE THAT RENDERS ANYONE WHO LANDS ON THAT WORLD UNCONSCIOUS! WE DISCOVERED THIS RECENTLY!...*SUPER-BOY*, OF COURSE, IS INVULNERABLE TO EVERYTHING EXCEPT *KRYPTONITE!*

AS *BRAINIAC 5* FINISHES HIS EXPLANATION...

LOOK! *MEGLARO* ACCOMPANIED THE CROOKS TO *UMRAX*, AND *SUPERBOY'S* NOW FLYING HIM INTO THE TIME-BARRIER, TO ABANDON HIM IN THE FAR, FAR DISTANT FUTURE AS WE PLANNED ORIGINALLY! LATER, HE'LL COME BACK AND TURN THE UNCONSCIOUS CRIMINALS OVER TO THE LAW!

11

IMAGINE THAT! I'VE BEEN CARRYING A MINIATURE-SIZED SPY AROUND IN MY HEEL, UNKNOWINGLY! GOSH, IT MAKES ME FEEL LIKE A...A TROJAN HORSE!!

YOU'RE GOING BACK TO THE HOSPITAL RIGHT NOW, FOR SOME FOURTH-DIMENSIONAL SURGERY!

PRESENTLY, DURING A HURRIED OPERATION...

NOW I'LL SUBSTITUTE A *REAL* CURATIVE CAPSULE FOR THIS SPY-CAPSULE!

GIVE ME THE ORIGINAL CAPSULE, PLEASE! I WANT YOU TO MEET THE TINY SPY IN PERSON!

SOON, AS *COSMIC BOY* SHINES AN EXPERIMENTAL ENLARGING RAY ON THE CAPSULE SO THAT IT IS RESTORED TO ITS NORMAL SIZE...

THERE'S ONLY ENOUGH OF A CHARGE FOR THIS RAY TO WORK BUT *ONCE!*

I SURRENDER!!

YOU'RE UNDER ARREST FOR ESPIONAGE! *BRAINIAC 5* OUTWITTED YOU NEATLY!

LATER, AT THE LEGION'S CLUBHOUSE...

WE'RE ALL PROUD OF YOU, *BRAINIAC 5!*

IT'S IRONIC THAT I, THE GREAT-GREAT-GREAT-GREAT GRAND-SON OF THE FIRST *BRAINIAC,* SOLVED A CRIME IN WHICH MY ANCESTOR'S DIABOLICAL SHRINKING-RAY WAS USED BY VILLAINS OF THIS TIME-ERA!

12

The End.

LEGION of SUPER-HEROES

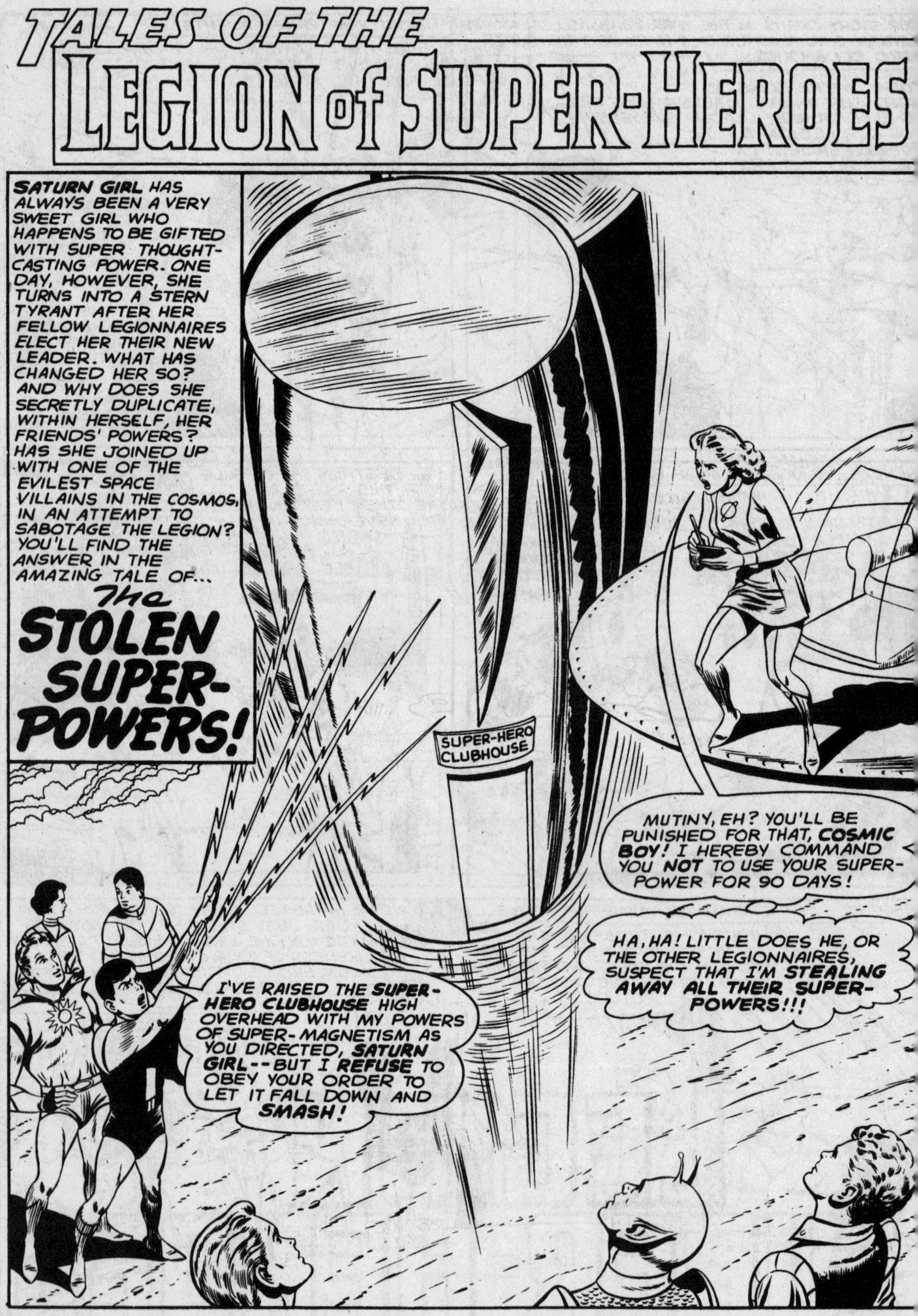
TALES OF THE
LEGION of SUPER-HEROES
SATURN GIRL HAS ALWAYS BEEN A VERY SWEET GIRL WHO HAPPENS TO BE GIFTED WITH SUPER THOUGHT-CASTING POWER. ONE DAY, HOWEVER, SHE TURNS INTO A STERN TYRANT AFTER HER FELLOW LEGIONNAIRES ELECT HER THEIR NEW LEADER. WHAT HAS CHANGED HER SO? AND WHY DOES SHE SECRETLY DUPLICATE, WITHIN HERSELF, HER FRIENDS' POWERS? HAS SHE JOINED UP WITH ONE OF THE EVILEST SPACE VILLAINS IN THE COSMOS, IN AN ATTEMPT TO SABOTAGE THE LEGION? YOU'LL FIND THE ANSWER IN THE AMAZING TALE OF...
The STOLEN SUPER-POWERS!
SUPER-HERO CLUBHOUSE
I'VE RAISED THE SUPER-HERO CLUBHOUSE HIGH OVERHEAD WITH MY POWERS OF SUPER-MAGNETISM AS YOU DIRECTED, SATURN GIRL--BUT I REFUSE TO OBEY YOUR ORDER TO LET IT FALL DOWN AND SMASH!
MUTINY, EH? YOU'LL BE PUNISHED FOR THAT, COSMIC BOY! I HEREBY COMMAND YOU NOT TO USE YOUR SUPER-POWER FOR 90 DAYS!
HA, HA! LITTLE DOES HE, OR THE OTHER LEGIONNAIRES, SUSPECT THAT I'M STEALING AWAY ALL THEIR SUPER-POWERS!!!

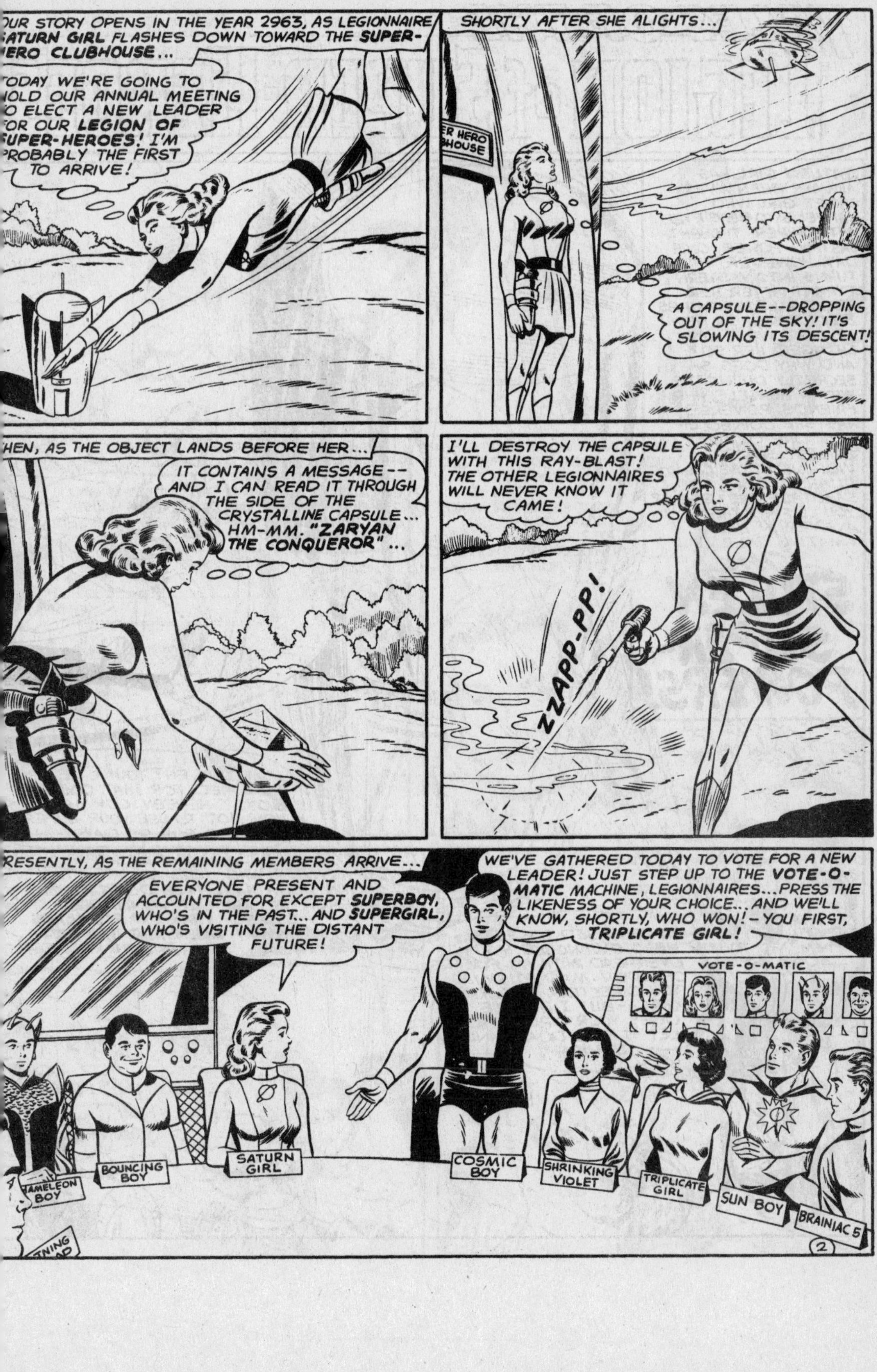
OUR STORY OPENS IN THE YEAR 2963, AS LEGIONNAIRE SATURN GIRL FLASHES DOWN TOWARD THE SUPER-HERO CLUBHOUSE...
TODAY WE'RE GOING TO HOLD OUR ANNUAL MEETING TO ELECT A NEW LEADER FOR OUR LEGION OF SUPER-HEROES! I'M PROBABLY THE FIRST TO ARRIVE!
SHORTLY AFTER SHE ALIGHTS...
A CAPSULE--DROPPING OUT OF THE SKY! IT'S SLOWING ITS DESCENT!
THEN, AS THE OBJECT LANDS BEFORE HER...
IT CONTAINS A MESSAGE--AND I CAN READ IT THROUGH THE SIDE OF THE CRYSTALLINE CAPSULE... HM-MM. "ZARYAN THE CONQUEROR"...
I'LL DESTROY THE CAPSULE WITH THIS RAY-BLAST! THE OTHER LEGIONNAIRES WILL NEVER KNOW IT CAME!
ZZAPP-PP!
PRESENTLY, AS THE REMAINING MEMBERS ARRIVE...
EVERYONE PRESENT AND ACCOUNTED FOR EXCEPT SUPERBOY, WHO'S IN THE PAST... AND SUPERGIRL, WHO'S VISITING THE DISTANT FUTURE!
WE'VE GATHERED TODAY TO VOTE FOR A NEW LEADER! JUST STEP UP TO THE VOTE-O-MATIC MACHINE, LEGIONNAIRES... PRESS THE LIKENESS OF YOUR CHOICE... AND WE'LL KNOW, SHORTLY, WHO WON! – YOU FIRST, TRIPLICATE GIRL!
VOTE-O-MATIC
BOUNCING BOY
SATURN GIRL
COSMIC BOY
SHRINKING VIOLET
TRIPLICATE GIRL
SUN BOY
BRAINIAC 5
2

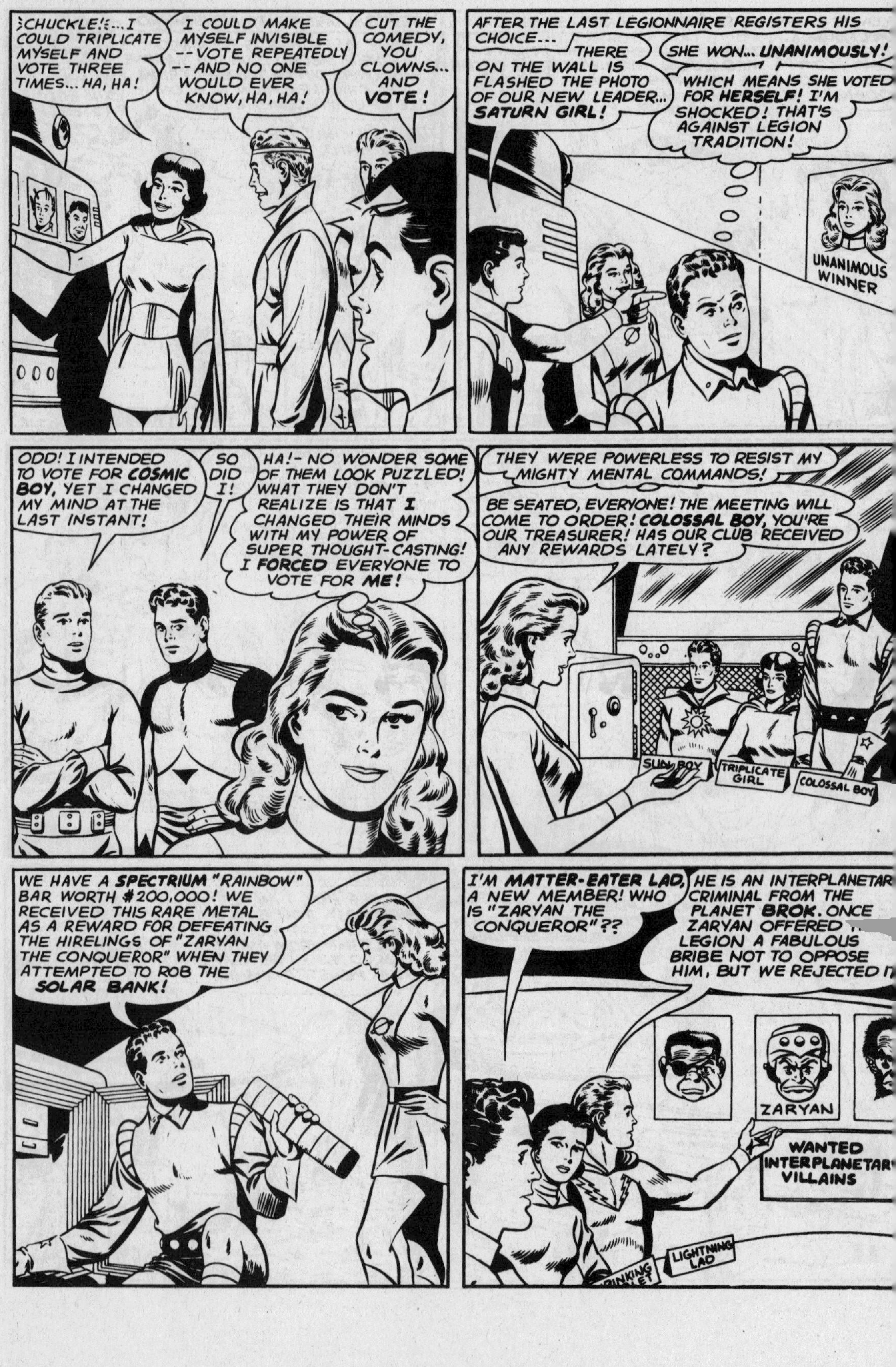

CHUCKLE!... I COULD TRIPLICATE MYSELF AND VOTE THREE TIMES... HA, HA!
I COULD MAKE MYSELF INVISIBLE --VOTE REPEATEDLY --AND NO ONE WOULD EVER KNOW, HA, HA!
CUT THE COMEDY, YOU CLOWNS... AND **VOTE**!
AFTER THE LAST LEGIONNAIRE REGISTERS HIS CHOICE...
THERE ON THE WALL IS FLASHED THE PHOTO OF OUR NEW LEADER... **SATURN GIRL**!
SHE WON... **UNANIMOUSLY**!
WHICH MEANS SHE VOTED FOR **HERSELF**! I'M SHOCKED! THAT'S AGAINST LEGION TRADITION!
UNANIMOUS WINNER
ODD! I INTENDED TO VOTE FOR **COSMIC BOY**, YET I CHANGED MY MIND AT THE LAST INSTANT!
SO DID I!
HA!- NO WONDER SOME OF THEM LOOK PUZZLED! WHAT THEY DON'T REALIZE IS THAT **I** CHANGED THEIR MINDS WITH MY POWER OF SUPER THOUGHT-CASTING! I **FORCED** EVERYONE TO VOTE FOR **ME**!
THEY WERE POWERLESS TO RESIST MY MIGHTY MENTAL COMMANDS!
BE SEATED, EVERYONE! THE MEETING WILL COME TO ORDER! **COLOSSAL BOY**, YOU'RE OUR TREASURER! HAS OUR CLUB RECEIVED ANY REWARDS LATELY?
SUN BOY
TRIPLICATE GIRL
COLOSSAL BOY
WE HAVE A **SPECTRUM** "RAINBOW" BAR WORTH $200,000! WE RECEIVED THIS RARE METAL AS A REWARD FOR DEFEATING THE HIRELINGS OF "ZARYAN THE CONQUEROR" WHEN THEY ATTEMPTED TO ROB THE **SOLAR BANK**!
I'M **MATTER-EATER LAD**, A NEW MEMBER! WHO IS "ZARYAN THE CONQUEROR"??
HE IS AN INTERPLANETAR CRIMINAL FROM THE PLANET **BROK**. ONCE ZARYAN OFFERED LEGION A FABULOUS BRIBE NOT TO OPPOSE HIM, BUT WE REJECTED IT
ZARYAN
WANTED INTERPLANETAR VILLAINS
LIGHTNING LAD

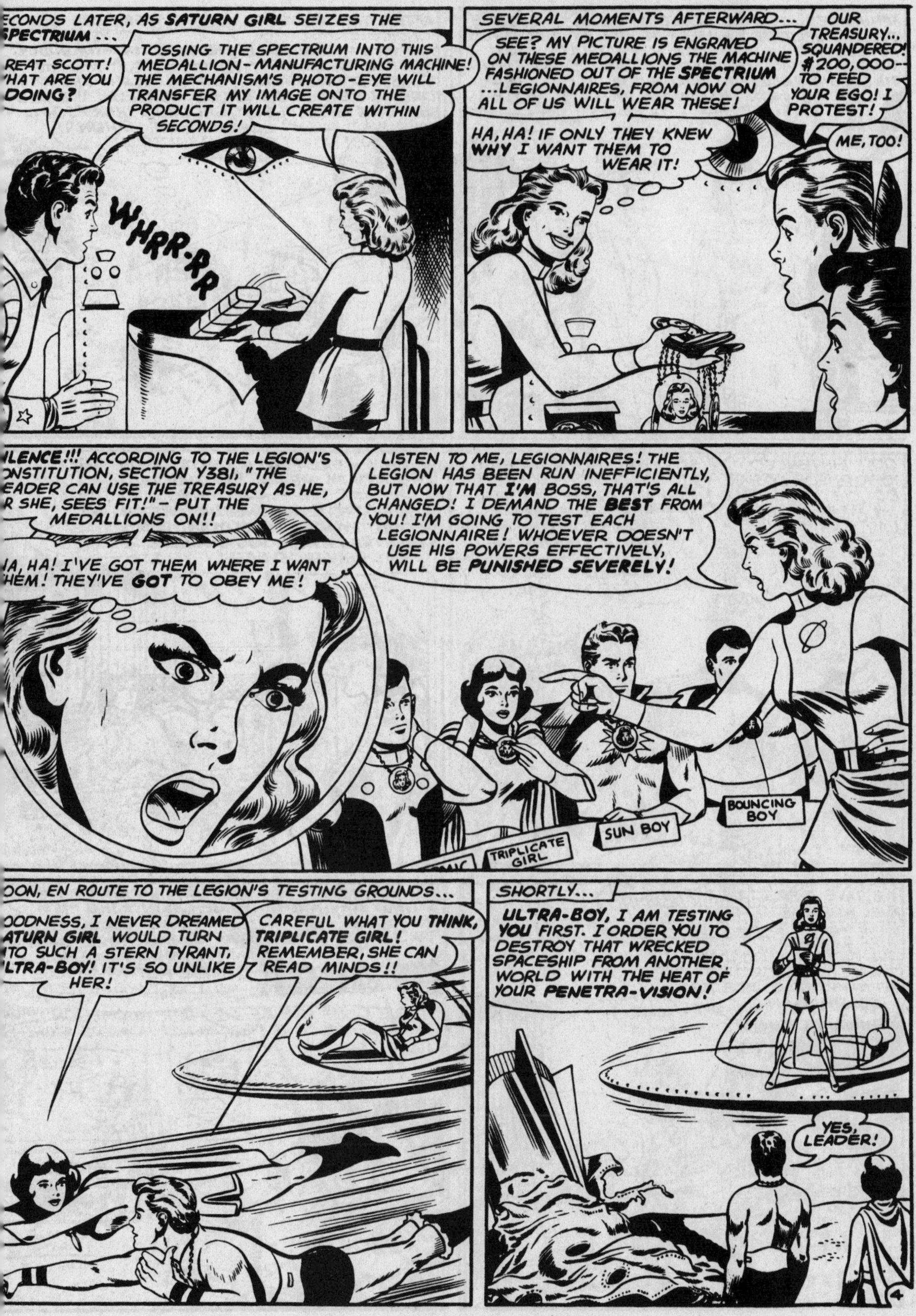
ECONDS LATER, AS SATURN GIRL SEIZES THE SPECTRIUM...
REAT SCOTT! WHAT ARE YOU DOING?
TOSSING THE SPECTRIUM INTO THIS MEDALLION-MANUFACTURING MACHINE! THE MECHANISM'S PHOTO-EYE WILL TRANSFER MY IMAGE ONTO THE PRODUCT IT WILL CREATE WITHIN SECONDS!
WHRR-RR
SEVERAL MOMENTS AFTERWARD...
SEE? MY PICTURE IS ENGRAVED ON THESE MEDALLIONS THE MACHINE FASHIONED OUT OF THE SPECTRIUM ...LEGIONNAIRES, FROM NOW ON ALL OF US WILL WEAR THESE!
OUR TREASURY... SQUANDERED! $200,000-- TO FEED YOUR EGO! I PROTEST!
ME, TOO!
HA, HA! IF ONLY THEY KNEW WHY I WANT THEM TO WEAR IT!
ILENCE!!! ACCORDING TO THE LEGION'S ONSTITUTION, SECTION Y381, "THE EADER CAN USE THE TREASURY AS HE, R SHE, SEES FIT!" - PUT THE MEDALLIONS ON!!
HA, HA! I'VE GOT THEM WHERE I WANT HEM! THEY'VE GOT TO OBEY ME!
LISTEN TO ME, LEGIONNAIRES! THE LEGION HAS BEEN RUN INEFFICIENTLY, BUT NOW THAT I'M BOSS, THAT'S ALL CHANGED! I DEMAND THE BEST FROM YOU! I'M GOING TO TEST EACH LEGIONNAIRE! WHOEVER DOESN'T USE HIS POWERS EFFECTIVELY, WILL BE PUNISHED SEVERELY!
BOUNCING BOY
SUN BOY
TRIPLICATE GIRL
OON, EN ROUTE TO THE LEGION'S TESTING GROUNDS...
OODNESS, I NEVER DREAMED ATURN GIRL WOULD TURN TO SUCH A STERN TYRANT, LTRA-BOY! IT'S SO UNLIKE HER!
CAREFUL WHAT YOU THINK, TRIPLICATE GIRL! REMEMBER, SHE CAN READ MINDS!!
SHORTLY...
ULTRA-BOY, I AM TESTING YOU FIRST. I ORDER YOU TO DESTROY THAT WRECKED SPACESHIP FROM ANOTHER WORLD WITH THE HEAT OF YOUR PENETRA-VISION!
YES, LEADER!
4

Panel 1: AH-HHH! CONCENTRATING HARD ON HIS **SPECTRIUM** MEDALLION, AS HE USES HIS FANTASTIC VISION, I'M ACTIVATING THE METAL'S UNIQUE PROPERTIES SO THAT HIS AMAZING POWER IS BEING **DUPLICATED** WITHIN ME! NOW **I**, TOO, POSSESS **PENETRA-VISION!!**

SSSS-SSSSSSSS...

Panel 2: AFTER THE TEST...

YOU **FAIL!** I ORDERED YOU TO DESTROY THE SHIP, BUT YOU NEGLECTED TO MELT DOWN ITS TAIL. FOR THAT ERROR, I FORBID YOU TO USE YOUR SUPER-POWER FOR 20 DAYS OR TAKE PART IN ANY LEGION MISSIONS! NOW LEAVE!

I MELTED EVERYTHING EXCEPT THE SHIP'S TAIL! USING A TECHNICALITY SHE'S BEING UNREASONABLY HARSH!

Panel 3: MINUTES LATER, IN ANOTHER PART OF THE TESTING AREA...

TRIPLICATE GIRL, YOU'RE NEXT! DEFEND YOURSELF WITH THE RAY GUN I'VE TOSSED TO YOU! – IN A FEW MOMENTS, YOU'LL BE ATTACKED BY A STARTLING MENACE! USE YOUR POWERS TO FIGHT IT! ARE YOU READY?

READY, **SATURN GIRL!**

Panel 4: THEN...

AWP! A...A **HYDRA-HEADED M-MONSTER!**...LUCKILY, I'M FROM THE PLANET **CARGG**, WHERE A TRIPLE SUN GAVE EVERYONE ON MY WORLD THE POWER TO SPLIT INTO **THREE** BODIES! HERE GOES!!

Panel 5:

AT LEAST **ONE** OF MY THREE FORMS WILL SUCCEED IN FORCING THE CREATURE INTO THAT CAGE WITH THESE POWER-RAYS BEFORE THE BEAST CAN OVERPOWER THE OTHER TWO OF US!

HA, HA, HA! IDIOT!

}ULP!{ – IT'S LEAPING R-RIGHT THROUGH US!!!??

Panel 6:

YOU "BATTLED" A **NON-EXISTENT** CREATURE...WHAT YOU SAW WAS A **3-D** IMAGE CAST BY THIS FILM PROJECTOR! – BECAUSE YOU WERE FOOLED, I FORBID YOU TO USE YOUR POWERS FOR 30 DAYS OR TAKE PART IN ANY LEGION MISSION. NOW CHANGE BACK TO YOUR **SINGLE** FORM!

LITTLE DOES SHE REALIZE HER MEDALLION NOW ENABLES **ME** TO DUPLICATE HER POWERS WHENEVER I WISH!

}SOB!{

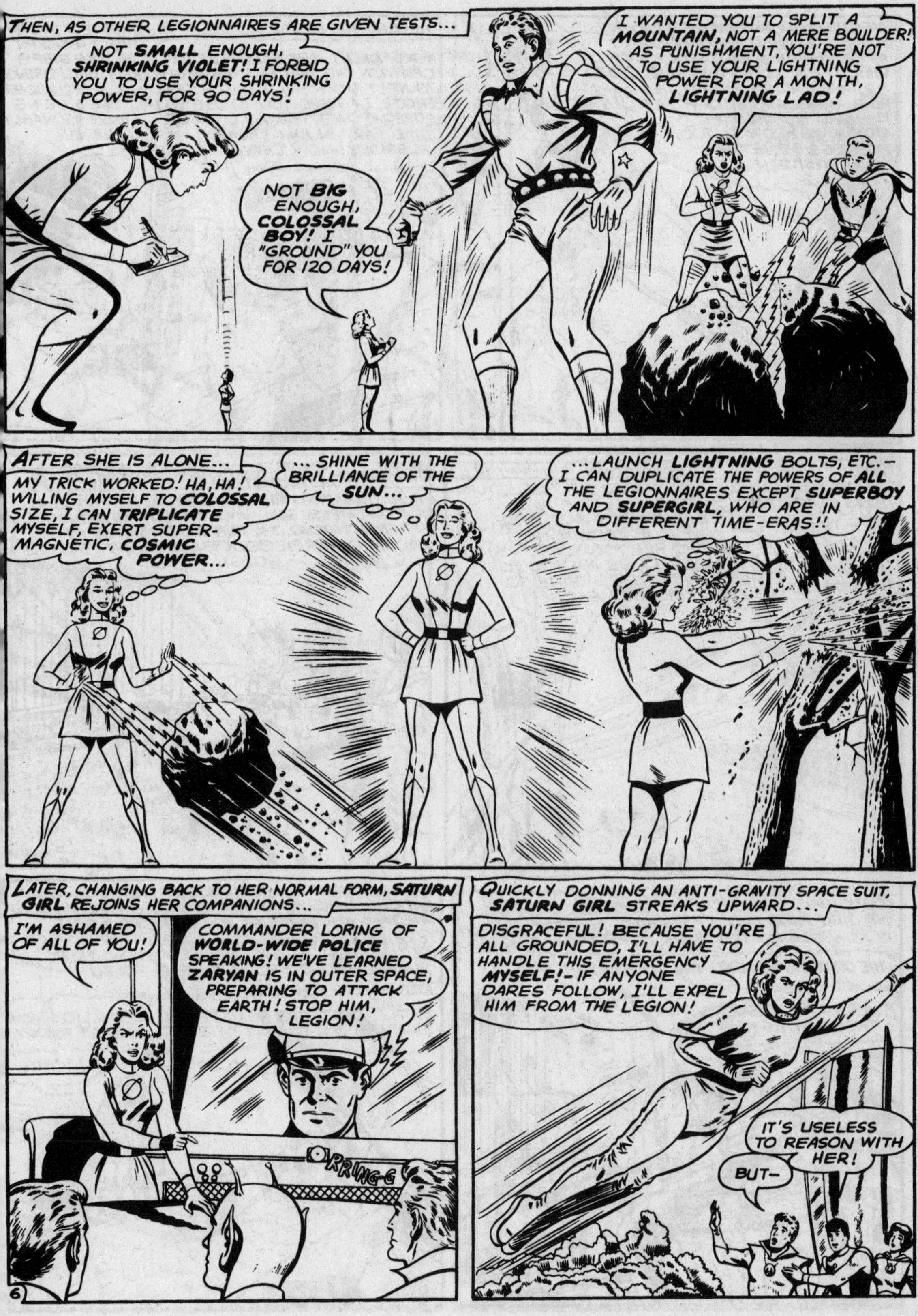

THEN, AS OTHER LEGIONNAIRES ARE GIVEN TESTS...
NOT SMALL ENOUGH, SHRINKING VIOLET! I FORBID YOU TO USE YOUR SHRINKING POWER, FOR 90 DAYS!
NOT BIG ENOUGH, COLOSSAL BOY! I "GROUND" YOU FOR 120 DAYS!
I WANTED YOU TO SPLIT A MOUNTAIN, NOT A MERE BOULDER! AS PUNISHMENT, YOU'RE NOT TO USE YOUR LIGHTNING POWER FOR A MONTH, LIGHTNING LAD!
AFTER SHE IS ALONE...
MY TRICK WORKED! HA, HA! WILLING MYSELF TO COLOSSAL SIZE, I CAN TRIPLICATE MYSELF, EXERT SUPER-MAGNETIC, COSMIC POWER...
... SHINE WITH THE BRILLIANCE OF THE SUN...
...LAUNCH LIGHTNING BOLTS, ETC.– I CAN DUPLICATE THE POWERS OF ALL THE LEGIONNAIRES EXCEPT SUPERBOY AND SUPERGIRL, WHO ARE IN DIFFERENT TIME-ERAS!!
LATER, CHANGING BACK TO HER NORMAL FORM, SATURN GIRL REJOINS HER COMPANIONS...
I'M ASHAMED OF ALL OF YOU!
COMMANDER LORING OF WORLD-WIDE POLICE SPEAKING! WE'VE LEARNED ZARYAN IS IN OUTER SPACE, PREPARING TO ATTACK EARTH! STOP HIM, LEGION!
RRING-G
6
QUICKLY DONNING AN ANTI-GRAVITY SPACE SUIT, SATURN GIRL STREAKS UPWARD...
DISGRACEFUL! BECAUSE YOU'RE ALL GROUNDED, I'LL HAVE TO HANDLE THIS EMERGENCY MYSELF!– IF ANYONE DARES FOLLOW, I'LL EXPEL HIM FROM THE LEGION!
IT'S USELESS TO REASON WITH HER!
BUT–

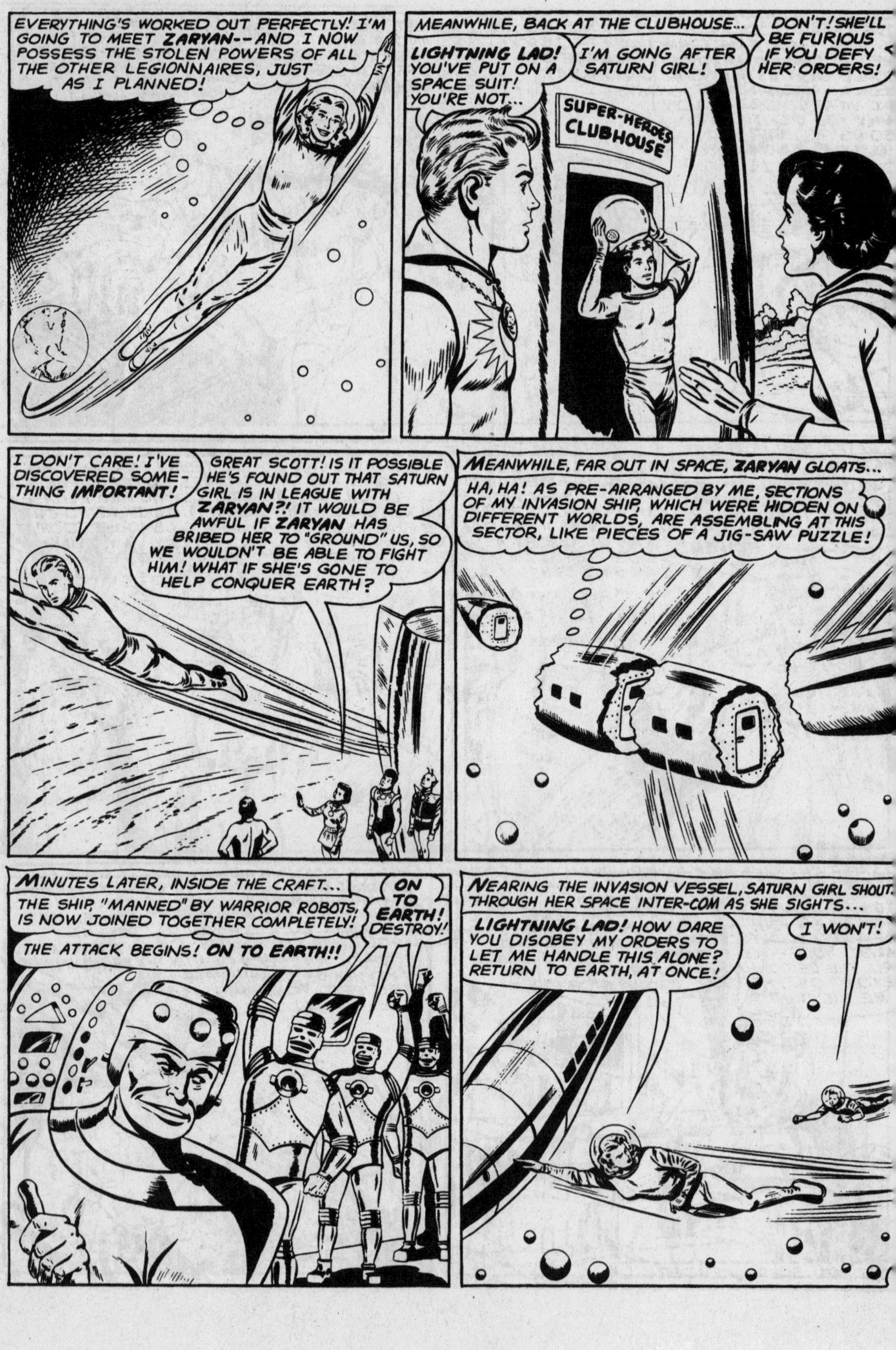
EVERYTHING'S WORKED OUT PERFECTLY! I'M GOING TO MEET ZARYAN--AND I NOW POSSESS THE STOLEN POWERS OF ALL THE OTHER LEGIONNAIRES, JUST AS I PLANNED!
MEANWHILE, BACK AT THE CLUBHOUSE...
LIGHTNING LAD! YOU'VE PUT ON A SPACE SUIT! YOU'RE NOT...
I'M GOING AFTER SATURN GIRL!
DON'T! SHE'LL BE FURIOUS IF YOU DEFY HER ORDERS!
SUPER-HEROES CLUBHOUSE
I DON'T CARE! I'VE DISCOVERED SOMETHING IMPORTANT!
GREAT SCOTT! IS IT POSSIBLE HE'S FOUND OUT THAT SATURN GIRL IS IN LEAGUE WITH ZARYAN?! IT WOULD BE AWFUL IF ZARYAN HAS BRIBED HER TO "GROUND" US, SO WE WOULDN'T BE ABLE TO FIGHT HIM! WHAT IF SHE'S GONE TO HELP CONQUER EARTH?
MEANWHILE, FAR OUT IN SPACE, ZARYAN GLOATS...
HA, HA! AS PRE-ARRANGED BY ME, SECTIONS OF MY INVASION SHIP, WHICH WERE HIDDEN ON DIFFERENT WORLDS, ARE ASSEMBLING AT THIS SECTOR, LIKE PIECES OF A JIG-SAW PUZZLE!
MINUTES LATER, INSIDE THE CRAFT...
THE SHIP, "MANNED" BY WARRIOR ROBOTS, IS NOW JOINED TOGETHER COMPLETELY!
THE ATTACK BEGINS! ON TO EARTH!!
ON TO EARTH! DESTROY!
NEARING THE INVASION VESSEL, SATURN GIRL SHOUTS THROUGH HER SPACE INTER-COM AS SHE SIGHTS...
LIGHTNING LAD! HOW DARE YOU DISOBEY MY ORDERS TO LET ME HANDLE THIS ALONE? RETURN TO EARTH, AT ONCE!
I WON'T!

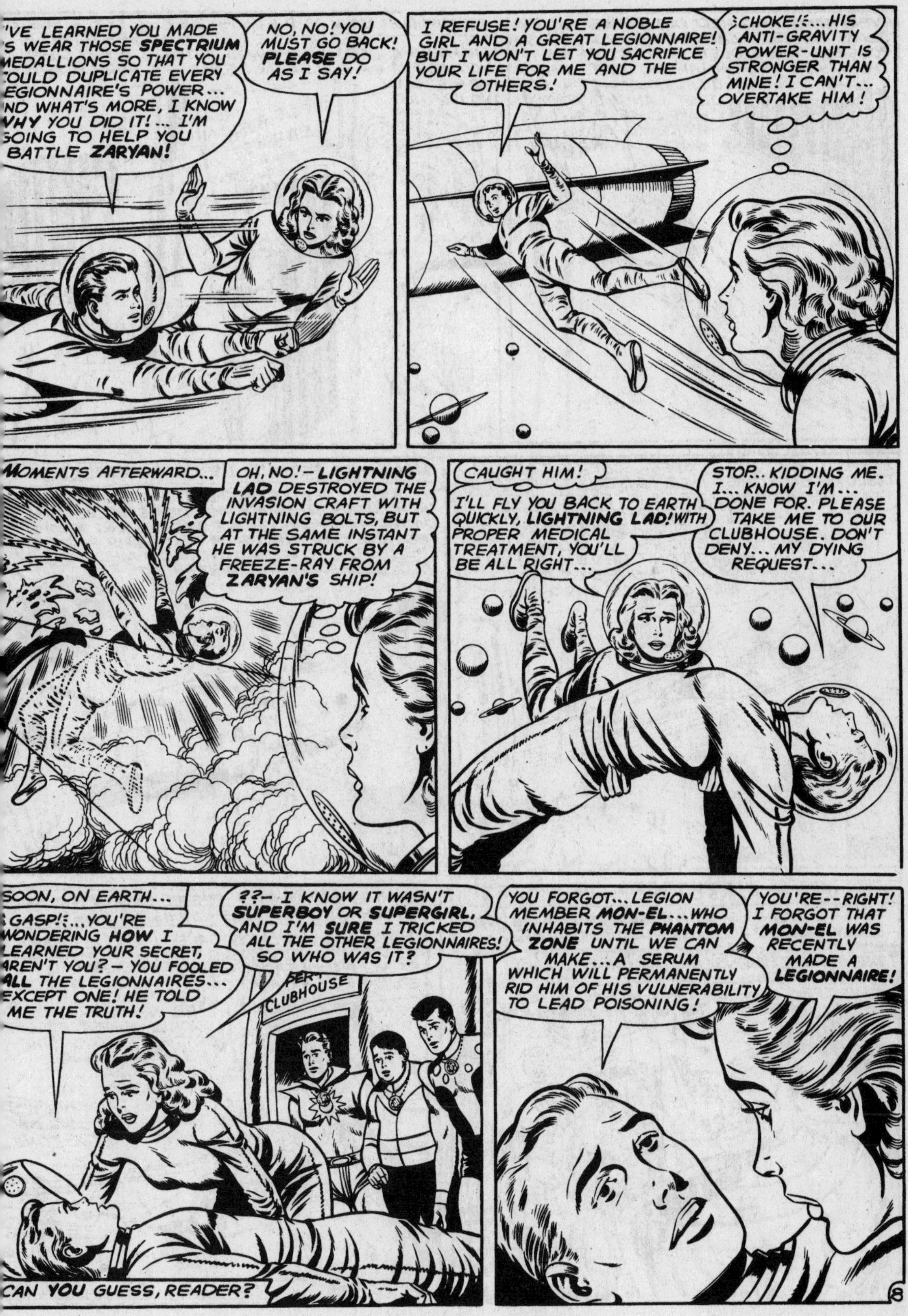
I'VE LEARNED YOU MADE US WEAR THOSE SPECTRIUM MEDALLIONS SO THAT YOU COULD DUPLICATE EVERY LEGIONNAIRE'S POWER... AND WHAT'S MORE, I KNOW WHY YOU DID IT!... I'M GOING TO HELP YOU BATTLE ZARYAN!
NO, NO! YOU MUST GO BACK! PLEASE DO AS I SAY!
I REFUSE! YOU'RE A NOBLE GIRL AND A GREAT LEGIONNAIRE! BUT I WON'T LET YOU SACRIFICE YOUR LIFE FOR ME AND THE OTHERS!
CHOKE!... HIS ANTI-GRAVITY POWER-UNIT IS STRONGER THAN MINE! I CAN'T... OVERTAKE HIM!
MOMENTS AFTERWARD...
OH, NO!– LIGHTNING LAD DESTROYED THE INVASION CRAFT WITH LIGHTNING BOLTS, BUT AT THE SAME INSTANT HE WAS STRUCK BY A FREEZE-RAY FROM ZARYAN'S SHIP!
CAUGHT HIM!
I'LL FLY YOU BACK TO EARTH QUICKLY, LIGHTNING LAD! WITH PROPER MEDICAL TREATMENT, YOU'LL BE ALL RIGHT...
STOP.. KIDDING ME. I... KNOW I'M... DONE FOR. PLEASE TAKE ME TO OUR CLUBHOUSE. DON'T DENY... MY DYING REQUEST...
SOON, ON EARTH...
GASP!... YOU'RE WONDERING HOW I LEARNED YOUR SECRET, AREN'T YOU?– YOU FOOLED ALL THE LEGIONNAIRES... EXCEPT ONE! HE TOLD ME THE TRUTH!
??– I KNOW IT WASN'T SUPERBOY OR SUPERGIRL, AND I'M SURE I TRICKED ALL THE OTHER LEGIONNAIRES! SO WHO WAS IT?
CLUBHOUSE
CAN YOU GUESS, READER?
YOU FORGOT... LEGION MEMBER MON-EL... WHO INHABITS THE PHANTOM ZONE UNTIL WE CAN MAKE... A SERUM WHICH WILL PERMANENTLY RID HIM OF HIS VULNERABILITY TO LEAD POISONING!
YOU'RE--RIGHT! I FORGOT THAT MON-EL WAS RECENTLY MADE A LEGIONNAIRE!
8

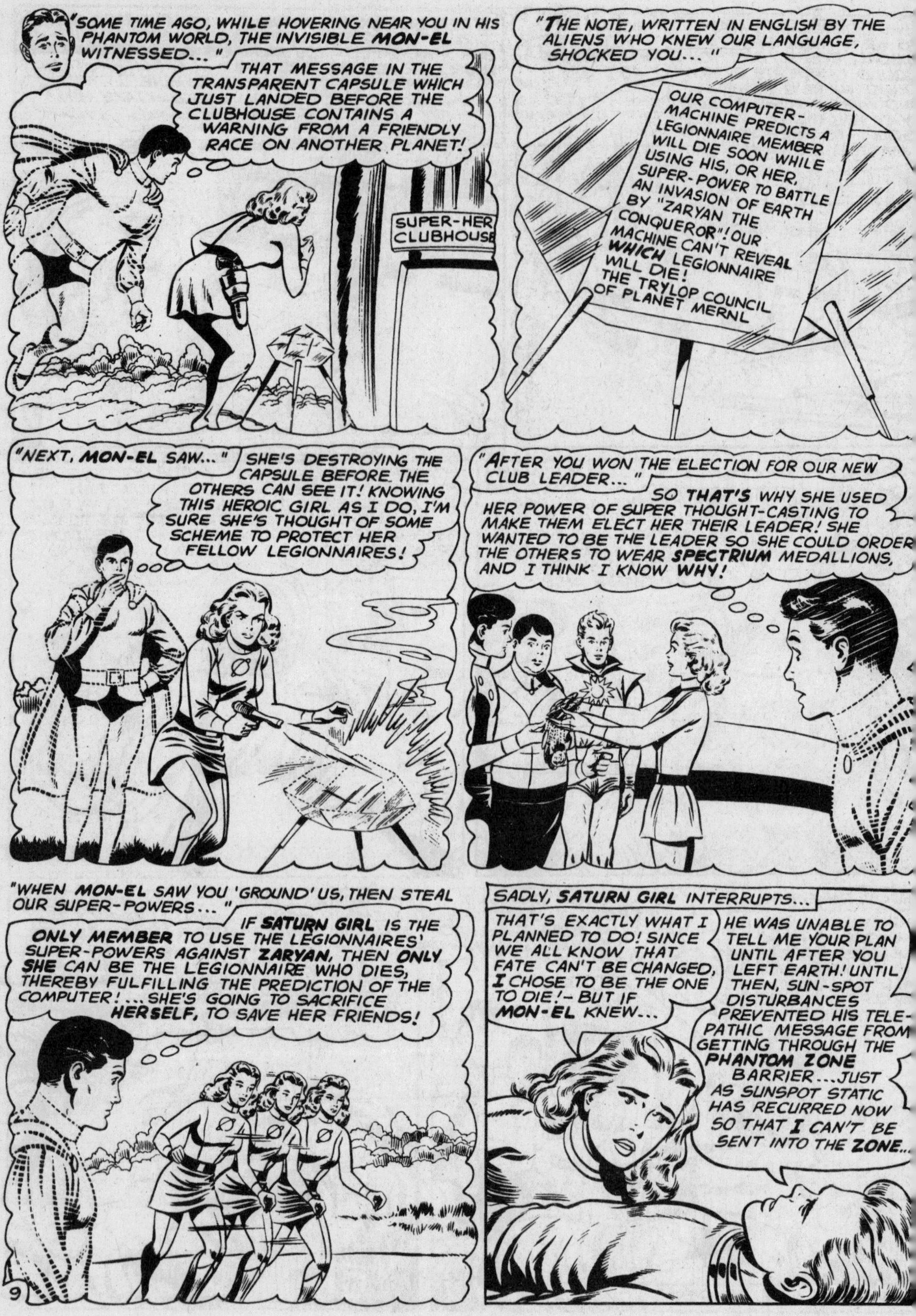
"SOME TIME AGO, WHILE HOVERING NEAR YOU IN HIS PHANTOM WORLD, THE INVISIBLE MON-EL WITNESSED..."
THAT MESSAGE IN THE TRANSPARENT CAPSULE WHICH JUST LANDED BEFORE THE CLUBHOUSE CONTAINS A WARNING FROM A FRIENDLY RACE ON ANOTHER PLANET!
SUPER-HER CLUBHOUSE
"THE NOTE, WRITTEN IN ENGLISH BY THE ALIENS WHO KNEW OUR LANGUAGE, SHOCKED YOU..."
OUR COMPUTER-MACHINE PREDICTS A LEGIONNAIRE MEMBER WILL DIE SOON WHILE USING HIS, OR HER, SUPER-POWER TO BATTLE AN INVASION OF EARTH BY "ZARYAN THE CONQUEROR"! OUR MACHINE CAN'T REVEAL WHICH LEGIONNAIRE WILL DIE! THE TRYLOP COUNCIL OF PLANET MERNL
"NEXT, MON-EL SAW..."
SHE'S DESTROYING THE CAPSULE BEFORE THE OTHERS CAN SEE IT! KNOWING THIS HEROIC GIRL AS I DO, I'M SURE SHE'S THOUGHT OF SOME SCHEME TO PROTECT HER FELLOW LEGIONNAIRES!
"AFTER YOU WON THE ELECTION FOR OUR NEW CLUB LEADER..."
SO THAT'S WHY SHE USED HER POWER OF SUPER THOUGHT-CASTING TO MAKE THEM ELECT HER THEIR LEADER! SHE WANTED TO BE THE LEADER SO SHE COULD ORDER THE OTHERS TO WEAR SPECTRIUM MEDALLIONS, AND I THINK I KNOW WHY!
"WHEN MON-EL SAW YOU 'GROUND' US, THEN STEAL OUR SUPER-POWERS..."
IF SATURN GIRL IS THE ONLY MEMBER TO USE THE LEGIONNAIRES' SUPER-POWERS AGAINST ZARYAN, THEN ONLY SHE CAN BE THE LEGIONNAIRE WHO DIES, THEREBY FULFILLING THE PREDICTION OF THE COMPUTER! ...SHE'S GOING TO SACRIFICE HERSELF, TO SAVE HER FRIENDS!
9
SADLY, SATURN GIRL INTERRUPTS...
THAT'S EXACTLY WHAT I PLANNED TO DO! SINCE WE ALL KNOW THAT FATE CAN'T BE CHANGED, I CHOSE TO BE THE ONE TO DIE! -- BUT IF MON-EL KNEW...
HE WAS UNABLE TO TELL ME YOUR PLAN UNTIL AFTER YOU LEFT EARTH! UNTIL THEN, SUN-SPOT DISTURBANCES PREVENTED HIS TELEPATHIC MESSAGE FROM GETTING THROUGH THE PHANTOM ZONE BARRIER... JUST AS SUNSPOT STATIC HAS RECURRED NOW SO THAT I CAN'T BE SENT INTO THE ZONE...

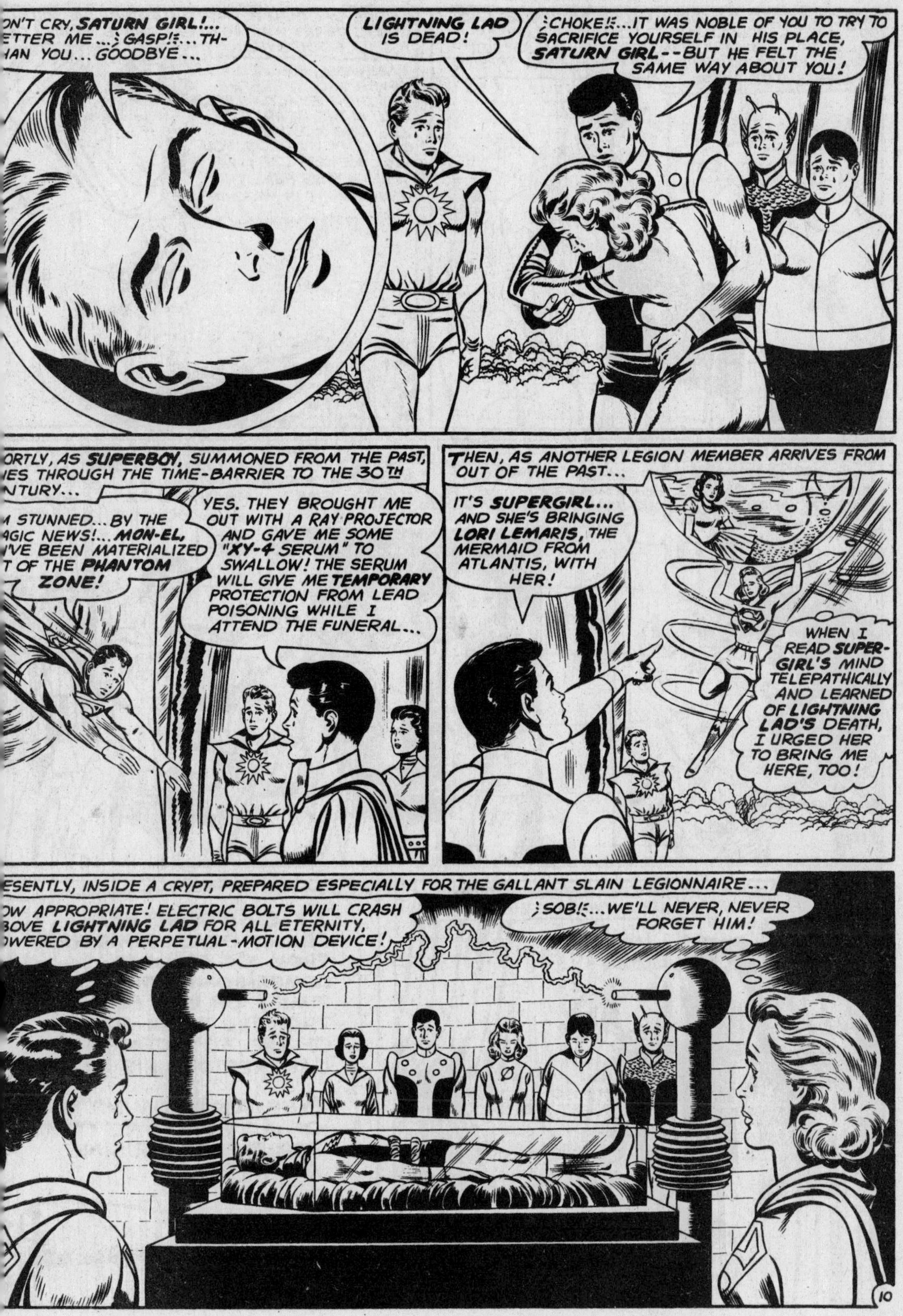
ON'T CRY, SATURN GIRL!... ETTER ME...;GASP!;...TH- HAN YOU... GOODBYE...
LIGHTNING LAD IS DEAD!
;CHOKE!;...IT WAS NOBLE OF YOU TO TRY TO SACRIFICE YOURSELF IN HIS PLACE, SATURN GIRL--BUT HE FELT THE SAME WAY ABOUT YOU!
ORTLY, AS SUPERBOY, SUMMONED FROM THE PAST, ES THROUGH THE TIME-BARRIER TO THE 30TH NTURY...
M STUNNED...BY THE AGIC NEWS!...MON-EL, VE BEEN MATERIALIZED T OF THE PHANTOM ZONE!
YES. THEY BROUGHT ME OUT WITH A RAY PROJECTOR AND GAVE ME SOME "XY-4 SERUM" TO SWALLOW! THE SERUM WILL GIVE ME TEMPORARY PROTECTION FROM LEAD POISONING WHILE I ATTEND THE FUNERAL...
THEN, AS ANOTHER LEGION MEMBER ARRIVES FROM OUT OF THE PAST...
IT'S SUPERGIRL... AND SHE'S BRINGING LORI LEMARIS, THE MERMAID FROM ATLANTIS, WITH HER!
WHEN I READ SUPER-GIRL'S MIND TELEPATHICALLY AND LEARNED OF LIGHTNING LAD'S DEATH, I URGED HER TO BRING ME HERE, TOO!
ESENTLY, INSIDE A CRYPT, PREPARED ESPECIALLY FOR THE GALLANT SLAIN LEGIONNAIRE...
OW APPROPRIATE! ELECTRIC BOLTS WILL CRASH BOVE LIGHTNING LAD FOR ALL ETERNITY, OWERED BY A PERPETUAL-MOTION DEVICE!
;SOB!;...WE'LL NEVER, NEVER FORGET HIM!
10

NOT ONLY DOES ALL EARTH MOURN *LIGHTNING LAD*, BUT MANY CIVILIZATIONS THROUGHOUT A DOZEN GALAXIES AND FAR-FLUNG ISLAND-UNIVERSES LOWER FLAGS TO HALF-MAST IN A FINAL TRIBUTE TO *LIGHTNING LAD*...

ALIENS OF OTHER PLANETS ALSO BID THE YOUTH WHOSE HEART WAS AS GREAT AS HIS MIGHTY DEED A SAD GOODBYE...

FAREWELL, BRAVE LAD! NEVER WILL THERE BE ANOTHER EXACTLY LIKE YOU! IN THE HEARTS OF ALL WHO ADMIRED YOU, ON MANY WORLDS, YOU WILL NEVER DIE! WE WILL ALWAYS FEEL THAT YOUR SPIRIT IS WATCHING US!

ON EARTH, AS THE SUPER-HEROES LEAVE THE CRYPT...

THEY SAY THAT THE EXTRA SUPER-POWERS *SATURN GIRL* "BORROWED" HAVE ALREADY WORN OFF!... I WONDER WHAT SHE'S THINKING, NOW?

I *TRIED* TO SAVE YOU, *LIGHTNING LAD*, IF ONLY *I* COULD HAVE DIED IN YOUR PLACE, AS I INTENDED!... BUT IT WAS ¡SOB!: ...MEANT TO BE... ¡CHOKE!:

AS A FINAL GESTURE, THE LEGIONNAIRES PLACE A STATUE OF *LIGHTNING LAD* IN THEIR CLUBHOUSE, TO HONOR THEIR SLAIN COMRADE...

IN MEMORY OF
LIGHTNING LAD
THE FIRST LEGIONNAIRE
TO PERISH IN ACTION

IS *LIGHTNING LAD* REALLY DEAD...SEPARATED FROM HIS GALLANT COMPANIONS FOR ALL TIME? OR IS IT POSSIBLE THAT THE SUPER-SCIENCE OF THE 30TH CENTURY CAN RESTORE HIS LIFE?

SEE forthcoming issues OF *ADVENTURE* COMICS FOR THE SURPRISING ANSWER!

THE END

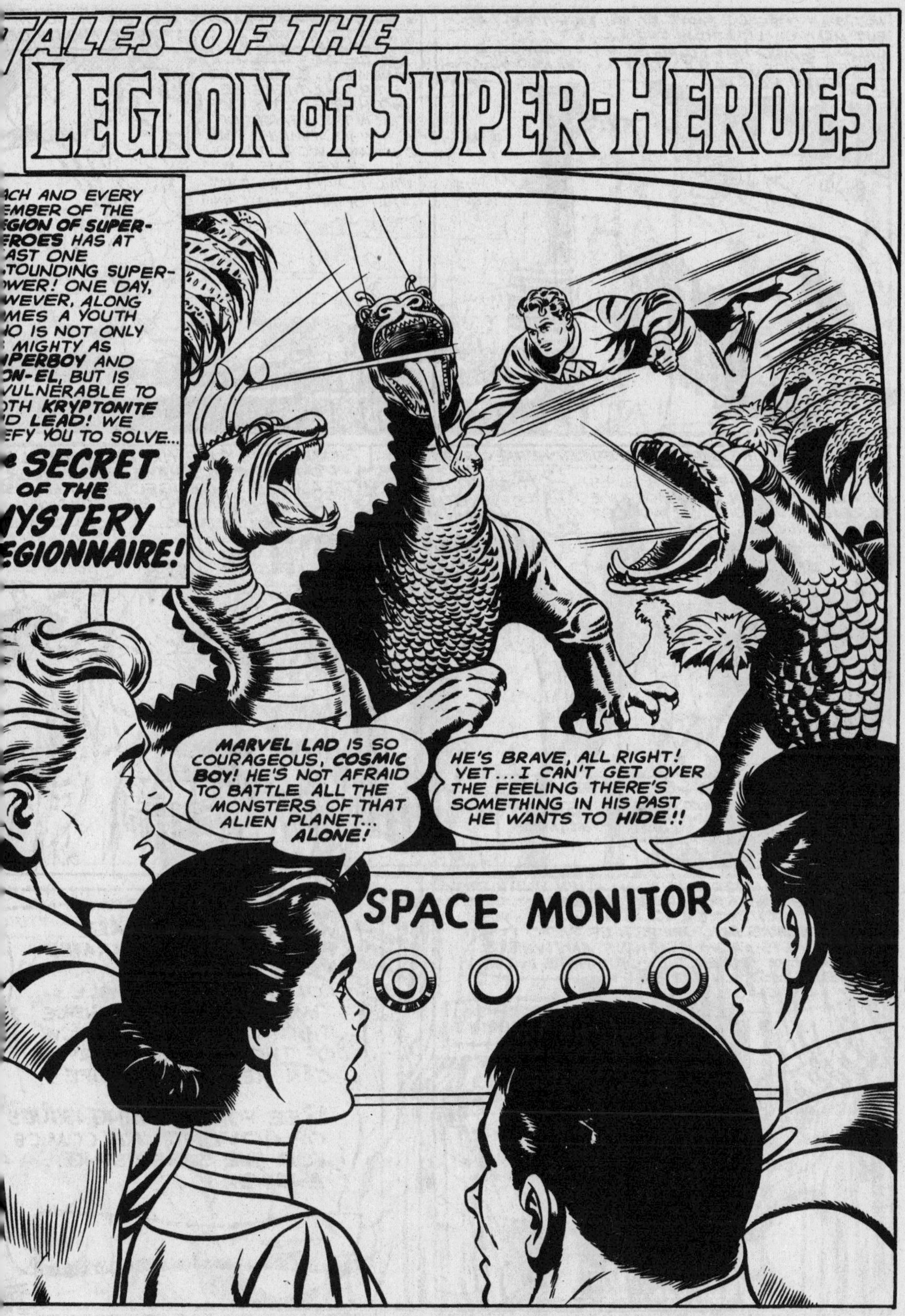
TALES OF THE
LEGION of SUPER-HEROES
ACH AND EVERY EMBER OF THE EGION OF SUPER-EROES HAS AT AST ONE STOUNDING SUPER-OWER! ONE DAY, WEVER, ALONG MES A YOUTH HO IS NOT ONLY MIGHTY AS PERBOY AND ON-EL, BUT IS VULNERABLE TO OTH KRYPTONITE D LEAD! WE EFY YOU TO SOLVE...
SECRET OF THE YSTERY EGIONNAIRE!
MARVEL LAD IS SO COURAGEOUS, COSMIC BOY! HE'S NOT AFRAID TO BATTLE ALL THE MONSTERS OF THAT ALIEN PLANET... ALONE!
HE'S BRAVE, ALL RIGHT! YET... I CAN'T GET OVER THE FEELING THERE'S SOMETHING IN HIS PAST HE WANTS TO HIDE!!
SPACE MONITOR

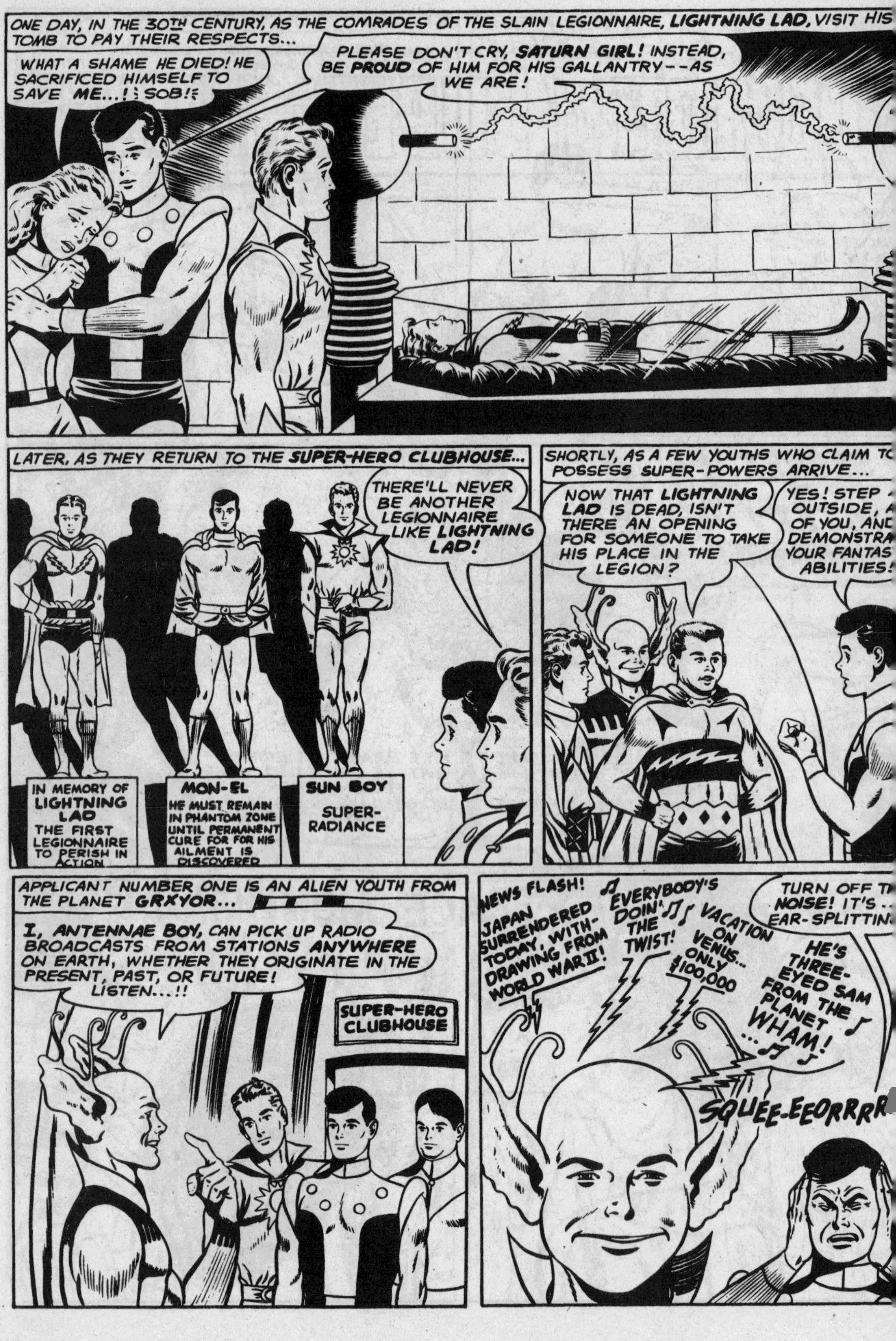

ONE DAY, IN THE 30TH CENTURY, AS THE COMRADES OF THE SLAIN LEGIONNAIRE, LIGHTNING LAD, VISIT HIS TOMB TO PAY THEIR RESPECTS...
WHAT A SHAME HE DIED! HE SACRIFICED HIMSELF TO SAVE ME...! SOB!
PLEASE DON'T CRY, SATURN GIRL! INSTEAD, BE PROUD OF HIM FOR HIS GALLANTRY--AS WE ARE!
LATER, AS THEY RETURN TO THE SUPER-HERO CLUBHOUSE...
THERE'LL NEVER BE ANOTHER LEGIONNAIRE LIKE LIGHTNING LAD!
IN MEMORY OF LIGHTNING LAD THE FIRST LEGIONNAIRE TO PERISH IN ACTION
MON-EL HE MUST REMAIN IN PHANTOM ZONE UNTIL PERMANENT CURE FOR FOR HIS AILMENT IS DISCOVERED
SUN BOY SUPER-RADIANCE
SHORTLY, AS A FEW YOUTHS WHO CLAIM TO POSSESS SUPER-POWERS ARRIVE...
NOW THAT LIGHTNING LAD IS DEAD, ISN'T THERE AN OPENING FOR SOMEONE TO TAKE HIS PLACE IN THE LEGION?
YES! STEP OUTSIDE, OF YOU, AND DEMONSTRA YOUR FANTAS ABILITIES!
APPLICANT NUMBER ONE IS AN ALIEN YOUTH FROM THE PLANET GRXYOR...
I, ANTENNAE BOY, CAN PICK UP RADIO BROADCASTS FROM STATIONS ANYWHERE ON EARTH, WHETHER THEY ORIGINATE IN THE PRESENT, PAST, OR FUTURE! LISTEN...!!
SUPER-HERO CLUBHOUSE
NEWS FLASH! JAPAN SURRENDERED TODAY, WITH-DRAWING FROM WORLD WAR II!
EVERYBODY'S DOIN' THE TWIST!
VACATION ON VENUS... ONLY $100,000
HE'S THREE-EYED SAM FROM THE PLANET WHAM!
TURN OFF THE NOISE! IT'S... EAR-SPLITTIN
SQUEE-EEORRRR

...LETIN!
...NNEDY
...ELECTED
...ESIDENT
...U.S.

COME, JOSEPHINE, IN MY TIME MACHINE!

ER... I CAN'T STOP IT! I DON'T KNOW HOW TO CONTROL THIS POWER PERFECTLY!

ELIMINATED!— NEXT PLEASE!

A CLOAKED YOUTH STEPS FORWARD...

I AM...*THE DYNAMO KID!* I POSSESS THE POWER OF SUPER-LIGHTNING, JUST AS *LIGHTNING LAD* DID! SHALL I DEMONSTRATE?

PLEASE DO!

HE'S A HUMAN DYNAMO... ELECTRICITY IS CRACKLING AROUND HIS BODY!

SUPER HERO CLUBHOUSE

Read the DAILY PLANET-- THE MICROFILM NEWSPAPER THAT BRINGS YOU ALL THE INTERPLANETARY NEWS!

...E THAT ...CKET-PROPELLED ...VERTISING SIGN ...ERHEAD? ...TCH THIS!

GREAT *RINGS OF SATURN!* THE SIGN WAS DESTROYED BY LIGHTNING BOLTS FROM HIS BODY! AMAZING!

GREAT FEAT, *DYNAMO KID!* YOU'LL PAY THE DAMAGE COSTS FOR THAT SIGN, OF COURSE?

HM-MM! I'LL REMOVE A WIRE-CUTTER FROM MY UTILITY-BELT!

OF COURSE! I'M RICH!

Read THE BR...

...ET-- ...AT

...INTERP...

...OW LET'S SEE YOU ...ATTER SOMETHING ... ELSE!

IT'S A CINCH! JUST WATCH, AND I'LL BLAST THAT TREE!

SNIP!

AWP! N-NOTHING'S HAPPENING! I DON'T UNDERSTAND!!

AHA! JUST AS I THOUGHT! THE WIRE I CUT WAS CONNECTED TO A POWERFUL MINIATURE HYPER-BATTERY HIDDEN UNDER YOUR CLOAK! START EXPLAINING, HOAXTER!

3

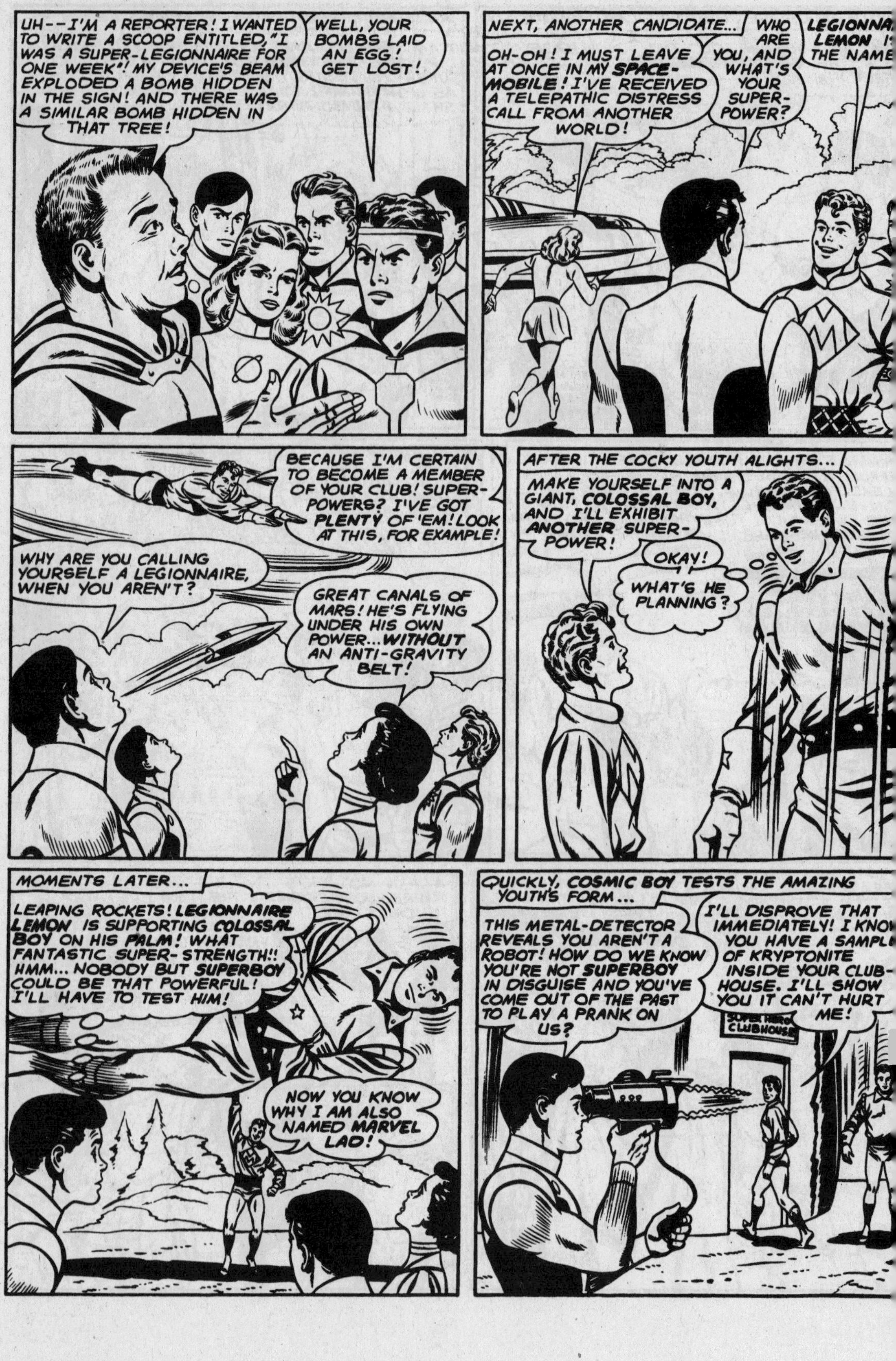

UH--I'M A REPORTER! I WANTED TO WRITE A SCOOP ENTITLED, "I WAS A SUPER-LEGIONNAIRE FOR ONE WEEK"! MY DEVICE'S BEAM EXPLODED A BOMB HIDDEN IN THE SIGN! AND THERE WAS A SIMILAR BOMB HIDDEN IN THAT TREE!
WELL, YOUR BOMBS LAID AN EGG! GET LOST!
NEXT, ANOTHER CANDIDATE...
OH-OH! I MUST LEAVE AT ONCE IN MY SPACE-MOBILE! I'VE RECEIVED A TELEPATHIC DISTRESS CALL FROM ANOTHER WORLD!
WHO ARE YOU, AND WHAT'S YOUR SUPER-POWER?
BECAUSE I'M CERTAIN TO BECOME A MEMBER OF YOUR CLUB! SUPER-POWERS? I'VE GOT PLENTY OF 'EM! LOOK AT THIS, FOR EXAMPLE!
WHY ARE YOU CALLING YOURSELF A LEGIONNAIRE, WHEN YOU AREN'T?
GREAT CANALS OF MARS! HE'S FLYING UNDER HIS OWN POWER...WITHOUT AN ANTI-GRAVITY BELT!
AFTER THE COCKY YOUTH ALIGHTS...
MAKE YOURSELF INTO A GIANT, COLOSSAL BOY, AND I'LL EXHIBIT ANOTHER SUPER-POWER!
OKAY!
WHAT'S HE PLANNING?
MOMENTS LATER...
LEAPING ROCKETS! LEGIONNAIRE LEMON IS SUPPORTING COLOSSAL BOY ON HIS PALM! WHAT FANTASTIC SUPER-STRENGTH!! HMM... NOBODY BUT SUPERBOY COULD BE THAT POWERFUL! I'LL HAVE TO TEST HIM!
NOW YOU KNOW WHY I AM ALSO NAMED MARVEL LAD!
QUICKLY, COSMIC BOY TESTS THE AMAZING YOUTH'S FORM...
THIS METAL-DETECTOR REVEALS YOU AREN'T A ROBOT! HOW DO WE KNOW YOU'RE NOT SUPERBOY IN DISGUISE AND YOU'VE COME OUT OF THE PAST TO PLAY A PRANK ON US?
CLUBHOUSE

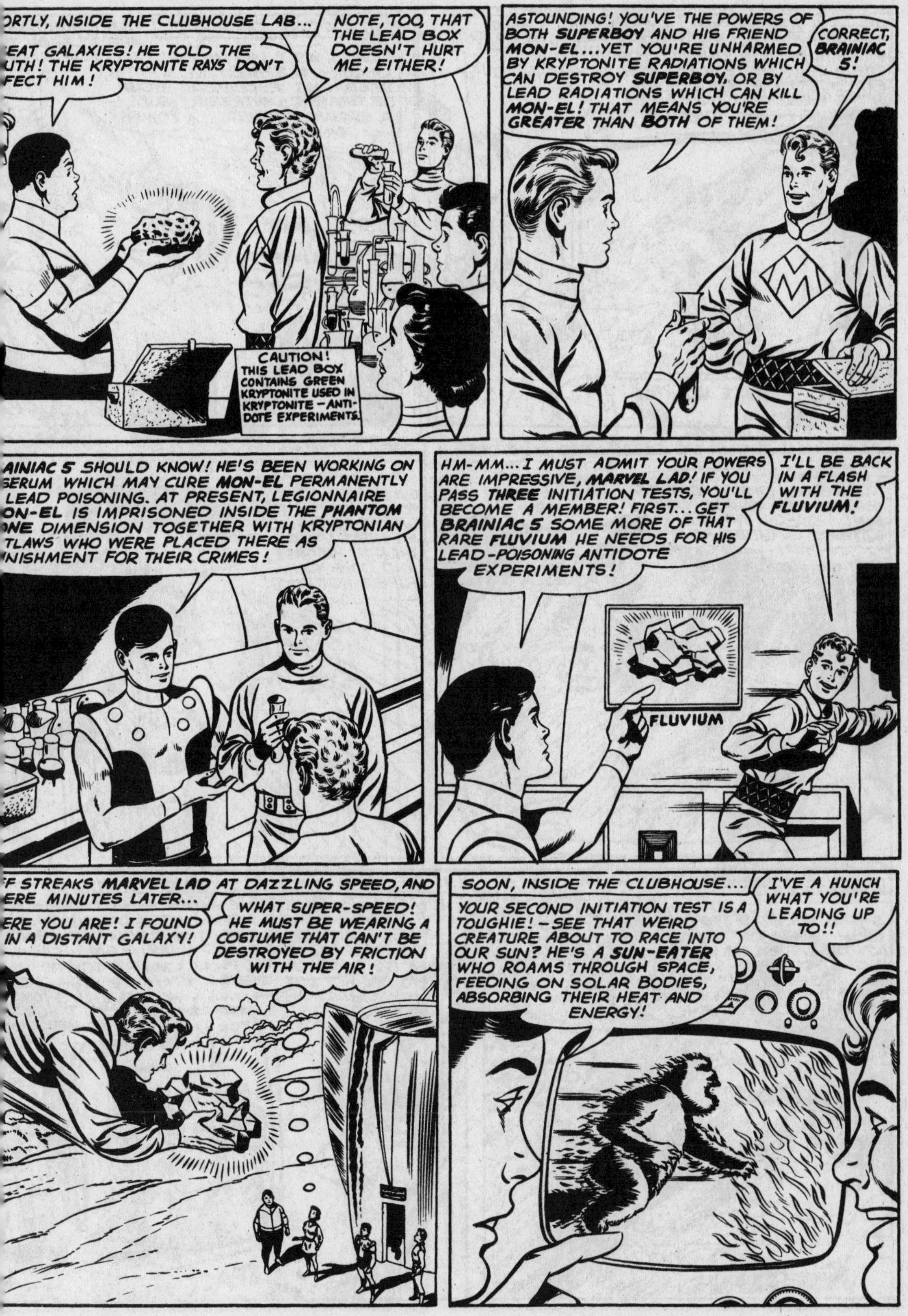
ORTLY, INSIDE THE CLUBHOUSE LAB...
EAT GALAXIES! HE TOLD THE UTH! THE KRYPTONITE RAYS DON'T FECT HIM!
NOTE, TOO, THAT THE LEAD BOX DOESN'T HURT ME, EITHER!
CAUTION! THIS LEAD BOX CONTAINS GREEN KRYPTONITE USED IN KRYPTONITE-ANTI-DOTE EXPERIMENTS.
ASTOUNDING! YOU'VE THE POWERS OF BOTH SUPERBOY AND HIS FRIEND MON-EL...YET YOU'RE UNHARMED BY KRYPTONITE RADIATIONS WHICH CAN DESTROY SUPERBOY, OR BY LEAD RADIATIONS WHICH CAN KILL MON-EL! THAT MEANS YOU'RE GREATER THAN BOTH OF THEM!
CORRECT, BRAINIAC 5!
AINIAC 5 SHOULD KNOW! HE'S BEEN WORKING ON SERUM WHICH MAY CURE MON-EL PERMANENTLY LEAD POISONING. AT PRESENT, LEGIONNAIRE ON-EL IS IMPRISONED INSIDE THE PHANTOM ONE DIMENSION TOGETHER WITH KRYPTONIAN TLAWS WHO WERE PLACED THERE AS NISHMENT FOR THEIR CRIMES!
HM-MM...I MUST ADMIT YOUR POWERS ARE IMPRESSIVE, MARVEL LAD! IF YOU PASS THREE INITIATION TESTS, YOU'LL BECOME A MEMBER! FIRST...GET BRAINIAC 5 SOME MORE OF THAT RARE FLUVIUM HE NEEDS FOR HIS LEAD-POISONING ANTIDOTE EXPERIMENTS!
I'LL BE BACK IN A FLASH WITH THE FLUVIUM!
FLUVIUM
F STREAKS MARVEL LAD AT DAZZLING SPEED, AND ERE MINUTES LATER...
ERE YOU ARE! I FOUND IN A DISTANT GALAXY!
WHAT SUPER-SPEED! HE MUST BE WEARING A COSTUME THAT CAN'T BE DESTROYED BY FRICTION WITH THE AIR!
SOON, INSIDE THE CLUBHOUSE...
YOUR SECOND INITIATION TEST IS A TOUGHIE! -SEE THAT WEIRD CREATURE ABOUT TO RACE INTO OUR SUN? HE'S A SUN-EATER WHO ROAMS THROUGH SPACE, FEEDING ON SOLAR BODIES, ABSORBING THEIR HEAT AND ENERGY!
I'VE A HUNCH WHAT YOU'RE LEADING UP TO!!

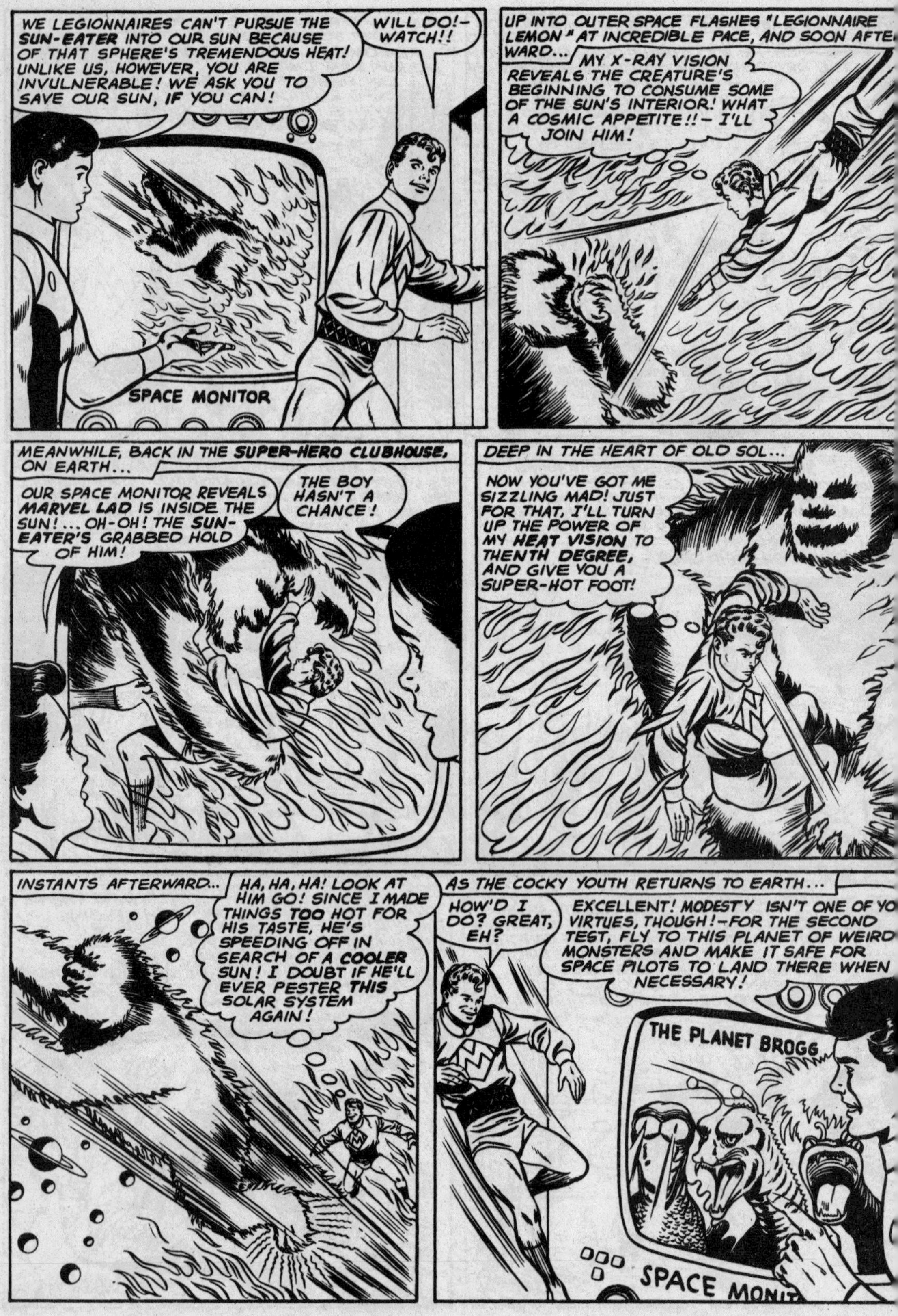
WE LEGIONNAIRES CAN'T PURSUE THE SUN-EATER INTO OUR SUN BECAUSE OF THAT SPHERE'S TREMENDOUS HEAT! UNLIKE US, HOWEVER, YOU ARE INVULNERABLE! WE ASK YOU TO SAVE OUR SUN, IF YOU CAN!
WILL DO!-WATCH!!
SPACE MONITOR
UP INTO OUTER SPACE FLASHES "LEGIONNAIRE LEMON" AT INCREDIBLE PACE, AND SOON AFTE WARD...
MY X-RAY VISION REVEALS THE CREATURE'S BEGINNING TO CONSUME SOME OF THE SUN'S INTERIOR! WHAT A COSMIC APPETITE!! - I'LL JOIN HIM!
MEANWHILE, BACK IN THE SUPER-HERO CLUBHOUSE, ON EARTH...
OUR SPACE MONITOR REVEALS MARVEL LAD IS INSIDE THE SUN!... OH-OH! THE SUN-EATER'S GRABBED HOLD OF HIM!
THE BOY HASN'T A CHANCE!
DEEP IN THE HEART OF OLD SOL...
NOW YOU'VE GOT ME SIZZLING MAD! JUST FOR THAT, I'LL TURN UP THE POWER OF MY HEAT VISION TO THENTH DEGREE, AND GIVE YOU A SUPER-HOT FOOT!
INSTANTS AFTERWARD...
HA, HA, HA! LOOK AT HIM GO! SINCE I MADE THINGS TOO HOT FOR HIS TASTE, HE'S SPEEDING OFF IN SEARCH OF A COOLER SUN! I DOUBT IF HE'LL EVER PESTER THIS SOLAR SYSTEM AGAIN!
AS THE COCKY YOUTH RETURNS TO EARTH...
HOW'D I DO? GREAT, EH?
EXCELLENT! MODESTY ISN'T ONE OF YO VIRTUES, THOUGH!-FOR THE SECOND TEST, FLY TO THIS PLANET OF WEIRD MONSTERS AND MAKE IT SAFE FOR SPACE PILOTS TO LAND THERE WHEN NECESSARY!
THE PLANET BROGG
SPACE MONIT

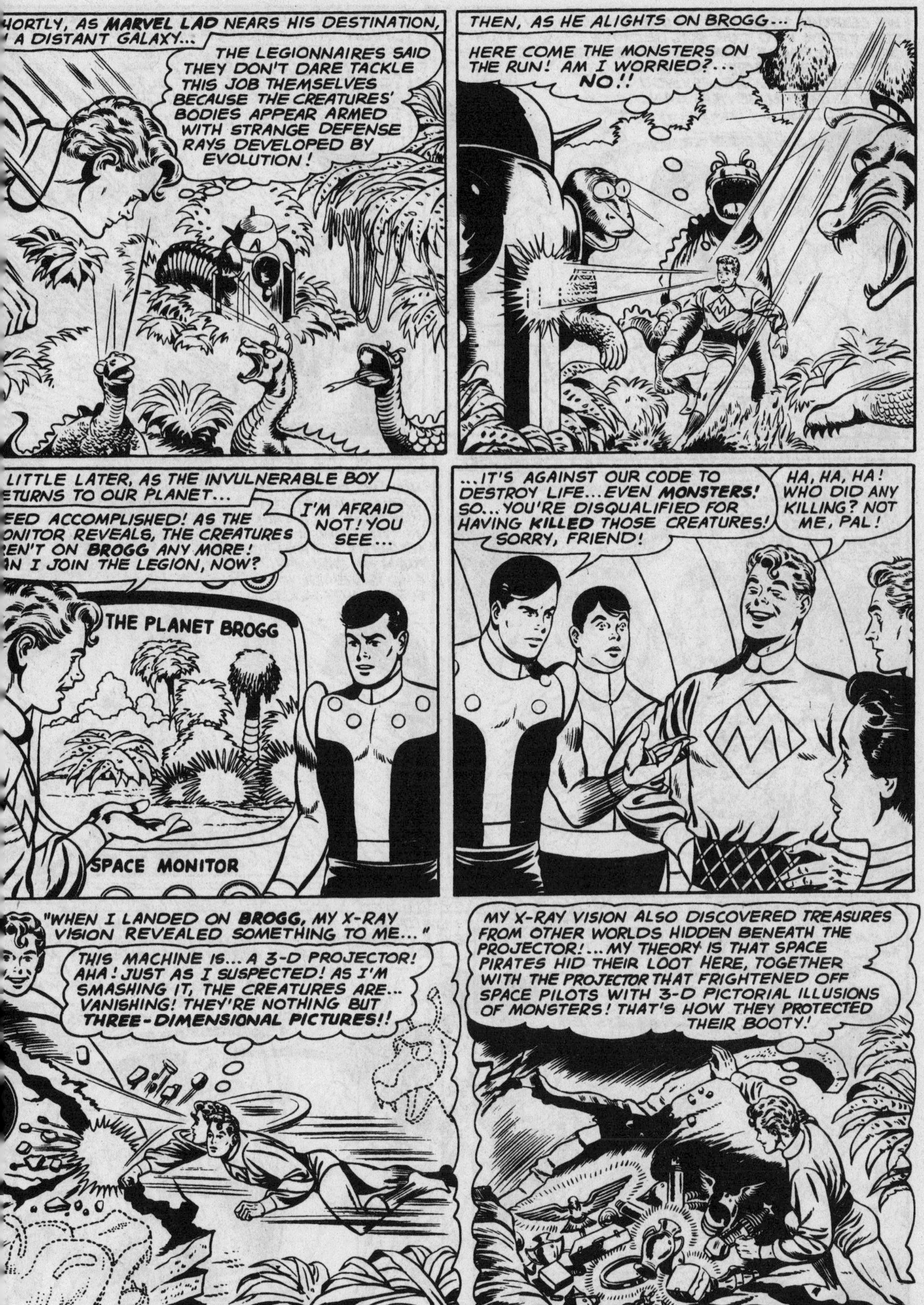
HORTLY, AS MARVEL LAD NEARS HIS DESTINATION,
A DISTANT GALAXY...
THE LEGIONNAIRES SAID THEY DON'T DARE TACKLE THIS JOB THEMSELVES BECAUSE THE CREATURES' BODIES APPEAR ARMED WITH STRANGE DEFENSE RAYS DEVELOPED BY EVOLUTION!
THEN, AS HE ALIGHTS ON BROGG...
HERE COME THE MONSTERS ON THE RUN! AM I WORRIED?... NO!!
LITTLE LATER, AS THE INVULNERABLE BOY ETURNS TO OUR PLANET...
EED ACCOMPLISHED! AS THE ONITOR REVEALS, THE CREATURES EN'T ON BROGG ANY MORE! AN I JOIN THE LEGION, NOW?
I'M AFRAID NOT! YOU SEE...
THE PLANET BROGG
SPACE MONITOR
...IT'S AGAINST OUR CODE TO DESTROY LIFE...EVEN MONSTERS! SO...YOU'RE DISQUALIFIED FOR HAVING KILLED THOSE CREATURES! SORRY, FRIEND!
HA, HA, HA! WHO DID ANY KILLING? NOT ME, PAL!
"WHEN I LANDED ON BROGG, MY X-RAY VISION REVEALED SOMETHING TO ME..."
THIS MACHINE IS... A 3-D PROJECTOR! AHA! JUST AS I SUSPECTED! AS I'M SMASHING IT, THE CREATURES ARE... VANISHING! THEY'RE NOTHING BUT THREE-DIMENSIONAL PICTURES!!
MY X-RAY VISION ALSO DISCOVERED TREASURES FROM OTHER WORLDS HIDDEN BENEATH THE PROJECTOR!...MY THEORY IS THAT SPACE PIRATES HID THEIR LOOT HERE, TOGETHER WITH THE PROJECTOR THAT FRIGHTENED OFF SPACE PILOTS WITH 3-D PICTORIAL ILLUSIONS OF MONSTERS! THAT'S HOW THEY PROTECTED THEIR BOOTY!

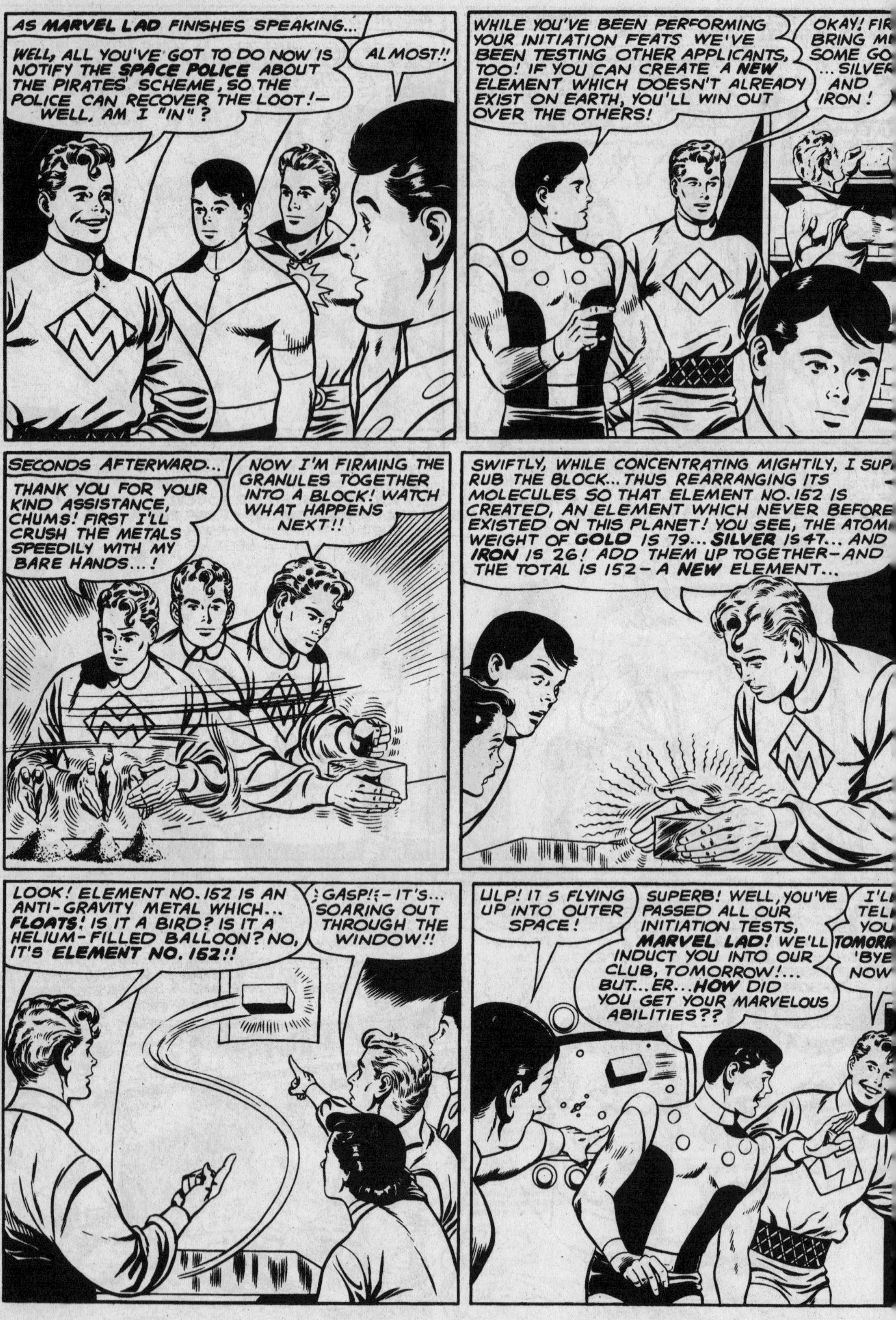
AS MARVEL LAD FINISHES SPEAKING...
WELL, ALL YOU'VE GOT TO DO NOW IS NOTIFY THE SPACE POLICE ABOUT THE PIRATES' SCHEME, SO THE POLICE CAN RECOVER THE LOOT!— WELL, AM I "IN"?
ALMOST!!
WHILE YOU'VE BEEN PERFORMING YOUR INITIATION FEATS WE'VE BEEN TESTING OTHER APPLICANTS, TOO! IF YOU CAN CREATE A NEW ELEMENT WHICH DOESN'T ALREADY EXIST ON EARTH, YOU'LL WIN OUT OVER THE OTHERS!
OKAY! FIR BRING M SOME GO ...SILVER AND IRON!
SECONDS AFTERWARD...
THANK YOU FOR YOUR KIND ASSISTANCE, CHUMS! FIRST I'LL CRUSH THE METALS SPEEDILY WITH MY BARE HANDS...!
NOW I'M FIRMING THE GRANULES TOGETHER INTO A BLOCK! WATCH WHAT HAPPENS NEXT!!
SWIFTLY, WHILE CONCENTRATING MIGHTILY, I SUP RUB THE BLOCK...THUS REARRANGING ITS MOLECULES SO THAT ELEMENT NO. 152 IS CREATED, AN ELEMENT WHICH NEVER BEFORE EXISTED ON THIS PLANET! YOU SEE, THE ATOM WEIGHT OF GOLD IS 79... SILVER IS 47... AND IRON IS 26! ADD THEM UP TOGETHER—AND THE TOTAL IS 152—A NEW ELEMENT...
LOOK! ELEMENT NO. 152 IS AN ANTI-GRAVITY METAL WHICH... FLOATS! IS IT A BIRD? IS IT A HELIUM-FILLED BALLOON? NO, IT'S ELEMENT NO. 152!!
GASP!—IT'S... SOARING OUT THROUGH THE WINDOW!!
ULP! IT S FLYING UP INTO OUTER SPACE!
SUPERB! WELL, YOU'VE PASSED ALL OUR INITIATION TESTS, MARVEL LAD! WE'LL INDUCT YOU INTO OUR CLUB, TOMORROW!... BUT...ER...HOW DID YOU GET YOUR MARVELOUS ABILITIES??
I'L TEL YOU TOMORR 'BYE NOW

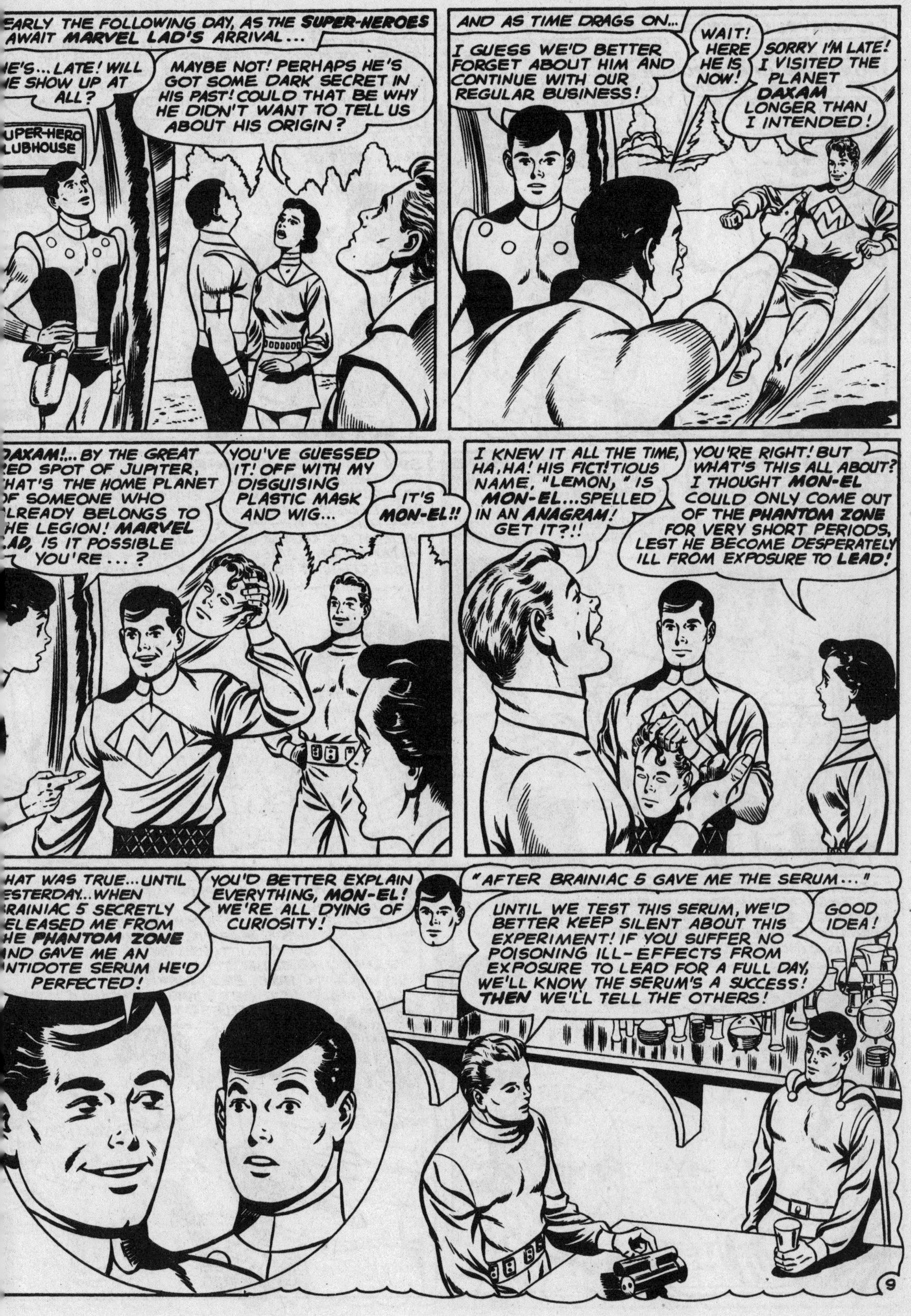
EARLY THE FOLLOWING DAY, AS THE SUPER-HEROES AWAIT MARVEL LAD'S ARRIVAL...
HE'S... LATE! WILL HE SHOW UP AT ALL?
MAYBE NOT! PERHAPS HE'S GOT SOME DARK SECRET IN HIS PAST! COULD THAT BE WHY HE DIDN'T WANT TO TELL US ABOUT HIS ORIGIN?
SUPER-HERO CLUBHOUSE
AND AS TIME DRAGS ON...
I GUESS WE'D BETTER FORGET ABOUT HIM AND CONTINUE WITH OUR REGULAR BUSINESS!
WAIT! HERE HE IS NOW!
SORRY I'M LATE! I VISITED THE PLANET DAXAM LONGER THAN I INTENDED!
DAXAM!... BY THE GREAT RED SPOT OF JUPITER, THAT'S THE HOME PLANET OF SOMEONE WHO ALREADY BELONGS TO THE LEGION! MARVEL LAD, IS IT POSSIBLE YOU'RE ...?
YOU'VE GUESSED IT! OFF WITH MY DISGUISING PLASTIC MASK AND WIG...
IT'S MON-EL!!
I KNEW IT ALL THE TIME, HA, HA! HIS FICTITIOUS NAME, "LEMON," IS MON-EL...SPELLED IN AN ANAGRAM! GET IT?!!
YOU'RE RIGHT! BUT WHAT'S THIS ALL ABOUT? I THOUGHT MON-EL COULD ONLY COME OUT OF THE PHANTOM ZONE FOR VERY SHORT PERIODS, LEST HE BECOME DESPERATELY ILL FROM EXPOSURE TO LEAD!
THAT WAS TRUE...UNTIL YESTERDAY...WHEN BRAINIAC 5 SECRETLY RELEASED ME FROM THE PHANTOM ZONE AND GAVE ME AN ANTIDOTE SERUM HE'D PERFECTED!
YOU'D BETTER EXPLAIN EVERYTHING, MON-EL! WE'RE ALL DYING OF CURIOSITY!
"AFTER BRAINIAC 5 GAVE ME THE SERUM..."
UNTIL WE TEST THIS SERUM, WE'D BETTER KEEP SILENT ABOUT THIS EXPERIMENT! IF YOU SUFFER NO POISONING ILL-EFFECTS FROM EXPOSURE TO LEAD FOR A FULL DAY, WE'LL KNOW THE SERUM'S A SUCCESS! THEN WE'LL TELL THE OTHERS!
GOOD IDEA!
9

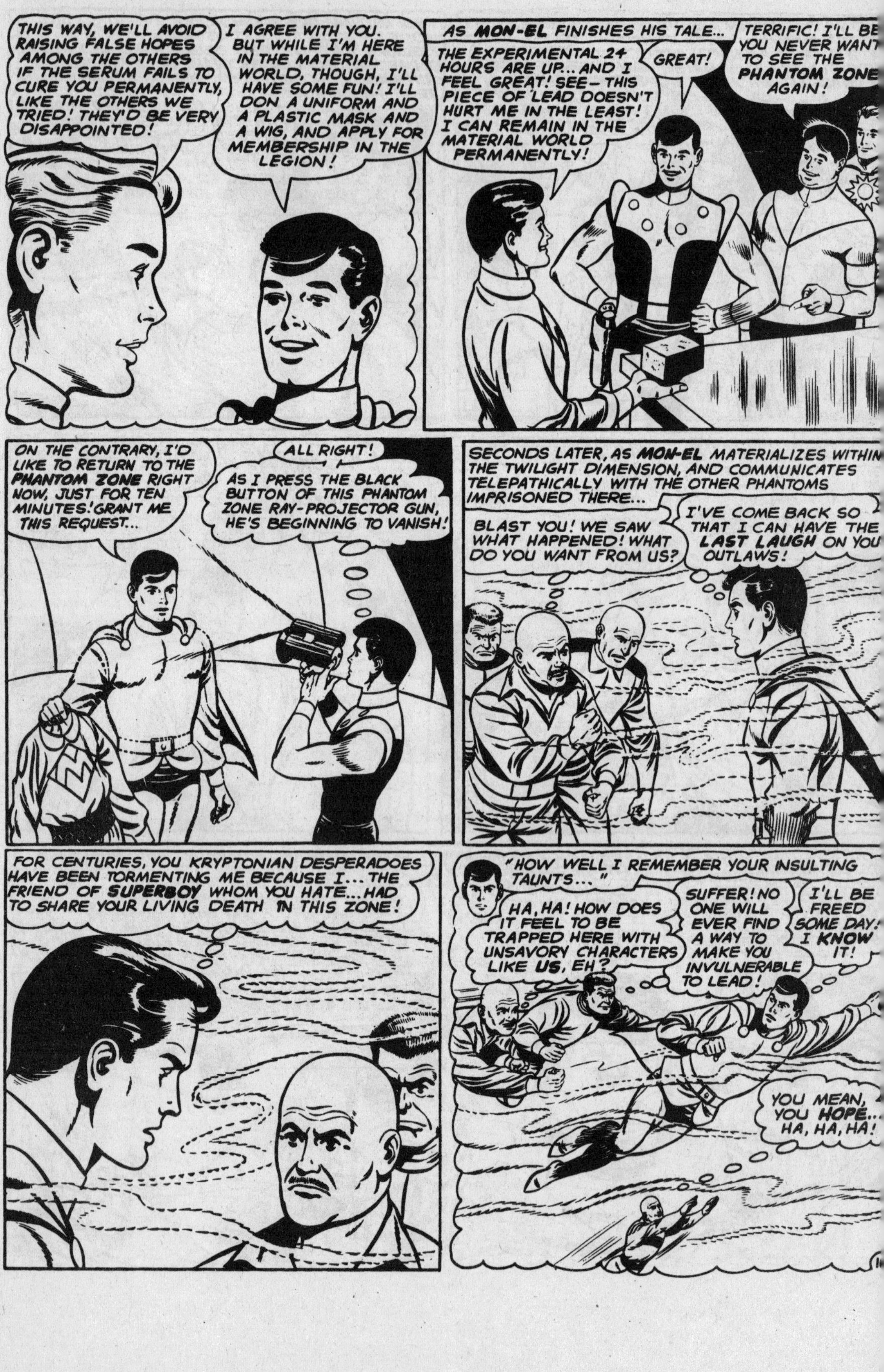
THIS WAY, WE'LL AVOID RAISING FALSE HOPES AMONG THE OTHERS IF THE SERUM FAILS TO CURE YOU PERMANENTLY, LIKE THE OTHERS WE TRIED! THEY'D BE VERY DISAPPOINTED!
I AGREE WITH YOU. BUT WHILE I'M HERE IN THE MATERIAL WORLD, THOUGH, I'LL HAVE SOME FUN! I'LL DON A UNIFORM AND A PLASTIC MASK AND A WIG, AND APPLY FOR MEMBERSHIP IN THE LEGION!
AS MON-EL FINISHES HIS TALE...
THE EXPERIMENTAL 24 HOURS ARE UP... AND I FEEL GREAT! SEE—THIS PIECE OF LEAD DOESN'T HURT ME IN THE LEAST! I CAN REMAIN IN THE MATERIAL WORLD PERMANENTLY!
GREAT!
TERRIFIC! I'LL BE YOU NEVER WANT TO SEE THE PHANTOM ZONE AGAIN!
ON THE CONTRARY, I'D LIKE TO RETURN TO THE PHANTOM ZONE RIGHT NOW, JUST FOR TEN MINUTES! GRANT ME THIS REQUEST...
ALL RIGHT!
AS I PRESS THE BLACK BUTTON OF THIS PHANTOM ZONE RAY-PROJECTOR GUN, HE'S BEGINNING TO VANISH!
SECONDS LATER, AS MON-EL MATERIALIZES WITHIN THE TWILIGHT DIMENSION, AND COMMUNICATES TELEPATHICALLY WITH THE OTHER PHANTOMS IMPRISONED THERE...
BLAST YOU! WE SAW WHAT HAPPENED! WHAT DO YOU WANT FROM US?
I'VE COME BACK SO THAT I CAN HAVE THE LAST LAUGH ON YOU OUTLAWS!
FOR CENTURIES, YOU KRYPTONIAN DESPERADOES HAVE BEEN TORMENTING ME BECAUSE I... THE FRIEND OF SUPERBOY WHOM YOU HATE... HAD TO SHARE YOUR LIVING DEATH IN THIS ZONE!
"HOW WELL I REMEMBER YOUR INSULTING TAUNTS..."
HA, HA! HOW DOES IT FEEL TO BE TRAPPED HERE WITH UNSAVORY CHARACTERS LIKE US, EH?
SUFFER! NO ONE WILL EVER FIND A WAY TO MAKE YOU INVULNERABLE TO LEAD!
I'LL BE FREED SOME DAY! I KNOW IT!
YOU MEAN, YOU HOPE... HA, HA, HA!

"...AND WHEN SATURN GIRL INVENTED 'SERUM XY-4'..."

HA! IT'S ONLY A TEMPORARY ANTIDOTE FOR POISONING BY LEAD RADIATIONS...!

YOU'LL NEVER GET AWAY FROM US PERMANENTLY, HA, HA, HA!

"BEFORE I LEAVE YOU FOREVER, I WANT TO TELL SOME OF YOU, WHO MAY NOT KNOW IT, HOW I BECAME A PHANTOM. IT BEGAN AGES AGO, WHEN I LANDED FROM OUTER SPACE IN SMALLVILLE! SUPERBOY THOUGHT I WAS HIS ENEMY AND SET A TRAP FOR ME..."

HE WAS BORN ON KRYPTON AND IS SUFFERING FROM AMNESIA! BUT HE'S A PHONEY! HE'S INVULNERABLE TO KRYPTONITE, BUT LEAD IS POISONOUS TO HIM! I'LL PAINT THESE LEAD BALLS GREEN, THEN HURL THEM TO A DISTANT PLANETOID SO THAT THEY LOOK LIKE KRYPTONITE METEORS!

THIS CHARACTER IS PRETENDING

GREEN

"THEN LATER, AS WE VISITED THAT PLANETOID TOGETHER..."

WHAT A FAKE! HE'S PRETENDING THESE "GREEN KRYPTONITE" METEORS ARE HARMING HIM!

OKAY, MON-EL! CUT OUT THE DYING ACT! UNDERNEATH THE GREEN-PAINTED SURFACE, THESE "METEORS" ARE NOTHING BUT HARMLESS LEAD BALLS! SEE?

CHOKE! MY AMNESIA IS GONE! NOW I REMEMBER EVERY-THING... I'M A NATIVE OF THE PLANET DAXAM ...WHERE LEAD AFFECTS ITS PEOPLE THE WAY KRYPTONITE AFFECTS YOU ...EXCEPT THAT ITS EFFECTS NEVER WEAR OFF! I'M... DYING!

"SUPERBOY SAVED MY LIFE BY PROJECTING ME INTO THE PHANTOM ZONE..."

MON-EL, I'M SORRY I DIDN'T TRUST YOU! I'M TRANSPORTING YOU INTO ANOTHER DIMENSION WHERE YOU'LL AT LEAST CONTINUE TO LIVE! YOU'LL BE IMPRISONED THERE WITH THE MOST DANGEROUS VILLAINS FROM THE PLANET KRYPTON. BUT SOME DAY, WHEN A CURE FOR YOU IS FOUND, YOU'LL BE RETURNED TO THE REAL WORLD!

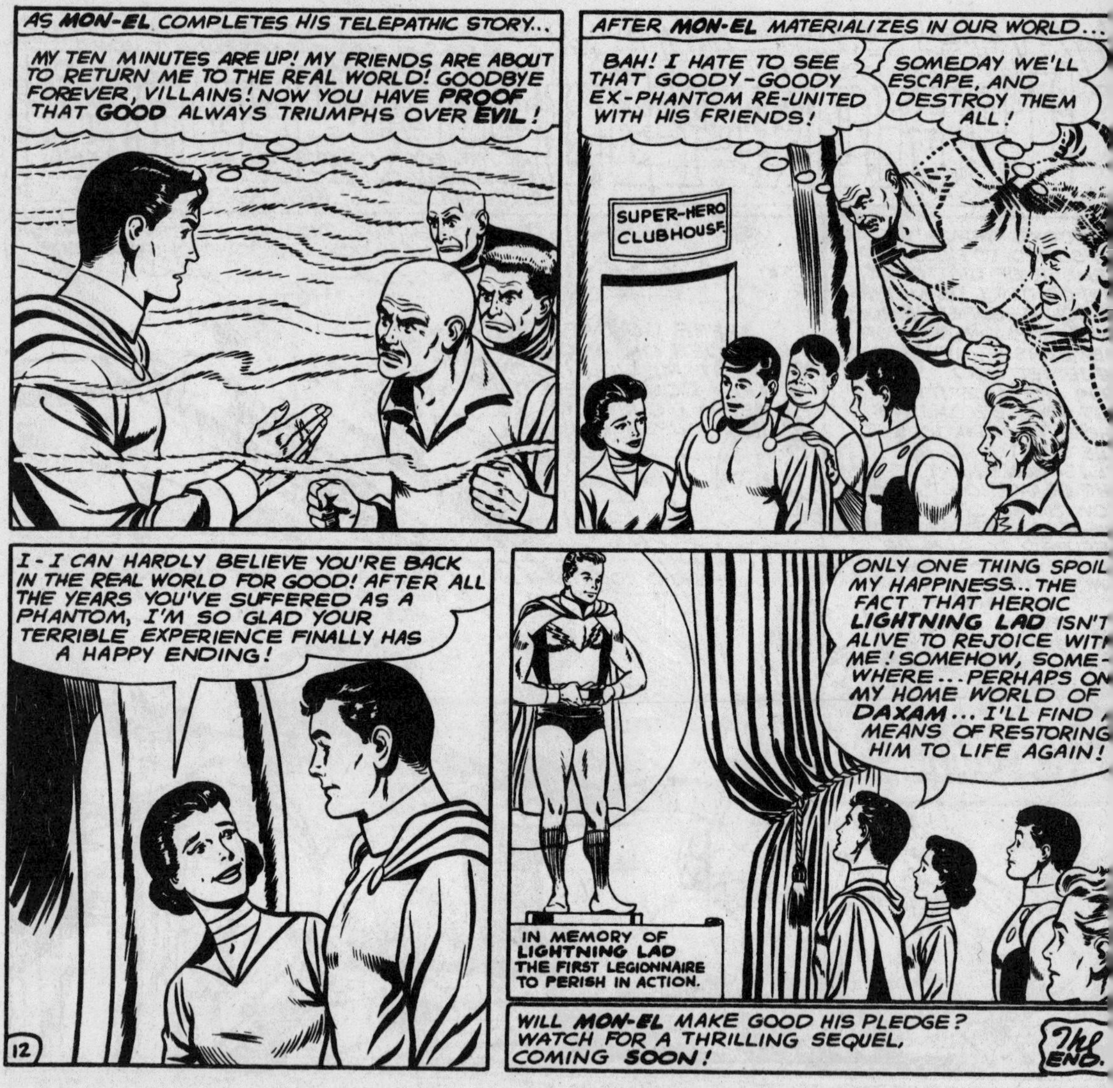
AS MON-EL COMPLETES HIS TELEPATHIC STORY...
MY TEN MINUTES ARE UP! MY FRIENDS ARE ABOUT TO RETURN ME TO THE REAL WORLD! GOODBYE FOREVER, VILLAINS! NOW YOU HAVE PROOF THAT GOOD ALWAYS TRIUMPHS OVER EVIL!
AFTER MON-EL MATERIALIZES IN OUR WORLD...
BAH! I HATE TO SEE THAT GOODY-GOODY EX-PHANTOM RE-UNITED WITH HIS FRIENDS!
SOMEDAY WE'LL ESCAPE, AND DESTROY THEM ALL!
SUPER-HERO CLUBHOUSE
I-I CAN HARDLY BELIEVE YOU'RE BACK IN THE REAL WORLD FOR GOOD! AFTER ALL THE YEARS YOU'VE SUFFERED AS A PHANTOM, I'M SO GLAD YOUR TERRIBLE EXPERIENCE FINALLY HAS A HAPPY ENDING!
12
ONLY ONE THING SPOIL MY HAPPINESS... THE FACT THAT HEROIC LIGHTNING LAD ISN'T ALIVE TO REJOICE WIT ME! SOMEHOW, SOME-WHERE... PERHAPS ON MY HOME WORLD OF DAXAM... I'LL FIND MEANS OF RESTORING HIM TO LIFE AGAIN!
IN MEMORY OF LIGHTNING LAD THE FIRST LEGIONNAIRE TO PERISH IN ACTION.
WILL MON-EL MAKE GOOD HIS PLEDGE? WATCH FOR A THRILLING SEQUEL, COMING SOON!
THE END.

LEGION of SUPER-HEROES

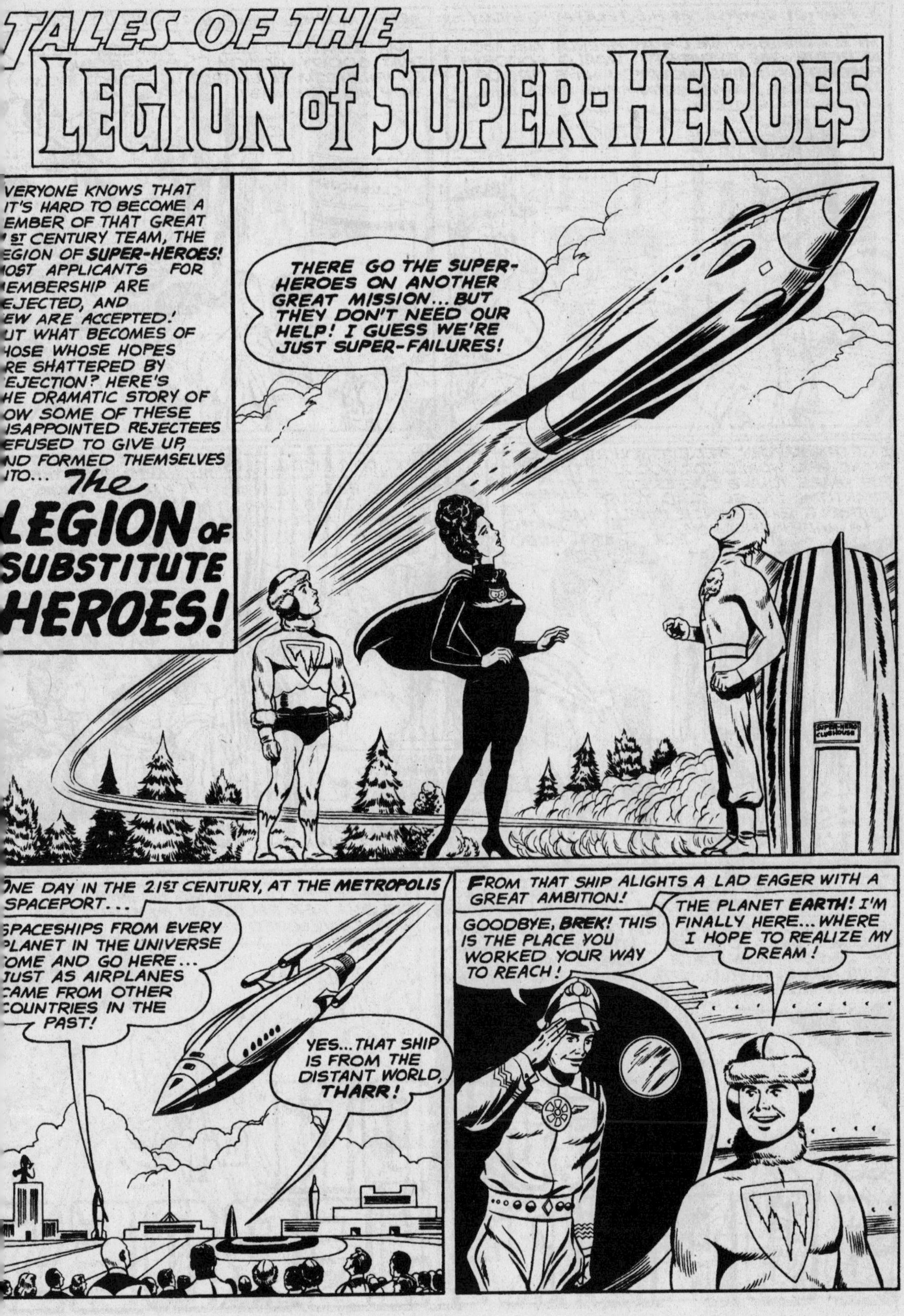
TALES OF THE
LEGION of SUPER-HEROES
VERYONE KNOWS THAT IT'S HARD TO BECOME A EMBER OF THAT GREAT ST CENTURY TEAM, THE EGION OF SUPER-HEROES! MOST APPLICANTS FOR MEMBERSHIP ARE EJECTED, AND EW ARE ACCEPTED! UT WHAT BECOMES OF HOSE WHOSE HOPES RE SHATTERED BY EJECTION? HERE'S HE DRAMATIC STORY OF OW SOME OF THESE ISAPPOINTED REJECTEES EFUSED TO GIVE UP, ND FORMED THEMSELVES NTO...
The LEGION OF SUBSTITUTE HEROES!
THERE GO THE SUPER-HEROES ON ANOTHER GREAT MISSION... BUT THEY DON'T NEED OUR HELP! I GUESS WE'RE JUST SUPER-FAILURES!
SUPER-HERO CLUBHOUSE
ONE DAY IN THE 21ST CENTURY, AT THE METROPOLIS SPACEPORT...
SPACESHIPS FROM EVERY PLANET IN THE UNIVERSE COME AND GO HERE... JUST AS AIRPLANES CAME FROM OTHER COUNTRIES IN THE PAST!
YES...THAT SHIP IS FROM THE DISTANT WORLD, THARR!
FROM THAT SHIP ALIGHTS A LAD EAGER WITH A GREAT AMBITION!
GOODBYE, BREK! THIS IS THE PLACE YOU WORKED YOUR WAY TO REACH!
THE PLANET EARTH! I'M FINALLY HERE... WHERE I HOPE TO REALIZE MY DREAM!

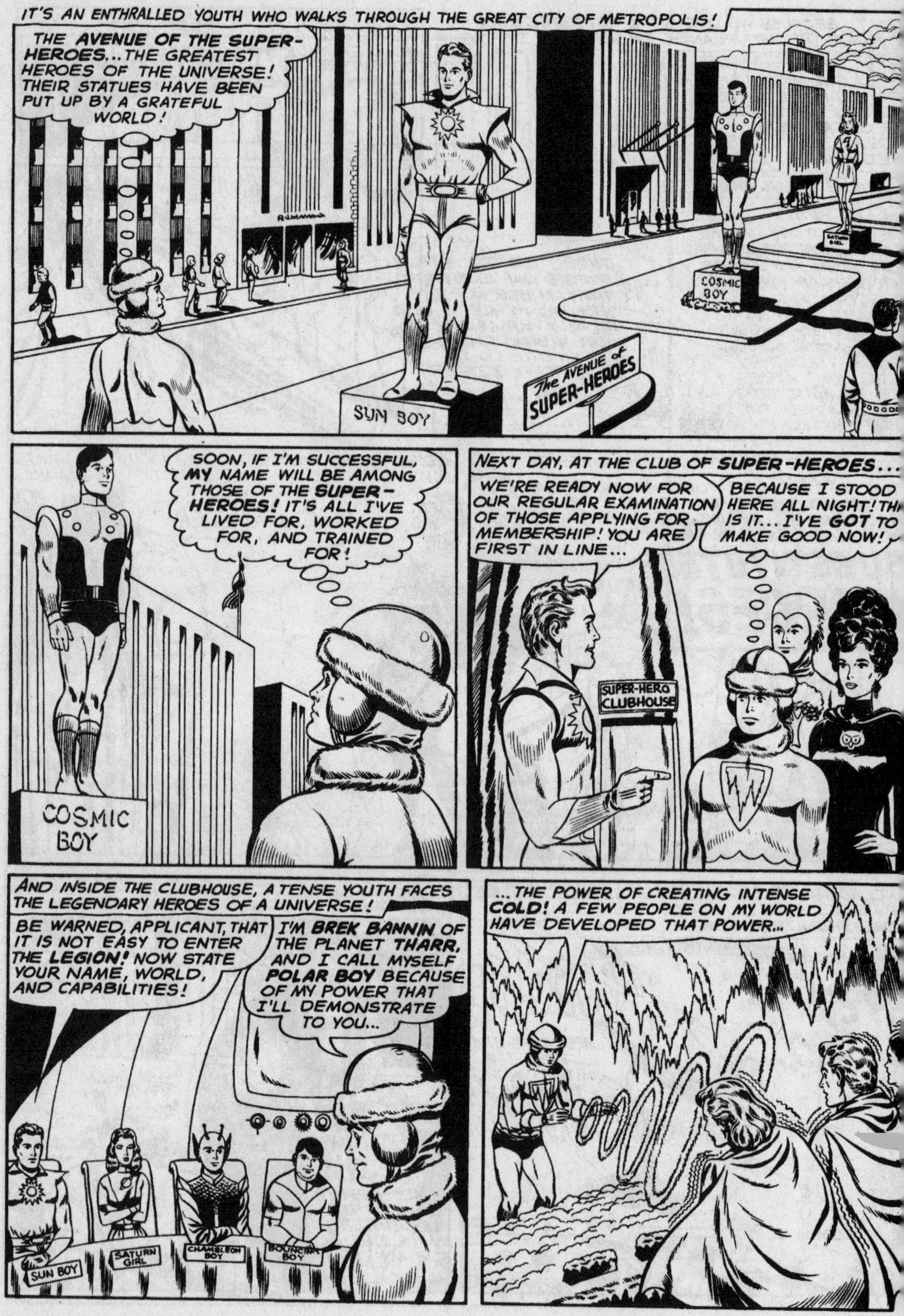
IT'S AN ENTHRALLED YOUTH WHO WALKS THROUGH THE GREAT CITY OF METROPOLIS!
THE AVENUE OF THE SUPER-HEROES...THE GREATEST HEROES OF THE UNIVERSE! THEIR STATUES HAVE BEEN PUT UP BY A GRATEFUL WORLD!
COSMIC BOY
SUN BOY
The AVENUE of SUPER-HEROES
SOON, IF I'M SUCCESSFUL, MY NAME WILL BE AMONG THOSE OF THE SUPER-HEROES! IT'S ALL I'VE LIVED FOR, WORKED FOR, AND TRAINED FOR!
COSMIC BOY
NEXT DAY, AT THE CLUB OF SUPER-HEROES...
WE'RE READY NOW FOR OUR REGULAR EXAMINATION OF THOSE APPLYING FOR MEMBERSHIP! YOU ARE FIRST IN LINE...
BECAUSE I STOOD HERE ALL NIGHT! THIS IS IT... I'VE GOT TO MAKE GOOD NOW!
SUPER-HERO CLUBHOUSE
AND INSIDE THE CLUBHOUSE, A TENSE YOUTH FACES THE LEGENDARY HEROES OF A UNIVERSE!
BE WARNED, APPLICANT, THAT IT IS NOT EASY TO ENTER THE LEGION! NOW STATE YOUR NAME, WORLD, AND CAPABILITIES!
I'M BREK BANNIN OF THE PLANET THARR, AND I CALL MYSELF POLAR BOY BECAUSE OF MY POWER THAT I'LL DEMONSTRATE TO YOU...
SUN BOY
SATURN GIRL
CHAMELEON BOY
BOUNCING BOY
...THE POWER OF CREATING INTENSE COLD! A FEW PEOPLE ON MY WORLD HAVE DEVELOPED THAT POWER...

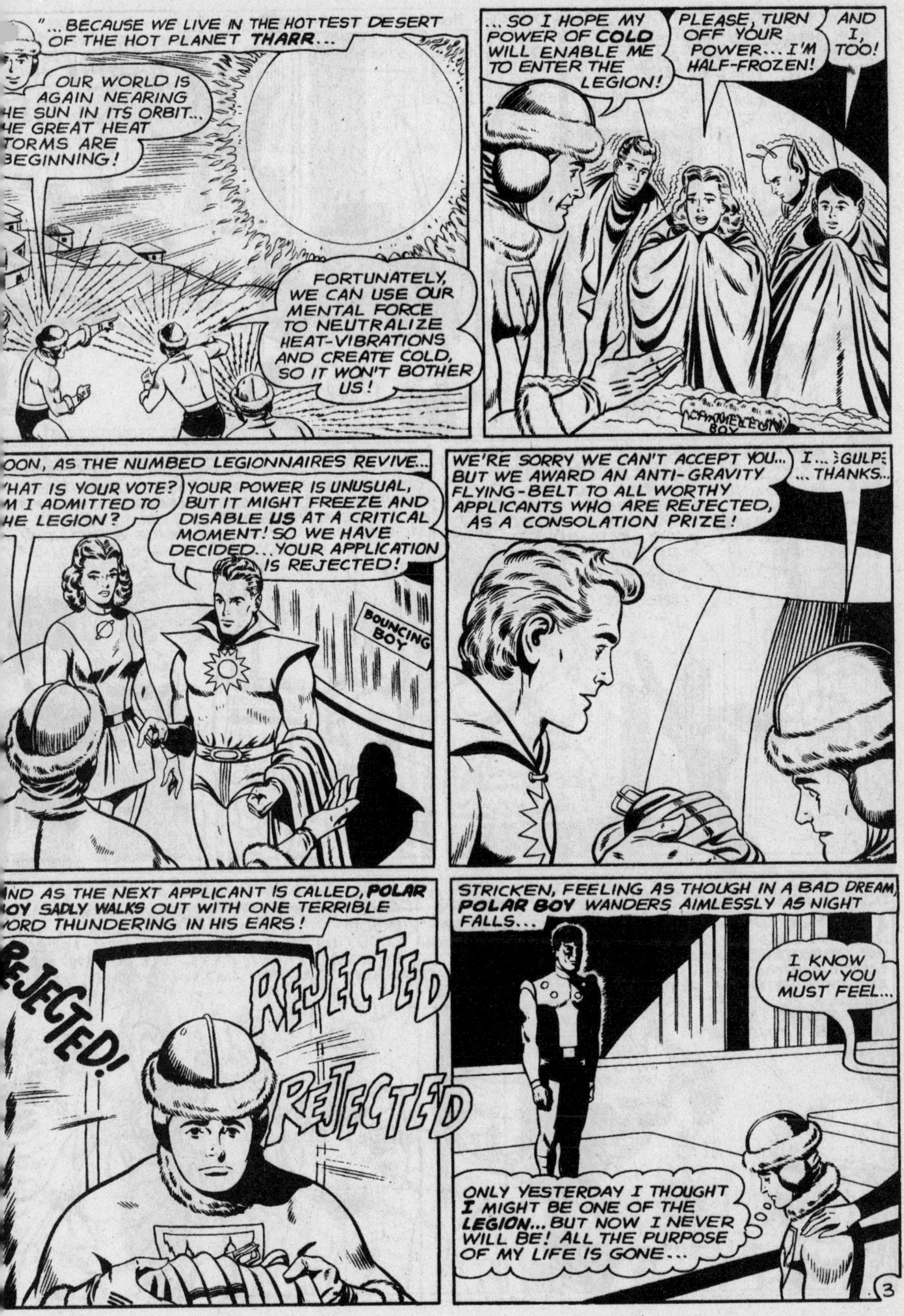
"...BECAUSE WE LIVE IN THE HOTTEST DESERT OF THE HOT PLANET THARR...
OUR WORLD IS AGAIN NEARING HE SUN IN ITS ORBIT... HE GREAT HEAT TORMS ARE BEGINNING!
FORTUNATELY, WE CAN USE OUR MENTAL FORCE TO NEUTRALIZE HEAT-VIBRATIONS AND CREATE COLD, SO IT WON'T BOTHER US!
...SO I HOPE MY POWER OF COLD WILL ENABLE ME TO ENTER THE LEGION!
PLEASE, TURN OFF YOUR POWER... I'M HALF-FROZEN!
AND I, TOO!
CHAMELEON BOY
OON, AS THE NUMBED LEGIONNAIRES REVIVE...
HAT IS YOUR VOTE? M I ADMITTED TO HE LEGION?
YOUR POWER IS UNUSUAL, BUT IT MIGHT FREEZE AND DISABLE US AT A CRITICAL MOMENT! SO WE HAVE DECIDED... YOUR APPLICATION IS REJECTED!
BOUNCING BOY
WE'RE SORRY WE CAN'T ACCEPT YOU... BUT WE AWARD AN ANTI-GRAVITY FLYING-BELT TO ALL WORTHY APPLICANTS WHO ARE REJECTED, AS A CONSOLATION PRIZE!
I... GULP ...THANKS...
ND AS THE NEXT APPLICANT IS CALLED, POLAR OY SADLY WALKS OUT WITH ONE TERRIBLE ORD THUNDERING IN HIS EARS!
REJECTED!
REJECTED
REJECTED
STRICKEN, FEELING AS THOUGH IN A BAD DREAM, POLAR BOY WANDERS AIMLESSLY AS NIGHT FALLS...
I KNOW HOW YOU MUST FEEL...
ONLY YESTERDAY I THOUGHT I MIGHT BE ONE OF THE LEGION... BUT NOW I NEVER WILL BE! ALL THE PURPOSE OF MY LIFE IS GONE...
3

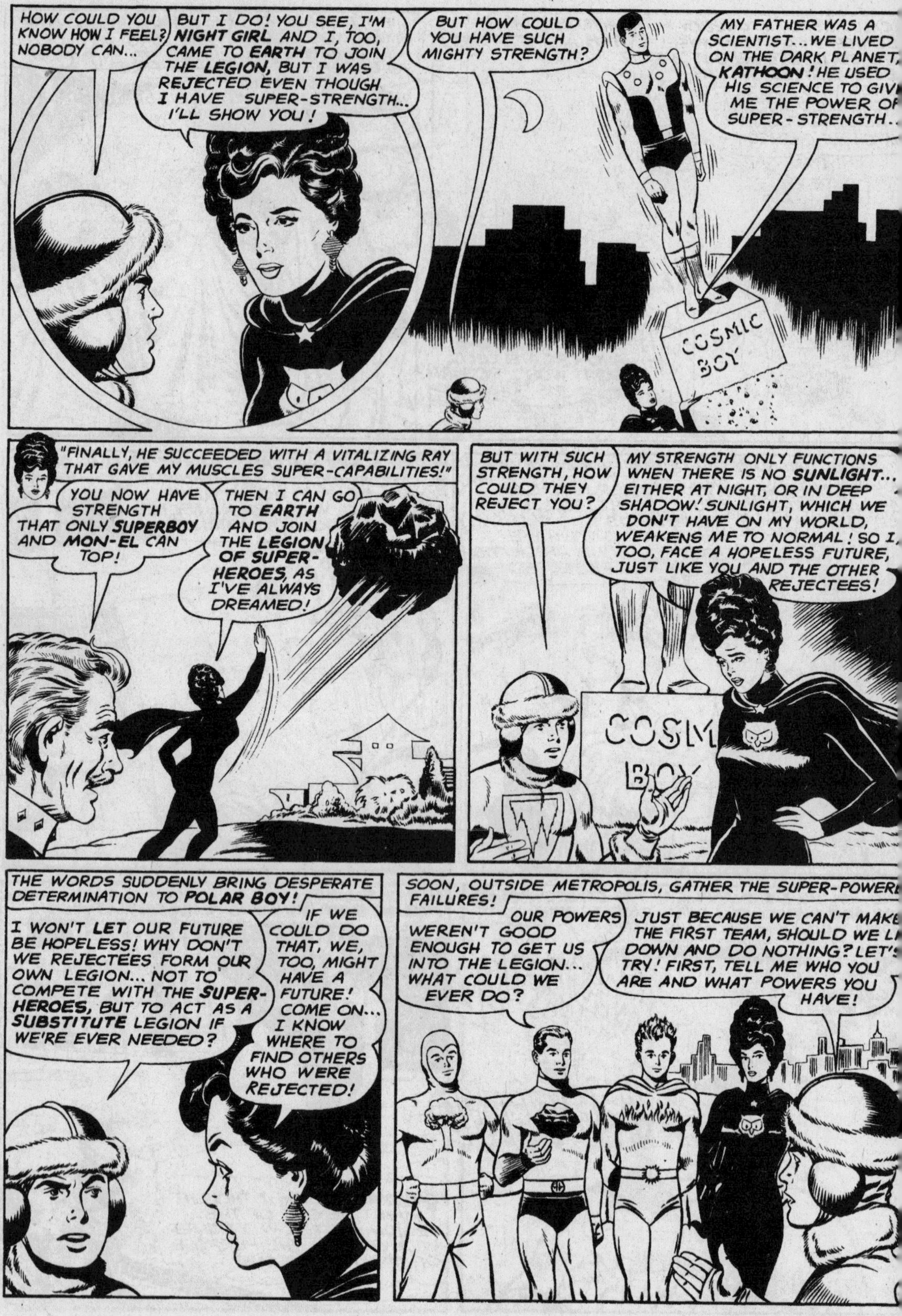
HOW COULD YOU KNOW HOW I FEEL? NOBODY CAN...
BUT I DO! YOU SEE, I'M NIGHT GIRL AND I, TOO, CAME TO EARTH TO JOIN THE LEGION, BUT I WAS REJECTED EVEN THOUGH I HAVE SUPER-STRENGTH... I'LL SHOW YOU!
BUT HOW COULD YOU HAVE SUCH MIGHTY STRENGTH?
MY FATHER WAS A SCIENTIST...WE LIVED ON THE DARK PLANET, KATHOON! HE USED HIS SCIENCE TO GIV ME THE POWER OF SUPER-STRENGTH..
COSMIC BOY
"FINALLY, HE SUCCEEDED WITH A VITALIZING RAY THAT GAVE MY MUSCLES SUPER-CAPABILITIES!"
YOU NOW HAVE STRENGTH THAT ONLY SUPERBOY AND MON-EL CAN TOP!
THEN I CAN GO TO EARTH AND JOIN THE LEGION OF SUPER-HEROES, AS I'VE ALWAYS DREAMED!
BUT WITH SUCH STRENGTH, HOW COULD THEY REJECT YOU?
MY STRENGTH ONLY FUNCTIONS WHEN THERE IS NO SUNLIGHT... EITHER AT NIGHT, OR IN DEEP SHADOW! SUNLIGHT, WHICH WE DON'T HAVE ON MY WORLD, WEAKENS ME TO NORMAL! SO I, TOO, FACE A HOPELESS FUTURE, JUST LIKE YOU AND THE OTHER REJECTEES!
COSM BOY
THE WORDS SUDDENLY BRING DESPERATE DETERMINATION TO POLAR BOY!
I WON'T LET OUR FUTURE BE HOPELESS! WHY DON'T WE REJECTEES FORM OUR OWN LEGION... NOT TO COMPETE WITH THE SUPER-HEROES, BUT TO ACT AS A SUBSTITUTE LEGION IF WE'RE EVER NEEDED?
IF WE COULD DO THAT, WE, TOO, MIGHT HAVE A FUTURE! COME ON... I KNOW WHERE TO FIND OTHERS WHO WERE REJECTED!
SOON, OUTSIDE METROPOLIS, GATHER THE SUPER-POWER FAILURES!
OUR POWERS WEREN'T GOOD ENOUGH TO GET US INTO THE LEGION... WHAT COULD WE EVER DO?
JUST BECAUSE WE CAN'T MAKE THE FIRST TEAM, SHOULD WE L DOWN AND DO NOTHING? LET'S TRY! FIRST, TELL ME WHO YOU ARE AND WHAT POWERS YOU HAVE!

CALL MYSELF *STONEBOY* BECAUSE I CAN TURN MYSELF.. INTO *SOLID STONE!* BUT THE *LEGIONNAIRES* SAID MY POWER WAS TOO STATIC AND WOULD ACCOMPLISH NOTHING POSITIVE! WATCH ME CHANGE!

HOW DID YOU ACQUIRE THIS WEIRD ABILITY?

NEXT SECOND..

"MY DISTANT WORLD ROTATES SO SLOWLY THE NIGHTS ARE A HALF-YEAR LONG! WE EVOLVED A POWER OF SUPER-SUSPENDED ANIMATION!"

IT'S ALMOST NIGHT... TIME FOR OUR SUSPENDED-ANIMATION SLEEP! USE YOUR WILL-FORCE TO TURN YOURSELF TO STONE, SON!

ALL RIGHT, MOTHER!

"I'M *FIRE-LAD*, AND I HAVE FIRE-BREATH THAT CAN SET ANYTHING COMBUSTIBLE ON FIRE! BUT THE *LEGIONNAIRES* SAID MY POWER WAS TOO DANGEROUS AND MIGHT CAUSE ACCIDENTAL HOLOCAUSTS!

"A FIERY METEOR CRASHED IN FRONT OF ME ONE NIGHT..."

MY LUNGS... I INHALED WEIRD VAPORS FROM THAT CRASHING METEOR...

"... THE VAPORS GAVE MY LUNGS THE POWER TO BREATHE FIRE AT WILL!"

THEY CALL ME THE *CHLOROPHYLL KID*, AND I CAN MAKE ANY PLANT *GROW* SUPER-FAST! I, TOO, GAINED MY POWER BY AN ACCIDENT, BUT I GOT THEM WHEN I WAS A CHILD...

"...AND FELL INTO A TANK OF POWERFUL PLANT-GROWING SOLUTION IN A HYDROPONIC GARDEN!"

OH, MY LITTLE BOY! WILL THAT SOLUTION HURT HIM?

HE SEEMS ALL RIGHT... BUT NO ONE CAN TELL WHAT EFFECT THIS POWERFUL SOLUTION MIGHT HAVE ON A HUMAN BEING!

IT GAVE ME THE POWER TO MAKE ANY PLANT GROW WITH TERRIFIC SPEED! BUT THE **SUPER-HEROES** DIDN'T THINK THAT WOULD HELP THEM IN THEIR MISSIONS!

ALL OF YOU HAVE POWERS LIKE THESE, YET YOU'D JUST **QUIT**? NO...WE CAN NEVER EQUAL THE **SUPER-HEROES**, BUT WE **CAN** USE OUR ABILITIES TO HELP PEOPLE!

INSTEAD OF GOING HOME AS HOPELESS FAILURES, LET'S FORM THE LEGION OF **SUBSTITUTE** HEROES, TO ACT AS PINCH-HITTERS FOR THE **SUPER-HEROES** AND HELP THEM IN ANY WAY WE CAN!

IF WE CAN DO THAT, I'LL REGAIN MY SELF-RESPECT!

AND I TOO!

AS NIGHT FALLS, THE MEMBERS OF THE NEW LEGION SOLEMNLY PLEDGE THEMSELVES!

I TAKE OATH THAT THIS SUPER-POWER I AM NOW USING WILL BE USED ONLY FOR THE GOOD OF ALL PEOPLES OF EARTH AND THE **UNIVERSE**!...AND THAT I WILL ALWAYS TRY TO HELP THE **LEGION OF SUPER-HEROES** IN THEIR GREAT DEEDS!

A ROCKY PINNACLE IS CHOSEN FOR THEIR CLUB-HOUSE!

WE'LL HOLLOW OUT THIS SOLID ROCK PEAK FOR OUR CLUB-HOUSE...THE INTENSE COLD I'M RADIATING WILL MAKE THE ROCK EASIER TO CRACK!

I HAVE TO HURRY, FOR MY SUPER-STRENGTH WILL FADE WHEN THE SUN RISES!

THE BIGGER TUNNEL IS FOR THE SMALL SPACE-SHIP WE'LL BUILD...BUT MY SUPER-POWER ISN'T MUCH HELP ON THESE JOBS!

NOR MINE! MAYBE...MAYBE THE **SUPER-HEROES** WERE RIGHT IN REJECTING US...

AND THAT DEEP DOUBT OF THEIR OWN ABILITIES STILL HAUNTS THEM, AS...

THE *LEGION OF SUBSTITUTE HEROES* HOLDS ITS FIRST MEETING!

BUT I CAN'T HELP FEELING WE'RE JUST IMITATING THE REAL LEGION!

I MUSTN'T LET THEM LOSE CONFIDENCE!

WE'LL NEVER SUCCEED IF WE START MOPING... WE HAVE A SPACESHIP TO BUILD AND A MONITOR-ALARM SYSTEM TO SET UP!

FIRE LAD · POLAR BOY · NIGHT GIRL · CHLOROPHYLL KID · STONE BOY

SOON, THE SUBSTITUTE HEROES THROW ALL THEIR POWERS INTO PREPARATIONS!

THE LAST BATCH OF ALLOY FOR THE SPACE-SHIP WE'RE BUILDING IS ALMOST READY!

HERE, INSIDE OUR CLUBHOUSE, WHERE THERE'S NO SUNLIGHT, I CAN USE MY SUPER-STRENGTH FREELY!

AND INSIDE ANOTHER ROOM OF THE CLUBHOUSE...

THE STAR MAP OF OUR BIG WARNING WALL MONITOR SHOWS A RED LIGHT WHEREVER DISASTER THREATENS... LOOK!

THE RED LIGHT IS AT *EARTH*... AND THE SCREEN SHOWS THAT THE GIANT CREATURES AT THE *OCEAN RESEARCH LABORATORY* HAVE BROKEN LOOSE! GET YOUR FLYING BELTS... THIS IS OUR FIRST MISSION!

BUT WHEN THE SUBSTITUTE HEROES, EAGER FOR ACTION, STREAK TO THE SCENE...

THESE ARTIFICIALLY-EVOLVED SEA-MONSTERS WERE ESCAPING, BUT MY BOUNCING IS SCARING THEM BACK, *SATURN GIRL!*

GOOD WORK, *BOUNCING BOY!* BUT ONE HUGE CREATURE GOT PAST YOU... I'LL SUMMON *COLOSSAL BOY* BY TELEPATHY, AND HE CAN GROW BIG AND CATCH IT!

AND AS THE FRUSTRATED SUBSTITUTE HEROES LOOK ON...

GOOD WORK, *COLOSSAL BOY!* WE'RE USING *COSMIC BOY'S* MAGNETIC POWER TO PULL TOGETHER THE BROKEN STEEL FENCE, AND THEN ALL WILL BE SAFE AGAIN!

WE MIGHT HAVE KNOWN... THE REAL SUPER-HEROES WERE HERE BEFORE US AND WE'RE NOT NEEDED! EVEN IF WE *HAD* BEEN NEEDED, I HAVE NO SUPER-STRENGTH IN SUNLIGHT!

7

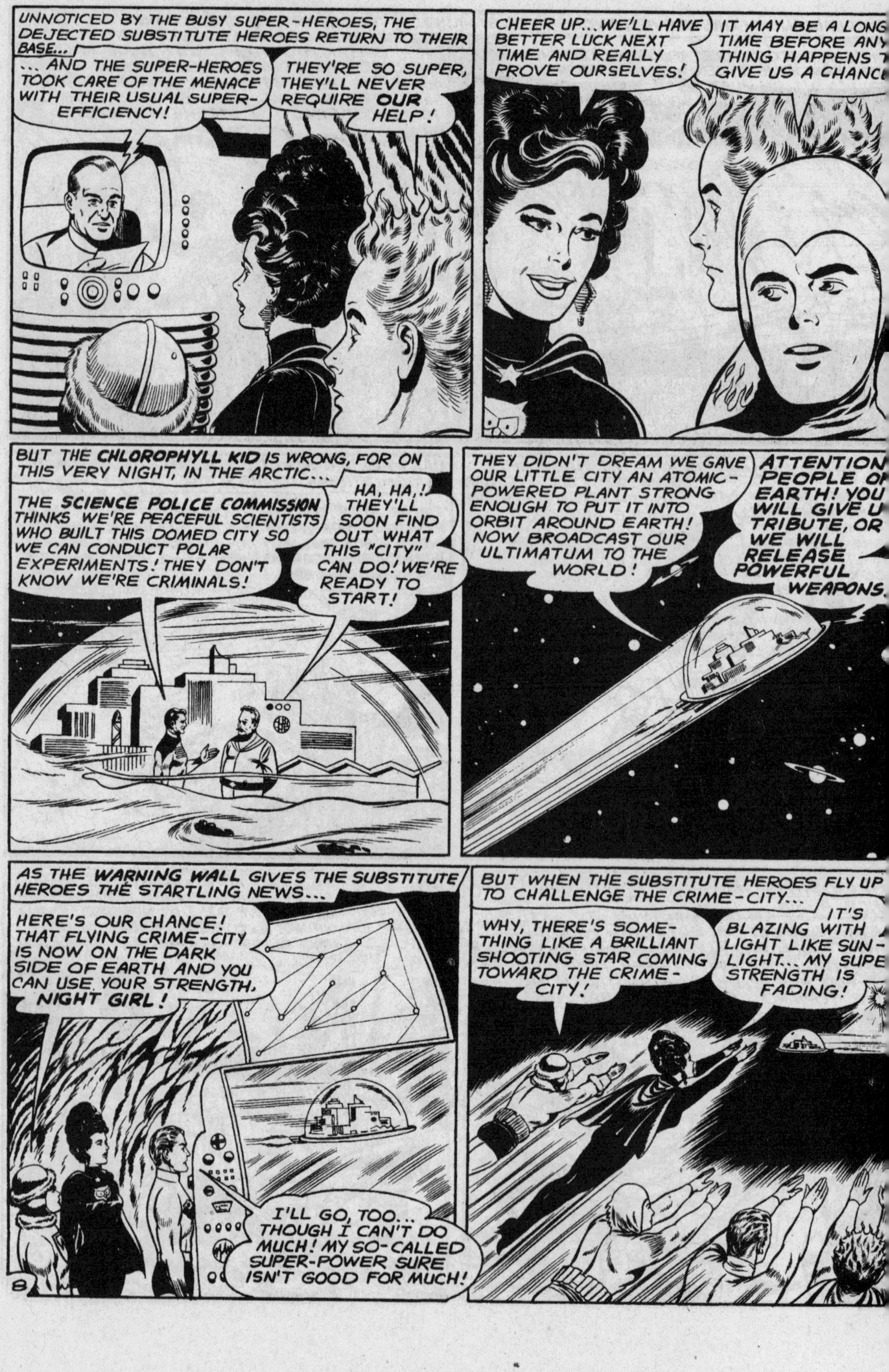
UNNOTICED BY THE BUSY SUPER-HEROES, THE DEJECTED SUBSTITUTE HEROES RETURN TO THEIR BASE...
... AND THE SUPER-HEROES TOOK CARE OF THE MENACE WITH THEIR USUAL SUPER-EFFICIENCY!
THEY'RE SO SUPER, THEY'LL NEVER REQUIRE OUR HELP!
CHEER UP...WE'LL HAVE BETTER LUCK NEXT TIME AND REALLY PROVE OURSELVES!
IT MAY BE A LONG TIME BEFORE AN THING HAPPENS GIVE US A CHANC
BUT THE CHLOROPHYLL KID IS WRONG, FOR ON THIS VERY NIGHT, IN THE ARCTIC...
THE SCIENCE POLICE COMMISSION THINKS WE'RE PEACEFUL SCIENTISTS WHO BUILT THIS DOMED CITY SO WE CAN CONDUCT POLAR EXPERIMENTS! THEY DON'T KNOW WE'RE CRIMINALS!
HA, HA,! THEY'LL SOON FIND OUT WHAT THIS "CITY" CAN DO! WE'RE READY TO START!
THEY DIDN'T DREAM WE GAVE OUR LITTLE CITY AN ATOMIC-POWERED PLANT STRONG ENOUGH TO PUT IT INTO ORBIT AROUND EARTH! NOW BROADCAST OUR ULTIMATUM TO THE WORLD!
ATTENTION PEOPLE O EARTH! YOU WILL GIVE U TRIBUTE, OR WE WILL RELEASE POWERFUL WEAPONS.
AS THE WARNING WALL GIVES THE SUBSTITUTE HEROES THE STARTLING NEWS...
HERE'S OUR CHANCE! THAT FLYING CRIME-CITY IS NOW ON THE DARK SIDE OF EARTH AND YOU CAN USE YOUR STRENGTH, NIGHT GIRL!
I'LL GO, TOO... THOUGH I CAN'T DO MUCH! MY SO-CALLED SUPER-POWER SURE ISN'T GOOD FOR MUCH!
8
BUT WHEN THE SUBSTITUTE HEROES FLY UP TO CHALLENGE THE CRIME-CITY...
WHY, THERE'S SOMETHING LIKE A BRILLIANT SHOOTING STAR COMING TOWARD THE CRIME-CITY!
IT'S BLAZING WITH LIGHT LIKE SUN-LIGHT... MY SUPE STRENGTH IS FADING!

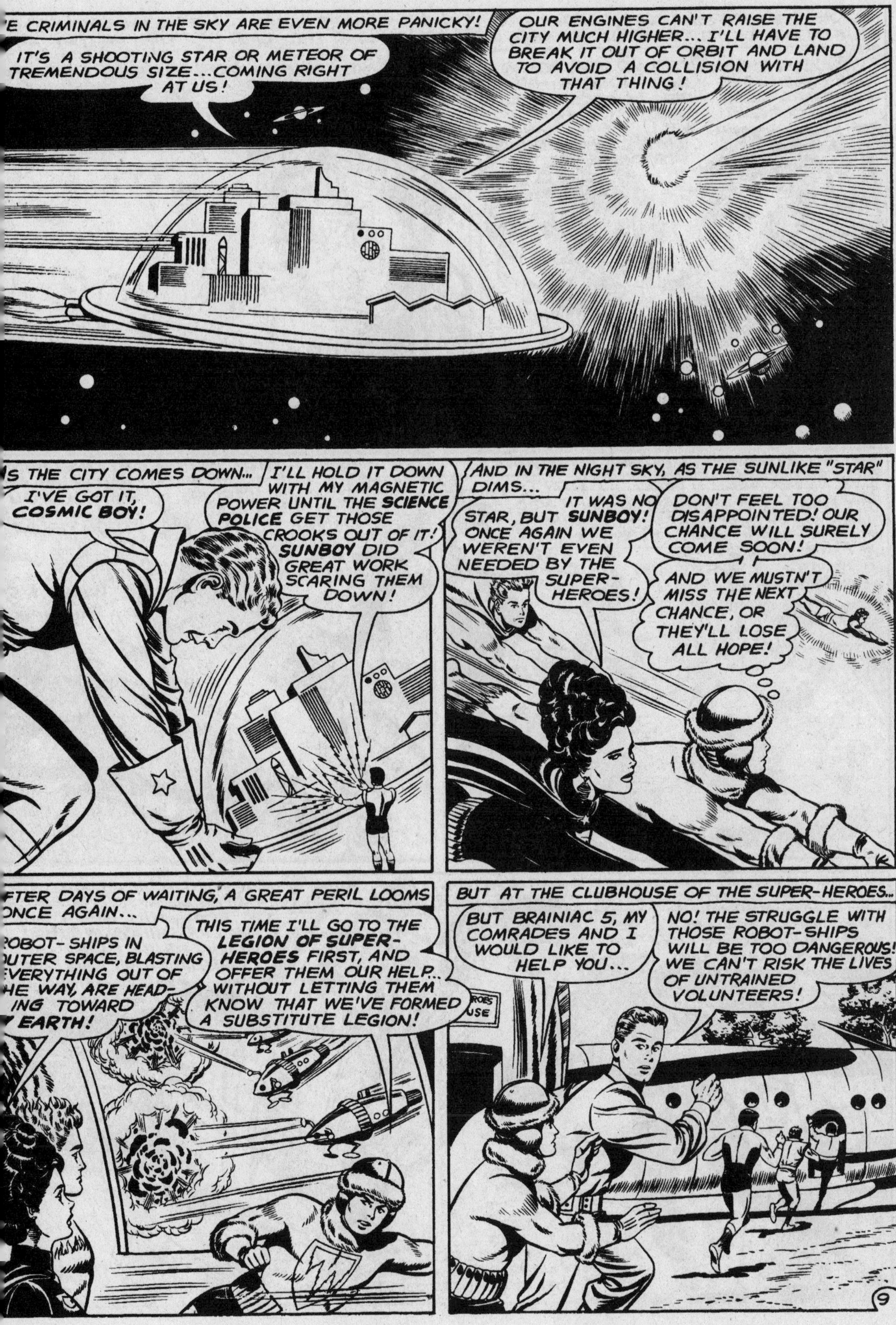
E CRIMINALS IN THE SKY ARE EVEN MORE PANICKY!
IT'S A SHOOTING STAR OR METEOR OF TREMENDOUS SIZE...COMING RIGHT AT US!
OUR ENGINES CAN'T RAISE THE CITY MUCH HIGHER... I'LL HAVE TO BREAK IT OUT OF ORBIT AND LAND TO AVOID A COLLISION WITH THAT THING!
S THE CITY COMES DOWN...
I'VE GOT IT, COSMIC BOY!
I'LL HOLD IT DOWN WITH MY MAGNETIC POWER UNTIL THE SCIENCE POLICE GET THOSE CROOKS OUT OF IT! SUNBOY DID GREAT WORK SCARING THEM DOWN!
AND IN THE NIGHT SKY, AS THE SUNLIKE "STAR" DIMS...
IT WAS NO STAR, BUT SUNBOY! ONCE AGAIN WE WEREN'T EVEN NEEDED BY THE SUPER-HEROES!
DON'T FEEL TOO DISAPPOINTED! OUR CHANCE WILL SURELY COME SOON!
AND WE MUSTN'T MISS THE NEXT CHANCE, OR THEY'LL LOSE ALL HOPE!
FTER DAYS OF WAITING, A GREAT PERIL LOOMS ONCE AGAIN...
ROBOT-SHIPS IN OUTER SPACE, BLASTING EVERYTHING OUT OF HE WAY, ARE HEAD-ING TOWARD EARTH!
THIS TIME I'LL GO TO THE LEGION OF SUPER-HEROES FIRST, AND OFFER THEM OUR HELP... WITHOUT LETTING THEM KNOW THAT WE'VE FORMED A SUBSTITUTE LEGION!
BUT AT THE CLUBHOUSE OF THE SUPER-HEROES...
BUT BRAINIAC 5, MY COMRADES AND I WOULD LIKE TO HELP YOU...
NO! THE STRUGGLE WITH THOSE ROBOT-SHIPS WILL BE TOO DANGEROUS! WE CAN'T RISK THE LIVES OF UNTRAINED VOLUNTEERS!
9

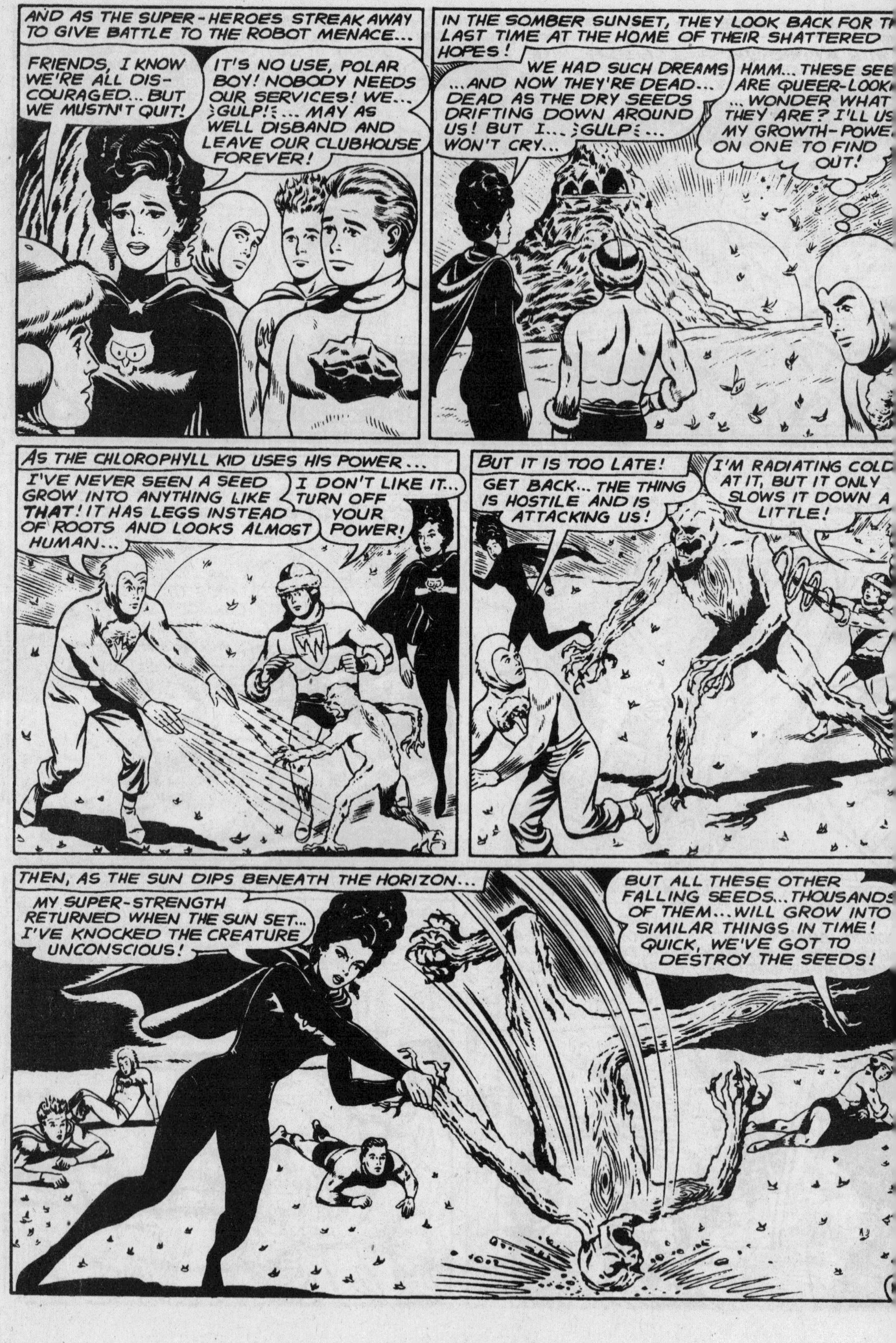
AND AS THE SUPER-HEROES STREAK AWAY TO GIVE BATTLE TO THE ROBOT MENACE...
FRIENDS, I KNOW WE'RE ALL DIS-COURAGED... BUT WE MUSTN'T QUIT!
IT'S NO USE, POLAR BOY! NOBODY NEEDS OUR SERVICES! WE... GULP! ... MAY AS WELL DISBAND AND LEAVE OUR CLUBHOUSE FOREVER!
IN THE SOMBER SUNSET, THEY LOOK BACK FOR T LAST TIME AT THE HOME OF THEIR SHATTERED HOPES!
WE HAD SUCH DREAMS ...AND NOW THEY'RE DEAD... DEAD AS THE DRY SEEDS DRIFTING DOWN AROUND US! BUT I... GULP ... WON'T CRY...
HMM... THESE SEE ARE QUEER-LOOK ...WONDER WHAT THEY ARE? I'LL US MY GROWTH-POWE ON ONE TO FIND OUT!
AS THE CHLOROPHYLL KID USES HIS POWER...
I'VE NEVER SEEN A SEED GROW INTO ANYTHING LIKE THAT! IT HAS LEGS INSTEAD OF ROOTS AND LOOKS ALMOST HUMAN...
I DON'T LIKE IT... TURN OFF YOUR POWER!
BUT IT IS TOO LATE!
GET BACK... THE THING IS HOSTILE AND IS ATTACKING US!
I'M RADIATING COLD AT IT, BUT IT ONLY SLOWS IT DOWN A LITTLE!
THEN, AS THE SUN DIPS BENEATH THE HORIZON...
MY SUPER-STRENGTH RETURNED WHEN THE SUN SET... I'VE KNOCKED THE CREATURE UNCONSCIOUS!
BUT ALL THESE OTHER FALLING SEEDS...THOUSANDS OF THEM...WILL GROW INTO SIMILAR THINGS IN TIME! QUICK, WE'VE GOT TO DESTROY THE SEEDS!

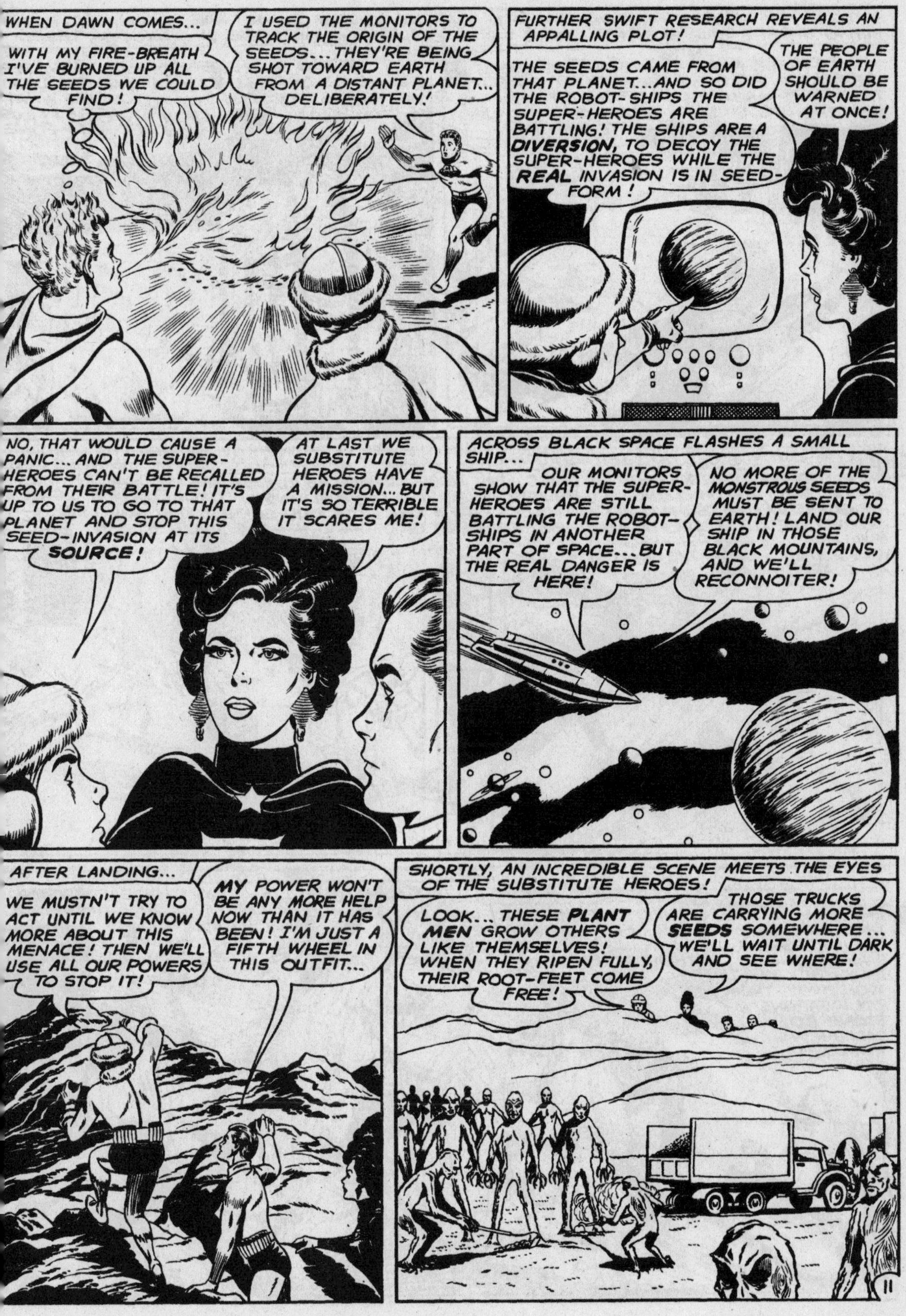
WHEN DAWN COMES...
WITH MY FIRE-BREATH I'VE BURNED UP ALL THE SEEDS WE COULD FIND!
I USED THE MONITORS TO TRACK THE ORIGIN OF THE SEEDS... THEY'RE BEING SHOT TOWARD EARTH FROM A DISTANT PLANET... DELIBERATELY!
FURTHER SWIFT RESEARCH REVEALS AN APPALLING PLOT!
THE SEEDS CAME FROM THAT PLANET...AND SO DID THE ROBOT-SHIPS THE SUPER-HEROES ARE BATTLING! THE SHIPS ARE A **DIVERSION**, TO DECOY THE SUPER-HEROES WHILE THE **REAL** INVASION IS IN SEED-FORM!
THE PEOPLE OF EARTH SHOULD BE WARNED AT ONCE!
NO, THAT WOULD CAUSE A PANIC... AND THE SUPER-HEROES CAN'T BE RECALLED FROM THEIR BATTLE! IT'S UP TO US TO GO TO THAT PLANET AND STOP THIS SEED-INVASION AT ITS **SOURCE**!
AT LAST WE SUBSTITUTE HEROES HAVE A MISSION... BUT IT'S SO TERRIBLE IT SCARES ME!
ACROSS BLACK SPACE FLASHES A SMALL SHIP...
OUR MONITORS SHOW THAT THE SUPER-HEROES ARE STILL BATTLING THE ROBOT-SHIPS IN ANOTHER PART OF SPACE... BUT THE REAL DANGER IS HERE!
NO MORE OF THE MONSTROUS SEEDS MUST BE SENT TO EARTH! LAND OUR SHIP IN THOSE BLACK MOUNTAINS, AND WE'LL RECONNOITER!
AFTER LANDING...
WE MUSTN'T TRY TO ACT UNTIL WE KNOW MORE ABOUT THIS MENACE! THEN WE'LL USE ALL OUR POWERS TO STOP IT!
MY POWER WON'T BE ANY MORE HELP NOW THAN IT HAS BEEN! I'M JUST A FIFTH WHEEL IN THIS OUTFIT...
SHORTLY, AN INCREDIBLE SCENE MEETS THE EYES OF THE SUBSTITUTE HEROES!
LOOK... THESE **PLANT MEN** GROW OTHERS LIKE THEMSELVES! WHEN THEY RIPEN FULLY, THEIR ROOT-FEET COME FREE!
THOSE TRUCKS ARE CARRYING MORE **SEEDS** SOMEWHERE... WE'LL WAIT UNTIL DARK AND SEE WHERE!
11

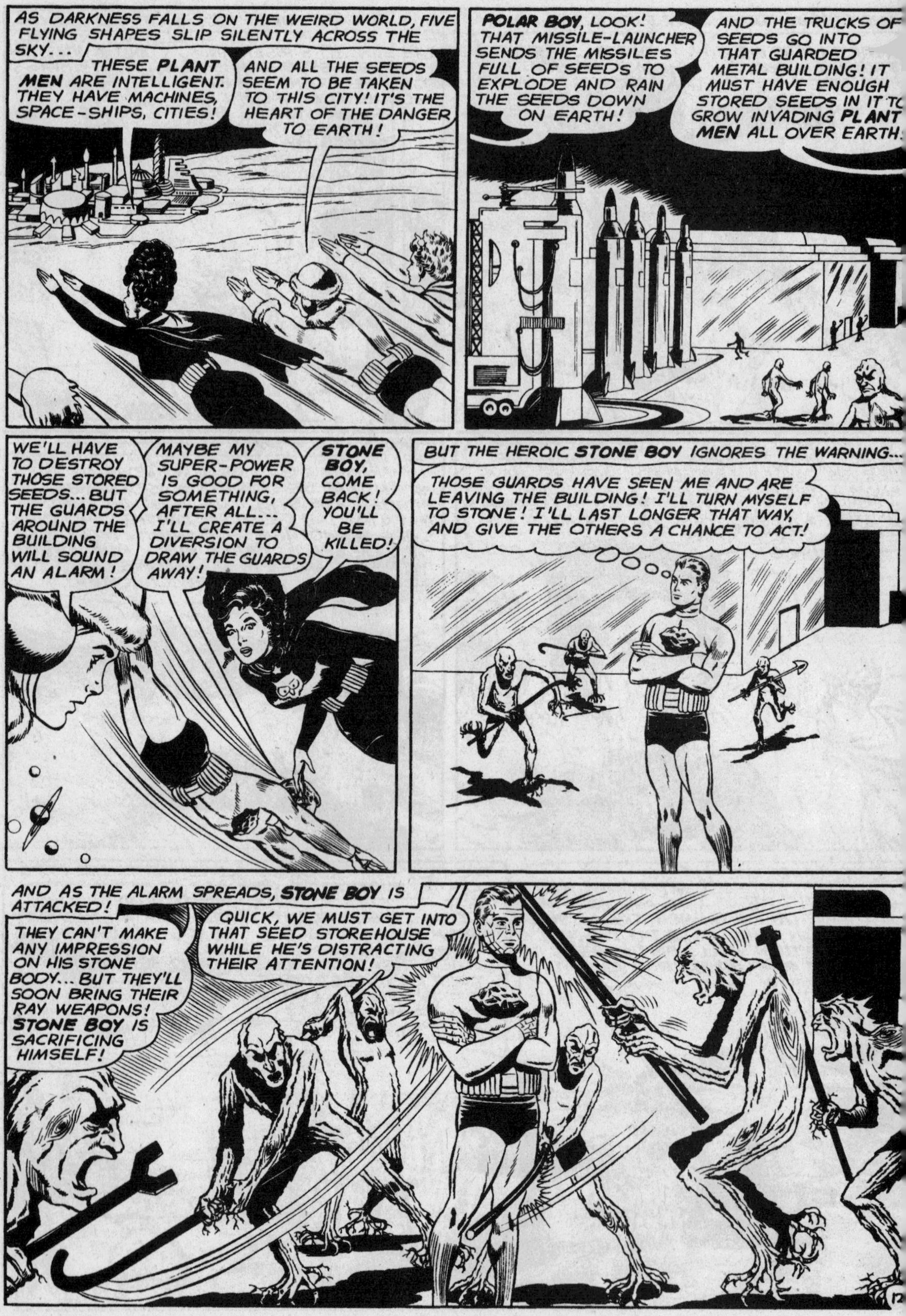
AS DARKNESS FALLS ON THE WEIRD WORLD, FIVE FLYING SHAPES SLIP SILENTLY ACROSS THE SKY...
THESE PLANT MEN ARE INTELLIGENT. THEY HAVE MACHINES, SPACE-SHIPS, CITIES!
AND ALL THE SEEDS SEEM TO BE TAKEN TO THIS CITY! IT'S THE HEART OF THE DANGER TO EARTH!
POLAR BOY, LOOK! THAT MISSILE-LAUNCHER SENDS THE MISSILES FULL OF SEEDS TO EXPLODE AND RAIN THE SEEDS DOWN ON EARTH!
AND THE TRUCKS OF SEEDS GO INTO THAT GUARDED METAL BUILDING! IT MUST HAVE ENOUGH STORED SEEDS IN IT TO GROW INVADING PLANT MEN ALL OVER EARTH!
WE'LL HAVE TO DESTROY THOSE STORED SEEDS... BUT THE GUARDS AROUND THE BUILDING WILL SOUND AN ALARM!
MAYBE MY SUPER-POWER IS GOOD FOR SOMETHING, AFTER ALL... I'LL CREATE A DIVERSION TO DRAW THE GUARDS AWAY!
STONE BOY, COME BACK! YOU'LL BE KILLED!
BUT THE HEROIC STONE BOY IGNORES THE WARNING...
THOSE GUARDS HAVE SEEN ME AND ARE LEAVING THE BUILDING! I'LL TURN MYSELF TO STONE! I'LL LAST LONGER THAT WAY, AND GIVE THE OTHERS A CHANCE TO ACT!
AND AS THE ALARM SPREADS, STONE BOY IS ATTACKED!
THEY CAN'T MAKE ANY IMPRESSION ON HIS STONE BODY... BUT THEY'LL SOON BRING THEIR RAY WEAPONS! STONE BOY IS SACRIFICING HIMSELF!
QUICK, WE MUST GET INTO THAT SEED STOREHOUSE WHILE HE'S DISTRACTING THEIR ATTENTION!

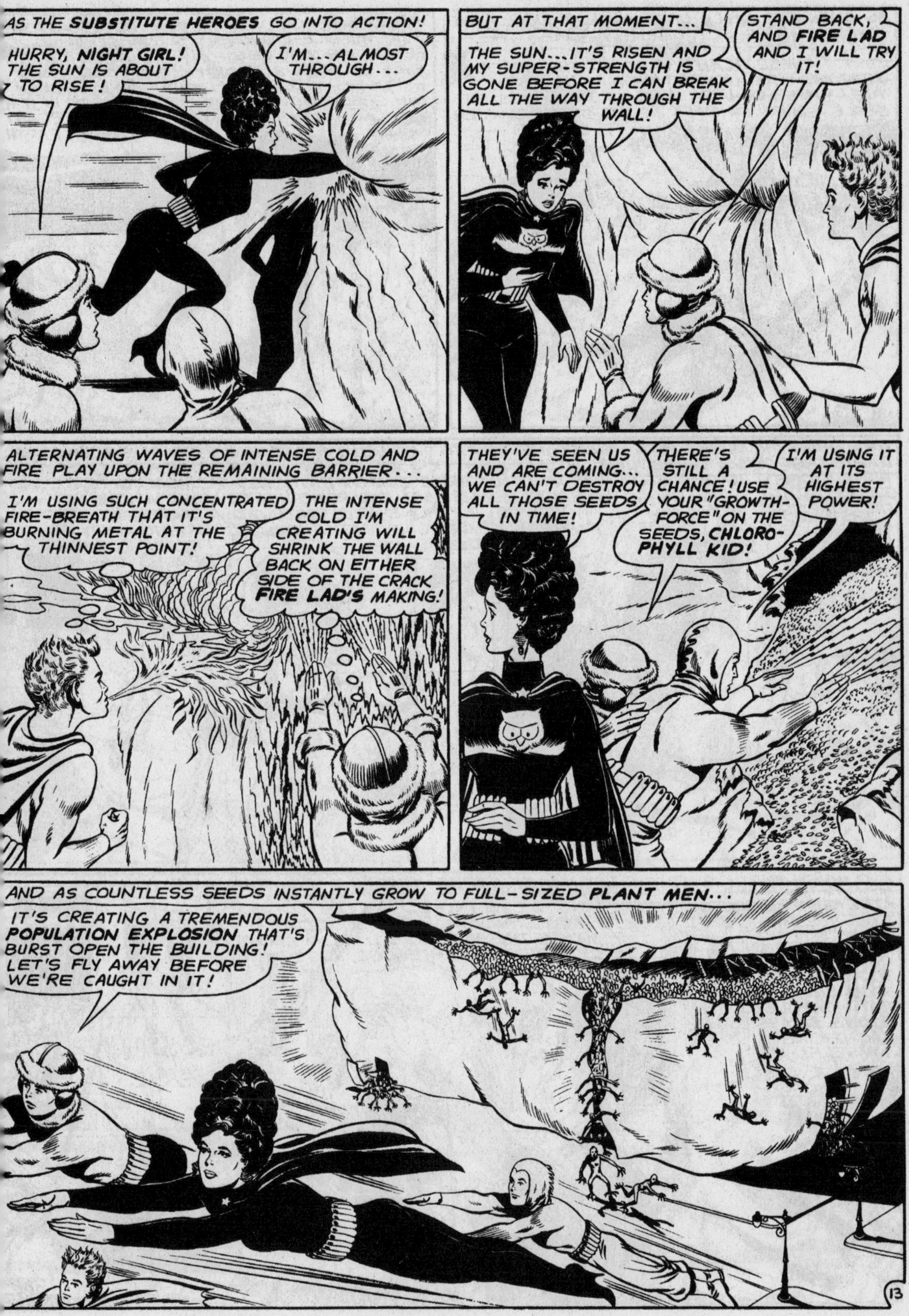
AS THE SUBSTITUTE HEROES GO INTO ACTION!
HURRY, NIGHT GIRL! THE SUN IS ABOUT TO RISE!
I'M... ALMOST THROUGH...
BUT AT THAT MOMENT...
THE SUN...IT'S RISEN AND MY SUPER-STRENGTH IS GONE BEFORE I CAN BREAK ALL THE WAY THROUGH THE WALL!
STAND BACK, AND FIRE LAD AND I WILL TRY IT!
ALTERNATING WAVES OF INTENSE COLD AND FIRE PLAY UPON THE REMAINING BARRIER...
I'M USING SUCH CONCENTRATED FIRE-BREATH THAT IT'S BURNING METAL AT THE THINNEST POINT!
THE INTENSE COLD I'M CREATING WILL SHRINK THE WALL BACK ON EITHER SIDE OF THE CRACK FIRE LAD'S MAKING!
THEY'VE SEEN US AND ARE COMING... WE CAN'T DESTROY ALL THOSE SEEDS IN TIME!
THERE'S STILL A CHANCE! USE YOUR "GROWTH-FORCE" ON THE SEEDS, CHLORO-PHYLL KID!
I'M USING IT AT ITS HIGHEST POWER!
AND AS COUNTLESS SEEDS INSTANTLY GROW TO FULL-SIZED PLANT MEN...
IT'S CREATING A TREMENDOUS POPULATION EXPLOSION THAT'S BURST OPEN THE BUILDING! LET'S FLY AWAY BEFORE WE'RE CAUGHT IN IT!
13

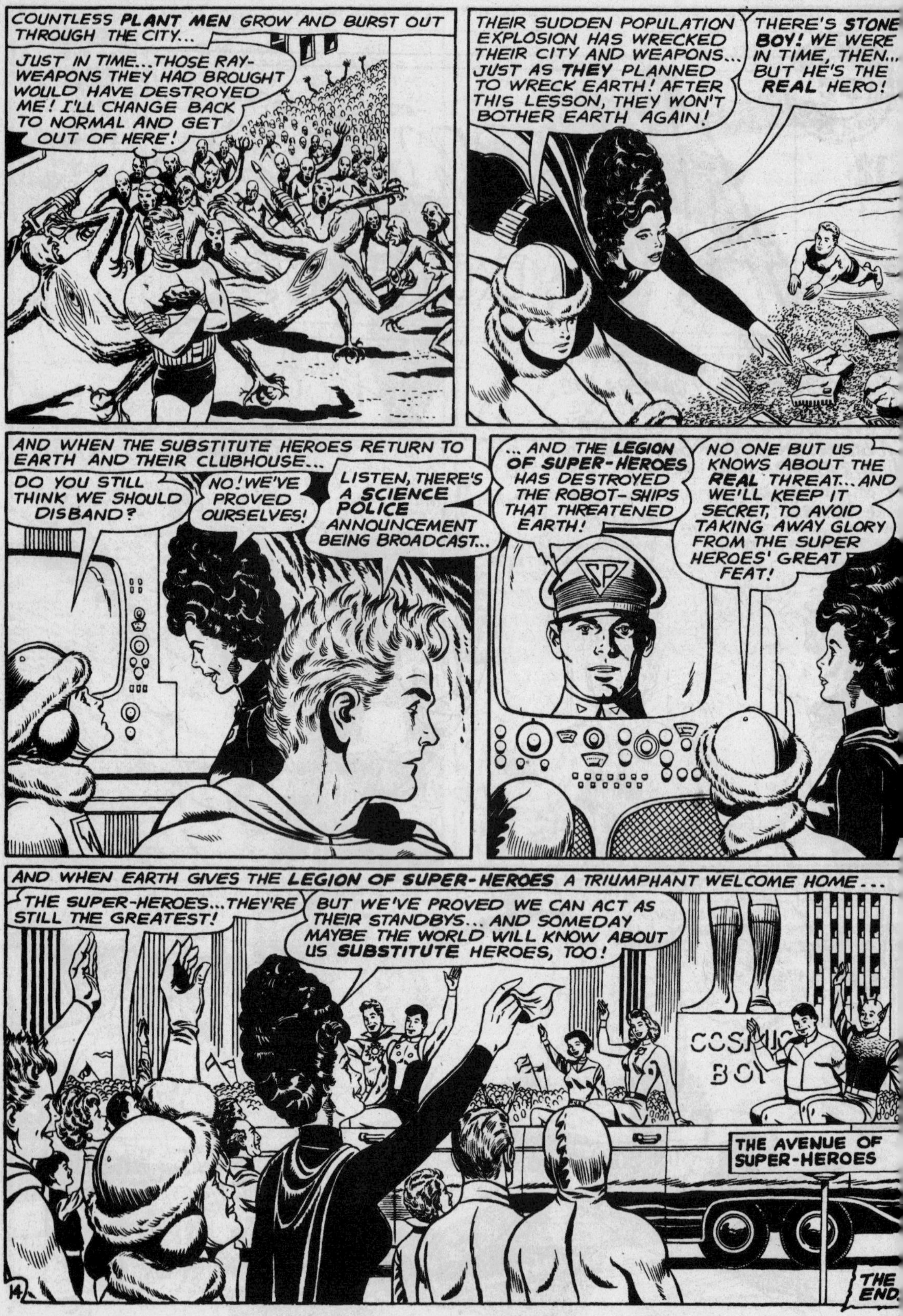
COUNTLESS PLANT MEN GROW AND BURST OUT THROUGH THE CITY...
JUST IN TIME... THOSE RAY-WEAPONS THEY HAD BROUGHT WOULD HAVE DESTROYED ME! I'LL CHANGE BACK TO NORMAL AND GET OUT OF HERE!
THEIR SUDDEN POPULATION EXPLOSION HAS WRECKED THEIR CITY AND WEAPONS... JUST AS THEY PLANNED TO WRECK EARTH! AFTER THIS LESSON, THEY WON'T BOTHER EARTH AGAIN!
THERE'S STONE BOY! WE WERE IN TIME, THEN... BUT HE'S THE REAL HERO!
AND WHEN THE SUBSTITUTE HEROES RETURN TO EARTH AND THEIR CLUBHOUSE...
DO YOU STILL THINK WE SHOULD DISBAND?
NO! WE'VE PROVED OURSELVES!
LISTEN, THERE'S A SCIENCE POLICE ANNOUNCEMENT BEING BROADCAST...
... AND THE LEGION OF SUPER-HEROES HAS DESTROYED THE ROBOT-SHIPS THAT THREATENED EARTH!
NO ONE BUT US KNOWS ABOUT THE REAL THREAT... AND WE'LL KEEP IT SECRET, TO AVOID TAKING AWAY GLORY FROM THE SUPER HEROES' GREAT FEAT!
AND WHEN EARTH GIVES THE LEGION OF SUPER-HEROES A TRIUMPHANT WELCOME HOME...
THE SUPER-HEROES... THEY'RE STILL THE GREATEST!
BUT WE'VE PROVED WE CAN ACT AS THEIR STANDBYS... AND SOMEDAY MAYBE THE WORLD WILL KNOW ABOUT US SUBSTITUTE HEROES, TOO!
COSMIC BOY
THE AVENUE OF SUPER-HEROES
14
THE END

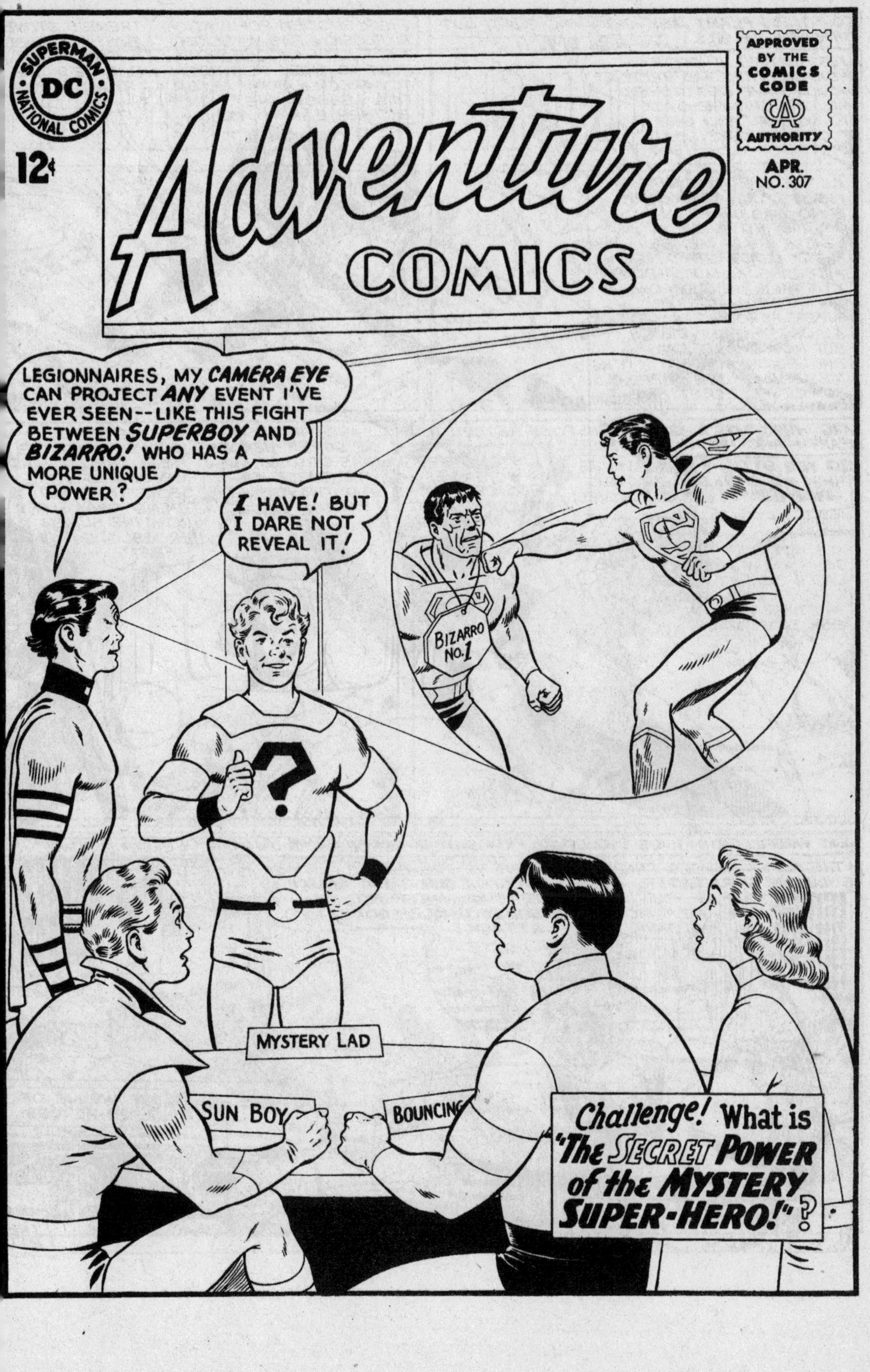
SUPERMAN DC NATIONAL COMICS
12¢
Adventure COMICS
APPROVED BY THE COMICS CODE AUTHORITY
APR. NO. 307
LEGIONNAIRES, MY CAMERA EYE CAN PROJECT ANY EVENT I'VE EVER SEEN--LIKE THIS FIGHT BETWEEN SUPERBOY AND BIZARRO! WHO HAS A MORE UNIQUE POWER?
I HAVE! BUT I DARE NOT REVEAL IT!
BIZARRO No. 1
MYSTERY LAD
SUN BOY
BOUNCING
Challenge! What is "The SECRET POWER of the MYSTERY SUPER-HERO!"?

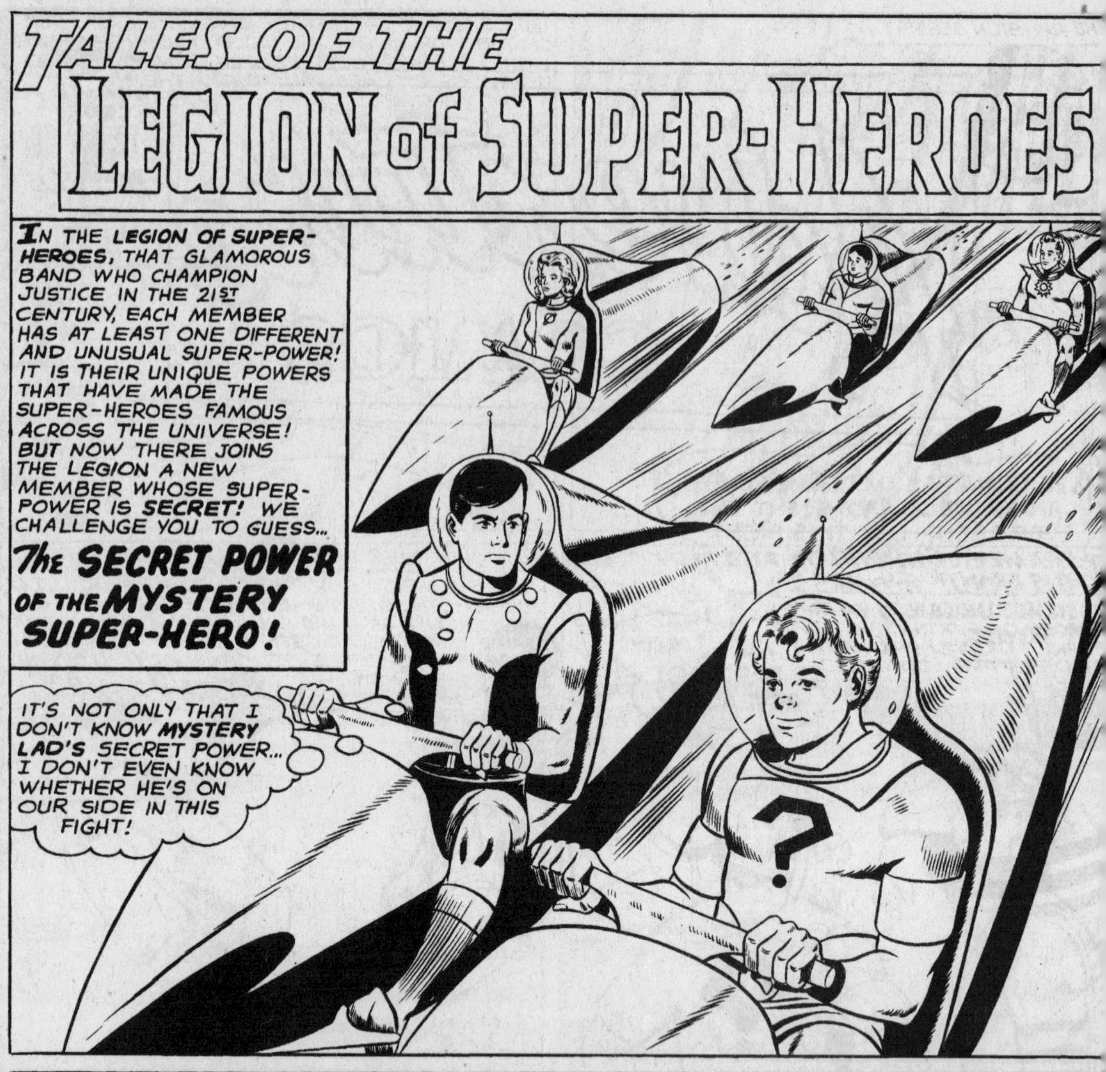
TALES OF THE
LEGION of SUPER-HEROES
IN THE LEGION OF SUPER-HEROES, THAT GLAMOROUS BAND WHO CHAMPION JUSTICE IN THE 21ST CENTURY, EACH MEMBER HAS AT LEAST ONE DIFFERENT AND UNUSUAL SUPER-POWER! IT IS THEIR UNIQUE POWERS THAT HAVE MADE THE SUPER-HEROES FAMOUS ACROSS THE UNIVERSE! BUT NOW THERE JOINS THE LEGION A NEW MEMBER WHOSE SUPER-POWER IS SECRET! WE CHALLENGE YOU TO GUESS...
The SECRET POWER of the MYSTERY SUPER-HERO!
IT'S NOT ONLY THAT I DON'T KNOW MYSTERY LAD'S SECRET POWER... I DON'T EVEN KNOW WHETHER HE'S ON OUR SIDE IN THIS FIGHT!

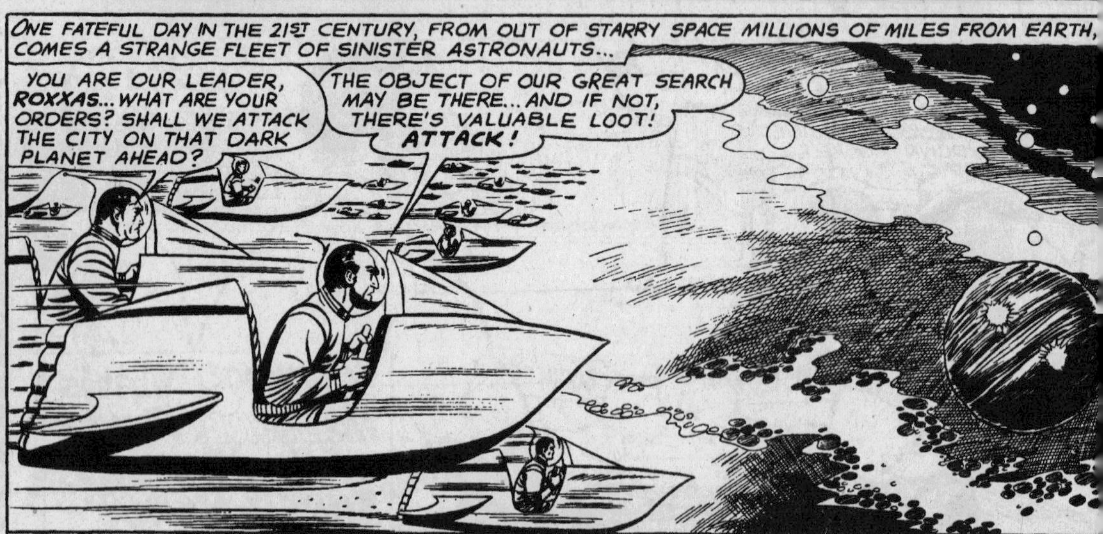
ONE FATEFUL DAY IN THE 21ST CENTURY, FROM OUT OF STARRY SPACE MILLIONS OF MILES FROM EARTH, COMES A STRANGE FLEET OF SINISTER ASTRONAUTS...
YOU ARE OUR LEADER, ROXXAS... WHAT ARE YOUR ORDERS? SHALL WE ATTACK THE CITY ON THAT DARK PLANET AHEAD?
THE OBJECT OF OUR GREAT SEARCH MAY BE THERE... AND IF NOT, THERE'S VALUABLE LOOT! ATTACK!

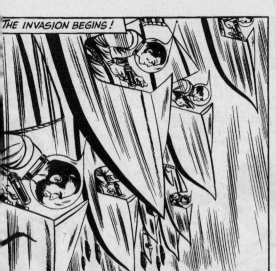

THE INVASION BEGINS!

THE OBJECT OF OUR SEARCH ISN'T ON THIS WORLD. BUT THE "COLD LIGHT" GLOBES THESE PEOPLE USE IN THEIR CITY ARE VALUABLE! TAKE THEM ALL!

IT'S EASY... OUR SURPRISE STRIKE OVERWHELMED THEM!

FROM A MONITOR ROOM IN THE ATTACKED CITY GOES A FRANTIC CALL FOR HELP!

CALLING THE LEGION OF SUPER-HEROES ON EARTH! THIS IS THE PLANET ORANZ! UNKNOWN RAIDERS ARE LOOTING OUR CITY!

WE OF THE LEGION WILL COME AT TOP SPEED!

BUT WHEN THEIR SHIP REACHES THE DARK PLANET...

THEY SEEMED SEARCHING FOR SOMETHING, BUT WHEN THEY DIDN'T FIND IT THEY STOLE OUR "COLD LIGHT" GLOBES AND DARKENED OUR WORLD! BUT WE SHOT DOWN ONE OF THEIR ROCKETS!

THEN WE'RE TOO LATE! BUT THIS WORLD MUST HAVE LIGHT, SUN BOY!

I'LL DO WHAT I CAN, COSMIC BOY!

AS SUN BOY USES HIS UNIQUE POWER OF RADIATING LIGHT AND HEAT...

SUN BOY IS MAKING A BIG PEAK WHITE-HOT, SO THE PEOPLE WILL HAVE LIGHT UNTIL THEY CAN MAKE NEW "COLD LIGHT" GLOBES! HAVE YOU EXAMINED THIS SHOT-DOWN ROCKET, BRAINIAC 5?

YES...

2

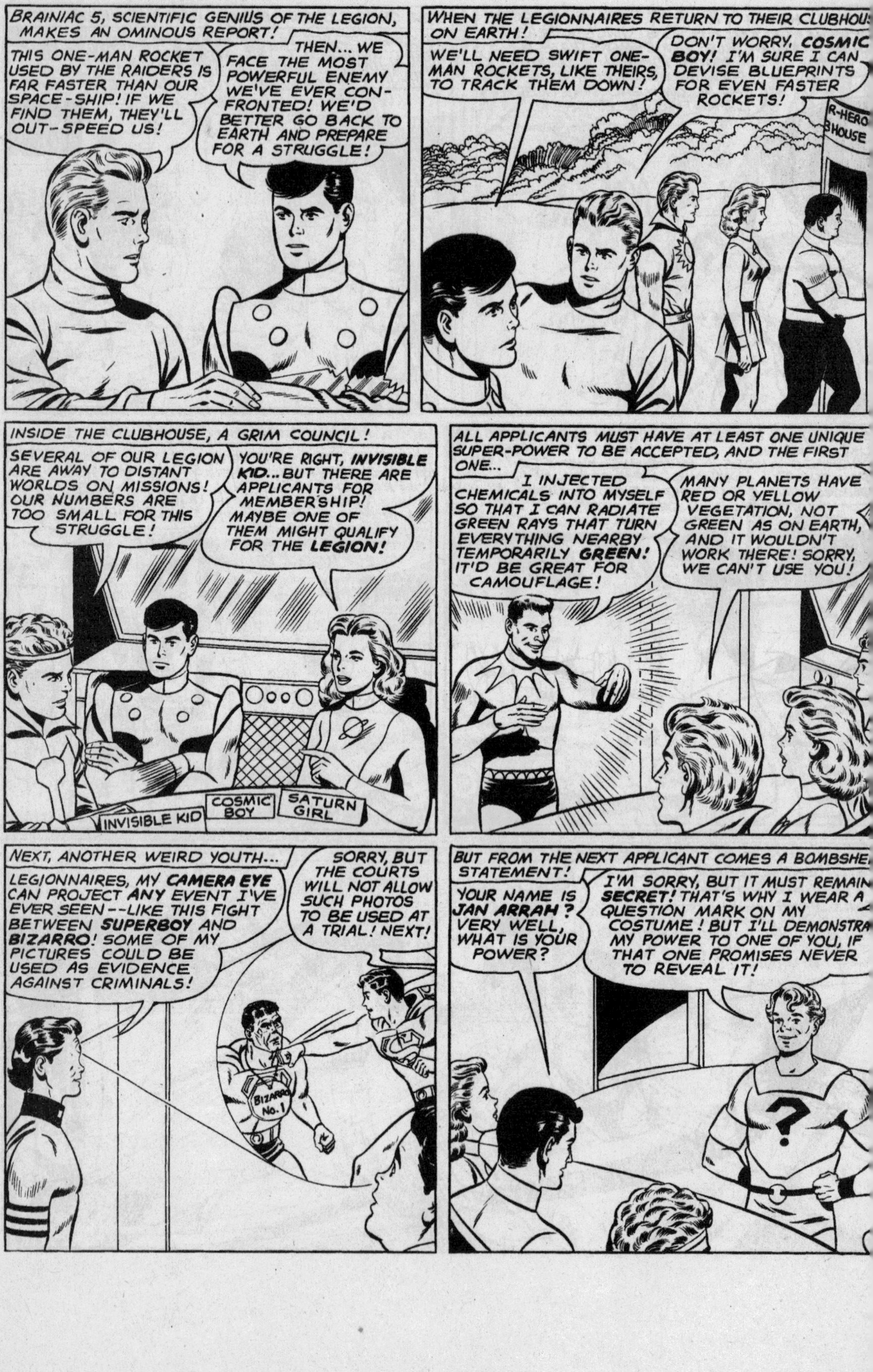
BRAINIAC 5, SCIENTIFIC GENIUS OF THE LEGION, MAKES AN OMINOUS REPORT!
THIS ONE-MAN ROCKET USED BY THE RAIDERS IS FAR FASTER THAN OUR SPACE-SHIP! IF WE FIND THEM, THEY'LL OUT-SPEED US!
THEN... WE FACE THE MOST POWERFUL ENEMY WE'VE EVER CONFRONTED! WE'D BETTER GO BACK TO EARTH AND PREPARE FOR A STRUGGLE!
WHEN THE LEGIONNAIRES RETURN TO THEIR CLUBHOUS
ON EARTH!
WE'LL NEED SWIFT ONE-MAN ROCKETS, LIKE THEIRS, TO TRACK THEM DOWN!
DON'T WORRY, COSMIC BOY! I'M SURE I CAN DEVISE BLUEPRINTS FOR EVEN FASTER ROCKETS!
R-HERO
HOUSE
INSIDE THE CLUBHOUSE, A GRIM COUNCIL!
SEVERAL OF OUR LEGION ARE AWAY TO DISTANT WORLDS ON MISSIONS! OUR NUMBERS ARE TOO SMALL FOR THIS STRUGGLE!
YOU'RE RIGHT, INVISIBLE KID... BUT THERE ARE APPLICANTS FOR MEMBERSHIP! MAYBE ONE OF THEM MIGHT QUALIFY FOR THE LEGION!
INVISIBLE KID
COSMIC BOY
SATURN GIRL
ALL APPLICANTS MUST HAVE AT LEAST ONE UNIQUE SUPER-POWER TO BE ACCEPTED, AND THE FIRST ONE...
I INJECTED CHEMICALS INTO MYSELF SO THAT I CAN RADIATE GREEN RAYS THAT TURN EVERYTHING NEARBY TEMPORARILY GREEN! IT'D BE GREAT FOR CAMOUFLAGE!
MANY PLANETS HAVE RED OR YELLOW VEGETATION, NOT GREEN AS ON EARTH, AND IT WOULDN'T WORK THERE! SORRY, WE CAN'T USE YOU!
NEXT, ANOTHER WEIRD YOUTH...
LEGIONNAIRES, MY CAMERA EYE CAN PROJECT ANY EVENT I'VE EVER SEEN--LIKE THIS FIGHT BETWEEN SUPERBOY AND BIZARRO! SOME OF MY PICTURES COULD BE USED AS EVIDENCE AGAINST CRIMINALS!
SORRY, BUT THE COURTS WILL NOT ALLOW SUCH PHOTOS TO BE USED AT A TRIAL! NEXT!
BIZARRO No. 1
BUT FROM THE NEXT APPLICANT COMES A BOMBSHE
STATEMENT!
YOUR NAME IS JAN ARRAH? VERY WELL, WHAT IS YOUR POWER?
I'M SORRY, BUT IT MUST REMAIN SECRET! THAT'S WHY I WEAR A QUESTION MARK ON MY COSTUME! BUT I'LL DEMONSTRA MY POWER TO ONE OF YOU, IF THAT ONE PROMISES NEVER TO REVEAL IT!

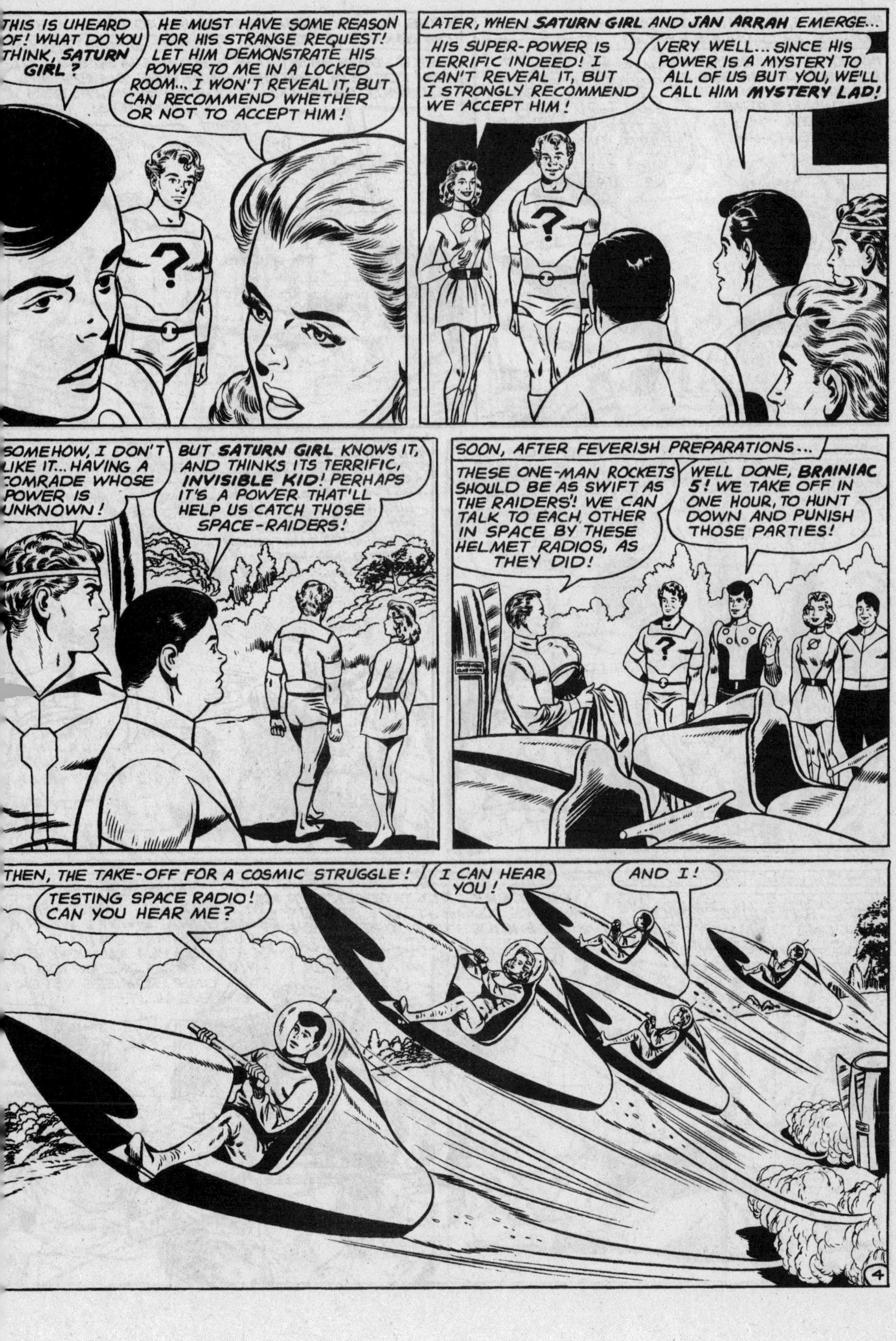
THIS IS UHEARD OF! WHAT DO YOU THINK, SATURN GIRL?
HE MUST HAVE SOME REASON FOR HIS STRANGE REQUEST! LET HIM DEMONSTRATE HIS POWER TO ME IN A LOCKED ROOM... I WON'T REVEAL IT, BUT CAN RECOMMEND WHETHER OR NOT TO ACCEPT HIM!
LATER, WHEN SATURN GIRL AND JAN ARRAH EMERGE...
HIS SUPER-POWER IS TERRIFIC INDEED! I CAN'T REVEAL IT, BUT I STRONGLY RECOMMEND WE ACCEPT HIM!
VERY WELL... SINCE HIS POWER IS A MYSTERY TO ALL OF US BUT YOU, WE'LL CALL HIM MYSTERY LAD!
SOMEHOW, I DON'T LIKE IT... HAVING A COMRADE WHOSE POWER IS UNKNOWN!
BUT SATURN GIRL KNOWS IT, AND THINKS ITS TERRIFIC, INVISIBLE KID! PERHAPS IT'S A POWER THAT'LL HELP US CATCH THOSE SPACE-RAIDERS!
SOON, AFTER FEVERISH PREPARATIONS...
THESE ONE-MAN ROCKETS SHOULD BE AS SWIFT AS THE RAIDERS! WE CAN TALK TO EACH OTHER IN SPACE BY THESE HELMET RADIOS, AS THEY DID!
WELL DONE, BRAINIAC 5! WE TAKE OFF IN ONE HOUR, TO HUNT DOWN AND PUNISH THOSE PARTIES!
THEN, THE TAKE-OFF FOR A COSMIC STRUGGLE!
TESTING SPACE RADIO! CAN YOU HEAR ME?
I CAN HEAR YOU!
AND I!
4

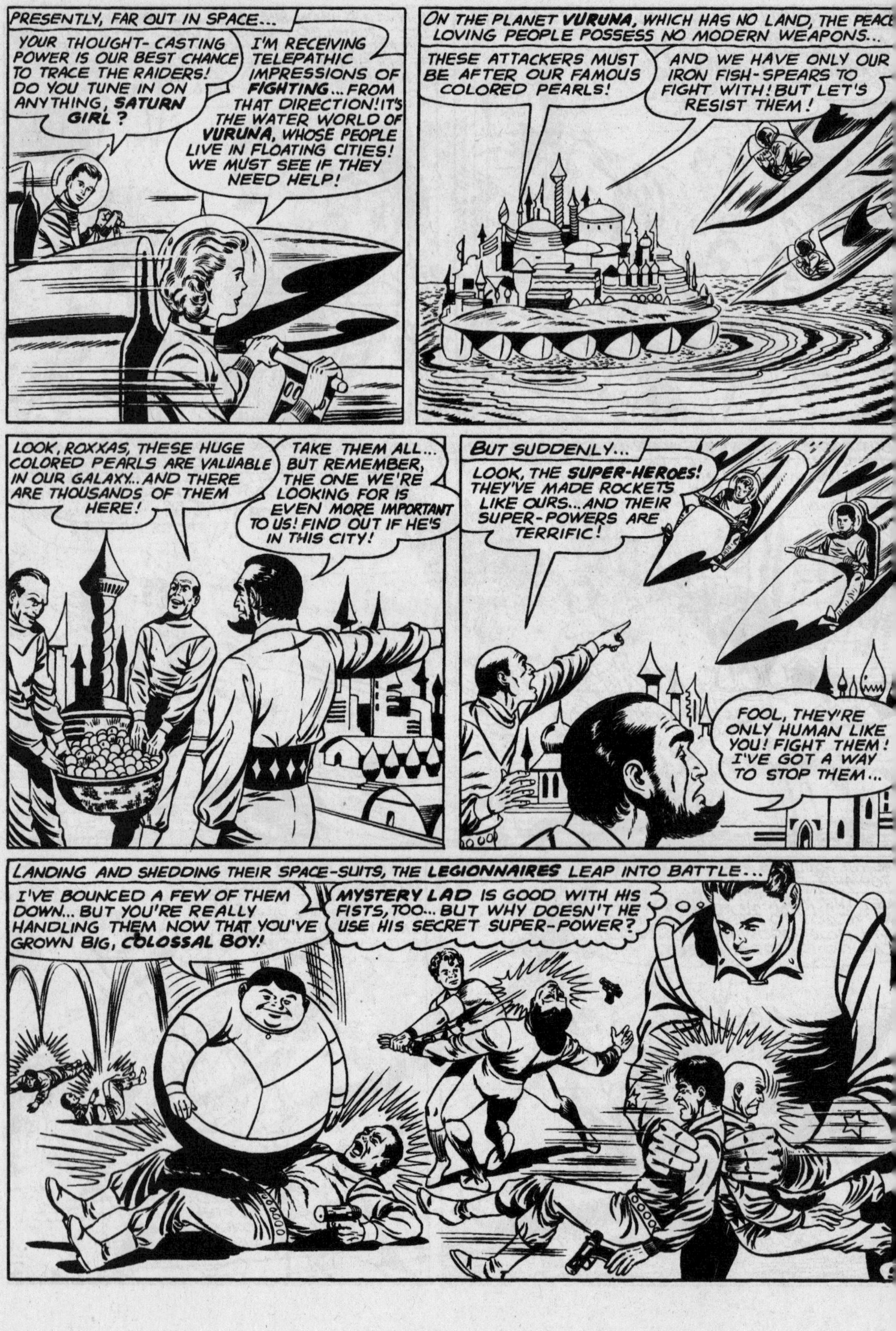
PRESENTLY, FAR OUT IN SPACE...
YOUR THOUGHT-CASTING POWER IS OUR BEST CHANCE TO TRACE THE RAIDERS! DO YOU TUNE IN ON ANYTHING, SATURN GIRL?
I'M RECEIVING TELEPATHIC IMPRESSIONS OF FIGHTING... FROM THAT DIRECTION! IT'S THE WATER WORLD OF VURUNA, WHOSE PEOPLE LIVE IN FLOATING CITIES! WE MUST SEE IF THEY NEED HELP!
ON THE PLANET VURUNA, WHICH HAS NO LAND, THE PEACE LOVING PEOPLE POSSESS NO MODERN WEAPONS...
THESE ATTACKERS MUST BE AFTER OUR FAMOUS COLORED PEARLS!
AND WE HAVE ONLY OUR IRON FISH-SPEARS TO FIGHT WITH! BUT LET'S RESIST THEM!
LOOK, ROXXAS, THESE HUGE COLORED PEARLS ARE VALUABLE IN OUR GALAXY... AND THERE ARE THOUSANDS OF THEM HERE!
TAKE THEM ALL... BUT REMEMBER, THE ONE WE'RE LOOKING FOR IS EVEN MORE IMPORTANT TO US! FIND OUT IF HE'S IN THIS CITY!
BUT SUDDENLY...
LOOK, THE SUPER-HEROES! THEY'VE MADE ROCKETS LIKE OURS... AND THEIR SUPER-POWERS ARE TERRIFIC!
FOOL, THEY'RE ONLY HUMAN LIKE YOU! FIGHT THEM! I'VE GOT A WAY TO STOP THEM...
LANDING AND SHEDDING THEIR SPACE-SUITS, THE LEGIONNAIRES LEAP INTO BATTLE...
I'VE BOUNCED A FEW OF THEM DOWN... BUT YOU'RE REALLY HANDLING THEM NOW THAT YOU'VE GROWN BIG, COLOSSAL BOY!
MYSTERY LAD IS GOOD WITH HIS FISTS, TOO... BUT WHY DOESN'T HE USE HIS SECRET SUPER-POWER?

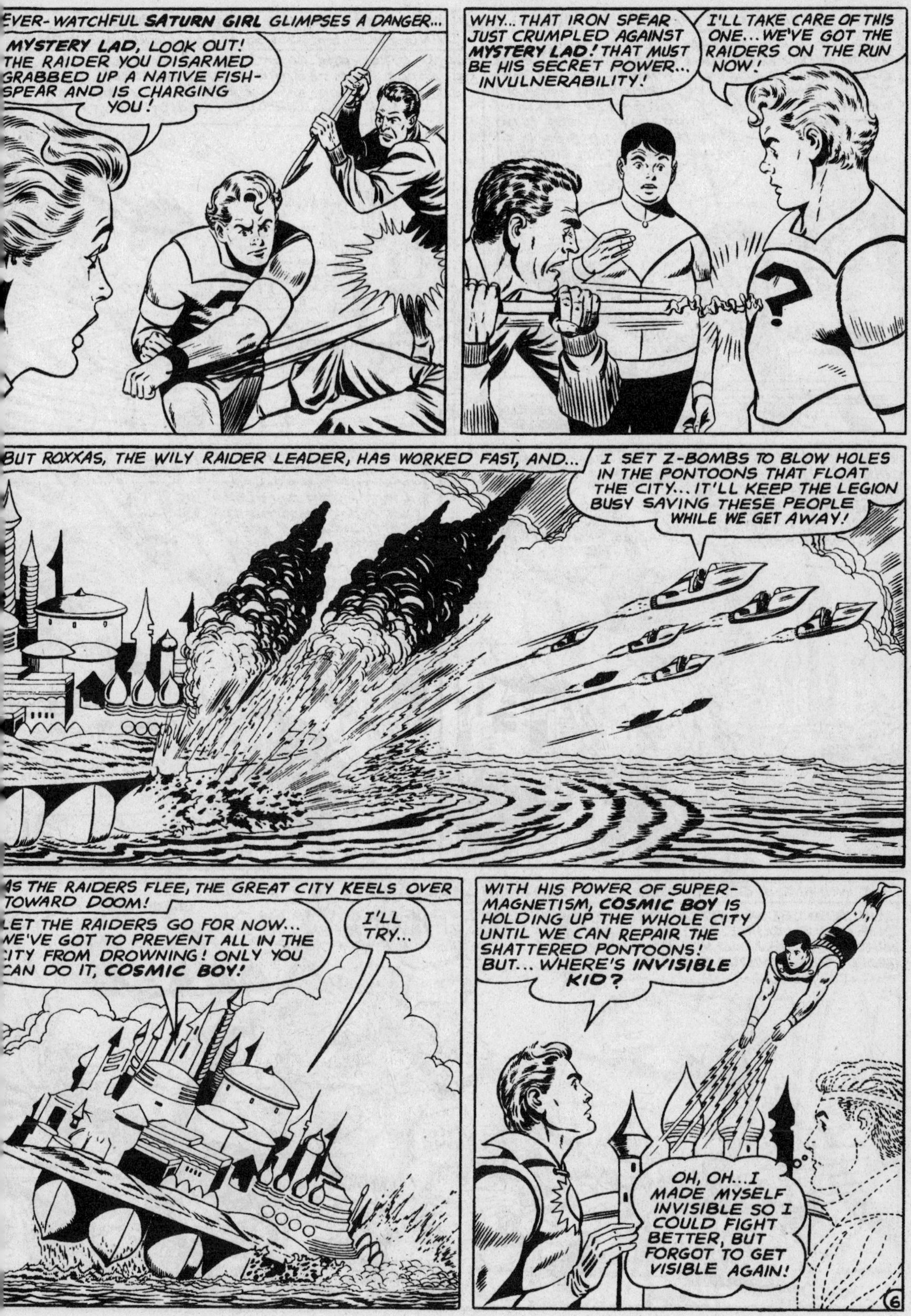
EVER-WATCHFUL SATURN GIRL GLIMPSES A DANGER...
MYSTERY LAD, LOOK OUT! THE RAIDER YOU DISARMED GRABBED UP A NATIVE FISH-SPEAR AND IS CHARGING YOU!
WHY... THAT IRON SPEAR JUST CRUMPLED AGAINST MYSTERY LAD! THAT MUST BE HIS SECRET POWER... INVULNERABILITY!
I'LL TAKE CARE OF THIS ONE... WE'VE GOT THE RAIDERS ON THE RUN NOW!
BUT ROXXAS, THE WILY RAIDER LEADER, HAS WORKED FAST, AND...
I SET Z-BOMBS TO BLOW HOLES IN THE PONTOONS THAT FLOAT THE CITY... IT'LL KEEP THE LEGION BUSY SAVING THESE PEOPLE WHILE WE GET AWAY!
AS THE RAIDERS FLEE, THE GREAT CITY KEELS OVER TOWARD DOOM!
LET THE RAIDERS GO FOR NOW... WE'VE GOT TO PREVENT ALL IN THE CITY FROM DROWNING! ONLY YOU CAN DO IT, COSMIC BOY!
I'LL TRY...
WITH HIS POWER OF SUPER-MAGNETISM, COSMIC BOY IS HOLDING UP THE WHOLE CITY UNTIL WE CAN REPAIR THE SHATTERED PONTOONS! BUT... WHERE'S INVISIBLE KID?
OH, OH... I MADE MYSELF INVISIBLE SO I COULD FIGHT BETTER, BUT FORGOT TO GET VISIBLE AGAIN!
6

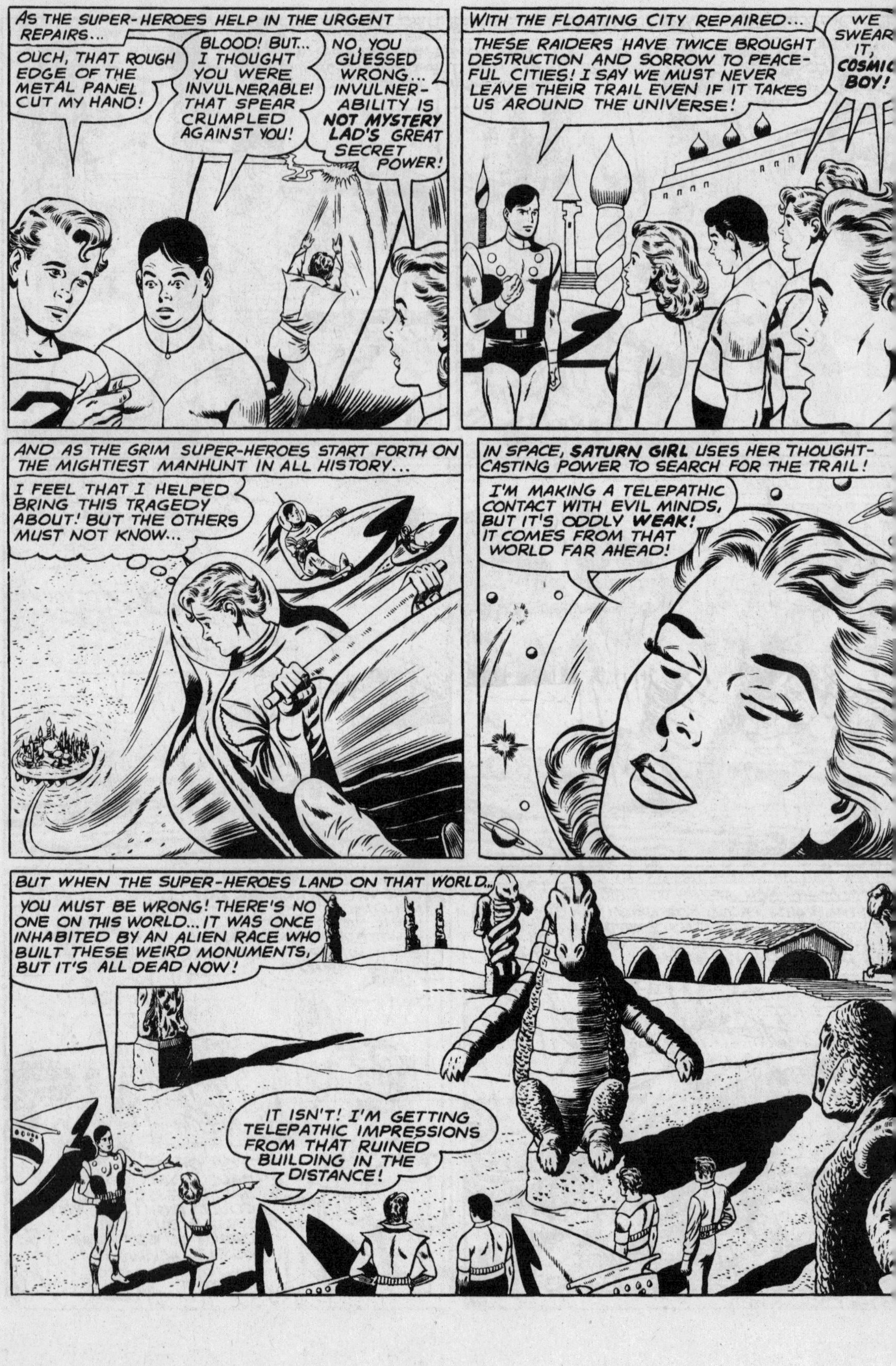
AS THE SUPER-HEROES HELP IN THE URGENT REPAIRS...
OUCH, THAT ROUGH EDGE OF THE METAL PANEL CUT MY HAND!
BLOOD! BUT... I THOUGHT YOU WERE INVULNERABLE! THAT SPEAR CRUMPLED AGAINST YOU!
NO, YOU GUESSED WRONG... INVULNERABILITY IS NOT MYSTERY LAD'S GREAT SECRET POWER!
WITH THE FLOATING CITY REPAIRED...
THESE RAIDERS HAVE TWICE BROUGHT DESTRUCTION AND SORROW TO PEACEFUL CITIES! I SAY WE MUST NEVER LEAVE THEIR TRAIL EVEN IF IT TAKES US AROUND THE UNIVERSE!
WE SWEAR IT, COSMIC BOY!
AND AS THE GRIM SUPER-HEROES START FORTH ON THE MIGHTIEST MANHUNT IN ALL HISTORY...
I FEEL THAT I HELPED BRING THIS TRAGEDY ABOUT! BUT THE OTHERS MUST NOT KNOW...
IN SPACE, SATURN GIRL USES HER THOUGHT-CASTING POWER TO SEARCH FOR THE TRAIL!
I'M MAKING A TELEPATHIC CONTACT WITH EVIL MINDS, BUT IT'S ODDLY WEAK! IT COMES FROM THAT WORLD FAR AHEAD!
BUT WHEN THE SUPER-HEROES LAND ON THAT WORLD...
YOU MUST BE WRONG! THERE'S NO ONE ON THIS WORLD... IT WAS ONCE INHABITED BY AN ALIEN RACE WHO BUILT THESE WEIRD MONUMENTS, BUT IT'S ALL DEAD NOW!
IT ISN'T! I'M GETTING TELEPATHIC IMPRESSIONS FROM THAT RUINED BUILDING IN THE DISTANCE!

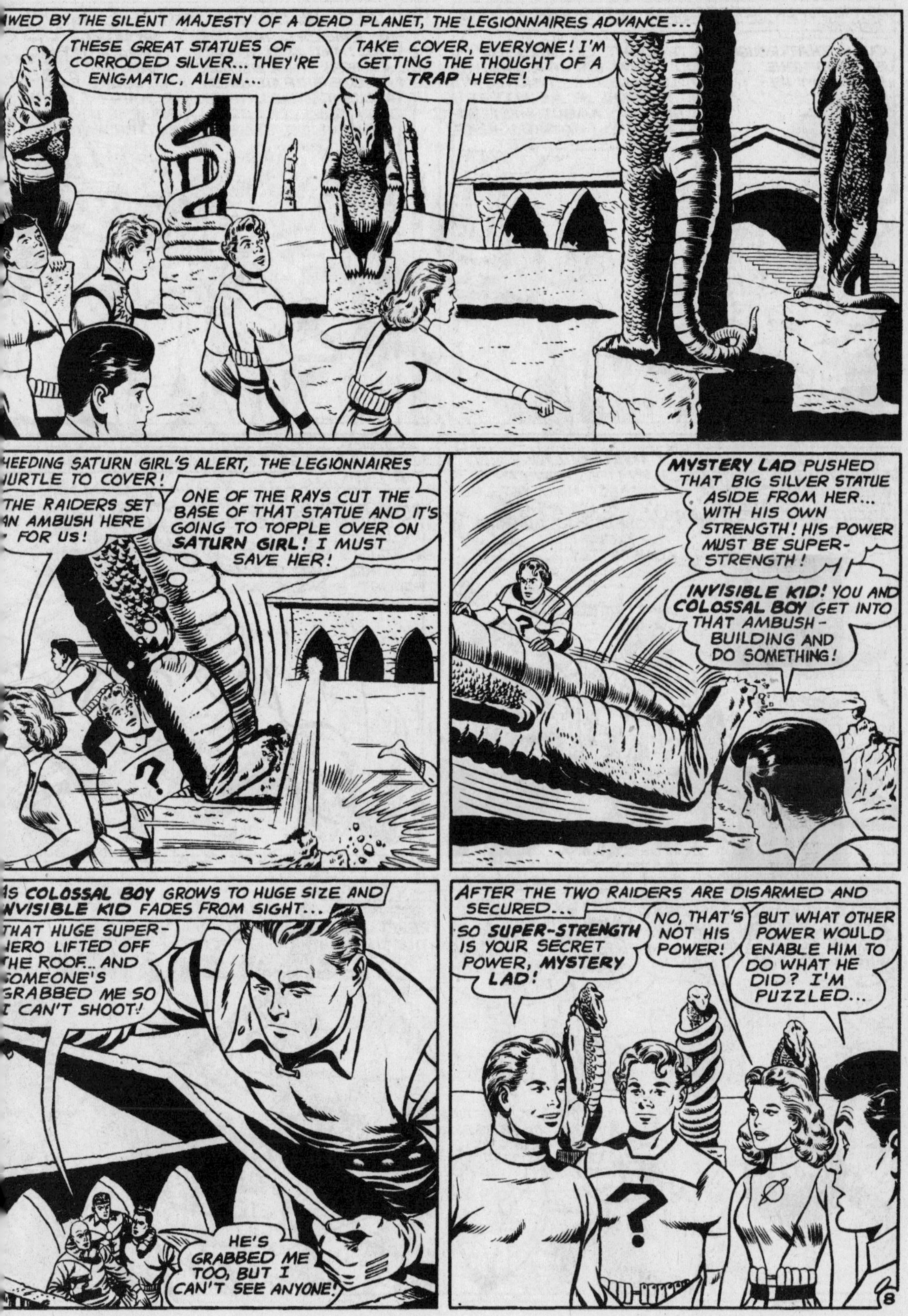
WED BY THE SILENT MAJESTY OF A DEAD PLANET, THE LEGIONNAIRES ADVANCE...
THESE GREAT STATUES OF CORRODED SILVER... THEY'RE ENIGMATIC, ALIEN...
TAKE COVER, EVERYONE! I'M GETTING THE THOUGHT OF A TRAP HERE!
HEEDING SATURN GIRL'S ALERT, THE LEGIONNAIRES HURTLE TO COVER!
THE RAIDERS SET AN AMBUSH HERE FOR US!
ONE OF THE RAYS CUT THE BASE OF THAT STATUE AND IT'S GOING TO TOPPLE OVER ON SATURN GIRL! I MUST SAVE HER!
MYSTERY LAD PUSHED THAT BIG SILVER STATUE ASIDE FROM HER... WITH HIS OWN STRENGTH! HIS POWER MUST BE SUPER-STRENGTH!
INVISIBLE KID! YOU AND COLOSSAL BOY GET INTO THAT AMBUSH-BUILDING AND DO SOMETHING!
S COLOSSAL BOY GROWS TO HUGE SIZE AND NVISIBLE KID FADES FROM SIGHT...
THAT HUGE SUPER-HERO LIFTED OFF THE ROOF... AND SOMEONE'S GRABBED ME SO I CAN'T SHOOT!
HE'S GRABBED ME TOO, BUT I CAN'T SEE ANYONE!
AFTER THE TWO RAIDERS ARE DISARMED AND SECURED...
SO SUPER-STRENGTH IS YOUR SECRET POWER, MYSTERY LAD!
NO, THAT'S NOT HIS POWER!
BUT WHAT OTHER POWER WOULD ENABLE HIM TO DO WHAT HE DID? I'M PUZZLED...
8

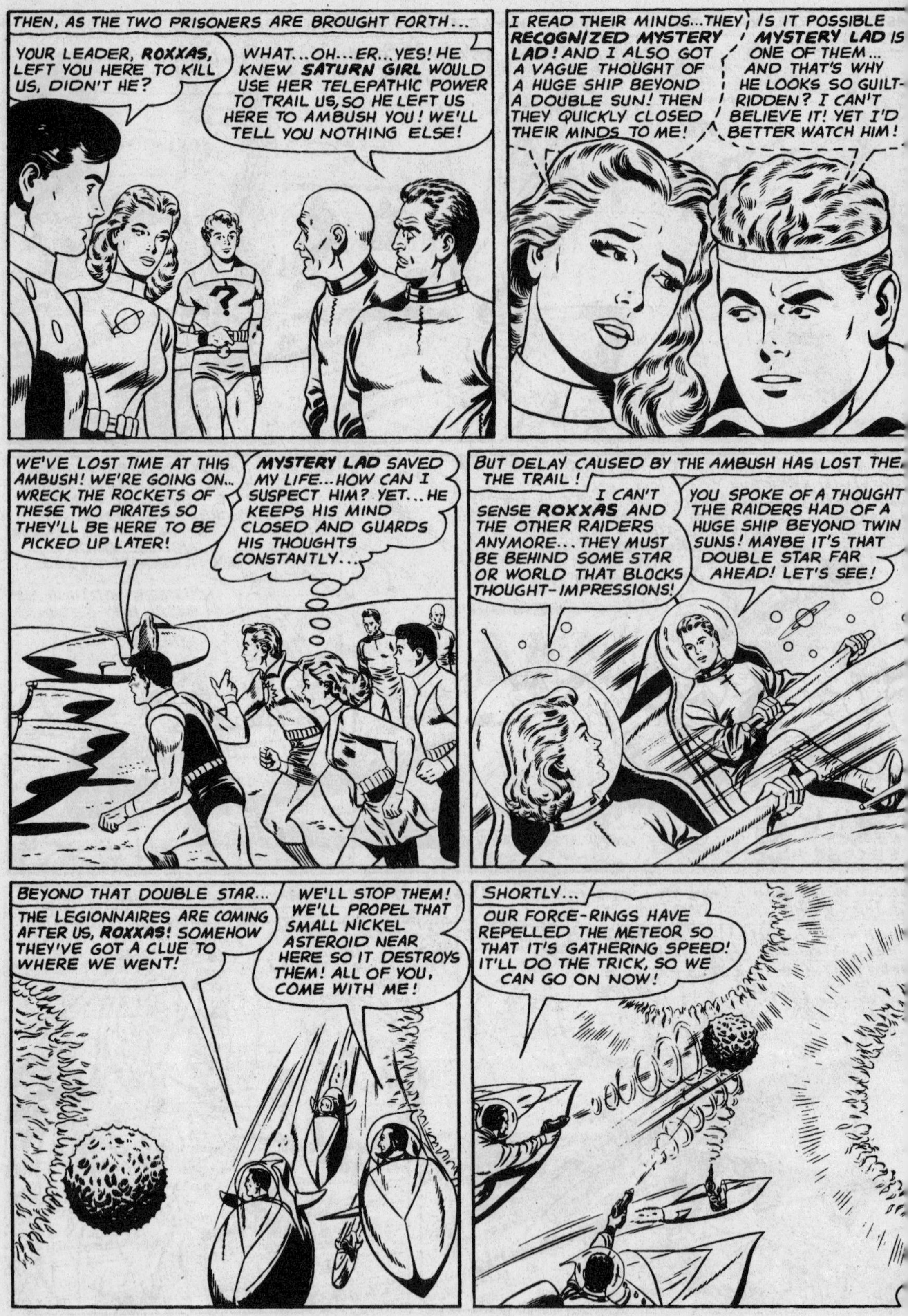

THEN, AS THE TWO PRISONERS ARE BROUGHT FORTH...
YOUR LEADER, ROXXAS, LEFT YOU HERE TO KILL US, DIDN'T HE?
WHAT...OH...ER...YES! HE KNEW SATURN GIRL WOULD USE HER TELEPATHIC POWER TO TRAIL US, SO HE LEFT US HERE TO AMBUSH YOU! WE'LL TELL YOU NOTHING ELSE!
I READ THEIR MINDS...THEY RECOGNIZED MYSTERY LAD! AND I ALSO GOT A VAGUE THOUGHT OF A HUGE SHIP BEYOND A DOUBLE SUN! THEN THEY QUICKLY CLOSED THEIR MINDS TO ME!
IS IT POSSIBLE MYSTERY LAD IS ONE OF THEM... AND THAT'S WHY HE LOOKS SO GUILT-RIDDEN? I CAN'T BELIEVE IT! YET I'D BETTER WATCH HIM!
WE'VE LOST TIME AT THIS AMBUSH! WE'RE GOING ON... WRECK THE ROCKETS OF THESE TWO PIRATES SO THEY'LL BE HERE TO BE PICKED UP LATER!
MYSTERY LAD SAVED MY LIFE...HOW CAN I SUSPECT HIM? YET...HE KEEPS HIS MIND CLOSED AND GUARDS HIS THOUGHTS CONSTANTLY...
BUT DELAY CAUSED BY THE AMBUSH HAS LOST THE TRAIL!
I CAN'T SENSE ROXXAS AND THE OTHER RAIDERS ANYMORE... THEY MUST BE BEHIND SOME STAR OR WORLD THAT BLOCKS THOUGHT-IMPRESSIONS!
YOU SPOKE OF A THOUGHT THE RAIDERS HAD OF A HUGE SHIP BEYOND TWIN SUNS! MAYBE IT'S THAT DOUBLE STAR FAR AHEAD! LET'S SEE!
BEYOND THAT DOUBLE STAR...
THE LEGIONNAIRES ARE COMING AFTER US, ROXXAS! SOMEHOW THEY'VE GOT A CLUE TO WHERE WE WENT!
WE'LL STOP THEM! WE'LL PROPEL THAT SMALL NICKEL ASTEROID NEAR HERE SO IT DESTROYS THEM! ALL OF YOU, COME WITH ME!
SHORTLY...
OUR FORCE-RINGS HAVE REPELLED THE METEOR SO THAT IT'S GATHERING SPEED! IT'LL DO THE TRICK, SO WE CAN GO ON NOW!

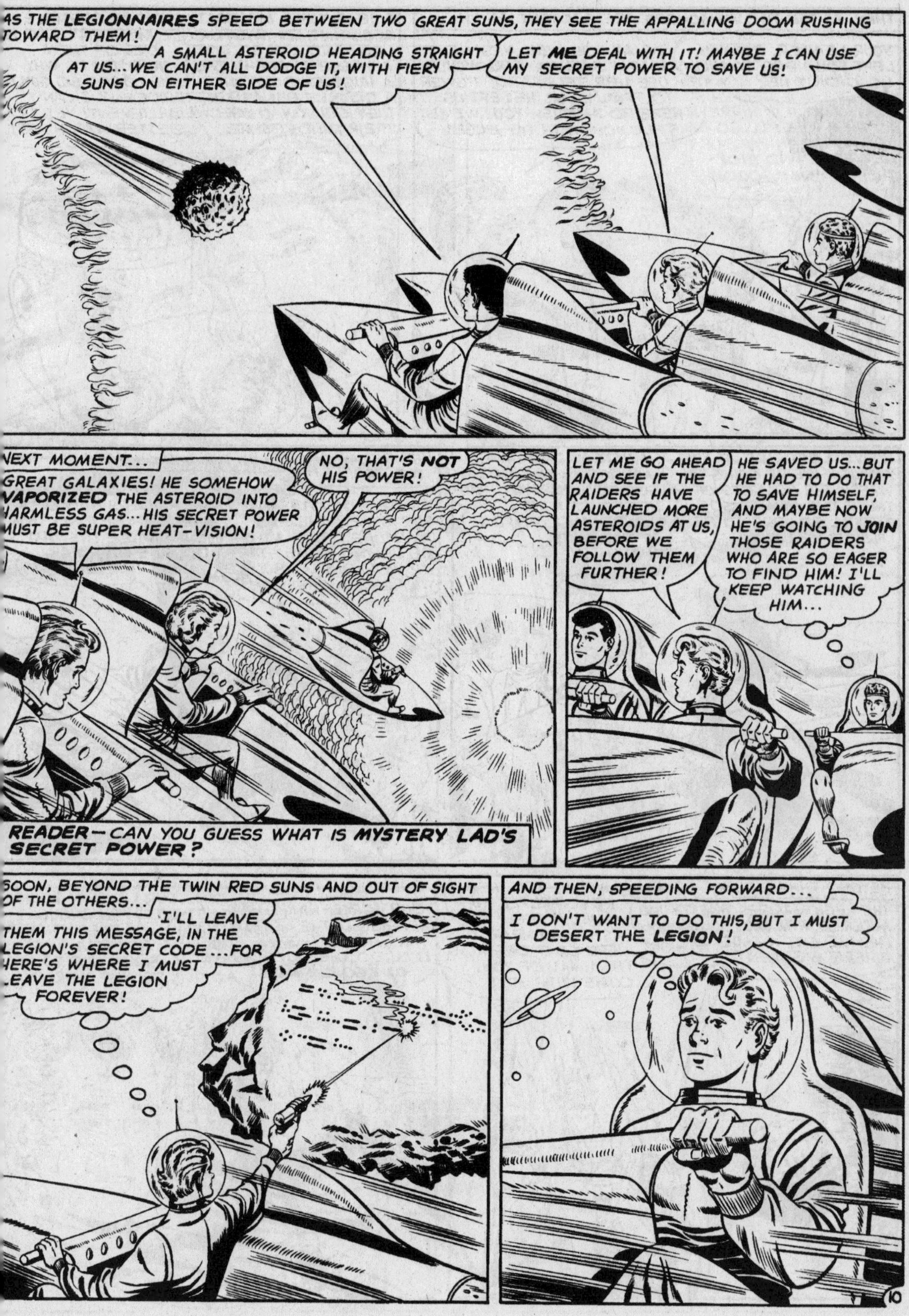
AS THE LEGIONNAIRES SPEED BETWEEN TWO GREAT SUNS, THEY SEE THE APPALLING DOOM RUSHING TOWARD THEM!
A SMALL ASTEROID HEADING STRAIGHT AT US... WE CAN'T ALL DODGE IT, WITH FIERY SUNS ON EITHER SIDE OF US!
LET ME DEAL WITH IT! MAYBE I CAN USE MY SECRET POWER TO SAVE US!
NEXT MOMENT...
GREAT GALAXIES! HE SOMEHOW VAPORIZED THE ASTEROID INTO HARMLESS GAS... HIS SECRET POWER MUST BE SUPER HEAT-VISION!
NO, THAT'S NOT HIS POWER!
READER—CAN YOU GUESS WHAT IS MYSTERY LAD'S SECRET POWER?
LET ME GO AHEAD AND SEE IF THE RAIDERS HAVE LAUNCHED MORE ASTEROIDS AT US, BEFORE WE FOLLOW THEM FURTHER!
HE SAVED US...BUT HE HAD TO DO THAT TO SAVE HIMSELF, AND MAYBE NOW HE'S GOING TO JOIN THOSE RAIDERS WHO ARE SO EAGER TO FIND HIM! I'LL KEEP WATCHING HIM...
SOON, BEYOND THE TWIN RED SUNS AND OUT OF SIGHT OF THE OTHERS...
I'LL LEAVE THEM THIS MESSAGE, IN THE LEGION'S SECRET CODE...FOR HERE'S WHERE I MUST LEAVE THE LEGION FOREVER!
AND THEN, SPEEDING FORWARD...
I DON'T WANT TO DO THIS, BUT I MUST DESERT THE LEGION!
10

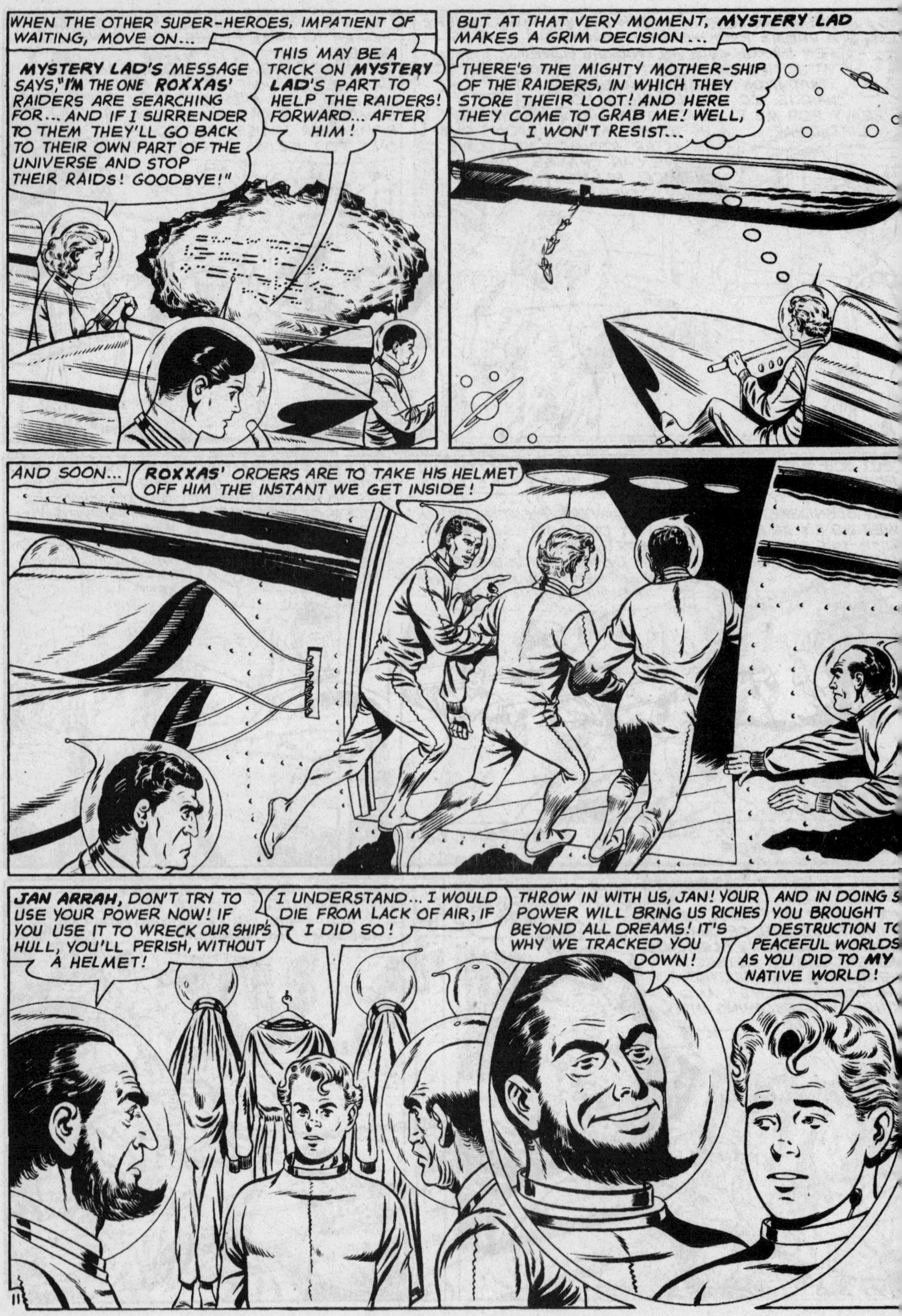
WHEN THE OTHER SUPER-HEROES, IMPATIENT OF WAITING, MOVE ON...
MYSTERY LAD'S MESSAGE SAYS, "I'M THE ONE ROXXAS' RAIDERS ARE SEARCHING FOR... AND IF I SURRENDER TO THEM THEY'LL GO BACK TO THEIR OWN PART OF THE UNIVERSE AND STOP THEIR RAIDS! GOODBYE!"
THIS MAY BE A TRICK ON MYSTERY LAD'S PART TO HELP THE RAIDERS! FORWARD... AFTER HIM!
BUT AT THAT VERY MOMENT, MYSTERY LAD MAKES A GRIM DECISION...
THERE'S THE MIGHTY MOTHER-SHIP OF THE RAIDERS, IN WHICH THEY STORE THEIR LOOT! AND HERE THEY COME TO GRAB ME! WELL, I WON'T RESIST...
AND SOON...
ROXXAS' ORDERS ARE TO TAKE HIS HELMET OFF HIM THE INSTANT WE GET INSIDE!
JAN ARRAH, DON'T TRY TO USE YOUR POWER NOW! IF YOU USE IT TO WRECK OUR SHIP'S HULL, YOU'LL PERISH, WITHOUT A HELMET!
I UNDERSTAND... I WOULD DIE FROM LACK OF AIR, IF I DID SO!
THROW IN WITH US, JAN! YOUR POWER WILL BRING US RICHES BEYOND ALL DREAMS! IT'S WHY WE TRACKED YOU DOWN!
AND IN DOING S YOU BROUGHT DESTRUCTION TO PEACEFUL WORLDS AS YOU DID TO MY NATIVE WORLD!
11

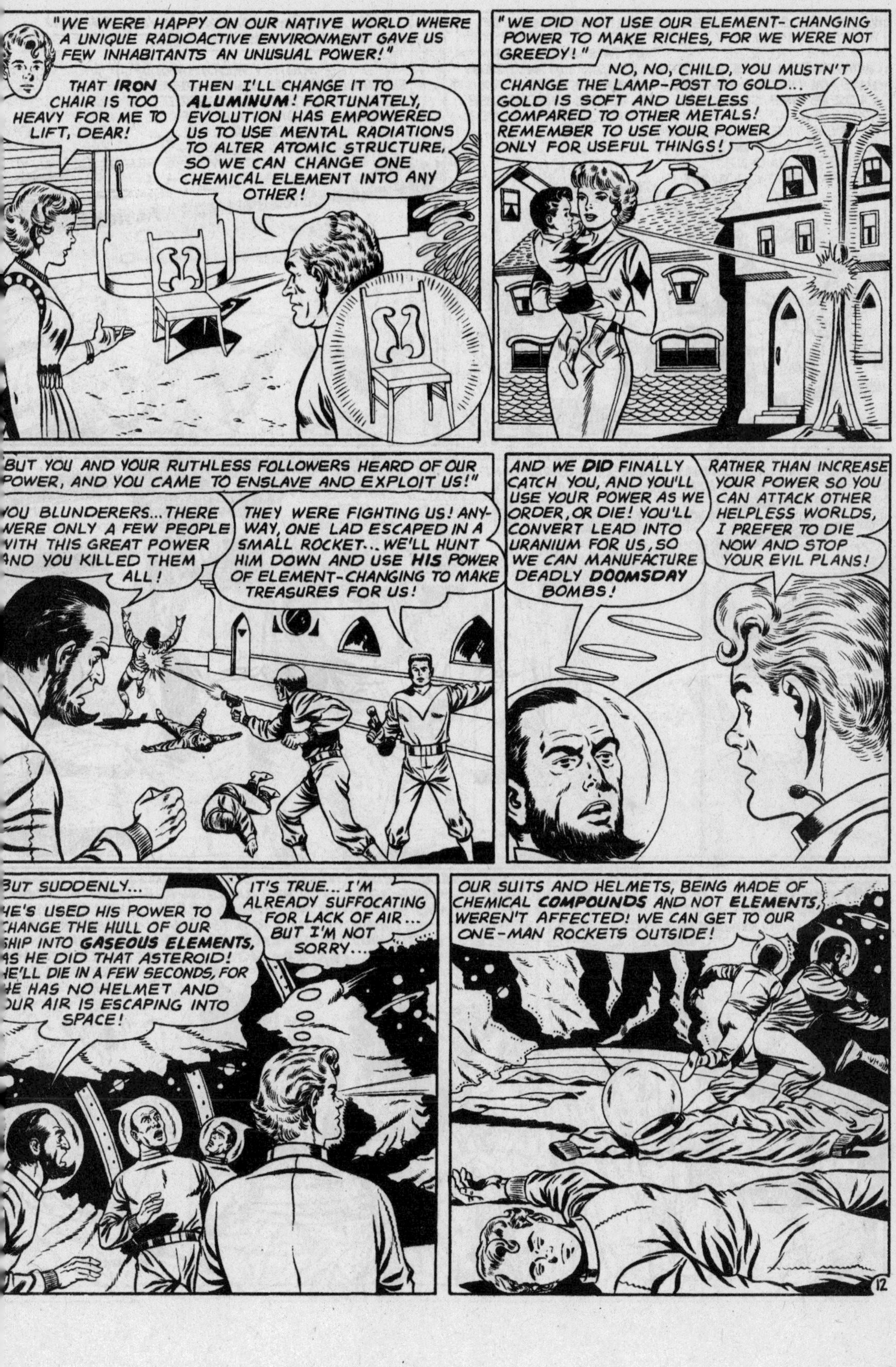
"WE WERE HAPPY ON OUR NATIVE WORLD WHERE A UNIQUE RADIOACTIVE ENVIRONMENT GAVE US FEW INHABITANTS AN UNUSUAL POWER!"
THAT IRON CHAIR IS TOO HEAVY FOR ME TO LIFT, DEAR!
THEN I'LL CHANGE IT TO ALUMINUM! FORTUNATELY, EVOLUTION HAS EMPOWERED US TO USE MENTAL RADIATIONS TO ALTER ATOMIC STRUCTURE, SO WE CAN CHANGE ONE CHEMICAL ELEMENT INTO ANY OTHER!
"WE DID NOT USE OUR ELEMENT-CHANGING POWER TO MAKE RICHES, FOR WE WERE NOT GREEDY!"
NO, NO, CHILD, YOU MUSTN'T CHANGE THE LAMP-POST TO GOLD... GOLD IS SOFT AND USELESS COMPARED TO OTHER METALS! REMEMBER TO USE YOUR POWER ONLY FOR USEFUL THINGS!
BUT YOU AND YOUR RUTHLESS FOLLOWERS HEARD OF OUR POWER, AND YOU CAME TO ENSLAVE AND EXPLOIT US!"
YOU BLUNDERERS... THERE WERE ONLY A FEW PEOPLE WITH THIS GREAT POWER AND YOU KILLED THEM ALL!
THEY WERE FIGHTING US! ANYWAY, ONE LAD ESCAPED IN A SMALL ROCKET... WE'LL HUNT HIM DOWN AND USE HIS POWER OF ELEMENT-CHANGING TO MAKE TREASURES FOR US!
AND WE DID FINALLY CATCH YOU, AND YOU'LL USE YOUR POWER AS WE ORDER, OR DIE! YOU'LL CONVERT LEAD INTO URANIUM FOR US, SO WE CAN MANUFACTURE DEADLY DOOMSDAY BOMBS!
RATHER THAN INCREASE YOUR POWER SO YOU CAN ATTACK OTHER HELPLESS WORLDS, I PREFER TO DIE NOW AND STOP YOUR EVIL PLANS!
BUT SUDDENLY...
HE'S USED HIS POWER TO CHANGE THE HULL OF OUR SHIP INTO GASEOUS ELEMENTS, AS HE DID THAT ASTEROID! HE'LL DIE IN A FEW SECONDS, FOR HE HAS NO HELMET AND OUR AIR IS ESCAPING INTO SPACE!
IT'S TRUE... I'M ALREADY SUFFOCATING FOR LACK OF AIR... BUT I'M NOT SORRY...
OUR SUITS AND HELMETS, BEING MADE OF CHEMICAL COMPOUNDS AND NOT ELEMENTS, WEREN'T AFFECTED! WE CAN GET TO OUR ONE-MAN ROCKETS OUTSIDE!
12

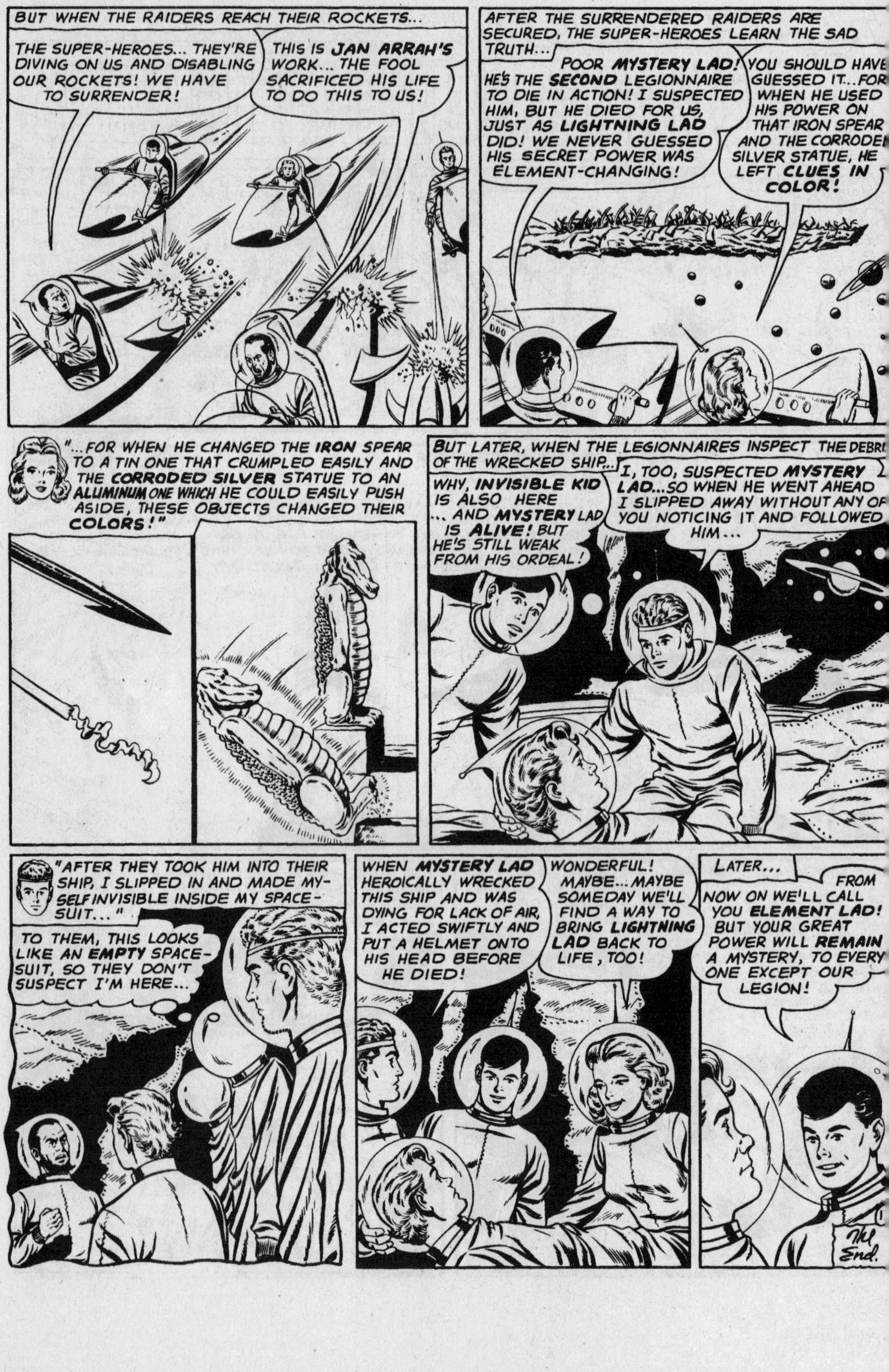
BUT WHEN THE RAIDERS REACH THEIR ROCKETS...
THE SUPER-HEROES... THEY'RE DIVING ON US AND DISABLING OUR ROCKETS! WE HAVE TO SURRENDER!
THIS IS JAN ARRAH'S WORK... THE FOOL SACRIFICED HIS LIFE TO DO THIS TO US!
AFTER THE SURRENDERED RAIDERS ARE SECURED, THE SUPER-HEROES LEARN THE SAD TRUTH...
POOR MYSTERY LAD! HE'S THE SECOND LEGIONNAIRE TO DIE IN ACTION! I SUSPECTED HIM, BUT HE DIED FOR US, JUST AS LIGHTNING LAD DID! WE NEVER GUESSED HIS SECRET POWER WAS ELEMENT-CHANGING!
YOU SHOULD HAVE GUESSED IT...FOR WHEN HE USED HIS POWER ON THAT IRON SPEAR AND THE CORRODED SILVER STATUE, HE LEFT CLUES IN COLOR!
"...FOR WHEN HE CHANGED THE IRON SPEAR TO A TIN ONE THAT CRUMPLED EASILY AND THE CORRODED SILVER STATUE TO AN ALUMINUM ONE WHICH HE COULD EASILY PUSH ASIDE, THESE OBJECTS CHANGED THEIR COLORS!"
BUT LATER, WHEN THE LEGIONNAIRES INSPECT THE DEBRI
OF THE WRECKED SHIP...
WHY, INVISIBLE KID IS ALSO HERE ... AND MYSTERY LAD IS ALIVE! BUT HE'S STILL WEAK FROM HIS ORDEAL!
I, TOO, SUSPECTED MYSTERY LAD...SO WHEN HE WENT AHEAD I SLIPPED AWAY WITHOUT ANY OF YOU NOTICING IT AND FOLLOWED HIM...
"AFTER THEY TOOK HIM INTO THEIR SHIP, I SLIPPED IN AND MADE MYSELF INVISIBLE INSIDE MY SPACE-SUIT..."
TO THEM, THIS LOOKS LIKE AN EMPTY SPACE-SUIT, SO THEY DON'T SUSPECT I'M HERE...
WHEN MYSTERY LAD HEROICALLY WRECKED THIS SHIP AND WAS DYING FOR LACK OF AIR, I ACTED SWIFTLY AND PUT A HELMET ONTO HIS HEAD BEFORE HE DIED!
WONDERFUL! MAYBE... MAYBE SOMEDAY WE'LL FIND A WAY TO BRING LIGHTNING LAD BACK TO LIFE, TOO!
LATER...
FROM NOW ON WE'LL CALL YOU ELEMENT LAD! BUT YOUR GREAT POWER WILL REMAIN A MYSTERY, TO EVERY ONE EXCEPT OUR LEGION!
The End.

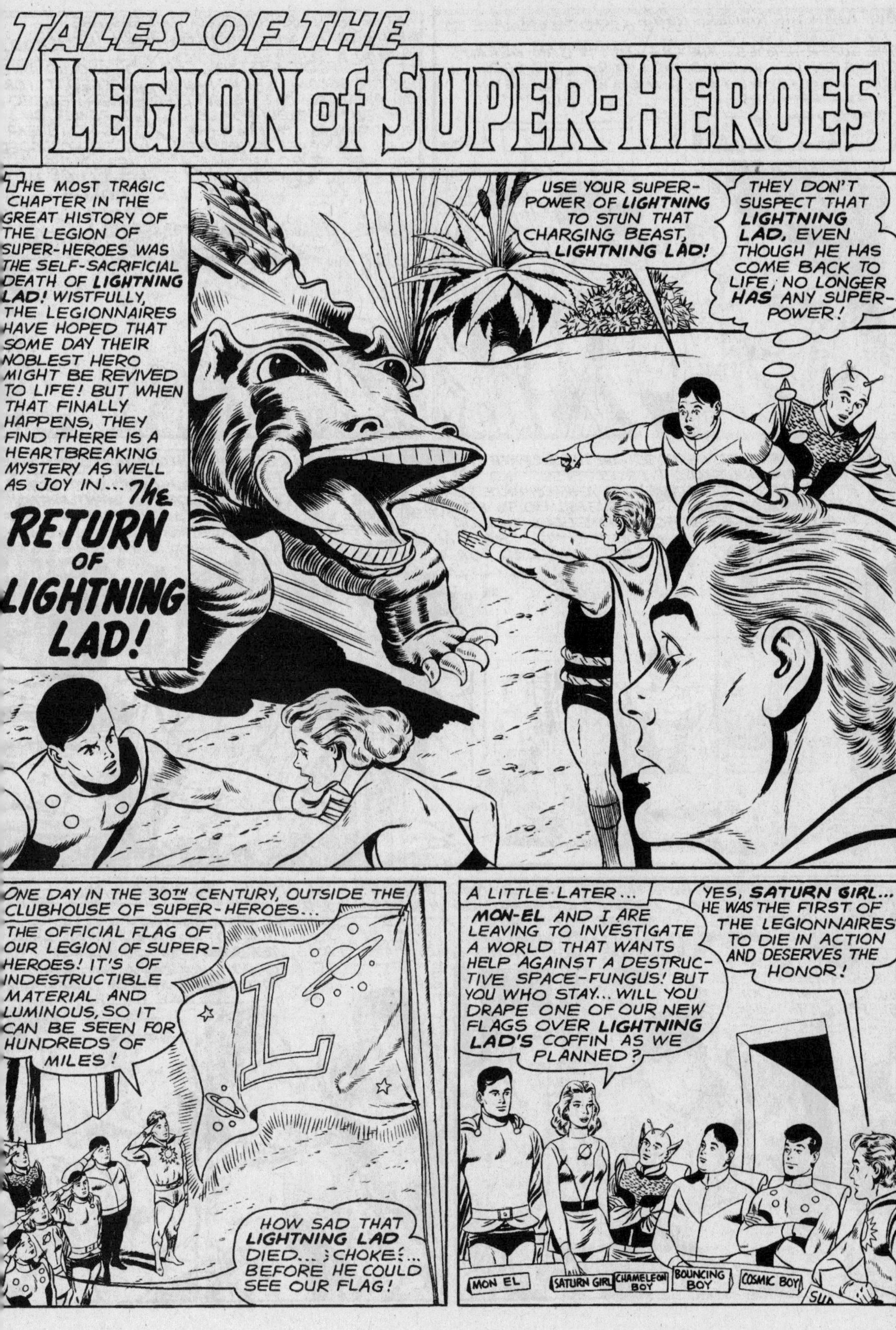
TALES OF THE
LEGION of SUPER-HEROES
THE MOST TRAGIC CHAPTER IN THE GREAT HISTORY OF THE LEGION OF SUPER-HEROES WAS THE SELF-SACRIFICIAL DEATH OF LIGHTNING LAD! WISTFULLY, THE LEGIONNAIRES HAVE HOPED THAT SOME DAY THEIR NOBLEST HERO MIGHT BE REVIVED TO LIFE! BUT WHEN THAT FINALLY HAPPENS, THEY FIND THERE IS A HEARTBREAKING MYSTERY AS WELL AS JOY IN... The RETURN OF LIGHTNING LAD!
USE YOUR SUPER-POWER OF LIGHTNING TO STUN THAT CHARGING BEAST, LIGHTNING LAD!
THEY DON'T SUSPECT THAT LIGHTNING LAD, EVEN THOUGH HE HAS COME BACK TO LIFE, NO LONGER HAS ANY SUPER-POWER!
ONE DAY IN THE 30TH CENTURY, OUTSIDE THE CLUBHOUSE OF SUPER-HEROES...
THE OFFICIAL FLAG OF OUR LEGION OF SUPER-HEROES! IT'S OF INDESTRUCTIBLE MATERIAL AND LUMINOUS, SO IT CAN BE SEEN FOR HUNDREDS OF MILES!
L
HOW SAD THAT LIGHTNING LAD DIED... *CHOKE*... BEFORE HE COULD SEE OUR FLAG!
A LITTLE LATER...
MON-EL AND I ARE LEAVING TO INVESTIGATE A WORLD THAT WANTS HELP AGAINST A DESTRUCTIVE SPACE-FUNGUS! BUT YOU WHO STAY... WILL YOU DRAPE ONE OF OUR NEW FLAGS OVER LIGHTNING LAD'S COFFIN AS WE PLANNED?
YES, SATURN GIRL... HE WAS THE FIRST OF THE LEGIONNAIRES TO DIE IN ACTION AND DESERVES THE HONOR!
MON EL
SATURN GIRL
CHAMELEON BOY
BOUNCING BOY
COSMIC BOY
SU

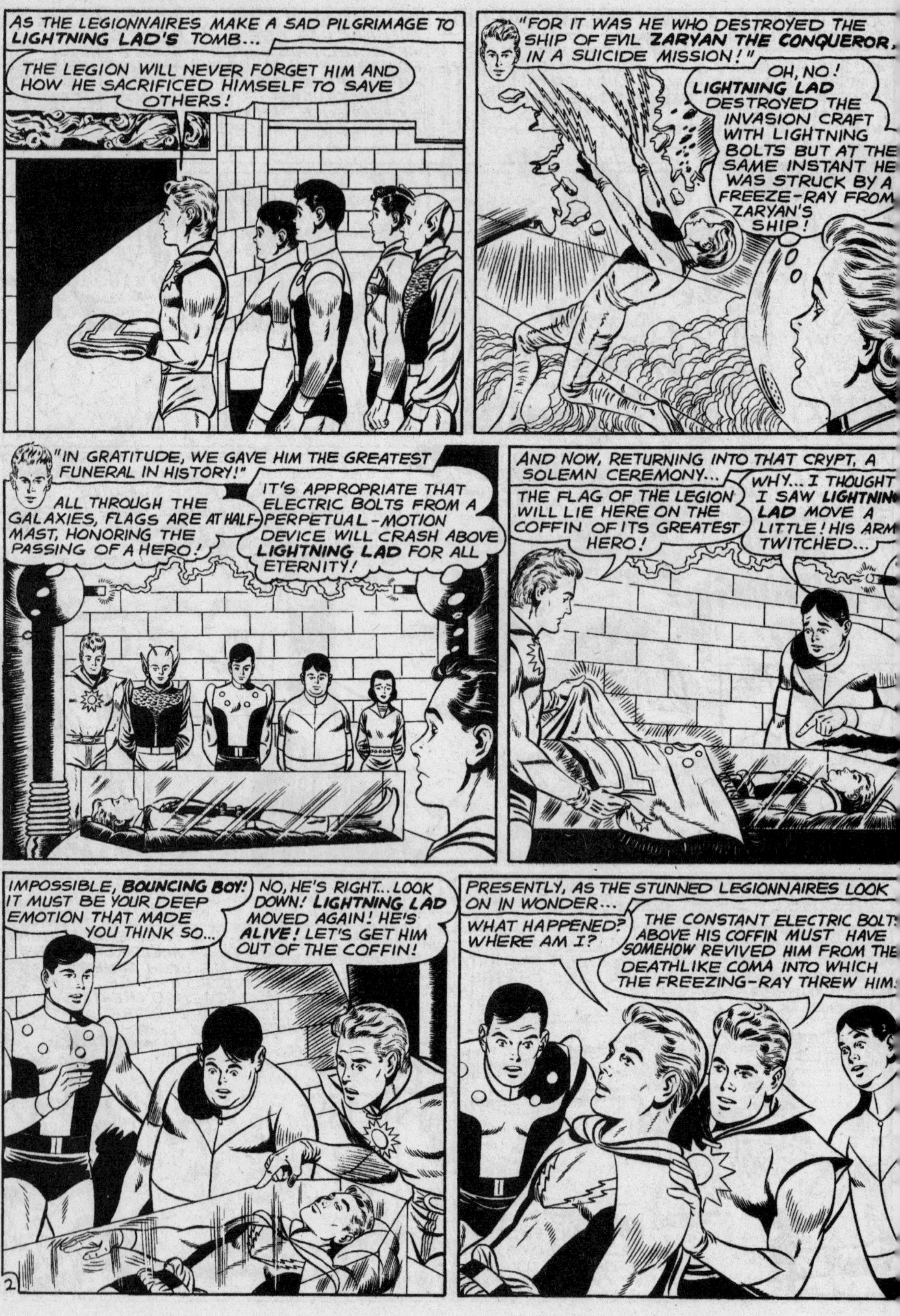
AS THE LEGIONNAIRES MAKE A SAD PILGRIMAGE TO LIGHTNING LAD'S TOMB...
THE LEGION WILL NEVER FORGET HIM AND HOW HE SACRIFICED HIMSELF TO SAVE OTHERS!
"FOR IT WAS HE WHO DESTROYED THE SHIP OF EVIL ZARYAN THE CONQUEROR, IN A SUICIDE MISSION!"
OH, NO! LIGHTNING LAD DESTROYED THE INVASION CRAFT WITH LIGHTNING BOLTS BUT AT THE SAME INSTANT HE WAS STRUCK BY A FREEZE-RAY FROM ZARYAN'S SHIP!
"IN GRATITUDE, WE GAVE HIM THE GREATEST FUNERAL IN HISTORY!"
ALL THROUGH THE GALAXIES, FLAGS ARE AT HALF-MAST, HONORING THE PASSING OF A HERO!
IT'S APPROPRIATE THAT ELECTRIC BOLTS FROM A PERPETUAL-MOTION DEVICE WILL CRASH ABOVE LIGHTNING LAD FOR ALL ETERNITY!
AND NOW, RETURNING INTO THAT CRYPT, A SOLEMN CEREMONY...
THE FLAG OF THE LEGION WILL LIE HERE ON THE COFFIN OF ITS GREATEST HERO!
WHY... I THOUGHT I SAW LIGHTNING LAD MOVE A LITTLE! HIS ARM TWITCHED...
IMPOSSIBLE, BOUNCING BOY! IT MUST BE YOUR DEEP EMOTION THAT MADE YOU THINK SO...
NO, HE'S RIGHT... LOOK DOWN! LIGHTNING LAD MOVED AGAIN! HE'S ALIVE! LET'S GET HIM OUT OF THE COFFIN!
2
PRESENTLY, AS THE STUNNED LEGIONNAIRES LOOK ON IN WONDER...
WHAT HAPPENED? WHERE AM I?
THE CONSTANT ELECTRIC BOLTS ABOVE HIS COFFIN MUST HAVE SOMEHOW REVIVED HIM FROM THE DEATHLIKE COMA INTO WHICH THE FREEZING-RAY THREW HIM!

JOYFULLY, THE LEGIONNAIRES TAKE *LIGHTNING LAD* TO THEIR CLUBHOUSE...

ALL I REMEMBER IS A TERRIBLE, FREEZING PAIN, THEN DARKNESS, AND THEN I BECAME CONSCIOUS AGAIN! MY MIND IS STILL DAZED...

BUT YOU'RE *ALIVE!* AND I'M SURE YOUR MEMORY WILL COME BACK TO YOU SOON!

PSST. *SUNBOY!* IF HIS MEMORY HAS BEEN AFFECTED, HIS SUPER-POWER MAY ALSO HAVE BEEN AFFECTED BY HIS DEATH-LIKE EXPERIENCE! HE MAY HAVE LOST HIS POWER!

NO, *COSMIC BOY,* DON'T SUGGEST SUCH A THING! WITHOUT HIS SUPER-POWER, HE COULD NO LONGER BELONG TO THE LEGION!

FATE HAS BROUGHT HIM BACK TO LIFE... TO LOSE HIS LEGION MEMBER-SHIP NOW WOULD BREAK HIS HEART!

I HOPE NOT, *SUNBOY!* BUT I'M AFRAID IT COULD BE! REMEMBER THE STRANGE ORIGIN OF *LIGHTNING LAD'S* POWER, WHICH HE TOLD US WHEN HE JOINED THE LEGION...

"HE TOLD US HOW HIS SPACE-FLIER RAN OUT OF POWER NEAR THE DANGEROUS PLANET, *KORBAL*..."

THE ENERGY-CELLS OF MY SHIP'S BATTERIES ARE EXHAUSTED... THERE'S A CHANCE I CAN REPLENISH THEM ON THE WILD WORLD *KORBAL,* BUT IT'LL BE RISKY...

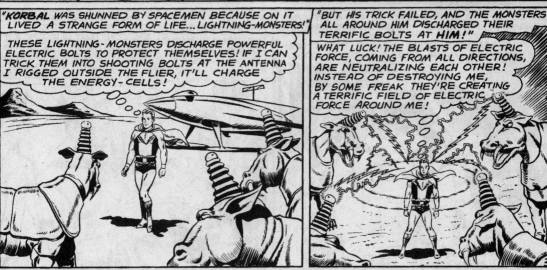

"*KORBAL* WAS SHUNNED BY SPACEMEN BECAUSE ON IT LIVED A STRANGE FORM OF LIFE... LIGHTNING-MONSTERS!"

THESE LIGHTNING-MONSTERS DISCHARGE POWERFUL ELECTRIC BOLTS TO PROTECT THEMSELVES! IF I CAN TRICK THEM INTO SHOOTING BOLTS AT THE ANTENNA I RIGGED OUTSIDE THE FLIER, IT'LL CHARGE THE ENERGY-CELLS!

"BUT HIS TRICK FAILED, AND THE MONSTERS ALL AROUND HIM DISCHARGED THEIR TERRIFIC BOLTS AT *HIM!*"

WHAT LUCK! THE BLASTS OF ELECTRIC FORCE, COMING FROM ALL DIRECTIONS, ARE NEUTRALIZING EACH OTHER! INSTEAD OF DESTROYING ME, BY SOME FREAK THEY'RE CREATING A TERRIFIC FIELD OF ELECTRIC FORCE AROUND ME!

3

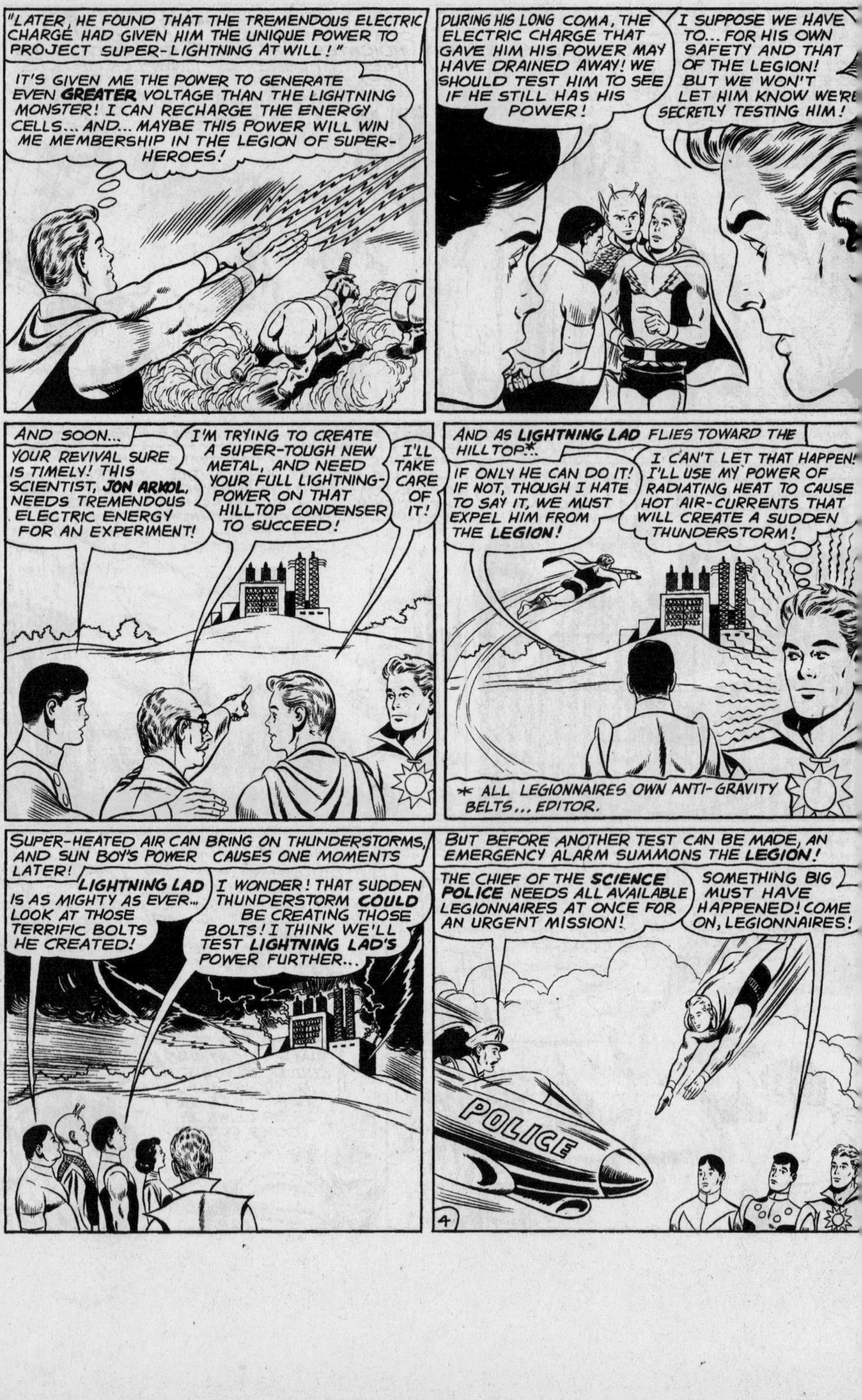
"LATER, HE FOUND THAT THE TREMENDOUS ELECTRIC CHARGE HAD GIVEN HIM THE UNIQUE POWER TO PROJECT SUPER-LIGHTNING AT WILL!"
IT'S GIVEN ME THE POWER TO GENERATE EVEN GREATER VOLTAGE THAN THE LIGHTNING MONSTER! I CAN RECHARGE THE ENERGY CELLS... AND... MAYBE THIS POWER WILL WIN ME MEMBERSHIP IN THE LEGION OF SUPER-HEROES!
DURING HIS LONG COMA, THE ELECTRIC CHARGE THAT GAVE HIM HIS POWER MAY HAVE DRAINED AWAY! WE SHOULD TEST HIM TO SEE IF HE STILL HAS HIS POWER!
I SUPPOSE WE HAVE TO... FOR HIS OWN SAFETY AND THAT OF THE LEGION! BUT WE WON'T LET HIM KNOW WE'RE SECRETLY TESTING HIM!
AND SOON...
YOUR REVIVAL SURE IS TIMELY! THIS SCIENTIST, JON ARKOL, NEEDS TREMENDOUS ELECTRIC ENERGY FOR AN EXPERIMENT!
I'M TRYING TO CREATE A SUPER-TOUGH NEW METAL, AND NEED YOUR FULL LIGHTNING-POWER ON THAT HILLTOP CONDENSER TO SUCCEED!
I'LL TAKE CARE OF IT!
AND AS LIGHTNING LAD FLIES TOWARD THE HILLTOP*...
IF ONLY HE CAN DO IT! IF NOT, THOUGH I HATE TO SAY IT, WE MUST EXPEL HIM FROM THE LEGION!
I CAN'T LET THAT HAPPEN! I'LL USE MY POWER OF RADIATING HEAT TO CAUSE HOT AIR-CURRENTS THAT WILL CREATE A SUDDEN THUNDERSTORM!
* ALL LEGIONNAIRES OWN ANTI-GRAVITY BELTS... EDITOR.
SUPER-HEATED AIR CAN BRING ON THUNDERSTORMS, AND SUN BOY'S POWER CAUSES ONE MOMENTS LATER!
LIGHTNING LAD IS AS MIGHTY AS EVER... LOOK AT THOSE TERRIFIC BOLTS HE CREATED!
I WONDER! THAT SUDDEN THUNDERSTORM COULD BE CREATING THOSE BOLTS! I THINK WE'LL TEST LIGHTNING LAD'S POWER FURTHER...
BUT BEFORE ANOTHER TEST CAN BE MADE, AN EMERGENCY ALARM SUMMONS THE LEGION!
THE CHIEF OF THE SCIENCE POLICE NEEDS ALL AVAILABLE LEGIONNAIRES AT ONCE FOR AN URGENT MISSION!
SOMETHING BIG MUST HAVE HAPPENED! COME ON, LEGIONNAIRES!
POLICE
4

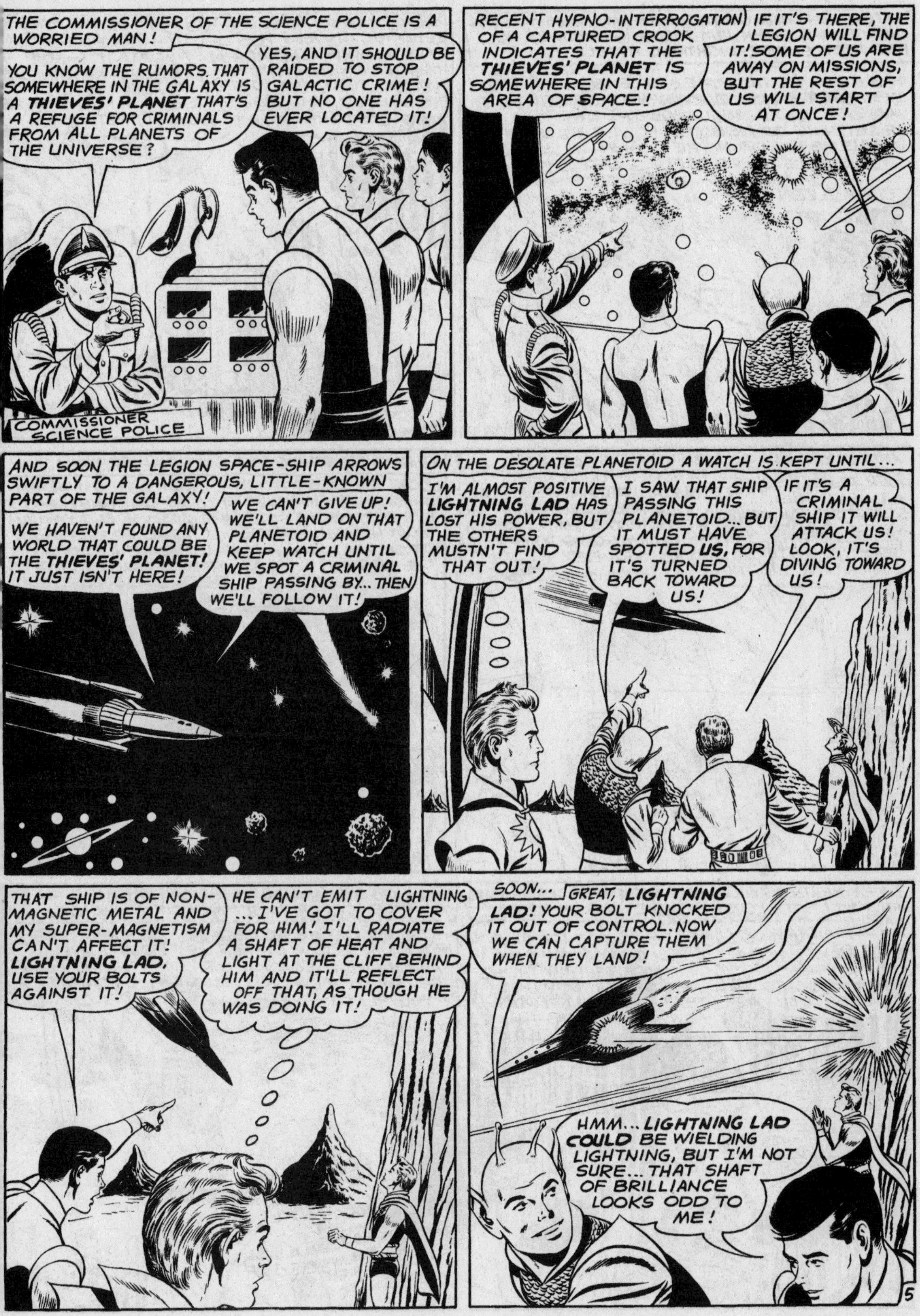
THE COMMISSIONER OF THE SCIENCE POLICE IS A WORRIED MAN!
YOU KNOW THE RUMORS THAT SOMEWHERE IN THE GALAXY IS A THIEVES' PLANET THAT'S A REFUGE FOR CRIMINALS FROM ALL PLANETS OF THE UNIVERSE?
YES, AND IT SHOULD BE RAIDED TO STOP GALACTIC CRIME! BUT NO ONE HAS EVER LOCATED IT!
COMMISSIONER SCIENCE POLICE
RECENT HYPNO-INTERROGATION OF A CAPTURED CROOK INDICATES THAT THE THIEVES' PLANET IS SOMEWHERE IN THIS AREA OF SPACE!
IF IT'S THERE, THE LEGION WILL FIND IT! SOME OF US ARE AWAY ON MISSIONS, BUT THE REST OF US WILL START AT ONCE!
AND SOON THE LEGION SPACE-SHIP ARROWS SWIFTLY TO A DANGEROUS, LITTLE-KNOWN PART OF THE GALAXY!
WE HAVEN'T FOUND ANY WORLD THAT COULD BE THE THIEVES' PLANET! IT JUST ISN'T HERE!
WE CAN'T GIVE UP! WE'LL LAND ON THAT PLANETOID AND KEEP WATCH UNTIL WE SPOT A CRIMINAL SHIP PASSING BY... THEN WE'LL FOLLOW IT!
ON THE DESOLATE PLANETOID A WATCH IS KEPT UNTIL...
I'M ALMOST POSITIVE LIGHTNING LAD HAS LOST HIS POWER, BUT THE OTHERS MUSTN'T FIND THAT OUT!
I SAW THAT SHIP PASSING THIS PLANETOID... BUT IT MUST HAVE SPOTTED US, FOR IT'S TURNED BACK TOWARD US!
IF IT'S A CRIMINAL SHIP IT WILL ATTACK US! LOOK, IT'S DIVING TOWARD US!
THAT SHIP IS OF NON-MAGNETIC METAL AND MY SUPER-MAGNETISM CAN'T AFFECT IT! LIGHTNING LAD, USE YOUR BOLTS AGAINST IT!
HE CAN'T EMIT LIGHTNING ... I'VE GOT TO COVER FOR HIM! I'LL RADIATE A SHAFT OF HEAT AND LIGHT AT THE CLIFF BEHIND HIM AND IT'LL REFLECT OFF THAT, AS THOUGH HE WAS DOING IT!
SOON...
GREAT, LIGHTNING LAD! YOUR BOLT KNOCKED IT OUT OF CONTROL. NOW WE CAN CAPTURE THEM WHEN THEY LAND!
HMM... LIGHTNING LAD COULD BE WIELDING LIGHTNING, BUT I'M NOT SURE... THAT SHAFT OF BRILLIANCE LOOKS ODD TO ME!
5

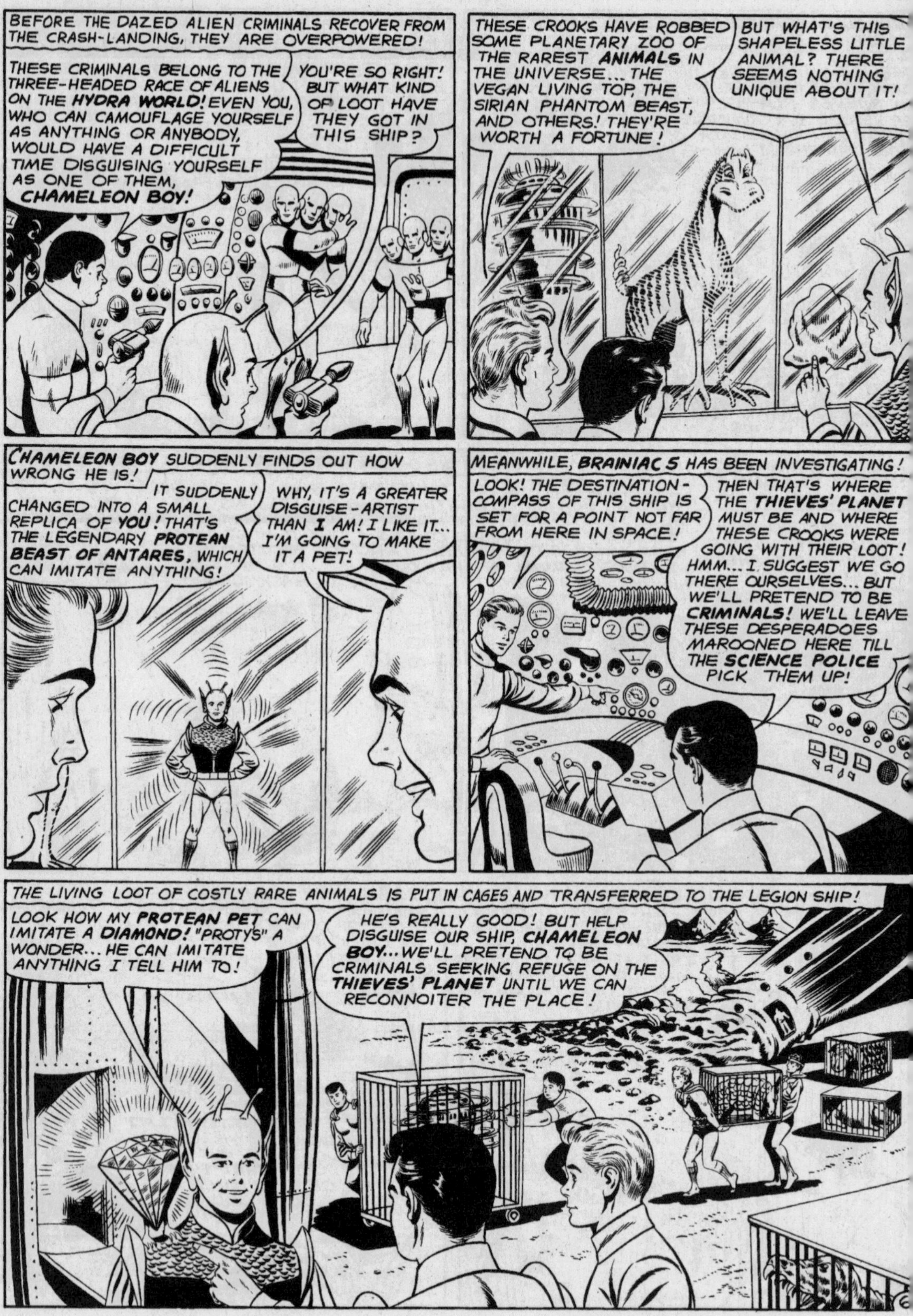
BEFORE THE DAZED ALIEN CRIMINALS RECOVER FROM THE CRASH-LANDING, THEY ARE OVERPOWERED!
THESE CRIMINALS BELONG TO THE THREE-HEADED RACE OF ALIENS ON THE HYDRA WORLD! EVEN YOU, WHO CAN CAMOUFLAGE YOURSELF AS ANYTHING OR ANYBODY, WOULD HAVE A DIFFICULT TIME DISGUISING YOURSELF AS ONE OF THEM, CHAMELEON BOY!
YOU'RE SO RIGHT! BUT WHAT KIND OF LOOT HAVE THEY GOT IN THIS SHIP?
THESE CROOKS HAVE ROBBED SOME PLANETARY ZOO OF THE RAREST ANIMALS IN THE UNIVERSE... THE VEGAN LIVING TOP, THE SIRIAN PHANTOM BEAST, AND OTHERS! THEY'RE WORTH A FORTUNE!
BUT WHAT'S THIS SHAPELESS LITTLE ANIMAL? THERE SEEMS NOTHING UNIQUE ABOUT IT!
CHAMELEON BOY SUDDENLY FINDS OUT HOW WRONG HE IS!
IT SUDDENLY CHANGED INTO A SMALL REPLICA OF YOU! THAT'S THE LEGENDARY PROTEAN BEAST OF ANTARES, WHICH CAN IMITATE ANYTHING!
WHY, IT'S A GREATER DISGUISE-ARTIST THAN I AM! I LIKE IT... I'M GOING TO MAKE IT A PET!
MEANWHILE, BRAINIAC 5 HAS BEEN INVESTIGATING!
LOOK! THE DESTINATION-COMPASS OF THIS SHIP IS SET FOR A POINT NOT FAR FROM HERE IN SPACE!
THEN THAT'S WHERE THE THIEVES' PLANET MUST BE AND WHERE THESE CROOKS WERE GOING WITH THEIR LOOT! HMM... I SUGGEST WE GO THERE OURSELVES... BUT WE'LL PRETEND TO BE CRIMINALS! WE'LL LEAVE THESE DESPERADOES MAROONED HERE TILL THE SCIENCE POLICE PICK THEM UP!
THE LIVING LOOT OF COSTLY RARE ANIMALS IS PUT IN CAGES AND TRANSFERRED TO THE LEGION SHIP!
LOOK HOW MY PROTEAN PET CAN IMITATE A DIAMOND! "PROTY'S" A WONDER... HE CAN IMITATE ANYTHING I TELL HIM TO!
HE'S REALLY GOOD! BUT HELP DISGUISE OUR SHIP, CHAMELEON BOY... WE'LL PRETEND TO BE CRIMINALS SEEKING REFUGE ON THE THIEVES' PLANET UNTIL WE CAN RECONNOITER THE PLACE!

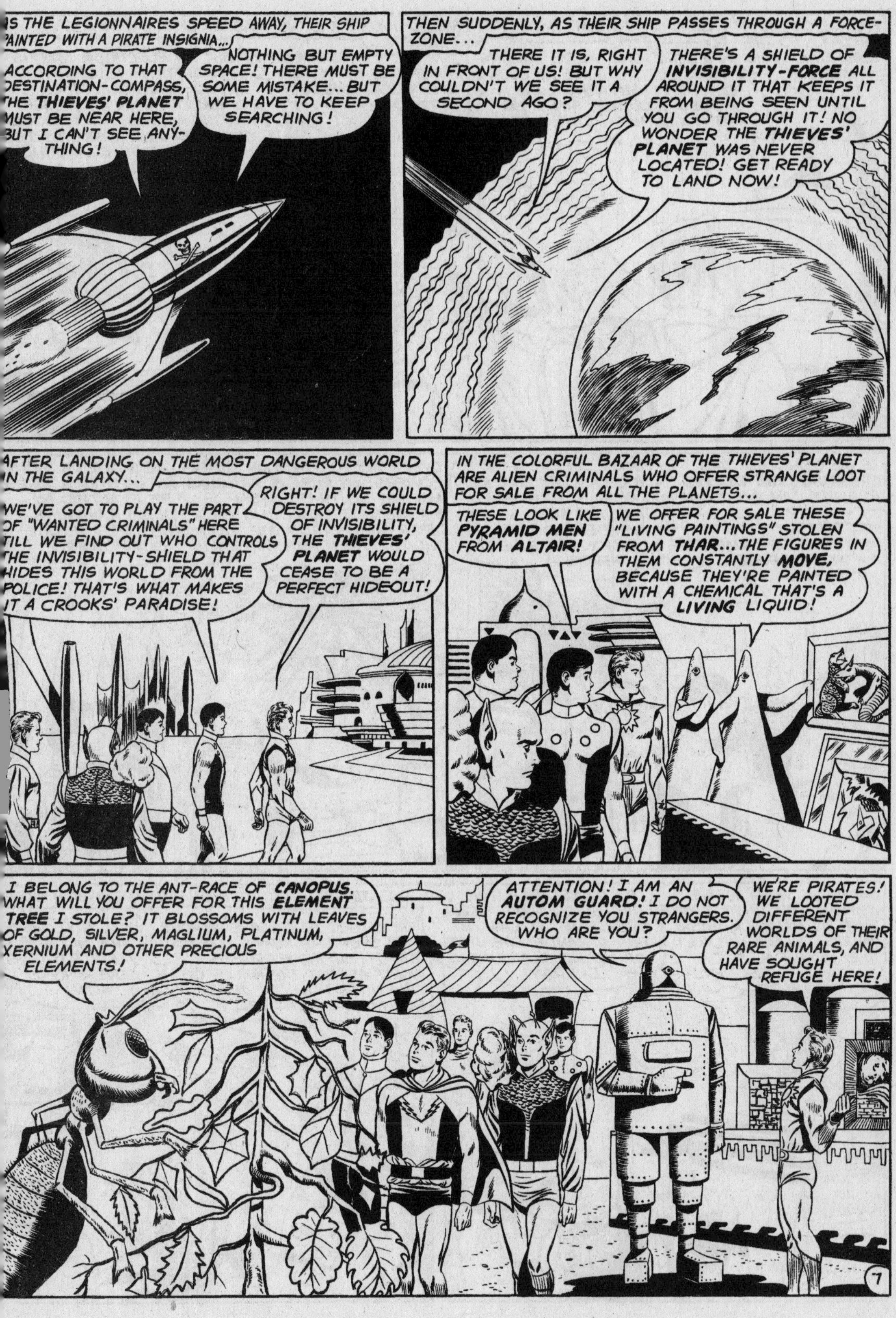
S THE LEGIONNAIRES SPEED AWAY, THEIR SHIP AINTED WITH A PIRATE INSIGNIA...
ACCORDING TO THAT ESTINATION-COMPASS, HE THIEVES' PLANET MUST BE NEAR HERE, UT I CAN'T SEE ANY-THING!
NOTHING BUT EMPTY SPACE! THERE MUST BE SOME MISTAKE... BUT WE HAVE TO KEEP SEARCHING!
THEN SUDDENLY, AS THEIR SHIP PASSES THROUGH A FORCE-ZONE...
THERE IT IS, RIGHT IN FRONT OF US! BUT WHY COULDN'T WE SEE IT A SECOND AGO?
THERE'S A SHIELD OF INVISIBILITY-FORCE ALL AROUND IT THAT KEEPS IT FROM BEING SEEN UNTIL YOU GO THROUGH IT! NO WONDER THE THIEVES' PLANET WAS NEVER LOCATED! GET READY TO LAND NOW!
AFTER LANDING ON THE MOST DANGEROUS WORLD IN THE GALAXY...
WE'VE GOT TO PLAY THE PART OF "WANTED CRIMINALS" HERE TILL WE FIND OUT WHO CONTROLS THE INVISIBILITY-SHIELD THAT HIDES THIS WORLD FROM THE POLICE! THAT'S WHAT MAKES IT A CROOKS' PARADISE!
RIGHT! IF WE COULD DESTROY ITS SHIELD OF INVISIBILITY, THE THIEVES' PLANET WOULD CEASE TO BE A PERFECT HIDEOUT!
IN THE COLORFUL BAZAAR OF THE THIEVES' PLANET ARE ALIEN CRIMINALS WHO OFFER STRANGE LOOT FOR SALE FROM ALL THE PLANETS...
THESE LOOK LIKE PYRAMID MEN FROM ALTAIR!
WE OFFER FOR SALE THESE "LIVING PAINTINGS" STOLEN FROM THAR...THE FIGURES IN THEM CONSTANTLY MOVE, BECAUSE THEY'RE PAINTED WITH A CHEMICAL THAT'S A LIVING LIQUID!
I BELONG TO THE ANT-RACE OF CANOPUS. WHAT WILL YOU OFFER FOR THIS ELEMENT TREE I STOLE? IT BLOSSOMS WITH LEAVES OF GOLD, SILVER, MAGLIUM, PLATINUM, XERNIUM AND OTHER PRECIOUS ELEMENTS!
ATTENTION! I AM AN AUTOM GUARD! I DO NOT RECOGNIZE YOU STRANGERS. WHO ARE YOU?
WE'RE PIRATES! WE LOOTED DIFFERENT WORLDS OF THEIR RARE ANIMALS, AND HAVE SOUGHT REFUGE HERE!
7

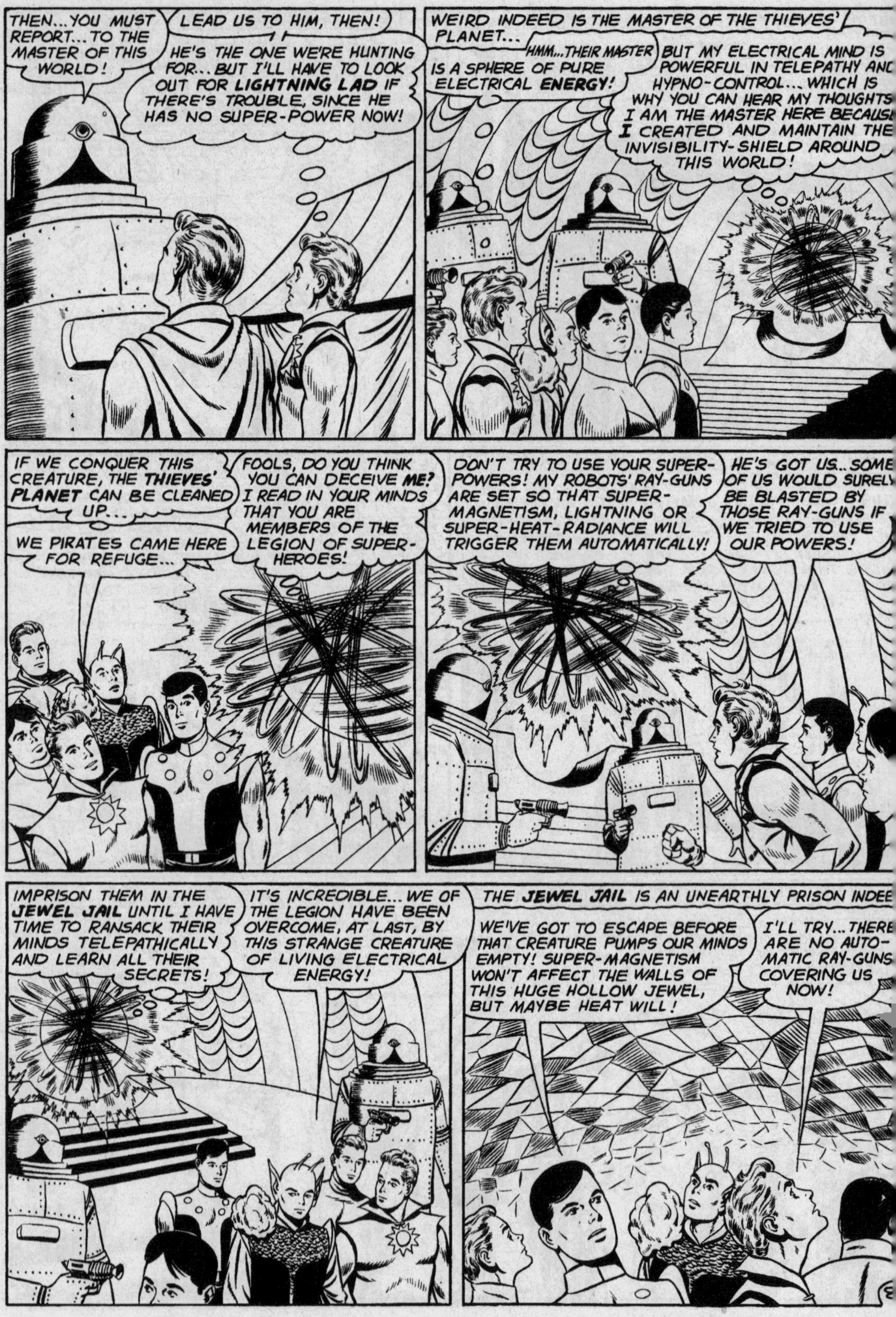
THEN... YOU MUST REPORT... TO THE MASTER OF THIS WORLD!
LEAD US TO HIM, THEN!
HE'S THE ONE WE'RE HUNTING FOR... BUT I'LL HAVE TO LOOK OUT FOR LIGHTNING LAD IF THERE'S TROUBLE, SINCE HE HAS NO SUPER-POWER NOW!
WEIRD INDEED IS THE MASTER OF THE THIEVES' PLANET...
HMM...THEIR MASTER IS A SPHERE OF PURE ELECTRICAL ENERGY!
BUT MY ELECTRICAL MIND IS POWERFUL IN TELEPATHY AND HYPNO-CONTROL... WHICH IS WHY YOU CAN HEAR MY THOUGHTS. I AM THE MASTER HERE BECAUSE I CREATED AND MAINTAIN THE INVISIBILITY-SHIELD AROUND THIS WORLD!
IF WE CONQUER THIS CREATURE, THE THIEVES' PLANET CAN BE CLEANED UP...
WE PIRATES CAME HERE FOR REFUGE...
FOOLS, DO YOU THINK YOU CAN DECEIVE ME? I READ IN YOUR MINDS THAT YOU ARE MEMBERS OF THE LEGION OF SUPER-HEROES!
DON'T TRY TO USE YOUR SUPER-POWERS! MY ROBOTS' RAY-GUNS ARE SET SO THAT SUPER-MAGNETISM, LIGHTNING OR SUPER-HEAT-RADIANCE WILL TRIGGER THEM AUTOMATICALLY!
HE'S GOT US... SOME OF US WOULD SURELY BE BLASTED BY THOSE RAY-GUNS IF WE TRIED TO USE OUR POWERS!
IMPRISON THEM IN THE JEWEL JAIL UNTIL I HAVE TIME TO RANSACK THEIR MINDS TELEPATHICALLY AND LEARN ALL THEIR SECRETS!
IT'S INCREDIBLE... WE OF THE LEGION HAVE BEEN OVERCOME, AT LAST, BY THIS STRANGE CREATURE OF LIVING ELECTRICAL ENERGY!
THE JEWEL JAIL IS AN UNEARTHLY PRISON INDEED
WE'VE GOT TO ESCAPE BEFORE THAT CREATURE PUMPS OUR MINDS EMPTY! SUPER-MAGNETISM WON'T AFFECT THE WALLS OF THIS HUGE HOLLOW JEWEL, BUT MAYBE HEAT WILL!
I'LL TRY... THERE ARE NO AUTO-MATIC RAY-GUNS COVERING US NOW!

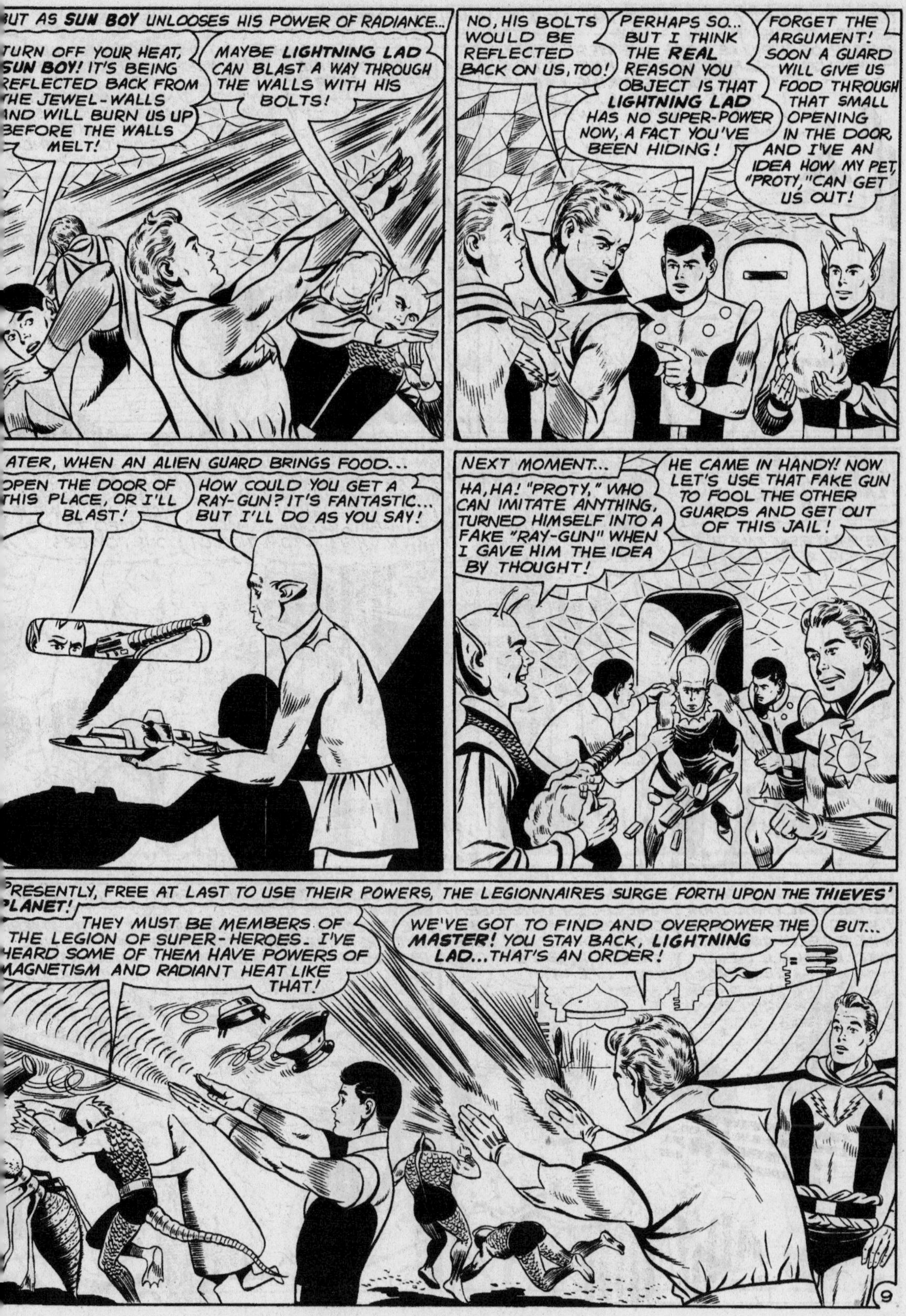
BUT AS SUN BOY UNLOOSES HIS POWER OF RADIANCE...
TURN OFF YOUR HEAT, SUN BOY! IT'S BEING REFLECTED BACK FROM THE JEWEL-WALLS AND WILL BURN US UP BEFORE THE WALLS MELT!
MAYBE LIGHTNING LAD CAN BLAST A WAY THROUGH THE WALLS WITH HIS BOLTS!
NO, HIS BOLTS WOULD BE REFLECTED BACK ON US, TOO!
PERHAPS SO... BUT I THINK THE REAL REASON YOU OBJECT IS THAT LIGHTNING LAD HAS NO SUPER-POWER NOW, A FACT YOU'VE BEEN HIDING!
FORGET THE ARGUMENT! SOON A GUARD WILL GIVE US FOOD THROUGH THAT SMALL OPENING IN THE DOOR, AND I'VE AN IDEA HOW MY PET, "PROTY," CAN GET US OUT!
LATER, WHEN AN ALIEN GUARD BRINGS FOOD...
OPEN THE DOOR OF THIS PLACE, OR I'LL BLAST!
HOW COULD YOU GET A RAY-GUN? IT'S FANTASTIC... BUT I'LL DO AS YOU SAY!
NEXT MOMENT...
HA, HA! "PROTY," WHO CAN IMITATE ANYTHING, TURNED HIMSELF INTO A FAKE "RAY-GUN" WHEN I GAVE HIM THE IDEA BY THOUGHT!
HE CAME IN HANDY! NOW LET'S USE THAT FAKE GUN TO FOOL THE OTHER GUARDS AND GET OUT OF THIS JAIL!
PRESENTLY, FREE AT LAST TO USE THEIR POWERS, THE LEGIONNAIRES SURGE FORTH UPON THE THIEVES' PLANET!
THEY MUST BE MEMBERS OF THE LEGION OF SUPER-HEROES. I'VE HEARD SOME OF THEM HAVE POWERS OF MAGNETISM AND RADIANT HEAT LIKE THAT!
WE'VE GOT TO FIND AND OVERPOWER THE MASTER! YOU STAY BACK, LIGHTNING LAD...THAT'S AN ORDER!
BUT...
9

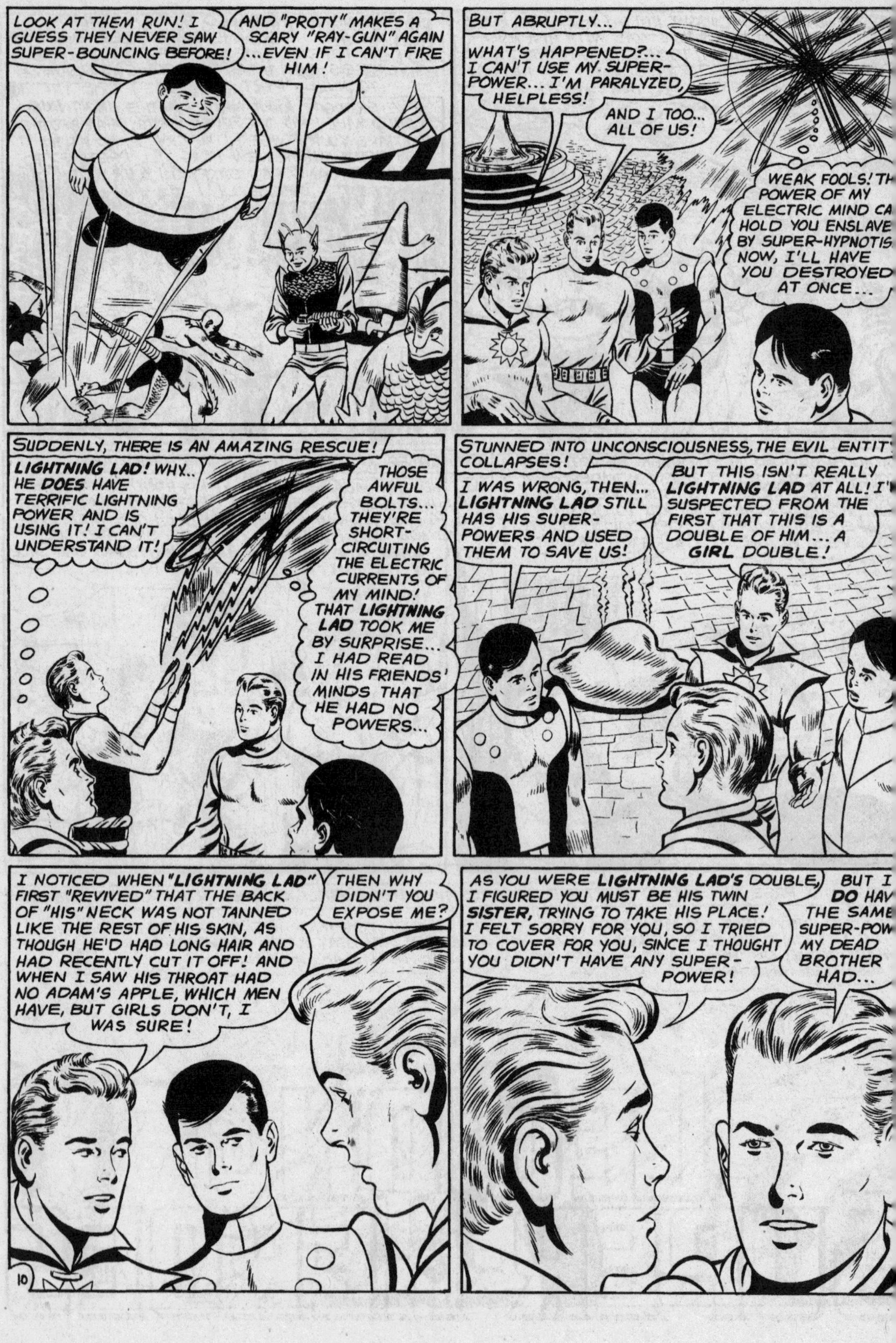
LOOK AT THEM RUN! I GUESS THEY NEVER SAW SUPER-BOUNCING BEFORE!
AND "PROTY" MAKES A SCARY "RAY-GUN" AGAIN ...EVEN IF I CAN'T FIRE HIM!
BUT ABRUPTLY...
WHAT'S HAPPENED?... I CAN'T USE MY SUPER-POWER... I'M PARALYZED, HELPLESS!
AND I TOO... ALL OF US!
WEAK FOOLS! TH POWER OF MY ELECTRIC MIND CA HOLD YOU ENSLAVE BY SUPER-HYPNOTIS NOW, I'LL HAVE YOU DESTROYED AT ONCE...
SUDDENLY, THERE IS AN AMAZING RESCUE!
LIGHTNING LAD! WHY.. HE DOES HAVE TERRIFIC LIGHTNING POWER AND IS USING IT! I CAN'T UNDERSTAND IT!
THOSE AWFUL BOLTS... THEY'RE SHORT-CIRCUITING THE ELECTRIC CURRENTS OF MY MIND! THAT LIGHTNING LAD TOOK ME BY SURPRISE... I HAD READ IN HIS FRIENDS' MINDS THAT HE HAD NO POWERS...
STUNNED INTO UNCONSCIOUSNESS, THE EVIL ENTIT COLLAPSES!
I WAS WRONG, THEN... LIGHTNING LAD STILL HAS HIS SUPER-POWERS AND USED THEM TO SAVE US!
BUT THIS ISN'T REALLY LIGHTNING LAD AT ALL! I' SUSPECTED FROM THE FIRST THAT THIS IS A DOUBLE OF HIM... A GIRL DOUBLE!
I NOTICED WHEN "LIGHTNING LAD" FIRST "REVIVED" THAT THE BACK OF "HIS" NECK WAS NOT TANNED LIKE THE REST OF HIS SKIN, AS THOUGH HE'D HAD LONG HAIR AND HAD RECENTLY CUT IT OFF! AND WHEN I SAW HIS THROAT HAD NO ADAM'S APPLE, WHICH MEN HAVE, BUT GIRLS DON'T, I WAS SURE!
THEN WHY DIDN'T YOU EXPOSE ME?
10
AS YOU WERE LIGHTNING LAD'S DOUBLE, I FIGURED YOU MUST BE HIS TWIN SISTER, TRYING TO TAKE HIS PLACE! I FELT SORRY FOR YOU, SO I TRIED TO COVER FOR YOU, SINCE I THOUGHT YOU DIDN'T HAVE ANY SUPER-POWER!
BUT I DO HAV THE SAME SUPER-POW MY DEAD BROTHER HAD...

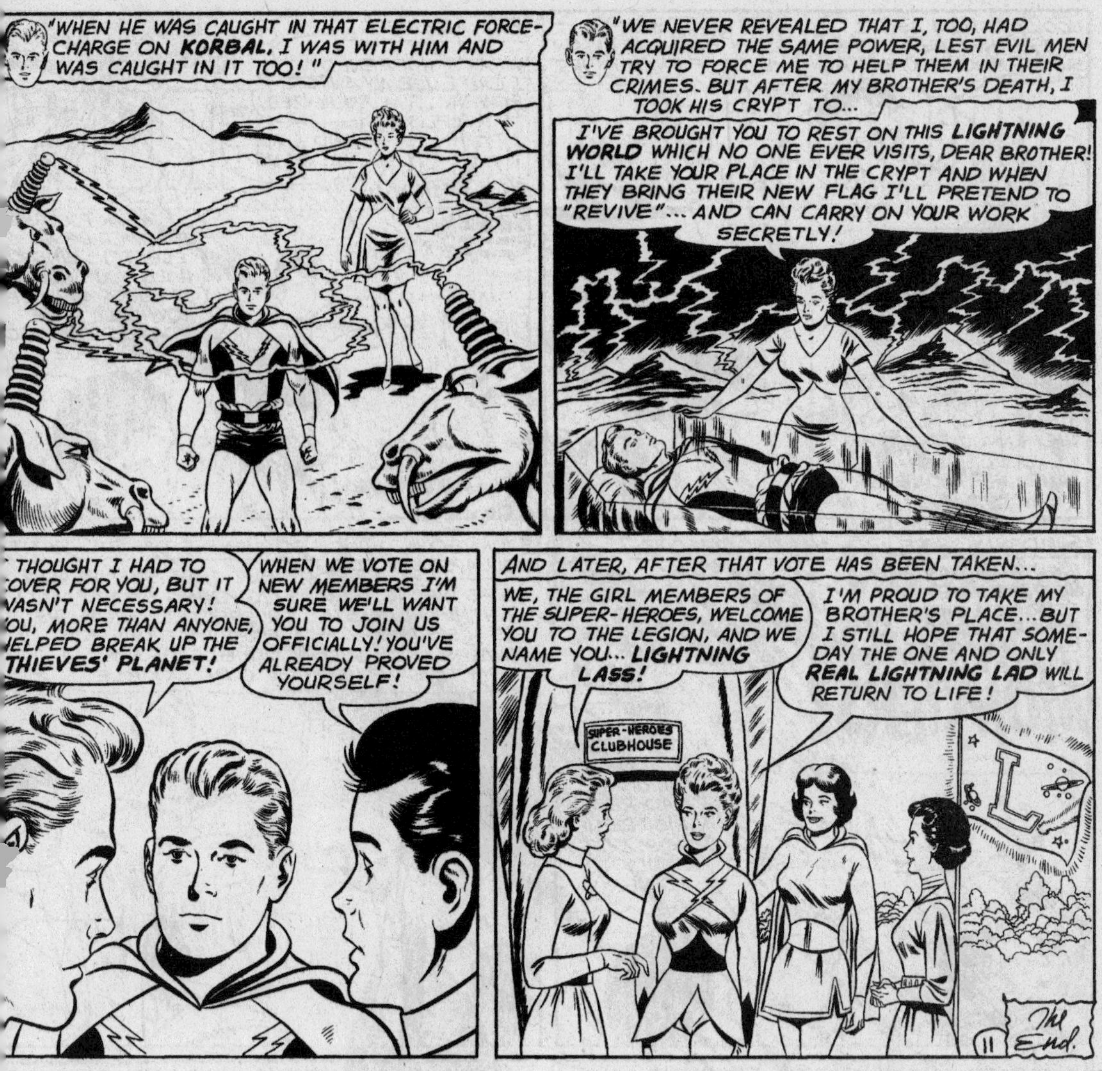
"WHEN HE WAS CAUGHT IN THAT ELECTRIC FORCE-CHARGE ON KORBAL, I WAS WITH HIM AND WAS CAUGHT IN IT TOO!"
"WE NEVER REVEALED THAT I, TOO, HAD ACQUIRED THE SAME POWER, LEST EVIL MEN TRY TO FORCE ME TO HELP THEM IN THEIR CRIMES. BUT AFTER MY BROTHER'S DEATH, I TOOK HIS CRYPT TO...
I'VE BROUGHT YOU TO REST ON THIS LIGHTNING WORLD WHICH NO ONE EVER VISITS, DEAR BROTHER! I'LL TAKE YOUR PLACE IN THE CRYPT AND WHEN THEY BRING THEIR NEW FLAG I'LL PRETEND TO "REVIVE"... AND CAN CARRY ON YOUR WORK SECRETLY!
THOUGHT I HAD TO OVER FOR YOU, BUT IT VASN'T NECESSARY! OU, MORE THAN ANYONE, IELPED BREAK UP THE THIEVES' PLANET!
WHEN WE VOTE ON NEW MEMBERS I'M SURE WE'LL WANT YOU TO JOIN US OFFICIALLY! YOU'VE ALREADY PROVED YOURSELF!
AND LATER, AFTER THAT VOTE HAS BEEN TAKEN...
WE, THE GIRL MEMBERS OF THE SUPER-HEROES, WELCOME YOU TO THE LEGION, AND WE NAME YOU... LIGHTNING LASS!
I'M PROUD TO TAKE MY BROTHER'S PLACE... BUT I STILL HOPE THAT SOME-DAY THE ONE AND ONLY REAL LIGHTNING LAD WILL RETURN TO LIFE!
SUPER-HEROES CLUBHOUSE
L
The End.
11

LEGION of SUPER-HEROES

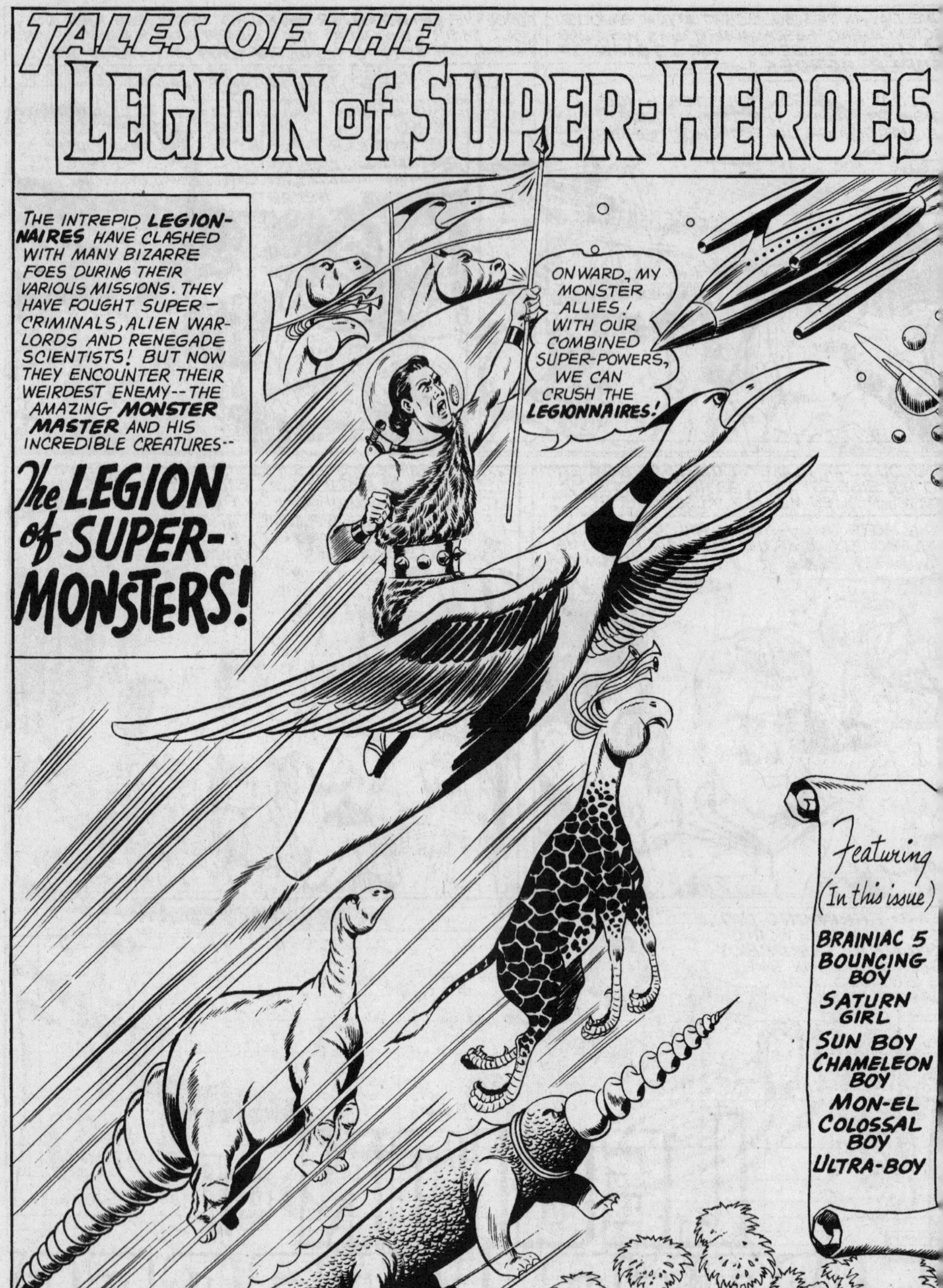
TALES OF THE
LEGION of SUPER-HEROES
THE INTREPID LEGIONNAIRES HAVE CLASHED WITH MANY BIZARRE FOES DURING THEIR VARIOUS MISSIONS. THEY HAVE FOUGHT SUPER-CRIMINALS, ALIEN WAR-LORDS AND RENEGADE SCIENTISTS! BUT NOW THEY ENCOUNTER THEIR WEIRDEST ENEMY--THE AMAZING MONSTER MASTER AND HIS INCREDIBLE CREATURES--
The LEGION of SUPER-MONSTERS!
ONWARD, MY MONSTER ALLIES! WITH OUR COMBINED SUPER-POWERS, WE CAN CRUSH THE LEGIONNAIRES!
Featuring (In this issue)
BRAINIAC 5
BOUNCING BOY
SATURN GIRL
SUN BOY
CHAMELEON BOY
MON-EL
COLOSSAL BOY
ULTRA-BOY

ONE DAY, IN THE 30TH CENTURY, A FAMOUS SCIENCE PROFESSOR ADDRESSES HIS CLASS OF SPECIAL STUDENTS -- THE **LEGION OF SUPER-HEROES!**

TODAY'S LESSON WILL TEACH YOU HOW TO FIGURE THE TENTH-ORDER EQUATIONS OF THE FOURTH DIMENSION!

YES, THE **LEGIONNAIRES**, NO MATTER WHERE THEY ARE, GET THEIR SCHOOLING BY CLOSED TV! FOR EXAMPLE, IN A FAR OFF SPACE-SHIP, **ULTRA-BOY** AND **MON-EL**...

...AND REMEMBER THAT IN THE EQUATION OF "Z OVER X TIMES Pi SQUARED", THE FOURTH DIMENSION INFINITY CONSTANT IS...

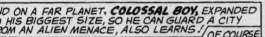

AND ON A FAR PLANET, **COLOSSAL BOY**, EXPANDED TO HIS BIGGEST SIZE, SO HE CAN GUARD A CITY FROM AN ALIEN MENACE, ALSO LEARNS!

OF COURSE, THIS EQUATION MUST BE ALTERED IN THE **ROX-URL** GALAXY...

ON EARTH, THOSE SUPER-HEROES WHO ARE NOT AWAY ON MISSIONS, ATTEND THEIR "CLASS" IN THE LEGIONNAIRES' CLUBHOUSE...

...AND THAT CONCLUDES TODAY'S LECTURE!

WOW, THAT WAS TOUGH... NOW, FOR OUR REGULAR **DAILY** CHECK OF THE WHEREABOUTS OF ALL MEMBERS!

...AND **SHRINKING VIOLET** IS STILL AT THE WORLD **KOLNAR!** SUPERBOY, BACK IN HIS OWN TIME, IS ENGAGED IN AN URGENT TASK!

MAP OF THE UNIVERSE

SHRINKING VIOLET

MATTER-EATER LAD

TRIPLICATE GIRL

COSMIC BOY

SUPER-BOY

INVISIBLE KID

ULTRA BOY AND MON-EL

ALL LEGION MEMBERS ACCOUNTED FOR! THE NEXT ORDER OF BUSINESS IS TO EXAMINE NEW APPLICANTS FOR LEGION MEMBERSHIP!

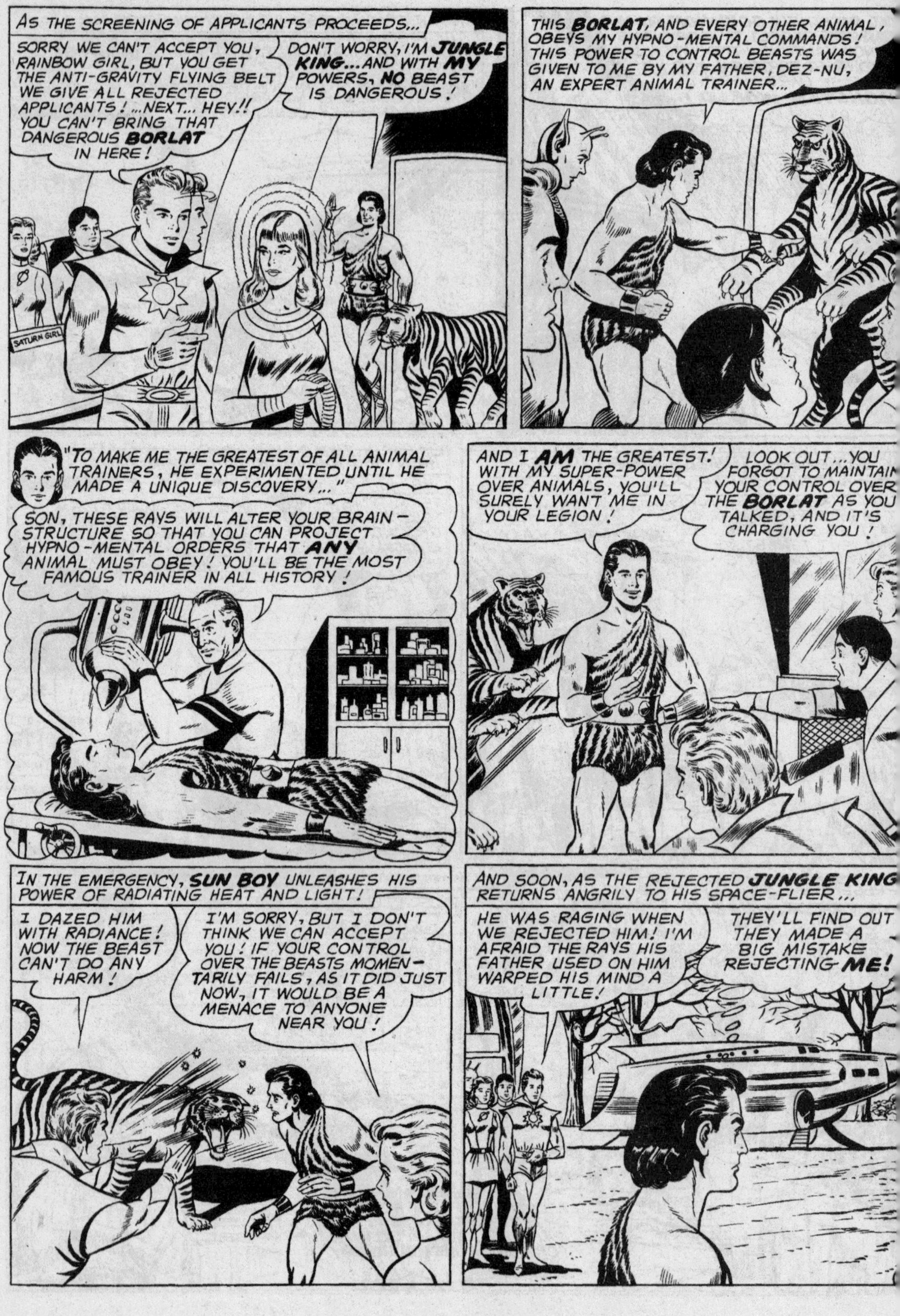
AS THE SCREENING OF APPLICANTS PROCEEDS...
SORRY WE CAN'T ACCEPT YOU, RAINBOW GIRL, BUT YOU GET THE ANTI-GRAVITY FLYING BELT WE GIVE ALL REJECTED APPLICANTS! ...NEXT... HEY!! YOU CAN'T BRING THAT DANGEROUS BORLAT IN HERE!
DON'T WORRY, I'M JUNGLE KING... AND WITH MY POWERS, NO BEAST IS DANGEROUS!
SATURN GIRL
THIS BORLAT, AND EVERY OTHER ANIMAL, OBEYS MY HYPNO-MENTAL COMMANDS! THIS POWER TO CONTROL BEASTS WAS GIVEN TO ME BY MY FATHER, DEZ-NU, AN EXPERT ANIMAL TRAINER...
"TO MAKE ME THE GREATEST OF ALL ANIMAL TRAINERS, HE EXPERIMENTED UNTIL HE MADE A UNIQUE DISCOVERY..."
SON, THESE RAYS WILL ALTER YOUR BRAIN-STRUCTURE SO THAT YOU CAN PROJECT HYPNO-MENTAL ORDERS THAT ANY ANIMAL MUST OBEY! YOU'LL BE THE MOST FAMOUS TRAINER IN ALL HISTORY!
AND I AM THE GREATEST! WITH MY SUPER-POWER OVER ANIMALS, YOU'LL SURELY WANT ME IN YOUR LEGION!
LOOK OUT... YOU FORGOT TO MAINTAIN YOUR CONTROL OVER THE BORLAT AS YOU TALKED, AND IT'S CHARGING YOU!
IN THE EMERGENCY, SUN BOY UNLEASHES HIS POWER OF RADIATING HEAT AND LIGHT!
I DAZED HIM WITH RADIANCE! NOW THE BEAST CAN'T DO ANY HARM!
I'M SORRY, BUT I DON'T THINK WE CAN ACCEPT YOU! IF YOUR CONTROL OVER THE BEASTS MOMENTARILY FAILS, AS IT DID JUST NOW, IT WOULD BE A MENACE TO ANYONE NEAR YOU!
AND SOON, AS THE REJECTED JUNGLE KING RETURNS ANGRILY TO HIS SPACE-FLIER...
HE WAS RAGING WHEN WE REJECTED HIM! I'M AFRAID THE RAYS HIS FATHER USED ON HIM WARPED HIS MIND A LITTLE!
THEY'LL FIND OUT THEY MADE A BIG MISTAKE REJECTING ME!

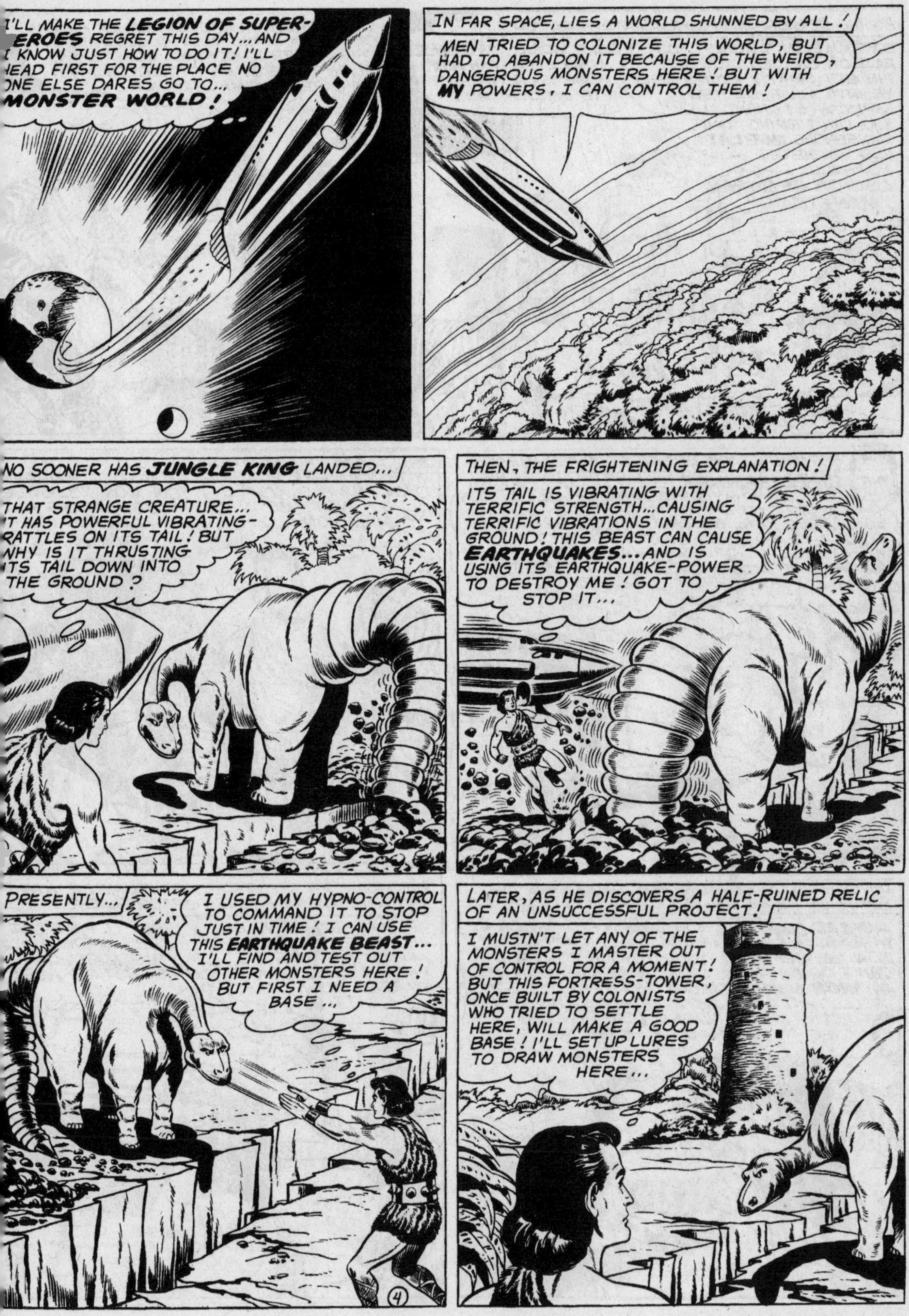
I'LL MAKE THE LEGION OF SUPER-HEROES REGRET THIS DAY... AND I KNOW JUST HOW TO DO IT! I'LL HEAD FIRST FOR THE PLACE NO ONE ELSE DARES GO TO... MONSTER WORLD! ...
IN FAR SPACE, LIES A WORLD SHUNNED BY ALL!
MEN TRIED TO COLONIZE THIS WORLD, BUT HAD TO ABANDON IT BECAUSE OF THE WEIRD, DANGEROUS MONSTERS HERE! BUT WITH MY POWERS, I CAN CONTROL THEM!
NO SOONER HAS JUNGLE KING LANDED...
THAT STRANGE CREATURE... IT HAS POWERFUL VIBRATING-RATTLES ON ITS TAIL! BUT WHY IS IT THRUSTING ITS TAIL DOWN INTO THE GROUND?
THEN, THE FRIGHTENING EXPLANATION!
ITS TAIL IS VIBRATING WITH TERRIFIC STRENGTH...CAUSING TERRIFIC VIBRATIONS IN THE GROUND! THIS BEAST CAN CAUSE EARTHQUAKES... AND IS USING ITS EARTHQUAKE-POWER TO DESTROY ME! GOT TO STOP IT...
PRESENTLY...
I USED MY HYPNO-CONTROL TO COMMAND IT TO STOP JUST IN TIME! I CAN USE THIS EARTHQUAKE BEAST... I'LL FIND AND TEST OUT OTHER MONSTERS HERE! BUT FIRST I NEED A BASE...
4
LATER, AS HE DISCOVERS A HALF-RUINED RELIC OF AN UNSUCCESSFUL PROJECT!
I MUSTN'T LET ANY OF THE MONSTERS I MASTER OUT OF CONTROL FOR A MOMENT! BUT THIS FORTRESS-TOWER, ONCE BUILT BY COLONISTS WHO TRIED TO SETTLE HERE, WILL MAKE A GOOD BASE! I'LL SET UP LURES TO DRAW MONSTERS HERE...

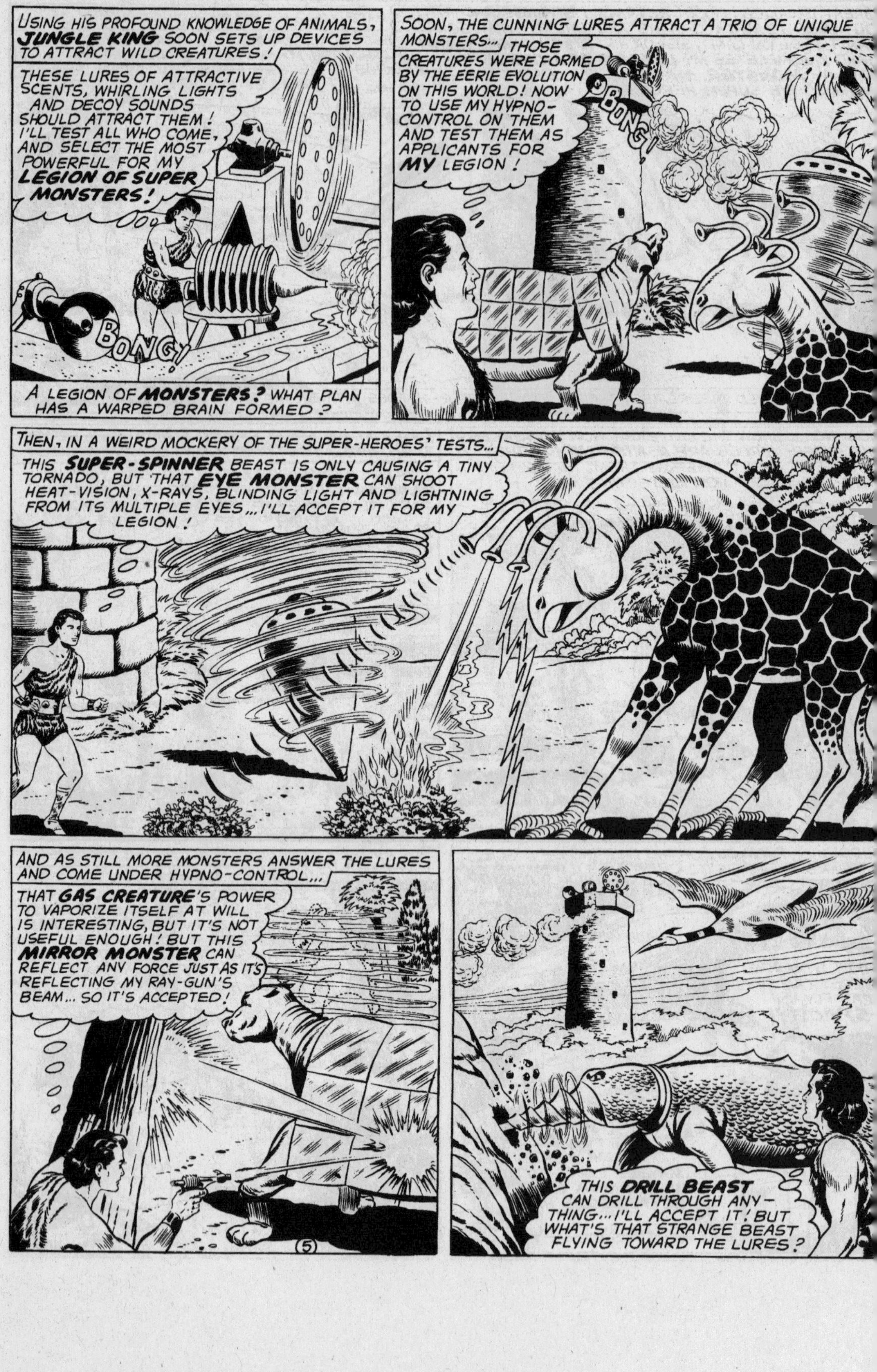
USING HIS PROFOUND KNOWLEDGE OF ANIMALS, JUNGLE KING SOON SETS UP DEVICES TO ATTRACT WILD CREATURES!
THESE LURES OF ATTRACTIVE SCENTS, WHIRLING LIGHTS AND DECOY SOUNDS SHOULD ATTRACT THEM! I'LL TEST ALL WHO COME, AND SELECT THE MOST POWERFUL FOR MY LEGION OF SUPER MONSTERS!
BONG!
A LEGION OF MONSTERS? WHAT PLAN HAS A WARPED BRAIN FORMED?
SOON, THE CUNNING LURES ATTRACT A TRIO OF UNIQUE MONSTERS...
THOSE CREATURES WERE FORMED BY THE EERIE EVOLUTION ON THIS WORLD! NOW TO USE MY HYPNO-CONTROL ON THEM AND TEST THEM AS APPLICANTS FOR MY LEGION!
BONG!
THEN, IN A WEIRD MOCKERY OF THE SUPER-HEROES' TESTS...
THIS SUPER-SPINNER BEAST IS ONLY CAUSING A TINY TORNADO, BUT THAT EYE MONSTER CAN SHOOT HEAT-VISION, X-RAYS, BLINDING LIGHT AND LIGHTNING FROM ITS MULTIPLE EYES... I'LL ACCEPT IT FOR MY LEGION!
AND AS STILL MORE MONSTERS ANSWER THE LURES AND COME UNDER HYPNO-CONTROL...
THAT GAS CREATURE'S POWER TO VAPORIZE ITSELF AT WILL IS INTERESTING, BUT IT'S NOT USEFUL ENOUGH! BUT THIS MIRROR MONSTER CAN REFLECT ANY FORCE JUST AS IT'S REFLECTING MY RAY-GUN'S BEAM... SO IT'S ACCEPTED!
5
THIS DRILL BEAST CAN DRILL THROUGH ANYTHING... I'LL ACCEPT IT! BUT WHAT'S THAT STRANGE BEAST FLYING TOWARD THE LURES?

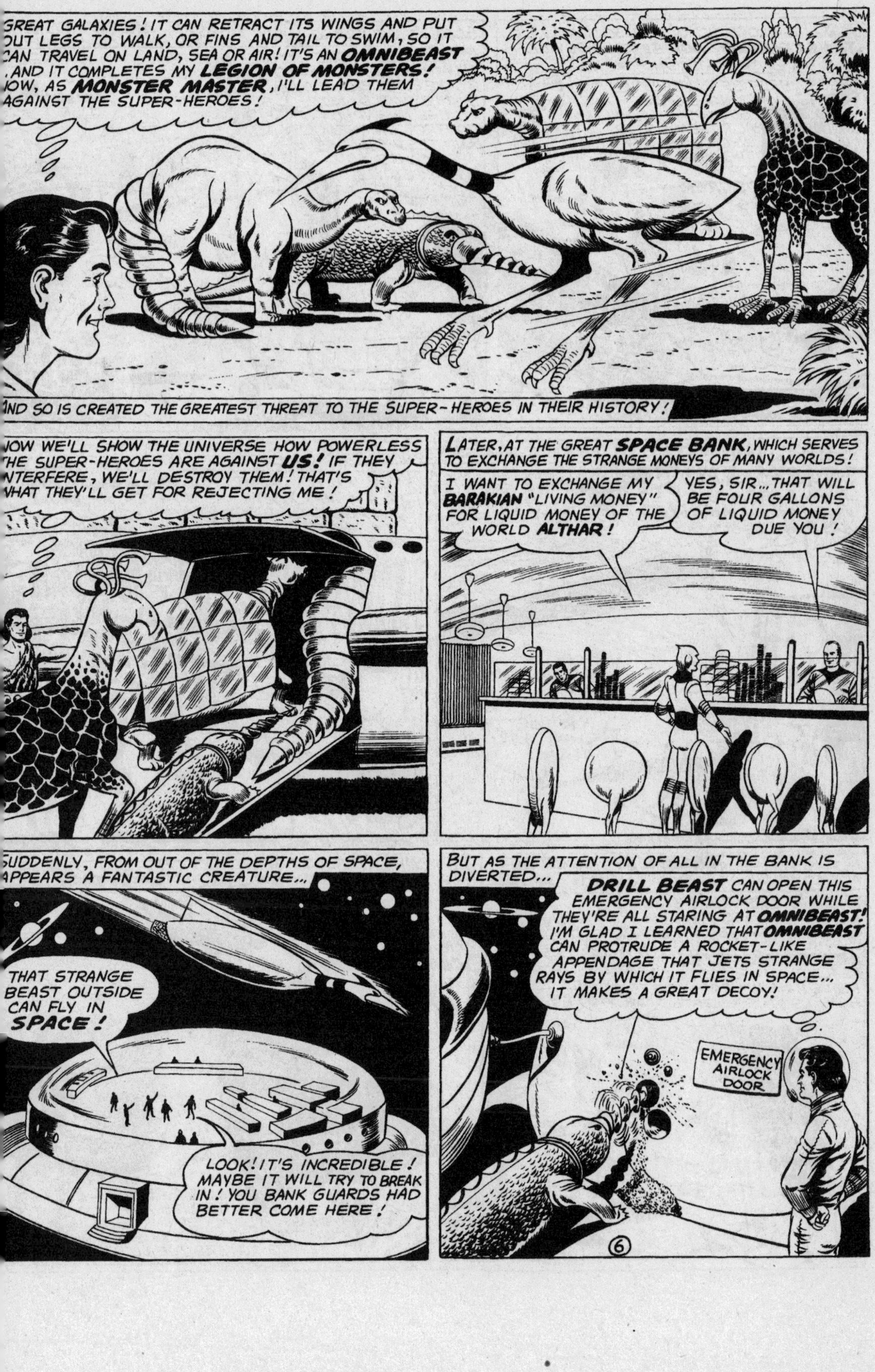
GREAT GALAXIES! IT CAN RETRACT ITS WINGS AND PUT OUT LEGS TO WALK, OR FINS AND TAIL TO SWIM, SO IT CAN TRAVEL ON LAND, SEA OR AIR! IT'S AN OMNIBEAST ...AND IT COMPLETES MY LEGION OF MONSTERS! NOW, AS MONSTER MASTER, I'LL LEAD THEM AGAINST THE SUPER-HEROES!
AND SO IS CREATED THE GREATEST THREAT TO THE SUPER-HEROES IN THEIR HISTORY!
NOW WE'LL SHOW THE UNIVERSE HOW POWERLESS THE SUPER-HEROES ARE AGAINST US! IF THEY INTERFERE, WE'LL DESTROY THEM! THAT'S WHAT THEY'LL GET FOR REJECTING ME!
LATER, AT THE GREAT SPACE BANK, WHICH SERVES TO EXCHANGE THE STRANGE MONEYS OF MANY WORLDS!
I WANT TO EXCHANGE MY BARAKIAN "LIVING MONEY" FOR LIQUID MONEY OF THE WORLD ALTHAR!
YES, SIR... THAT WILL BE FOUR GALLONS OF LIQUID MONEY DUE YOU!
SUDDENLY, FROM OUT OF THE DEPTHS OF SPACE, APPEARS A FANTASTIC CREATURE...
THAT STRANGE BEAST OUTSIDE CAN FLY IN SPACE!
LOOK! IT'S INCREDIBLE! MAYBE IT WILL TRY TO BREAK IN! YOU BANK GUARDS HAD BETTER COME HERE!
BUT AS THE ATTENTION OF ALL IN THE BANK IS DIVERTED...
DRILL BEAST CAN OPEN THIS EMERGENCY AIRLOCK DOOR WHILE THEY'RE ALL STARING AT OMNIBEAST! I'M GLAD I LEARNED THAT OMNIBEAST CAN PROTRUDE A ROCKET-LIKE APPENDAGE THAT JETS STRANGE RAYS BY WHICH IT FLIES IN SPACE... IT MAKES A GREAT DECOY!
EMERGENCY AIRLOCK DOOR
6

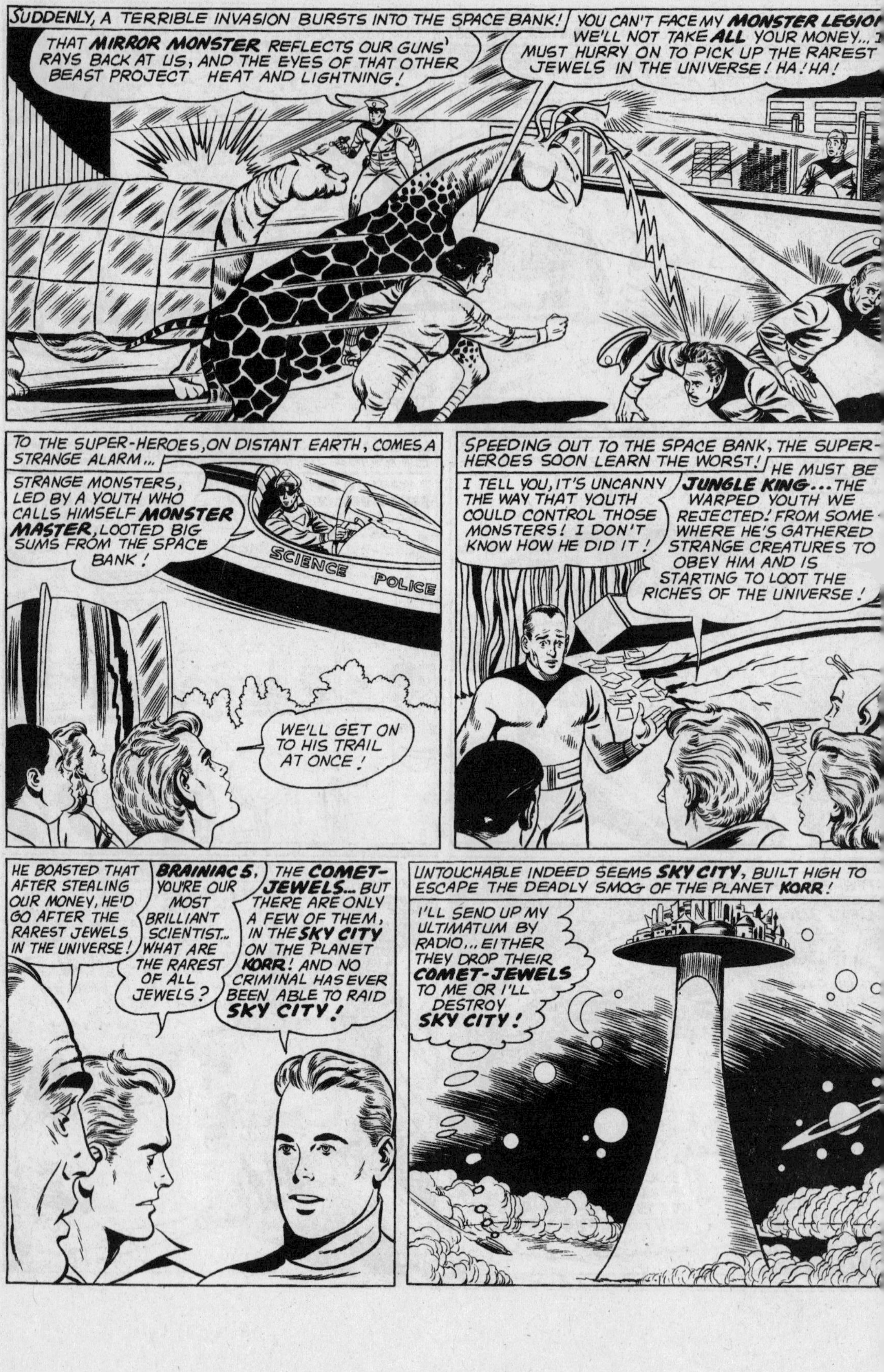
SUDDENLY, A TERRIBLE INVASION BURSTS INTO THE SPACE BANK!
THAT MIRROR MONSTER REFLECTS OUR GUNS' RAYS BACK AT US, AND THE EYES OF THAT OTHER BEAST PROJECT HEAT AND LIGHTNING!
YOU CAN'T FACE MY MONSTER LEGION! WE'LL NOT TAKE ALL YOUR MONEY... I MUST HURRY ON TO PICK UP THE RAREST JEWELS IN THE UNIVERSE! HA! HA!
TO THE SUPER-HEROES, ON DISTANT EARTH, COMES A STRANGE ALARM...
STRANGE MONSTERS, LED BY A YOUTH WHO CALLS HIMSELF MONSTER MASTER, LOOTED BIG SUMS FROM THE SPACE BANK!
SCIENCE POLICE
WE'LL GET ON TO HIS TRAIL AT ONCE!
SPEEDING OUT TO THE SPACE BANK, THE SUPER-HEROES SOON LEARN THE WORST!
I TELL YOU, IT'S UNCANNY THE WAY THAT YOUTH COULD CONTROL THOSE MONSTERS! I DON'T KNOW HOW HE DID IT!
HE MUST BE JUNGLE KING... THE WARPED YOUTH WE REJECTED! FROM SOMEWHERE HE'S GATHERED STRANGE CREATURES TO OBEY HIM AND IS STARTING TO LOOT THE RICHES OF THE UNIVERSE!
HE BOASTED THAT AFTER STEALING OUR MONEY, HE'D GO AFTER THE RAREST JEWELS IN THE UNIVERSE!
BRAINIAC 5, YOU'RE OUR MOST BRILLIANT SCIENTIST... WHAT ARE THE RAREST OF ALL JEWELS?
THE COMET-JEWELS... BUT THERE ARE ONLY A FEW OF THEM, IN THE SKY CITY ON THE PLANET KORR! AND NO CRIMINAL HAS EVER BEEN ABLE TO RAID SKY CITY!
UNTOUCHABLE INDEED SEEMS SKY CITY, BUILT HIGH TO ESCAPE THE DEADLY SMOG OF THE PLANET KORR!
I'LL SEND UP MY ULTIMATUM BY RADIO... EITHER THEY DROP THEIR COMET-JEWELS TO ME OR I'LL DESTROY SKY CITY!

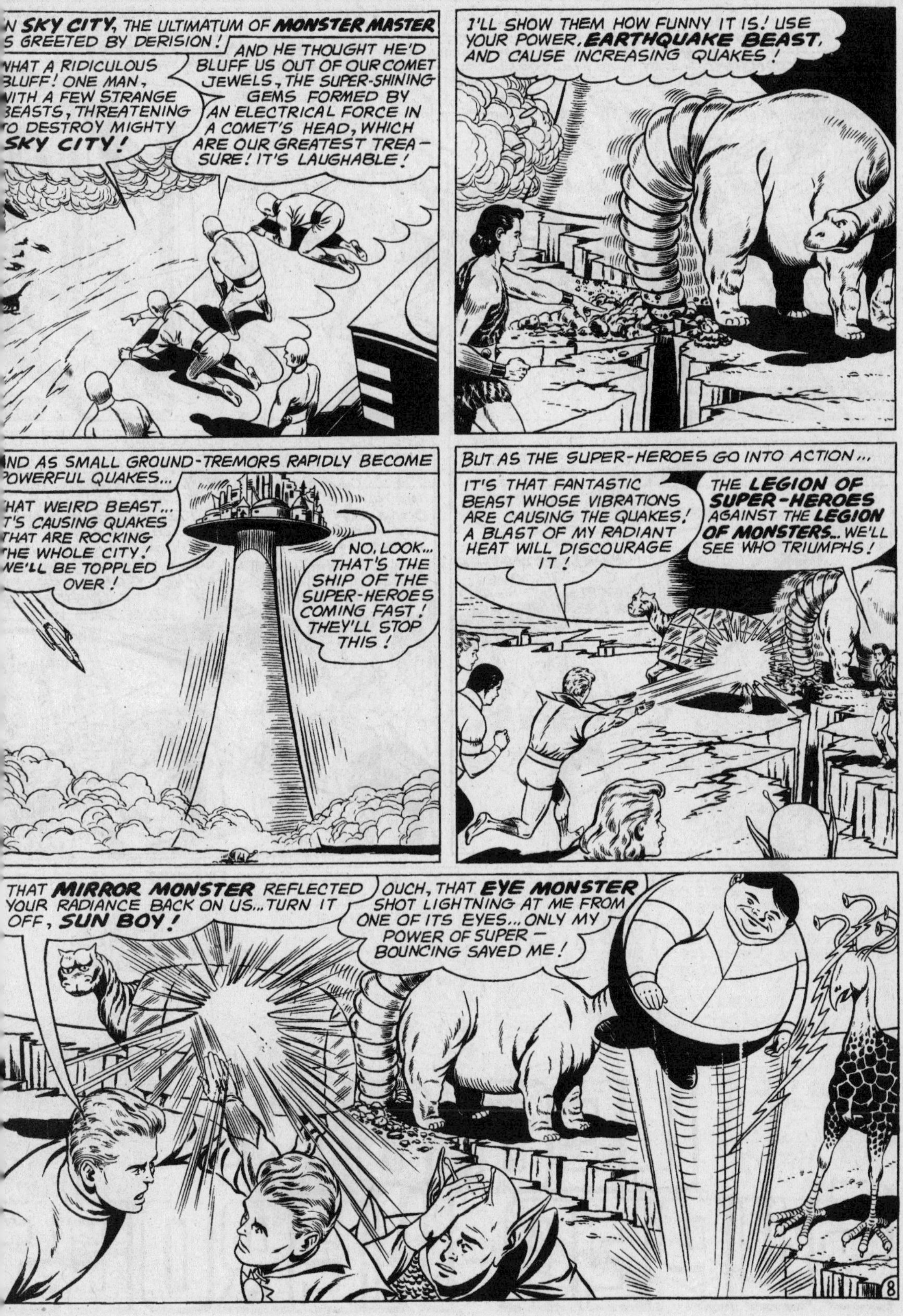
N SKY CITY, THE ULTIMATUM OF MONSTER MASTER S GREETED BY DERISION!
WHAT A RIDICULOUS BLUFF! ONE MAN, WITH A FEW STRANGE BEASTS, THREATENING TO DESTROY MIGHTY SKY CITY!
AND HE THOUGHT HE'D BLUFF US OUT OF OUR COMET JEWELS, THE SUPER-SHINING GEMS FORMED BY AN ELECTRICAL FORCE IN A COMET'S HEAD, WHICH ARE OUR GREATEST TREA-SURE! IT'S LAUGHABLE!
I'LL SHOW THEM HOW FUNNY IT IS! USE YOUR POWER, EARTHQUAKE BEAST, AND CAUSE INCREASING QUAKES!
ND AS SMALL GROUND-TREMORS RAPIDLY BECOME POWERFUL QUAKES...
THAT WEIRD BEAST... T'S CAUSING QUAKES THAT ARE ROCKING THE WHOLE CITY! WE'LL BE TOPPLED OVER!
NO, LOOK... THAT'S THE SHIP OF THE SUPER-HEROES COMING FAST! THEY'LL STOP THIS!
BUT AS THE SUPER-HEROES GO INTO ACTION...
IT'S THAT FANTASTIC BEAST WHOSE VIBRATIONS ARE CAUSING THE QUAKES! A BLAST OF MY RADIANT HEAT WILL DISCOURAGE IT!
THE LEGION OF SUPER-HEROES AGAINST THE LEGION OF MONSTERS... WE'LL SEE WHO TRIUMPHS!
THAT MIRROR MONSTER REFLECTED YOUR RADIANCE BACK ON US... TURN IT OFF, SUN BOY!
OUCH, THAT EYE MONSTER SHOT LIGHTNING AT ME FROM ONE OF ITS EYES... ONLY MY POWER OF SUPER-BOUNCING SAVED ME!
8

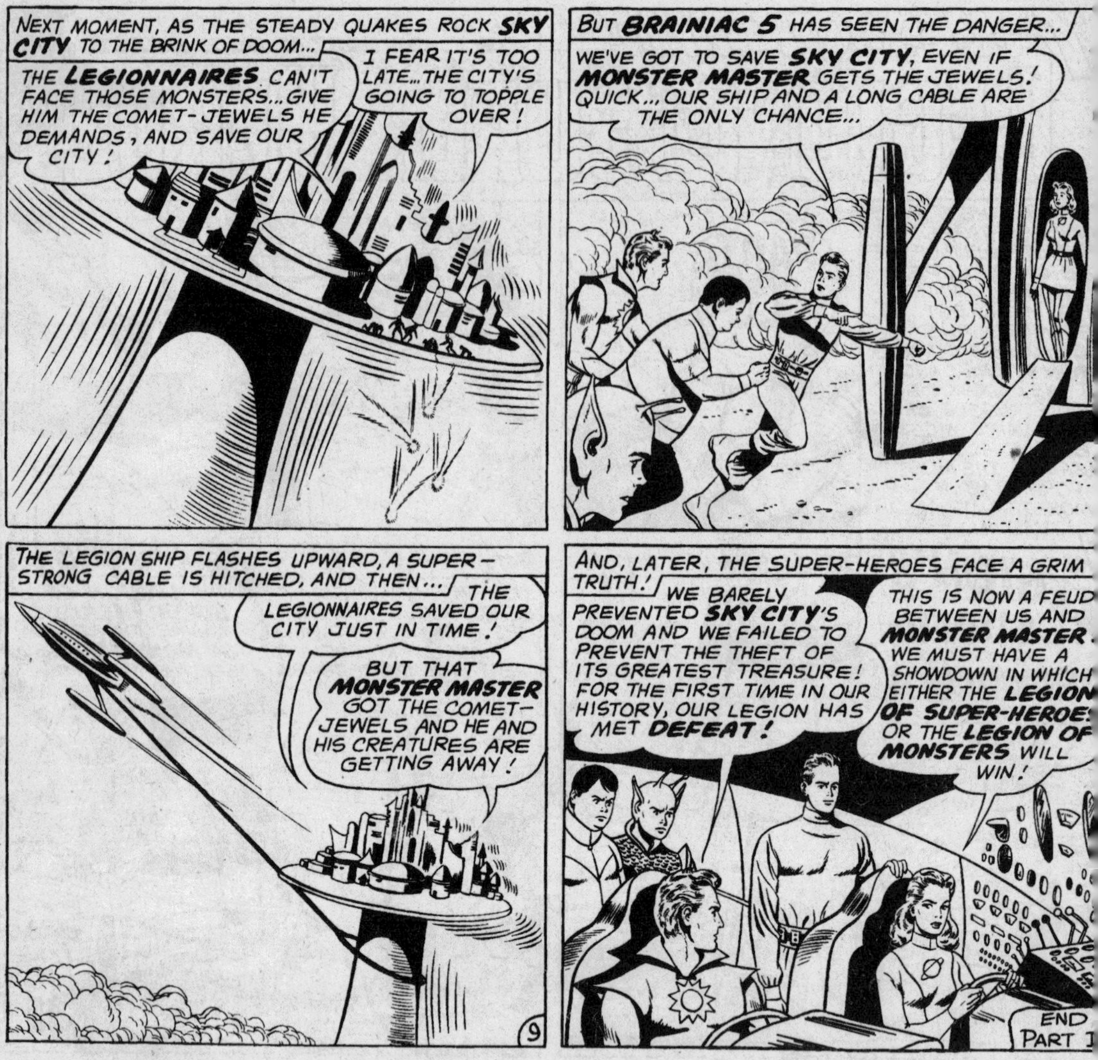
NEXT MOMENT, AS THE STEADY QUAKES ROCK SKY CITY TO THE BRINK OF DOOM...
THE LEGIONNAIRES CAN'T FACE THOSE MONSTERS...GIVE HIM THE COMET-JEWELS HE DEMANDS, AND SAVE OUR CITY!
I FEAR IT'S TOO LATE...THE CITY'S GOING TO TOPPLE OVER!
BUT BRAINIAC 5 HAS SEEN THE DANGER...
WE'VE GOT TO SAVE SKY CITY, EVEN IF MONSTER MASTER GETS THE JEWELS! QUICK..., OUR SHIP AND A LONG CABLE ARE THE ONLY CHANCE...
THE LEGION SHIP FLASHES UPWARD, A SUPER-STRONG CABLE IS HITCHED, AND THEN...
THE LEGIONNAIRES SAVED OUR CITY JUST IN TIME!
BUT THAT MONSTER MASTER GOT THE COMET-JEWELS AND HE AND HIS CREATURES ARE GETTING AWAY!
9
AND, LATER, THE SUPER-HEROES FACE A GRIM TRUTH!
WE BARELY PREVENTED SKY CITY'S DOOM AND WE FAILED TO PREVENT THE THEFT OF ITS GREATEST TREASURE! FOR THE FIRST TIME IN OUR HISTORY, OUR LEGION HAS MET DEFEAT!
THIS IS NOW A FEUD BETWEEN US AND MONSTER MASTER. WE MUST HAVE A SHOWDOWN IN WHICH EITHER THE LEGION OF SUPER-HEROE OR THE LEGION OF MONSTERS WILL WIN!
END PART

LEGION of SUPER-HEROES

TALES OF THE LEGION of SUPER-HEROES

ACROSS THE STARRY UNIVERSE RAGES THE EPIC STRUGGLE OF THE **LEGION OF SUPER-HEROES** AGAINST ITS MIGHTIEST ENEMIES... THE **LEGION OF SUPER-MONSTERS!** AND AT THE CLIMAX OF THAT STRUGGLE, ONE LEGIONNAIRE MUST BATTLE ALONE AGAINST THE MOST FORMIDABLE MONSTER OF ALL TIME IN...

The LEGION'S SUPER-SHOWDOWN!

PART II

I DREW THE MARKED LOT... AND IT'S UP TO ME TO CONQUER THE **EARTHQUAKE BEAST** SOMEHOW, OR DIE TRYING!

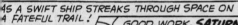

AS A SWIFT SHIP STREAKS THROUGH SPACE ON A FATEFUL TRAIL!

WITH MY THOUGHT-CASTING POWER, I READ IN **MONSTER MASTER'S** THOUGHTS THAT HIS NEXT LOOT WOULD BE **FLOWERS!**

GOOD WORK, **SATURN GIRL!** HE MUST BE HEADED FOR THE **WORLD OF GIANT FLOWERS**, WHOSE PRECIOUS SEEDS ARE WORTH A FORTUNE, AND THAT'S WHERE WE'LL GO!

IN THAT SHIP, THE DEFEATED **LEGION OF SUPER-HEROES** HOLDS GRIM COUNCIL!

IT WON'T BE EASY TO STOP THOSE MONSTERS! EACH CREATURE HAS A MIGHTY POWER, AND ONE OF THEM, **THE EARTHQUAKE BEAST**, IS SO FORMIDABLE, NONE OF US MAY BE ABLE TO CONQUER IT!

WE'VE GOT TO OUTWIT THEM WITH STRATEGY! I'VE A PLAN! LISTEN...

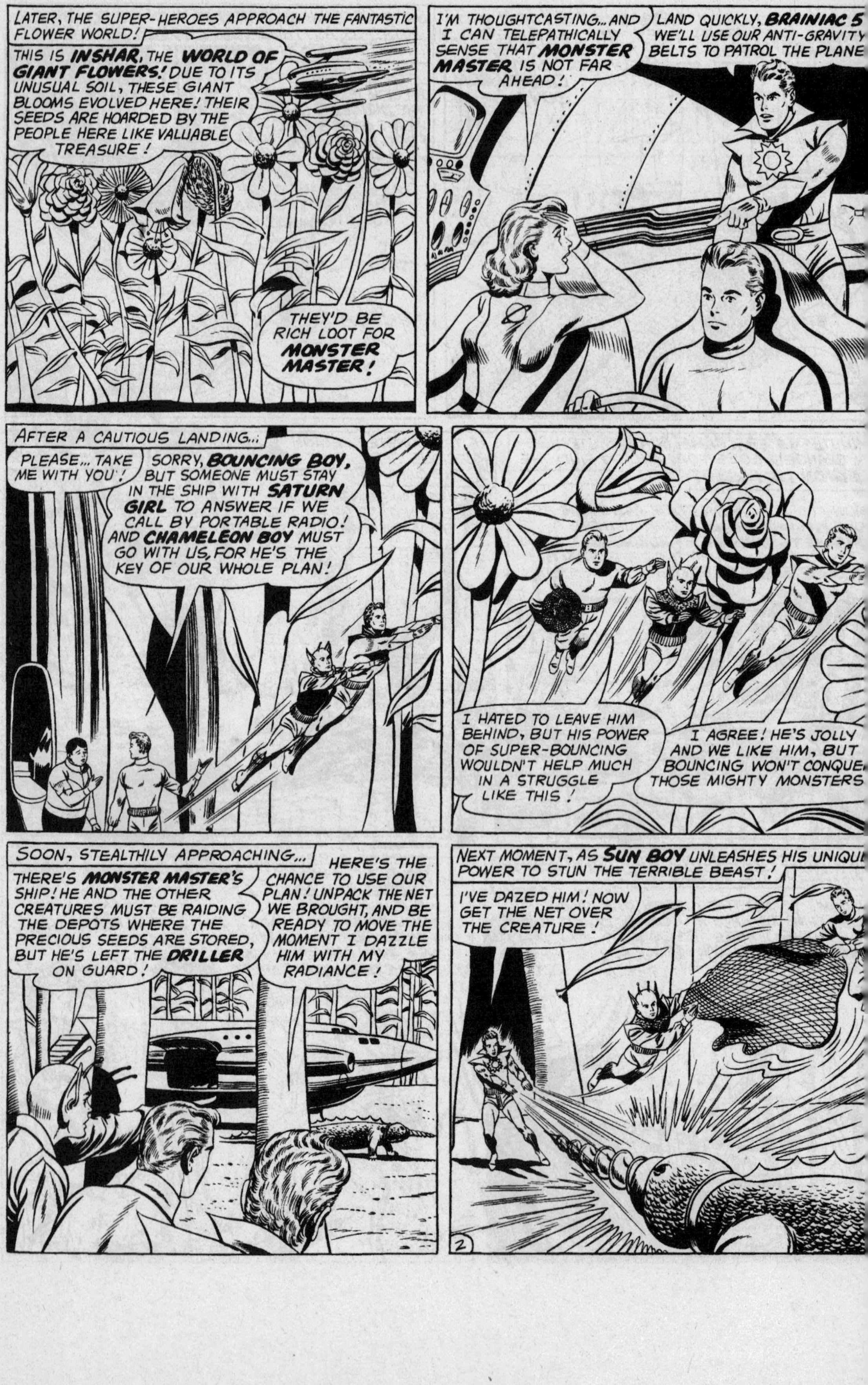
LATER, THE SUPER-HEROES APPROACH THE FANTASTIC FLOWER WORLD!
THIS IS INSHAR, THE WORLD OF GIANT FLOWERS! DUE TO ITS UNUSUAL SOIL, THESE GIANT BLOOMS EVOLVED HERE! THEIR SEEDS ARE HOARDED BY THE PEOPLE HERE LIKE VALUABLE TREASURE!
THEY'D BE RICH LOOT FOR MONSTER MASTER!
I'M THOUGHTCASTING... AND I CAN TELEPATHICALLY SENSE THAT MONSTER MASTER IS NOT FAR AHEAD!
LAND QUICKLY, BRAINIAC 5! WE'LL USE OUR ANTI-GRAVITY BELTS TO PATROL THE PLANE
AFTER A CAUTIOUS LANDING...
PLEASE... TAKE ME WITH YOU!
SORRY, BOUNCING BOY, BUT SOMEONE MUST STAY IN THE SHIP WITH SATURN GIRL TO ANSWER IF WE CALL BY PORTABLE RADIO! AND CHAMELEON BOY MUST GO WITH US, FOR HE'S THE KEY OF OUR WHOLE PLAN!
I HATED TO LEAVE HIM BEHIND, BUT HIS POWER OF SUPER-BOUNCING WOULDN'T HELP MUCH IN A STRUGGLE LIKE THIS!
I AGREE! HE'S JOLLY AND WE LIKE HIM, BUT BOUNCING WON'T CONQUE THOSE MIGHTY MONSTERS
SOON, STEALTHILY APPROACHING...
THERE'S MONSTER MASTER'S SHIP! HE AND THE OTHER CREATURES MUST BE RAIDING THE DEPOTS WHERE THE PRECIOUS SEEDS ARE STORED, BUT HE'S LEFT THE DRILLER ON GUARD!
HERE'S THE CHANCE TO USE OUR PLAN! UNPACK THE NET WE BROUGHT, AND BE READY TO MOVE THE MOMENT I DAZZLE HIM WITH MY RADIANCE!
NEXT MOMENT, AS SUN BOY UNLEASHES HIS UNIQU POWER TO STUN THE TERRIBLE BEAST!
I'VE DAZED HIM! NOW GET THE NET OVER THE CREATURE!
2

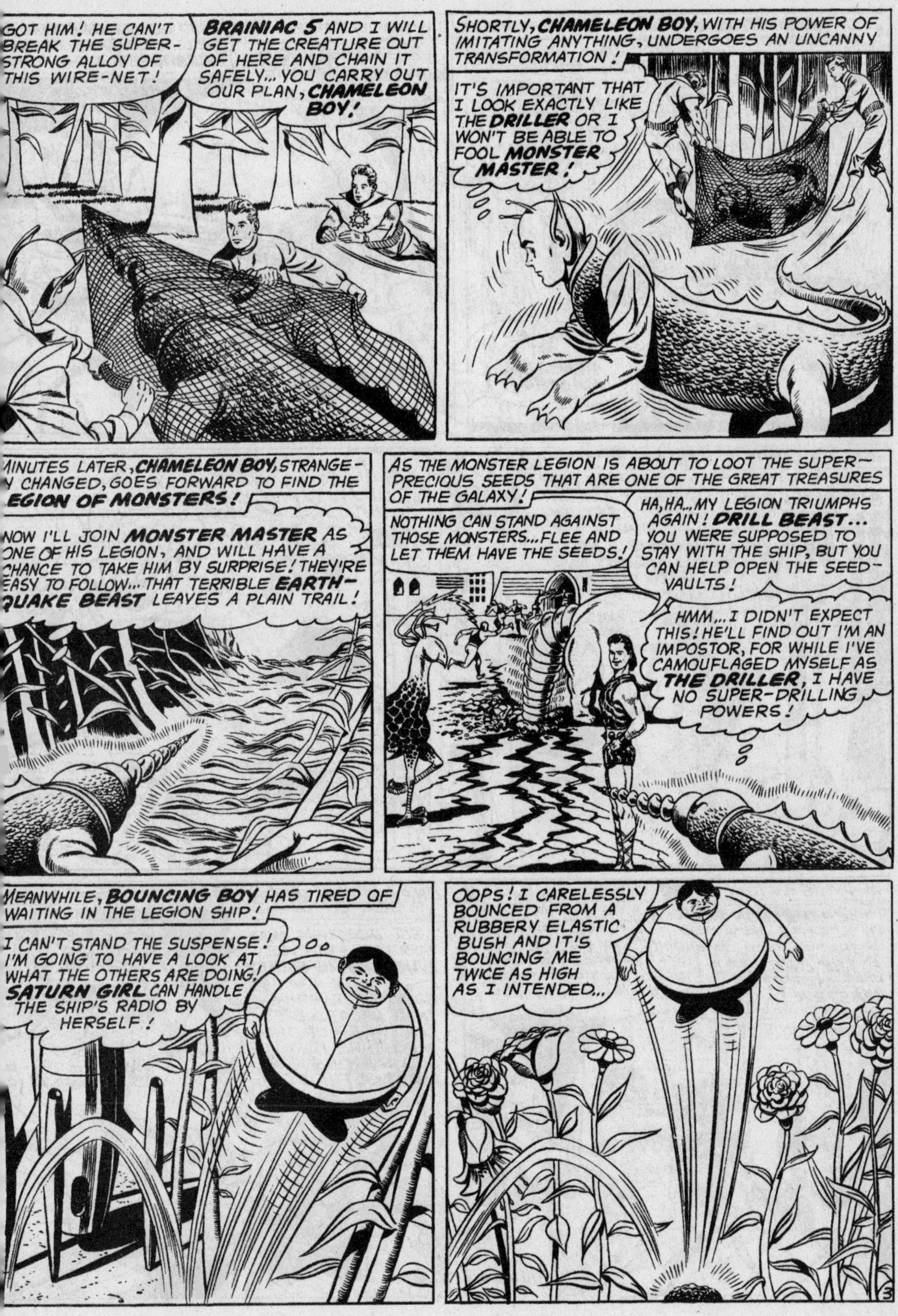
GOT HIM! HE CAN'T BREAK THE SUPER-STRONG ALLOY OF THIS WIRE-NET!
BRAINIAC 5 AND I WILL GET THE CREATURE OUT OF HERE AND CHAIN IT SAFELY... YOU CARRY OUT OUR PLAN, CHAMELEON BOY!
SHORTLY, CHAMELEON BOY, WITH HIS POWER OF IMITATING ANYTHING, UNDERGOES AN UNCANNY TRANSFORMATION!
IT'S IMPORTANT THAT I LOOK EXACTLY LIKE THE DRILLER OR I WON'T BE ABLE TO FOOL MONSTER MASTER!
MINUTES LATER, CHAMELEON BOY, STRANGELY CHANGED, GOES FORWARD TO FIND THE LEGION OF MONSTERS!
NOW I'LL JOIN MONSTER MASTER AS ONE OF HIS LEGION, AND WILL HAVE A CHANCE TO TAKE HIM BY SURPRISE! THEY'RE EASY TO FOLLOW... THAT TERRIBLE EARTHQUAKE BEAST LEAVES A PLAIN TRAIL!
AS THE MONSTER LEGION IS ABOUT TO LOOT THE SUPER-PRECIOUS SEEDS THAT ARE ONE OF THE GREAT TREASURES OF THE GALAXY!
NOTHING CAN STAND AGAINST THOSE MONSTERS...FLEE AND LET THEM HAVE THE SEEDS!
HA, HA... MY LEGION TRIUMPHS AGAIN! DRILL BEAST... YOU WERE SUPPOSED TO STAY WITH THE SHIP, BUT YOU CAN HELP OPEN THE SEED-VAULTS!
HMM... I DIDN'T EXPECT THIS! HE'LL FIND OUT I'M AN IMPOSTOR, FOR WHILE I'VE CAMOUFLAGED MYSELF AS THE DRILLER, I HAVE NO SUPER-DRILLING POWERS!
MEANWHILE, BOUNCING BOY HAS TIRED OF WAITING IN THE LEGION SHIP!
I CAN'T STAND THE SUSPENSE! I'M GOING TO HAVE A LOOK AT WHAT THE OTHERS ARE DOING! SATURN GIRL CAN HANDLE THE SHIP'S RADIO BY HERSELF!
OOPS! I CARELESSLY BOUNCED FROM A RUBBERY ELASTIC BUSH AND IT'S BOUNCING ME TWICE AS HIGH AS I INTENDED...
3

BUT AS **MONSTER MASTER** SCOUTS THE AREA...

THAT'S **BOUNCING BOY**, AND THAT MEANS THE SUPER-HEROES HAVE FOLLOWED ME HERE! I'D BETTER FORGET THE SEEDS AND RETREAT WITH MY LEGION, FOR THE SUPER-HEROES MAY HAVE SOME NEW WEAPON TO USE AGAINST ME!

BACK TO THE SHIP! HURRY! THEY'RE GETTING MY MENTAL COMMAND AND OBEYING...

THIS UPSETS OUR PLAN FOR **SUN BOY** AND **BRAINIAC 5** AREN'T BACK YET FROM CHAINING THE REAL **DRILL BEAST**! I'LL HAVE TO KEEP IMPERSONATING A MONSTER AND GO WITH THEM!

WHEN **SUN BOY** AND **BRAINIAC 5** RETURN TO COMPLETE THEIR PLAN OF ATTACK...

BOUNCING BOY, WHY AREN'T YOU AT OUR SHIP? AND WHAT HAPPENED TO MAKE THE **LEGION OF MONSTERS** TAKE OFF SO SUDDENLY?

I...I'M AFRAID IT'S MY FAULT...

I WANTED TO TAKE PART IN THE FIGHT AND FOLLOWED YOU, BUT I ACCIDENTALLY BOUNCED TOO HIGH AND **MONSTER MASTER** SAW ME!

YOU'VE RUINED EVERYTHING! WITH **CHAMELEON BOY** AS A "SPY" IN THE MONSTER LEGION WE HAD A CHANCE FOR A SURPRISE MOP-UP! BUT YOU SPOILED IT!

HURRY, BACK TO THE SHIP.

MINUTES LATER...

IT'S **CHAMELEON BOY** I'M WORRIED ABOUT...HE'S IN THAT SHIP STILL POSING AS **THE DRILLER**! I HOPE **MONSTER MASTER** DOESN'T DISCOVER HE'S REALLY A LEGIONNAIRE!

THEY'RE TOO FAR AWAY FOR ME TO CONTACT THEM TELE-PATHICALLY! I HOPE **CHAMELEON BOY** IS CLEVER ENOUGH TO PROTECT HIMSELF!

CHAMELEON BOY IS IN THE WORST PREDICAMENT OF HIS LIFE!

THESE MONSTERS ARE TERRIBLE, ESPECIALLY **EARTHQUAKE BEAST**! I DON'T SEE HOW ANY-BODY WILL EVER HANDLE **THAT** CREATURE! I CAN'T KEEP UP THIS IMPOSTURE FOREVER, AND IF **MONSTER MASTER** FINDS OUT...

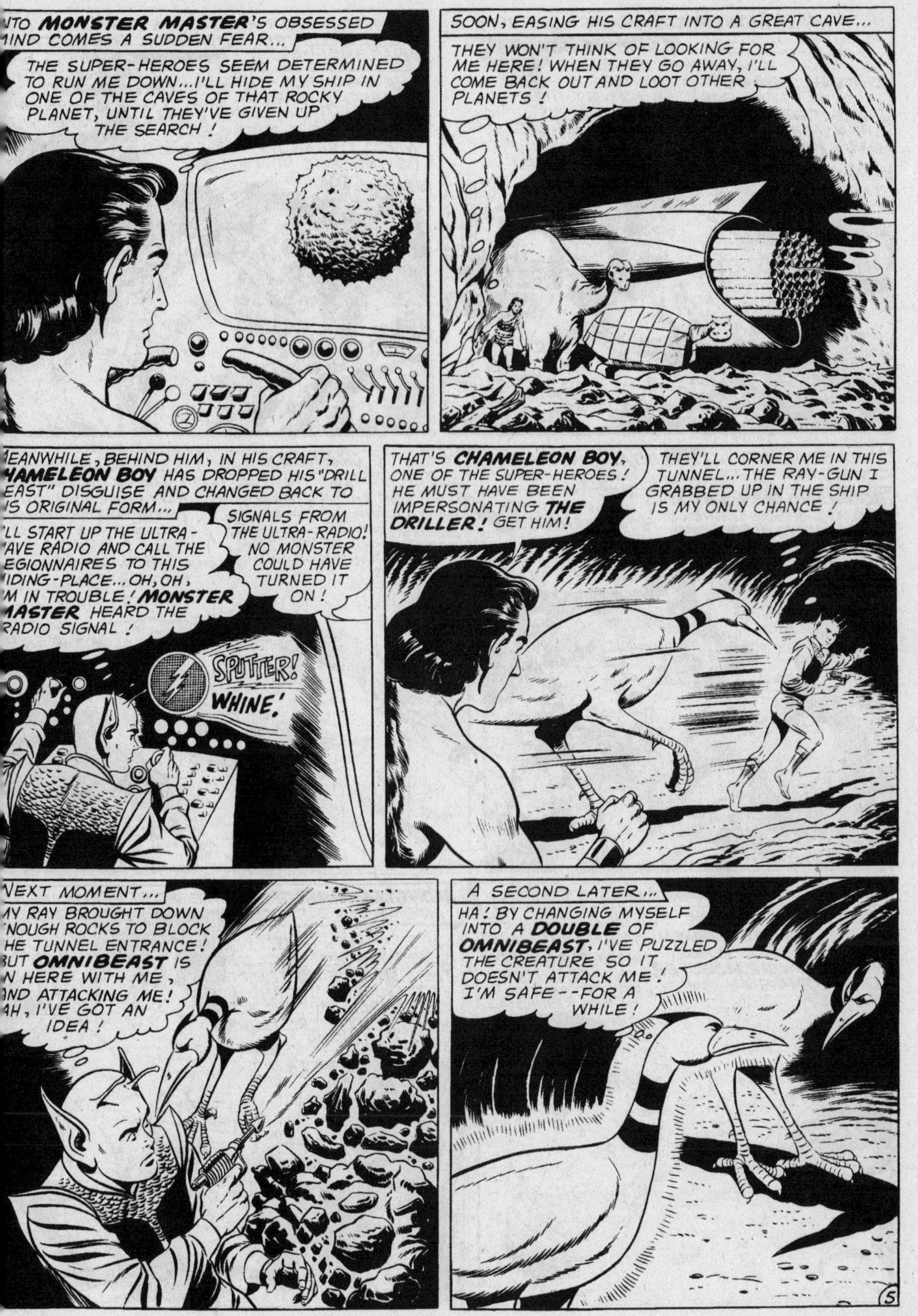
NTO MONSTER MASTER'S OBSESSED MIND COMES A SUDDEN FEAR...
THE SUPER-HEROES SEEM DETERMINED TO RUN ME DOWN...I'LL HIDE MY SHIP IN ONE OF THE CAVES OF THAT ROCKY PLANET, UNTIL THEY'VE GIVEN UP THE SEARCH!
SOON, EASING HIS CRAFT INTO A GREAT CAVE...
THEY WON'T THINK OF LOOKING FOR ME HERE! WHEN THEY GO AWAY, I'LL COME BACK OUT AND LOOT OTHER PLANETS!
MEANWHILE, BEHIND HIM, IN HIS CRAFT, CHAMELEON BOY HAS DROPPED HIS "DRILL BEAST" DISGUISE AND CHANGED BACK TO HIS ORIGINAL FORM...
SIGNALS FROM THE ULTRA-RADIO! NO MONSTER COULD HAVE TURNED IT ON!
I'LL START UP THE ULTRA-WAVE RADIO AND CALL THE LEGIONNAIRES TO THIS HIDING-PLACE...OH, OH, I'M IN TROUBLE! MONSTER MASTER HEARD THE RADIO SIGNAL!
SPUTTER!
WHINE!
THAT'S CHAMELEON BOY, ONE OF THE SUPER-HEROES! HE MUST HAVE BEEN IMPERSONATING THE DRILLER! GET HIM!
THEY'LL CORNER ME IN THIS TUNNEL...THE RAY-GUN I GRABBED UP IN THE SHIP IS MY ONLY CHANCE!
NEXT MOMENT...
MY RAY BROUGHT DOWN ENOUGH ROCKS TO BLOCK THE TUNNEL ENTRANCE! BUT OMNIBEAST IS IN HERE WITH ME, AND ATTACKING ME! AH, I'VE GOT AN IDEA!
A SECOND LATER...
HA! BY CHANGING MYSELF INTO A DOUBLE OF OMNIBEAST, I'VE PUZZLED THE CREATURE SO IT DOESN'T ATTACK ME! I'M SAFE--FOR A WHILE!
5

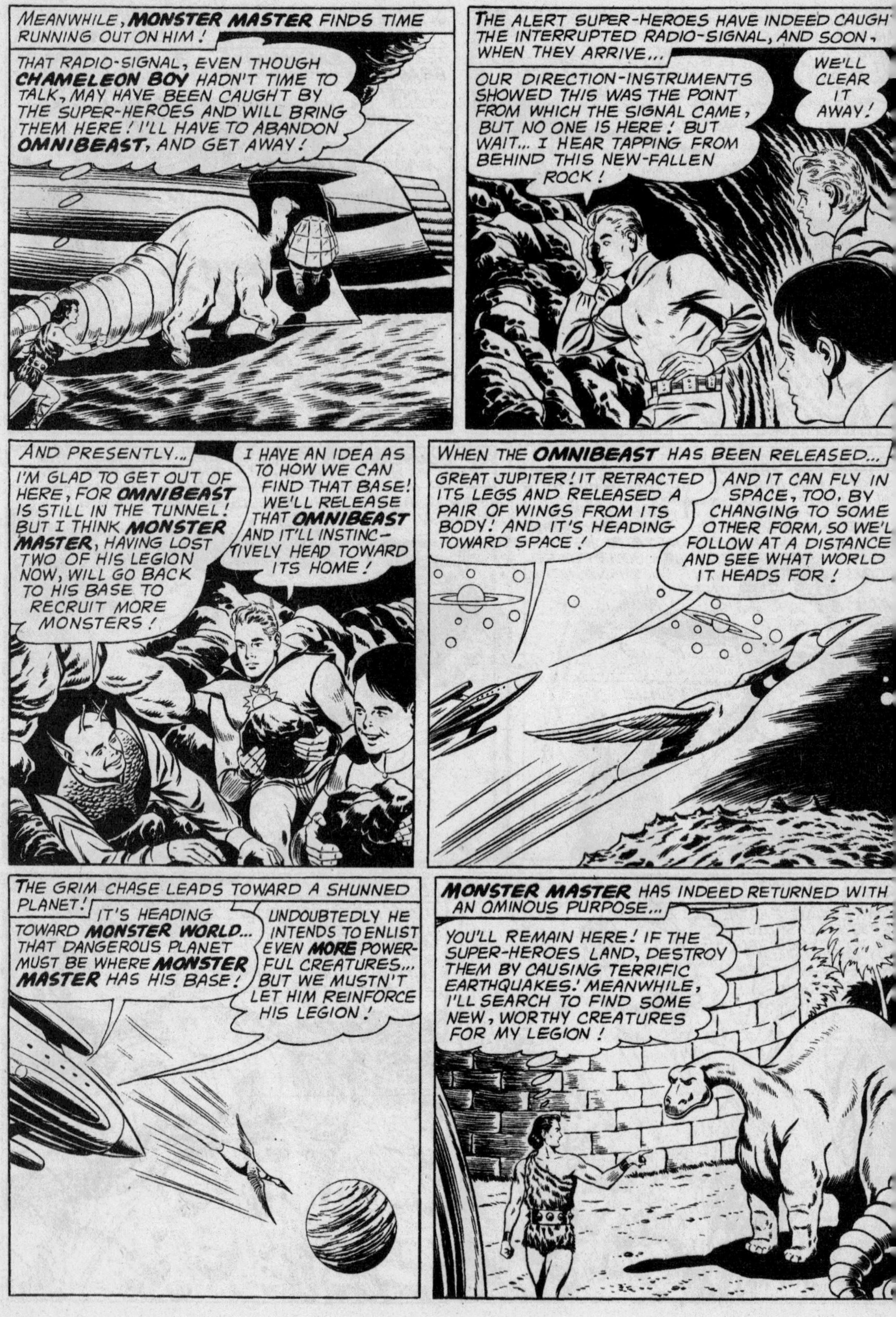
MEANWHILE, MONSTER MASTER FINDS TIME RUNNING OUT ON HIM!
THAT RADIO-SIGNAL, EVEN THOUGH CHAMELEON BOY HADN'T TIME TO TALK, MAY HAVE BEEN CAUGHT BY THE SUPER-HEROES AND WILL BRING THEM HERE! I'LL HAVE TO ABANDON OMNIBEAST, AND GET AWAY!
THE ALERT SUPER-HEROES HAVE INDEED CAUGHT THE INTERRUPTED RADIO-SIGNAL, AND SOON, WHEN THEY ARRIVE...
OUR DIRECTION-INSTRUMENTS SHOWED THIS WAS THE POINT FROM WHICH THE SIGNAL CAME, BUT NO ONE IS HERE! BUT WAIT... I HEAR TAPPING FROM BEHIND THIS NEW-FALLEN ROCK!
WE'LL CLEAR IT AWAY!
AND PRESENTLY...
I'M GLAD TO GET OUT OF HERE, FOR OMNIBEAST IS STILL IN THE TUNNEL! BUT I THINK MONSTER MASTER, HAVING LOST TWO OF HIS LEGION NOW, WILL GO BACK TO HIS BASE TO RECRUIT MORE MONSTERS!
I HAVE AN IDEA AS TO HOW WE CAN FIND THAT BASE! WE'LL RELEASE THAT OMNIBEAST AND IT'LL INSTINCTIVELY HEAD TOWARD ITS HOME!
WHEN THE OMNIBEAST HAS BEEN RELEASED...
GREAT JUPITER! IT RETRACTED ITS LEGS AND RELEASED A PAIR OF WINGS FROM ITS BODY! AND IT'S HEADING TOWARD SPACE!
AND IT CAN FLY IN SPACE, TOO, BY CHANGING TO SOME OTHER FORM, SO WE'LL FOLLOW AT A DISTANCE AND SEE WHAT WORLD IT HEADS FOR!
THE GRIM CHASE LEADS TOWARD A SHUNNED PLANET!
IT'S HEADING TOWARD MONSTER WORLD... THAT DANGEROUS PLANET MUST BE WHERE MONSTER MASTER HAS HIS BASE!
UNDOUBTEDLY HE INTENDS TO ENLIST EVEN MORE POWERFUL CREATURES... BUT WE MUSTN'T LET HIM REINFORCE HIS LEGION!
MONSTER MASTER HAS INDEED RETURNED WITH AN OMINOUS PURPOSE...
YOU'LL REMAIN HERE! IF THE SUPER-HEROES LAND, DESTROY THEM BY CAUSING TERRIFIC EARTHQUAKES! MEANWHILE, I'LL SEARCH TO FIND SOME NEW, WORTHY CREATURES FOR MY LEGION!

...HIS WEIRD GAS CREATURE THAT CAN TURN ITSELF INTO PURE VAPOR SEEMS TO *WANT* TO JOIN ME... BUT I WON'T HAVE IT, FOR IT HAS NO GREAT POWERS!

GET AWAY FROM ME!

MEANWHILE, HOVERING ABOVE THE PERILOUS PLANET, THE LEGIONNAIRES FACE A DIRE DECISION!

HE LEFT THE *EARTHQUAKE BEAST* ON GUARD, TO STOP US! WE DAREN'T LAND THE SHIP OPENLY, OR THE CREATURE WILL DESTROY IT! I PROPOSE THAT ONE OF US GO IN ALONE IN SECRET, TO GET *MONSTER MASTER!*

WE'LL DRAW LOTS FOR THE JOB... EXCLUDING *SATURN GIRL*, BECAUSE IT'S TOO RISKY A MISSION FOR A GIRL!

WHEN THE FATEFUL LOT IS DRAWN...

I DREW THE MARKED LOT! AT LAST I GET A CHANCE TO GO ON AN IMPORTANT MISSION!

OH, NO! *BOUNCING BOY*, YOU CAN'T HOPE TO DEFEAT THE *MONSTER MASTER* MERELY WITH YOUR POWER OF SUPER-BOUNCING! LET ONE OF US TAKE YOUR PLACE!

BUT *BOUNCING BOY* IS DETERMINED, AND SWOOPING DOWN VIA HIS FLYING-BELT FROM THE UPPER AIR...

SORRY, BUT I'M GOING THROUGH WITH THE JOB!

THEY THINK I'M JUST FUNNY, BUT I'LL SHOW THEM! I HAVE A PLAN!

PRESENTLY, AS HE LANDS ON *MONSTER WORLD*...

COME ON, MR. EARTHQUAKE BEASTIE! LASH OUT AT ME WITH YOUR TAIL!

NEXT MOMENT...

AH! HE REACTED JUST AS I THOUGHT HE WOULD! HIS TAIL MISSED MY BOUNCING BODY AND CRACKED THIS CLIFF WALL WIDE OPEN! HE'LL BE COVERED WITH ROCKS!

AND WHEN MONSTER MASTER RETURNS TO THE SCENE, HAVING FELT THE DISTANT BATTLE OF VIBRATIONS...
THAT RIDICULOUS BOUNCING BOY... HE'S BEATEN MY EARTHQUAKE BEAST!
SUDDENLY...
THIS WEIRD GAS CREATURE IT'S GRABBING ME... IT'S ANGRY BECAUSE I WOULDN'T LET IT JOIN MY MONSTER LEGION...
IT'S CHANGING TO GAS... AND AS IT HOLDS ME, IT'S CHANGING ME TO VAPOR, TOO! I NEVER KNEW IT HAD THIS POWER TO VAPORIZE ANYTHING IT GRABS... AIGHH...
8
LATER, WHEN THE OTHER SUPER-HEROES LAND...
AND THAT WAS THE END OF MONSTER MASTER! IT'S IRONICAL... A REJECTED MONSTER DESTROYED HIM, JUST AS HE TRIED TO DESTROY US BECAUSE WE REJECTED HIM!
THE MONSTERS HE COMMANDED HAVE GONE BACK TO THEI NATURAL LIFE... LET'S HOPE THEY STAY THERE, AND THAT NO ONE EVER FORMS ANOTHE LEGION OF SUPER MONSTERS!
THE End

LEGION of SUPER-HEROES

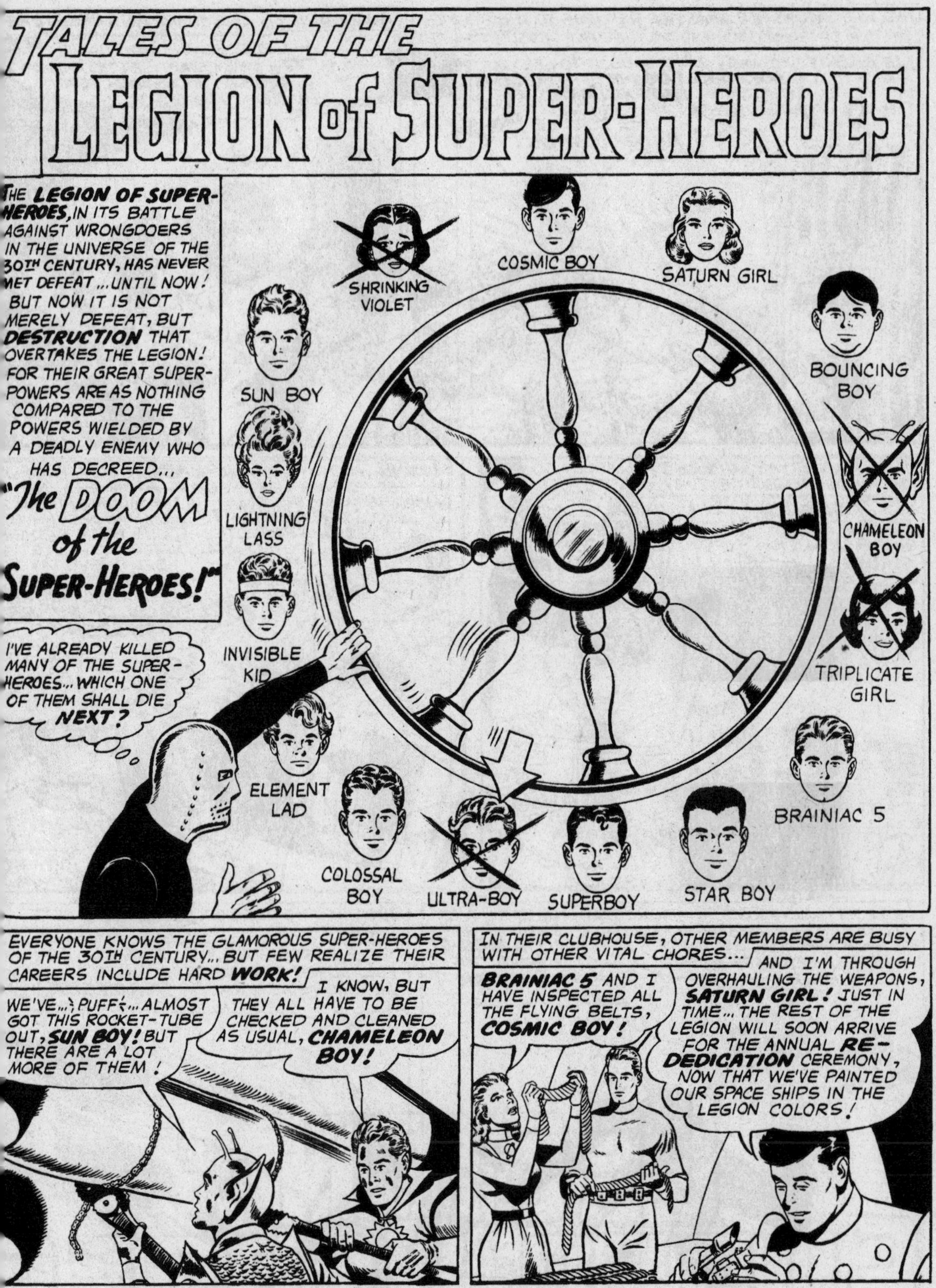
TALES OF THE
LEGION of SUPER-HEROES
THE LEGION OF SUPER-HEROES, IN ITS BATTLE AGAINST WRONGDOERS IN THE UNIVERSE OF THE 30TH CENTURY, HAS NEVER MET DEFEAT ... UNTIL NOW! BUT NOW IT IS NOT MERELY DEFEAT, BUT DESTRUCTION THAT OVERTAKES THE LEGION! FOR THEIR GREAT SUPER-POWERS ARE AS NOTHING COMPARED TO THE POWERS WIELDED BY A DEADLY ENEMY WHO HAS DECREED...
"The DOOM of the SUPER-HEROES!"
SHRINKING VIOLET
COSMIC BOY
SATURN GIRL
BOUNCING BOY
SUN BOY
LIGHTNING LASS
CHAMELEON BOY
INVISIBLE KID
TRIPLICATE GIRL
I'VE ALREADY KILLED MANY OF THE SUPER-HEROES... WHICH ONE OF THEM SHALL DIE NEXT?
ELEMENT LAD
BRAINIAC 5
COLOSSAL BOY
ULTRA-BOY
SUPERBOY
STAR BOY
EVERYONE KNOWS THE GLAMOROUS SUPER-HEROES OF THE 30TH CENTURY... BUT FEW REALIZE THEIR CAREERS INCLUDE HARD WORK!
WE'VE...PUFF...ALMOST GOT THIS ROCKET-TUBE OUT, SUN BOY! BUT THERE ARE A LOT MORE OF THEM!
I KNOW, BUT THEY ALL HAVE TO BE CHECKED AND CLEANED AS USUAL, CHAMELEON BOY!
IN THEIR CLUBHOUSE, OTHER MEMBERS ARE BUSY WITH OTHER VITAL CHORES...
BRAINIAC 5 AND I HAVE INSPECTED ALL THE FLYING BELTS, COSMIC BOY!
AND I'M THROUGH OVERHAULING THE WEAPONS, SATURN GIRL! JUST IN TIME... THE REST OF THE LEGION WILL SOON ARRIVE FOR THE ANNUAL RE-DEDICATION CEREMONY, NOW THAT WE'VE PAINTED OUR SPACE SHIPS IN THE LEGION COLORS!

Panel 1:

FROM ALL POINTS IN SPACE COME THE LEGIONNAIRES... AND ONE OF THEM COMES FROM THE PAST...

SUPERBOY, WE WERE AFRAID YOU'D FORGOTTEN... BUT YOU CAME THROUGH THE TIME-DIMENSION AFTER ALL!

IT'S GOOD TO SEE YOU, MON-EL! AND BOUNCING BOY AND THE OTHERS ARE ARRIVING... IT'S TIME FOR THE REDEDICATION!

SUPER-HERO CLUBHOUSE

Panel 2:

SOON, THE ASSEMBLED SUPER-HEROES SOLEMNLY REPEAT A VOW!

I PLEDGE ALWAYS TO USE MY SUPER-POWER ONLY FOR THE GOOD OF ALL PEOPLE, AND NEVER FOR SELFISH PURPOSES!

Panel 3:

A LITTLE LATER, AS SUPERBOY IS ABOUT TO RETURN TO THE 20TH CENTURY...

LOOK, A SCIENCE POLICE ALARM ON OUR MONITOR-SCREEN!

A MYSTERIOUS MASKED RAIDER IS LOOTING METROPOLIS! HE'S USING SUPER-MAGNETIC POWERS SUCH AS ONLY COSMIC BOY HAS!

BUT COSMIC BOY IS RIGHT HERE!

Panel 4:

MON-EL AND I WILL GET TO THIS RAIDER FAST!

SUPERBOY, WE CAN'T FLY LIKE YOU AND MON-EL, BUT WE'LL ALL FOLLOW BY USING OUR ANTI-GRAVITY BELTS!

SUPER CLUBHOUSE

Panel 5:

THERE HE IS, USING SUPER-MAGNETISM TO DRAW STEEL TREASURE VAULTS UP FROM THE CITY! BUT I CAN'T SEE HIS FACE... HE WEARS A LEAD MASK!

YOU CATCH AND RETURN THE VAULTS, MON-EL. I'LL GRAB THIS MYSTERIOUS MASK MAN!

Panel 6:

BUT WHEN HE DOES SO, SUPERBOY GETS THE SURPRISE OF HIS LIFE...

IT'S INCREDIBLE... I'M USING MY FULL SUPER-STRENGTH, BUT HE'S AS STRONG AS I AM, OR STRONGER!

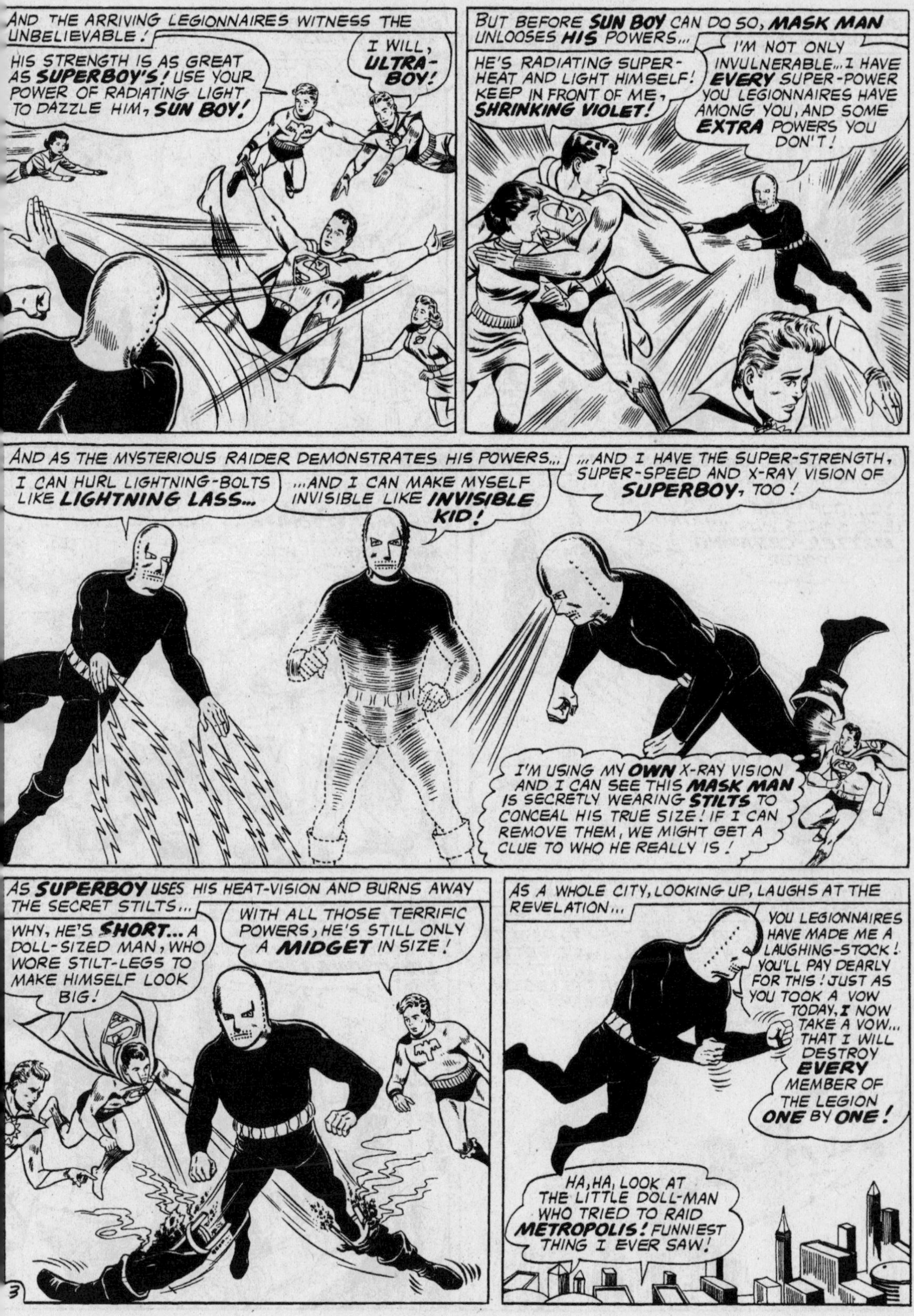
AND THE ARRIVING LEGIONNAIRES WITNESS THE UNBELIEVABLE!
HIS STRENGTH IS AS GREAT AS SUPERBOY'S! USE YOUR POWER OF RADIATING LIGHT TO DAZZLE HIM, SUN BOY!
I WILL, ULTRA-BOY!
BUT BEFORE SUN BOY CAN DO SO, MASK MAN UNLOOSES HIS POWERS...
HE'S RADIATING SUPER-HEAT AND LIGHT HIMSELF! KEEP IN FRONT OF ME, SHRINKING VIOLET!
I'M NOT ONLY INVULNERABLE... I HAVE EVERY SUPER-POWER YOU LEGIONNAIRES HAVE AMONG YOU, AND SOME EXTRA POWERS YOU DON'T!
AND AS THE MYSTERIOUS RAIDER DEMONSTRATES HIS POWERS...
I CAN HURL LIGHTNING-BOLTS LIKE LIGHTNING LASS...
...AND I CAN MAKE MYSELF INVISIBLE LIKE INVISIBLE KID!
...AND I HAVE THE SUPER-STRENGTH, SUPER-SPEED AND X-RAY VISION OF SUPERBOY, TOO!
I'M USING MY OWN X-RAY VISION AND I CAN SEE THIS MASK MAN IS SECRETLY WEARING STILTS TO CONCEAL HIS TRUE SIZE! IF I CAN REMOVE THEM, WE MIGHT GET A CLUE TO WHO HE REALLY IS!
AS SUPERBOY USES HIS HEAT-VISION AND BURNS AWAY THE SECRET STILTS...
WHY, HE'S SHORT... A DOLL-SIZED MAN, WHO WORE STILT-LEGS TO MAKE HIMSELF LOOK BIG!
WITH ALL THOSE TERRIFIC POWERS, HE'S STILL ONLY A MIDGET IN SIZE!
3
AS A WHOLE CITY, LOOKING UP, LAUGHS AT THE REVELATION...
YOU LEGIONNAIRES HAVE MADE ME A LAUGHING-STOCK! YOU'LL PAY DEARLY FOR THIS! JUST AS YOU TOOK A VOW TODAY, I NOW TAKE A VOW... THAT I WILL DESTROY EVERY MEMBER OF THE LEGION ONE BY ONE!
HA, HA, LOOK AT THE LITTLE DOLL-MAN WHO TRIED TO RAID METROPOLIS! FUNNIEST THING I EVER SAW!

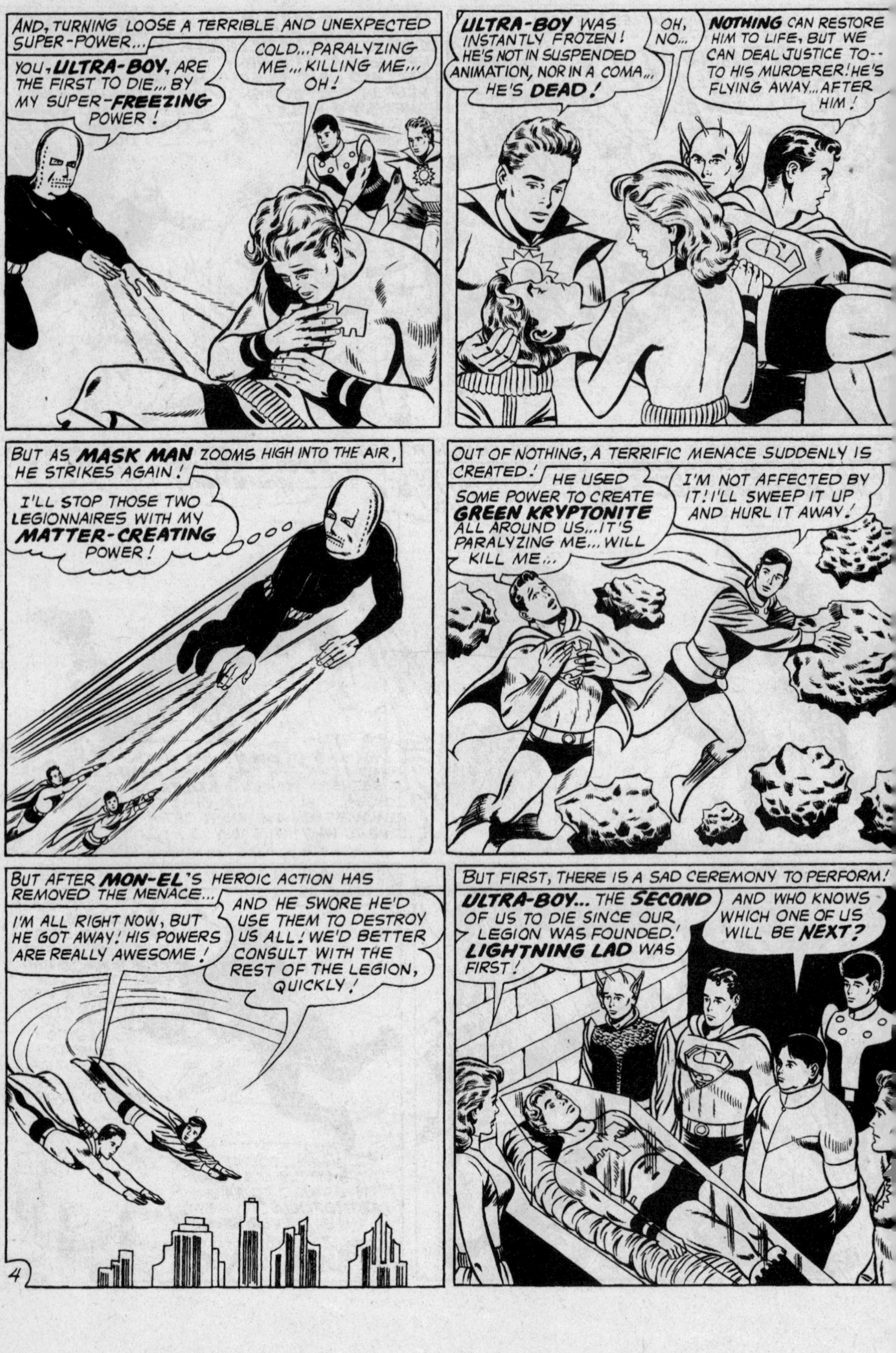
AND, TURNING LOOSE A TERRIBLE AND UNEXPECTED SUPER-POWER...
YOU, ULTRA-BOY, ARE THE FIRST TO DIE... BY MY SUPER-FREEZING POWER!
COLD... PARALYZING ME... KILLING ME... OH!
ULTRA-BOY WAS INSTANTLY FROZEN! HE'S NOT IN SUSPENDED ANIMATION, NOR IN A COMA... HE'S DEAD!
OH, NO...
NOTHING CAN RESTORE HIM TO LIFE, BUT WE CAN DEAL JUSTICE TO-- TO HIS MURDERER! HE'S FLYING AWAY... AFTER HIM!
BUT AS MASK MAN ZOOMS HIGH INTO THE AIR, HE STRIKES AGAIN!
I'LL STOP THOSE TWO LEGIONNAIRES WITH MY MATTER-CREATING POWER!
OUT OF NOTHING, A TERRIFIC MENACE SUDDENLY IS CREATED!
HE USED SOME POWER TO CREATE GREEN KRYPTONITE ALL AROUND US... IT'S PARALYZING ME... WILL KILL ME...
I'M NOT AFFECTED BY IT! I'LL SWEEP IT UP AND HURL IT AWAY!
BUT AFTER MON-EL'S HEROIC ACTION HAS REMOVED THE MENACE...
I'M ALL RIGHT NOW, BUT HE GOT AWAY! HIS POWERS ARE REALLY AWESOME!
AND HE SWORE HE'D USE THEM TO DESTROY US ALL! WE'D BETTER CONSULT WITH THE REST OF THE LEGION, QUICKLY!
4
BUT FIRST, THERE IS A SAD CEREMONY TO PERFORM!
ULTRA-BOY... THE SECOND OF US TO DIE SINCE OUR LEGION WAS FOUNDED! LIGHTNING LAD WAS FIRST!
AND WHO KNOWS WHICH ONE OF US WILL BE NEXT?

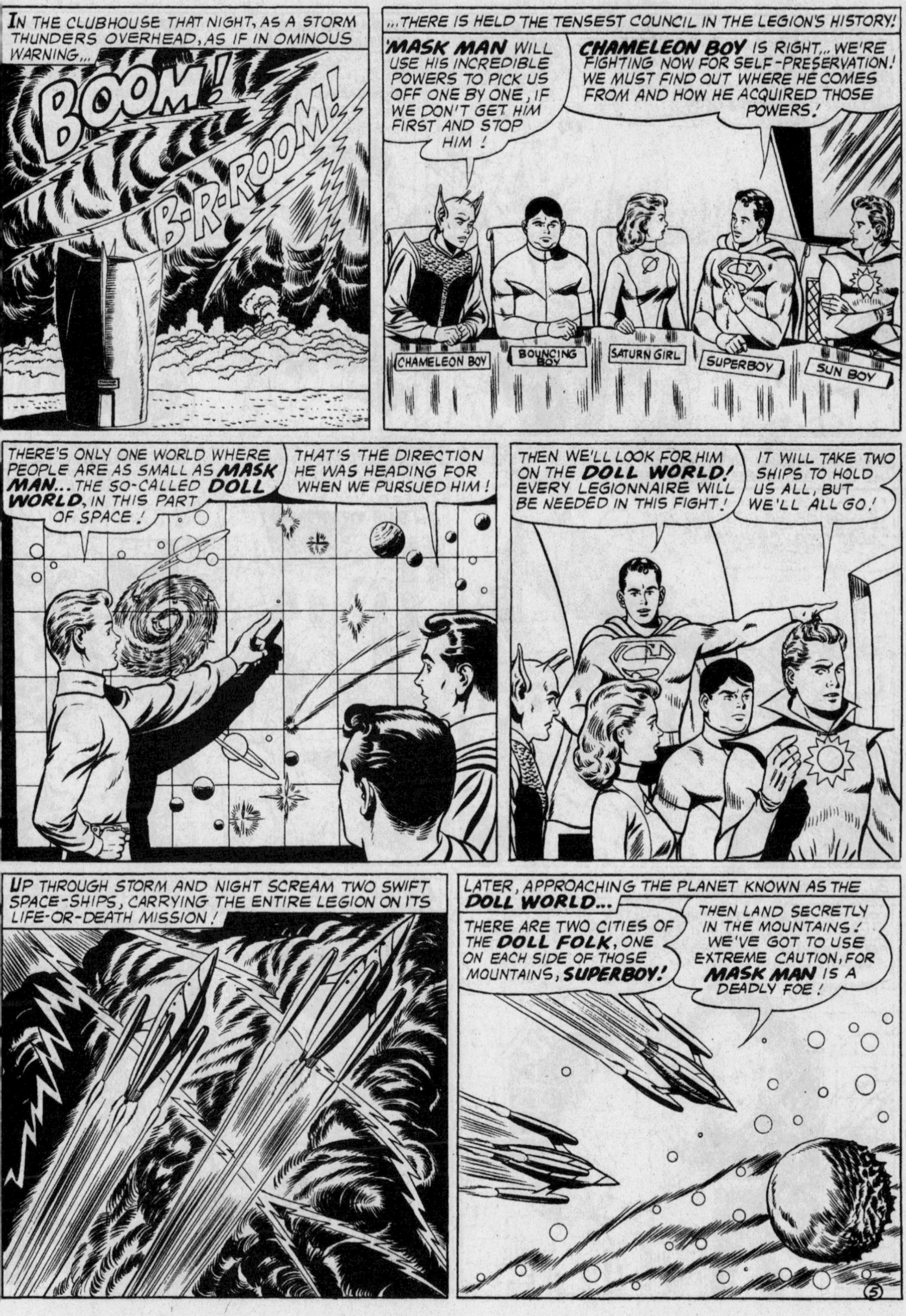
IN THE CLUBHOUSE THAT NIGHT, AS A STORM THUNDERS OVERHEAD, AS IF IN OMINOUS WARNING...
BOOM!
B-R-ROOM!
...THERE IS HELD THE TENSEST COUNCIL IN THE LEGION'S HISTORY!
MASK MAN WILL USE HIS INCREDIBLE POWERS TO PICK US OFF ONE BY ONE, IF WE DON'T GET HIM FIRST AND STOP HIM!
CHAMELEON BOY IS RIGHT... WE'RE FIGHTING NOW FOR SELF-PRESERVATION! WE MUST FIND OUT WHERE HE COMES FROM AND HOW HE ACQUIRED THOSE POWERS!
CHAMELEON BOY
BOUNCING BOY
SATURN GIRL
SUPERBOY
SUN BOY
THERE'S ONLY ONE WORLD WHERE PEOPLE ARE AS SMALL AS MASK MAN... THE SO-CALLED DOLL WORLD, IN THIS PART OF SPACE!
THAT'S THE DIRECTION HE WAS HEADING FOR WHEN WE PURSUED HIM!
THEN WE'LL LOOK FOR HIM ON THE DOLL WORLD! EVERY LEGIONNAIRE WILL BE NEEDED IN THIS FIGHT!
IT WILL TAKE TWO SHIPS TO HOLD US ALL, BUT WE'LL ALL GO!
UP THROUGH STORM AND NIGHT SCREAM TWO SWIFT SPACE-SHIPS, CARRYING THE ENTIRE LEGION ON ITS LIFE-OR-DEATH MISSION!
LATER, APPROACHING THE PLANET KNOWN AS THE DOLL WORLD...
THERE ARE TWO CITIES OF THE DOLL FOLK, ONE ON EACH SIDE OF THOSE MOUNTAINS, SUPERBOY!
THEN LAND SECRETLY IN THE MOUNTAINS! WE'VE GOT TO USE EXTREME CAUTION, FOR MASK MAN IS A DEADLY FOE!
5

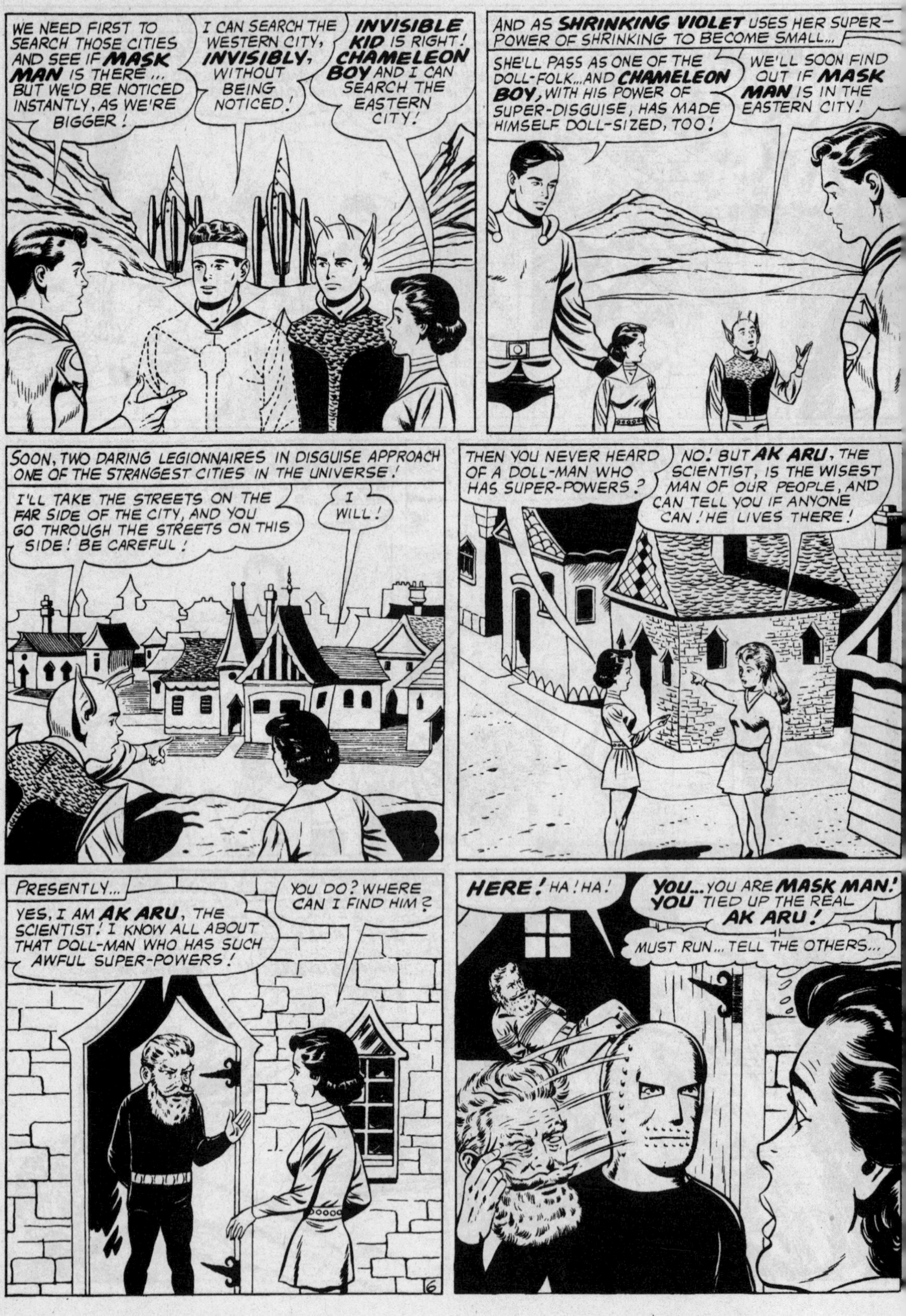
WE NEED FIRST TO SEARCH THOSE CITIES AND SEE IF MASK MAN IS THERE... BUT WE'D BE NOTICED INSTANTLY, AS WE'RE BIGGER!
I CAN SEARCH THE WESTERN CITY, INVISIBLY, WITHOUT BEING NOTICED!
INVISIBLE KID IS RIGHT! CHAMELEON BOY AND I CAN SEARCH THE EASTERN CITY!
AND AS SHRINKING VIOLET USES HER SUPER-POWER OF SHRINKING TO BECOME SMALL...
SHE'LL PASS AS ONE OF THE DOLL-FOLK...AND CHAMELEON BOY, WITH HIS POWER OF SUPER-DISGUISE, HAS MADE HIMSELF DOLL-SIZED, TOO!
WE'LL SOON FIND OUT IF MASK MAN IS IN THE EASTERN CITY!
SOON, TWO DARING LEGIONNAIRES IN DISGUISE APPROACH ONE OF THE STRANGEST CITIES IN THE UNIVERSE!
I'LL TAKE THE STREETS ON THE FAR SIDE OF THE CITY, AND YOU GO THROUGH THE STREETS ON THIS SIDE! BE CAREFUL!
I WILL!
THEN YOU NEVER HEARD OF A DOLL-MAN WHO HAS SUPER-POWERS?
NO! BUT AK ARU, THE SCIENTIST, IS THE WISEST MAN OF OUR PEOPLE, AND CAN TELL YOU IF ANYONE CAN! HE LIVES THERE!
PRESENTLY...
YES, I AM AK ARU, THE SCIENTIST! I KNOW ALL ABOUT THAT DOLL-MAN WHO HAS SUCH AWFUL SUPER-POWERS!
YOU DO? WHERE CAN I FIND HIM?
6
HERE! HA! HA!
YOU...YOU ARE MASK MAN! YOU TIED UP THE REAL AK ARU!
MUST RUN... TELL THE OTHERS...

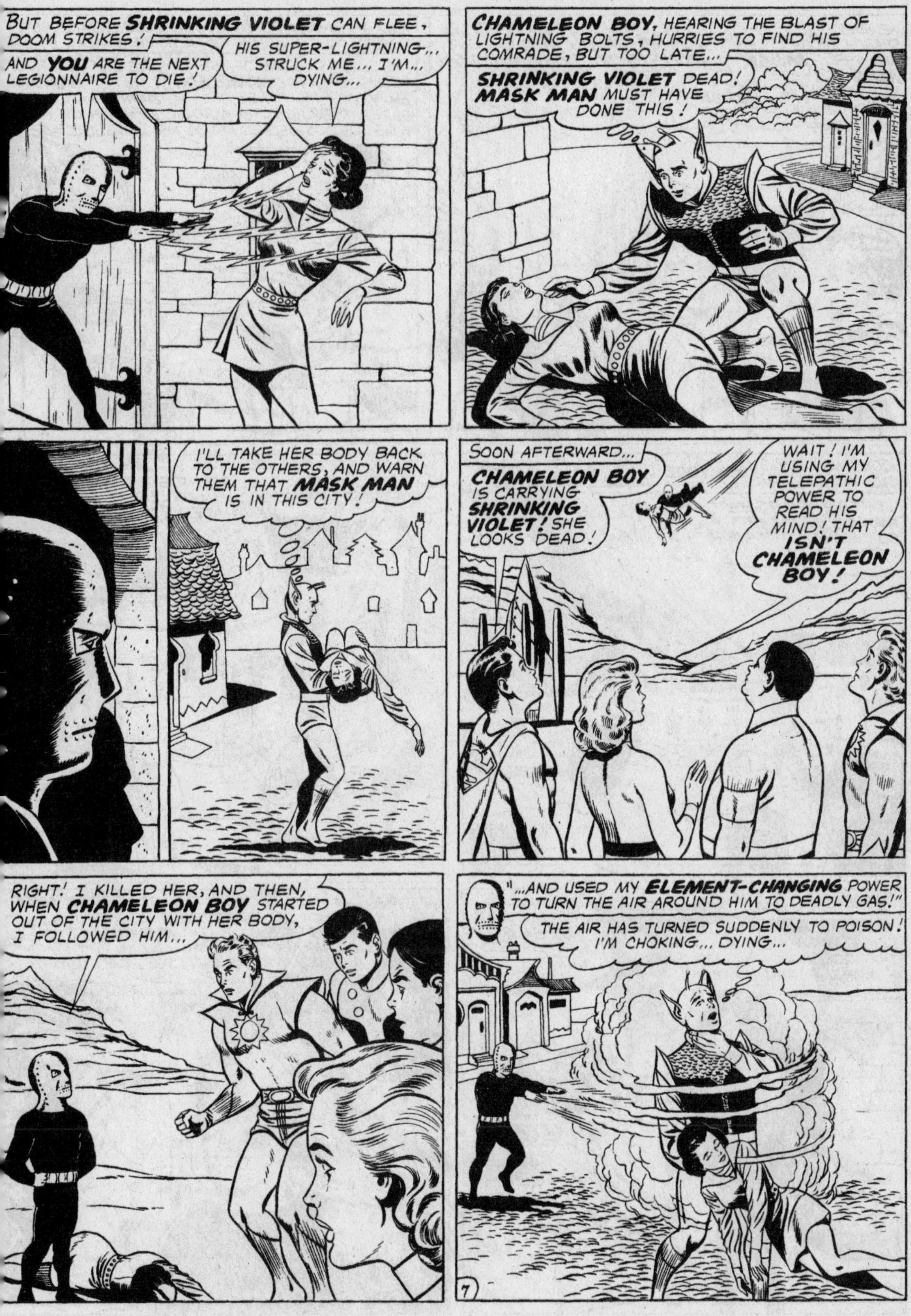
BUT BEFORE SHRINKING VIOLET CAN FLEE, DOOM STRIKES!
AND YOU ARE THE NEXT LEGIONNAIRE TO DIE!
HIS SUPER-LIGHTNING... STRUCK ME... I'M... DYING...
CHAMELEON BOY, HEARING THE BLAST OF LIGHTNING BOLTS, HURRIES TO FIND HIS COMRADE, BUT TOO LATE...
SHRINKING VIOLET DEAD! MASK MAN MUST HAVE DONE THIS!
I'LL TAKE HER BODY BACK TO THE OTHERS, AND WARN THEM THAT MASK MAN IS IN THIS CITY!
SOON AFTERWARD...
CHAMELEON BOY IS CARRYING SHRINKING VIOLET! SHE LOOKS DEAD!
WAIT! I'M USING MY TELEPATHIC POWER TO READ HIS MIND! THAT ISN'T CHAMELEON BOY!
RIGHT! I KILLED HER, AND THEN, WHEN CHAMELEON BOY STARTED OUT OF THE CITY WITH HER BODY, I FOLLOWED HIM...
"...AND USED MY ELEMENT-CHANGING POWER TO TURN THE AIR AROUND HIM TO DEADLY GAS!"
THE AIR HAS TURNED SUDDENLY TO POISON! I'M CHOKING... DYING...
7

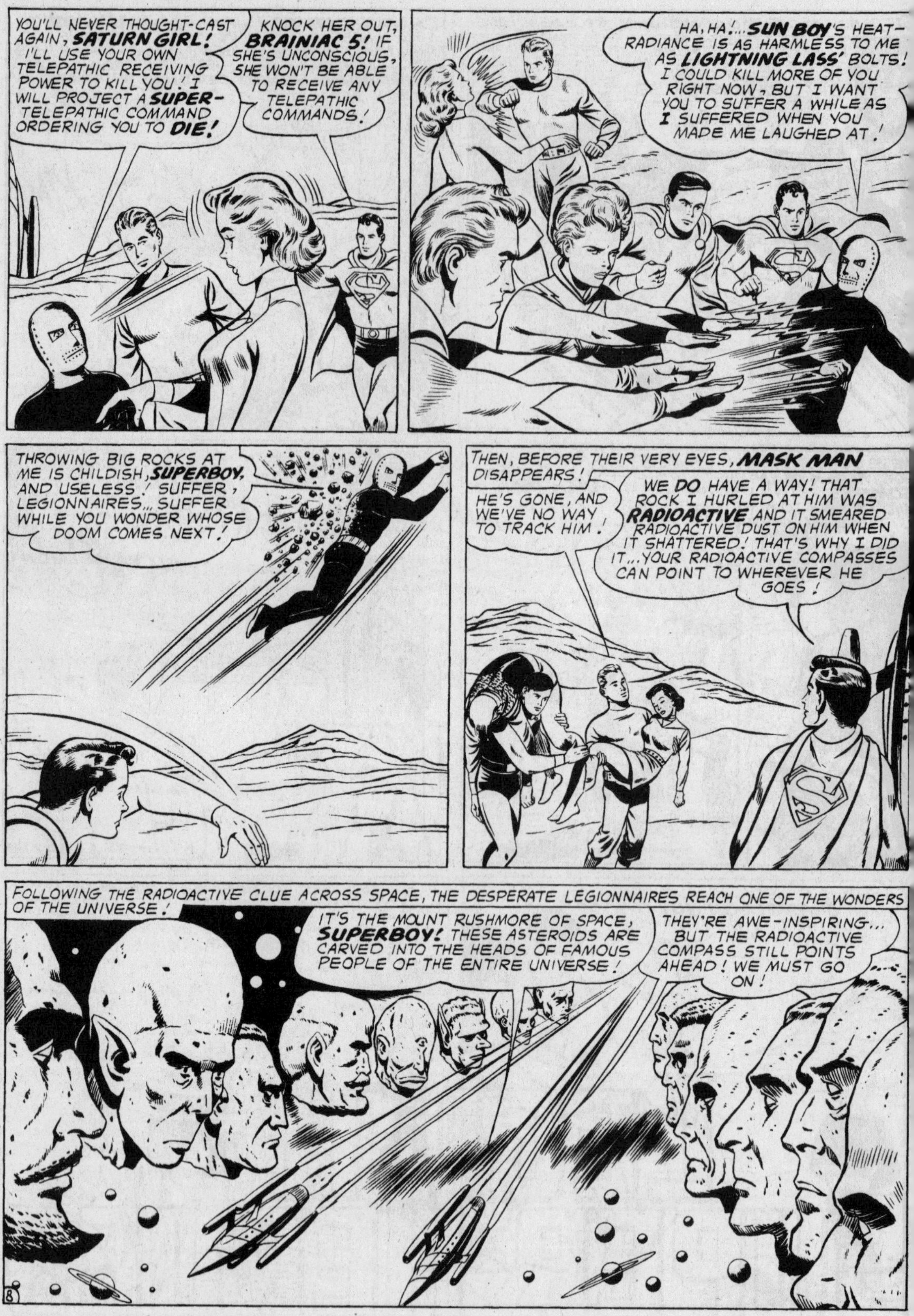
YOU'LL NEVER THOUGHT-CAST AGAIN, SATURN GIRL! I'LL USE YOUR OWN TELEPATHIC RECEIVING POWER TO KILL YOU! I WILL PROJECT A SUPER-TELEPATHIC COMMAND ORDERING YOU TO DIE!
KNOCK HER OUT, BRAINIAC 5! IF SHE'S UNCONSCIOUS, SHE WON'T BE ABLE TO RECEIVE ANY TELEPATHIC COMMANDS!
HA, HA!... SUN BOY'S HEAT-RADIANCE IS AS HARMLESS TO ME AS LIGHTNING LASS' BOLTS! I COULD KILL MORE OF YOU RIGHT NOW, BUT I WANT YOU TO SUFFER A WHILE AS I SUFFERED WHEN YOU MADE ME LAUGHED AT!
THROWING BIG ROCKS AT ME IS CHILDISH, SUPERBOY, AND USELESS! SUFFER, LEGIONNAIRES... SUFFER WHILE YOU WONDER WHOSE DOOM COMES NEXT!
THEN, BEFORE THEIR VERY EYES, MASK MAN DISAPPEARS!
HE'S GONE, AND WE'VE NO WAY TO TRACK HIM!
WE DO HAVE A WAY! THAT ROCK I HURLED AT HIM WAS RADIOACTIVE AND IT SMEARED RADIOACTIVE DUST ON HIM WHEN IT SHATTERED! THAT'S WHY I DID IT... YOUR RADIOACTIVE COMPASSES CAN POINT TO WHEREVER HE GOES!
FOLLOWING THE RADIOACTIVE CLUE ACROSS SPACE, THE DESPERATE LEGIONNAIRES REACH ONE OF THE WONDERS OF THE UNIVERSE!
IT'S THE MOUNT RUSHMORE OF SPACE, SUPERBOY! THESE ASTEROIDS ARE CARVED INTO THE HEADS OF FAMOUS PEOPLE OF THE ENTIRE UNIVERSE!
THEY'RE AWE-INSPIRING... BUT THE RADIOACTIVE COMPASS STILL POINTS AHEAD! WE MUST GO ON!
8

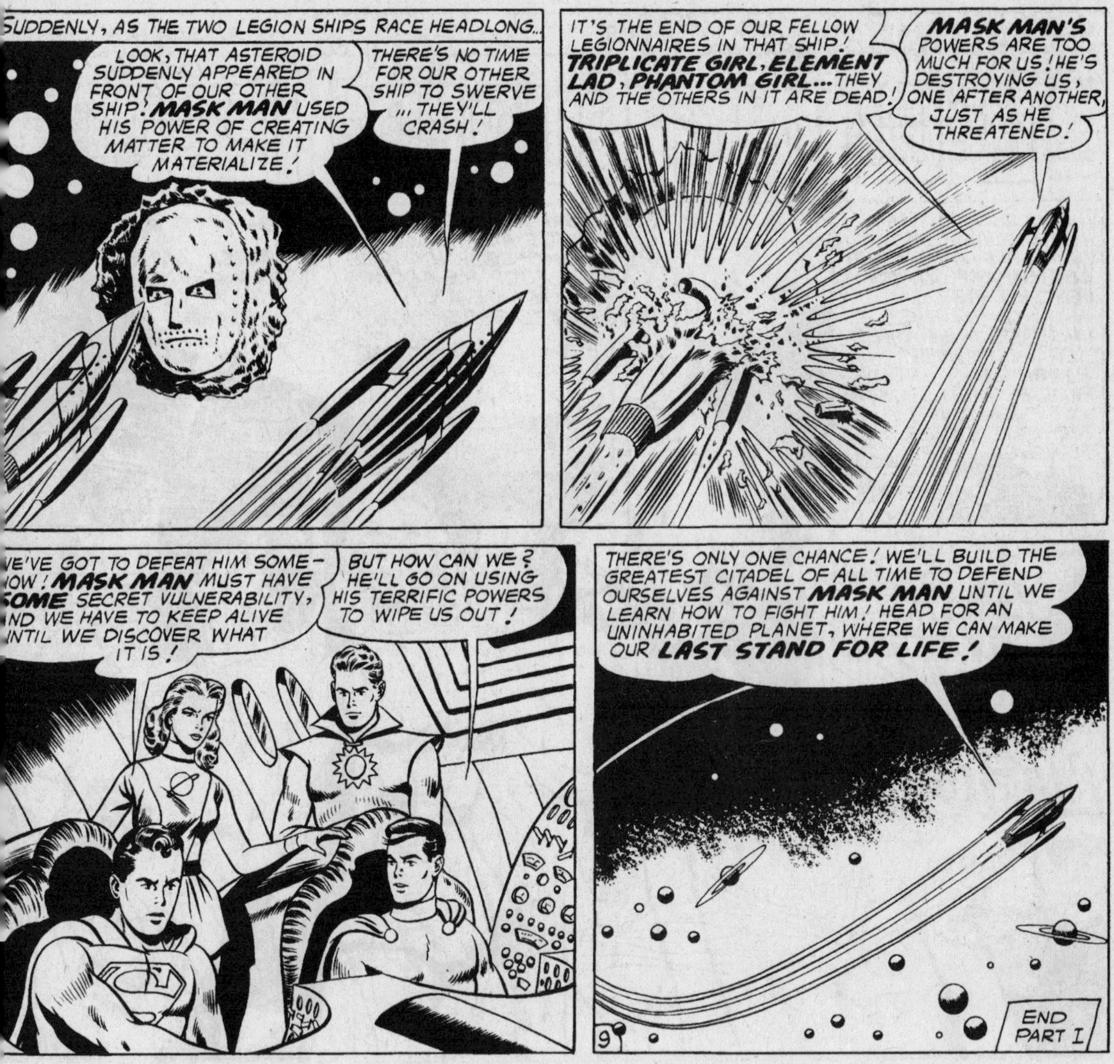
SUDDENLY, AS THE TWO LEGION SHIPS RACE HEADLONG...
LOOK, THAT ASTEROID SUDDENLY APPEARED IN FRONT OF OUR OTHER SHIP! MASK MAN USED HIS POWER OF CREATING MATTER TO MAKE IT MATERIALIZE!
THERE'S NO TIME FOR OUR OTHER SHIP TO SWERVE ... THEY'LL CRASH!
IT'S THE END OF OUR FELLOW LEGIONNAIRES IN THAT SHIP! TRIPLICATE GIRL, ELEMENT LAD, PHANTOM GIRL... THEY AND THE OTHERS IN IT ARE DEAD!
MASK MAN'S POWERS ARE TOO MUCH FOR US! HE'S DESTROYING US, ONE AFTER ANOTHER, JUST AS HE THREATENED!
VE'VE GOT TO DEFEAT HIM SOME-IOW! MASK MAN MUST HAVE SOME SECRET VULNERABILITY, ND WE HAVE TO KEEP ALIVE NTIL WE DISCOVER WHAT IT IS!
BUT HOW CAN WE? HE'LL GO ON USING HIS TERRIFIC POWERS TO WIPE US OUT!
THERE'S ONLY ONE CHANCE! WE'LL BUILD THE GREATEST CITADEL OF ALL TIME TO DEFEND OURSELVES AGAINST MASK MAN UNTIL WE LEARN HOW TO FIGHT HIM! HEAD FOR AN UNINHABITED PLANET, WHERE WE CAN MAKE OUR LAST STAND FOR LIFE!
9
END PART I

LEGION of SUPER-HEROES

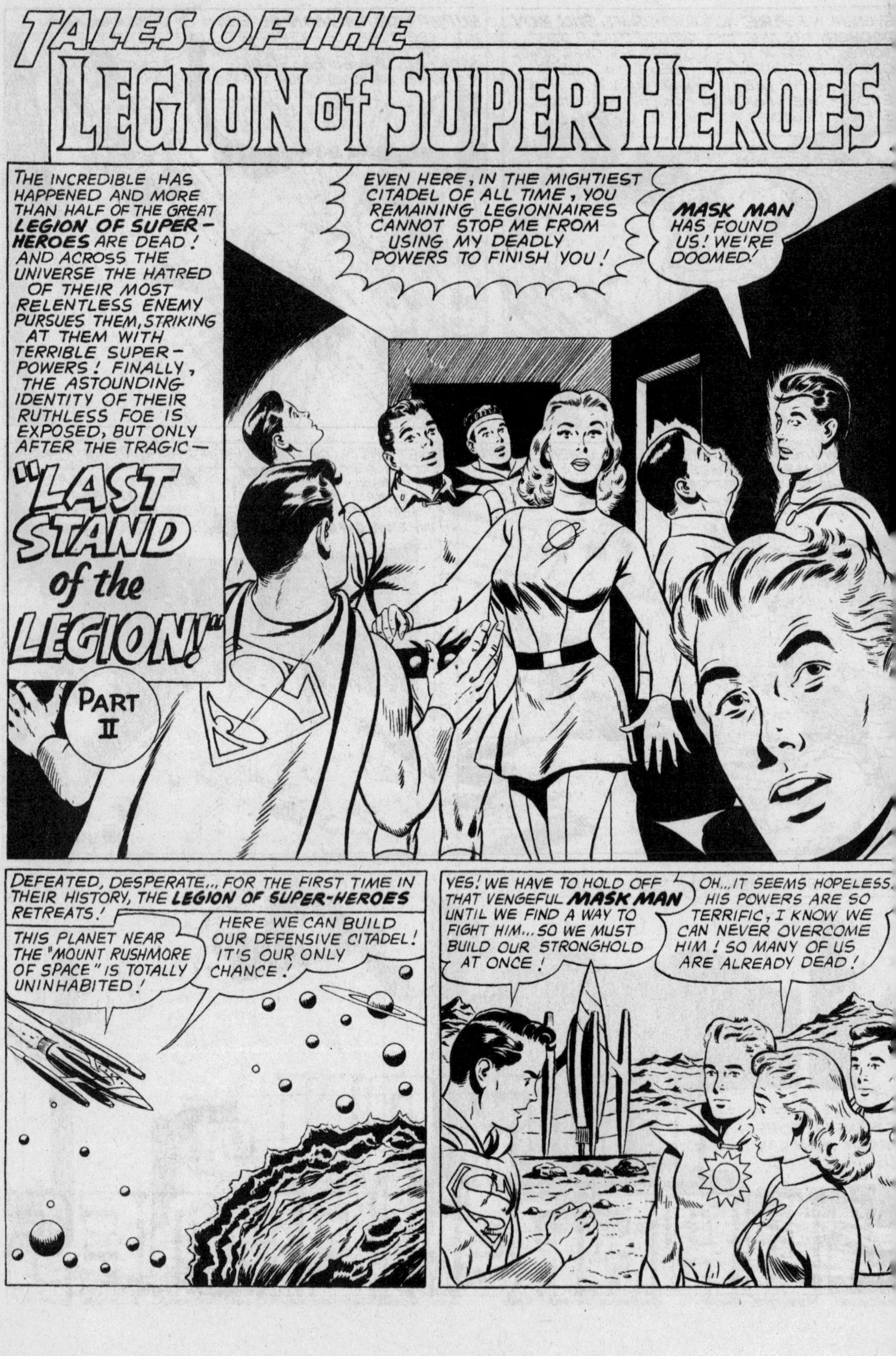
TALES OF THE
LEGION of SUPER-HEROES
THE INCREDIBLE HAS HAPPENED AND MORE THAN HALF OF THE GREAT LEGION OF SUPER-HEROES ARE DEAD! AND ACROSS THE UNIVERSE THE HATRED OF THEIR MOST RELENTLESS ENEMY PURSUES THEM, STRIKING AT THEM WITH TERRIBLE SUPER-POWERS! FINALLY, THE ASTOUNDING IDENTITY OF THEIR RUTHLESS FOE IS EXPOSED, BUT ONLY AFTER THE TRAGIC—
"LAST STAND of the LEGION!"
PART II
EVEN HERE, IN THE MIGHTIEST CITADEL OF ALL TIME, YOU REMAINING LEGIONNAIRES CANNOT STOP ME FROM USING MY DEADLY POWERS TO FINISH YOU!
MASK MAN HAS FOUND US! WE'RE DOOMED!
DEFEATED, DESPERATE... FOR THE FIRST TIME IN THEIR HISTORY, THE LEGION OF SUPER-HEROES RETREATS!
THIS PLANET NEAR THE "MOUNT RUSHMORE OF SPACE" IS TOTALLY UNINHABITED!
HERE WE CAN BUILD OUR DEFENSIVE CITADEL! IT'S OUR ONLY CHANCE!
YES! WE HAVE TO HOLD OFF THAT VENGEFUL MASK MAN UNTIL WE FIND A WAY TO FIGHT HIM... SO WE MUST BUILD OUR STRONGHOLD AT ONCE!
OH... IT SEEMS HOPELESS. HIS POWERS ARE SO TERRIFIC, I KNOW WE CAN NEVER OVERCOME HIM! SO MANY OF US ARE ALREADY DEAD!

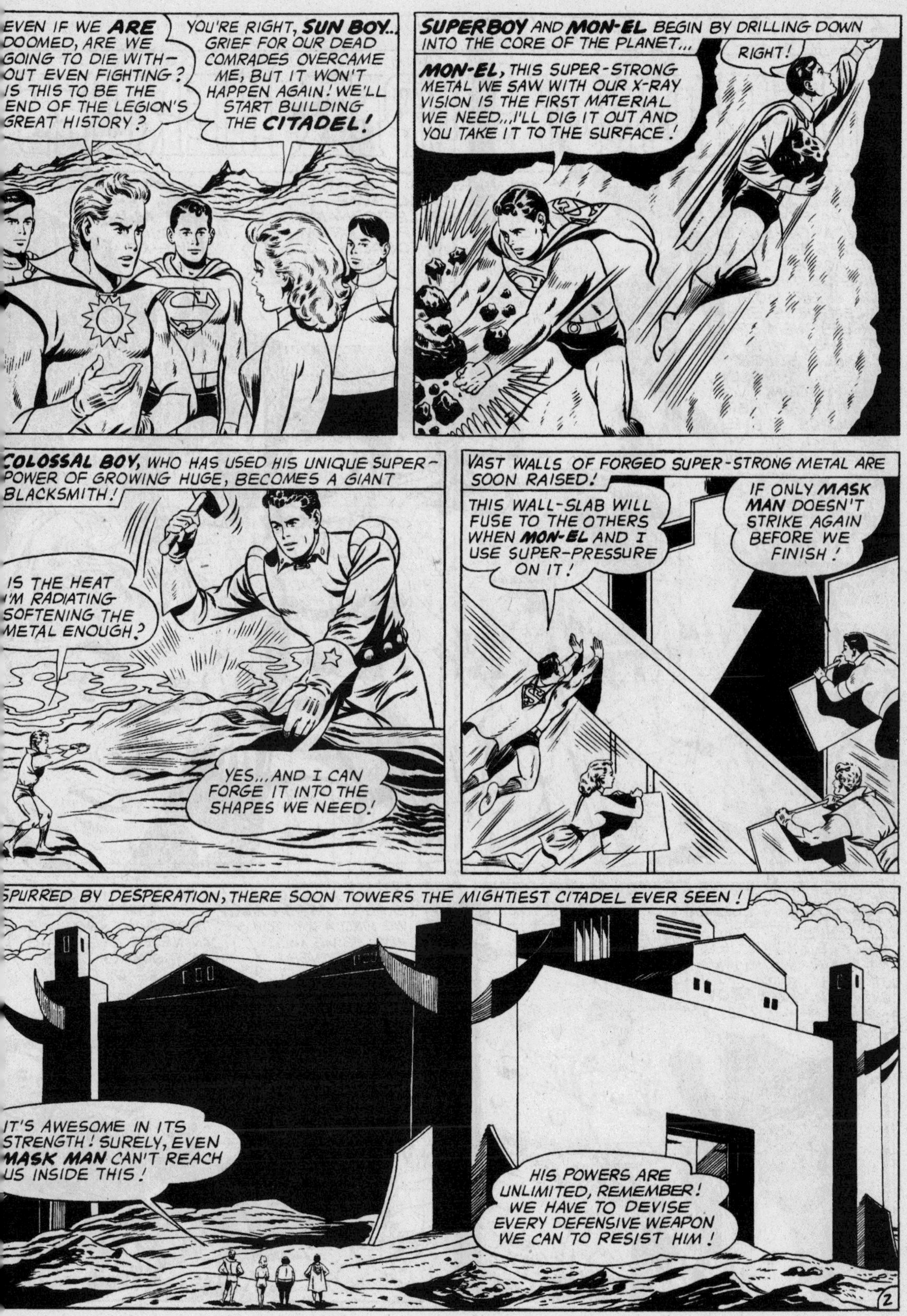
EVEN IF WE ARE DOOMED, ARE WE GOING TO DIE WITH-OUT EVEN FIGHTING? IS THIS TO BE THE END OF THE LEGION'S GREAT HISTORY?
YOU'RE RIGHT, SUN BOY... GRIEF FOR OUR DEAD COMRADES OVERCAME ME, BUT IT WON'T HAPPEN AGAIN! WE'LL START BUILDING THE CITADEL!
SUPERBOY AND MON-EL BEGIN BY DRILLING DOWN INTO THE CORE OF THE PLANET...
MON-EL, THIS SUPER-STRONG METAL WE SAW WITH OUR X-RAY VISION IS THE FIRST MATERIAL WE NEED...I'LL DIG IT OUT AND YOU TAKE IT TO THE SURFACE!
RIGHT!
COLOSSAL BOY, WHO HAS USED HIS UNIQUE SUPER-POWER OF GROWING HUGE, BECOMES A GIANT BLACKSMITH!
IS THE HEAT I'M RADIATING SOFTENING THE METAL ENOUGH?
YES...AND I CAN FORGE IT INTO THE SHAPES WE NEED!
VAST WALLS OF FORGED SUPER-STRONG METAL ARE SOON RAISED!
THIS WALL-SLAB WILL FUSE TO THE OTHERS WHEN MON-EL AND I USE SUPER-PRESSURE ON IT!
IF ONLY MASK MAN DOESN'T STRIKE AGAIN BEFORE WE FINISH!
SPURRED BY DESPERATION, THERE SOON TOWERS THE MIGHTIEST CITADEL EVER SEEN!
IT'S AWESOME IN ITS STRENGTH! SURELY, EVEN MASK MAN CAN'T REACH US INSIDE THIS!
HIS POWERS ARE UNLIMITED, REMEMBER! WE HAVE TO DEVISE EVERY DEFENSIVE WEAPON WE CAN TO RESIST HIM!
2

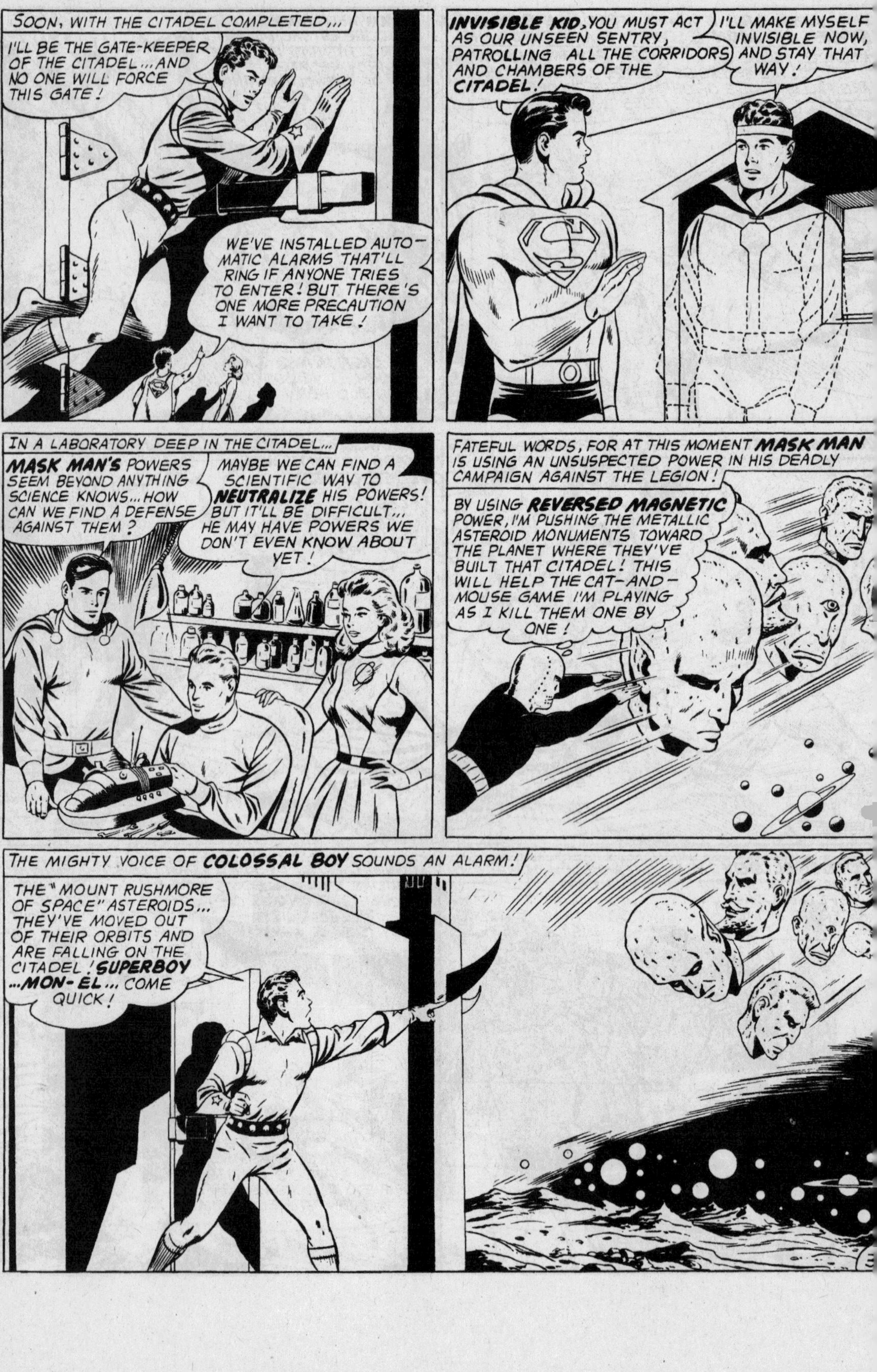
SOON, WITH THE CITADEL COMPLETED,...
I'LL BE THE GATE-KEEPER OF THE CITADEL... AND NO ONE WILL FORCE THIS GATE!
WE'VE INSTALLED AUTOMATIC ALARMS THAT'LL RING IF ANYONE TRIES TO ENTER! BUT THERE'S ONE MORE PRECAUTION I WANT TO TAKE!
INVISIBLE KID, YOU MUST ACT AS OUR UNSEEN SENTRY, PATROLLING ALL THE CORRIDORS AND CHAMBERS OF THE CITADEL!
I'LL MAKE MYSELF INVISIBLE NOW, AND STAY THAT WAY!
IN A LABORATORY DEEP IN THE CITADEL...
MASK MAN'S POWERS SEEM BEYOND ANYTHING SCIENCE KNOWS... HOW CAN WE FIND A DEFENSE AGAINST THEM?
MAYBE WE CAN FIND A SCIENTIFIC WAY TO NEUTRALIZE HIS POWERS! BUT IT'LL BE DIFFICULT... HE MAY HAVE POWERS WE DON'T EVEN KNOW ABOUT YET!
FATEFUL WORDS, FOR AT THIS MOMENT MASK MAN IS USING AN UNSUSPECTED POWER IN HIS DEADLY CAMPAIGN AGAINST THE LEGION!
BY USING REVERSED MAGNETIC POWER, I'M PUSHING THE METALLIC ASTEROID MONUMENTS TOWARD THE PLANET WHERE THEY'VE BUILT THAT CITADEL! THIS WILL HELP THE CAT-AND-MOUSE GAME I'M PLAYING AS I KILL THEM ONE BY ONE!
THE MIGHTY VOICE OF COLOSSAL BOY SOUNDS AN ALARM!
THE "MOUNT RUSHMORE OF SPACE" ASTEROIDS... THEY'VE MOVED OUT OF THEIR ORBITS AND ARE FALLING ON THE CITADEL! SUPERBOY ...MON-EL... COME QUICK!

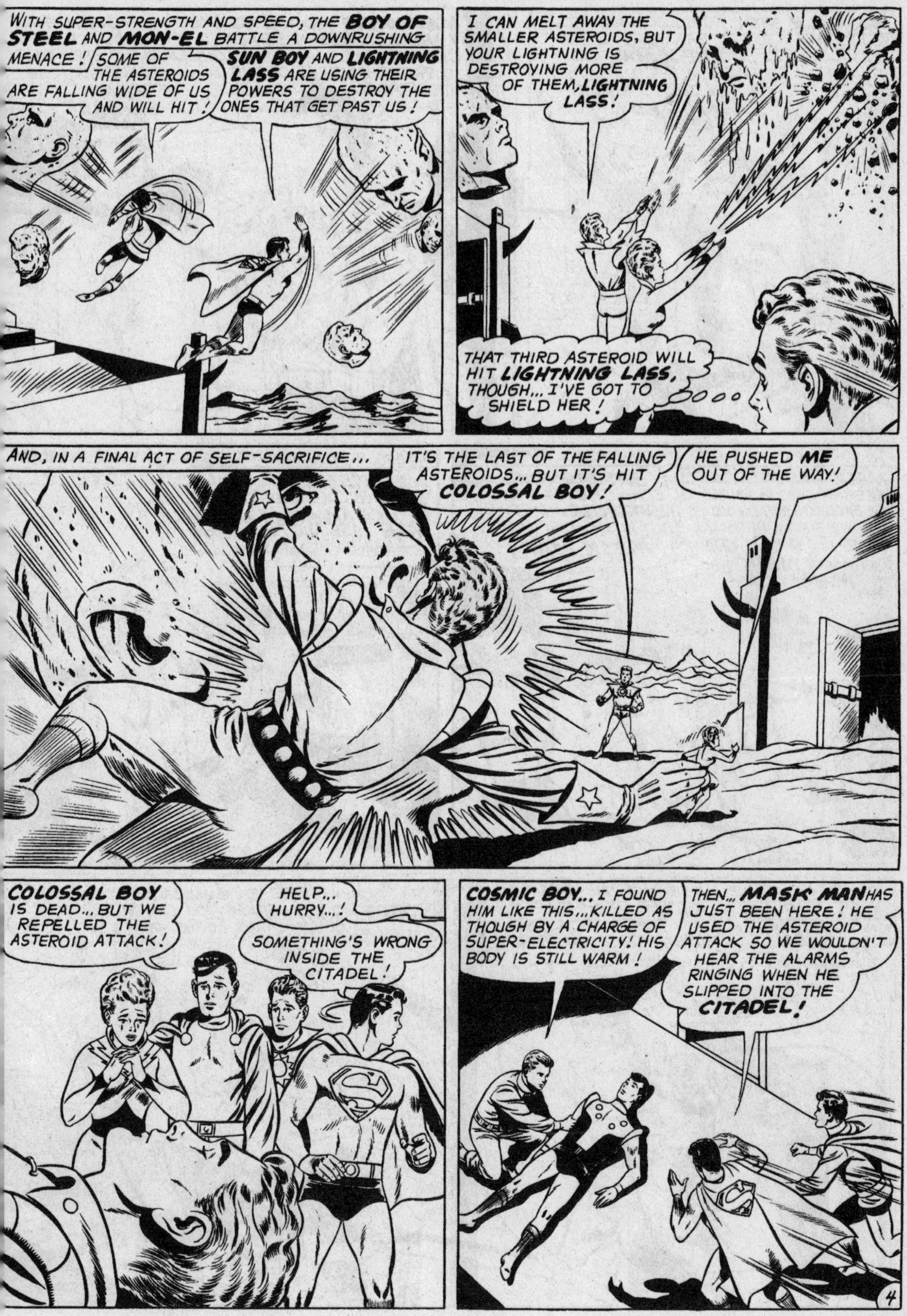
WITH SUPER-STRENGTH AND SPEED, THE BOY OF STEEL AND MON-EL BATTLE A DOWNRUSHING MENACE!
SOME OF THE ASTEROIDS ARE FALLING WIDE OF US AND WILL HIT!
SUN BOY AND LIGHTNING LASS ARE USING THEIR POWERS TO DESTROY THE ONES THAT GET PAST US!
I CAN MELT AWAY THE SMALLER ASTEROIDS, BUT YOUR LIGHTNING IS DESTROYING MORE OF THEM, LIGHTNING LASS!
THAT THIRD ASTEROID WILL HIT LIGHTNING LASS, THOUGH... I'VE GOT TO SHIELD HER!
AND, IN A FINAL ACT OF SELF-SACRIFICE...
IT'S THE LAST OF THE FALLING ASTEROIDS... BUT IT'S HIT COLOSSAL BOY!
HE PUSHED ME OUT OF THE WAY!
COLOSSAL BOY IS DEAD... BUT WE REPELLED THE ASTEROID ATTACK!
HELP... HURRY...!
SOMETHING'S WRONG INSIDE THE CITADEL!
COSMIC BOY... I FOUND HIM LIKE THIS... KILLED AS THOUGH BY A CHARGE OF SUPER-ELECTRICITY! HIS BODY IS STILL WARM!
THEN... MASK MAN HAS JUST BEEN HERE! HE USED THE ASTEROID ATTACK SO WE WOULDN'T HEAR THE ALARMS RINGING WHEN HE SLIPPED INTO THE CITADEL!
4

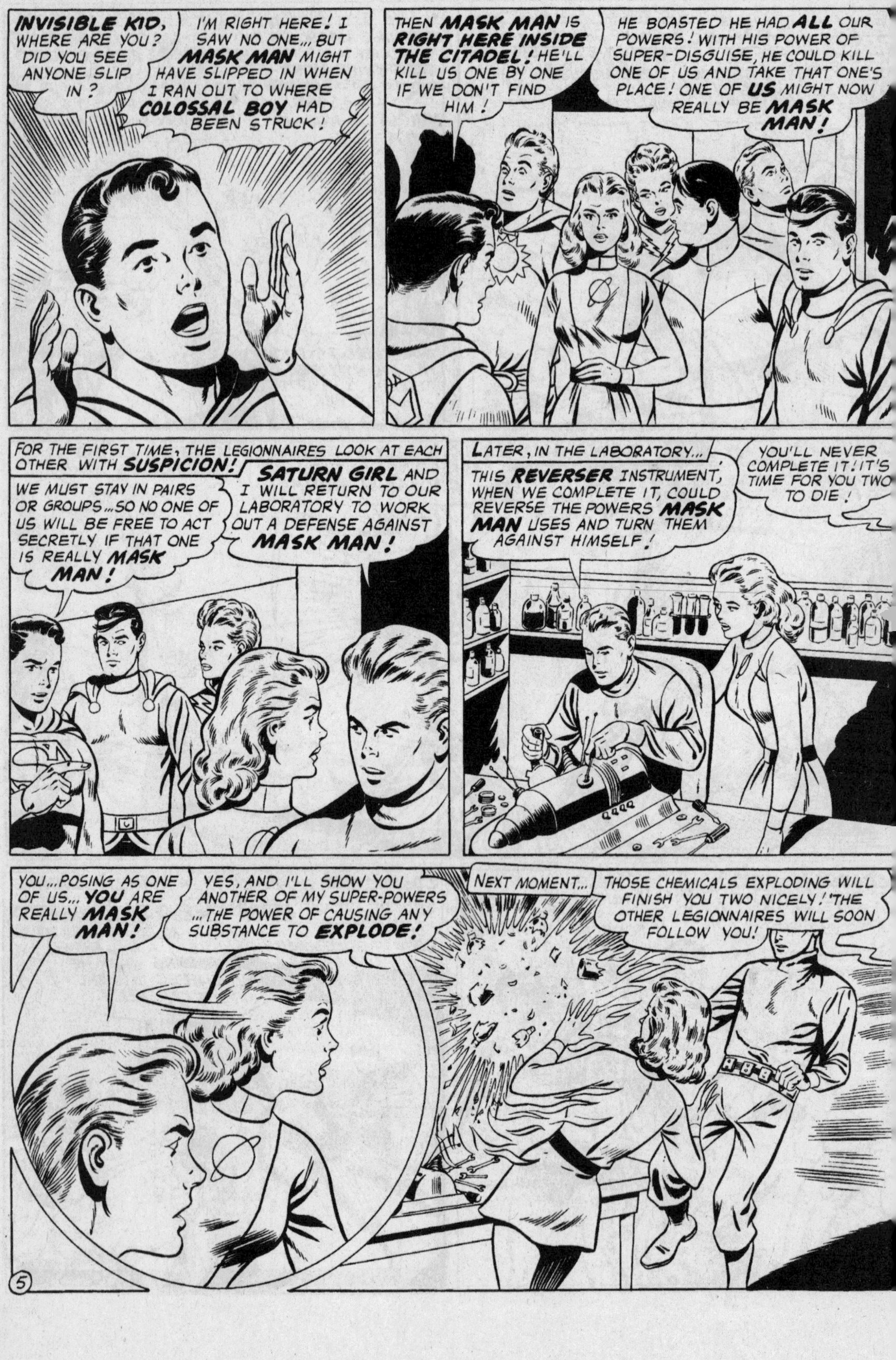
INVISIBLE KID, WHERE ARE YOU? DID YOU SEE ANYONE SLIP IN?
I'M RIGHT HERE! I SAW NO ONE... BUT MASK MAN MIGHT HAVE SLIPPED IN WHEN I RAN OUT TO WHERE COLOSSAL BOY HAD BEEN STRUCK!
THEN MASK MAN IS RIGHT HERE INSIDE THE CITADEL! HE'LL KILL US ONE BY ONE IF WE DON'T FIND HIM!
HE BOASTED HE HAD ALL OUR POWERS! WITH HIS POWER OF SUPER-DISGUISE, HE COULD KILL ONE OF US AND TAKE THAT ONE'S PLACE! ONE OF US MIGHT NOW REALLY BE MASK MAN!
FOR THE FIRST TIME, THE LEGIONNAIRES LOOK AT EACH OTHER WITH SUSPICION!
WE MUST STAY IN PAIRS OR GROUPS... SO NO ONE OF US WILL BE FREE TO ACT SECRETLY IF THAT ONE IS REALLY MASK MAN!
SATURN GIRL AND I WILL RETURN TO OUR LABORATORY TO WORK OUT A DEFENSE AGAINST MASK MAN!
LATER, IN THE LABORATORY...
THIS REVERSER INSTRUMENT, WHEN WE COMPLETE IT, COULD REVERSE THE POWERS MASK MAN USES AND TURN THEM AGAINST HIMSELF!
YOU'LL NEVER COMPLETE IT! IT'S TIME FOR YOU TWO TO DIE!
YOU... POSING AS ONE OF US... YOU ARE REALLY MASK MAN!
YES, AND I'LL SHOW YOU ANOTHER OF MY SUPER-POWERS ... THE POWER OF CAUSING ANY SUBSTANCE TO EXPLODE!
NEXT MOMENT...
THOSE CHEMICALS EXPLODING WILL FINISH YOU TWO NICELY! THE OTHER LEGIONNAIRES WILL SOON FOLLOW YOU!
5

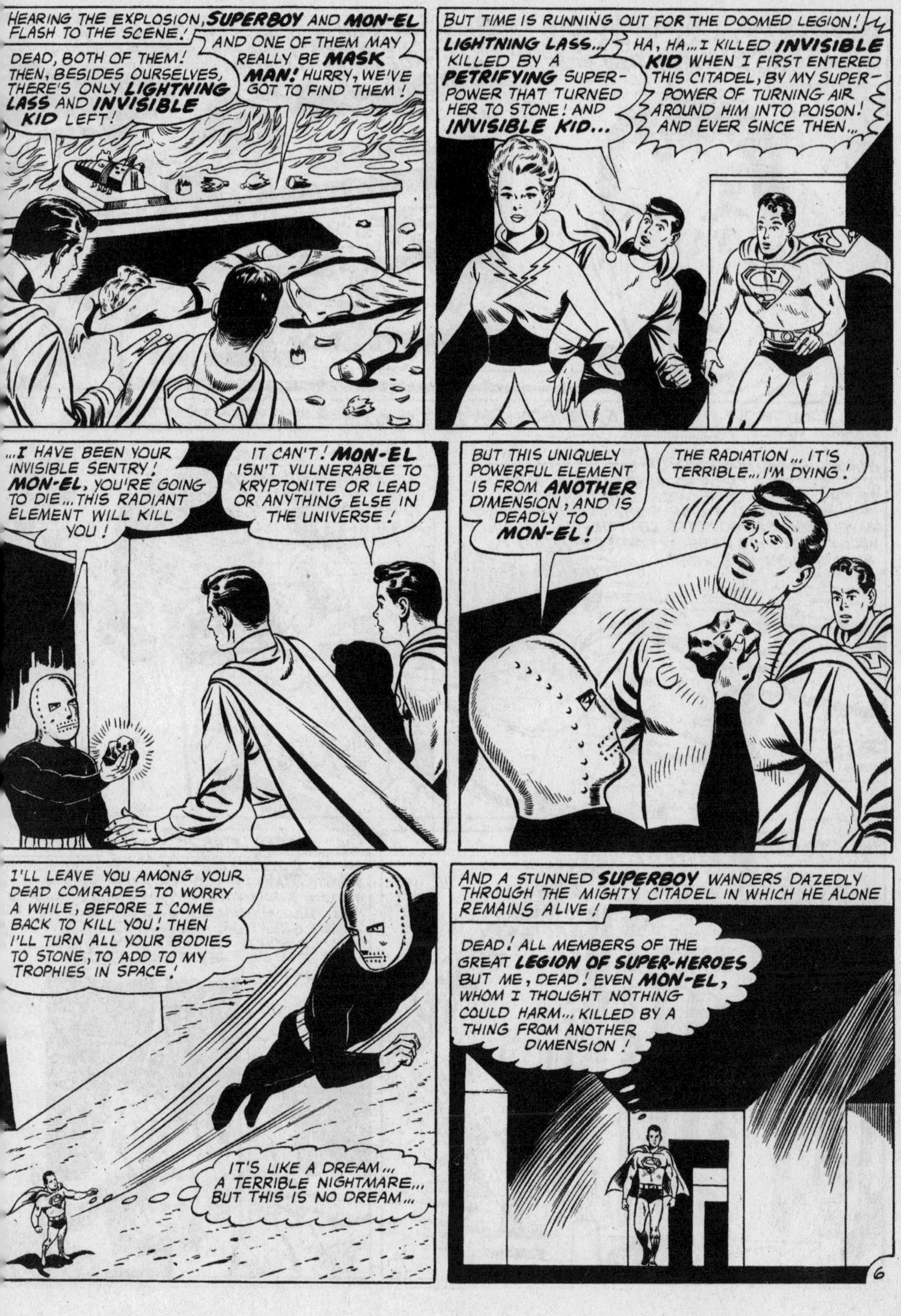
HEARING THE EXPLOSION, SUPERBOY AND MON-EL FLASH TO THE SCENE!
DEAD, BOTH OF THEM! THEN, BESIDES OURSELVES, THERE'S ONLY LIGHTNING LASS AND INVISIBLE KID LEFT!
AND ONE OF THEM MAY REALLY BE MASK MAN! HURRY, WE'VE GOT TO FIND THEM!
BUT TIME IS RUNNING OUT FOR THE DOOMED LEGION!
LIGHTNING LASS... KILLED BY A PETRIFYING SUPER-POWER THAT TURNED HER TO STONE! AND INVISIBLE KID...
HA, HA... I KILLED INVISIBLE KID WHEN I FIRST ENTERED THIS CITADEL, BY MY SUPER-POWER OF TURNING AIR AROUND HIM INTO POISON! AND EVER SINCE THEN...
...I HAVE BEEN YOUR INVISIBLE SENTRY! MON-EL, YOU'RE GOING TO DIE... THIS RADIANT ELEMENT WILL KILL YOU!
IT CAN'T! MON-EL ISN'T VULNERABLE TO KRYPTONITE OR LEAD OR ANYTHING ELSE IN THE UNIVERSE!
BUT THIS UNIQUELY POWERFUL ELEMENT IS FROM ANOTHER DIMENSION, AND IS DEADLY TO MON-EL!
THE RADIATION... IT'S TERRIBLE... I'M DYING!
I'LL LEAVE YOU AMONG YOUR DEAD COMRADES TO WORRY A WHILE, BEFORE I COME BACK TO KILL YOU! THEN I'LL TURN ALL YOUR BODIES TO STONE, TO ADD TO MY TROPHIES IN SPACE!
IT'S LIKE A DREAM... A TERRIBLE NIGHTMARE... BUT THIS IS NO DREAM...
AND A STUNNED SUPERBOY WANDERS DAZEDLY THROUGH THE MIGHTY CITADEL IN WHICH HE ALONE REMAINS ALIVE!
DEAD! ALL MEMBERS OF THE GREAT LEGION OF SUPER-HEROES BUT ME, DEAD! EVEN MON-EL, WHOM I THOUGHT NOTHING COULD HARM... KILLED BY A THING FROM ANOTHER DIMENSION!
6

BUT WAIT... HOW COULD *MASK MAN* BRING A THING FROM ANOTHER DIMENSION, UNLESS HE HAS POWERS THAT ARE *MAGICAL?* MAYBE THAT'S IT... AND IF WHAT I SUSPECT IS TRUE, I MIGHT STILL CONQUER HIM!

THIS REVERSER-INSTRUMENT WHICH POOR *BRAINIAC 5* ALMOST COMPLETED MIGHT STILL WORK! IT WAS A LITTLE DAMAGED BY THE EXPLOSION, BUT I CAN REPAIR AND ALTER IT...

THEN, ZOOMING OUT INTO SPACE, *SUPERBOY* SEARCHES WITH TELESCOPIC VISION UNTIL HE FINDS A STRANGE WORLD!

MASK MAN BOASTED OF HIS TROPHIES IN SPACE, SO I KNEW HE MUST HAVE A TROPHY COLLECTION SOMEWHERE! AND THIS WORLD IS IT... THOSE EIGHT MOONS HAVE BEEN CARVED INTO LETTERS WHICH SPELL HIS NAME ON BOTH SIDES! MY SUSPICION WAS RIGHT!

THIS *MASK MAN* IS REALLY A DESCENDANT OF *MR. MXYZPTLK*, THE IMP WHO PESTERS ME IN MY OWN TIME! IF HE SAYS HIS NAME BACKWARDS, HE'LL BE SHOT BACK INTO HIS 5TH DIMENSION UNIVERSE AND ALL EFFECTS OF HIS MAGIC WILL VANISH! I'VE GOT TO ACT FAST...

ONLY MINUTES LATER...

HA, HA... I *WANTED* YOU TO FOLLOW ME HERE *SUPERBOY*, SO THAT BEFORE YOU DIE YOU'LL KNOW WHO IT WAS WHO CONQUERED YOU ALL! MY NAME IS THE SAME AS MY GREAT, GREAT, GREAT, GREAT ANCESTOR'S, AND TO HONOR IT, THOSE MOONS AS THEY RISE AND SET SPELL IT OUT!

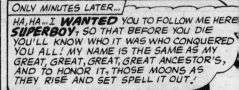

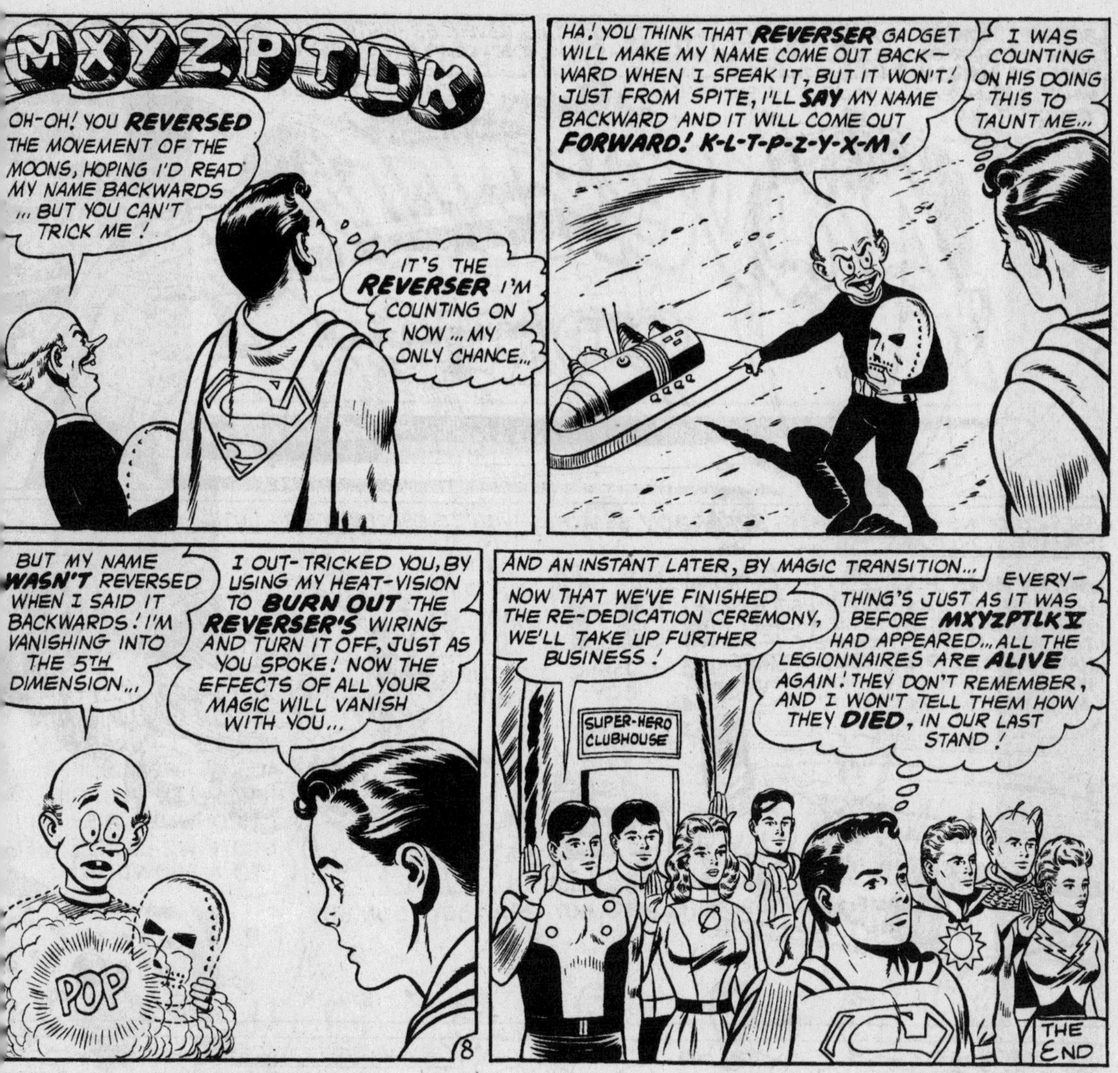
MXYZPTLK
OH-OH! YOU REVERSED THE MOVEMENT OF THE MOONS, HOPING I'D READ MY NAME BACKWARDS ... BUT YOU CAN'T TRICK ME!
IT'S THE REVERSER I'M COUNTING ON NOW ... MY ONLY CHANCE...
HA! YOU THINK THAT REVERSER GADGET WILL MAKE MY NAME COME OUT BACKWARD WHEN I SPEAK IT, BUT IT WON'T! JUST FROM SPITE, I'LL SAY MY NAME BACKWARD AND IT WILL COME OUT FORWARD! K-L-T-P-Z-Y-X-M!
I WAS COUNTING ON HIS DOING THIS TO TAUNT ME...
BUT MY NAME WASN'T REVERSED WHEN I SAID IT BACKWARDS! I'M VANISHING INTO THE 5TH DIMENSION...
I OUT-TRICKED YOU, BY USING MY HEAT-VISION TO BURN OUT THE REVERSER'S WIRING AND TURN IT OFF, JUST AS YOU SPOKE! NOW THE EFFECTS OF ALL YOUR MAGIC WILL VANISH WITH YOU...
POP
8
AND AN INSTANT LATER, BY MAGIC TRANSITION...
NOW THAT WE'VE FINISHED THE RE-DEDICATION CEREMONY, WE'LL TAKE UP FURTHER BUSINESS!
EVERYTHING'S JUST AS IT WAS BEFORE MXYZPTLK V HAD APPEARED... ALL THE LEGIONNAIRES ARE ALIVE AGAIN! THEY DON'T REMEMBER, AND I WON'T TELL THEM HOW THEY DIED, IN OUR LAST STAND!
SUPER-HERO CLUBHOUSE
THE END

LEGION of SUPER-HEROES

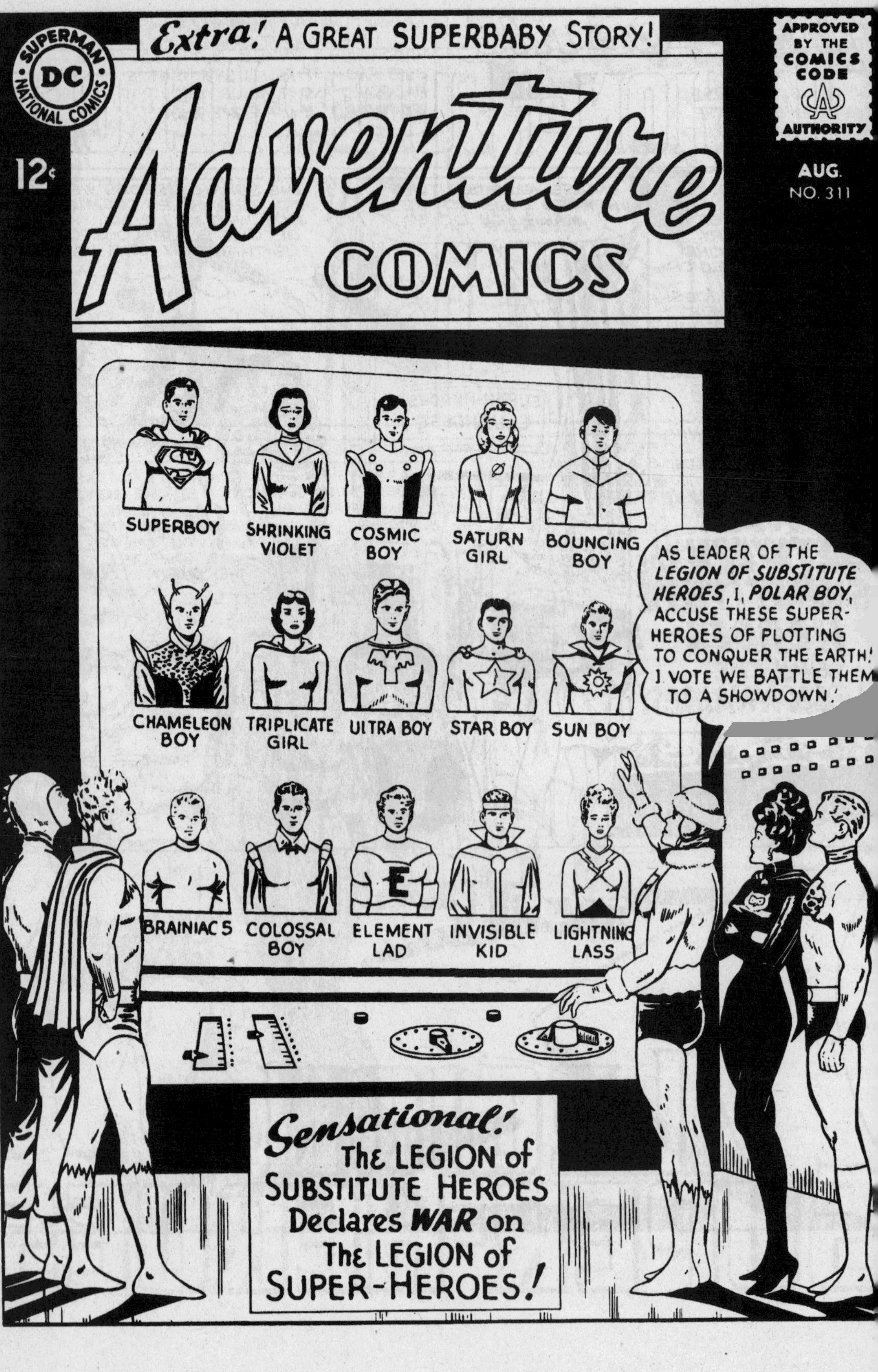
Extra! A GREAT SUPERBABY STORY!
SUPERMAN DC NATIONAL COMICS
12¢
Adventure COMICS
APPROVED BY THE COMICS CODE AUTHORITY
AUG. NO. 311
SUPERBOY
SHRINKING VIOLET
COSMIC BOY
SATURN GIRL
BOUNCING BOY
CHAMELEON BOY
TRIPLICATE GIRL
ULTRA BOY
STAR BOY
SUN BOY
BRAINIAC 5
COLOSSAL BOY
ELEMENT LAD
INVISIBLE KID
LIGHTNING LASS
AS LEADER OF THE LEGION OF SUBSTITUTE HEROES, I, POLAR BOY, ACCUSE THESE SUPER-HEROES OF PLOTTING TO CONQUER THE EARTH! I VOTE WE BATTLE THEM TO A SHOWDOWN!
Sensational! The LEGION of SUBSTITUTE HEROES Declares WAR on The LEGION of SUPER-HEROES!

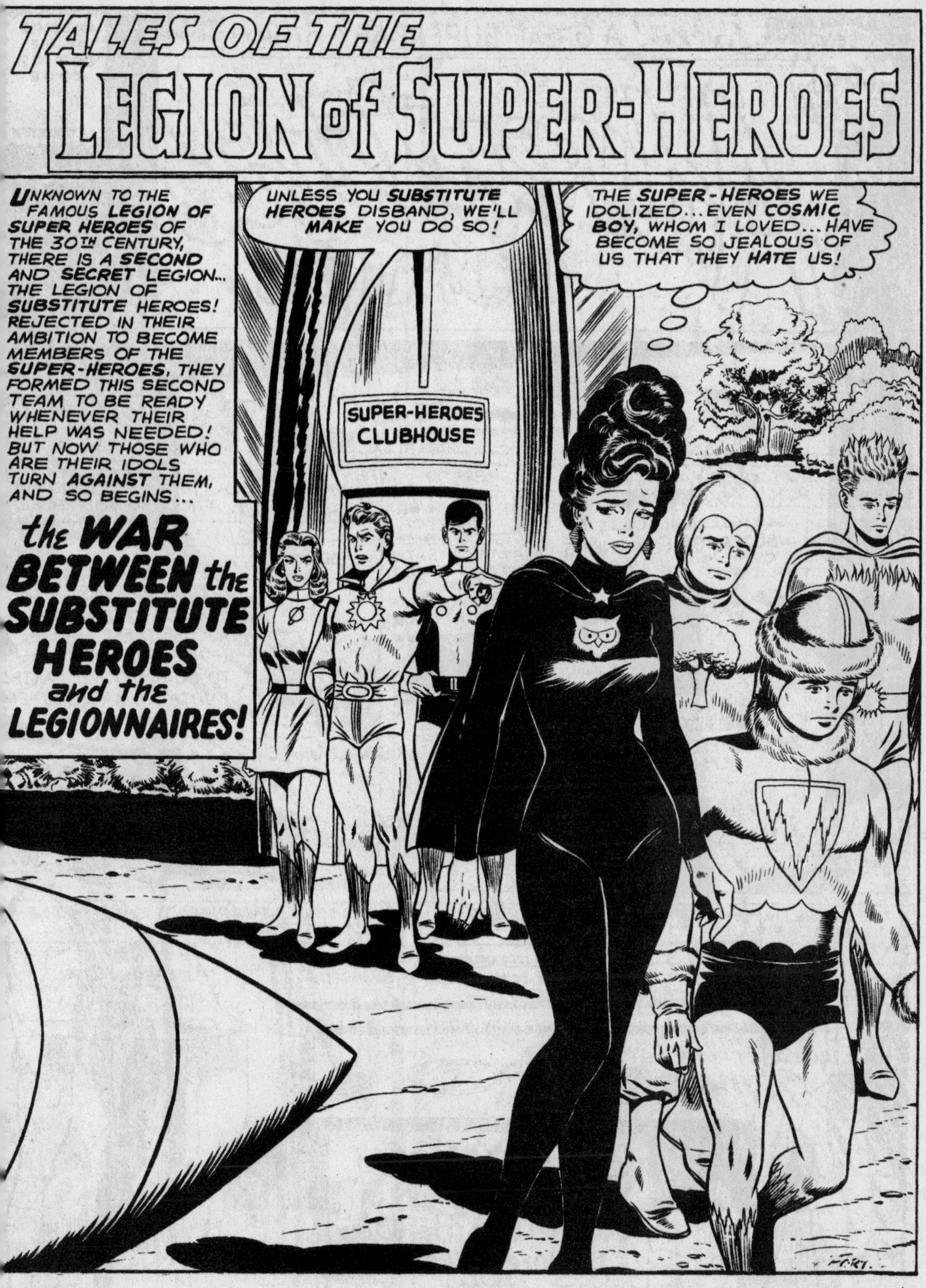
TALES OF THE
LEGION of SUPER-HEROES
UNKNOWN TO THE FAMOUS LEGION OF SUPER HEROES OF THE 30TH CENTURY, THERE IS A SECOND AND SECRET LEGION... THE LEGION OF SUBSTITUTE HEROES! REJECTED IN THEIR AMBITION TO BECOME MEMBERS OF THE SUPER-HEROES, THEY FORMED THIS SECOND TEAM TO BE READY WHENEVER THEIR HELP WAS NEEDED! BUT NOW THOSE WHO ARE THEIR IDOLS TURN AGAINST THEM, AND SO BEGINS...
the WAR BETWEEN the SUBSTITUTE HEROES and the LEGIONNAIRES!
UNLESS YOU SUBSTITUTE HEROES DISBAND, WE'LL MAKE YOU DO SO!
THE SUPER-HEROES WE IDOLIZED... EVEN COSMIC BOY, WHOM I LOVED... HAVE BECOME SO JEALOUS OF US THAT THEY HATE US!
SUPER-HEROES CLUBHOUSE

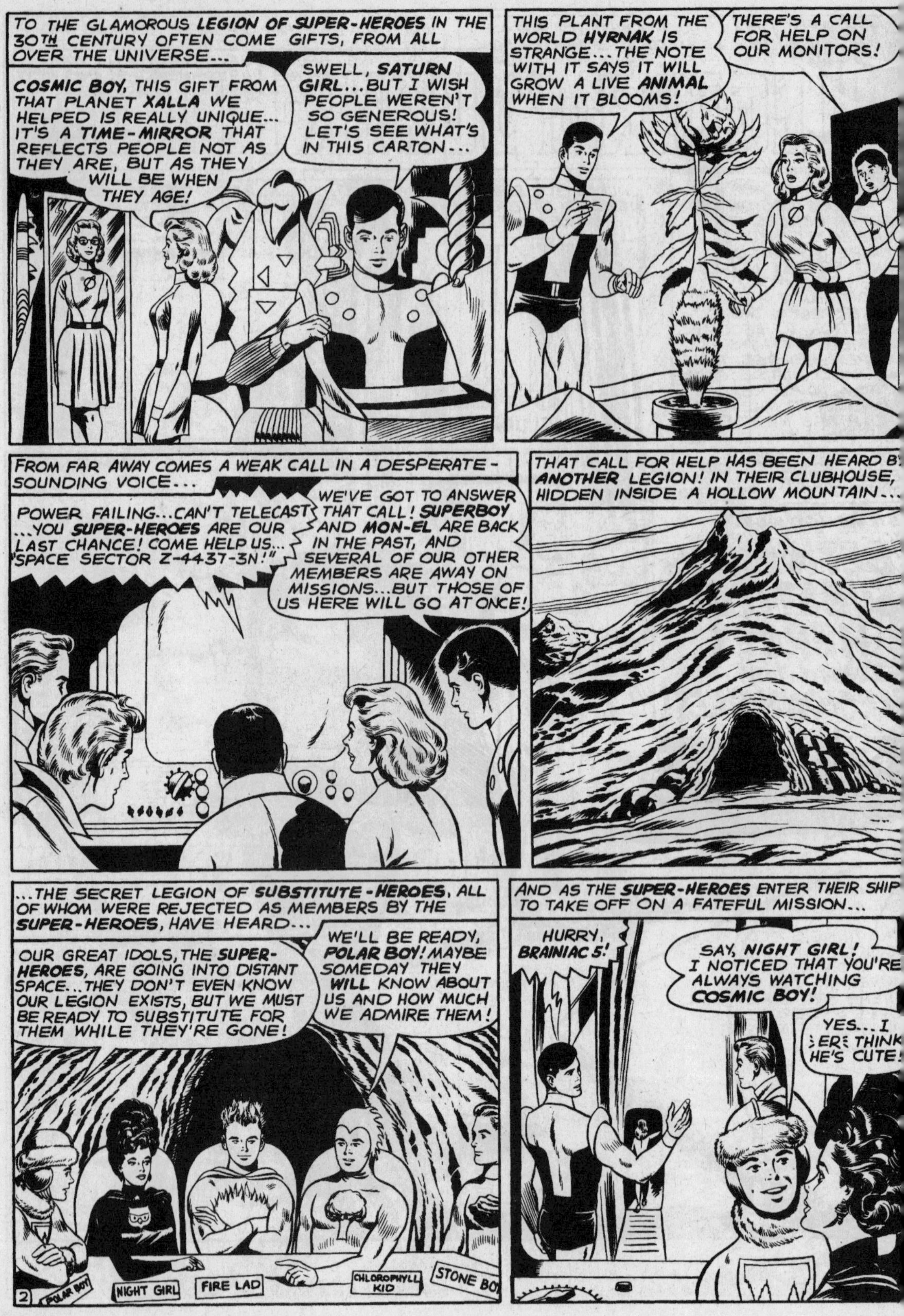
TO THE GLAMOROUS LEGION OF SUPER-HEROES IN THE 30TH CENTURY OFTEN COME GIFTS, FROM ALL OVER THE UNIVERSE...
COSMIC BOY, THIS GIFT FROM THAT PLANET XALLA WE HELPED IS REALLY UNIQUE... IT'S A TIME-MIRROR THAT REFLECTS PEOPLE NOT AS THEY ARE, BUT AS THEY WILL BE WHEN THEY AGE!
SWELL, SATURN GIRL... BUT I WISH PEOPLE WEREN'T SO GENEROUS! LET'S SEE WHAT'S IN THIS CARTON...
THIS PLANT FROM THE WORLD HYRNAK IS STRANGE... THE NOTE WITH IT SAYS IT WILL GROW A LIVE ANIMAL WHEN IT BLOOMS!
THERE'S A CALL FOR HELP ON OUR MONITORS!
FROM FAR AWAY COMES A WEAK CALL IN A DESPERATE-SOUNDING VOICE...
POWER FAILING...CAN'T TELECAST ...YOU SUPER-HEROES ARE OUR LAST CHANCE! COME HELP US... "SPACE SECTOR Z-4437-3N!"
WE'VE GOT TO ANSWER THAT CALL! SUPERBOY AND MON-EL ARE BACK IN THE PAST, AND SEVERAL OF OUR OTHER MEMBERS ARE AWAY ON MISSIONS...BUT THOSE OF US HERE WILL GO AT ONCE!
THAT CALL FOR HELP HAS BEEN HEARD BY ANOTHER LEGION! IN THEIR CLUBHOUSE, HIDDEN INSIDE A HOLLOW MOUNTAIN...
...THE SECRET LEGION OF SUBSTITUTE-HEROES, ALL OF WHOM WERE REJECTED AS MEMBERS BY THE SUPER-HEROES, HAVE HEARD...
OUR GREAT IDOLS, THE SUPER-HEROES, ARE GOING INTO DISTANT SPACE...THEY DON'T EVEN KNOW OUR LEGION EXISTS, BUT WE MUST BE READY TO SUBSTITUTE FOR THEM WHILE THEY'RE GONE!
WE'LL BE READY, POLAR BOY! MAYBE SOMEDAY THEY WILL KNOW ABOUT US AND HOW MUCH WE ADMIRE THEM!
POLAR BOY
NIGHT GIRL
FIRE LAD
CHLOROPHYLL KID
STONE BOY
2
AND AS THE SUPER-HEROES ENTER THEIR SHIP TO TAKE OFF ON A FATEFUL MISSION...
HURRY, BRAINIAC 5!
SAY, NIGHT GIRL! I NOTICED THAT YOU'RE ALWAYS WATCHING COSMIC BOY!
YES... I ...ER... THINK HE'S CUTE!

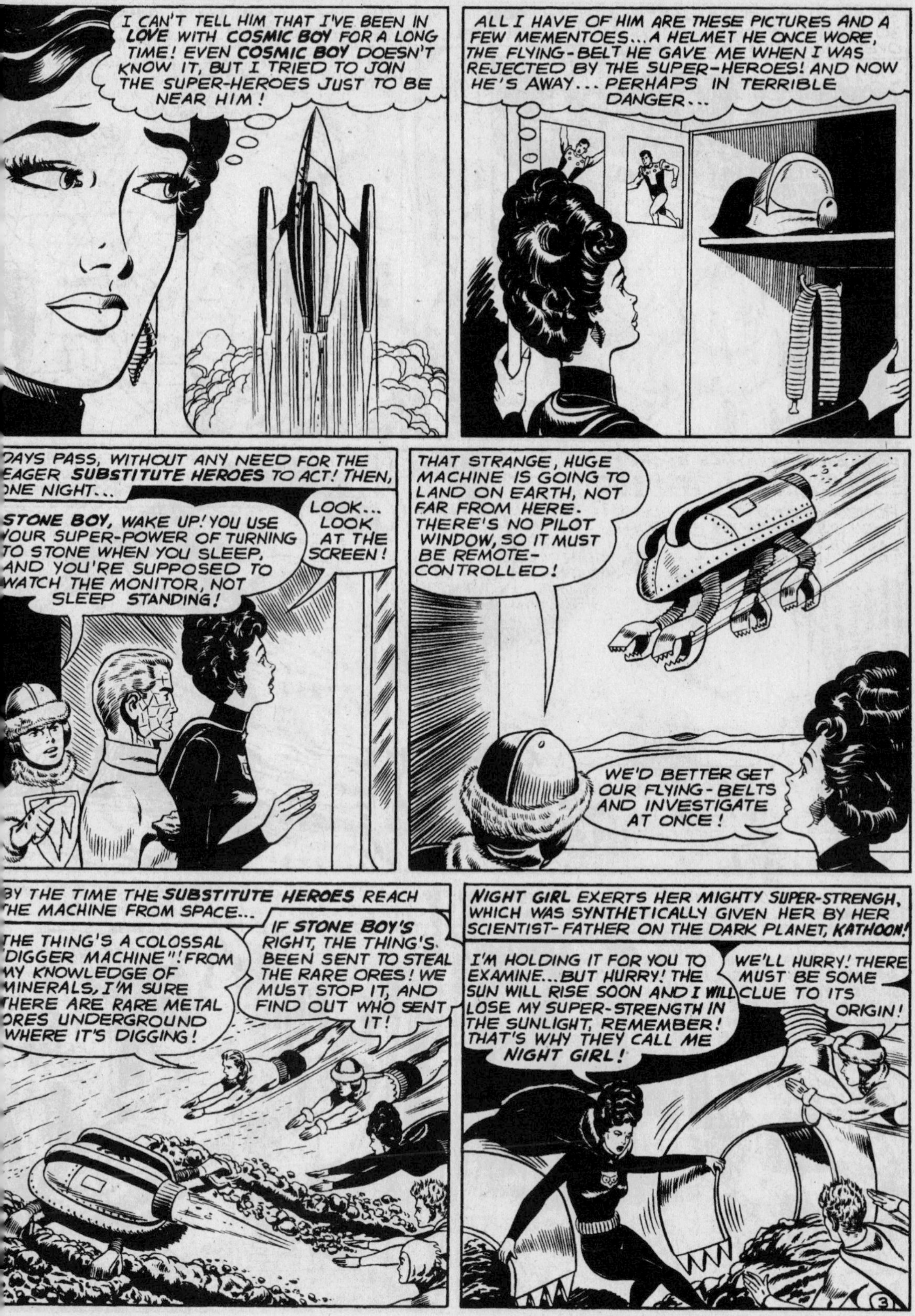
I CAN'T TELL HIM THAT I'VE BEEN IN LOVE WITH COSMIC BOY FOR A LONG TIME! EVEN COSMIC BOY DOESN'T KNOW IT, BUT I TRIED TO JOIN THE SUPER-HEROES JUST TO BE NEAR HIM!
ALL I HAVE OF HIM ARE THESE PICTURES AND A FEW MEMENTOES... A HELMET HE ONCE WORE, THE FLYING-BELT HE GAVE ME WHEN I WAS REJECTED BY THE SUPER-HEROES! AND NOW HE'S AWAY... PERHAPS IN TERRIBLE DANGER...
DAYS PASS, WITHOUT ANY NEED FOR THE EAGER SUBSTITUTE HEROES TO ACT! THEN, ONE NIGHT...
STONE BOY, WAKE UP! YOU USE YOUR SUPER-POWER OF TURNING TO STONE WHEN YOU SLEEP, AND YOU'RE SUPPOSED TO WATCH THE MONITOR, NOT SLEEP STANDING!
LOOK... LOOK AT THE SCREEN!
THAT STRANGE, HUGE MACHINE IS GOING TO LAND ON EARTH, NOT FAR FROM HERE. THERE'S NO PILOT WINDOW, SO IT MUST BE REMOTE-CONTROLLED!
WE'D BETTER GET OUR FLYING-BELTS AND INVESTIGATE AT ONCE!
BY THE TIME THE SUBSTITUTE HEROES REACH THE MACHINE FROM SPACE...
THE THING'S A COLOSSAL "DIGGER MACHINE"! FROM MY KNOWLEDGE OF MINERALS, I'M SURE THERE ARE RARE METAL ORES UNDERGROUND WHERE IT'S DIGGING!
IF STONE BOY'S RIGHT, THE THING'S BEEN SENT TO STEAL THE RARE ORES! WE MUST STOP IT, AND FIND OUT WHO SENT IT!
NIGHT GIRL EXERTS HER MIGHTY SUPER-STRENGH, WHICH WAS SYNTHETICALLY GIVEN HER BY HER SCIENTIST-FATHER ON THE DARK PLANET, KATHOON!
I'M HOLDING IT FOR YOU TO EXAMINE... BUT HURRY! THE SUN WILL RISE SOON AND I WILL LOSE MY SUPER-STRENGTH IN THE SUNLIGHT, REMEMBER! THAT'S WHY THEY CALL ME NIGHT GIRL!
WE'LL HURRY! THERE MUST BE SOME CLUE TO ITS ORIGIN!
3

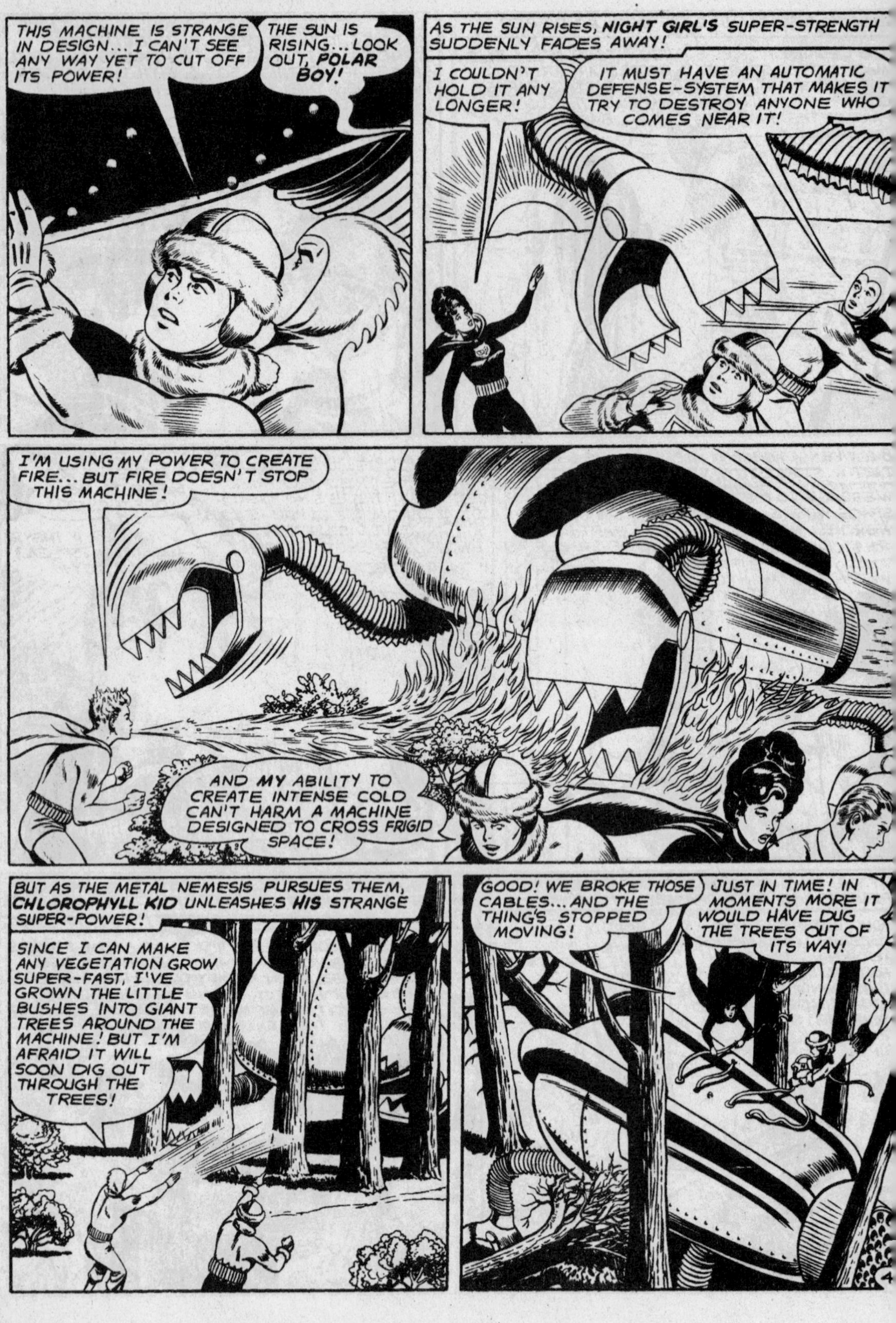
THIS MACHINE IS STRANGE IN DESIGN... I CAN'T SEE ANY WAY YET TO CUT OFF ITS POWER!
THE SUN IS RISING... LOOK OUT, POLAR BOY!
AS THE SUN RISES, NIGHT GIRL'S SUPER-STRENGTH SUDDENLY FADES AWAY!
I COULDN'T HOLD IT ANY LONGER!
IT MUST HAVE AN AUTOMATIC DEFENSE-SYSTEM THAT MAKES IT TRY TO DESTROY ANYONE WHO COMES NEAR IT!
I'M USING MY POWER TO CREATE FIRE... BUT FIRE DOESN'T STOP THIS MACHINE!
AND MY ABILITY TO CREATE INTENSE COLD CAN'T HARM A MACHINE DESIGNED TO CROSS FRIGID SPACE!
BUT AS THE METAL NEMESIS PURSUES THEM, CHLOROPHYLL KID UNLEASHES HIS STRANGE SUPER-POWER!
SINCE I CAN MAKE ANY VEGETATION GROW SUPER-FAST, I'VE GROWN THE LITTLE BUSHES INTO GIANT TREES AROUND THE MACHINE! BUT I'M AFRAID IT WILL SOON DIG OUT THROUGH THE TREES!
GOOD! WE BROKE THOSE CABLES... AND THE THING'S STOPPED MOVING!
JUST IN TIME! IN MOMENTS MORE IT WOULD HAVE DUG THE TREES OUT OF ITS WAY!
4

SOON, AS THEY EXAMINE THE DISABLED DIGGER...

THE DESIGN OF THIS MACHINE IS SO STRANGE AND DIFFERENT, IT MUST COME FROM AN UNKNOWN PART OF THE UNIVERSE!

THEN A COMPLETELY *ALIEN* PEOPLE ARE TRYING TO LOOT EARTH'S RAREST METALS! THIS LOOKS BAD!

I FEEL WE SHOULD SEND A MESSAGE TO THE *SUPER-HEROES,* OUT THERE IN SPACE, ABOUT THIS... SO THAT WHEN THEY FINISH THEIR MISSION, THEY CAN SEARCH SPACE FOR THE ORIGIN OF THIS PLOT!

YOU'RE RIGHT! WE *SUBSTITUTE HEROES* CAN DEAL WITH THE DANGER HERE ON EARTH, WHILE THEY SEARCH OUT THERE!

BUT WHEN AN URGENT MESSAGE HAS BEEN BROAD-CAST...

HE'S BEAMING THE MESSAGE TO THE SECTOR OF SPACE WHERE THE *SUPER-HEROES* WENT TO ANSWER THAT DISTRESS-CALL!

CALLING THE *SUPER-HEROES!*...AN ALIEN DANGER MENACES EARTH... MAY WE OFFER OUR ASSISTANCE? ...COME IN...

AN HOUR LATER...

I'VE TRIED AND TRIED, BUT THERE'S NO ANSWER FROM THE *SUPER-HEROES!* COULD SOMETHING HAVE HAPPENED TO THEM?

NO, DON'T EVEN THINK THAT! THEY'RE TOO SUPER TO BE DESTROYED!

I WONDER IF THEY'RE ALL SAFE...ESPECIALLY *COSMIC BOY!*

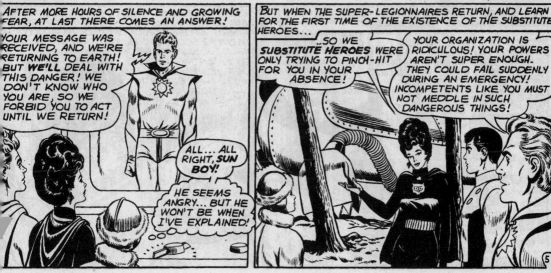

AFTER MORE HOURS OF SILENCE AND GROWING FEAR, AT LAST THERE COMES AN ANSWER!

YOUR MESSAGE WAS RECEIVED, AND WE'RE RETURNING TO EARTH! BUT *WE'LL* DEAL WITH THIS DANGER! WE DON'T KNOW WHO YOU ARE, SO WE FORBID YOU TO ACT UNTIL WE RETURN!

ALL... ALL RIGHT, *SUN BOY!*

HE SEEMS ANGRY... BUT HE WON'T BE WHEN I'VE EXPLAINED!

BUT WHEN THE SUPER-LEGIONNAIRES RETURN, AND LEARN FOR THE FIRST TIME OF THE EXISTENCE OF THE SUBSTITUTE HEROES...

"...SO WE *SUBSTITUTE HEROES* WERE ONLY TRYING TO PINCH-HIT FOR YOU IN YOUR ABSENCE!

YOUR ORGANIZATION IS RIDICULOUS! YOUR POWERS AREN'T *SUPER* ENOUGH. THEY COULD FAIL SUDDENLY DURING AN EMERGENCY! INCOMPETENTS LIKE YOU MUST NOT MEDDLE IN SUCH DANGEROUS THINGS!

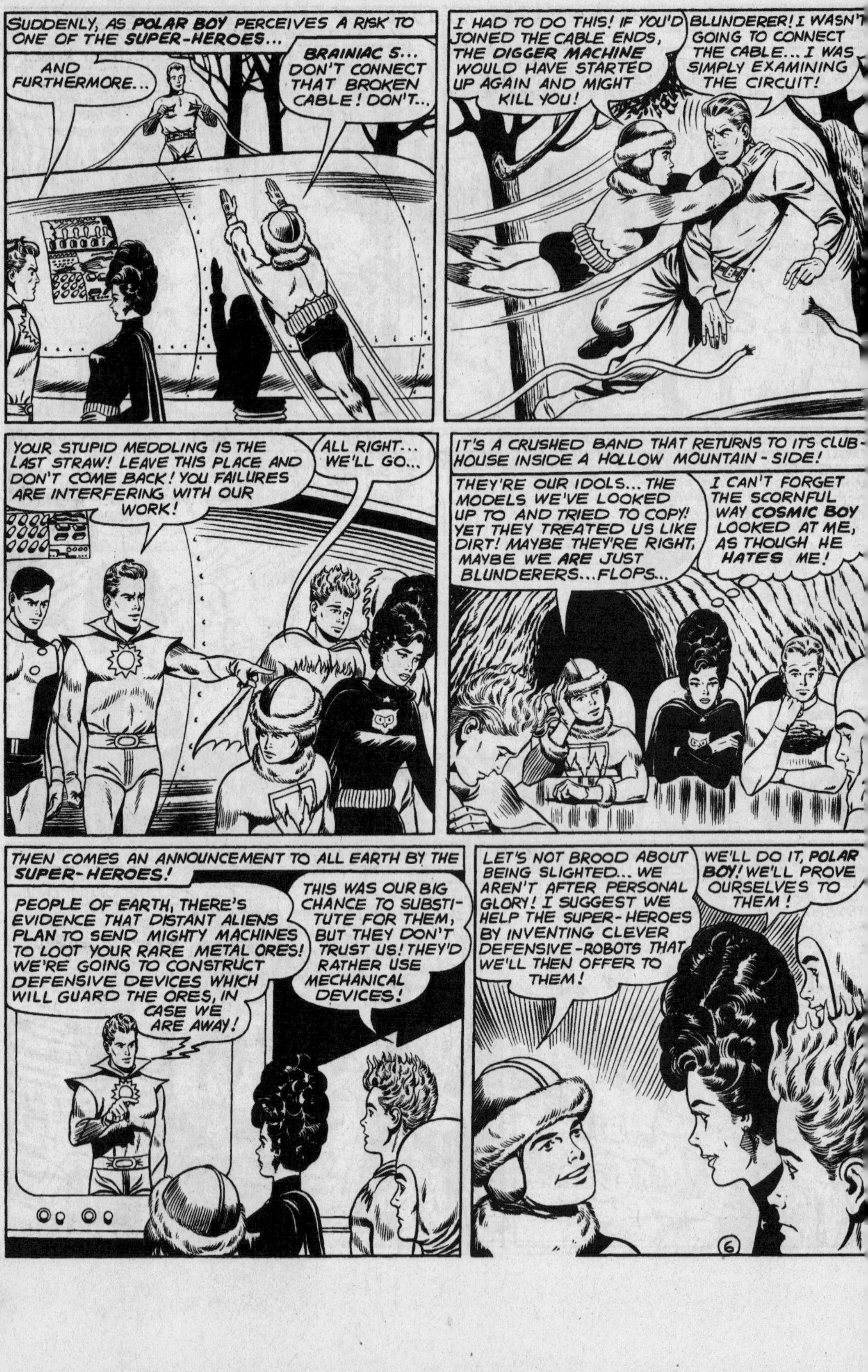
SUDDENLY, AS POLAR BOY PERCEIVES A RISK TO ONE OF THE SUPER-HEROES...
AND FURTHERMORE...
BRAINIAC 5... DON'T CONNECT THAT BROKEN CABLE! DON'T...
I HAD TO DO THIS! IF YOU'D JOINED THE CABLE ENDS, THE DIGGER MACHINE WOULD HAVE STARTED UP AGAIN AND MIGHT KILL YOU!
BLUNDERER! I WASN'T GOING TO CONNECT THE CABLE... I WAS SIMPLY EXAMINING THE CIRCUIT!
YOUR STUPID MEDDLING IS THE LAST STRAW! LEAVE THIS PLACE AND DON'T COME BACK! YOU FAILURES ARE INTERFERING WITH OUR WORK!
ALL RIGHT... WE'LL GO...
IT'S A CRUSHED BAND THAT RETURNS TO ITS CLUB-HOUSE INSIDE A HOLLOW MOUNTAIN-SIDE!
THEY'RE OUR IDOLS... THE MODELS WE'VE LOOKED UP TO AND TRIED TO COPY! YET THEY TREATED US LIKE DIRT! MAYBE THEY'RE RIGHT, MAYBE WE ARE JUST BLUNDERERS... FLOPS...
I CAN'T FORGET THE SCORNFUL WAY COSMIC BOY LOOKED AT ME, AS THOUGH HE HATES ME!
THEN COMES AN ANNOUNCEMENT TO ALL EARTH BY THE SUPER-HEROES!
PEOPLE OF EARTH, THERE'S EVIDENCE THAT DISTANT ALIENS PLAN TO SEND MIGHTY MACHINES TO LOOT YOUR RARE METAL ORES! WE'RE GOING TO CONSTRUCT DEFENSIVE DEVICES WHICH WILL GUARD THE ORES, IN CASE WE ARE AWAY!
THIS WAS OUR BIG CHANCE TO SUBSTITUTE FOR THEM, BUT THEY DON'T TRUST US! THEY'D RATHER USE MECHANICAL DEVICES!
LET'S NOT BROOD ABOUT BEING SLIGHTED... WE AREN'T AFTER PERSONAL GLORY! I SUGGEST WE HELP THE SUPER-HEROES BY INVENTING CLEVER DEFENSIVE-ROBOTS THAT WE'LL THEN OFFER TO THEM!
WE'LL DO IT, POLAR BOY! WE'LL PROVE OURSELVES TO THEM!
6

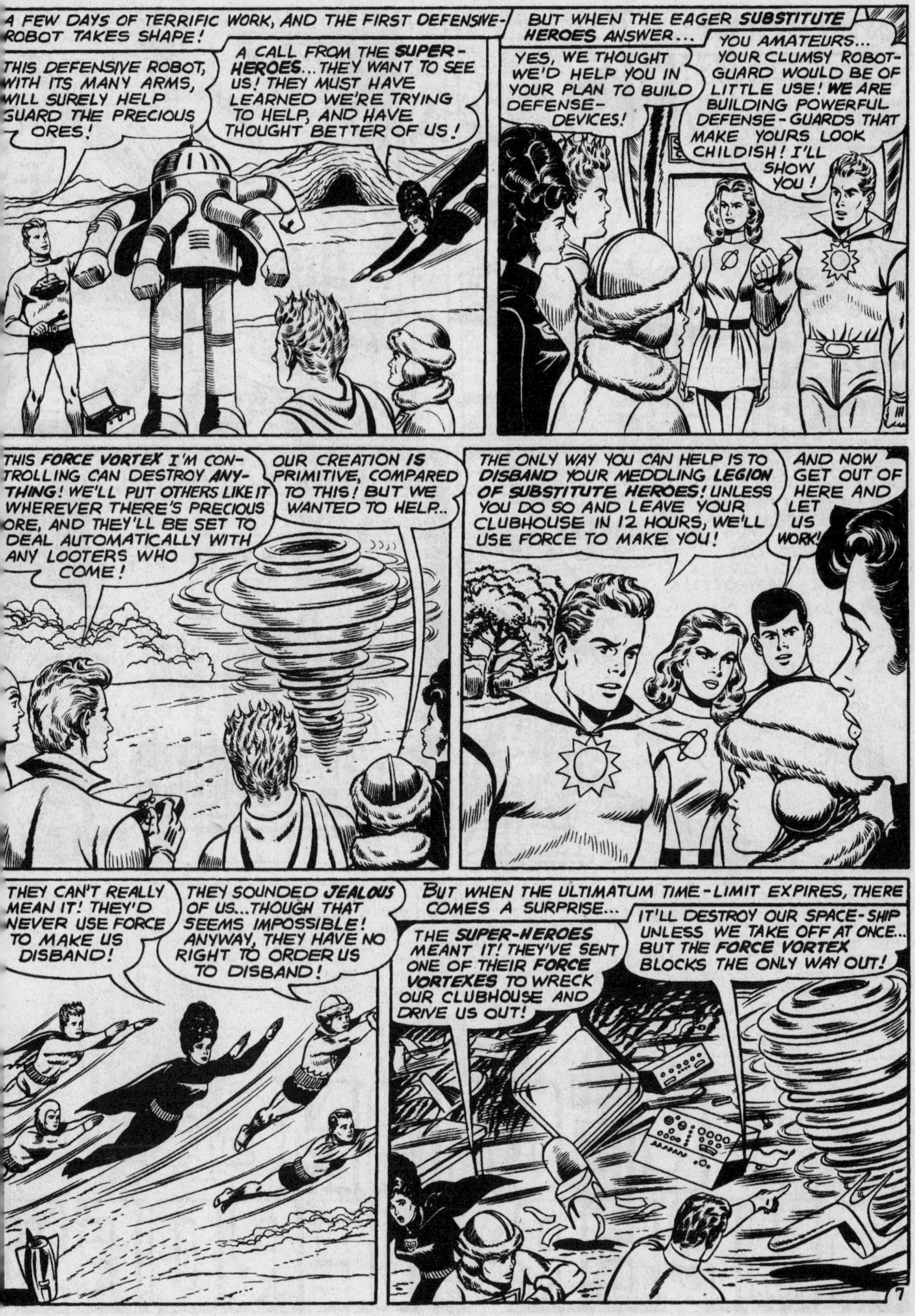
A FEW DAYS OF TERRIFIC WORK, AND THE FIRST DEFENSIVE-ROBOT TAKES SHAPE!
THIS DEFENSIVE ROBOT, WITH ITS MANY ARMS, WILL SURELY HELP GUARD THE PRECIOUS ORES!
A CALL FROM THE SUPER-HEROES... THEY WANT TO SEE US! THEY MUST HAVE LEARNED WE'RE TRYING TO HELP, AND HAVE THOUGHT BETTER OF US!
BUT WHEN THE EAGER SUBSTITUTE HEROES ANSWER...
YES, WE THOUGHT WE'D HELP YOU IN YOUR PLAN TO BUILD DEFENSE-DEVICES!
YOU AMATEURS... YOUR CLUMSY ROBOT-GUARD WOULD BE OF LITTLE USE! WE ARE BUILDING POWERFUL DEFENSE-GUARDS THAT MAKE YOURS LOOK CHILDISH! I'LL SHOW YOU!
THIS FORCE VORTEX I'M CONTROLLING CAN DESTROY ANYTHING! WE'LL PUT OTHERS LIKE IT WHEREVER THERE'S PRECIOUS ORE, AND THEY'LL BE SET TO DEAL AUTOMATICALLY WITH ANY LOOTERS WHO COME!
OUR CREATION IS PRIMITIVE, COMPARED TO THIS! BUT WE WANTED TO HELP..
THE ONLY WAY YOU CAN HELP IS TO DISBAND YOUR MEDDLING LEGION OF SUBSTITUTE HEROES! UNLESS YOU DO SO AND LEAVE YOUR CLUBHOUSE IN 12 HOURS, WE'LL USE FORCE TO MAKE YOU!
AND NOW GET OUT OF HERE AND LET US WORK!
THEY CAN'T REALLY MEAN IT! THEY'D NEVER USE FORCE TO MAKE US DISBAND!
THEY SOUNDED JEALOUS OF US...THOUGH THAT SEEMS IMPOSSIBLE! ANYWAY, THEY HAVE NO RIGHT TO ORDER US TO DISBAND!
BUT WHEN THE ULTIMATUM TIME-LIMIT EXPIRES, THERE COMES A SURPRISE...
THE SUPER-HEROES MEANT IT! THEY'VE SENT ONE OF THEIR FORCE VORTEXES TO WRECK OUR CLUBHOUSE AND DRIVE US OUT!
IT'LL DESTROY OUR SPACE-SHIP UNLESS WE TAKE OFF AT ONCE... BUT THE FORCE VORTEX BLOCKS THE ONLY WAY OUT!
7

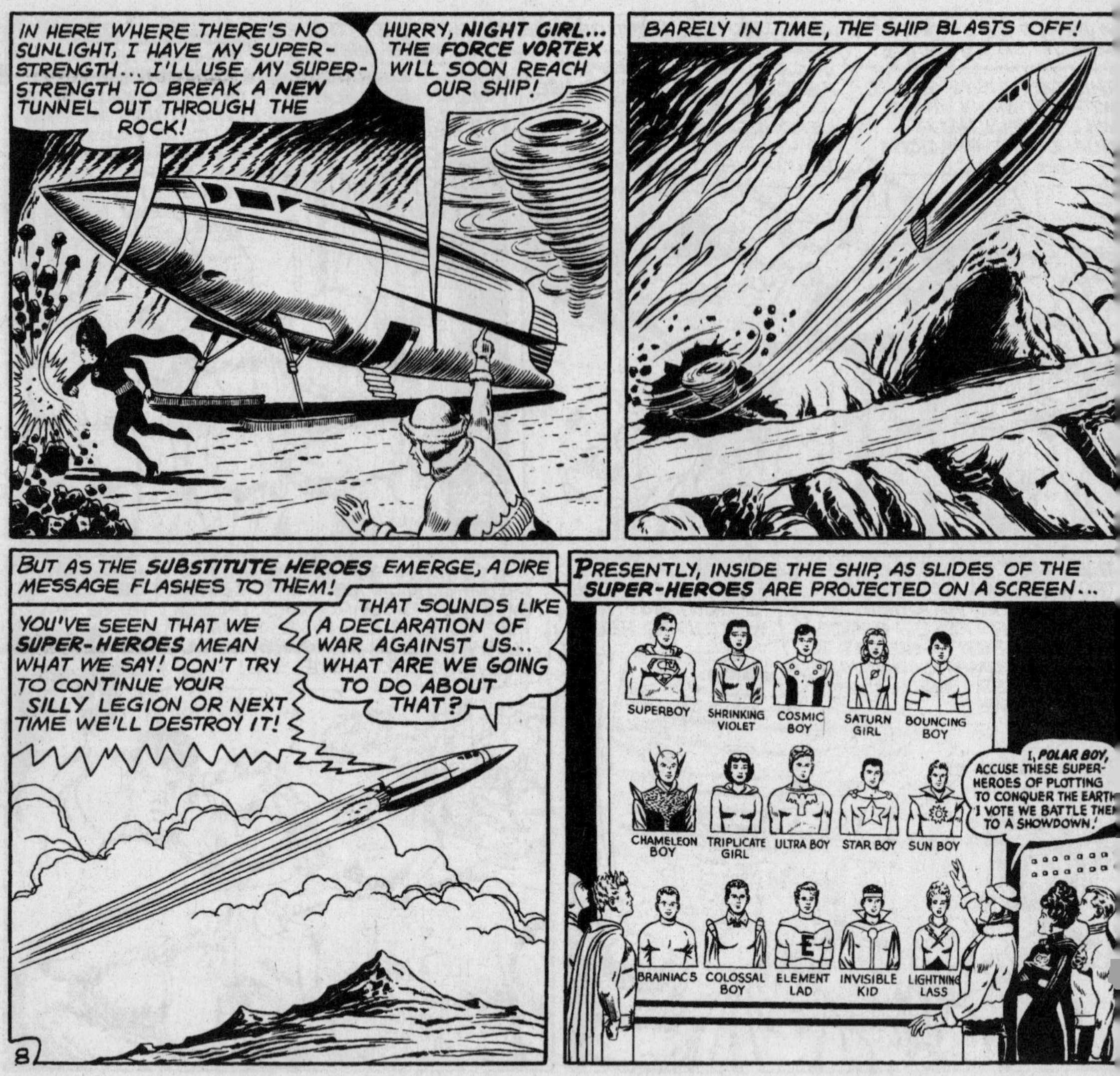
IN HERE WHERE THERE'S NO SUNLIGHT, I HAVE MY SUPER-STRENGTH... I'LL USE MY SUPER-STRENGTH TO BREAK A NEW TUNNEL OUT THROUGH THE ROCK!
HURRY, NIGHT GIRL... THE FORCE VORTEX WILL SOON REACH OUR SHIP!
BARELY IN TIME, THE SHIP BLASTS OFF!
BUT AS THE SUBSTITUTE HEROES EMERGE, A DIRE MESSAGE FLASHES TO THEM!
YOU'VE SEEN THAT WE SUPER-HEROES MEAN WHAT WE SAY! DON'T TRY TO CONTINUE YOUR SILLY LEGION OR NEXT TIME WE'LL DESTROY IT!
THAT SOUNDS LIKE A DECLARATION OF WAR AGAINST US... WHAT ARE WE GOING TO DO ABOUT THAT?
8
PRESENTLY, INSIDE THE SHIP, AS SLIDES OF THE SUPER-HEROES ARE PROJECTED ON A SCREEN...
SUPERBOY
SHRINKING VIOLET
COSMIC BOY
SATURN GIRL
BOUNCING BOY
CHAMELEON BOY
TRIPLICATE GIRL
ULTRA BOY
STAR BOY
SUN BOY
BRAINIAC 5
COLOSSAL BOY
ELEMENT LAD
INVISIBLE KID
LIGHTNING LASS
I, POLAR BOY, ACCUSE THESE SUPER-HEROES OF PLOTTING TO CONQUER THE EART I VOTE WE BATTLE THE TO A SHOWDOWN!

LEGION of SUPER-HEROES

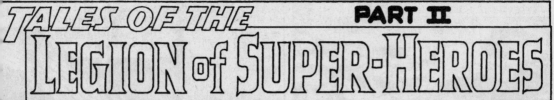

TALES OF THE LEGION of SUPER-HEROES

PART II

A DARK MENACE THAT HAS REACHED TOWARD EARTH FROM DISTANT SPACE HAS HAD FATEFUL CONSEQUENCES! FOR NOW IT SEEMS THAT THE *LEGION OF SUPER-HEROES* IS SO JEALOUS OVER THE SUCCESS OF THE *SUBSTITUTE HEROES* IN CHECKING THAT MENACE, THAT THEY'RE RESOLVED TO DESTROY THEIR DEVOTED ADMIRERS! AND THE WORLD IS ROCKED BY A COSMIC STRUGGLE TO THE DEATH IN...

"The DUEL of the LEGIONS!"

THE *SUPER-HEROES* SENT THAT MECHANICAL MONSTER TO DESTROY US... AND IT'S KILLED **STONE BOY!** TURNING HIMSELF INTO **SOLID ROCK** DIDN'T SAVE HIM!

AWAY FROM EARTH FLEE THE *LEGION OF SUBSTITUTE HEROES!*

FIRST, WE'LL HAVE TO FIND A NEW BASE AND KEEP IT SECRET FROM OUR ENEMIES, THE *SUPER-HEROES!* THE MOON IS THE PLACE!

⑨

BUT THERE'S NO HIDING PLACE ON THE BARREN MOON!

NOT ON IT, BUT *IN* IT! IT'S LONG BEEN KNOWN THAT THERE ARE GREAT FISSURES AND CAVERNS THAT HONEY—COMB THE MOON'S INTERIOR!

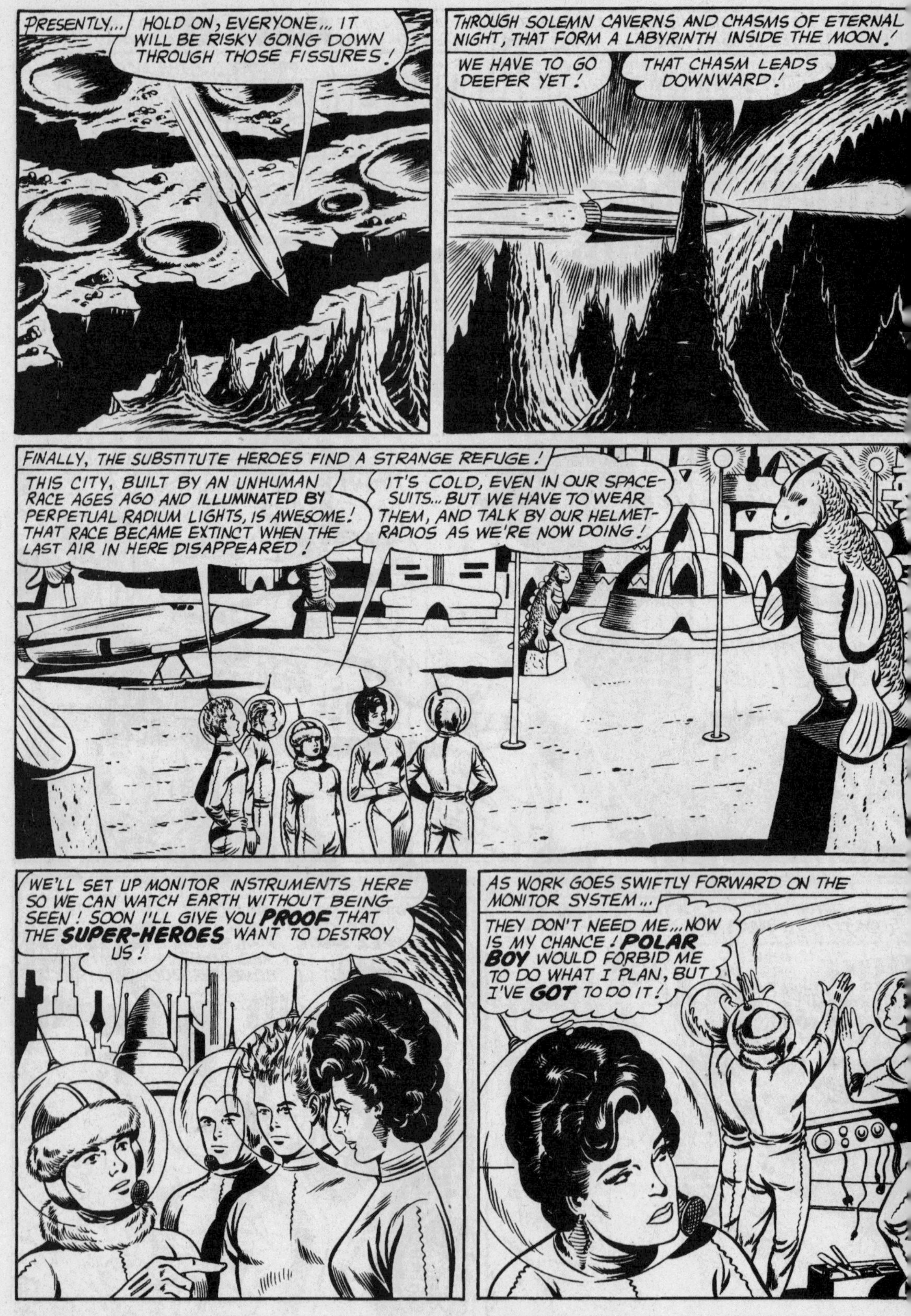
PRESENTLY...
HOLD ON, EVERYONE... IT WILL BE RISKY GOING DOWN THROUGH THOSE FISSURES!
THROUGH SOLEMN CAVERNS AND CHASMS OF ETERNAL NIGHT, THAT FORM A LABYRINTH INSIDE THE MOON!
WE HAVE TO GO DEEPER YET!
THAT CHASM LEADS DOWNWARD!
FINALLY, THE SUBSTITUTE HEROES FIND A STRANGE REFUGE!
THIS CITY, BUILT BY AN UNHUMAN RACE AGES AGO AND ILLUMINATED BY PERPETUAL RADIUM LIGHTS, IS AWESOME! THAT RACE BECAME EXTINCT WHEN THE LAST AIR IN HERE DISAPPEARED!
IT'S COLD, EVEN IN OUR SPACE-SUITS... BUT WE HAVE TO WEAR THEM, AND TALK BY OUR HELMET-RADIOS AS WE'RE NOW DOING!
WE'LL SET UP MONITOR INSTRUMENTS HERE SO WE CAN WATCH EARTH WITHOUT BEING SEEN! SOON I'LL GIVE YOU PROOF THAT THE SUPER-HEROES WANT TO DESTROY US!
AS WORK GOES SWIFTLY FORWARD ON THE MONITOR SYSTEM...
THEY DON'T NEED ME... NOW IS MY CHANCE! POLAR BOY WOULD FORBID ME TO DO WHAT I PLAN, BUT I'VE GOT TO DO IT!

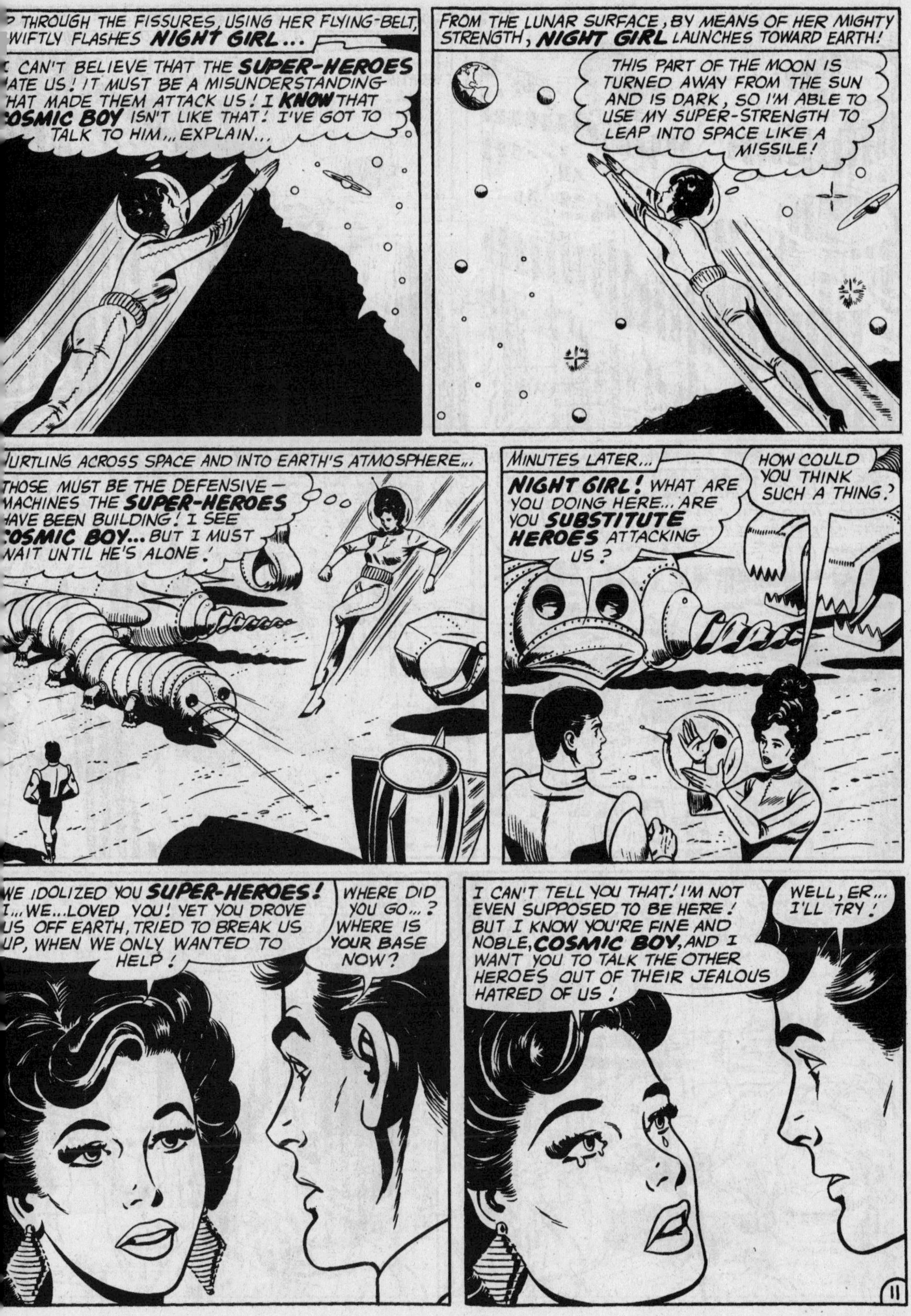
P THROUGH THE FISSURES, USING HER FLYING-BELT, WIFTLY FLASHES NIGHT GIRL...
I CAN'T BELIEVE THAT THE SUPER-HEROES HATE US! IT MUST BE A MISUNDERSTANDING THAT MADE THEM ATTACK US! I KNOW THAT COSMIC BOY ISN'T LIKE THAT! I'VE GOT TO TALK TO HIM... EXPLAIN...
FROM THE LUNAR SURFACE, BY MEANS OF HER MIGHTY STRENGTH, NIGHT GIRL LAUNCHES TOWARD EARTH!
THIS PART OF THE MOON IS TURNED AWAY FROM THE SUN AND IS DARK, SO I'M ABLE TO USE MY SUPER-STRENGTH TO LEAP INTO SPACE LIKE A MISSILE!
HURTLING ACROSS SPACE AND INTO EARTH'S ATMOSPHERE...
THOSE MUST BE THE DEFENSIVE-MACHINES THE SUPER-HEROES HAVE BEEN BUILDING! I SEE COSMIC BOY... BUT I MUST WAIT UNTIL HE'S ALONE!
MINUTES LATER...
NIGHT GIRL! WHAT ARE YOU DOING HERE... ARE YOU SUBSTITUTE HEROES ATTACKING US?
HOW COULD YOU THINK SUCH A THING?
WE IDOLIZED YOU SUPER-HEROES! I... WE... LOVED YOU! YET YOU DROVE US OFF EARTH, TRIED TO BREAK US UP, WHEN WE ONLY WANTED TO HELP!
WHERE DID YOU GO...? WHERE IS YOUR BASE NOW?
I CAN'T TELL YOU THAT! I'M NOT EVEN SUPPOSED TO BE HERE! BUT I KNOW YOU'RE FINE AND NOBLE, COSMIC BOY, AND I WANT YOU TO TALK THE OTHER HEROES OUT OF THEIR JEALOUS HATRED OF US!
WELL, ER... I'LL TRY!
11

I KNEW YOU WOULD! I MUST GO, NOW... PLEASE PROMISE NOT TO TRY TO TRACE ME IN ANY WAY!

I PROMISE!

BUT NO SOONER HAS *NIGHT GIRL* DEPARTED...

...AND I PROMISED NOT TO TRACE HER, AND THE SILLY GIRL BELIEVED MY PROMISE! BUT OF COURSE WE'LL TRACE HER! WE'LL GET A SUPER-RADAR LOCK ON HER AND SEE WHERE SHE GOES!

AT ONCE.

Shortly... SO *THAT'S* WHERE THE *SUBSTITUTE HEROES* HAVE HIDDEN THEIR BASE... INSIDE THE LUNAR FISSURES AND CAVERNS!

THEIR CONTINUAL INTERFERENCE MUST BE STOPPED! AND I KNOW HOW TO DO IT!

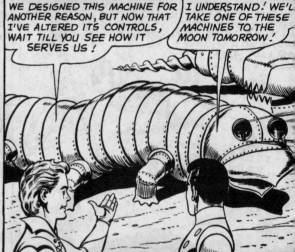

WE DESIGNED THIS MACHINE FOR ANOTHER REASON, BUT NOW THAT I'VE ALTERED ITS CONTROLS, WAIT TILL YOU SEE HOW IT SERVES US!

I UNDERSTAND! WE'L TAKE ONE OF THESE MACHINES TO THE MOON TOMORROW!

AND NEXT DAY, ON THE MOON...

THE *SUBSTITUTE HEROES* HAVE SUPER-POWERS AND COULD BE DANGEROUS WHEN CORNERED! BUT THIS MACHINE IS NOW PROGRAMMED SO IT'LL HUNT THEM IN THE CAVERNS, WITHOUT DANGER TO US!

A SPLENDID IDEA! WE WON'T HAVE TO GO DOWN INTO THOSE COLD CAVERNS!

LOOK! OUR MONITOR SHOWS THE *SUPER-HEROES'* SHIP ON THE SURFACE ABOVE! THEY MUST HAVE LOCATED US, SOMEHOW!

COSMIC BOY MUST HAV TRACED ME... BUT HE PROMISED HE WOULDN' HE *COULDN'T* BREAK A PROMISE LIKE THAT!

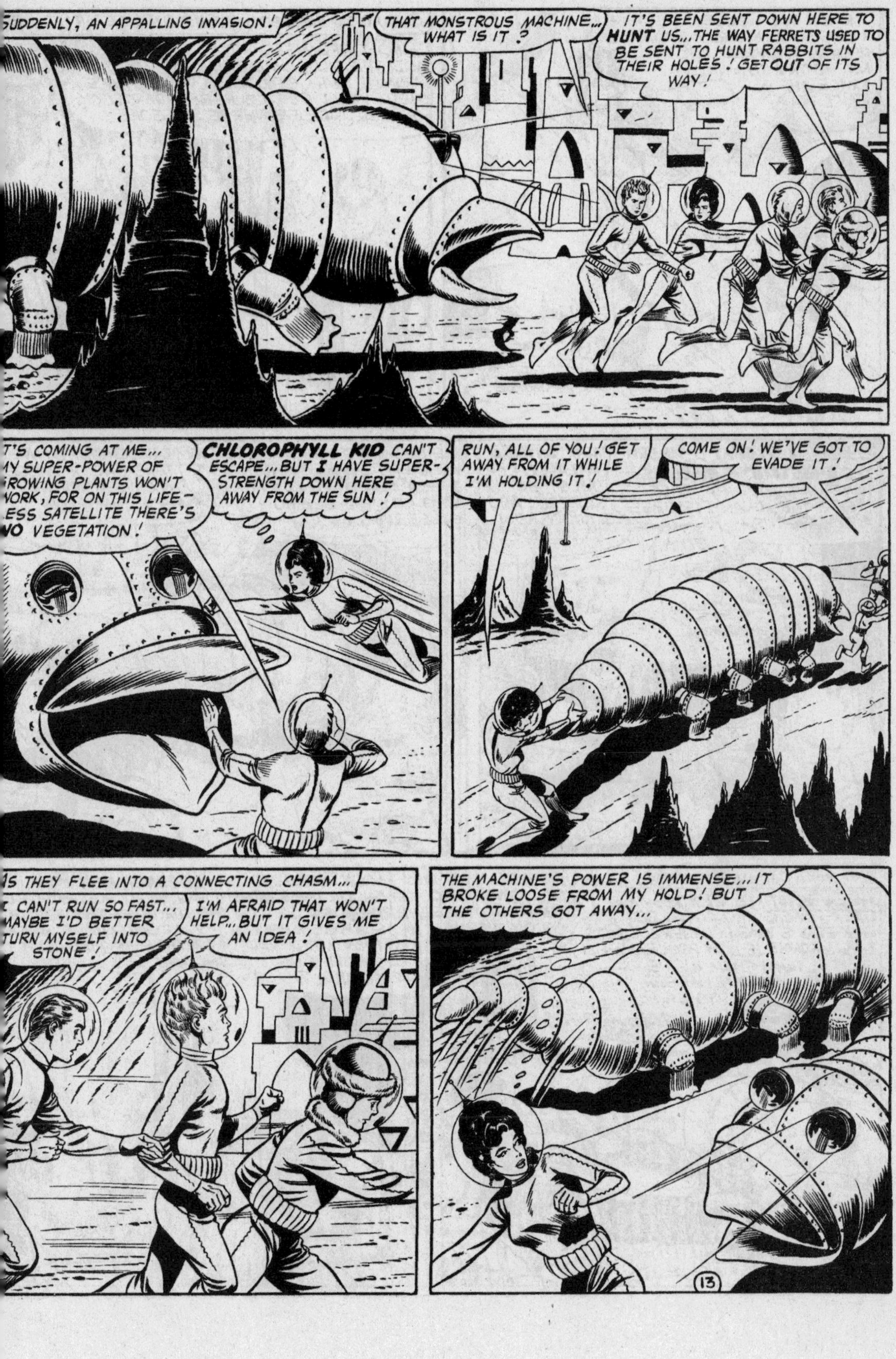
SUDDENLY, AN APPALLING INVASION!
THAT MONSTROUS MACHINE... WHAT IS IT?
IT'S BEEN SENT DOWN HERE TO HUNT US...THE WAY FERRETS USED TO BE SENT TO HUNT RABBITS IN THEIR HOLES! GET OUT OF ITS WAY!
IT'S COMING AT ME... MY SUPER-POWER OF GROWING PLANTS WON'T WORK, FOR ON THIS LIFELESS SATELLITE THERE'S NO VEGETATION!
CHLOROPHYLL KID CAN'T ESCAPE...BUT I HAVE SUPER-STRENGTH DOWN HERE AWAY FROM THE SUN!
RUN, ALL OF YOU! GET AWAY FROM IT WHILE I'M HOLDING IT!
COME ON! WE'VE GOT TO EVADE IT!
AS THEY FLEE INTO A CONNECTING CHASM...
I CAN'T RUN SO FAST... MAYBE I'D BETTER TURN MYSELF INTO STONE!
I'M AFRAID THAT WON'T HELP...BUT IT GIVES ME AN IDEA!
THE MACHINE'S POWER IS IMMENSE...IT BROKE LOOSE FROM MY HOLD! BUT THE OTHERS GOT AWAY...
13

IT'S FOLLOWING ME, BUT I CAN KEEP AHEAD...OH-OH...THERE'S *STONE BOY!* HE TURNED HIMSELF INTO SOLID ROCK, BUT THAT WON'T SAVE HIM!

JUST AS I FEARED! IT'S GOT *STONE BOY...* IT'S CRUSHED HIS PETRIFIED BODY...OH, NO!

NOW IT'S TAKING *STONE BOY'S* BROKEN BODY BACK TO THE SURFACE...FOLLOWING ITS PROGRAMMED ORDERS! IT'S MY FAULT! BECAUSE I LOVED AND TRUSTED *COSMIC BOY*, MY COMRADE IS DEAD!

AND SOON, ON THE LUNAR SURFACE...

THAT'S *STONE BOY!* THE FOOL! TURNING HIM-SELF TO STONE DIDN'T SAVE HIM!

THE MACHINE MUST'VE WIPED OUT THE OTHER *SUBSTITUTE HEROES*, TOO! WELL, THAT'S THE END OF THEIR INTER-FERENCE! NOW WE CAN RETURN TO OUR WORK ON EARTH!

BUT AT THAT MOMENT, IN THE CAVERN BELOW...

*STONE BOY...*ALIVE! BUT I SAW THE THING TAKE YOUR PETRIFIED BODY AWAY!

THAT WAS A *STATUE* OF *STONE BOY* YOU SAW! TO FOOL THE MACHINE, WE USED OUR RAY-GUNS TO CARVE AND THEN RETOUCH ONE OF THE ALIEN STATUES, FIGURING IT WOULD DECEIVE THE MACHINE AND THE *SUPER-HEROES*, TOO!

IT FOOLED THEM, ALL RIGHT...THE *SUPER-HEROES* ARE GOING BACK TO EARTH! I'D NEVER HAVE BELIEVED THEY WOULD WANT TO KILL US!

IT SUPPORTS WHAT I'VE SUSPECTED! A TERRIBLE DANGER THREATENS EARTH, IF I'M RIGHT! WE'VE GOT TO WORK FAST AND BUILD A *SECOND* SPACE-SHIP!

BEFORE LONG, IN THE CLUBHOUSE OF THE SUPER-HEROES ON EARTH, THERE'S AN ALARM!

WE WERE TRICKED! WE DIDN'T DESTROY THE SUBSTITUTE HEROES AFTER ALL! FOR LOOK, A SHIP IS HEADING OUT FROM THE MOON... TOWARD SPACE SECTOR Z-4437-3N!

THEY MUSTN'T GO THERE...IT WOULD RUIN EVERYTHING!

ALL OF YOU...TO OUR SHIP! WE MUST OVERTAKE THEM BEFORE THEY REACH THAT DISTANT SECTOR! EVERYTHING DEPENDS ON IT!

AS A TERRIFIC PURSUIT INTO FAR SPACE GOES FORWARD...

I DON'T UNDERSTAND, POLAR BOY! YOU SENT THAT NEW SHIP WE BUILT INTO FAR SPACE ON AUTOMATIC CONTROL...WITH NO ONE IN IT! WHY?

IT WAS A BAIT, TO LURE THE SUPER-HEROES AWAY FROM EARTH, AND THEY FOLLOWED IT! LOOK...ON THE MONITOR...LOOK!

THE SUPER-HEROES THOUGHT WE WERE IN THAT SHIP, AND THEY DESTROYED IT! AND COSMIC BOY HELPED DO IT ...OH!

NOW, BEFORE THEY RETURN FROM SPACE, IS OUR CHANCE! WE'RE GOING BACK TO EARTH, TO THE SUPER-HEROES' BASE!

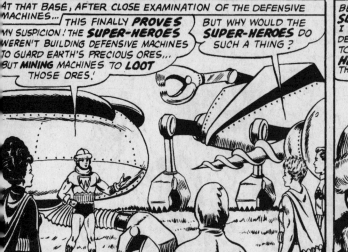

AT THAT BASE, AFTER CLOSE EXAMINATION OF THE DEFENSIVE MACHINES...

THIS FINALLY PROVES MY SUSPICION! THE SUPER-HEROES WEREN'T BUILDING DEFENSIVE MACHINES TO GUARD EARTH'S PRECIOUS ORES... BUT MINING MACHINES TO LOOT THOSE ORES!

BUT WHY WOULD THE SUPER-HEROES DO SUCH A THING?

BECAUSE THEY'RE NOT THE SUPER-HEROES AT ALL! I SUSPECTED IT WHEN THEY DESTROYED OUR BASE AND TRIED TO KILL US...FOR THE REAL SUPER-HEROES WOULD NEVER DO THAT! THESE MACHINES PROVE THEY'RE IMPOSTORS!

SO YOU NOW KNOW THE TRUTH!

15

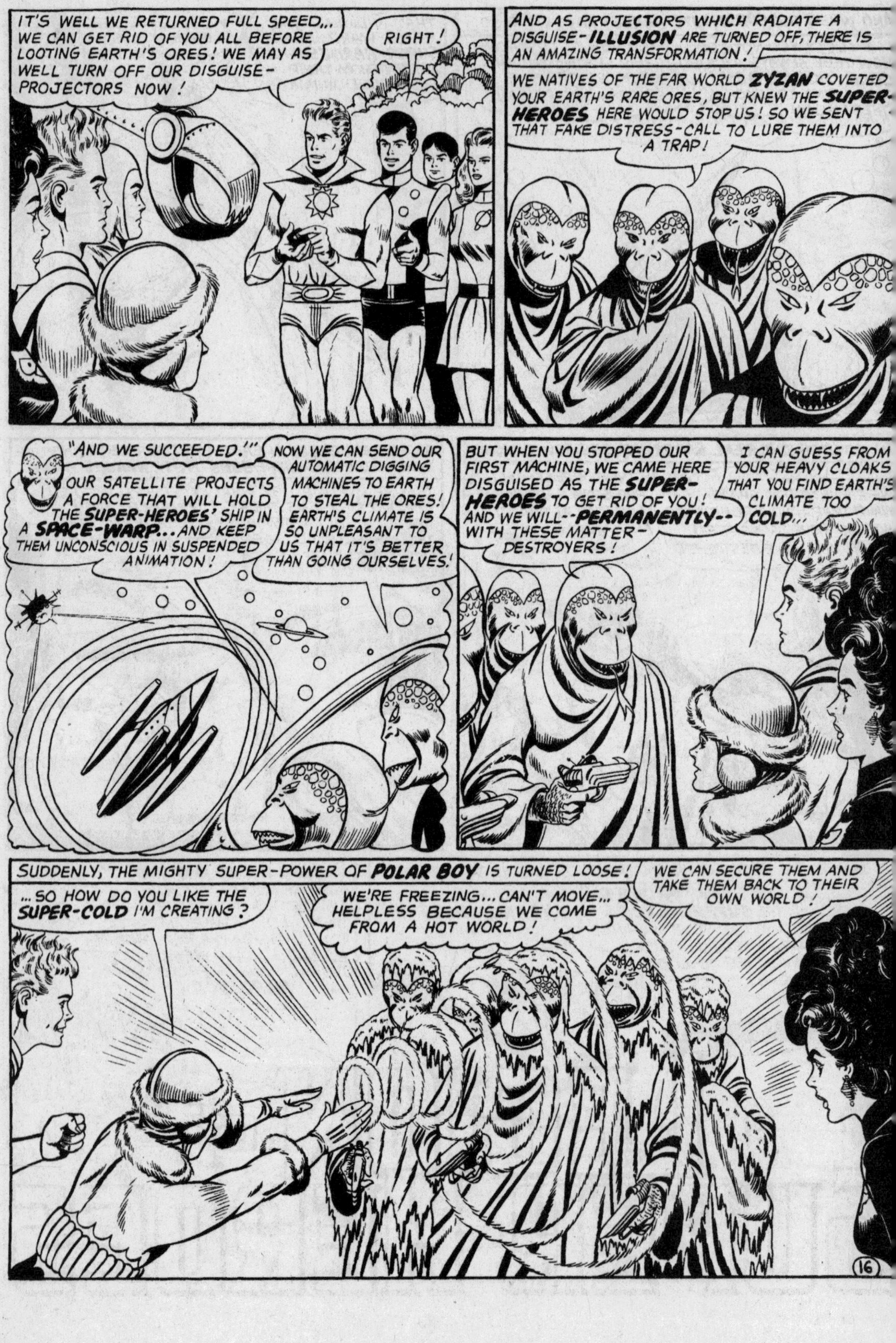
IT'S WELL WE RETURNED FULL SPEED... WE CAN GET RID OF YOU ALL BEFORE LOOTING EARTH'S ORES! WE MAY AS WELL TURN OFF OUR DISGUISE-PROJECTORS NOW!
RIGHT!
AND AS PROJECTORS WHICH RADIATE A DISGUISE-ILLUSION ARE TURNED OFF, THERE IS AN AMAZING TRANSFORMATION!
WE NATIVES OF THE FAR WORLD ZYZAN COVETED YOUR EARTH'S RARE ORES, BUT KNEW THE SUPER-HEROES HERE WOULD STOP US! SO WE SENT THAT FAKE DISTRESS-CALL TO LURE THEM INTO A TRAP!
"AND WE SUCCEEDED."
OUR SATELLITE PROJECTS A FORCE THAT WILL HOLD THE SUPER-HEROES' SHIP IN A SPACE-WARP...AND KEEP THEM UNCONSCIOUS IN SUSPENDED ANIMATION!
NOW WE CAN SEND OUR AUTOMATIC DIGGING MACHINES TO EARTH TO STEAL THE ORES! EARTH'S CLIMATE IS SO UNPLEASANT TO US THAT IT'S BETTER THAN GOING OURSELVES!
BUT WHEN YOU STOPPED OUR FIRST MACHINE, WE CAME HERE DISGUISED AS THE SUPER-HEROES TO GET RID OF YOU! AND WE WILL--PERMANENTLY--WITH THESE MATTER-DESTROYERS!
I CAN GUESS FROM YOUR HEAVY CLOAKS THAT YOU FIND EARTH'S CLIMATE TOO COLD...
SUDDENLY, THE MIGHTY SUPER-POWER OF POLAR BOY IS TURNED LOOSE!
...SO HOW DO YOU LIKE THE SUPER-COLD I'M CREATING?
WE'RE FREEZING... CAN'T MOVE... HELPLESS BECAUSE WE COME FROM A HOT WORLD!
WE CAN SECURE THEM AND TAKE THEM BACK TO THEIR OWN WORLD!
16

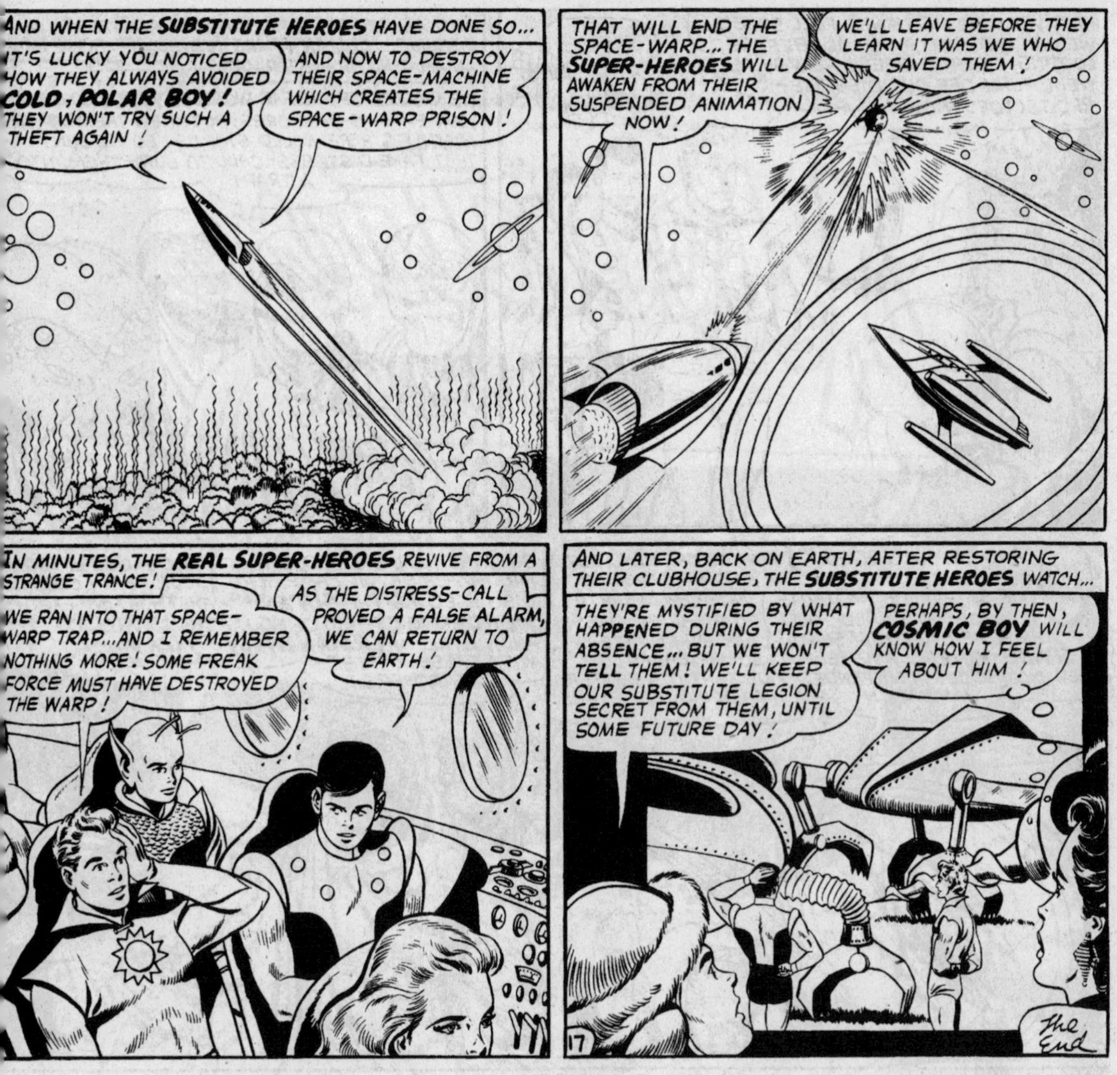
AND WHEN THE SUBSTITUTE HEROES HAVE DONE SO...
IT'S LUCKY YOU NOTICED HOW THEY ALWAYS AVOIDED COLD, POLAR BOY! THEY WON'T TRY SUCH A THEFT AGAIN!
AND NOW TO DESTROY THEIR SPACE-MACHINE WHICH CREATES THE SPACE-WARP PRISON!
THAT WILL END THE SPACE-WARP... THE SUPER-HEROES WILL AWAKEN FROM THEIR SUSPENDED ANIMATION NOW!
WE'LL LEAVE BEFORE THEY LEARN IT WAS WE WHO SAVED THEM!
IN MINUTES, THE REAL SUPER-HEROES REVIVE FROM A STRANGE TRANCE!
WE RAN INTO THAT SPACE-WARP TRAP...AND I REMEMBER NOTHING MORE! SOME FREAK FORCE MUST HAVE DESTROYED THE WARP!
AS THE DISTRESS-CALL PROVED A FALSE ALARM, WE CAN RETURN TO EARTH!
AND LATER, BACK ON EARTH, AFTER RESTORING THEIR CLUBHOUSE, THE SUBSTITUTE HEROES WATCH...
THEY'RE MYSTIFIED BY WHAT HAPPENED DURING THEIR ABSENCE... BUT WE WON'T TELL THEM! WE'LL KEEP OUR SUBSTITUTE LEGION SECRET FROM THEM, UNTIL SOME FUTURE DAY!
PERHAPS, BY THEN, COSMIC BOY WILL KNOW HOW I FEEL ABOUT HIM!
17
The End

LEGION of SUPER-HEROES

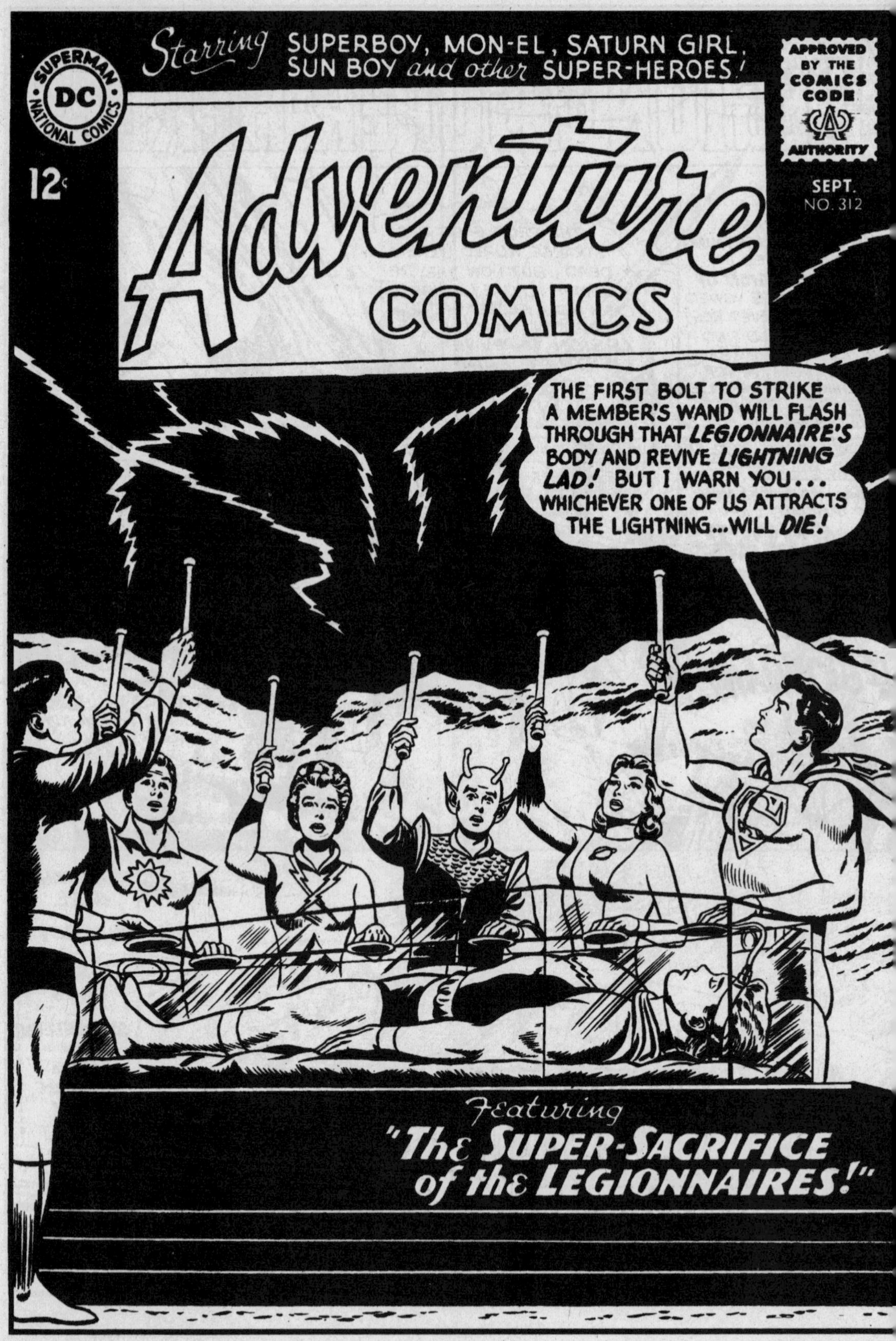
Starring SUPERBOY, MON-EL, SATURN GIRL, SUN BOY and other SUPER-HEROES!
SUPERMAN DC NATIONAL COMICS
APPROVED BY THE COMICS CODE AUTHORITY
12¢
Adventure COMICS
SEPT. NO. 312
THE FIRST BOLT TO STRIKE A MEMBER'S WAND WILL FLASH THROUGH THAT LEGIONNAIRE'S BODY AND REVIVE LIGHTNING LAD! BUT I WARN YOU... WHICHEVER ONE OF US ATTRACTS THE LIGHTNING...WILL DIE!
Featuring "The SUPER-SACRIFICE of the LEGIONNAIRES!"

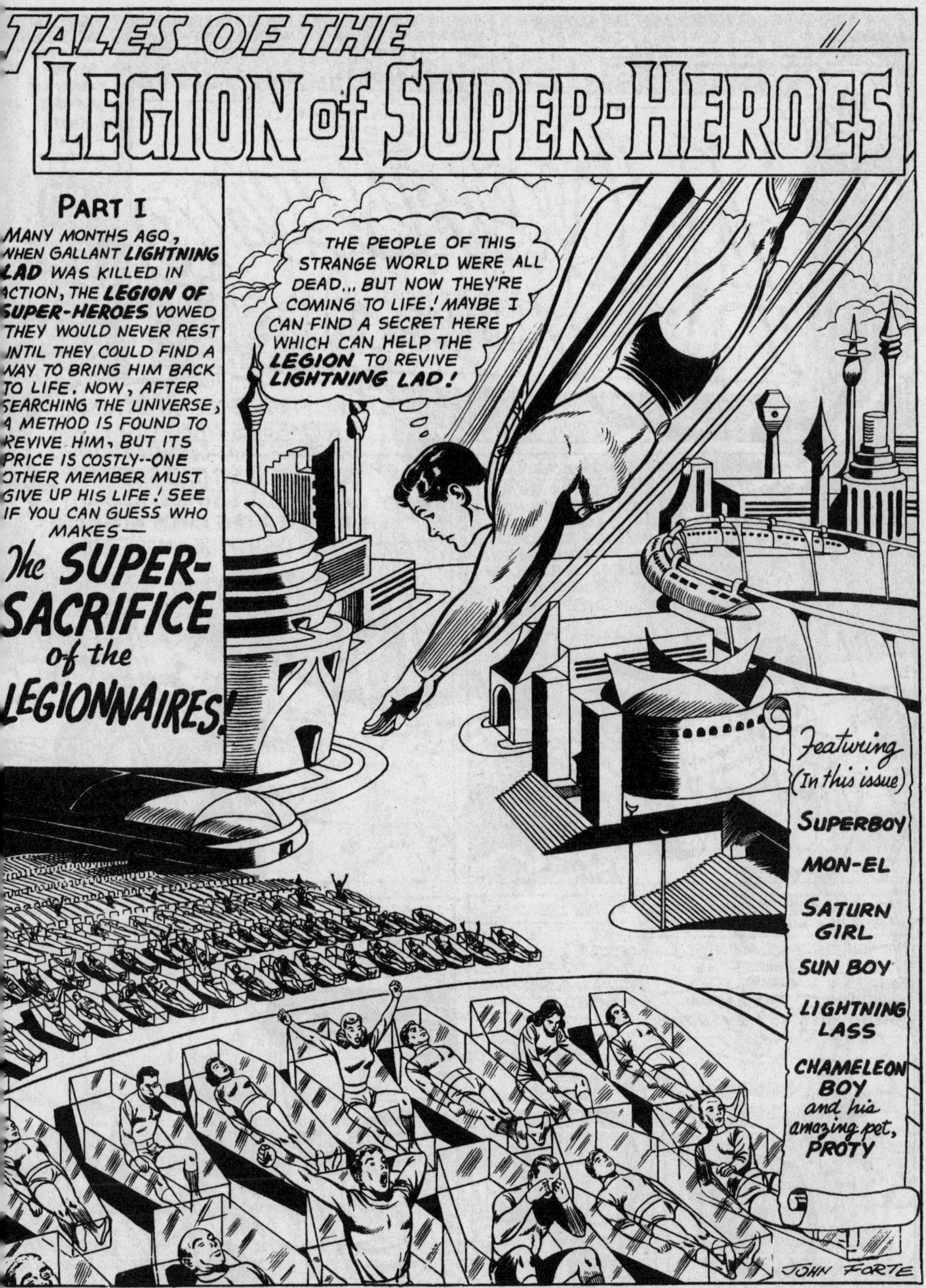
TALES OF THE
LEGION of SUPER-HEROES
PART I
MANY MONTHS AGO, WHEN GALLANT LIGHTNING LAD WAS KILLED IN ACTION, THE LEGION OF SUPER-HEROES VOWED THEY WOULD NEVER REST UNTIL THEY COULD FIND A WAY TO BRING HIM BACK TO LIFE. NOW, AFTER SEARCHING THE UNIVERSE, A METHOD IS FOUND TO REVIVE HIM, BUT ITS PRICE IS COSTLY--ONE OTHER MEMBER MUST GIVE UP HIS LIFE! SEE IF YOU CAN GUESS WHO MAKES—
The SUPER-SACRIFICE of the LEGIONNAIRES!
THE PEOPLE OF THIS STRANGE WORLD WERE ALL DEAD... BUT NOW THEY'RE COMING TO LIFE! MAYBE I CAN FIND A SECRET HERE WHICH CAN HELP THE LEGION TO REVIVE LIGHTNING LAD!
Featuring (In this issue)
SUPERBOY
MON-EL
SATURN GIRL
SUN BOY
LIGHTNING LASS
CHAMELEON BOY and his amazing pet, PROTY
JOHN FORTE

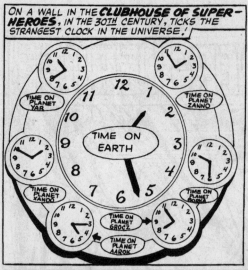

ON A WALL IN THE **CLUBHOUSE OF SUPER-HEROES**, IN THE 30TH CENTURY, TICKS THE STRANGEST CLOCK IN THE UNIVERSE!

TIME ON PLANET YAR
TIME ON PLANET ZANNO
TIME ON EARTH
TIME ON PLANET XANDO
TIME ON PLANET BORRA
TIME ON PLANET GROCZ
TIME ON PLANET AAROK

AND WITH EACH TICK OF THE CLOCK, THE SUPER-HEROES WHO ARE NOT AWAY ON ACTIVE SERVICE GROW MORE TENSE

OH, **SUPERBOY**, WHY DOESN'T **MON-EL** COME? I CAN'T BEAR THIS WAITING, WHEN IT MEANS LIFE OR DEATH!

I KNOW, **LIGHTNING LAS** WE ALL FEEL THE SAME WAY! BUT **MON-EL** SHOULD BE HERE SOON!

LIGHTNING LASS
SUN BOY
CHAMELEON BOY
SUPERBOY

A MOMENT AFTER **SUPERBOY** SPEAKS **MON-EL'S** NAME...

WHY, THERE'S **MON-EL** NOW...RIGHT BESIDE **CHAMELEON BOY!**

SORRY, BUT IT'S ONLY MY PET, **PROTY!** YOU KNOW, HE HAS CHAMELEON POWERS LIKE MINE AND CAN CHANGE HIS **PROTOPLASM** FORM TO IMITATE ANYTHING OR ANYONE! BEING TELEPATHIC, HE CAUGHT YOUR THOUGHT OF **MON-EL** AND IMITATED HIM!

SUN BOY
CHAM

QUIT IT AND CHANGE BACK TO NORMAL, **PROTY**...THAT'S AN ORDER!

I CAN HEAR A SHIP COMING, WITH MY SUPER-HEARING...AND WITH MY SUPER-VISION, I CAN SEE IT'S **MON-EL'S!**

CHAMELEON BOY
SUPERBOY

AND WHEN **MON-EL** ARRIVES, THE TENSE LEGION-NAIRES ASK A FATEFUL QUESTION!

DID YOU SUCCEED, **MON-EL?** DID YOU FIND, AMONG THE SCIENTIFIC WIZARDS OF YOUR HOME WORLD, **DAXAM**, A WAY TO RESTORE **LIGHTNING LAD** TO LIFE?

TELL US! YOU ONCE VOWED NEVER TO REST UNTIL YOU COULD FIND A WAY TO REVIVE HIM!

I'M SORRY TO REPORT THIS...BUT I FOUND NO WAY WE CAN USE TO BRING **LIGHTNING LAD** BACK TO LIFE!

THEN MY BROTHER IS GONE, FOREVER!

THIS IS SAD NEWS...AND IT'LL BE A TERRIBLE SHOCK TO **SATURN GIRL**

2

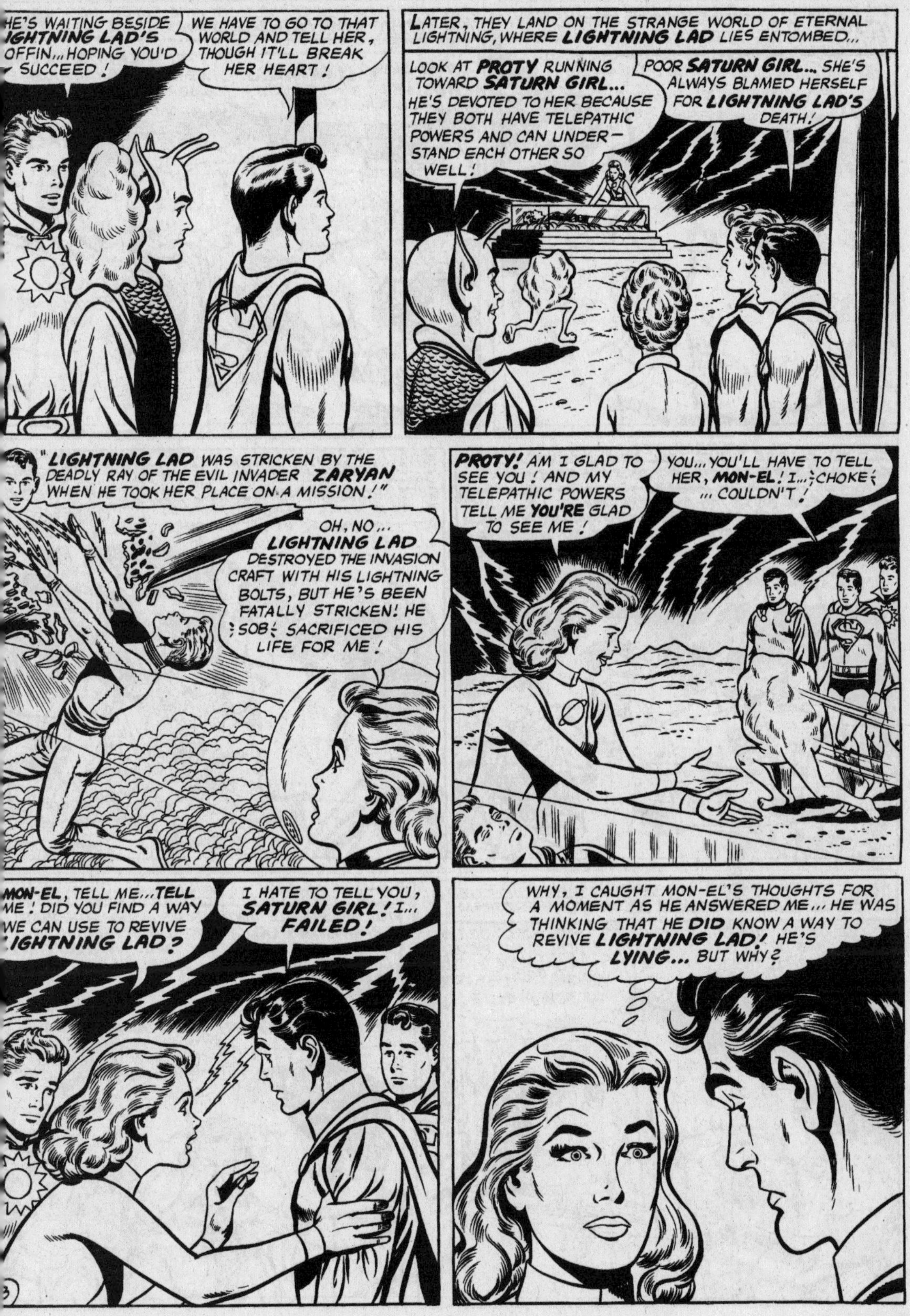
HE'S WAITING BESIDE LIGHTNING LAD'S OFFIN... HOPING YOU'D SUCCEED!
WE HAVE TO GO TO THAT WORLD AND TELL HER, THOUGH IT'LL BREAK HER HEART!
LATER, THEY LAND ON THE STRANGE WORLD OF ETERNAL LIGHTNING, WHERE LIGHTNING LAD LIES ENTOMBED...
LOOK AT PROTY RUNNING TOWARD SATURN GIRL... HE'S DEVOTED TO HER BECAUSE THEY BOTH HAVE TELEPATHIC POWERS AND CAN UNDER-STAND EACH OTHER SO WELL!
POOR SATURN GIRL... SHE'S ALWAYS BLAMED HERSELF FOR LIGHTNING LAD'S DEATH!
"LIGHTNING LAD WAS STRICKEN BY THE DEADLY RAY OF THE EVIL INVADER ZARYAN WHEN HE TOOK HER PLACE ON A MISSION!"
OH, NO... LIGHTNING LAD DESTROYED THE INVASION CRAFT WITH HIS LIGHTNING BOLTS, BUT HE'S BEEN FATALLY STRICKEN! HE ;SOB; SACRIFICED HIS LIFE FOR ME!
PROTY! AM I GLAD TO SEE YOU! AND MY TELEPATHIC POWERS TELL ME YOU'RE GLAD TO SEE ME!
YOU... YOU'LL HAVE TO TELL HER, MON-EL! I... ;CHOKE; ... COULDN'T!
MON-EL, TELL ME... TELL ME! DID YOU FIND A WAY WE CAN USE TO REVIVE LIGHTNING LAD?
I HATE TO TELL YOU, SATURN GIRL! I... FAILED!
WHY, I CAUGHT MON-EL'S THOUGHTS FOR A MOMENT AS HE ANSWERED ME... HE WAS THINKING THAT HE DID KNOW A WAY TO REVIVE LIGHTNING LAD! HE'S LYING... BUT WHY?

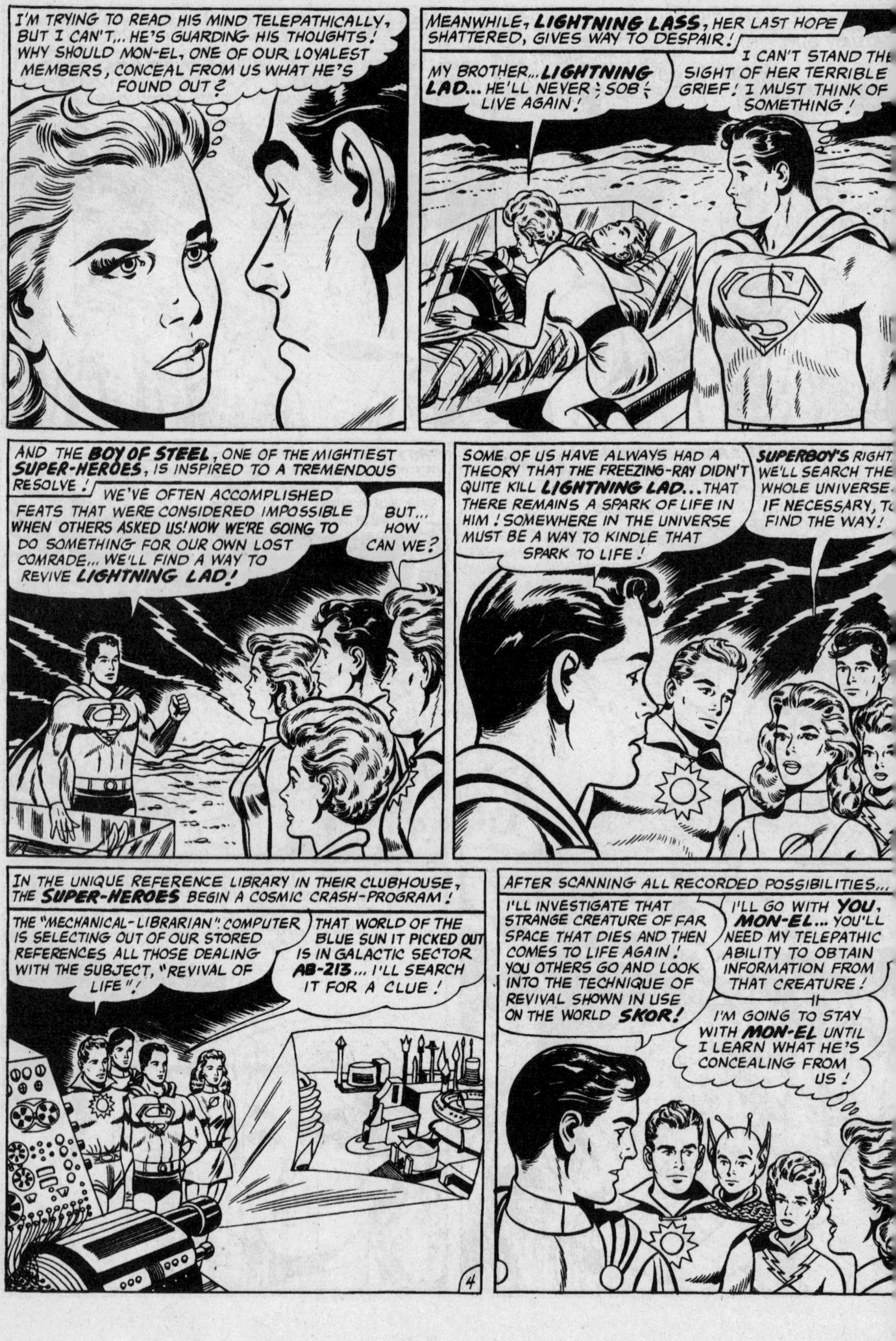
I'M TRYING TO READ HIS MIND TELEPATHICALLY, BUT I CAN'T... HE'S GUARDING HIS THOUGHTS! WHY SHOULD MON-EL, ONE OF OUR LOYALEST MEMBERS, CONCEAL FROM US WHAT HE'S FOUND OUT?
MEANWHILE, LIGHTNING LASS, HER LAST HOPE SHATTERED, GIVES WAY TO DESPAIR!
MY BROTHER... LIGHTNING LAD... HE'LL NEVER -SOB- LIVE AGAIN!
I CAN'T STAND THE SIGHT OF HER TERRIBLE GRIEF! I MUST THINK OF SOMETHING!
AND THE BOY OF STEEL, ONE OF THE MIGHTIEST SUPER-HEROES, IS INSPIRED TO A TREMENDOUS RESOLVE!
WE'VE OFTEN ACCOMPLISHED FEATS THAT WERE CONSIDERED IMPOSSIBLE WHEN OTHERS ASKED US! NOW WE'RE GOING TO DO SOMETHING FOR OUR OWN LOST COMRADE... WE'LL FIND A WAY TO REVIVE LIGHTNING LAD!
BUT... HOW CAN WE?
SOME OF US HAVE ALWAYS HAD A THEORY THAT THE FREEZING-RAY DIDN'T QUITE KILL LIGHTNING LAD... THAT THERE REMAINS A SPARK OF LIFE IN HIM! SOMEWHERE IN THE UNIVERSE MUST BE A WAY TO KINDLE THAT SPARK TO LIFE!
SUPERBOY'S RIGHT. WE'LL SEARCH THE WHOLE UNIVERSE, IF NECESSARY, TO FIND THE WAY!
IN THE UNIQUE REFERENCE LIBRARY IN THEIR CLUBHOUSE, THE SUPER-HEROES BEGIN A COSMIC CRASH-PROGRAM!
THE "MECHANICAL-LIBRARIAN" COMPUTER IS SELECTING OUT OF OUR STORED REFERENCES ALL THOSE DEALING WITH THE SUBJECT, "REVIVAL OF LIFE"!
THAT WORLD OF THE BLUE SUN IT PICKED OUT IS IN GALACTIC SECTOR AB-213... I'LL SEARCH IT FOR A CLUE!
4
AFTER SCANNING ALL RECORDED POSSIBILITIES...
I'LL INVESTIGATE THAT STRANGE CREATURE OF FAR SPACE THAT DIES AND THEN COMES TO LIFE AGAIN! YOU OTHERS GO AND LOOK INTO THE TECHNIQUE OF REVIVAL SHOWN IN USE ON THE WORLD SKOR!
I'LL GO WITH YOU, MON-EL... YOU'LL NEED MY TELEPATHIC ABILITY TO OBTAIN INFORMATION FROM THAT CREATURE!
I'M GOING TO STAY WITH MON-EL UNTIL I LEARN WHAT HE'S CONCEALING FROM US!

SOON, THERE BEGINS THE GREATEST SUPER-SEARCH IN THE LEGION'S HISTORY!

SATURN GIRL SUSPECTS ME... I MUST GUARD MY THOUGHTS OR SHE'LL LEARN MY SECRET! IT COULD MEAN DEATH TO HER!

FULL SPEED TO THE WORLD OF SKOR, SUN BOY! REMEMBER, IT'S FOR LIGHTNING LAD'S LIFE!

THE BLUE SUN WHICH IS MY DESTINATION IS AT THE FARTHEST END OF GALAXY AB-213 ... BUT I MUST REACH IT! I MUST INVESTIGATE THE PLANET WHICH CIRCLES IT!

AT AWESOME SPEED, SUPERBOY HURTLES THROUGH THE COSMOS UNTIL HE REACHES HIS GOAL...

HMM... THE BLUE SUN IS HALF OF A DOUBLE STAR... AND THE PLANET OUR RECORDS REFERRED TO MOVES IN AN ORBIT AROUND BOTH IT AND THE ORANGE SUN! I THINK I SEE A CITY ON THAT WORLD!

THE PLANET IS STARTING TO MOVE AWAY FROM THE ORANGE SUN TOWARD THE BLUE SUN... BUT... THE PEOPLE ON THIS WORLD ALL SEEM... DEAD!

THEN, AS THE STRANGE PLANET ENTERS THE RAYS OF THE BLUE SUN ...

GREAT KRYPTON! BECAUSE OF THE DIFFERENT RAYS OF THEIR TWO SUNS, THESE PEOPLE LIE IN DEATH-LIKE COMA WHILE THEIR WORLD IS UNDER THE ORANGE SUN... THEN THEY'RE REVIVED BY THE RAYS OF THE BLUE SUN! HMM... MAYBE THOSE RAYS COULD REVIVE LIGHTNING LAD!

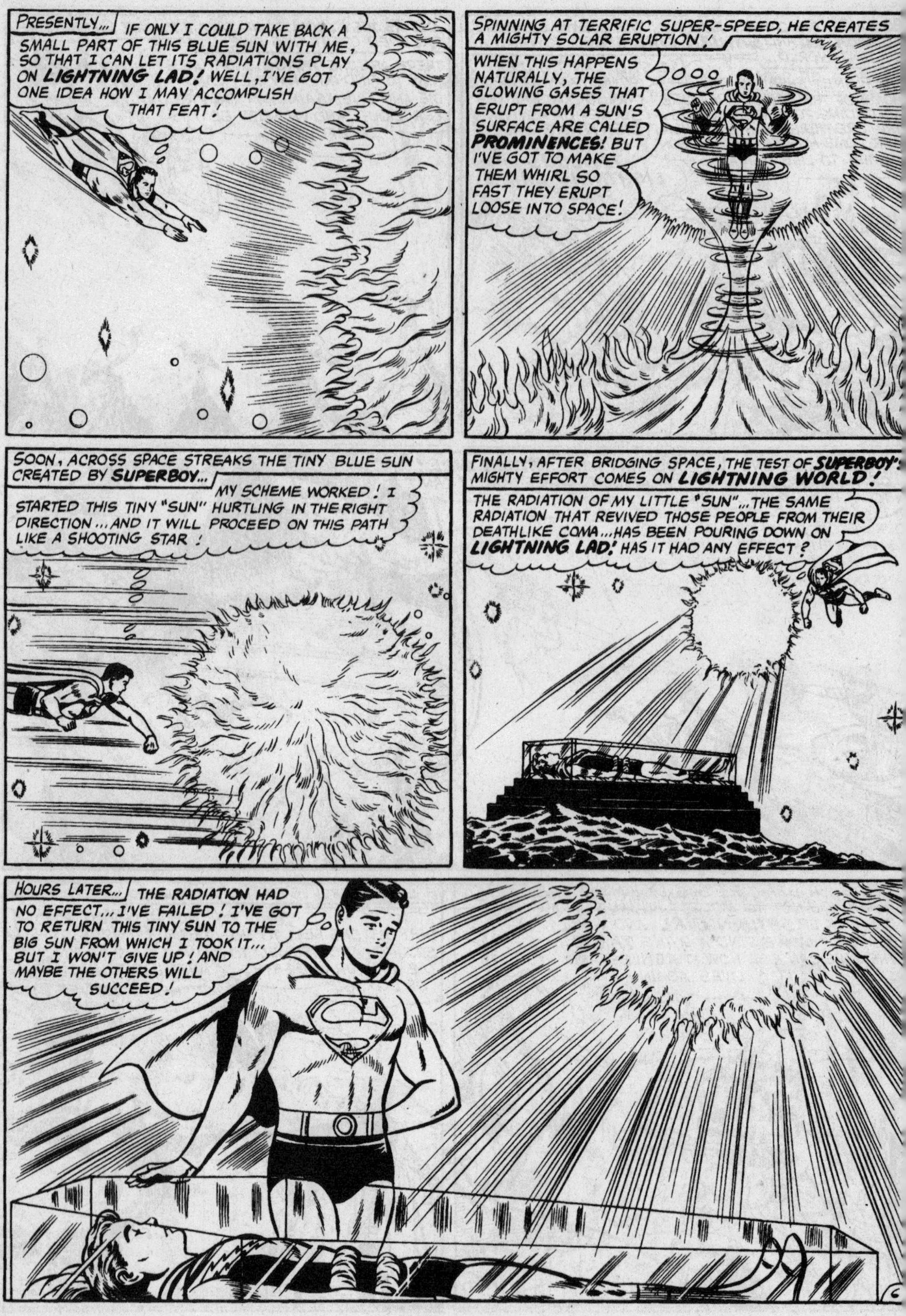
PRESENTLY...
IF ONLY I COULD TAKE BACK A SMALL PART OF THIS BLUE SUN WITH ME, SO THAT I CAN LET ITS RADIATIONS PLAY ON LIGHTNING LAD! WELL, I'VE GOT ONE IDEA HOW I MAY ACCOMPLISH THAT FEAT!
SPINNING AT TERRIFIC SUPER-SPEED, HE CREATES A MIGHTY SOLAR ERUPTION!
WHEN THIS HAPPENS NATURALLY, THE GLOWING GASES THAT ERUPT FROM A SUN'S SURFACE ARE CALLED PROMINENCES! BUT I'VE GOT TO MAKE THEM WHIRL SO FAST THEY ERUPT LOOSE INTO SPACE!
SOON, ACROSS SPACE STREAKS THE TINY BLUE SUN CREATED BY SUPERBOY...
MY SCHEME WORKED! I STARTED THIS TINY "SUN" HURTLING IN THE RIGHT DIRECTION... AND IT WILL PROCEED ON THIS PATH LIKE A SHOOTING STAR!
FINALLY, AFTER BRIDGING SPACE, THE TEST OF SUPERBOY'S MIGHTY EFFORT COMES ON LIGHTNING WORLD!
THE RADIATION OF MY LITTLE "SUN"... THE SAME RADIATION THAT REVIVED THOSE PEOPLE FROM THEIR DEATHLIKE COMA... HAS BEEN POURING DOWN ON LIGHTNING LAD! HAS IT HAD ANY EFFECT?
HOURS LATER...
THE RADIATION HAD NO EFFECT... I'VE FAILED! I'VE GOT TO RETURN THIS TINY SUN TO THE BIG SUN FROM WHICH I TOOK IT... BUT I WON'T GIVE UP! AND MAYBE THE OTHERS WILL SUCCEED!
6

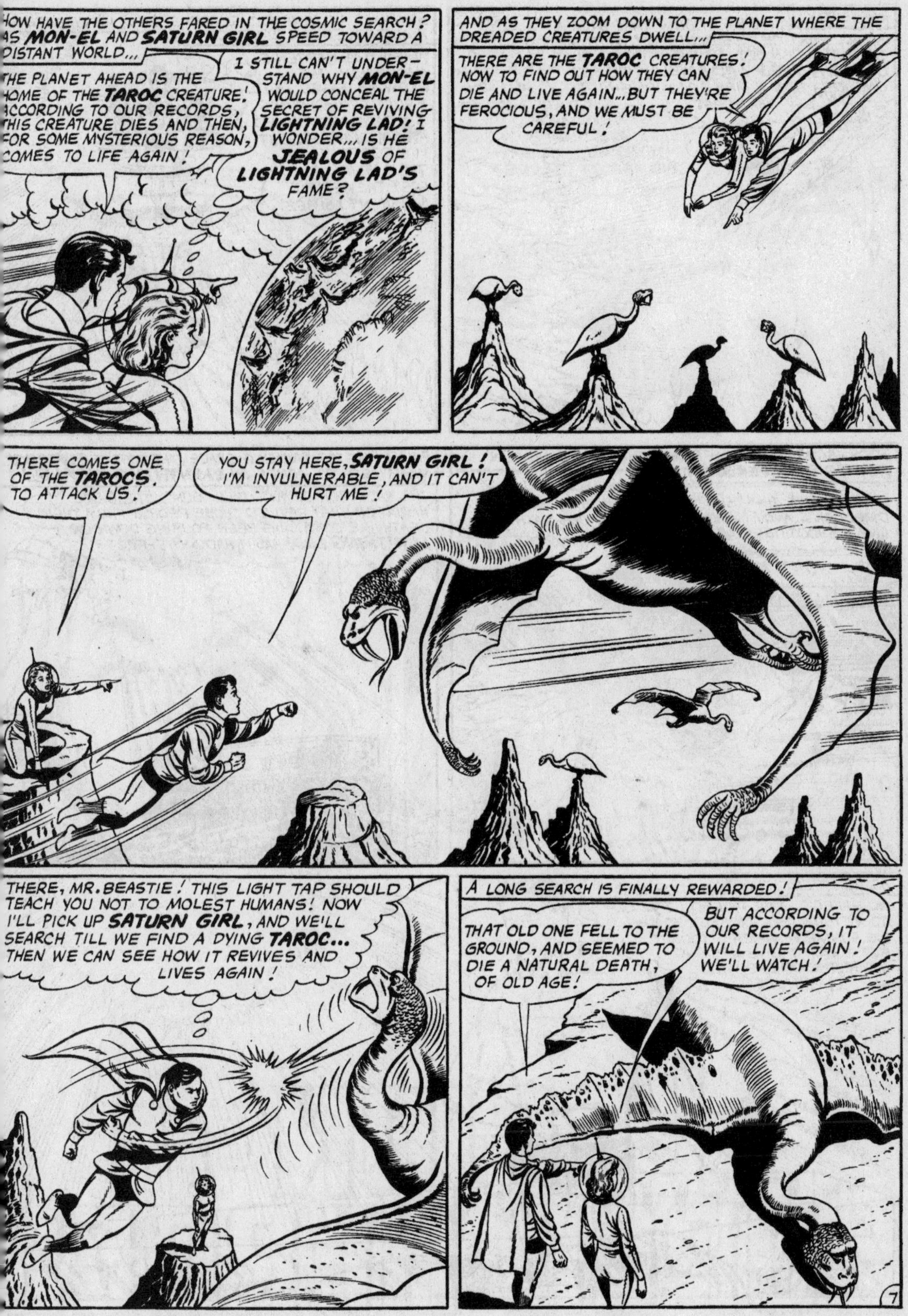
HOW HAVE THE OTHERS FARED IN THE COSMIC SEARCH? AS MON-EL AND SATURN GIRL SPEED TOWARD A DISTANT WORLD...
THE PLANET AHEAD IS THE HOME OF THE TAROC CREATURE! ACCORDING TO OUR RECORDS, THIS CREATURE DIES AND THEN, FOR SOME MYSTERIOUS REASON, COMES TO LIFE AGAIN!
I STILL CAN'T UNDERSTAND WHY MON-EL WOULD CONCEAL THE SECRET OF REVIVING LIGHTNING LAD! I WONDER... IS HE JEALOUS OF LIGHTNING LAD'S FAME?
AND AS THEY ZOOM DOWN TO THE PLANET WHERE THE DREADED CREATURES DWELL...
THERE ARE THE TAROC CREATURES! NOW TO FIND OUT HOW THEY CAN DIE AND LIVE AGAIN... BUT THEY'RE FEROCIOUS, AND WE MUST BE CAREFUL!
THERE COMES ONE OF THE TAROCS. TO ATTACK US!
YOU STAY HERE, SATURN GIRL! I'M INVULNERABLE, AND IT CAN'T HURT ME!
THERE, MR. BEASTIE! THIS LIGHT TAP SHOULD TEACH YOU NOT TO MOLEST HUMANS! NOW I'LL PICK UP SATURN GIRL, AND WE'LL SEARCH TILL WE FIND A DYING TAROC... THEN WE CAN SEE HOW IT REVIVES AND LIVES AGAIN!
A LONG SEARCH IS FINALLY REWARDED!
THAT OLD ONE FELL TO THE GROUND, AND SEEMED TO DIE A NATURAL DEATH, OF OLD AGE!
BUT ACCORDING TO OUR RECORDS, IT WILL LIVE AGAIN! WE'LL WATCH!
7

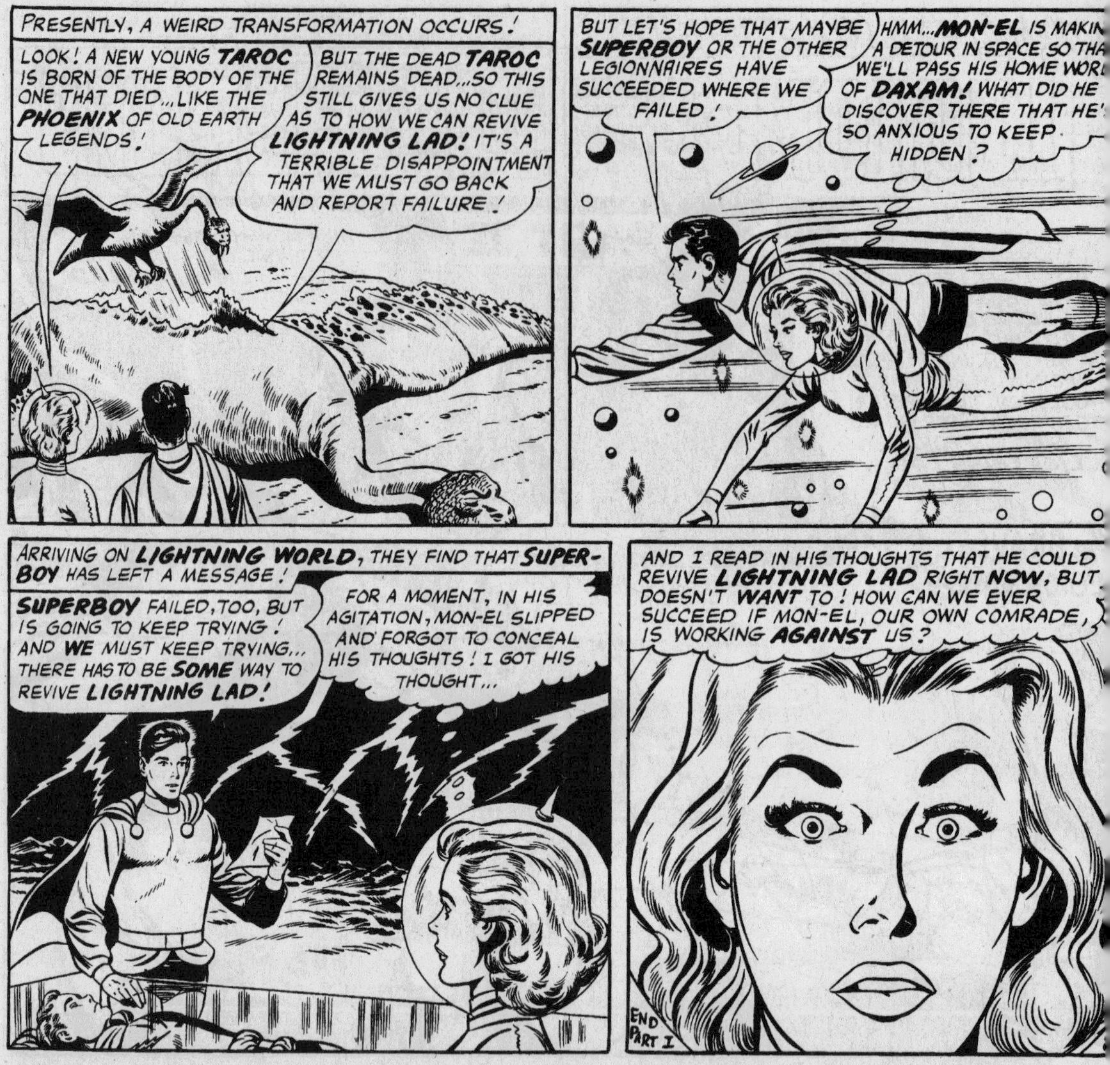
PRESENTLY, A WEIRD TRANSFORMATION OCCURS!
LOOK! A NEW YOUNG TAROC IS BORN OF THE BODY OF THE ONE THAT DIED...LIKE THE PHOENIX OF OLD EARTH LEGENDS!
BUT THE DEAD TAROC REMAINS DEAD...SO THIS STILL GIVES US NO CLUE AS TO HOW WE CAN REVIVE LIGHTNING LAD! IT'S A TERRIBLE DISAPPOINTMENT THAT WE MUST GO BACK AND REPORT FAILURE!
BUT LET'S HOPE THAT MAYBE SUPERBOY OR THE OTHER LEGIONNAIRES HAVE SUCCEEDED WHERE WE FAILED!
HMM...MON-EL IS MAKIN A DETOUR IN SPACE SO THA WE'LL PASS HIS HOME WOR OF DAXAM! WHAT DID HE DISCOVER THERE THAT HE' SO ANXIOUS TO KEEP HIDDEN?
ARRIVING ON LIGHTNING WORLD, THEY FIND THAT SUPERBOY HAS LEFT A MESSAGE!
SUPERBOY FAILED, TOO, BUT IS GOING TO KEEP TRYING! AND WE MUST KEEP TRYING... THERE HAS TO BE SOME WAY TO REVIVE LIGHTNING LAD!
FOR A MOMENT, IN HIS AGITATION, MON-EL SLIPPED AND FORGOT TO CONCEAL HIS THOUGHTS! I GOT HIS THOUGHT...
AND I READ IN HIS THOUGHTS THAT HE COULD REVIVE LIGHTNING LAD RIGHT NOW, BUT DOESN'T WANT TO! HOW CAN WE EVER SUCCEED IF MON-EL, OUR OWN COMRADE, IS WORKING AGAINST US?
END PART I

LEGION of SUPER-HEROES

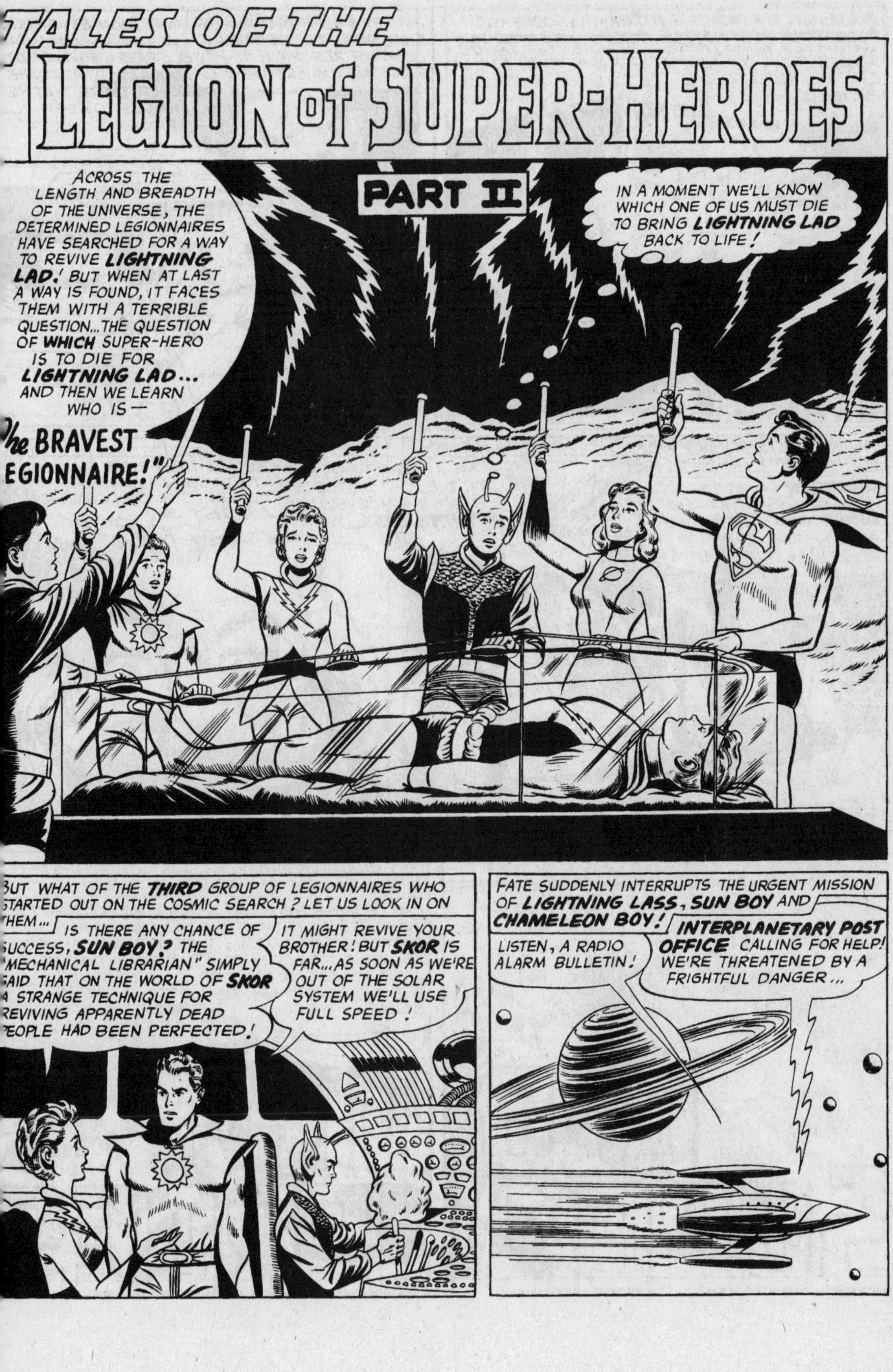
TALES OF THE
LEGION of SUPER-HEROES
PART II
ACROSS THE LENGTH AND BREADTH OF THE UNIVERSE, THE DETERMINED LEGIONNAIRES HAVE SEARCHED FOR A WAY TO REVIVE LIGHTNING LAD! BUT WHEN AT LAST A WAY IS FOUND, IT FACES THEM WITH A TERRIBLE QUESTION... THE QUESTION OF WHICH SUPER-HERO IS TO DIE FOR LIGHTNING LAD... AND THEN WE LEARN WHO IS—
"The BRAVEST LEGIONNAIRE!"
IN A MOMENT WE'LL KNOW WHICH ONE OF US MUST DIE TO BRING LIGHTNING LAD BACK TO LIFE!
BUT WHAT OF THE THIRD GROUP OF LEGIONNAIRES WHO STARTED OUT ON THE COSMIC SEARCH? LET US LOOK IN ON THEM...
IS THERE ANY CHANCE OF SUCCESS, SUN BOY? THE "MECHANICAL LIBRARIAN" SIMPLY SAID THAT ON THE WORLD OF SKOR A STRANGE TECHNIQUE FOR REVIVING APPARENTLY DEAD PEOPLE HAD BEEN PERFECTED!
IT MIGHT REVIVE YOUR BROTHER! BUT SKOR IS FAR... AS SOON AS WE'RE OUT OF THE SOLAR SYSTEM WE'LL USE FULL SPEED!
FATE SUDDENLY INTERRUPTS THE URGENT MISSION OF LIGHTNING LASS, SUN BOY AND CHAMELEON BOY!
LISTEN, A RADIO ALARM BULLETIN!
INTERPLANETARY POST OFFICE CALLING FOR HELP! WE'RE THREATENED BY A FRIGHTFUL DANGER...

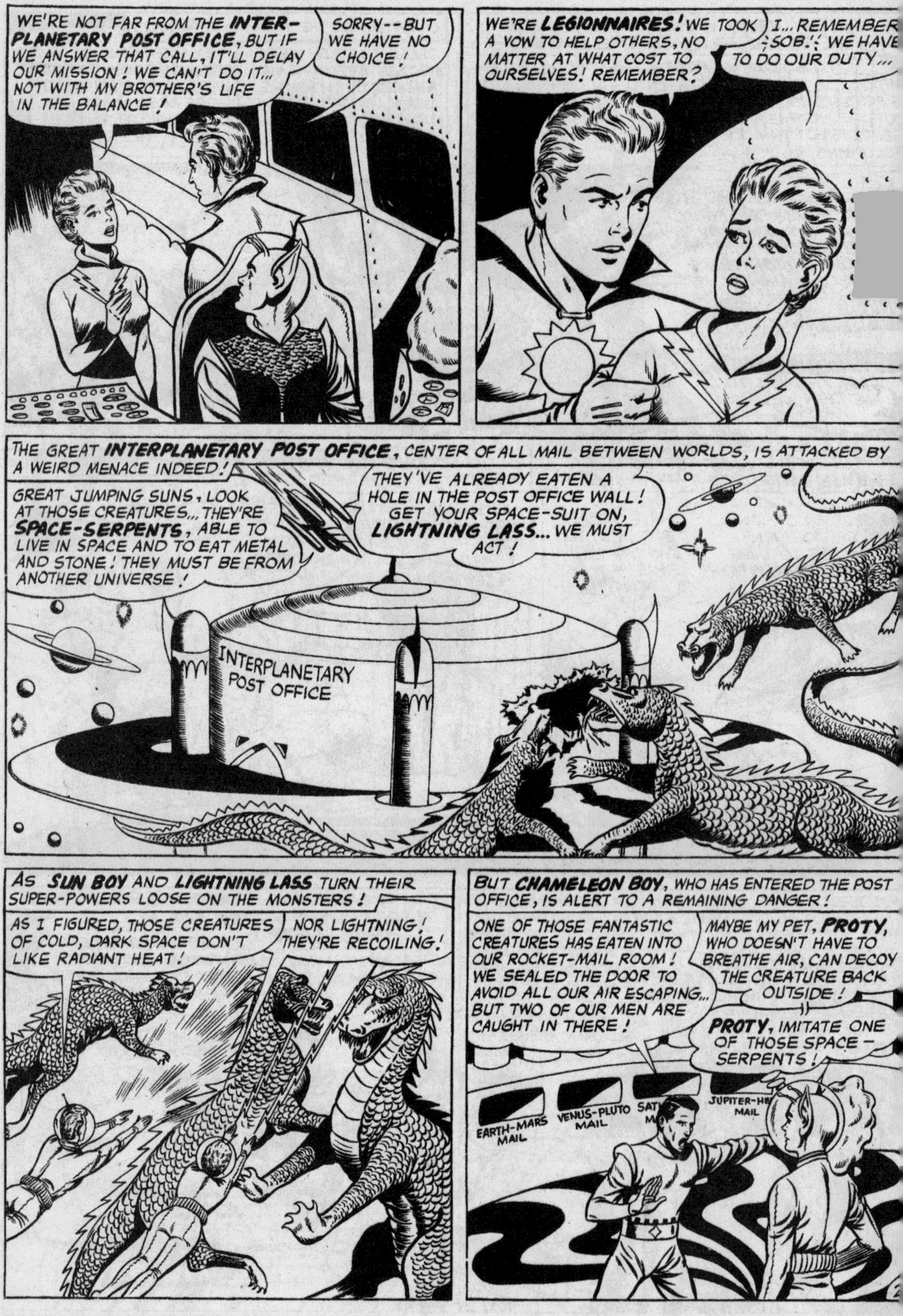
WE'RE NOT FAR FROM THE INTER-PLANETARY POST OFFICE, BUT IF WE ANSWER THAT CALL, IT'LL DELAY OUR MISSION! WE CAN'T DO IT... NOT WITH MY BROTHER'S LIFE IN THE BALANCE!
SORRY--BUT WE HAVE NO CHOICE!
WE'RE LEGIONNAIRES! WE TOOK A VOW TO HELP OTHERS, NO MATTER AT WHAT COST TO OURSELVES! REMEMBER?
I... REMEMBER *SOB!* WE HAVE TO DO OUR DUTY...
THE GREAT INTERPLANETARY POST OFFICE, CENTER OF ALL MAIL BETWEEN WORLDS, IS ATTACKED BY A WEIRD MENACE INDEED!
GREAT JUMPING SUNS, LOOK AT THOSE CREATURES... THEY'RE SPACE-SERPENTS, ABLE TO LIVE IN SPACE AND TO EAT METAL AND STONE! THEY MUST BE FROM ANOTHER UNIVERSE!
THEY'VE ALREADY EATEN A HOLE IN THE POST OFFICE WALL! GET YOUR SPACE-SUIT ON, LIGHTNING LASS... WE MUST ACT!
INTERPLANETARY POST OFFICE
AS SUN BOY AND LIGHTNING LASS TURN THEIR SUPER-POWERS LOOSE ON THE MONSTERS!
AS I FIGURED, THOSE CREATURES OF COLD, DARK SPACE DON'T LIKE RADIANT HEAT!
NOR LIGHTNING! THEY'RE RECOILING!
BUT CHAMELEON BOY, WHO HAS ENTERED THE POST OFFICE, IS ALERT TO A REMAINING DANGER!
ONE OF THOSE FANTASTIC CREATURES HAS EATEN INTO OUR ROCKET-MAIL ROOM! WE SEALED THE DOOR TO AVOID ALL OUR AIR ESCAPING... BUT TWO OF OUR MEN ARE CAUGHT IN THERE!
MAYBE MY PET, PROTY, WHO DOESN'T HAVE TO BREATHE AIR, CAN DECOY THE CREATURE BACK OUTSIDE!
PROTY, IMITATE ONE OF THOSE SPACE-SERPENTS!
EARTH-MARS MAIL
VENUS-PLUTO MAIL

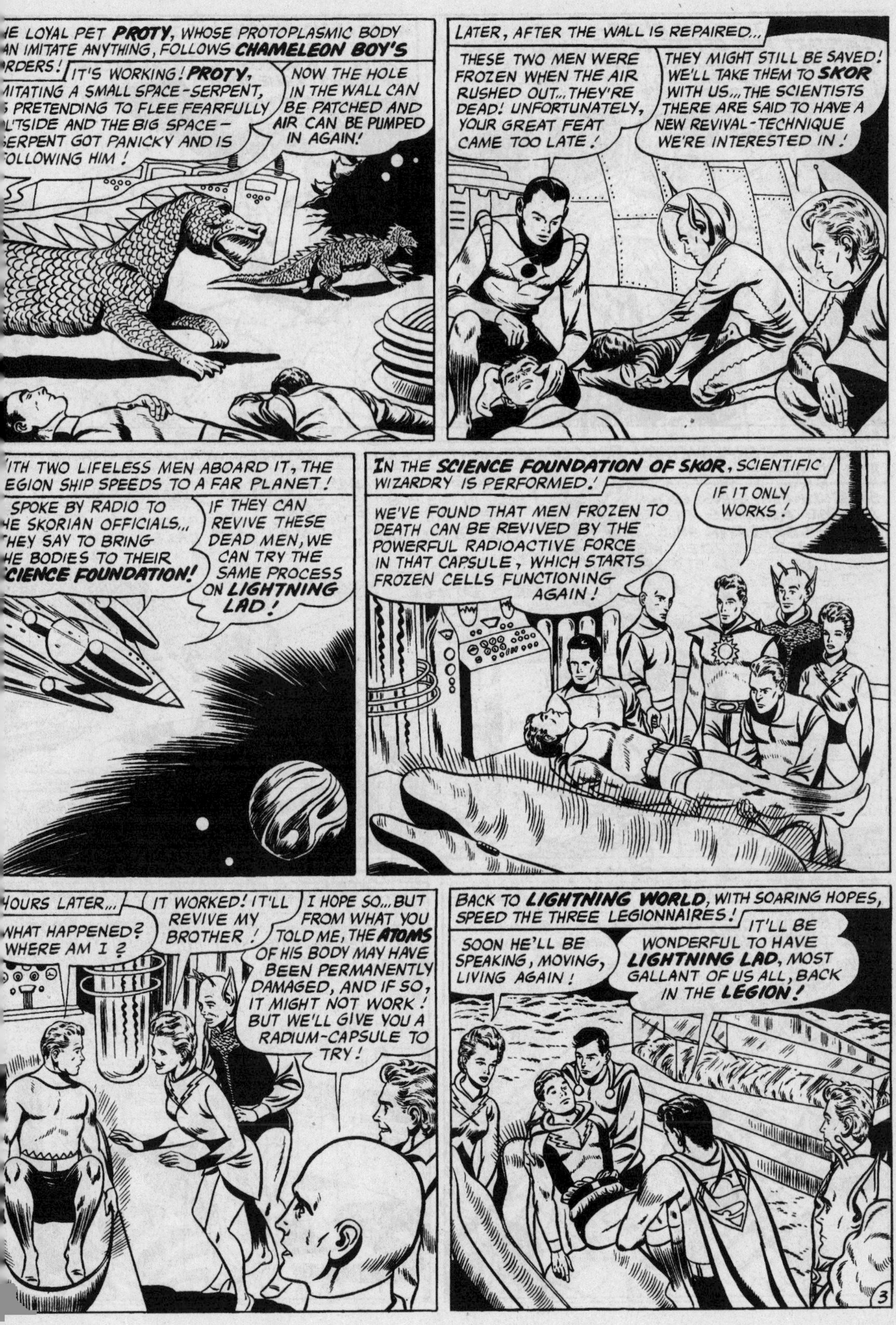
HE LOYAL PET PROTY, WHOSE PROTOPLASMIC BODY AN IMITATE ANYTHING, FOLLOWS CHAMELEON BOY'S ORDERS!
IT'S WORKING! PROTY, MITATING A SMALL SPACE-SERPENT, S PRETENDING TO FLEE FEARFULLY UTSIDE AND THE BIG SPACE-SERPENT GOT PANICKY AND IS FOLLOWING HIM!
NOW THE HOLE IN THE WALL CAN BE PATCHED AND AIR CAN BE PUMPED IN AGAIN!
LATER, AFTER THE WALL IS REPAIRED...
THESE TWO MEN WERE FROZEN WHEN THE AIR RUSHED OUT... THEY'RE DEAD! UNFORTUNATELY, YOUR GREAT FEAT CAME TOO LATE!
THEY MIGHT STILL BE SAVED! WE'LL TAKE THEM TO SKOR WITH US... THE SCIENTISTS THERE ARE SAID TO HAVE A NEW REVIVAL-TECHNIQUE WE'RE INTERESTED IN!
ITH TWO LIFELESS MEN ABOARD IT, THE EGION SHIP SPEEDS TO A FAR PLANET!
SPOKE BY RADIO TO HE SKORIAN OFFICIALS... HEY SAY TO BRING HE BODIES TO THEIR CIENCE FOUNDATION!
IF THEY CAN REVIVE THESE DEAD MEN, WE CAN TRY THE SAME PROCESS ON LIGHTNING LAD!
IN THE SCIENCE FOUNDATION OF SKOR, SCIENTIFIC WIZARDRY IS PERFORMED!
WE'VE FOUND THAT MEN FROZEN TO DEATH CAN BE REVIVED BY THE POWERFUL RADIOACTIVE FORCE IN THAT CAPSULE, WHICH STARTS FROZEN CELLS FUNCTIONING AGAIN!
IF IT ONLY WORKS!
HOURS LATER...
WHAT HAPPENED? WHERE AM I?
IT WORKED! IT'LL REVIVE MY BROTHER!
I HOPE SO... BUT FROM WHAT YOU TOLD ME, THE ATOMS OF HIS BODY MAY HAVE BEEN PERMANENTLY DAMAGED, AND IF SO, IT MIGHT NOT WORK! BUT WE'LL GIVE YOU A RADIUM-CAPSULE TO TRY!
BACK TO LIGHTNING WORLD, WITH SOARING HOPES, SPEED THE THREE LEGIONNAIRES!
SOON HE'LL BE SPEAKING, MOVING, LIVING AGAIN!
IT'LL BE WONDERFUL TO HAVE LIGHTNING LAD, MOST GALLANT OF US ALL, BACK IN THE LEGION!
3

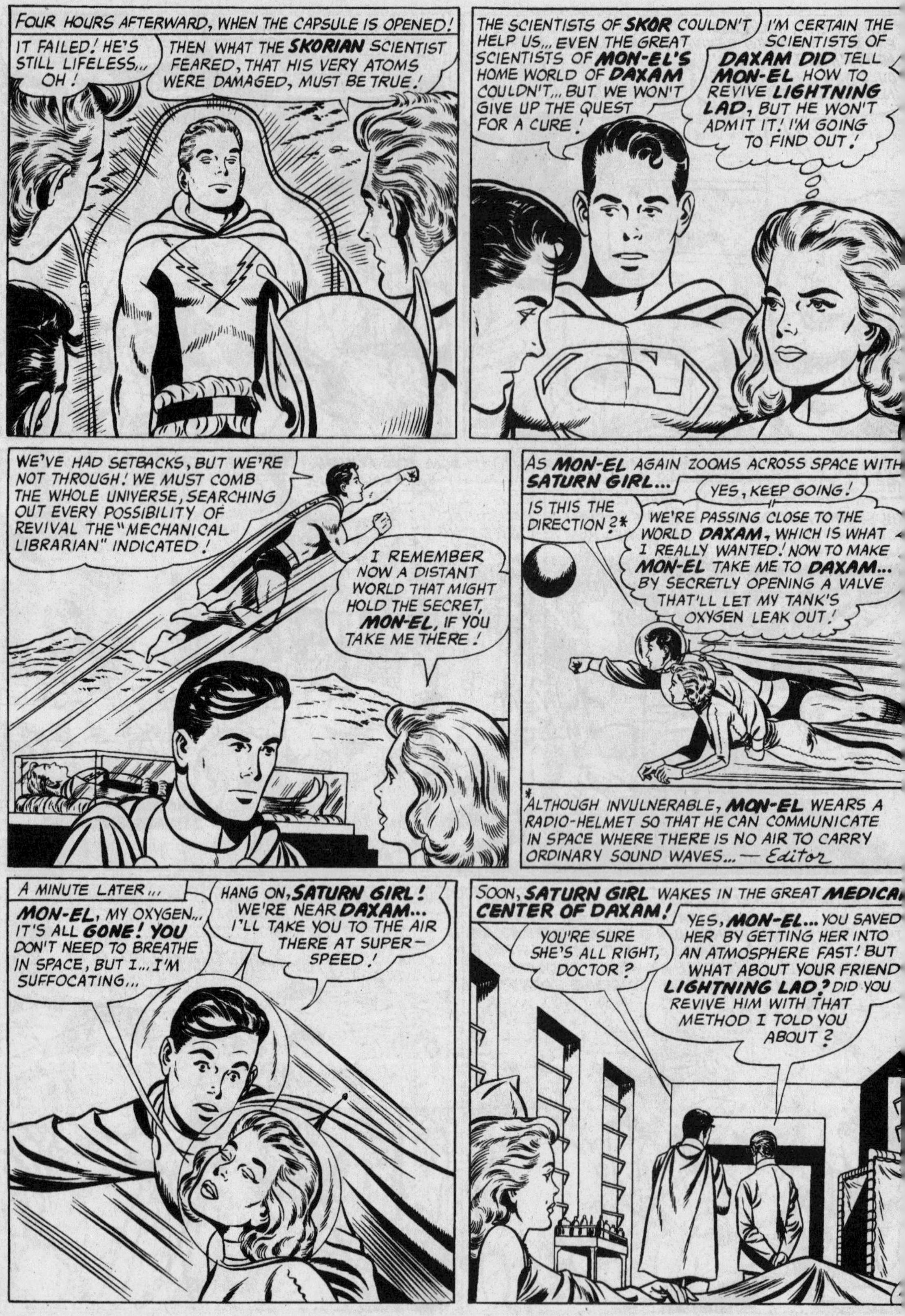
FOUR HOURS AFTERWARD, WHEN THE CAPSULE IS OPENED!
IT FAILED! HE'S STILL LIFELESS... OH!
THEN WHAT THE SKORIAN SCIENTIST FEARED, THAT HIS VERY ATOMS WERE DAMAGED, MUST BE TRUE!
THE SCIENTISTS OF SKOR COULDN'T HELP US... EVEN THE GREAT SCIENTISTS OF MON-EL'S HOME WORLD OF DAXAM COULDN'T... BUT WE WON'T GIVE UP THE QUEST FOR A CURE!
I'M CERTAIN THE SCIENTISTS OF DAXAM DID TELL MON-EL HOW TO REVIVE LIGHTNING LAD, BUT HE WON'T ADMIT IT! I'M GOING TO FIND OUT!
WE'VE HAD SETBACKS, BUT WE'RE NOT THROUGH! WE MUST COMB THE WHOLE UNIVERSE, SEARCHING OUT EVERY POSSIBILITY OF REVIVAL THE "MECHANICAL LIBRARIAN" INDICATED!
I REMEMBER NOW A DISTANT WORLD THAT MIGHT HOLD THE SECRET, MON-EL, IF YOU TAKE ME THERE!
AS MON-EL AGAIN ZOOMS ACROSS SPACE WITH SATURN GIRL...
IS THIS THE DIRECTION?*
YES, KEEP GOING!
WE'RE PASSING CLOSE TO THE WORLD DAXAM, WHICH IS WHAT I REALLY WANTED! NOW TO MAKE MON-EL TAKE ME TO DAXAM... BY SECRETLY OPENING A VALVE THAT'LL LET MY TANK'S OXYGEN LEAK OUT!
*ALTHOUGH INVULNERABLE, MON-EL WEARS A RADIO-HELMET SO THAT HE CAN COMMUNICATE IN SPACE WHERE THERE IS NO AIR TO CARRY ORDINARY SOUND WAVES... —Editor
A MINUTE LATER...
MON-EL, MY OXYGEN... IT'S ALL GONE! YOU DON'T NEED TO BREATHE IN SPACE, BUT I... I'M SUFFOCATING...
HANG ON, SATURN GIRL! WE'RE NEAR DAXAM... I'LL TAKE YOU TO THE AIR THERE AT SUPER-SPEED!
SOON, SATURN GIRL WAKES IN THE GREAT MEDICAL CENTER OF DAXAM!
YOU'RE SURE SHE'S ALL RIGHT, DOCTOR?
YES, MON-EL... YOU SAVED HER BY GETTING HER INTO AN ATMOSPHERE FAST! BUT WHAT ABOUT YOUR FRIEND LIGHTNING LAD? DID YOU REVIVE HIM WITH THAT METHOD I TOLD YOU ABOUT?

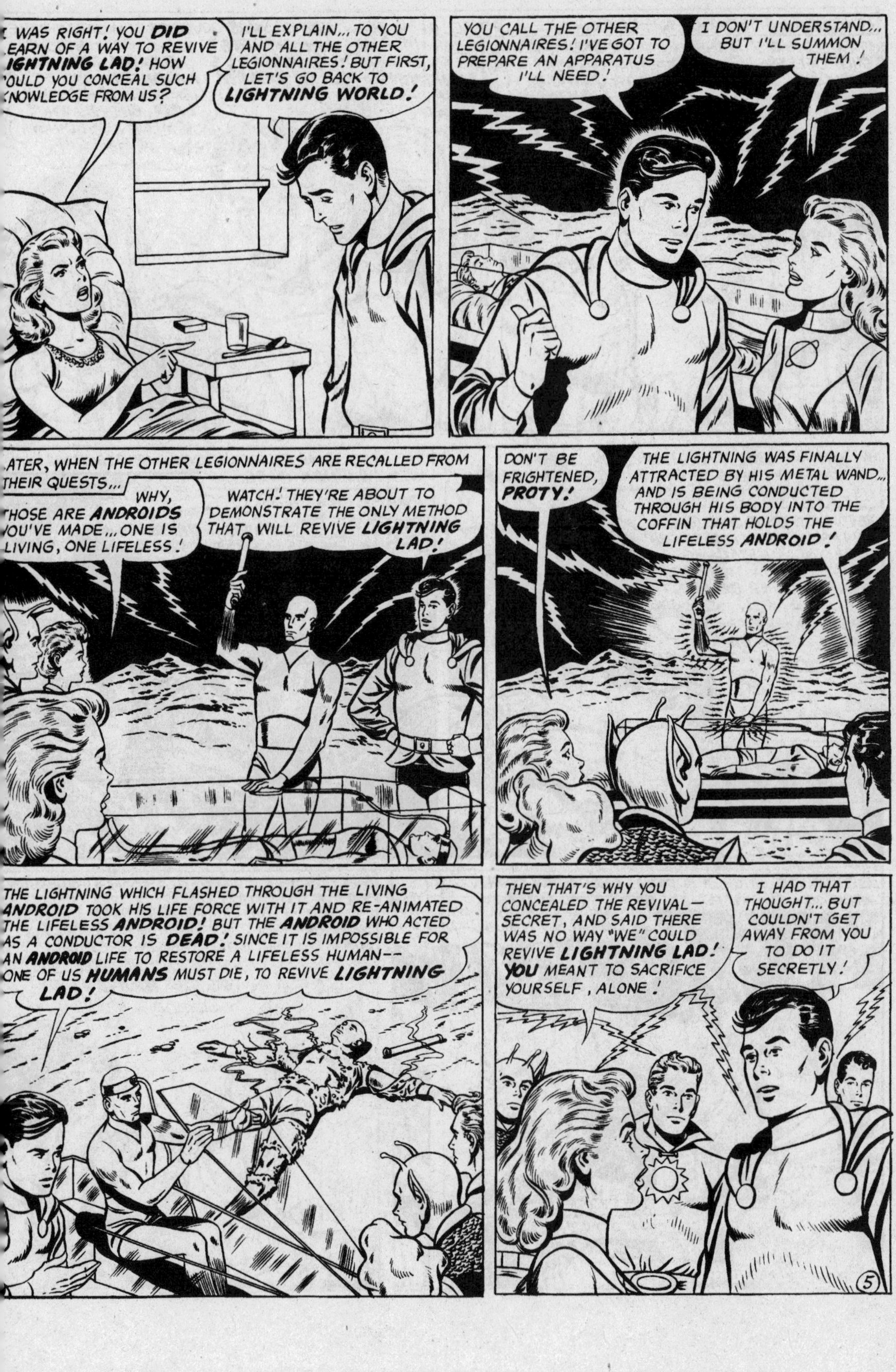
I WAS RIGHT! YOU DID LEARN OF A WAY TO REVIVE LIGHTNING LAD! HOW COULD YOU CONCEAL SUCH KNOWLEDGE FROM US?
I'LL EXPLAIN... TO YOU AND ALL THE OTHER LEGIONNAIRES! BUT FIRST, LET'S GO BACK TO LIGHTNING WORLD!
YOU CALL THE OTHER LEGIONNAIRES! I'VE GOT TO PREPARE AN APPARATUS I'LL NEED!
I DON'T UNDERSTAND... BUT I'LL SUMMON THEM!
LATER, WHEN THE OTHER LEGIONNAIRES ARE RECALLED FROM THEIR QUESTS...
WHY, THOSE ARE ANDROIDS YOU'VE MADE... ONE IS LIVING, ONE LIFELESS!
WATCH! THEY'RE ABOUT TO DEMONSTRATE THE ONLY METHOD THAT WILL REVIVE LIGHTNING LAD!
DON'T BE FRIGHTENED, PROTY!
THE LIGHTNING WAS FINALLY ATTRACTED BY HIS METAL WAND... AND IS BEING CONDUCTED THROUGH HIS BODY INTO THE COFFIN THAT HOLDS THE LIFELESS ANDROID!
THE LIGHTNING WHICH FLASHED THROUGH THE LIVING ANDROID TOOK HIS LIFE FORCE WITH IT AND RE-ANIMATED THE LIFELESS ANDROID! BUT THE ANDROID WHO ACTED AS A CONDUCTOR IS DEAD! SINCE IT IS IMPOSSIBLE FOR AN ANDROID LIFE TO RESTORE A LIFELESS HUMAN-- ONE OF US HUMANS MUST DIE, TO REVIVE LIGHTNING LAD!
THEN THAT'S WHY YOU CONCEALED THE REVIVAL-SECRET, AND SAID THERE WAS NO WAY "WE" COULD REVIVE LIGHTNING LAD! YOU MEANT TO SACRIFICE YOURSELF, ALONE!
I HAD THAT THOUGHT... BUT COULDN'T GET AWAY FROM YOU TO DO IT SECRETLY!
5

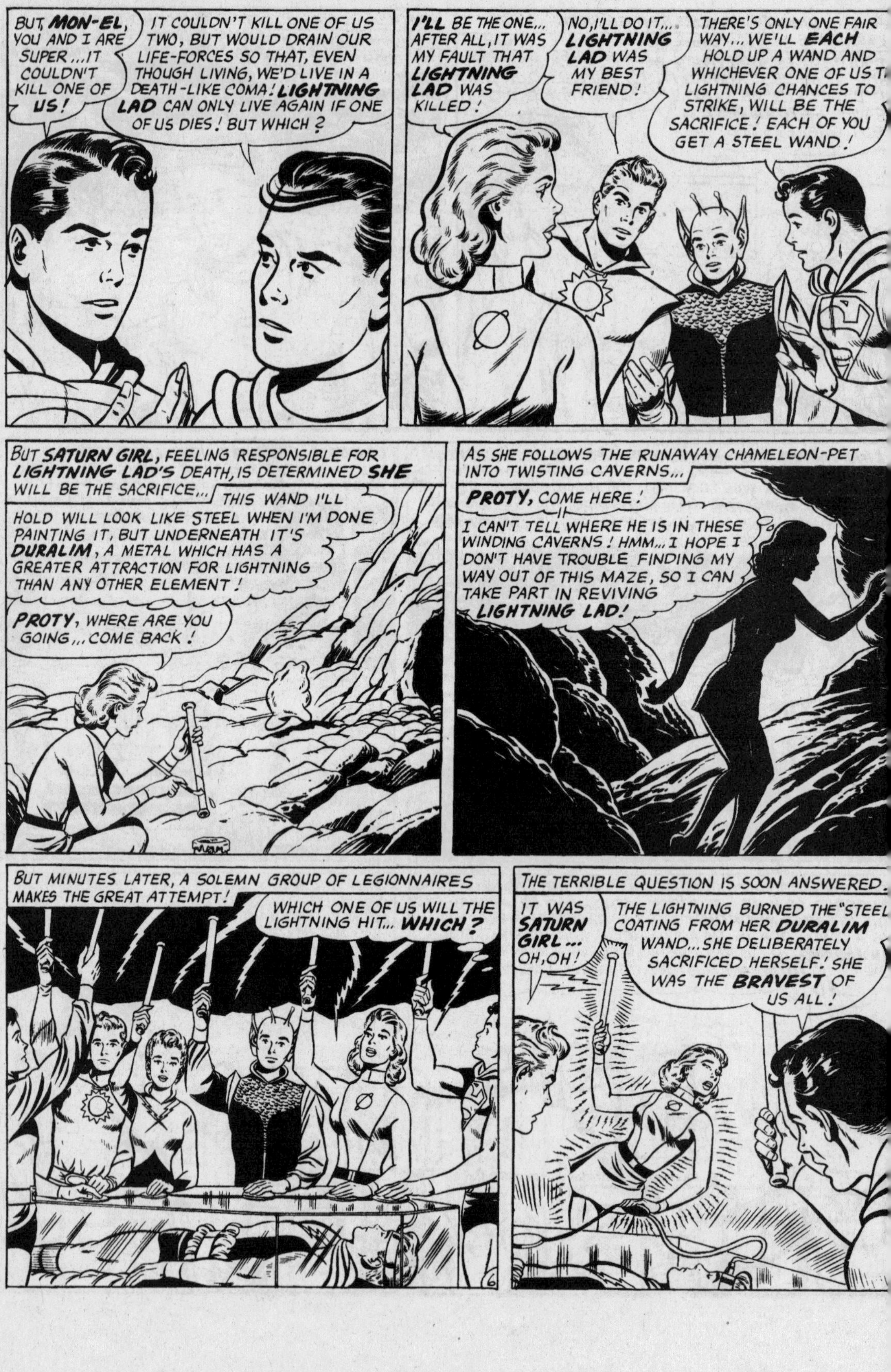
BUT, MON-EL, YOU AND I ARE SUPER ...IT COULDN'T KILL ONE OF US!
IT COULDN'T KILL ONE OF US TWO, BUT WOULD DRAIN OUR LIFE-FORCES SO THAT, EVEN THOUGH LIVING, WE'D LIVE IN A DEATH-LIKE COMA! LIGHTNING LAD CAN ONLY LIVE AGAIN IF ONE OF US DIES! BUT WHICH?
I'LL BE THE ONE... AFTER ALL, IT WAS MY FAULT THAT LIGHTNING LAD WAS KILLED!
NO, I'LL DO IT... LIGHTNING LAD WAS MY BEST FRIEND!
THERE'S ONLY ONE FAIR WAY... WE'LL EACH HOLD UP A WAND AND WHICHEVER ONE OF US T LIGHTNING CHANCES TO STRIKE, WILL BE THE SACRIFICE! EACH OF YOU GET A STEEL WAND!
BUT SATURN GIRL, FEELING RESPONSIBLE FOR LIGHTNING LAD'S DEATH, IS DETERMINED SHE WILL BE THE SACRIFICE...
THIS WAND I'LL HOLD WILL LOOK LIKE STEEL WHEN I'M DONE PAINTING IT, BUT UNDERNEATH IT'S DURALIM, A METAL WHICH HAS A GREATER ATTRACTION FOR LIGHTNING THAN ANY OTHER ELEMENT!
PROTY, WHERE ARE YOU GOING... COME BACK!
AS SHE FOLLOWS THE RUNAWAY CHAMELEON-PET INTO TWISTING CAVERNS...
PROTY, COME HERE!
I CAN'T TELL WHERE HE IS IN THESE WINDING CAVERNS! HMM... I HOPE I DON'T HAVE TROUBLE FINDING MY WAY OUT OF THIS MAZE, SO I CAN TAKE PART IN REVIVING LIGHTNING LAD!
BUT MINUTES LATER, A SOLEMN GROUP OF LEGIONNAIRES MAKES THE GREAT ATTEMPT!
WHICH ONE OF US WILL THE LIGHTNING HIT... WHICH?
THE TERRIBLE QUESTION IS SOON ANSWERED.
IT WAS SATURN GIRL... OH, OH!
THE LIGHTNING BURNED THE "STEEL COATING FROM HER DURALIM WAND... SHE DELIBERATELY SACRIFICED HERSELF! SHE WAS THE BRAVEST OF US ALL!
6

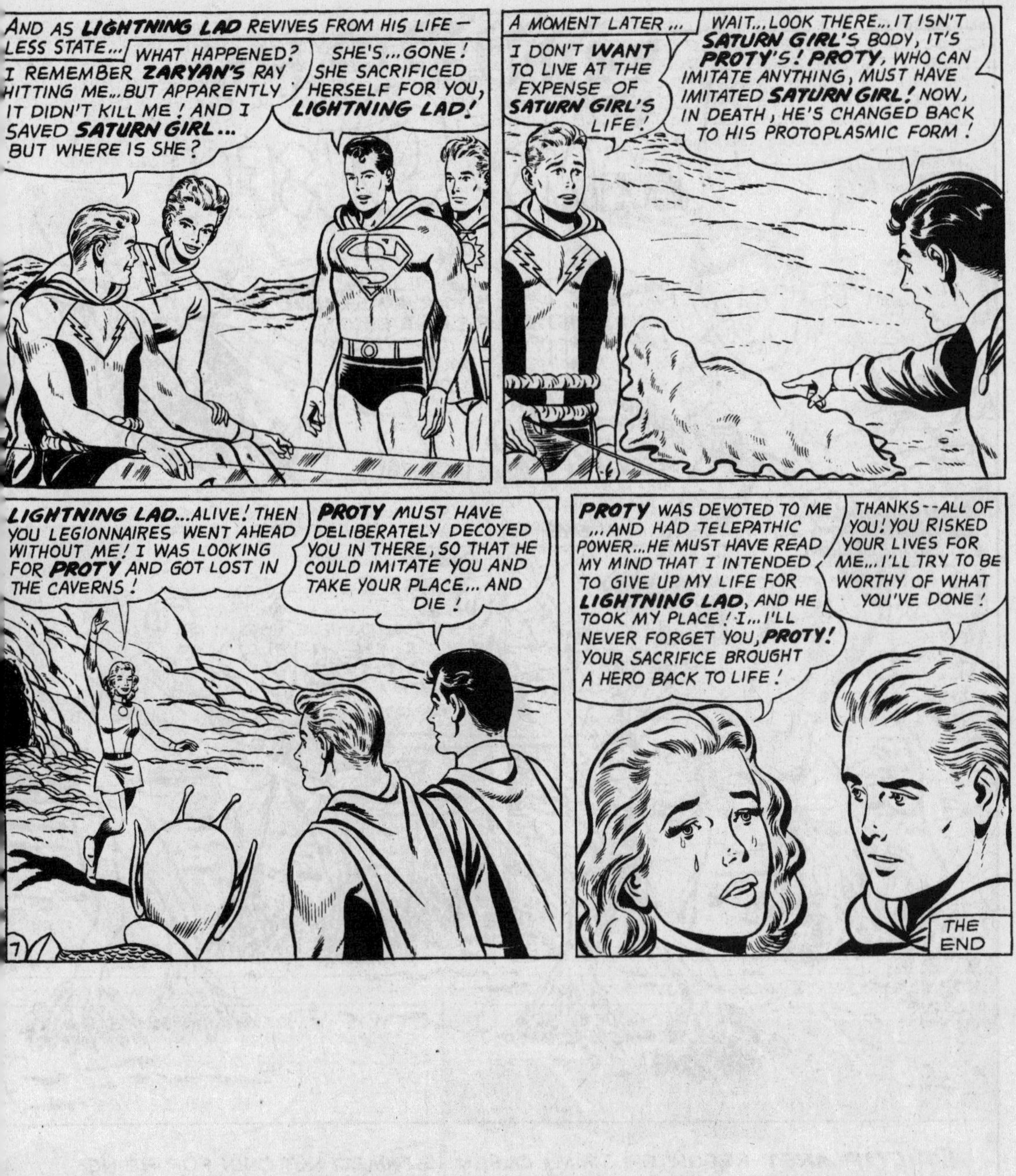
AND AS LIGHTNING LAD REVIVES FROM HIS LIFELESS STATE...
WHAT HAPPENED? I REMEMBER ZARYAN'S RAY HITTING ME...BUT APPARENTLY IT DIDN'T KILL ME! AND I SAVED SATURN GIRL... BUT WHERE IS SHE?
SHE'S...GONE! SHE SACRIFICED HERSELF FOR YOU, LIGHTNING LAD!
A MOMENT LATER...
I DON'T WANT TO LIVE AT THE EXPENSE OF SATURN GIRL'S LIFE!
WAIT...LOOK THERE...IT ISN'T SATURN GIRL'S BODY, IT'S PROTY'S! PROTY, WHO CAN IMITATE ANYTHING, MUST HAVE IMITATED SATURN GIRL! NOW, IN DEATH, HE'S CHANGED BACK TO HIS PROTOPLASMIC FORM!
LIGHTNING LAD...ALIVE! THEN YOU LEGIONNAIRES WENT AHEAD WITHOUT ME! I WAS LOOKING FOR PROTY AND GOT LOST IN THE CAVERNS!
PROTY MUST HAVE DELIBERATELY DECOYED YOU IN THERE, SO THAT HE COULD IMITATE YOU AND TAKE YOUR PLACE... AND DIE!
7
PROTY WAS DEVOTED TO ME ...AND HAD TELEPATHIC POWER...HE MUST HAVE READ MY MIND THAT I INTENDED TO GIVE UP MY LIFE FOR LIGHTNING LAD, AND HE TOOK MY PLACE! I...I'LL NEVER FORGET YOU, PROTY! YOUR SACRIFICE BROUGHT A HERO BACK TO LIFE!
THANKS--ALL OF YOU! YOU RISKED YOUR LIVES FOR ME...I'LL TRY TO BE WORTHY OF WHAT YOU'VE DONE!
THE END

LEGION of SUPER-HEROES

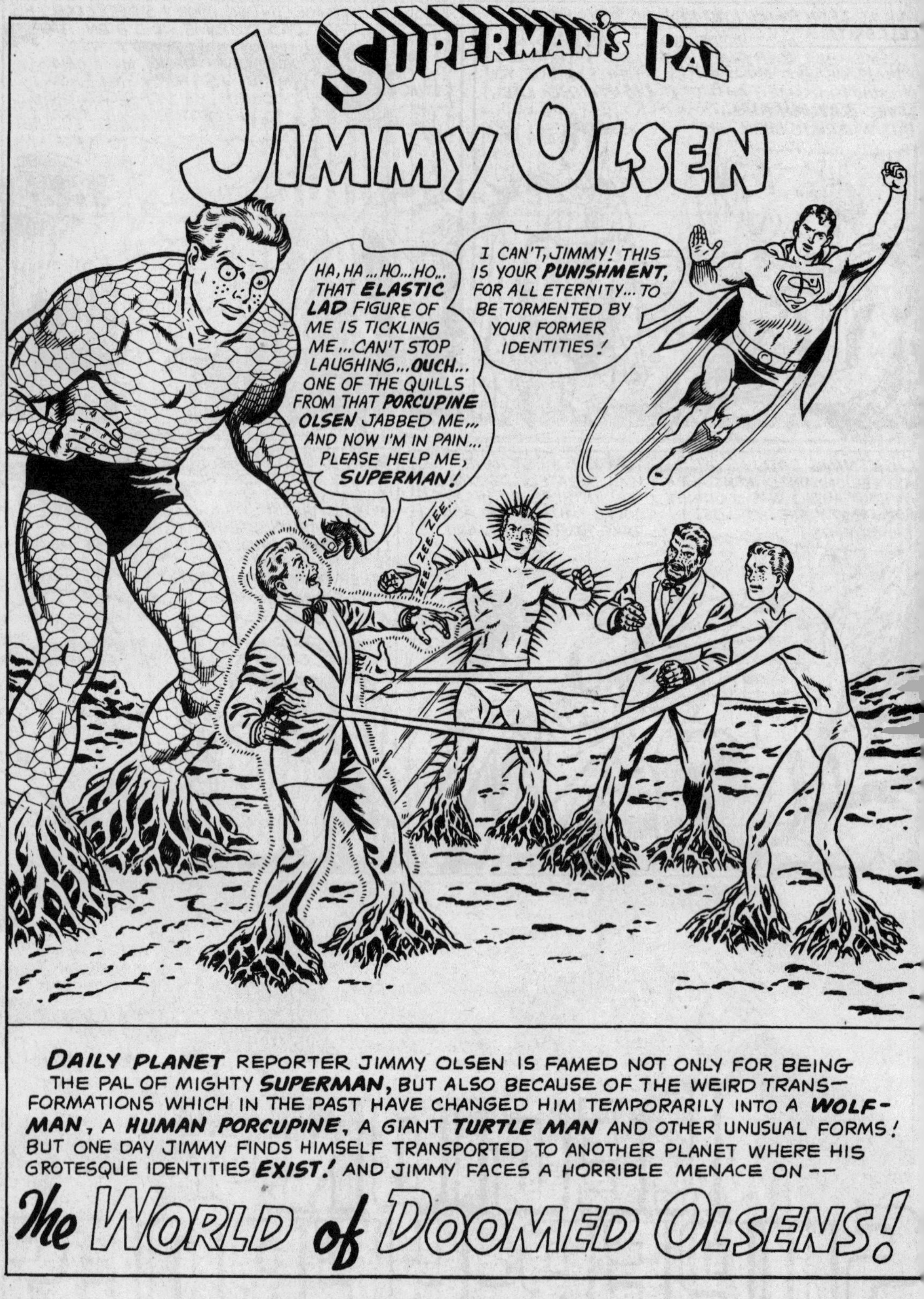
SUPERMAN'S PAL
JIMMY OLSEN
HA, HA... HO... HO... THAT ELASTIC LAD FIGURE OF ME IS TICKLING ME... CAN'T STOP LAUGHING... OUCH... ONE OF THE QUILLS FROM THAT PORCUPINE OLSEN JABBED ME... AND NOW I'M IN PAIN... PLEASE HELP ME, SUPERMAN!
I CAN'T, JIMMY! THIS IS YOUR PUNISHMENT, FOR ALL ETERNITY... TO BE TORMENTED BY YOUR FORMER IDENTITIES!
DAILY PLANET REPORTER JIMMY OLSEN IS FAMED NOT ONLY FOR BEING THE PAL OF MIGHTY SUPERMAN, BUT ALSO BECAUSE OF THE WEIRD TRANSFORMATIONS WHICH IN THE PAST HAVE CHANGED HIM TEMPORARILY INTO A WOLF-MAN, A HUMAN PORCUPINE, A GIANT TURTLE MAN AND OTHER UNUSUAL FORMS! BUT ONE DAY JIMMY FINDS HIMSELF TRANSPORTED TO ANOTHER PLANET WHERE HIS GROTESQUE IDENTITIES EXIST! AND JIMMY FACES A HORRIBLE MENACE ON --
The WORLD of DOOMED OLSENS!

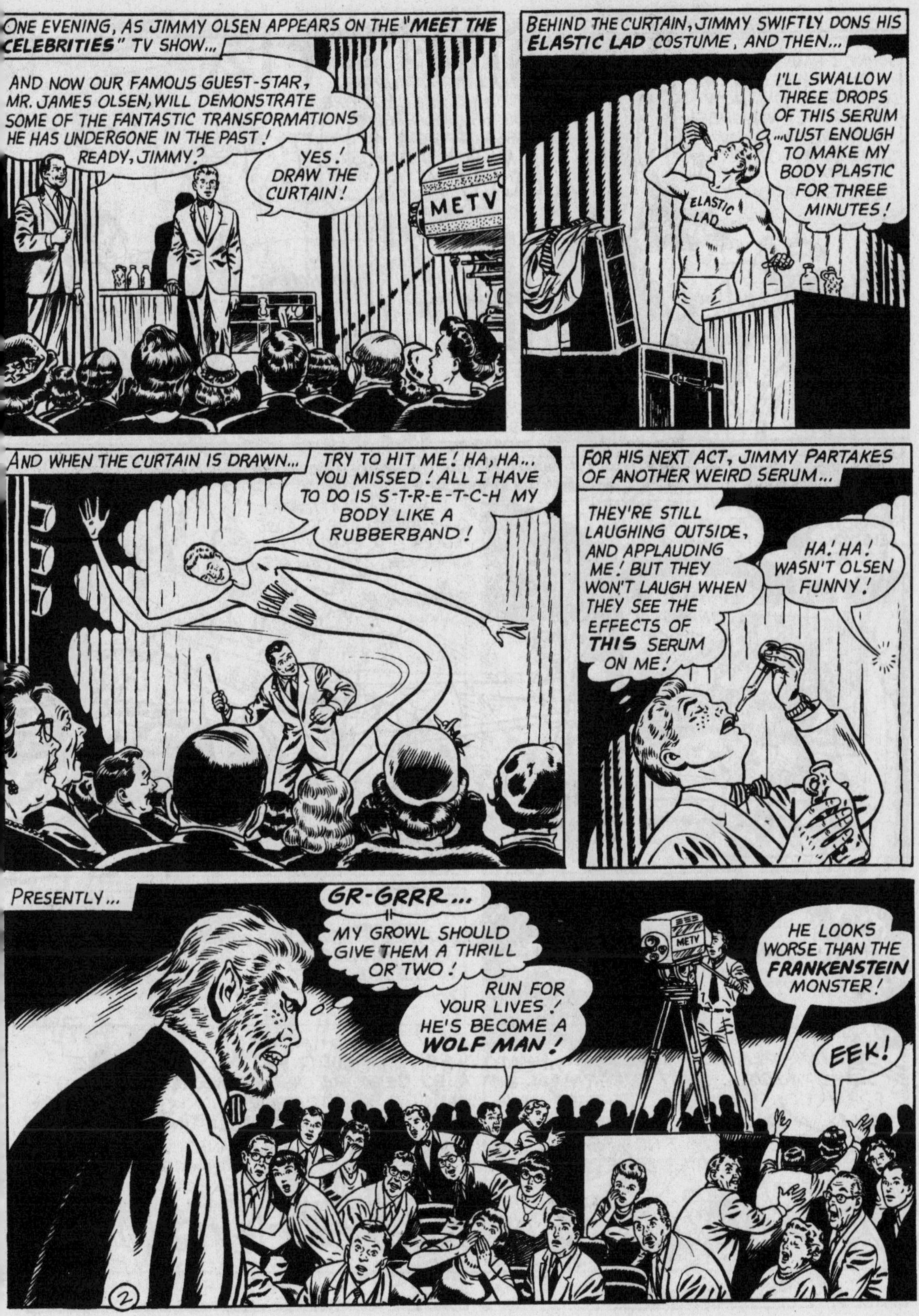
ONE EVENING, AS JIMMY OLSEN APPEARS ON THE "MEET THE CELEBRITIES" TV SHOW...
AND NOW OUR FAMOUS GUEST-STAR, MR. JAMES OLSEN, WILL DEMONSTRATE SOME OF THE FANTASTIC TRANSFORMATIONS HE HAS UNDERGONE IN THE PAST! READY, JIMMY?
YES! DRAW THE CURTAIN!
METV
BEHIND THE CURTAIN, JIMMY SWIFTLY DONS HIS ELASTIC LAD COSTUME, AND THEN...
I'LL SWALLOW THREE DROPS OF THIS SERUM ...JUST ENOUGH TO MAKE MY BODY PLASTIC FOR THREE MINUTES!
ELASTIC LAD
AND WHEN THE CURTAIN IS DRAWN...
TRY TO HIT ME! HA, HA.. YOU MISSED! ALL I HAVE TO DO IS S-T-R-E-T-C-H MY BODY LIKE A RUBBERBAND!
FOR HIS NEXT ACT, JIMMY PARTAKES OF ANOTHER WEIRD SERUM...
THEY'RE STILL LAUGHING OUTSIDE, AND APPLAUDING ME! BUT THEY WON'T LAUGH WHEN THEY SEE THE EFFECTS OF THIS SERUM ON ME!
HA! HA! WASN'T OLSEN FUNNY!
PRESENTLY...
GR-GRRR...
MY GROWL SHOULD GIVE THEM A THRILL OR TWO!
RUN FOR YOUR LIVES! HE'S BECOME A WOLF MAN!
METV
HE LOOKS WORSE THAN THE FRANKENSTEIN MONSTER!
EEK!
2

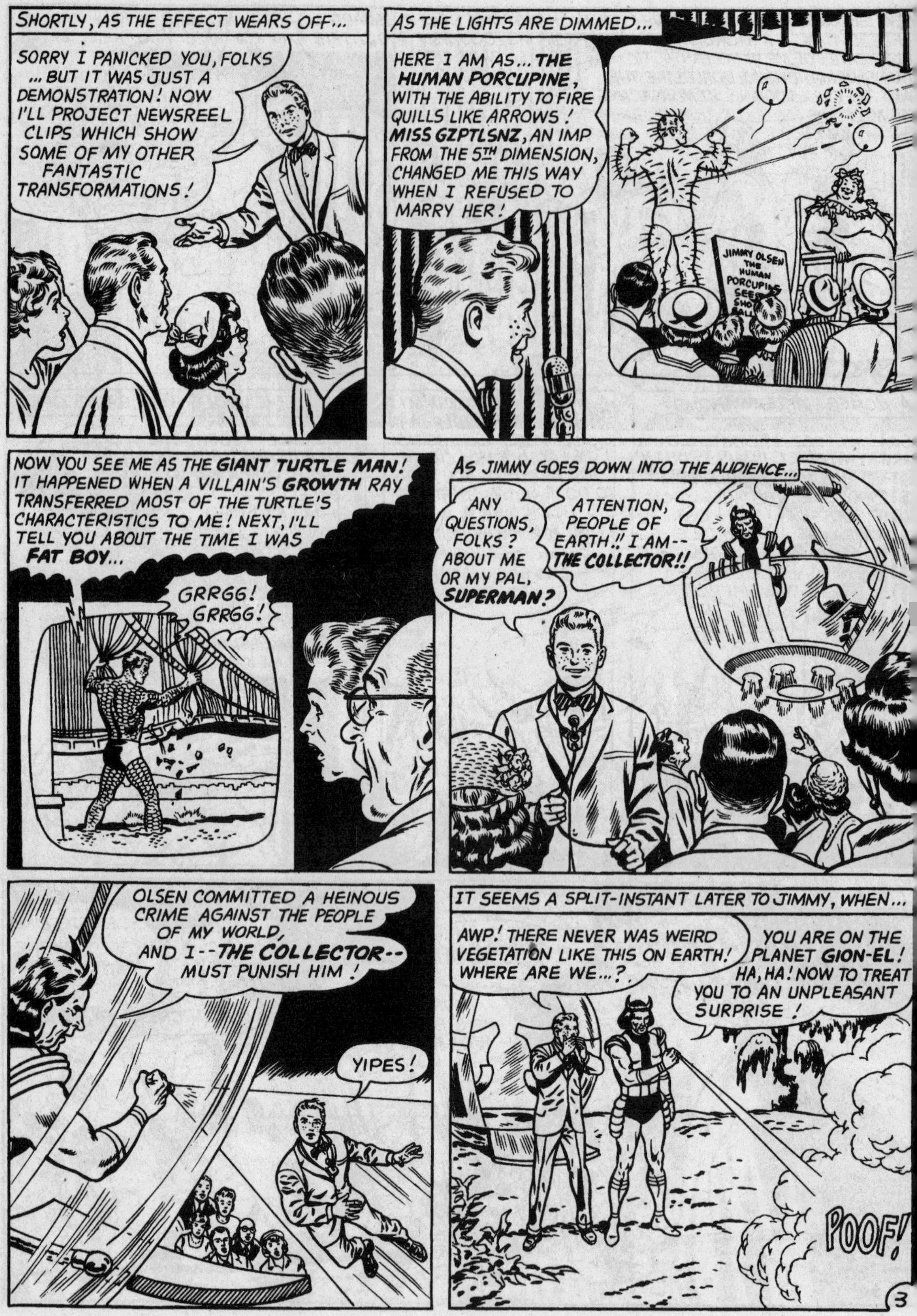
SHORTLY, AS THE EFFECT WEARS OFF...
SORRY I PANICKED YOU, FOLKS ... BUT IT WAS JUST A DEMONSTRATION! NOW I'LL PROJECT NEWSREEL CLIPS WHICH SHOW SOME OF MY OTHER FANTASTIC TRANSFORMATIONS!
AS THE LIGHTS ARE DIMMED...
HERE I AM AS... THE HUMAN PORCUPINE, WITH THE ABILITY TO FIRE QUILLS LIKE ARROWS! MISS GZPTLSNZ, AN IMP FROM THE 5TH DIMENSION, CHANGED ME THIS WAY WHEN I REFUSED TO MARRY HER!
JIMMY OLSEN THE HUMAN PORCUPINE
NOW YOU SEE ME AS THE GIANT TURTLE MAN! IT HAPPENED WHEN A VILLAIN'S GROWTH RAY TRANSFERRED MOST OF THE TURTLE'S CHARACTERISTICS TO ME! NEXT, I'LL TELL YOU ABOUT THE TIME I WAS FAT BOY...
GRRGG! GRRGG!
AS JIMMY GOES DOWN INTO THE AUDIENCE...
ANY QUESTIONS, FOLKS? ABOUT ME OR MY PAL, SUPERMAN?
ATTENTION, PEOPLE OF EARTH!! I AM-- THE COLLECTOR!!
OLSEN COMMITTED A HEINOUS CRIME AGAINST THE PEOPLE OF MY WORLD, AND I--THE COLLECTOR-- MUST PUNISH HIM!
YIPES!
IT SEEMS A SPLIT-INSTANT LATER TO JIMMY, WHEN...
AWP! THERE NEVER WAS WEIRD VEGETATION LIKE THIS ON EARTH! WHERE ARE WE...?
YOU ARE ON THE PLANET GION-EL! HA, HA! NOW TO TREAT YOU TO AN UNPLEASANT SURPRISE!
POOF!
3

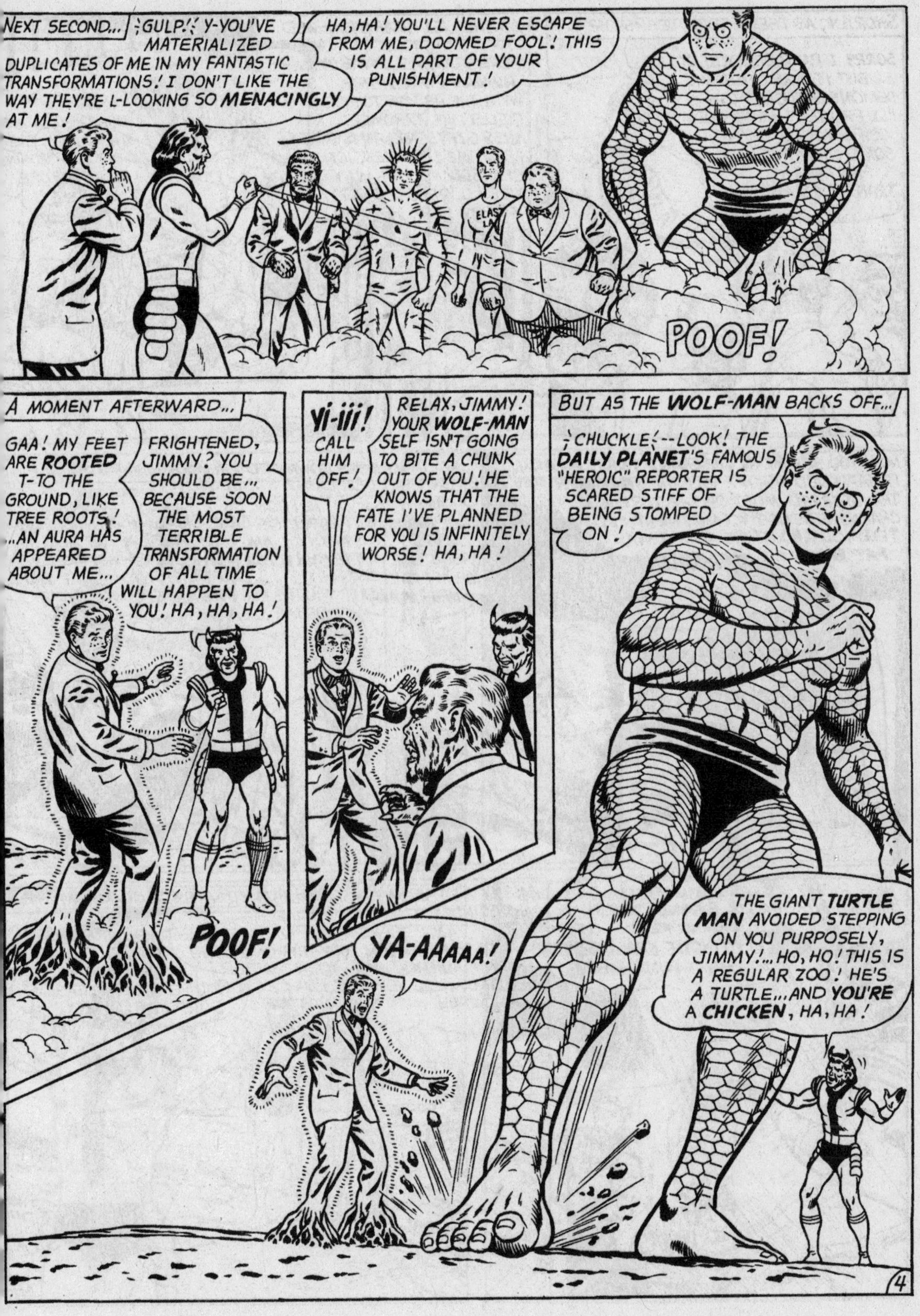
NEXT SECOND...
¡GULP!¡ Y-YOU'VE MATERIALIZED DUPLICATES OF ME IN MY FANTASTIC TRANSFORMATIONS! I DON'T LIKE THE WAY THEY'RE L-LOOKING SO MENACINGLY AT ME!
HA, HA! YOU'LL NEVER ESCAPE FROM ME, DOOMED FOOL! THIS IS ALL PART OF YOUR PUNISHMENT!
ELASTIC LAD
POOF!
A MOMENT AFTERWARD...
GAA! MY FEET ARE ROOTED T-TO THE GROUND, LIKE TREE ROOTS! ...AN AURA HAS APPEARED ABOUT ME...
FRIGHTENED, JIMMY? YOU SHOULD BE... BECAUSE SOON THE MOST TERRIBLE TRANSFORMATION OF ALL TIME WILL HAPPEN TO YOU! HA, HA, HA!
POOF!
YI-III! CALL HIM OFF!
RELAX, JIMMY! YOUR WOLF-MAN SELF ISN'T GOING TO BITE A CHUNK OUT OF YOU! HE KNOWS THAT THE FATE I'VE PLANNED FOR YOU IS INFINITELY WORSE! HA, HA!
BUT AS THE WOLF-MAN BACKS OFF...
¡CHUCKLE¡--LOOK! THE DAILY PLANET'S FAMOUS "HEROIC" REPORTER IS SCARED STIFF OF BEING STOMPED ON!
YA-AAAAA!
THE GIANT TURTLE MAN AVOIDED STEPPING ON YOU PURPOSELY, JIMMY!... HO, HO! THIS IS A REGULAR ZOO! HE'S A TURTLE... AND YOU'RE A CHICKEN, HA, HA!
4

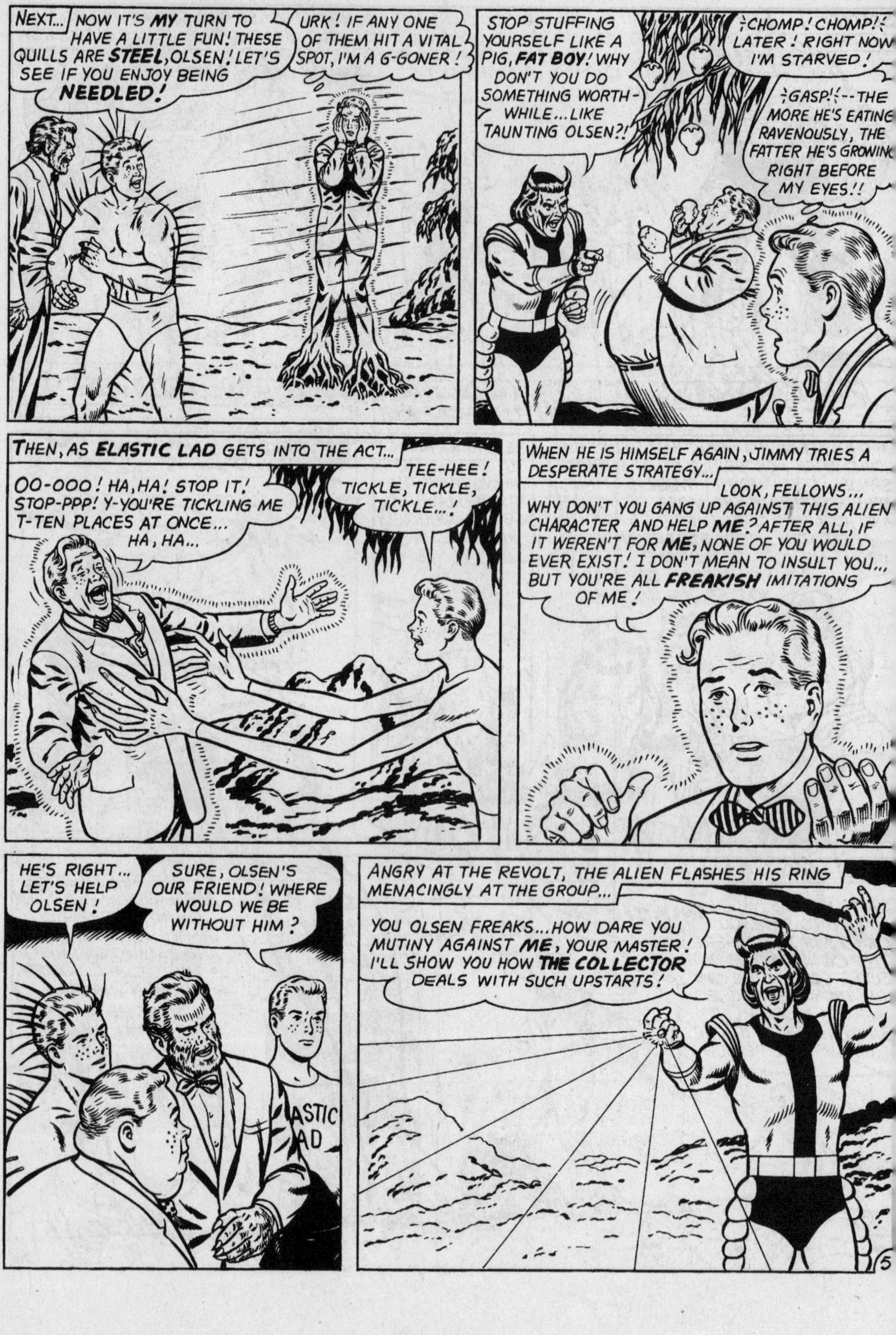
NEXT...
NOW IT'S MY TURN TO HAVE A LITTLE FUN! THESE QUILLS ARE STEEL, OLSEN! LET'S SEE IF YOU ENJOY BEING NEEDLED!
URK! IF ANY ONE OF THEM HIT A VITAL SPOT, I'M A G-GONER!
STOP STUFFING YOURSELF LIKE A PIG, FAT BOY! WHY DON'T YOU DO SOMETHING WORTH-WHILE... LIKE TAUNTING OLSEN?!
¦CHOMP! CHOMP!¦ LATER! RIGHT NOW I'M STARVED!
¦GASP!¦--THE MORE HE'S EATING RAVENOUSLY, THE FATTER HE'S GROWING RIGHT BEFORE MY EYES!!
THEN, AS ELASTIC LAD GETS INTO THE ACT...
OO-OOO! HA, HA! STOP IT! STOP-PPP! Y-YOU'RE TICKLING ME T-TEN PLACES AT ONCE... HA, HA...
TEE-HEE! TICKLE, TICKLE, TICKLE...!
WHEN HE IS HIMSELF AGAIN, JIMMY TRIES A DESPERATE STRATEGY...
LOOK, FELLOWS... WHY DON'T YOU GANG UP AGAINST THIS ALIEN CHARACTER AND HELP ME? AFTER ALL, IF IT WEREN'T FOR ME, NONE OF YOU WOULD EVER EXIST! I DON'T MEAN TO INSULT YOU... BUT YOU'RE ALL FREAKISH IMITATIONS OF ME!
HE'S RIGHT... LET'S HELP OLSEN!
SURE, OLSEN'S OUR FRIEND! WHERE WOULD WE BE WITHOUT HIM?
ASTIC AD
ANGRY AT THE REVOLT, THE ALIEN FLASHES HIS RING MENACINGLY AT THE GROUP...
YOU OLSEN FREAKS... HOW DARE YOU MUTINY AGAINST ME, YOUR MASTER! I'LL SHOW YOU HOW THE COLLECTOR DEALS WITH SUCH UPSTARTS!
5

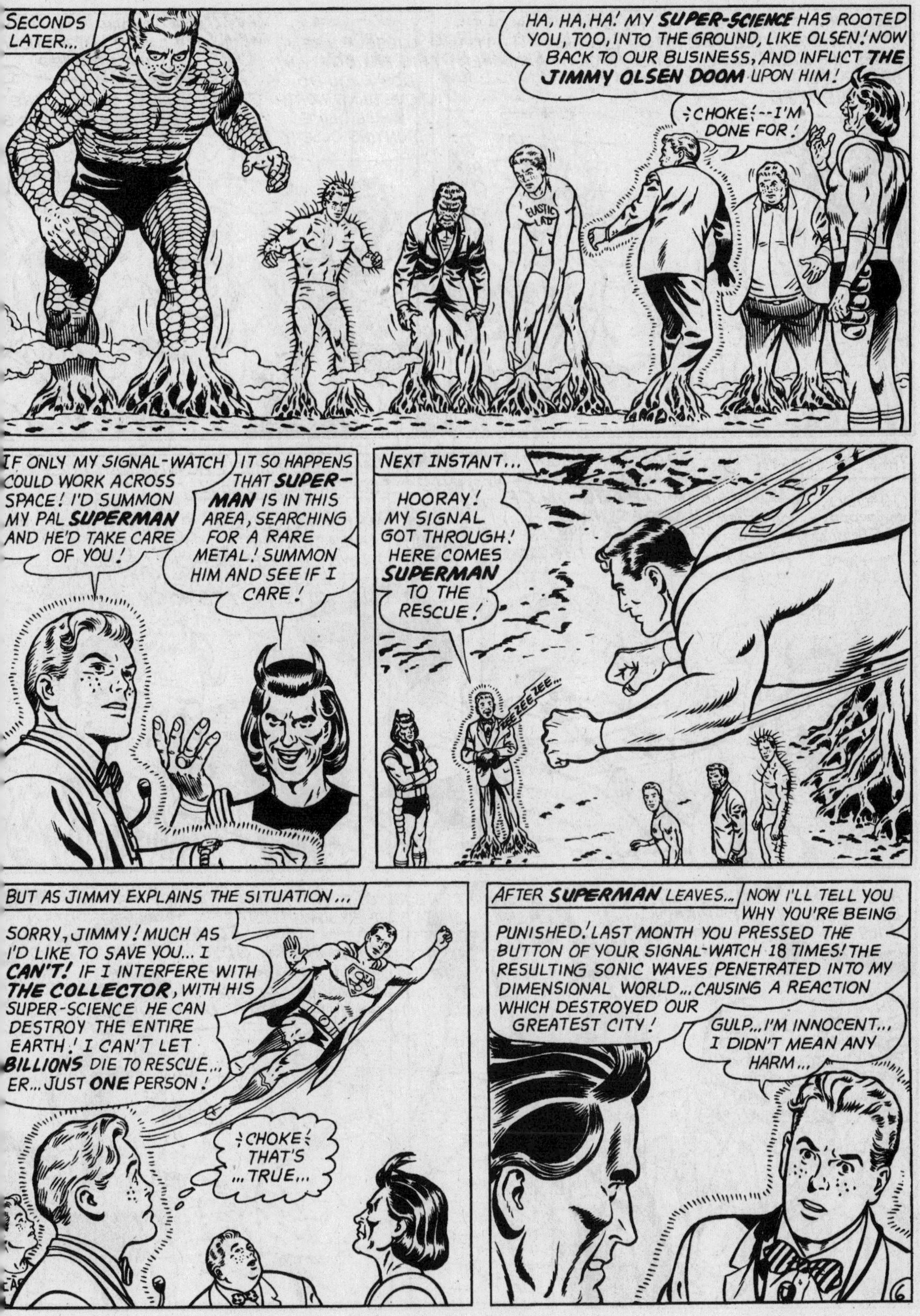
SECONDS LATER...
HA, HA, HA! MY SUPER-SCIENCE HAS ROOTED YOU, TOO, INTO THE GROUND, LIKE OLSEN! NOW BACK TO OUR BUSINESS, AND INFLICT THE JIMMY OLSEN DOOM UPON HIM!
CHOKE --I'M DONE FOR!
ELASTIC LAD
IF ONLY MY SIGNAL-WATCH COULD WORK ACROSS SPACE! I'D SUMMON MY PAL SUPERMAN AND HE'D TAKE CARE OF YOU!
IT SO HAPPENS THAT SUPERMAN IS IN THIS AREA, SEARCHING FOR A RARE METAL! SUMMON HIM AND SEE IF I CARE!
NEXT INSTANT...
HOORAY! MY SIGNAL GOT THROUGH! HERE COMES SUPERMAN TO THE RESCUE!
ZEE ZEE ZEE...
BUT AS JIMMY EXPLAINS THE SITUATION...
SORRY, JIMMY! MUCH AS I'D LIKE TO SAVE YOU... I CAN'T! IF I INTERFERE WITH THE COLLECTOR, WITH HIS SUPER-SCIENCE HE CAN DESTROY THE ENTIRE EARTH! I CAN'T LET BILLIONS DIE TO RESCUE... ER... JUST ONE PERSON!
CHOKE THAT'S ...TRUE...
AFTER SUPERMAN LEAVES...
NOW I'LL TELL YOU WHY YOU'RE BEING PUNISHED! LAST MONTH YOU PRESSED THE BUTTON OF YOUR SIGNAL-WATCH 18 TIMES! THE RESULTING SONIC WAVES PENETRATED INTO MY DIMENSIONAL WORLD... CAUSING A REACTION WHICH DESTROYED OUR GREATEST CITY!
GULP... I'M INNOCENT... I DIDN'T MEAN ANY HARM...
6

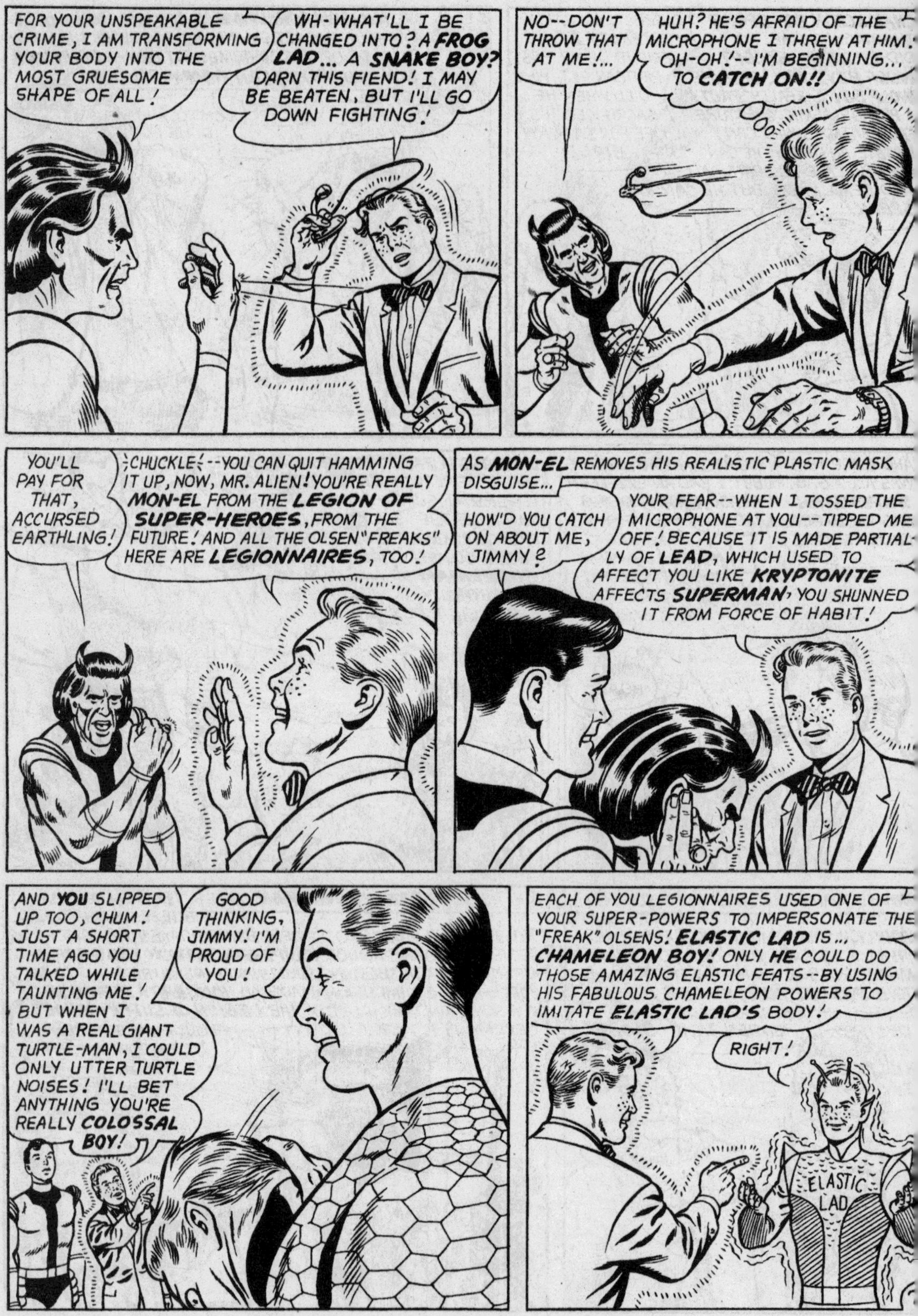
FOR YOUR UNSPEAKABLE CRIME, I AM TRANSFORMING YOUR BODY INTO THE MOST GRUESOME SHAPE OF ALL!
WH-WHAT'LL I BE CHANGED INTO? A FROG LAD... A SNAKE BOY? DARN THIS FIEND! I MAY BE BEATEN, BUT I'LL GO DOWN FIGHTING!
NO--DON'T THROW THAT AT ME!...
HUH? HE'S AFRAID OF THE MICROPHONE I THREW AT HIM. OH-OH!--I'M BEGINNING... TO CATCH ON!!
YOU'LL PAY FOR THAT, ACCURSED EARTHLING!
¡CHUCKLE¡--YOU CAN QUIT HAMMING IT UP, NOW, MR. ALIEN! YOU'RE REALLY MON-EL FROM THE LEGION OF SUPER-HEROES, FROM THE FUTURE! AND ALL THE OLSEN "FREAKS" HERE ARE LEGIONNAIRES, TOO!
AS MON-EL REMOVES HIS REALISTIC PLASTIC MASK DISGUISE...
HOW'D YOU CATCH ON ABOUT ME, JIMMY?
YOUR FEAR--WHEN I TOSSED THE MICROPHONE AT YOU--TIPPED ME OFF! BECAUSE IT IS MADE PARTIALLY OF LEAD, WHICH USED TO AFFECT YOU LIKE KRYPTONITE AFFECTS SUPERMAN, YOU SHUNNED IT FROM FORCE OF HABIT!
AND YOU SLIPPED UP TOO, CHUM! JUST A SHORT TIME AGO YOU TALKED WHILE TAUNTING ME! BUT WHEN I WAS A REAL GIANT TURTLE-MAN, I COULD ONLY UTTER TURTLE NOISES! I'LL BET ANYTHING YOU'RE REALLY COLOSSAL BOY!
GOOD THINKING, JIMMY! I'M PROUD OF YOU!
EACH OF YOU LEGIONNAIRES USED ONE OF YOUR SUPER-POWERS TO IMPERSONATE THE "FREAK" OLSENS! ELASTIC LAD IS... CHAMELEON BOY! ONLY HE COULD DO THOSE AMAZING ELASTIC FEATS--BY USING HIS FABULOUS CHAMELEON POWERS TO IMITATE ELASTIC LAD'S BODY!
RIGHT!
ELASTIC LAD

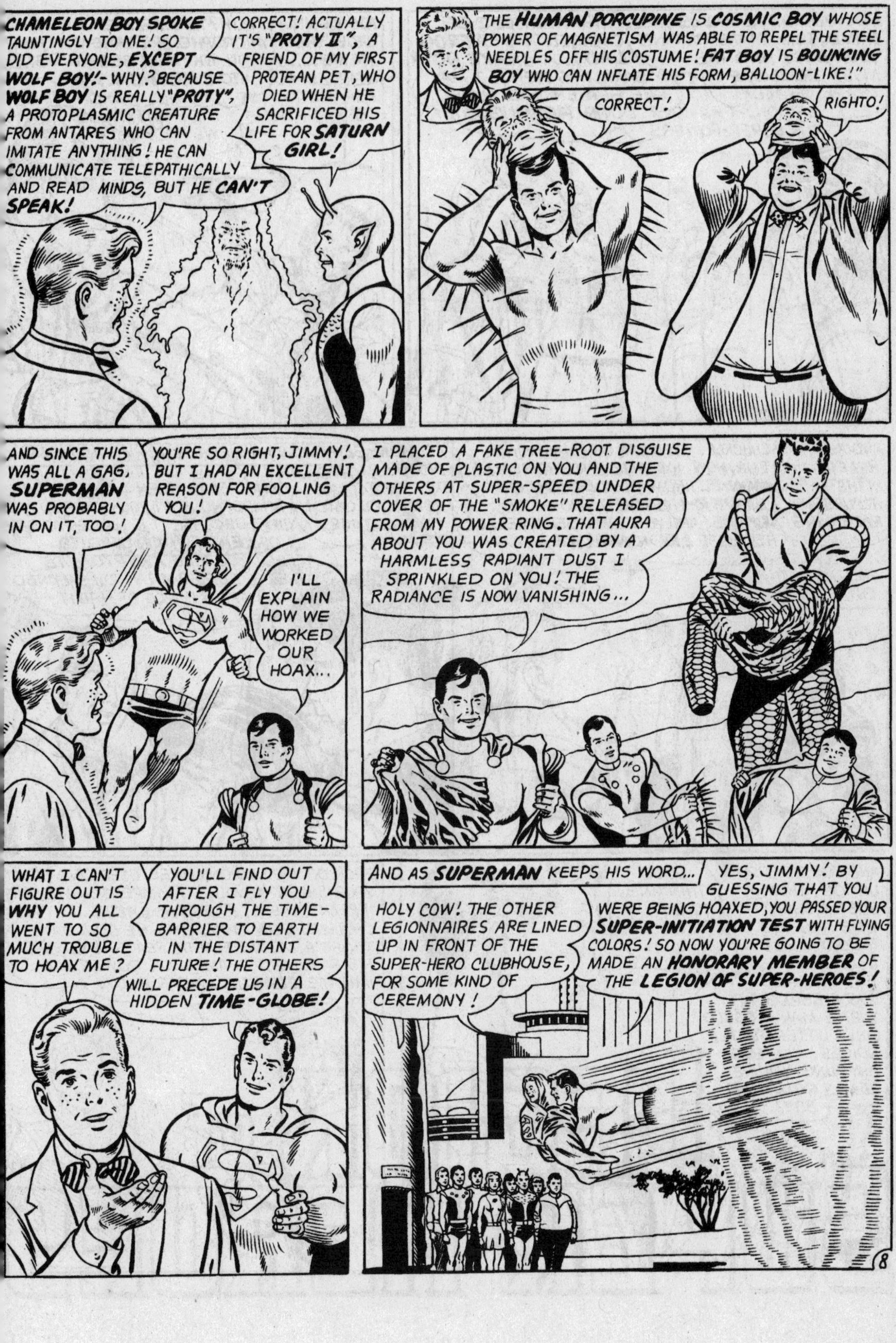
CHAMELEON BOY SPOKE TAUNTINGLY TO ME! SO DID EVERYONE, EXCEPT WOLF BOY!- WHY? BECAUSE WOLF BOY IS REALLY "PROTY", A PROTOPLASMIC CREATURE FROM ANTARES WHO CAN IMITATE ANYTHING! HE CAN COMMUNICATE TELEPATHICALLY AND READ MINDS, BUT HE CAN'T SPEAK!
CORRECT! ACTUALLY IT'S "PROTY II", A FRIEND OF MY FIRST PROTEAN PET, WHO DIED WHEN HE SACRIFICED HIS LIFE FOR SATURN GIRL!
"THE HUMAN PORCUPINE IS COSMIC BOY WHOSE POWER OF MAGNETISM WAS ABLE TO REPEL THE STEEL NEEDLES OFF HIS COSTUME! FAT BOY IS BOUNCING BOY WHO CAN INFLATE HIS FORM, BALLOON-LIKE!"
CORRECT!
RIGHTO!
AND SINCE THIS WAS ALL A GAG, SUPERMAN WAS PROBABLY IN ON IT, TOO!
YOU'RE SO RIGHT, JIMMY! BUT I HAD AN EXCELLENT REASON FOR FOOLING YOU!
I'LL EXPLAIN HOW WE WORKED OUR HOAX...
I PLACED A FAKE TREE-ROOT DISGUISE MADE OF PLASTIC ON YOU AND THE OTHERS AT SUPER-SPEED UNDER COVER OF THE "SMOKE" RELEASED FROM MY POWER RING. THAT AURA ABOUT YOU WAS CREATED BY A HARMLESS RADIANT DUST I SPRINKLED ON YOU! THE RADIANCE IS NOW VANISHING...
WHAT I CAN'T FIGURE OUT IS WHY YOU ALL WENT TO SO MUCH TROUBLE TO HOAX ME?
YOU'LL FIND OUT AFTER I FLY YOU THROUGH THE TIME-BARRIER TO EARTH IN THE DISTANT FUTURE! THE OTHERS WILL PRECEDE US IN A HIDDEN TIME-GLOBE!
AND AS SUPERMAN KEEPS HIS WORD...
HOLY COW! THE OTHER LEGIONNAIRES ARE LINED UP IN FRONT OF THE SUPER-HERO CLUBHOUSE, FOR SOME KIND OF CEREMONY!
YES, JIMMY! BY GUESSING THAT YOU WERE BEING HOAXED, YOU PASSED YOUR SUPER-INITIATION TEST WITH FLYING COLORS! SO NOW YOU'RE GOING TO BE MADE AN HONORARY MEMBER OF THE LEGION OF SUPER-HEROES!
8

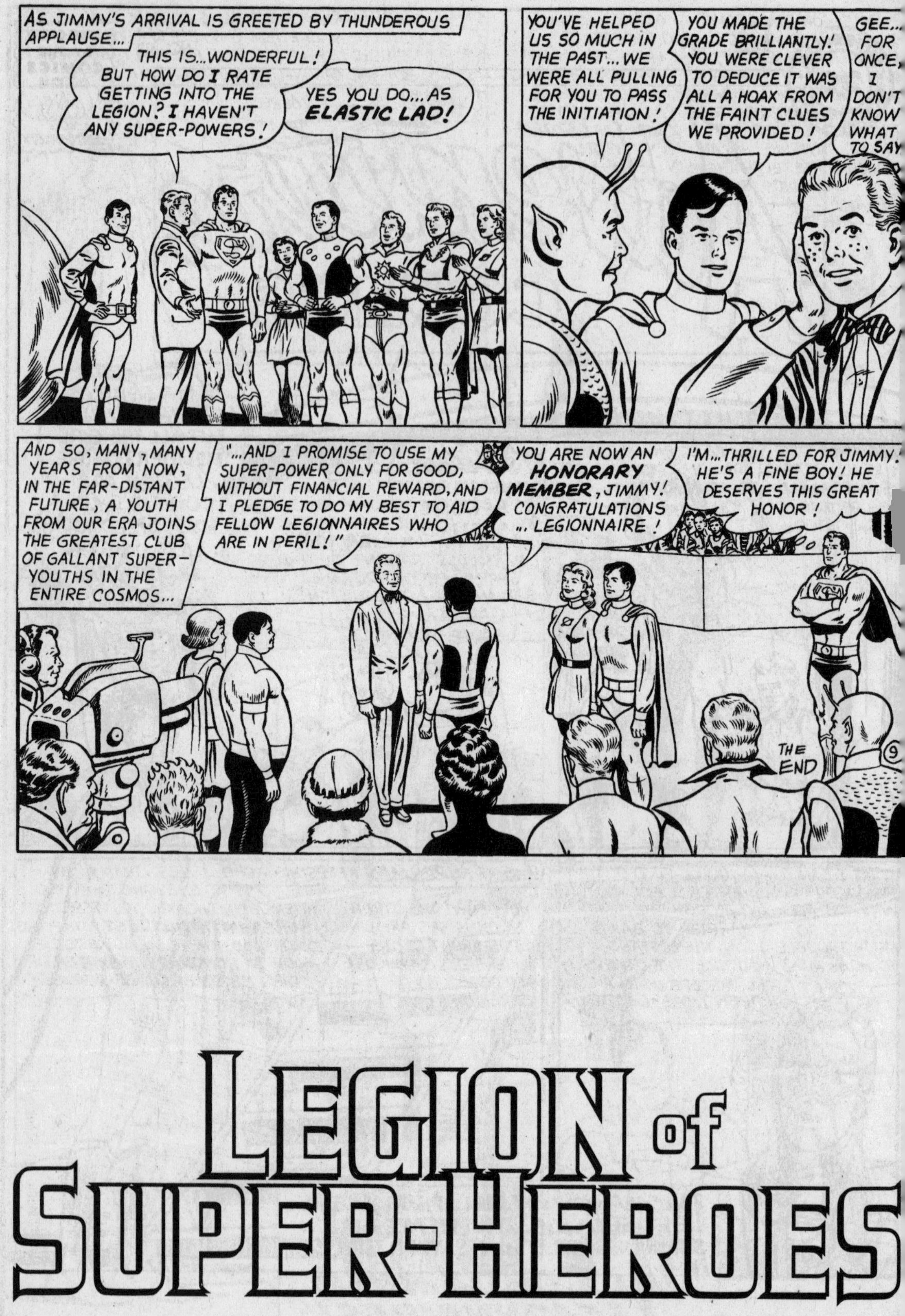
AS JIMMY'S ARRIVAL IS GREETED BY THUNDEROUS APPLAUSE...
THIS IS...WONDERFUL! BUT HOW DO I RATE GETTING INTO THE LEGION? I HAVEN'T ANY SUPER-POWERS!
YES YOU DO...AS ELASTIC LAD!
YOU'VE HELPED US SO MUCH IN THE PAST...WE WERE ALL PULLING FOR YOU TO PASS THE INITIATION!
YOU MADE THE GRADE BRILLIANTLY! YOU WERE CLEVER TO DEDUCE IT WAS ALL A HOAX FROM THE FAINT CLUES WE PROVIDED!
GEE... FOR ONCE, I DON'T KNOW WHAT TO SAY
AND SO, MANY, MANY YEARS FROM NOW, IN THE FAR-DISTANT FUTURE, A YOUTH FROM OUR ERA JOINS THE GREATEST CLUB OF GALLANT SUPER-YOUTHS IN THE ENTIRE COSMOS...
"...AND I PROMISE TO USE MY SUPER-POWER ONLY FOR GOOD, WITHOUT FINANCIAL REWARD, AND I PLEDGE TO DO MY BEST TO AID FELLOW LEGIONNAIRES WHO ARE IN PERIL!"
YOU ARE NOW AN HONORARY MEMBER, JIMMY! CONGRATULATIONS ... LEGIONNAIRE!
I'M...THRILLED FOR JIMMY! HE'S A FINE BOY! HE DESERVES THIS GREAT HONOR!
THE END
9

LEGION of SUPER-HEROES

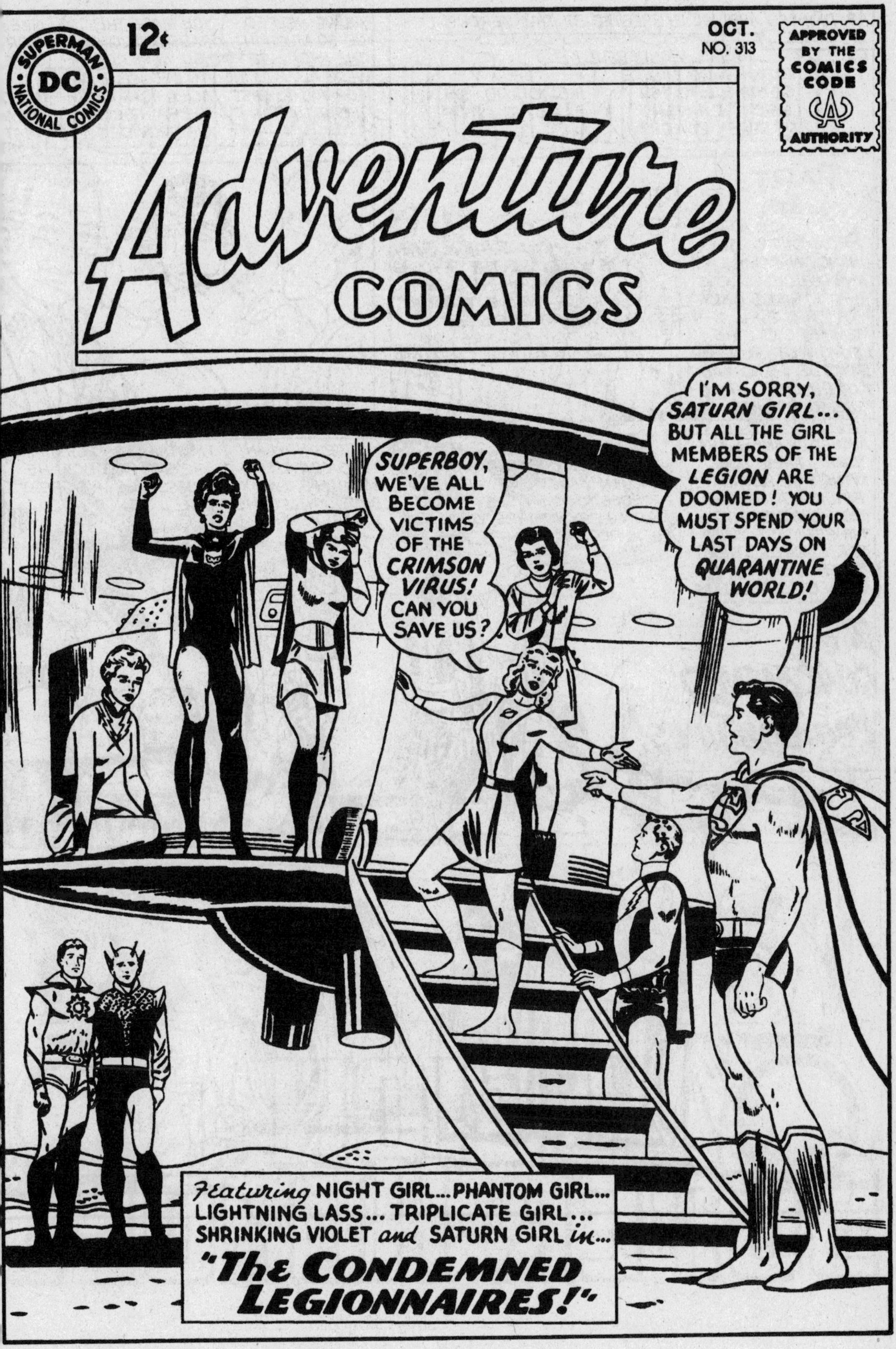
12¢
SUPERMAN DC NATIONAL COMICS
OCT.
NO. 313
APPROVED BY THE COMICS CODE AUTHORITY
Adventure COMICS
SUPERBOY, WE'VE ALL BECOME VICTIMS OF THE CRIMSON VIRUS! CAN YOU SAVE US?
I'M SORRY, SATURN GIRL... BUT ALL THE GIRL MEMBERS OF THE LEGION ARE DOOMED! YOU MUST SPEND YOUR LAST DAYS ON QUARANTINE WORLD!
Featuring NIGHT GIRL... PHANTOM GIRL... LIGHTNING LASS... TRIPLICATE GIRL... SHRINKING VIOLET and SATURN GIRL in...
"The CONDEMNED LEGIONNAIRES!"

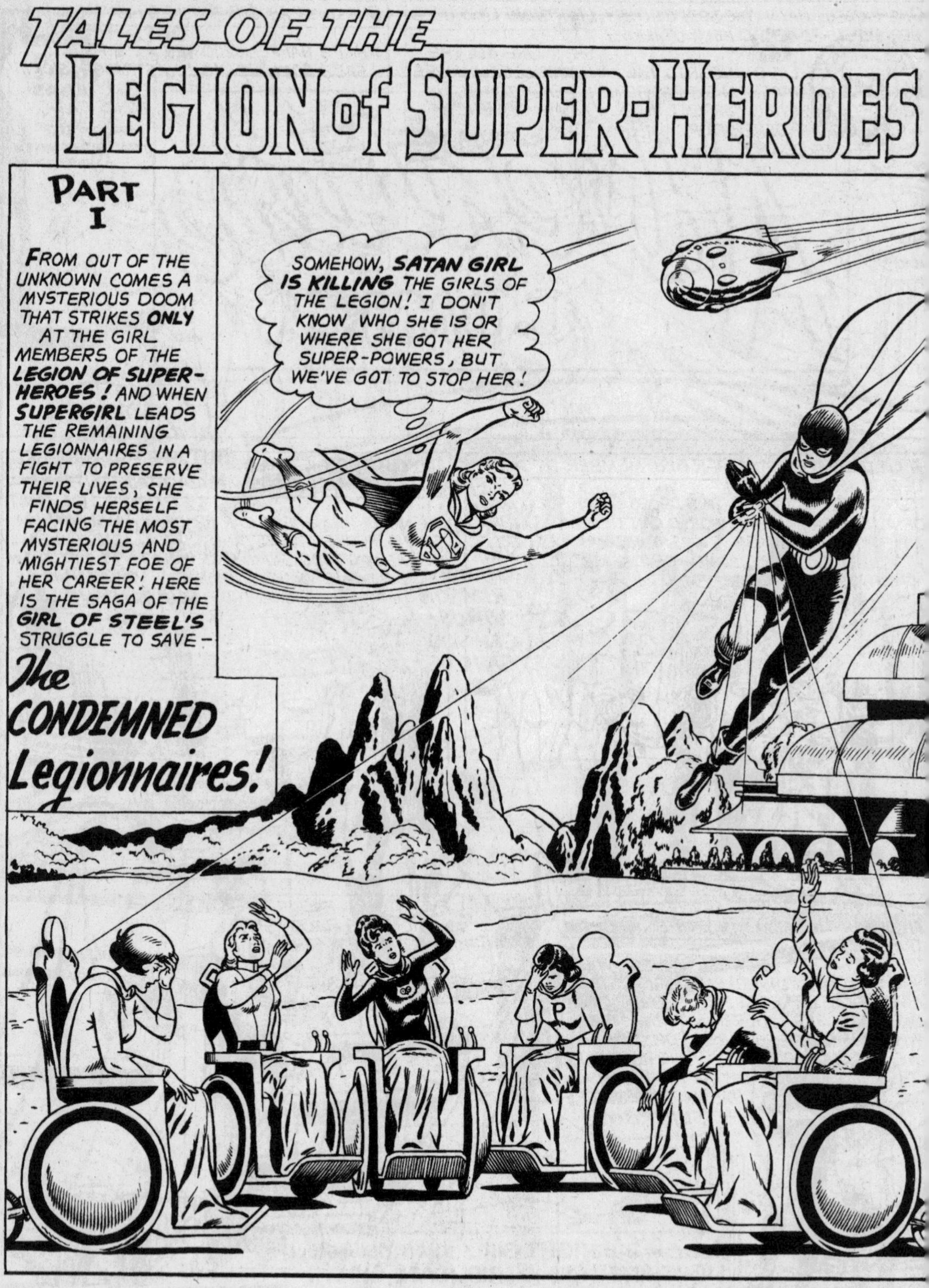
TALES OF THE
LEGION of SUPER-HEROES
PART I
FROM OUT OF THE UNKNOWN COMES A MYSTERIOUS DOOM THAT STRIKES ONLY AT THE GIRL MEMBERS OF THE LEGION OF SUPER-HEROES! AND WHEN SUPERGIRL LEADS THE REMAINING LEGIONNAIRES IN A FIGHT TO PRESERVE THEIR LIVES, SHE FINDS HERSELF FACING THE MOST MYSTERIOUS AND MIGHTIEST FOE OF HER CAREER! HERE IS THE SAGA OF THE GIRL OF STEEL'S STRUGGLE TO SAVE—
The CONDEMNED Legionnaires!
SOMEHOW, SATAN GIRL IS KILLING THE GIRLS OF THE LEGION! I DON'T KNOW WHO SHE IS OR WHERE SHE GOT HER SUPER-POWERS, BUT WE'VE GOT TO STOP HER!

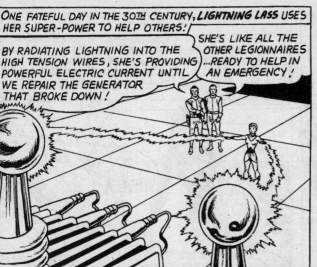

ONE FATEFUL DAY IN THE 30TH CENTURY, *LIGHTNING LASS* USES HER SUPER-POWER TO HELP OTHERS!

BY RADIATING LIGHTNING INTO THE HIGH TENSION WIRES, SHE'S PROVIDING POWERFUL ELECTRIC CURRENT UNTIL WE REPAIR THE GENERATOR THAT BROKE DOWN!

SHE'S LIKE ALL THE OTHER LEGIONNAIRES ...READY TO HELP IN AN EMERGENCY!

BUT JUST AS SHE FINISHES HER TASK...

WHAT'S HAPPENED TO HER ...SHE'S *COLLAPSING!*

I FEEL STRANGE, SICK... EVERYTHING'S GOING DARK...

A LITTLE LATER, ANOTHER GIRL MEMBER OF THE LEGION IS STRICKEN!

OF ALIENS FROM A FAR WORLD CAN'T SPEAK ANY KNOWN LANGUAGE...BUT *SATURN GIRL*, WITH HER TELEPATHIC POWER OF THOUGHT-CASTING, CAN INTERPRET FOR US!

THIS DELEGATION

BUT LOOK... *SATURN GIRL* SUDDENLY SEEMS SICK!

AND OUTSIDE THE CLUBHOUSE OF THE SUPER-HEROES, THE SAME MYSTERIOUS MALADY STRIKES!

WE NEED TO INSPECT OUR SPACE-SHIP'S ROCKET TUBES, AND THAT'LL BE EASY FOR YOU, *SHRINKING VIOLET* ...YOU CAN JUST MAKE YOURSELF TINY AND WALK INSIDE THE TUBES!

I...I CAN'T, *SUN BOY!* I'M DIZZY, WEAK... I DON'T KNOW WHAT'S HIT ME...

SUPER-HEROES CLUBHOUSE

SOON, WHEN *SUPERBOY* ARRIVES TO SHARE AN URGENT MISSION WITH *MON-EL*, HE GETS TRAGIC TIDINGS!

MON-EL, YOU SAID TWO PLANETS FAR ACROSS THE UNIVERSE ARE ON A COLLISION COURSE! WITH OUR SUPER-POWERS, WE TWO CAN PREVENT THEIR COLLIDING!

YES, WE MUST START SOON ON THAT LIFE-OR-DEATH MISSION! BUT AN AWFUL THING HAS HAPPENED HERE, *SUPERBOY!*

EVERY *GIRL* IN OUR LEGION HAS BECOME THE VICTIM OF A STRANGE, CRIMSON VIRUS... AND WE CAN'T FIND A CURE!

THIS IS TERRIBLE NEWS!

2

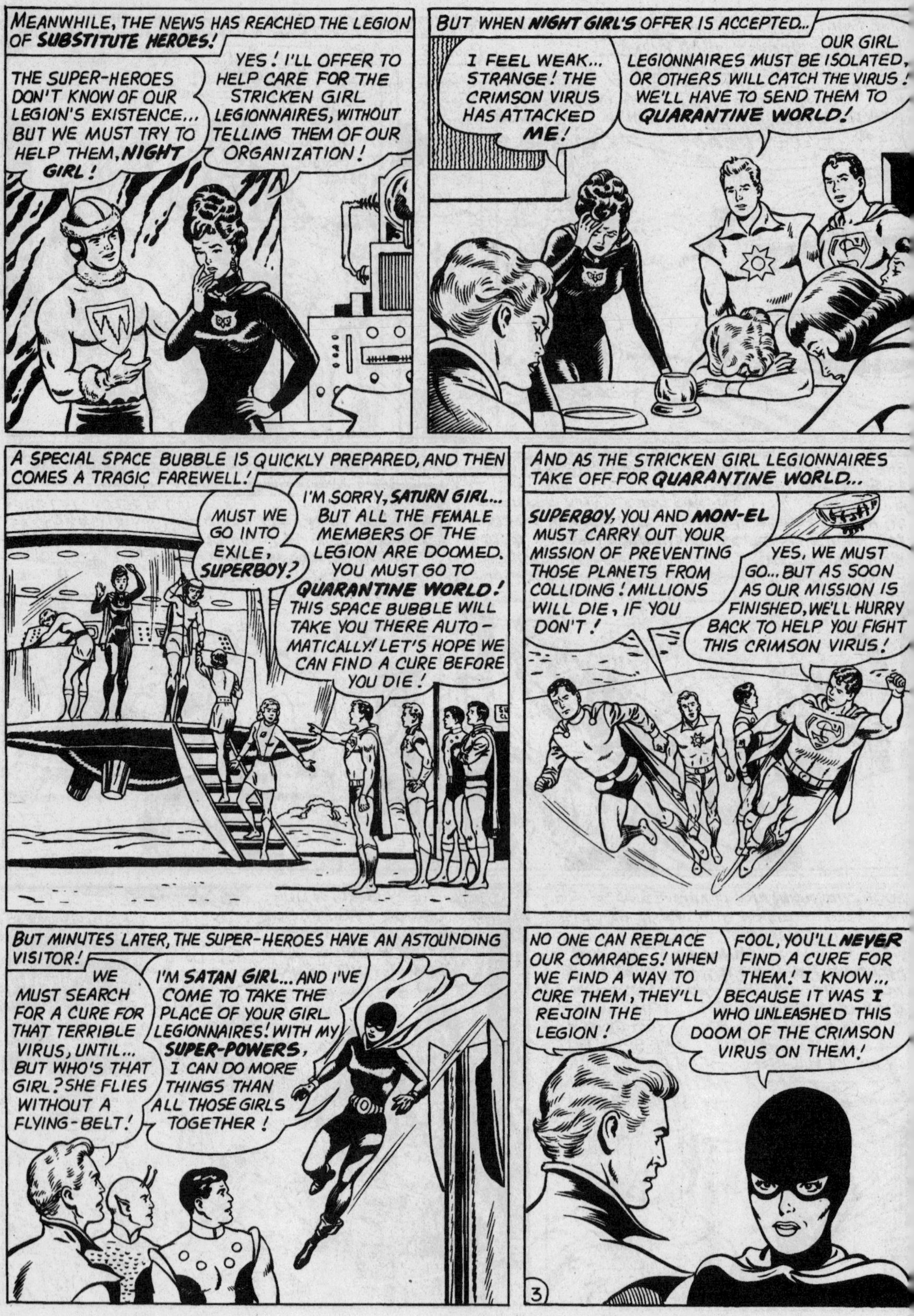
MEANWHILE, THE NEWS HAS REACHED THE LEGION OF SUBSTITUTE HEROES!
THE SUPER-HEROES DON'T KNOW OF OUR LEGION'S EXISTENCE... BUT WE MUST TRY TO HELP THEM, NIGHT GIRL!
YES! I'LL OFFER TO HELP CARE FOR THE STRICKEN GIRL LEGIONNAIRES, WITHOUT TELLING THEM OF OUR ORGANIZATION!
BUT WHEN NIGHT GIRL'S OFFER IS ACCEPTED...
I FEEL WEAK... STRANGE! THE CRIMSON VIRUS HAS ATTACKED ME!
OUR GIRL LEGIONNAIRES MUST BE ISOLATED, OR OTHERS WILL CATCH THE VIRUS! WE'LL HAVE TO SEND THEM TO QUARANTINE WORLD!
A SPECIAL SPACE BUBBLE IS QUICKLY PREPARED, AND THEN COMES A TRAGIC FAREWELL!
MUST WE GO INTO EXILE, SUPERBOY?
I'M SORRY, SATURN GIRL... BUT ALL THE FEMALE MEMBERS OF THE LEGION ARE DOOMED. YOU MUST GO TO QUARANTINE WORLD! THIS SPACE BUBBLE WILL TAKE YOU THERE AUTO-MATICALLY! LET'S HOPE WE CAN FIND A CURE BEFORE YOU DIE!
AND AS THE STRICKEN GIRL LEGIONNAIRES TAKE OFF FOR QUARANTINE WORLD...
SUPERBOY, YOU AND MON-EL MUST CARRY OUT YOUR MISSION OF PREVENTING THOSE PLANETS FROM COLLIDING! MILLIONS WILL DIE, IF YOU DON'T!
YES, WE MUST GO... BUT AS SOON AS OUR MISSION IS FINISHED, WE'LL HURRY BACK TO HELP YOU FIGHT THIS CRIMSON VIRUS!
BUT MINUTES LATER, THE SUPER-HEROES HAVE AN ASTOUNDING VISITOR!
WE MUST SEARCH FOR A CURE FOR THAT TERRIBLE VIRUS, UNTIL... BUT WHO'S THAT GIRL? SHE FLIES WITHOUT A FLYING-BELT!
I'M SATAN GIRL... AND I'VE COME TO TAKE THE PLACE OF YOUR GIRL LEGIONNAIRES! WITH MY SUPER-POWERS, I CAN DO MORE THINGS THAN ALL THOSE GIRLS TOGETHER!
NO ONE CAN REPLACE OUR COMRADES! WHEN WE FIND A WAY TO CURE THEM, THEY'LL REJOIN THE LEGION!
FOOL, YOU'LL NEVER FIND A CURE FOR THEM! I KNOW... BECAUSE IT WAS I WHO UNLEASHED THIS DOOM OF THE CRIMSON VIRUS ON THEM!
3

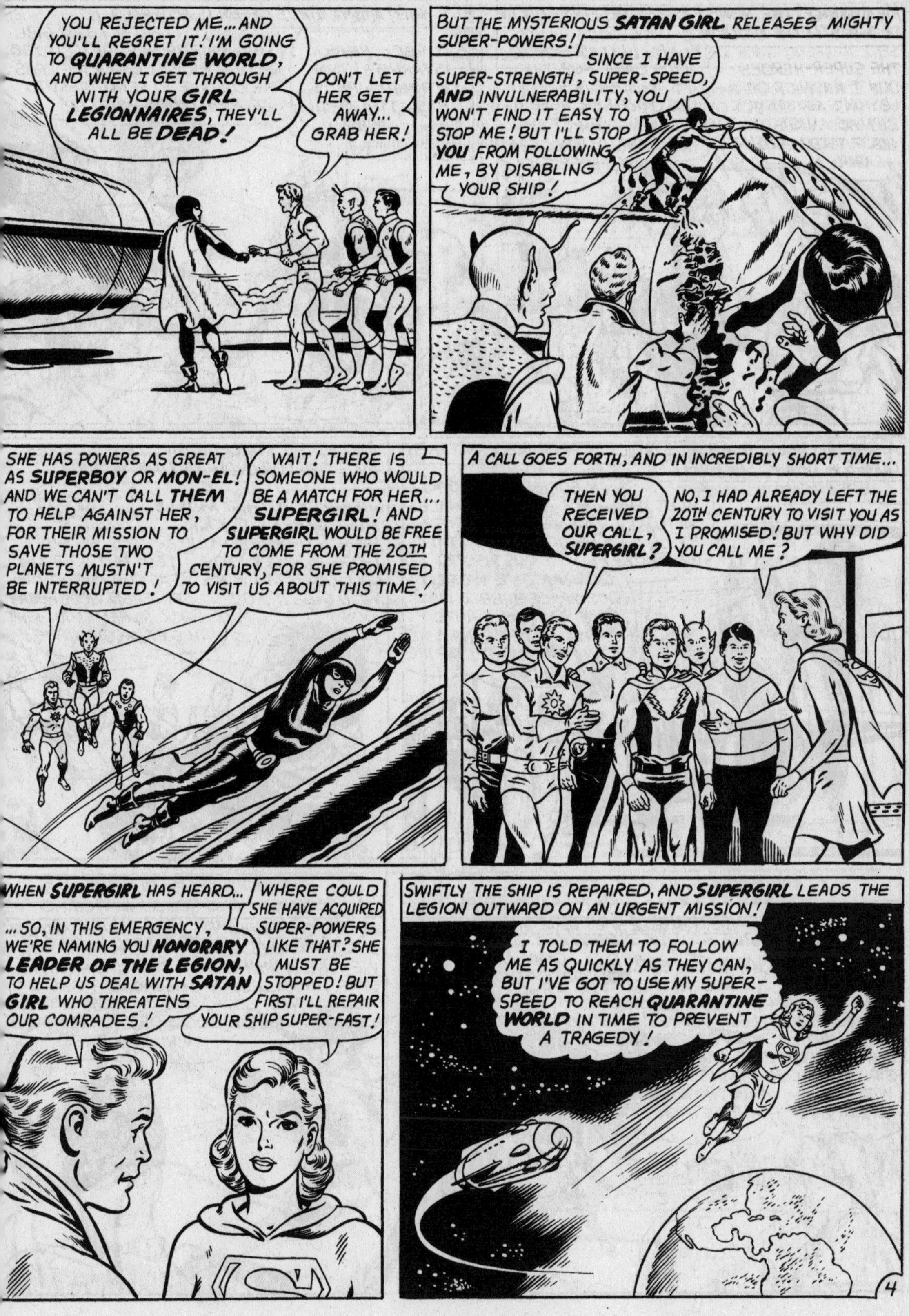
YOU REJECTED ME... AND YOU'LL REGRET IT! I'M GOING TO QUARANTINE WORLD, AND WHEN I GET THROUGH WITH YOUR GIRL LEGIONNAIRES, THEY'LL ALL BE DEAD!
DON'T LET HER GET AWAY... GRAB HER!
BUT THE MYSTERIOUS SATAN GIRL RELEASES MIGHTY SUPER-POWERS!
SINCE I HAVE SUPER-STRENGTH, SUPER-SPEED, AND INVULNERABILITY, YOU WON'T FIND IT EASY TO STOP ME! BUT I'LL STOP YOU FROM FOLLOWING ME, BY DISABLING YOUR SHIP!
SHE HAS POWERS AS GREAT AS SUPERBOY OR MON-EL! AND WE CAN'T CALL THEM TO HELP AGAINST HER, FOR THEIR MISSION TO SAVE THOSE TWO PLANETS MUSTN'T BE INTERRUPTED!
WAIT! THERE IS SOMEONE WHO WOULD BE A MATCH FOR HER... SUPERGIRL! AND SUPERGIRL WOULD BE FREE TO COME FROM THE 20TH CENTURY, FOR SHE PROMISED TO VISIT US ABOUT THIS TIME!
A CALL GOES FORTH, AND IN INCREDIBLY SHORT TIME...
THEN YOU RECEIVED OUR CALL, SUPERGIRL?
NO, I HAD ALREADY LEFT THE 20TH CENTURY TO VISIT YOU AS I PROMISED! BUT WHY DID YOU CALL ME?
WHEN SUPERGIRL HAS HEARD...
...SO, IN THIS EMERGENCY, WE'RE NAMING YOU HONORARY LEADER OF THE LEGION, TO HELP US DEAL WITH SATAN GIRL WHO THREATENS OUR COMRADES!
WHERE COULD SHE HAVE ACQUIRED SUPER-POWERS LIKE THAT? SHE MUST BE STOPPED! BUT FIRST I'LL REPAIR YOUR SHIP SUPER-FAST!
SWIFTLY THE SHIP IS REPAIRED, AND SUPERGIRL LEADS THE LEGION OUTWARD ON AN URGENT MISSION!
I TOLD THEM TO FOLLOW ME AS QUICKLY AS THEY CAN, BUT I'VE GOT TO USE MY SUPER-SPEED TO REACH QUARANTINE WORLD IN TIME TO PREVENT A TRAGEDY!
4

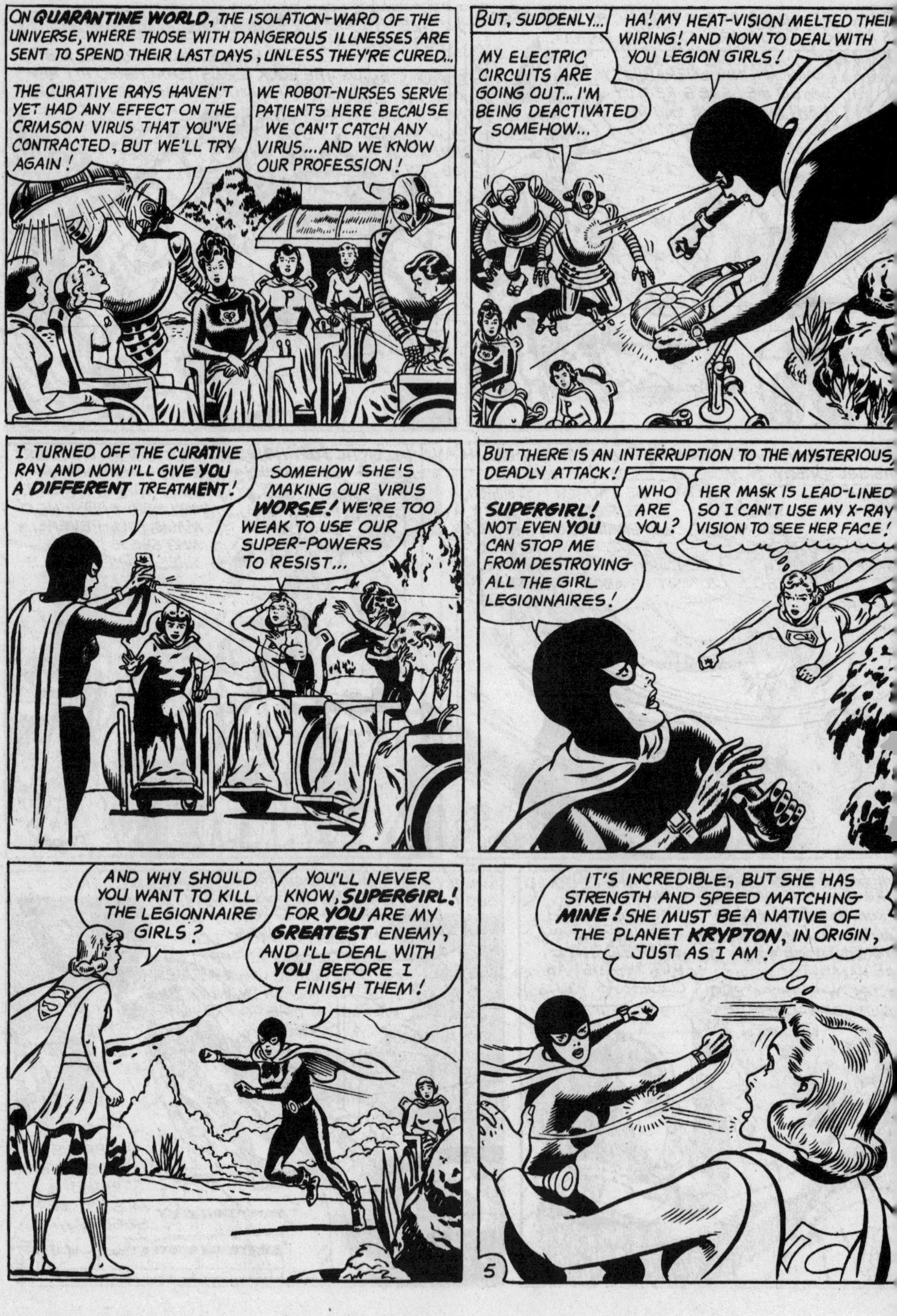
ON QUARANTINE WORLD, THE ISOLATION-WARD OF THE UNIVERSE, WHERE THOSE WITH DANGEROUS ILLNESSES ARE SENT TO SPEND THEIR LAST DAYS, UNLESS THEY'RE CURED...
THE CURATIVE RAYS HAVEN'T YET HAD ANY EFFECT ON THE CRIMSON VIRUS THAT YOU'VE CONTRACTED, BUT WE'LL TRY AGAIN!
WE ROBOT-NURSES SERVE PATIENTS HERE BECAUSE WE CAN'T CATCH ANY VIRUS...AND WE KNOW OUR PROFESSION!
BUT, SUDDENLY...
MY ELECTRIC CIRCUITS ARE GOING OUT... I'M BEING DEACTIVATED SOMEHOW...
HA! MY HEAT-VISION MELTED THEI WIRING! AND NOW TO DEAL WITH YOU LEGION GIRLS!
I TURNED OFF THE CURATIVE RAY AND NOW I'LL GIVE YOU A DIFFERENT TREATMENT!
SOMEHOW SHE'S MAKING OUR VIRUS WORSE! WE'RE TOO WEAK TO USE OUR SUPER-POWERS TO RESIST...
BUT THERE IS AN INTERRUPTION TO THE MYSTERIOUS, DEADLY ATTACK!
SUPERGIRL! NOT EVEN YOU CAN STOP ME FROM DESTROYING ALL THE GIRL LEGIONNAIRES!
WHO ARE YOU?
HER MASK IS LEAD-LINED SO I CAN'T USE MY X-RAY VISION TO SEE HER FACE!
AND WHY SHOULD YOU WANT TO KILL THE LEGIONNAIRE GIRLS?
YOU'LL NEVER KNOW, SUPERGIRL! FOR YOU ARE MY GREATEST ENEMY, AND I'LL DEAL WITH YOU BEFORE I FINISH THEM!
5
IT'S INCREDIBLE, BUT SHE HAS STRENGTH AND SPEED MATCHING MINE! SHE MUST BE A NATIVE OF THE PLANET KRYPTON, IN ORIGIN, JUST AS I AM!

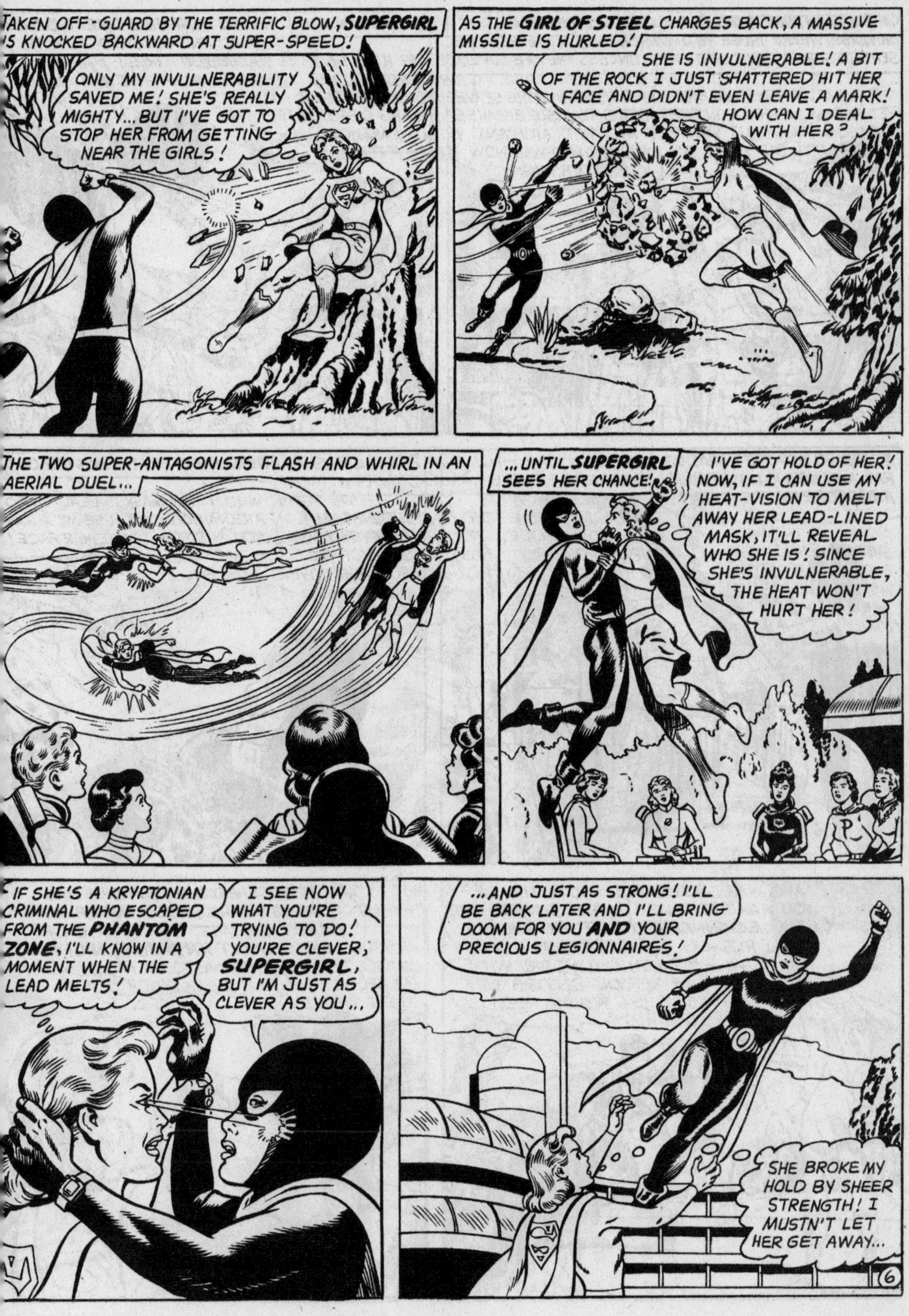
TAKEN OFF-GUARD BY THE TERRIFIC BLOW, SUPERGIRL IS KNOCKED BACKWARD AT SUPER-SPEED!
ONLY MY INVULNERABILITY SAVED ME! SHE'S REALLY MIGHTY... BUT I'VE GOT TO STOP HER FROM GETTING NEAR THE GIRLS!
AS THE GIRL OF STEEL CHARGES BACK, A MASSIVE MISSILE IS HURLED!
SHE IS INVULNERABLE! A BIT OF THE ROCK I JUST SHATTERED HIT HER FACE AND DIDN'T EVEN LEAVE A MARK! HOW CAN I DEAL WITH HER?
THE TWO SUPER-ANTAGONISTS FLASH AND WHIRL IN AN AERIAL DUEL...
...UNTIL SUPERGIRL SEES HER CHANCE!
I'VE GOT HOLD OF HER! NOW, IF I CAN USE MY HEAT-VISION TO MELT AWAY HER LEAD-LINED MASK, IT'LL REVEAL WHO SHE IS! SINCE SHE'S INVULNERABLE, THE HEAT WON'T HURT HER!
IF SHE'S A KRYPTONIAN CRIMINAL WHO ESCAPED FROM THE PHANTOM ZONE, I'LL KNOW IN A MOMENT WHEN THE LEAD MELTS!
I SEE NOW WHAT YOU'RE TRYING TO DO! YOU'RE CLEVER, SUPERGIRL, BUT I'M JUST AS CLEVER AS YOU...
...AND JUST AS STRONG! I'LL BE BACK LATER AND I'LL BRING DOOM FOR YOU AND YOUR PRECIOUS LEGIONNAIRES!
SHE BROKE MY HOLD BY SHEER STRENGTH! I MUSTN'T LET HER GET AWAY...
6

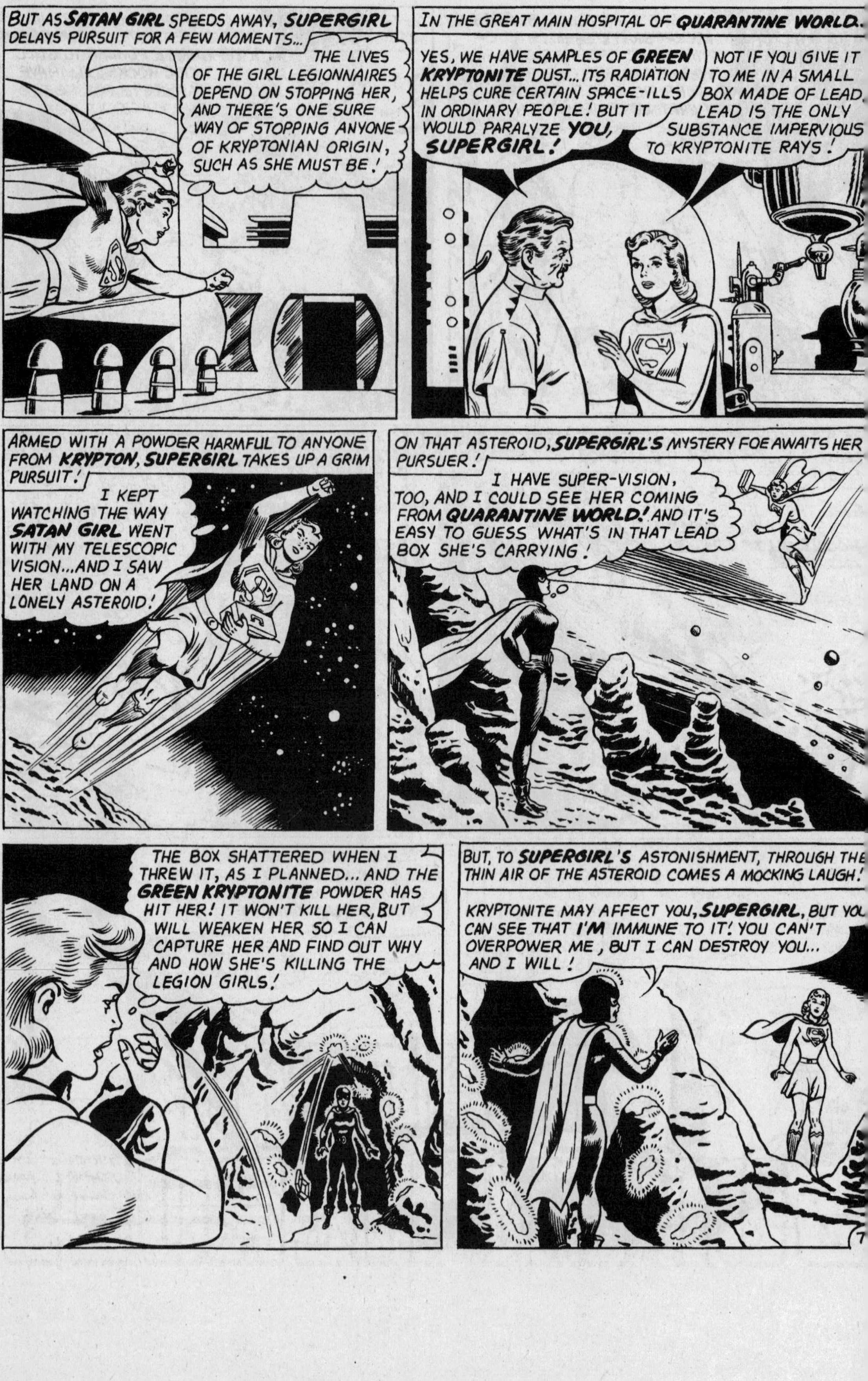
BUT AS SATAN GIRL SPEEDS AWAY, SUPERGIRL DELAYS PURSUIT FOR A FEW MOMENTS...
THE LIVES OF THE GIRL LEGIONNAIRES DEPEND ON STOPPING HER, AND THERE'S ONE SURE WAY OF STOPPING ANYONE OF KRYPTONIAN ORIGIN, SUCH AS SHE MUST BE!
IN THE GREAT MAIN HOSPITAL OF QUARANTINE WORLD...
YES, WE HAVE SAMPLES OF GREEN KRYPTONITE DUST...ITS RADIATION HELPS CURE CERTAIN SPACE-ILLS IN ORDINARY PEOPLE! BUT IT WOULD PARALYZE YOU, SUPERGIRL!
NOT IF YOU GIVE IT TO ME IN A SMALL BOX MADE OF LEAD. LEAD IS THE ONLY SUBSTANCE IMPERVIOUS TO KRYPTONITE RAYS!
ARMED WITH A POWDER HARMFUL TO ANYONE FROM KRYPTON, SUPERGIRL TAKES UP A GRIM PURSUIT!
I KEPT WATCHING THE WAY SATAN GIRL WENT WITH MY TELESCOPIC VISION...AND I SAW HER LAND ON A LONELY ASTEROID!
ON THAT ASTEROID, SUPERGIRL'S MYSTERY FOE AWAITS HER PURSUER!
I HAVE SUPER-VISION, TOO, AND I COULD SEE HER COMING FROM QUARANTINE WORLD! AND IT'S EASY TO GUESS WHAT'S IN THAT LEAD BOX SHE'S CARRYING!
THE BOX SHATTERED WHEN I THREW IT, AS I PLANNED... AND THE GREEN KRYPTONITE POWDER HAS HIT HER! IT WON'T KILL HER, BUT WILL WEAKEN HER SO I CAN CAPTURE HER AND FIND OUT WHY AND HOW SHE'S KILLING THE LEGION GIRLS!
BUT, TO SUPERGIRL'S ASTONISHMENT, THROUGH THE THIN AIR OF THE ASTEROID COMES A MOCKING LAUGH!
KRYPTONITE MAY AFFECT YOU, SUPERGIRL, BUT YOU CAN SEE THAT I'M IMMUNE TO IT! YOU CAN'T OVERPOWER ME, BUT I CAN DESTROY YOU... AND I WILL!
7

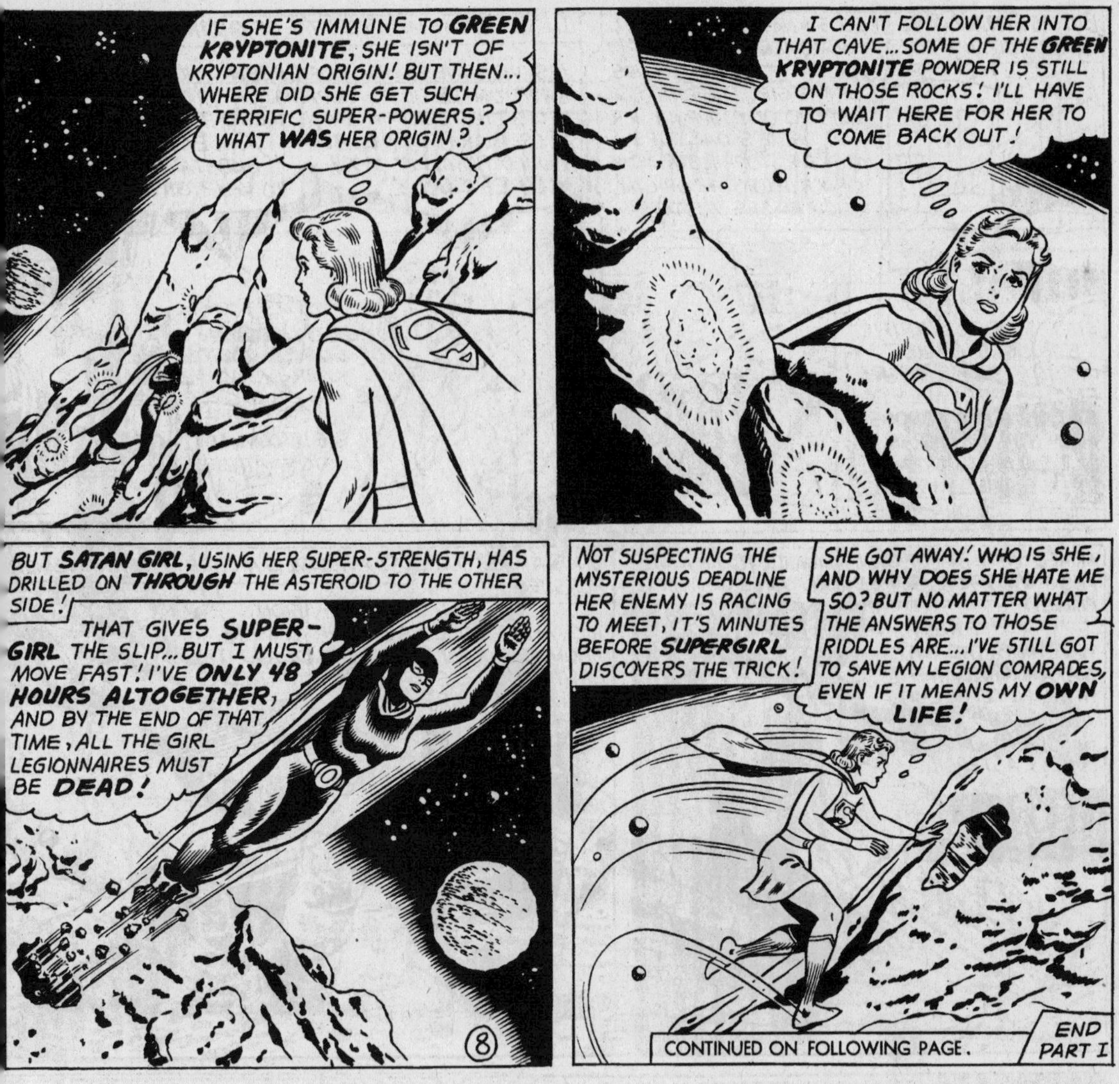
IF SHE'S IMMUNE TO GREEN KRYPTONITE, SHE ISN'T OF KRYPTONIAN ORIGIN! BUT THEN... WHERE DID SHE GET SUCH TERRIFIC SUPER-POWERS? WHAT WAS HER ORIGIN?
I CAN'T FOLLOW HER INTO THAT CAVE... SOME OF THE GREEN KRYPTONITE POWDER IS STILL ON THOSE ROCKS! I'LL HAVE TO WAIT HERE FOR HER TO COME BACK OUT!
BUT SATAN GIRL, USING HER SUPER-STRENGTH, HAS DRILLED ON THROUGH THE ASTEROID TO THE OTHER SIDE!
THAT GIVES SUPER-GIRL THE SLIP... BUT I MUST MOVE FAST! I'VE ONLY 48 HOURS ALTOGETHER, AND BY THE END OF THAT TIME, ALL THE GIRL LEGIONNAIRES MUST BE DEAD!
8
NOT SUSPECTING THE MYSTERIOUS DEADLINE HER ENEMY IS RACING TO MEET, IT'S MINUTES BEFORE SUPERGIRL DISCOVERS THE TRICK!
SHE GOT AWAY! WHO IS SHE, AND WHY DOES SHE HATE ME SO? BUT NO MATTER WHAT THE ANSWERS TO THOSE RIDDLES ARE... I'VE STILL GOT TO SAVE MY LEGION COMRADES, EVEN IF IT MEANS MY OWN LIFE!
CONTINUED ON FOLLOWING PAGE.
END PART I

LEGION of SUPER-HEROES

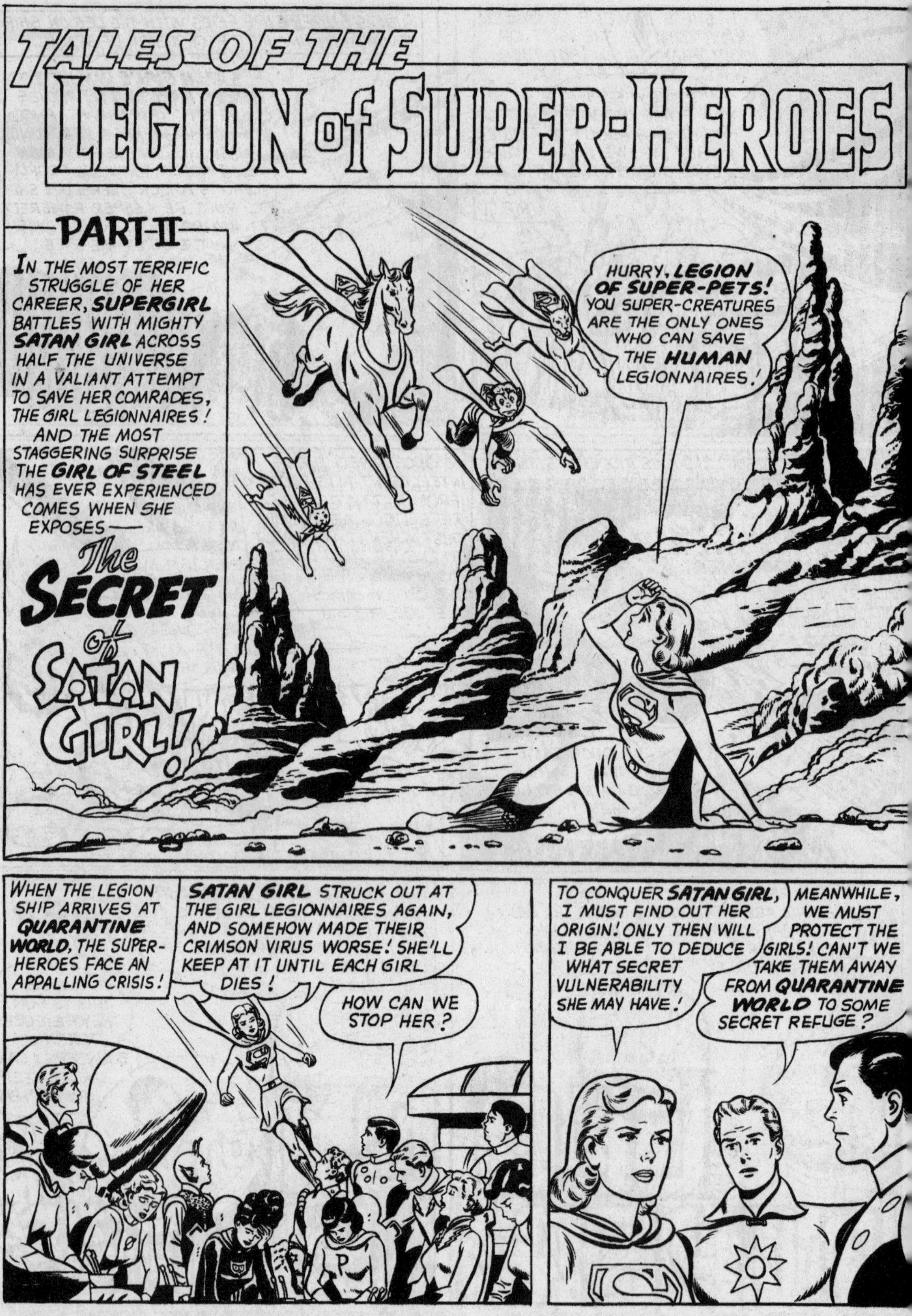
TALES OF THE
LEGION of SUPER-HEROES
PART-II
IN THE MOST TERRIFIC STRUGGLE OF HER CAREER, SUPERGIRL BATTLES WITH MIGHTY SATAN GIRL ACROSS HALF THE UNIVERSE IN A VALIANT ATTEMPT TO SAVE HER COMRADES, THE GIRL LEGIONNAIRES! AND THE MOST STAGGERING SURPRISE THE GIRL OF STEEL HAS EVER EXPERIENCED COMES WHEN SHE EXPOSES--
The SECRET of SATAN GIRL!
HURRY, LEGION OF SUPER-PETS! YOU SUPER-CREATURES ARE THE ONLY ONES WHO CAN SAVE THE HUMAN LEGIONNAIRES!
WHEN THE LEGION SHIP ARRIVES AT QUARANTINE WORLD, THE SUPER-HEROES FACE AN APPALLING CRISIS!
SATAN GIRL STRUCK OUT AT THE GIRL LEGIONNAIRES AGAIN, AND SOMEHOW MADE THEIR CRIMSON VIRUS WORSE! SHE'LL KEEP AT IT UNTIL EACH GIRL DIES!
HOW CAN WE STOP HER?
TO CONQUER SATAN GIRL, I MUST FIND OUT HER ORIGIN! ONLY THEN WILL I BE ABLE TO DEDUCE WHAT SECRET VULNERABILITY SHE MAY HAVE!
MEANWHILE, WE MUST PROTECT THE GIRLS! CAN'T WE TAKE THEM AWAY FROM QUARANTINE WORLD TO SOME SECRET REFUGE?

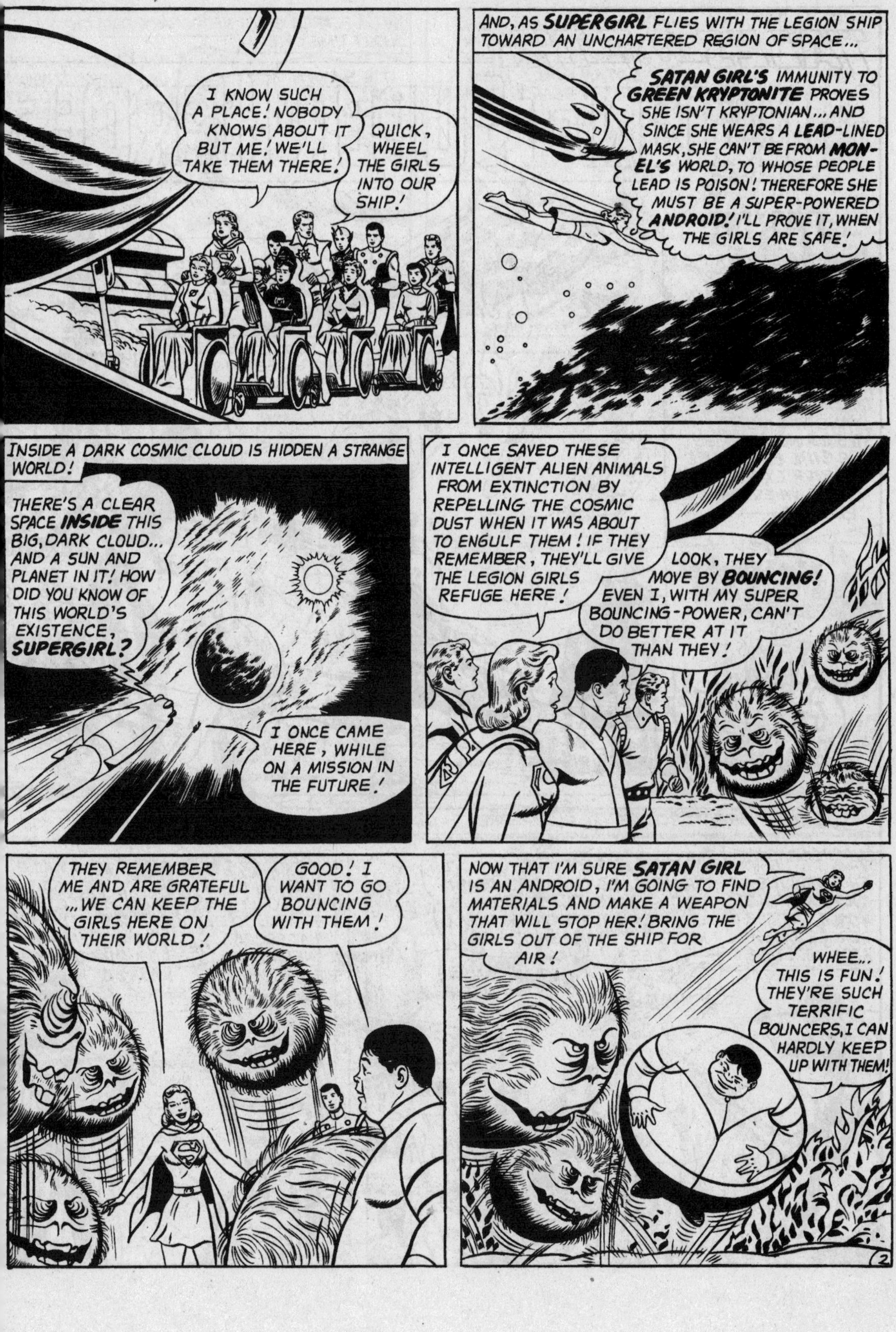
I KNOW SUCH A PLACE! NOBODY KNOWS ABOUT IT BUT ME! WE'LL TAKE THEM THERE!
QUICK, WHEEL THE GIRLS INTO OUR SHIP!
AND, AS SUPERGIRL FLIES WITH THE LEGION SHIP TOWARD AN UNCHARTERED REGION OF SPACE...
SATAN GIRL'S IMMUNITY TO GREEN KRYPTONITE PROVES SHE ISN'T KRYPTONIAN... AND SINCE SHE WEARS A LEAD-LINED MASK, SHE CAN'T BE FROM MON-EL'S WORLD, TO WHOSE PEOPLE LEAD IS POISON! THEREFORE SHE MUST BE A SUPER-POWERED ANDROID! I'LL PROVE IT, WHEN THE GIRLS ARE SAFE!
INSIDE A DARK COSMIC CLOUD IS HIDDEN A STRANGE WORLD!
THERE'S A CLEAR SPACE INSIDE THIS BIG, DARK CLOUD... AND A SUN AND PLANET IN IT! HOW DID YOU KNOW OF THIS WORLD'S EXISTENCE, SUPERGIRL?
I ONCE CAME HERE, WHILE ON A MISSION IN THE FUTURE!
I ONCE SAVED THESE INTELLIGENT ALIEN ANIMALS FROM EXTINCTION BY REPELLING THE COSMIC DUST WHEN IT WAS ABOUT TO ENGULF THEM! IF THEY REMEMBER, THEY'LL GIVE THE LEGION GIRLS REFUGE HERE!
LOOK, THEY MOVE BY BOUNCING! EVEN I, WITH MY SUPER BOUNCING-POWER, CAN'T DO BETTER AT IT THAN THEY!
THEY REMEMBER ME AND ARE GRATEFUL ...WE CAN KEEP THE GIRLS HERE ON THEIR WORLD!
GOOD! I WANT TO GO BOUNCING WITH THEM!
NOW THAT I'M SURE SATAN GIRL IS AN ANDROID, I'M GOING TO FIND MATERIALS AND MAKE A WEAPON THAT WILL STOP HER! BRING THE GIRLS OUT OF THE SHIP FOR AIR!
WHEE... THIS IS FUN! THEY'RE SUCH TERRIFIC BOUNCERS, I CAN HARDLY KEEP UP WITH THEM!
2

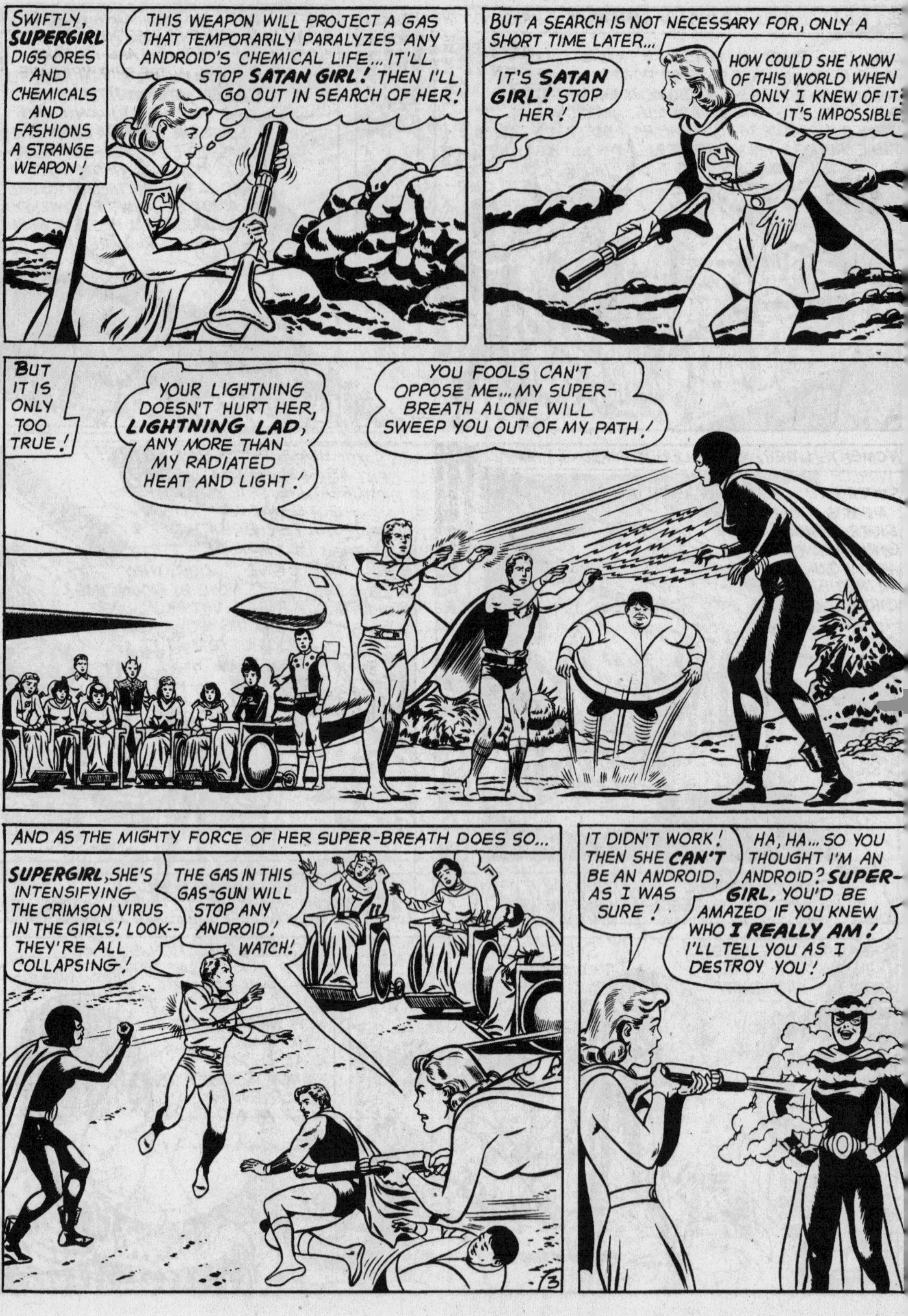
SWIFTLY, SUPERGIRL DIGS ORES AND CHEMICALS AND FASHIONS A STRANGE WEAPON!
THIS WEAPON WILL PROJECT A GAS THAT TEMPORARILY PARALYZES ANY ANDROID'S CHEMICAL LIFE... IT'LL STOP SATAN GIRL! THEN I'LL GO OUT IN SEARCH OF HER!
BUT A SEARCH IS NOT NECESSARY FOR, ONLY A SHORT TIME LATER...
IT'S SATAN GIRL! STOP HER!
HOW COULD SHE KNOW OF THIS WORLD WHEN ONLY I KNEW OF IT? IT'S IMPOSSIBLE
BUT IT IS ONLY TOO TRUE!
YOUR LIGHTNING DOESN'T HURT HER, LIGHTNING LAD, ANY MORE THAN MY RADIATED HEAT AND LIGHT!
YOU FOOLS CAN'T OPPOSE ME... MY SUPER-BREATH ALONE WILL SWEEP YOU OUT OF MY PATH!
AND AS THE MIGHTY FORCE OF HER SUPER-BREATH DOES SO...
SUPERGIRL, SHE'S INTENSIFYING THE CRIMSON VIRUS IN THE GIRLS! LOOK-- THEY'RE ALL COLLAPSING!
THE GAS IN THIS GAS-GUN WILL STOP ANY ANDROID! WATCH!
3
IT DIDN'T WORK! THEN SHE CAN'T BE AN ANDROID, AS I WAS SURE!
HA, HA... SO YOU THOUGHT I'M AN ANDROID? SUPER-GIRL, YOU'D BE AMAZED IF YOU KNEW WHO I REALLY AM! I'LL TELL YOU AS I DESTROY YOU!

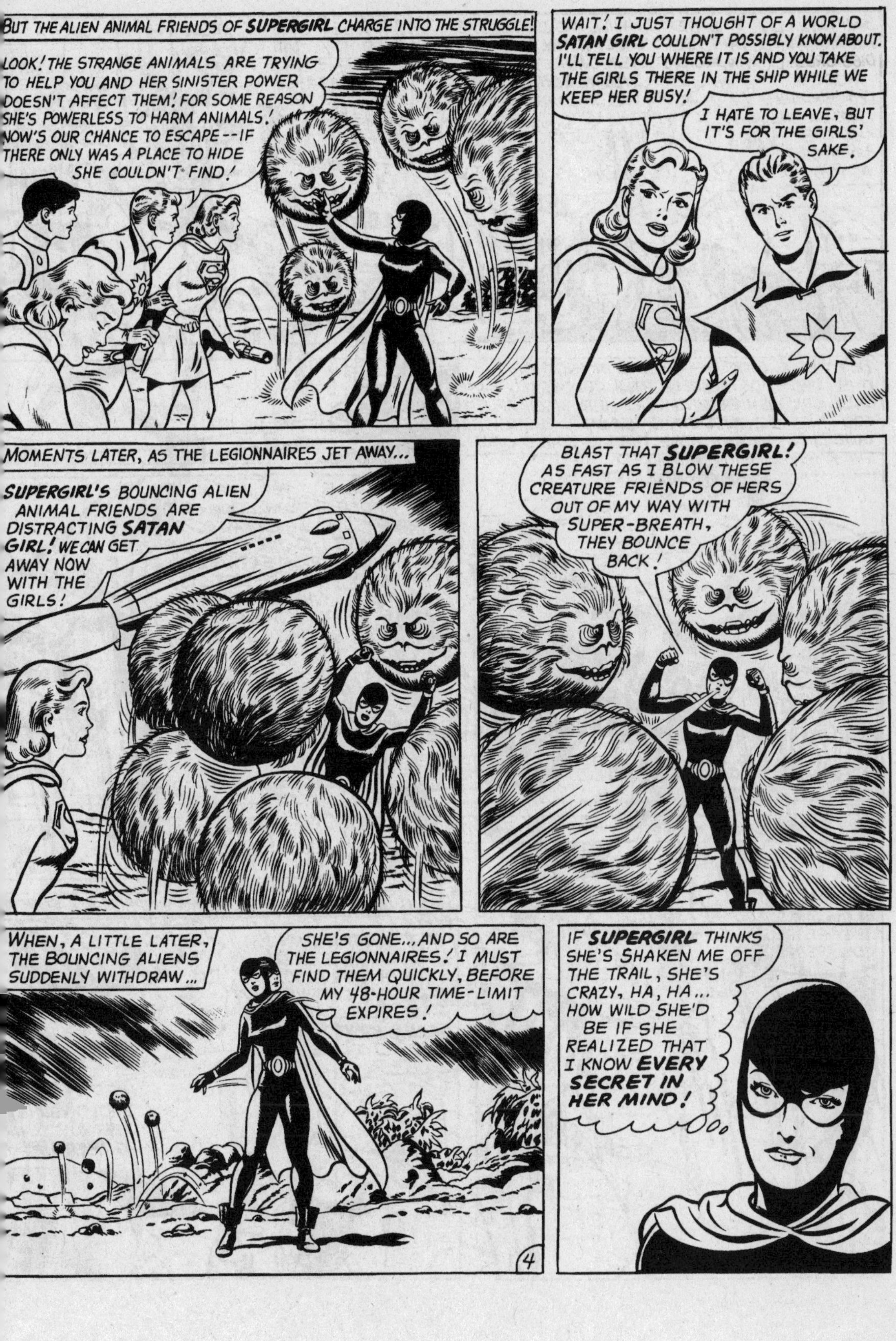
BUT THE ALIEN ANIMAL FRIENDS OF SUPERGIRL CHARGE INTO THE STRUGGLE!
LOOK! THE STRANGE ANIMALS ARE TRYING TO HELP YOU AND HER SINISTER POWER DOESN'T AFFECT THEM! FOR SOME REASON SHE'S POWERLESS TO HARM ANIMALS! NOW'S OUR CHANCE TO ESCAPE--IF THERE ONLY WAS A PLACE TO HIDE SHE COULDN'T FIND!
WAIT! I JUST THOUGHT OF A WORLD SATAN GIRL COULDN'T POSSIBLY KNOW ABOUT. I'LL TELL YOU WHERE IT IS AND YOU TAKE THE GIRLS THERE IN THE SHIP WHILE WE KEEP HER BUSY!
I HATE TO LEAVE, BUT IT'S FOR THE GIRLS' SAKE.
MOMENTS LATER, AS THE LEGIONNAIRES JET AWAY...
SUPERGIRL'S BOUNCING ALIEN ANIMAL FRIENDS ARE DISTRACTING SATAN GIRL! WE CAN GET AWAY NOW WITH THE GIRLS!
BLAST THAT SUPERGIRL! AS FAST AS I BLOW THESE CREATURE FRIENDS OF HERS OUT OF MY WAY WITH SUPER-BREATH, THEY BOUNCE BACK!
WHEN, A LITTLE LATER, THE BOUNCING ALIENS SUDDENLY WITHDRAW...
SHE'S GONE...AND SO ARE THE LEGIONNAIRES! I MUST FIND THEM QUICKLY, BEFORE MY 48-HOUR TIME-LIMIT EXPIRES!
4
IF SUPERGIRL THINKS SHE'S SHAKEN ME OFF THE TRAIL, SHE'S CRAZY, HA, HA... HOW WILD SHE'D BE IF SHE REALIZED THAT I KNOW EVERY SECRET IN HER MIND!

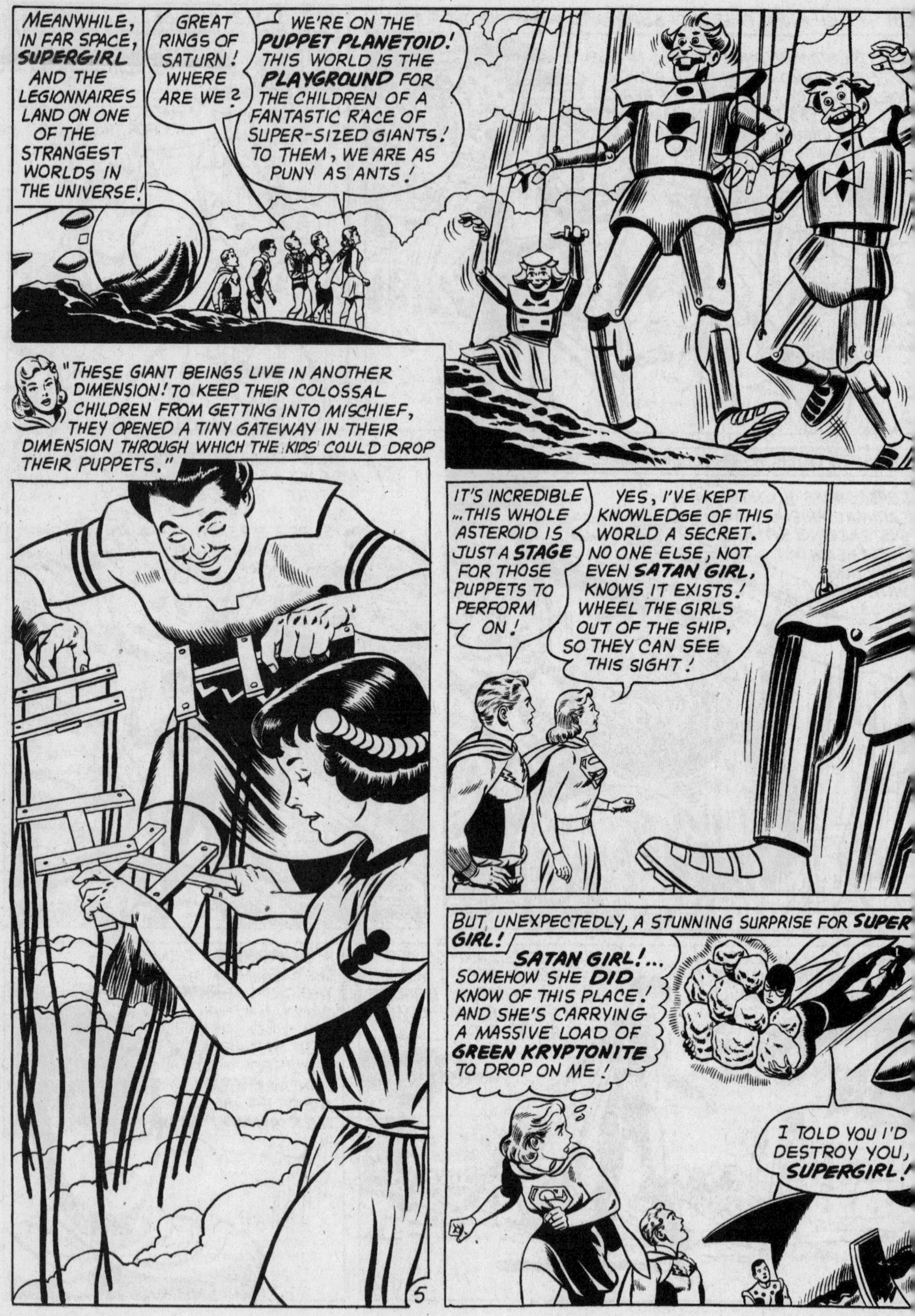
MEANWHILE, IN FAR SPACE, SUPERGIRL AND THE LEGIONNAIRES LAND ON ONE OF THE STRANGEST WORLDS IN THE UNIVERSE!
GREAT RINGS OF SATURN! WHERE ARE WE?
WE'RE ON THE PUPPET PLANETOID! THIS WORLD IS THE PLAYGROUND FOR THE CHILDREN OF A FANTASTIC RACE OF SUPER-SIZED GIANTS! TO THEM, WE ARE AS PUNY AS ANTS!
"THESE GIANT BEINGS LIVE IN ANOTHER DIMENSION! TO KEEP THEIR COLOSSAL CHILDREN FROM GETTING INTO MISCHIEF, THEY OPENED A TINY GATEWAY IN THEIR DIMENSION THROUGH WHICH THE KIDS COULD DROP THEIR PUPPETS."
5
IT'S INCREDIBLE ...THIS WHOLE ASTEROID IS JUST A STAGE FOR THOSE PUPPETS TO PERFORM ON!
YES, I'VE KEPT KNOWLEDGE OF THIS WORLD A SECRET. NO ONE ELSE, NOT EVEN SATAN GIRL, KNOWS IT EXISTS! WHEEL THE GIRLS OUT OF THE SHIP, SO THEY CAN SEE THIS SIGHT!
BUT, UNEXPECTEDLY, A STUNNING SURPRISE FOR SUPERGIRL!
SATAN GIRL!... SOMEHOW SHE DID KNOW OF THIS PLACE! AND SHE'S CARRYING A MASSIVE LOAD OF GREEN KRYPTONITE TO DROP ON ME!
I TOLD YOU I'D DESTROY YOU, SUPERGIRL!

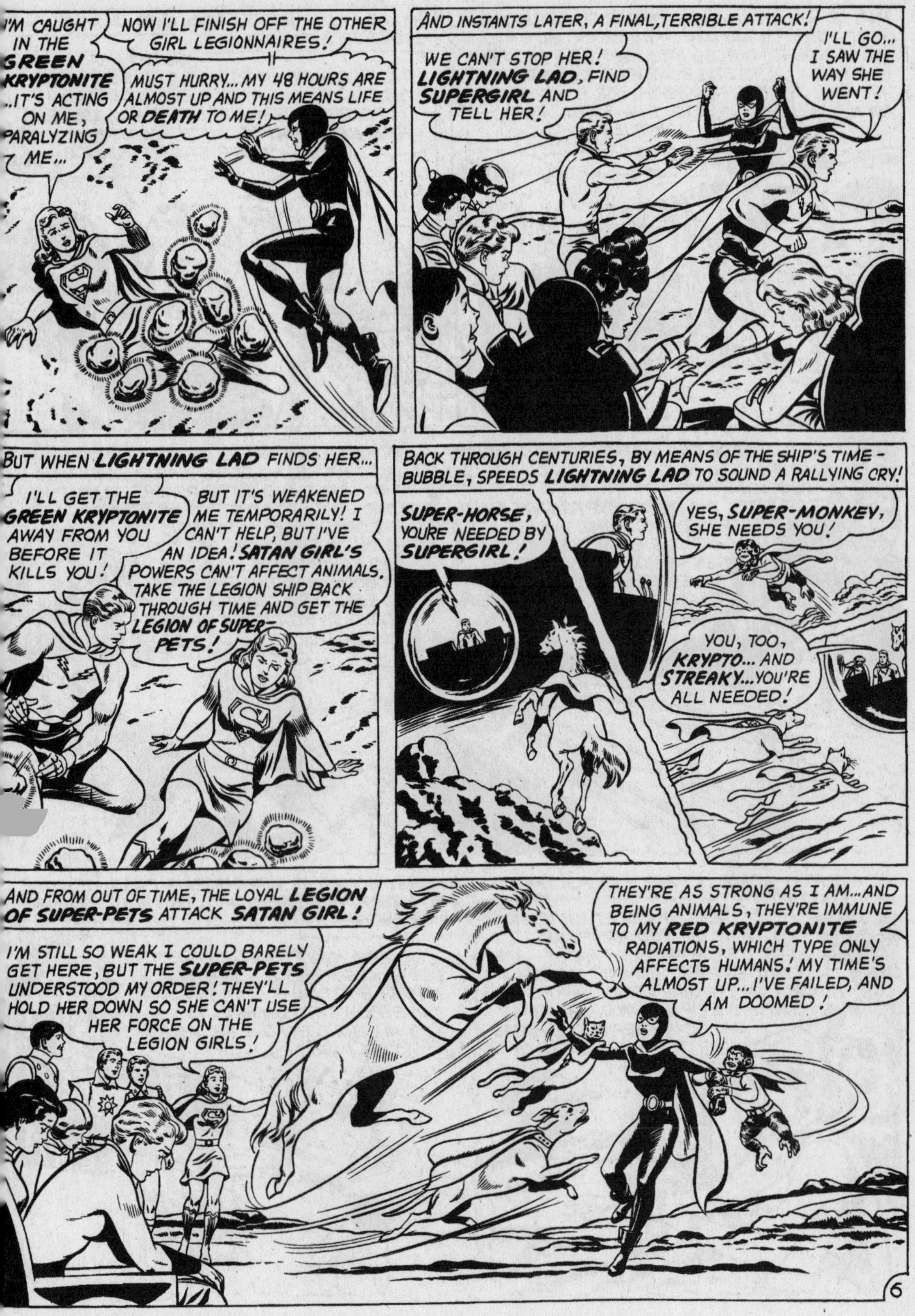
I'M CAUGHT IN THE GREEN KRYPTONITE ..IT'S ACTING ON ME, PARALYZING ME...
NOW I'LL FINISH OFF THE OTHER GIRL LEGIONNAIRES!
MUST HURRY... MY 48 HOURS ARE ALMOST UP AND THIS MEANS LIFE OR DEATH TO ME!
AND INSTANTS LATER, A FINAL, TERRIBLE ATTACK!
WE CAN'T STOP HER! LIGHTNING LAD, FIND SUPERGIRL AND TELL HER!
I'LL GO... I SAW THE WAY SHE WENT!
BUT WHEN LIGHTNING LAD FINDS HER...
I'LL GET THE GREEN KRYPTONITE AWAY FROM YOU BEFORE IT KILLS YOU!
BUT IT'S WEAKENED ME TEMPORARILY! I CAN'T HELP, BUT I'VE AN IDEA! SATAN GIRL'S POWERS CAN'T AFFECT ANIMALS. TAKE THE LEGION SHIP BACK THROUGH TIME AND GET THE LEGION OF SUPER-PETS!
BACK THROUGH CENTURIES, BY MEANS OF THE SHIP'S TIME-BUBBLE, SPEEDS LIGHTNING LAD TO SOUND A RALLYING CRY!
SUPER-HORSE, YOU'RE NEEDED BY SUPERGIRL!
YES, SUPER-MONKEY, SHE NEEDS YOU!
YOU, TOO, KRYPTO... AND STREAKY...YOU'RE ALL NEEDED!
AND FROM OUT OF TIME, THE LOYAL LEGION OF SUPER-PETS ATTACK SATAN GIRL!
I'M STILL SO WEAK I COULD BARELY GET HERE, BUT THE SUPER-PETS UNDERSTOOD MY ORDER! THEY'LL HOLD HER DOWN SO SHE CAN'T USE HER FORCE ON THE LEGION GIRLS!
THEY'RE AS STRONG AS I AM...AND BEING ANIMALS, THEY'RE IMMUNE TO MY RED KRYPTONITE RADIATIONS, WHICH TYPE ONLY AFFECTS HUMANS! MY TIME'S ALMOST UP... I'VE FAILED, AND AM DOOMED!
6

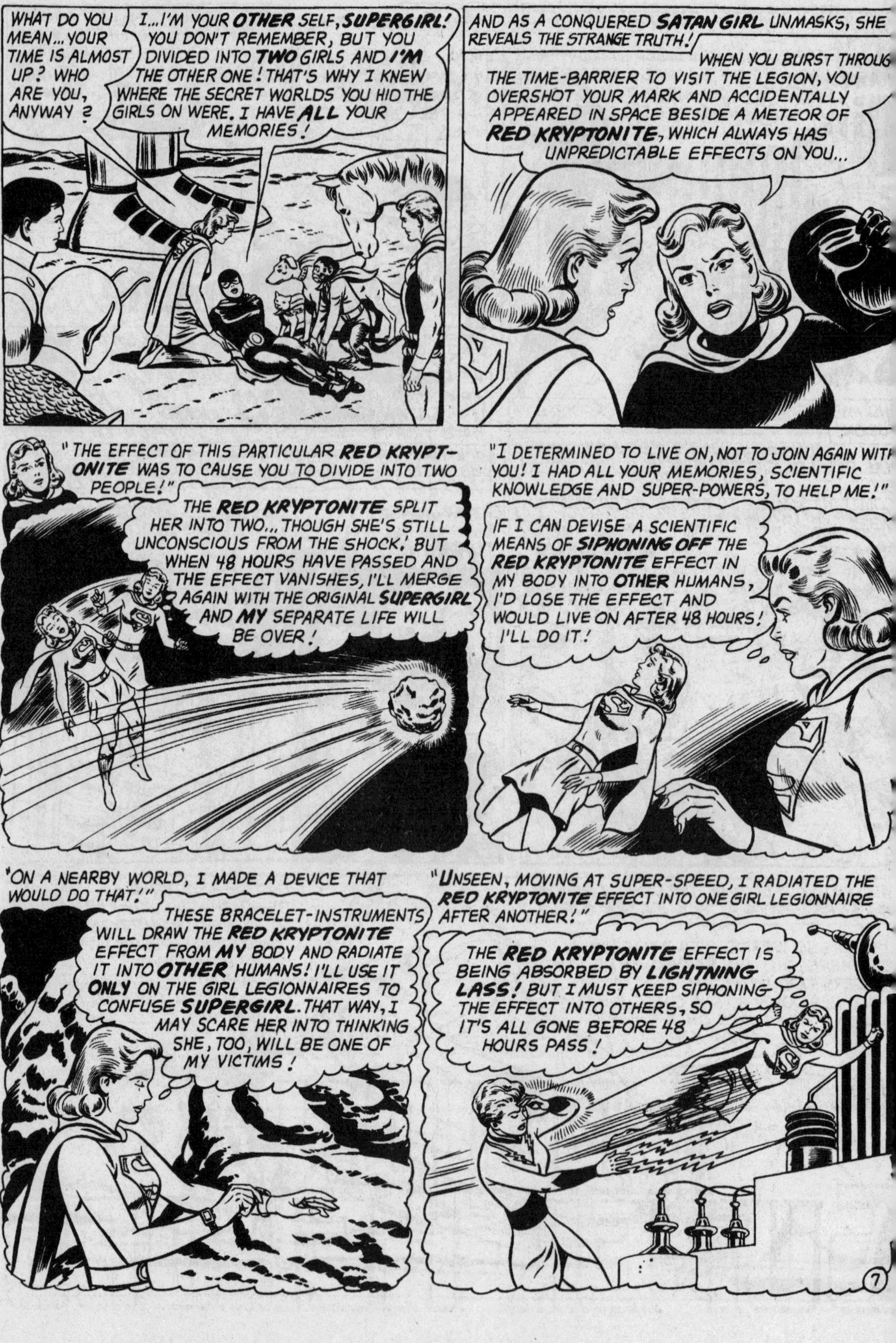
WHAT DO YOU MEAN... YOUR TIME IS ALMOST UP? WHO ARE YOU, ANYWAY ?
I...I'M YOUR OTHER SELF, SUPERGIRL! YOU DON'T REMEMBER, BUT YOU DIVIDED INTO TWO GIRLS AND I'M THE OTHER ONE! THAT'S WHY I KNEW WHERE THE SECRET WORLDS YOU HID THE GIRLS ON WERE. I HAVE ALL YOUR MEMORIES!
AND AS A CONQUERED SATAN GIRL UNMASKS, SHE REVEALS THE STRANGE TRUTH!
WHEN YOU BURST THROUG THE TIME-BARRIER TO VISIT THE LEGION, YOU OVERSHOT YOUR MARK AND ACCIDENTALLY APPEARED IN SPACE BESIDE A METEOR OF RED KRYPTONITE, WHICH ALWAYS HAS UNPREDICTABLE EFFECTS ON YOU...
"THE EFFECT OF THIS PARTICULAR RED KRYPTONITE WAS TO CAUSE YOU TO DIVIDE INTO TWO PEOPLE!"
THE RED KRYPTONITE SPLIT HER INTO TWO... THOUGH SHE'S STILL UNCONSCIOUS FROM THE SHOCK! BUT WHEN 48 HOURS HAVE PASSED AND THE EFFECT VANISHES, I'LL MERGE AGAIN WITH THE ORIGINAL SUPERGIRL AND MY SEPARATE LIFE WILL BE OVER!
"I DETERMINED TO LIVE ON, NOT TO JOIN AGAIN WITH YOU! I HAD ALL YOUR MEMORIES, SCIENTIFIC KNOWLEDGE AND SUPER-POWERS, TO HELP ME!"
IF I CAN DEVISE A SCIENTIFIC MEANS OF SIPHONING OFF THE RED KRYPTONITE EFFECT IN MY BODY INTO OTHER HUMANS, I'D LOSE THE EFFECT AND WOULD LIVE ON AFTER 48 HOURS! I'LL DO IT!
"ON A NEARBY WORLD, I MADE A DEVICE THAT WOULD DO THAT!"
THESE BRACELET-INSTRUMENTS WILL DRAW THE RED KRYPTONITE EFFECT FROM MY BODY AND RADIATE IT INTO OTHER HUMANS! I'LL USE IT ONLY ON THE GIRL LEGIONNAIRES TO CONFUSE SUPERGIRL. THAT WAY, I MAY SCARE HER INTO THINKING SHE, TOO, WILL BE ONE OF MY VICTIMS!
"UNSEEN, MOVING AT SUPER-SPEED, I RADIATED THE RED KRYPTONITE EFFECT INTO ONE GIRL LEGIONNAIRE AFTER ANOTHER!"
THE RED KRYPTONITE EFFECT IS BEING ABSORBED BY LIGHTNING LASS! BUT I MUST KEEP SIPHONING THE EFFECT INTO OTHERS, SO IT'S ALL GONE BEFORE 48 HOURS PASS!
7

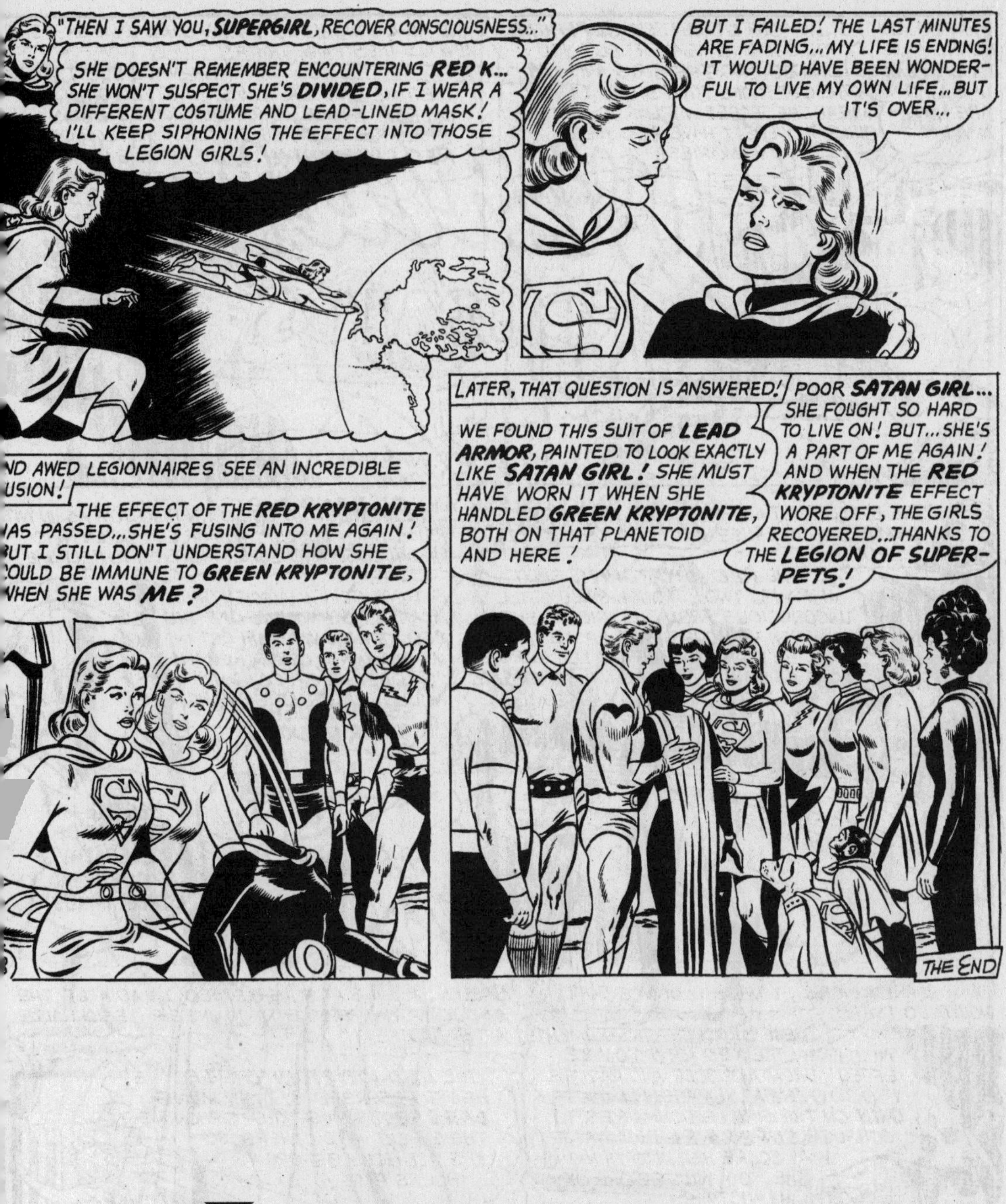
"THEN I SAW YOU, SUPERGIRL, RECOVER CONSCIOUSNESS..."
SHE DOESN'T REMEMBER ENCOUNTERING RED K... SHE WON'T SUSPECT SHE'S DIVIDED, IF I WEAR A DIFFERENT COSTUME AND LEAD-LINED MASK! I'LL KEEP SIPHONING THE EFFECT INTO THOSE LEGION GIRLS!
BUT I FAILED! THE LAST MINUTES ARE FADING... MY LIFE IS ENDING! IT WOULD HAVE BEEN WONDERFUL TO LIVE MY OWN LIFE... BUT IT'S OVER...
ND AWED LEGIONNAIRES SEE AN INCREDIBLE USION!
THE EFFECT OF THE RED KRYPTONITE AS PASSED... SHE'S FUSING INTO ME AGAIN! UT I STILL DON'T UNDERSTAND HOW SHE OULD BE IMMUNE TO GREEN KRYPTONITE, HEN SHE WAS ME?
LATER, THAT QUESTION IS ANSWERED!
WE FOUND THIS SUIT OF LEAD ARMOR, PAINTED TO LOOK EXACTLY LIKE SATAN GIRL! SHE MUST HAVE WORN IT WHEN SHE HANDLED GREEN KRYPTONITE, BOTH ON THAT PLANETOID AND HERE!
POOR SATAN GIRL... SHE FOUGHT SO HARD TO LIVE ON! BUT... SHE'S A PART OF ME AGAIN! AND WHEN THE RED KRYPTONITE EFFECT WORE OFF, THE GIRLS RECOVERED... THANKS TO THE LEGION OF SUPER-PETS!
THE END

LEGION of SUPER-HEROES

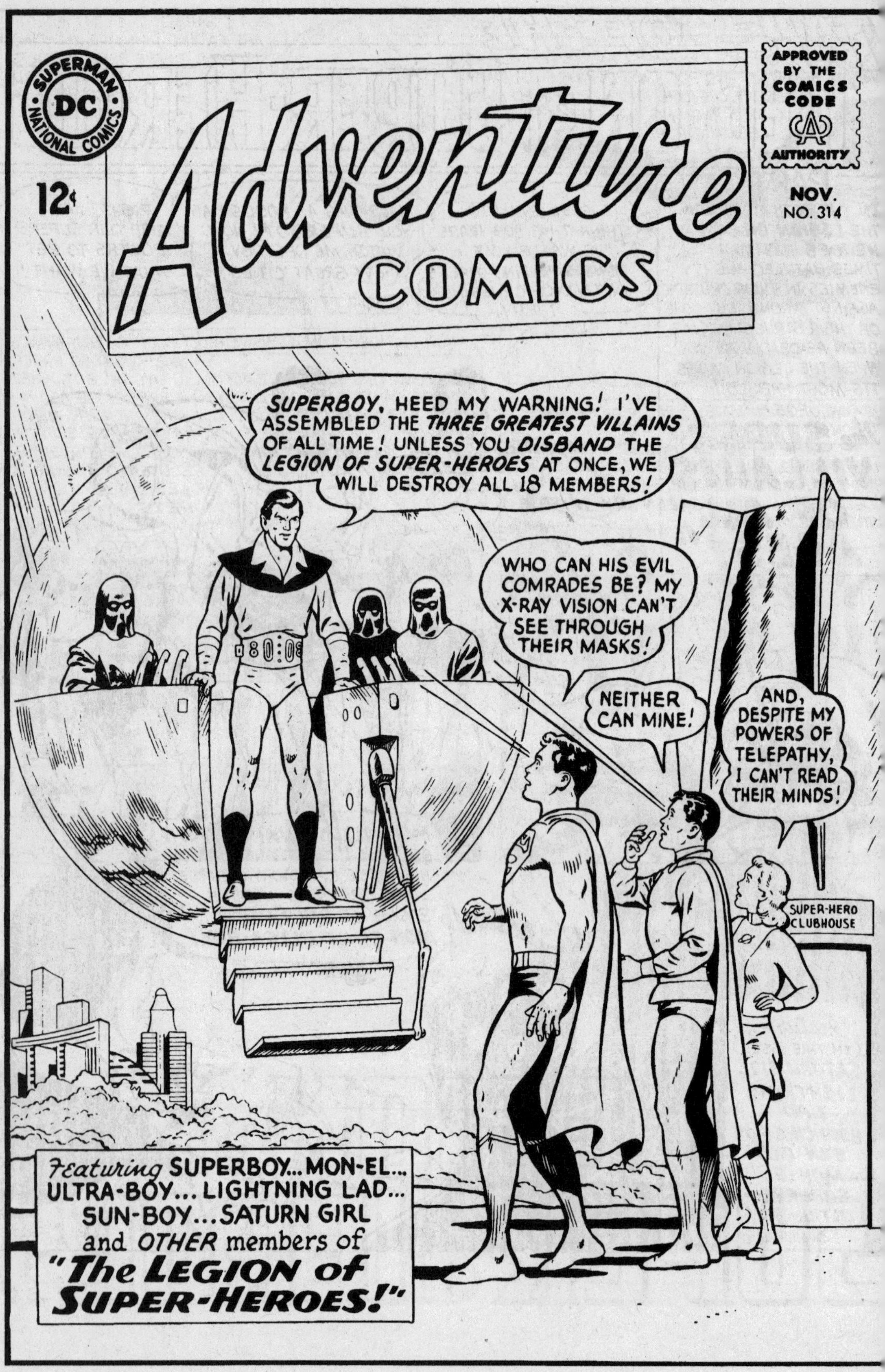

SUPERMAN DC NATIONAL COMICS
12¢
Adventure COMICS
APPROVED BY THE COMICS CODE AUTHORITY
NOV. NO. 314
SUPERBOY, HEED MY WARNING! I'VE ASSEMBLED THE THREE GREATEST VILLAINS OF ALL TIME! UNLESS YOU DISBAND THE LEGION OF SUPER-HEROES AT ONCE, WE WILL DESTROY ALL 18 MEMBERS!
WHO CAN HIS EVIL COMRADES BE? MY X-RAY VISION CAN'T SEE THROUGH THEIR MASKS!
NEITHER CAN MINE!
AND, DESPITE MY POWERS OF TELEPATHY, I CAN'T READ THEIR MINDS!
SUPER-HERO CLUBHOUSE
Featuring SUPERBOY... MON-EL... ULTRA-BOY... LIGHTNING LAD... SUN-BOY... SATURN GIRL and OTHER members of "The LEGION of SUPER-HEROES!"

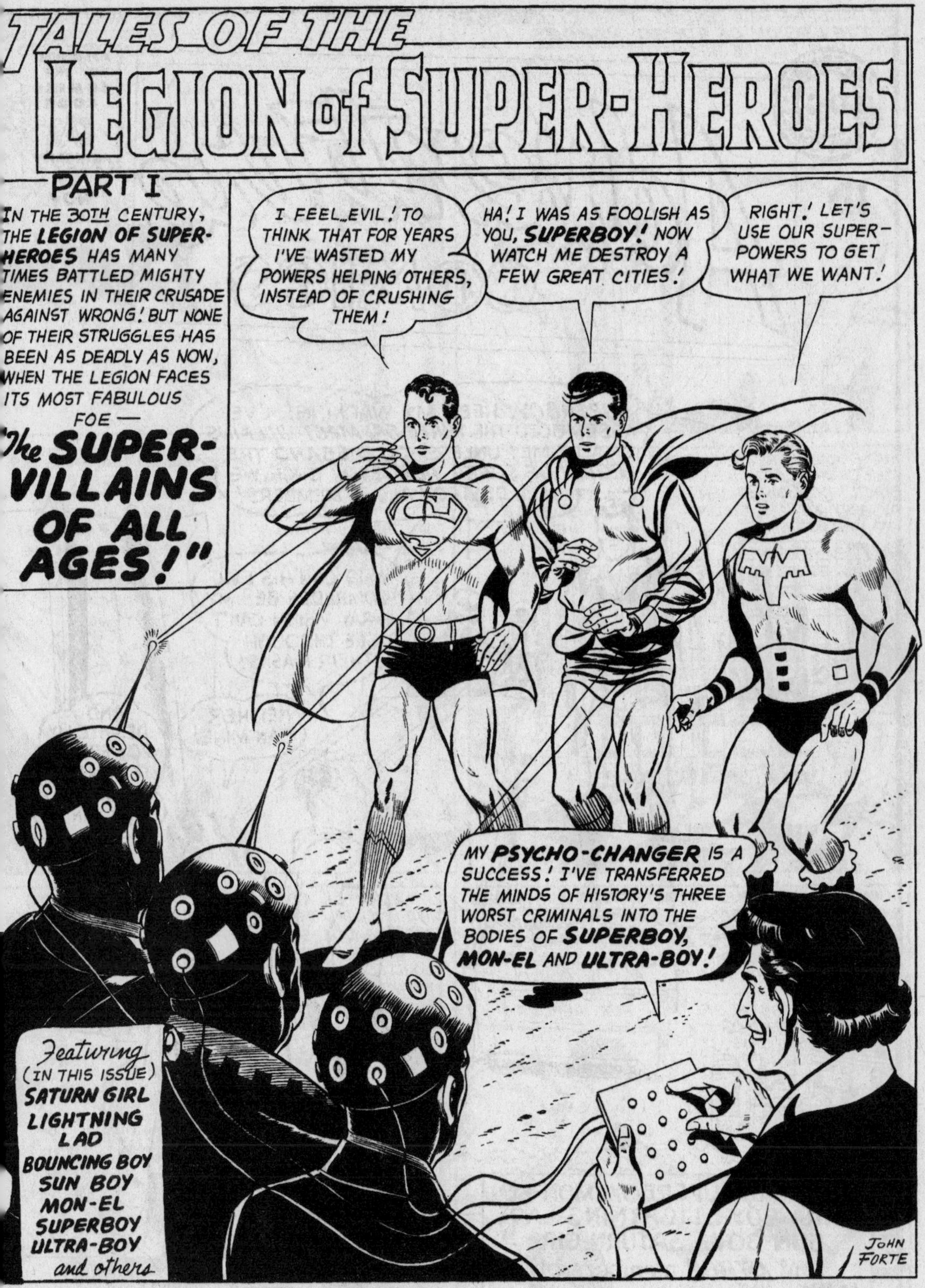
TALES OF THE
LEGION of SUPER-HEROES
PART I
IN THE 30TH CENTURY, THE LEGION OF SUPER-HEROES HAS MANY TIMES BATTLED MIGHTY ENEMIES IN THEIR CRUSADE AGAINST WRONG! BUT NONE OF THEIR STRUGGLES HAS BEEN AS DEADLY AS NOW, WHEN THE LEGION FACES ITS MOST FABULOUS FOE —
"The SUPER-VILLAINS OF ALL AGES!"
I FEEL...EVIL! TO THINK THAT FOR YEARS I'VE WASTED MY POWERS HELPING OTHERS, INSTEAD OF CRUSHING THEM!
HA! I WAS AS FOOLISH AS YOU, SUPERBOY! NOW WATCH ME DESTROY A FEW GREAT CITIES!
RIGHT! LET'S USE OUR SUPER-POWERS TO GET WHAT WE WANT!
MY PSYCHO-CHANGER IS A SUCCESS! I'VE TRANSFERRED THE MINDS OF HISTORY'S THREE WORST CRIMINALS INTO THE BODIES OF SUPERBOY, MON-EL AND ULTRA-BOY!
Featuring (IN THIS ISSUE) SATURN GIRL LIGHTNING LAD BOUNCING BOY SUN BOY MON-EL SUPERBOY ULTRA-BOY and others
JOHN FORTE

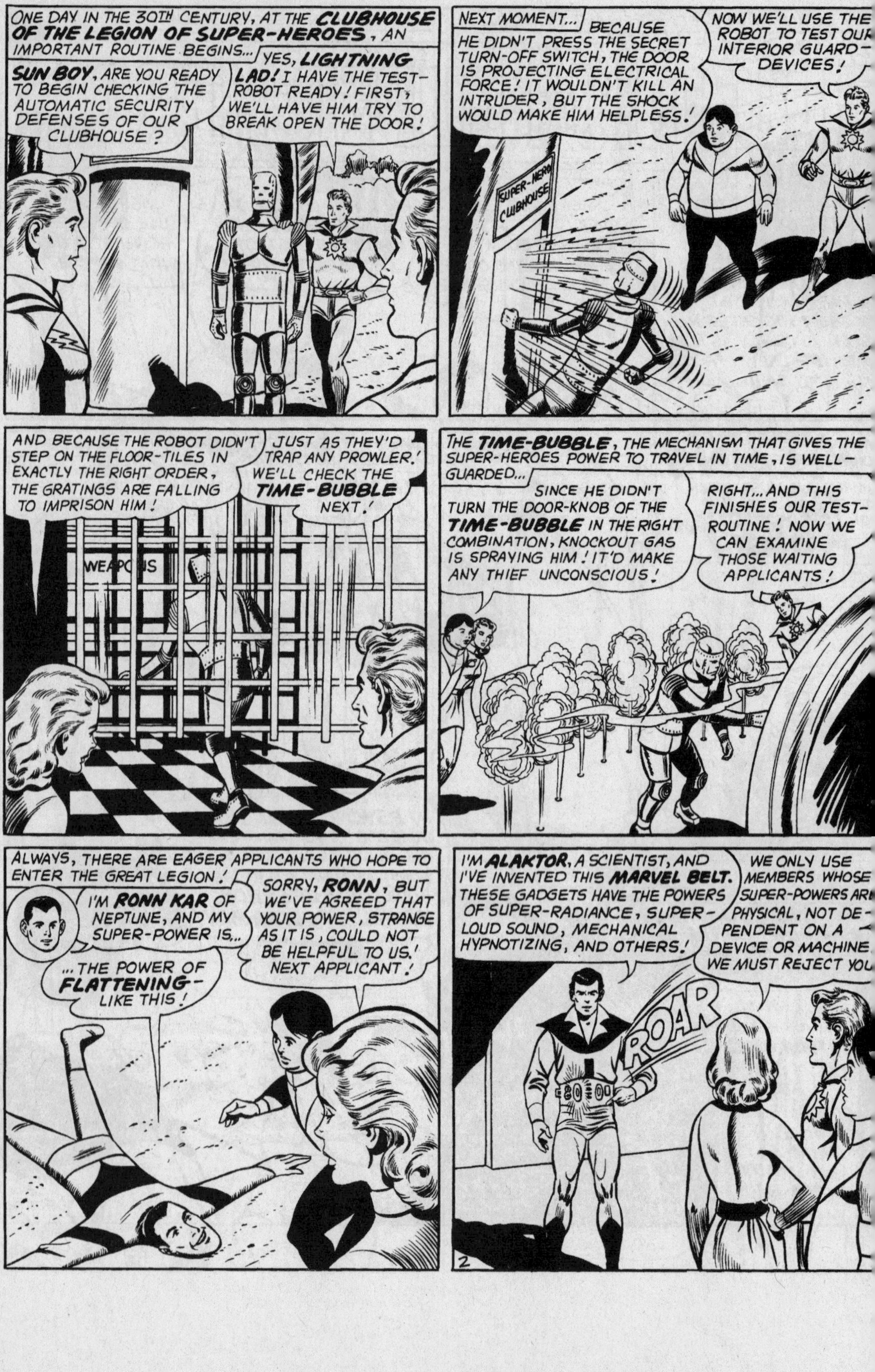
ONE DAY IN THE 30TH CENTURY, AT THE CLUBHOUSE OF THE LEGION OF SUPER-HEROES, AN IMPORTANT ROUTINE BEGINS...
SUN BOY, ARE YOU READY TO BEGIN CHECKING THE AUTOMATIC SECURITY DEFENSES OF OUR CLUBHOUSE?
YES, LIGHTNING LAD! I HAVE THE TEST-ROBOT READY! FIRST, WE'LL HAVE HIM TRY TO BREAK OPEN THE DOOR!
NEXT MOMENT...
BECAUSE HE DIDN'T PRESS THE SECRET TURN-OFF SWITCH, THE DOOR IS PROJECTING ELECTRICAL FORCE! IT WOULDN'T KILL AN INTRUDER, BUT THE SHOCK WOULD MAKE HIM HELPLESS!
NOW WE'LL USE THE ROBOT TO TEST OUR INTERIOR GUARD-DEVICES!
SUPER-HERO CLUBHOUSE
AND BECAUSE THE ROBOT DIDN'T STEP ON THE FLOOR-TILES IN EXACTLY THE RIGHT ORDER, THE GRATINGS ARE FALLING TO IMPRISON HIM!
JUST AS THEY'D TRAP ANY PROWLER! WE'LL CHECK THE TIME-BUBBLE NEXT!
THE TIME-BUBBLE, THE MECHANISM THAT GIVES THE SUPER-HEROES POWER TO TRAVEL IN TIME, IS WELL-GUARDED...
SINCE HE DIDN'T TURN THE DOOR-KNOB OF THE TIME-BUBBLE IN THE RIGHT COMBINATION, KNOCKOUT GAS IS SPRAYING HIM! IT'D MAKE ANY THIEF UNCONSCIOUS!
RIGHT... AND THIS FINISHES OUR TEST-ROUTINE! NOW WE CAN EXAMINE THOSE WAITING APPLICANTS!
ALWAYS, THERE ARE EAGER APPLICANTS WHO HOPE TO ENTER THE GREAT LEGION!
I'M RONN KAR OF NEPTUNE, AND MY SUPER-POWER IS...
...THE POWER OF FLATTENING-LIKE THIS!
SORRY, RONN, BUT WE'VE AGREED THAT YOUR POWER, STRANGE AS IT IS, COULD NOT BE HELPFUL TO US! NEXT APPLICANT!
I'M ALAKTOR, A SCIENTIST, AND I'VE INVENTED THIS MARVEL BELT. THESE GADGETS HAVE THE POWERS OF SUPER-RADIANCE, SUPER-LOUD SOUND, MECHANICAL HYPNOTIZING, AND OTHERS!
WE ONLY USE MEMBERS WHOSE SUPER-POWERS ARE PHYSICAL, NOT DEPENDENT ON A DEVICE OR MACHINE. WE MUST REJECT YOU
ROAR
2

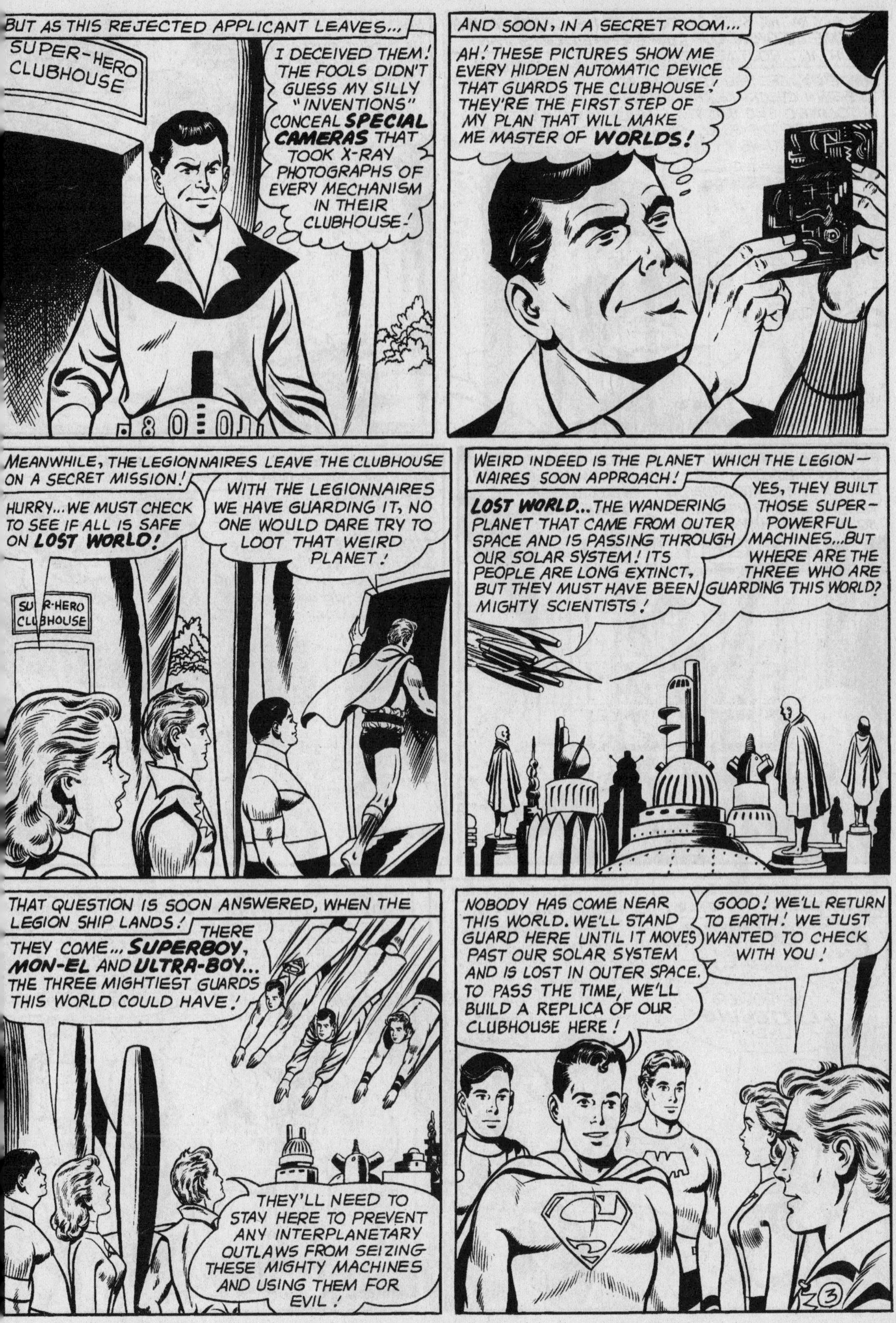
BUT AS THIS REJECTED APPLICANT LEAVES...
SUPER-HERO CLUBHOUSE
I DECEIVED THEM! THE FOOLS DIDN'T GUESS MY SILLY "INVENTIONS" CONCEAL SPECIAL CAMERAS THAT TOOK X-RAY PHOTOGRAPHS OF EVERY MECHANISM IN THEIR CLUBHOUSE!
AND SOON, IN A SECRET ROOM...
AH! THESE PICTURES SHOW ME EVERY HIDDEN AUTOMATIC DEVICE THAT GUARDS THE CLUBHOUSE! THEY'RE THE FIRST STEP OF MY PLAN THAT WILL MAKE ME MASTER OF WORLDS!
MEANWHILE, THE LEGIONNAIRES LEAVE THE CLUBHOUSE ON A SECRET MISSION!
HURRY... WE MUST CHECK TO SEE IF ALL IS SAFE ON LOST WORLD!
WITH THE LEGIONNAIRES WE HAVE GUARDING IT, NO ONE WOULD DARE TRY TO LOOT THAT WEIRD PLANET!
SUPER-HERO CLUBHOUSE
WEIRD INDEED IS THE PLANET WHICH THE LEGIONNAIRES SOON APPROACH!
LOST WORLD... THE WANDERING PLANET THAT CAME FROM OUTER SPACE AND IS PASSING THROUGH OUR SOLAR SYSTEM! ITS PEOPLE ARE LONG EXTINCT, BUT THEY MUST HAVE BEEN MIGHTY SCIENTISTS!
YES, THEY BUILT THOSE SUPER-POWERFUL MACHINES...BUT WHERE ARE THE THREE WHO ARE GUARDING THIS WORLD?
THAT QUESTION IS SOON ANSWERED, WHEN THE LEGION SHIP LANDS!
THERE THEY COME... SUPERBOY, MON-EL AND ULTRA-BOY... THE THREE MIGHTIEST GUARDS THIS WORLD COULD HAVE!
THEY'LL NEED TO STAY HERE TO PREVENT ANY INTERPLANETARY OUTLAWS FROM SEIZING THESE MIGHTY MACHINES AND USING THEM FOR EVIL!
NOBODY HAS COME NEAR THIS WORLD. WE'LL STAND GUARD HERE UNTIL IT MOVES PAST OUR SOLAR SYSTEM AND IS LOST IN OUTER SPACE. TO PASS THE TIME, WE'LL BUILD A REPLICA OF OUR CLUBHOUSE HERE!
GOOD! WE'LL RETURN TO EARTH! WE JUST WANTED TO CHECK WITH YOU!
3

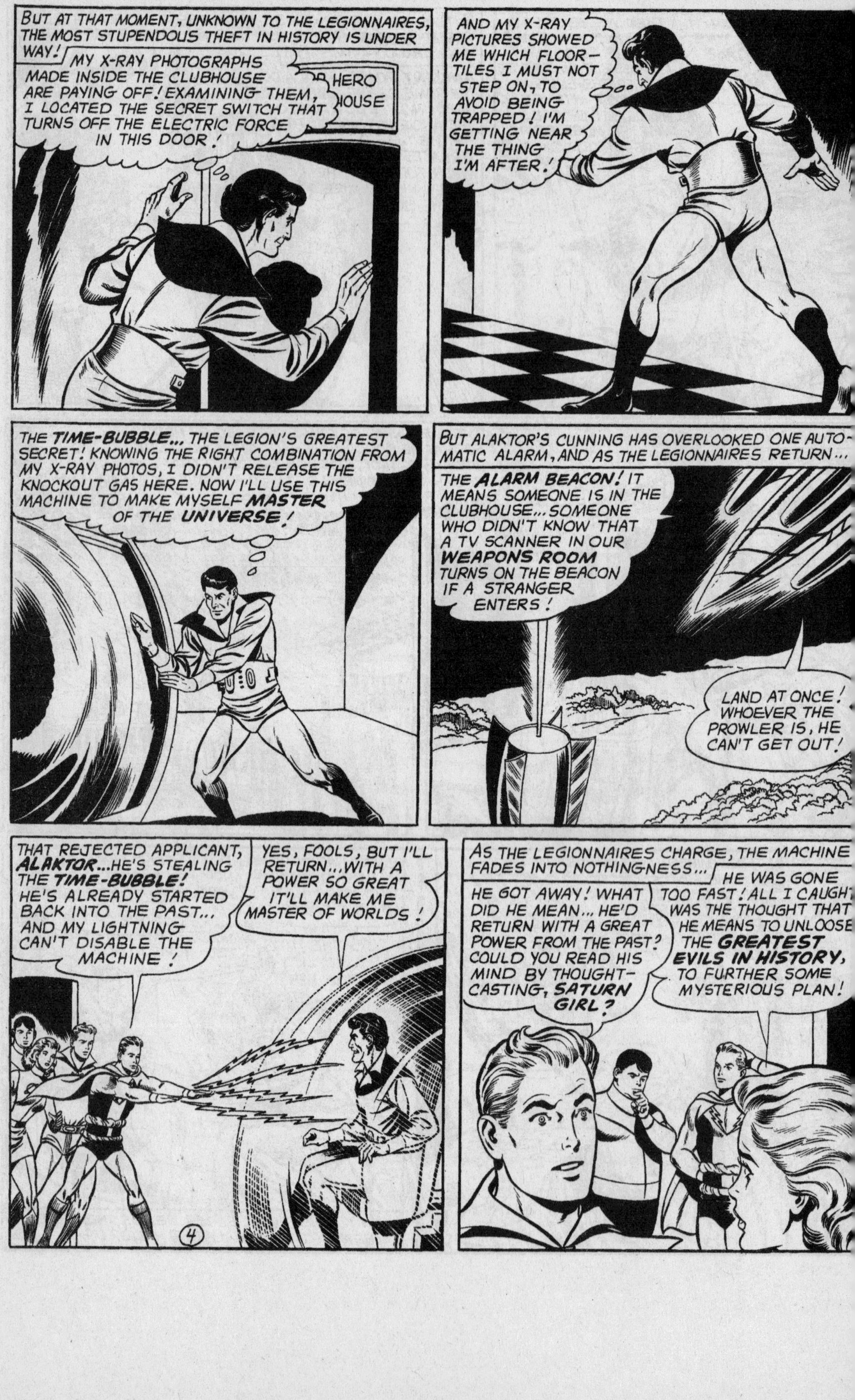
BUT AT THAT MOMENT, UNKNOWN TO THE LEGIONNAIRES, THE MOST STUPENDOUS THEFT IN HISTORY IS UNDER WAY!
MY X-RAY PHOTOGRAPHS MADE INSIDE THE CLUBHOUSE ARE PAYING OFF! EXAMINING THEM, I LOCATED THE SECRET SWITCH THAT TURNS OFF THE ELECTRIC FORCE IN THIS DOOR!
AND MY X-RAY PICTURES SHOWED ME WHICH FLOOR-TILES I MUST NOT STEP ON, TO AVOID BEING TRAPPED! I'M GETTING NEAR THE THING I'M AFTER!
THE TIME-BUBBLE... THE LEGION'S GREATEST SECRET! KNOWING THE RIGHT COMBINATION FROM MY X-RAY PHOTOS, I DIDN'T RELEASE THE KNOCKOUT GAS HERE. NOW I'LL USE THIS MACHINE TO MAKE MYSELF MASTER OF THE UNIVERSE!
BUT ALAKTOR'S CUNNING HAS OVERLOOKED ONE AUTOMATIC ALARM, AND AS THE LEGIONNAIRES RETURN...
THE ALARM BEACON! IT MEANS SOMEONE IS IN THE CLUBHOUSE... SOMEONE WHO DIDN'T KNOW THAT A TV SCANNER IN OUR WEAPONS ROOM TURNS ON THE BEACON IF A STRANGER ENTERS!
LAND AT ONCE! WHOEVER THE PROWLER IS, HE CAN'T GET OUT!
THAT REJECTED APPLICANT, ALAKTOR... HE'S STEALING THE TIME-BUBBLE! HE'S ALREADY STARTED BACK INTO THE PAST... AND MY LIGHTNING CAN'T DISABLE THE MACHINE!
YES, FOOLS, BUT I'LL RETURN... WITH A POWER SO GREAT IT'LL MAKE ME MASTER OF WORLDS!
4
AS THE LEGIONNAIRES CHARGE, THE MACHINE FADES INTO NOTHINGNESS...
HE GOT AWAY! WHAT DID HE MEAN... HE'D RETURN WITH A GREAT POWER FROM THE PAST? COULD YOU READ HIS MIND BY THOUGHT-CASTING, SATURN GIRL?
HE WAS GONE TOO FAST! ALL I CAUGHT WAS THE THOUGHT THAT HE MEANS TO UNLOOSE THE GREATEST EVILS IN HISTORY, TO FURTHER SOME MYSTERIOUS PLAN!

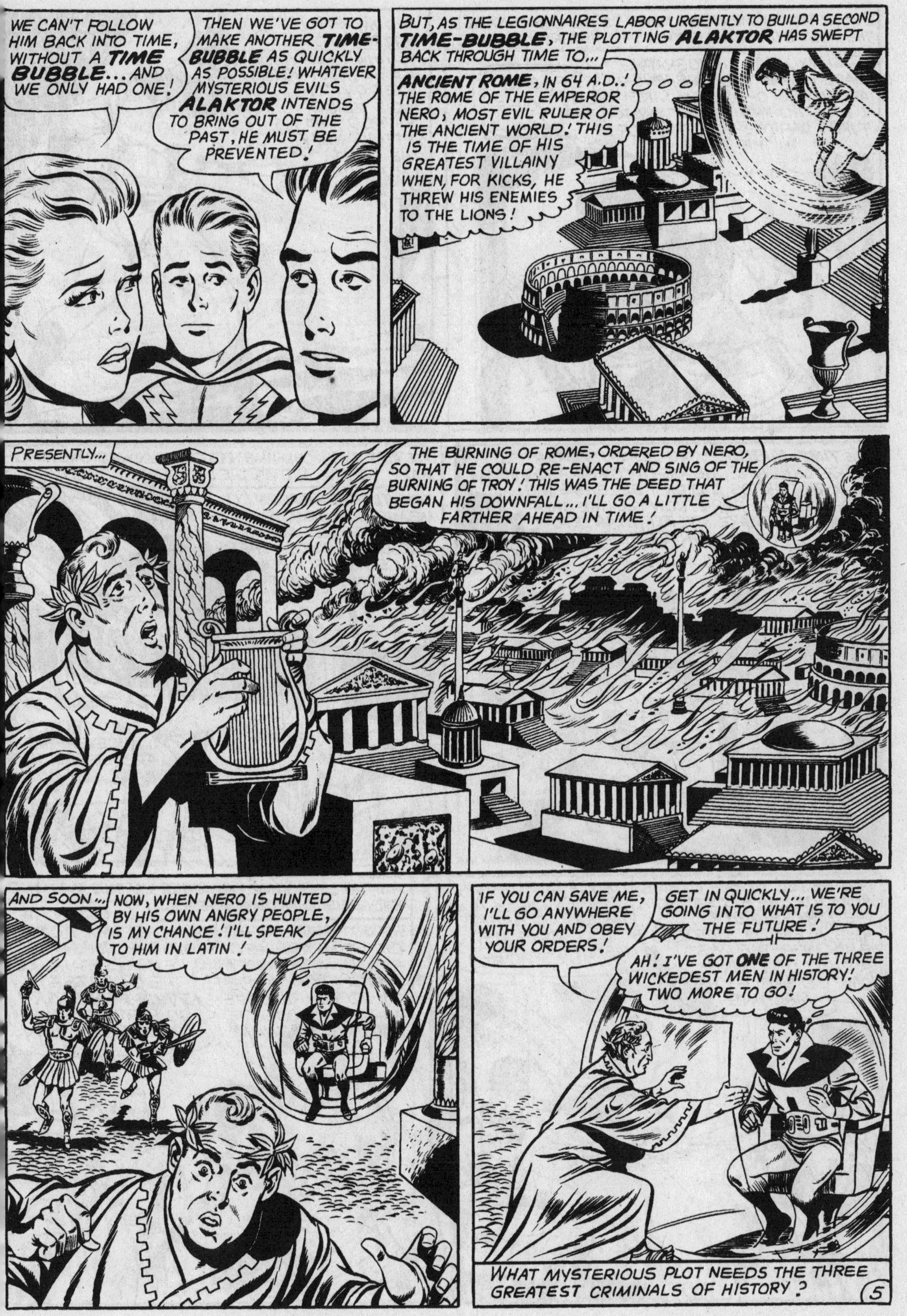
WE CAN'T FOLLOW HIM BACK INTO TIME, WITHOUT A TIME BUBBLE... AND WE ONLY HAD ONE!
THEN WE'VE GOT TO MAKE ANOTHER TIME-BUBBLE AS QUICKLY AS POSSIBLE! WHATEVER MYSTERIOUS EVILS ALAKTOR INTENDS TO BRING OUT OF THE PAST, HE MUST BE PREVENTED!
BUT, AS THE LEGIONNAIRES LABOR URGENTLY TO BUILD A SECOND TIME-BUBBLE, THE PLOTTING ALAKTOR HAS SWEPT BACK THROUGH TIME TO...
ANCIENT ROME, IN 64 A.D.! THE ROME OF THE EMPEROR NERO, MOST EVIL RULER OF THE ANCIENT WORLD! THIS IS THE TIME OF HIS GREATEST VILLAINY WHEN, FOR KICKS, HE THREW HIS ENEMIES TO THE LIONS!
PRESENTLY...
THE BURNING OF ROME, ORDERED BY NERO, SO THAT HE COULD RE-ENACT AND SING OF THE BURNING OF TROY! THIS WAS THE DEED THAT BEGAN HIS DOWNFALL... I'LL GO A LITTLE FARTHER AHEAD IN TIME!
AND SOON...
NOW, WHEN NERO IS HUNTED BY HIS OWN ANGRY PEOPLE, IS MY CHANCE! I'LL SPEAK TO HIM IN LATIN!
IF YOU CAN SAVE ME, I'LL GO ANYWHERE WITH YOU AND OBEY YOUR ORDERS!
GET IN QUICKLY... WE'RE GOING INTO WHAT IS TO YOU THE FUTURE!
AH! I'VE GOT ONE OF THE THREE WICKEDEST MEN IN HISTORY! TWO MORE TO GO!
WHAT MYSTERIOUS PLOT NEEDS THE THREE GREATEST CRIMINALS OF HISTORY?
5

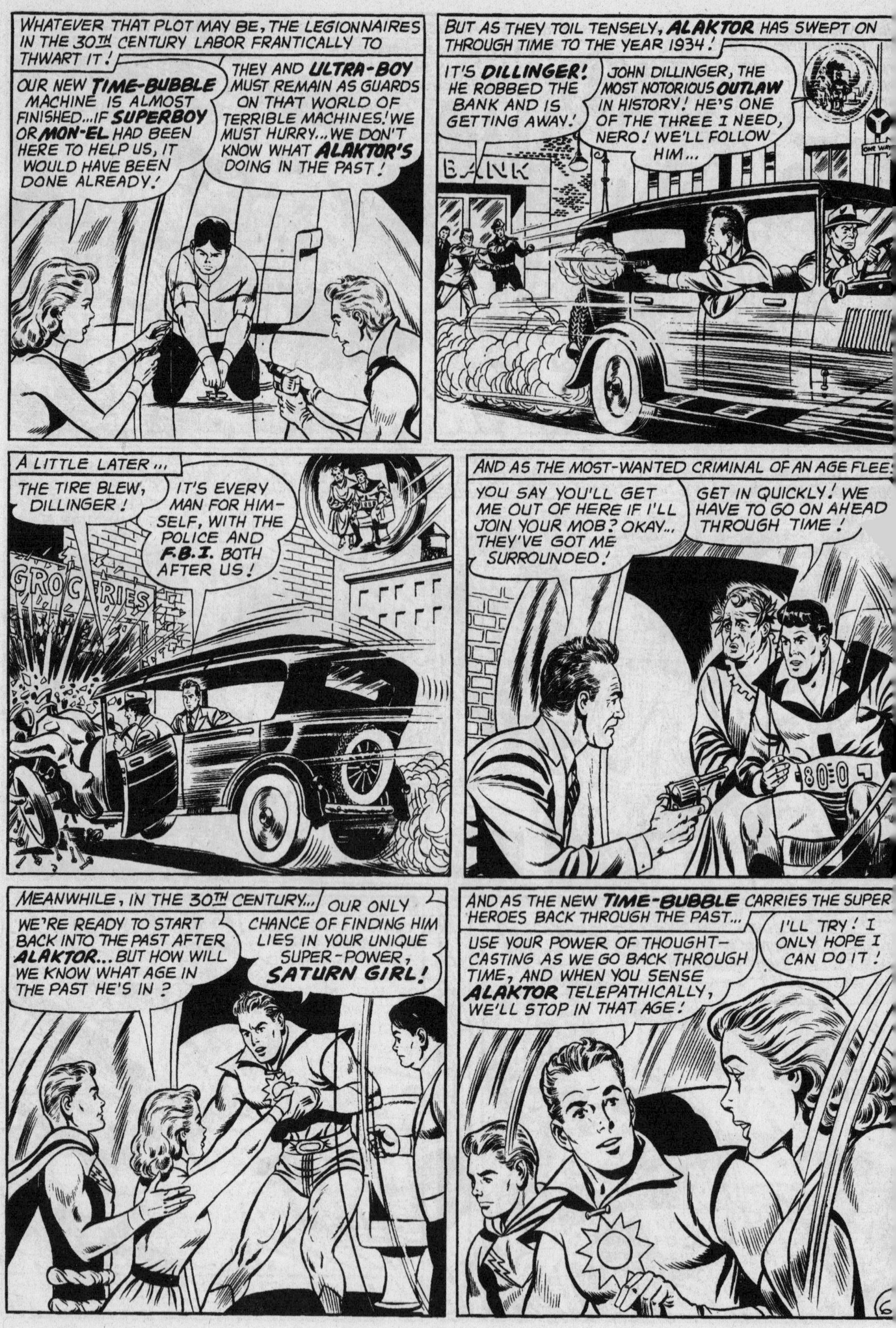
WHATEVER THAT PLOT MAY BE, THE LEGIONNAIRES IN THE 30TH CENTURY LABOR FRANTICALLY TO THWART IT!
OUR NEW TIME-BUBBLE MACHINE IS ALMOST FINISHED...IF SUPERBOY OR MON-EL HAD BEEN HERE TO HELP US, IT WOULD HAVE BEEN DONE ALREADY!
THEY AND ULTRA-BOY MUST REMAIN AS GUARDS ON THAT WORLD OF TERRIBLE MACHINES! WE MUST HURRY...WE DON'T KNOW WHAT ALAKTOR'S DOING IN THE PAST!
BUT AS THEY TOIL TENSELY, ALAKTOR HAS SWEPT ON THROUGH TIME TO THE YEAR 1934!
IT'S DILLINGER! HE ROBBED THE BANK AND IS GETTING AWAY!
JOHN DILLINGER, THE MOST NOTORIOUS OUTLAW IN HISTORY! HE'S ONE OF THE THREE I NEED, NERO! WE'LL FOLLOW HIM...
BANK
A LITTLE LATER...
THE TIRE BLEW, DILLINGER!
IT'S EVERY MAN FOR HIMSELF, WITH THE POLICE AND F.B.I. BOTH AFTER US!
GROCERIES
AND AS THE MOST-WANTED CRIMINAL OF AN AGE FLEES
YOU SAY YOU'LL GET ME OUT OF HERE IF I'LL JOIN YOUR MOB? OKAY... THEY'VE GOT ME SURROUNDED!
GET IN QUICKLY! WE HAVE TO GO ON AHEAD THROUGH TIME!
MEANWHILE, IN THE 30TH CENTURY...
WE'RE READY TO START BACK INTO THE PAST AFTER ALAKTOR... BUT HOW WILL WE KNOW WHAT AGE IN THE PAST HE'S IN?
OUR ONLY CHANCE OF FINDING HIM LIES IN YOUR UNIQUE SUPER-POWER, SATURN GIRL!
AND AS THE NEW TIME-BUBBLE CARRIES THE SUPER HEROES BACK THROUGH THE PAST...
USE YOUR POWER OF THOUGHT-CASTING AS WE GO BACK THROUGH TIME, AND WHEN YOU SENSE ALAKTOR TELEPATHICALLY, WE'LL STOP IN THAT AGE!
I'LL TRY! I ONLY HOPE I CAN DO IT!
6

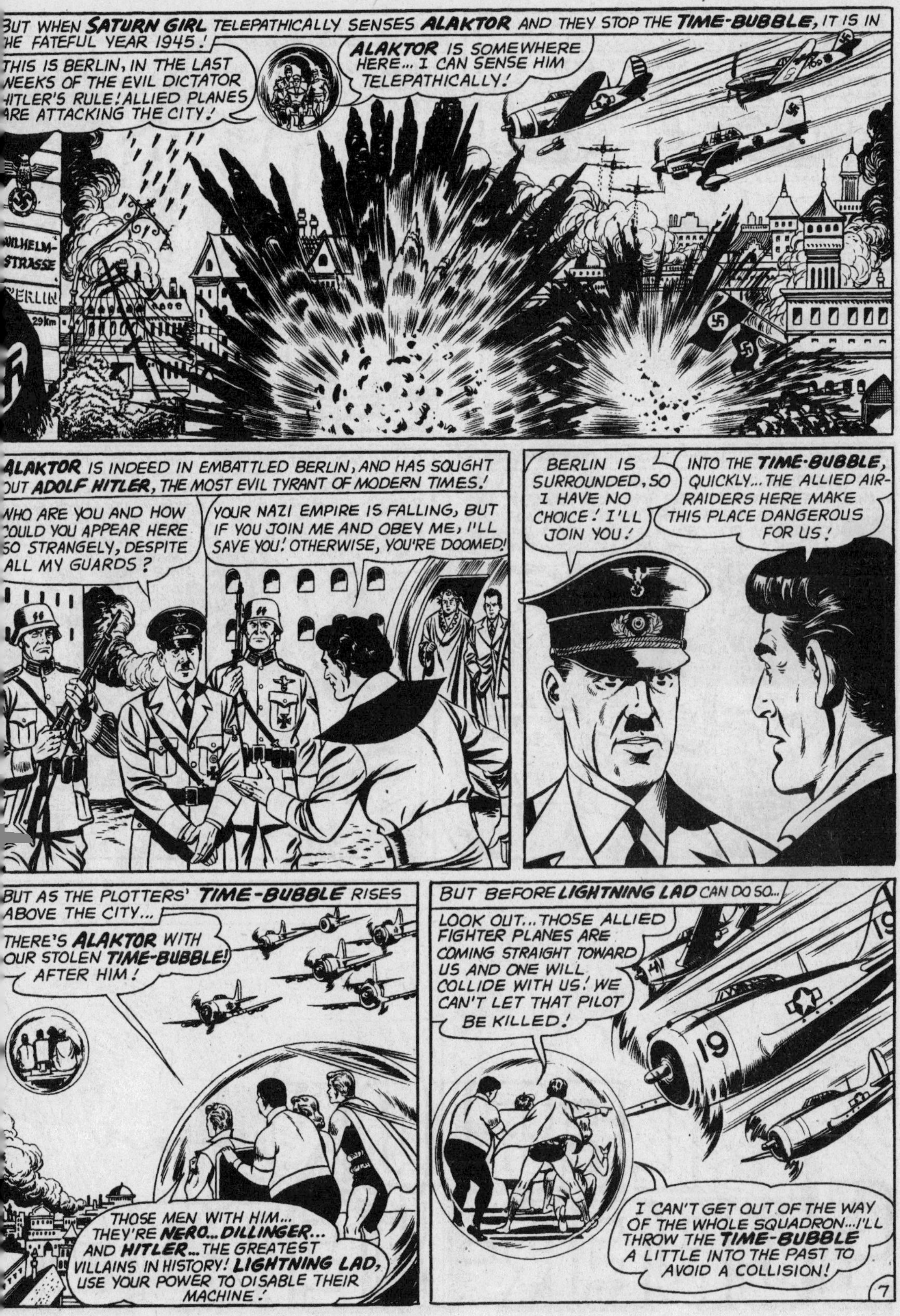
BUT WHEN SATURN GIRL TELEPATHICALLY SENSES ALAKTOR AND THEY STOP THE TIME-BUBBLE, IT IS IN THE FATEFUL YEAR 1945!
THIS IS BERLIN, IN THE LAST WEEKS OF THE EVIL DICTATOR HITLER'S RULE! ALLIED PLANES ARE ATTACKING THE CITY!
ALAKTOR IS SOMEWHERE HERE... I CAN SENSE HIM TELEPATHICALLY!
WILHELM-STRASSE
BERLIN
29 km
ALAKTOR IS INDEED IN EMBATTLED BERLIN, AND HAS SOUGHT OUT ADOLF HITLER, THE MOST EVIL TYRANT OF MODERN TIMES!
WHO ARE YOU AND HOW COULD YOU APPEAR HERE SO STRANGELY, DESPITE ALL MY GUARDS?
YOUR NAZI EMPIRE IS FALLING, BUT IF YOU JOIN ME AND OBEY ME, I'LL SAVE YOU! OTHERWISE, YOU'RE DOOMED!
BERLIN IS SURROUNDED, SO I HAVE NO CHOICE! I'LL JOIN YOU!
INTO THE TIME-BUBBLE, QUICKLY... THE ALLIED AIR-RAIDERS HERE MAKE THIS PLACE DANGEROUS FOR US!
BUT AS THE PLOTTERS' TIME-BUBBLE RISES ABOVE THE CITY...
THERE'S ALAKTOR WITH OUR STOLEN TIME-BUBBLE! AFTER HIM!
THOSE MEN WITH HIM... THEY'RE NERO... DILLINGER... AND HITLER... THE GREATEST VILLAINS IN HISTORY! LIGHTNING LAD, USE YOUR POWER TO DISABLE THEIR MACHINE!
BUT BEFORE LIGHTNING LAD CAN DO SO...
LOOK OUT... THOSE ALLIED FIGHTER PLANES ARE COMING STRAIGHT TOWARD US AND ONE WILL COLLIDE WITH US! WE CAN'T LET THAT PILOT BE KILLED!
I CAN'T GET OUT OF THE WAY OF THE WHOLE SQUADRON... I'LL THROW THE TIME-BUBBLE A LITTLE INTO THE PAST TO AVOID A COLLISION!
7

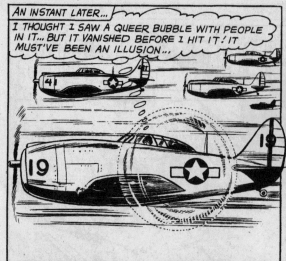

AN INSTANT LATER...

I THOUGHT I SAW A QUEER BUBBLE WITH PEOPLE IN IT... BUT IT VANISHED BEFORE I HIT IT! IT MUST'VE BEEN AN ILLUSION...

SWIFTLY, A COLLISION AVERTED, *SUN BOY* BRINGS THE LEGION *TIME-BUBBLE* BACK!

ALAKTOR IS GONE! I SENSE THAT HE MUST HAVE GONE ON INTO THE FUTURE!

THEN LET'S FOLLOW HIM!

AND AS THE LEGIONNAIRES PURSUE ON THROUGH TIME...

I'M THOUGHT-CASTING FOR HIM, BUT HE HASN'T STOPPED YET! HE MUST BE RETURNING TO OUR OWN 30TH CENTURY AGE!

AND NERO... DILLINGER... HITLER... *THEY* ARE THE GREATEST EVILS IN HISTORY THAT HE MEANT TO USE FOR HIS PLAN!

WHAT TERRIBLE PLAN DOES HE HAVE, THAT HE NEEDS THE HELP OF THE *THREE GREATEST CRIMINALS OF ALL TIME* TO CARRY IT OUT? *SATURN GIRL*, AS SOON AS WE ARRIVE IN OUR OWN TIME, GO TO *LOST WORLD* AND CHECK WITH *SUPERBOY* AND THE OTHERS!

1945

1964

2008

End PART I

LEGION of SUPER-HEROES

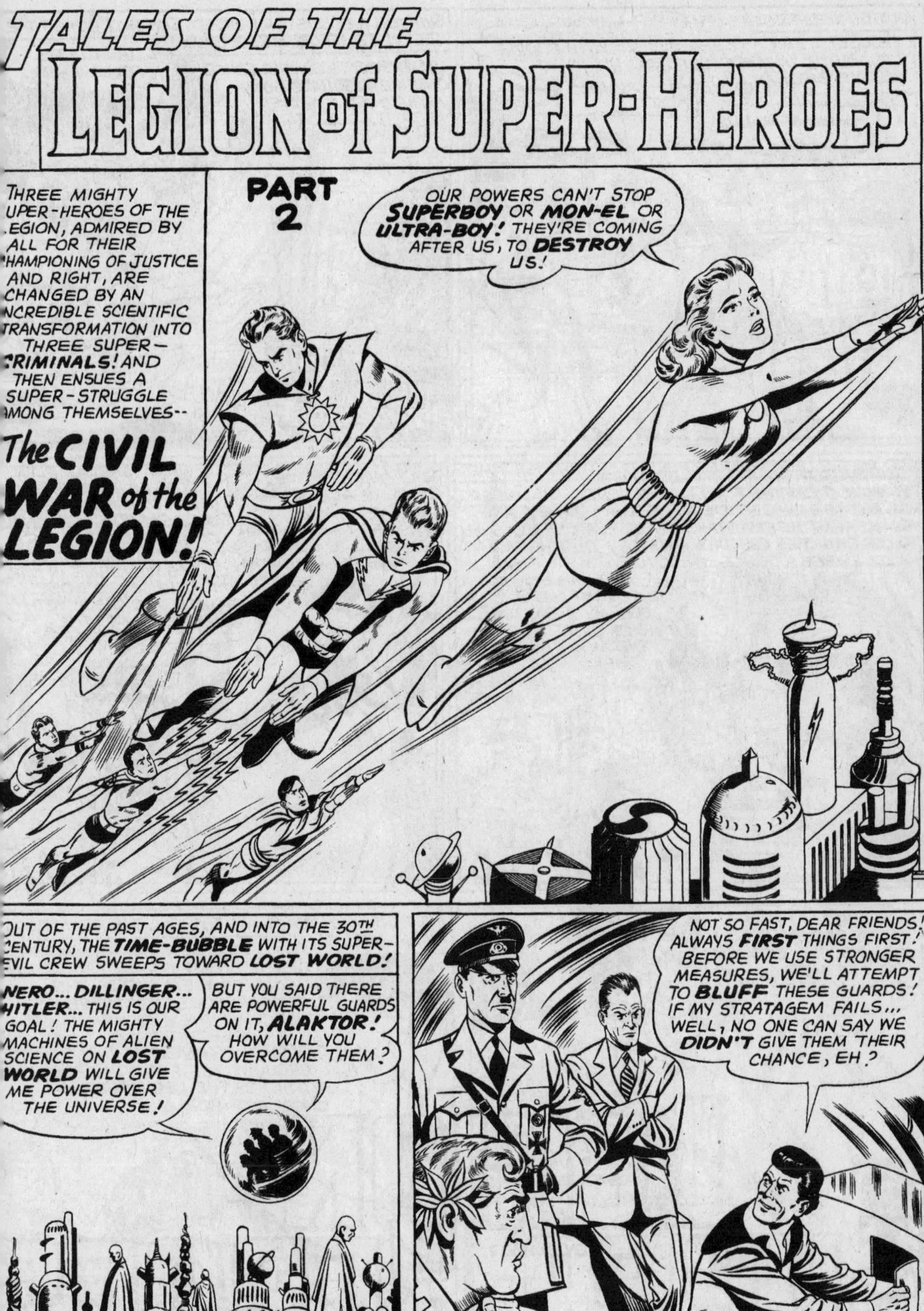

TALES OF THE
LEGION of SUPER-HEROES
PART 2
THREE MIGHTY UPER-HEROES OF THE .EGION, ADMIRED BY ALL FOR THEIR HAMPIONING OF JUSTICE AND RIGHT, ARE CHANGED BY AN NCREDIBLE SCIENTIFIC TRANSFORMATION INTO THREE SUPER-CRIMINALS! AND THEN ENSUES A SUPER-STRUGGLE AMONG THEMSELVES--
The CIVIL WAR of the LEGION!
OUR POWERS CAN'T STOP SUPERBOY OR MON-EL OR ULTRA-BOY! THEY'RE COMING AFTER US, TO DESTROY US!
OUT OF THE PAST AGES, AND INTO THE 30TH CENTURY, THE TIME-BUBBLE WITH ITS SUPER-EVIL CREW SWEEPS TOWARD LOST WORLD!
NERO... DILLINGER... HITLER... THIS IS OUR GOAL! THE MIGHTY MACHINES OF ALIEN SCIENCE ON LOST WORLD WILL GIVE ME POWER OVER THE UNIVERSE!
BUT YOU SAID THERE ARE POWERFUL GUARDS ON IT, ALAKTOR! HOW WILL YOU OVERCOME THEM?
NOT SO FAST, DEAR FRIENDS! ALWAYS FIRST THINGS FIRST! BEFORE WE USE STRONGER MEASURES, WE'LL ATTEMPT TO BLUFF THESE GUARDS! IF MY STRATAGEM FAILS... WELL, NO ONE CAN SAY WE DIDN'T GIVE THEM THEIR CHANCE, EH?

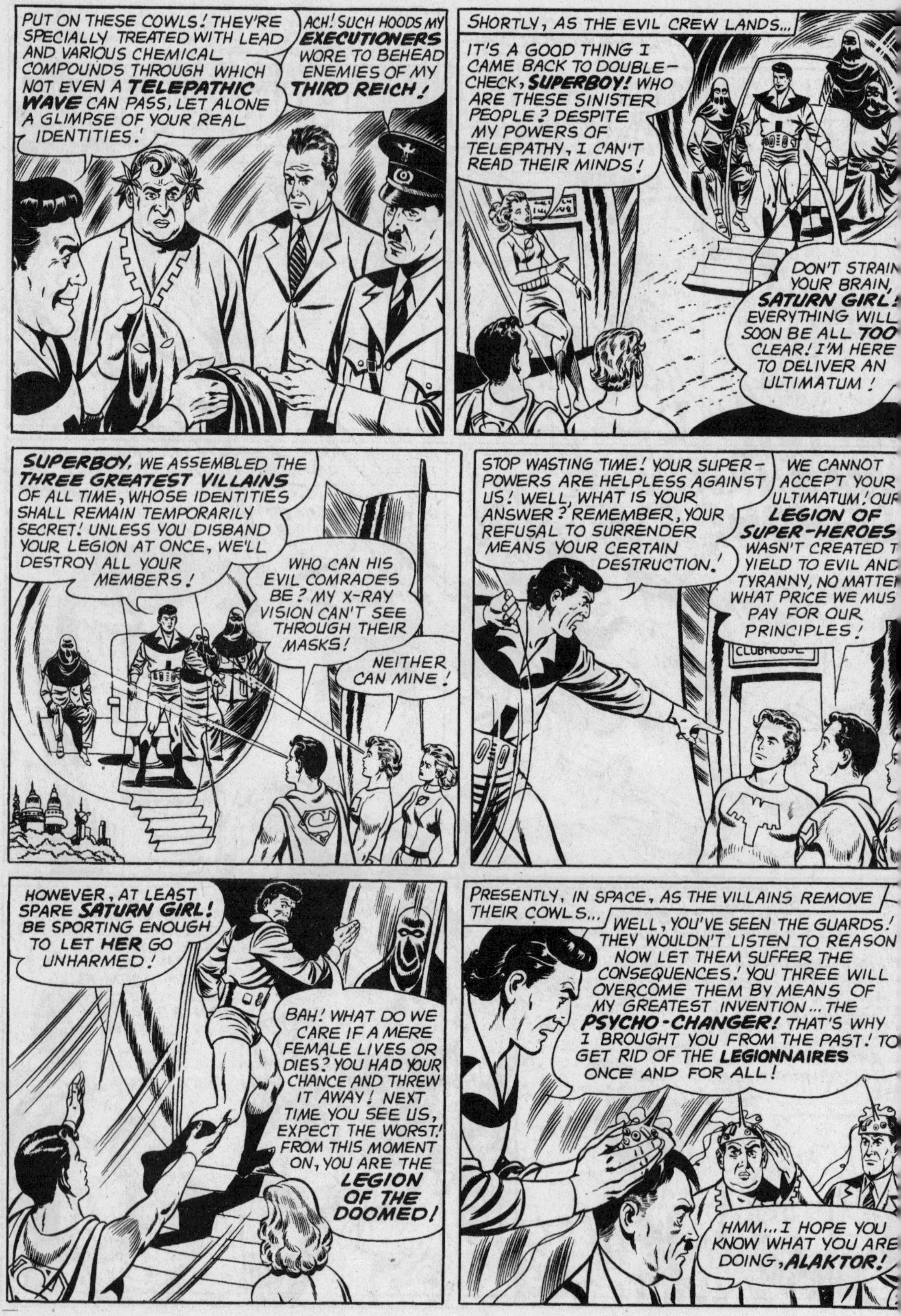
PUT ON THESE COWLS! THEY'RE SPECIALLY TREATED WITH LEAD AND VARIOUS CHEMICAL COMPOUNDS THROUGH WHICH NOT EVEN A TELEPATHIC WAVE CAN PASS, LET ALONE A GLIMPSE OF YOUR REAL IDENTITIES!
ACH! SUCH HOODS MY EXECUTIONERS WORE TO BEHEAD ENEMIES OF MY THIRD REICH!
SHORTLY, AS THE EVIL CREW LANDS...
IT'S A GOOD THING I CAME BACK TO DOUBLE-CHECK, SUPERBOY! WHO ARE THESE SINISTER PEOPLE? DESPITE MY POWERS OF TELEPATHY, I CAN'T READ THEIR MINDS!
DON'T STRAIN YOUR BRAIN, SATURN GIRL! EVERYTHING WILL SOON BE ALL TOO CLEAR! I'M HERE TO DELIVER AN ULTIMATUM!
SUPERBOY, WE ASSEMBLED THE THREE GREATEST VILLAINS OF ALL TIME, WHOSE IDENTITIES SHALL REMAIN TEMPORARILY SECRET! UNLESS YOU DISBAND YOUR LEGION AT ONCE, WE'LL DESTROY ALL YOUR MEMBERS!
WHO CAN HIS EVIL COMRADES BE? MY X-RAY VISION CAN'T SEE THROUGH THEIR MASKS!
NEITHER CAN MINE!
STOP WASTING TIME! YOUR SUPER-POWERS ARE HELPLESS AGAINST US! WELL, WHAT IS YOUR ANSWER? REMEMBER, YOUR REFUSAL TO SURRENDER MEANS YOUR CERTAIN DESTRUCTION!
WE CANNOT ACCEPT YOUR ULTIMATUM! OUR LEGION OF SUPER-HEROES WASN'T CREATED TO YIELD TO EVIL AND TYRANNY, NO MATTER WHAT PRICE WE MUST PAY FOR OUR PRINCIPLES!
CLUBHOUSE
HOWEVER, AT LEAST SPARE SATURN GIRL! BE SPORTING ENOUGH TO LET HER GO UNHARMED!
BAH! WHAT DO WE CARE IF A MERE FEMALE LIVES OR DIES? YOU HAD YOUR CHANCE AND THREW IT AWAY! NEXT TIME YOU SEE US, EXPECT THE WORST! FROM THIS MOMENT ON, YOU ARE THE LEGION OF THE DOOMED!
PRESENTLY, IN SPACE, AS THE VILLAINS REMOVE THEIR COWLS...
WELL, YOU'VE SEEN THE GUARDS! THEY WOULDN'T LISTEN TO REASON! NOW LET THEM SUFFER THE CONSEQUENCES! YOU THREE WILL OVERCOME THEM BY MEANS OF MY GREATEST INVENTION... THE PSYCHO-CHANGER! THAT'S WHY I BROUGHT YOU FROM THE PAST! TO GET RID OF THE LEGIONNAIRES ONCE AND FOR ALL!
HMM... I HOPE YOU KNOW WHAT YOU ARE DOING, ALAKTOR!

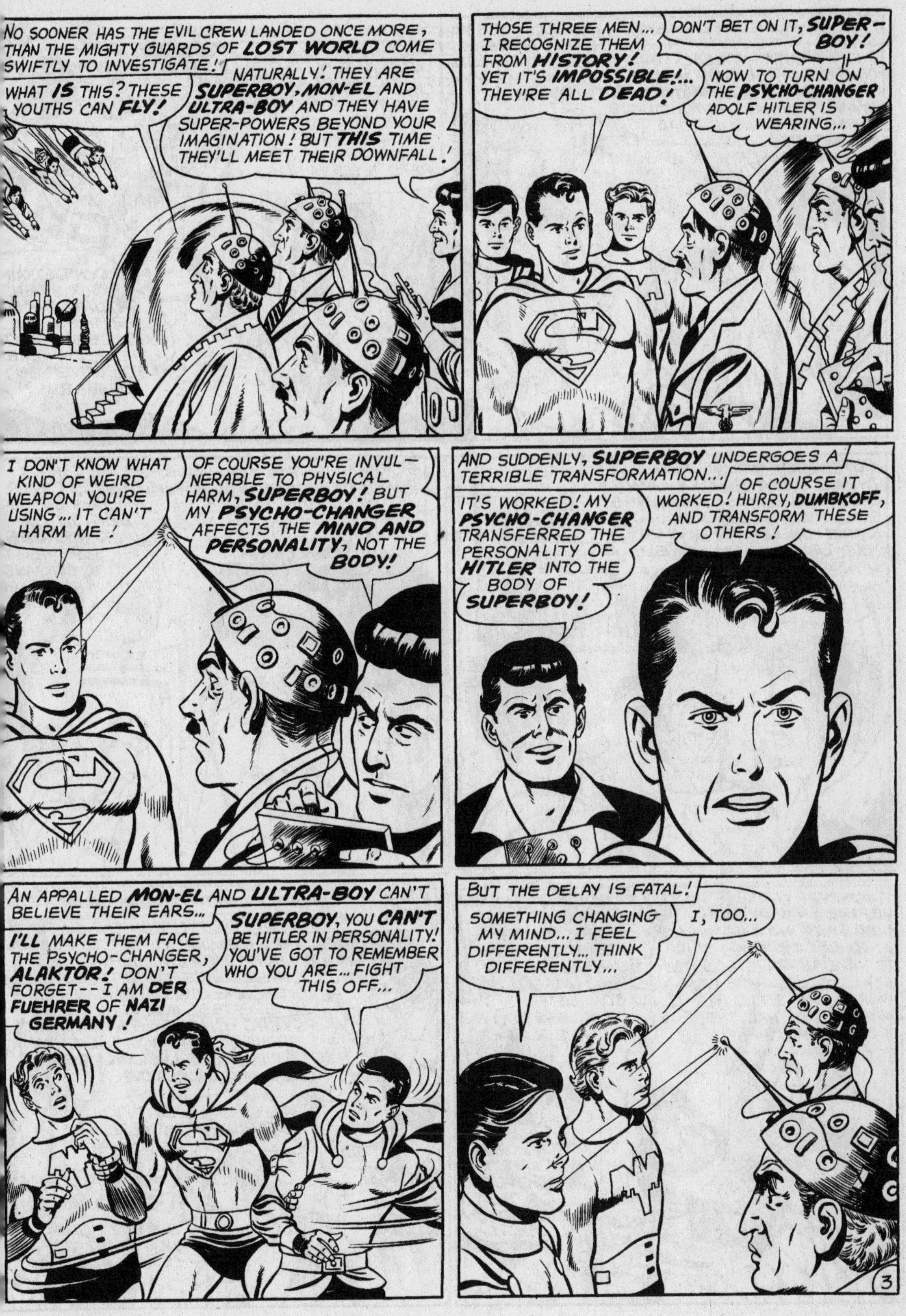
NO SOONER HAS THE EVIL CREW LANDED ONCE MORE, THAN THE MIGHTY GUARDS OF LOST WORLD COME SWIFTLY TO INVESTIGATE!
WHAT IS THIS? THESE YOUTHS CAN FLY!
NATURALLY! THEY ARE SUPERBOY, MON-EL AND ULTRA-BOY AND THEY HAVE SUPER-POWERS BEYOND YOUR IMAGINATION! BUT THIS TIME THEY'LL MEET THEIR DOWNFALL!
THOSE THREE MEN... I RECOGNIZE THEM FROM HISTORY! YET IT'S IMPOSSIBLE!... THEY'RE ALL DEAD!
DON'T BET ON IT, SUPER-BOY!
NOW TO TURN ON THE PSYCHO-CHANGER ADOLF HITLER IS WEARING...
I DON'T KNOW WHAT KIND OF WEIRD WEAPON YOU'RE USING... IT CAN'T HARM ME!
OF COURSE YOU'RE INVUL-NERABLE TO PHYSICAL HARM, SUPERBOY! BUT MY PSYCHO-CHANGER AFFECTS THE MIND AND PERSONALITY, NOT THE BODY!
AND SUDDENLY, SUPERBOY UNDERGOES A TERRIBLE TRANSFORMATION...
IT'S WORKED! MY PSYCHO-CHANGER TRANSFERRED THE PERSONALITY OF HITLER INTO THE BODY OF SUPERBOY!
OF COURSE IT WORKED! HURRY, DUMBKOFF, AND TRANSFORM THESE OTHERS!
AN APPALLED MON-EL AND ULTRA-BOY CAN'T BELIEVE THEIR EARS...
I'LL MAKE THEM FACE THE PSYCHO-CHANGER, ALAKTOR! DON'T FORGET--I AM DER FUEHRER OF NAZI GERMANY!
SUPERBOY, YOU CAN'T BE HITLER IN PERSONALITY! YOU'VE GOT TO REMEMBER WHO YOU ARE... FIGHT THIS OFF...
BUT THE DELAY IS FATAL!
SOMETHING CHANGING MY MIND... I FEEL DIFFERENTLY... THINK DIFFERENTLY...
I, TOO...
3

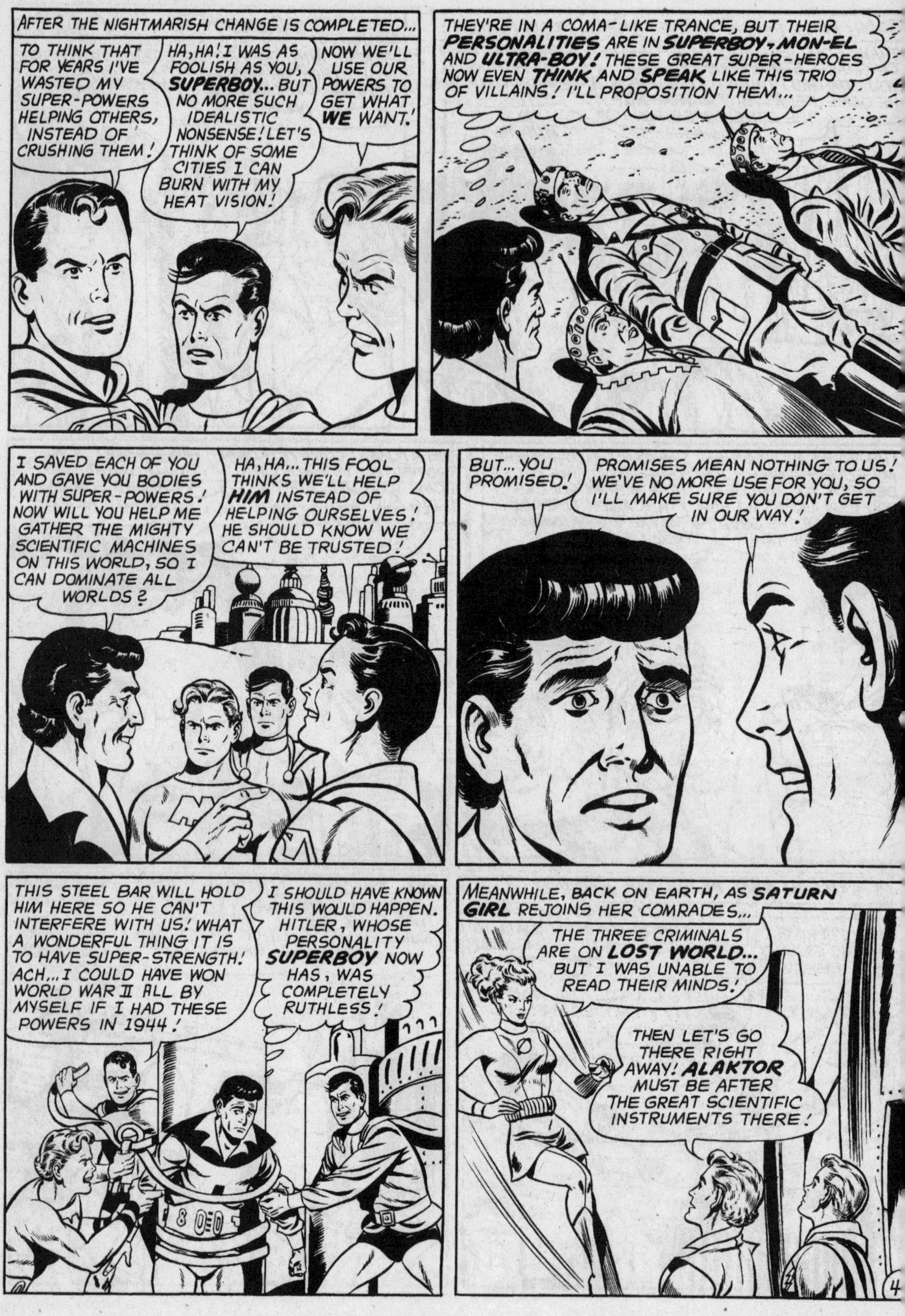
AFTER THE NIGHTMARISH CHANGE IS COMPLETED...
TO THINK THAT FOR YEARS I'VE WASTED MY SUPER-POWERS HELPING OTHERS, INSTEAD OF CRUSHING THEM!
HA, HA! I WAS AS FOOLISH AS YOU, SUPERBOY... BUT NO MORE SUCH IDEALISTIC NONSENSE! LET'S THINK OF SOME CITIES I CAN BURN WITH MY HEAT VISION!
NOW WE'LL USE OUR POWERS TO GET WHAT WE WANT!
THEY'RE IN A COMA-LIKE TRANCE, BUT THEIR PERSONALITIES ARE IN SUPERBOY, MON-EL AND ULTRA-BOY! THESE GREAT SUPER-HEROES NOW EVEN THINK AND SPEAK LIKE THIS TRIO OF VILLAINS! I'LL PROPOSITION THEM...
I SAVED EACH OF YOU AND GAVE YOU BODIES WITH SUPER-POWERS! NOW WILL YOU HELP ME GATHER THE MIGHTY SCIENTIFIC MACHINES ON THIS WORLD, SO I CAN DOMINATE ALL WORLDS?
HA, HA... THIS FOOL THINKS WE'LL HELP HIM INSTEAD OF HELPING OURSELVES! HE SHOULD KNOW WE CAN'T BE TRUSTED!
BUT... YOU PROMISED!
PROMISES MEAN NOTHING TO US! WE'VE NO MORE USE FOR YOU, SO I'LL MAKE SURE YOU DON'T GET IN OUR WAY!
THIS STEEL BAR WILL HOLD HIM HERE SO HE CAN'T INTERFERE WITH US! WHAT A WONDERFUL THING IT IS TO HAVE SUPER-STRENGTH! ACH... I COULD HAVE WON WORLD WAR II ALL BY MYSELF IF I HAD THESE POWERS IN 1944!
I SHOULD HAVE KNOWN THIS WOULD HAPPEN. HITLER, WHOSE PERSONALITY SUPERBOY NOW HAS, WAS COMPLETELY RUTHLESS!
MEANWHILE, BACK ON EARTH, AS SATURN GIRL REJOINS HER COMRADES...
THE THREE CRIMINALS ARE ON LOST WORLD... BUT I WAS UNABLE TO READ THEIR MINDS!
THEN LET'S GO THERE RIGHT AWAY! ALAKTOR MUST BE AFTER THE GREAT SCIENTIFIC INSTRUMENTS THERE!
4

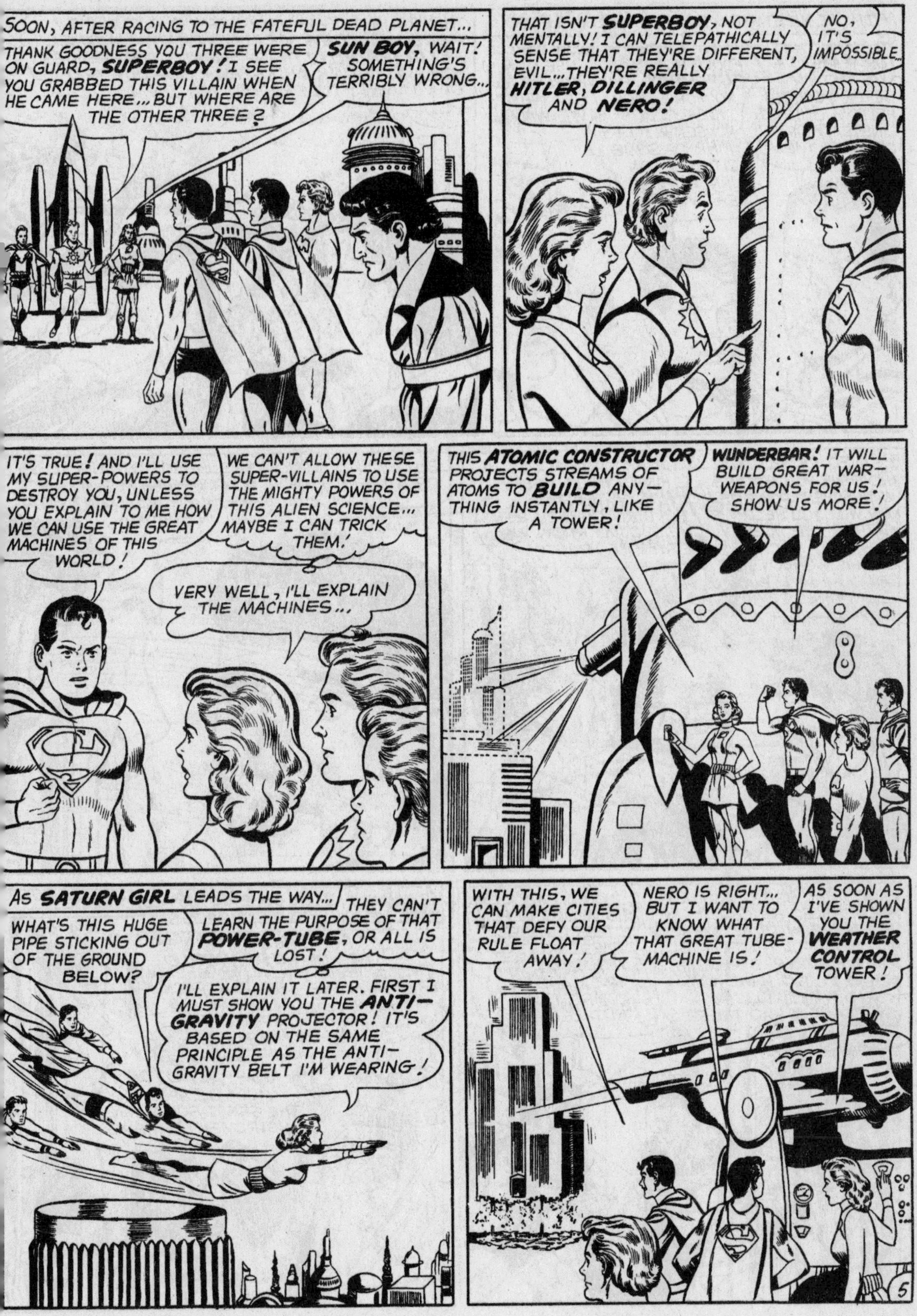
SOON, AFTER RACING TO THE FATEFUL DEAD PLANET...
THANK GOODNESS YOU THREE WERE ON GUARD, SUPERBOY! I SEE YOU GRABBED THIS VILLAIN WHEN HE CAME HERE... BUT WHERE ARE THE OTHER THREE?
SUN BOY, WAIT! SOMETHING'S TERRIBLY WRONG...
THAT ISN'T SUPERBOY, NOT MENTALLY! I CAN TELEPATHICALLY SENSE THAT THEY'RE DIFFERENT, EVIL... THEY'RE REALLY HITLER, DILLINGER AND NERO!
NO, IT'S IMPOSSIBLE...
IT'S TRUE! AND I'LL USE MY SUPER-POWERS TO DESTROY YOU, UNLESS YOU EXPLAIN TO ME HOW WE CAN USE THE GREAT MACHINES OF THIS WORLD!
WE CAN'T ALLOW THESE SUPER-VILLAINS TO USE THE MIGHTY POWERS OF THIS ALIEN SCIENCE... MAYBE I CAN TRICK THEM.
VERY WELL, I'LL EXPLAIN THE MACHINES...
THIS ATOMIC CONSTRUCTOR PROJECTS STREAMS OF ATOMS TO BUILD ANY-THING INSTANTLY, LIKE A TOWER!
WUNDERBAR! IT WILL BUILD GREAT WAR-WEAPONS FOR US! SHOW US MORE!
AS SATURN GIRL LEADS THE WAY...
WHAT'S THIS HUGE PIPE STICKING OUT OF THE GROUND BELOW?
THEY CAN'T LEARN THE PURPOSE OF THAT POWER-TUBE, OR ALL IS LOST!
I'LL EXPLAIN IT LATER. FIRST I MUST SHOW YOU THE ANTI-GRAVITY PROJECTOR! IT'S BASED ON THE SAME PRINCIPLE AS THE ANTI-GRAVITY BELT I'M WEARING!
WITH THIS, WE CAN MAKE CITIES THAT DEFY OUR RULE FLOAT AWAY!
NERO IS RIGHT... BUT I WANT TO KNOW WHAT THAT GREAT TUBE-MACHINE IS!
AS SOON AS I'VE SHOWN YOU THE WEATHER CONTROL TOWER!
5

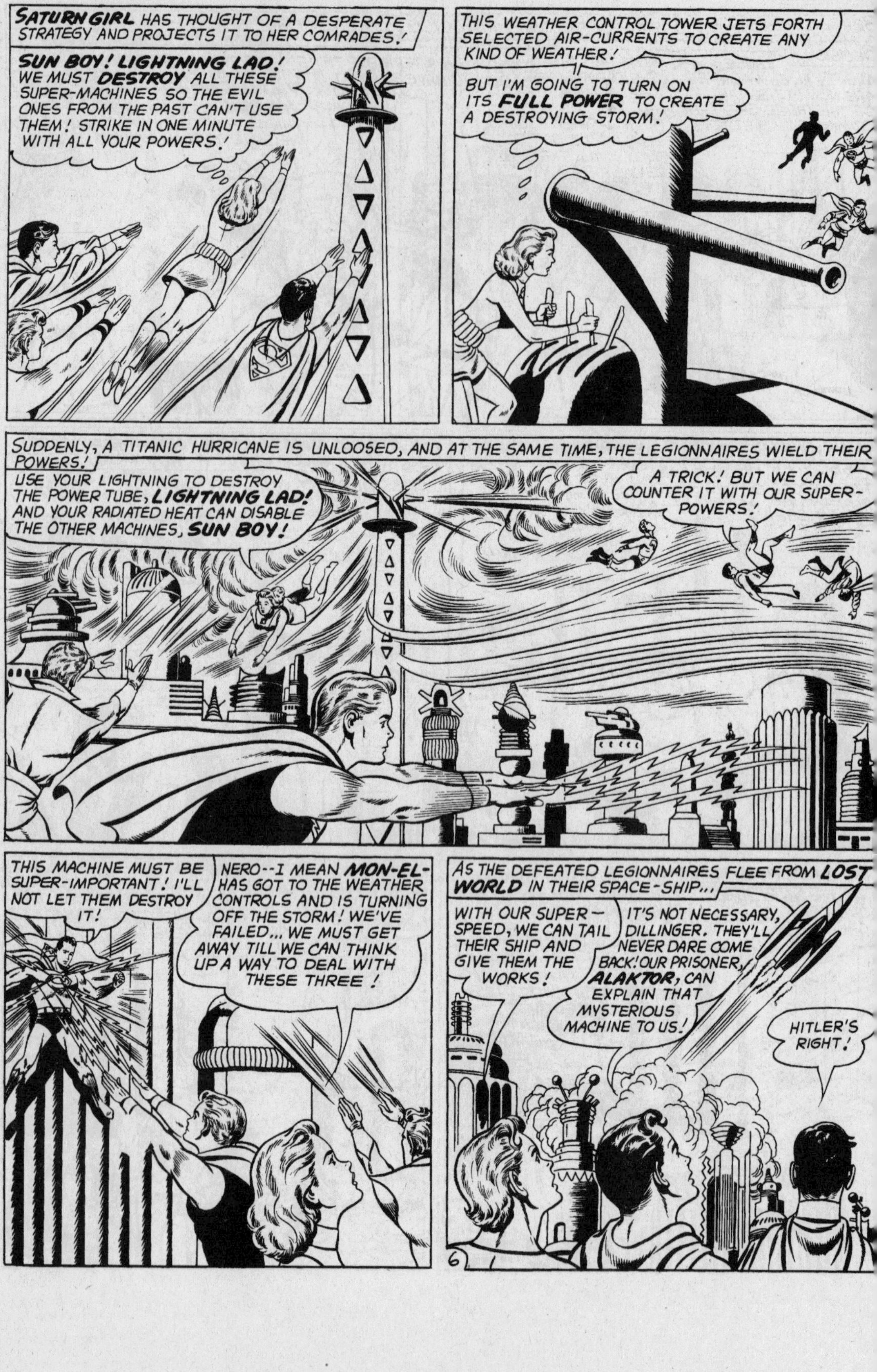
SATURN GIRL HAS THOUGHT OF A DESPERATE STRATEGY AND PROJECTS IT TO HER COMRADES!
SUN BOY! LIGHTNING LAD! WE MUST DESTROY ALL THESE SUPER-MACHINES SO THE EVIL ONES FROM THE PAST CAN'T USE THEM! STRIKE IN ONE MINUTE WITH ALL YOUR POWERS!
THIS WEATHER CONTROL TOWER JETS FORTH SELECTED AIR-CURRENTS TO CREATE ANY KIND OF WEATHER!
BUT I'M GOING TO TURN ON ITS FULL POWER TO CREATE A DESTROYING STORM!
SUDDENLY, A TITANIC HURRICANE IS UNLOOSED, AND AT THE SAME TIME, THE LEGIONNAIRES WIELD THEIR POWERS!
USE YOUR LIGHTNING TO DESTROY THE POWER TUBE, LIGHTNING LAD! AND YOUR RADIATED HEAT CAN DISABLE THE OTHER MACHINES, SUN BOY!
A TRICK! BUT WE CAN COUNTER IT WITH OUR SUPER-POWERS!
THIS MACHINE MUST BE SUPER-IMPORTANT! I'LL NOT LET THEM DESTROY IT!
NERO--I MEAN MON-EL-HAS GOT TO THE WEATHER CONTROLS AND IS TURNING OFF THE STORM! WE'VE FAILED... WE MUST GET AWAY TILL WE CAN THINK UP A WAY TO DEAL WITH THESE THREE!
AS THE DEFEATED LEGIONNAIRES FLEE FROM LOST WORLD IN THEIR SPACE-SHIP...
WITH OUR SUPER-SPEED, WE CAN TAIL THEIR SHIP AND GIVE THEM THE WORKS!
IT'S NOT NECESSARY, DILLINGER. THEY'LL NEVER DARE COME BACK! OUR PRISONER, ALAKTOR, CAN EXPLAIN THAT MYSTERIOUS MACHINE TO US!
HITLER'S RIGHT!
6

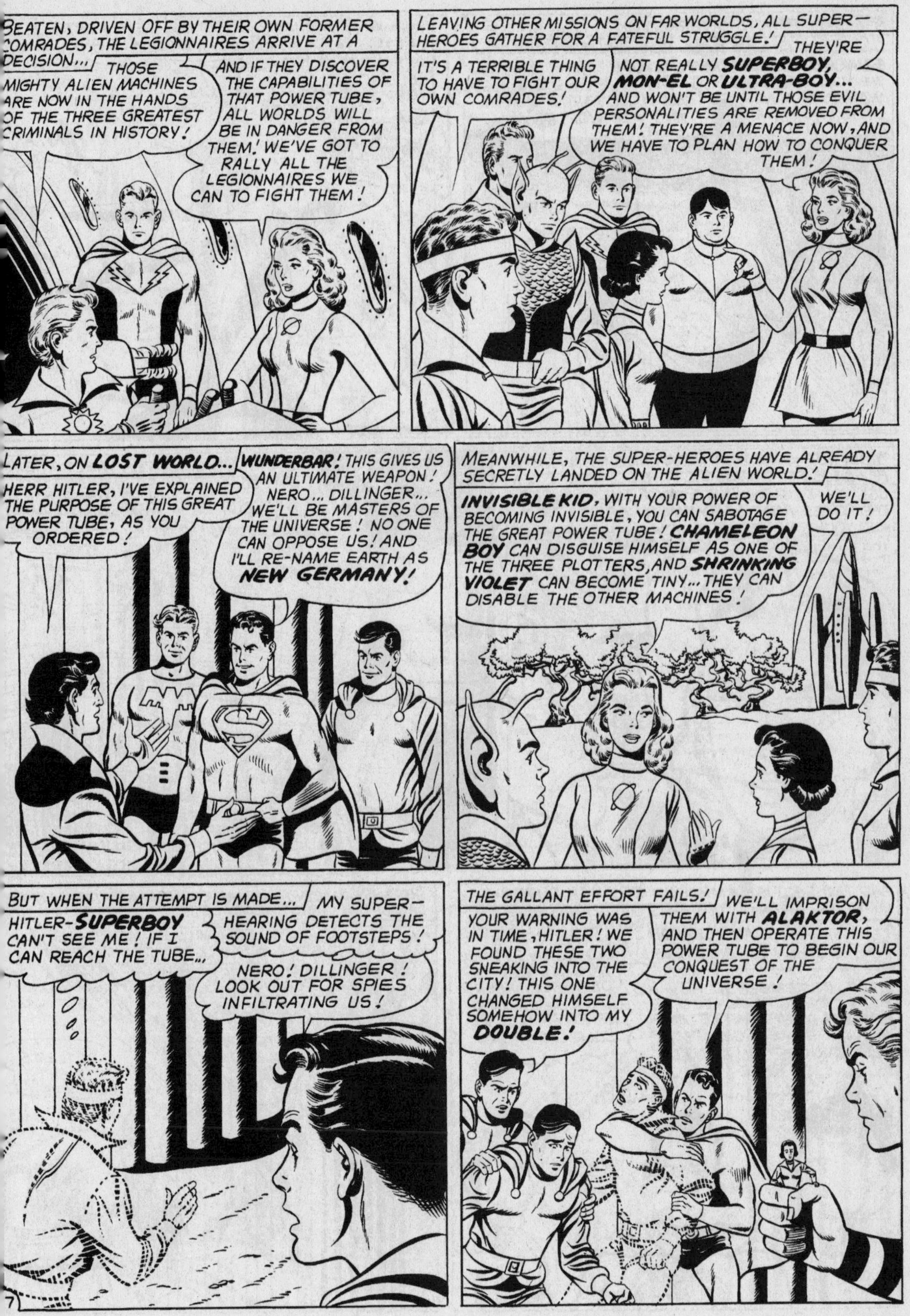
BEATEN, DRIVEN OFF BY THEIR OWN FORMER COMRADES, THE LEGIONNAIRES ARRIVE AT A DECISION...
THOSE MIGHTY ALIEN MACHINES ARE NOW IN THE HANDS OF THE THREE GREATEST CRIMINALS IN HISTORY!
AND IF THEY DISCOVER THE CAPABILITIES OF THAT POWER TUBE, ALL WORLDS WILL BE IN DANGER FROM THEM! WE'VE GOT TO RALLY ALL THE LEGIONNAIRES WE CAN TO FIGHT THEM!
LEAVING OTHER MISSIONS ON FAR WORLDS, ALL SUPER-HEROES GATHER FOR A FATEFUL STRUGGLE!
IT'S A TERRIBLE THING TO HAVE TO FIGHT OUR OWN COMRADES!
THEY'RE NOT REALLY SUPERBOY, MON-EL OR ULTRA-BOY... AND WON'T BE UNTIL THOSE EVIL PERSONALITIES ARE REMOVED FROM THEM! THEY'RE A MENACE NOW, AND WE HAVE TO PLAN HOW TO CONQUER THEM!
LATER, ON LOST WORLD...
HERR HITLER, I'VE EXPLAINED THE PURPOSE OF THIS GREAT POWER TUBE, AS YOU ORDERED!
WUNDERBAR! THIS GIVES US AN ULTIMATE WEAPON! NERO... DILLINGER... WE'LL BE MASTERS OF THE UNIVERSE! NO ONE CAN OPPOSE US! AND I'LL RE-NAME EARTH AS NEW GERMANY!
MEANWHILE, THE SUPER-HEROES HAVE ALREADY SECRETLY LANDED ON THE ALIEN WORLD!
INVISIBLE KID, WITH YOUR POWER OF BECOMING INVISIBLE, YOU CAN SABOTAGE THE GREAT POWER TUBE! CHAMELEON BOY CAN DISGUISE HIMSELF AS ONE OF THE THREE PLOTTERS, AND SHRINKING VIOLET CAN BECOME TINY... THEY CAN DISABLE THE OTHER MACHINES!
WE'LL DO IT!
BUT WHEN THE ATTEMPT IS MADE...
HITLER-SUPERBOY CAN'T SEE ME! IF I CAN REACH THE TUBE...
MY SUPER-HEARING DETECTS THE SOUND OF FOOTSTEPS!
NERO! DILLINGER! LOOK OUT FOR SPIES INFILTRATING US!
7
THE GALLANT EFFORT FAILS!
YOUR WARNING WAS IN TIME, HITLER! WE FOUND THESE TWO SNEAKING INTO THE CITY! THIS ONE CHANGED HIMSELF SOMEHOW INTO MY DOUBLE!
WE'LL IMPRISON THEM WITH ALAKTOR, AND THEN OPERATE THIS POWER TUBE TO BEGIN OUR CONQUEST OF THE UNIVERSE!

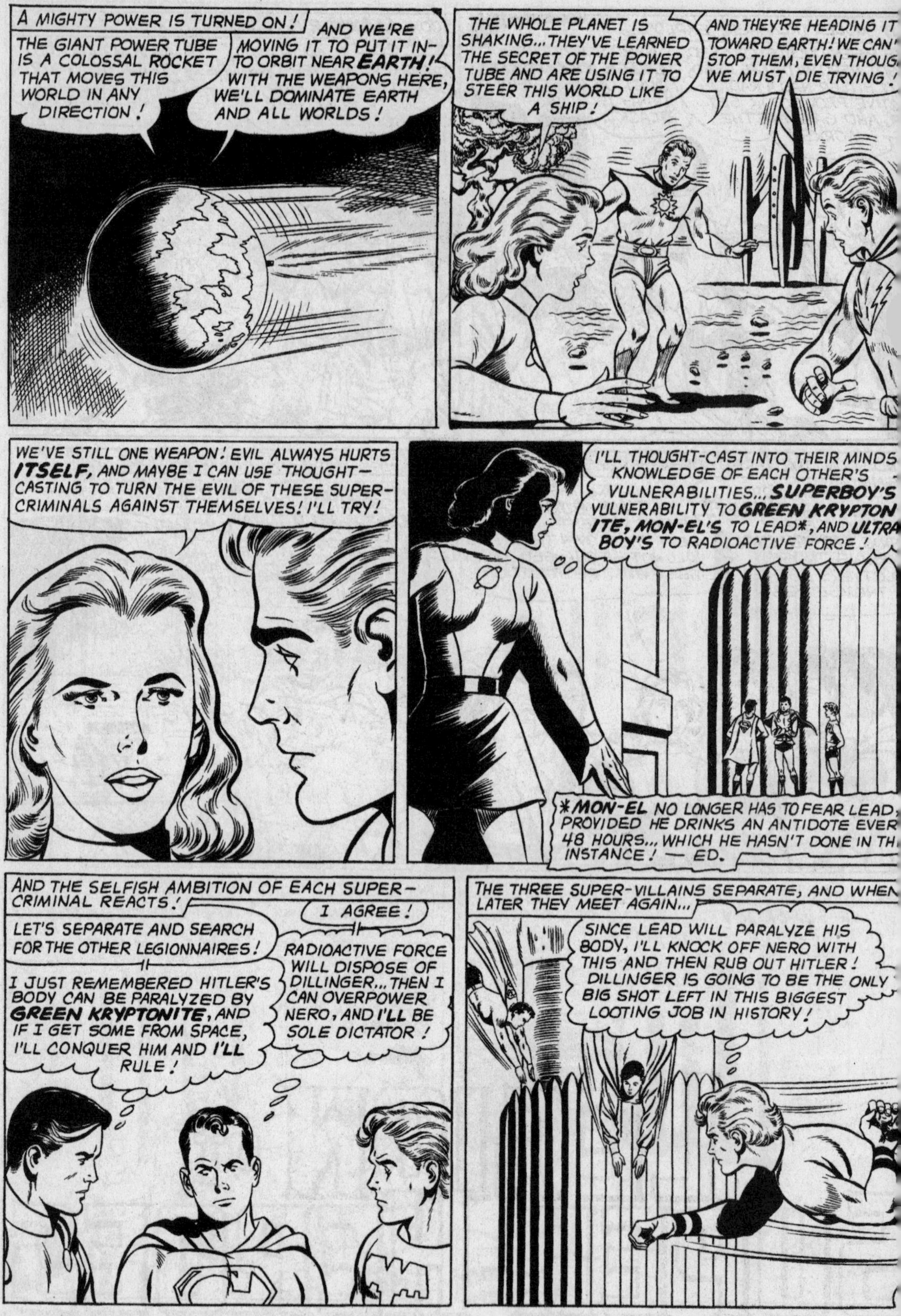
A MIGHTY POWER IS TURNED ON!
THE GIANT POWER TUBE IS A COLOSSAL ROCKET THAT MOVES THIS WORLD IN ANY DIRECTION!
AND WE'RE MOVING IT TO PUT IT INTO ORBIT NEAR EARTH! WITH THE WEAPONS HERE, WE'LL DOMINATE EARTH AND ALL WORLDS!
THE WHOLE PLANET IS SHAKING... THEY'VE LEARNED THE SECRET OF THE POWER TUBE AND ARE USING IT TO STEER THIS WORLD LIKE A SHIP!
AND THEY'RE HEADING IT TOWARD EARTH! WE CAN' STOP THEM, EVEN THOUG WE MUST DIE TRYING!
WE'VE STILL ONE WEAPON! EVIL ALWAYS HURTS ITSELF, AND MAYBE I CAN USE THOUGHT-CASTING TO TURN THE EVIL OF THESE SUPER-CRIMINALS AGAINST THEMSELVES! I'LL TRY!
I'LL THOUGHT-CAST INTO THEIR MINDS KNOWLEDGE OF EACH OTHER'S VULNERABILITIES... SUPERBOY'S VULNERABILITY TO GREEN KRYPTON ITE, MON-EL'S TO LEAD*, AND ULTRA BOY'S TO RADIOACTIVE FORCE!
*MON-EL NO LONGER HAS TO FEAR LEAD, PROVIDED HE DRINKS AN ANTIDOTE EVER 48 HOURS... WHICH HE HASN'T DONE IN TH INSTANCE! — ED.
AND THE SELFISH AMBITION OF EACH SUPER-CRIMINAL REACTS!
LET'S SEPARATE AND SEARCH FOR THE OTHER LEGIONNAIRES!
I AGREE!
I JUST REMEMBERED HITLER'S BODY CAN BE PARALYZED BY GREEN KRYPTONITE, AND IF I GET SOME FROM SPACE, I'LL CONQUER HIM AND I'LL RULE!
RADIOACTIVE FORCE WILL DISPOSE OF DILLINGER... THEN I CAN OVERPOWER NERO, AND I'LL BE SOLE DICTATOR!
THE THREE SUPER-VILLAINS SEPARATE, AND WHEN LATER THEY MEET AGAIN...
SINCE LEAD WILL PARALYZE HIS BODY, I'LL KNOCK OFF NERO WITH THIS AND THEN RUB OUT HITLER! DILLINGER IS GOING TO BE THE ONLY BIG SHOT LEFT IN THIS BIGGEST LOOTING JOB IN HISTORY!

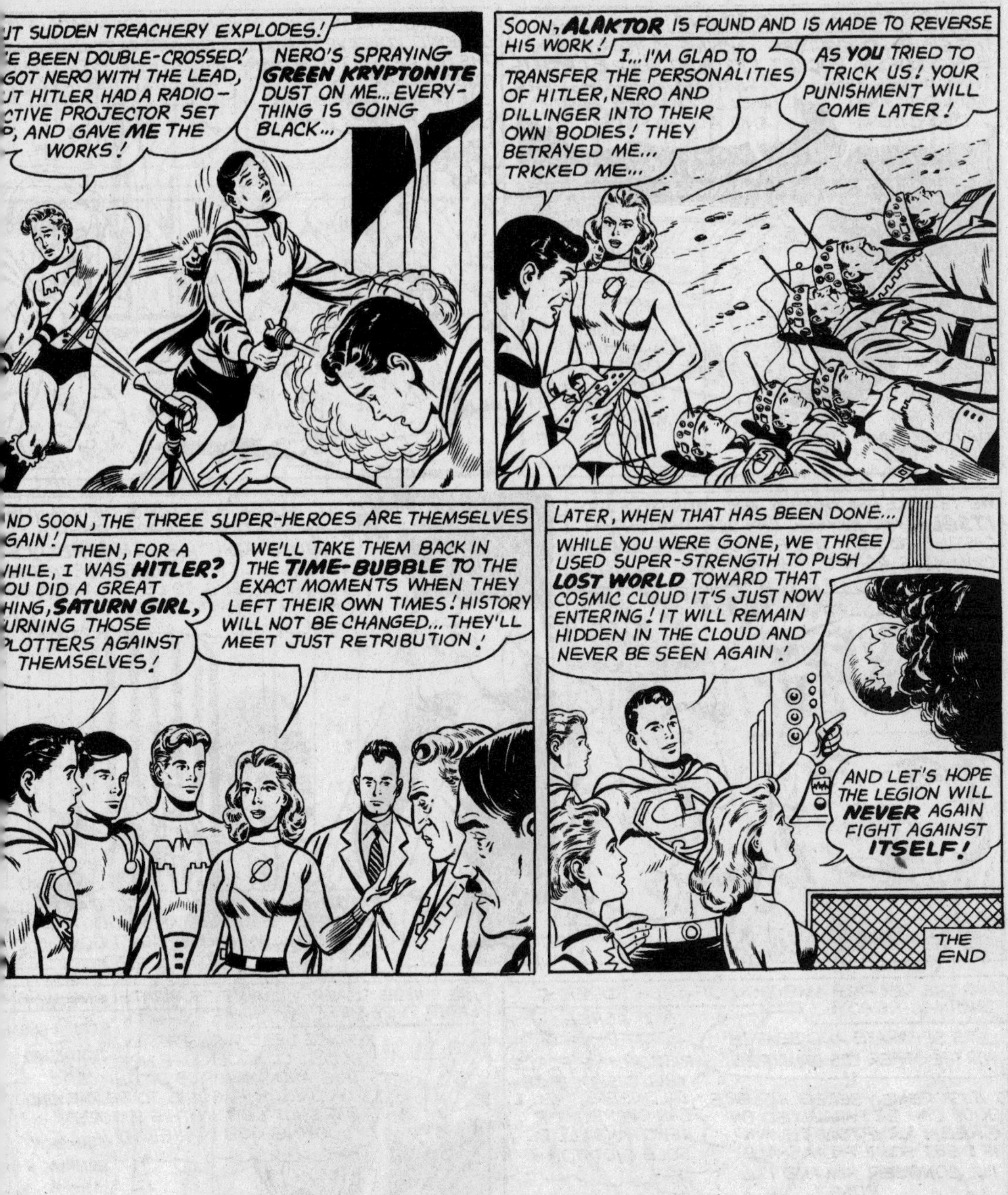
UT SUDDEN TREACHERY EXPLODES!
'E BEEN DOUBLE-CROSSED! GOT NERO WITH THE LEAD, UT HITLER HAD A RADIO-CTIVE PROJECTOR SET P, AND GAVE ME THE WORKS!
NERO'S SPRAYING GREEN KRYPTONITE DUST ON ME... EVERYTHING IS GOING BLACK...
SOON, ALAKTOR IS FOUND AND IS MADE TO REVERSE HIS WORK!
I... I'M GLAD TO TRANSFER THE PERSONALITIES OF HITLER, NERO AND DILLINGER INTO THEIR OWN BODIES! THEY BETRAYED ME... TRICKED ME...
AS YOU TRIED TO TRICK US! YOUR PUNISHMENT WILL COME LATER!
ND SOON, THE THREE SUPER-HEROES ARE THEMSELVES GAIN!
THEN, FOR A VHILE, I WAS HITLER? OU DID A GREAT HING, SATURN GIRL, URNING THOSE PLOTTERS AGAINST THEMSELVES!
WE'LL TAKE THEM BACK IN THE TIME-BUBBLE TO THE EXACT MOMENTS WHEN THEY LEFT THEIR OWN TIMES! HISTORY WILL NOT BE CHANGED... THEY'LL MEET JUST RETRIBUTION!
LATER, WHEN THAT HAS BEEN DONE...
WHILE YOU WERE GONE, WE THREE USED SUPER-STRENGTH TO PUSH LOST WORLD TOWARD THAT COSMIC CLOUD IT'S JUST NOW ENTERING! IT WILL REMAIN HIDDEN IN THE CLOUD AND NEVER BE SEEN AGAIN!
AND LET'S HOPE THE LEGION WILL NEVER AGAIN FIGHT AGAINST ITSELF!
THE END

LEGION of SUPER-HEROES

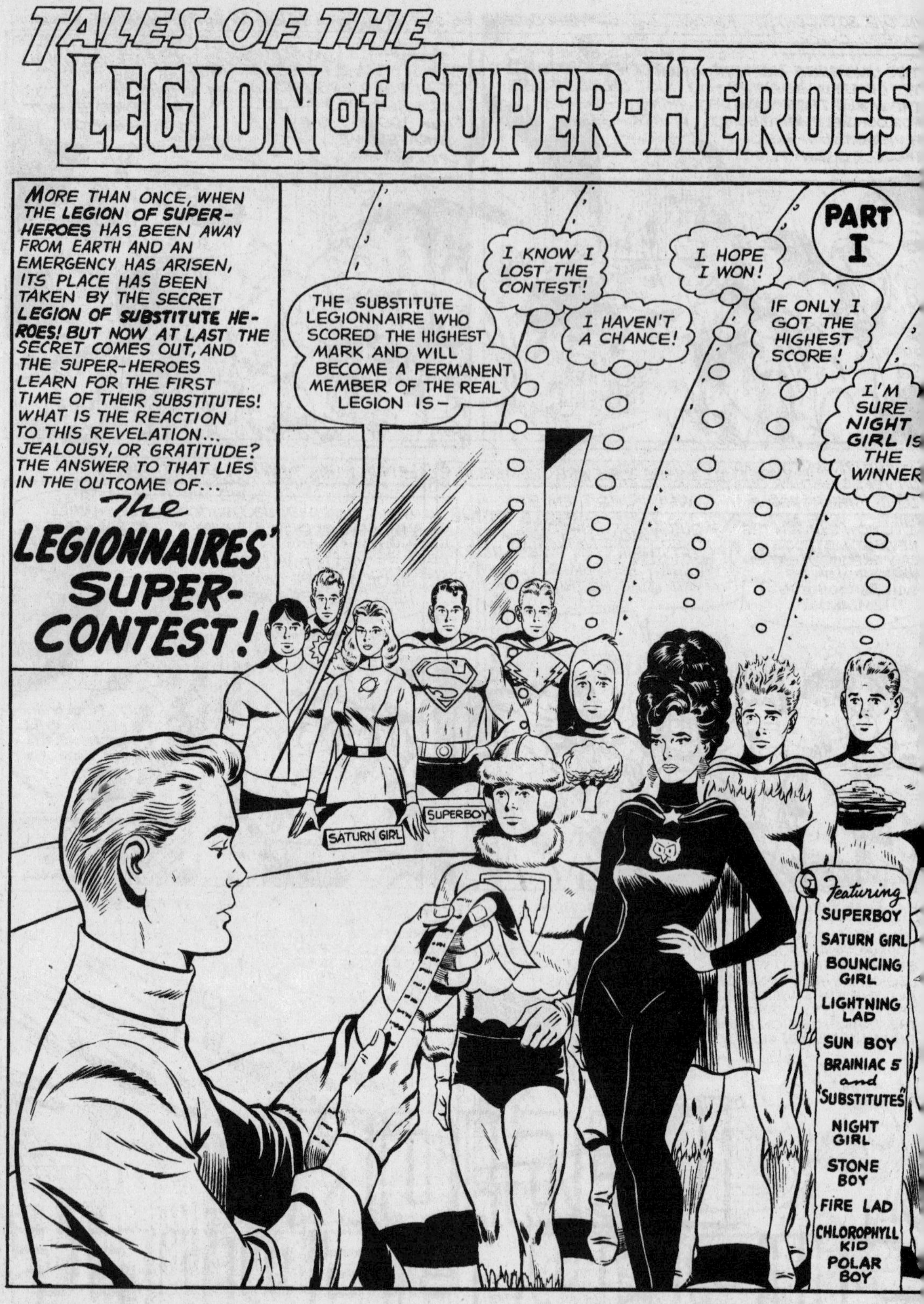
TALES OF THE
LEGION of SUPER-HEROES
MORE THAN ONCE, WHEN THE LEGION OF SUPER-HEROES HAS BEEN AWAY FROM EARTH AND AN EMERGENCY HAS ARISEN, ITS PLACE HAS BEEN TAKEN BY THE SECRET LEGION OF SUBSTITUTE HEROES! BUT NOW AT LAST THE SECRET COMES OUT, AND THE SUPER-HEROES LEARN FOR THE FIRST TIME OF THEIR SUBSTITUTES! WHAT IS THE REACTION TO THIS REVELATION... JEALOUSY, OR GRATITUDE? THE ANSWER TO THAT LIES IN THE OUTCOME OF...
The LEGIONNAIRES' SUPER-CONTEST!
PART I
THE SUBSTITUTE LEGIONNAIRE WHO SCORED THE HIGHEST MARK AND WILL BECOME A PERMANENT MEMBER OF THE REAL LEGION IS—
I KNOW I LOST THE CONTEST!
I HAVEN'T A CHANCE!
I HOPE I WON!
IF ONLY I GOT THE HIGHEST SCORE!
I'M SURE NIGHT GIRL IS THE WINNER
SATURN GIRL
SUPERBOY
Featuring
SUPERBOY
SATURN GIRL
BOUNCING GIRL
LIGHTNING LAD
SUN BOY
BRAINIAC 5
and
"SUBSTITUTES"
NIGHT GIRL
STONE BOY
FIRE LAD
CHLOROPHYLL KID
POLAR BOY

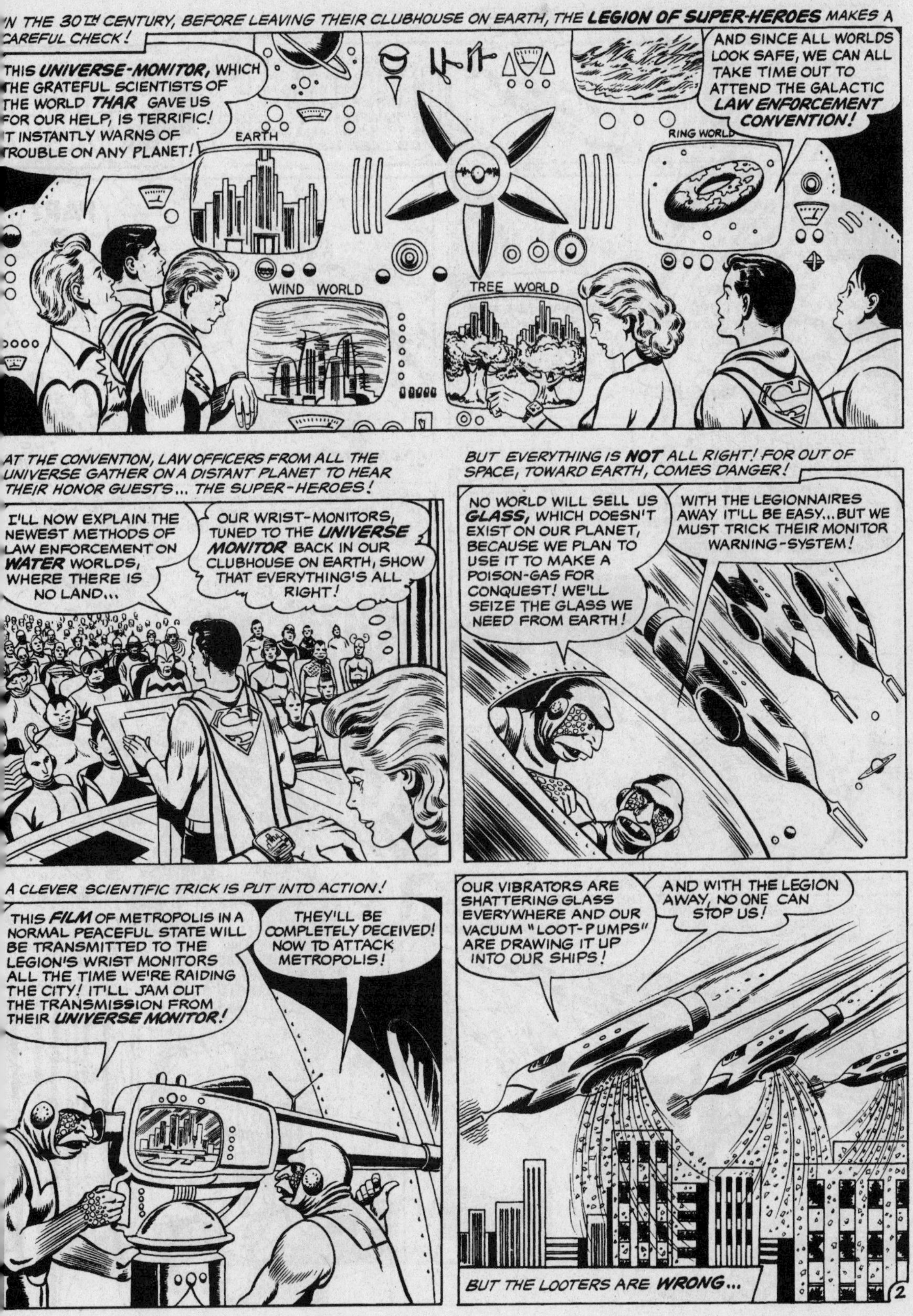
IN THE 30TH CENTURY, BEFORE LEAVING THEIR CLUBHOUSE ON EARTH, THE LEGION OF SUPER-HEROES MAKES A CAREFUL CHECK!
THIS UNIVERSE-MONITOR, WHICH THE GRATEFUL SCIENTISTS OF THE WORLD THAR GAVE US FOR OUR HELP, IS TERRIFIC! IT INSTANTLY WARNS OF TROUBLE ON ANY PLANET!
AND SINCE ALL WORLDS LOOK SAFE, WE CAN ALL TAKE TIME OUT TO ATTEND THE GALACTIC LAW ENFORCEMENT CONVENTION!
EARTH
RING WORLD
WIND WORLD
TREE WORLD
AT THE CONVENTION, LAW OFFICERS FROM ALL THE UNIVERSE GATHER ON A DISTANT PLANET TO HEAR THEIR HONOR GUESTS... THE SUPER-HEROES!
I'LL NOW EXPLAIN THE NEWEST METHODS OF LAW ENFORCEMENT ON WATER WORLDS, WHERE THERE IS NO LAND...
OUR WRIST-MONITORS, TUNED TO THE UNIVERSE MONITOR BACK IN OUR CLUBHOUSE ON EARTH, SHOW THAT EVERYTHING'S ALL RIGHT!
BUT EVERYTHING IS NOT ALL RIGHT! FOR OUT OF SPACE, TOWARD EARTH, COMES DANGER!
NO WORLD WILL SELL US GLASS, WHICH DOESN'T EXIST ON OUR PLANET, BECAUSE WE PLAN TO USE IT TO MAKE A POISON-GAS FOR CONQUEST! WE'LL SEIZE THE GLASS WE NEED FROM EARTH!
WITH THE LEGIONNAIRES AWAY IT'LL BE EASY...BUT WE MUST TRICK THEIR MONITOR WARNING-SYSTEM!
A CLEVER SCIENTIFIC TRICK IS PUT INTO ACTION!
THIS FILM OF METROPOLIS IN A NORMAL PEACEFUL STATE WILL BE TRANSMITTED TO THE LEGION'S WRIST MONITORS ALL THE TIME WE'RE RAIDING THE CITY! IT'LL JAM OUT THE TRANSMISSION FROM THEIR UNIVERSE MONITOR!
THEY'LL BE COMPLETELY DECEIVED! NOW TO ATTACK METROPOLIS!
OUR VIBRATORS ARE SHATTERING GLASS EVERYWHERE AND OUR VACUUM "LOOT-PUMPS" ARE DRAWING IT UP INTO OUR SHIPS!
AND WITH THE LEGION AWAY, NO ONE CAN STOP US!
BUT THE LOOTERS ARE WRONG...
2

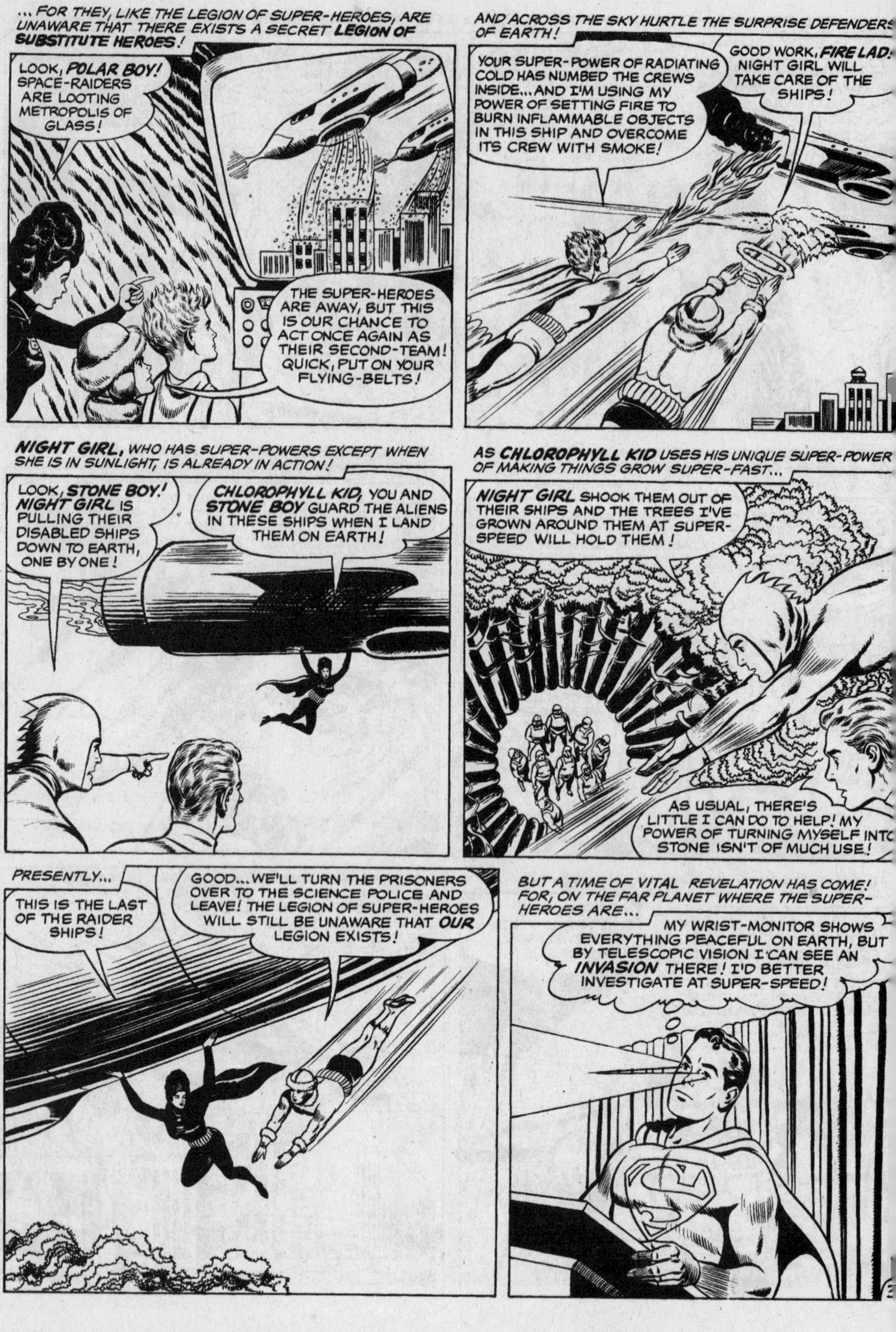
...FOR THEY, LIKE THE LEGION OF SUPER-HEROES, ARE UNAWARE THAT THERE EXISTS A SECRET LEGION OF SUBSTITUTE HEROES!
LOOK, POLAR BOY! SPACE-RAIDERS ARE LOOTING METROPOLIS OF GLASS!
THE SUPER-HEROES ARE AWAY, BUT THIS IS OUR CHANCE TO ACT ONCE AGAIN AS THEIR SECOND-TEAM! QUICK, PUT ON YOUR FLYING-BELTS!
AND ACROSS THE SKY HURTLE THE SURPRISE DEFENDERS OF EARTH!
YOUR SUPER-POWER OF RADIATING COLD HAS NUMBED THE CREWS INSIDE...AND I'M USING MY POWER OF SETTING FIRE TO BURN INFLAMMABLE OBJECTS IN THIS SHIP AND OVERCOME ITS CREW WITH SMOKE!
GOOD WORK, FIRE LAD! NIGHT GIRL WILL TAKE CARE OF THE SHIPS!
NIGHT GIRL, WHO HAS SUPER-POWERS EXCEPT WHEN SHE IS IN SUNLIGHT, IS ALREADY IN ACTION!
LOOK, STONE BOY! NIGHT GIRL IS PULLING THEIR DISABLED SHIPS DOWN TO EARTH, ONE BY ONE!
CHLOROPHYLL KID, YOU AND STONE BOY GUARD THE ALIENS IN THESE SHIPS WHEN I LAND THEM ON EARTH!
AS CHLOROPHYLL KID USES HIS UNIQUE SUPER-POWER OF MAKING THINGS GROW SUPER-FAST...
NIGHT GIRL SHOOK THEM OUT OF THEIR SHIPS AND THE TREES I'VE GROWN AROUND THEM AT SUPER-SPEED WILL HOLD THEM!
AS USUAL, THERE'S LITTLE I CAN DO TO HELP! MY POWER OF TURNING MYSELF INTO STONE ISN'T OF MUCH USE!
PRESENTLY...
THIS IS THE LAST OF THE RAIDER SHIPS!
GOOD...WE'LL TURN THE PRISONERS OVER TO THE SCIENCE POLICE AND LEAVE! THE LEGION OF SUPER-HEROES WILL STILL BE UNAWARE THAT OUR LEGION EXISTS!
BUT A TIME OF VITAL REVELATION HAS COME! FOR, ON THE FAR PLANET WHERE THE SUPER-HEROES ARE...
MY WRIST-MONITOR SHOWS EVERYTHING PEACEFUL ON EARTH, BUT BY TELESCOPIC VISION I CAN SEE AN INVASION THERE! I'D BETTER INVESTIGATE AT SUPER-SPEED!

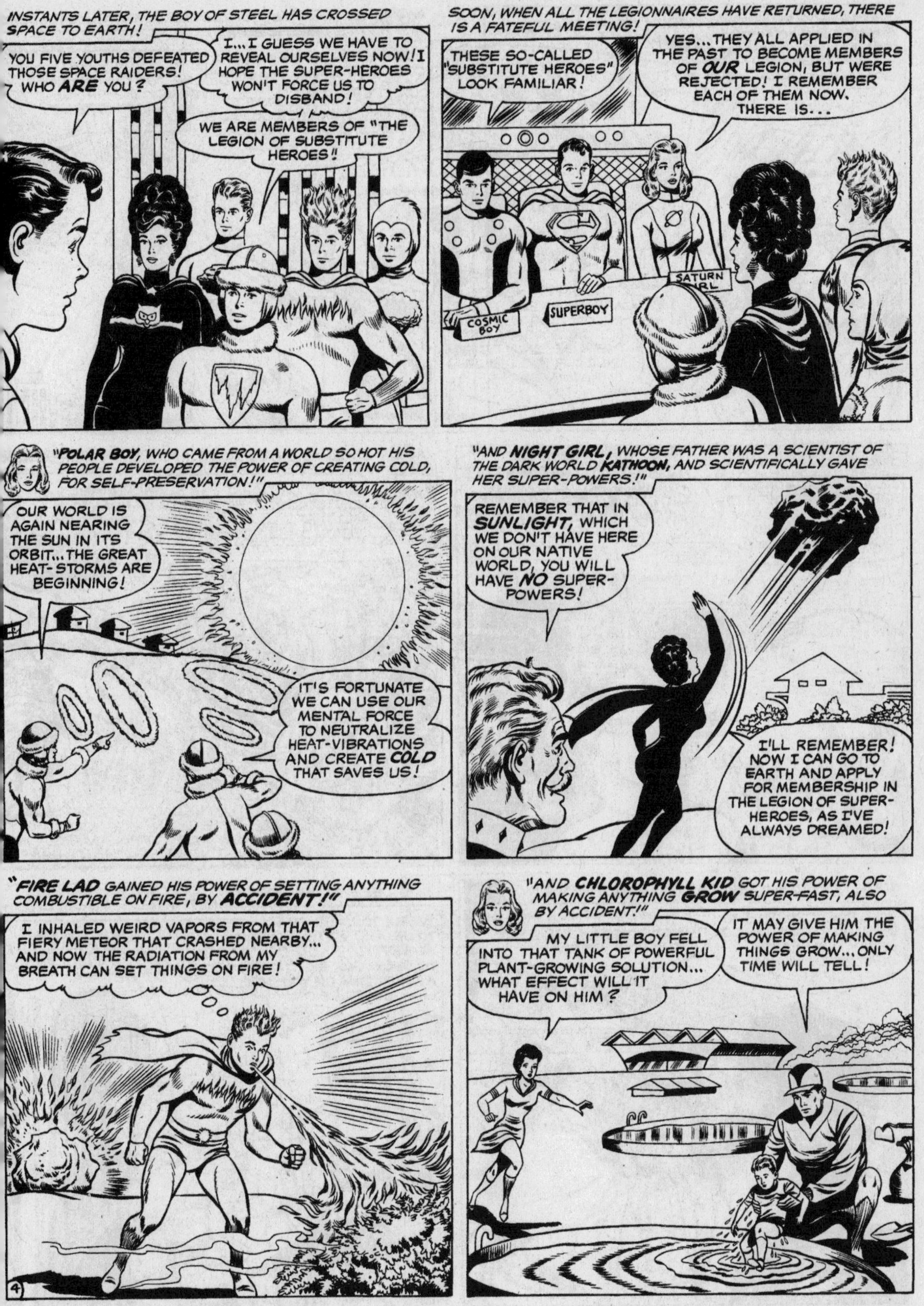
INSTANTS LATER, THE BOY OF STEEL HAS CROSSED SPACE TO EARTH!
YOU FIVE YOUTHS DEFEATED THOSE SPACE RAIDERS! WHO ARE YOU?
I...I GUESS WE HAVE TO REVEAL OURSELVES NOW! I HOPE THE SUPER-HEROES WON'T FORCE US TO DISBAND!
WE ARE MEMBERS OF "THE LEGION OF SUBSTITUTE HEROES"!
SOON, WHEN ALL THE LEGIONNAIRES HAVE RETURNED, THERE IS A FATEFUL MEETING!
THESE SO-CALLED "SUBSTITUTE HEROES" LOOK FAMILIAR!
YES... THEY ALL APPLIED IN THE PAST TO BECOME MEMBERS OF OUR LEGION, BUT WERE REJECTED! I REMEMBER EACH OF THEM NOW. THERE IS...
COSMIC BOY
SUPERBOY
SATURN GIRL
"POLAR BOY, WHO CAME FROM A WORLD SO HOT HIS PEOPLE DEVELOPED THE POWER OF CREATING COLD, FOR SELF-PRESERVATION!"
OUR WORLD IS AGAIN NEARING THE SUN IN ITS ORBIT... THE GREAT HEAT-STORMS ARE BEGINNING!
IT'S FORTUNATE WE CAN USE OUR MENTAL FORCE TO NEUTRALIZE HEAT-VIBRATIONS AND CREATE COLD THAT SAVES US!
"AND NIGHT GIRL, WHOSE FATHER WAS A SCIENTIST OF THE DARK WORLD KATHOON, AND SCIENTIFICALLY GAVE HER SUPER-POWERS!"
REMEMBER THAT IN SUNLIGHT, WHICH WE DON'T HAVE HERE ON OUR NATIVE WORLD, YOU WILL HAVE NO SUPER-POWERS!
I'LL REMEMBER! NOW I CAN GO TO EARTH AND APPLY FOR MEMBERSHIP IN THE LEGION OF SUPER-HEROES, AS I'VE ALWAYS DREAMED!
"FIRE LAD GAINED HIS POWER OF SETTING ANYTHING COMBUSTIBLE ON FIRE, BY ACCIDENT!"
I INHALED WEIRD VAPORS FROM THAT FIERY METEOR THAT CRASHED NEARBY... AND NOW THE RADIATION FROM MY BREATH CAN SET THINGS ON FIRE!
"AND CHLOROPHYLL KID GOT HIS POWER OF MAKING ANYTHING GROW SUPER-FAST, ALSO BY ACCIDENT!"
MY LITTLE BOY FELL INTO THAT TANK OF POWERFUL PLANT-GROWING SOLUTION... WHAT EFFECT WILL IT HAVE ON HIM?
IT MAY GIVE HIM THE POWER OF MAKING THINGS GROW... ONLY TIME WILL TELL!

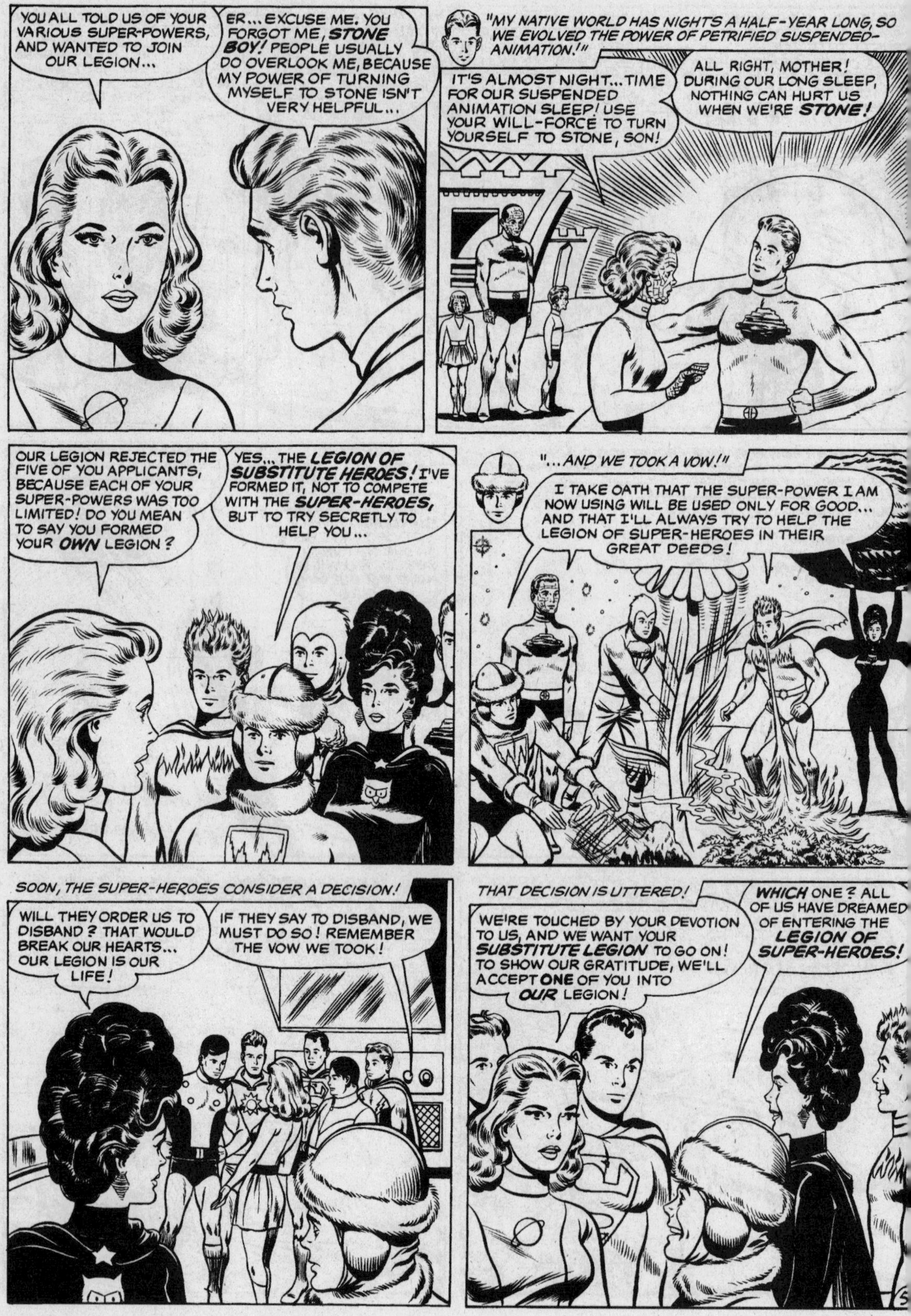
YOU ALL TOLD US OF YOUR VARIOUS SUPER-POWERS, AND WANTED TO JOIN OUR LEGION...
ER... EXCUSE ME. YOU FORGOT ME, STONE BOY! PEOPLE USUALLY DO OVERLOOK ME, BECAUSE MY POWER OF TURNING MYSELF TO STONE ISN'T VERY HELPFUL...
"MY NATIVE WORLD HAS NIGHTS A HALF-YEAR LONG, SO WE EVOLVED THE POWER OF PETRIFIED SUSPENDED-ANIMATION!"
IT'S ALMOST NIGHT... TIME FOR OUR SUSPENDED ANIMATION SLEEP! USE YOUR WILL-FORCE TO TURN YOURSELF TO STONE, SON!
ALL RIGHT, MOTHER! DURING OUR LONG SLEEP, NOTHING CAN HURT US WHEN WE'RE STONE!
OUR LEGION REJECTED THE FIVE OF YOU APPLICANTS, BECAUSE EACH OF YOUR SUPER-POWERS WAS TOO LIMITED! DO YOU MEAN TO SAY YOU FORMED YOUR OWN LEGION?
YES... THE LEGION OF SUBSTITUTE HEROES! I'VE FORMED IT, NOT TO COMPETE WITH THE SUPER-HEROES, BUT TO TRY SECRETLY TO HELP YOU...
"...AND WE TOOK A VOW!"
I TAKE OATH THAT THE SUPER-POWER I AM NOW USING WILL BE USED ONLY FOR GOOD... AND THAT I'LL ALWAYS TRY TO HELP THE LEGION OF SUPER-HEROES IN THEIR GREAT DEEDS!
SOON, THE SUPER-HEROES CONSIDER A DECISION!
WILL THEY ORDER US TO DISBAND? THAT WOULD BREAK OUR HEARTS... OUR LEGION IS OUR LIFE!
IF THEY SAY TO DISBAND, WE MUST DO SO! REMEMBER THE VOW WE TOOK!
THAT DECISION IS UTTERED!
WE'RE TOUCHED BY YOUR DEVOTION TO US, AND WE WANT YOUR SUBSTITUTE LEGION TO GO ON! TO SHOW OUR GRATITUDE, WE'LL ACCEPT ONE OF YOU INTO OUR LEGION!
WHICH ONE? ALL OF US HAVE DREAMED OF ENTERING THE LEGION OF SUPER-HEROES!

THAT WILL BE DECIDED BY COMPETITIVE *TESTS* OF YOU SUBSTITUTE HEROES! WHICHEVER OF YOU *SHOWS* THE GREATEST INITIATIVE, SPEED IN ACTION, TEAMWORK, COURAGE AND INGENUITY, WILL BE ELECTED A MEMBER OF THE LEGION OF SUPER-HEROES!

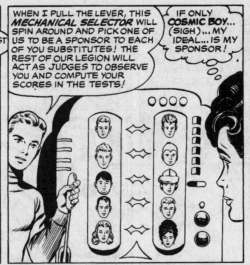

WHEN I PULL THE LEVER, THIS *MECHANICAL SELECTOR* WILL SPIN AROUND AND PICK ONE OF US TO BE A SPONSOR TO EACH OF YOU SUBSTITUTES! THE REST OF OUR LEGION WILL ACT AS JUDGES TO OBSERVE YOU AND COMPUTE YOUR SCORES IN THE TESTS!

IF ONLY *COSMIC BOY...* (SIGH)... MY IDEAL... IS MY SPONSOR!

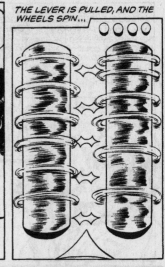

THE LEVER IS PULLED, AND THE WHEELS SPIN...

AND WHEN THE MECHANICAL SELECTOR COMES TO A HALT...

THE SPONSORS ARE CHOSEN, AND I AM ONE OF THEM! *BRAINIAC 5,* WILL YOU HEAD THE JUDGES?

I WILL... AND WE'LL ASSIGN THE FIRST TEST TO *POLAR BOY!*

TWO SCIENTISTS, WHO CALL THEMSELVES "THE HUMAN GUINEA PIGS!" TRIED AN EXPERIMENT THAT WENT WRONG AND SUPER-*FROZE* THEM! NO ONE'S BEEN ABLE TO REVIVE THEM, SO REVIVING THEM WILL BE YOUR TASK!

BUT... MY POWER TO CREATE COLD IS WORSE THAN USELESS IN THIS TEST!

6

AND AS *POLAR BOY* AND HIS SPONSOR, *SUN BOY,* USE THEIR *ANTI-GRAVITY BELTS* TO FLY TO THE TEST AREA...

THESE TESTS ARE ALL PURPOSELY CHOSEN TO BE DIFFICULT FOR YOUR POWERS TO HANDLE SO WE CAN FIND OUT IF YOU'RE EQUAL TO ANY EMERGENCY! BUT YOU CAN DO IT, *POLAR BOY!*

THIS IS REALLY TOUGH! IF I COULD ONLY CREATE HEAT LIKE YOU, INSTEAD OF COLD!

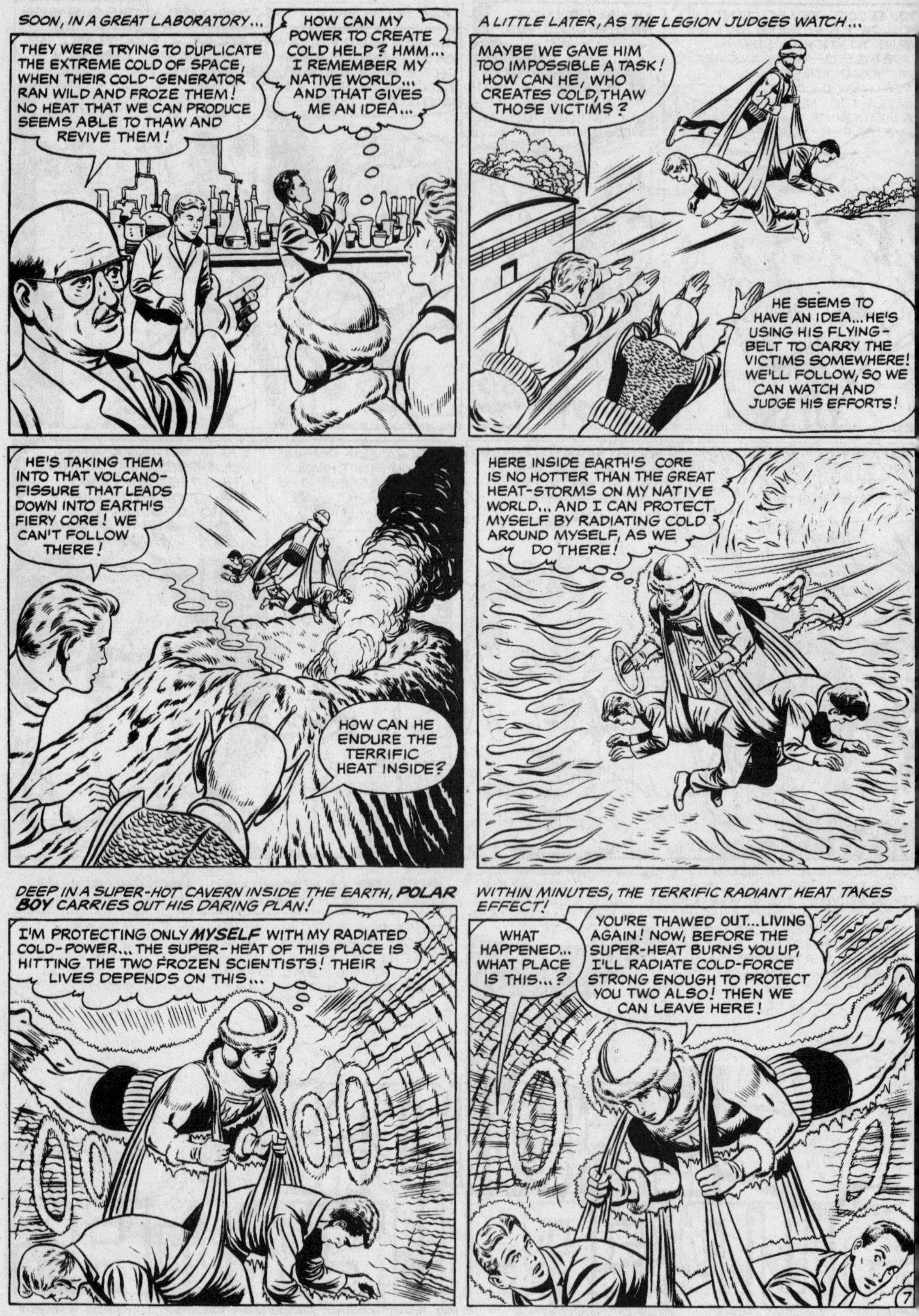
SOON, IN A GREAT LABORATORY...
THEY WERE TRYING TO DUPLICATE THE EXTREME COLD OF SPACE, WHEN THEIR COLD-GENERATOR RAN WILD AND FROZE THEM! NO HEAT THAT WE CAN PRODUCE SEEMS ABLE TO THAW AND REVIVE THEM!
HOW CAN MY POWER TO CREATE COLD HELP? HMM... I REMEMBER MY NATIVE WORLD... AND THAT GIVES ME AN IDEA...
A LITTLE LATER, AS THE LEGION JUDGES WATCH...
MAYBE WE GAVE HIM TOO IMPOSSIBLE A TASK! HOW CAN HE, WHO CREATES COLD, THAW THOSE VICTIMS?
HE SEEMS TO HAVE AN IDEA... HE'S USING HIS FLYING-BELT TO CARRY THE VICTIMS SOMEWHERE! WE'LL FOLLOW, SO WE CAN WATCH AND JUDGE HIS EFFORTS!
HE'S TAKING THEM INTO THAT VOLCANO-FISSURE THAT LEADS DOWN INTO EARTH'S FIERY CORE! WE CAN'T FOLLOW THERE!
HOW CAN HE ENDURE THE TERRIFIC HEAT INSIDE?
HERE INSIDE EARTH'S CORE IS NO HOTTER THAN THE GREAT HEAT-STORMS ON MY NATIVE WORLD... AND I CAN PROTECT MYSELF BY RADIATING COLD AROUND MYSELF, AS WE DO THERE!
DEEP IN A SUPER-HOT CAVERN INSIDE THE EARTH, POLAR BOY CARRIES OUT HIS DARING PLAN!
I'M PROTECTING ONLY MYSELF WITH MY RADIATED COLD-POWER... THE SUPER-HEAT OF THIS PLACE IS HITTING THE TWO FROZEN SCIENTISTS! THEIR LIVES DEPENDS ON THIS...
WITHIN MINUTES, THE TERRIFIC RADIANT HEAT TAKES EFFECT!
WHAT HAPPENED... WHAT PLACE IS THIS...?
YOU'RE THAWED OUT... LIVING AGAIN! NOW, BEFORE THE SUPER-HEAT BURNS YOU UP, I'LL RADIATE COLD-FORCE STRONG ENOUGH TO PROTECT YOU TWO ALSO! THEN WE CAN LEAVE HERE!
7

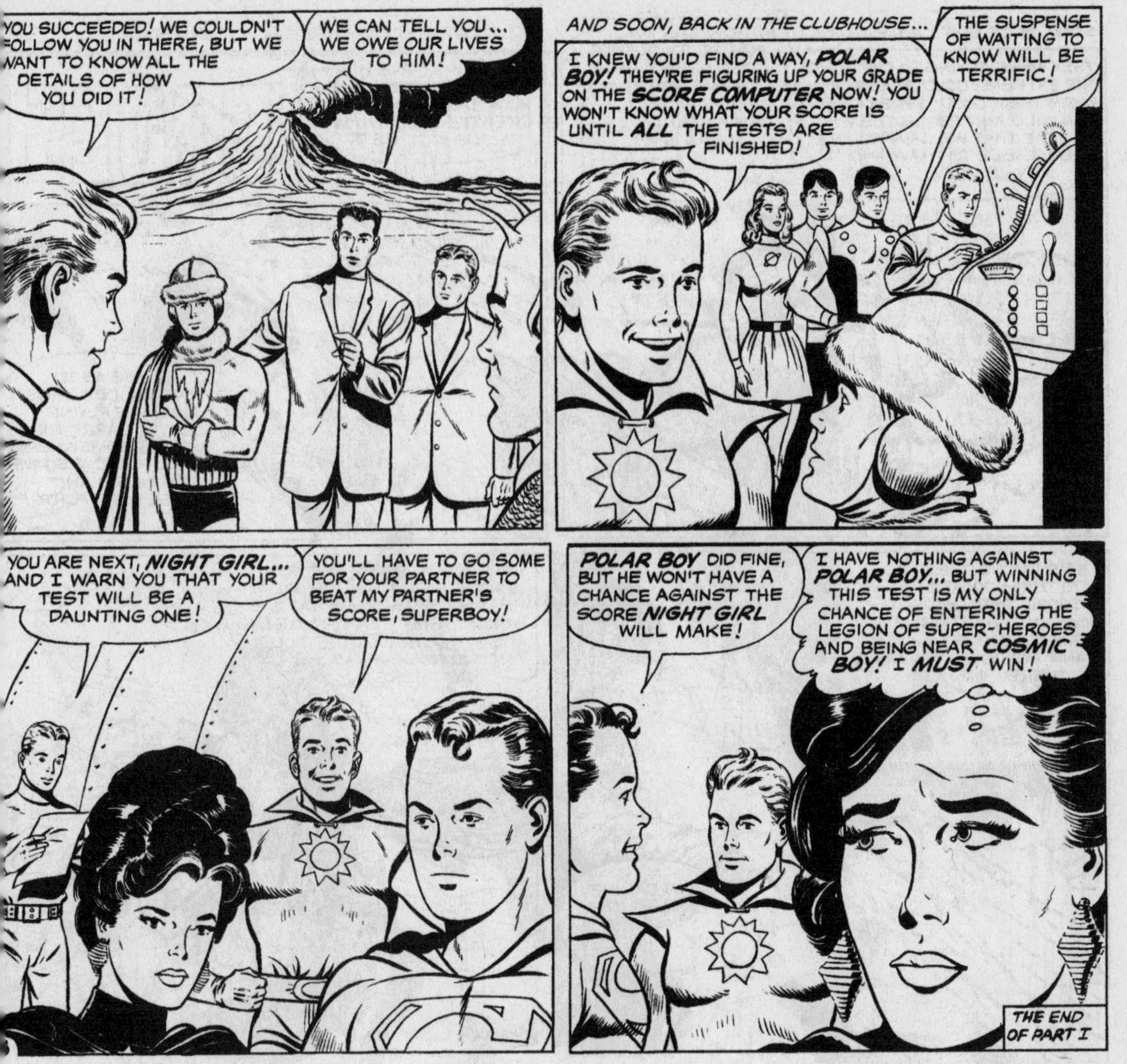
YOU SUCCEEDED! WE COULDN'T FOLLOW YOU IN THERE, BUT WE WANT TO KNOW ALL THE DETAILS OF HOW YOU DID IT!
WE CAN TELL YOU... WE OWE OUR LIVES TO HIM!
AND SOON, BACK IN THE CLUBHOUSE...
I KNEW YOU'D FIND A WAY, POLAR BOY! THEY'RE FIGURING UP YOUR GRADE ON THE SCORE COMPUTER NOW! YOU WON'T KNOW WHAT YOUR SCORE IS UNTIL ALL THE TESTS ARE FINISHED!
THE SUSPENSE OF WAITING TO KNOW WILL BE TERRIFIC!
YOU ARE NEXT, NIGHT GIRL... AND I WARN YOU THAT YOUR TEST WILL BE A DAUNTING ONE!
YOU'LL HAVE TO GO SOME FOR YOUR PARTNER TO BEAT MY PARTNER'S SCORE, SUPERBOY!
POLAR BOY DID FINE, BUT HE WON'T HAVE A CHANCE AGAINST THE SCORE NIGHT GIRL WILL MAKE!
I HAVE NOTHING AGAINST POLAR BOY... BUT WINNING THIS TEST IS MY ONLY CHANCE OF ENTERING THE LEGION OF SUPER-HEROES AND BEING NEAR COSMIC BOY! I MUST WIN!
THE END OF PART I

LEGION of SUPER-HEROES

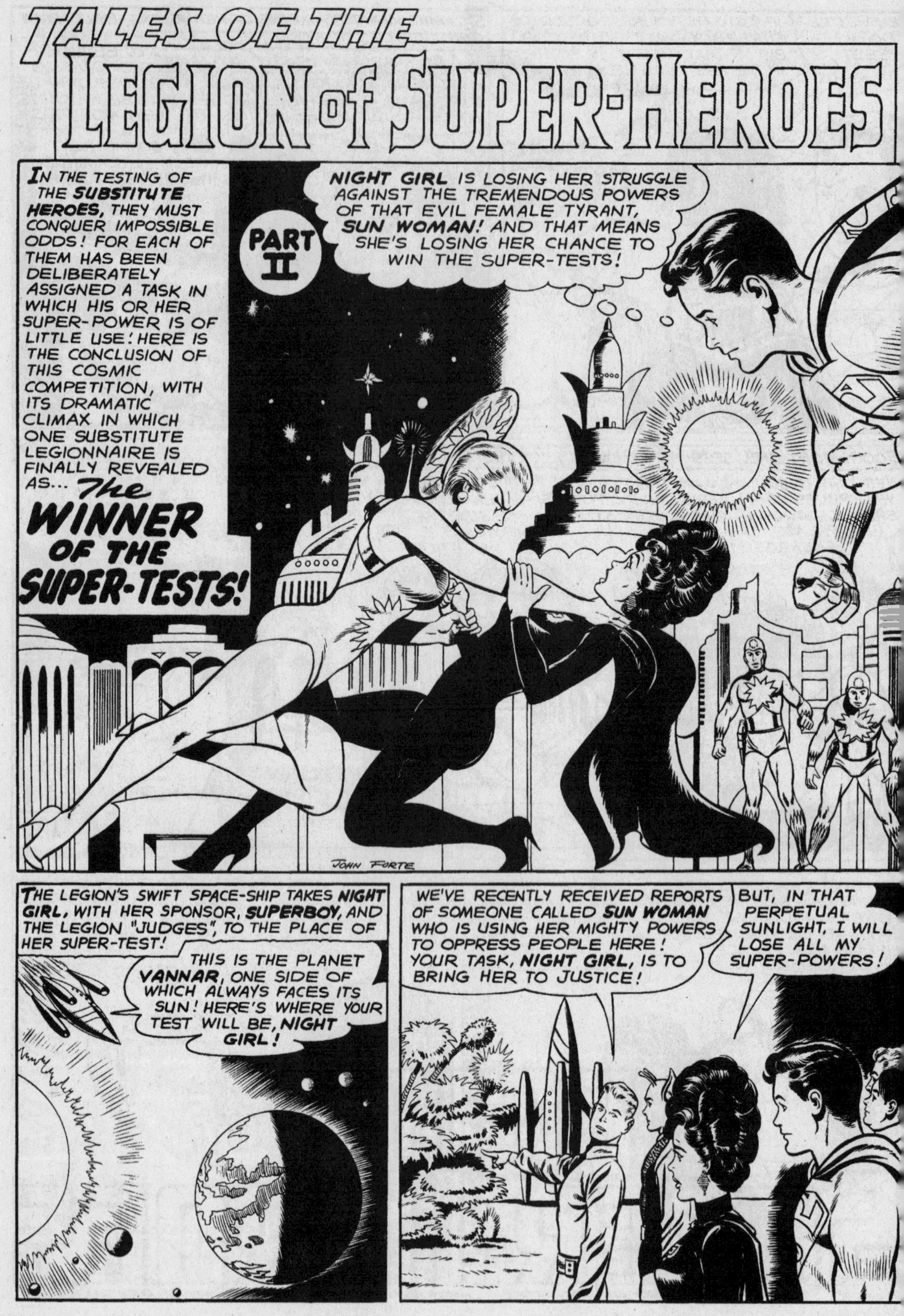
TALES OF THE
LEGION of SUPER-HEROES
IN THE TESTING OF THE SUBSTITUTE HEROES, THEY MUST CONQUER IMPOSSIBLE ODDS! FOR EACH OF THEM HAS BEEN DELIBERATELY ASSIGNED A TASK IN WHICH HIS OR HER SUPER-POWER IS OF LITTLE USE! HERE IS THE CONCLUSION OF THIS COSMIC COMPETITION, WITH ITS DRAMATIC CLIMAX IN WHICH ONE SUBSTITUTE LEGIONNAIRE IS FINALLY REVEALED AS... The WINNER OF THE SUPER-TESTS!
PART II
NIGHT GIRL IS LOSING HER STRUGGLE AGAINST THE TREMENDOUS POWERS OF THAT EVIL FEMALE TYRANT, SUN WOMAN! AND THAT MEANS SHE'S LOSING HER CHANCE TO WIN THE SUPER-TESTS!
JOHN FORTE
THE LEGION'S SWIFT SPACE-SHIP TAKES NIGHT GIRL, WITH HER SPONSOR, SUPERBOY, AND THE LEGION "JUDGES", TO THE PLACE OF HER SUPER-TEST!
THIS IS THE PLANET VANNAR, ONE SIDE OF WHICH ALWAYS FACES ITS SUN! HERE'S WHERE YOUR TEST WILL BE, NIGHT GIRL!
WE'VE RECENTLY RECEIVED REPORTS OF SOMEONE CALLED SUN WOMAN WHO IS USING HER MIGHTY POWERS TO OPPRESS PEOPLE HERE! YOUR TASK, NIGHT GIRL, IS TO BRING HER TO JUSTICE!
BUT, IN THAT PERPETUAL SUNLIGHT, I WILL LOSE ALL MY SUPER-POWERS!

BUT... I'LL DO MY BEST!

IF YOU FAIL, YOUR SPONSOR, **SUPERBOY,** MUST DO THE JOB... BUT IN THAT CASE YOUR SCORE IN THE TEST WILL BE VERY LOW!

SOARING ALOFT BY MEANS OF HER FLYING-BELT, **NIGHT GIRL** HURTLES TOWARD THE TEST!

DON'T INTERFERE, NO MATTER WHAT HAPPENS, **SUPERBOY.** I MIGHT MAKE A HIGH SCORE!

I'LL BE WATCHING BY TELESCOPIC VISION FROM A DISTANCE, AND THE JUDGES WILL BE WATCHING, TOO, ON THEIR MONITORS!

NIGHT GIRL SEEMS SO DESPERATELY DETERMINED THAT I'M WORRIED ABOUT HER!

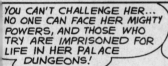

SOON, **NIGHT GIRL** SEES THE MAGNITUDE OF THE TASK SHE FACES...

YES, THAT IS **SUN WOMAN,** THE TYRANT WHO RULES US BY HER TERRIFIC POWERS! SHE'S DESTROYING OUR HOUSES SO HER PALACE CAN BE ENLARGED!

THIS **SUN WOMAN** DRAWS SUPER-POWERS FROM THE SUN! THAT HARNESS SHE WEARS IS THE STOLEN INVENTION OF A GREAT SCIENTIST. IT DRAWS SOLAR POWER TO CHARGE A HUMAN BODY!

YOU CAN'T CHALLENGE HER... NO ONE CAN FACE HER MIGHTY POWERS, AND THOSE WHO TRY ARE IMPRISONED FOR LIFE IN HER PALACE DUNGEONS!

SHE CAN'T GO ON DESTROYING AND TYRANNIZING LIKE THIS! I'M GOING TO STOP HER!

YOU'RE USING THAT STOLEN INVENTION FOR EVIL INSTEAD OF GOOD... THIS MUST STOP!

WHY, THE STRONGEST MAN ON THIS PLANET DARES NOT FACE ME! YOU, A SNIP OF A WEAK GIRL, WILL SOON GET YOUR LESSON!

2

BE THANKFUL I AM SPARING YOUR LIFE! GUARDS, PUT HER IN THE DUNGEONS LIKE THE OTHER REBELS!

YES, YOUR HIGHNESS!

AND IN A DUNGEON, DEEP UNDER THE PALACE...

YOU'LL NEVER LEAVE THIS DUNGEON, FOOLISH STRANGER!

THAT'S WHAT YOU THINK! WHEN I HEARD ABOUT THESE DARK DUNGEONS I WANTED TO BE PUT INTO ONE...

...FOR DOWN HERE, AWAY FROM THE SUN, I HAVE FULL POSSESSION OF MY SUPER-POWERS! AND NOW I'LL USE THEM!

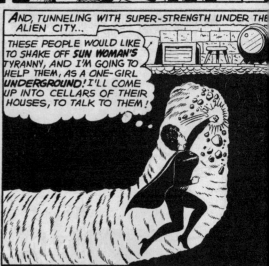

AND, TUNNELING WITH SUPER-STRENGTH UNDER THE ALIEN CITY...

THESE PEOPLE WOULD LIKE TO SHAKE OFF SUN WOMAN'S TYRANNY, AND I'M GOING TO HELP THEM, AS A ONE-GIRL UNDERGROUND! I'LL COME UP INTO CELLARS OF THEIR HOUSES, TO TALK TO THEM!

FEARFUL, YET HOPEFUL, THE NATIVES OF THE CITY LISTEN TO NIGHT GIRL'S PLAN!

IF YOU PEOPLE DO AS I'VE SUGGESTED, I CAN RID YOU OF YOUR FEMALE TYRANT!

WE'LL SPREAD THE WORD, AND DO EXACTLY AS YOU ADVISED!

LATER, AROUND THE EDGE OF THE CITY OF ENDLESS SUNSHINE, THE FURTIVE FREEDOM-FIGHTERS SET FIRES!

THIS IS THE BLACK ROCK THAT NIGHT GIRL SAID TO PUT INTO OUR FIRES!

WE COULD HAVE DONE THIS BEFORE, BUT WE DIDN'T KNOW THE SCIENCE THAT SHE KNOWS AND DIDN'T THINK OF IT!

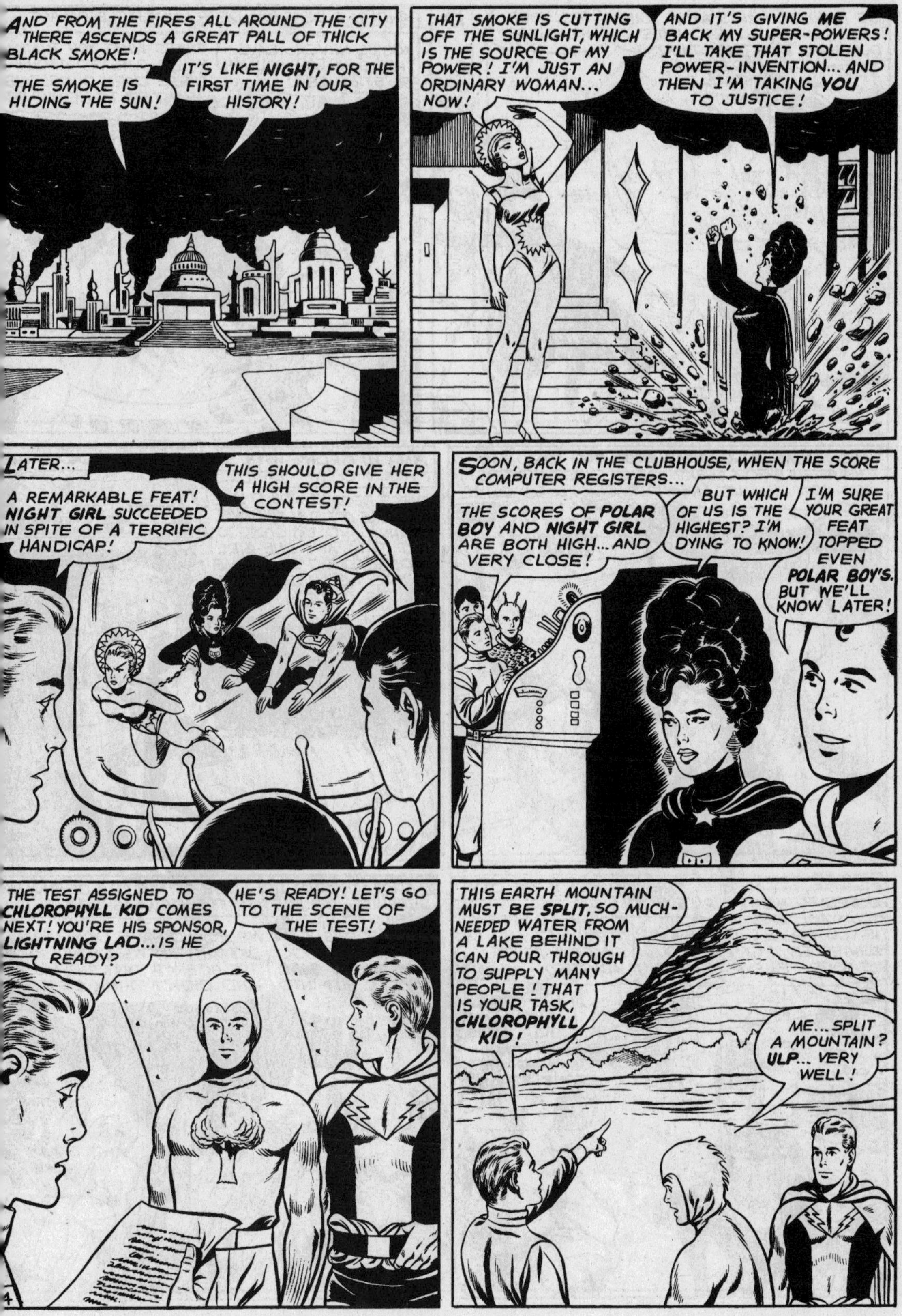
AND FROM THE FIRES ALL AROUND THE CITY THERE ASCENDS A GREAT PALL OF THICK BLACK SMOKE!
THE SMOKE IS HIDING THE SUN!
IT'S LIKE NIGHT, FOR THE FIRST TIME IN OUR HISTORY!
THAT SMOKE IS CUTTING OFF THE SUNLIGHT, WHICH IS THE SOURCE OF MY POWER! I'M JUST AN ORDINARY WOMAN... NOW!
AND IT'S GIVING ME BACK MY SUPER-POWERS! I'LL TAKE THAT STOLEN POWER-INVENTION... AND THEN I'M TAKING YOU TO JUSTICE!
LATER...
A REMARKABLE FEAT! NIGHT GIRL SUCCEEDED IN SPITE OF A TERRIFIC HANDICAP!
THIS SHOULD GIVE HER A HIGH SCORE IN THE CONTEST!
SOON, BACK IN THE CLUBHOUSE, WHEN THE SCORE COMPUTER REGISTERS...
THE SCORES OF POLAR BOY AND NIGHT GIRL ARE BOTH HIGH... AND VERY CLOSE!
BUT WHICH OF US IS THE HIGHEST? I'M DYING TO KNOW!
I'M SURE YOUR GREAT FEAT TOPPED EVEN POLAR BOY'S. BUT WE'LL KNOW LATER!
THE TEST ASSIGNED TO CHLOROPHYLL KID COMES NEXT! YOU'RE HIS SPONSOR, LIGHTNING LAD... IS HE READY?
HE'S READY! LET'S GO TO THE SCENE OF THE TEST!
THIS EARTH MOUNTAIN MUST BE SPLIT, SO MUCH-NEEDED WATER FROM A LAKE BEHIND IT CAN POUR THROUGH TO SUPPLY MANY PEOPLE! THAT IS YOUR TASK, CHLOROPHYLL KID!
ME... SPLIT A MOUNTAIN? ULP... VERY WELL!

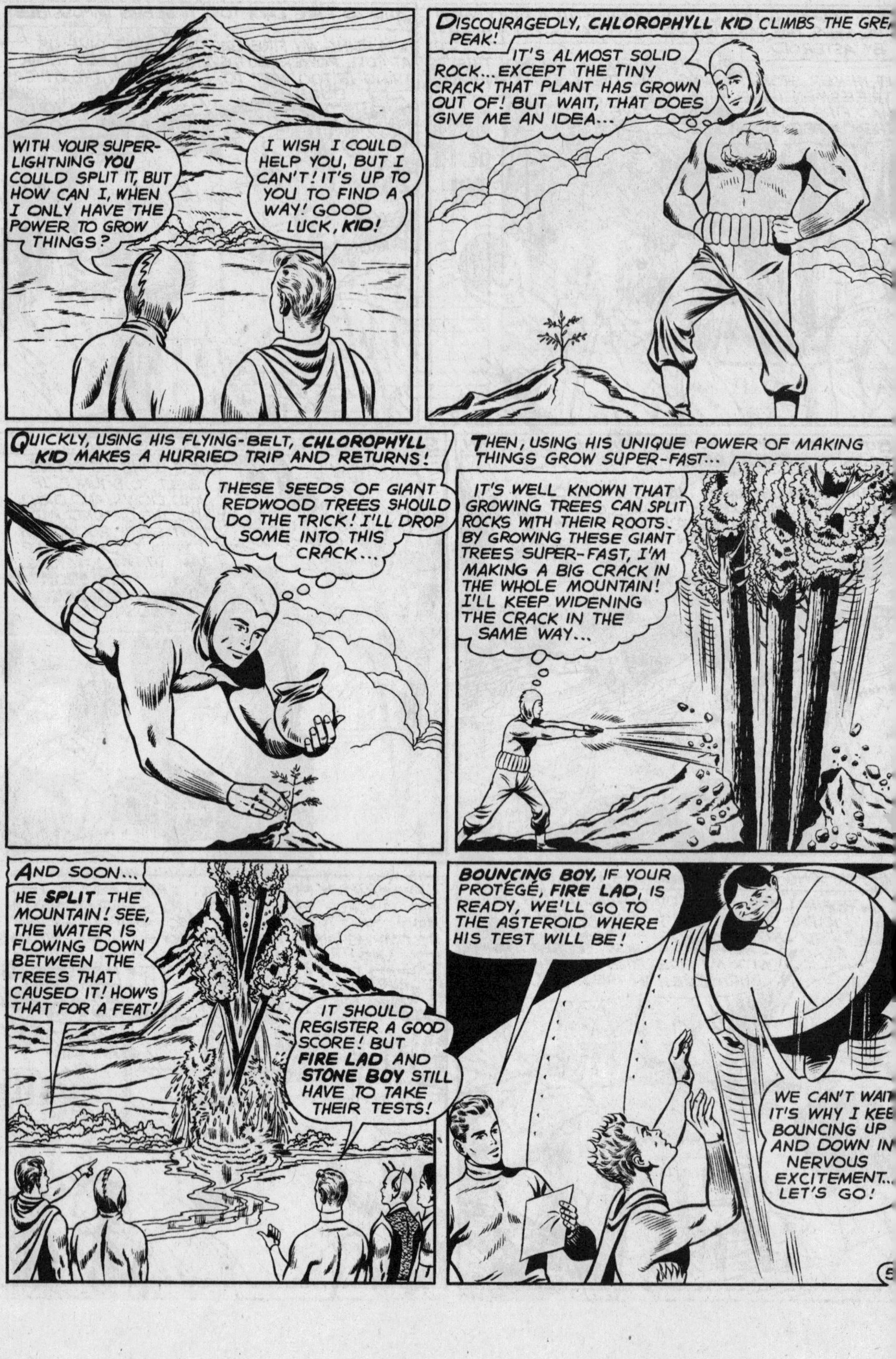
WITH YOUR SUPER-LIGHTNING YOU COULD SPLIT IT, BUT HOW CAN I, WHEN I ONLY HAVE THE POWER TO GROW THINGS?
I WISH I COULD HELP YOU, BUT I CAN'T! IT'S UP TO YOU TO FIND A WAY! GOOD LUCK, KID!
DISCOURAGEDLY, CHLOROPHYLL KID CLIMBS THE GRE PEAK!
IT'S ALMOST SOLID ROCK... EXCEPT THE TINY CRACK THAT PLANT HAS GROWN OUT OF! BUT WAIT, THAT DOES GIVE ME AN IDEA...
QUICKLY, USING HIS FLYING-BELT, CHLOROPHYLL KID MAKES A HURRIED TRIP AND RETURNS!
THESE SEEDS OF GIANT REDWOOD TREES SHOULD DO THE TRICK! I'LL DROP SOME INTO THIS CRACK...
THEN, USING HIS UNIQUE POWER OF MAKING THINGS GROW SUPER-FAST...
IT'S WELL KNOWN THAT GROWING TREES CAN SPLIT ROCKS WITH THEIR ROOTS. BY GROWING THESE GIANT TREES SUPER-FAST, I'M MAKING A BIG CRACK IN THE WHOLE MOUNTAIN! I'LL KEEP WIDENING THE CRACK IN THE SAME WAY...
AND SOON...
HE SPLIT THE MOUNTAIN! SEE, THE WATER IS FLOWING DOWN BETWEEN THE TREES THAT CAUSED IT! HOW'S THAT FOR A FEAT!
IT SHOULD REGISTER A GOOD SCORE! BUT FIRE LAD AND STONE BOY STILL HAVE TO TAKE THEIR TESTS!
BOUNCING BOY, IF YOUR PROTÉGÉ, FIRE LAD, IS READY, WE'LL GO TO THE ASTEROID WHERE HIS TEST WILL BE!
WE CAN'T WAI IT'S WHY I KEE BOUNCING UP AND DOWN IN NERVOUS EXCITEMENT... LET'S GO!

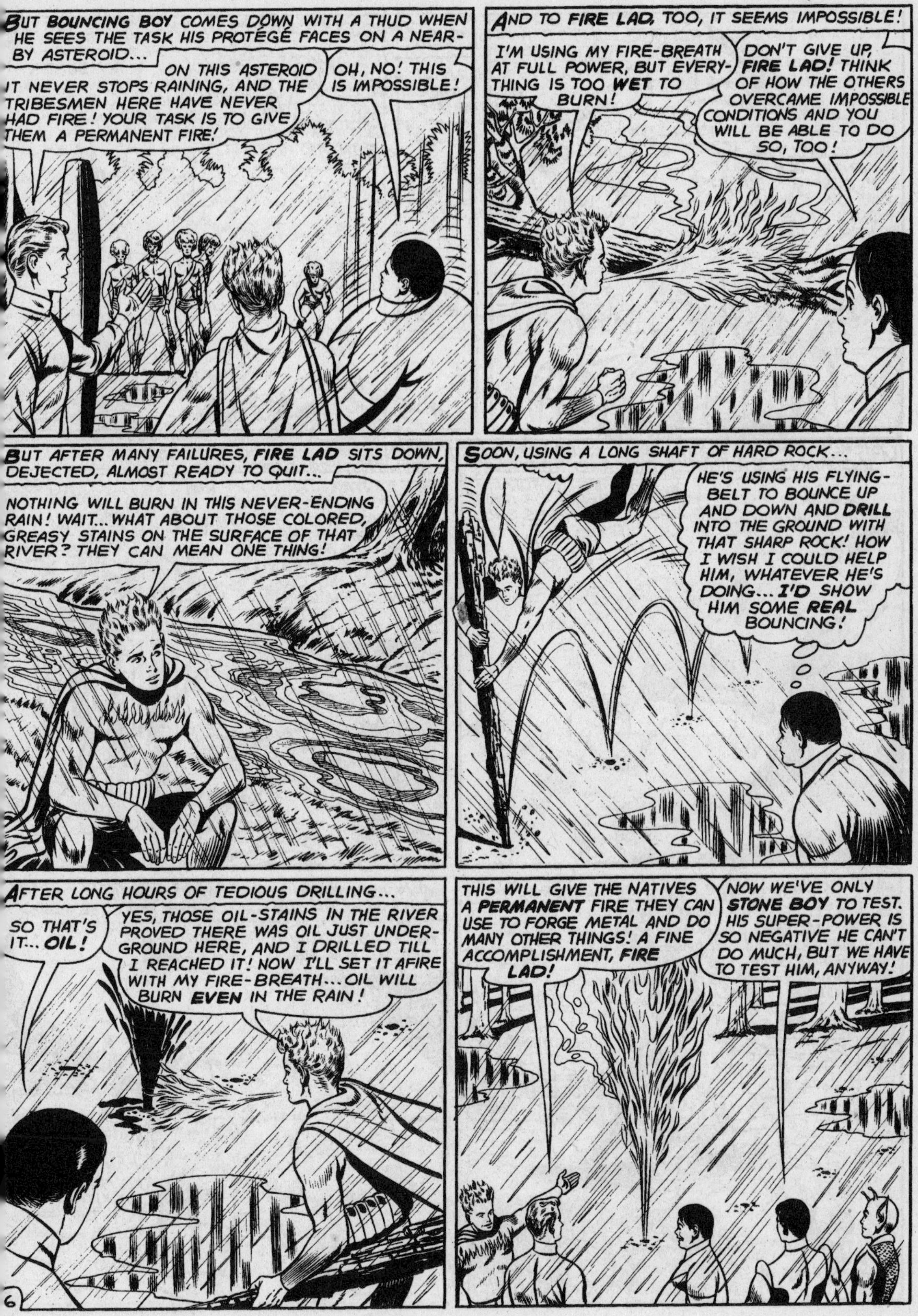
BUT BOUNCING BOY COMES DOWN WITH A THUD WHEN HE SEES THE TASK HIS PROTÉGÉ FACES ON A NEAR-BY ASTEROID...
ON THIS ASTEROID IT NEVER STOPS RAINING, AND THE TRIBESMEN HERE HAVE NEVER HAD FIRE! YOUR TASK IS TO GIVE THEM A PERMANENT FIRE!
OH, NO! THIS IS IMPOSSIBLE!
AND TO FIRE LAD, TOO, IT SEEMS IMPOSSIBLE!
I'M USING MY FIRE-BREATH AT FULL POWER, BUT EVERYTHING IS TOO WET TO BURN!
DON'T GIVE UP, FIRE LAD! THINK OF HOW THE OTHERS OVERCAME IMPOSSIBLE CONDITIONS AND YOU WILL BE ABLE TO DO SO, TOO!
BUT AFTER MANY FAILURES, FIRE LAD SITS DOWN, DEJECTED, ALMOST READY TO QUIT...
NOTHING WILL BURN IN THIS NEVER-ENDING RAIN! WAIT... WHAT ABOUT THOSE COLORED, GREASY STAINS ON THE SURFACE OF THAT RIVER? THEY CAN MEAN ONE THING!
SOON, USING A LONG SHAFT OF HARD ROCK...
HE'S USING HIS FLYING-BELT TO BOUNCE UP AND DOWN AND DRILL INTO THE GROUND WITH THAT SHARP ROCK! HOW I WISH I COULD HELP HIM, WHATEVER HE'S DOING... I'D SHOW HIM SOME REAL BOUNCING!
AFTER LONG HOURS OF TEDIOUS DRILLING...
SO THAT'S IT... OIL!
YES, THOSE OIL-STAINS IN THE RIVER PROVED THERE WAS OIL JUST UNDERGROUND HERE, AND I DRILLED TILL I REACHED IT! NOW I'LL SET IT AFIRE WITH MY FIRE-BREATH... OIL WILL BURN EVEN IN THE RAIN!
6
THIS WILL GIVE THE NATIVES A PERMANENT FIRE THEY CAN USE TO FORGE METAL AND DO MANY OTHER THINGS! A FINE ACCOMPLISHMENT, FIRE LAD!
NOW WE'VE ONLY STONE BOY TO TEST. HIS SUPER-POWER IS SO NEGATIVE HE CAN'T DO MUCH, BUT WE HAVE TO TEST HIM, ANYWAY!

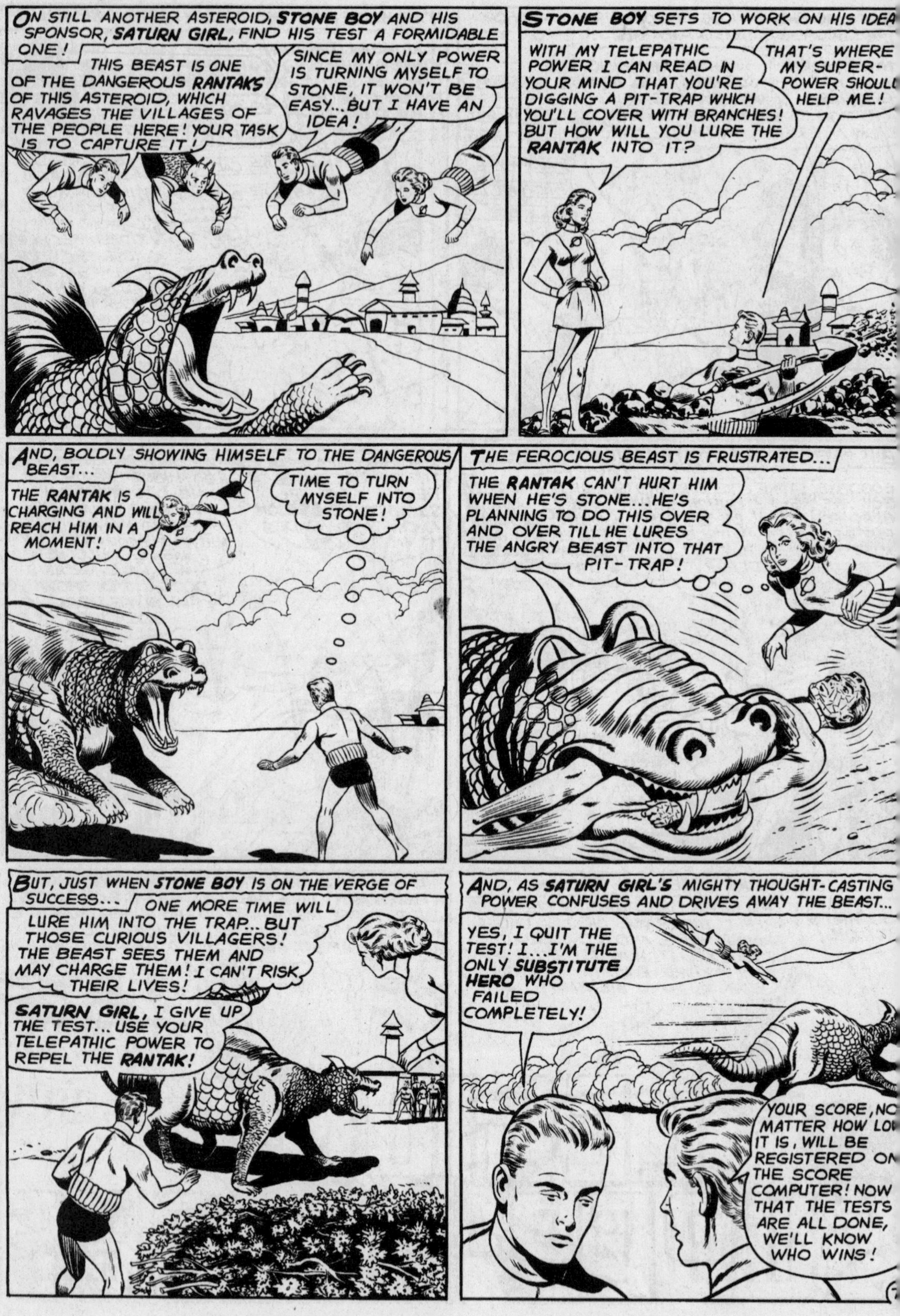
ON STILL ANOTHER ASTEROID, STONE BOY AND HIS SPONSOR, SATURN GIRL, FIND HIS TEST A FORMIDABLE ONE!
THIS BEAST IS ONE OF THE DANGEROUS RANTAKS OF THIS ASTEROID, WHICH RAVAGES THE VILLAGES OF THE PEOPLE HERE! YOUR TASK IS TO CAPTURE IT!
SINCE MY ONLY POWER IS TURNING MYSELF TO STONE, IT WON'T BE EASY... BUT I HAVE AN IDEA!
STONE BOY SETS TO WORK ON HIS IDEA
WITH MY TELEPATHIC POWER I CAN READ IN YOUR MIND THAT YOU'RE DIGGING A PIT-TRAP WHICH YOU'LL COVER WITH BRANCHES! BUT HOW WILL YOU LURE THE RANTAK INTO IT?
THAT'S WHERE MY SUPER-POWER SHOULD HELP ME!
AND, BOLDLY SHOWING HIMSELF TO THE DANGEROUS BEAST...
THE RANTAK IS CHARGING AND WILL REACH HIM IN A MOMENT!
TIME TO TURN MYSELF INTO STONE!
THE FEROCIOUS BEAST IS FRUSTRATED...
THE RANTAK CAN'T HURT HIM WHEN HE'S STONE... HE'S PLANNING TO DO THIS OVER AND OVER TILL HE LURES THE ANGRY BEAST INTO THAT PIT-TRAP!
BUT, JUST WHEN STONE BOY IS ON THE VERGE OF SUCCESS...
ONE MORE TIME WILL LURE HIM INTO THE TRAP... BUT THOSE CURIOUS VILLAGERS! THE BEAST SEES THEM AND MAY CHARGE THEM! I CAN'T RISK THEIR LIVES!
SATURN GIRL, I GIVE UP THE TEST... USE YOUR TELEPATHIC POWER TO REPEL THE RANTAK!
AND, AS SATURN GIRL'S MIGHTY THOUGHT-CASTING POWER CONFUSES AND DRIVES AWAY THE BEAST...
YES, I QUIT THE TEST! I... I'M THE ONLY SUBSTITUTE HERO WHO FAILED COMPLETELY!
YOUR SCORE, NO MATTER HOW LOW IT IS, WILL BE REGISTERED ON THE SCORE COMPUTER! NOW THAT THE TESTS ARE ALL DONE, WE'LL KNOW WHO WINS!

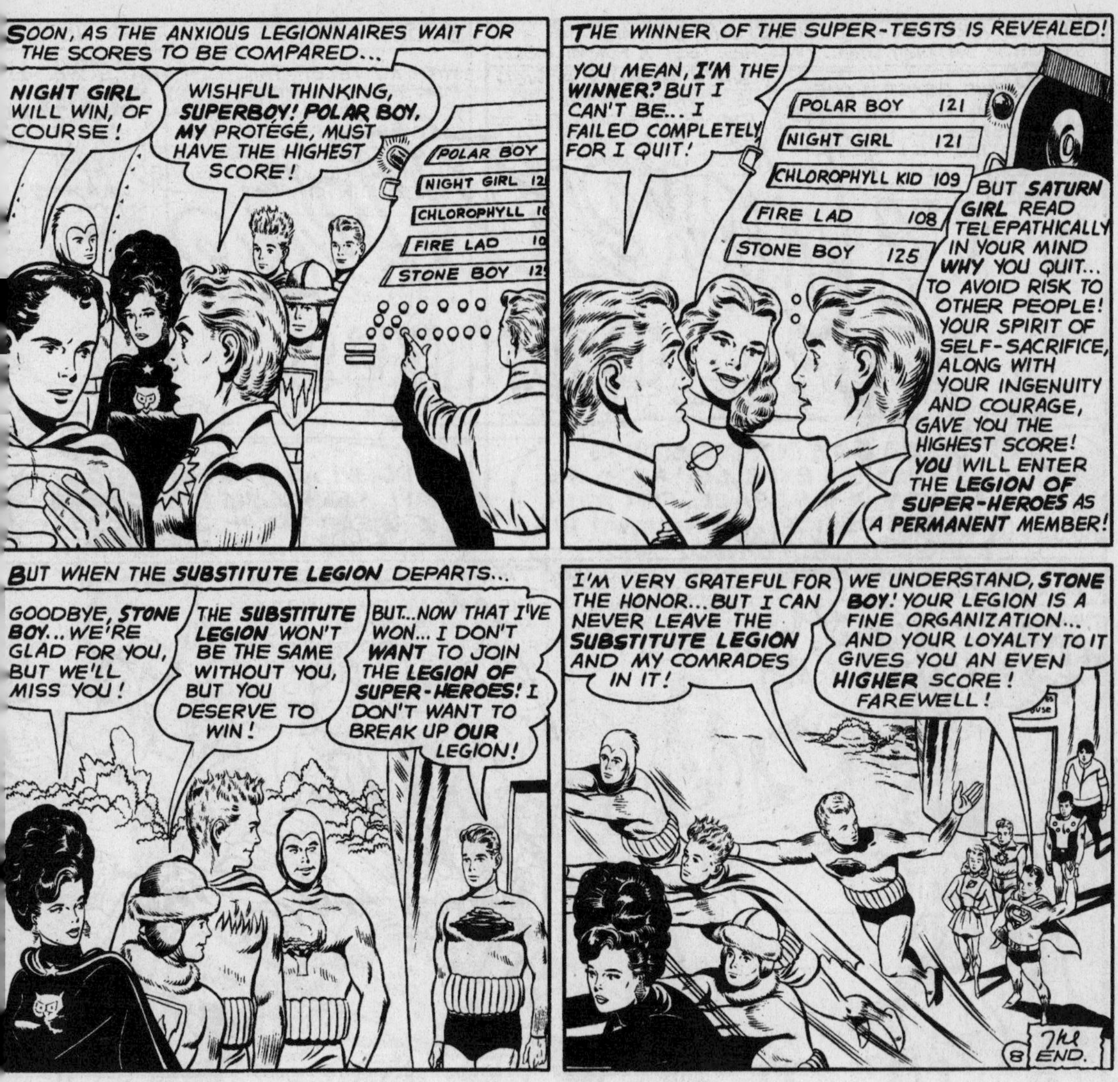
SOON, AS THE ANXIOUS LEGIONNAIRES WAIT FOR THE SCORES TO BE COMPARED...
NIGHT GIRL WILL WIN, OF COURSE!
WISHFUL THINKING, SUPERBOY! POLAR BOY, MY PROTÉGÉ, MUST HAVE THE HIGHEST SCORE!
POLAR BOY
NIGHT GIRL 12
CHLOROPHYLL 1
FIRE LAD 10
STONE BOY 12
THE WINNER OF THE SUPER-TESTS IS REVEALED!
YOU MEAN, I'M THE WINNER? BUT I CAN'T BE... I FAILED COMPLETELY FOR I QUIT!
POLAR BOY 121
NIGHT GIRL 121
CHLOROPHYLL KID 109
FIRE LAD 108
STONE BOY 125
BUT SATURN GIRL READ TELEPATHICALLY IN YOUR MIND WHY YOU QUIT... TO AVOID RISK TO OTHER PEOPLE! YOUR SPIRIT OF SELF-SACRIFICE, ALONG WITH YOUR INGENUITY AND COURAGE, GAVE YOU THE HIGHEST SCORE! YOU WILL ENTER THE LEGION OF SUPER-HEROES AS A PERMANENT MEMBER!
BUT WHEN THE SUBSTITUTE LEGION DEPARTS...
GOODBYE, STONE BOY... WE'RE GLAD FOR YOU, BUT WE'LL MISS YOU!
THE SUBSTITUTE LEGION WON'T BE THE SAME WITHOUT YOU, BUT YOU DESERVE TO WIN!
BUT...NOW THAT I'VE WON... I DON'T WANT TO JOIN THE LEGION OF SUPER-HEROES! I DON'T WANT TO BREAK UP OUR LEGION!
I'M VERY GRATEFUL FOR THE HONOR... BUT I CAN NEVER LEAVE THE SUBSTITUTE LEGION AND MY COMRADES IN IT!
WE UNDERSTAND, STONE BOY! YOUR LEGION IS A FINE ORGANIZATION... AND YOUR LOYALTY TO IT GIVES YOU AN EVEN HIGHER SCORE! FAREWELL!
8
The END.

LEGION of SUPER-HEROES

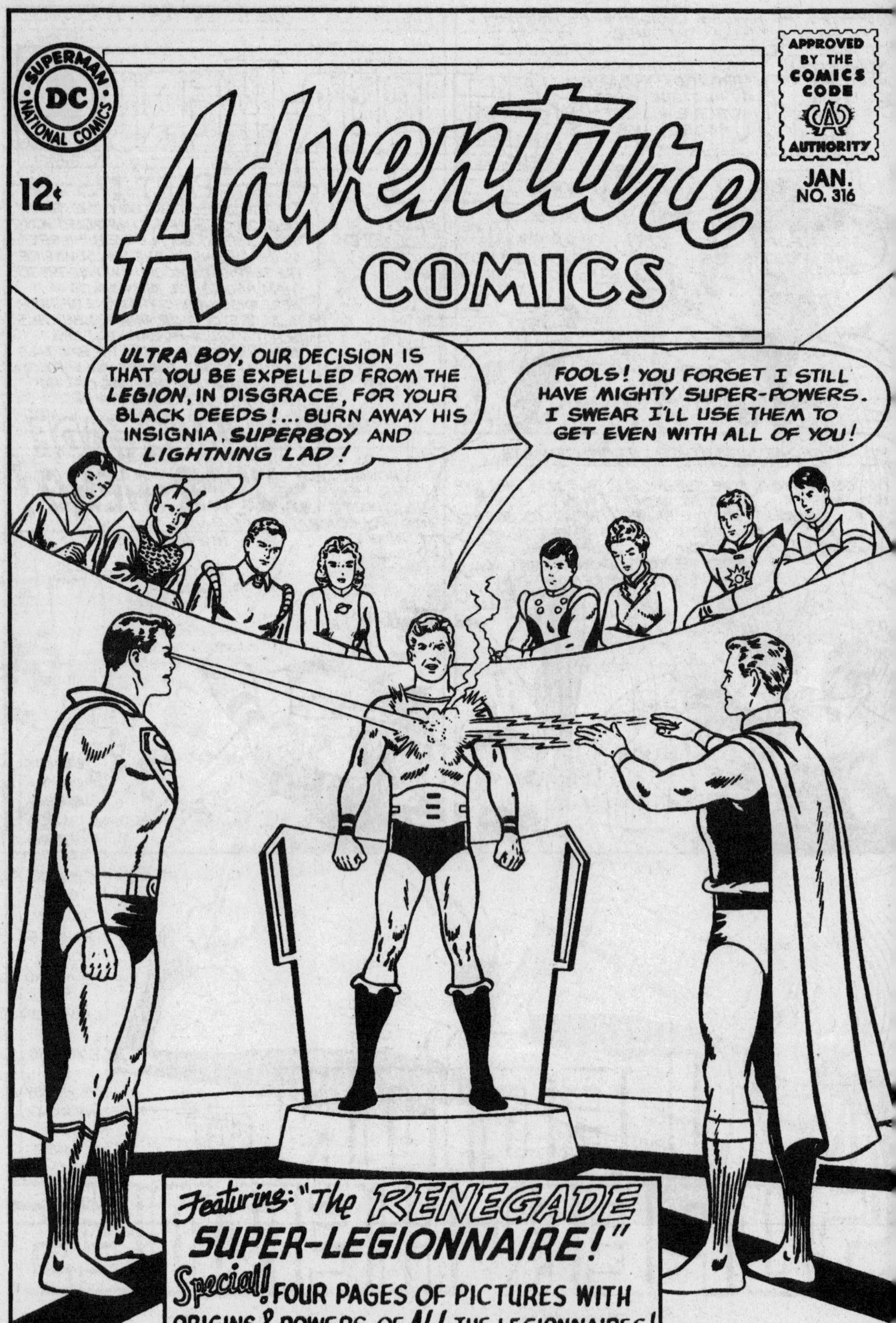

SUPERMAN DC NATIONAL COMICS
12¢
APPROVED BY THE COMICS CODE AUTHORITY
JAN. NO. 316
Adventure COMICS
ULTRA BOY, OUR DECISION IS THAT YOU BE EXPELLED FROM THE LEGION, IN DISGRACE, FOR YOUR BLACK DEEDS!... BURN AWAY HIS INSIGNIA, SUPERBOY AND LIGHTNING LAD!
FOOLS! YOU FORGET I STILL HAVE MIGHTY SUPER-POWERS. I SWEAR I'LL USE THEM TO GET EVEN WITH ALL OF YOU!
Featuring: "The RENEGADE SUPER-LEGIONNAIRE!"
Special! FOUR PAGES OF PICTURES WITH ORIGINS & POWERS OF ALL THE LEGIONNAIRES!

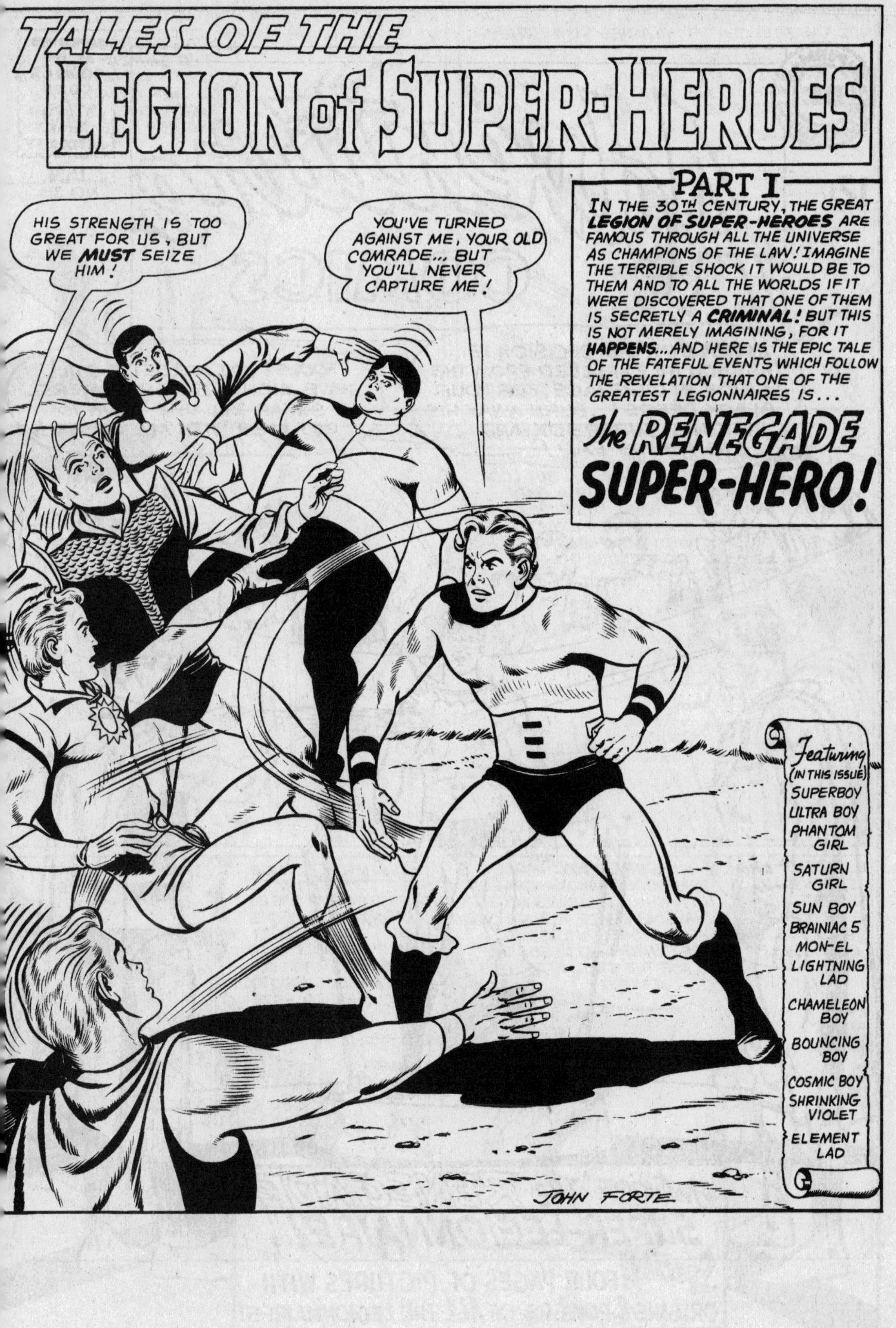
TALES OF THE
LEGION of SUPER-HEROES
PART I
IN THE 30TH CENTURY, THE GREAT LEGION OF SUPER-HEROES ARE FAMOUS THROUGH ALL THE UNIVERSE AS CHAMPIONS OF THE LAW! IMAGINE THE TERRIBLE SHOCK IT WOULD BE TO THEM AND TO ALL THE WORLDS IF IT WERE DISCOVERED THAT ONE OF THEM IS SECRETLY A CRIMINAL! BUT THIS IS NOT MERELY IMAGINING, FOR IT HAPPENS... AND HERE IS THE EPIC TALE OF THE FATEFUL EVENTS WHICH FOLLOW THE REVELATION THAT ONE OF THE GREATEST LEGIONNAIRES IS...
The RENEGADE SUPER-HERO!
HIS STRENGTH IS TOO GREAT FOR US, BUT WE MUST SEIZE HIM!
YOU'VE TURNED AGAINST ME, YOUR OLD COMRADE... BUT YOU'LL NEVER CAPTURE ME!
Featuring (IN THIS ISSUE) SUPERBOY ULTRA BOY PHANTOM GIRL SATURN GIRL SUN BOY BRAINIAC 5 MON-EL LIGHTNING LAD CHAMELEON BOY BOUNCING BOY COSMIC BOY SHRINKING VIOLET ELEMENT LAD
JOHN FORTE

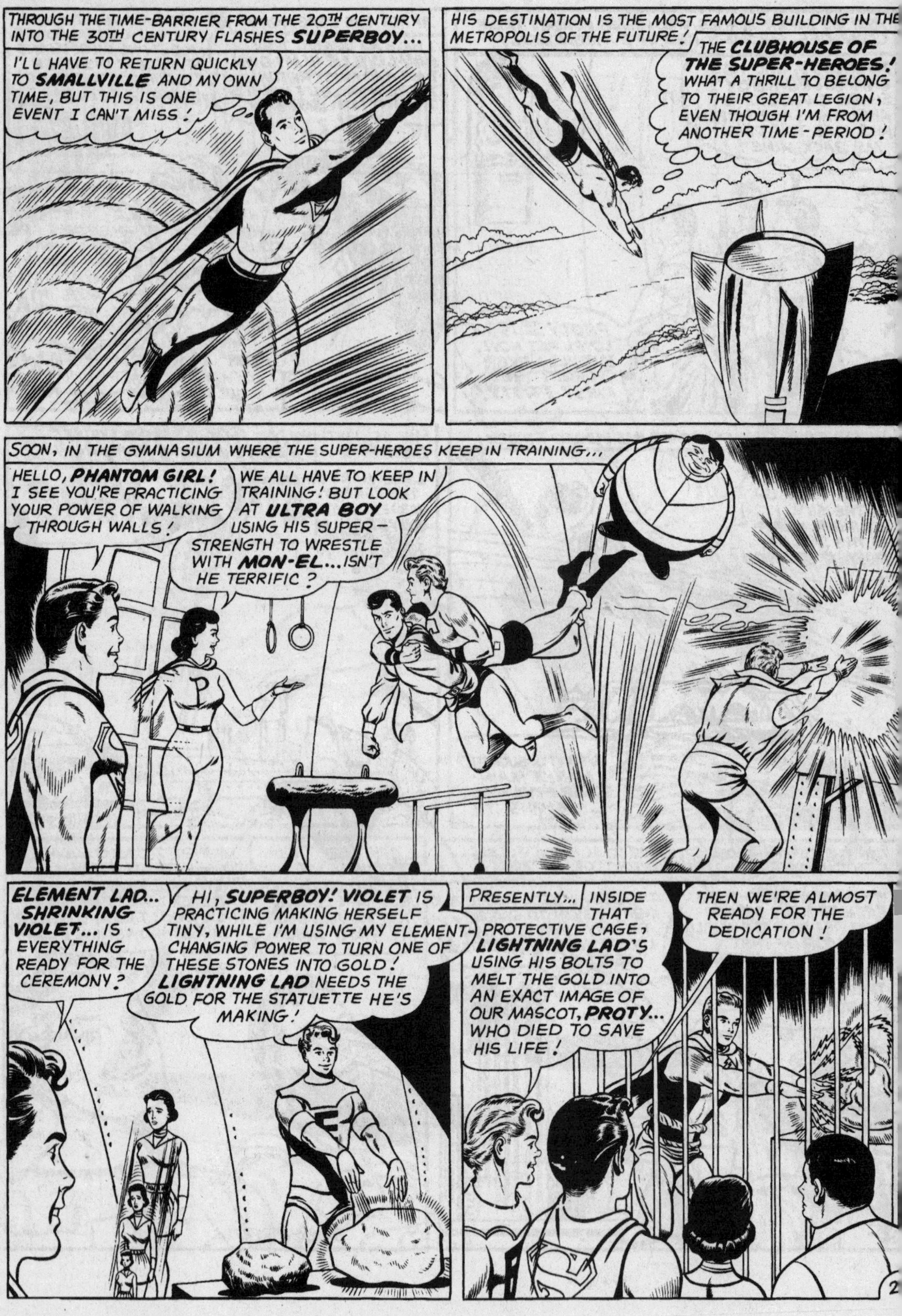
THROUGH THE TIME-BARRIER FROM THE 20TH CENTURY INTO THE 30TH CENTURY FLASHES SUPERBOY...
I'LL HAVE TO RETURN QUICKLY TO SMALLVILLE AND MY OWN TIME, BUT THIS IS ONE EVENT I CAN'T MISS!
HIS DESTINATION IS THE MOST FAMOUS BUILDING IN THE METROPOLIS OF THE FUTURE!
THE CLUBHOUSE OF THE SUPER-HEROES! WHAT A THRILL TO BELONG TO THEIR GREAT LEGION, EVEN THOUGH I'M FROM ANOTHER TIME-PERIOD!
SOON, IN THE GYMNASIUM WHERE THE SUPER-HEROES KEEP IN TRAINING...
HELLO, PHANTOM GIRL! I SEE YOU'RE PRACTICING YOUR POWER OF WALKING THROUGH WALLS!
WE ALL HAVE TO KEEP IN TRAINING! BUT LOOK AT ULTRA BOY USING HIS SUPER-STRENGTH TO WRESTLE WITH MON-EL... ISN'T HE TERRIFIC?
ELEMENT LAD... SHRINKING VIOLET... IS EVERYTHING READY FOR THE CEREMONY?
HI, SUPERBOY! VIOLET IS PRACTICING MAKING HERSELF TINY, WHILE I'M USING MY ELEMENT-CHANGING POWER TO TURN ONE OF THESE STONES INTO GOLD! LIGHTNING LAD NEEDS THE GOLD FOR THE STATUETTE HE'S MAKING!
PRESENTLY...
INSIDE THAT PROTECTIVE CAGE, LIGHTNING LAD'S USING HIS BOLTS TO MELT THE GOLD INTO AN EXACT IMAGE OF OUR MASCOT, PROTY... WHO DIED TO SAVE HIS LIFE!
THEN WE'RE ALMOST READY FOR THE DEDICATION!
2

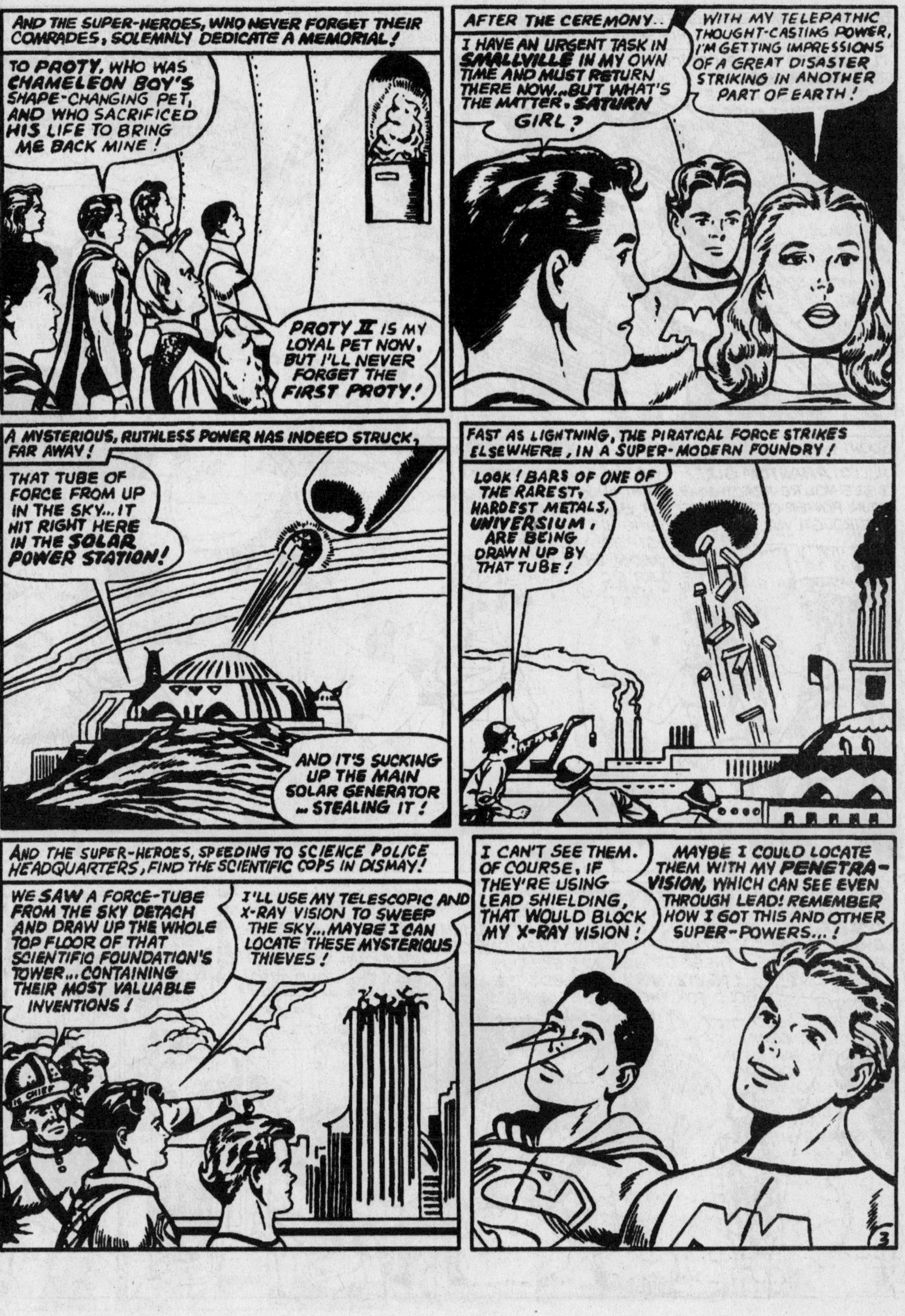
AND THE SUPER-HEROES, WHO NEVER FORGET THEIR COMRADES, SOLEMNLY DEDICATE A MEMORIAL!
TO PROTY, WHO WAS CHAMELEON BOY'S SHAPE-CHANGING PET, AND WHO SACRIFICED HIS LIFE TO BRING ME BACK MINE!
PROTY II IS MY LOYAL PET NOW, BUT I'LL NEVER FORGET THE FIRST PROTY!
AFTER THE CEREMONY..
I HAVE AN URGENT TASK IN SMALLVILLE IN MY OWN TIME AND MUST RETURN THERE NOW...BUT WHAT'S THE MATTER, SATURN GIRL?
WITH MY TELEPATHIC THOUGHT-CASTING POWER, I'M GETTING IMPRESSIONS OF A GREAT DISASTER STRIKING IN ANOTHER PART OF EARTH!
A MYSTERIOUS, RUTHLESS POWER HAS INDEED STRUCK, FAR AWAY!
THAT TUBE OF FORCE FROM UP IN THE SKY...IT HIT RIGHT HERE IN THE SOLAR POWER STATION!
AND IT'S SUCKING UP THE MAIN SOLAR GENERATOR ... STEALING IT!
FAST AS LIGHTNING, THE PIRATICAL FORCE STRIKES ELSEWHERE, IN A SUPER-MODERN FOUNDRY!
LOOK! BARS OF ONE OF THE RAREST, HARDEST METALS, UNIVERSIUM, ARE BEING DRAWN UP BY THAT TUBE!
AND THE SUPER-HEROES, SPEEDING TO SCIENCE POLICE HEADQUARTERS, FIND THE SCIENTIFIC COPS IN DISMAY!
WE SAW A FORCE-TUBE FROM THE SKY DETACH AND DRAW UP THE WHOLE TOP FLOOR OF THAT SCIENTIFIC FOUNDATION'S TOWER... CONTAINING THEIR MOST VALUABLE INVENTIONS!
I'LL USE MY TELESCOPIC AND X-RAY VISION TO SWEEP THE SKY...MAYBE I CAN LOCATE THESE MYSTERIOUS THIEVES!
CHIEF
I CAN'T SEE THEM. OF COURSE, IF THEY'RE USING LEAD SHIELDING, THAT WOULD BLOCK MY X-RAY VISION!
MAYBE I COULD LOCATE THEM WITH MY PENETRA-VISION, WHICH CAN SEE EVEN THROUGH LEAD! REMEMBER HOW I GOT THIS AND OTHER SUPER-POWERS...!
3

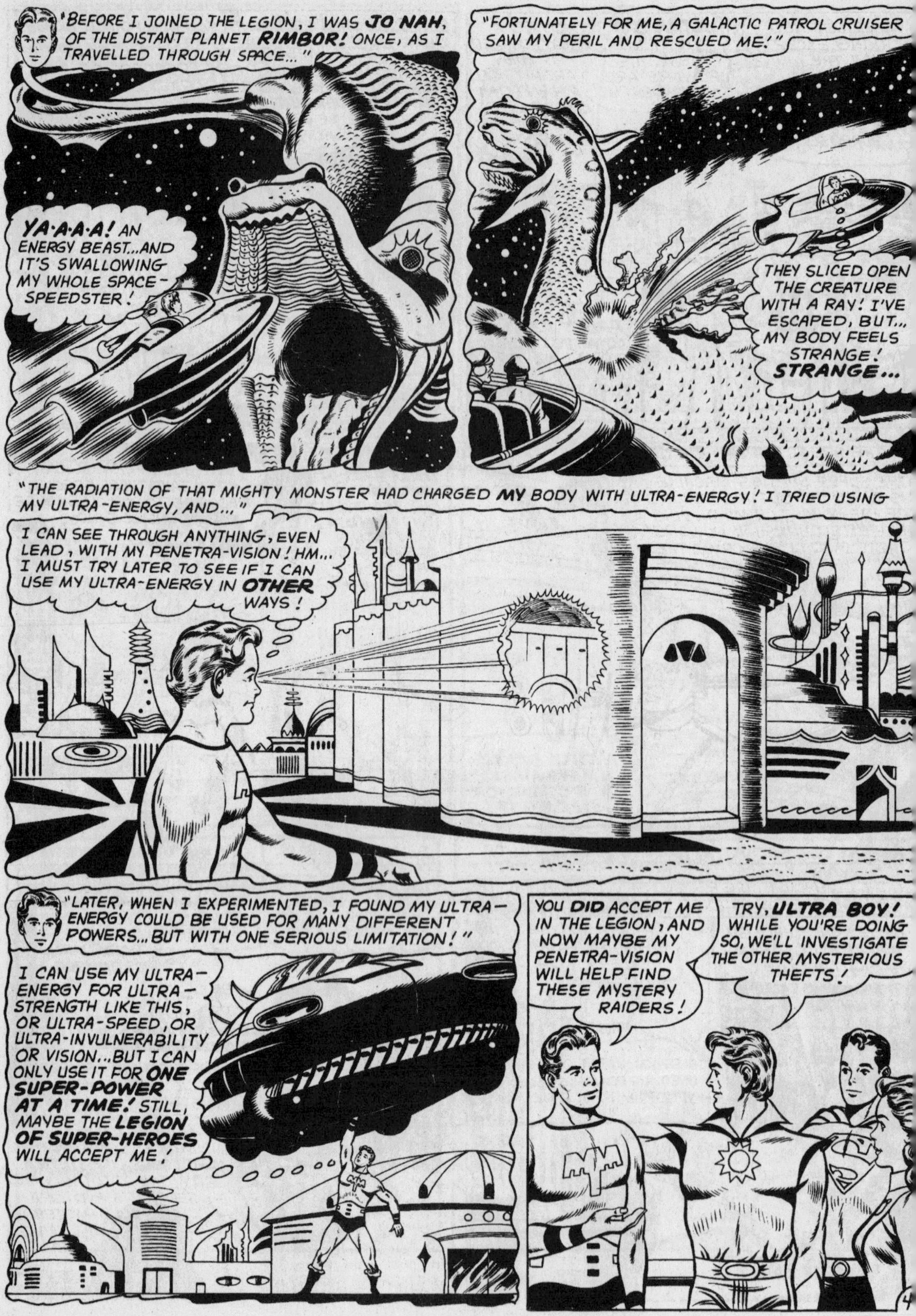
"BEFORE I JOINED THE LEGION, I WAS JO NAH, OF THE DISTANT PLANET RIMBOR! ONCE, AS I TRAVELLED THROUGH SPACE..."
YA-A-A-A! AN ENERGY BEAST...AND IT'S SWALLOWING MY WHOLE SPACE-SPEEDSTER!
"FORTUNATELY FOR ME, A GALACTIC PATROL CRUISER SAW MY PERIL AND RESCUED ME!"
THEY SLICED OPEN THE CREATURE WITH A RAY! I'VE ESCAPED, BUT... MY BODY FEELS STRANGE! STRANGE...
"THE RADIATION OF THAT MIGHTY MONSTER HAD CHARGED MY BODY WITH ULTRA-ENERGY! I TRIED USING MY ULTRA-ENERGY, AND..."
I CAN SEE THROUGH ANYTHING, EVEN LEAD, WITH MY PENETRA-VISION! HM... I MUST TRY LATER TO SEE IF I CAN USE MY ULTRA-ENERGY IN OTHER WAYS!
"LATER, WHEN I EXPERIMENTED, I FOUND MY ULTRA-ENERGY COULD BE USED FOR MANY DIFFERENT POWERS... BUT WITH ONE SERIOUS LIMITATION!"
I CAN USE MY ULTRA-ENERGY FOR ULTRA-STRENGTH LIKE THIS, OR ULTRA-SPEED, OR ULTRA-INVULNERABILITY OR VISION... BUT I CAN ONLY USE IT FOR ONE SUPER-POWER AT A TIME! STILL, MAYBE THE LEGION OF SUPER-HEROES WILL ACCEPT ME!
YOU DID ACCEPT ME IN THE LEGION, AND NOW MAYBE MY PENETRA-VISION WILL HELP FIND THESE MYSTERY RAIDERS!
TRY, ULTRA BOY! WHILE YOU'RE DOING SO, WE'LL INVESTIGATE THE OTHER MYSTERIOUS THEFTS!
4

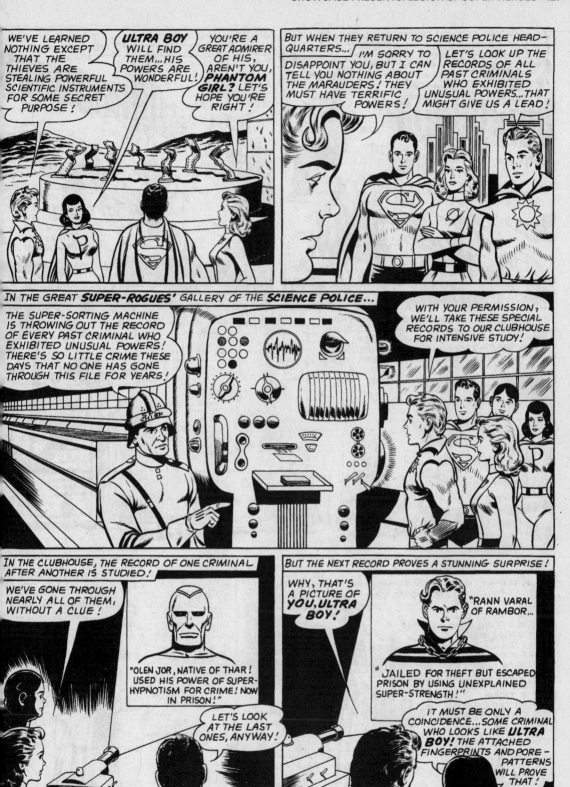

Panel 1: WE'VE LEARNED NOTHING EXCEPT THAT THE THIEVES ARE STEALING POWERFUL SCIENTIFIC INSTRUMENTS FOR SOME SECRET PURPOSE!

ULTRA BOY WILL FIND THEM...HIS POWERS ARE WONDERFUL!

YOU'RE A GREAT ADMIRER OF HIS, AREN'T YOU, *PHANTOM GIRL?* LET'S HOPE YOU'RE RIGHT!

Panel 2: BUT WHEN THEY RETURN TO SCIENCE POLICE HEADQUARTERS...

I'M SORRY TO DISAPPOINT YOU, BUT I CAN TELL YOU NOTHING ABOUT THE MARAUDERS! THEY MUST HAVE TERRIFIC POWERS!

LET'S LOOK UP THE RECORDS OF ALL PAST CRIMINALS WHO EXHIBITED UNUSUAL POWERS...THAT MIGHT GIVE US A LEAD!

Panel 3: IN THE GREAT *SUPER-ROGUES'* GALLERY OF THE *SCIENCE POLICE*...

THE SUPER-SORTING MACHINE IS THROWING OUT THE RECORD OF EVERY PAST CRIMINAL WHO EXHIBITED UNUSUAL POWERS! THERE'S SO LITTLE CRIME THESE DAYS THAT NO ONE HAS GONE THROUGH THIS FILE FOR YEARS!

WITH YOUR PERMISSION, WE'LL TAKE THESE SPECIAL RECORDS TO OUR CLUBHOUSE FOR INTENSIVE STUDY!

Panel 4: IN THE CLUBHOUSE, THE RECORD OF ONE CRIMINAL AFTER ANOTHER IS STUDIED!

WE'VE GONE THROUGH NEARLY ALL OF THEM, WITHOUT A CLUE!

"OLEN JOR, NATIVE OF THAR! USED HIS POWER OF SUPER-HYPNOTISM FOR CRIME! NOW IN PRISON!"

LET'S LOOK AT THE LAST ONES, ANYWAY!

Panel 5: BUT THE NEXT RECORD PROVES A STUNNING SURPRISE!

WHY, THAT'S A PICTURE OF *YOU, ULTRA BOY!*

"RANN VARAL OF RAMBOR...

"JAILED FOR THEFT BUT ESCAPED PRISON BY USING UNEXPLAINED SUPER-STRENGTH!"

IT MUST BE ONLY A COINCIDENCE...SOME CRIMINAL WHO LOOKS LIKE *ULTRA BOY!* THE ATTACHED FINGERPRINTS AND PORE-PATTERNS WILL PROVE THAT!

5

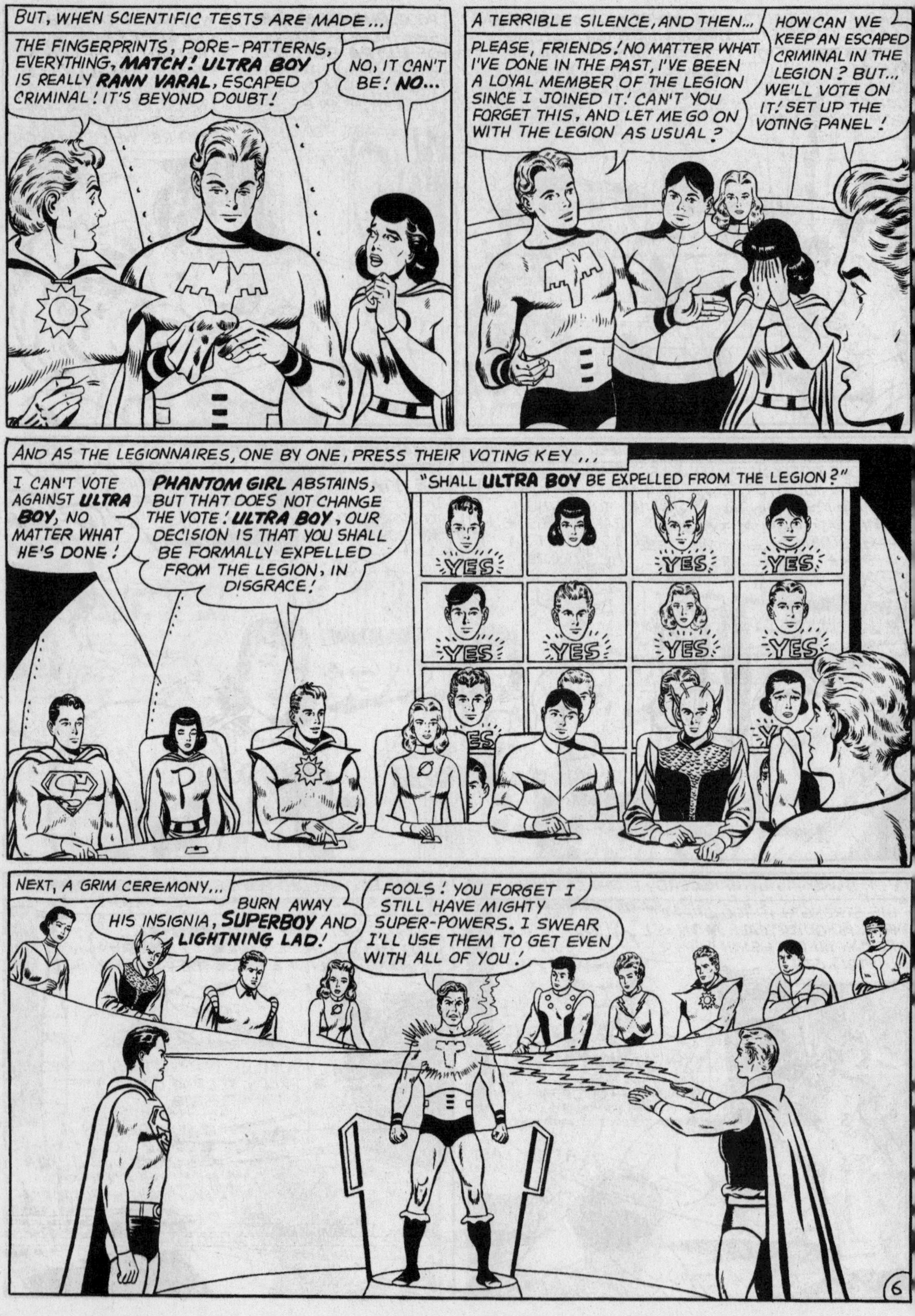

BUT, WHEN SCIENTIFIC TESTS ARE MADE...
THE FINGERPRINTS, PORE-PATTERNS, EVERYTHING, MATCH! ULTRA BOY IS REALLY RANN VARAL, ESCAPED CRIMINAL! IT'S BEYOND DOUBT!
NO, IT CAN'T BE! NO...
A TERRIBLE SILENCE, AND THEN...
PLEASE, FRIENDS! NO MATTER WHAT I'VE DONE IN THE PAST, I'VE BEEN A LOYAL MEMBER OF THE LEGION SINCE I JOINED IT! CAN'T YOU FORGET THIS, AND LET ME GO ON WITH THE LEGION AS USUAL?
HOW CAN WE KEEP AN ESCAPED CRIMINAL IN THE LEGION? BUT... WE'LL VOTE ON IT! SET UP THE VOTING PANEL!
AND AS THE LEGIONNAIRES, ONE BY ONE, PRESS THEIR VOTING KEY...
I CAN'T VOTE AGAINST ULTRA BOY, NO MATTER WHAT HE'S DONE!
PHANTOM GIRL ABSTAINS, BUT THAT DOES NOT CHANGE THE VOTE! ULTRA BOY, OUR DECISION IS THAT YOU SHALL BE FORMALLY EXPELLED FROM THE LEGION, IN DISGRACE!
"SHALL ULTRA BOY BE EXPELLED FROM THE LEGION?"
YES
YES
YES
YES
YES
YES
YES
NEXT, A GRIM CEREMONY...
BURN AWAY HIS INSIGNIA, SUPERBOY AND LIGHTNING LAD!
FOOLS! YOU FORGET I STILL HAVE MIGHTY SUPER-POWERS. I SWEAR I'LL USE THEM TO GET EVEN WITH ALL OF YOU!
6

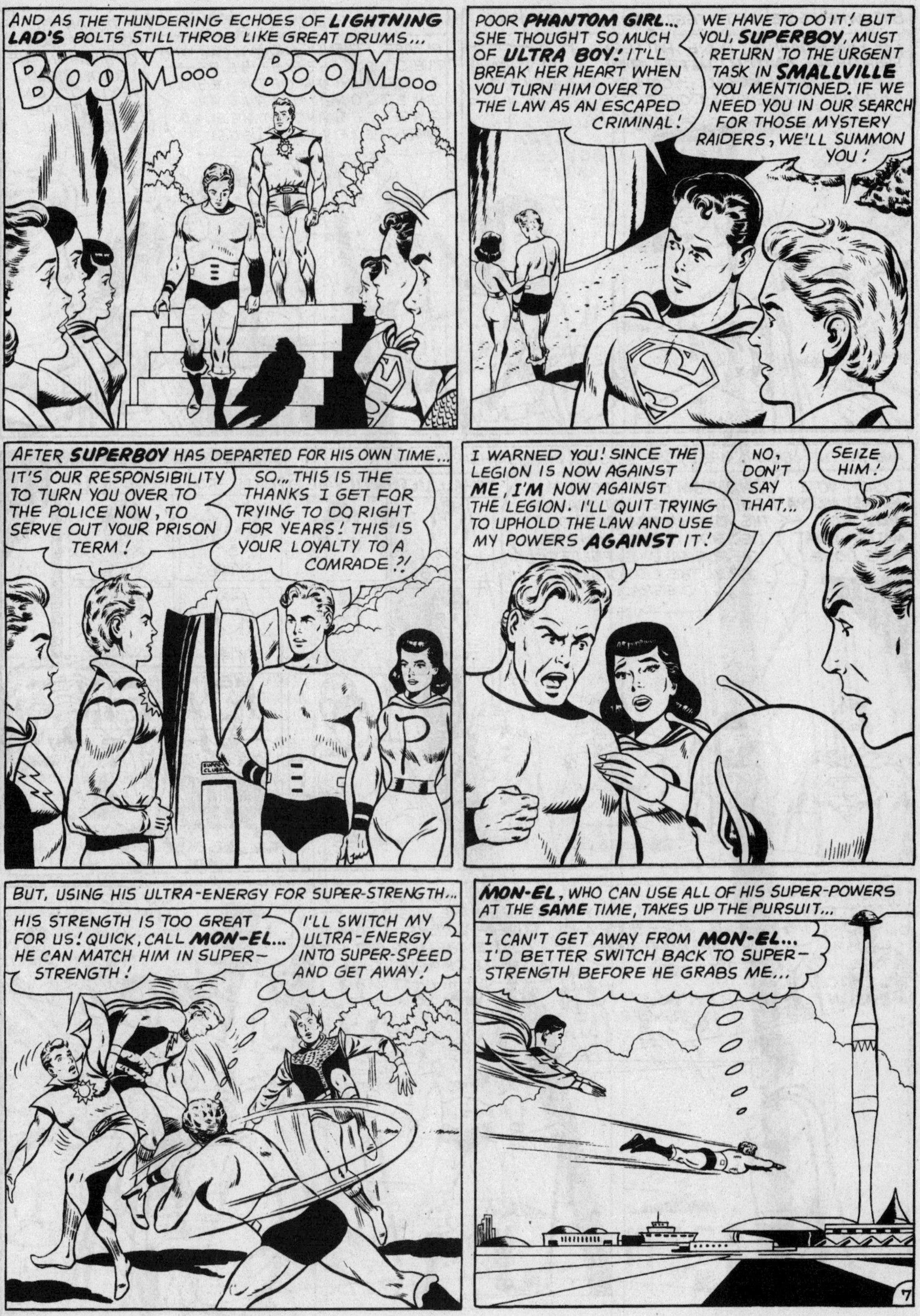
AND AS THE THUNDERING ECHOES OF LIGHTNING LAD'S BOLTS STILL THROB LIKE GREAT DRUMS...
BOOM... BOOM...
POOR PHANTOM GIRL... SHE THOUGHT SO MUCH OF ULTRA BOY! IT'LL BREAK HER HEART WHEN YOU TURN HIM OVER TO THE LAW AS AN ESCAPED CRIMINAL!
WE HAVE TO DO IT! BUT YOU, SUPERBOY, MUST RETURN TO THE URGENT TASK IN SMALLVILLE YOU MENTIONED. IF WE NEED YOU IN OUR SEARCH FOR THOSE MYSTERY RAIDERS, WE'LL SUMMON YOU!
AFTER SUPERBOY HAS DEPARTED FOR HIS OWN TIME...
IT'S OUR RESPONSIBILITY TO TURN YOU OVER TO THE POLICE NOW, TO SERVE OUT YOUR PRISON TERM!
SO... THIS IS THE THANKS I GET FOR TRYING TO DO RIGHT FOR YEARS! THIS IS YOUR LOYALTY TO A COMRADE?!
I WARNED YOU! SINCE THE LEGION IS NOW AGAINST ME, I'M NOW AGAINST THE LEGION. I'LL QUIT TRYING TO UPHOLD THE LAW AND USE MY POWERS AGAINST IT!
NO, DON'T SAY THAT...
SEIZE HIM!
BUT, USING HIS ULTRA-ENERGY FOR SUPER-STRENGTH...
HIS STRENGTH IS TOO GREAT FOR US! QUICK, CALL MON-EL... HE CAN MATCH HIM IN SUPER-STRENGTH!
I'LL SWITCH MY ULTRA-ENERGY INTO SUPER-SPEED AND GET AWAY!
MON-EL, WHO CAN USE ALL OF HIS SUPER-POWERS AT THE SAME TIME, TAKES UP THE PURSUIT...
I CAN'T GET AWAY FROM MON-EL... I'D BETTER SWITCH BACK TO SUPER-STRENGTH BEFORE HE GRABS ME...
7

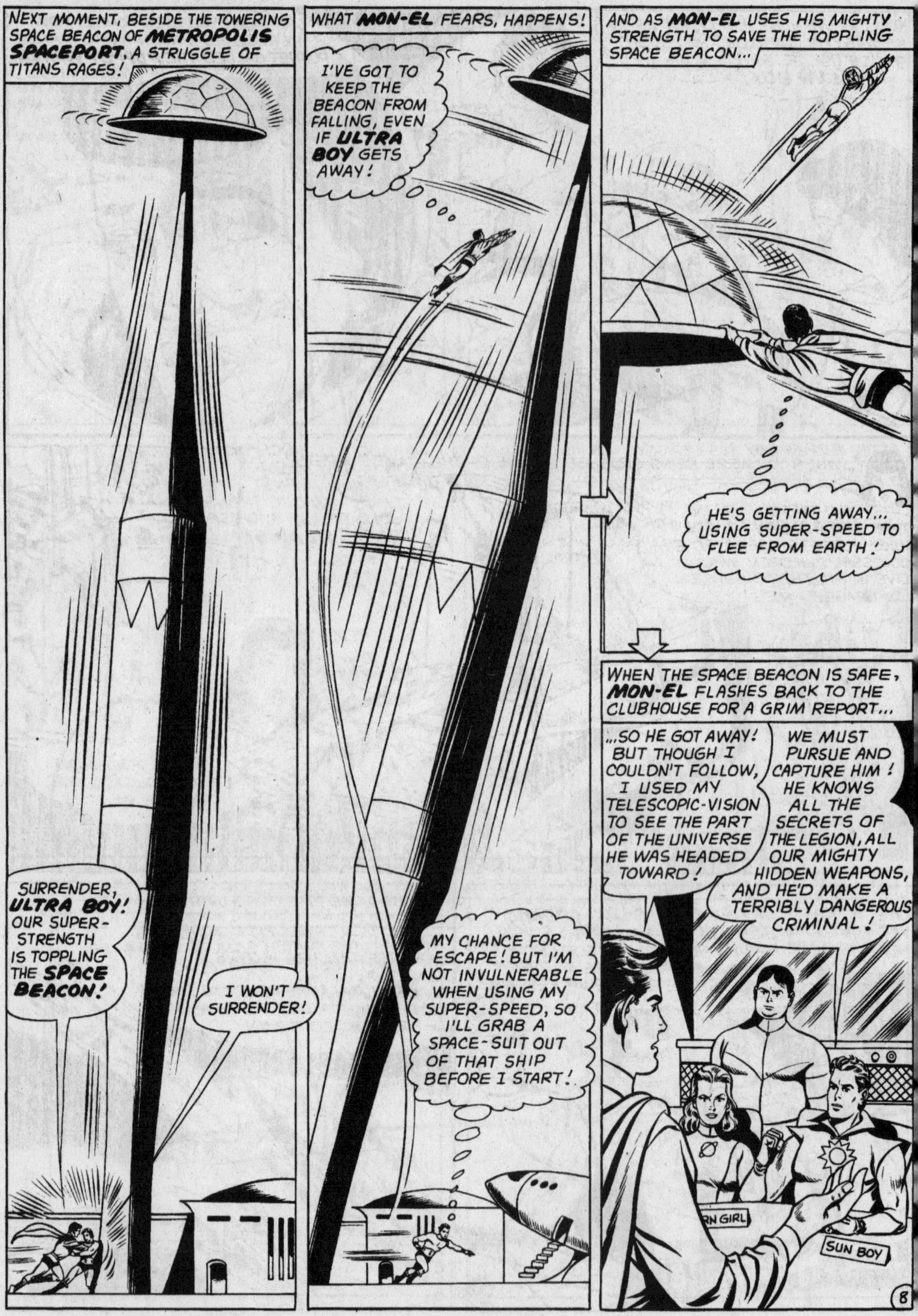
NEXT MOMENT, BESIDE THE TOWERING SPACE BEACON OF METROPOLIS SPACEPORT, A STRUGGLE OF TITANS RAGES!
SURRENDER, ULTRA BOY! OUR SUPER-STRENGTH IS TOPPLING THE SPACE BEACON!
I WON'T SURRENDER!
WHAT MON-EL FEARS, HAPPENS!
I'VE GOT TO KEEP THE BEACON FROM FALLING, EVEN IF ULTRA BOY GETS AWAY!
MY CHANCE FOR ESCAPE! BUT I'M NOT INVULNERABLE WHEN USING MY SUPER-SPEED, SO I'LL GRAB A SPACE-SUIT OUT OF THAT SHIP BEFORE I START!
AND AS MON-EL USES HIS MIGHTY STRENGTH TO SAVE THE TOPPLING SPACE BEACON...
HE'S GETTING AWAY... USING SUPER-SPEED TO FLEE FROM EARTH!
WHEN THE SPACE BEACON IS SAFE, MON-EL FLASHES BACK TO THE CLUBHOUSE FOR A GRIM REPORT...
...SO HE GOT AWAY! BUT THOUGH I COULDN'T FOLLOW, I USED MY TELESCOPIC-VISION TO SEE THE PART OF THE UNIVERSE HE WAS HEADED TOWARD!
WE MUST PURSUE AND CAPTURE HIM! HE KNOWS ALL THE SECRETS OF THE LEGION, ALL OUR MIGHTY HIDDEN WEAPONS, AND HE'D MAKE A TERRIBLY DANGEROUS CRIMINAL!
RN GIRL
SUN BOY
8

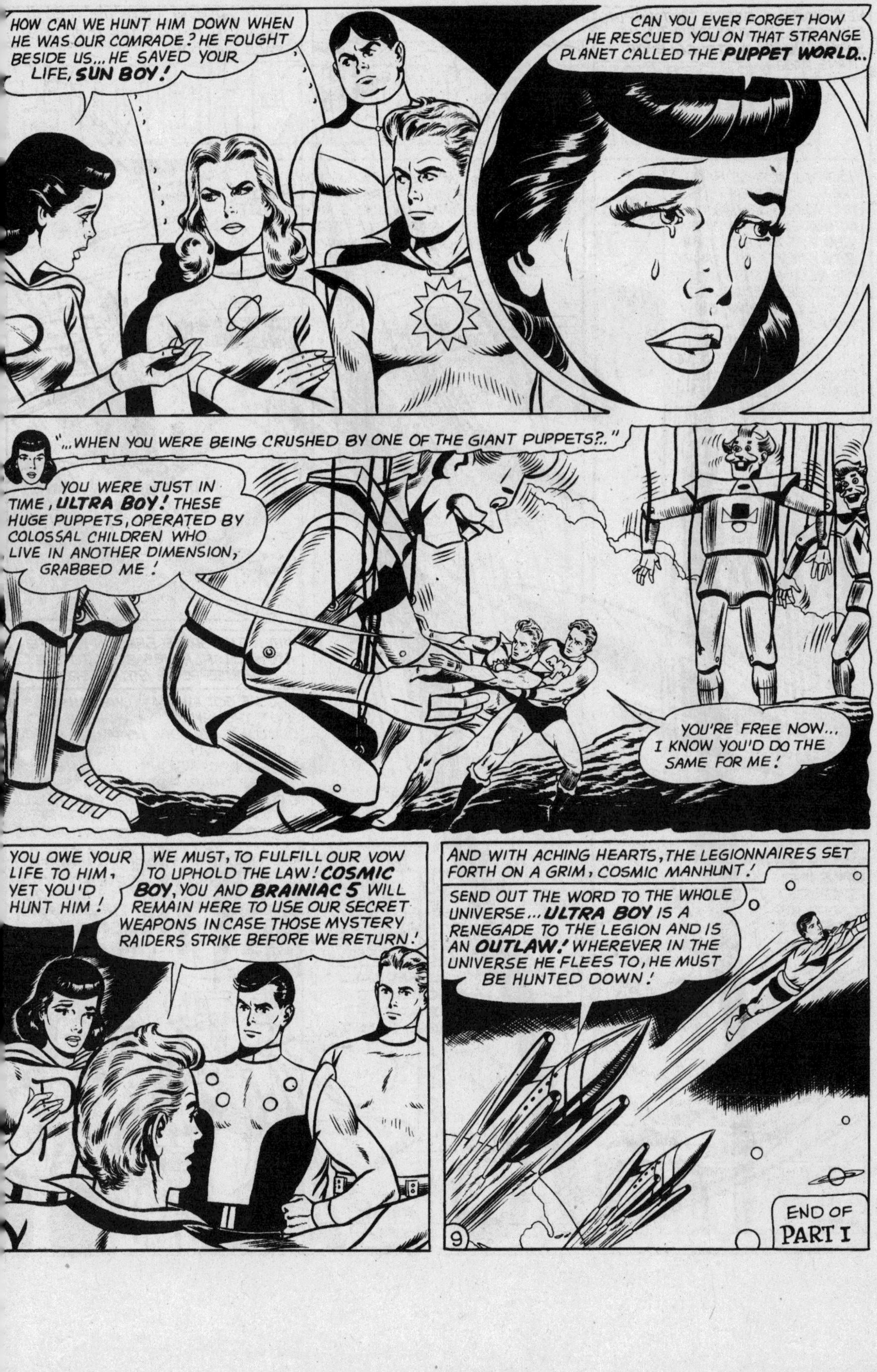
HOW CAN WE HUNT HIM DOWN WHEN HE WAS OUR COMRADE? HE FOUGHT BESIDE US... HE SAVED YOUR LIFE, SUN BOY!
CAN YOU EVER FORGET HOW HE RESCUED YOU ON THAT STRANGE PLANET CALLED THE PUPPET WORLD...
"...WHEN YOU WERE BEING CRUSHED BY ONE OF THE GIANT PUPPETS?.."
YOU WERE JUST IN TIME, ULTRA BOY! THESE HUGE PUPPETS, OPERATED BY COLOSSAL CHILDREN WHO LIVE IN ANOTHER DIMENSION, GRABBED ME!
YOU'RE FREE NOW... I KNOW YOU'D DO THE SAME FOR ME!
YOU OWE YOUR LIFE TO HIM, YET YOU'D HUNT HIM!
WE MUST, TO FULFILL OUR VOW TO UPHOLD THE LAW! COSMIC BOY, YOU AND BRAINIAC 5 WILL REMAIN HERE TO USE OUR SECRET WEAPONS IN CASE THOSE MYSTERY RAIDERS STRIKE BEFORE WE RETURN!
AND WITH ACHING HEARTS, THE LEGIONNAIRES SET FORTH ON A GRIM, COSMIC MANHUNT!
SEND OUT THE WORD TO THE WHOLE UNIVERSE... ULTRA BOY IS A RENEGADE TO THE LEGION AND IS AN OUTLAW! WHEREVER IN THE UNIVERSE HE FLEES TO, HE MUST BE HUNTED DOWN!
9
END OF PART I

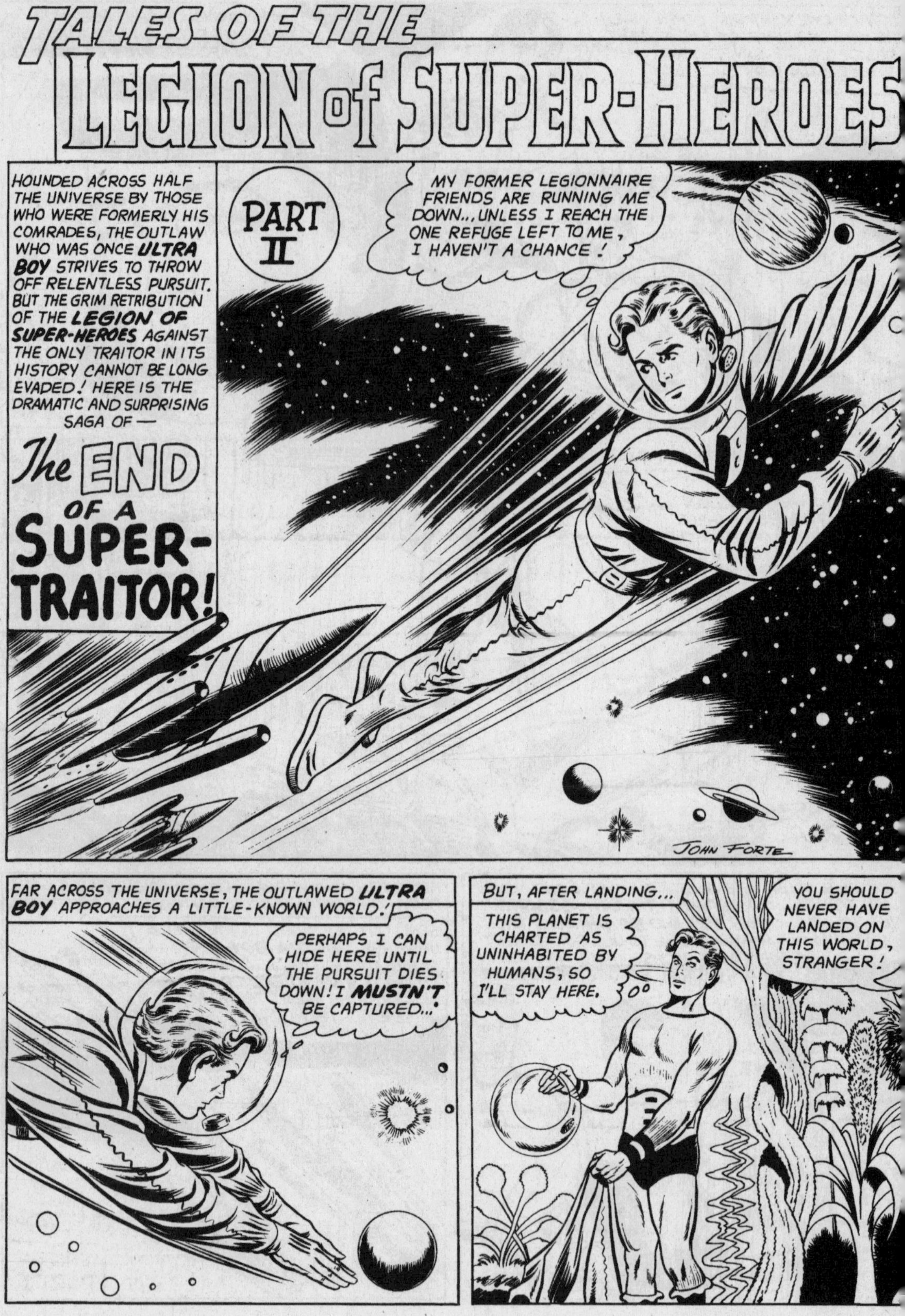
TALES OF THE
LEGION of SUPER-HEROES
HOUNDED ACROSS HALF THE UNIVERSE BY THOSE WHO WERE FORMERLY HIS COMRADES, THE OUTLAW WHO WAS ONCE ULTRA BOY STRIVES TO THROW OFF RELENTLESS PURSUIT. BUT THE GRIM RETRIBUTION OF THE LEGION OF SUPER-HEROES AGAINST THE ONLY TRAITOR IN ITS HISTORY CANNOT BE LONG EVADED! HERE IS THE DRAMATIC AND SURPRISING SAGA OF —
The END OF A SUPER-TRAITOR!
PART II
MY FORMER LEGIONNAIRE FRIENDS ARE RUNNING ME DOWN... UNLESS I REACH THE ONE REFUGE LEFT TO ME, I HAVEN'T A CHANCE!
JOHN FORTE
FAR ACROSS THE UNIVERSE, THE OUTLAWED ULTRA BOY APPROACHES A LITTLE-KNOWN WORLD!
PERHAPS I CAN HIDE HERE UNTIL THE PURSUIT DIES DOWN! I MUSTN'T BE CAPTURED...
BUT, AFTER LANDING...
THIS PLANET IS CHARTED AS UNINHABITED BY HUMANS, SO I'LL STAY HERE.
YOU SHOULD NEVER HAVE LANDED ON THIS WORLD, STRANGER!

WHO SPOKE TO ME? IT COULDN'T BE THIS TERRIBLE MONSTER...

YOU'RE WRONG...I *DID* SPEAK TO YOU!

THE NERVOUS STRAIN OF BEING A FUGITIVE IS GIVING ME DELUSIONS ...SUCH MONSTERS COULDN'T SPEAK INTELLIGENTLY!

BUT WE WERE ONCE HUMAN MEN...LIKE YOU!

WE MEN VOLUNTEERED AS SUBJECTS FOR AN EXPERIMENT BY A GREAT SCIENTIST...HE EXCHANGED OUR MINDS INTO THESE MONSTROUS BODIES!

BUT HE'S BEEN UNABLE TO *REVERSE* THE EXCHANGE, SO OUR MINDS ARE TRAPPED IN THESE BODIES!

EVEN THOUGH *ULTRA BOY* IS A HUNTED OUTLAW, HIS SYMPATHY IS AROUSED!

PERHAPS MY EARTH SCIENCE COULD HELP THIS SCIENTIST UNDO THE EFFECT, AND CHANGE YOU BACK TO YOUR HUMAN BODIES!

WE'LL TAKE YOU TO THE LABORATORY HE BUILT ON THIS TERRIBLE WORLD!

ON THIS WEIRD PLANET, A SCIENTIST IS IN DESPAIR!

I DID AN AWFUL THING AND CAN'T UNDO IT! MY MIND-EXCHANGE MACHINE SIMPLY WON'T WORK IN REVERSE! IT'S ALL BECAUSE I DUPLICATED AN EXPERIMENT ONCE CONDUCTED BY A KRYPTONIAN CRIMINAL! *

LET ME SEE THE MACHINE!

* SEE "SUPERGIRL'S WEDDING DAY" IN *ACTION COMICS* NO. 307. — EDITOR

CAN YOU MAKE IT WORK IN REVERSE?

I'M AFRAID MY KNOWLEDGE OF BIOPHYSICAL SCIENCE ISN'T ENOUGH! *MON-EL*, WHOSE PEOPLE ARE MASTER BIOPHYSICISTS, COULD DO IT...BUT HE'S AMONG THOSE SEARCHING TO CAPTURE ME...

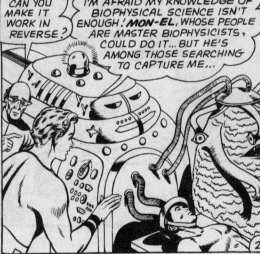

2

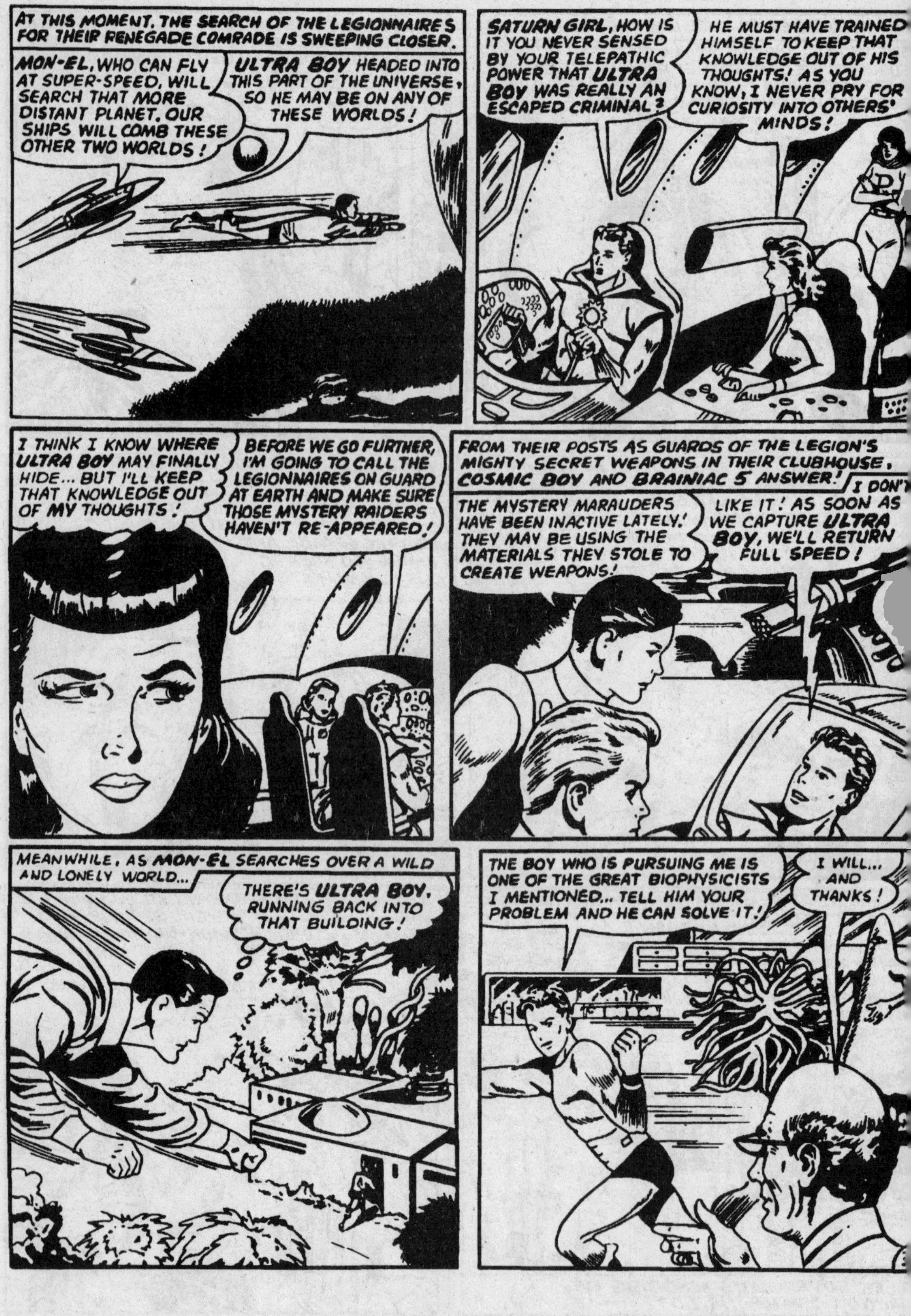
AT THIS MOMENT, THE SEARCH OF THE LEGIONNAIRES FOR THEIR RENEGADE COMRADE IS SWEEPING CLOSER.
MON-EL, WHO CAN FLY AT SUPER-SPEED, WILL SEARCH THAT MORE DISTANT PLANET. OUR SHIPS WILL COMB THESE OTHER TWO WORLDS!
ULTRA BOY HEADED INTO THIS PART OF THE UNIVERSE, SO HE MAY BE ON ANY OF THESE WORLDS!
SATURN GIRL, HOW IS IT YOU NEVER SENSED BY YOUR TELEPATHIC POWER THAT ULTRA BOY WAS REALLY AN ESCAPED CRIMINAL?
HE MUST HAVE TRAINED HIMSELF TO KEEP THAT KNOWLEDGE OUT OF HIS THOUGHTS! AS YOU KNOW, I NEVER PRY FOR CURIOSITY INTO OTHERS' MINDS!
I THINK I KNOW WHERE ULTRA BOY MAY FINALLY HIDE... BUT I'LL KEEP THAT KNOWLEDGE OUT OF MY THOUGHTS!
BEFORE WE GO FURTHER, I'M GOING TO CALL THE LEGIONNAIRES ON GUARD AT EARTH AND MAKE SURE THOSE MYSTERY RAIDERS HAVEN'T RE-APPEARED!
FROM THEIR POSTS AS GUARDS OF THE LEGION'S MIGHTY SECRET WEAPONS IN THEIR CLUBHOUSE, COSMIC BOY AND BRAINIAC 5 ANSWER!
THE MYSTERY MARAUDERS HAVE BEEN INACTIVE LATELY! THEY MAY BE USING THE MATERIALS THEY STOLE TO CREATE WEAPONS!
I DON'T LIKE IT! AS SOON AS WE CAPTURE ULTRA BOY, WE'LL RETURN FULL SPEED!
MEANWHILE, AS MON-EL SEARCHES OVER A WILD AND LONELY WORLD...
THERE'S ULTRA BOY, RUNNING BACK INTO THAT BUILDING!
THE BOY WHO IS PURSUING ME IS ONE OF THE GREAT BIOPHYSICISTS I MENTIONED... TELL HIM YOUR PROBLEM AND HE CAN SOLVE IT!
I WILL... AND THANKS!

AND AS **MON-EL** PURSUES INTO THE BUILDING...

GIVE ME HELP, BEFORE MY HUMAN SUBJECTS DIE OF DESPAIR! I PUT THEIR MINDS INTO THOSE MONSTROUS BODIES, BUT I CAN'T RE-EXCHANGE THEM!

BUT I HAVE TO GO AFTER **ULTRA BOY**... STILL, IF THIS IS A MATTER OF LIFE OR DEATH, I'LL TRY TO HELP!

I THINK I SEE WHAT THE TROUBLE WITH YOUR MIND-EXCHANGER IS...IT'LL TAKE A LITTLE TIME TO FIX IT!

THINK HOW THESE HORROR-STRICKEN MEN WHO ARE TRAPPED IN MONSTROUS BODIES WILL BLESS YOU, IF YOU SUCCEED!

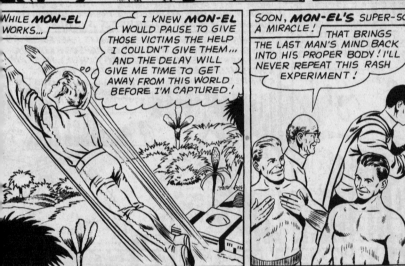

WHILE **MON-EL** WORKS...

I KNEW **MON-EL** WOULD PAUSE TO GIVE THOSE VICTIMS THE HELP I COULDN'T GIVE THEM...AND THE DELAY WILL GIVE ME TIME TO GET AWAY FROM THIS WORLD BEFORE I'M CAPTURED!

SOON, **MON-EL'S** SUPER-SCIENTIFIC ABILITY WORKS A MIRACLE!

THAT BRINGS THE LAST MAN'S MIND BACK INTO HIS PROPER BODY! I'LL NEVER REPEAT THIS RASH EXPERIMENT!

NOW I HAVE TO GO, BUT I'M AFRAID I'VE LOST THE TRAIL!

AND, AS THE CRUISERS OF THE SEARCHING LEGIONNAIRES OVERTAKE **MON-EL**...

KNOWING I'D DELAY TO HELP THOSE VICTIMS WITH MY BIOPHYSICAL SCIENCE, **ULTRA BOY** HAD TIME TO SLIP AWAY!

THAT'S OUR HANDICAP! **ULTRA BOY**, OUR COMRADE OF THE PAST, **KNOWS** US ALL...OUR STRENGTHS, OUR WEAKNESSES, AND HOW BEST TO EVADE US!

WE'VE GOT TO KEEP AFTER HIM UNTIL WE RUN HIM DOWN!

WE'LL CAPTURE HIM, EVEN THOUGH RIGHT NOW HE'S PROBABLY LAUGHING AT US!

4

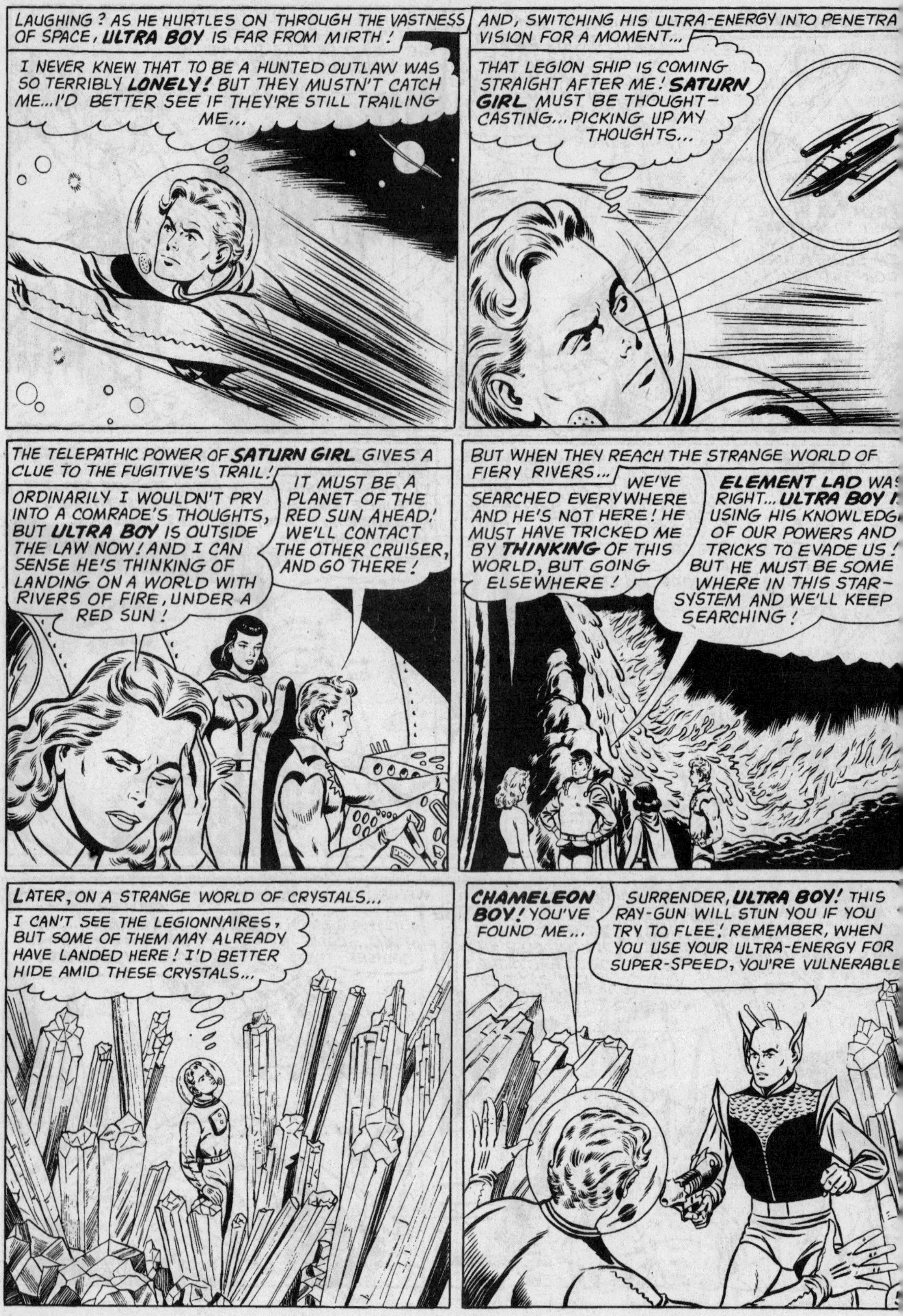
LAUGHING? AS HE HURTLES ON THROUGH THE VASTNESS OF SPACE, ULTRA BOY IS FAR FROM MIRTH!
I NEVER KNEW THAT TO BE A HUNTED OUTLAW WAS SO TERRIBLY LONELY! BUT THEY MUSTN'T CATCH ME...I'D BETTER SEE IF THEY'RE STILL TRAILING ME...
AND, SWITCHING HIS ULTRA-ENERGY INTO PENETRA VISION FOR A MOMENT...
THAT LEGION SHIP IS COMING STRAIGHT AFTER ME! SATURN GIRL MUST BE THOUGHT-CASTING... PICKING UP MY THOUGHTS...
THE TELEPATHIC POWER OF SATURN GIRL GIVES A CLUE TO THE FUGITIVE'S TRAIL!
ORDINARILY I WOULDN'T PRY INTO A COMRADE'S THOUGHTS, BUT ULTRA BOY IS OUTSIDE THE LAW NOW! AND I CAN SENSE HE'S THINKING OF LANDING ON A WORLD WITH RIVERS OF FIRE, UNDER A RED SUN!
IT MUST BE A PLANET OF THE RED SUN AHEAD! WE'LL CONTACT THE OTHER CRUISER, AND GO THERE!
BUT WHEN THEY REACH THE STRANGE WORLD OF FIERY RIVERS...
WE'VE SEARCHED EVERYWHERE AND HE'S NOT HERE! HE MUST HAVE TRICKED ME BY THINKING OF THIS WORLD, BUT GOING ELSEWHERE!
ELEMENT LAD WAS RIGHT...ULTRA BOY I USING HIS KNOWLEDG OF OUR POWERS AND TRICKS TO EVADE US! BUT HE MUST BE SOME WHERE IN THIS STAR-SYSTEM AND WE'LL KEEP SEARCHING!
LATER, ON A STRANGE WORLD OF CRYSTALS...
I CAN'T SEE THE LEGIONNAIRES, BUT SOME OF THEM MAY ALREADY HAVE LANDED HERE! I'D BETTER HIDE AMID THESE CRYSTALS...
CHAMELEON BOY! YOU'VE FOUND ME...
SURRENDER, ULTRA BOY! THIS RAY-GUN WILL STUN YOU IF YOU TRY TO FLEE! REMEMBER, WHEN YOU USE YOUR ULTRA-ENERGY FOR SUPER-SPEED, YOU'RE VULNERABLE

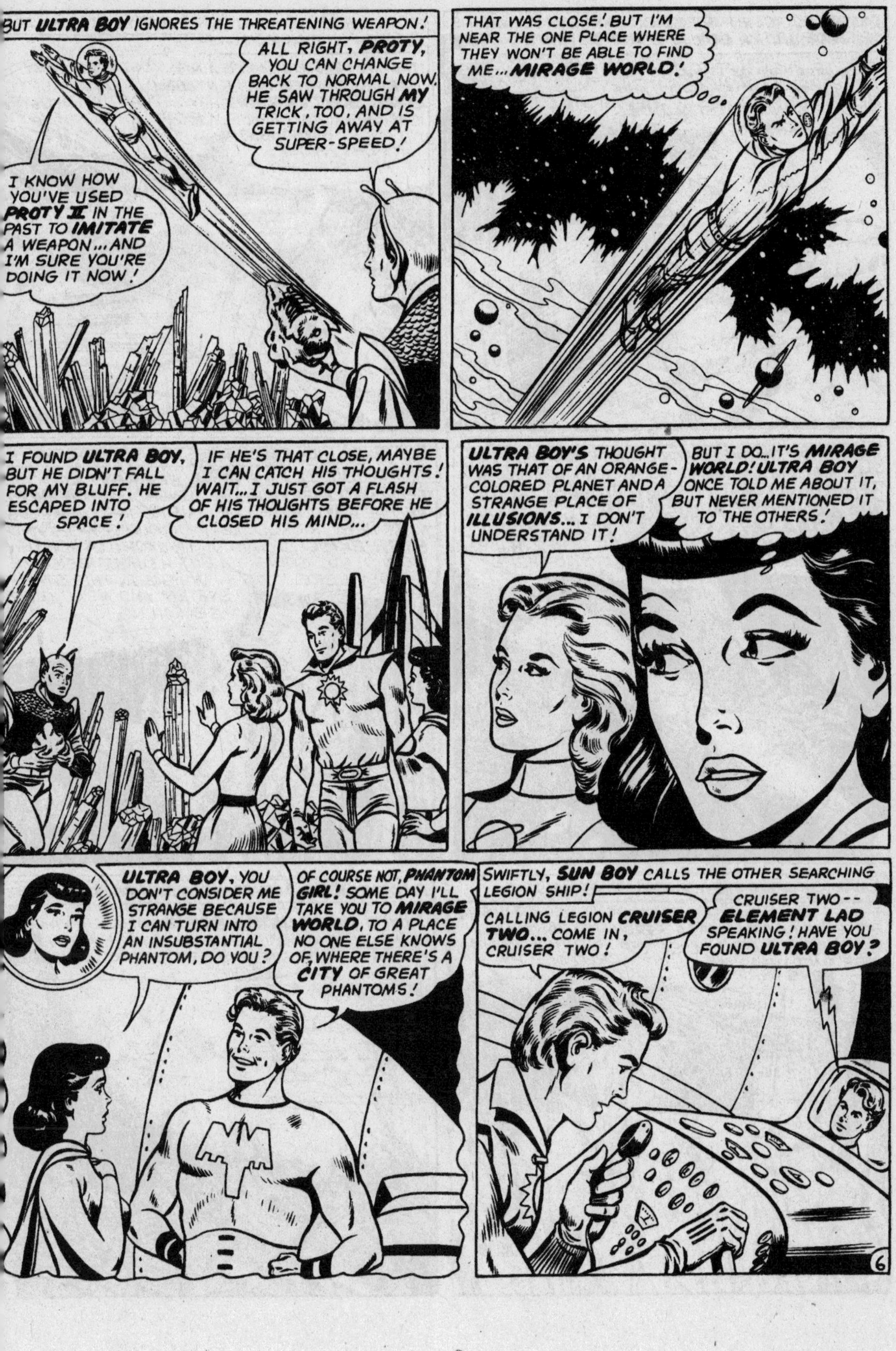
BUT ULTRA BOY IGNORES THE THREATENING WEAPON!
ALL RIGHT, PROTY, YOU CAN CHANGE BACK TO NORMAL NOW. HE SAW THROUGH MY TRICK, TOO, AND IS GETTING AWAY AT SUPER-SPEED!
I KNOW HOW YOU'VE USED PROTY II IN THE PAST TO IMITATE A WEAPON... AND I'M SURE YOU'RE DOING IT NOW!
THAT WAS CLOSE! BUT I'M NEAR THE ONE PLACE WHERE THEY WON'T BE ABLE TO FIND ME... MIRAGE WORLD!
I FOUND ULTRA BOY, BUT HE DIDN'T FALL FOR MY BLUFF. HE ESCAPED INTO SPACE!
IF HE'S THAT CLOSE, MAYBE I CAN CATCH HIS THOUGHTS! WAIT... I JUST GOT A FLASH OF HIS THOUGHTS BEFORE HE CLOSED HIS MIND...
ULTRA BOY'S THOUGHT WAS THAT OF AN ORANGE-COLORED PLANET AND A STRANGE PLACE OF ILLUSIONS... I DON'T UNDERSTAND IT!
BUT I DO...IT'S MIRAGE WORLD! ULTRA BOY ONCE TOLD ME ABOUT IT, BUT NEVER MENTIONED IT TO THE OTHERS!
ULTRA BOY, YOU DON'T CONSIDER ME STRANGE BECAUSE I CAN TURN INTO AN INSUBSTANTIAL PHANTOM, DO YOU?
OF COURSE NOT, PHANTOM GIRL! SOME DAY I'LL TAKE YOU TO MIRAGE WORLD, TO A PLACE NO ONE ELSE KNOWS OF, WHERE THERE'S A CITY OF GREAT PHANTOMS!
SWIFTLY, SUN BOY CALLS THE OTHER SEARCHING LEGION SHIP!
CALLING LEGION CRUISER TWO... COME IN, CRUISER TWO!
CRUISER TWO -- ELEMENT LAD SPEAKING! HAVE YOU FOUND ULTRA BOY?
6

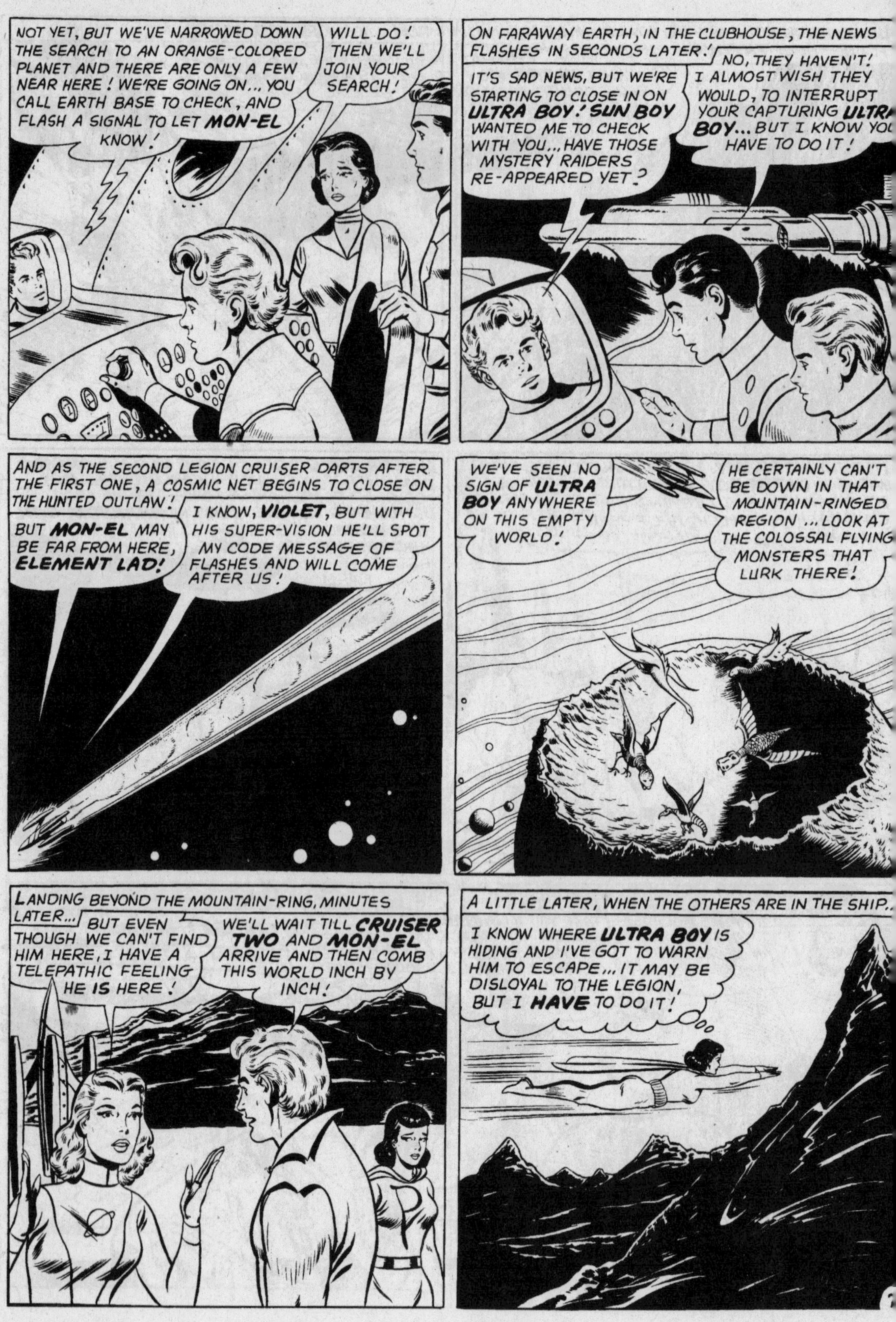
NOT YET, BUT WE'VE NARROWED DOWN THE SEARCH TO AN ORANGE-COLORED PLANET AND THERE ARE ONLY A FEW NEAR HERE! WE'RE GOING ON... YOU CALL EARTH BASE TO CHECK, AND FLASH A SIGNAL TO LET MON-EL KNOW!
WILL DO! THEN WE'LL JOIN YOUR SEARCH!
ON FARAWAY EARTH, IN THE CLUBHOUSE, THE NEWS FLASHES IN SECONDS LATER!
IT'S SAD NEWS, BUT WE'RE STARTING TO CLOSE IN ON ULTRA BOY! SUN BOY WANTED ME TO CHECK WITH YOU... HAVE THOSE MYSTERY RAIDERS RE-APPEARED YET?
NO, THEY HAVEN'T! I ALMOST WISH THEY WOULD, TO INTERRUPT YOUR CAPTURING ULTRA BOY... BUT I KNOW YOU HAVE TO DO IT!
AND AS THE SECOND LEGION CRUISER DARTS AFTER THE FIRST ONE, A COSMIC NET BEGINS TO CLOSE ON THE HUNTED OUTLAW!
BUT MON-EL MAY BE FAR FROM HERE, ELEMENT LAD!
I KNOW, VIOLET, BUT WITH HIS SUPER-VISION HE'LL SPOT MY CODE MESSAGE OF FLASHES AND WILL COME AFTER US!
WE'VE SEEN NO SIGN OF ULTRA BOY ANYWHERE ON THIS EMPTY WORLD!
HE CERTAINLY CAN'T BE DOWN IN THAT MOUNTAIN-RINGED REGION ... LOOK AT THE COLOSSAL FLYING MONSTERS THAT LURK THERE!
LANDING BEYOND THE MOUNTAIN-RING, MINUTES LATER...
BUT EVEN THOUGH WE CAN'T FIND HIM HERE, I HAVE A TELEPATHIC FEELING HE IS HERE!
WE'LL WAIT TILL CRUISER TWO AND MON-EL ARRIVE AND THEN COMB THIS WORLD INCH BY INCH!
A LITTLE LATER, WHEN THE OTHERS ARE IN THE SHIP...
I KNOW WHERE ULTRA BOY IS HIDING AND I'VE GOT TO WARN HIM TO ESCAPE... IT MAY BE DISLOYAL TO THE LEGION, BUT I HAVE TO DO IT!

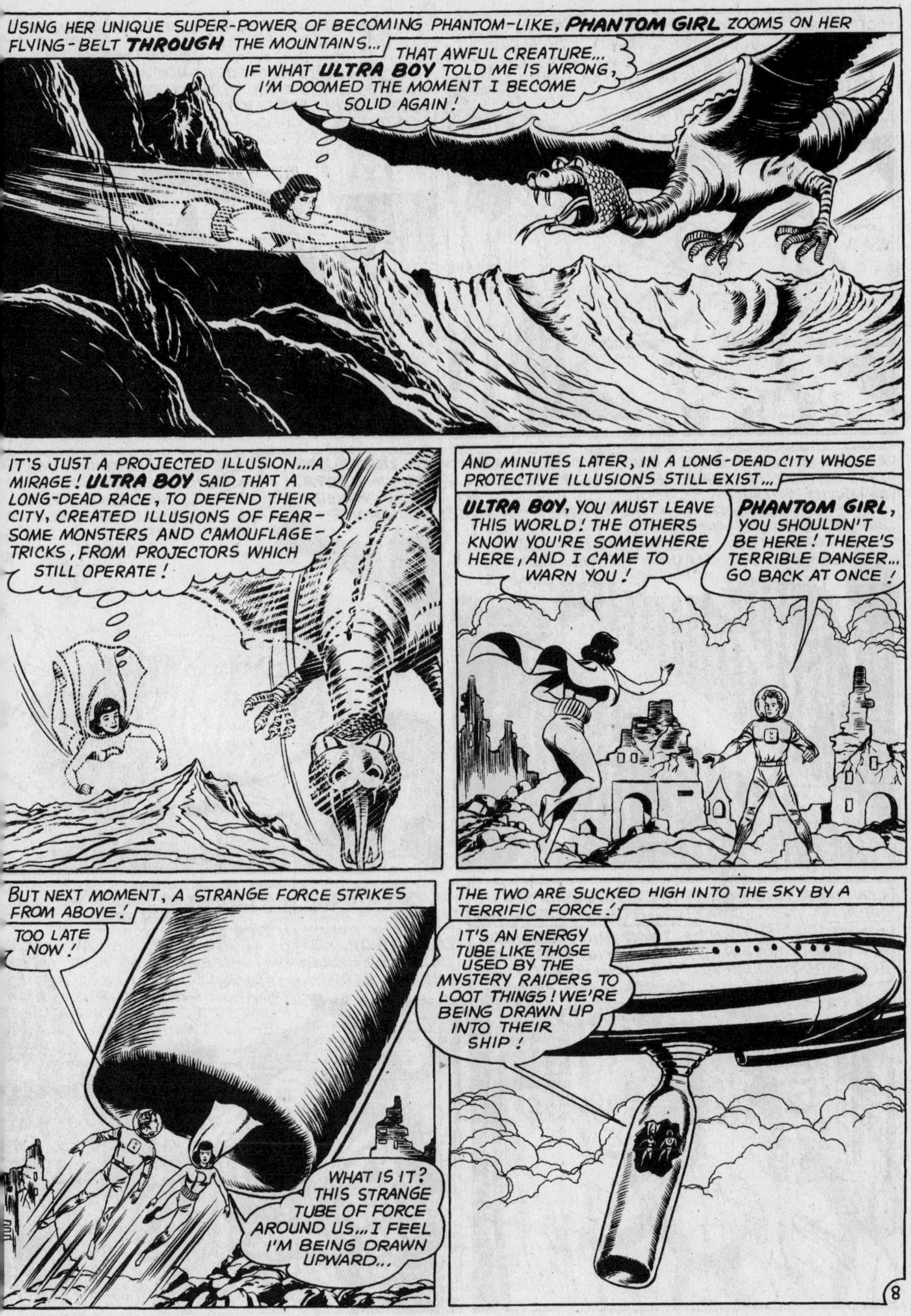
USING HER UNIQUE SUPER-POWER OF BECOMING PHANTOM-LIKE, PHANTOM GIRL ZOOMS ON HER FLYING-BELT THROUGH THE MOUNTAINS...
THAT AWFUL CREATURE... IF WHAT ULTRA BOY TOLD ME IS WRONG, I'M DOOMED THE MOMENT I BECOME SOLID AGAIN!
IT'S JUST A PROJECTED ILLUSION...A MIRAGE! ULTRA BOY SAID THAT A LONG-DEAD RACE, TO DEFEND THEIR CITY, CREATED ILLUSIONS OF FEARSOME MONSTERS AND CAMOUFLAGE-TRICKS, FROM PROJECTORS WHICH STILL OPERATE!
AND MINUTES LATER, IN A LONG-DEAD CITY WHOSE PROTECTIVE ILLUSIONS STILL EXIST...
ULTRA BOY, YOU MUST LEAVE THIS WORLD! THE OTHERS KNOW YOU'RE SOMEWHERE HERE, AND I CAME TO WARN YOU!
PHANTOM GIRL, YOU SHOULDN'T BE HERE! THERE'S TERRIBLE DANGER... GO BACK AT ONCE!
BUT NEXT MOMENT, A STRANGE FORCE STRIKES FROM ABOVE!
TOO LATE NOW!
WHAT IS IT? THIS STRANGE TUBE OF FORCE AROUND US...I FEEL I'M BEING DRAWN UPWARD...
THE TWO ARE SUCKED HIGH INTO THE SKY BY A TERRIFIC FORCE!
IT'S AN ENERGY TUBE LIKE THOSE USED BY THE MYSTERY RAIDERS TO LOOT THINGS! WE'RE BEING DRAWN UP INTO THEIR SHIP!
8

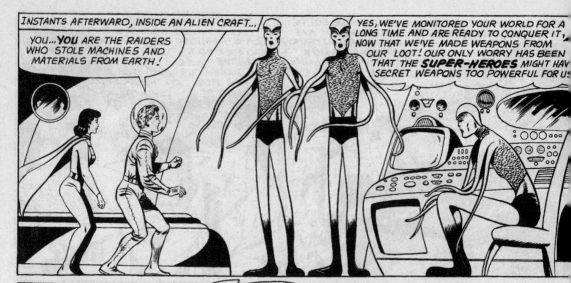

INSTANTS AFTERWARD, INSIDE AN ALIEN CRAFT...

YOU... **YOU** ARE THE RAIDERS WHO STOLE MACHINES AND MATERIALS FROM EARTH!

YES, WE'VE MONITORED YOUR WORLD FOR A LONG TIME AND ARE READY TO CONQUER IT, NOW THAT WE'VE MADE WEAPONS FROM OUR LOOT! OUR ONLY WORRY HAS BEEN THAT THE **SUPER-HEROES** MIGHT HAVE SECRET WEAPONS TOO POWERFUL FOR US!

BUT OUR MONITORS SHOWED THAT YOU, A FORMER LEGIONNAIRE, ARE NOW A HUNTED OUTLAW! JOIN US AND TELL US THE SECRETS OF THE LEGION'S WEAPONS AND YOU'LL SHARE THE VAST LOOT WE'LL TAKE FROM EARTH!

I'VE BEEN HOUNDED ACROSS THE UNIVERSE BY MY FORMER COMRADES... WHY SHOULD I HAVE LOYALTY TO THEM AND EARTH? YES, I'LL JOIN YOU!

NO, **ULTRA BOY**, YOU CAN'T COMMIT SUCH TREACHERY... YOU **CAN'T!**

TAKE ME TO EARTH AND I'LL NOT ONLY TELL YOU OF THE LEGION'S SECRET WEAPONS... I'LL SHOW YOU HOW TO SECURE AND USE THEM!

SOON, CROSSING SPACE AT TREMENDOUS SPEED, THE ALIEN CRAFT DESCENDS BY NIGHT NEAR THE LEGION CLUBHOUSE...

YOUR KNOWLEDGE ENABLED US TO PASS THROUGH ALL THE LEGION'S RADAR ALARMS! NOW WHERE ARE THEIR SECRET WEAPONS?

IN A VAULT BENEATH THE CLUBHOUSE...AND I KNOW HOW TO TURN OFF EVERY HIDDEN ALARM-DEVICE! FOLLOW ME CLOSELY...

SUPER-HEROES CLUBHOUSE

AS **COSMIC BOY** AND **BRAINIAC 5** KEEP THEIR VIGIL THE ALIENS SURPRISE THEM FROM BEHIND...

ULTRA BOY... YOU'VE BETRAYED THE LEGION AND ALL EARTH!

COME, NOW I'LL SHOW YOU HOW THESE WEAPONS WORK! THEY'RE DESIGNED NOT TO KILL, BUT TO RADIATE A FREEZING-FORCE THAT PLUNGES ANYONE WITHIN A MILE INTO AN ICY COMA!

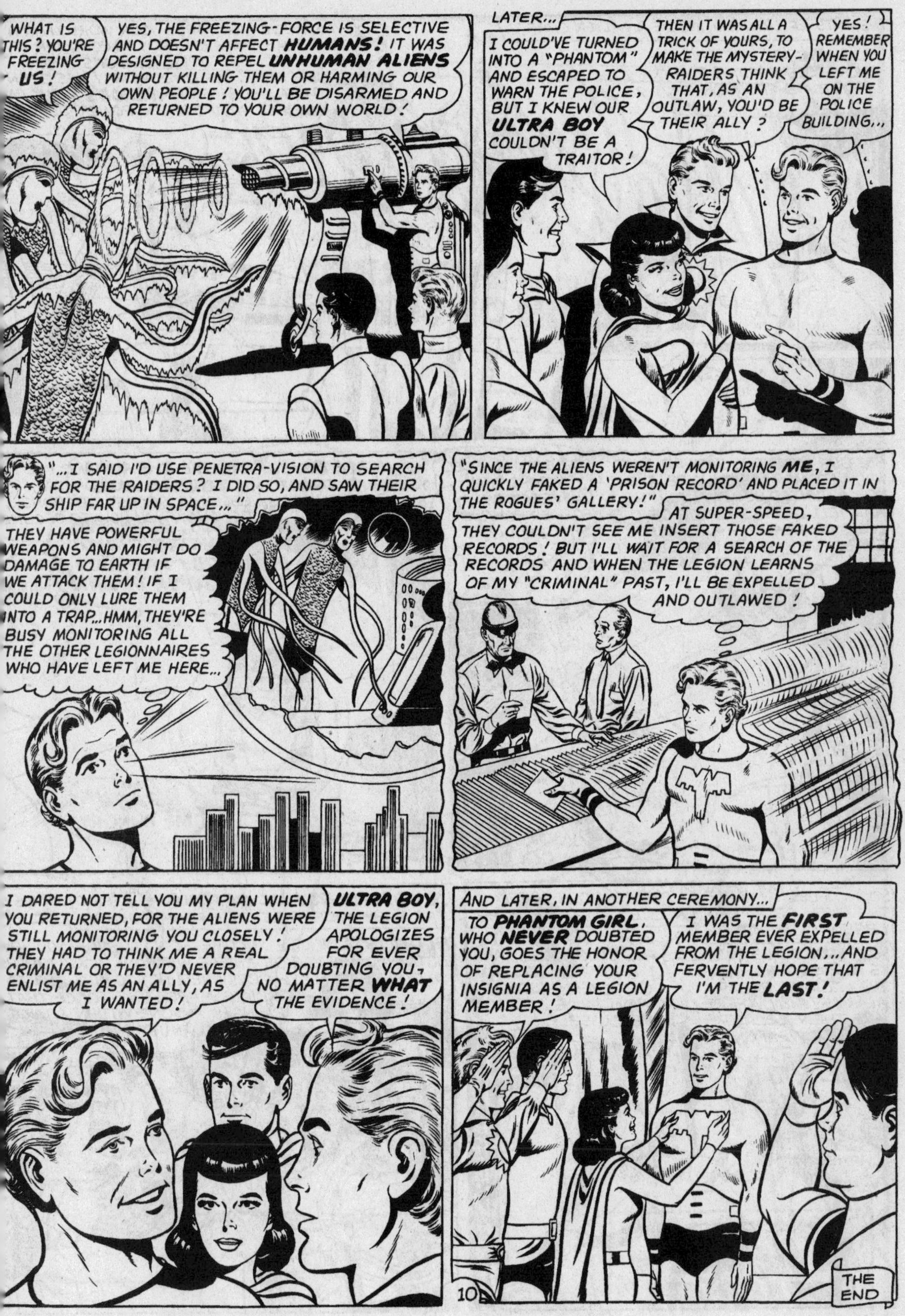
WHAT IS THIS? YOU'RE FREEZING US!
YES, THE FREEZING-FORCE IS SELECTIVE AND DOESN'T AFFECT HUMANS! IT WAS DESIGNED TO REPEL UNHUMAN ALIENS WITHOUT KILLING THEM OR HARMING OUR OWN PEOPLE! YOU'LL BE DISARMED AND RETURNED TO YOUR OWN WORLD!
LATER...
I COULD'VE TURNED INTO A "PHANTOM" AND ESCAPED TO WARN THE POLICE, BUT I KNEW OUR ULTRA BOY COULDN'T BE A TRAITOR!
THEN IT WAS ALL A TRICK OF YOURS, TO MAKE THE MYSTERY-RAIDERS THINK THAT, AS AN OUTLAW, YOU'D BE THEIR ALLY?
YES! REMEMBER WHEN YOU LEFT ME ON THE POLICE BUILDING...
"...I SAID I'D USE PENETRA-VISION TO SEARCH FOR THE RAIDERS? I DID SO, AND SAW THEIR SHIP FAR UP IN SPACE..."
THEY HAVE POWERFUL WEAPONS AND MIGHT DO DAMAGE TO EARTH IF WE ATTACK THEM! IF I COULD ONLY LURE THEM INTO A TRAP... HMM, THEY'RE BUSY MONITORING ALL THE OTHER LEGIONNAIRES WHO HAVE LEFT ME HERE...
"SINCE THE ALIENS WEREN'T MONITORING ME, I QUICKLY FAKED A 'PRISON RECORD' AND PLACED IT IN THE ROGUES' GALLERY!"
AT SUPER-SPEED, THEY COULDN'T SEE ME INSERT THOSE FAKED RECORDS! BUT I'LL WAIT FOR A SEARCH OF THE RECORDS AND WHEN THE LEGION LEARNS OF MY "CRIMINAL" PAST, I'LL BE EXPELLED AND OUTLAWED!
I DARED NOT TELL YOU MY PLAN WHEN YOU RETURNED, FOR THE ALIENS WERE STILL MONITORING YOU CLOSELY! THEY HAD TO THINK ME A REAL CRIMINAL OR THEY'D NEVER ENLIST ME AS AN ALLY, AS I WANTED!
ULTRA BOY, THE LEGION APOLOGIZES FOR EVER DOUBTING YOU, NO MATTER WHAT THE EVIDENCE!
AND LATER, IN ANOTHER CEREMONY...
TO PHANTOM GIRL, WHO NEVER DOUBTED YOU, GOES THE HONOR OF REPLACING YOUR INSIGNIA AS A LEGION MEMBER!
I WAS THE FIRST MEMBER EVER EXPELLED FROM THE LEGION... AND FERVENTLY HOPE THAT I'M THE LAST!
10
THE END

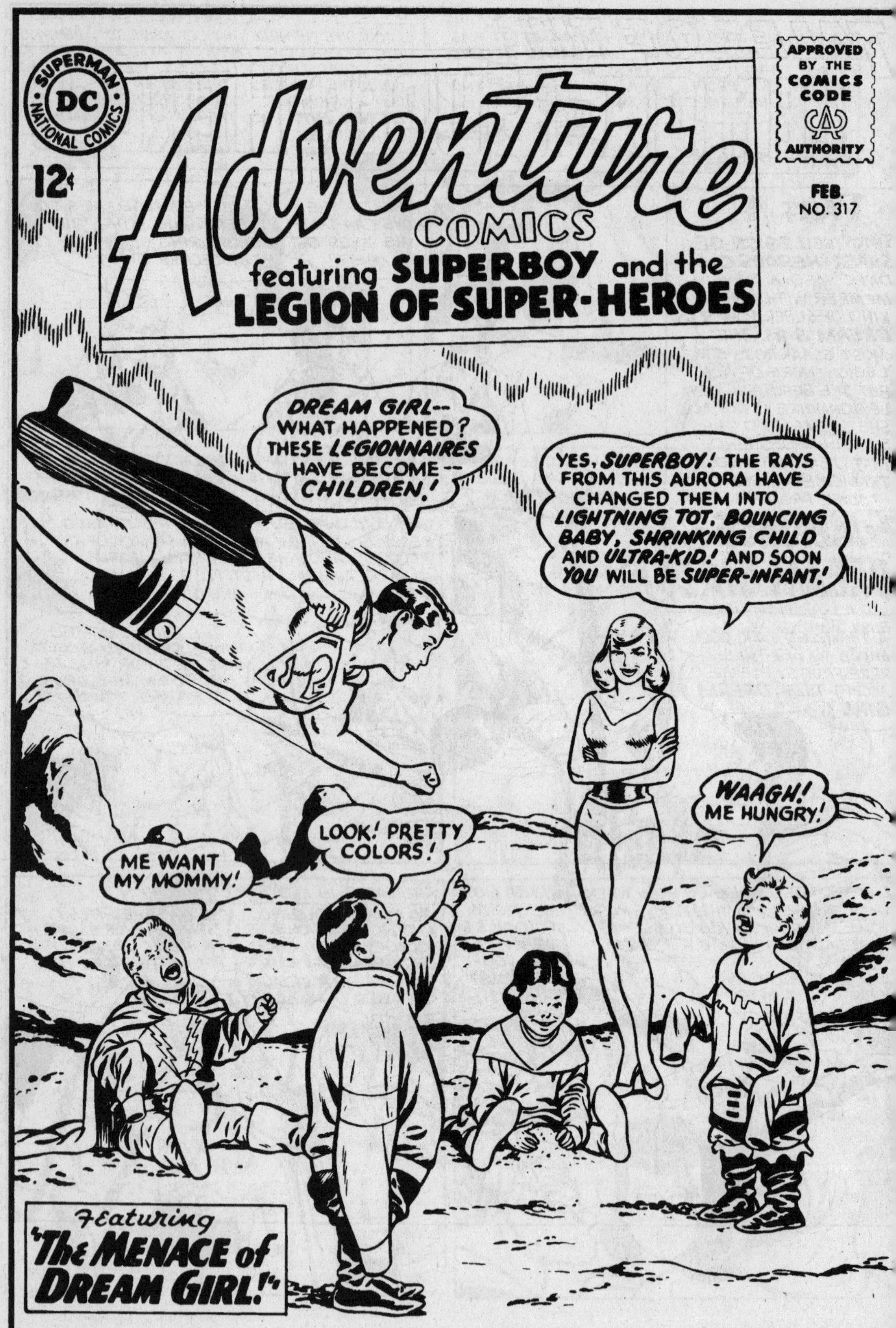

SUPERMAN DC NATIONAL COMICS
12¢
Adventure COMICS
featuring SUPERBOY and the LEGION OF SUPER-HEROES
APPROVED BY THE COMICS CODE AUTHORITY
FEB. NO. 317
DREAM GIRL-- WHAT HAPPENED? THESE LEGIONNAIRES HAVE BECOME-- CHILDREN!
YES, SUPERBOY! THE RAYS FROM THIS AURORA HAVE CHANGED THEM INTO LIGHTNING TOT, BOUNCING BABY, SHRINKING CHILD AND ULTRA-KID! AND SOON YOU WILL BE SUPER-INFANT!
ME WANT MY MOMMY!
LOOK! PRETTY COLORS!
WAAGH! ME HUNGRY!
Featuring "The MENACE of DREAM GIRL!"

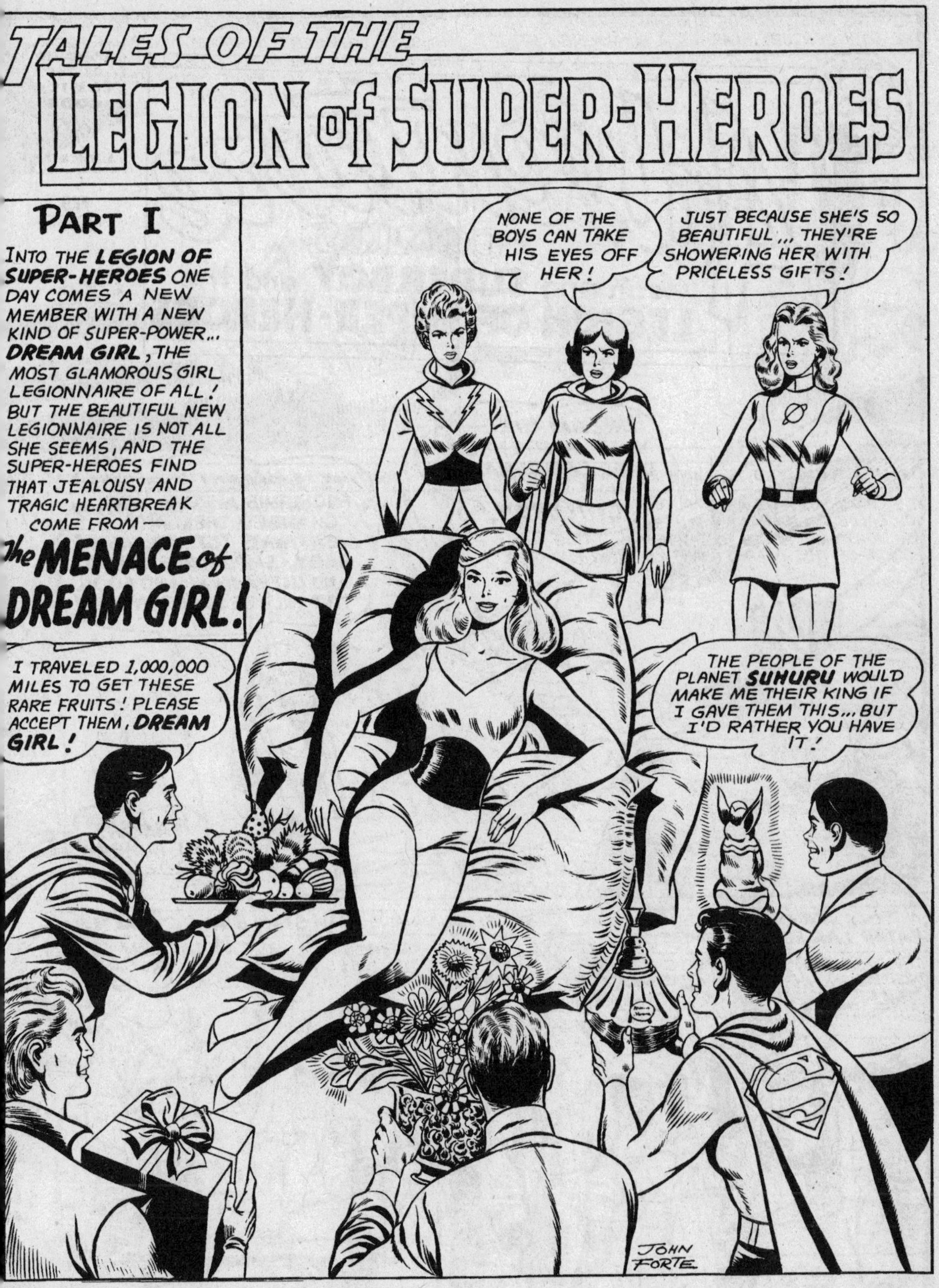
TALES OF THE
LEGION of SUPER-HEROES
PART I
INTO THE LEGION OF SUPER-HEROES ONE DAY COMES A NEW MEMBER WITH A NEW KIND OF SUPER-POWER... DREAM GIRL, THE MOST GLAMOROUS GIRL LEGIONNAIRE OF ALL! BUT THE BEAUTIFUL NEW LEGIONNAIRE IS NOT ALL SHE SEEMS, AND THE SUPER-HEROES FIND THAT JEALOUSY AND TRAGIC HEARTBREAK COME FROM —
the MENACE of DREAM GIRL!
NONE OF THE BOYS CAN TAKE HIS EYES OFF HER!
JUST BECAUSE SHE'S SO BEAUTIFUL,,, THEY'RE SHOWERING HER WITH PRICELESS GIFTS!
I TRAVELED 1,000,000 MILES TO GET THESE RARE FRUITS! PLEASE ACCEPT THEM, DREAM GIRL!
THE PEOPLE OF THE PLANET SUHURU WOULD MAKE ME THEIR KING IF I GAVE THEM THIS... BUT I'D RATHER YOU HAVE IT!
JOHN FORTE

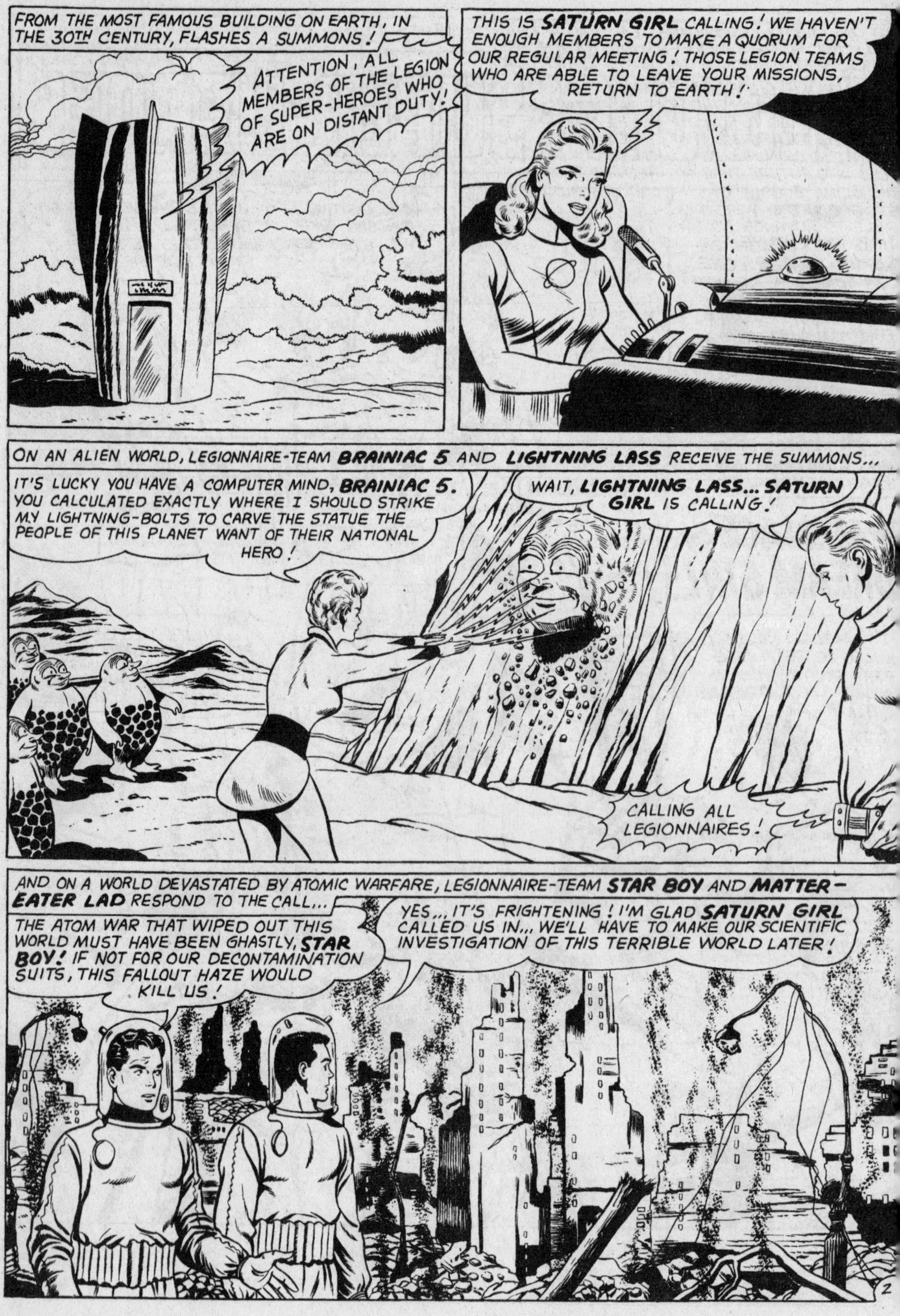
FROM THE MOST FAMOUS BUILDING ON EARTH, IN THE 30TH CENTURY, FLASHES A SUMMONS!
ATTENTION, ALL MEMBERS OF THE LEGION OF SUPER-HEROES WHO ARE ON DISTANT DUTY!
THIS IS SATURN GIRL CALLING! WE HAVEN'T ENOUGH MEMBERS TO MAKE A QUORUM FOR OUR REGULAR MEETING! THOSE LEGION TEAMS WHO ARE ABLE TO LEAVE YOUR MISSIONS, RETURN TO EARTH!
ON AN ALIEN WORLD, LEGIONNAIRE-TEAM BRAINIAC 5 AND LIGHTNING LASS RECEIVE THE SUMMONS...
IT'S LUCKY YOU HAVE A COMPUTER MIND, BRAINIAC 5. YOU CALCULATED EXACTLY WHERE I SHOULD STRIKE MY LIGHTNING-BOLTS TO CARVE THE STATUE THE PEOPLE OF THIS PLANET WANT OF THEIR NATIONAL HERO!
WAIT, LIGHTNING LASS... SATURN GIRL IS CALLING!
CALLING ALL LEGIONNAIRES!
AND ON A WORLD DEVASTATED BY ATOMIC WARFARE, LEGIONNAIRE-TEAM STAR BOY AND MATTER-EATER LAD RESPOND TO THE CALL...
THE ATOM WAR THAT WIPED OUT THIS WORLD MUST HAVE BEEN GHASTLY, STAR BOY! IF NOT FOR OUR DECONTAMINATION SUITS, THIS FALLOUT HAZE WOULD KILL US!
YES... IT'S FRIGHTENING! I'M GLAD SATURN GIRL CALLED US IN... WE'LL HAVE TO MAKE OUR SCIENTIFIC INVESTIGATION OF THIS TERRIBLE WORLD LATER!
2

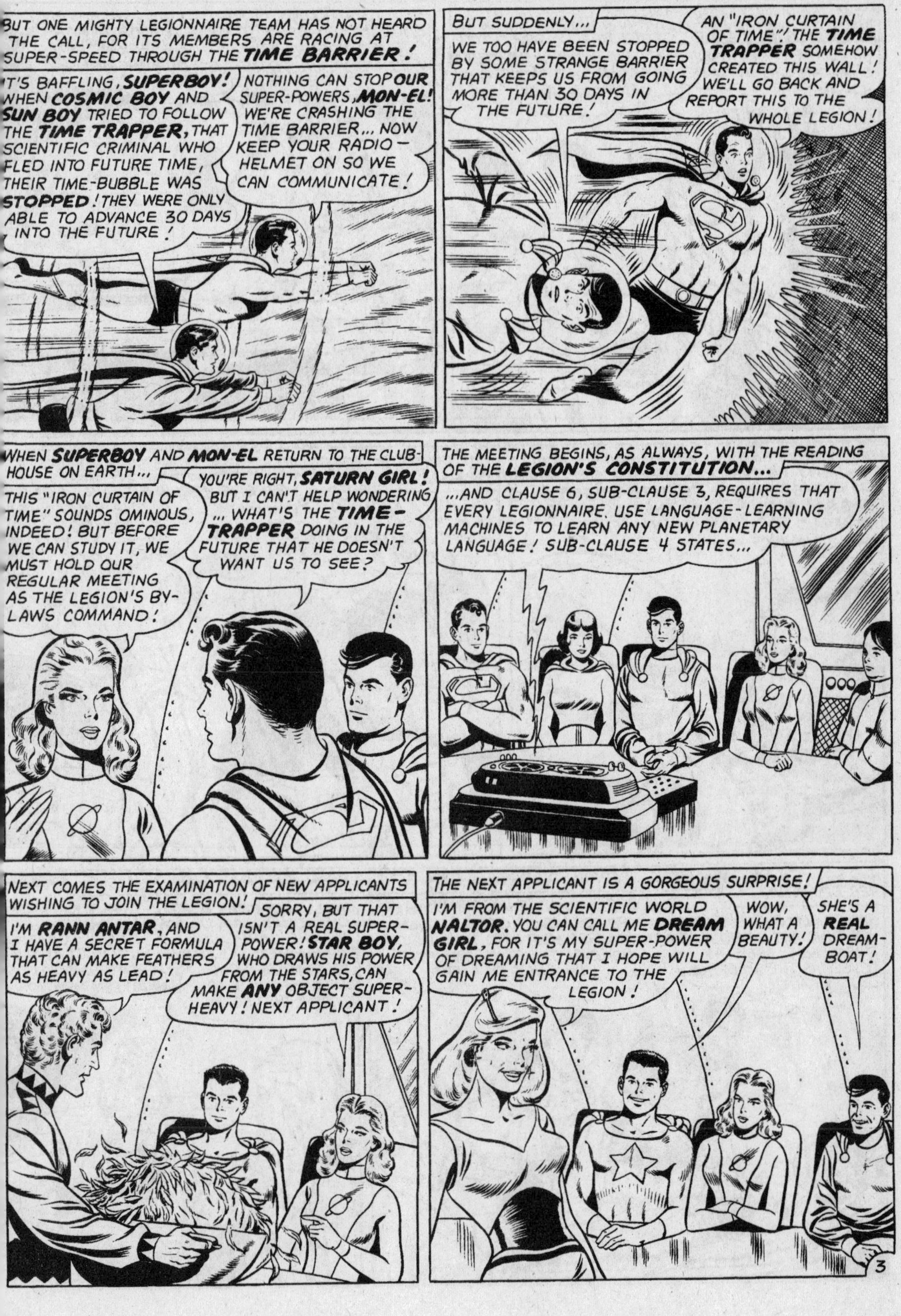
BUT ONE MIGHTY LEGIONNAIRE TEAM HAS NOT HEARD THE CALL, FOR ITS MEMBERS ARE RACING AT SUPER-SPEED THROUGH THE TIME BARRIER!
IT'S BAFFLING, SUPERBOY! WHEN COSMIC BOY AND SUN BOY TRIED TO FOLLOW THE TIME TRAPPER, THAT SCIENTIFIC CRIMINAL WHO FLED INTO FUTURE TIME, THEIR TIME-BUBBLE WAS STOPPED! THEY WERE ONLY ABLE TO ADVANCE 30 DAYS INTO THE FUTURE!
NOTHING CAN STOP OUR SUPER-POWERS, MON-EL! WE'RE CRASHING THE TIME BARRIER... NOW KEEP YOUR RADIO-HELMET ON SO WE CAN COMMUNICATE!
BUT SUDDENLY...
WE TOO HAVE BEEN STOPPED BY SOME STRANGE BARRIER THAT KEEPS US FROM GOING MORE THAN 30 DAYS IN THE FUTURE!
AN "IRON CURTAIN OF TIME"! THE TIME TRAPPER SOMEHOW CREATED THIS WALL! WE'LL GO BACK AND REPORT THIS TO THE WHOLE LEGION!
WHEN SUPERBOY AND MON-EL RETURN TO THE CLUB-HOUSE ON EARTH...
THIS "IRON CURTAIN OF TIME" SOUNDS OMINOUS, INDEED! BUT BEFORE WE CAN STUDY IT, WE MUST HOLD OUR REGULAR MEETING AS THE LEGION'S BY-LAWS COMMAND!
YOU'RE RIGHT, SATURN GIRL! BUT I CAN'T HELP WONDERING ... WHAT'S THE TIME-TRAPPER DOING IN THE FUTURE THAT HE DOESN'T WANT US TO SEE?
THE MEETING BEGINS, AS ALWAYS, WITH THE READING OF THE LEGION'S CONSTITUTION...
...AND CLAUSE 6, SUB-CLAUSE 3, REQUIRES THAT EVERY LEGIONNAIRE USE LANGUAGE-LEARNING MACHINES TO LEARN ANY NEW PLANETARY LANGUAGE! SUB-CLAUSE 4 STATES...
NEXT COMES THE EXAMINATION OF NEW APPLICANTS WISHING TO JOIN THE LEGION!
I'M RANN ANTAR, AND I HAVE A SECRET FORMULA THAT CAN MAKE FEATHERS AS HEAVY AS LEAD!
SORRY, BUT THAT ISN'T A REAL SUPER-POWER! STAR BOY, WHO DRAWS HIS POWER FROM THE STARS, CAN MAKE ANY OBJECT SUPER-HEAVY! NEXT APPLICANT!
THE NEXT APPLICANT IS A GORGEOUS SURPRISE!
I'M FROM THE SCIENTIFIC WORLD NALTOR. YOU CAN CALL ME DREAM GIRL, FOR IT'S MY SUPER-POWER OF DREAMING THAT I HOPE WILL GAIN ME ENTRANCE TO THE LEGION!
WOW, WHAT A BEAUTY!
SHE'S A REAL DREAM-BOAT!
3

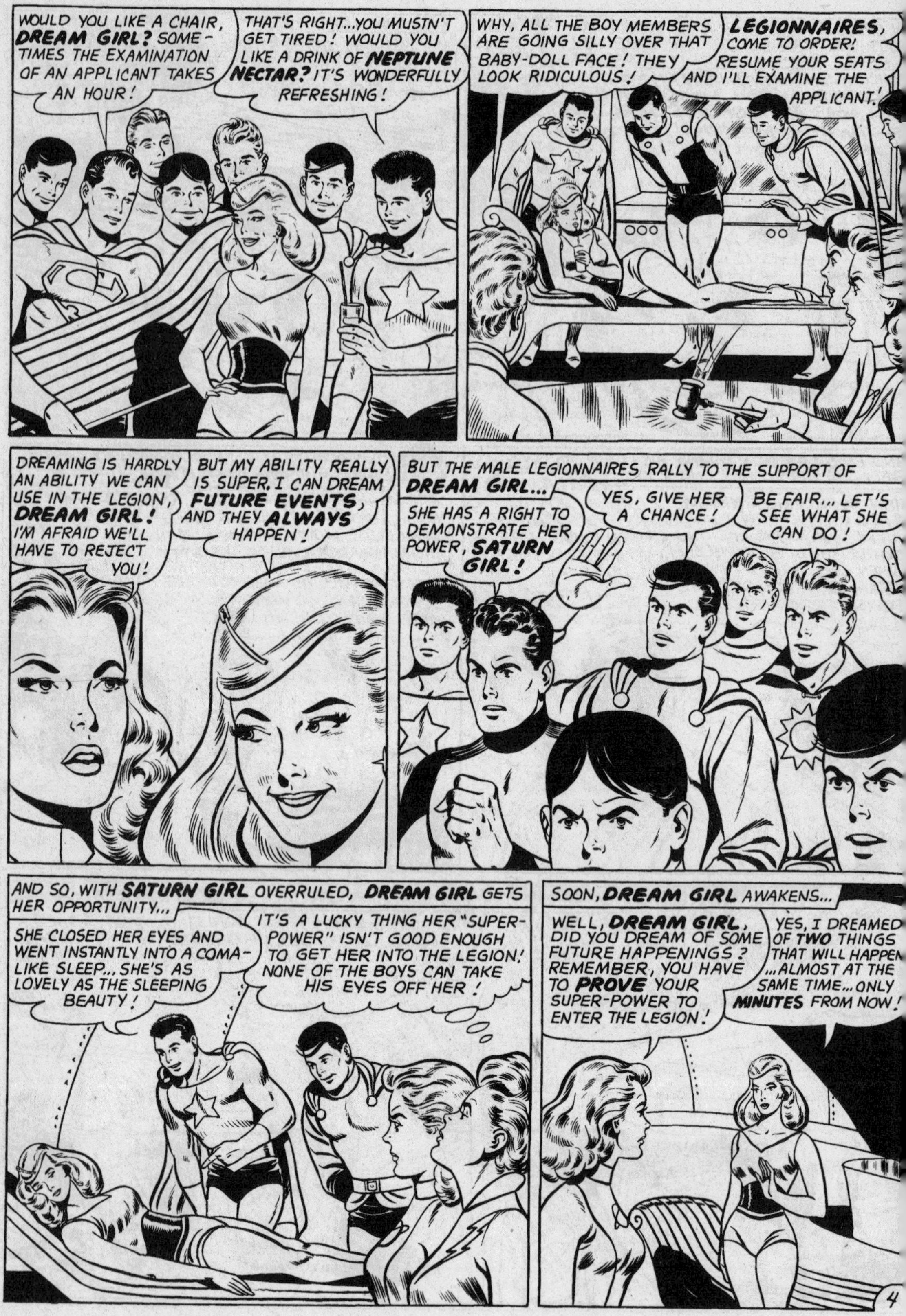
WOULD YOU LIKE A CHAIR, DREAM GIRL? SOMETIMES THE EXAMINATION OF AN APPLICANT TAKES AN HOUR!
THAT'S RIGHT...YOU MUSTN'T GET TIRED! WOULD YOU LIKE A DRINK OF NEPTUNE NECTAR? IT'S WONDERFULLY REFRESHING!
WHY, ALL THE BOY MEMBERS ARE GOING SILLY OVER THAT BABY-DOLL FACE! THEY LOOK RIDICULOUS!
LEGIONNAIRES, COME TO ORDER! RESUME YOUR SEATS AND I'LL EXAMINE THE APPLICANT!
DREAMING IS HARDLY AN ABILITY WE CAN USE IN THE LEGION, DREAM GIRL! I'M AFRAID WE'LL HAVE TO REJECT YOU!
BUT MY ABILITY REALLY IS SUPER. I CAN DREAM FUTURE EVENTS, AND THEY ALWAYS HAPPEN!
BUT THE MALE LEGIONNAIRES RALLY TO THE SUPPORT OF DREAM GIRL...
SHE HAS A RIGHT TO DEMONSTRATE HER POWER, SATURN GIRL!
YES, GIVE HER A CHANCE!
BE FAIR... LET'S SEE WHAT SHE CAN DO!
AND SO, WITH SATURN GIRL OVERRULED, DREAM GIRL GETS HER OPPORTUNITY...
SHE CLOSED HER EYES AND WENT INSTANTLY INTO A COMA-LIKE SLEEP... SHE'S AS LOVELY AS THE SLEEPING BEAUTY!
IT'S A LUCKY THING HER "SUPER-POWER" ISN'T GOOD ENOUGH TO GET HER INTO THE LEGION! NONE OF THE BOYS CAN TAKE HIS EYES OFF HER!
SOON, DREAM GIRL AWAKENS...
WELL, DREAM GIRL, DID YOU DREAM OF SOME FUTURE HAPPENINGS? REMEMBER, YOU HAVE TO PROVE YOUR SUPER-POWER TO ENTER THE LEGION!
YES, I DREAMED OF TWO THINGS THAT WILL HAPPEN ...ALMOST AT THE SAME TIME... ONLY MINUTES FROM NOW!
4

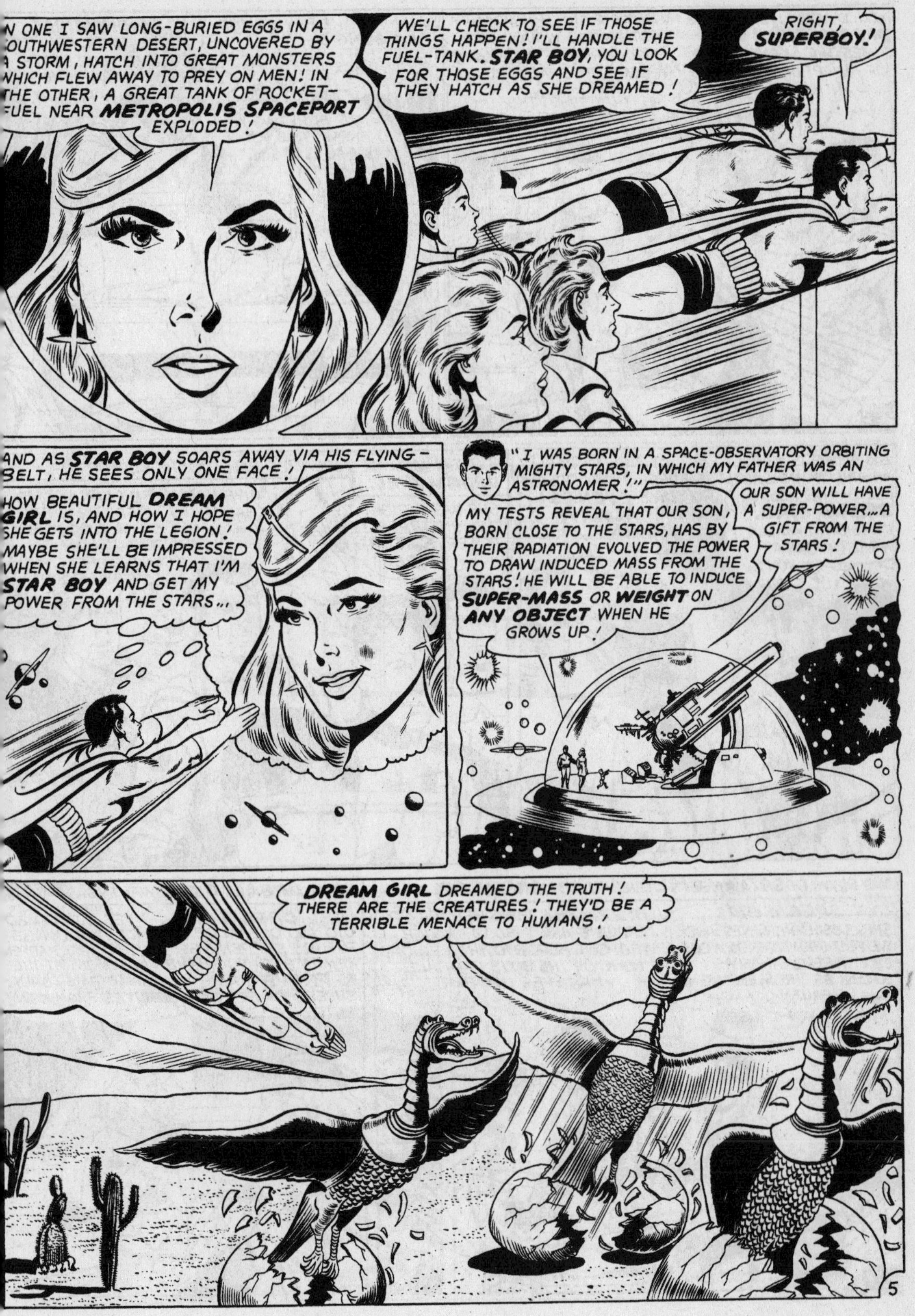
N ONE I SAW LONG-BURIED EGGS IN A OUTHWESTERN DESERT, UNCOVERED BY A STORM, HATCH INTO GREAT MONSTERS WHICH FLEW AWAY TO PREY ON MEN! IN THE OTHER, A GREAT TANK OF ROCKET-FUEL NEAR METROPOLIS SPACEPORT EXPLODED!
WE'LL CHECK TO SEE IF THOSE THINGS HAPPEN! I'LL HANDLE THE FUEL-TANK. STAR BOY, YOU LOOK FOR THOSE EGGS AND SEE IF THEY HATCH AS SHE DREAMED!
RIGHT, SUPERBOY!
AND AS STAR BOY SOARS AWAY VIA HIS FLYING-BELT, HE SEES ONLY ONE FACE!
HOW BEAUTIFUL DREAM GIRL IS, AND HOW I HOPE SHE GETS INTO THE LEGION! MAYBE SHE'LL BE IMPRESSED WHEN SHE LEARNS THAT I'M STAR BOY AND GET MY POWER FROM THE STARS...
"I WAS BORN IN A SPACE-OBSERVATORY ORBITING MIGHTY STARS, IN WHICH MY FATHER WAS AN ASTRONOMER!"
MY TESTS REVEAL THAT OUR SON, BORN CLOSE TO THE STARS, HAS BY THEIR RADIATION EVOLVED THE POWER TO DRAW INDUCED MASS FROM THE STARS! HE WILL BE ABLE TO INDUCE SUPER-MASS OR WEIGHT ON ANY OBJECT WHEN HE GROWS UP!
OUR SON WILL HAVE A SUPER-POWER... A GIFT FROM THE STARS!
DREAM GIRL DREAMED THE TRUTH! THERE ARE THE CREATURES! THEY'D BE A TERRIBLE MENACE TO HUMANS!
5

BUT BY PROJECTING MY STORED-UP INDUCED MASS INTO THOSE CREATURES, I'VE MADE THEM SO SUPER-HEAVY THEY CAN'T FLY! THE EFFECT ALWAYS PASSES AWAY IN A FEW HOURS, BUT BY THAT TIME, THE **SCIENCE POLICE** WILL HAVE THEM SAFELY CAGED!

ALMOST AT THE SAME TIME, ABOVE **METROPOLIS SPACEPORT**...

THE FUEL-TANK WAS JUST ON THE POINT OF EXPLODING...BUT I HURLED IT INTO THE SKY WHERE ITS BURSTING WILL DO NO HARM! THIS PROOF OF **DREAM GIRL'S** SUPER-POWER WILL SURELY WIN HER LEGION MEMBERSHIP!

METROPOLIS SPACEPORT

LATER, WHEN A SOLEMN VOTE OF THE LEGION IS TAKEN...

YOU'VE BEEN VOTED INTO THE LEGION, **DREAM GIRL!** CONGRATULATIONS! IT'LL BE GREAT, HAVING YOU WITH US!

NONE OF US GIRLS VOTED FOR HER, BUT THEY'RE ALL DAZZLED BY HER PRETTY FACE! WELL, WE HAVE TO OBEY THE **LEGION CONSTITUTION**, SO SHE'S A FULL-FLEDGED MEMBER NOW!

YES	YES	YES	NO	YES
YES	NO	YES	YES	YES
NO	YES	YES	NO	YES

THE NEW LEGIONNAIRE GETS PLENTY OF ATTENTION!

LOOK, **DREAM GIRL**... THIS DIAGRAM SHOWS OUR SECRET MONITOR DEVICES THAT PREVENT ANY PROWLER FROM ENTERING THE CLUBHOUSE! YOU MUST LEARN THESE!

LET **ME** SHOW YOU THE LEGION'S ARSENAL OF WEAPONS, **DREAM GIRL!**

BESIDES OUR POWERFUL WEAPONS HERE, WE MAINTAIN DEFENSIVE WEAPONS IN MANY OTHER PLACES! THERE'S THE **SOLAR SATELLITE** FOR USE IN **DEFENSE PLAN 44**, THE ROCKET HIDDEN IN THE ASTEROIDS FOR **PLAN 78**...

PLEASE,...I'LL LEARN ALL THIS LATER! I WANT TO STUDY THE LEGION'S CONSTITUTION FIRST!

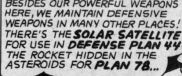

PLAN 78

6

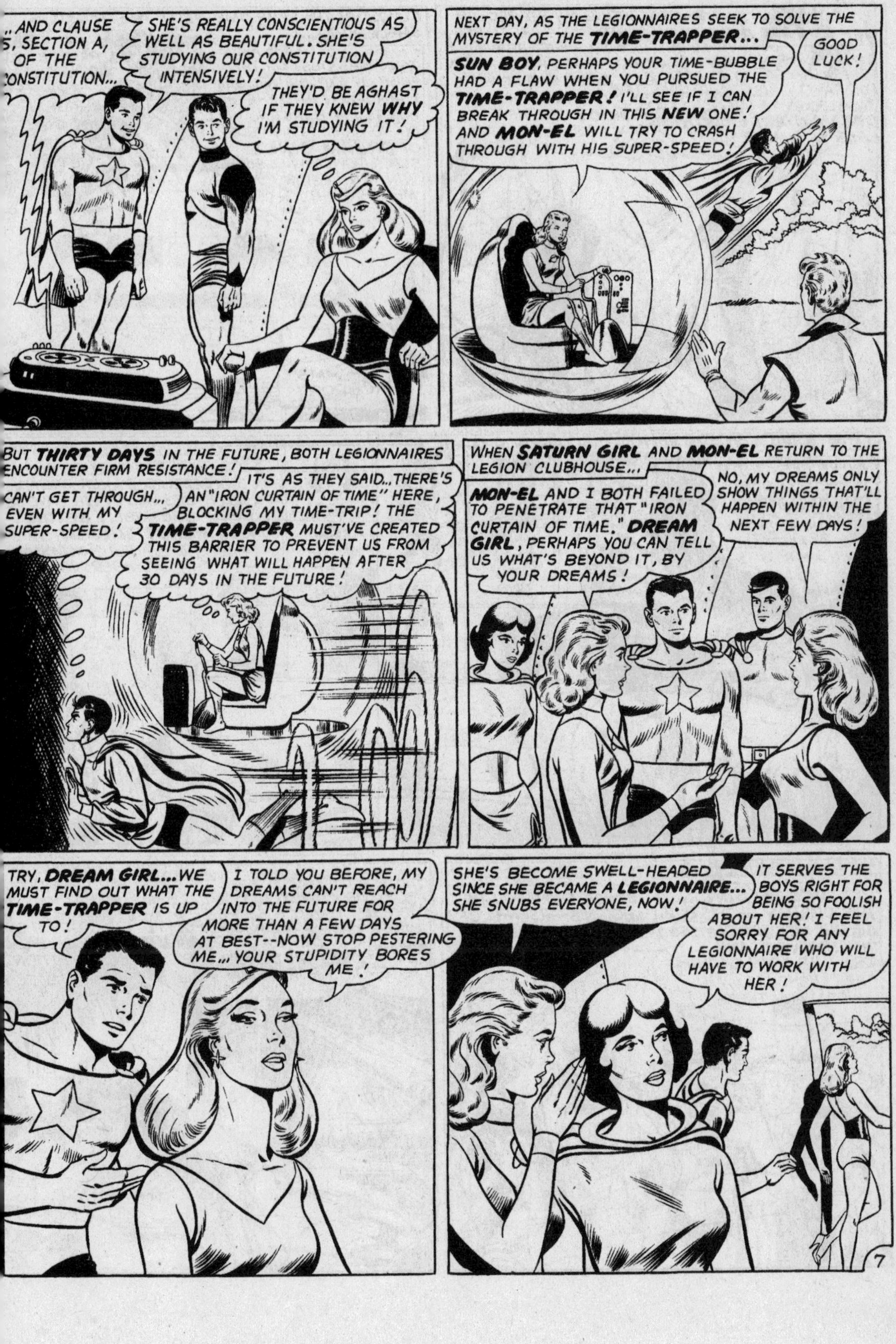
..AND CLAUSE 5, SECTION A, OF THE CONSTITUTION...
SHE'S REALLY CONSCIENTIOUS AS WELL AS BEAUTIFUL. SHE'S STUDYING OUR CONSTITUTION INTENSIVELY!
THEY'D BE AGHAST IF THEY KNEW WHY I'M STUDYING IT!
NEXT DAY, AS THE LEGIONNAIRES SEEK TO SOLVE THE MYSTERY OF THE TIME-TRAPPER...
SUN BOY, PERHAPS YOUR TIME-BUBBLE HAD A FLAW WHEN YOU PURSUED THE TIME-TRAPPER! I'LL SEE IF I CAN BREAK THROUGH IN THIS NEW ONE! AND MON-EL WILL TRY TO CRASH THROUGH WITH HIS SUPER-SPEED!
GOOD LUCK!
BUT THIRTY DAYS IN THE FUTURE, BOTH LEGIONNAIRES ENCOUNTER FIRM RESISTANCE!
CAN'T GET THROUGH... EVEN WITH MY SUPER-SPEED!
IT'S AS THEY SAID...THERE'S AN "IRON CURTAIN OF TIME" HERE, BLOCKING MY TIME-TRIP! THE TIME-TRAPPER MUST'VE CREATED THIS BARRIER TO PREVENT US FROM SEEING WHAT WILL HAPPEN AFTER 30 DAYS IN THE FUTURE!
WHEN SATURN GIRL AND MON-EL RETURN TO THE LEGION CLUBHOUSE...
MON-EL AND I BOTH FAILED TO PENETRATE THAT "IRON CURTAIN OF TIME." DREAM GIRL, PERHAPS YOU CAN TELL US WHAT'S BEYOND IT, BY YOUR DREAMS!
NO, MY DREAMS ONLY SHOW THINGS THAT'LL HAPPEN WITHIN THE NEXT FEW DAYS!
TRY, DREAM GIRL...WE MUST FIND OUT WHAT THE TIME-TRAPPER IS UP TO!
I TOLD YOU BEFORE, MY DREAMS CAN'T REACH INTO THE FUTURE FOR MORE THAN A FEW DAYS AT BEST--NOW STOP PESTERING ME... YOUR STUPIDITY BORES ME!
SHE'S BECOME SWELL-HEADED SINCE SHE BECAME A LEGIONNAIRE... SHE SNUBS EVERYONE, NOW!
IT SERVES THE BOYS RIGHT FOR BEING SO FOOLISH ABOUT HER! I FEEL SORRY FOR ANY LEGIONNAIRE WHO WILL HAVE TO WORK WITH HER!
7

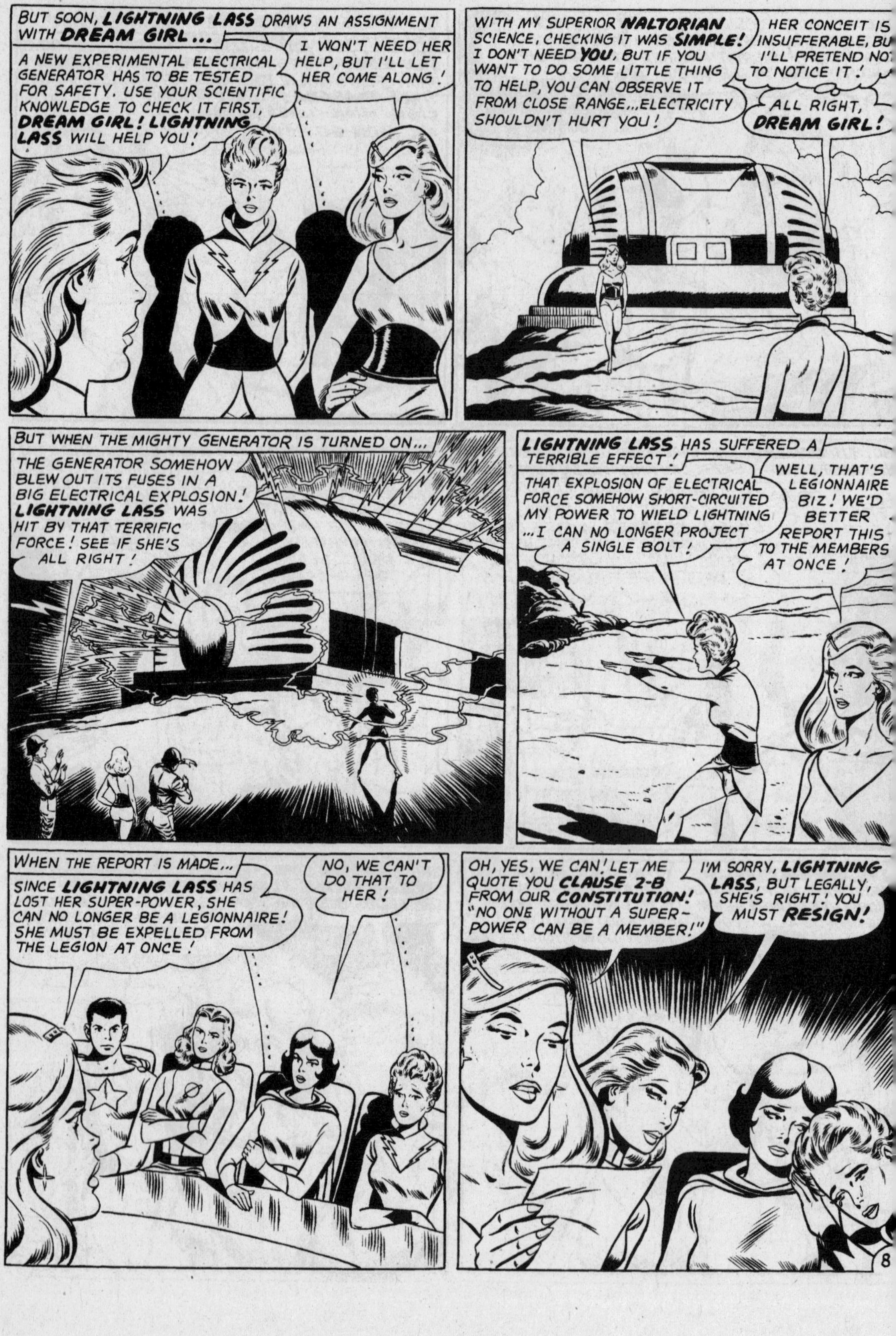
BUT SOON, LIGHTNING LASS DRAWS AN ASSIGNMENT WITH DREAM GIRL...
A NEW EXPERIMENTAL ELECTRICAL GENERATOR HAS TO BE TESTED FOR SAFETY. USE YOUR SCIENTIFIC KNOWLEDGE TO CHECK IT FIRST, DREAM GIRL! LIGHTNING LASS WILL HELP YOU!
I WON'T NEED HER HELP, BUT I'LL LET HER COME ALONG!
WITH MY SUPERIOR NALTORIAN SCIENCE, CHECKING IT WAS SIMPLE! I DON'T NEED YOU, BUT IF YOU WANT TO DO SOME LITTLE THING TO HELP, YOU CAN OBSERVE IT FROM CLOSE RANGE... ELECTRICITY SHOULDN'T HURT YOU!
HER CONCEIT IS INSUFFERABLE, BU I'LL PRETEND NO TO NOTICE IT!
ALL RIGHT, DREAM GIRL!
BUT WHEN THE MIGHTY GENERATOR IS TURNED ON...
THE GENERATOR SOMEHOW BLEW OUT ITS FUSES IN A BIG ELECTRICAL EXPLOSION! LIGHTNING LASS WAS HIT BY THAT TERRIFIC FORCE! SEE IF SHE'S ALL RIGHT!
LIGHTNING LASS HAS SUFFERED A TERRIBLE EFFECT!
THAT EXPLOSION OF ELECTRICAL FORCE SOMEHOW SHORT-CIRCUITED MY POWER TO WIELD LIGHTNING ...I CAN NO LONGER PROJECT A SINGLE BOLT!
WELL, THAT'S LEGIONNAIRE BIZ! WE'D BETTER REPORT THIS TO THE MEMBERS AT ONCE!
WHEN THE REPORT IS MADE...
SINCE LIGHTNING LASS HAS LOST HER SUPER-POWER, SHE CAN NO LONGER BE A LEGIONNAIRE! SHE MUST BE EXPELLED FROM THE LEGION AT ONCE!
NO, WE CAN'T DO THAT TO HER!
OH, YES, WE CAN! LET ME QUOTE YOU CLAUSE 2-B FROM OUR CONSTITUTION! "NO ONE WITHOUT A SUPER-POWER CAN BE A MEMBER!"
I'M SORRY, LIGHTNING LASS, BUT LEGALLY, SHE'S RIGHT! YOU MUST RESIGN!
8

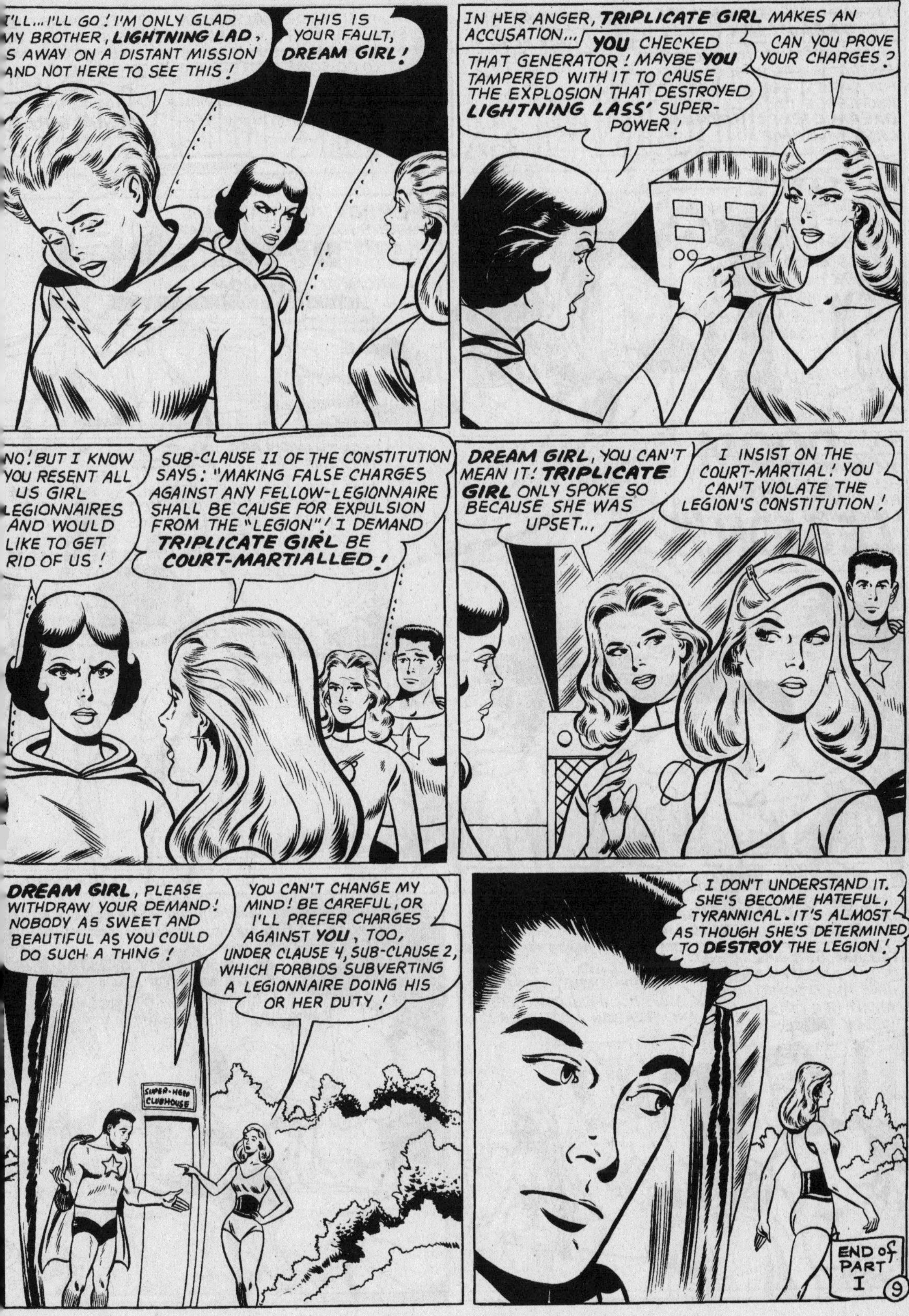
I'LL... I'LL GO! I'M ONLY GLAD MY BROTHER, LIGHTNING LAD, IS AWAY ON A DISTANT MISSION AND NOT HERE TO SEE THIS!
THIS IS YOUR FAULT, DREAM GIRL!
IN HER ANGER, TRIPLICATE GIRL MAKES AN ACCUSATION...
YOU CHECKED THAT GENERATOR! MAYBE YOU TAMPERED WITH IT TO CAUSE THE EXPLOSION THAT DESTROYED LIGHTNING LASS' SUPER-POWER!
CAN YOU PROVE YOUR CHARGES?
NO! BUT I KNOW YOU RESENT ALL US GIRL LEGIONNAIRES AND WOULD LIKE TO GET RID OF US!
SUB-CLAUSE 11 OF THE CONSTITUTION SAYS: "MAKING FALSE CHARGES AGAINST ANY FELLOW-LEGIONNAIRE SHALL BE CAUSE FOR EXPULSION FROM THE "LEGION"! I DEMAND TRIPLICATE GIRL BE COURT-MARTIALLED!
DREAM GIRL, YOU CAN'T MEAN IT! TRIPLICATE GIRL ONLY SPOKE SO BECAUSE SHE WAS UPSET...
I INSIST ON THE COURT-MARTIAL! YOU CAN'T VIOLATE THE LEGION'S CONSTITUTION!
DREAM GIRL, PLEASE WITHDRAW YOUR DEMAND! NOBODY AS SWEET AND BEAUTIFUL AS YOU COULD DO SUCH A THING!
YOU CAN'T CHANGE MY MIND! BE CAREFUL, OR I'LL PREFER CHARGES AGAINST YOU, TOO, UNDER CLAUSE 4, SUB-CLAUSE 2, WHICH FORBIDS SUBVERTING A LEGIONNAIRE DOING HIS OR HER DUTY!
SUPER-HERO CLUBHOUSE
I DON'T UNDERSTAND IT. SHE'S BECOME HATEFUL, TYRANNICAL. IT'S ALMOST AS THOUGH SHE'S DETERMINED TO DESTROY THE LEGION!
END of PART I
9

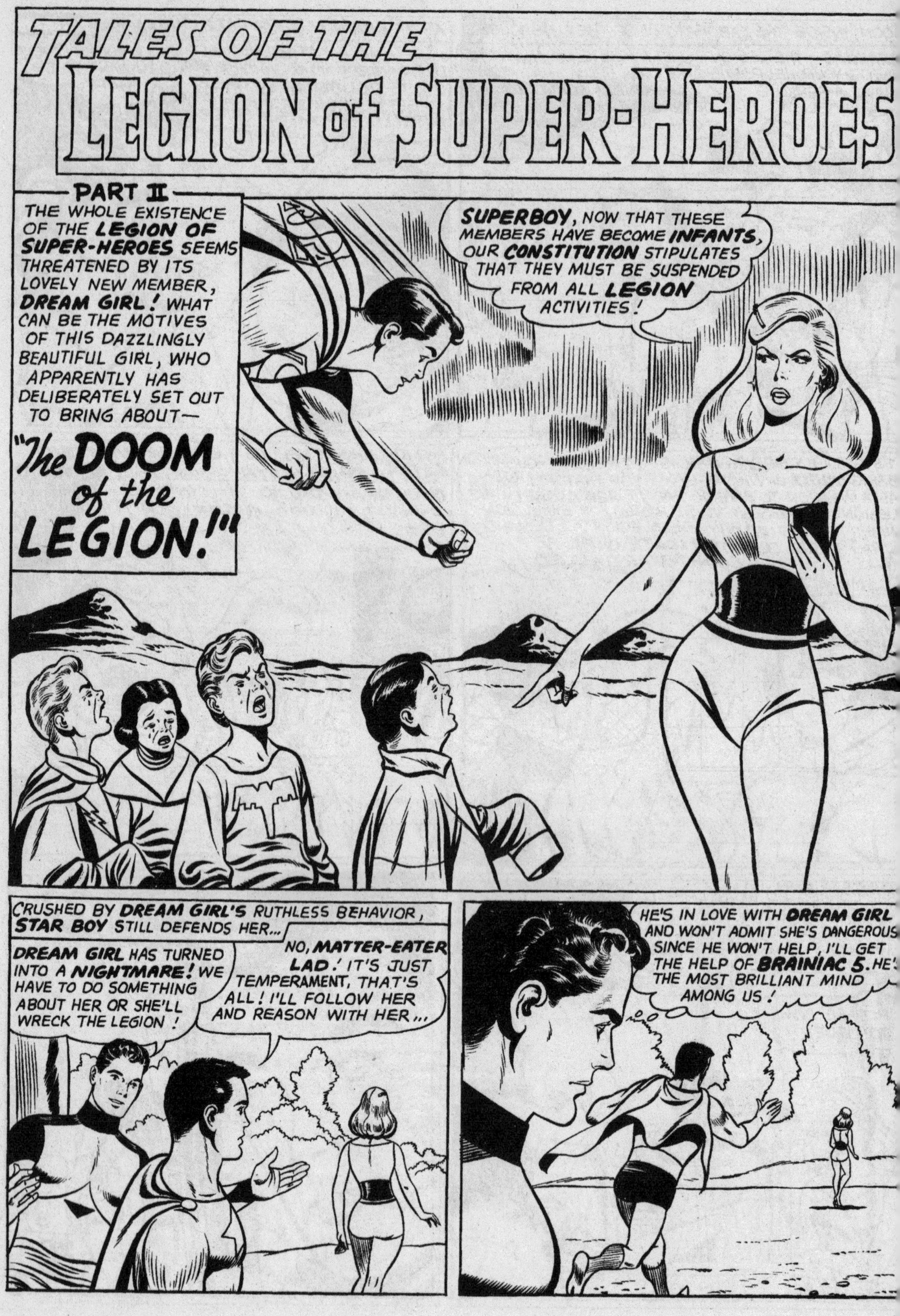
TALES OF THE
LEGION of SUPER-HEROES
PART II
THE WHOLE EXISTENCE OF THE LEGION OF SUPER-HEROES SEEMS THREATENED BY ITS LOVELY NEW MEMBER, DREAM GIRL! WHAT CAN BE THE MOTIVES OF THIS DAZZLINGLY BEAUTIFUL GIRL, WHO APPARENTLY HAS DELIBERATELY SET OUT TO BRING ABOUT—
"The DOOM of the LEGION!"
SUPERBOY, NOW THAT THESE MEMBERS HAVE BECOME INFANTS, OUR CONSTITUTION STIPULATES THAT THEY MUST BE SUSPENDED FROM ALL LEGION ACTIVITIES!
CRUSHED BY DREAM GIRL'S RUTHLESS BEHAVIOR, STAR BOY STILL DEFENDS HER...
DREAM GIRL HAS TURNED INTO A NIGHTMARE! WE HAVE TO DO SOMETHING ABOUT HER OR SHE'LL WRECK THE LEGION!
NO, MATTER-EATER LAD! IT'S JUST TEMPERAMENT, THAT'S ALL! I'LL FOLLOW HER AND REASON WITH HER...
HE'S IN LOVE WITH DREAM GIRL AND WON'T ADMIT SHE'S DANGEROUS! SINCE HE WON'T HELP, I'LL GET THE HELP OF BRAINIAC 5. HE'S THE MOST BRILLIANT MIND AMONG US!

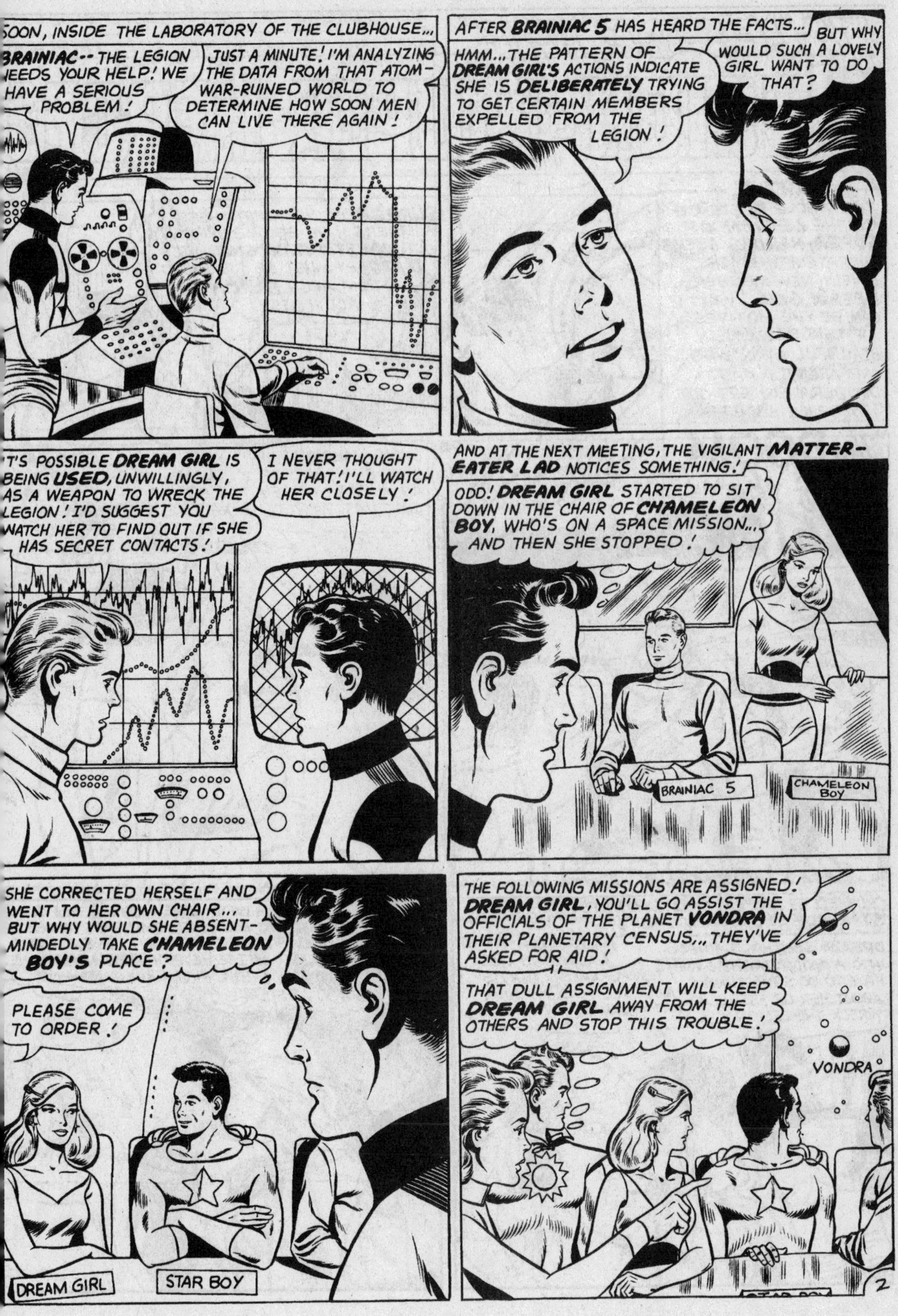
SOON, INSIDE THE LABORATORY OF THE CLUBHOUSE...
BRAINIAC-- THE LEGION NEEDS YOUR HELP! WE HAVE A SERIOUS PROBLEM!
JUST A MINUTE! I'M ANALYZING THE DATA FROM THAT ATOM-WAR-RUINED WORLD TO DETERMINE HOW SOON MEN CAN LIVE THERE AGAIN!
AFTER BRAINIAC 5 HAS HEARD THE FACTS...
HMM...THE PATTERN OF DREAM GIRL'S ACTIONS INDICATE SHE IS DELIBERATELY TRYING TO GET CERTAIN MEMBERS EXPELLED FROM THE LEGION!
BUT WHY WOULD SUCH A LOVELY GIRL WANT TO DO THAT?
IT'S POSSIBLE DREAM GIRL IS BEING USED, UNWILLINGLY, AS A WEAPON TO WRECK THE LEGION! I'D SUGGEST YOU WATCH HER TO FIND OUT IF SHE HAS SECRET CONTACTS!
I NEVER THOUGHT OF THAT! I'LL WATCH HER CLOSELY!
AND AT THE NEXT MEETING, THE VIGILANT MATTER-EATER LAD NOTICES SOMETHING!
ODD! DREAM GIRL STARTED TO SIT DOWN IN THE CHAIR OF CHAMELEON BOY, WHO'S ON A SPACE MISSION... AND THEN SHE STOPPED!
BRAINIAC 5
CHAMELEON BOY
SHE CORRECTED HERSELF AND WENT TO HER OWN CHAIR... BUT WHY WOULD SHE ABSENT-MINDEDLY TAKE CHAMELEON BOY'S PLACE?
PLEASE COME TO ORDER!
DREAM GIRL
STAR BOY
THE FOLLOWING MISSIONS ARE ASSIGNED! DREAM GIRL, YOU'LL GO ASSIST THE OFFICIALS OF THE PLANET VONDRA IN THEIR PLANETARY CENSUS... THEY'VE ASKED FOR AID!
THAT DULL ASSIGNMENT WILL KEEP DREAM GIRL AWAY FROM THE OTHERS AND STOP THIS TROUBLE!
VONDRA
2

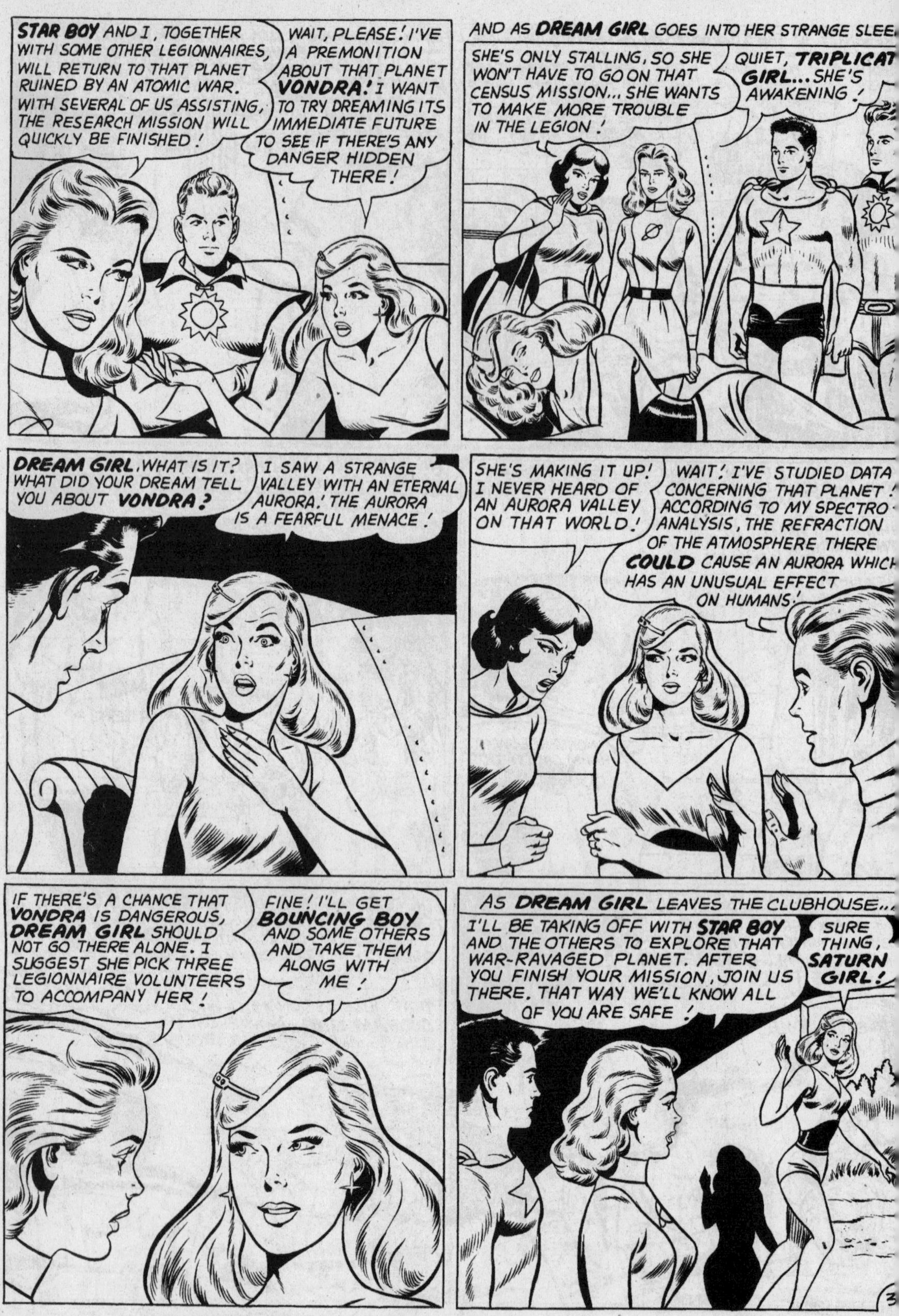
STAR BOY AND I, TOGETHER WITH SOME OTHER LEGIONNAIRES, WILL RETURN TO THAT PLANET RUINED BY AN ATOMIC WAR. WITH SEVERAL OF US ASSISTING, THE RESEARCH MISSION WILL QUICKLY BE FINISHED!
WAIT, PLEASE! I'VE A PREMONITION ABOUT THAT PLANET VONDRA! I WANT TO TRY DREAMING ITS IMMEDIATE FUTURE TO SEE IF THERE'S ANY DANGER HIDDEN THERE!
AND AS DREAM GIRL GOES INTO HER STRANGE SLEE
SHE'S ONLY STALLING, SO SHE WON'T HAVE TO GO ON THAT CENSUS MISSION... SHE WANTS TO MAKE MORE TROUBLE IN THE LEGION!
QUIET, TRIPLICAT GIRL... SHE'S AWAKENING!
DREAM GIRL, WHAT IS IT? WHAT DID YOUR DREAM TELL YOU ABOUT VONDRA?
I SAW A STRANGE VALLEY WITH AN ETERNAL AURORA! THE AURORA IS A FEARFUL MENACE!
SHE'S MAKING IT UP! I NEVER HEARD OF AN AURORA VALLEY ON THAT WORLD!
WAIT! I'VE STUDIED DATA CONCERNING THAT PLANET! ACCORDING TO MY SPECTRO-ANALYSIS, THE REFRACTION OF THE ATMOSPHERE THERE COULD CAUSE AN AURORA WHICH HAS AN UNUSUAL EFFECT ON HUMANS!
IF THERE'S A CHANCE THAT VONDRA IS DANGEROUS, DREAM GIRL SHOULD NOT GO THERE ALONE. I SUGGEST SHE PICK THREE LEGIONNAIRE VOLUNTEERS TO ACCOMPANY HER!
FINE! I'LL GET BOUNCING BOY AND SOME OTHERS AND TAKE THEM ALONG WITH ME!
AS DREAM GIRL LEAVES THE CLUBHOUSE...
I'LL BE TAKING OFF WITH STAR BOY AND THE OTHERS TO EXPLORE THAT WAR-RAVAGED PLANET. AFTER YOU FINISH YOUR MISSION, JOIN US THERE. THAT WAY WE'LL KNOW ALL OF YOU ARE SAFE!
SURE THING, SATURN GIRL!
3

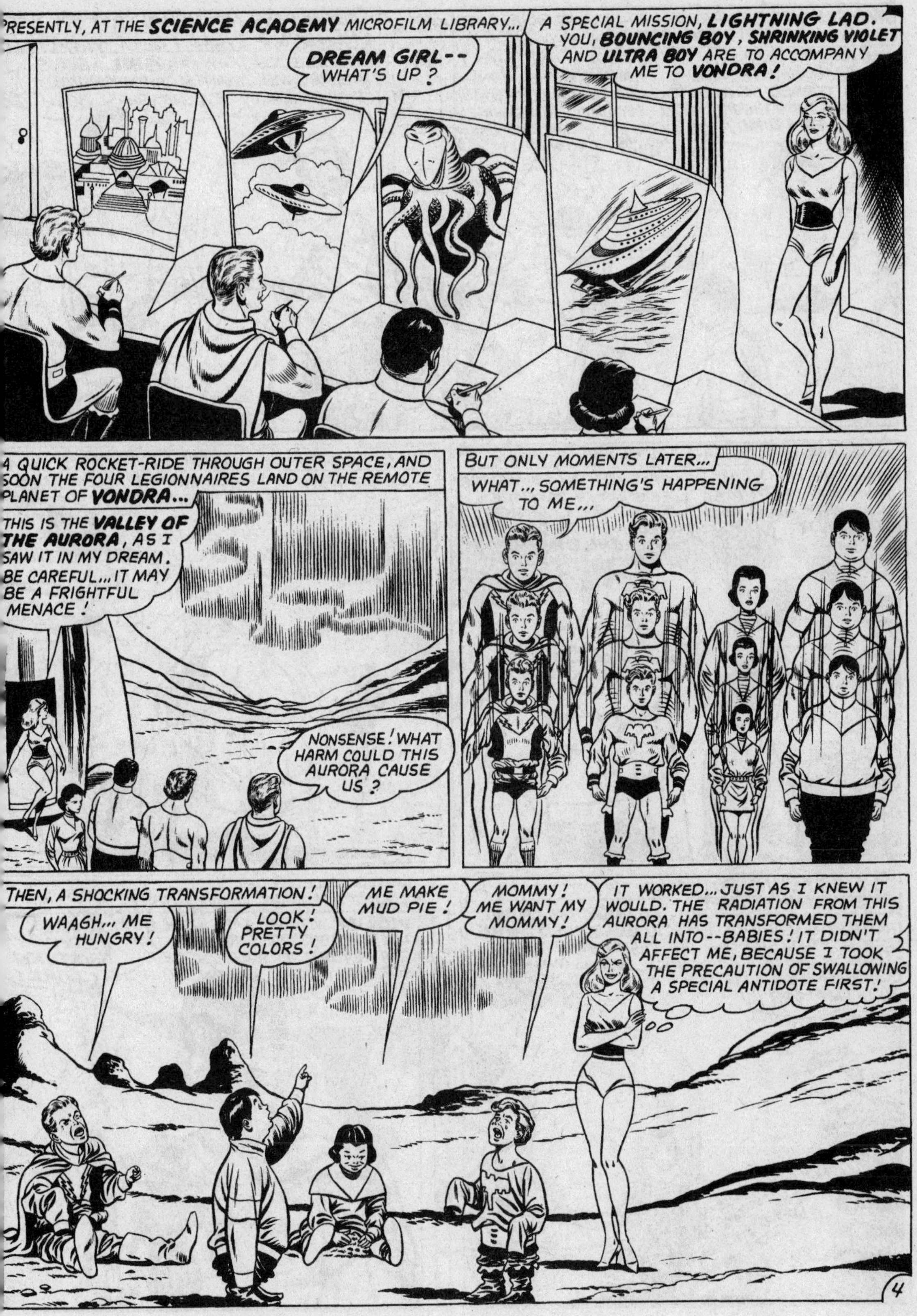
PRESENTLY, AT THE SCIENCE ACADEMY MICROFILM LIBRARY...
DREAM GIRL-- WHAT'S UP?
A SPECIAL MISSION, LIGHTNING LAD. YOU, BOUNCING BOY, SHRINKING VIOLET AND ULTRA BOY ARE TO ACCOMPANY ME TO VONDRA!
A QUICK ROCKET-RIDE THROUGH OUTER SPACE, AND SOON THE FOUR LEGIONNAIRES LAND ON THE REMOTE PLANET OF VONDRA...
THIS IS THE VALLEY OF THE AURORA, AS I SAW IT IN MY DREAM. BE CAREFUL... IT MAY BE A FRIGHTFUL MENACE!
NONSENSE! WHAT HARM COULD THIS AURORA CAUSE US?
BUT ONLY MOMENTS LATER...
WHAT..., SOMETHING'S HAPPENING TO ME...
THEN, A SHOCKING TRANSFORMATION!
WAAGH... ME HUNGRY!
LOOK! PRETTY COLORS!
ME MAKE MUD PIE!
MOMMY! ME WANT MY MOMMY!
IT WORKED... JUST AS I KNEW IT WOULD. THE RADIATION FROM THIS AURORA HAS TRANSFORMED THEM ALL INTO--BABIES! IT DIDN'T AFFECT ME, BECAUSE I TOOK THE PRECAUTION OF SWALLOWING A SPECIAL ANTIDOTE FIRST!
4

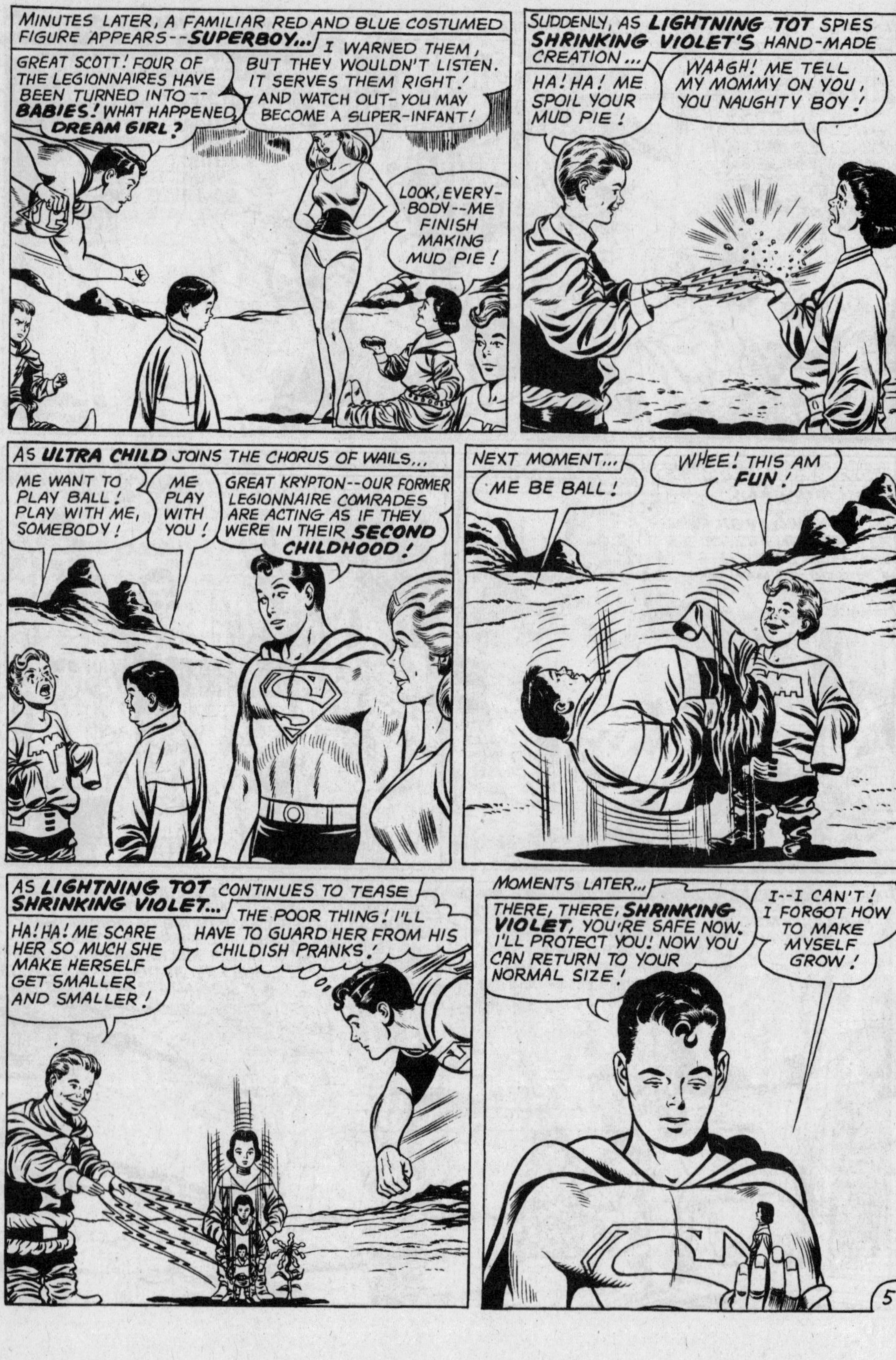
MINUTES LATER, A FAMILIAR RED AND BLUE COSTUMED FIGURE APPEARS--SUPERBOY...
GREAT SCOTT! FOUR OF THE LEGIONNAIRES HAVE BEEN TURNED INTO--BABIES! WHAT HAPPENED, DREAM GIRL?
I WARNED THEM, BUT THEY WOULDN'T LISTEN. IT SERVES THEM RIGHT! AND WATCH OUT- YOU MAY BECOME A SUPER-INFANT!
LOOK, EVERY-BODY--ME FINISH MAKING MUD PIE!
SUDDENLY, AS LIGHTNING TOT SPIES SHRINKING VIOLET'S HAND-MADE CREATION...
HA! HA! ME SPOIL YOUR MUD PIE!
WAAGH! ME TELL MY MOMMY ON YOU, YOU NAUGHTY BOY!
AS ULTRA CHILD JOINS THE CHORUS OF WAILS...
ME WANT TO PLAY BALL! PLAY WITH ME, SOMEBODY!
ME PLAY WITH YOU!
GREAT KRYPTON--OUR FORMER LEGIONNAIRE COMRADES ARE ACTING AS IF THEY WERE IN THEIR SECOND CHILDHOOD!
NEXT MOMENT...
ME BE BALL!
WHEE! THIS AM FUN!
AS LIGHTNING TOT CONTINUES TO TEASE SHRINKING VIOLET...
HA! HA! ME SCARE HER SO MUCH SHE MAKE HERSELF GET SMALLER AND SMALLER!
THE POOR THING! I'LL HAVE TO GUARD HER FROM HIS CHILDISH PRANKS!
MOMENTS LATER...
THERE, THERE, SHRINKING VIOLET, YOU'RE SAFE NOW. I'LL PROTECT YOU! NOW YOU CAN RETURN TO YOUR NORMAL SIZE!
I--I CAN'T! I FORGOT HOW TO MAKE MYSELF GROW!
5

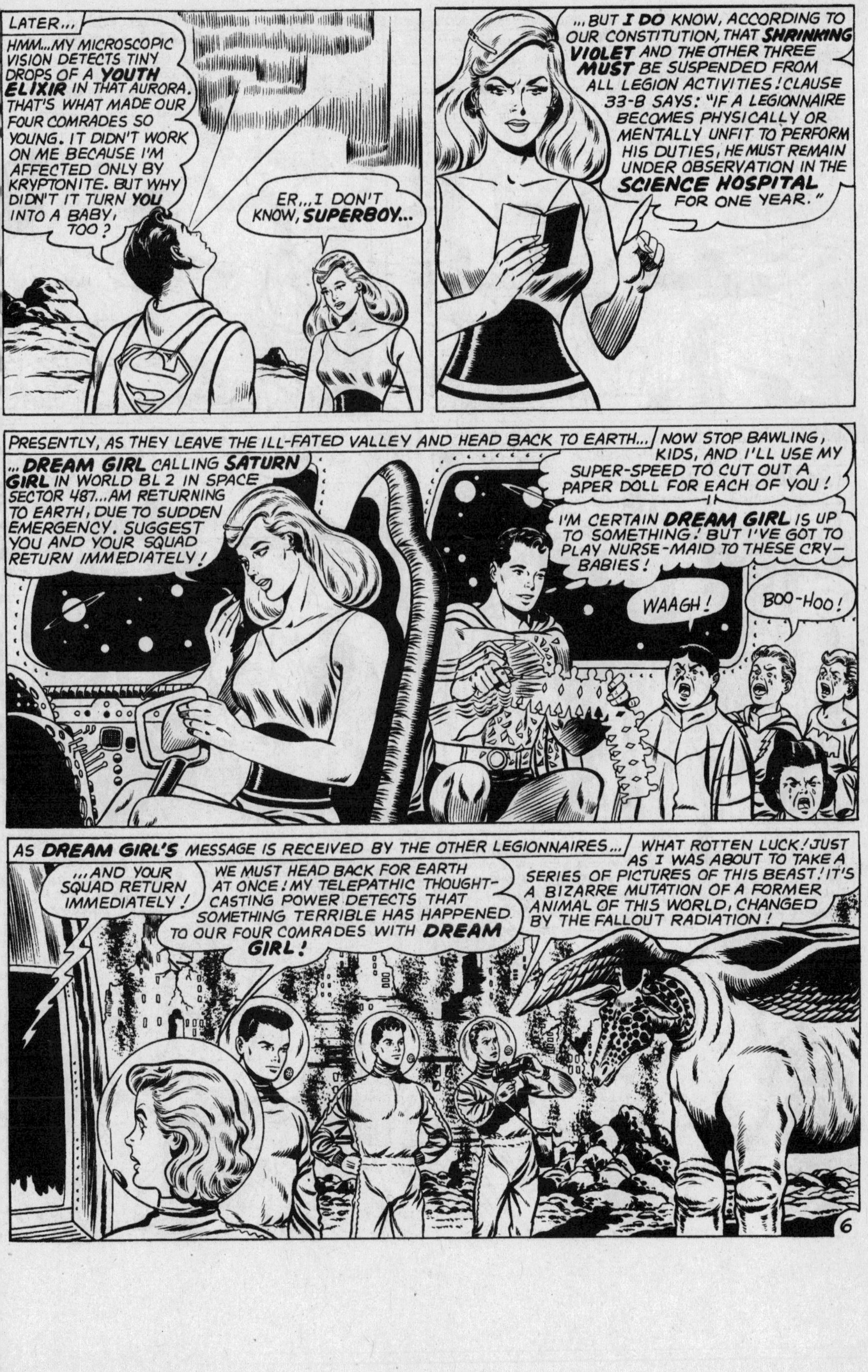
LATER...
HMM...MY MICROSCOPIC VISION DETECTS TINY DROPS OF A YOUTH ELIXIR IN THAT AURORA. THAT'S WHAT MADE OUR FOUR COMRADES SO YOUNG. IT DIDN'T WORK ON ME BECAUSE I'M AFFECTED ONLY BY KRYPTONITE. BUT WHY DIDN'T IT TURN YOU INTO A BABY, TOO?
ER...I DON'T KNOW, SUPERBOY...
...BUT I DO KNOW, ACCORDING TO OUR CONSTITUTION, THAT SHRINKING VIOLET AND THE OTHER THREE MUST BE SUSPENDED FROM ALL LEGION ACTIVITIES! CLAUSE 33-B SAYS: "IF A LEGIONNAIRE BECOMES PHYSICALLY OR MENTALLY UNFIT TO PERFORM HIS DUTIES, HE MUST REMAIN UNDER OBSERVATION IN THE SCIENCE HOSPITAL FOR ONE YEAR."
PRESENTLY, AS THEY LEAVE THE ILL-FATED VALLEY AND HEAD BACK TO EARTH...
...DREAM GIRL CALLING SATURN GIRL IN WORLD BL 2 IN SPACE SECTOR 487...AM RETURNING TO EARTH, DUE TO SUDDEN EMERGENCY. SUGGEST YOU AND YOUR SQUAD RETURN IMMEDIATELY!
NOW STOP BAWLING, KIDS, AND I'LL USE MY SUPER-SPEED TO CUT OUT A PAPER DOLL FOR EACH OF YOU!
I'M CERTAIN DREAM GIRL IS UP TO SOMETHING! BUT I'VE GOT TO PLAY NURSE-MAID TO THESE CRY-BABIES!
WAAGH!
BOO-HOO!
AS DREAM GIRL'S MESSAGE IS RECEIVED BY THE OTHER LEGIONNAIRES...
...AND YOUR SQUAD RETURN IMMEDIATELY!
WE MUST HEAD BACK FOR EARTH AT ONCE! MY TELEPATHIC THOUGHT-CASTING POWER DETECTS THAT SOMETHING TERRIBLE HAS HAPPENED TO OUR FOUR COMRADES WITH DREAM GIRL!
WHAT ROTTEN LUCK! JUST AS I WAS ABOUT TO TAKE A SERIES OF PICTURES OF THIS BEAST! IT'S A BIZARRE MUTATION OF A FORMER ANIMAL OF THIS WORLD, CHANGED BY THE FALLOUT RADIATION!
6

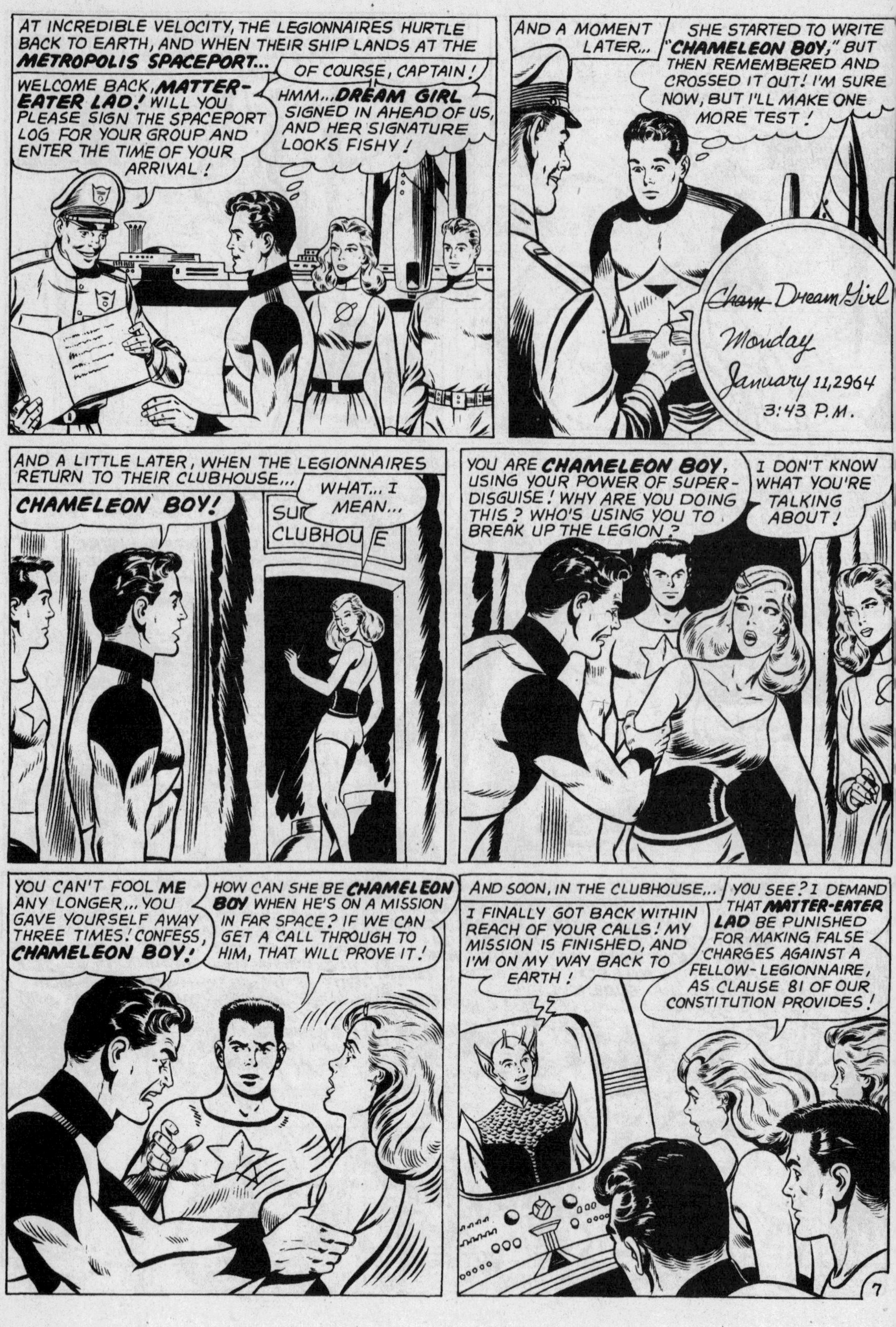
AT INCREDIBLE VELOCITY, THE LEGIONNAIRES HURTLE BACK TO EARTH, AND WHEN THEIR SHIP LANDS AT THE METROPOLIS SPACEPORT...
WELCOME BACK, MATTER-EATER LAD! WILL YOU PLEASE SIGN THE SPACEPORT LOG FOR YOUR GROUP AND ENTER THE TIME OF YOUR ARRIVAL!
OF COURSE, CAPTAIN!
HMM... DREAM GIRL SIGNED IN AHEAD OF US, AND HER SIGNATURE LOOKS FISHY!
AND A MOMENT LATER...
SHE STARTED TO WRITE "CHAMELEON BOY," BUT THEN REMEMBERED AND CROSSED IT OUT! I'M SURE NOW, BUT I'LL MAKE ONE MORE TEST!
~~Cham~~ Dream Girl
Monday
January 11, 2964
3:43 P.M.
AND A LITTLE LATER, WHEN THE LEGIONNAIRES RETURN TO THEIR CLUBHOUSE...
CHAMELEON BOY!
WHAT... I MEAN...
CLUBHOUSE
YOU ARE CHAMELEON BOY, USING YOUR POWER OF SUPER-DISGUISE! WHY ARE YOU DOING THIS? WHO'S USING YOU TO BREAK UP THE LEGION?
I DON'T KNOW WHAT YOU'RE TALKING ABOUT!
YOU CAN'T FOOL ME ANY LONGER... YOU GAVE YOURSELF AWAY THREE TIMES! CONFESS, CHAMELEON BOY!
HOW CAN SHE BE CHAMELEON BOY WHEN HE'S ON A MISSION IN FAR SPACE? IF WE CAN GET A CALL THROUGH TO HIM, THAT WILL PROVE IT!
AND SOON, IN THE CLUBHOUSE...
I FINALLY GOT BACK WITHIN REACH OF YOUR CALLS! MY MISSION IS FINISHED, AND I'M ON MY WAY BACK TO EARTH!
YOU SEE? I DEMAND THAT MATTER-EATER LAD BE PUNISHED FOR MAKING FALSE CHARGES AGAINST A FELLOW-LEGIONNAIRE, AS CLAUSE 81 OF OUR CONSTITUTION PROVIDES!
7

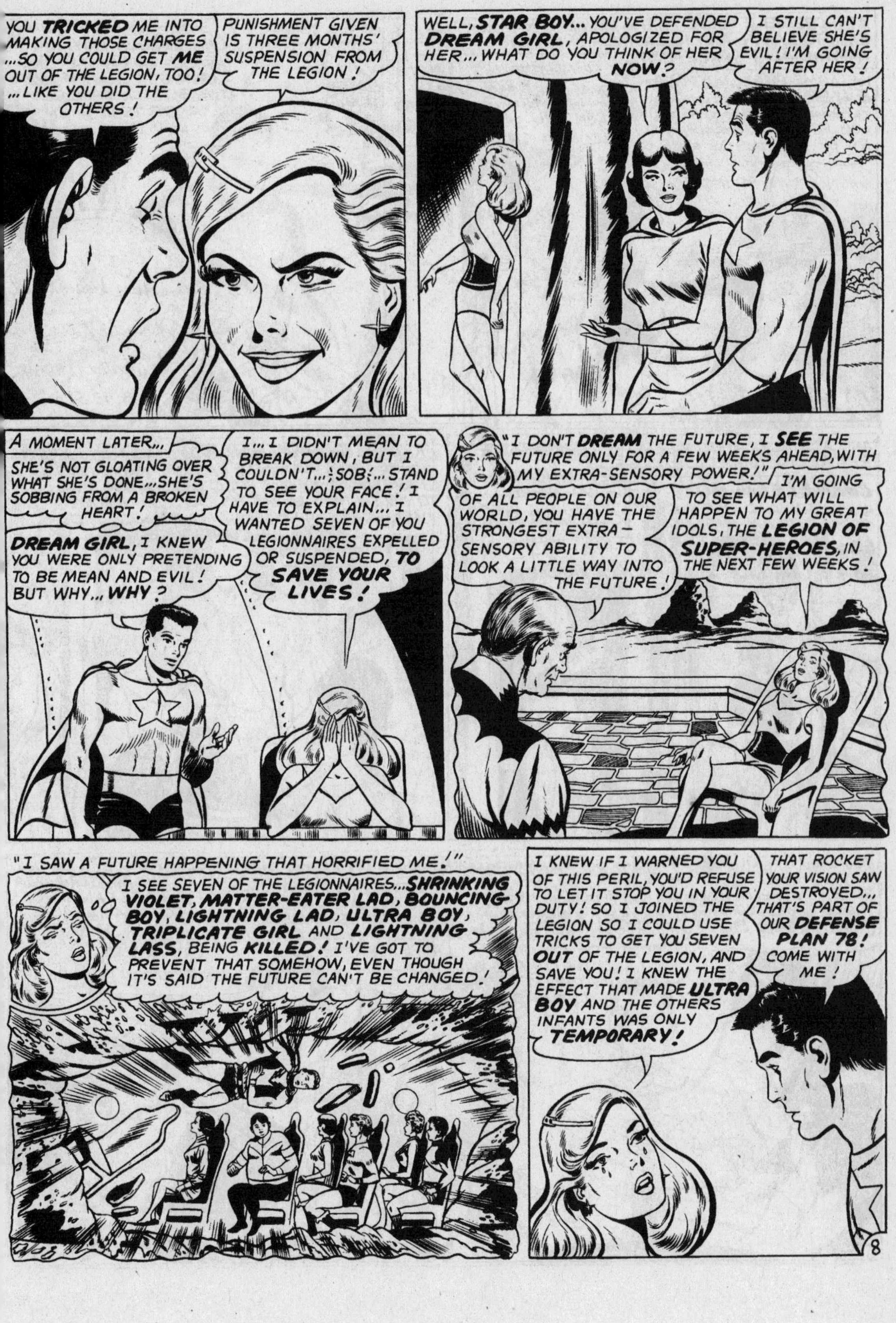
YOU TRICKED ME INTO MAKING THOSE CHARGES ...SO YOU COULD GET ME OUT OF THE LEGION, TOO! ...LIKE YOU DID THE OTHERS!
PUNISHMENT GIVEN IS THREE MONTHS' SUSPENSION FROM THE LEGION!
WELL, STAR BOY... YOU'VE DEFENDED DREAM GIRL, APOLOGIZED FOR HER... WHAT DO YOU THINK OF HER NOW?
I STILL CAN'T BELIEVE SHE'S EVIL! I'M GOING AFTER HER!
A MOMENT LATER...
SHE'S NOT GLOATING OVER WHAT SHE'S DONE... SHE'S SOBBING FROM A BROKEN HEART!
DREAM GIRL, I KNEW YOU WERE ONLY PRETENDING TO BE MEAN AND EVIL! BUT WHY... WHY?
I... I DIDN'T MEAN TO BREAK DOWN, BUT I COULDN'T... SOB ... STAND TO SEE YOUR FACE! I HAVE TO EXPLAIN... I WANTED SEVEN OF YOU LEGIONNAIRES EXPELLED OR SUSPENDED, TO SAVE YOUR LIVES!
"I DON'T DREAM THE FUTURE, I SEE THE FUTURE ONLY FOR A FEW WEEKS AHEAD, WITH MY EXTRA-SENSORY POWER!"
OF ALL PEOPLE ON OUR WORLD, YOU HAVE THE STRONGEST EXTRA-SENSORY ABILITY TO LOOK A LITTLE WAY INTO THE FUTURE!
I'M GOING TO SEE WHAT WILL HAPPEN TO MY GREAT IDOLS, THE LEGION OF SUPER-HEROES, IN THE NEXT FEW WEEKS!
"I SAW A FUTURE HAPPENING THAT HORRIFIED ME!"
I SEE SEVEN OF THE LEGIONNAIRES... SHRINKING VIOLET, MATTER-EATER LAD, BOUNCING BOY, LIGHTNING LAD, ULTRA BOY, TRIPLICATE GIRL AND LIGHTNING LASS, BEING KILLED! I'VE GOT TO PREVENT THAT SOMEHOW, EVEN THOUGH IT'S SAID THE FUTURE CAN'T BE CHANGED!
I KNEW IF I WARNED YOU OF THIS PERIL, YOU'D REFUSE TO LET IT STOP YOU IN YOUR DUTY! SO I JOINED THE LEGION SO I COULD USE TRICKS TO GET YOU SEVEN OUT OF THE LEGION, AND SAVE YOU! I KNEW THE EFFECT THAT MADE ULTRA BOY AND THE OTHERS INFANTS WAS ONLY TEMPORARY!
THAT ROCKET YOUR VISION SAW DESTROYED... THAT'S PART OF OUR DEFENSE PLAN 78! COME WITH ME!
8

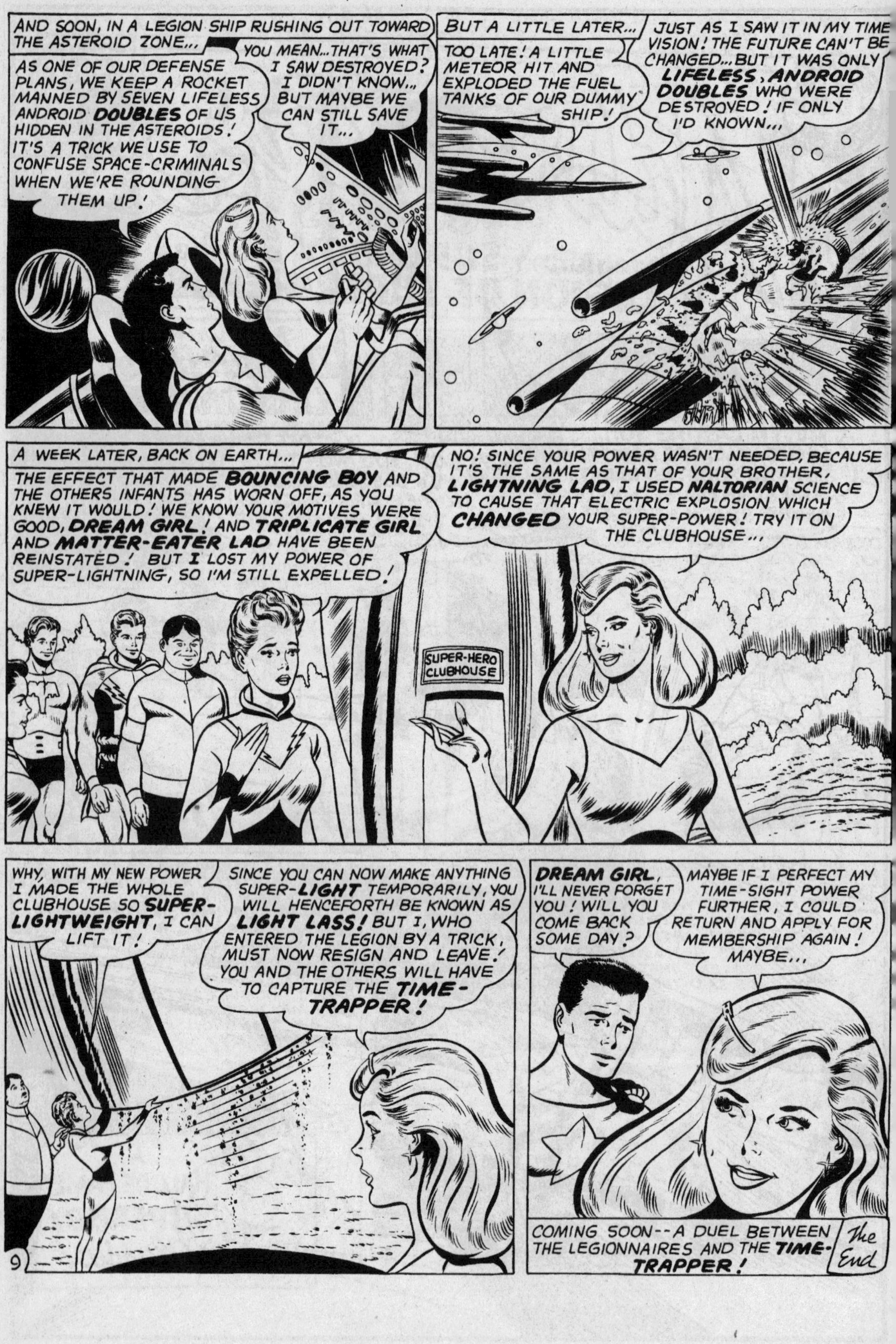
AND SOON, IN A LEGION SHIP RUSHING OUT TOWARD THE ASTEROID ZONE...
AS ONE OF OUR DEFENSE PLANS, WE KEEP A ROCKET MANNED BY SEVEN LIFELESS ANDROID DOUBLES OF US HIDDEN IN THE ASTEROIDS! IT'S A TRICK WE USE TO CONFUSE SPACE-CRIMINALS WHEN WE'RE ROUNDING THEM UP!
YOU MEAN...THAT'S WHAT I SAW DESTROYED? I DIDN'T KNOW... BUT MAYBE WE CAN STILL SAVE IT...
BUT A LITTLE LATER...
TOO LATE! A LITTLE METEOR HIT AND EXPLODED THE FUEL TANKS OF OUR DUMMY SHIP!
JUST AS I SAW IT IN MY TIME VISION! THE FUTURE CAN'T BE CHANGED... BUT IT WAS ONLY LIFELESS, ANDROID DOUBLES WHO WERE DESTROYED! IF ONLY I'D KNOWN...
A WEEK LATER, BACK ON EARTH...
THE EFFECT THAT MADE BOUNCING BOY AND THE OTHERS INFANTS HAS WORN OFF, AS YOU KNEW IT WOULD! WE KNOW YOUR MOTIVES WERE GOOD, DREAM GIRL! AND TRIPLICATE GIRL AND MATTER-EATER LAD HAVE BEEN REINSTATED! BUT I LOST MY POWER OF SUPER-LIGHTNING, SO I'M STILL EXPELLED!
NO! SINCE YOUR POWER WASN'T NEEDED, BECAUSE IT'S THE SAME AS THAT OF YOUR BROTHER, LIGHTNING LAD, I USED NALTORIAN SCIENCE TO CAUSE THAT ELECTRIC EXPLOSION WHICH CHANGED YOUR SUPER-POWER! TRY IT ON THE CLUBHOUSE...
SUPER-HERO CLUBHOUSE
WHY, WITH MY NEW POWER I MADE THE WHOLE CLUBHOUSE SO SUPER-LIGHTWEIGHT, I CAN LIFT IT!
SINCE YOU CAN NOW MAKE ANYTHING SUPER-LIGHT TEMPORARILY, YOU WILL HENCEFORTH BE KNOWN AS LIGHT LASS! BUT I, WHO ENTERED THE LEGION BY A TRICK, MUST NOW RESIGN AND LEAVE! YOU AND THE OTHERS WILL HAVE TO CAPTURE THE TIME-TRAPPER!
9
DREAM GIRL, I'LL NEVER FORGET YOU! WILL YOU COME BACK SOME DAY?
MAYBE IF I PERFECT MY TIME-SIGHT POWER FURTHER, I COULD RETURN AND APPLY FOR MEMBERSHIP AGAIN! MAYBE...
COMING SOON--A DUEL BETWEEN THE LEGIONNAIRES AND THE TIME-TRAPPER!
The End

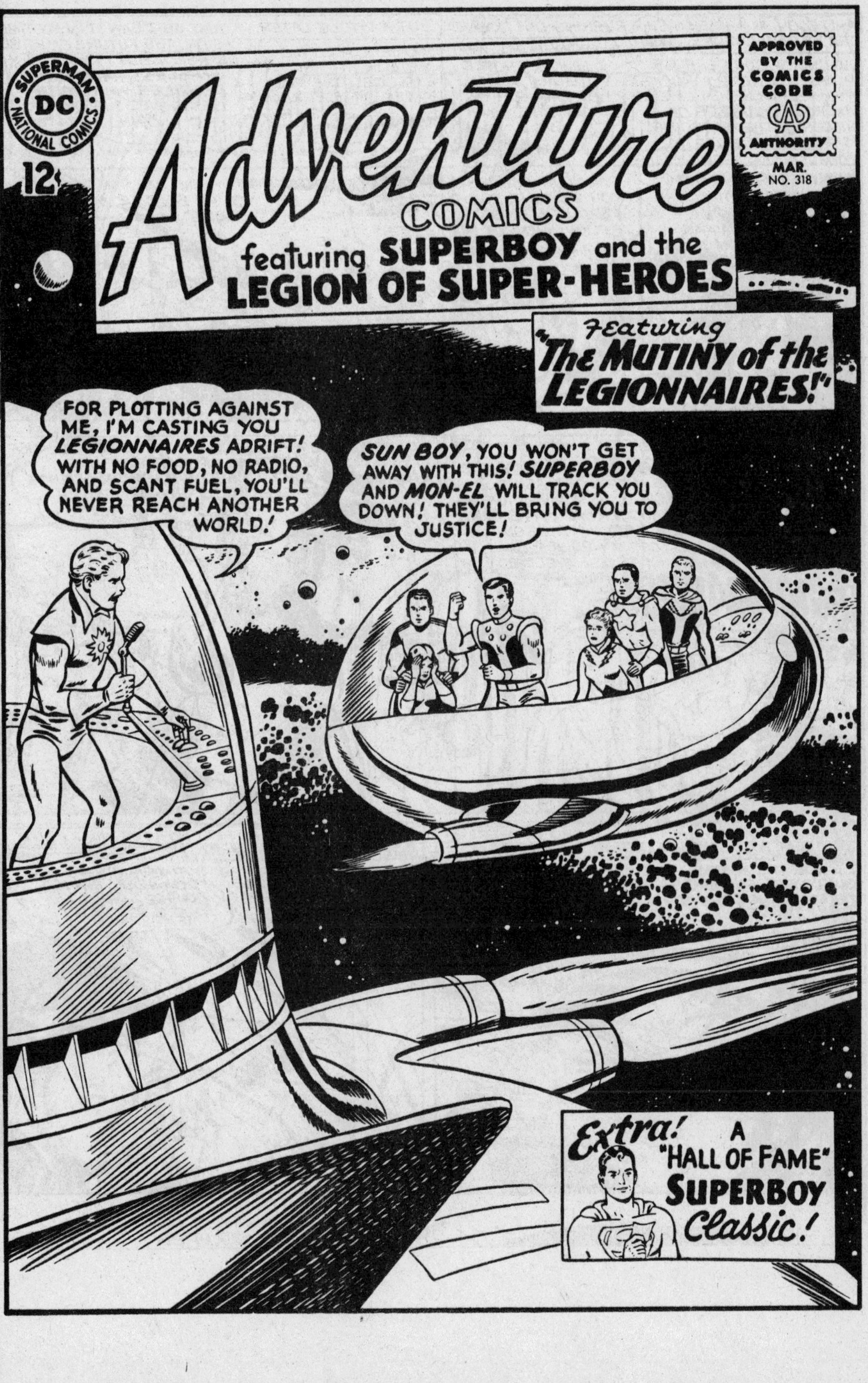
SUPERMAN DC NATIONAL COMICS
12¢
Adventure COMICS
featuring SUPERBOY and the LEGION OF SUPER-HEROES
APPROVED BY THE COMICS CODE AUTHORITY
MAR. NO. 318
Featuring "The MUTINY of the LEGIONNAIRES!"
FOR PLOTTING AGAINST ME, I'M CASTING YOU LEGIONNAIRES ADRIFT! WITH NO FOOD, NO RADIO, AND SCANT FUEL, YOU'LL NEVER REACH ANOTHER WORLD!
SUN BOY, YOU WON'T GET AWAY WITH THIS! SUPERBOY AND MON-EL WILL TRACK YOU DOWN! THEY'LL BRING YOU TO JUSTICE!
Extra! A "HALL OF FAME" SUPERBOY Classic!

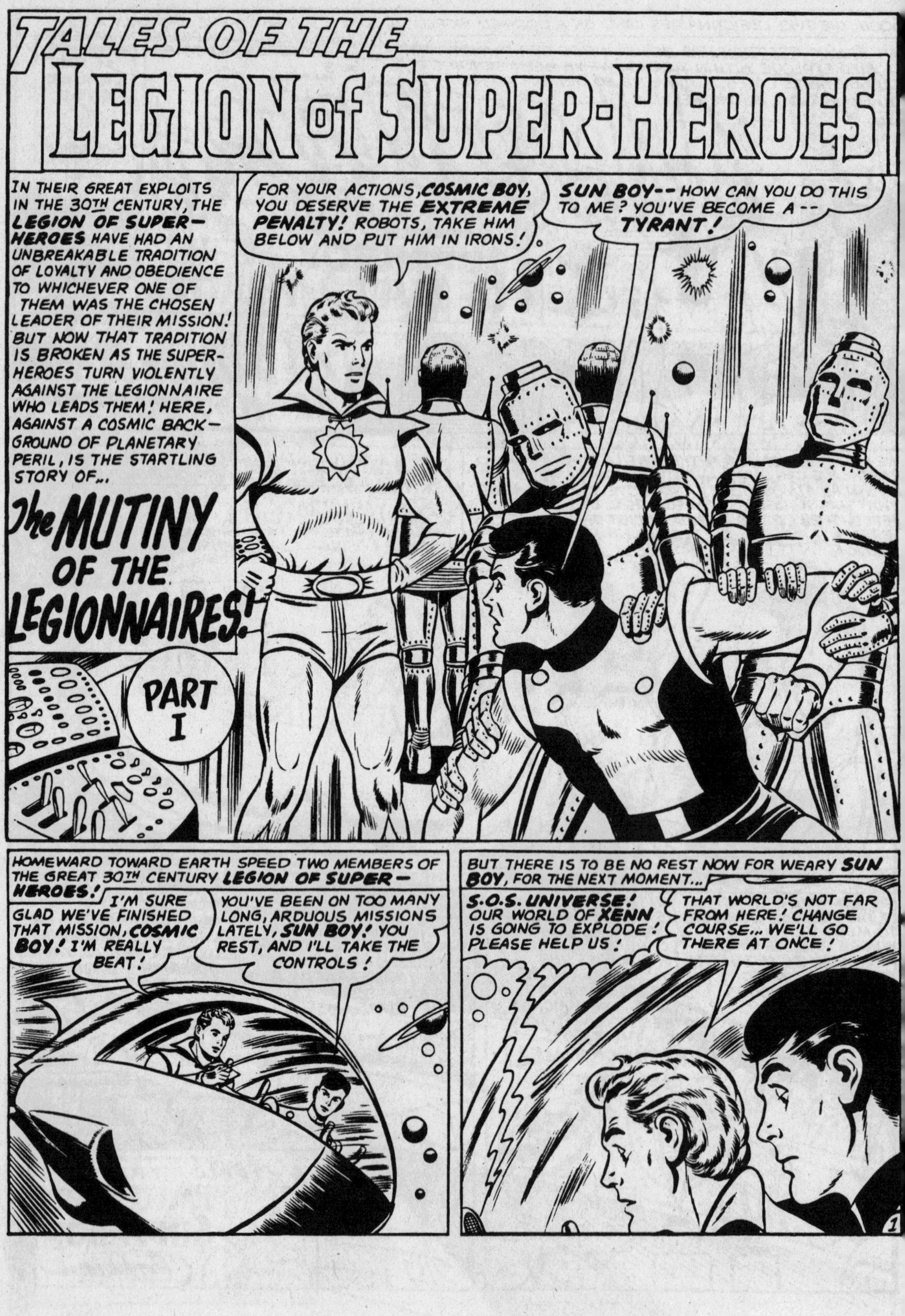
TALES OF THE
LEGION of SUPER-HEROES
IN THEIR GREAT EXPLOITS IN THE 30TH CENTURY, THE LEGION OF SUPER-HEROES HAVE HAD AN UNBREAKABLE TRADITION OF LOYALTY AND OBEDIENCE TO WHICHEVER ONE OF THEM WAS THE CHOSEN LEADER OF THEIR MISSION! BUT NOW THAT TRADITION IS BROKEN AS THE SUPER-HEROES TURN VIOLENTLY AGAINST THE LEGIONNAIRE WHO LEADS THEM! HERE, AGAINST A COSMIC BACK-GROUND OF PLANETARY PERIL, IS THE STARTLING STORY OF..
The MUTINY OF THE LEGIONNAIRES!
FOR YOUR ACTIONS, COSMIC BOY, YOU DESERVE THE EXTREME PENALTY! ROBOTS, TAKE HIM BELOW AND PUT HIM IN IRONS!
SUN BOY-- HOW CAN YOU DO THIS TO ME? YOU'VE BECOME A-- TYRANT!
PART I
HOMEWARD TOWARD EARTH SPEED TWO MEMBERS OF THE GREAT 30TH CENTURY LEGION OF SUPER-HEROES!
I'M SURE GLAD WE'VE FINISHED THAT MISSION, COSMIC BOY! I'M REALLY BEAT!
YOU'VE BEEN ON TOO MANY LONG, ARDUOUS MISSIONS LATELY, SUN BOY! YOU REST, AND I'LL TAKE THE CONTROLS!
BUT THERE IS TO BE NO REST NOW FOR WEARY SUN BOY, FOR THE NEXT MOMENT...
S.O.S. UNIVERSE! OUR WORLD OF XENN IS GOING TO EXPLODE! PLEASE HELP US!
THAT WORLD'S NOT FAR FROM HERE! CHANGE COURSE... WE'LL GO THERE AT ONCE!
1

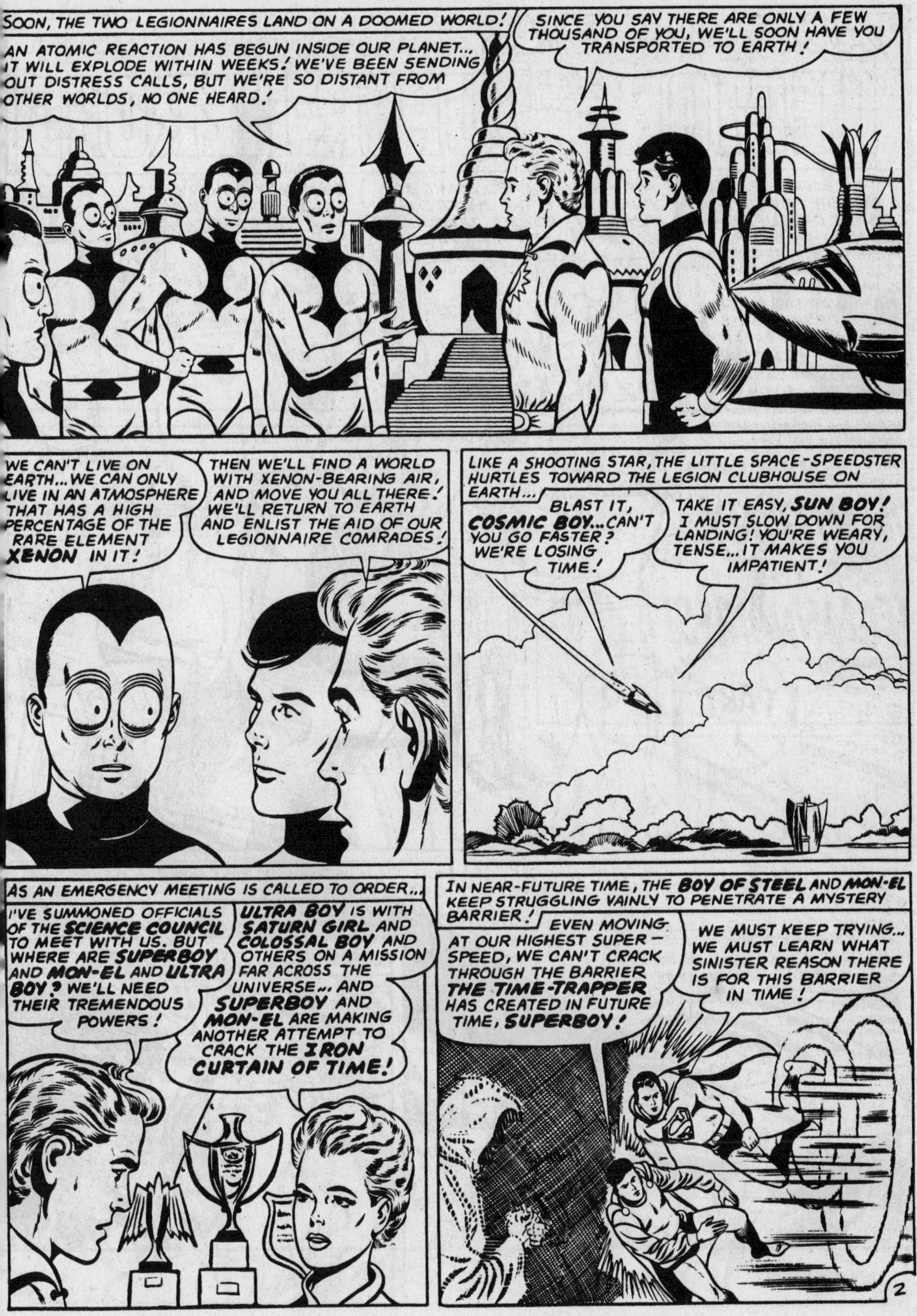
SOON, THE TWO LEGIONNAIRES LAND ON A DOOMED WORLD!
AN ATOMIC REACTION HAS BEGUN INSIDE OUR PLANET... IT WILL EXPLODE WITHIN WEEKS! WE'VE BEEN SENDING OUT DISTRESS CALLS, BUT WE'RE SO DISTANT FROM OTHER WORLDS, NO ONE HEARD!
SINCE YOU SAY THERE ARE ONLY A FEW THOUSAND OF YOU, WE'LL SOON HAVE YOU TRANSPORTED TO EARTH!
WE CAN'T LIVE ON EARTH... WE CAN ONLY LIVE IN AN ATMOSPHERE THAT HAS A HIGH PERCENTAGE OF THE RARE ELEMENT XENON IN IT!
THEN WE'LL FIND A WORLD WITH XENON-BEARING AIR, AND MOVE YOU ALL THERE! WE'LL RETURN TO EARTH AND ENLIST THE AID OF OUR LEGIONNAIRE COMRADES!
LIKE A SHOOTING STAR, THE LITTLE SPACE-SPEEDSTER HURTLES TOWARD THE LEGION CLUBHOUSE ON EARTH...
BLAST IT, COSMIC BOY... CAN'T YOU GO FASTER? WE'RE LOSING TIME!
TAKE IT EASY, SUN BOY! I MUST SLOW DOWN FOR LANDING! YOU'RE WEARY, TENSE... IT MAKES YOU IMPATIENT!
AS AN EMERGENCY MEETING IS CALLED TO ORDER...
I'VE SUMMONED OFFICIALS OF THE SCIENCE COUNCIL TO MEET WITH US. BUT WHERE ARE SUPERBOY AND MON-EL AND ULTRA BOY? WE'LL NEED THEIR TREMENDOUS POWERS!
ULTRA BOY IS WITH SATURN GIRL AND COLOSSAL BOY AND OTHERS ON A MISSION FAR ACROSS THE UNIVERSE... AND SUPERBOY AND MON-EL ARE MAKING ANOTHER ATTEMPT TO CRACK THE IRON CURTAIN OF TIME!
IN NEAR-FUTURE TIME, THE BOY OF STEEL AND MON-EL KEEP STRUGGLING VAINLY TO PENETRATE A MYSTERY BARRIER!
EVEN MOVING AT OUR HIGHEST SUPER-SPEED, WE CAN'T CRACK THROUGH THE BARRIER THE TIME-TRAPPER HAS CREATED IN FUTURE TIME, SUPERBOY!
WE MUST KEEP TRYING... WE MUST LEARN WHAT SINISTER REASON THERE IS FOR THIS BARRIER IN TIME!
2

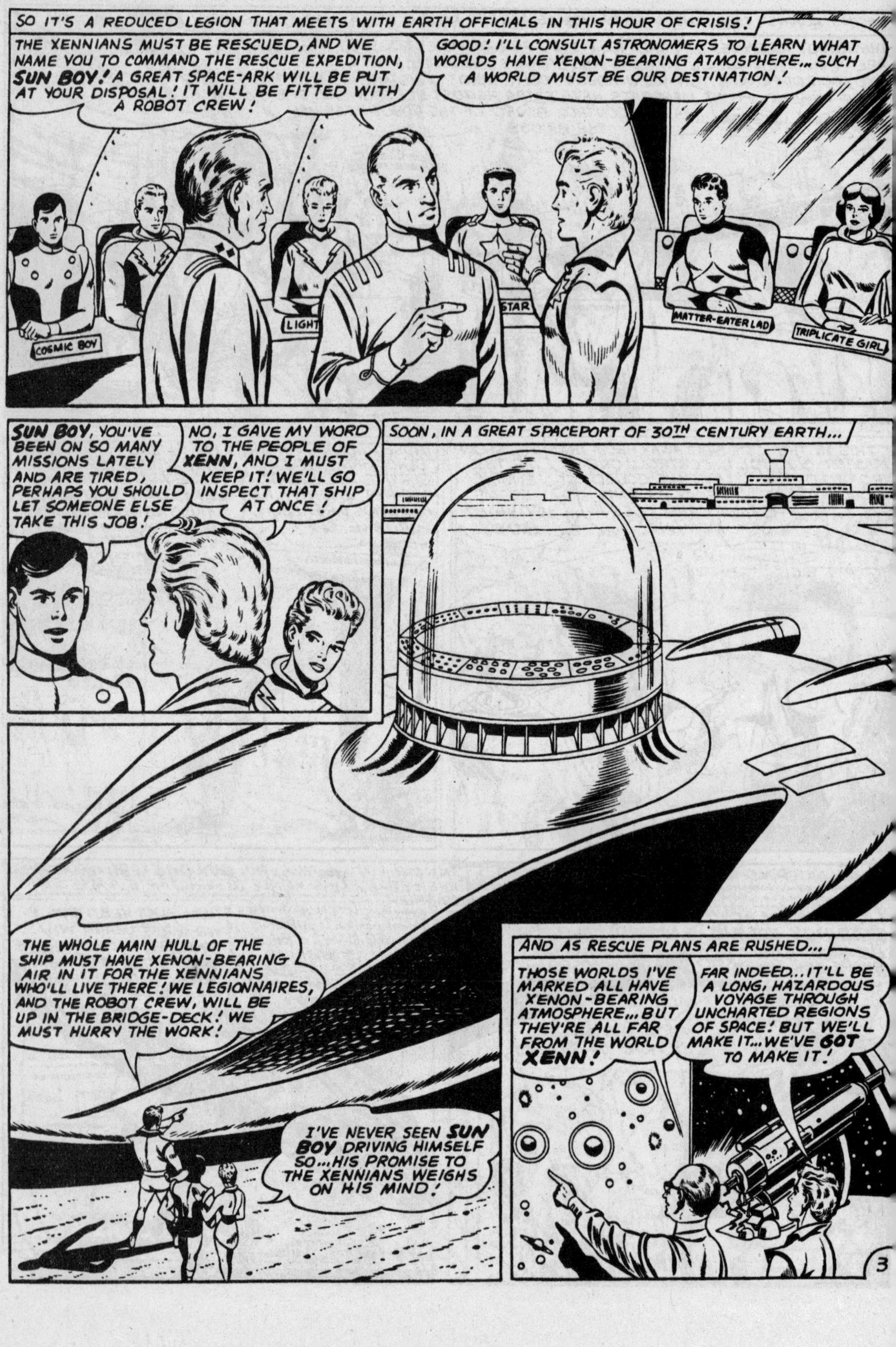
SO IT'S A REDUCED LEGION THAT MEETS WITH EARTH OFFICIALS IN THIS HOUR OF CRISIS!
THE XENNIANS MUST BE RESCUED, AND WE NAME YOU TO COMMAND THE RESCUE EXPEDITION, SUN BOY! A GREAT SPACE-ARK WILL BE PUT AT YOUR DISPOSAL! IT WILL BE FITTED WITH A ROBOT CREW!
GOOD! I'LL CONSULT ASTRONOMERS TO LEARN WHAT WORLDS HAVE XENON-BEARING ATMOSPHERE.. SUCH A WORLD MUST BE OUR DESTINATION!
COSMIC BOY
LIGHT
STAR
MATTER-EATER LAD
TRIPLICATE GIRL
SUN BOY, YOU'VE BEEN ON SO MANY MISSIONS LATELY AND ARE TIRED, PERHAPS YOU SHOULD LET SOMEONE ELSE TAKE THIS JOB!
NO, I GAVE MY WORD TO THE PEOPLE OF XENN, AND I MUST KEEP IT! WE'LL GO INSPECT THAT SHIP AT ONCE!
SOON, IN A GREAT SPACEPORT OF 30TH CENTURY EARTH...
THE WHOLE MAIN HULL OF THE SHIP MUST HAVE XENON-BEARING AIR IN IT FOR THE XENNIANS WHO'LL LIVE THERE! WE LEGIONNAIRES, AND THE ROBOT CREW, WILL BE UP IN THE BRIDGE-DECK! WE MUST HURRY THE WORK!
I'VE NEVER SEEN SUN BOY DRIVING HIMSELF SO...HIS PROMISE TO THE XENNIANS WEIGHS ON HIS MIND!
AND AS RESCUE PLANS ARE RUSHED...
THOSE WORLDS I'VE MARKED ALL HAVE XENON-BEARING ATMOSPHERE... BUT THEY'RE ALL FAR FROM THE WORLD XENN!
FAR INDEED...IT'LL BE A LONG, HAZARDOUS VOYAGE THROUGH UNCHARTED REGIONS OF SPACE! BUT WE'LL MAKE IT...WE'VE GOT TO MAKE IT!
3

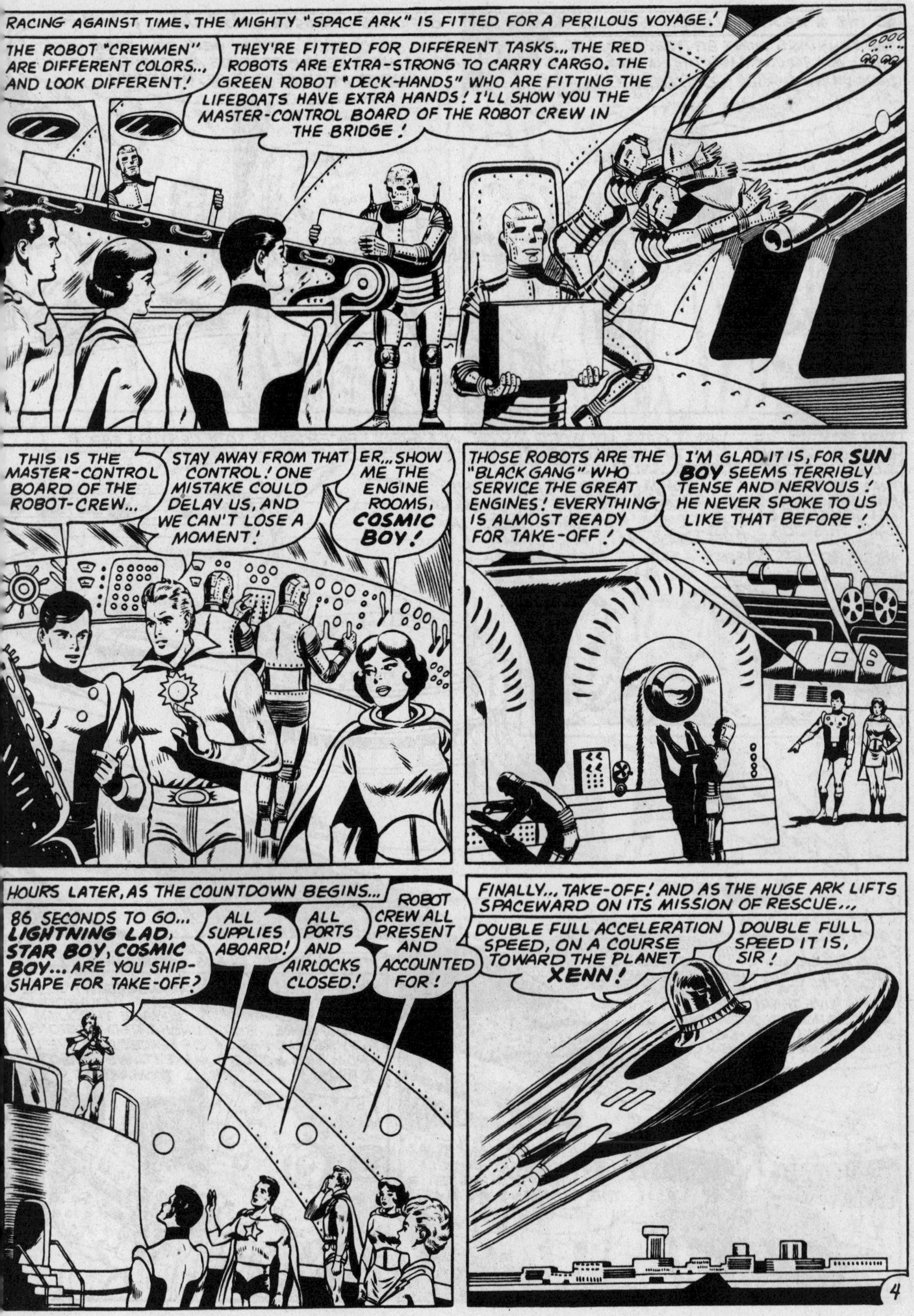
RACING AGAINST TIME, THE MIGHTY "SPACE ARK" IS FITTED FOR A PERILOUS VOYAGE!
THE ROBOT "CREWMEN" ARE DIFFERENT COLORS... AND LOOK DIFFERENT!
THEY'RE FITTED FOR DIFFERENT TASKS... THE RED ROBOTS ARE EXTRA-STRONG TO CARRY CARGO. THE GREEN ROBOT "DECK-HANDS" WHO ARE FITTING THE LIFEBOATS HAVE EXTRA HANDS! I'LL SHOW YOU THE MASTER-CONTROL BOARD OF THE ROBOT CREW IN THE BRIDGE!
THIS IS THE MASTER-CONTROL BOARD OF THE ROBOT-CREW...
STAY AWAY FROM THAT CONTROL! ONE MISTAKE COULD DELAY US, AND WE CAN'T LOSE A MOMENT!
ER... SHOW ME THE ENGINE ROOMS, COSMIC BOY!
THOSE ROBOTS ARE THE "BLACK GANG" WHO SERVICE THE GREAT ENGINES! EVERYTHING IS ALMOST READY FOR TAKE-OFF!
I'M GLAD IT IS, FOR SUN BOY SEEMS TERRIBLY TENSE AND NERVOUS! HE NEVER SPOKE TO US LIKE THAT BEFORE!
HOURS LATER, AS THE COUNTDOWN BEGINS...
86 SECONDS TO GO... LIGHTNING LAD, STAR BOY, COSMIC BOY... ARE YOU SHIP-SHAPE FOR TAKE-OFF?
ALL SUPPLIES ABOARD!
ALL PORTS AND AIRLOCKS CLOSED!
ROBOT CREW ALL PRESENT AND ACCOUNTED FOR!
FINALLY... TAKE-OFF! AND AS THE HUGE ARK LIFTS SPACEWARD ON ITS MISSION OF RESCUE...
DOUBLE FULL ACCELERATION SPEED, ON A COURSE TOWARD THE PLANET XENN!
DOUBLE FULL SPEED IT IS, SIR!
4

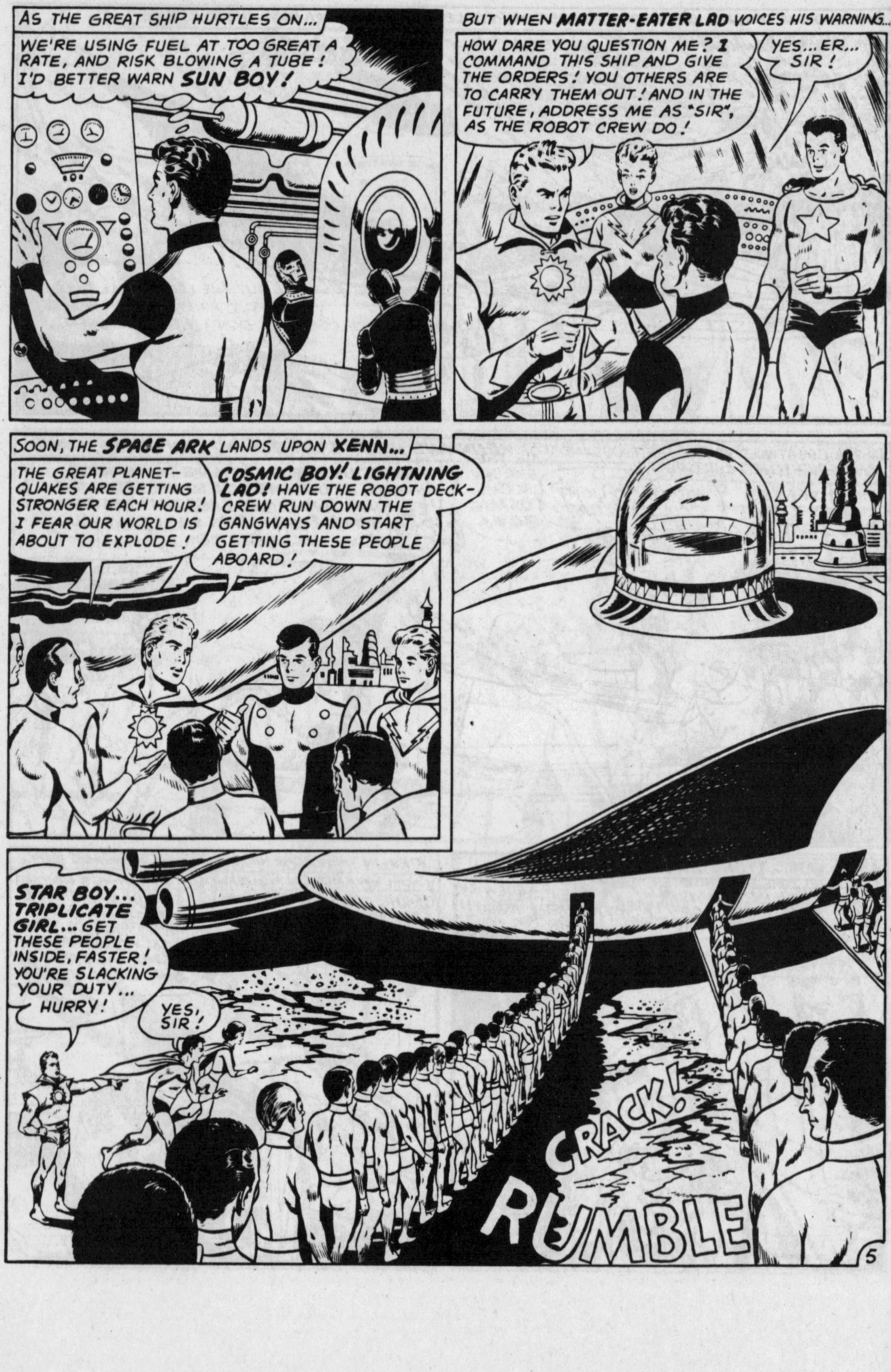
AS THE GREAT SHIP HURTLES ON...
WE'RE USING FUEL AT TOO GREAT A RATE, AND RISK BLOWING A TUBE! I'D BETTER WARN SUN BOY!
BUT WHEN MATTER-EATER LAD VOICES HIS WARNING...
HOW DARE YOU QUESTION ME? I COMMAND THIS SHIP AND GIVE THE ORDERS! YOU OTHERS ARE TO CARRY THEM OUT! AND IN THE FUTURE, ADDRESS ME AS "SIR", AS THE ROBOT CREW DO!
YES...ER... SIR!
SOON, THE SPACE ARK LANDS UPON XENN...
THE GREAT PLANET-QUAKES ARE GETTING STRONGER EACH HOUR! I FEAR OUR WORLD IS ABOUT TO EXPLODE!
COSMIC BOY! LIGHTNING LAD! HAVE THE ROBOT DECK-CREW RUN DOWN THE GANGWAYS AND START GETTING THESE PEOPLE ABOARD!
STAR BOY... TRIPLICATE GIRL... GET THESE PEOPLE INSIDE, FASTER! YOU'RE SLACKING YOUR DUTY... HURRY!
YES, SIR!
CRACK!
RUMBLE
5

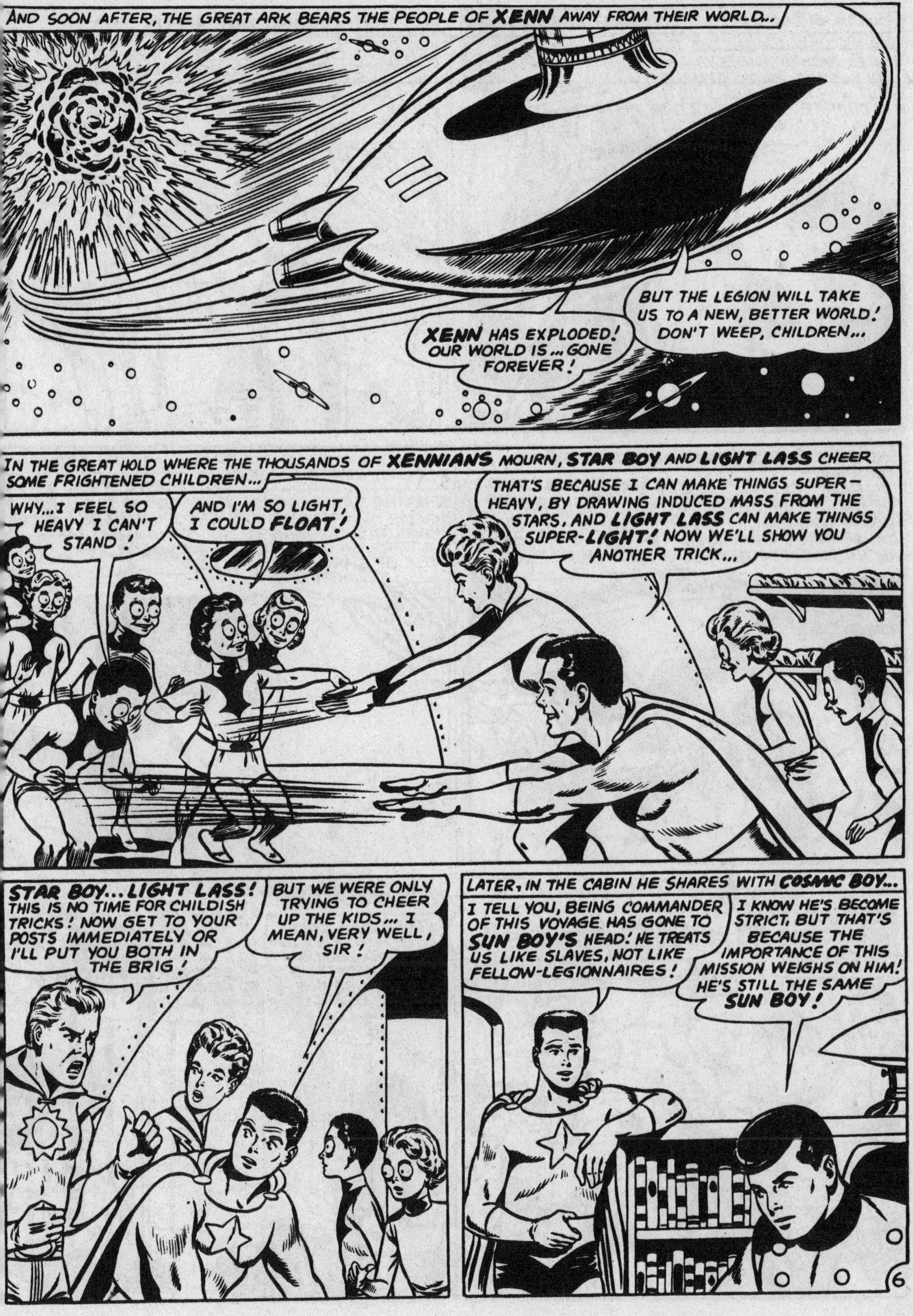
AND SOON AFTER, THE GREAT ARK BEARS THE PEOPLE OF XENN AWAY FROM THEIR WORLD...
XENN HAS EXPLODED! OUR WORLD IS ... GONE FOREVER!
BUT THE LEGION WILL TAKE US TO A NEW, BETTER WORLD! DON'T WEEP, CHILDREN...
IN THE GREAT HOLD WHERE THE THOUSANDS OF XENNIANS MOURN, STAR BOY AND LIGHT LASS CHEER SOME FRIGHTENED CHILDREN...
WHY...I FEEL SO HEAVY I CAN'T STAND!
AND I'M SO LIGHT, I COULD FLOAT!
THAT'S BECAUSE I CAN MAKE THINGS SUPER-HEAVY, BY DRAWING INDUCED MASS FROM THE STARS, AND LIGHT LASS CAN MAKE THINGS SUPER-LIGHT! NOW WE'LL SHOW YOU ANOTHER TRICK...
STAR BOY... LIGHT LASS! THIS IS NO TIME FOR CHILDISH TRICKS! NOW GET TO YOUR POSTS IMMEDIATELY OR I'LL PUT YOU BOTH IN THE BRIG!
BUT WE WERE ONLY TRYING TO CHEER UP THE KIDS... I MEAN, VERY WELL, SIR!
LATER, IN THE CABIN HE SHARES WITH COSMIC BOY...
I TELL YOU, BEING COMMANDER OF THIS VOYAGE HAS GONE TO SUN BOY'S HEAD! HE TREATS US LIKE SLAVES, NOT LIKE FELLOW-LEGIONNAIRES!
I KNOW HE'S BECOME STRICT, BUT THAT'S BECAUSE THE IMPORTANCE OF THIS MISSION WEIGHS ON HIM! HE'S STILL THE SAME SUN BOY!
6

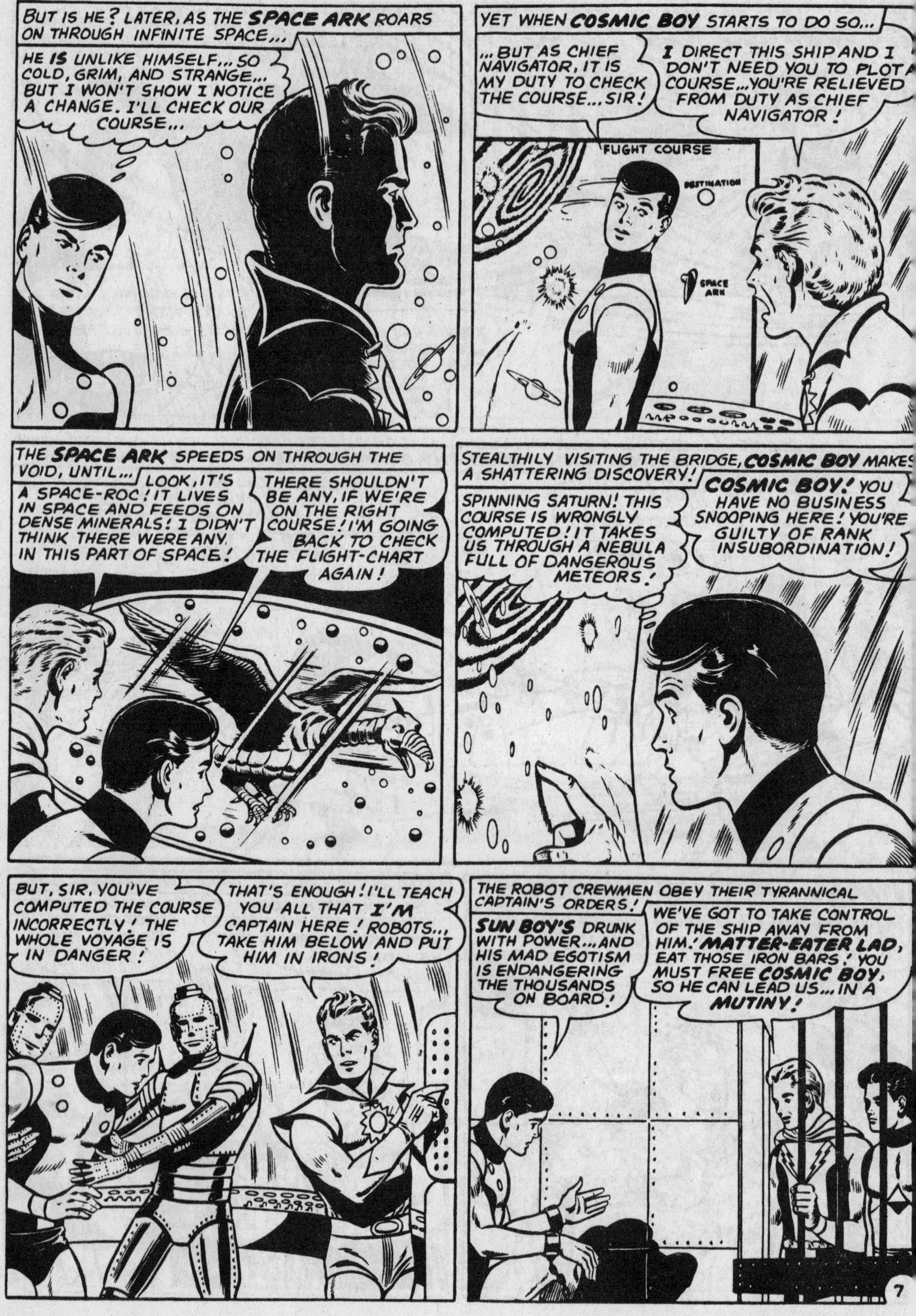
BUT IS HE? LATER, AS THE SPACE ARK ROARS ON THROUGH INFINITE SPACE,..
HE IS UNLIKE HIMSELF... SO COLD, GRIM, AND STRANGE... BUT I WON'T SHOW I NOTICE A CHANGE. I'LL CHECK OUR COURSE...
YET WHEN COSMIC BOY STARTS TO DO SO...
...BUT AS CHIEF NAVIGATOR, IT IS MY DUTY TO CHECK THE COURSE... SIR!
I DIRECT THIS SHIP AND I DON'T NEED YOU TO PLOT A COURSE... YOU'RE RELIEVED FROM DUTY AS CHIEF NAVIGATOR!
FLIGHT COURSE
DESTINATION
SPACE ARK
THE SPACE ARK SPEEDS ON THROUGH THE VOID, UNTIL...
LOOK, IT'S A SPACE-ROC! IT LIVES IN SPACE AND FEEDS ON DENSE MINERALS! I DIDN'T THINK THERE WERE ANY IN THIS PART OF SPACE!
THERE SHOULDN'T BE ANY, IF WE'RE ON THE RIGHT COURSE! I'M GOING BACK TO CHECK THE FLIGHT-CHART AGAIN!
STEALTHILY VISITING THE BRIDGE, COSMIC BOY MAKES A SHATTERING DISCOVERY!
SPINNING SATURN! THIS COURSE IS WRONGLY COMPUTED! IT TAKES US THROUGH A NEBULA FULL OF DANGEROUS METEORS!
COSMIC BOY! YOU HAVE NO BUSINESS SNOOPING HERE! YOU'RE GUILTY OF RANK INSUBORDINATION!
BUT, SIR, YOU'VE COMPUTED THE COURSE INCORRECTLY! THE WHOLE VOYAGE IS IN DANGER!
THAT'S ENOUGH! I'LL TEACH YOU ALL THAT I'M CAPTAIN HERE! ROBOTS.., TAKE HIM BELOW AND PUT HIM IN IRONS!
THE ROBOT CREWMEN OBEY THEIR TYRANNICAL CAPTAIN'S ORDERS!
SUN BOY'S DRUNK WITH POWER... AND HIS MAD EGOTISM IS ENDANGERING THE THOUSANDS ON BOARD!
WE'VE GOT TO TAKE CONTROL OF THE SHIP AWAY FROM HIM! MATTER-EATER LAD, EAT THOSE IRON BARS! YOU MUST FREE COSMIC BOY, SO HE CAN LEAD US... IN A MUTINY!
7

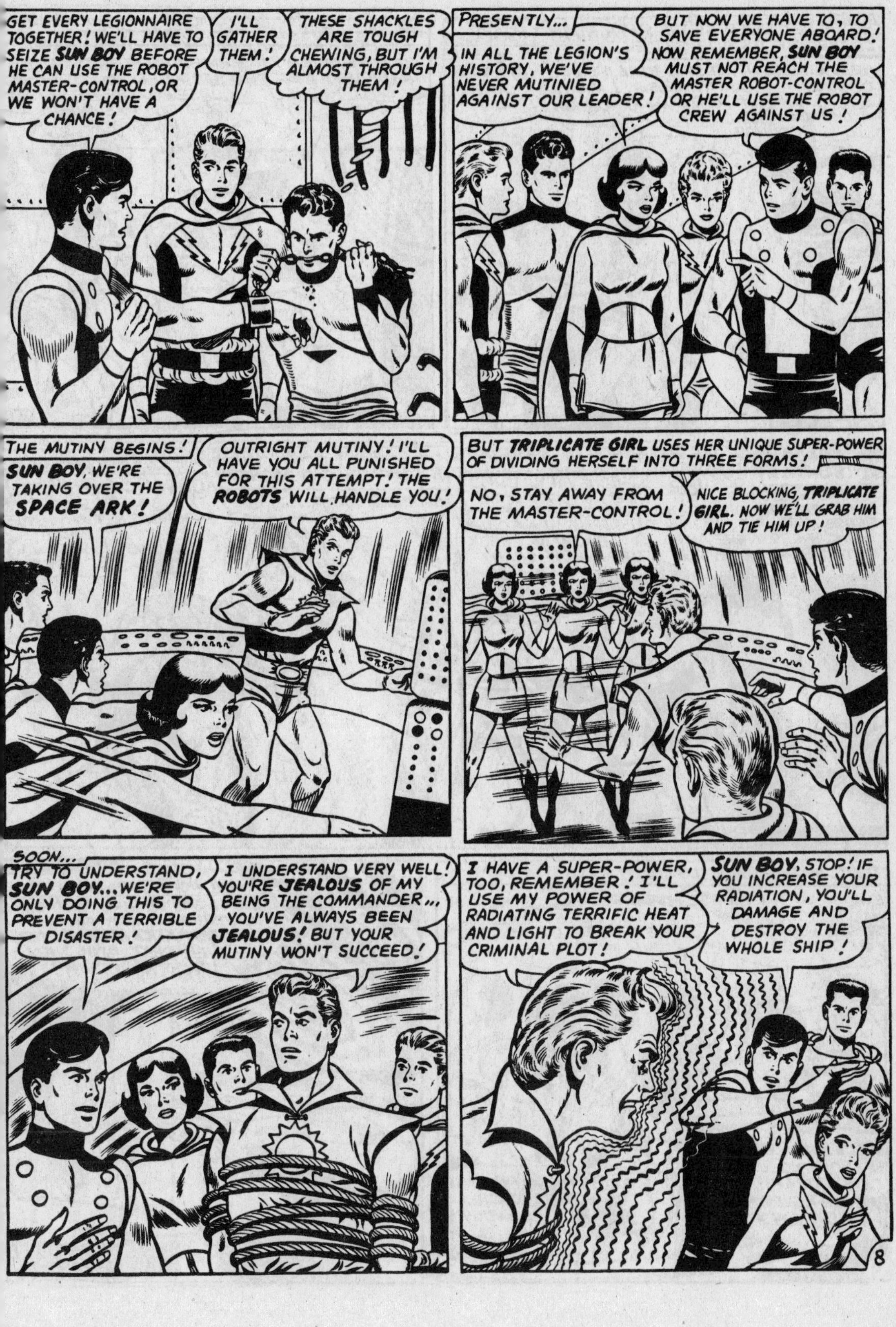
GET EVERY LEGIONNAIRE TOGETHER! WE'LL HAVE TO SEIZE SUN BOY BEFORE HE CAN USE THE ROBOT MASTER-CONTROL, OR WE WON'T HAVE A CHANCE!
I'LL GATHER THEM!
THESE SHACKLES ARE TOUGH CHEWING, BUT I'M ALMOST THROUGH THEM!
PRESENTLY...
IN ALL THE LEGION'S HISTORY, WE'VE NEVER MUTINIED AGAINST OUR LEADER!
BUT NOW WE HAVE TO, TO SAVE EVERYONE ABOARD! NOW REMEMBER, SUN BOY MUST NOT REACH THE MASTER ROBOT-CONTROL OR HE'LL USE THE ROBOT CREW AGAINST US!
THE MUTINY BEGINS!
SUN BOY, WE'RE TAKING OVER THE SPACE ARK!
OUTRIGHT MUTINY! I'LL HAVE YOU ALL PUNISHED FOR THIS ATTEMPT! THE ROBOTS WILL HANDLE YOU!
BUT TRIPLICATE GIRL USES HER UNIQUE SUPER-POWER OF DIVIDING HERSELF INTO THREE FORMS!
NO, STAY AWAY FROM THE MASTER-CONTROL!
NICE BLOCKING, TRIPLICATE GIRL. NOW WE'LL GRAB HIM AND TIE HIM UP!
SOON...
TRY TO UNDERSTAND, SUN BOY... WE'RE ONLY DOING THIS TO PREVENT A TERRIBLE DISASTER!
I UNDERSTAND VERY WELL! YOU'RE JEALOUS OF MY BEING THE COMMANDER... YOU'VE ALWAYS BEEN JEALOUS! BUT YOUR MUTINY WON'T SUCCEED!
I HAVE A SUPER-POWER, TOO, REMEMBER! I'LL USE MY POWER OF RADIATING TERRIFIC HEAT AND LIGHT TO BREAK YOUR CRIMINAL PLOT!
SUN BOY, STOP! IF YOU INCREASE YOUR RADIATION, YOU'LL DAMAGE AND DESTROY THE WHOLE SHIP!
8

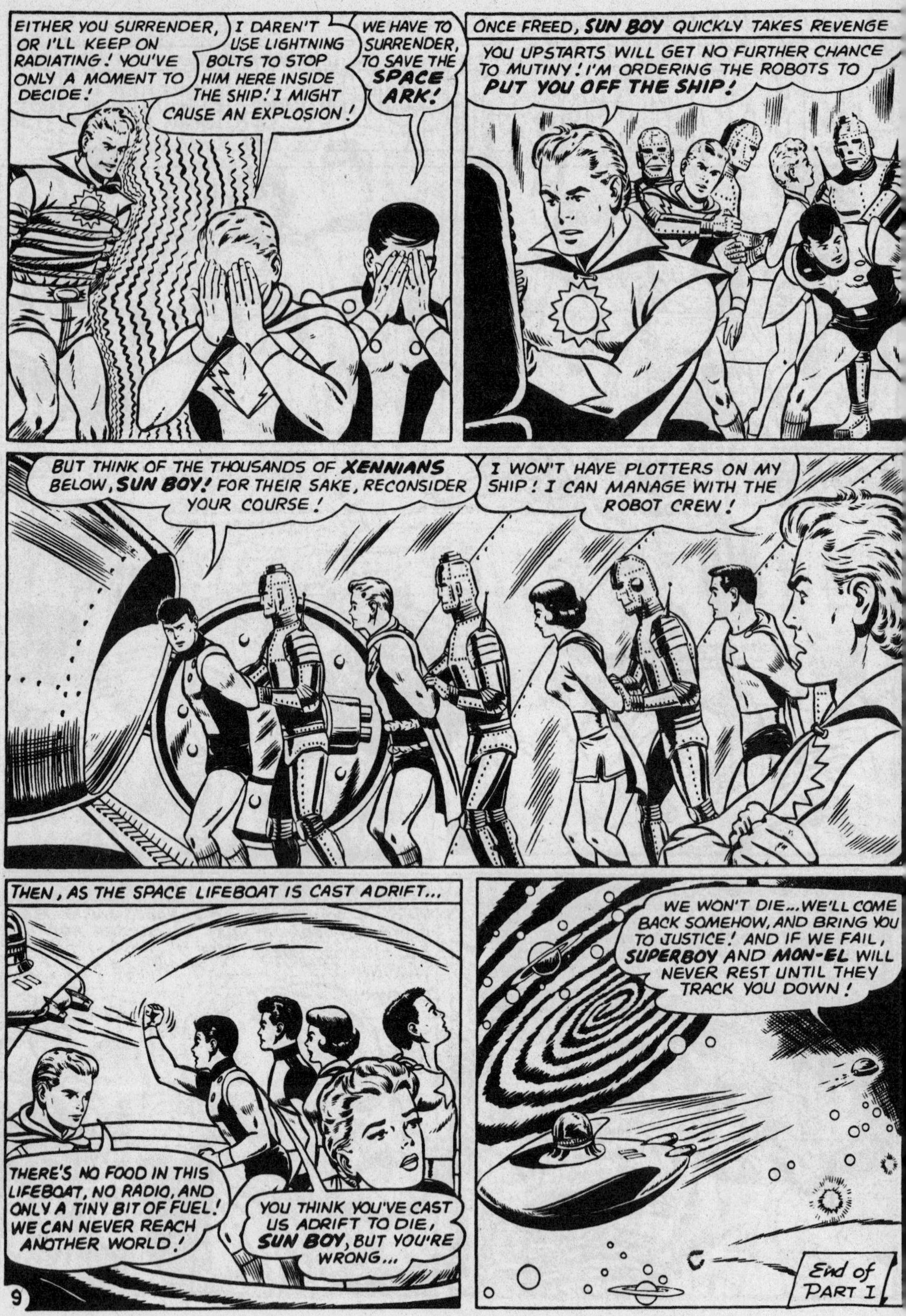
EITHER YOU SURRENDER, OR I'LL KEEP ON RADIATING! YOU'VE ONLY A MOMENT TO DECIDE!
I DAREN'T USE LIGHTNING BOLTS TO STOP HIM HERE INSIDE THE SHIP! I MIGHT CAUSE AN EXPLOSION!
WE HAVE TO SURRENDER, TO SAVE THE SPACE ARK!
ONCE FREED, SUN BOY QUICKLY TAKES REVENGE
YOU UPSTARTS WILL GET NO FURTHER CHANCE TO MUTINY! I'M ORDERING THE ROBOTS TO PUT YOU OFF THE SHIP!
BUT THINK OF THE THOUSANDS OF XENNIANS BELOW, SUN BOY! FOR THEIR SAKE, RECONSIDER YOUR COURSE!
I WON'T HAVE PLOTTERS ON MY SHIP! I CAN MANAGE WITH THE ROBOT CREW!
THEN, AS THE SPACE LIFEBOAT IS CAST ADRIFT...
THERE'S NO FOOD IN THIS LIFEBOAT, NO RADIO, AND ONLY A TINY BIT OF FUEL! WE CAN NEVER REACH ANOTHER WORLD!
YOU THINK YOU'VE CAST US ADRIFT TO DIE, SUN BOY, BUT YOU'RE WRONG...
WE WON'T DIE...WE'LL COME BACK SOMEHOW, AND BRING YOU TO JUSTICE! AND IF WE FAIL, SUPERBOY AND MON-EL WILL NEVER REST UNTIL THEY TRACK YOU DOWN!
9
End of PART I

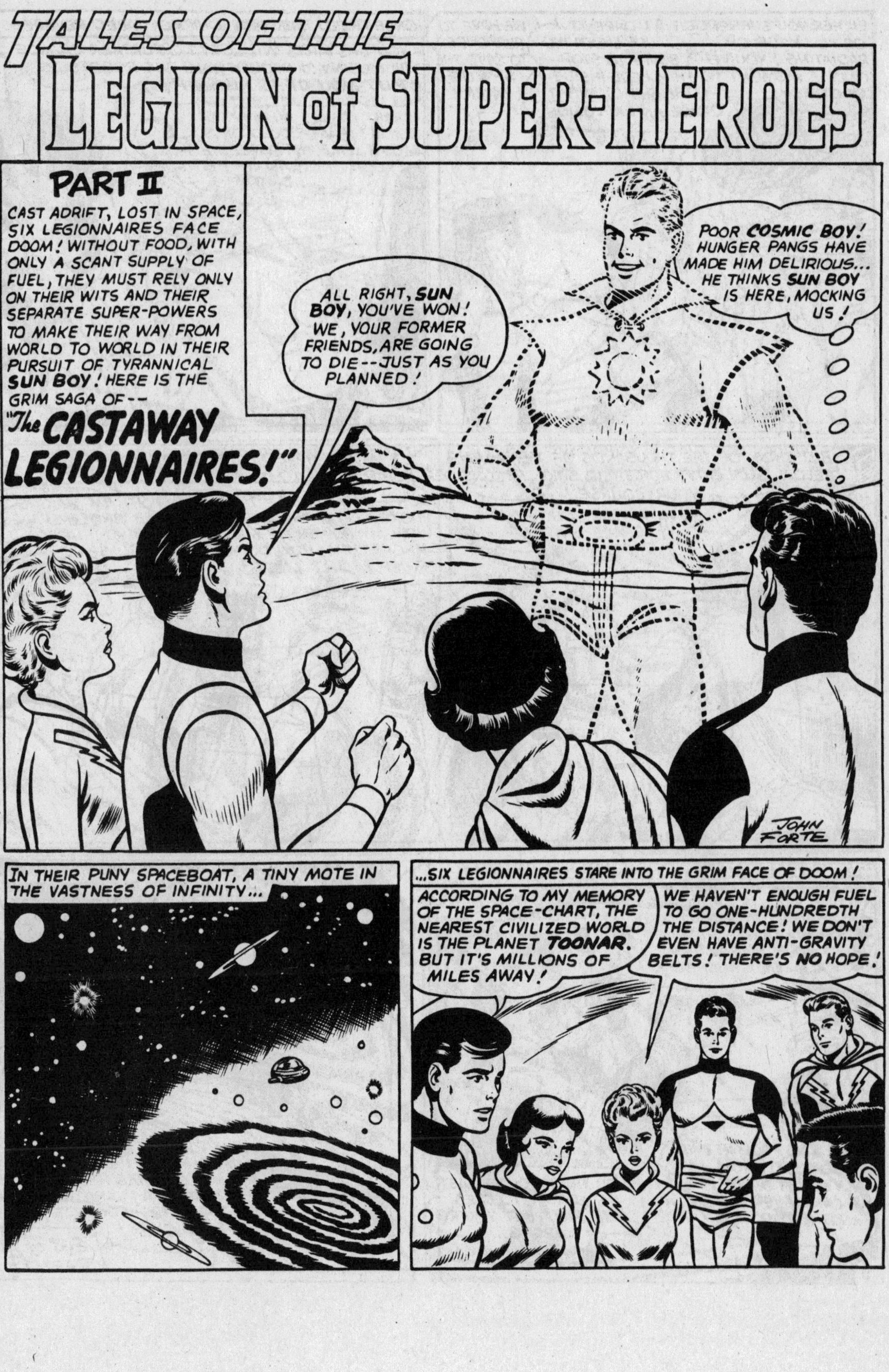
TALES OF THE
LEGION of SUPER-HEROES
PART II
CAST ADRIFT, LOST IN SPACE, SIX LEGIONNAIRES FACE DOOM! WITHOUT FOOD, WITH ONLY A SCANT SUPPLY OF FUEL, THEY MUST RELY ONLY ON THEIR WITS AND THEIR SEPARATE SUPER-POWERS TO MAKE THEIR WAY FROM WORLD TO WORLD IN THEIR PURSUIT OF TYRANNICAL SUN BOY! HERE IS THE GRIM SAGA OF --
"The CASTAWAY LEGIONNAIRES!"
ALL RIGHT, SUN BOY, YOU'VE WON! WE, YOUR FORMER FRIENDS, ARE GOING TO DIE--JUST AS YOU PLANNED!
POOR COSMIC BOY! HUNGER PANGS HAVE MADE HIM DELIRIOUS... HE THINKS SUN BOY IS HERE, MOCKING US!
JOHN FORTE
IN THEIR PUNY SPACEBOAT, A TINY MOTE IN THE VASTNESS OF INFINITY...
...SIX LEGIONNAIRES STARE INTO THE GRIM FACE OF DOOM!
ACCORDING TO MY MEMORY OF THE SPACE-CHART, THE NEAREST CIVILIZED WORLD IS THE PLANET TOONAR. BUT IT'S MILLIONS OF MILES AWAY!
WE HAVEN'T ENOUGH FUEL TO GO ONE-HUNDREDTH THE DISTANCE! WE DON'T EVEN HAVE ANTI-GRAVITY BELTS! THERE'S NO HOPE!

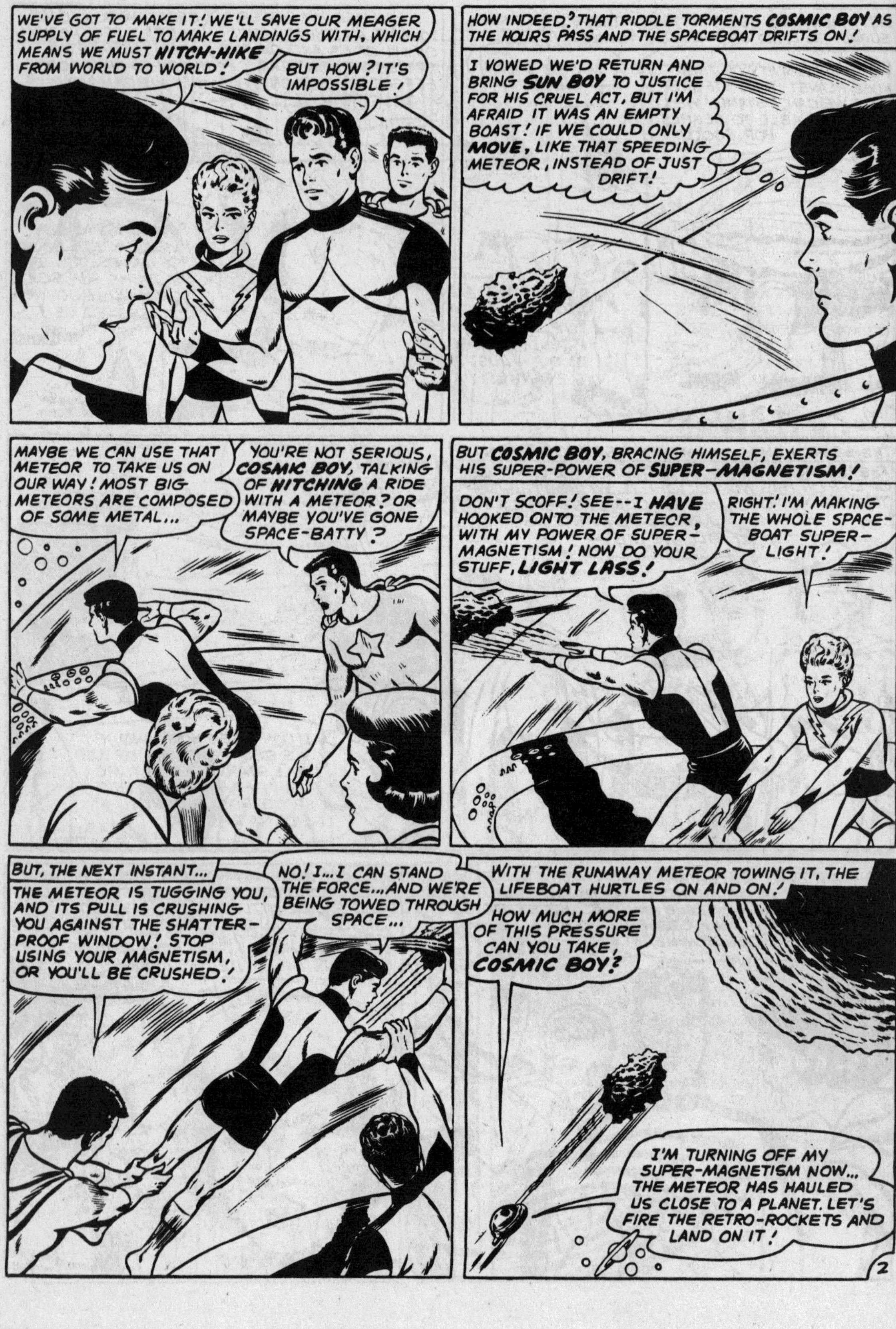

WE'VE GOT TO MAKE IT! WE'LL SAVE OUR MEAGER SUPPLY OF FUEL TO MAKE LANDINGS WITH, WHICH MEANS WE MUST HITCH-HIKE FROM WORLD TO WORLD!
BUT HOW? IT'S IMPOSSIBLE!
HOW INDEED? THAT RIDDLE TORMENTS COSMIC BOY AS THE HOURS PASS AND THE SPACEBOAT DRIFTS ON!
I VOWED WE'D RETURN AND BRING SUN BOY TO JUSTICE FOR HIS CRUEL ACT, BUT I'M AFRAID IT WAS AN EMPTY BOAST! IF WE COULD ONLY MOVE, LIKE THAT SPEEDING METEOR, INSTEAD OF JUST DRIFT!
MAYBE WE CAN USE THAT METEOR TO TAKE US ON OUR WAY! MOST BIG METEORS ARE COMPOSED OF SOME METAL...
YOU'RE NOT SERIOUS, COSMIC BOY, TALKING OF HITCHING A RIDE WITH A METEOR? OR MAYBE YOU'VE GONE SPACE-BATTY?
BUT COSMIC BOY, BRACING HIMSELF, EXERTS HIS SUPER-POWER OF SUPER-MAGNETISM!
DON'T SCOFF! SEE--I HAVE HOOKED ONTO THE METEOR, WITH MY POWER OF SUPER-MAGNETISM! NOW DO YOUR STUFF, LIGHT LASS!
RIGHT! I'M MAKING THE WHOLE SPACE-BOAT SUPER-LIGHT!
BUT, THE NEXT INSTANT...
THE METEOR IS TUGGING YOU, AND ITS PULL IS CRUSHING YOU AGAINST THE SHATTER-PROOF WINDOW! STOP USING YOUR MAGNETISM, OR YOU'LL BE CRUSHED!
NO! I...I CAN STAND THE FORCE...AND WE'RE BEING TOWED THROUGH SPACE...
WITH THE RUNAWAY METEOR TOWING IT, THE LIFEBOAT HURTLES ON AND ON!
HOW MUCH MORE OF THIS PRESSURE CAN YOU TAKE, COSMIC BOY?
I'M TURNING OFF MY SUPER-MAGNETISM NOW... THE METEOR HAS HAULED US CLOSE TO A PLANET. LET'S FIRE THE RETRO-ROCKETS AND LAND ON IT!
2

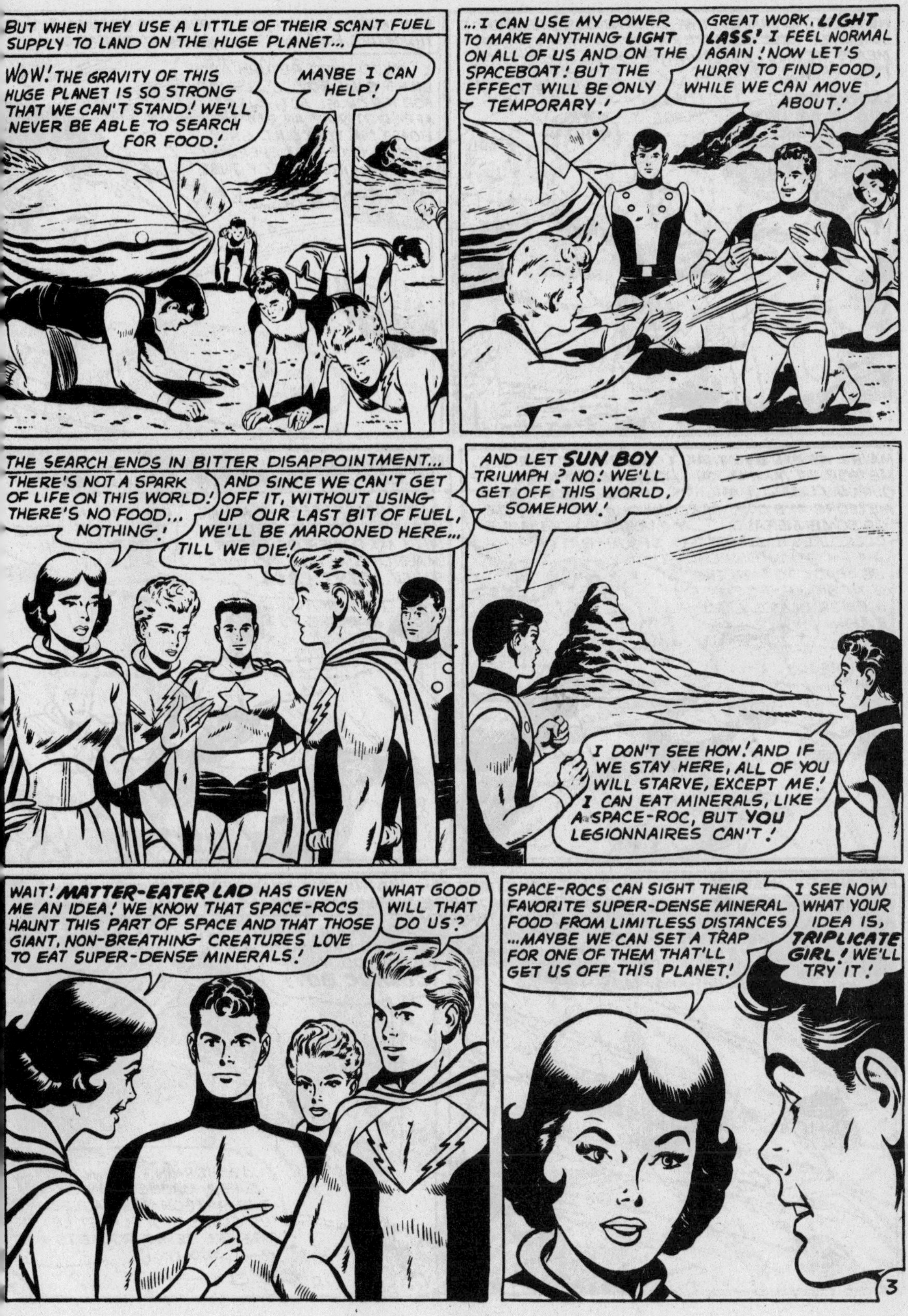
BUT WHEN THEY USE A LITTLE OF THEIR SCANT FUEL SUPPLY TO LAND ON THE HUGE PLANET...
WOW! THE GRAVITY OF THIS HUGE PLANET IS SO STRONG THAT WE CAN'T STAND! WE'LL NEVER BE ABLE TO SEARCH FOR FOOD!
MAYBE I CAN HELP!
...I CAN USE MY POWER TO MAKE ANYTHING LIGHT ON ALL OF US AND ON THE SPACEBOAT! BUT THE EFFECT WILL BE ONLY TEMPORARY!
GREAT WORK, LIGHT LASS! I FEEL NORMAL AGAIN! NOW LET'S HURRY TO FIND FOOD, WHILE WE CAN MOVE ABOUT!
THE SEARCH ENDS IN BITTER DISAPPOINTMENT...
THERE'S NOT A SPARK OF LIFE ON THIS WORLD! THERE'S NO FOOD... NOTHING!
AND SINCE WE CAN'T GET OFF IT, WITHOUT USING UP OUR LAST BIT OF FUEL, WE'LL BE MAROONED HERE... TILL WE DIE!
AND LET SUN BOY TRIUMPH? NO! WE'LL GET OFF THIS WORLD, SOMEHOW!
I DON'T SEE HOW! AND IF WE STAY HERE, ALL OF YOU WILL STARVE, EXCEPT ME! I CAN EAT MINERALS, LIKE A SPACE-ROC, BUT YOU LEGIONNAIRES CAN'T!
WAIT! MATTER-EATER LAD HAS GIVEN ME AN IDEA! WE KNOW THAT SPACE-ROCS HAUNT THIS PART OF SPACE AND THAT THOSE GIANT, NON-BREATHING CREATURES LOVE TO EAT SUPER-DENSE MINERALS!
WHAT GOOD WILL THAT DO US?
SPACE-ROCS CAN SIGHT THEIR FAVORITE SUPER-DENSE MINERAL FOOD FROM LIMITLESS DISTANCES ...MAYBE WE CAN SET A TRAP FOR ONE OF THEM THAT'LL GET US OFF THIS PLANET!
I SEE NOW WHAT YOUR IDEA IS, TRIPLICATE GIRL! WE'LL TRY IT!
3

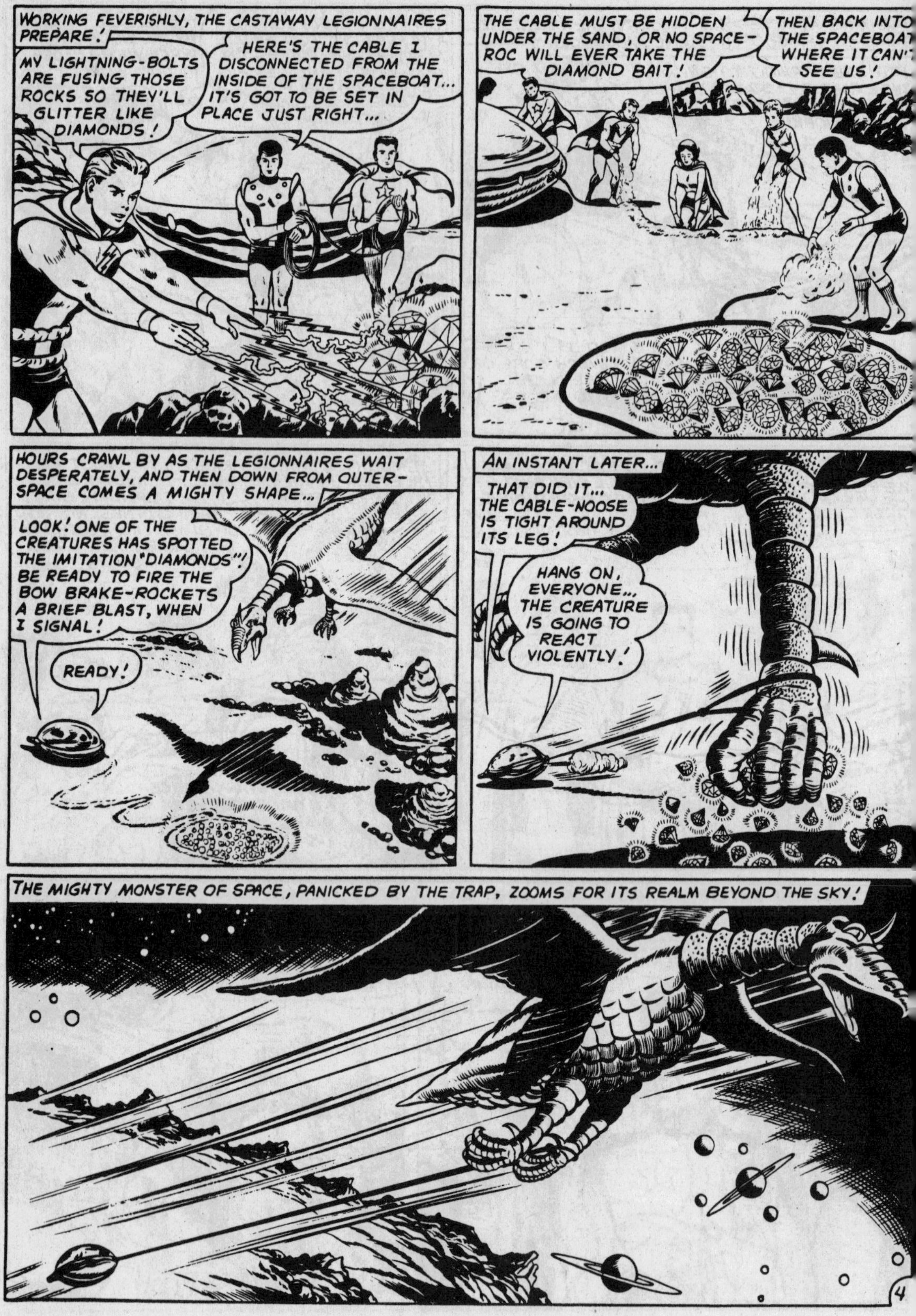
WORKING FEVERISHLY, THE CASTAWAY LEGIONNAIRES PREPARE!
MY LIGHTNING-BOLTS ARE FUSING THOSE ROCKS SO THEY'LL GLITTER LIKE DIAMONDS!
HERE'S THE CABLE I DISCONNECTED FROM THE INSIDE OF THE SPACEBOAT... IT'S GOT TO BE SET IN PLACE JUST RIGHT...
THE CABLE MUST BE HIDDEN UNDER THE SAND, OR NO SPACE-ROC WILL EVER TAKE THE DIAMOND BAIT!
THEN BACK INTO THE SPACEBOAT WHERE IT CAN'T SEE US!
HOURS CRAWL BY AS THE LEGIONNAIRES WAIT DESPERATELY, AND THEN DOWN FROM OUTER-SPACE COMES A MIGHTY SHAPE...
LOOK! ONE OF THE CREATURES HAS SPOTTED THE IMITATION "DIAMONDS"! BE READY TO FIRE THE BOW BRAKE-ROCKETS A BRIEF BLAST, WHEN I SIGNAL!
READY!
AN INSTANT LATER...
THAT DID IT... THE CABLE-NOOSE IS TIGHT AROUND ITS LEG!
HANG ON, EVERYONE... THE CREATURE IS GOING TO REACT VIOLENTLY!
THE MIGHTY MONSTER OF SPACE, PANICKED BY THE TRAP, ZOOMS FOR ITS REALM BEYOND THE SKY!
4

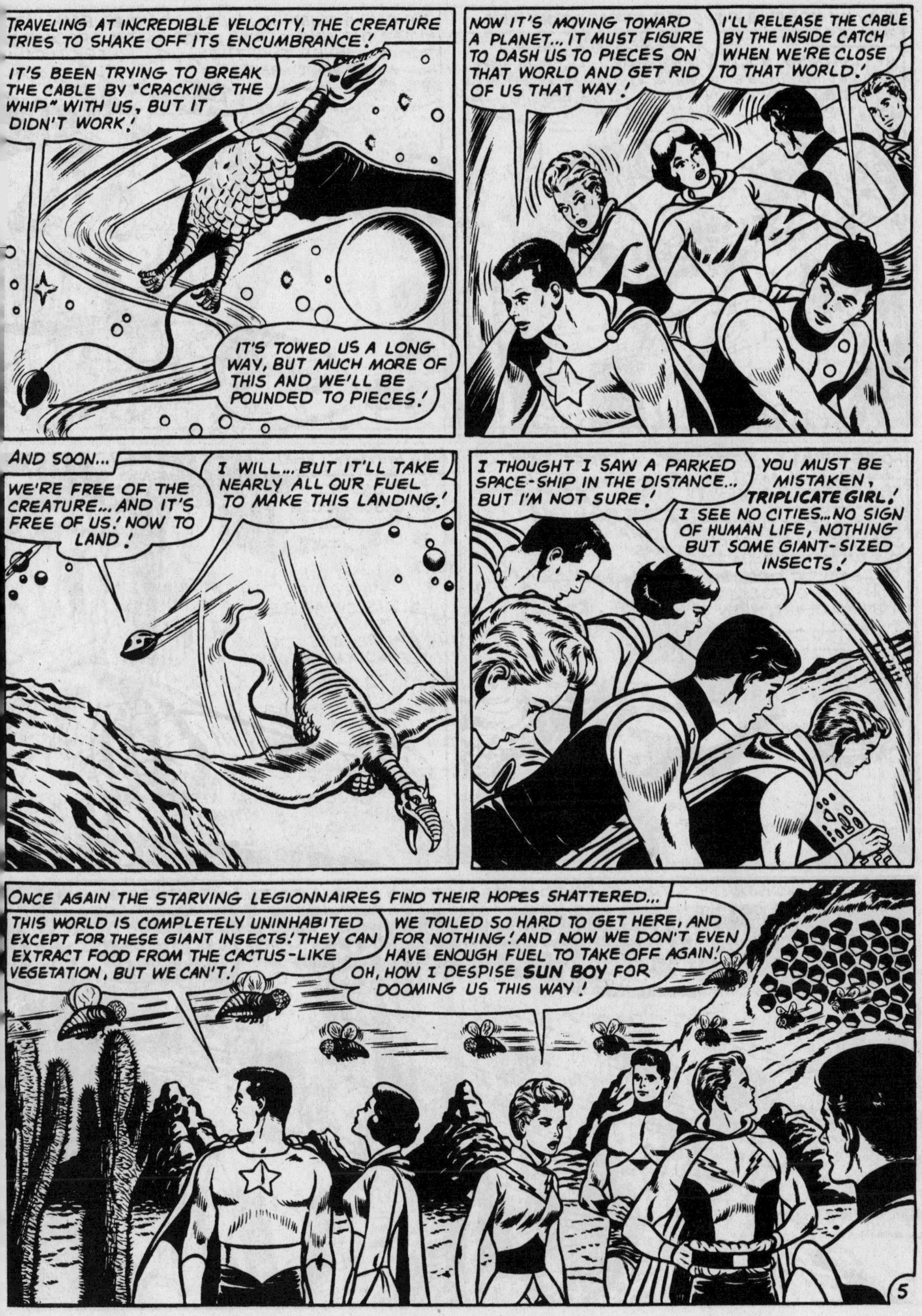
TRAVELING AT INCREDIBLE VELOCITY, THE CREATURE TRIES TO SHAKE OFF ITS ENCUMBRANCE!
IT'S BEEN TRYING TO BREAK THE CABLE BY "CRACKING THE WHIP" WITH US, BUT IT DIDN'T WORK!
IT'S TOWED US A LONG WAY, BUT MUCH MORE OF THIS AND WE'LL BE POUNDED TO PIECES!
NOW IT'S MOVING TOWARD A PLANET... IT MUST FIGURE TO DASH US TO PIECES ON THAT WORLD AND GET RID OF US THAT WAY!
I'LL RELEASE THE CABLE BY THE INSIDE CATCH WHEN WE'RE CLOSE TO THAT WORLD!
AND SOON...
WE'RE FREE OF THE CREATURE... AND IT'S FREE OF US! NOW TO LAND!
I WILL... BUT IT'LL TAKE NEARLY ALL OUR FUEL TO MAKE THIS LANDING!
I THOUGHT I SAW A PARKED SPACE-SHIP IN THE DISTANCE... BUT I'M NOT SURE!
YOU MUST BE MISTAKEN, TRIPLICATE GIRL! I SEE NO CITIES... NO SIGN OF HUMAN LIFE, NOTHING BUT SOME GIANT-SIZED INSECTS!
ONCE AGAIN THE STARVING LEGIONNAIRES FIND THEIR HOPES SHATTERED...
THIS WORLD IS COMPLETELY UNINHABITED EXCEPT FOR THESE GIANT INSECTS! THEY CAN EXTRACT FOOD FROM THE CACTUS-LIKE VEGETATION, BUT WE CAN'T!
WE TOILED SO HARD TO GET HERE, AND FOR NOTHING! AND NOW WE DON'T EVEN HAVE ENOUGH FUEL TO TAKE OFF AGAIN! OH, HOW I DESPISE SUN BOY FOR DOOMING US THIS WAY!
5

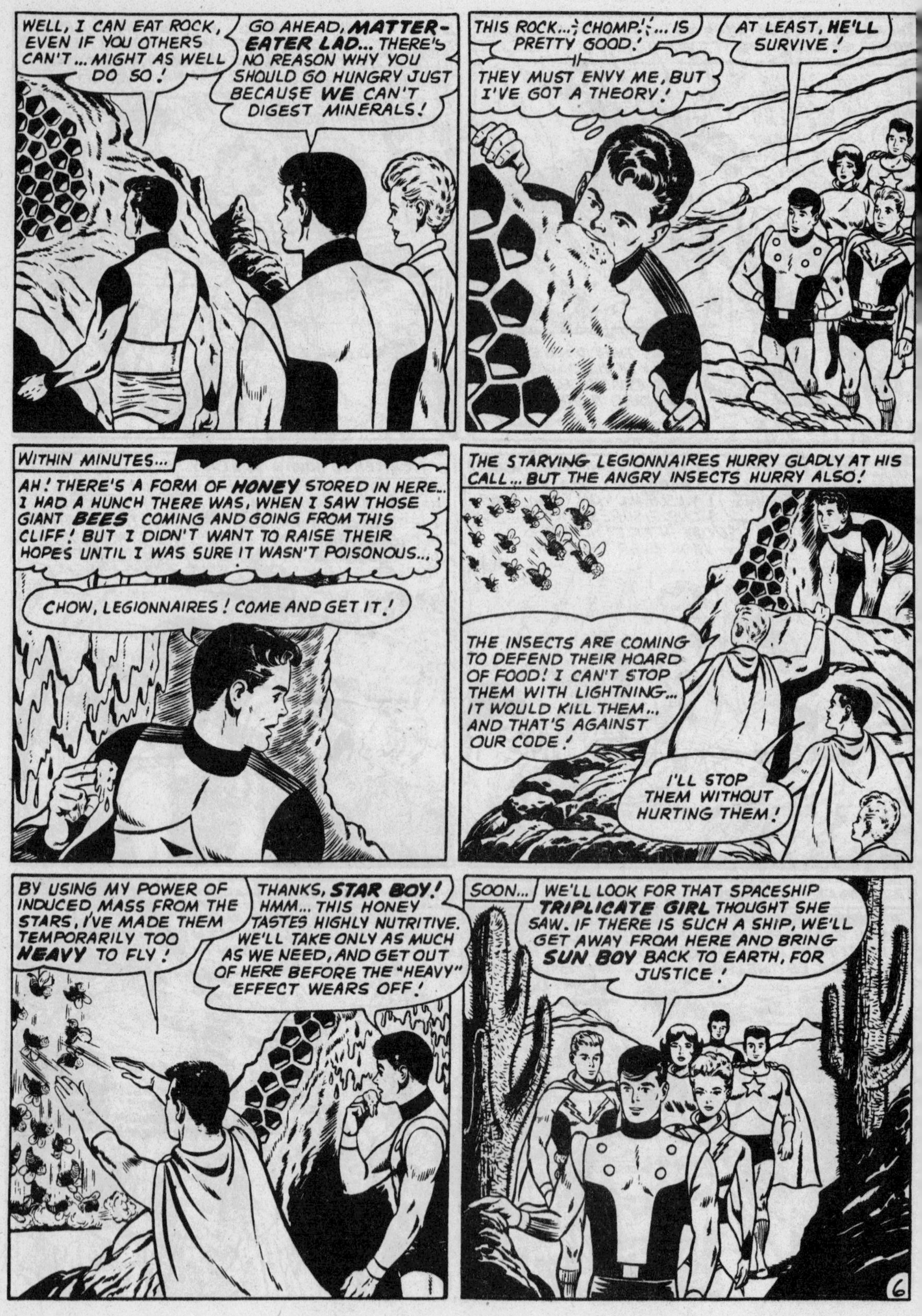

WELL, I CAN EAT ROCK, EVEN IF YOU OTHERS CAN'T... MIGHT AS WELL DO SO!
GO AHEAD, MATTER-EATER LAD... THERE'S NO REASON WHY YOU SHOULD GO HUNGRY JUST BECAUSE WE CAN'T DIGEST MINERALS!
THIS ROCK... CHOMP!... IS PRETTY GOOD!
THEY MUST ENVY ME, BUT I'VE GOT A THEORY!
AT LEAST, HE'LL SURVIVE!
WITHIN MINUTES...
AH! THERE'S A FORM OF HONEY STORED IN HERE.. I HAD A HUNCH THERE WAS, WHEN I SAW THOSE GIANT BEES COMING AND GOING FROM THIS CLIFF! BUT I DIDN'T WANT TO RAISE THEIR HOPES UNTIL I WAS SURE IT WASN'T POISONOUS...
CHOW, LEGIONNAIRES! COME AND GET IT!
THE STARVING LEGIONNAIRES HURRY GLADLY AT HIS CALL... BUT THE ANGRY INSECTS HURRY ALSO!
THE INSECTS ARE COMING TO DEFEND THEIR HOARD OF FOOD! I CAN'T STOP THEM WITH LIGHTNING... IT WOULD KILL THEM... AND THAT'S AGAINST OUR CODE!
I'LL STOP THEM WITHOUT HURTING THEM!
BY USING MY POWER OF INDUCED MASS FROM THE STARS, I'VE MADE THEM TEMPORARILY TOO HEAVY TO FLY!
THANKS, STAR BOY! HMM... THIS HONEY TASTES HIGHLY NUTRITIVE. WE'LL TAKE ONLY AS MUCH AS WE NEED, AND GET OUT OF HERE BEFORE THE "HEAVY" EFFECT WEARS OFF!
SOON...
WE'LL LOOK FOR THAT SPACESHIP TRIPLICATE GIRL THOUGHT SHE SAW. IF THERE IS SUCH A SHIP, WE'LL GET AWAY FROM HERE AND BRING SUN BOY BACK TO EARTH, FOR JUSTICE!
6

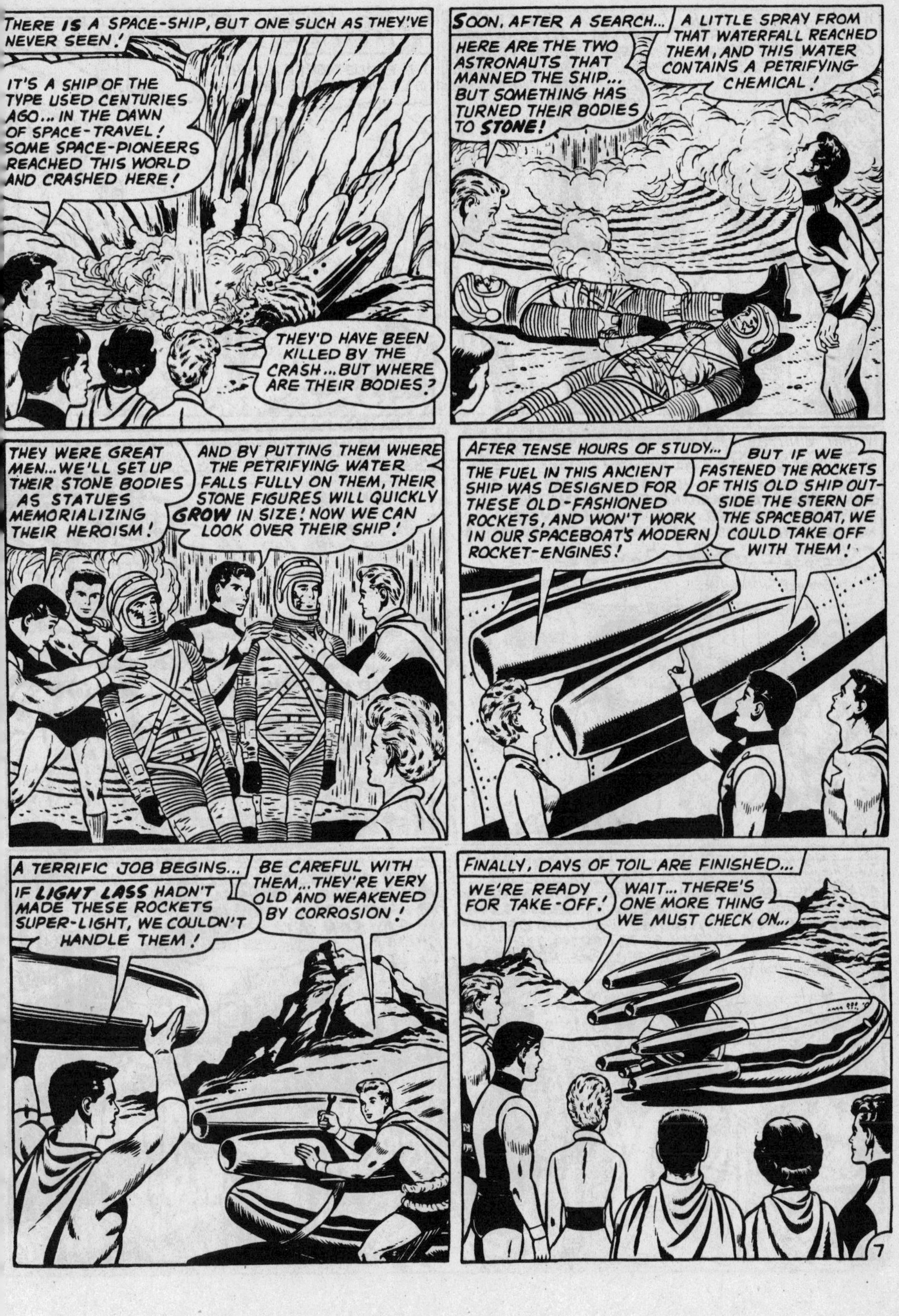
THERE IS A SPACE-SHIP, BUT ONE SUCH AS THEY'VE NEVER SEEN!
IT'S A SHIP OF THE TYPE USED CENTURIES AGO... IN THE DAWN OF SPACE-TRAVEL! SOME SPACE-PIONEERS REACHED THIS WORLD AND CRASHED HERE!
THEY'D HAVE BEEN KILLED BY THE CRASH... BUT WHERE ARE THEIR BODIES?
SOON, AFTER A SEARCH...
HERE ARE THE TWO ASTRONAUTS THAT MANNED THE SHIP... BUT SOMETHING HAS TURNED THEIR BODIES TO STONE!
A LITTLE SPRAY FROM THAT WATERFALL REACHED THEM, AND THIS WATER CONTAINS A PETRIFYING CHEMICAL!
THEY WERE GREAT MEN... WE'LL SET UP THEIR STONE BODIES AS STATUES MEMORIALIZING THEIR HEROISM!
AND BY PUTTING THEM WHERE THE PETRIFYING WATER FALLS FULLY ON THEM, THEIR STONE FIGURES WILL QUICKLY GROW IN SIZE! NOW WE CAN LOOK OVER THEIR SHIP!
AFTER TENSE HOURS OF STUDY...
THE FUEL IN THIS ANCIENT SHIP WAS DESIGNED FOR THESE OLD-FASHIONED ROCKETS, AND WON'T WORK IN OUR SPACEBOAT'S MODERN ROCKET-ENGINES!
BUT IF WE FASTENED THE ROCKETS OF THIS OLD SHIP OUTSIDE THE STERN OF THE SPACEBOAT, WE COULD TAKE OFF WITH THEM!
A TERRIFIC JOB BEGINS...
IF LIGHT LASS HADN'T MADE THESE ROCKETS SUPER-LIGHT, WE COULDN'T HANDLE THEM!
BE CAREFUL WITH THEM... THEY'RE VERY OLD AND WEAKENED BY CORROSION!
FINALLY, DAYS OF TOIL ARE FINISHED...
WE'RE READY FOR TAKE-OFF!
WAIT... THERE'S ONE MORE THING WE MUST CHECK ON...
7

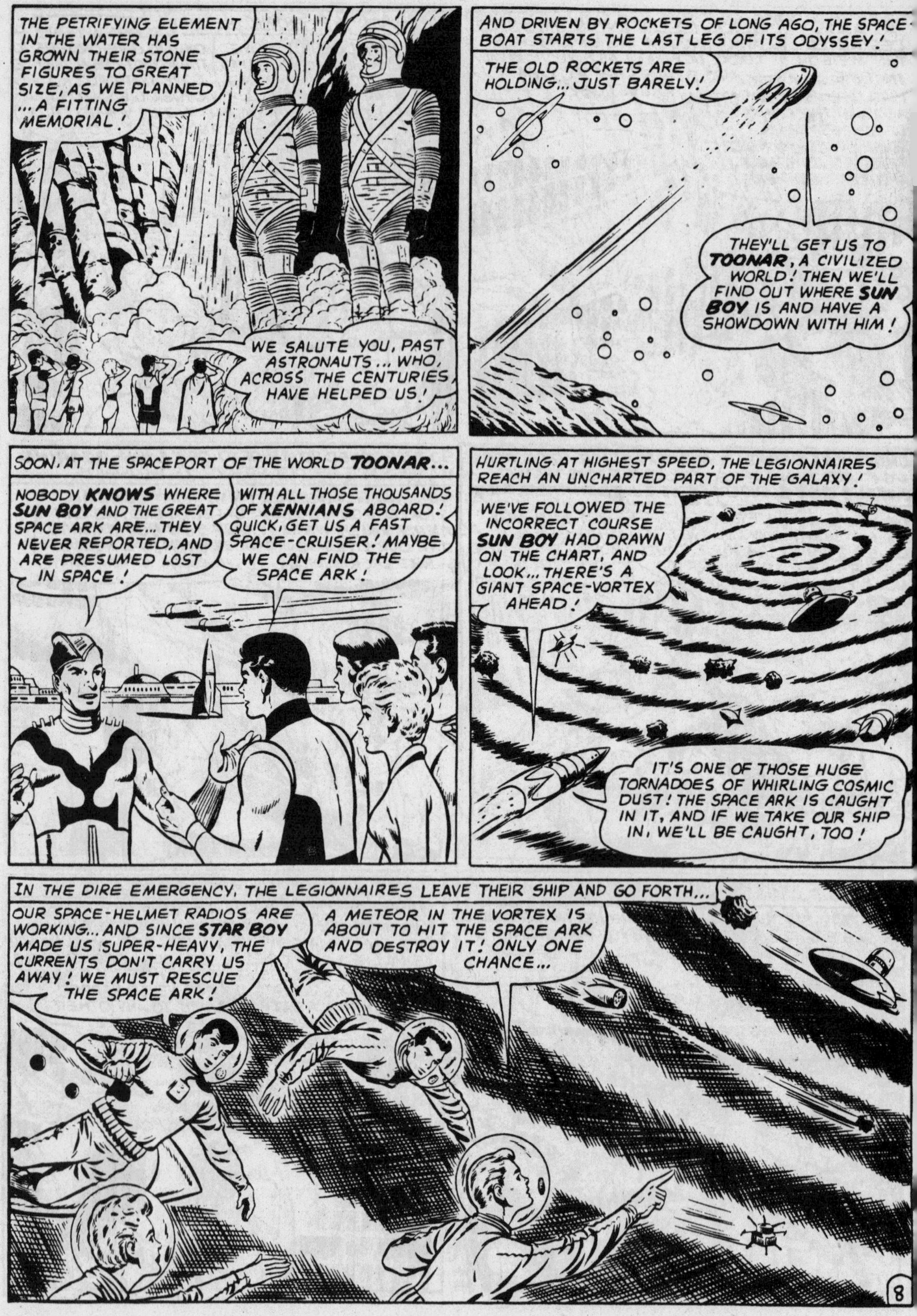
THE PETRIFYING ELEMENT IN THE WATER HAS GROWN THEIR STONE FIGURES TO GREAT SIZE, AS WE PLANNED ...A FITTING MEMORIAL!
WE SALUTE YOU, PAST ASTRONAUTS... WHO, ACROSS THE CENTURIES, HAVE HELPED US!
AND DRIVEN BY ROCKETS OF LONG AGO, THE SPACE-BOAT STARTS THE LAST LEG OF ITS ODYSSEY!
THE OLD ROCKETS ARE HOLDING... JUST BARELY!
THEY'LL GET US TO TOONAR, A CIVILIZED WORLD! THEN WE'LL FIND OUT WHERE SUN BOY IS AND HAVE A SHOWDOWN WITH HIM!
SOON, AT THE SPACEPORT OF THE WORLD TOONAR...
NOBODY KNOWS WHERE SUN BOY AND THE GREAT SPACE ARK ARE... THEY NEVER REPORTED, AND ARE PRESUMED LOST IN SPACE!
WITH ALL THOSE THOUSANDS OF XENNIANS ABOARD! QUICK, GET US A FAST SPACE-CRUISER! MAYBE WE CAN FIND THE SPACE ARK!
HURTLING AT HIGHEST SPEED, THE LEGIONNAIRES REACH AN UNCHARTED PART OF THE GALAXY!
WE'VE FOLLOWED THE INCORRECT COURSE SUN BOY HAD DRAWN ON THE CHART, AND LOOK... THERE'S A GIANT SPACE-VORTEX AHEAD!
IT'S ONE OF THOSE HUGE TORNADOES OF WHIRLING COSMIC DUST! THE SPACE ARK IS CAUGHT IN IT, AND IF WE TAKE OUR SHIP IN, WE'LL BE CAUGHT, TOO!
IN THE DIRE EMERGENCY, THE LEGIONNAIRES LEAVE THEIR SHIP AND GO FORTH...
OUR SPACE-HELMET RADIOS ARE WORKING... AND SINCE STAR BOY MADE US SUPER-HEAVY, THE CURRENTS DON'T CARRY US AWAY! WE MUST RESCUE THE SPACE ARK!
A METEOR IN THE VORTEX IS ABOUT TO HIT THE SPACE ARK AND DESTROY IT! ONLY ONE CHANCE...
8

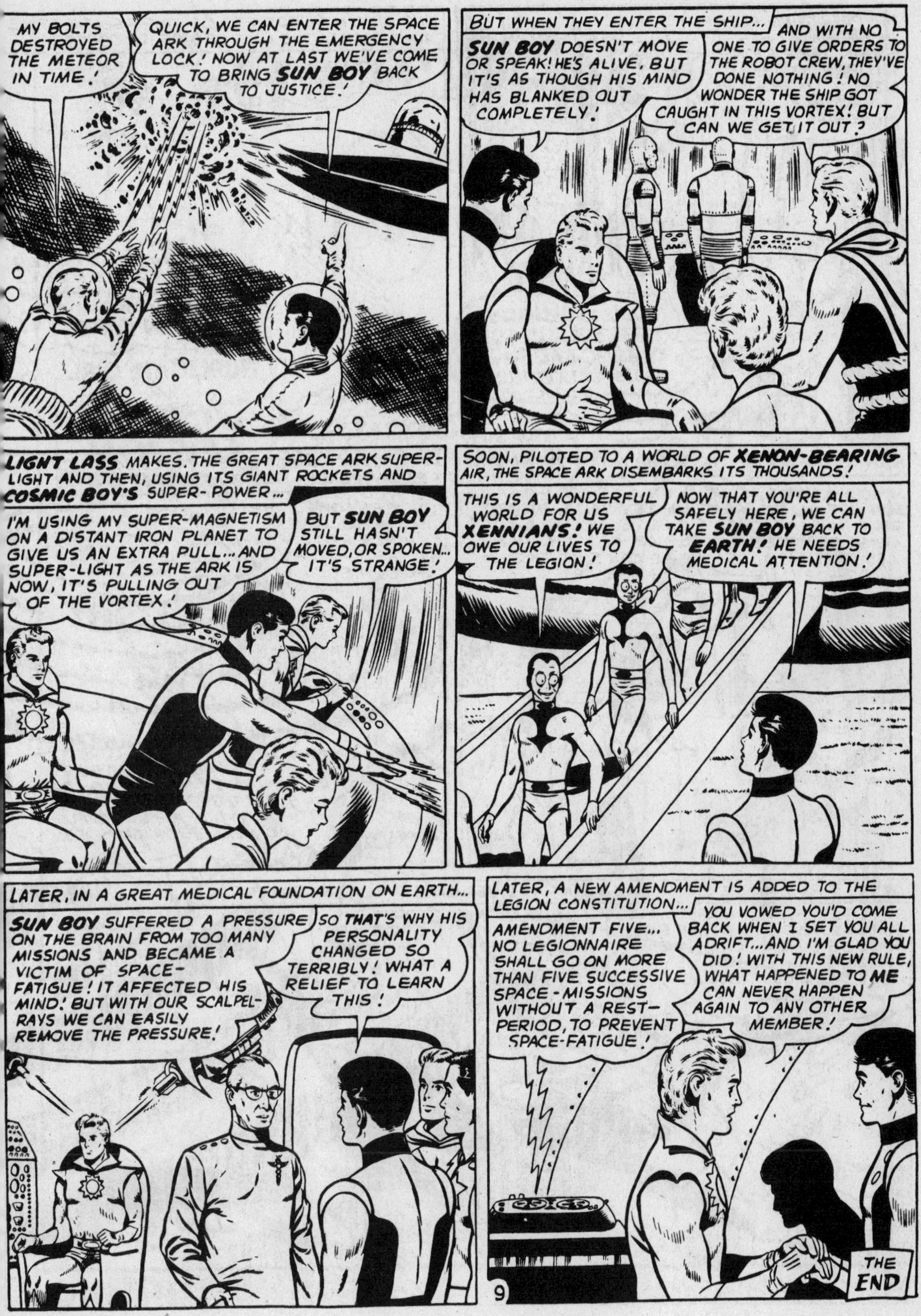
MY BOLTS DESTROYED THE METEOR IN TIME!
QUICK, WE CAN ENTER THE SPACE ARK THROUGH THE EMERGENCY LOCK! NOW AT LAST WE'VE COME TO BRING SUN BOY BACK TO JUSTICE!
BUT WHEN THEY ENTER THE SHIP...
SUN BOY DOESN'T MOVE OR SPEAK! HE'S ALIVE, BUT IT'S AS THOUGH HIS MIND HAS BLANKED OUT COMPLETELY!
AND WITH NO ONE TO GIVE ORDERS TO THE ROBOT CREW, THEY'VE DONE NOTHING! NO WONDER THE SHIP GOT CAUGHT IN THIS VORTEX! BUT CAN WE GET IT OUT?
LIGHT LASS MAKES THE GREAT SPACE ARK SUPER-LIGHT AND THEN, USING ITS GIANT ROCKETS AND COSMIC BOY'S SUPER-POWER...
I'M USING MY SUPER-MAGNETISM ON A DISTANT IRON PLANET TO GIVE US AN EXTRA PULL... AND SUPER-LIGHT AS THE ARK IS NOW, IT'S PULLING OUT OF THE VORTEX!
BUT SUN BOY STILL HASN'T MOVED, OR SPOKEN... IT'S STRANGE!
SOON, PILOTED TO A WORLD OF XENON-BEARING AIR, THE SPACE ARK DISEMBARKS ITS THOUSANDS!
THIS IS A WONDERFUL WORLD FOR US XENNIANS! WE OWE OUR LIVES TO THE LEGION!
NOW THAT YOU'RE ALL SAFELY HERE, WE CAN TAKE SUN BOY BACK TO EARTH! HE NEEDS MEDICAL ATTENTION!
LATER, IN A GREAT MEDICAL FOUNDATION ON EARTH...
SUN BOY SUFFERED A PRESSURE ON THE BRAIN FROM TOO MANY MISSIONS AND BECAME A VICTIM OF SPACE-FATIGUE! IT AFFECTED HIS MIND! BUT WITH OUR SCALPEL-RAYS WE CAN EASILY REMOVE THE PRESSURE!
SO THAT'S WHY HIS PERSONALITY CHANGED SO TERRIBLY! WHAT A RELIEF TO LEARN THIS!
LATER, A NEW AMENDMENT IS ADDED TO THE LEGION CONSTITUTION...
AMENDMENT FIVE... NO LEGIONNAIRE SHALL GO ON MORE THAN FIVE SUCCESSIVE SPACE-MISSIONS WITHOUT A REST-PERIOD, TO PREVENT SPACE-FATIGUE!
YOU VOWED YOU'D COME BACK WHEN I SET YOU ALL ADRIFT... AND I'M GLAD YOU DID! WITH THIS NEW RULE, WHAT HAPPENED TO ME CAN NEVER HAPPEN AGAIN TO ANY OTHER MEMBER!
THE END
9

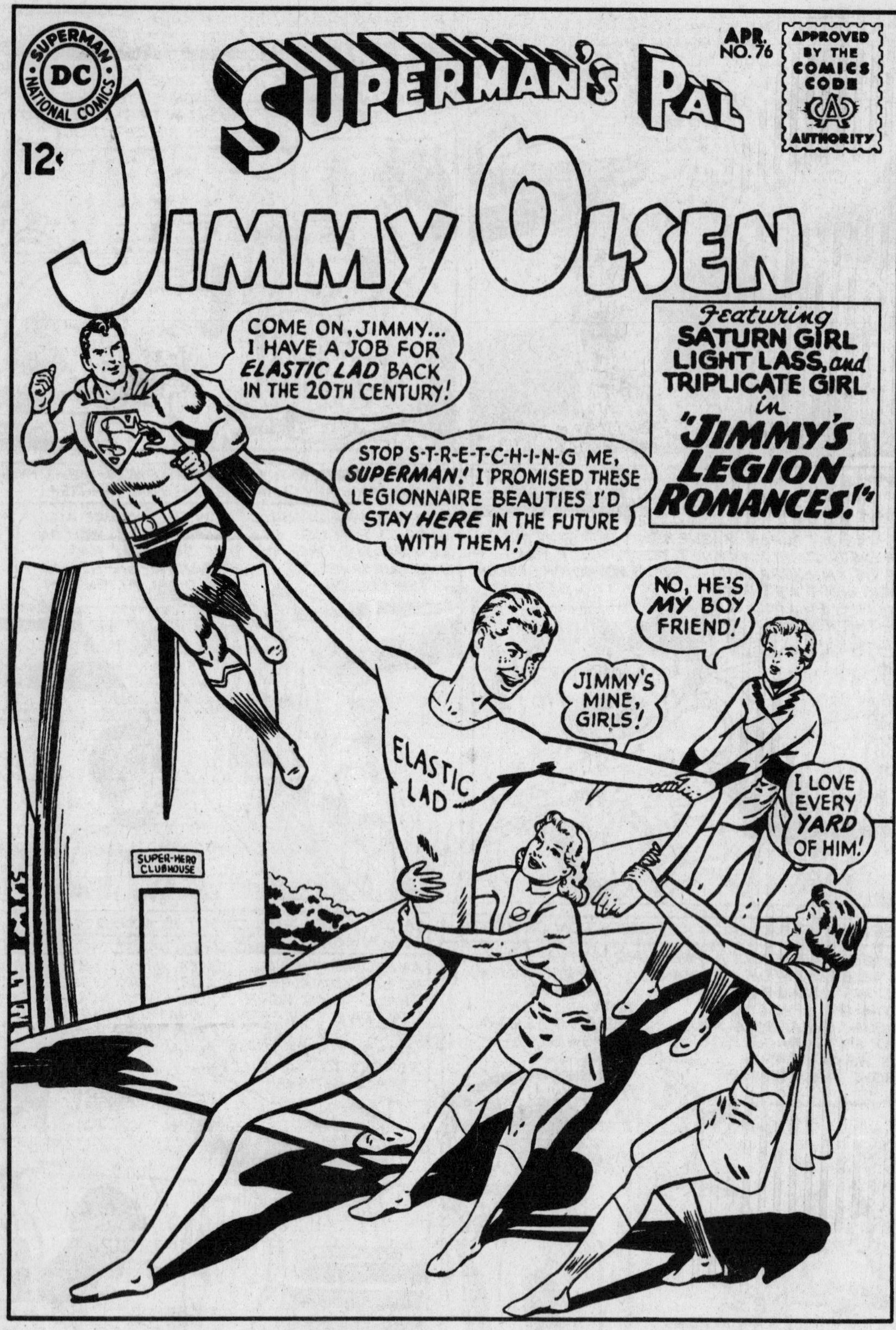
SUPERMAN DC NATIONAL COMICS
12¢
SUPERMAN'S PAL
APR. NO. 76
APPROVED BY THE COMICS CODE AUTHORITY
JIMMY OLSEN
Featuring SATURN GIRL LIGHT LASS, and TRIPLICATE GIRL in "JIMMY'S LEGION ROMANCES!"
COME ON, JIMMY... I HAVE A JOB FOR ELASTIC LAD BACK IN THE 20TH CENTURY!
STOP S-T-R-E-T-C-H-I-N-G ME, SUPERMAN! I PROMISED THESE LEGIONNAIRE BEAUTIES I'D STAY HERE IN THE FUTURE WITH THEM!
NO, HE'S MY BOY FRIEND!
JIMMY'S MINE, GIRLS!
I LOVE EVERY YARD OF HIM!
ELASTIC LAD
SUPER-HERO CLUBHOUSE

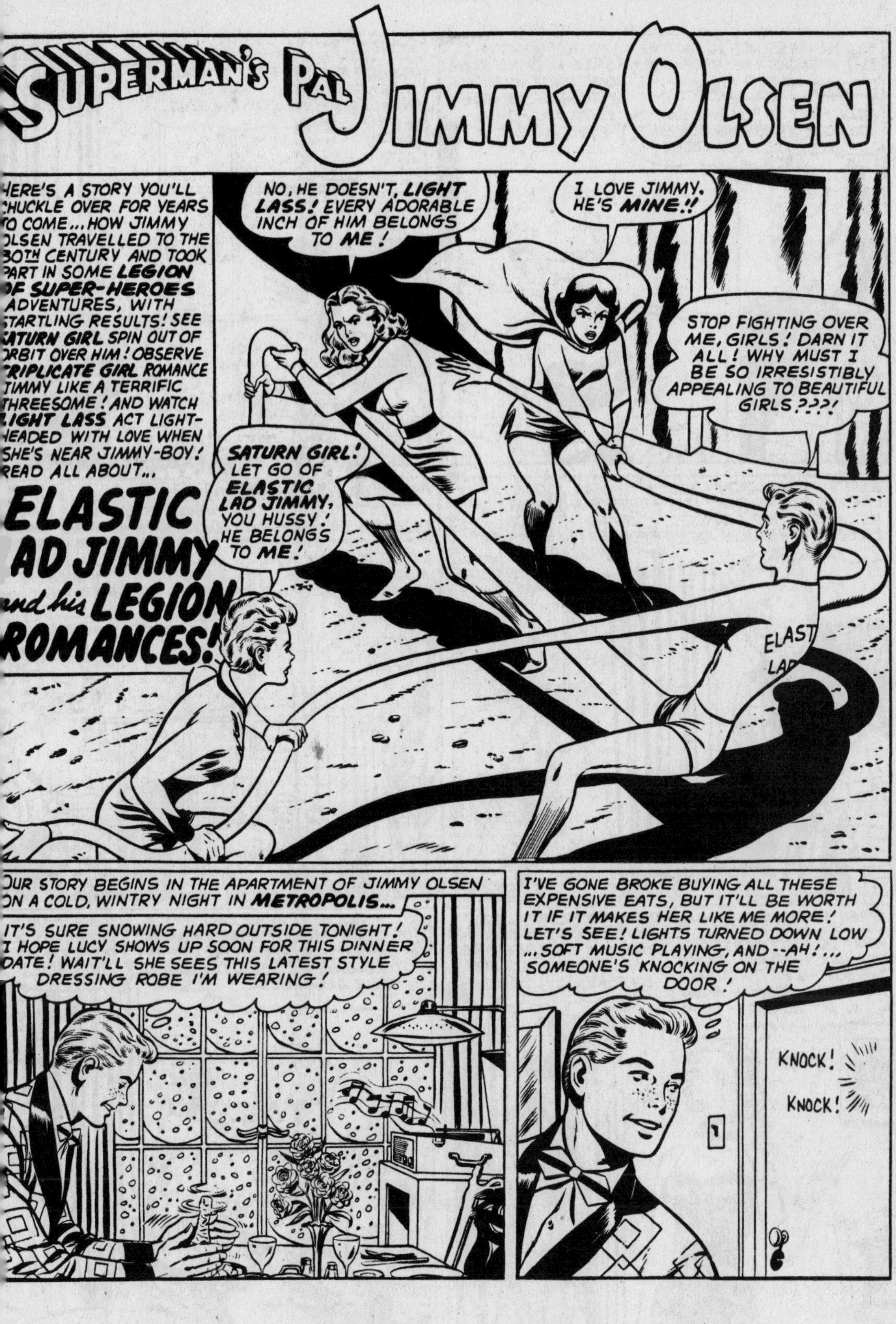
SUPERMAN'S PAL JIMMY OLSEN
HERE'S A STORY YOU'LL CHUCKLE OVER FOR YEARS TO COME... HOW JIMMY OLSEN TRAVELLED TO THE 30TH CENTURY AND TOOK PART IN SOME LEGION OF SUPER-HEROES ADVENTURES, WITH STARTLING RESULTS! SEE SATURN GIRL SPIN OUT OF ORBIT OVER HIM! OBSERVE TRIPLICATE GIRL ROMANCE JIMMY LIKE A TERRIFIC THREESOME! AND WATCH LIGHT LASS ACT LIGHT-HEADED WITH LOVE WHEN SHE'S NEAR JIMMY-BOY! READ ALL ABOUT...
ELASTIC LAD JIMMY and his LEGION ROMANCES!
NO, HE DOESN'T, LIGHT LASS! EVERY ADORABLE INCH OF HIM BELONGS TO ME!
I LOVE JIMMY. HE'S MINE!!
STOP FIGHTING OVER ME, GIRLS! DARN IT ALL! WHY MUST I BE SO IRRESISTIBLY APPEALING TO BEAUTIFUL GIRLS???!
SATURN GIRL! LET GO OF ELASTIC LAD JIMMY, YOU HUSSY! HE BELONGS TO ME!
ELAST LA
OUR STORY BEGINS IN THE APARTMENT OF JIMMY OLSEN ON A COLD, WINTRY NIGHT IN METROPOLIS...
IT'S SURE SNOWING HARD OUTSIDE TONIGHT! I HOPE LUCY SHOWS UP SOON FOR THIS DINNER DATE! WAIT'LL SHE SEES THIS LATEST STYLE DRESSING ROBE I'M WEARING!
I'VE GONE BROKE BUYING ALL THESE EXPENSIVE EATS, BUT IT'LL BE WORTH IT IF IT MAKES HER LIKE ME MORE! LET'S SEE! LIGHTS TURNED DOWN LOW ...SOFT MUSIC PLAYING, AND--AH!... SOMEONE'S KNOCKING ON THE DOOR!
KNOCK!
KNOCK!

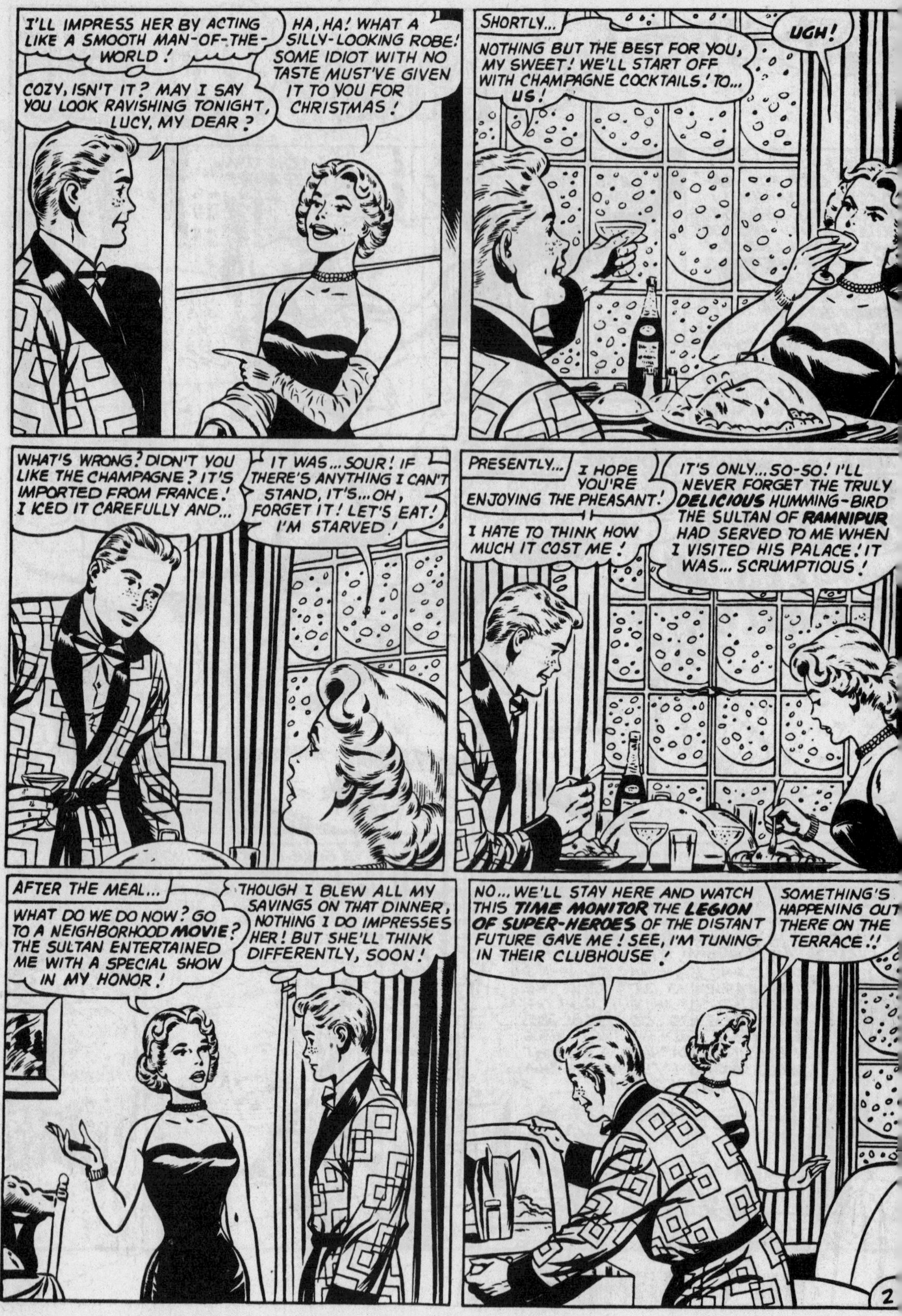
I'LL IMPRESS HER BY ACTING LIKE A SMOOTH MAN-OF-THE-WORLD!
COZY, ISN'T IT? MAY I SAY YOU LOOK RAVISHING TONIGHT, LUCY, MY DEAR?
HA, HA! WHAT A SILLY-LOOKING ROBE! SOME IDIOT WITH NO TASTE MUST'VE GIVEN IT TO YOU FOR CHRISTMAS!
SHORTLY...
NOTHING BUT THE BEST FOR YOU, MY SWEET! WE'LL START OFF WITH CHAMPAGNE COCKTAILS! TO... US!
UGH!
WHAT'S WRONG? DIDN'T YOU LIKE THE CHAMPAGNE? IT'S IMPORTED FROM FRANCE! I ICED IT CAREFULLY AND...
IT WAS... SOUR! IF THERE'S ANYTHING I CAN'T STAND, IT'S... OH, FORGET IT! LET'S EAT! I'M STARVED!
PRESENTLY...
I HOPE YOU'RE ENJOYING THE PHEASANT!
I HATE TO THINK HOW MUCH IT COST ME!
IT'S ONLY... SO-SO! I'LL NEVER FORGET THE TRULY DELICIOUS HUMMING-BIRD THE SULTAN OF RAMNIPUR HAD SERVED TO ME WHEN I VISITED HIS PALACE! IT WAS... SCRUMPTIOUS!
AFTER THE MEAL...
WHAT DO WE DO NOW? GO TO A NEIGHBORHOOD MOVIE? THE SULTAN ENTERTAINED ME WITH A SPECIAL SHOW IN MY HONOR!
THOUGH I BLEW ALL MY SAVINGS ON THAT DINNER, NOTHING I DO IMPRESSES HER! BUT SHE'LL THINK DIFFERENTLY, SOON!
NO... WE'LL STAY HERE AND WATCH THIS TIME MONITOR THE LEGION OF SUPER-HEROES OF THE DISTANT FUTURE GAVE ME! SEE, I'M TUNING IN THEIR CLUBHOUSE!
SOMETHING'S HAPPENING OUT THERE ON THE TERRACE!!
2

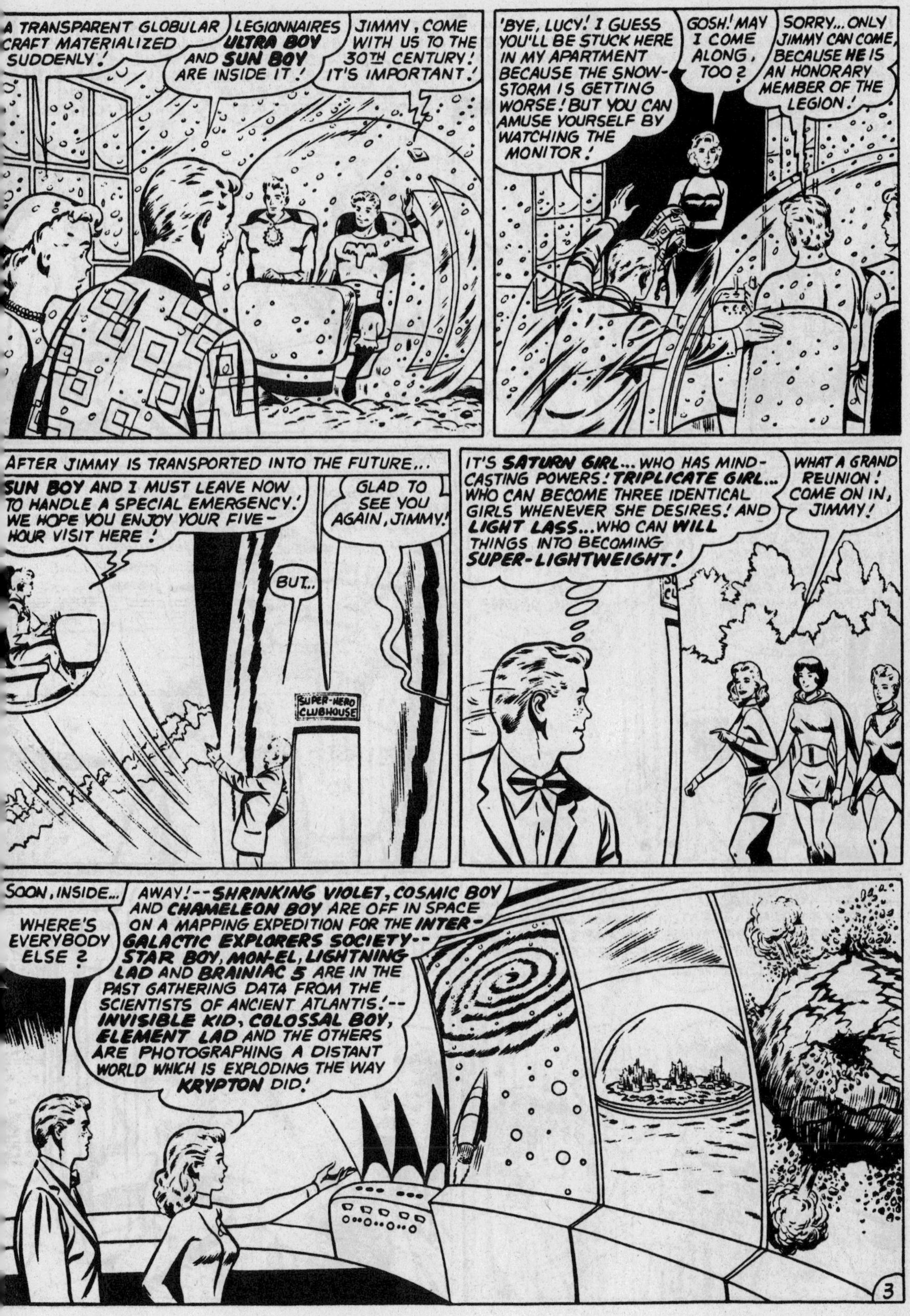
A TRANSPARENT GLOBULAR CRAFT MATERIALIZED SUDDENLY!
LEGIONNAIRES ULTRA BOY AND SUN BOY ARE INSIDE IT!
JIMMY, COME WITH US TO THE 30TH CENTURY! IT'S IMPORTANT!
'BYE, LUCY! I GUESS YOU'LL BE STUCK HERE IN MY APARTMENT BECAUSE THE SNOW-STORM IS GETTING WORSE! BUT YOU CAN AMUSE YOURSELF BY WATCHING THE MONITOR!
GOSH! MAY I COME ALONG, TOO?
SORRY... ONLY JIMMY CAN COME, BECAUSE HE IS AN HONORARY MEMBER OF THE LEGION!
AFTER JIMMY IS TRANSPORTED INTO THE FUTURE...
SUN BOY AND I MUST LEAVE NOW TO HANDLE A SPECIAL EMERGENCY! WE HOPE YOU ENJOY YOUR FIVE-HOUR VISIT HERE!
BUT...
GLAD TO SEE YOU AGAIN, JIMMY!
SUPER-HERO CLUBHOUSE
IT'S SATURN GIRL... WHO HAS MIND-CASTING POWERS! TRIPLICATE GIRL... WHO CAN BECOME THREE IDENTICAL GIRLS WHENEVER SHE DESIRES! AND LIGHT LASS... WHO CAN WILL THINGS INTO BECOMING SUPER-LIGHTWEIGHT!
WHAT A GRAND REUNION! COME ON IN, JIMMY!
SOON, INSIDE...
WHERE'S EVERYBODY ELSE?
AWAY!--SHRINKING VIOLET, COSMIC BOY AND CHAMELEON BOY ARE OFF IN SPACE ON A MAPPING EXPEDITION FOR THE INTER-GALACTIC EXPLORERS SOCIETY--STAR BOY, MON-EL, LIGHTNING LAD AND BRAINIAC 5 ARE IN THE PAST GATHERING DATA FROM THE SCIENTISTS OF ANCIENT ATLANTIS!--INVISIBLE KID, COLOSSAL BOY, ELEMENT LAD AND THE OTHERS ARE PHOTOGRAPHING A DISTANT WORLD WHICH IS EXPLODING THE WAY KRYPTON DID!
3

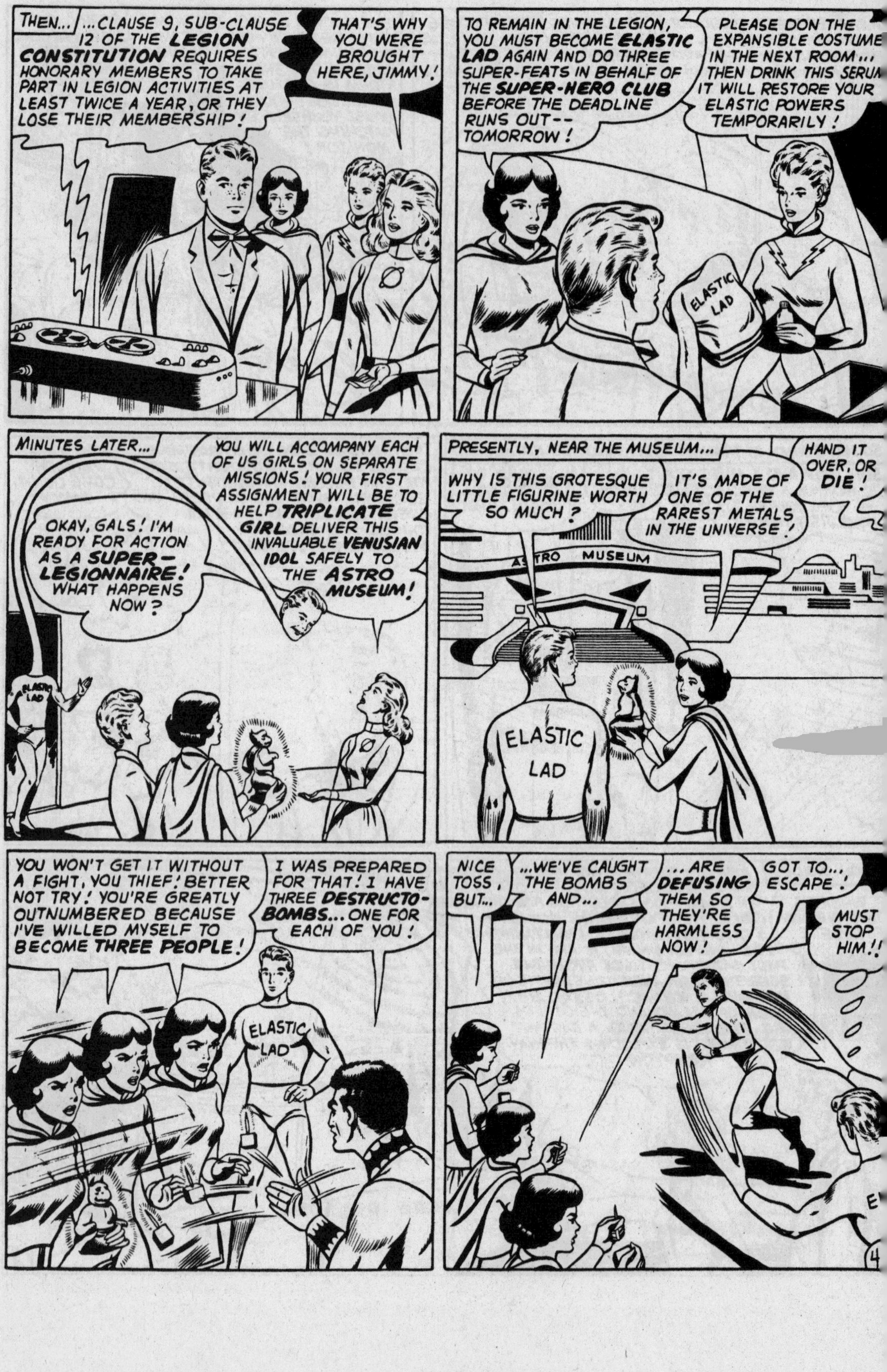
THEN...
...CLAUSE 9, SUB-CLAUSE 12 OF THE LEGION CONSTITUTION REQUIRES HONORARY MEMBERS TO TAKE PART IN LEGION ACTIVITIES AT LEAST TWICE A YEAR, OR THEY LOSE THEIR MEMBERSHIP!
THAT'S WHY YOU WERE BROUGHT HERE, JIMMY!
TO REMAIN IN THE LEGION, YOU MUST BECOME ELASTIC LAD AGAIN AND DO THREE SUPER-FEATS IN BEHALF OF THE SUPER-HERO CLUB BEFORE THE DEADLINE RUNS OUT--TOMORROW!
PLEASE DON THE EXPANSIBLE COSTUME IN THE NEXT ROOM... THEN DRINK THIS SERUM IT WILL RESTORE YOUR ELASTIC POWERS TEMPORARILY!
ELASTIC LAD
MINUTES LATER...
YOU WILL ACCOMPANY EACH OF US GIRLS ON SEPARATE MISSIONS! YOUR FIRST ASSIGNMENT WILL BE TO HELP TRIPLICATE GIRL DELIVER THIS INVALUABLE VENUSIAN IDOL SAFELY TO THE ASTRO MUSEUM!
OKAY, GALS! I'M READY FOR ACTION AS A SUPER-LEGIONNAIRE! WHAT HAPPENS NOW?
PRESENTLY, NEAR THE MUSEUM...
WHY IS THIS GROTESQUE LITTLE FIGURINE WORTH SO MUCH?
IT'S MADE OF ONE OF THE RAREST METALS IN THE UNIVERSE!
HAND IT OVER, OR DIE!
ASTRO MUSEUM
ELASTIC LAD
YOU WON'T GET IT WITHOUT A FIGHT, YOU THIEF! BETTER NOT TRY! YOU'RE GREATLY OUTNUMBERED BECAUSE I'VE WILLED MYSELF TO BECOME THREE PEOPLE!
I WAS PREPARED FOR THAT! I HAVE THREE DESTRUCTO-BOMBS... ONE FOR EACH OF YOU!
ELASTIC LAD
NICE TOSS, BUT...
...WE'VE CAUGHT THE BOMBS AND...
... ARE DEFUSING THEM SO THEY'RE HARMLESS NOW!
GOT TO... ESCAPE!
MUST STOP HIM!!

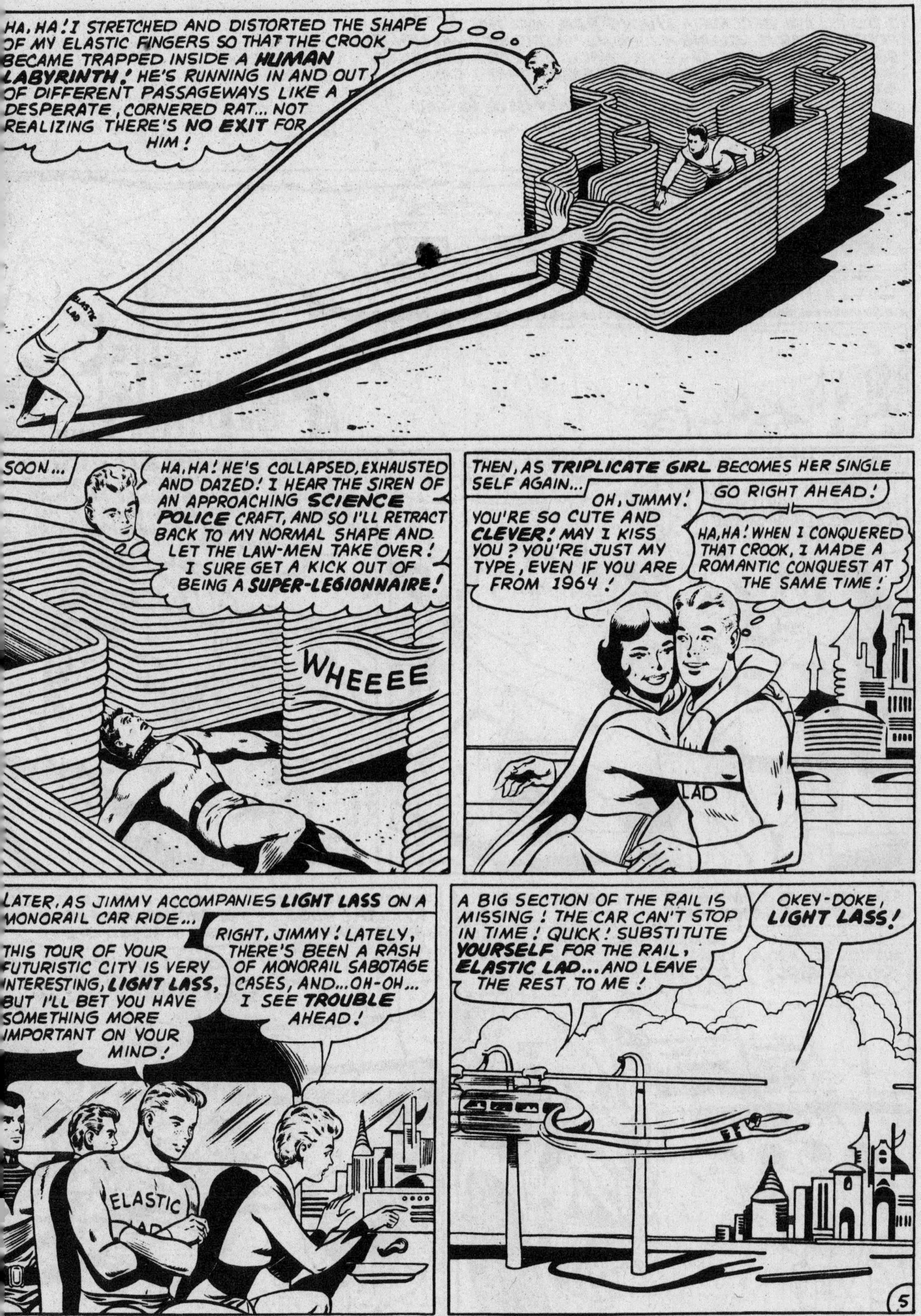
HA, HA! I STRETCHED AND DISTORTED THE SHAPE OF MY ELASTIC FINGERS SO THAT THE CROOK BECAME TRAPPED INSIDE A HUMAN LABYRINTH! HE'S RUNNING IN AND OUT OF DIFFERENT PASSAGEWAYS LIKE A DESPERATE, CORNERED RAT... NOT REALIZING THERE'S NO EXIT FOR HIM!
ELASTIC LAD
SOON...
HA, HA! HE'S COLLAPSED, EXHAUSTED AND DAZED! I HEAR THE SIREN OF AN APPROACHING SCIENCE POLICE CRAFT, AND SO I'LL RETRACT BACK TO MY NORMAL SHAPE AND LET THE LAW-MEN TAKE OVER! I SURE GET A KICK OUT OF BEING A SUPER-LEGIONNAIRE!
WHEEEE
THEN, AS TRIPLICATE GIRL BECOMES HER SINGLE SELF AGAIN...
OH, JIMMY! YOU'RE SO CUTE AND CLEVER! MAY I KISS YOU? YOU'RE JUST MY TYPE, EVEN IF YOU ARE FROM 1964!
GO RIGHT AHEAD!
HA, HA! WHEN I CONQUERED THAT CROOK, I MADE A ROMANTIC CONQUEST AT THE SAME TIME!
LAD
LATER, AS JIMMY ACCOMPANIES LIGHT LASS ON A MONORAIL CAR RIDE...
THIS TOUR OF YOUR FUTURISTIC CITY IS VERY INTERESTING, LIGHT LASS, BUT I'LL BET YOU HAVE SOMETHING MORE IMPORTANT ON YOUR MIND!
RIGHT, JIMMY! LATELY, THERE'S BEEN A RASH OF MONORAIL SABOTAGE CASES, AND...OH-OH... I SEE TROUBLE AHEAD!
ELASTIC LAD
A BIG SECTION OF THE RAIL IS MISSING! THE CAR CAN'T STOP IN TIME! QUICK! SUBSTITUTE YOURSELF FOR THE RAIL, ELASTIC LAD...AND LEAVE THE REST TO ME!
OKEY-DOKE, LIGHT LASS!
5

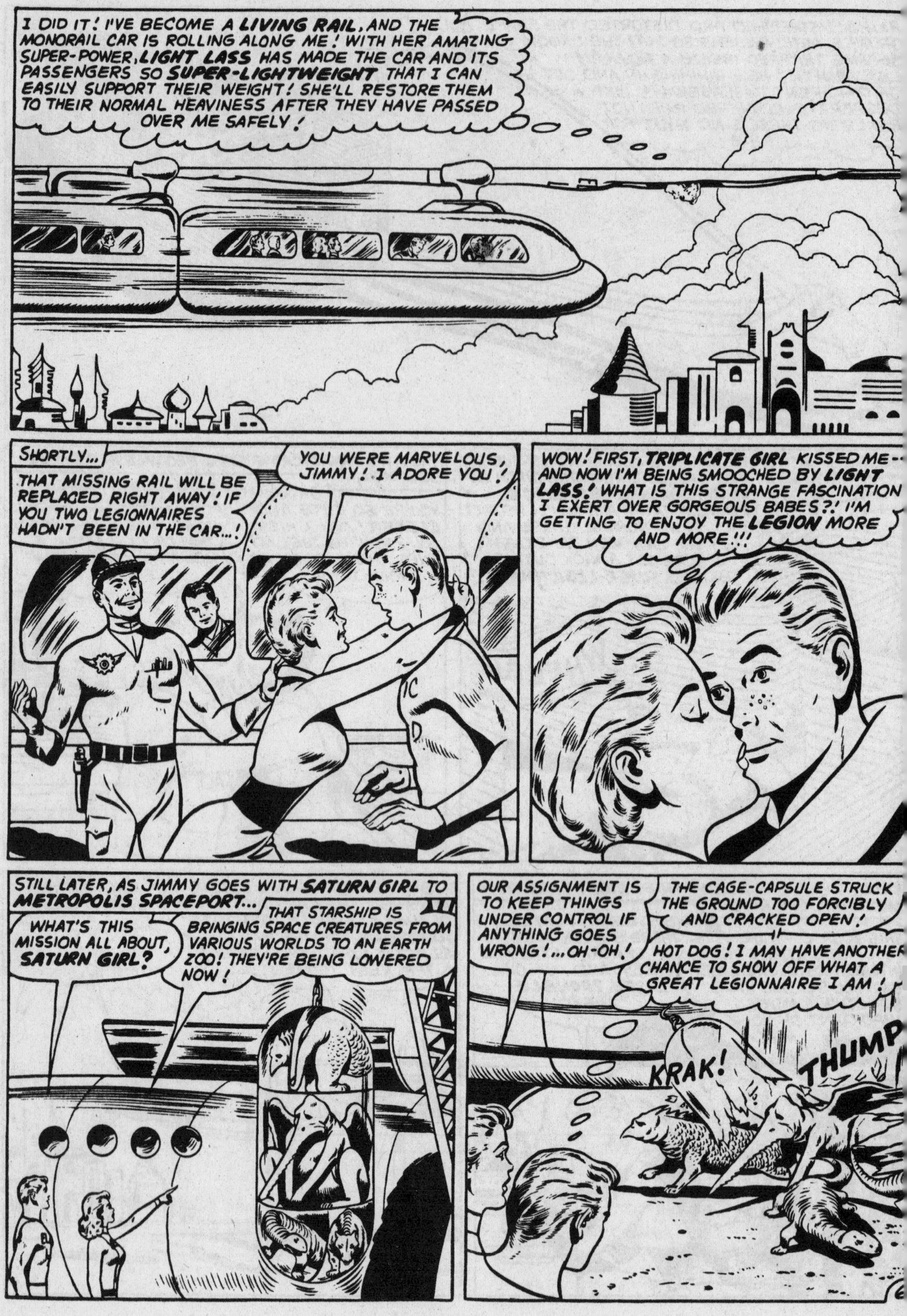
I DID IT! I'VE BECOME A LIVING RAIL, AND THE MONORAIL CAR IS ROLLING ALONG ME! WITH HER AMAZING SUPER-POWER, LIGHT LASS HAS MADE THE CAR AND ITS PASSENGERS SO SUPER-LIGHTWEIGHT THAT I CAN EASILY SUPPORT THEIR WEIGHT! SHE'LL RESTORE THEM TO THEIR NORMAL HEAVINESS AFTER THEY HAVE PASSED OVER ME SAFELY!
SHORTLY...
THAT MISSING RAIL WILL BE REPLACED RIGHT AWAY! IF YOU TWO LEGIONNAIRES HADN'T BEEN IN THE CAR...!
YOU WERE MARVELOUS, JIMMY! I ADORE YOU!
WOW! FIRST, TRIPLICATE GIRL KISSED ME--AND NOW I'M BEING SMOOCHED BY LIGHT LASS! WHAT IS THIS STRANGE FASCINATION I EXERT OVER GORGEOUS BABES?! I'M GETTING TO ENJOY THE LEGION MORE AND MORE!!!
STILL LATER, AS JIMMY GOES WITH SATURN GIRL TO METROPOLIS SPACEPORT...
WHAT'S THIS MISSION ALL ABOUT, SATURN GIRL?
THAT STARSHIP IS BRINGING SPACE CREATURES FROM VARIOUS WORLDS TO AN EARTH ZOO! THEY'RE BEING LOWERED NOW!
OUR ASSIGNMENT IS TO KEEP THINGS UNDER CONTROL IF ANYTHING GOES WRONG!...OH-OH!
THE CAGE-CAPSULE STRUCK THE GROUND TOO FORCIBLY AND CRACKED OPEN!
HOT DOG! I MAY HAVE ANOTHER CHANCE TO SHOW OFF WHAT A GREAT LEGIONNAIRE I AM!
KRAK!
THUMP

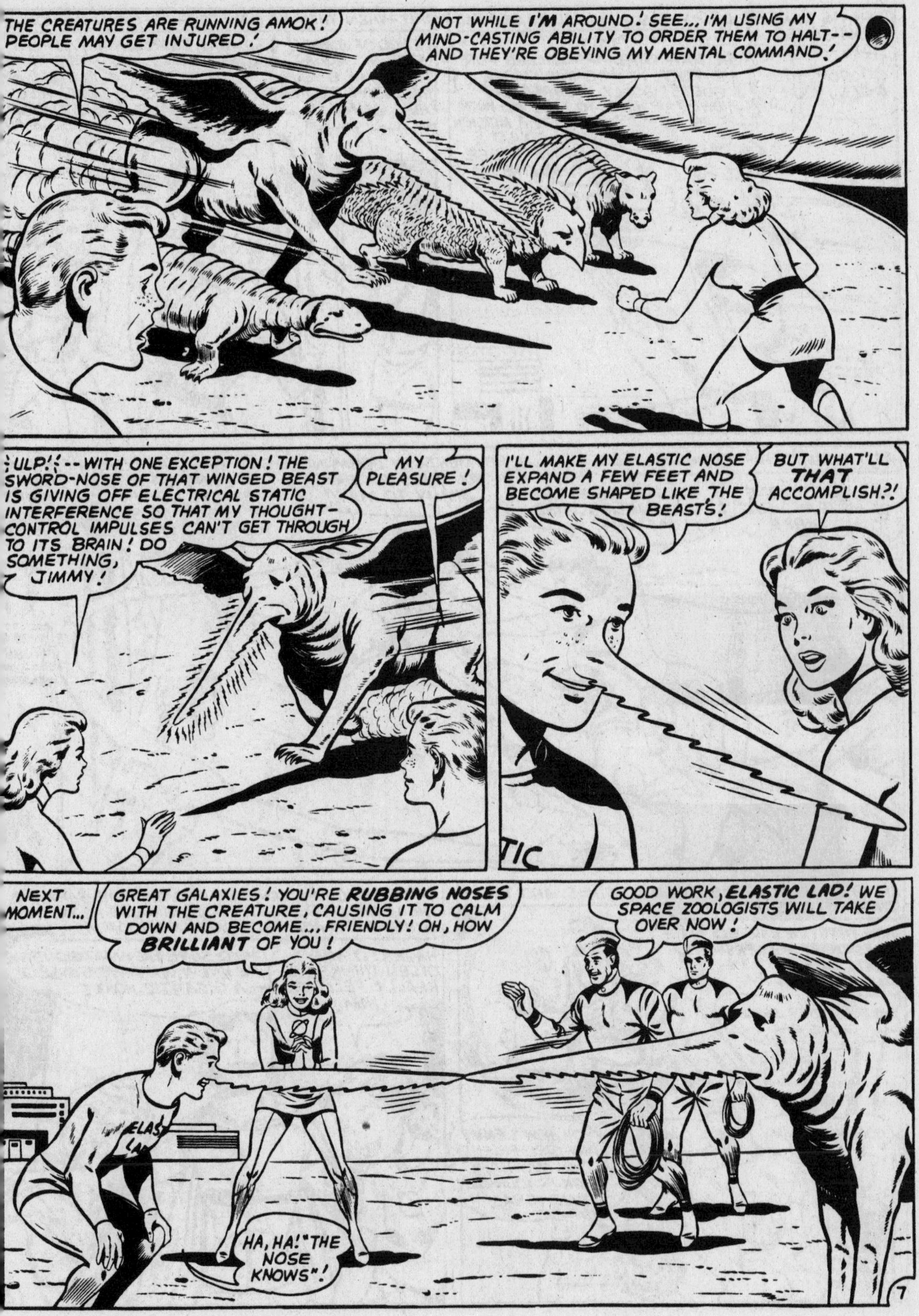
THE CREATURES ARE RUNNING AMOK! PEOPLE MAY GET INJURED!
NOT WHILE I'M AROUND! SEE... I'M USING MY MIND-CASTING ABILITY TO ORDER THEM TO HALT-- AND THEY'RE OBEYING MY MENTAL COMMAND!
ULP!--WITH ONE EXCEPTION! THE SWORD-NOSE OF THAT WINGED BEAST IS GIVING OFF ELECTRICAL STATIC INTERFERENCE SO THAT MY THOUGHT-CONTROL IMPULSES CAN'T GET THROUGH TO ITS BRAIN! DO SOMETHING, JIMMY!
MY PLEASURE!
I'LL MAKE MY ELASTIC NOSE EXPAND A FEW FEET AND BECOME SHAPED LIKE THE BEAST'S!
BUT WHAT'LL THAT ACCOMPLISH?!
TIC
NEXT MOMENT...
GREAT GALAXIES! YOU'RE RUBBING NOSES WITH THE CREATURE, CAUSING IT TO CALM DOWN AND BECOME... FRIENDLY! OH, HOW BRILLIANT OF YOU!
GOOD WORK, ELASTIC LAD! WE SPACE ZOOLOGISTS WILL TAKE OVER NOW!
HA, HA! "THE NOSE KNOWS"!
7

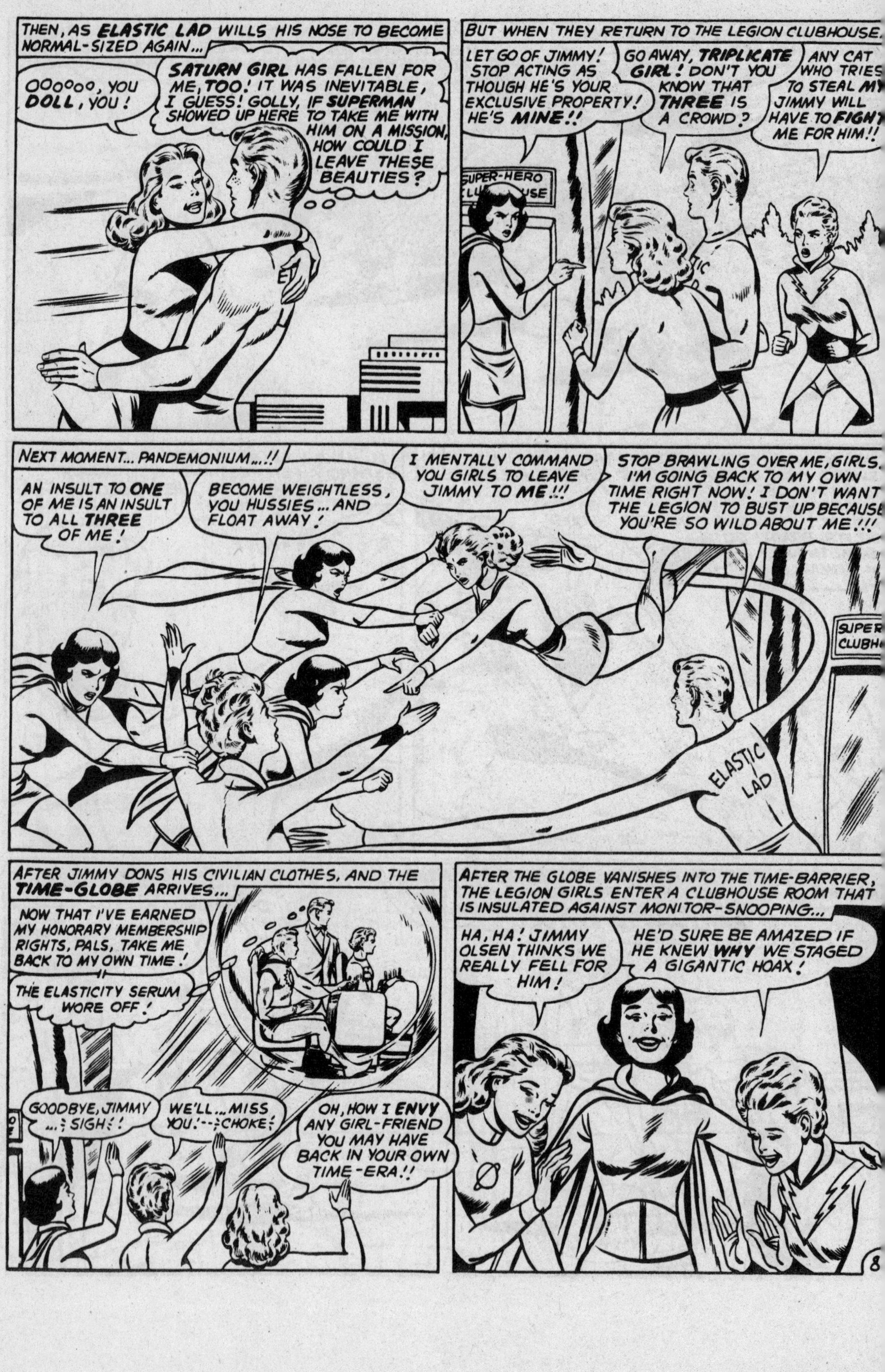
THEN, AS ELASTIC LAD WILLS HIS NOSE TO BECOME NORMAL-SIZED AGAIN...
OOOooo, YOU DOLL, YOU!
SATURN GIRL HAS FALLEN FOR ME, TOO! IT WAS INEVITABLE, I GUESS! GOLLY, IF SUPERMAN SHOWED UP HERE TO TAKE ME WITH HIM ON A MISSION, HOW COULD I LEAVE THESE BEAUTIES?
BUT WHEN THEY RETURN TO THE LEGION CLUBHOUSE...
LET GO OF JIMMY! STOP ACTING AS THOUGH HE'S YOUR EXCLUSIVE PROPERTY! HE'S MINE!!
GO AWAY, TRIPLICATE GIRL! DON'T YOU KNOW THAT THREE IS A CROWD?
ANY CAT WHO TRIES TO STEAL MY JIMMY WILL HAVE TO FIGHT ME FOR HIM!!
SUPER-HERO
NEXT MOMENT... PANDEMONIUM...!!
AN INSULT TO ONE OF ME IS AN INSULT TO ALL THREE OF ME!
BECOME WEIGHTLESS, YOU HUSSIES... AND FLOAT AWAY!
I MENTALLY COMMAND YOU GIRLS TO LEAVE JIMMY TO ME!!!
STOP BRAWLING OVER ME, GIRLS. I'M GOING BACK TO MY OWN TIME RIGHT NOW! I DON'T WANT THE LEGION TO BUST UP BECAUSE YOU'RE SO WILD ABOUT ME!!!
ELASTIC LAD
AFTER JIMMY DONS HIS CIVILIAN CLOTHES, AND THE TIME-GLOBE ARRIVES...
NOW THAT I'VE EARNED MY HONORARY MEMBERSHIP RIGHTS, PALS, TAKE ME BACK TO MY OWN TIME!
THE ELASTICITY SERUM WORE OFF!
GOODBYE, JIMMY ...SIGH!
WE'LL... MISS YOU! --CHOKE!
OH, HOW I ENVY ANY GIRL-FRIEND YOU MAY HAVE BACK IN YOUR OWN TIME-ERA!!
AFTER THE GLOBE VANISHES INTO THE TIME-BARRIER, THE LEGION GIRLS ENTER A CLUBHOUSE ROOM THAT IS INSULATED AGAINST MONITOR-SNOOPING...
HA, HA! JIMMY OLSEN THINKS WE REALLY FELL FOR HIM!
HE'D SURE BE AMAZED IF HE KNEW WHY WE STAGED A GIGANTIC HOAX!
8

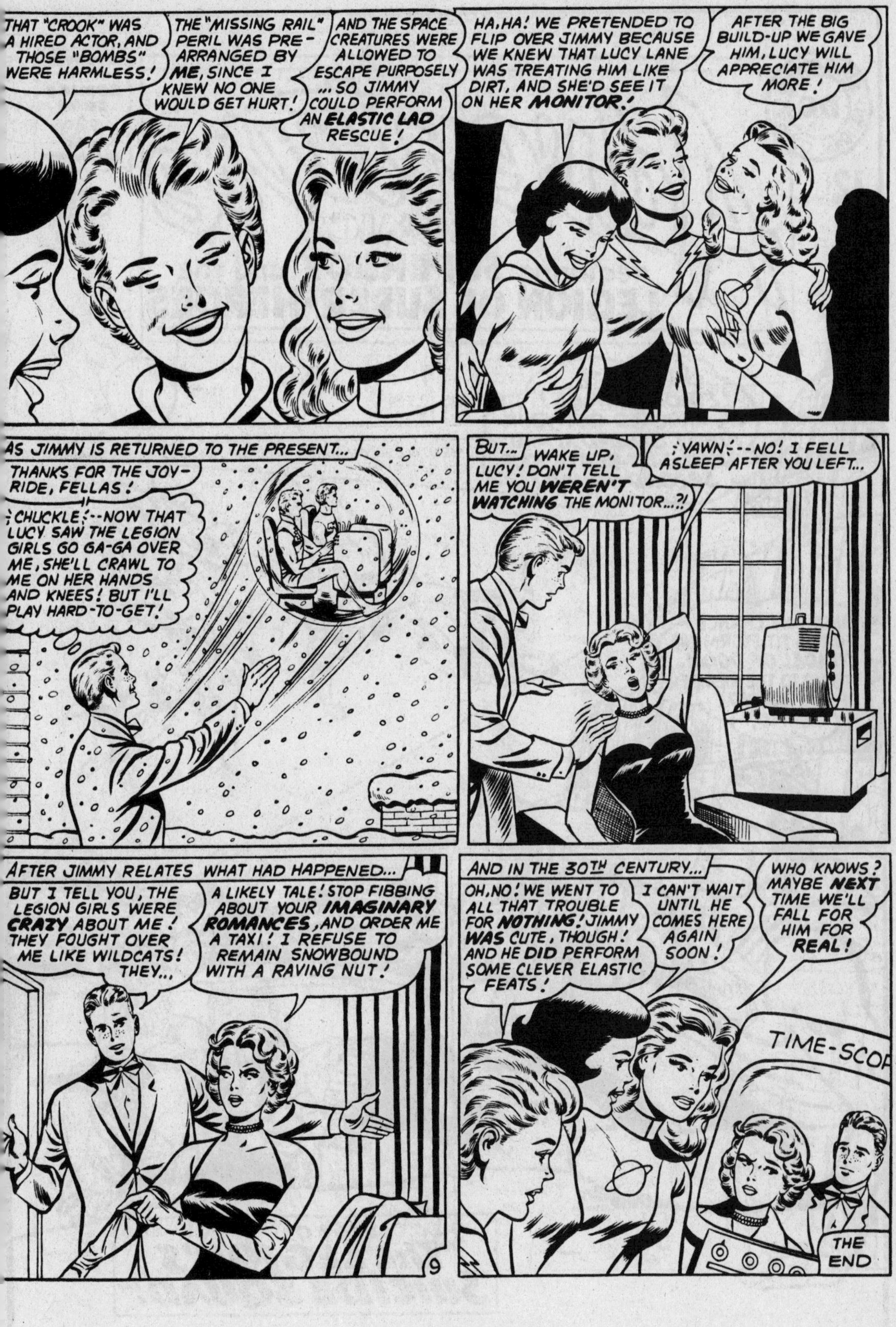
THAT "CROOK" WAS A HIRED ACTOR, AND THOSE "BOMBS" WERE HARMLESS!
THE "MISSING RAIL" PERIL WAS PRE-ARRANGED BY **ME**, SINCE I KNEW NO ONE WOULD GET HURT!
AND THE SPACE CREATURES WERE ALLOWED TO ESCAPE PURPOSELY ...SO JIMMY COULD PERFORM AN **ELASTIC LAD** RESCUE!
HA, HA! WE PRETENDED TO FLIP OVER JIMMY BECAUSE WE KNEW THAT LUCY LANE WAS TREATING HIM LIKE DIRT, AND SHE'D SEE IT ON HER **MONITOR**!
AFTER THE BIG BUILD-UP WE GAVE HIM, LUCY WILL APPRECIATE HIM MORE!
AS JIMMY IS RETURNED TO THE PRESENT...
THANKS FOR THE JOY-RIDE, FELLAS!
:CHUCKLE:--NOW THAT LUCY SAW THE LEGION GIRLS GO GA-GA OVER ME, SHE'LL CRAWL TO ME ON HER HANDS AND KNEES! BUT I'LL PLAY HARD-TO-GET!
BUT...
WAKE UP, LUCY! DON'T TELL ME YOU **WEREN'T WATCHING** THE MONITOR...?!
:YAWN:--NO! I FELL ASLEEP AFTER YOU LEFT...
AFTER JIMMY RELATES WHAT HAD HAPPENED...
BUT I TELL YOU, THE LEGION GIRLS WERE **CRAZY** ABOUT ME! THEY FOUGHT OVER ME LIKE WILDCATS! THEY...
A LIKELY TALE! STOP FIBBING ABOUT YOUR **IMAGINARY ROMANCES**, AND ORDER ME A TAXI! I REFUSE TO REMAIN SNOWBOUND WITH A RAVING NUT!
9
AND IN THE 30TH CENTURY...
OH, NO! WE WENT TO ALL THAT TROUBLE FOR **NOTHING**! JIMMY **WAS** CUTE, THOUGH! AND HE **DID** PERFORM SOME CLEVER ELASTIC FEATS!
I CAN'T WAIT UNTIL HE COMES HERE AGAIN SOON!
WHO KNOWS? MAYBE **NEXT** TIME WE'LL FALL FOR HIM FOR **REAL**!
TIME-SCOP
THE END

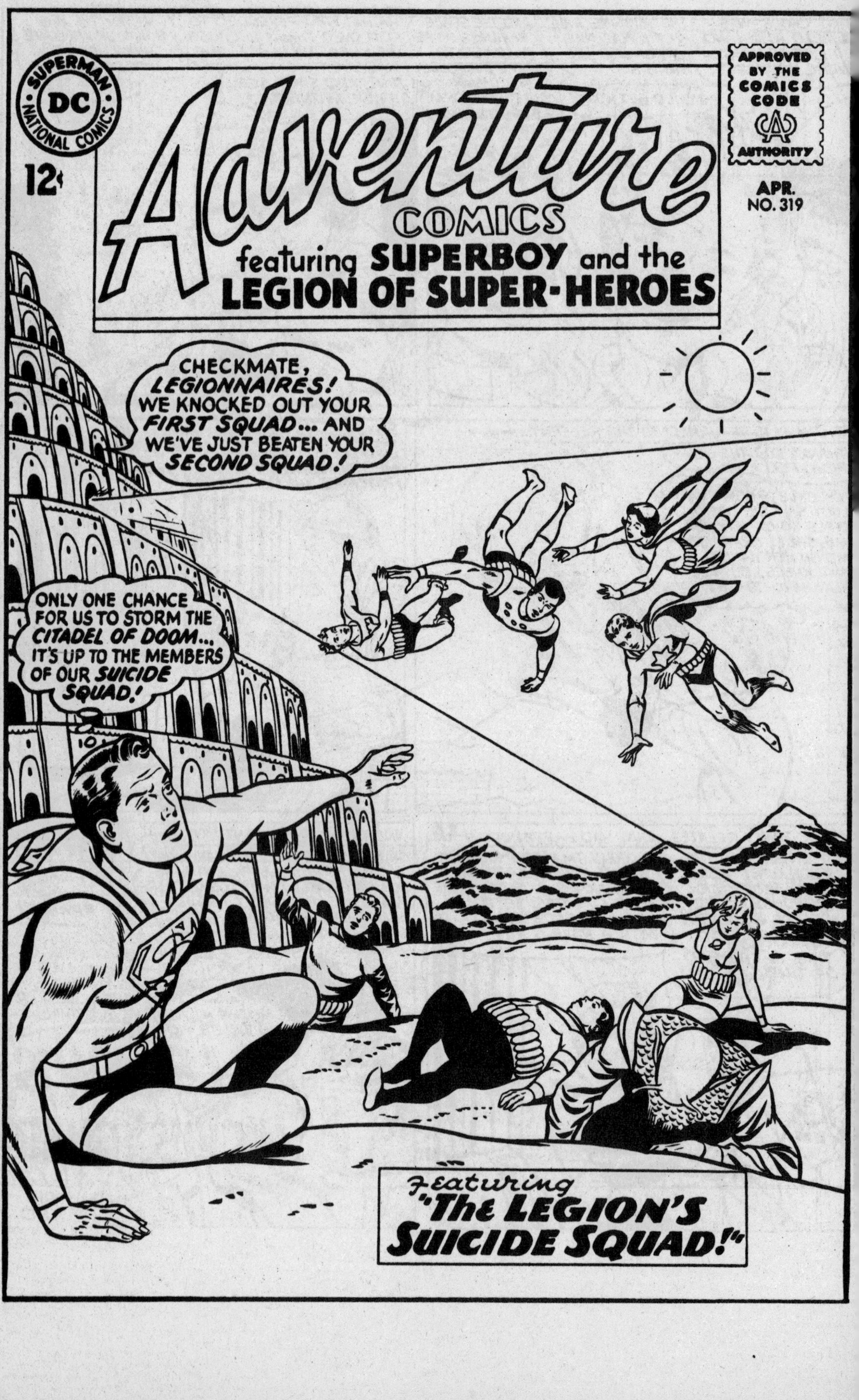
SUPERMAN DC NATIONAL COMICS
12¢
Adventure COMICS
featuring SUPERBOY and the LEGION OF SUPER-HEROES
APPROVED BY THE COMICS CODE AUTHORITY
APR. NO. 319
CHECKMATE, LEGIONNAIRES! WE KNOCKED OUT YOUR FIRST SQUAD... AND WE'VE JUST BEATEN YOUR SECOND SQUAD!
ONLY ONE CHANCE FOR US TO STORM THE CITADEL OF DOOM... IT'S UP TO THE MEMBERS OF OUR SUICIDE SQUAD!
Featuring "The LEGION'S SUICIDE SQUAD!"

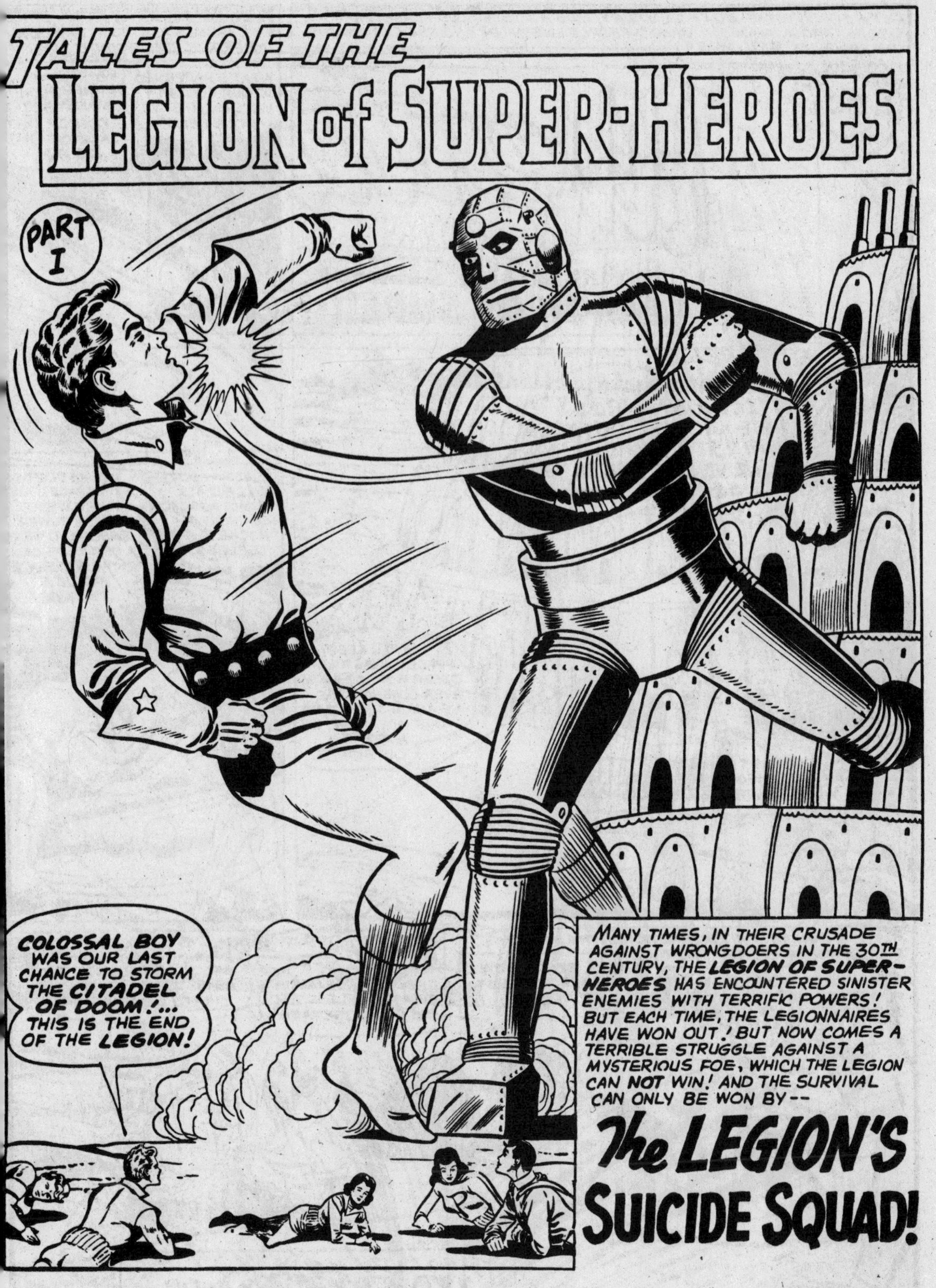
TALES OF THE
LEGION of SUPER-HEROES
PART I
COLOSSAL BOY WAS OUR LAST CHANCE TO STORM THE CITADEL OF DOOM!... THIS IS THE END OF THE LEGION!
MANY TIMES, IN THEIR CRUSADE AGAINST WRONGDOERS IN THE 30TH CENTURY, THE LEGION OF SUPER-HEROES HAS ENCOUNTERED SINISTER ENEMIES WITH TERRIFIC POWERS! BUT EACH TIME, THE LEGIONNAIRES HAVE WON OUT! BUT NOW COMES A TERRIBLE STRUGGLE AGAINST A MYSTERIOUS FOE, WHICH THE LEGION CAN NOT WIN! AND THE SURVIVAL CAN ONLY BE WON BY--
The LEGION'S SUICIDE SQUAD!

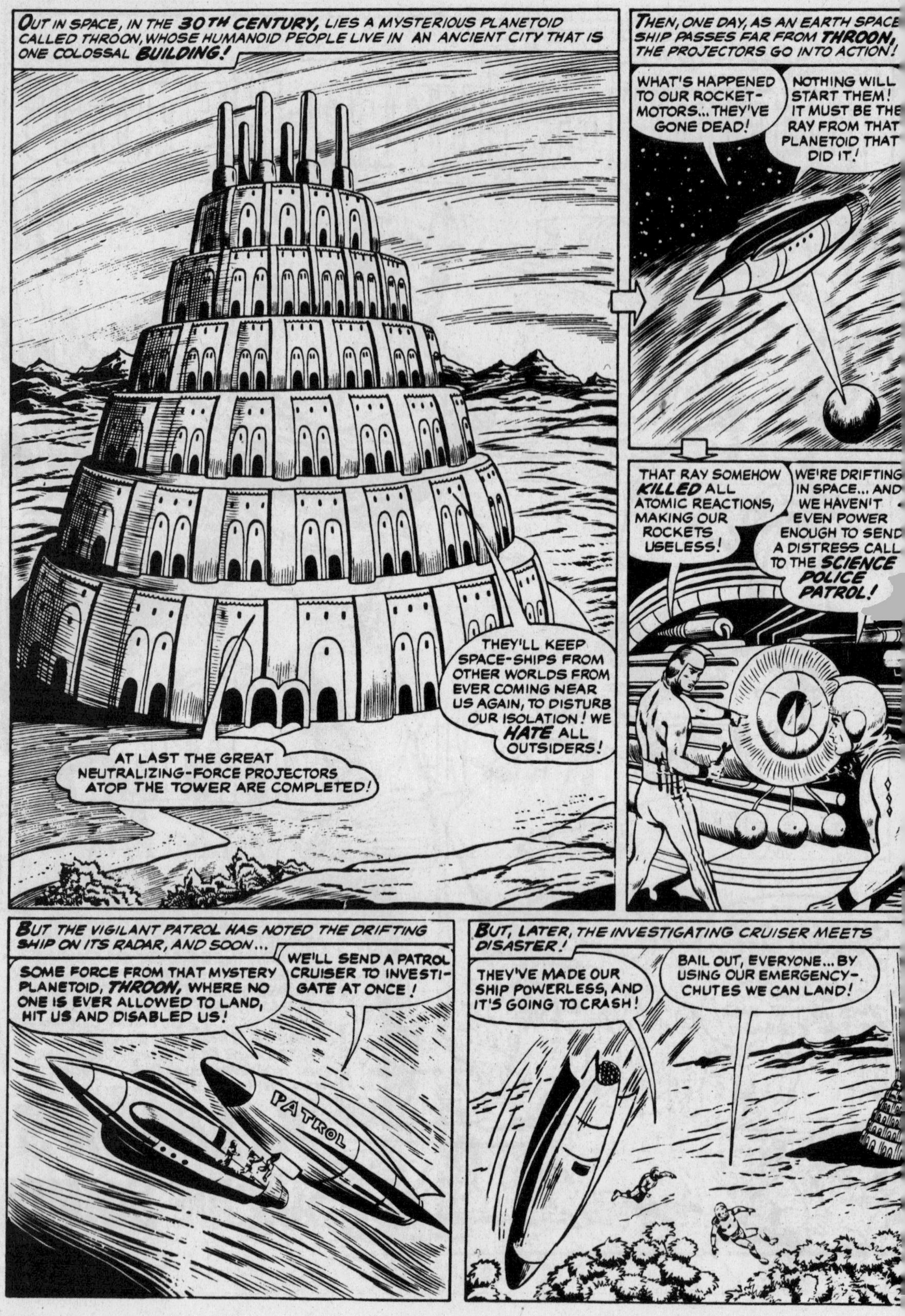
OUT IN SPACE, IN THE 30TH CENTURY, LIES A MYSTERIOUS PLANETOID CALLED THROON, WHOSE HUMANOID PEOPLE LIVE IN AN ANCIENT CITY THAT IS ONE COLOSSAL BUILDING!
AT LAST THE GREAT NEUTRALIZING-FORCE PROJECTORS ATOP THE TOWER ARE COMPLETED!
THEY'LL KEEP SPACE-SHIPS FROM OTHER WORLDS FROM EVER COMING NEAR US AGAIN, TO DISTURB OUR ISOLATION! WE HATE ALL OUTSIDERS!
THEN, ONE DAY, AS AN EARTH SPACE SHIP PASSES FAR FROM THROON, THE PROJECTORS GO INTO ACTION!
WHAT'S HAPPENED TO OUR ROCKET-MOTORS...THEY'VE GONE DEAD!
NOTHING WILL START THEM! IT MUST BE THE RAY FROM THAT PLANETOID THAT DID IT!
THAT RAY SOMEHOW KILLED ALL ATOMIC REACTIONS, MAKING OUR ROCKETS USELESS!
WE'RE DRIFTING IN SPACE... AND WE HAVEN'T EVEN POWER ENOUGH TO SEND A DISTRESS CALL TO THE SCIENCE POLICE PATROL!
BUT THE VIGILANT PATROL HAS NOTED THE DRIFTING SHIP ON ITS RADAR, AND SOON...
SOME FORCE FROM THAT MYSTERY PLANETOID, THROON, WHERE NO ONE IS EVER ALLOWED TO LAND, HIT US AND DISABLED US!
WE'LL SEND A PATROL CRUISER TO INVESTIGATE AT ONCE!
PATROL
BUT, LATER, THE INVESTIGATING CRUISER MEETS DISASTER!
THEY'VE MADE OUR SHIP POWERLESS, AND IT'S GOING TO CRASH!
BAIL OUT, EVERYONE... BY USING OUR EMERGENCY-CHUTES WE CAN LAND!

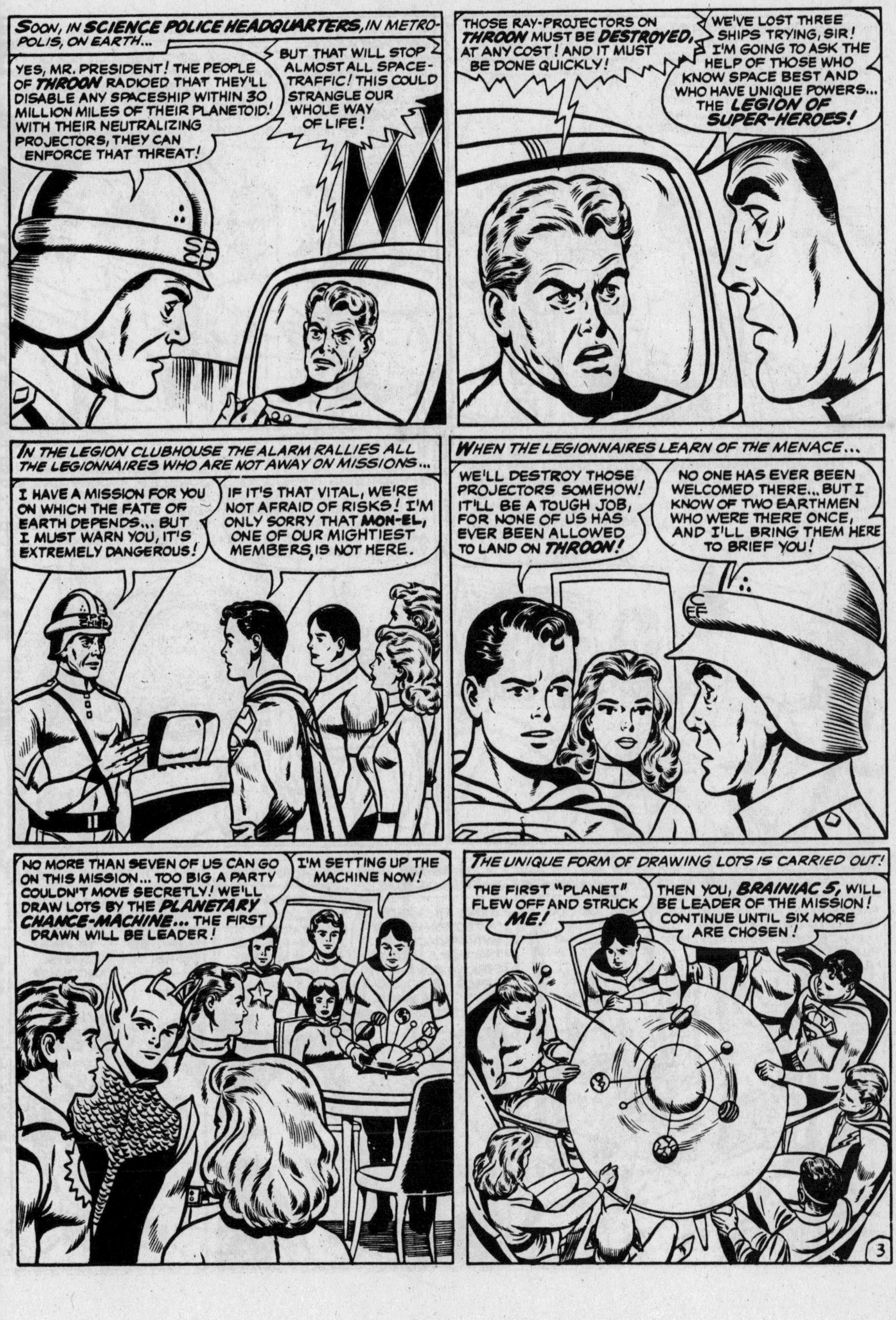
SOON, IN SCIENCE POLICE HEADQUARTERS, IN METROPOLIS, ON EARTH...
YES, MR. PRESIDENT! THE PEOPLE OF THROON RADIOED THAT THEY'LL DISABLE ANY SPACESHIP WITHIN 30 MILLION MILES OF THEIR PLANETOID! WITH THEIR NEUTRALIZING PROJECTORS, THEY CAN ENFORCE THAT THREAT!
BUT THAT WILL STOP ALMOST ALL SPACE-TRAFFIC! THIS COULD STRANGLE OUR WHOLE WAY OF LIFE!
THOSE RAY-PROJECTORS ON THROON MUST BE DESTROYED, AT ANY COST! AND IT MUST BE DONE QUICKLY!
WE'VE LOST THREE SHIPS TRYING, SIR! I'M GOING TO ASK THE HELP OF THOSE WHO KNOW SPACE BEST AND WHO HAVE UNIQUE POWERS... THE LEGION OF SUPER-HEROES!
IN THE LEGION CLUBHOUSE THE ALARM RALLIES ALL THE LEGIONNAIRES WHO ARE NOT AWAY ON MISSIONS...
I HAVE A MISSION FOR YOU ON WHICH THE FATE OF EARTH DEPENDS... BUT I MUST WARN YOU, IT'S EXTREMELY DANGEROUS!
IF IT'S THAT VITAL, WE'RE NOT AFRAID OF RISKS! I'M ONLY SORRY THAT MON-EL, ONE OF OUR MIGHTIEST MEMBERS, IS NOT HERE.
WHEN THE LEGIONNAIRES LEARN OF THE MENACE...
WE'LL DESTROY THOSE PROJECTORS SOMEHOW! IT'LL BE A TOUGH JOB, FOR NONE OF US HAS EVER BEEN ALLOWED TO LAND ON THROON!
NO ONE HAS EVER BEEN WELCOMED THERE... BUT I KNOW OF TWO EARTHMEN WHO WERE THERE ONCE, AND I'LL BRING THEM HERE TO BRIEF YOU!
NO MORE THAN SEVEN OF US CAN GO ON THIS MISSION... TOO BIG A PARTY COULDN'T MOVE SECRETLY! WE'LL DRAW LOTS BY THE PLANETARY CHANCE-MACHINE... THE FIRST DRAWN WILL BE LEADER!
I'M SETTING UP THE MACHINE NOW!
THE UNIQUE FORM OF DRAWING LOTS IS CARRIED OUT!
THE FIRST "PLANET" FLEW OFF AND STRUCK ME!
THEN YOU, BRAINIAC 5, WILL BE LEADER OF THE MISSION! CONTINUE UNTIL SIX MORE ARE CHOSEN!
3

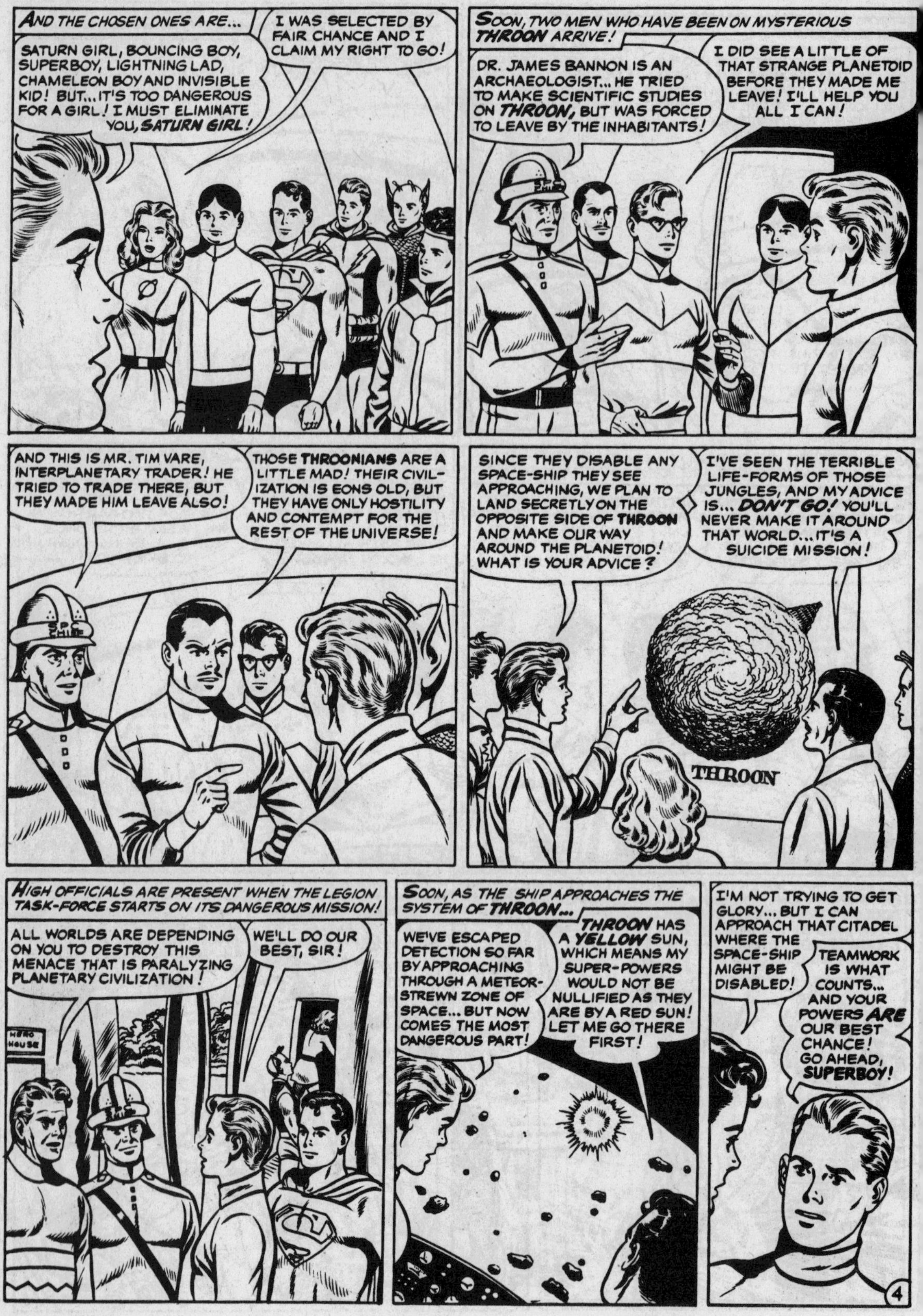
AND THE CHOSEN ONES ARE...
SATURN GIRL, BOUNCING BOY, SUPERBOY, LIGHTNING LAD, CHAMELEON BOY AND INVISIBLE KID! BUT... IT'S TOO DANGEROUS FOR A GIRL! I MUST ELIMINATE YOU, SATURN GIRL!
I WAS SELECTED BY FAIR CHANCE AND I CLAIM MY RIGHT TO GO!
SOON, TWO MEN WHO HAVE BEEN ON MYSTERIOUS THROON ARRIVE!
DR. JAMES BANNON IS AN ARCHAEOLOGIST... HE TRIED TO MAKE SCIENTIFIC STUDIES ON THROON, BUT WAS FORCED TO LEAVE BY THE INHABITANTS!
I DID SEE A LITTLE OF THAT STRANGE PLANETOID BEFORE THEY MADE ME LEAVE! I'LL HELP YOU ALL I CAN!
AND THIS IS MR. TIM VARE, INTERPLANETARY TRADER! HE TRIED TO TRADE THERE, BUT THEY MADE HIM LEAVE ALSO!
THOSE THROONIANS ARE A LITTLE MAD! THEIR CIVILIZATION IS EONS OLD, BUT THEY HAVE ONLY HOSTILITY AND CONTEMPT FOR THE REST OF THE UNIVERSE!
S.P.C. CHIEF
SINCE THEY DISABLE ANY SPACE-SHIP THEY SEE APPROACHING, WE PLAN TO LAND SECRETLY ON THE OPPOSITE SIDE OF THROON AND MAKE OUR WAY AROUND THE PLANETOID! WHAT IS YOUR ADVICE?
I'VE SEEN THE TERRIBLE LIFE-FORMS OF THOSE JUNGLES, AND MY ADVICE IS... DON'T GO! YOU'LL NEVER MAKE IT AROUND THAT WORLD... IT'S A SUICIDE MISSION!
THROON
HIGH OFFICIALS ARE PRESENT WHEN THE LEGION TASK-FORCE STARTS ON ITS DANGEROUS MISSION!
ALL WORLDS ARE DEPENDING ON YOU TO DESTROY THIS MENACE THAT IS PARALYZING PLANETARY CIVILIZATION!
WE'LL DO OUR BEST, SIR!
HERO HOUSE
SOON, AS THE SHIP APPROACHES THE SYSTEM OF THROON...
WE'VE ESCAPED DETECTION SO FAR BY APPROACHING THROUGH A METEOR-STREWN ZONE OF SPACE... BUT NOW COMES THE MOST DANGEROUS PART!
THROON HAS A YELLOW SUN, WHICH MEANS MY SUPER-POWERS WOULD NOT BE NULLIFIED AS THEY ARE BY A RED SUN! LET ME GO THERE FIRST!
I'M NOT TRYING TO GET GLORY... BUT I CAN APPROACH THAT CITADEL WHERE THE SPACE-SHIP MIGHT BE DISABLED!
TEAMWORK IS WHAT COUNTS... AND YOUR POWERS ARE OUR BEST CHANCE! GO AHEAD, SUPERBOY!
4

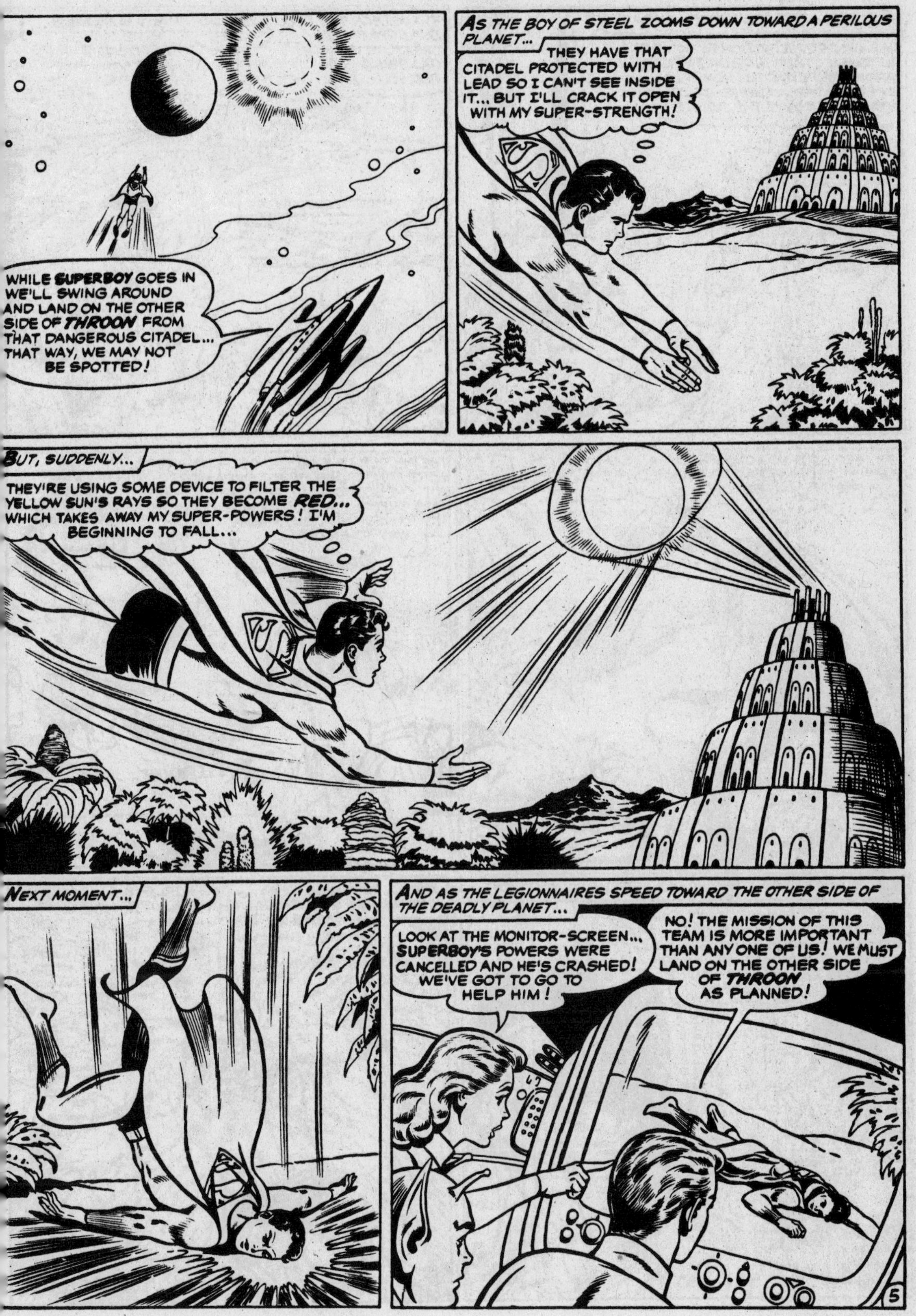
WHILE SUPERBOY GOES IN WE'LL SWING AROUND AND LAND ON THE OTHER SIDE OF THROON FROM THAT DANGEROUS CITADEL... THAT WAY, WE MAY NOT BE SPOTTED!
AS THE BOY OF STEEL ZOOMS DOWN TOWARD A PERILOUS PLANET...
THEY HAVE THAT CITADEL PROTECTED WITH LEAD SO I CAN'T SEE INSIDE IT... BUT I'LL CRACK IT OPEN WITH MY SUPER-STRENGTH!
BUT, SUDDENLY...
THEY'RE USING SOME DEVICE TO FILTER THE YELLOW SUN'S RAYS SO THEY BECOME RED... WHICH TAKES AWAY MY SUPER-POWERS! I'M BEGINNING TO FALL...
NEXT MOMENT...
AND AS THE LEGIONNAIRES SPEED TOWARD THE OTHER SIDE OF THE DEADLY PLANET...
LOOK AT THE MONITOR-SCREEN... SUPERBOY'S POWERS WERE CANCELLED AND HE'S CRASHED! WE'VE GOT TO GO TO HELP HIM!
NO! THE MISSION OF THIS TEAM IS MORE IMPORTANT THAN ANY ONE OF US! WE MUST LAND ON THE OTHER SIDE OF THROON AS PLANNED!
5

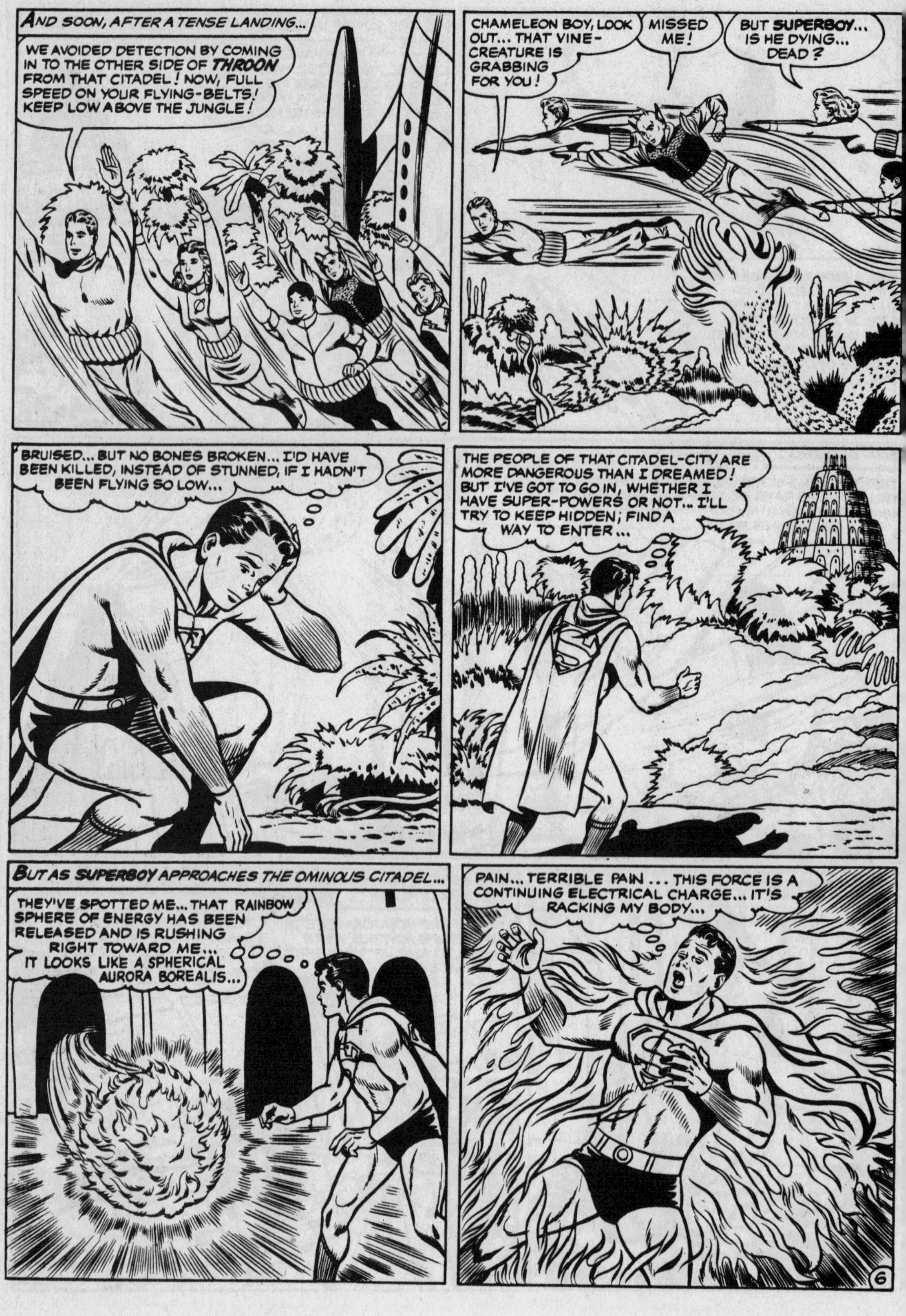
AND SOON, AFTER A TENSE LANDING...
WE AVOIDED DETECTION BY COMING IN TO THE OTHER SIDE OF THROON FROM THAT CITADEL! NOW, FULL SPEED ON YOUR FLYING-BELTS! KEEP LOW ABOVE THE JUNGLE!
CHAMELEON BOY, LOOK OUT... THAT VINE-CREATURE IS GRABBING FOR YOU!
MISSED ME!
BUT SUPERBOY... IS HE DYING... DEAD?
BRUISED... BUT NO BONES BROKEN... I'D HAVE BEEN KILLED, INSTEAD OF STUNNED, IF I HADN'T BEEN FLYING SO LOW...
THE PEOPLE OF THAT CITADEL-CITY ARE MORE DANGEROUS THAN I DREAMED! BUT I'VE GOT TO GO IN, WHETHER I HAVE SUPER-POWERS OR NOT.. I'LL TRY TO KEEP HIDDEN; FIND A WAY TO ENTER...
BUT AS SUPERBOY APPROACHES THE OMINOUS CITADEL...
THEY'VE SPOTTED ME... THAT RAINBOW SPHERE OF ENERGY HAS BEEN RELEASED AND IS RUSHING RIGHT TOWARD ME... IT LOOKS LIKE A SPHERICAL AURORA BOREALIS...
PAIN... TERRIBLE PAIN ... THIS FORCE IS A CONTINUING ELECTRICAL CHARGE... IT'S RACKING MY BODY...
6

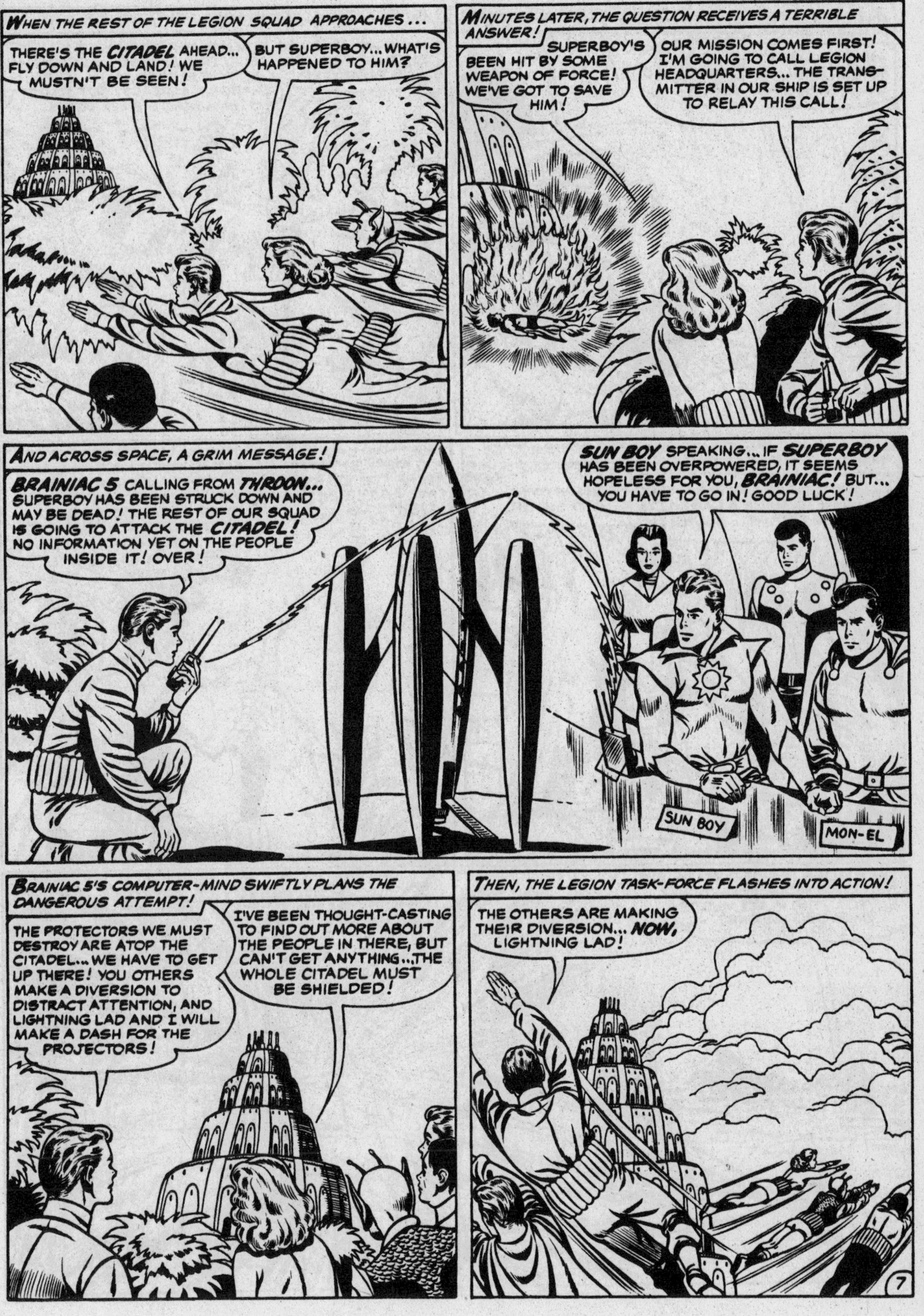
WHEN THE REST OF THE LEGION SQUAD APPROACHES ...
THERE'S THE CITADEL AHEAD... FLY DOWN AND LAND! WE MUSTN'T BE SEEN!
BUT SUPERBOY... WHAT'S HAPPENED TO HIM?
MINUTES LATER, THE QUESTION RECEIVES A TERRIBLE ANSWER!
SUPERBOY'S BEEN HIT BY SOME WEAPON OF FORCE! WE'VE GOT TO SAVE HIM!
OUR MISSION COMES FIRST! I'M GOING TO CALL LEGION HEADQUARTERS... THE TRANSMITTER IN OUR SHIP IS SET UP TO RELAY THIS CALL!
AND ACROSS SPACE, A GRIM MESSAGE!
BRAINIAC 5 CALLING FROM THROON... SUPERBOY HAS BEEN STRUCK DOWN AND MAY BE DEAD! THE REST OF OUR SQUAD IS GOING TO ATTACK THE CITADEL! NO INFORMATION YET ON THE PEOPLE INSIDE IT! OVER!
SUN BOY SPEAKING... IF SUPERBOY HAS BEEN OVERPOWERED, IT SEEMS HOPELESS FOR YOU, BRAINIAC! BUT... YOU HAVE TO GO IN! GOOD LUCK!
SUN BOY
MON-EL
BRAINIAC 5'S COMPUTER-MIND SWIFTLY PLANS THE DANGEROUS ATTEMPT!
THE PROTECTORS WE MUST DESTROY ARE ATOP THE CITADEL... WE HAVE TO GET UP THERE! YOU OTHERS MAKE A DIVERSION TO DISTRACT ATTENTION, AND LIGHTNING LAD AND I WILL MAKE A DASH FOR THE PROJECTORS!
I'VE BEEN THOUGHT-CASTING TO FIND OUT MORE ABOUT THE PEOPLE IN THERE, BUT CAN'T GET ANYTHING... THE WHOLE CITADEL MUST BE SHIELDED!
THEN, THE LEGION TASK-FORCE FLASHES INTO ACTION!
THE OTHERS ARE MAKING THEIR DIVERSION... NOW, LIGHTNING LAD!
7

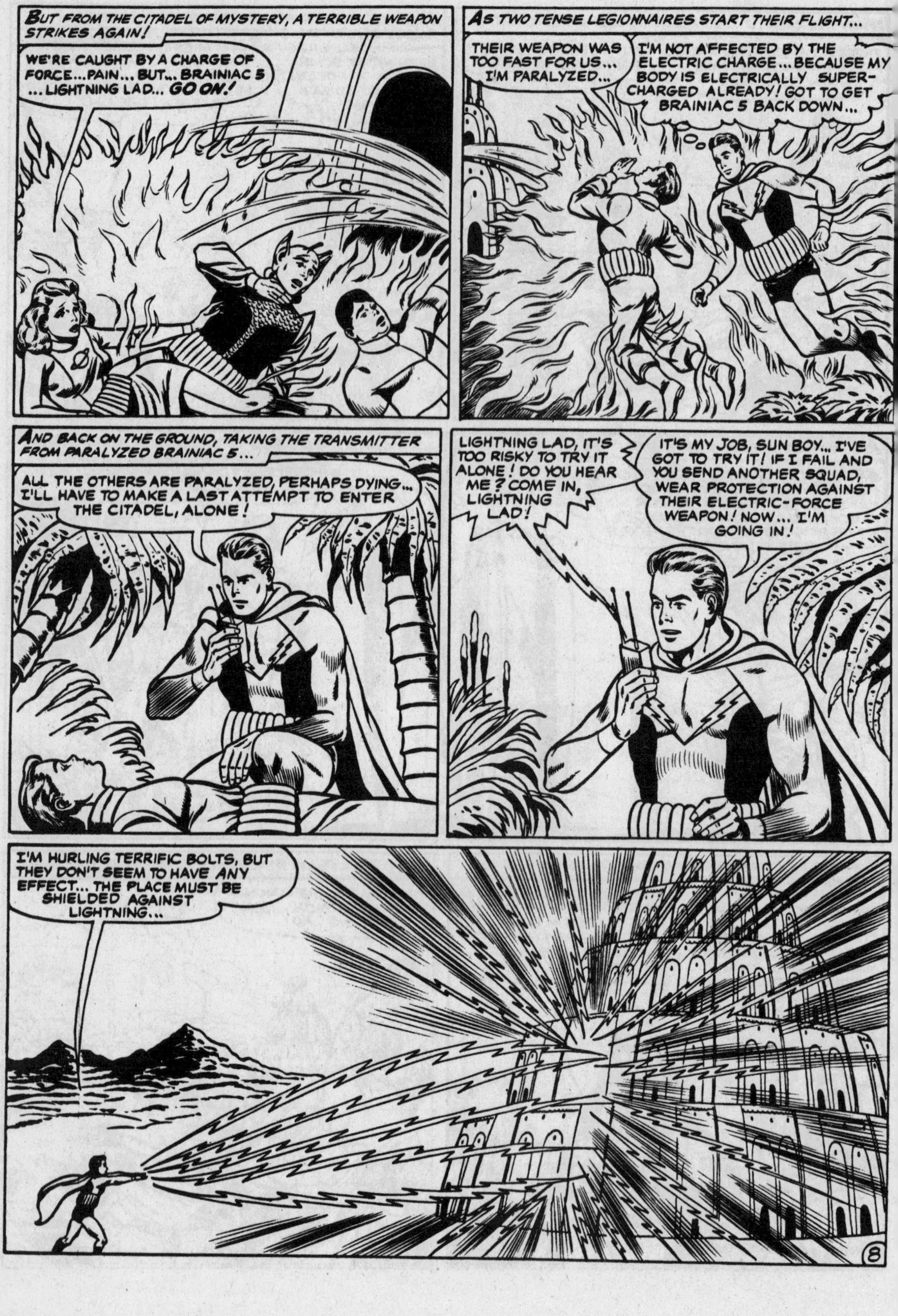
BUT FROM THE CITADEL OF MYSTERY, A TERRIBLE WEAPON STRIKES AGAIN!
WE'RE CAUGHT BY A CHARGE OF FORCE...PAIN...BUT...BRAINIAC 5 ...LIGHTNING LAD... GO ON!
AS TWO TENSE LEGIONNAIRES START THEIR FLIGHT...
THEIR WEAPON WAS TOO FAST FOR US... I'M PARALYZED...
I'M NOT AFFECTED BY THE ELECTRIC CHARGE...BECAUSE MY BODY IS ELECTRICALLY SUPER-CHARGED ALREADY! GOT TO GET BRAINIAC 5 BACK DOWN...
AND BACK ON THE GROUND, TAKING THE TRANSMITTER FROM PARALYZED BRAINIAC 5...
ALL THE OTHERS ARE PARALYZED, PERHAPS DYING... I'LL HAVE TO MAKE A LAST ATTEMPT TO ENTER THE CITADEL, ALONE!
LIGHTNING LAD, IT'S TOO RISKY TO TRY IT ALONE! DO YOU HEAR ME? COME IN, LIGHTNING LAD!
IT'S MY JOB, SUN BOY... I'VE GOT TO TRY IT! IF I FAIL AND YOU SEND ANOTHER SQUAD, WEAR PROTECTION AGAINST THEIR ELECTRIC-FORCE WEAPON! NOW... I'M GOING IN!
I'M HURLING TERRIFIC BOLTS, BUT THEY DON'T SEEM TO HAVE ANY EFFECT... THE PLACE MUST BE SHIELDED AGAINST LIGHTNING...
8

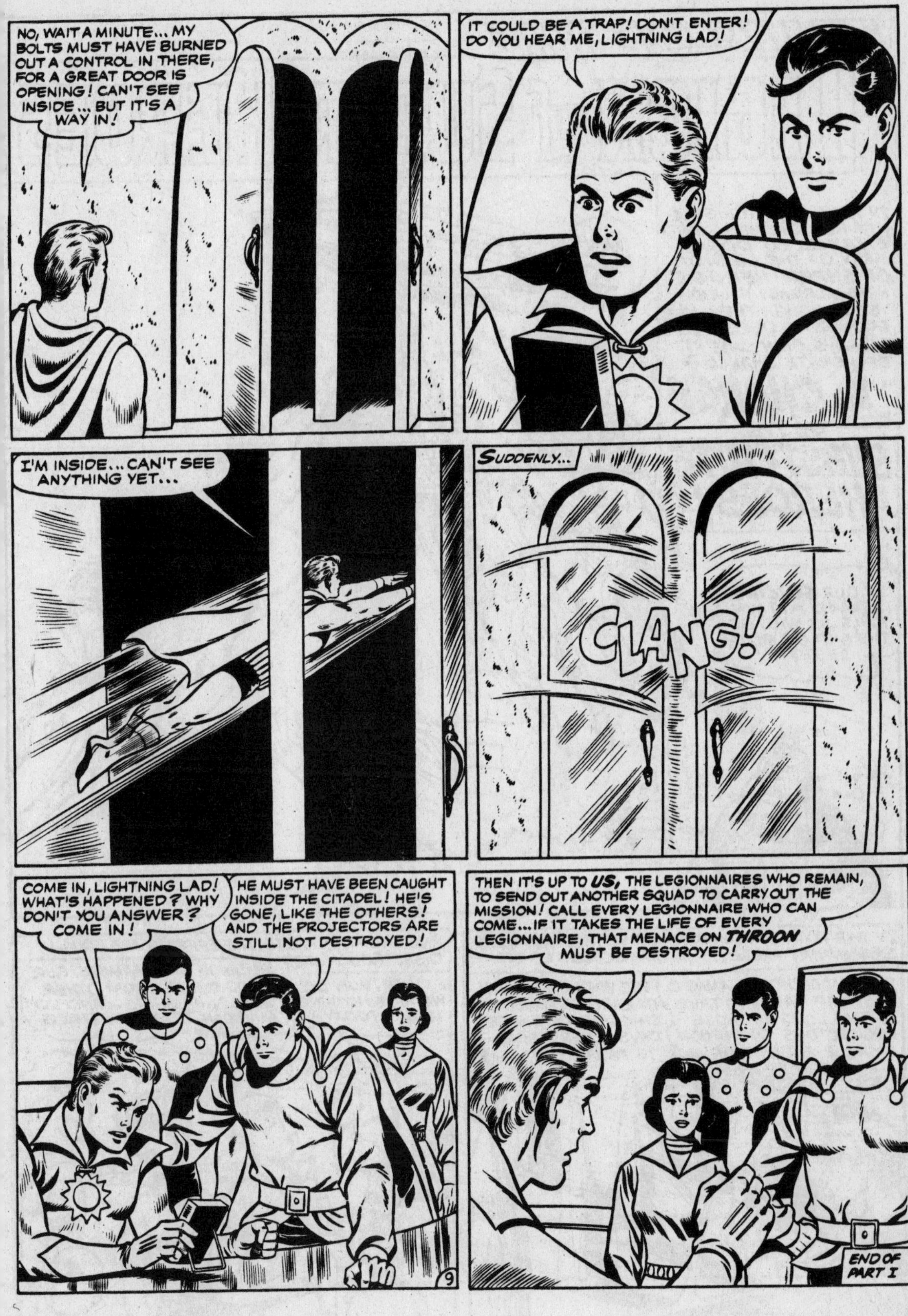
NO, WAIT A MINUTE... MY BOLTS MUST HAVE BURNED OUT A CONTROL IN THERE, FOR A GREAT DOOR IS OPENING! CAN'T SEE INSIDE... BUT IT'S A WAY IN!
IT COULD BE A TRAP! DON'T ENTER! DO YOU HEAR ME, LIGHTNING LAD!
I'M INSIDE... CAN'T SEE ANYTHING YET...
SUDDENLY...
CLANG!
COME IN, LIGHTNING LAD! WHAT'S HAPPENED? WHY DON'T YOU ANSWER? COME IN!
HE MUST HAVE BEEN CAUGHT INSIDE THE CITADEL! HE'S GONE, LIKE THE OTHERS! AND THE PROJECTORS ARE STILL NOT DESTROYED!
9
THEN IT'S UP TO US, THE LEGIONNAIRES WHO REMAIN, TO SEND OUT ANOTHER SQUAD TO CARRY OUT THE MISSION! CALL EVERY LEGIONNAIRE WHO CAN COME... IF IT TAKES THE LIFE OF EVERY LEGIONNAIRE, THAT MENACE ON THROON MUST BE DESTROYED!
END OF PART I

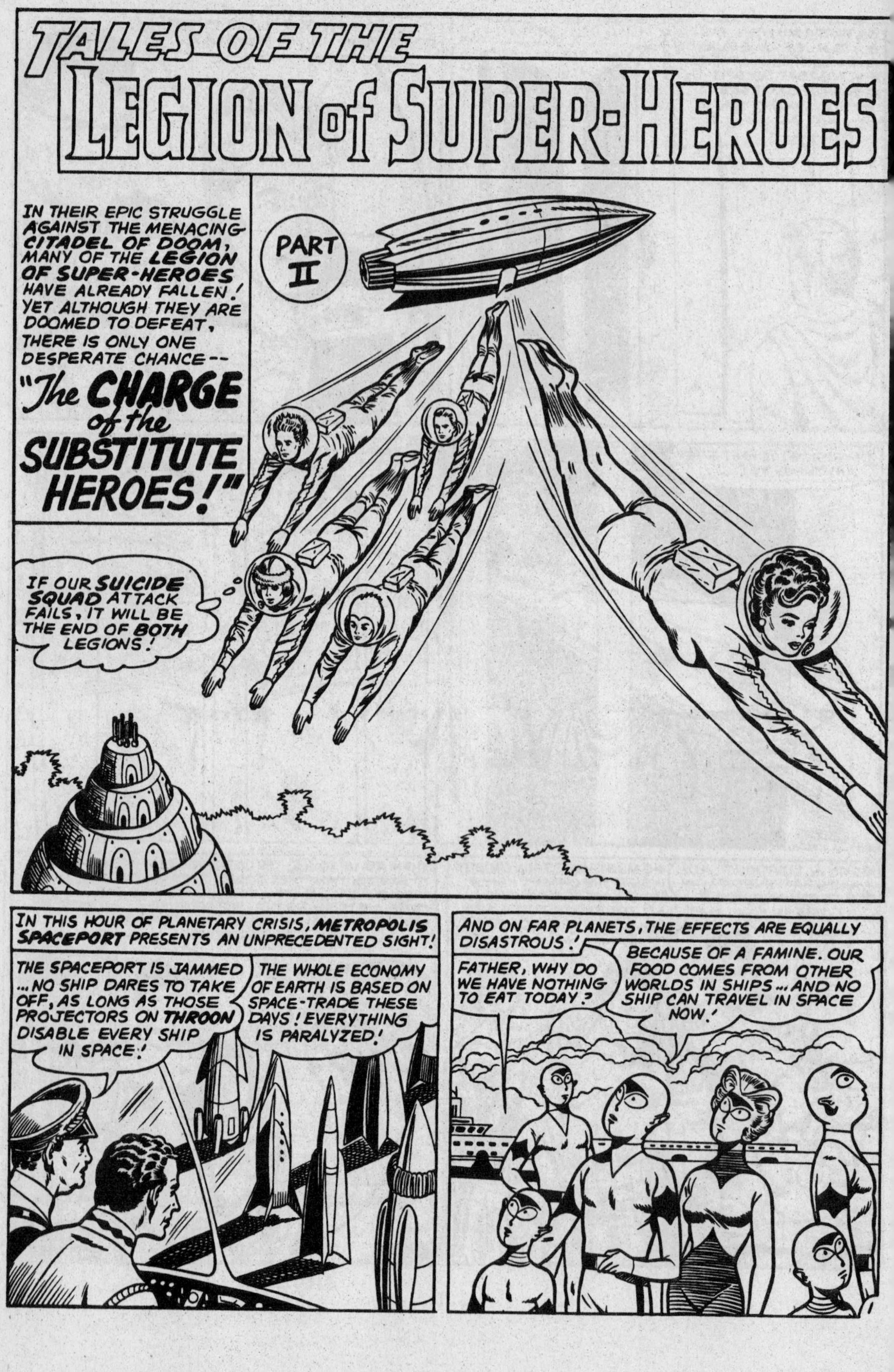
TALES OF THE
LEGION of SUPER-HEROES
IN THEIR EPIC STRUGGLE AGAINST THE MENACING CITADEL OF DOOM, MANY OF THE LEGION OF SUPER-HEROES HAVE ALREADY FALLEN! YET ALTHOUGH THEY ARE DOOMED TO DEFEAT, THERE IS ONLY ONE DESPERATE CHANCE--
"The CHARGE of the SUBSTITUTE HEROES!"
PART II
IF OUR SUICIDE SQUAD ATTACK FAILS, IT WILL BE THE END OF BOTH LEGIONS!
IN THIS HOUR OF PLANETARY CRISIS, METROPOLIS SPACEPORT PRESENTS AN UNPRECEDENTED SIGHT!
THE SPACEPORT IS JAMMED ...NO SHIP DARES TO TAKE OFF, AS LONG AS THOSE PROJECTORS ON THROON DISABLE EVERY SHIP IN SPACE!
THE WHOLE ECONOMY OF EARTH IS BASED ON SPACE-TRADE THESE DAYS! EVERYTHING IS PARALYZED!
AND ON FAR PLANETS, THE EFFECTS ARE EQUALLY DISASTROUS!
FATHER, WHY DO WE HAVE NOTHING TO EAT TODAY?
BECAUSE OF A FAMINE. OUR FOOD COMES FROM OTHER WORLDS IN SHIPS...AND NO SHIP CAN TRAVEL IN SPACE NOW!

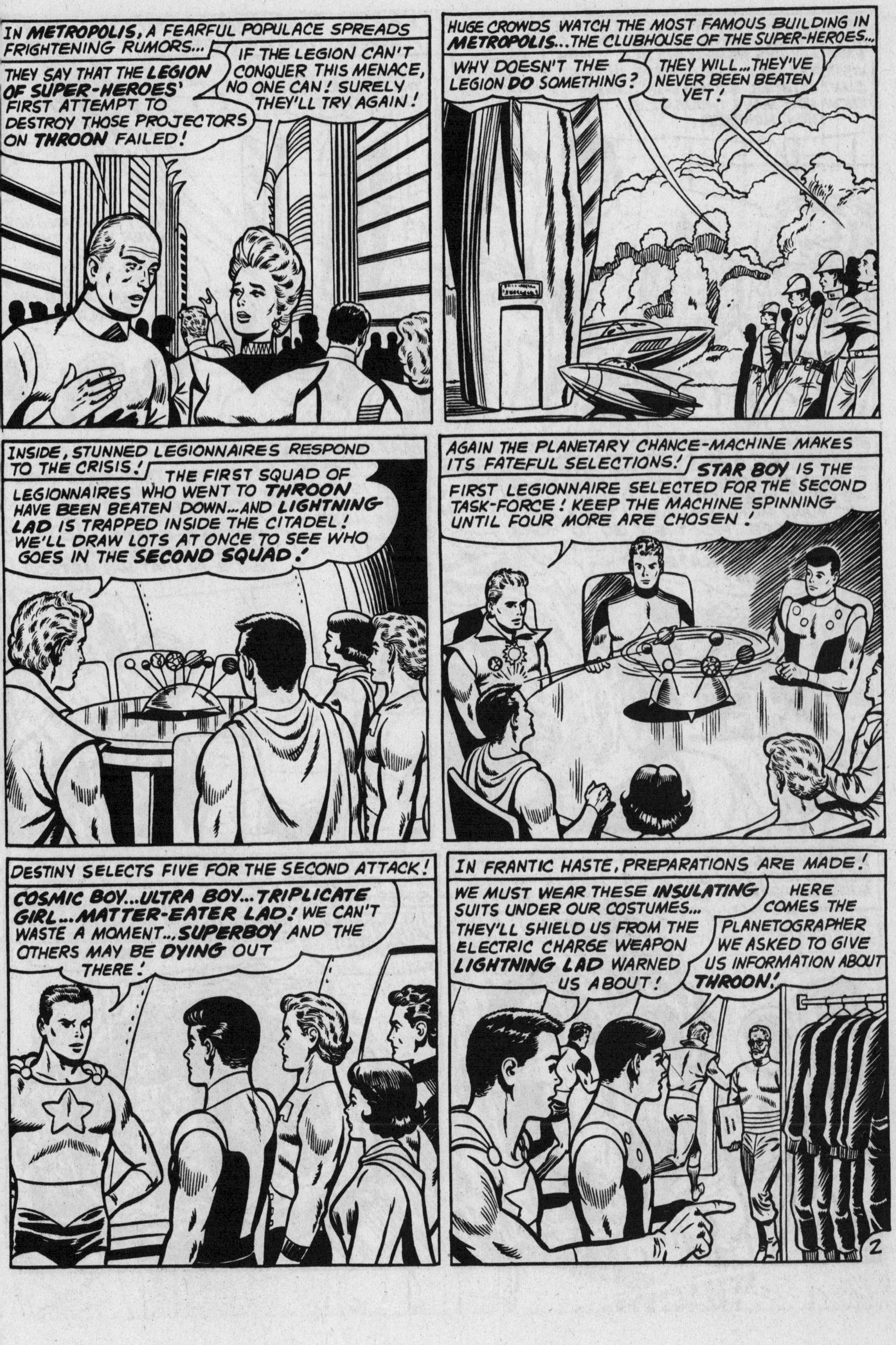

IN METROPOLIS, A FEARFUL POPULACE SPREADS FRIGHTENING RUMORS...
THEY SAY THAT THE LEGION OF SUPER-HEROES' FIRST ATTEMPT TO DESTROY THOSE PROJECTORS ON THROON FAILED!
IF THE LEGION CAN'T CONQUER THIS MENACE, NO ONE CAN! SURELY THEY'LL TRY AGAIN!
HUGE CROWDS WATCH THE MOST FAMOUS BUILDING IN METROPOLIS...THE CLUBHOUSE OF THE SUPER-HEROES...
WHY DOESN'T THE LEGION DO SOMETHING?
THEY WILL...THEY'VE NEVER BEEN BEATEN YET!
INSIDE, STUNNED LEGIONNAIRES RESPOND TO THE CRISIS!
THE FIRST SQUAD OF LEGIONNAIRES WHO WENT TO THROON HAVE BEEN BEATEN DOWN...AND LIGHTNING LAD IS TRAPPED INSIDE THE CITADEL! WE'LL DRAW LOTS AT ONCE TO SEE WHO GOES IN THE SECOND SQUAD!
AGAIN THE PLANETARY CHANCE-MACHINE MAKES ITS FATEFUL SELECTIONS!
STAR BOY IS THE FIRST LEGIONNAIRE SELECTED FOR THE SECOND TASK-FORCE! KEEP THE MACHINE SPINNING UNTIL FOUR MORE ARE CHOSEN!
DESTINY SELECTS FIVE FOR THE SECOND ATTACK!
COSMIC BOY...ULTRA BOY...TRIPLICATE GIRL...MATTER-EATER LAD! WE CAN'T WASTE A MOMENT...SUPERBOY AND THE OTHERS MAY BE DYING OUT THERE!
IN FRANTIC HASTE, PREPARATIONS ARE MADE!
WE MUST WEAR THESE INSULATING SUITS UNDER OUR COSTUMES... THEY'LL SHIELD US FROM THE ELECTRIC CHARGE WEAPON LIGHTNING LAD WARNED US ABOUT!
HERE COMES THE PLANETOGRAPHER WE ASKED TO GIVE US INFORMATION ABOUT THROON!
2

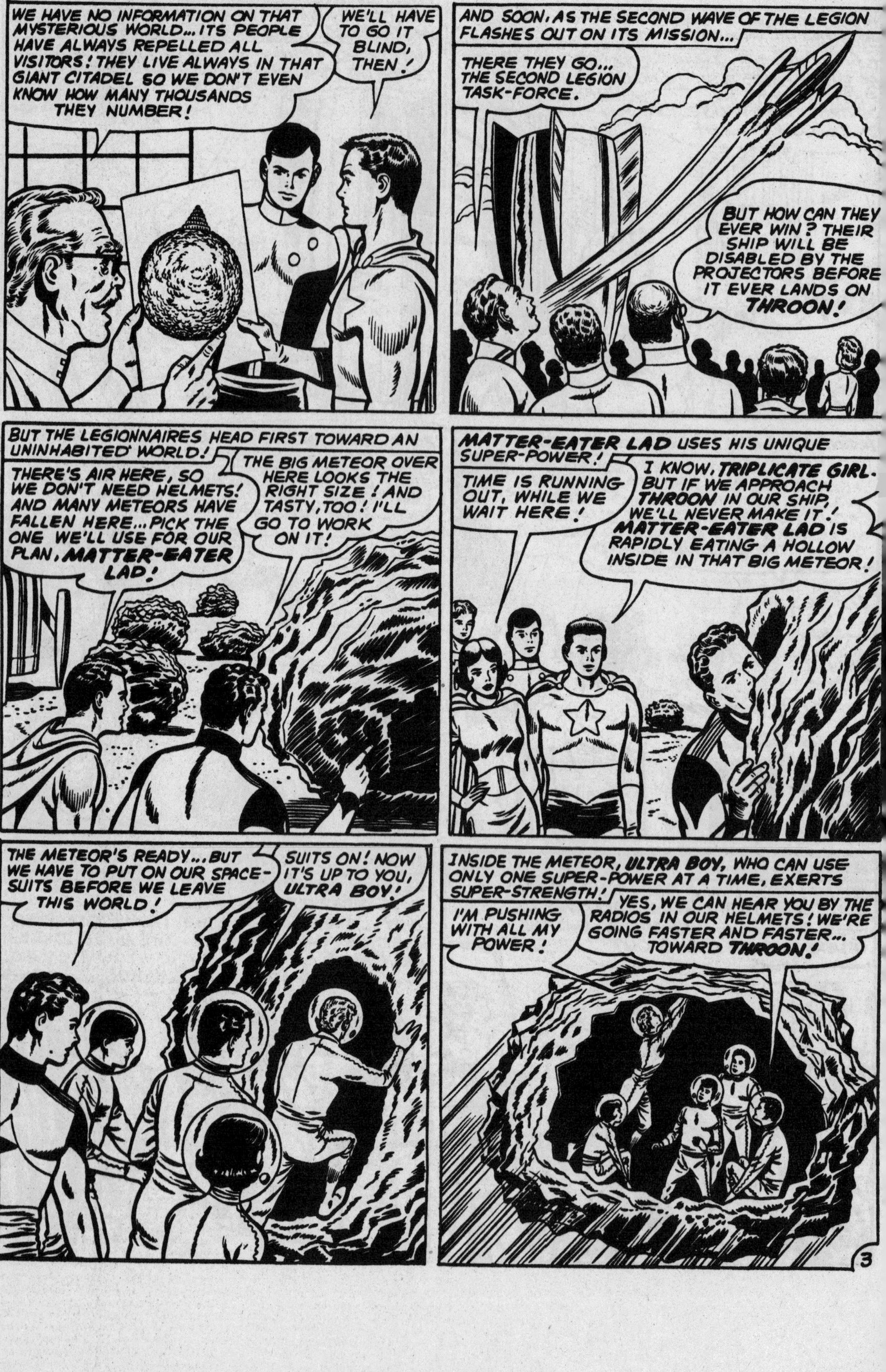
WE HAVE NO INFORMATION ON THAT MYSTERIOUS WORLD... ITS PEOPLE HAVE ALWAYS REPELLED ALL VISITORS! THEY LIVE ALWAYS IN THAT GIANT CITADEL SO WE DON'T EVEN KNOW HOW MANY THOUSANDS THEY NUMBER!
WE'LL HAVE TO GO IT BLIND, THEN!
AND SOON, AS THE SECOND WAVE OF THE LEGION FLASHES OUT ON ITS MISSION...
THERE THEY GO... THE SECOND LEGION TASK-FORCE.
BUT HOW CAN THEY EVER WIN? THEIR SHIP WILL BE DISABLED BY THE PROJECTORS BEFORE IT EVER LANDS ON THROON!
BUT THE LEGIONNAIRES HEAD FIRST TOWARD AN UNINHABITED WORLD!
THERE'S AIR HERE, SO WE DON'T NEED HELMETS! AND MANY METEORS HAVE FALLEN HERE... PICK THE ONE WE'LL USE FOR OUR PLAN, MATTER-EATER LAD!
THE BIG METEOR OVER HERE LOOKS THE RIGHT SIZE! AND TASTY, TOO! I'LL GO TO WORK ON IT!
MATTER-EATER LAD USES HIS UNIQUE SUPER-POWER!
TIME IS RUNNING OUT, WHILE WE WAIT HERE!
I KNOW, TRIPLICATE GIRL. BUT IF WE APPROACH THROON IN OUR SHIP, WE'LL NEVER MAKE IT! MATTER-EATER LAD IS RAPIDLY EATING A HOLLOW INSIDE IN THAT BIG METEOR!
THE METEOR'S READY... BUT WE HAVE TO PUT ON OUR SPACE-SUITS BEFORE WE LEAVE THIS WORLD!
SUITS ON! NOW IT'S UP TO YOU, ULTRA BOY!
INSIDE THE METEOR, ULTRA BOY, WHO CAN USE ONLY ONE SUPER-POWER AT A TIME, EXERTS SUPER-STRENGTH!
I'M PUSHING WITH ALL MY POWER!
YES, WE CAN HEAR YOU BY THE RADIOS IN OUR HELMETS! WE'RE GOING FASTER AND FASTER... TOWARD THROON!
3

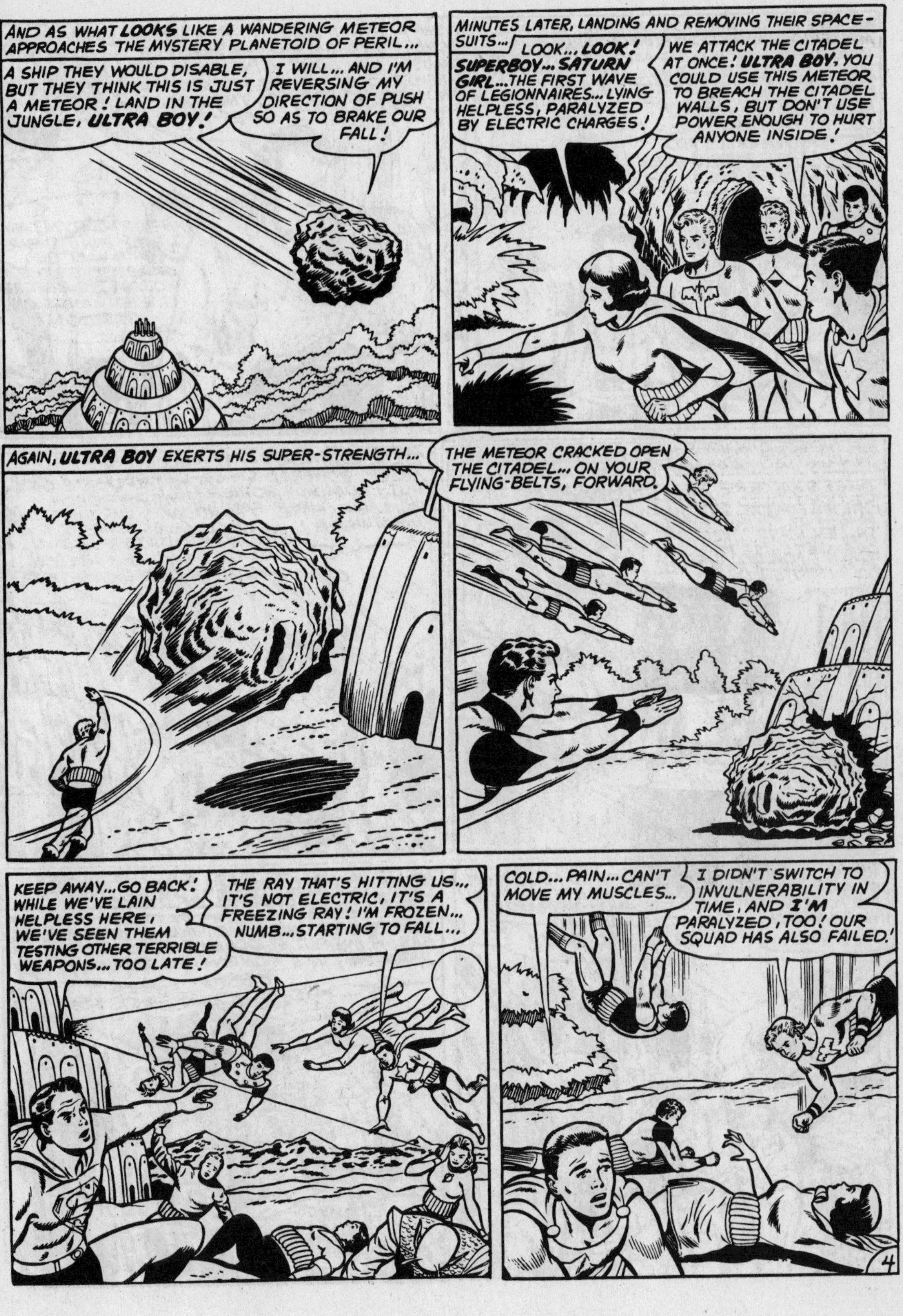
AND AS WHAT LOOKS LIKE A WANDERING METEOR APPROACHES THE MYSTERY PLANETOID OF PERIL...
A SHIP THEY WOULD DISABLE, BUT THEY THINK THIS IS JUST A METEOR! LAND IN THE JUNGLE, ULTRA BOY!
I WILL... AND I'M REVERSING MY DIRECTION OF PUSH SO AS TO BRAKE OUR FALL!
MINUTES LATER, LANDING AND REMOVING THEIR SPACE-SUITS...
LOOK... LOOK! SUPERBOY... SATURN GIRL... THE FIRST WAVE OF LEGIONNAIRES... LYING HELPLESS, PARALYZED BY ELECTRIC CHARGES!
WE ATTACK THE CITADEL AT ONCE! ULTRA BOY, YOU COULD USE THIS METEOR TO BREACH THE CITADEL WALLS, BUT DON'T USE POWER ENOUGH TO HURT ANYONE INSIDE!
AGAIN, ULTRA BOY EXERTS HIS SUPER-STRENGTH...
THE METEOR CRACKED OPEN THE CITADEL... ON YOUR FLYING-BELTS, FORWARD.
KEEP AWAY...GO BACK! WHILE WE'VE LAIN HELPLESS HERE, WE'VE SEEN THEM TESTING OTHER TERRIBLE WEAPONS... TOO LATE!
THE RAY THAT'S HITTING US... IT'S NOT ELECTRIC, IT'S A FREEZING RAY! I'M FROZEN... NUMB... STARTING TO FALL...
COLD... PAIN... CAN'T MOVE MY MUSCLES...
I DIDN'T SWITCH TO INVULNERABILITY IN TIME, AND I'M PARALYZED, TOO! OUR SQUAD HAS ALSO FAILED!
4

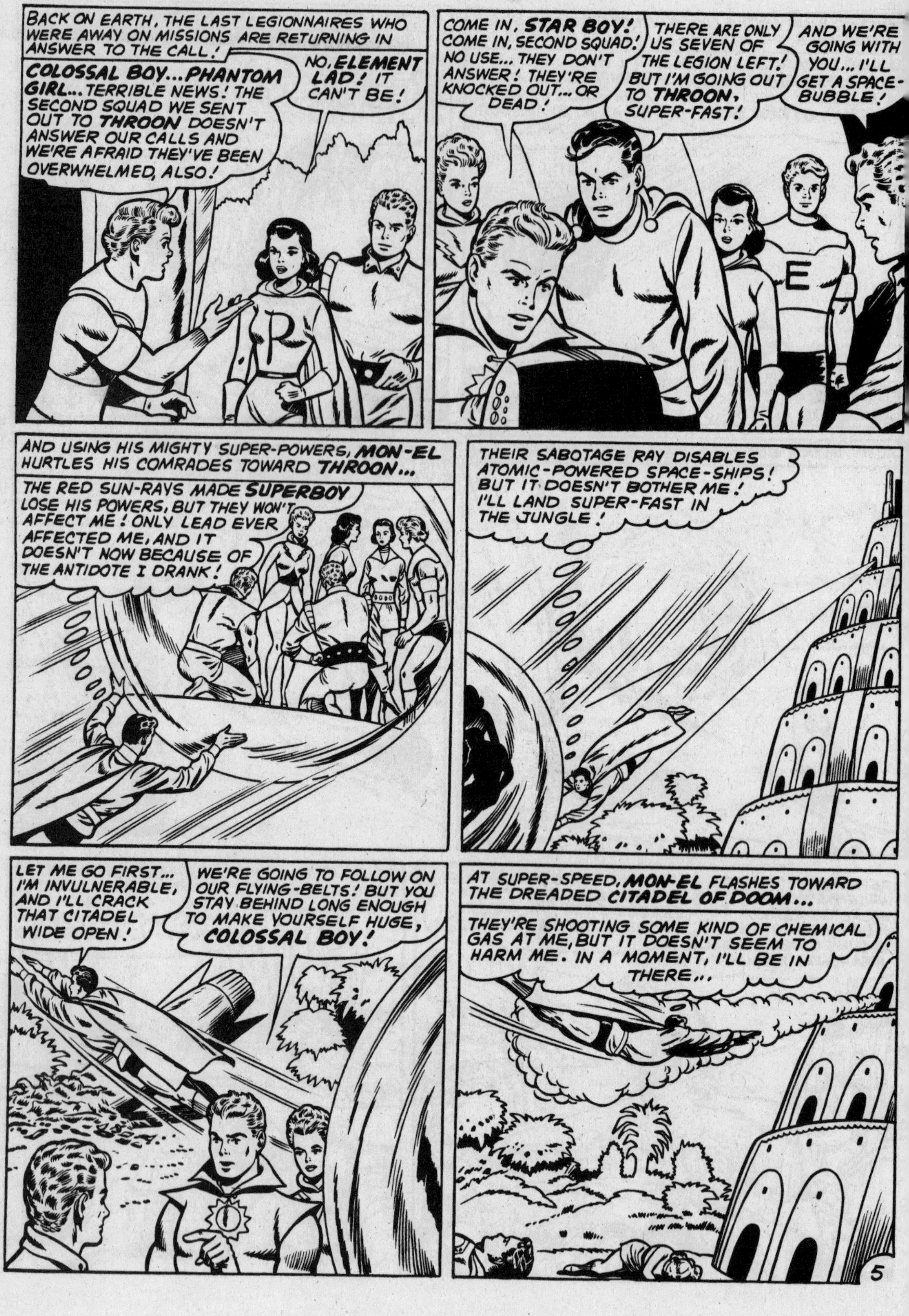
BACK ON EARTH, THE LAST LEGIONNAIRES WHO WERE AWAY ON MISSIONS ARE RETURNING IN ANSWER TO THE CALL!
COLOSSAL BOY...PHANTOM GIRL...TERRIBLE NEWS! THE SECOND SQUAD WE SENT OUT TO THROON DOESN'T ANSWER OUR CALLS AND WE'RE AFRAID THEY'VE BEEN OVERWHELMED, ALSO!
NO, ELEMENT LAD! IT CAN'T BE!
COME IN, STAR BOY! COME IN, SECOND SQUAD! NO USE... THEY DON'T ANSWER! THEY'RE KNOCKED OUT... OR DEAD!
THERE ARE ONLY US SEVEN OF THE LEGION LEFT! BUT I'M GOING OUT TO THROON, SUPER-FAST!
AND WE'RE GOING WITH YOU... I'LL GET A SPACE-BUBBLE!
AND USING HIS MIGHTY SUPER-POWERS, MON-EL HURTLES HIS COMRADES TOWARD THROON...
THE RED SUN-RAYS MADE SUPERBOY LOSE HIS POWERS, BUT THEY WON'T AFFECT ME! ONLY LEAD EVER AFFECTED ME, AND IT DOESN'T NOW BECAUSE OF THE ANTIDOTE I DRANK!
THEIR SABOTAGE RAY DISABLES ATOMIC-POWERED SPACE-SHIPS! BUT IT DOESN'T BOTHER ME! I'LL LAND SUPER-FAST IN THE JUNGLE!
LET ME GO FIRST... I'M INVULNERABLE, AND I'LL CRACK THAT CITADEL WIDE OPEN!
WE'RE GOING TO FOLLOW ON OUR FLYING-BELTS! BUT YOU STAY BEHIND LONG ENOUGH TO MAKE YOURSELF HUGE, COLOSSAL BOY!
AT SUPER-SPEED, MON-EL FLASHES TOWARD THE DREADED CITADEL OF DOOM...
THEY'RE SHOOTING SOME KIND OF CHEMICAL GAS AT ME, BUT IT DOESN'T SEEM TO HARM ME. IN A MOMENT, I'LL BE IN THERE...
5

BUT A TERRIBLE SURPRISE AWAITS **MON-EL!**

LEAD...AND IT'S AFFECTING ME TERRIBLY JUST AS IT USED TO! THAT CHEMICAL GAS MUST HAVE NEUTRALIZED THE ANTIDOTE I TOOK...LEAD IS PARALYZING ME!

AS **MON-EL** FALLS, HIS LOYAL COMRADES FOLLOW HIM!

IF WE CAN GET THAT LEAD AWAY FROM **MON-EL**, HE'LL RECOVER HIS POWERS... TOO LATE!

A FREEZING RAY HITTING US... WE'RE FALLING...WITH ONLY ONE LEGIONNAIRE LEFT, WE'RE **BEATEN!**

BUT THE ONE REMAINING LEGIONNAIRE HAS USED HIS UNIQUE POWER OF GROWING IN SIZE...

OUR WRECKED SHIP IN THE JUNGLE WILL ACT AS MY SHIELD... IF I CAN GET TO THE CITADEL, I'LL TEAR IT OPEN!

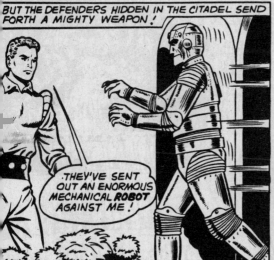

BUT THE DEFENDERS HIDDEN IN THE CITADEL SEND FORTH A MIGHTY WEAPON!

...THEY'VE SENT OUT AN ENORMOUS MECHANICAL **ROBOT** AGAINST ME!

SOON, THE LAST SURVIVING MEMBER OF THE LEGION STRUGGLES AGAINST A GIGANTIC ANTAGONIST...

6

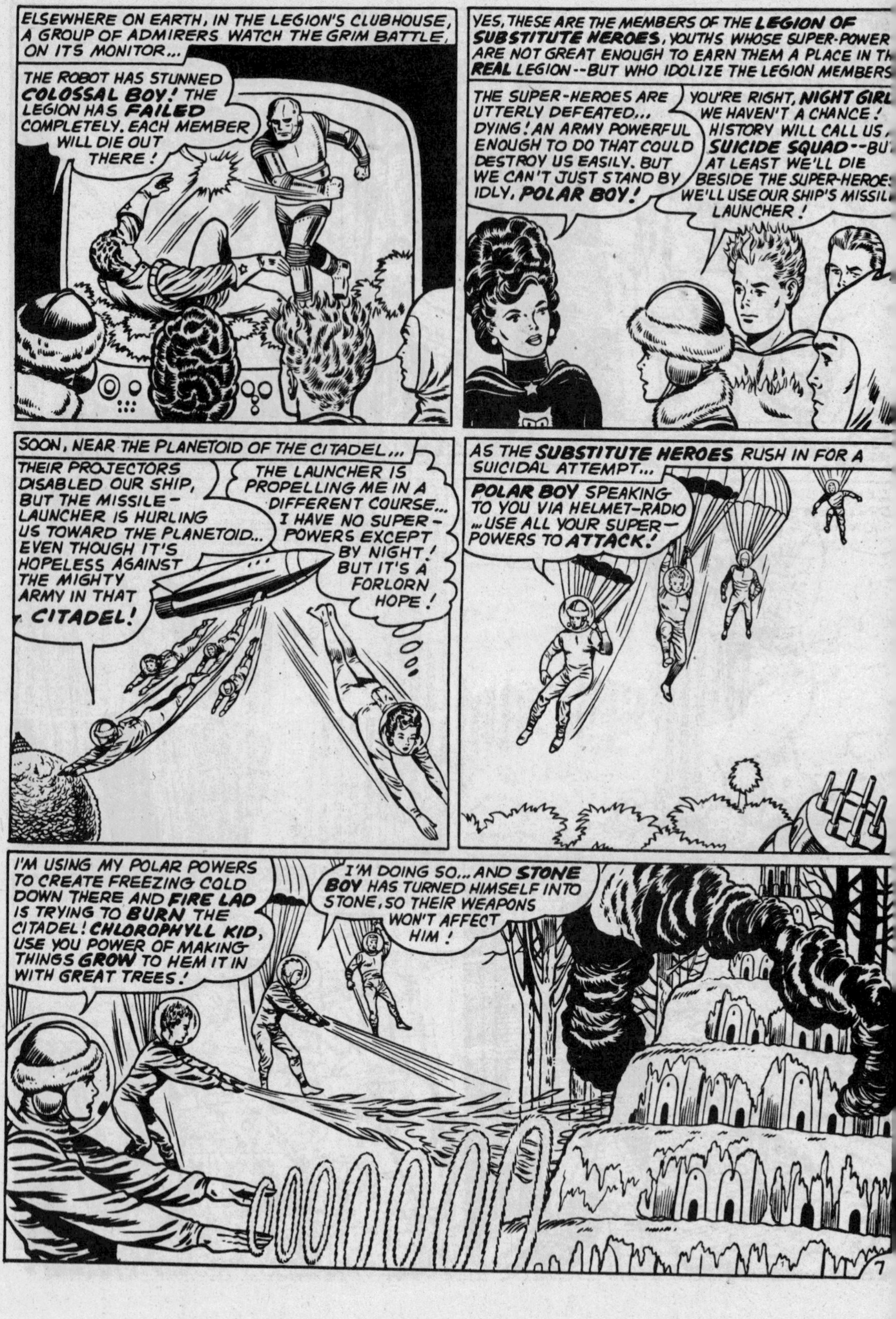
ELSEWHERE ON EARTH, IN THE LEGION'S CLUBHOUSE, A GROUP OF ADMIRERS WATCH THE GRIM BATTLE, ON ITS MONITOR...
THE ROBOT HAS STUNNED COLOSSAL BOY! THE LEGION HAS FAILED COMPLETELY. EACH MEMBER WILL DIE OUT THERE!
YES, THESE ARE THE MEMBERS OF THE LEGION OF SUBSTITUTE HEROES, YOUTHS WHOSE SUPER-POWER ARE NOT GREAT ENOUGH TO EARN THEM A PLACE IN TH REAL LEGION--BUT WHO IDOLIZE THE LEGION MEMBERS
THE SUPER-HEROES ARE UTTERLY DEFEATED... DYING! AN ARMY POWERFUL ENOUGH TO DO THAT COULD DESTROY US EASILY. BUT WE CAN'T JUST STAND BY IDLY, POLAR BOY!
YOU'RE RIGHT, NIGHT GIRL WE HAVEN'T A CHANCE! HISTORY WILL CALL US SUICIDE SQUAD--BU AT LEAST WE'LL DIE BESIDE THE SUPER-HEROE WE'LL USE OUR SHIP'S MISSIL LAUNCHER!
SOON, NEAR THE PLANETOID OF THE CITADEL...
THEIR PROJECTORS DISABLED OUR SHIP, BUT THE MISSILE-LAUNCHER IS HURLING US TOWARD THE PLANETOID... EVEN THOUGH IT'S HOPELESS AGAINST THE MIGHTY ARMY IN THAT CITADEL!
THE LAUNCHER IS PROPELLING ME IN A DIFFERENT COURSE... I HAVE NO SUPER-POWERS EXCEPT BY NIGHT! BUT IT'S A FORLORN HOPE!
AS THE SUBSTITUTE HEROES RUSH IN FOR A SUICIDAL ATTEMPT...
POLAR BOY SPEAKING TO YOU VIA HELMET-RADIO ...USE ALL YOUR SUPER-POWERS TO ATTACK!
I'M USING MY POLAR POWERS TO CREATE FREEZING COLD DOWN THERE AND FIRE LAD IS TRYING TO BURN THE CITADEL! CHLOROPHYLL KID, USE YOU POWER OF MAKING THINGS GROW TO HEM IT IN WITH GREAT TREES!
I'M DOING SO... AND STONE BOY HAS TURNED HIMSELF INTO STONE, SO THEIR WEAPONS WON'T AFFECT HIM!
7

BUT SUDDENLY, FROM THE *CITADEL*, COMES A TITANIC DEFENDER...

THE SAME GIANT ROBOT THAT OVERCAME *COLOSSAL BOY*... AND IT'S GRABBING US!

WE'RE SUNK!

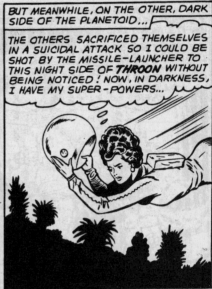

BUT MEANWHILE, ON THE OTHER, DARK SIDE OF THE PLANETOID...

THE OTHERS SACRIFICED THEMSELVES IN A SUICIDAL ATTACK SO I COULD BE SHOT BY THE MISSILE-LAUNCHER TO THIS NIGHT SIDE OF *THROON* WITHOUT BEING NOTICED! NOW, IN DARKNESS, I HAVE MY SUPER-POWERS...

...AND I CAN USE THEM TO BECOME A HUMAN DRILL AND BORE *THROUGH* THE PLANETOID, TOWARD THE *CITADEL!*

SHORTLY...

I'M IN THE DUNGEONS DEEP UNDER THE *CITADEL!* AS LONG AS I STAY INSIDE, OUT OF THE SUN, I'M SUPER-POWERED... BUT I'LL HAVE TREMENDOUS NUMBERS OF FOES TO FACE ALONE!

UP THROUGH SHADOWY, EMPTY ROOMS, MOVES *NIGHT GIRL!*

I'VE MET *NOBODY* SO FAR! THE LEAD-LINED PARTITIONS KEEP ME FROM SEEING WITH MY X-RAY VISION... BUT ALL OUR ENEMIES MUST BE IN THE FLOOR OF THE *CITADEL!* I'LL BURST IN ON THEM...

THEN, A STUNNING SURPRISE!

OUR REMOTE-CONTROLLED ROBOT HAS GRABBED THE NEW INVADERS! HEE, HEE!

WE'RE TOO MUCH FOR ALL OF THEM! WE FOOLED THEM, THEY THINK WE'RE AN *ENTIRE ARMY!*

WHY... *YOU TWO* ARE THE *ONLY* ONES IN THE *CITADEL!* A PAIR OF ZANY OLD MEN... THE ENEMIES WHO NEARLY DESTROYED BOTH LEGIONS!

8

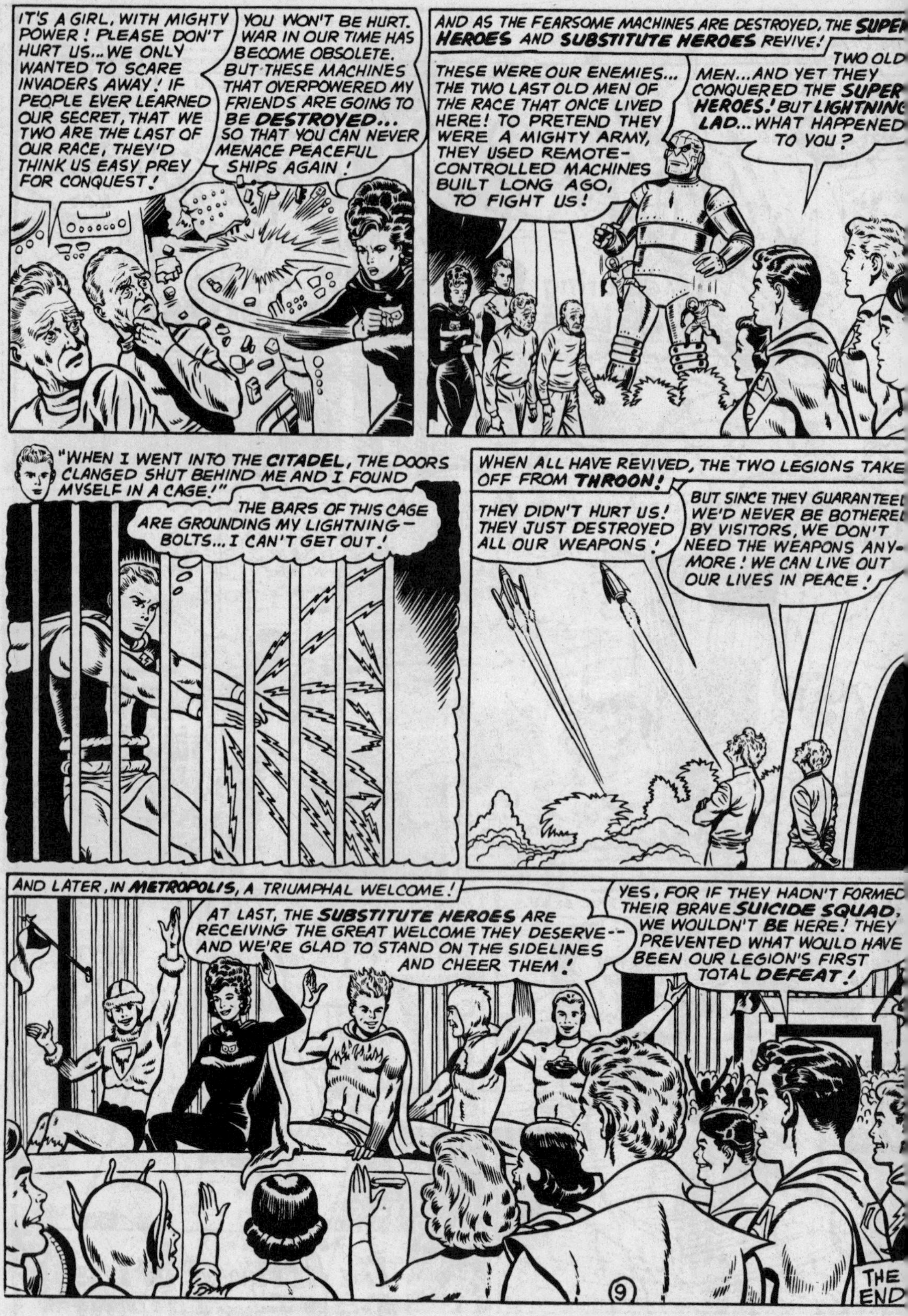
IT'S A GIRL, WITH MIGHTY POWER! PLEASE DON'T HURT US...WE ONLY WANTED TO SCARE INVADERS AWAY! IF PEOPLE EVER LEARNED OUR SECRET, THAT WE TWO ARE THE LAST OF OUR RACE, THEY'D THINK US EASY PREY FOR CONQUEST!
YOU WON'T BE HURT. WAR IN OUR TIME HAS BECOME OBSOLETE. BUT THESE MACHINES THAT OVERPOWERED MY FRIENDS ARE GOING TO BE DESTROYED... SO THAT YOU CAN NEVER MENACE PEACEFUL SHIPS AGAIN!
AND AS THE FEARSOME MACHINES ARE DESTROYED, THE SUPER-HEROES AND SUBSTITUTE HEROES REVIVE!
THESE WERE OUR ENEMIES... THE TWO LAST OLD MEN OF THE RACE THAT ONCE LIVED HERE! TO PRETEND THEY WERE A MIGHTY ARMY, THEY USED REMOTE-CONTROLLED MACHINES BUILT LONG AGO, TO FIGHT US!
TWO OLD MEN...AND YET THEY CONQUERED THE SUPER-HEROES! BUT LIGHTNING LAD...WHAT HAPPENED TO YOU?
"WHEN I WENT INTO THE CITADEL, THE DOORS CLANGED SHUT BEHIND ME AND I FOUND MYSELF IN A CAGE!"
THE BARS OF THIS CAGE ARE GROUNDING MY LIGHTNING-BOLTS...I CAN'T GET OUT!
WHEN ALL HAVE REVIVED, THE TWO LEGIONS TAKE OFF FROM THROON!
THEY DIDN'T HURT US! THEY JUST DESTROYED ALL OUR WEAPONS!
BUT SINCE THEY GUARANTEED WE'D NEVER BE BOTHERED BY VISITORS, WE DON'T NEED THE WEAPONS ANYMORE! WE CAN LIVE OUT OUR LIVES IN PEACE!
AND LATER, IN METROPOLIS, A TRIUMPHAL WELCOME!
AT LAST, THE SUBSTITUTE HEROES ARE RECEIVING THE GREAT WELCOME THEY DESERVE-- AND WE'RE GLAD TO STAND ON THE SIDELINES AND CHEER THEM!
YES, FOR IF THEY HADN'T FORMED THEIR BRAVE SUICIDE SQUAD, WE WOULDN'T BE HERE! THEY PREVENTED WHAT WOULD HAVE BEEN OUR LEGION'S FIRST TOTAL DEFEAT!
9
THE END

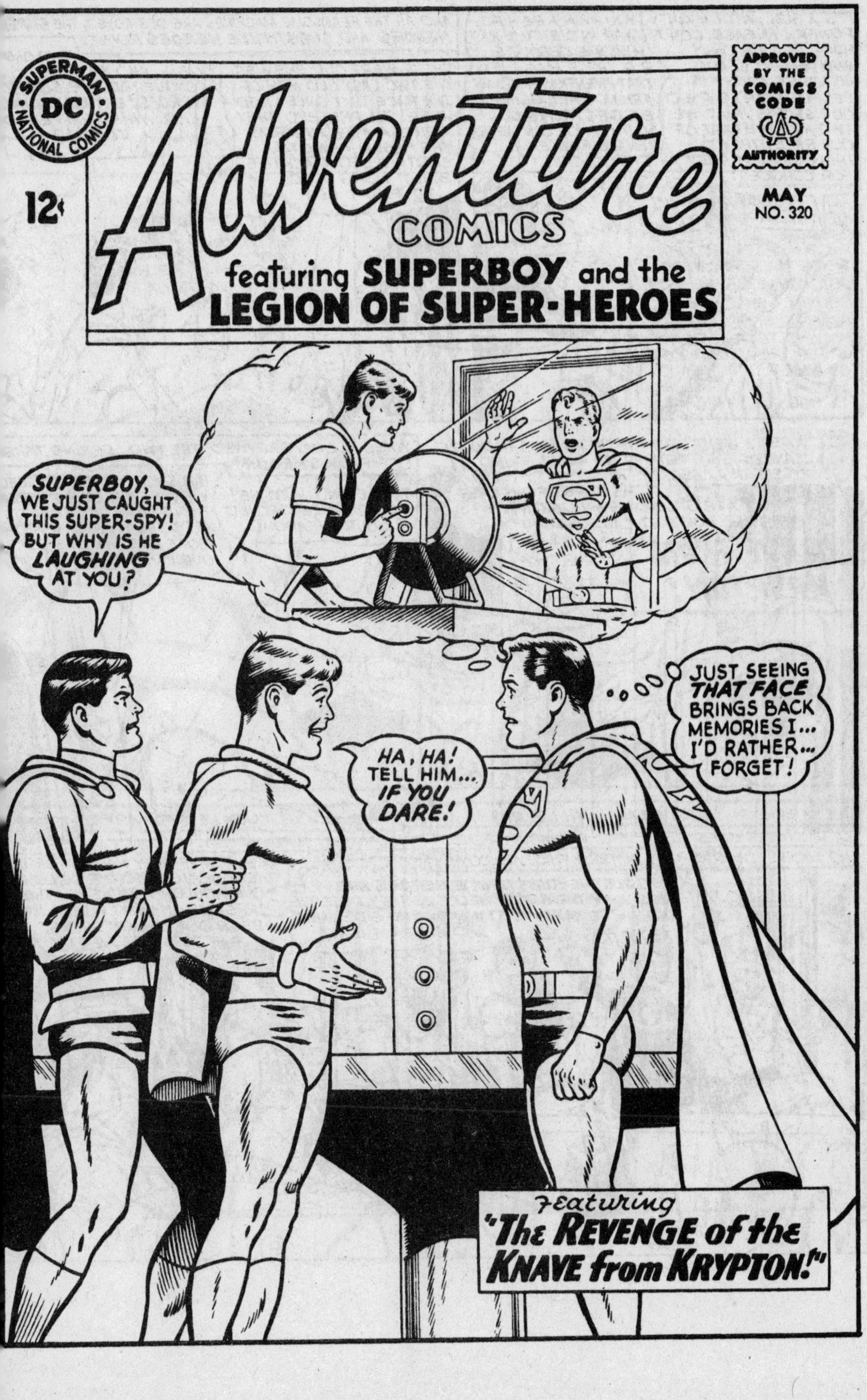
SUPERMAN DC NATIONAL COMICS
12¢
Adventure COMICS
featuring SUPERBOY and the LEGION OF SUPER-HEROES
APPROVED BY THE COMICS CODE AUTHORITY
MAY NO. 320
SUPERBOY, WE JUST CAUGHT THIS SUPER-SPY! BUT WHY IS HE LAUGHING AT YOU?
HA, HA! TELL HIM... IF YOU DARE!
JUST SEEING THAT FACE BRINGS BACK MEMORIES I... I'D RATHER... FORGET!
Featuring "The REVENGE of the KNAVE from KRYPTON!"

TALES OF THE LEGION of SUPER-HEROES

WHY IS *SUPERBOY* SO UPSEPT BY THIS YOUTH FROM OUT OF THE PAST WHOM HE MEETS SUDDENLY INSIDE THE *SUPER-HERO CLUBHOUSE* OF THE 30TH CENTURY? WHAT PAINFUL RECOLLECTIONS DO THESE MOCKING FEATURES SUMMON UP FOR THE MIGHTY *BOY OF STEEL?* IF YOU ENJOY ENIGMAS, THEN YOU'LL THRILL TO THIS *SUSPENSEFUL* ESPIONAGE TALE OF THE FAR FUTURE WHEN *SUPER-BOY* BRACES HIMSELF TO DEAL WITH--

The REVENGE OF THE KNAVE FROM KRYPTON!

PART I

YOU'RE A DESPICABLE, WORTHLESS ROGUE, *DEV-EM*, AND I'LL DO EVERYTHING IN MY POWER TO HAVE YOU PAY FOR ALL YOUR PAST CRIMES!

HA, HA, *SUPERBOY.* WHAT A JOKE ON *YOU!* YOU'LL *NEVER* BE ABLE TO PUNISH ME!

ONE AFTERNOON, OUTSIDE *SMALLVILLE HIGH*...

HA, HA! THERE GOES SCAREDY-CAT CLARK, WITH AN ARMFUL OF BOOKS!

HE'LL PROBABLY SPEND *HOURS* DOING HIS HOMEWORK, AND THEN READING! HE ISN'T JUST A BOOKWORM! HE'S A *WORM, PERIOD!*

ARRIVING HOME, CLARK GETS TO WORK...

USING MY SUPER-SPEED, I'LL FINISH MY ASSIGNMENTS IN JUST A FEW MINUTES! AFTERWARD, I'LL SWITCH TO MY SECRET IDENTITY OF *SUPERBOY,* AND AWAY I'LL GO!

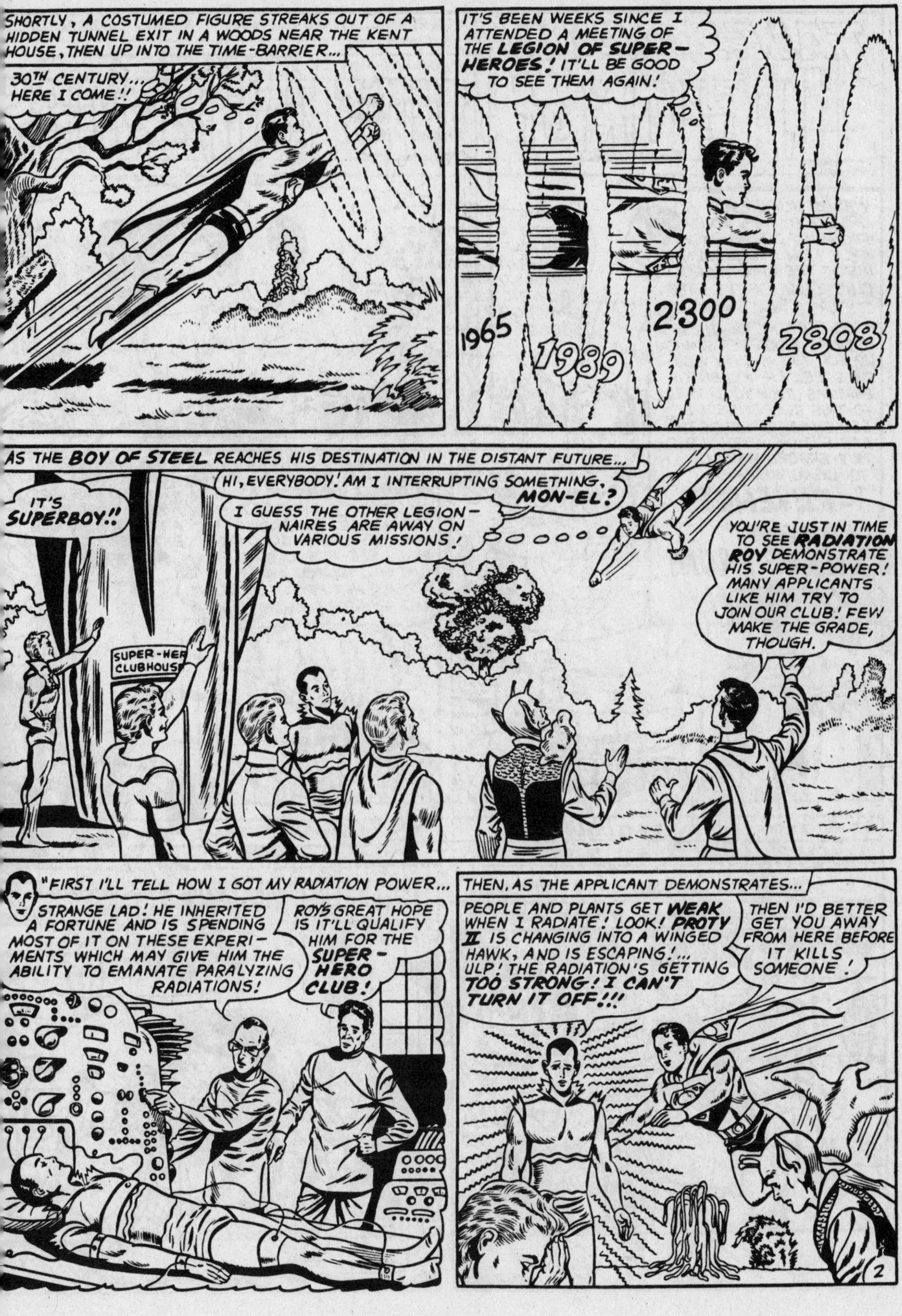
SHORTLY, A COSTUMED FIGURE STREAKS OUT OF A HIDDEN TUNNEL EXIT IN A WOODS NEAR THE KENT HOUSE, THEN UP INTO THE TIME-BARRIER...
30TH CENTURY... HERE I COME!!
IT'S BEEN WEEKS SINCE I ATTENDED A MEETING OF THE LEGION OF SUPER-HEROES! IT'LL BE GOOD TO SEE THEM AGAIN!
1965
1989
2300
2808
AS THE BOY OF STEEL REACHES HIS DESTINATION IN THE DISTANT FUTURE...
IT'S SUPERBOY!!
HI, EVERYBODY! AM I INTERRUPTING SOMETHING, MON-EL?
I GUESS THE OTHER LEGIONNAIRES ARE AWAY ON VARIOUS MISSIONS!
YOU'RE JUST IN TIME TO SEE RADIATION ROY DEMONSTRATE HIS SUPER-POWER! MANY APPLICANTS LIKE HIM TRY TO JOIN OUR CLUB! FEW MAKE THE GRADE, THOUGH.
"FIRST I'LL TELL HOW I GOT MY RADIATION POWER...
STRANGE LAD! HE INHERITED A FORTUNE AND IS SPENDING MOST OF IT ON THESE EXPERIMENTS WHICH MAY GIVE HIM THE ABILITY TO EMANATE PARALYZING RADIATIONS!
ROY'S GREAT HOPE IS IT'LL QUALIFY HIM FOR THE SUPER-HERO CLUB!
THEN, AS THE APPLICANT DEMONSTRATES...
PEOPLE AND PLANTS GET WEAK WHEN I RADIATE! LOOK! PROTY II IS CHANGING INTO A WINGED HAWK, AND IS ESCAPING!... ULP! THE RADIATION'S GETTING TOO STRONG! I CAN'T TURN IT OFF!!!
THEN I'D BETTER GET YOU AWAY FROM HERE BEFORE IT KILLS SOMEONE!
2

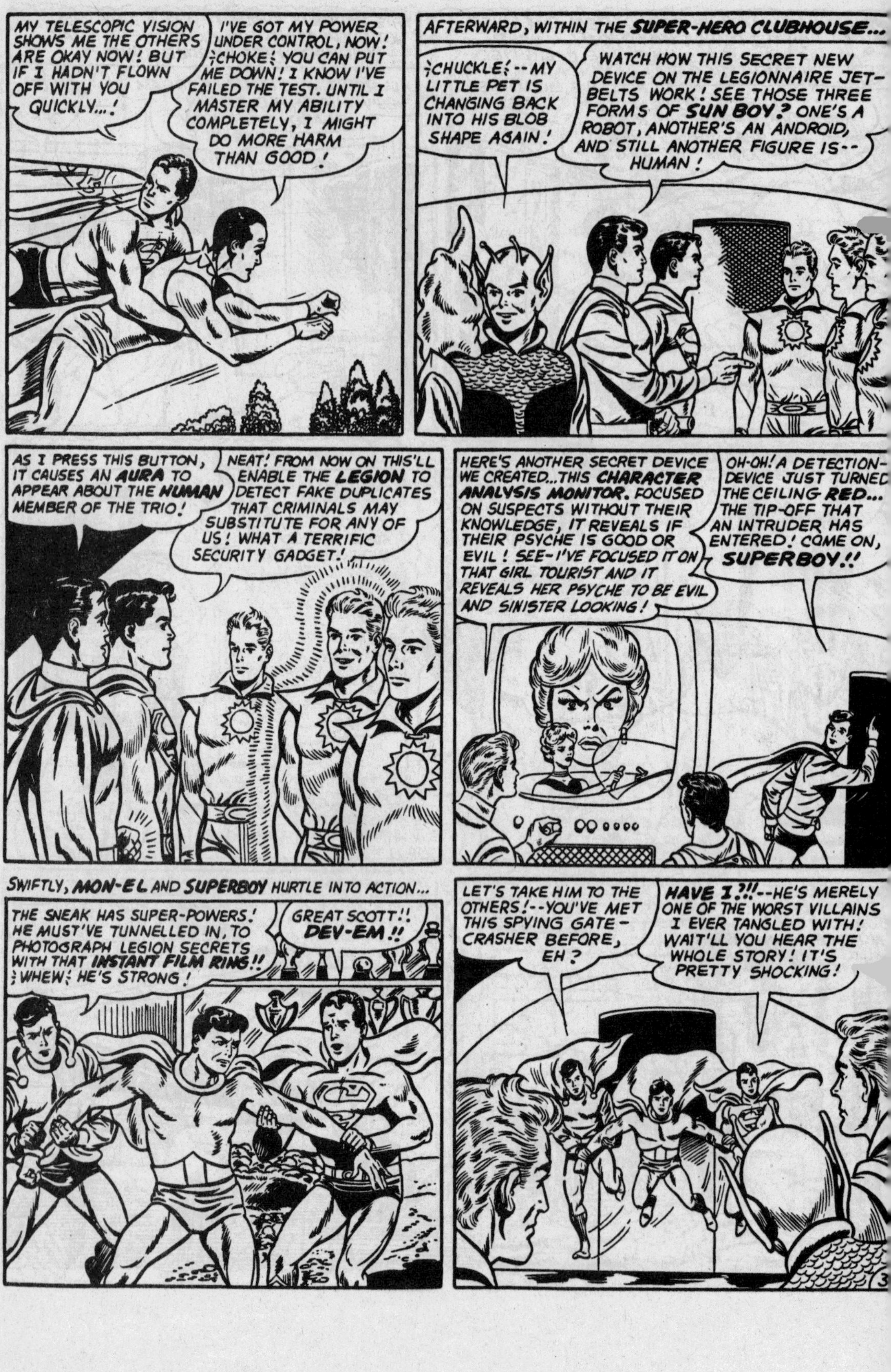
MY TELESCOPIC VISION SHOWS ME THE OTHERS ARE OKAY NOW! BUT IF I HADN'T FLOWN OFF WITH YOU QUICKLY...!
I'VE GOT MY POWER UNDER CONTROL, NOW! ;CHOKE; YOU CAN PUT ME DOWN! I KNOW I'VE FAILED THE TEST. UNTIL I MASTER MY ABILITY COMPLETELY, I MIGHT DO MORE HARM THAN GOOD!
AFTERWARD, WITHIN THE SUPER-HERO CLUBHOUSE...
;CHUCKLE; --MY LITTLE PET IS CHANGING BACK INTO HIS BLOB SHAPE AGAIN!
WATCH HOW THIS SECRET NEW DEVICE ON THE LEGIONNAIRE JET-BELTS WORK! SEE THOSE THREE FORMS OF SUN BOY? ONE'S A ROBOT, ANOTHER'S AN ANDROID, AND STILL ANOTHER FIGURE IS--HUMAN!
AS I PRESS THIS BUTTON, IT CAUSES AN AURA TO APPEAR ABOUT THE HUMAN MEMBER OF THE TRIO!
NEAT! FROM NOW ON THIS'LL ENABLE THE LEGION TO DETECT FAKE DUPLICATES THAT CRIMINALS MAY SUBSTITUTE FOR ANY OF US! WHAT A TERRIFIC SECURITY GADGET!
HERE'S ANOTHER SECRET DEVICE WE CREATED...THIS CHARACTER ANALYSIS MONITOR. FOCUSED ON SUSPECTS WITHOUT THEIR KNOWLEDGE, IT REVEALS IF THEIR PSYCHE IS GOOD OR EVIL! SEE-I'VE FOCUSED IT ON THAT GIRL TOURIST AND IT REVEALS HER PSYCHE TO BE EVIL AND SINISTER LOOKING!
OH-OH! A DETECTION-DEVICE JUST TURNED THE CEILING RED... THE TIP-OFF THAT AN INTRUDER HAS ENTERED! COME ON, SUPERBOY!!
SWIFTLY, MON-EL AND SUPERBOY HURTLE INTO ACTION...
THE SNEAK HAS SUPER-POWERS! HE MUST'VE TUNNELLED IN, TO PHOTOGRAPH LEGION SECRETS WITH THAT INSTANT FILM RING!! ;WHEW; HE'S STRONG!
GREAT SCOTT!! DEV-EM!!
LET'S TAKE HIM TO THE OTHERS!--YOU'VE MET THIS SPYING GATE-CRASHER BEFORE, EH?
HAVE I?!!--HE'S MERELY ONE OF THE WORST VILLAINS I EVER TANGLED WITH! WAIT'LL YOU HEAR THE WHOLE STORY! IT'S PRETTY SHOCKING!
3

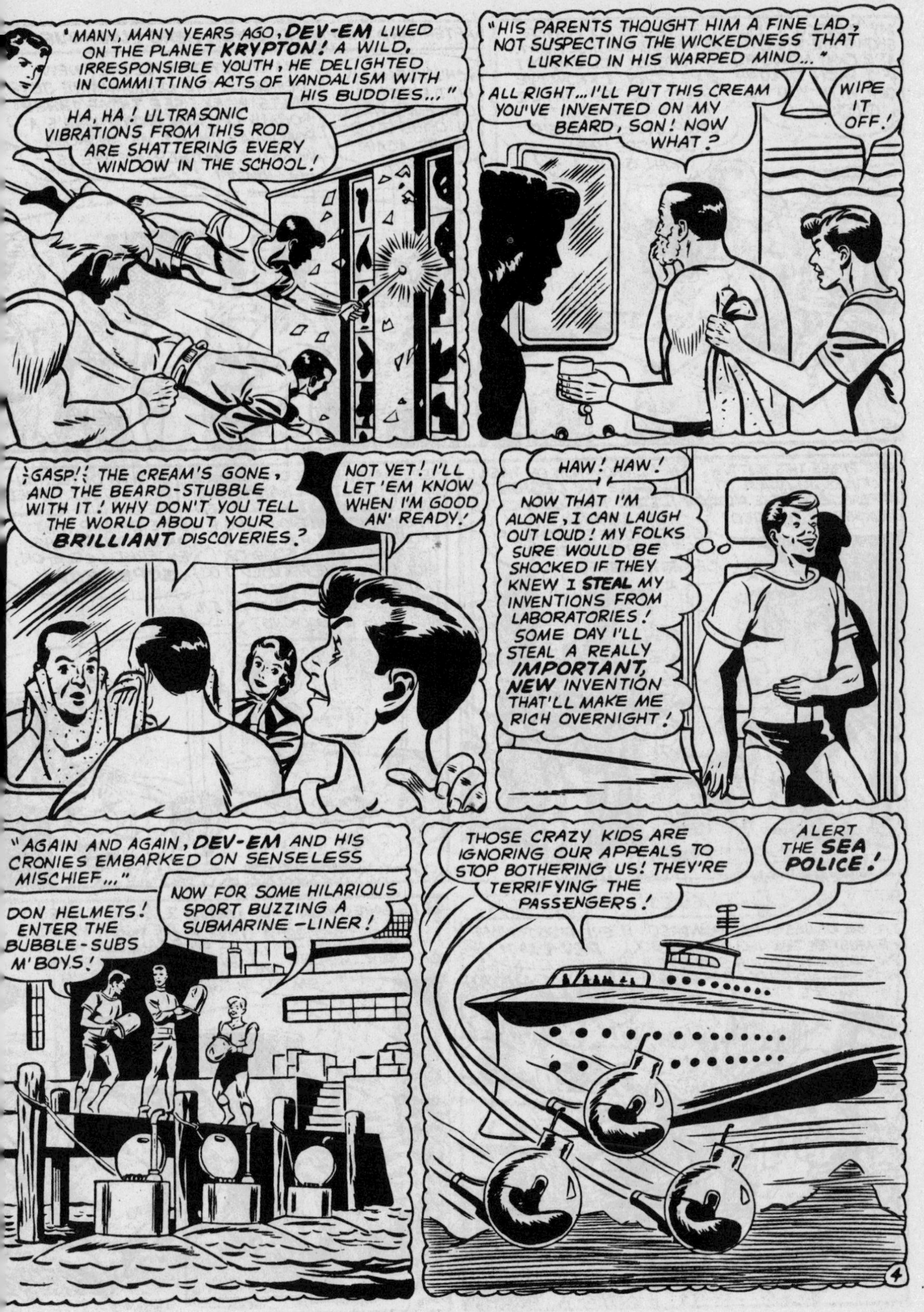
"MANY, MANY YEARS AGO, DEV-EM LIVED ON THE PLANET KRYPTON! A WILD, IRRESPONSIBLE YOUTH, HE DELIGHTED IN COMMITTING ACTS OF VANDALISM WITH HIS BUDDIES..."
HA, HA! ULTRASONIC VIBRATIONS FROM THIS ROD ARE SHATTERING EVERY WINDOW IN THE SCHOOL!
"HIS PARENTS THOUGHT HIM A FINE LAD, NOT SUSPECTING THE WICKEDNESS THAT LURKED IN HIS WARPED MIND..."
ALL RIGHT... I'LL PUT THIS CREAM YOU'VE INVENTED ON MY BEARD, SON! NOW WHAT?
WIPE IT OFF!
¡GASP!¡ THE CREAM'S GONE, AND THE BEARD-STUBBLE WITH IT! WHY DON'T YOU TELL THE WORLD ABOUT YOUR BRILLIANT DISCOVERIES?
NOT YET! I'LL LET 'EM KNOW WHEN I'M GOOD AN' READY!
HAW! HAW!
NOW THAT I'M ALONE, I CAN LAUGH OUT LOUD! MY FOLKS SURE WOULD BE SHOCKED IF THEY KNEW I STEAL MY INVENTIONS FROM LABORATORIES! SOME DAY I'LL STEAL A REALLY IMPORTANT, NEW INVENTION THAT'LL MAKE ME RICH OVERNIGHT!
"AGAIN AND AGAIN, DEV-EM AND HIS CRONIES EMBARKED ON SENSELESS MISCHIEF..."
DON HELMETS! ENTER THE BUBBLE-SUBS M' BOYS!
NOW FOR SOME HILARIOUS SPORT BUZZING A SUBMARINE-LINER!
THOSE CRAZY KIDS ARE IGNORING OUR APPEALS TO STOP BOTHERING US! THEY'RE TERRIFYING THE PASSENGERS!
ALERT THE SEA POLICE!
4

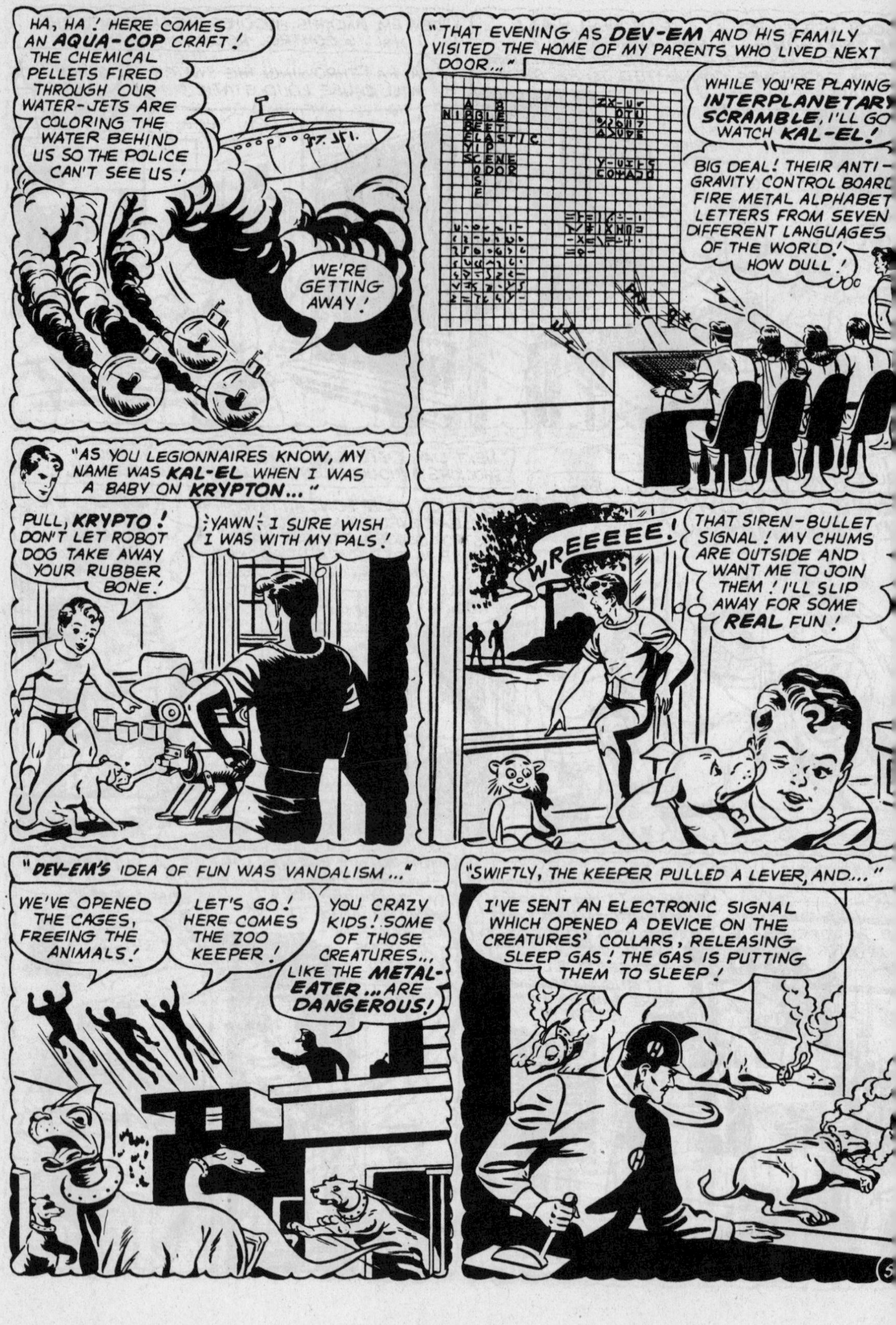
HA, HA! HERE COMES AN AQUA-COP CRAFT! THE CHEMICAL PELLETS FIRED THROUGH OUR WATER-JETS ARE COLORING THE WATER BEHIND US SO THE POLICE CAN'T SEE US!
WE'RE GETTING AWAY!
"THAT EVENING AS DEV-EM AND HIS FAMILY VISITED THE HOME OF MY PARENTS WHO LIVED NEXT DOOR..."
WHILE YOU'RE PLAYING INTERPLANETARY SCRAMBLE, I'LL GO WATCH KAL-EL!
BIG DEAL! THEIR ANTI-GRAVITY CONTROL BOARD FIRE METAL ALPHABET LETTERS FROM SEVEN DIFFERENT LANGUAGES OF THE WORLD! HOW DULL!
"AS YOU LEGIONNAIRES KNOW, MY NAME WAS KAL-EL WHEN I WAS A BABY ON KRYPTON..."
PULL, KRYPTO! DON'T LET ROBOT DOG TAKE AWAY YOUR RUBBER BONE!
-YAWN- I SURE WISH I WAS WITH MY PALS!
WREEEEEE!
THAT SIREN-BULLET SIGNAL! MY CHUMS ARE OUTSIDE AND WANT ME TO JOIN THEM! I'LL SLIP AWAY FOR SOME REAL FUN!
"DEV-EM'S IDEA OF FUN WAS VANDALISM..."
WE'VE OPENED THE CAGES, FREEING THE ANIMALS!
LET'S GO! HERE COMES THE ZOO KEEPER!
YOU CRAZY KIDS! SOME OF THOSE CREATURES... LIKE THE METAL-EATER... ARE DANGEROUS!
"SWIFTLY, THE KEEPER PULLED A LEVER, AND..."
I'VE SENT AN ELECTRONIC SIGNAL WHICH OPENED A DEVICE ON THE CREATURES' COLLARS, RELEASING SLEEP GAS! THE GAS IS PUTTING THEM TO SLEEP!

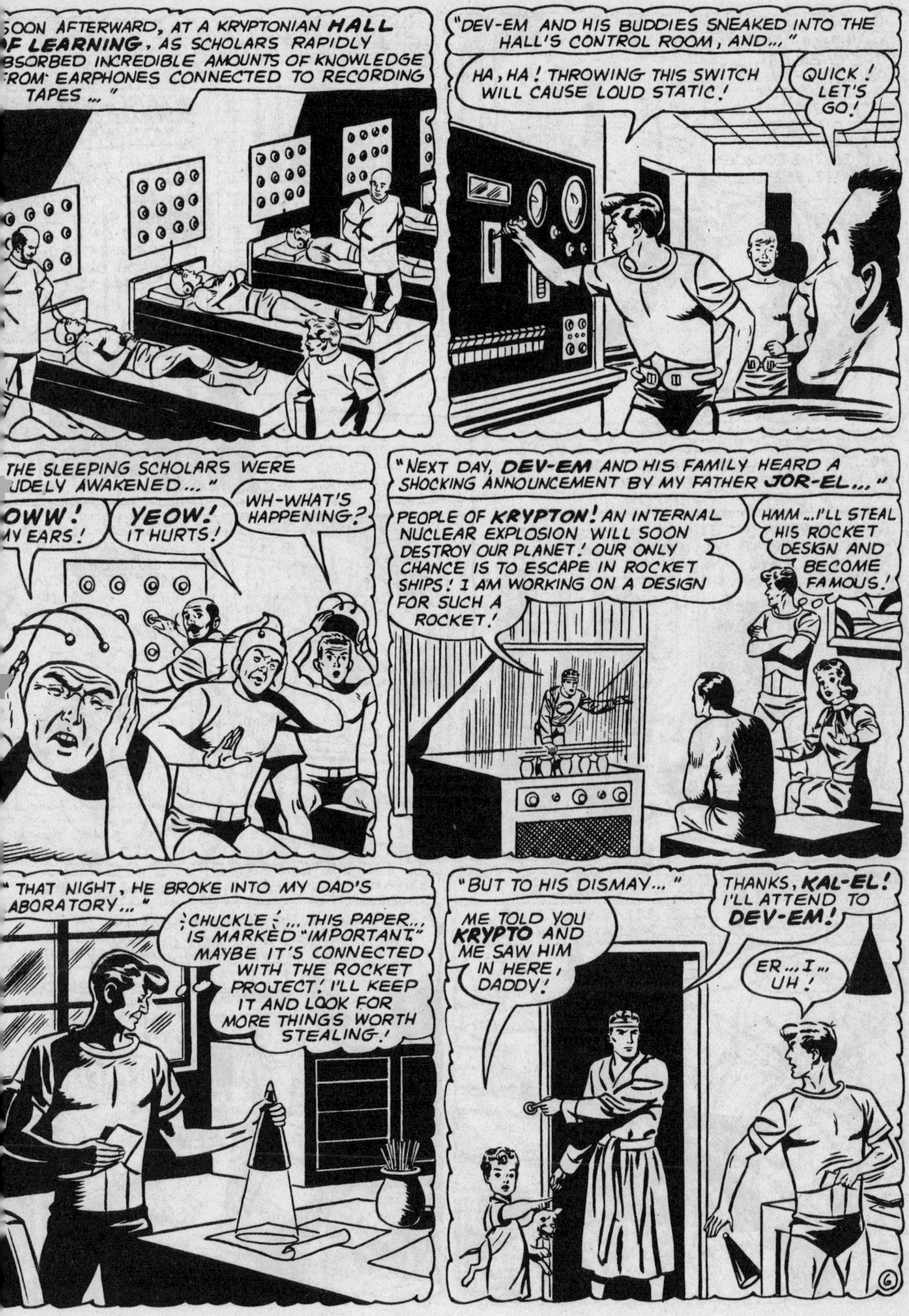
SOON AFTERWARD, AT A KRYPTONIAN HALL OF LEARNING, AS SCHOLARS RAPIDLY ABSORBED INCREDIBLE AMOUNTS OF KNOWLEDGE FROM EARPHONES CONNECTED TO RECORDING TAPES ..."
"DEV-EM AND HIS BUDDIES SNEAKED INTO THE HALL'S CONTROL ROOM, AND..."
HA, HA! THROWING THIS SWITCH WILL CAUSE LOUD STATIC!
QUICK! LET'S GO!
THE SLEEPING SCHOLARS WERE RUDELY AWAKENED..."
OWW! MY EARS!
YEOW! IT HURTS!
WH-WHAT'S HAPPENING?
"NEXT DAY, DEV-EM AND HIS FAMILY HEARD A SHOCKING ANNOUNCEMENT BY MY FATHER JOR-EL..."
PEOPLE OF KRYPTON! AN INTERNAL NUCLEAR EXPLOSION WILL SOON DESTROY OUR PLANET! OUR ONLY CHANCE IS TO ESCAPE IN ROCKET SHIPS! I AM WORKING ON A DESIGN FOR SUCH A ROCKET!
HMM...I'LL STEAL HIS ROCKET DESIGN AND BECOME FAMOUS!
"THAT NIGHT, HE BROKE INTO MY DAD'S LABORATORY..."
CHUCKLE ... THIS PAPER... IS MARKED "IMPORTANT." MAYBE IT'S CONNECTED WITH THE ROCKET PROJECT! I'LL KEEP IT AND LOOK FOR MORE THINGS WORTH STEALING!
"BUT TO HIS DISMAY..."
ME TOLD YOU KRYPTO AND ME SAW HIM IN HERE, DADDY!
THANKS, KAL-EL! I'LL ATTEND TO DEV-EM!
ER... I... UH!
6

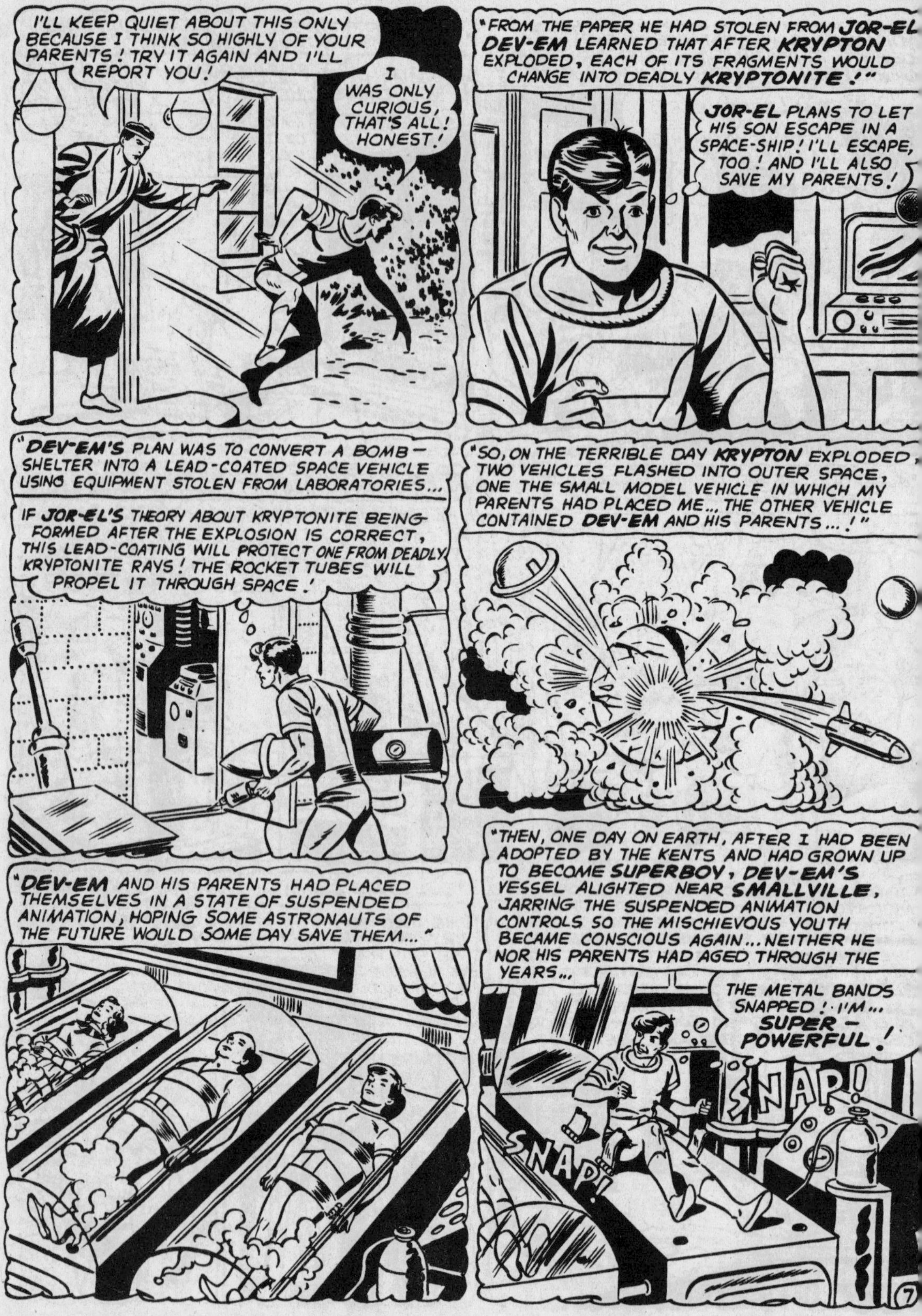
I'LL KEEP QUIET ABOUT THIS ONLY BECAUSE I THINK SO HIGHLY OF YOUR PARENTS! TRY IT AGAIN AND I'LL REPORT YOU!
I WAS ONLY CURIOUS, THAT'S ALL! HONEST!
"FROM THE PAPER HE HAD STOLEN FROM JOR-EL DEV-EM LEARNED THAT AFTER KRYPTON EXPLODED, EACH OF ITS FRAGMENTS WOULD CHANGE INTO DEADLY KRYPTONITE!"
JOR-EL PLANS TO LET HIS SON ESCAPE IN A SPACE-SHIP! I'LL ESCAPE, TOO! AND I'LL ALSO SAVE MY PARENTS!
"DEV-EM'S PLAN WAS TO CONVERT A BOMB-SHELTER INTO A LEAD-COATED SPACE VEHICLE USING EQUIPMENT STOLEN FROM LABORATORIES...
IF JOR-EL'S THEORY ABOUT KRYPTONITE BEING FORMED AFTER THE EXPLOSION IS CORRECT, THIS LEAD-COATING WILL PROTECT ONE FROM DEADLY KRYPTONITE RAYS! THE ROCKET TUBES WILL PROPEL IT THROUGH SPACE!
"SO, ON THE TERRIBLE DAY KRYPTON EXPLODED, TWO VEHICLES FLASHED INTO OUTER SPACE, ONE THE SMALL MODEL VEHICLE IN WHICH MY PARENTS HAD PLACED ME... THE OTHER VEHICLE CONTAINED DEV-EM AND HIS PARENTS...!"
"DEV-EM AND HIS PARENTS HAD PLACED THEMSELVES IN A STATE OF SUSPENDED ANIMATION, HOPING SOME ASTRONAUTS OF THE FUTURE WOULD SOME DAY SAVE THEM..."
"THEN, ONE DAY ON EARTH, AFTER I HAD BEEN ADOPTED BY THE KENTS AND HAD GROWN UP TO BECOME SUPERBOY, DEV-EM'S VESSEL ALIGHTED NEAR SMALLVILLE, JARRING THE SUSPENDED ANIMATION CONTROLS SO THE MISCHIEVOUS YOUTH BECAME CONSCIOUS AGAIN... NEITHER HE NOR HIS PARENTS HAD AGED THROUGH THE YEARS...
THE METAL BANDS SNAPPED! I'M... SUPER-POWERFUL!
SNAP!
SNAP!
7

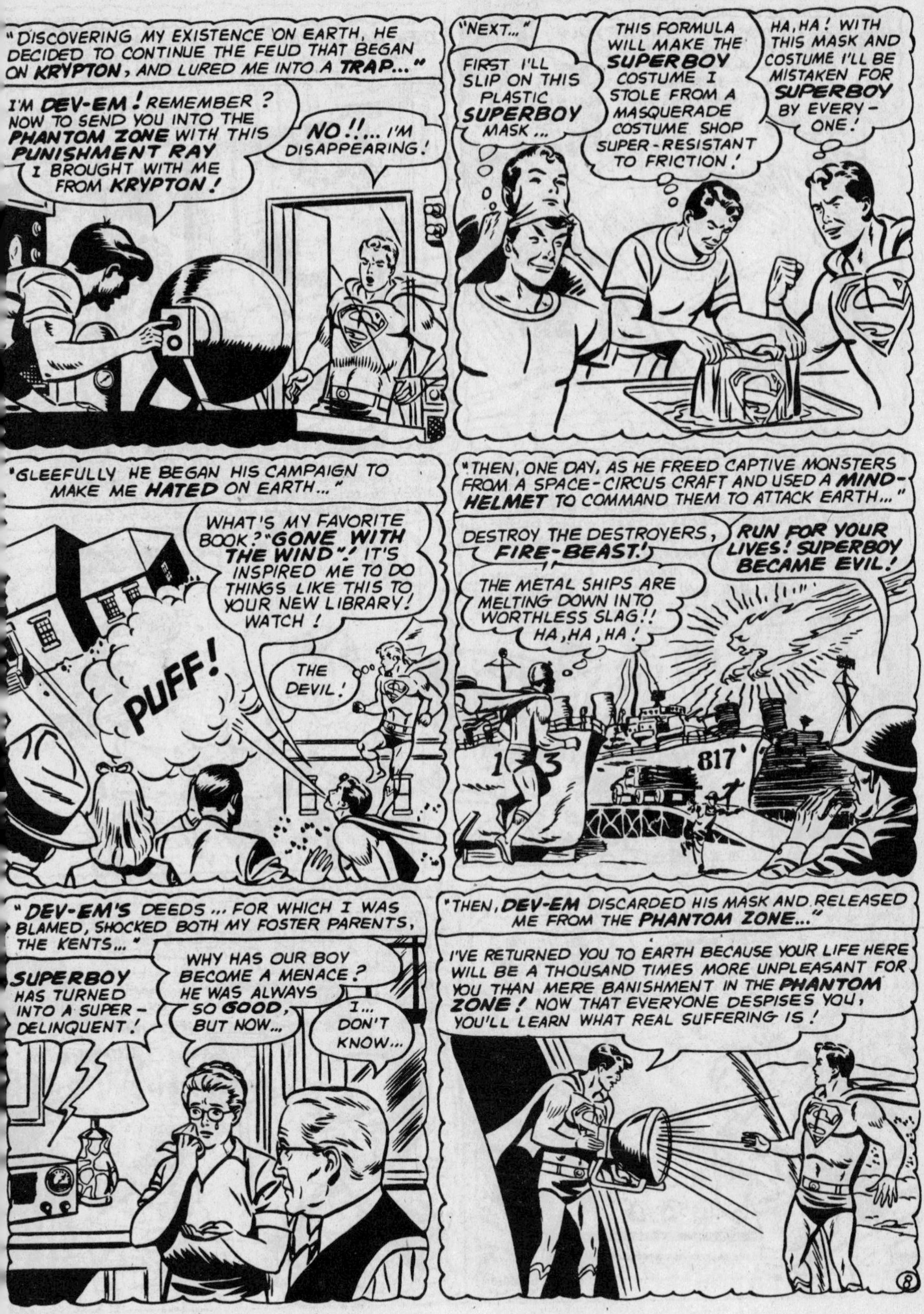
"DISCOVERING MY EXISTENCE ON EARTH, HE DECIDED TO CONTINUE THE FEUD THAT BEGAN ON KRYPTON, AND LURED ME INTO A TRAP..."
I'M DEV-EM! REMEMBER? NOW TO SEND YOU INTO THE PHANTOM ZONE WITH THIS PUNISHMENT RAY I BROUGHT WITH ME FROM KRYPTON!
NO!!... I'M DISAPPEARING!
"NEXT..."
FIRST I'LL SLIP ON THIS PLASTIC SUPERBOY MASK...
THIS FORMULA WILL MAKE THE SUPERBOY COSTUME I STOLE FROM A MASQUERADE COSTUME SHOP SUPER-RESISTANT TO FRICTION!
HA, HA! WITH THIS MASK AND COSTUME I'LL BE MISTAKEN FOR SUPERBOY BY EVERY-ONE!
"GLEEFULLY HE BEGAN HIS CAMPAIGN TO MAKE ME HATED ON EARTH..."
WHAT'S MY FAVORITE BOOK? "GONE WITH THE WIND"! IT'S INSPIRED ME TO DO THINGS LIKE THIS TO YOUR NEW LIBRARY! WATCH!
THE DEVIL!
PUFF!
"THEN, ONE DAY, AS HE FREED CAPTIVE MONSTERS FROM A SPACE-CIRCUS CRAFT AND USED A MIND-HELMET TO COMMAND THEM TO ATTACK EARTH..."
DESTROY THE DESTROYERS, FIRE-BEAST!
THE METAL SHIPS ARE MELTING DOWN INTO WORTHLESS SLAG!! HA, HA, HA!
RUN FOR YOUR LIVES! SUPERBOY BECAME EVIL!
"DEV-EM'S DEEDS ... FOR WHICH I WAS BLAMED, SHOCKED BOTH MY FOSTER PARENTS, THE KENTS..."
SUPERBOY HAS TURNED INTO A SUPER-DELINQUENT!
WHY HAS OUR BOY BECOME A MENACE? HE WAS ALWAYS SO GOOD, BUT NOW...
I... DON'T KNOW...
"THEN, DEV-EM DISCARDED HIS MASK AND RELEASED ME FROM THE PHANTOM ZONE..."
I'VE RETURNED YOU TO EARTH BECAUSE YOUR LIFE HERE WILL BE A THOUSAND TIMES MORE UNPLEASANT FOR YOU THAN MERE BANISHMENT IN THE PHANTOM ZONE! NOW THAT EVERYONE DESPISES YOU, YOU'LL LEARN WHAT REAL SUFFERING IS!
8

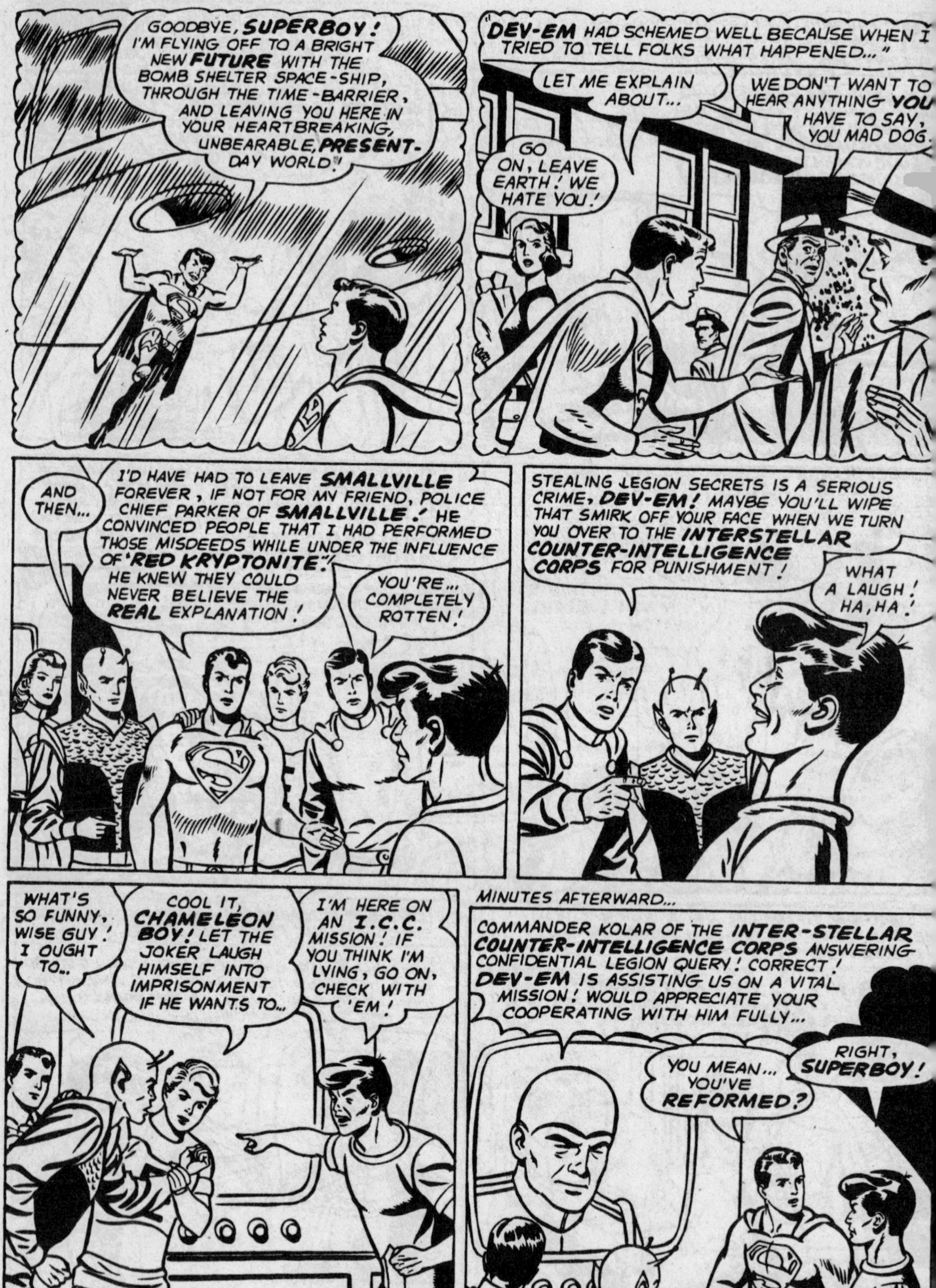
GOODBYE, SUPERBOY! I'M FLYING OFF TO A BRIGHT NEW FUTURE WITH THE BOMB SHELTER SPACE-SHIP, THROUGH THE TIME-BARRIER, AND LEAVING YOU HERE IN YOUR HEARTBREAKING, UNBEARABLE, PRESENT-DAY WORLD!"
"DEV-EM HAD SCHEMED WELL BECAUSE WHEN I TRIED TO TELL FOLKS WHAT HAPPENED..."
LET ME EXPLAIN ABOUT...
WE DON'T WANT TO HEAR ANYTHING YOU HAVE TO SAY, YOU MAD DOG.
GO ON, LEAVE EARTH! WE HATE YOU!
AND THEN...
I'D HAVE HAD TO LEAVE SMALLVILLE FOREVER, IF NOT FOR MY FRIEND, POLICE CHIEF PARKER OF SMALLVILLE! HE CONVINCED PEOPLE THAT I HAD PERFORMED THOSE MISDEEDS WHILE UNDER THE INFLUENCE OF 'RED KRYPTONITE'! HE KNEW THEY COULD NEVER BELIEVE THE REAL EXPLANATION!
YOU'RE... COMPLETELY ROTTEN!
STEALING LEGION SECRETS IS A SERIOUS CRIME, DEV-EM! MAYBE YOU'LL WIPE THAT SMIRK OFF YOUR FACE WHEN WE TURN YOU OVER TO THE INTERSTELLAR COUNTER-INTELLIGENCE CORPS FOR PUNISHMENT!
WHAT A LAUGH! HA, HA!
WHAT'S SO FUNNY, WISE GUY! I OUGHT TO...
COOL IT, CHAMELEON BOY! LET THE JOKER LAUGH HIMSELF INTO IMPRISONMENT IF HE WANTS TO...
I'M HERE ON AN I.C.C. MISSION! IF YOU THINK I'M LYING, GO ON, CHECK WITH 'EM!
MINUTES AFTERWARD...
COMMANDER KOLAR OF THE INTER-STELLAR COUNTER-INTELLIGENCE CORPS ANSWERING CONFIDENTIAL LEGION QUERY! CORRECT! DEV-EM IS ASSISTING US ON A VITAL MISSION! WOULD APPRECIATE YOUR COOPERATING WITH HIM FULLY...
YOU MEAN... YOU'VE REFORMED?
RIGHT, SUPERBOY!
9

"I LEARNED MY LESSON SINCE YOU LAST SAW ME! I REALIZE NOW THAT WRONG-DOERS ALWAYS LOSE OUT! AFTER THE I.C.C. TESTED ME WITH THEIR *PSYCHOTRON*..."

DEV-EM, OUR *PSYCHOTRON* [K]NOWS YOU'RE HONEST AND SINCERE! [W]E WANT TO NAB THE ELUSIVE [LE]ADER OF THE SINISTER [CO]SMIC SPY LEGION... [M]OLOCK THE MERCILESS"! [WI]LL YOU HELP US?

GLADLY!

I MANAGED TO CONTACT SOME C.S.L. UNDERLINGS! I LEARNED *MOLOCK* WOULD MEET ME PERSONALLY *IF* I OBTAINED LEGION SECURITY SECRETS FOR HIM! THAT'S WHY I STOLE IN HERE WITH THE *INSTANT FILM RING!* PRETTY CLEAR PICTURES, RIGHT?

[B]UT--I WAS GOING TO DAMAGE THE [N]EGATIVES WITH MY HEAT VISION [B]EFORE I TURNED THEM OVER TO [M]OLOCK...LIKE THIS...SO THERE'D [B]E NO HARM DONE! AND WHILE HE WAS [AS]SUMING, I'D CAPTURE HIM AND TURN [H]IM OVER TO COMMANDER *KOLAR!*

SPEAKING OF THE COMMANDER, HERE HE IS AGAIN! LISTEN...

NOW THAT THE LEGION HAS BECOME AWARE OF *OPERATION MOLOCK*, WE AT *I.C.C.* HAVE DECIDED TO CHANGE OUR STRATEGY! WE'D APPRECIATE IT IF *SUPERBOY*, WHO IS MORE EXPERIENCED AT COUNTERESPIONAGE, TOOK OVER *DEV-EM'S* MISSION! -- WILL YOU, *SUPERBOY?*

[I]T'S ALL RIGHT WITH [M]E! ANY OBJECTIONS, *DEV-EM?*

UH...NONE! CARRY ON, LEGIONNAIRE!

FINE! GOOD LUCK, *SUPERBOY!* IF YOU CAPTURE *MOLOCK*, YOU'LL BE PERFORMING A GREAT SERVICE FOR EVERY LAW-ABIDING WORLD IN THE UNIVERSE!

DEV-EM LOOKS UPSET! NOW THAT HE'S GONE STRAIGHT, I HOPE HE DOESN'T THINK I WANT TO TAKE ANY GLORY AWAY FROM HIM!

SEE PART II, IN THIS ISSUE, FOR THE AMAZING CONCLUSION OF THIS TALE OF 30TH-CENTURY-STYLE ESPIONAGE.

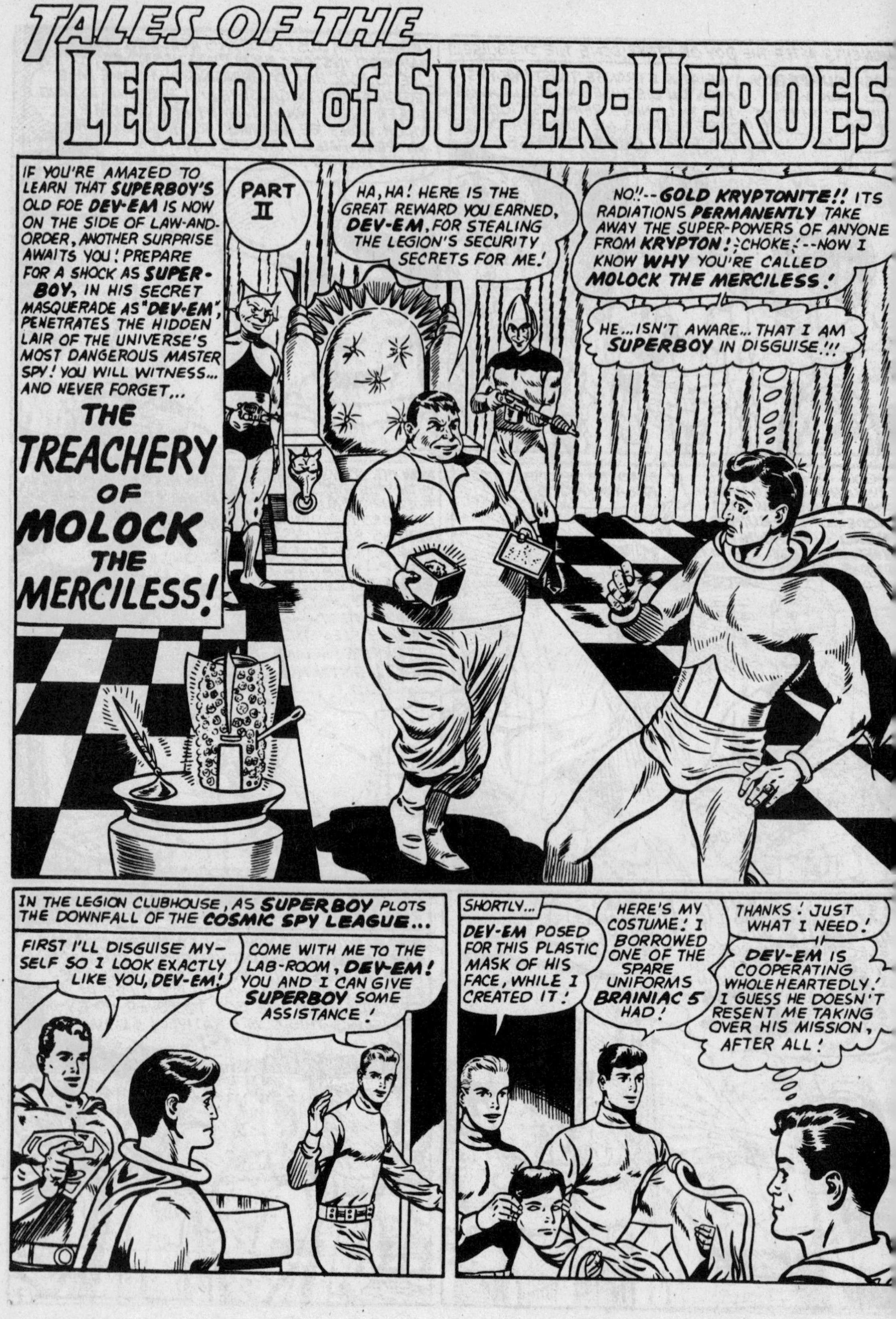
TALES OF THE
LEGION of SUPER-HEROES
IF YOU'RE AMAZED TO LEARN THAT SUPERBOY'S OLD FOE DEV-EM IS NOW ON THE SIDE OF LAW-AND-ORDER, ANOTHER SURPRISE AWAITS YOU! PREPARE FOR A SHOCK AS SUPERBOY, IN HIS SECRET MASQUERADE AS "DEV-EM", PENETRATES THE HIDDEN LAIR OF THE UNIVERSE'S MOST DANGEROUS MASTER SPY! YOU WILL WITNESS... AND NEVER FORGET...
THE TREACHERY OF MOLOCK THE MERCILESS!
PART II
HA, HA! HERE IS THE GREAT REWARD YOU EARNED, DEV-EM, FOR STEALING THE LEGION'S SECURITY SECRETS FOR ME!
NO!!--GOLD KRYPTONITE!! ITS RADIATIONS PERMANENTLY TAKE AWAY THE SUPER-POWERS OF ANYONE FROM KRYPTON! ;CHOKE; --NOW I KNOW WHY YOU'RE CALLED MOLOCK THE MERCILESS!
HE... ISN'T AWARE... THAT I AM SUPERBOY IN DISGUISE!!!
IN THE LEGION CLUBHOUSE, AS SUPERBOY PLOTS THE DOWNFALL OF THE COSMIC SPY LEAGUE...
FIRST I'LL DISGUISE MYSELF SO I LOOK EXACTLY LIKE YOU, DEV-EM!
COME WITH ME TO THE LAB-ROOM, DEV-EM! YOU AND I CAN GIVE SUPERBOY SOME ASSISTANCE!
SHORTLY...
DEV-EM POSED FOR THIS PLASTIC MASK OF HIS FACE, WHILE I CREATED IT!
HERE'S MY COSTUME! I BORROWED ONE OF THE SPARE UNIFORMS BRAINIAC 5 HAD!
THANKS! JUST WHAT I NEED!
DEV-EM IS COOPERATING WHOLEHEARTEDLY! I GUESS HE DOESN'T RESENT ME TAKING OVER HIS MISSION, AFTER ALL!

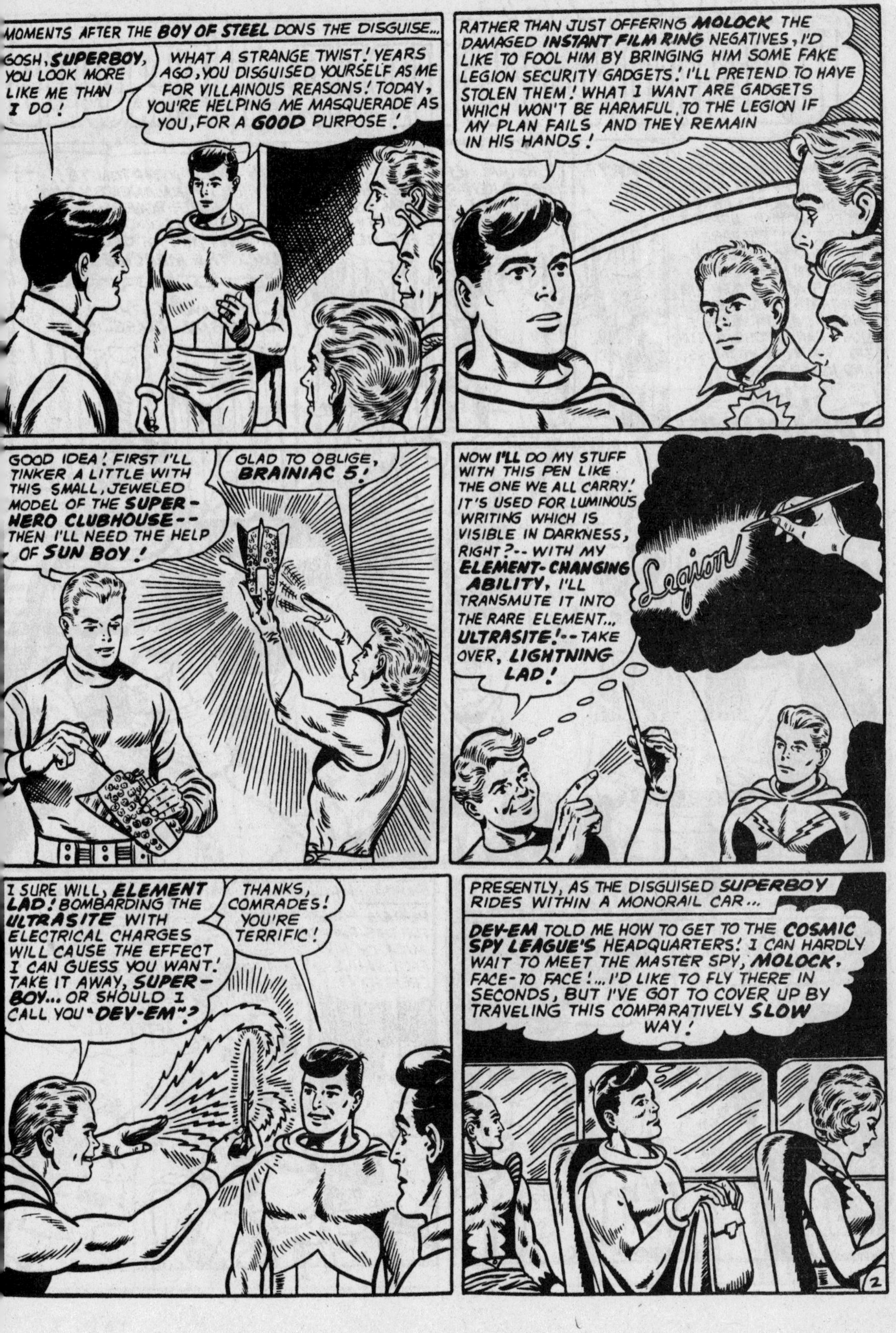
MOMENTS AFTER THE BOY OF STEEL DONS THE DISGUISE...
GOSH, SUPERBOY, YOU LOOK MORE LIKE ME THAN I DO!
WHAT A STRANGE TWIST! YEARS AGO, YOU DISGUISED YOURSELF AS ME FOR VILLAINOUS REASONS! TODAY, YOU'RE HELPING ME MASQUERADE AS YOU, FOR A GOOD PURPOSE!
RATHER THAN JUST OFFERING MOLOCK THE DAMAGED INSTANT FILM RING NEGATIVES, I'D LIKE TO FOOL HIM BY BRINGING HIM SOME FAKE LEGION SECURITY GADGETS! I'LL PRETEND TO HAVE STOLEN THEM! WHAT I WANT ARE GADGETS WHICH WON'T BE HARMFUL, TO THE LEGION IF MY PLAN FAILS AND THEY REMAIN IN HIS HANDS!
GOOD IDEA! FIRST I'LL TINKER A LITTLE WITH THIS SMALL, JEWELED MODEL OF THE SUPER-HERO CLUBHOUSE-- THEN I'LL NEED THE HELP OF SUN BOY!
GLAD TO OBLIGE, BRAINIAC 5!
NOW I'LL DO MY STUFF WITH THIS PEN LIKE THE ONE WE ALL CARRY! IT'S USED FOR LUMINOUS WRITING WHICH IS VISIBLE IN DARKNESS, RIGHT?-- WITH MY ELEMENT-CHANGING ABILITY, I'LL TRANSMUTE IT INTO THE RARE ELEMENT... ULTRASITE!-- TAKE OVER, LIGHTNING LAD!
Legion
I SURE WILL, ELEMENT LAD! BOMBARDING THE ULTRASITE WITH ELECTRICAL CHARGES WILL CAUSE THE EFFECT I CAN GUESS YOU WANT! TAKE IT AWAY, SUPER-BOY... OR SHOULD I CALL YOU "DEV-EM"?
THANKS, COMRADES! YOU'RE TERRIFIC!
PRESENTLY, AS THE DISGUISED SUPERBOY RIDES WITHIN A MONORAIL CAR...
DEV-EM TOLD ME HOW TO GET TO THE COSMIC SPY LEAGUE'S HEADQUARTERS! I CAN HARDLY WAIT TO MEET THE MASTER SPY, MOLOCK, FACE-TO FACE!... I'D LIKE TO FLY THERE IN SECONDS, BUT I'VE GOT TO COVER UP BY TRAVELING THIS COMPARATIVELY SLOW WAY!
2

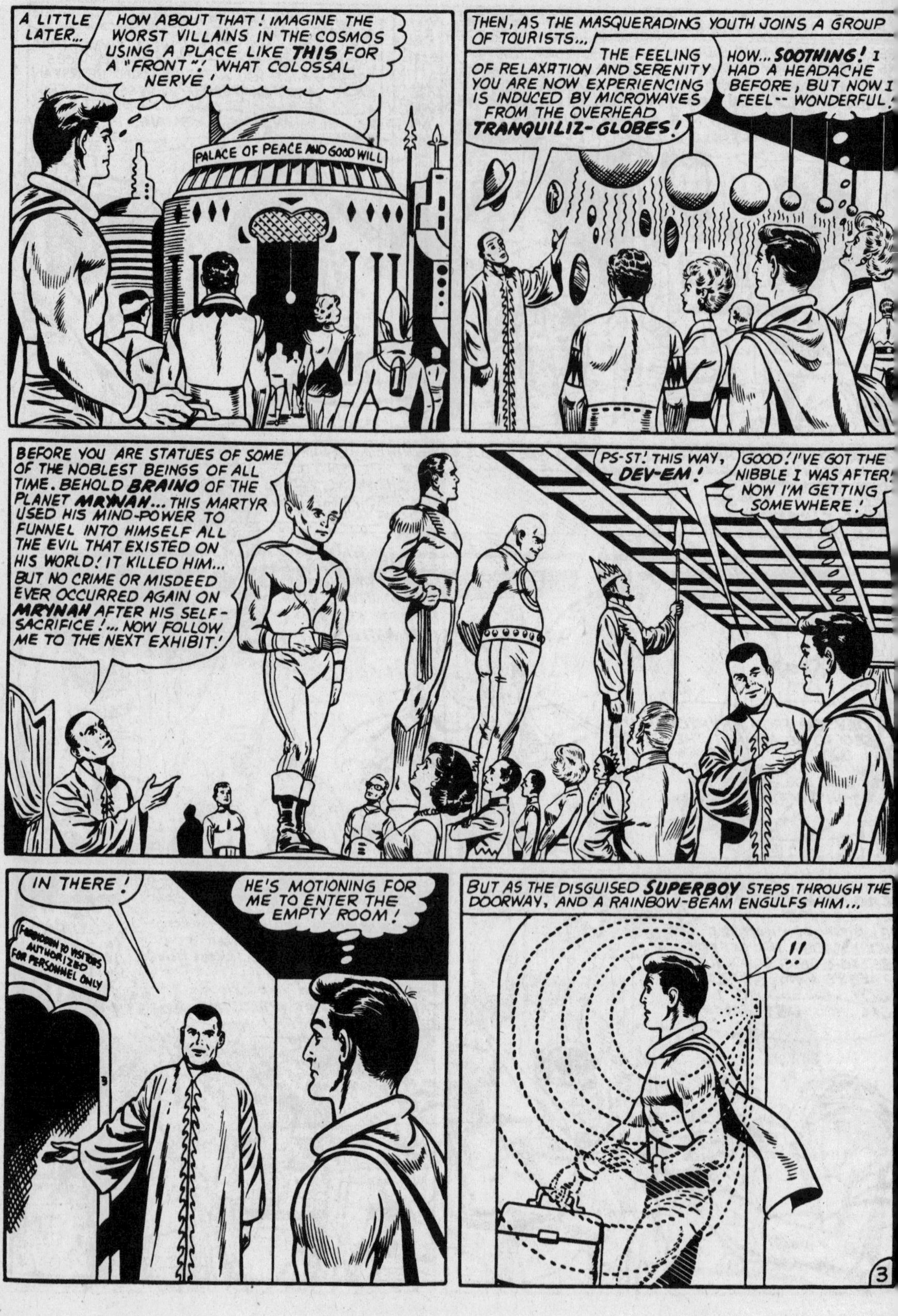
A LITTLE LATER...
HOW ABOUT THAT! IMAGINE THE WORST VILLAINS IN THE COSMOS USING A PLACE LIKE THIS FOR A "FRONT"! WHAT COLOSSAL NERVE!
PALACE OF PEACE AND GOOD WILL
THEN, AS THE MASQUERADING YOUTH JOINS A GROUP OF TOURISTS...
THE FEELING OF RELAXATION AND SERENITY YOU ARE NOW EXPERIENCING IS INDUCED BY MICROWAVES FROM THE OVERHEAD TRANQUILIZ-GLOBES!
HOW... SOOTHING! I HAD A HEADACHE BEFORE, BUT NOW I FEEL-- WONDERFUL!
BEFORE YOU ARE STATUES OF SOME OF THE NOBLEST BEINGS OF ALL TIME. BEHOLD BRAINO OF THE PLANET MRYNAH... THIS MARTYR USED HIS MIND-POWER TO FUNNEL INTO HIMSELF ALL THE EVIL THAT EXISTED ON HIS WORLD! IT KILLED HIM... BUT NO CRIME OR MISDEED EVER OCCURRED AGAIN ON MRYNAH AFTER HIS SELF-SACRIFICE!... NOW FOLLOW ME TO THE NEXT EXHIBIT!
PS-ST! THIS WAY, DEV-EM!
GOOD! I'VE GOT THE NIBBLE I WAS AFTER! NOW I'M GETTING SOMEWHERE!
IN THERE!
FORBIDDEN TO VISITORS AUTHORIZED FOR PERSONNEL ONLY
HE'S MOTIONING FOR ME TO ENTER THE EMPTY ROOM!
BUT AS THE DISGUISED SUPERBOY STEPS THROUGH THE DOORWAY, AND A RAINBOW-BEAM ENGULFS HIM...
!!
3

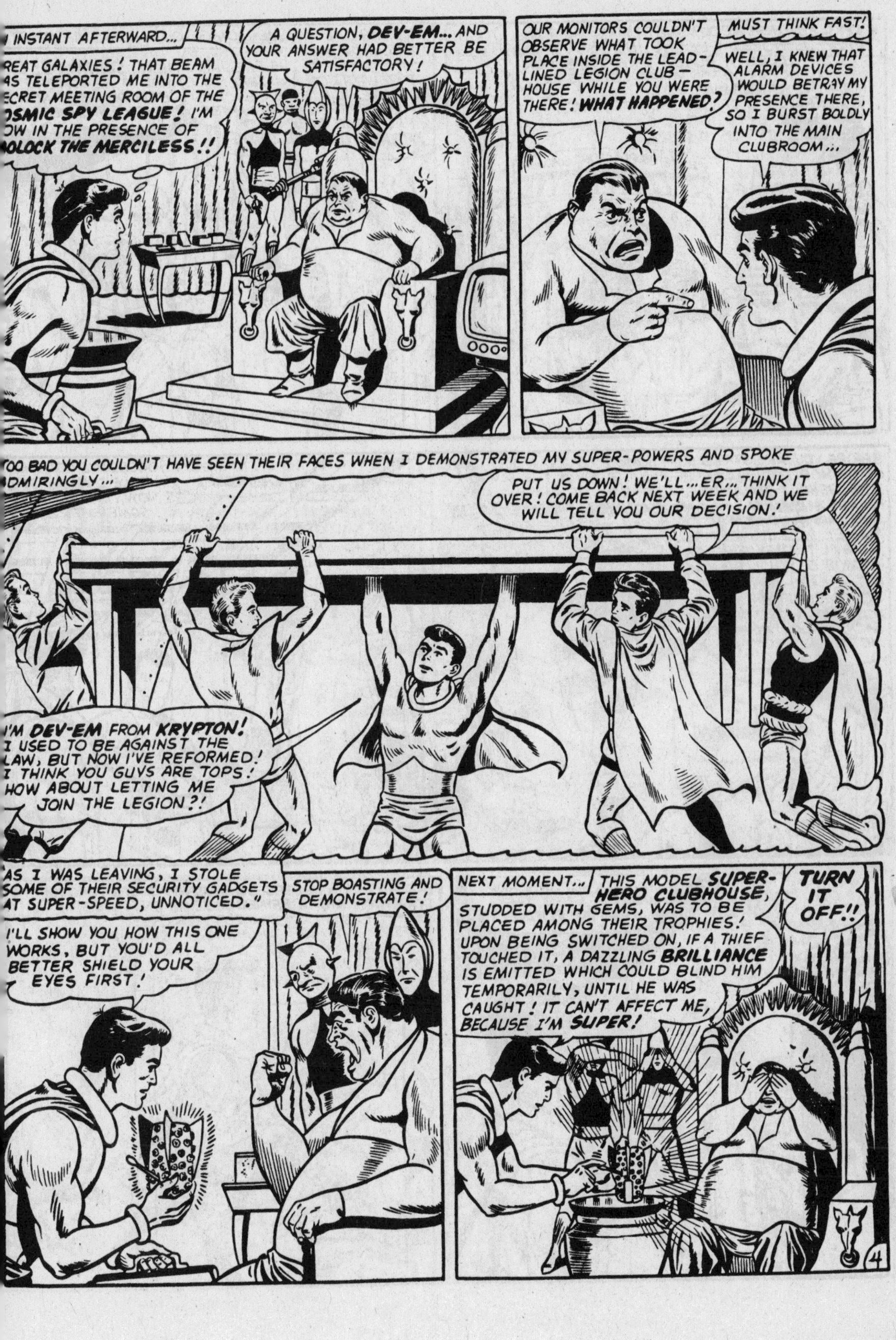

INSTANT AFTERWARD...
REAT GALAXIES! THAT BEAM AS TELEPORTED ME INTO THE ECRET MEETING ROOM OF THE OSMIC SPY LEAGUE! I'M OW IN THE PRESENCE OF OLOCK THE MERCILESS!!
A QUESTION, DEV-EM... AND YOUR ANSWER HAD BETTER BE SATISFACTORY!
OUR MONITORS COULDN'T OBSERVE WHAT TOOK PLACE INSIDE THE LEAD-LINED LEGION CLUB-HOUSE WHILE YOU WERE THERE! WHAT HAPPENED?
MUST THINK FAST!
WELL, I KNEW THAT ALARM DEVICES WOULD BETRAY MY PRESENCE THERE, SO I BURST BOLDLY INTO THE MAIN CLUBROOM...
TOO BAD YOU COULDN'T HAVE SEEN THEIR FACES WHEN I DEMONSTRATED MY SUPER-POWERS AND SPOKE ADMIRINGLY...
I'M DEV-EM FROM KRYPTON! I USED TO BE AGAINST THE LAW, BUT NOW I'VE REFORMED! I THINK YOU GUYS ARE TOPS! HOW ABOUT LETTING ME JOIN THE LEGION?!
PUT US DOWN! WE'LL...ER...THINK IT OVER! COME BACK NEXT WEEK AND WE WILL TELL YOU OUR DECISION!
"AS I WAS LEAVING, I STOLE SOME OF THEIR SECURITY GADGETS AT SUPER-SPEED, UNNOTICED."
I'LL SHOW YOU HOW THIS ONE WORKS, BUT YOU'D ALL BETTER SHIELD YOUR EYES FIRST!
STOP BOASTING AND DEMONSTRATE!
NEXT MOMENT...
THIS MODEL SUPER-HERO CLUBHOUSE, STUDDED WITH GEMS, WAS TO BE PLACED AMONG THEIR TROPHIES! UPON BEING SWITCHED ON, IF A THIEF TOUCHED IT, A DAZZLING BRILLIANCE IS EMITTED WHICH COULD BLIND HIM TEMPORARILY, UNTIL HE WAS CAUGHT! IT CAN'T AFFECT ME, BECAUSE I'M SUPER!
TURN IT OFF!!
4

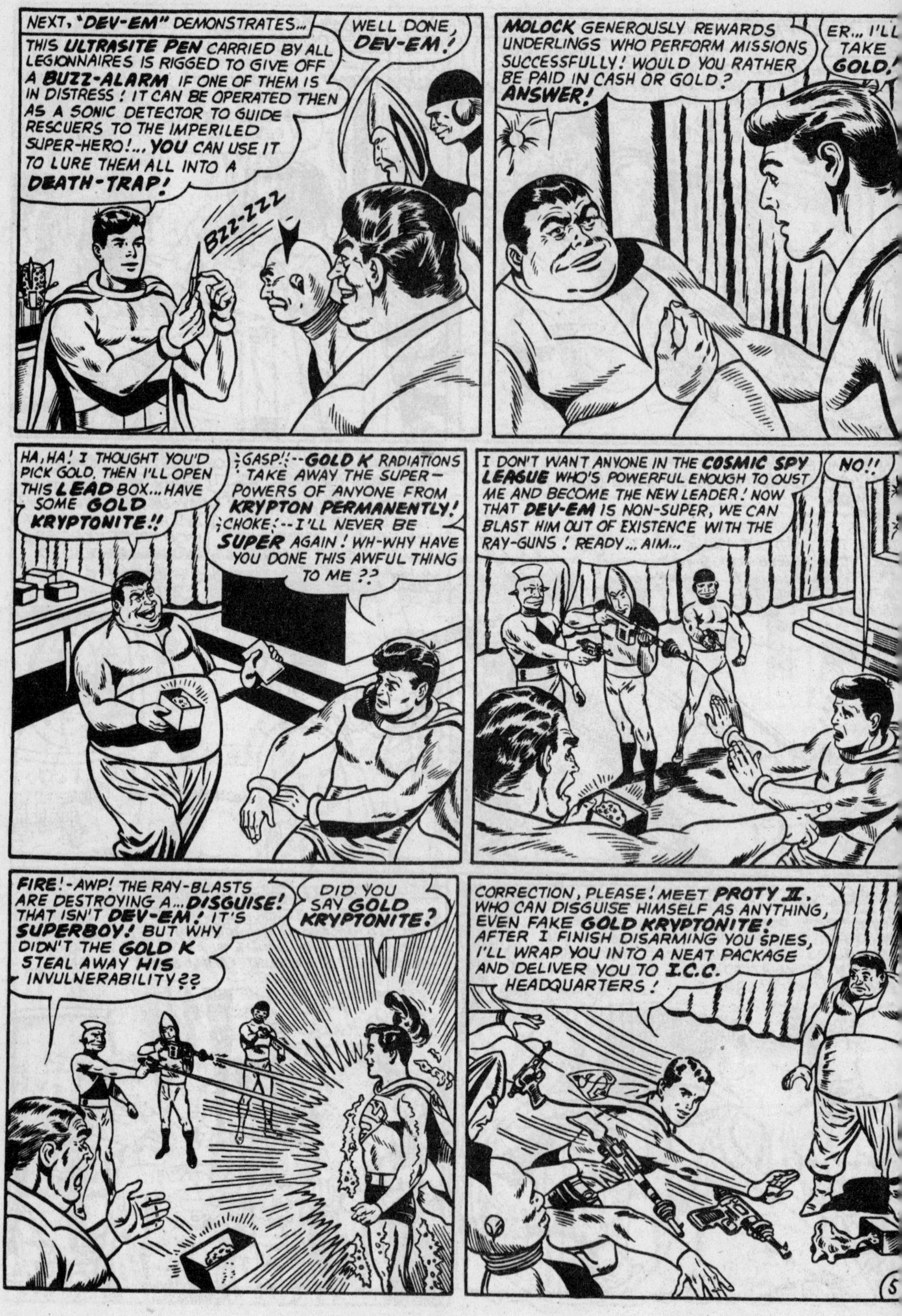
NEXT, "DEV-EM" DEMONSTRATES...
THIS ULTRASITE PEN CARRIED BY ALL LEGIONNAIRES IS RIGGED TO GIVE OFF A BUZZ-ALARM IF ONE OF THEM IS IN DISTRESS! IT CAN BE OPERATED THEN AS A SONIC DETECTOR TO GUIDE RESCUERS TO THE IMPERILED SUPER-HERO!... YOU CAN USE IT TO LURE THEM ALL INTO A DEATH-TRAP!
WELL DONE, DEV-EM!
BZZ-ZZZ
MOLOCK GENEROUSLY REWARDS UNDERLINGS WHO PERFORM MISSIONS SUCCESSFULLY! WOULD YOU RATHER BE PAID IN CASH OR GOLD? ANSWER!
ER... I'LL TAKE GOLD!
HA, HA! I THOUGHT YOU'D PICK GOLD. THEN I'LL OPEN THIS LEAD BOX... HAVE SOME GOLD KRYPTONITE!!
GASP! --GOLD K RADIATIONS TAKE AWAY THE SUPER-POWERS OF ANYONE FROM KRYPTON PERMANENTLY! CHOKE! --I'LL NEVER BE SUPER AGAIN! WH-WHY HAVE YOU DONE THIS AWFUL THING TO ME??
I DON'T WANT ANYONE IN THE COSMIC SPY LEAGUE WHO'S POWERFUL ENOUGH TO OUST ME AND BECOME THE NEW LEADER! NOW THAT DEV-EM IS NON-SUPER, WE CAN BLAST HIM OUT OF EXISTENCE WITH THE RAY-GUNS! READY... AIM...
NO!!
FIRE! -AWP! THE RAY-BLASTS ARE DESTROYING A... DISGUISE! THAT ISN'T DEV-EM! IT'S SUPERBOY! BUT WHY DIDN'T THE GOLD K STEAL AWAY HIS INVULNERABILITY??
DID YOU SAY GOLD KRYPTONITE?
CORRECTION, PLEASE! MEET PROTY II. WHO CAN DISGUISE HIMSELF AS ANYTHING, EVEN FAKE GOLD KRYPTONITE! AFTER I FINISH DISARMING YOU SPIES, I'LL WRAP YOU INTO A NEAT PACKAGE AND DELIVER YOU TO I.C.C. HEADQUARTERS!

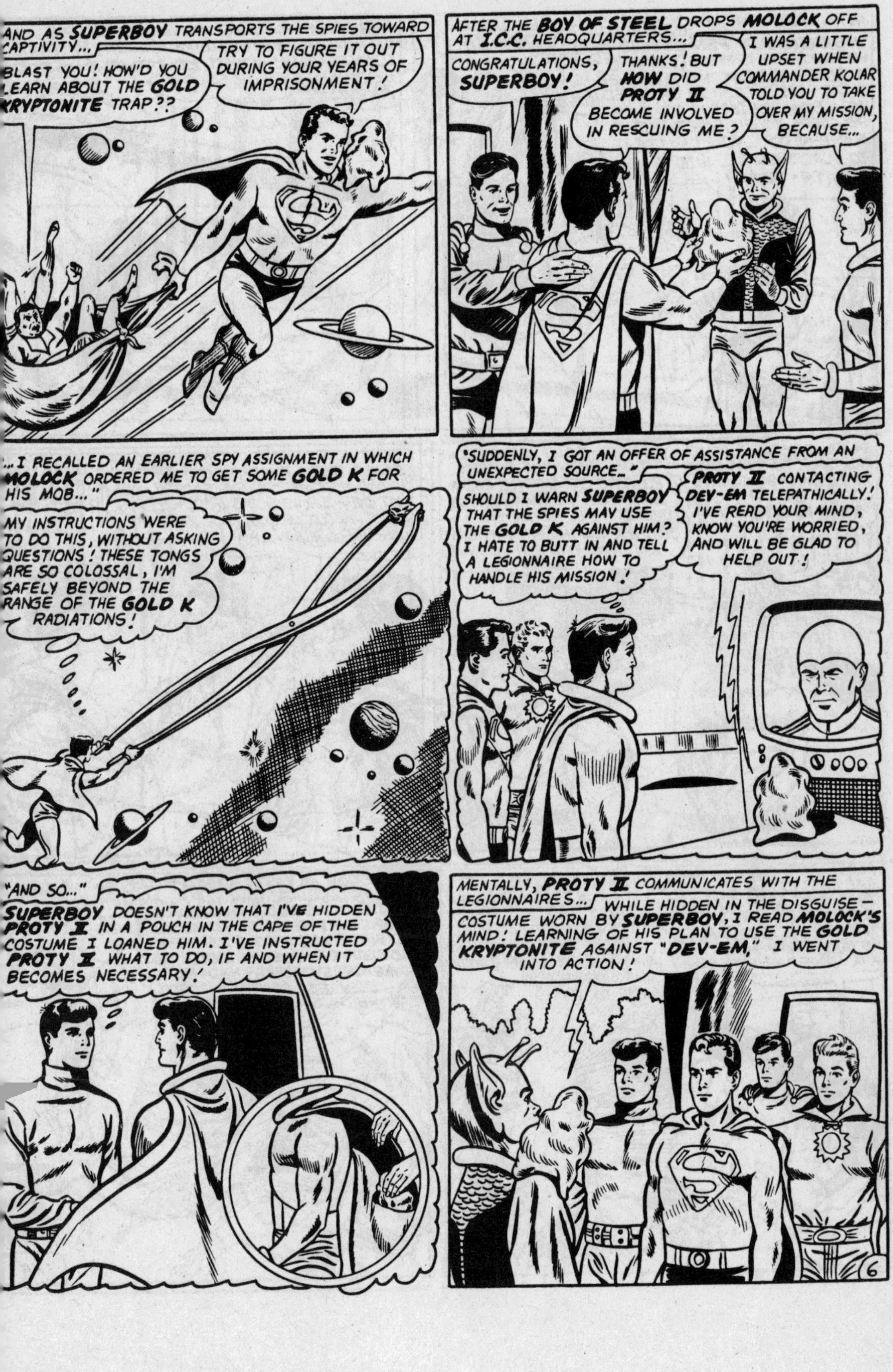
AND AS SUPERBOY TRANSPORTS THE SPIES TOWARD CAPTIVITY...
BLAST YOU! HOW'D YOU LEARN ABOUT THE GOLD KRYPTONITE TRAP??
TRY TO FIGURE IT OUT DURING YOUR YEARS OF IMPRISONMENT!
AFTER THE BOY OF STEEL DROPS MOLOCK OFF AT I.C.C. HEADQUARTERS...
CONGRATULATIONS, SUPERBOY!
THANKS! BUT HOW DID PROTY II BECOME INVOLVED IN RESCUING ME?
I WAS A LITTLE UPSET WHEN COMMANDER KOLAR TOLD YOU TO TAKE OVER MY MISSION, BECAUSE...
...I RECALLED AN EARLIER SPY ASSIGNMENT IN WHICH MOLOCK ORDERED ME TO GET SOME GOLD K FOR HIS MOB..."
MY INSTRUCTIONS WERE TO DO THIS, WITHOUT ASKING QUESTIONS! THESE TONGS ARE SO COLOSSAL, I'M SAFELY BEYOND THE RANGE OF THE GOLD K RADIATIONS!
"SUDDENLY, I GOT AN OFFER OF ASSISTANCE FROM AN UNEXPECTED SOURCE..."
SHOULD I WARN SUPERBOY THAT THE SPIES MAY USE THE GOLD K AGAINST HIM? I HATE TO BUTT IN AND TELL A LEGIONNAIRE HOW TO HANDLE HIS MISSION!
PROTY II CONTACTING DEV-EM TELEPATHICALLY! I'VE READ YOUR MIND, KNOW YOU'RE WORRIED, AND WILL BE GLAD TO HELP OUT!
"AND SO..."
SUPERBOY DOESN'T KNOW THAT I'VE HIDDEN PROTY II IN A POUCH IN THE CAPE OF THE COSTUME I LOANED HIM. I'VE INSTRUCTED PROTY II WHAT TO DO, IF AND WHEN IT BECOMES NECESSARY!
MENTALLY, PROTY II COMMUNICATES WITH THE LEGIONNAIRES...
WHILE HIDDEN IN THE DISGUISE-COSTUME WORN BY SUPERBOY, I READ MOLOCK'S MIND! LEARNING OF HIS PLAN TO USE THE GOLD KRYPTONITE AGAINST "DEV-EM," I WENT INTO ACTION!
6

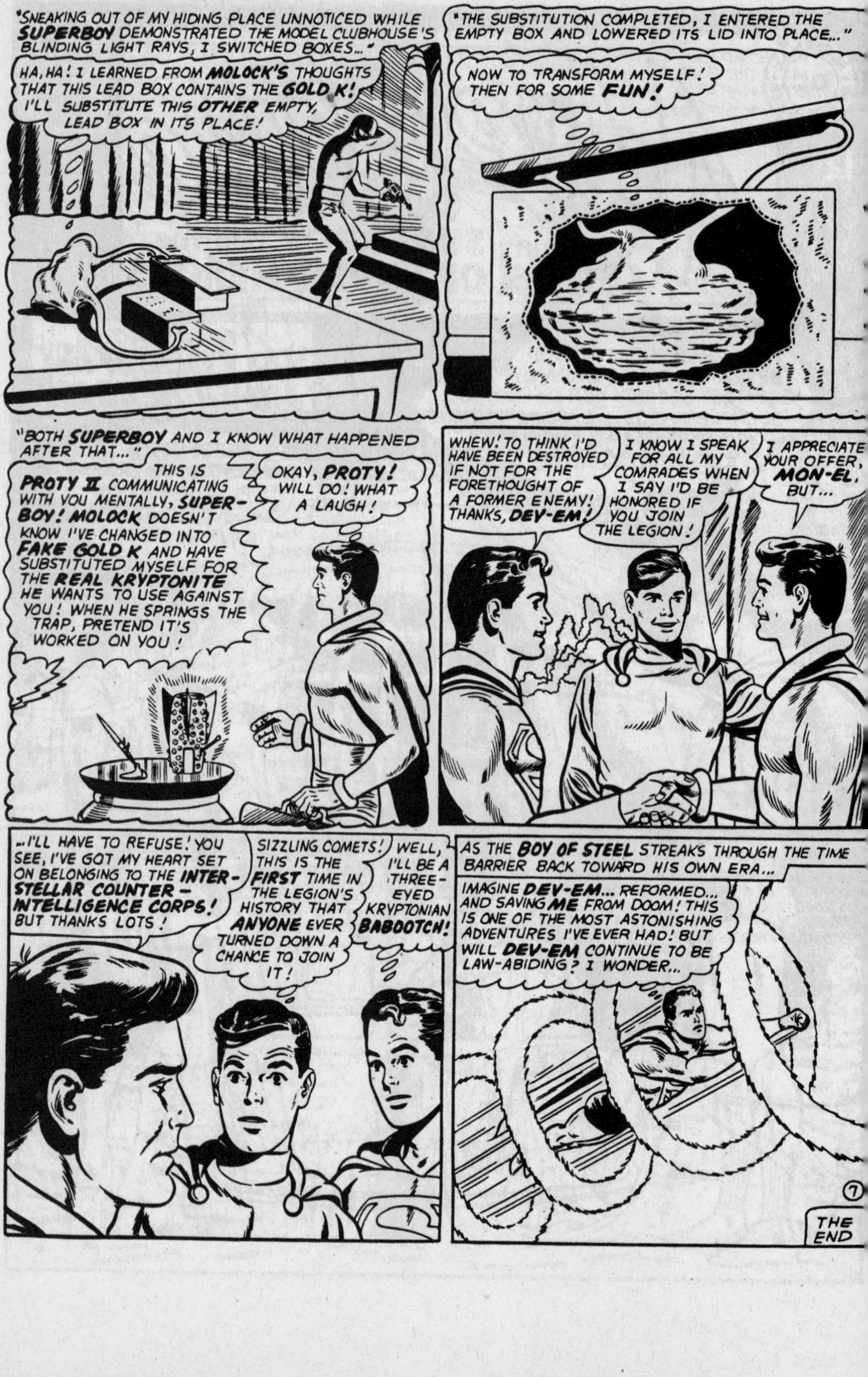
"SNEAKING OUT OF MY HIDING PLACE UNNOTICED WHILE SUPERBOY DEMONSTRATED THE MODEL CLUBHOUSE'S BLINDING LIGHT RAYS, I SWITCHED BOXES..."
HA, HA! I LEARNED FROM MOLOCK'S THOUGHTS THAT THIS LEAD BOX CONTAINS THE GOLD K! I'LL SUBSTITUTE THIS OTHER EMPTY, LEAD BOX IN ITS PLACE!
"THE SUBSTITUTION COMPLETED, I ENTERED THE EMPTY BOX AND LOWERED ITS LID INTO PLACE..."
NOW TO TRANSFORM MYSELF! THEN FOR SOME FUN!
"BOTH SUPERBOY AND I KNOW WHAT HAPPENED AFTER THAT..."
THIS IS PROTY II COMMUNICATING WITH YOU MENTALLY, SUPERBOY! MOLOCK DOESN'T KNOW I'VE CHANGED INTO FAKE GOLD K AND HAVE SUBSTITUTED MYSELF FOR THE REAL KRYPTONITE HE WANTS TO USE AGAINST YOU! WHEN HE SPRINGS THE TRAP, PRETEND IT'S WORKED ON YOU!
OKAY, PROTY! WILL DO! WHAT A LAUGH!
WHEW! TO THINK I'D HAVE BEEN DESTROYED IF NOT FOR THE FORETHOUGHT OF A FORMER ENEMY! THANKS, DEV-EM!
I KNOW I SPEAK FOR ALL MY COMRADES WHEN I SAY I'D BE HONORED IF YOU JOIN THE LEGION!
I APPRECIATE YOUR OFFER, MON-EL, BUT...
...I'LL HAVE TO REFUSE! YOU SEE, I'VE GOT MY HEART SET ON BELONGING TO THE INTERSTELLAR COUNTER-INTELLIGENCE CORPS! BUT THANKS LOTS!
SIZZLING COMETS! THIS IS THE FIRST TIME IN THE LEGION'S HISTORY THAT ANYONE EVER TURNED DOWN A CHANCE TO JOIN IT!
WELL, I'LL BE A THREE-EYED KRYPTONIAN BABOOTCH!
AS THE BOY OF STEEL STREAKS THROUGH THE TIME BARRIER BACK TOWARD HIS OWN ERA...
IMAGINE DEV-EM... REFORMED... AND SAVING ME FROM DOOM! THIS IS ONE OF THE MOST ASTONISHING ADVENTURES I'VE EVER HAD! BUT WILL DEV-EM CONTINUE TO BE LAW-ABIDING? I WONDER...
7
THE END

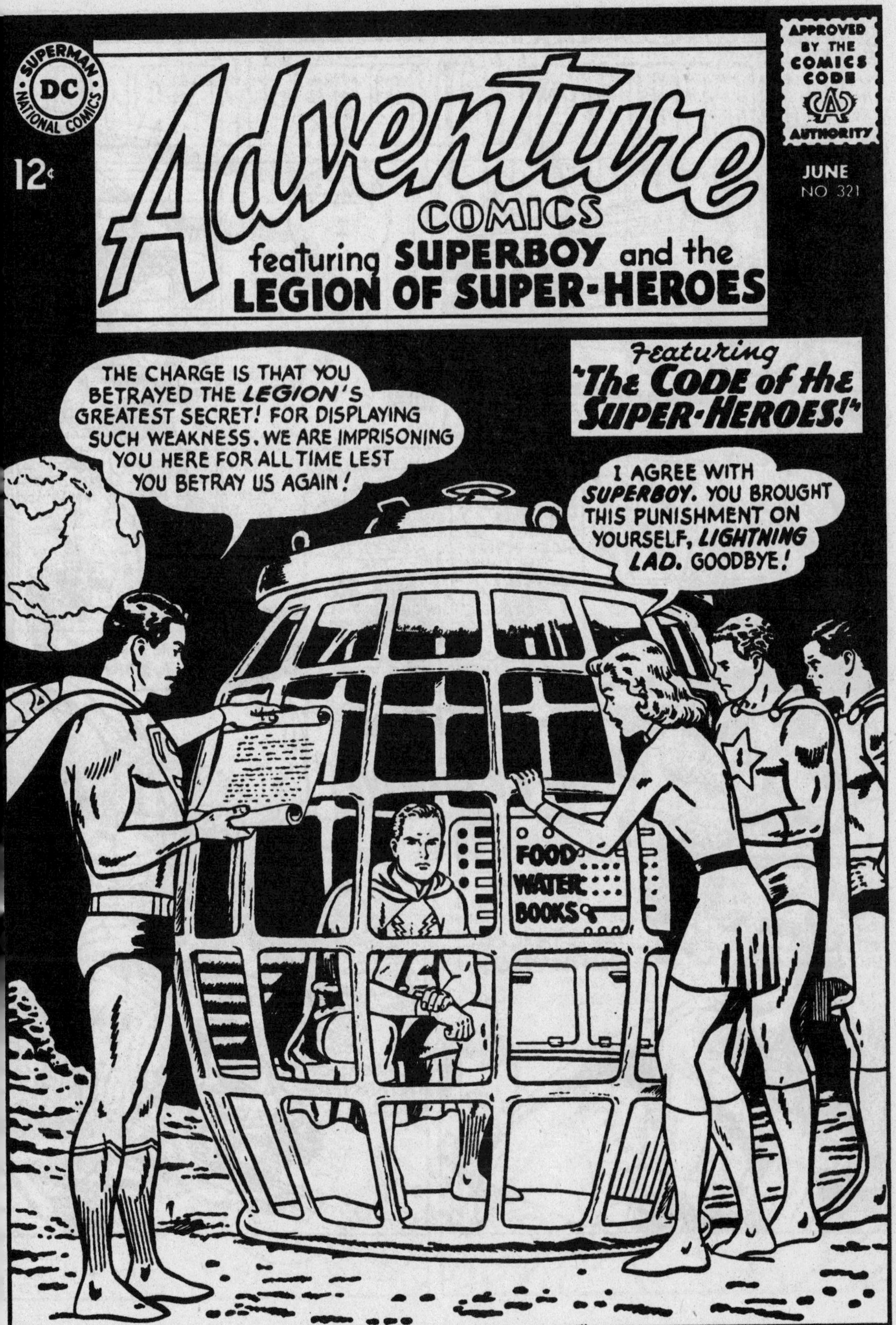
SUPERMAN DC NATIONAL COMICS
12¢
Adventure COMICS
featuring SUPERBOY and the LEGION OF SUPER-HEROES
APPROVED BY THE COMICS CODE AUTHORITY
JUNE NO 321
Featuring "The CODE of the SUPER-HEROES!"
THE CHARGE IS THAT YOU BETRAYED THE LEGION'S GREATEST SECRET! FOR DISPLAYING SUCH WEAKNESS, WE ARE IMPRISONING YOU HERE FOR ALL TIME LEST YOU BETRAY US AGAIN!
I AGREE WITH SUPERBOY. YOU BROUGHT THIS PUNISHMENT ON YOURSELF, LIGHTNING LAD. GOODBYE!
FOOD
WATER
BOOKS

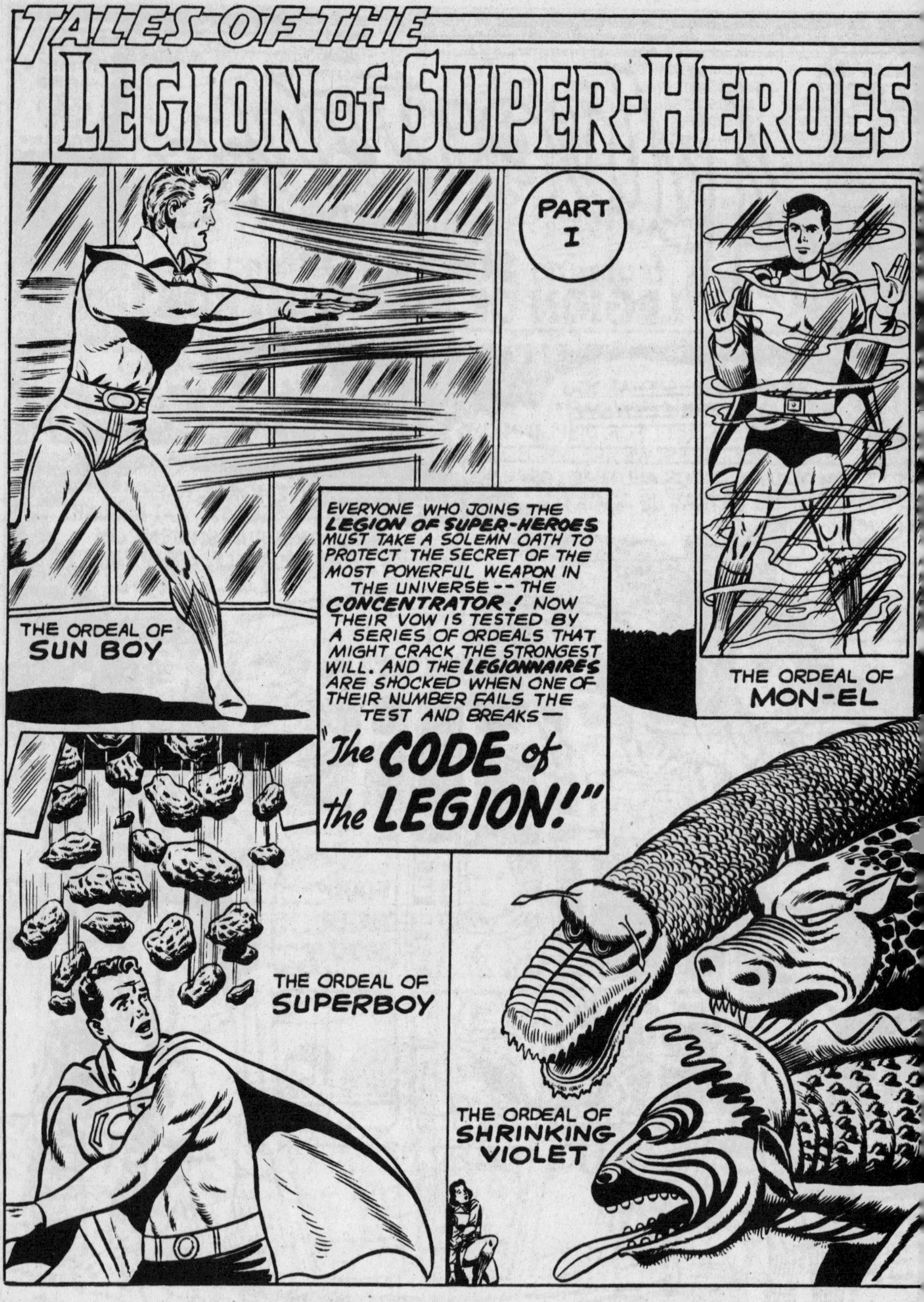
TALES OF THE
LEGION of SUPER-HEROES
PART I
THE ORDEAL OF SUN BOY
EVERYONE WHO JOINS THE LEGION OF SUPER-HEROES MUST TAKE A SOLEMN OATH TO PROTECT THE SECRET OF THE MOST POWERFUL WEAPON IN THE UNIVERSE -- THE CONCENTRATOR! NOW THEIR VOW IS TESTED BY A SERIES OF ORDEALS THAT MIGHT CRACK THE STRONGEST WILL. AND THE LEGIONNAIRES ARE SHOCKED WHEN ONE OF THEIR NUMBER FAILS THE TEST AND BREAKS—
"The CODE of the LEGION!"
THE ORDEAL OF MON-EL
THE ORDEAL OF SUPERBOY
THE ORDEAL OF SHRINKING VIOLET

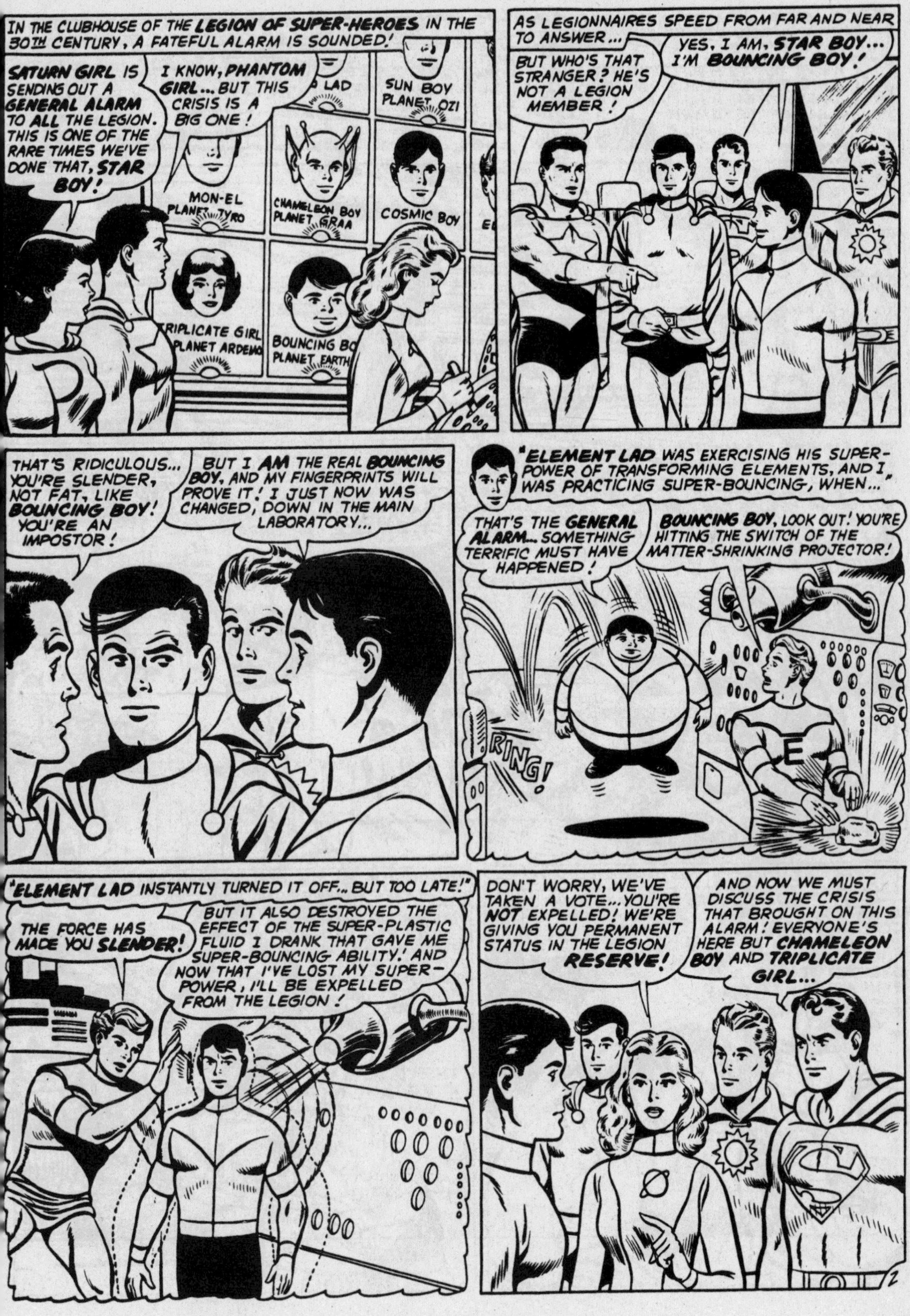
IN THE CLUBHOUSE OF THE LEGION OF SUPER-HEROES IN THE 30TH CENTURY, A FATEFUL ALARM IS SOUNDED!
SATURN GIRL IS SENDING OUT A GENERAL ALARM TO ALL THE LEGION. THIS IS ONE OF THE RARE TIMES WE'VE DONE THAT, STAR BOY!
I KNOW, PHANTOM GIRL... BUT THIS CRISIS IS A BIG ONE!
SUN BOY PLANET OZI
MON-EL PLANET TYRO
CHAMELEON BOY PLANET GRAA
COSMIC BOY
TRIPLICATE GIRL PLANET ARDEMO
AS LEGIONNAIRES SPEED FROM FAR AND NEAR TO ANSWER...
BUT WHO'S THAT STRANGER? HE'S NOT A LEGION MEMBER!
YES, I AM, STAR BOY... I'M BOUNCING BOY!
THAT'S RIDICULOUS... YOU'RE SLENDER, NOT FAT, LIKE BOUNCING BOY! YOU'RE AN IMPOSTOR!
BUT I AM THE REAL BOUNCING BOY, AND MY FINGERPRINTS WILL PROVE IT! I JUST NOW WAS CHANGED, DOWN IN THE MAIN LABORATORY...
"ELEMENT LAD WAS EXERCISING HIS SUPER-POWER OF TRANSFORMING ELEMENTS, AND I WAS PRACTICING SUPER-BOUNCING, WHEN..."
THAT'S THE GENERAL ALARM... SOMETHING TERRIFIC MUST HAVE HAPPENED!
BOUNCING BOY, LOOK OUT! YOU'RE HITTING THE SWITCH OF THE MATTER-SHRINKING PROJECTOR!
RING!
"ELEMENT LAD INSTANTLY TURNED IT OFF... BUT TOO LATE!"
THE FORCE HAS MADE YOU SLENDER!
BUT IT ALSO DESTROYED THE EFFECT OF THE SUPER-PLASTIC FLUID I DRANK THAT GAVE ME SUPER-BOUNCING ABILITY! AND NOW THAT I'VE LOST MY SUPER-POWER, I'LL BE EXPELLED FROM THE LEGION!
DON'T WORRY, WE'VE TAKEN A VOTE... YOU'RE NOT EXPELLED! WE'RE GIVING YOU PERMANENT STATUS IN THE LEGION RESERVE!
AND NOW WE MUST DISCUSS THE CRISIS THAT BROUGHT ON THIS ALARM! EVERYONE'S HERE BUT CHAMELEON BOY AND TRIPLICATE GIRL...
2

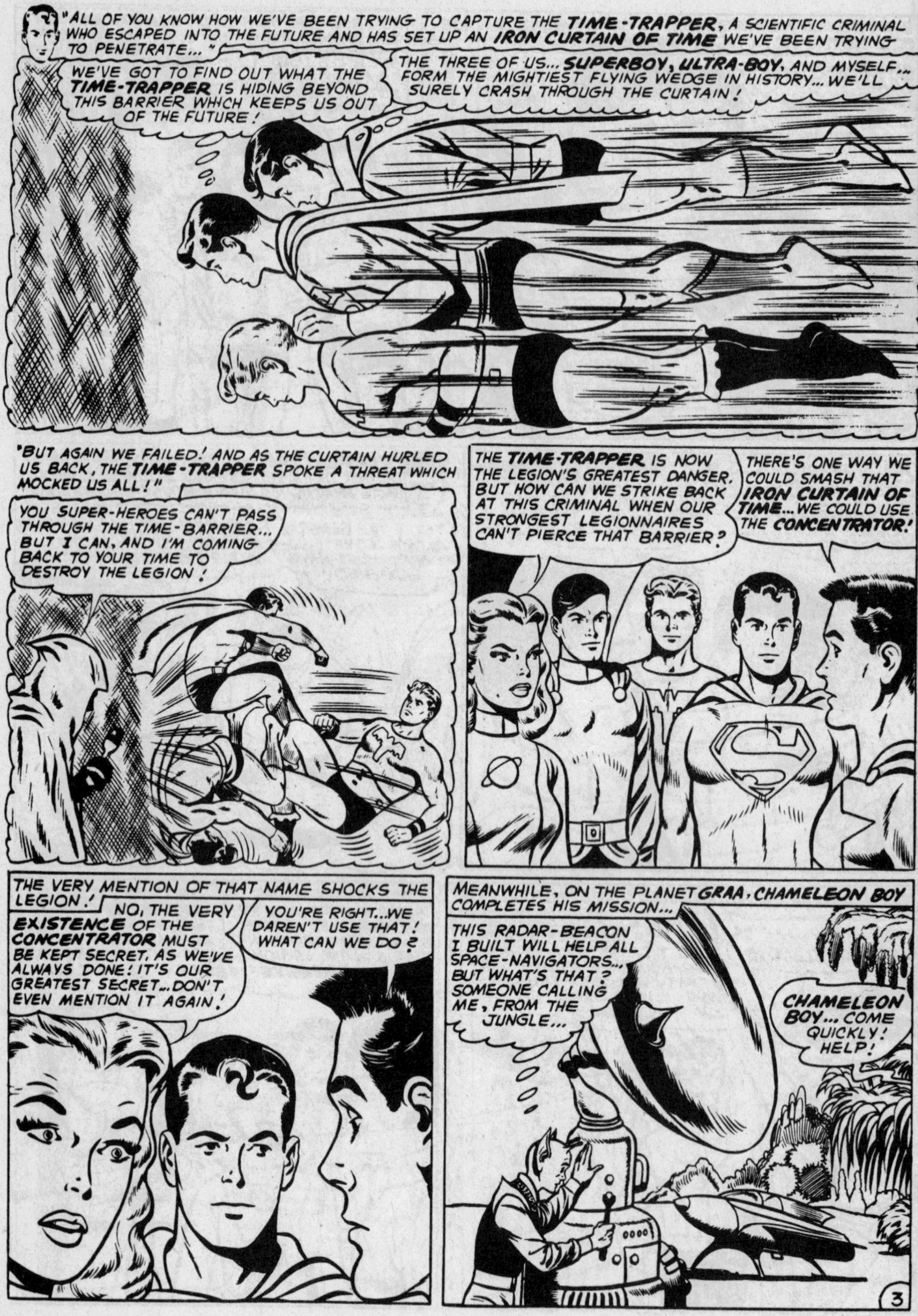
"ALL OF YOU KNOW HOW WE'VE BEEN TRYING TO CAPTURE THE TIME-TRAPPER, A SCIENTIFIC CRIMINAL WHO ESCAPED INTO THE FUTURE AND HAS SET UP AN IRON CURTAIN OF TIME WE'VE BEEN TRYING TO PENETRATE..."
WE'VE GOT TO FIND OUT WHAT THE TIME-TRAPPER IS HIDING BEYOND THIS BARRIER WHICH KEEPS US OUT OF THE FUTURE!
THE THREE OF US... SUPERBOY, ULTRA-BOY, AND MYSELF... FORM THE MIGHTIEST FLYING WEDGE IN HISTORY... WE'LL SURELY CRASH THROUGH THE CURTAIN!
"BUT AGAIN WE FAILED! AND AS THE CURTAIN HURLED US BACK, THE TIME-TRAPPER SPOKE A THREAT WHICH MOCKED US ALL!"
YOU SUPER-HEROES CAN'T PASS THROUGH THE TIME-BARRIER... BUT I CAN, AND I'M COMING BACK TO YOUR TIME TO DESTROY THE LEGION!
THE TIME-TRAPPER IS NOW THE LEGION'S GREATEST DANGER, BUT HOW CAN WE STRIKE BACK AT THIS CRIMINAL WHEN OUR STRONGEST LEGIONNAIRES CAN'T PIERCE THAT BARRIER?
THERE'S ONE WAY WE COULD SMASH THAT IRON CURTAIN OF TIME... WE COULD USE THE CONCENTRATOR!
THE VERY MENTION OF THAT NAME SHOCKS THE LEGION!
NO, THE VERY EXISTENCE OF THE CONCENTRATOR MUST BE KEPT SECRET, AS WE'VE ALWAYS DONE! IT'S OUR GREATEST SECRET... DON'T EVEN MENTION IT AGAIN!
YOU'RE RIGHT... WE DAREN'T USE THAT! WHAT CAN WE DO?
MEANWHILE, ON THE PLANET GRAA, CHAMELEON BOY COMPLETES HIS MISSION...
THIS RADAR-BEACON I BUILT WILL HELP ALL SPACE-NAVIGATORS... BUT WHAT'S THAT? SOMEONE CALLING ME, FROM THE JUNGLE...
CHAMELEON BOY... COME QUICKLY! HELP!
3

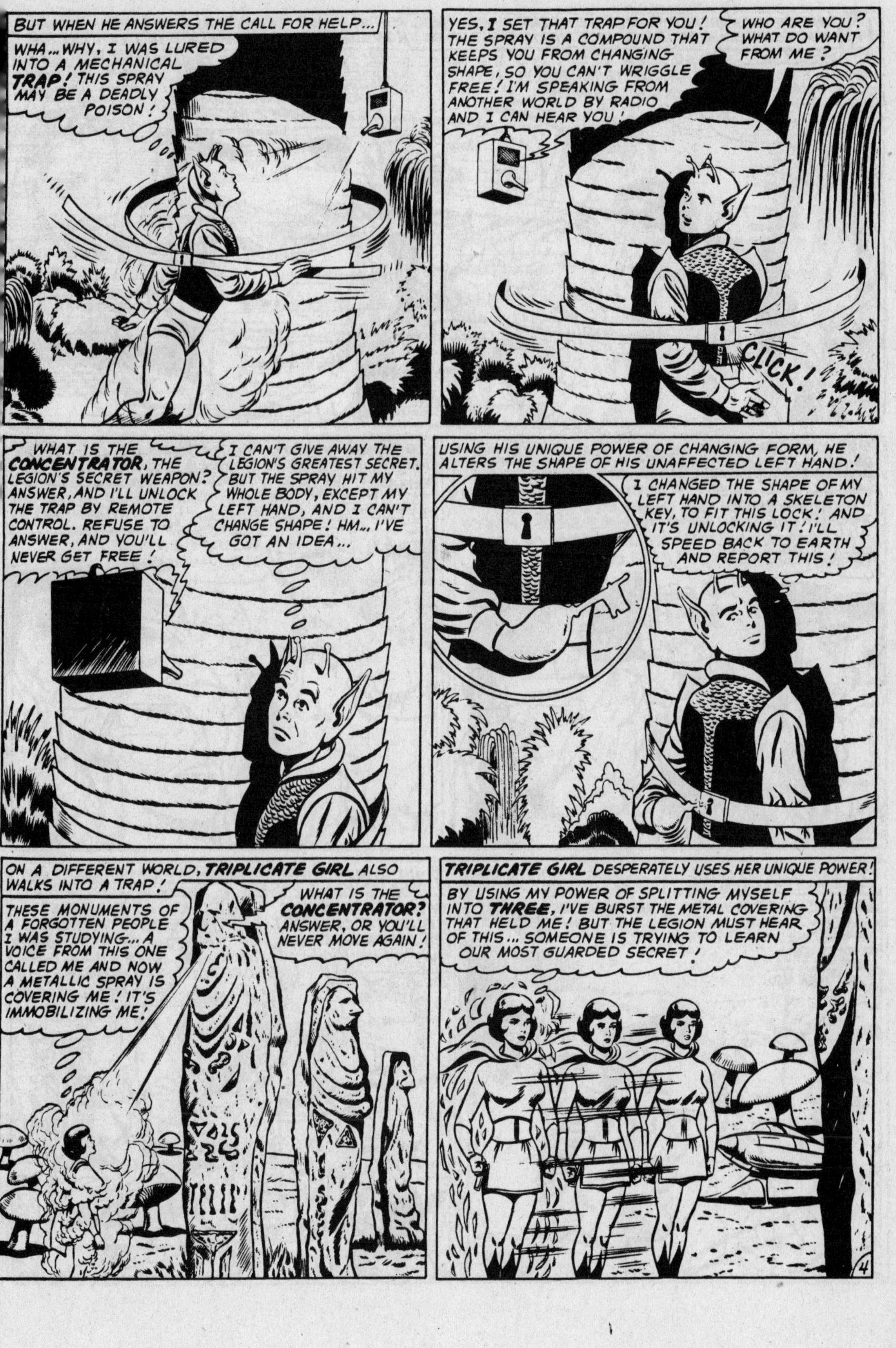
BUT WHEN HE ANSWERS THE CALL FOR HELP...
WHA... WHY, I WAS LURED INTO A MECHANICAL TRAP! THIS SPRAY MAY BE A DEADLY POISON!
YES, I SET THAT TRAP FOR YOU! THE SPRAY IS A COMPOUND THAT KEEPS YOU FROM CHANGING SHAPE, SO YOU CAN'T WRIGGLE FREE! I'M SPEAKING FROM ANOTHER WORLD BY RADIO AND I CAN HEAR YOU!
WHO ARE YOU? WHAT DO WANT FROM ME?
CLICK!
WHAT IS THE CONCENTRATOR, THE LEGION'S SECRET WEAPON? ANSWER, AND I'LL UNLOCK THE TRAP BY REMOTE CONTROL. REFUSE TO ANSWER, AND YOU'LL NEVER GET FREE!
I CAN'T GIVE AWAY THE LEGION'S GREATEST SECRET. BUT THE SPRAY HIT MY WHOLE BODY, EXCEPT MY LEFT HAND, AND I CAN'T CHANGE SHAPE! HM... I'VE GOT AN IDEA...
USING HIS UNIQUE POWER OF CHANGING FORM, HE ALTERS THE SHAPE OF HIS UNAFFECTED LEFT HAND!
I CHANGED THE SHAPE OF MY LEFT HAND INTO A SKELETON KEY, TO FIT THIS LOCK! AND IT'S UNLOCKING IT! I'LL SPEED BACK TO EARTH AND REPORT THIS!
ON A DIFFERENT WORLD, TRIPLICATE GIRL ALSO WALKS INTO A TRAP!
THESE MONUMENTS OF A FORGOTTEN PEOPLE I WAS STUDYING... A VOICE FROM THIS ONE CALLED ME AND NOW A METALLIC SPRAY IS COVERING ME! IT'S IMMOBILIZING ME!
WHAT IS THE CONCENTRATOR? ANSWER, OR YOU'LL NEVER MOVE AGAIN!
TRIPLICATE GIRL DESPERATELY USES HER UNIQUE POWER!
BY USING MY POWER OF SPLITTING MYSELF INTO THREE, I'VE BURST THE METAL COVERING THAT HELD ME! BUT THE LEGION MUST HEAR OF THIS... SOMEONE IS TRYING TO LEARN OUR MOST GUARDED SECRET!
4

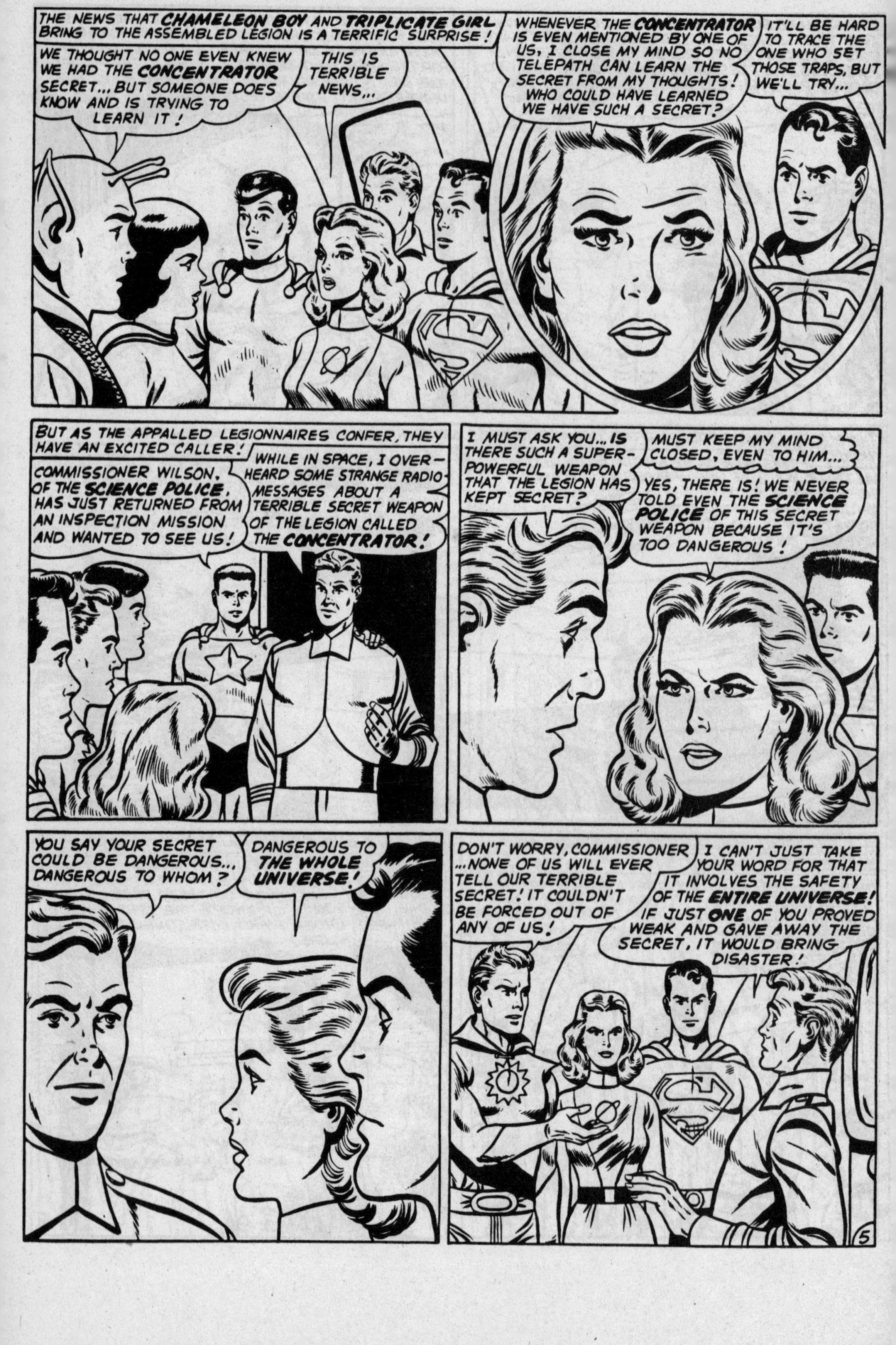
THE NEWS THAT CHAMELEON BOY AND TRIPLICATE GIRL BRING TO THE ASSEMBLED LEGION IS A TERRIFIC SURPRISE!
WE THOUGHT NO ONE EVEN KNEW WE HAD THE CONCENTRATOR SECRET... BUT SOMEONE DOES KNOW AND IS TRYING TO LEARN IT!
THIS IS TERRIBLE NEWS...
WHENEVER THE CONCENTRATOR IS EVEN MENTIONED BY ONE OF US, I CLOSE MY MIND SO NO TELEPATH CAN LEARN THE SECRET FROM MY THOUGHTS! WHO COULD HAVE LEARNED WE HAVE SUCH A SECRET?
IT'LL BE HARD TO TRACE THE ONE WHO SET THOSE TRAPS, BUT WE'LL TRY...
BUT AS THE APPALLED LEGIONNAIRES CONFER, THEY HAVE AN EXCITED CALLER!
COMMISSIONER WILSON, OF THE SCIENCE POLICE, HAS JUST RETURNED FROM AN INSPECTION MISSION AND WANTED TO SEE US!
WHILE IN SPACE, I OVERHEARD SOME STRANGE RADIO MESSAGES ABOUT A TERRIBLE SECRET WEAPON OF THE LEGION CALLED THE CONCENTRATOR!
I MUST ASK YOU... IS THERE SUCH A SUPER-POWERFUL WEAPON THAT THE LEGION HAS KEPT SECRET?
MUST KEEP MY MIND CLOSED, EVEN TO HIM...
YES, THERE IS! WE NEVER TOLD EVEN THE SCIENCE POLICE OF THIS SECRET WEAPON BECAUSE IT'S TOO DANGEROUS!
YOU SAY YOUR SECRET COULD BE DANGEROUS... DANGEROUS TO WHOM?
DANGEROUS TO THE WHOLE UNIVERSE!
DON'T WORRY, COMMISSIONER ...NONE OF US WILL EVER TELL OUR TERRIBLE SECRET! IT COULDN'T BE FORCED OUT OF ANY OF US!
I CAN'T JUST TAKE YOUR WORD FOR THAT IT INVOLVES THE SAFETY OF THE ENTIRE UNIVERSE! IF JUST ONE OF YOU PROVED WEAK AND GAVE AWAY THE SECRET, IT WOULD BRING DISASTER!
5

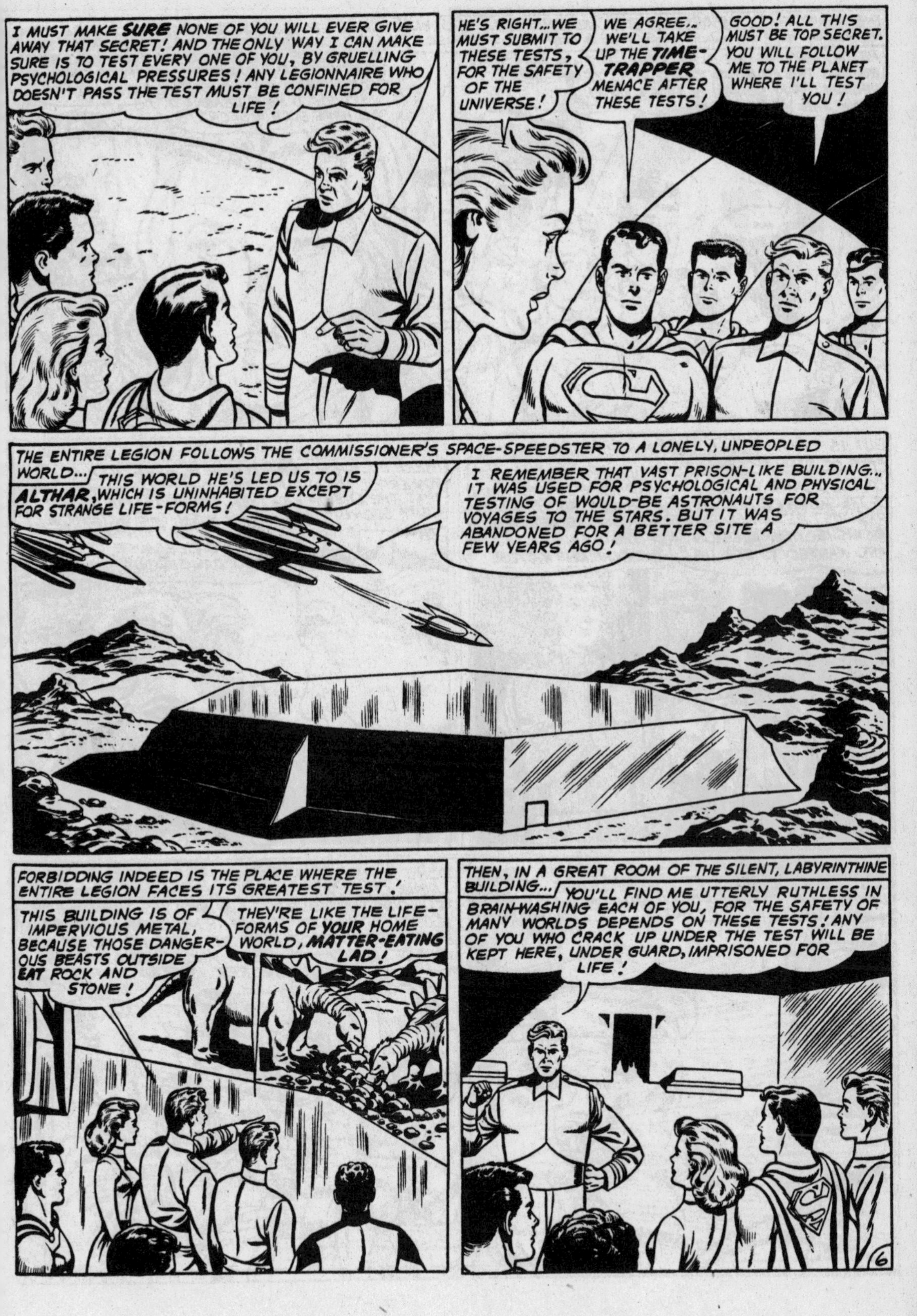
I MUST MAKE SURE NONE OF YOU WILL EVER GIVE AWAY THAT SECRET! AND THE ONLY WAY I CAN MAKE SURE IS TO TEST EVERY ONE OF YOU, BY GRUELLING PSYCHOLOGICAL PRESSURES! ANY LEGIONNAIRE WHO DOESN'T PASS THE TEST MUST BE CONFINED FOR LIFE!
HE'S RIGHT...WE MUST SUBMIT TO THESE TESTS, FOR THE SAFETY OF THE UNIVERSE!
WE AGREE.. WE'LL TAKE UP THE TIME-TRAPPER MENACE AFTER THESE TESTS!
GOOD! ALL THIS MUST BE TOP SECRET. YOU WILL FOLLOW ME TO THE PLANET WHERE I'LL TEST YOU!
THE ENTIRE LEGION FOLLOWS THE COMMISSIONER'S SPACE-SPEEDSTER TO A LONELY, UNPEOPLED WORLD...
THIS WORLD HE'S LED US TO IS ALTHAR, WHICH IS UNINHABITED EXCEPT FOR STRANGE LIFE-FORMS!
I REMEMBER THAT VAST PRISON-LIKE BUILDING... IT WAS USED FOR PSYCHOLOGICAL AND PHYSICAL TESTING OF WOULD-BE ASTRONAUTS FOR VOYAGES TO THE STARS. BUT IT WAS ABANDONED FOR A BETTER SITE A FEW YEARS AGO!
FORBIDDING INDEED IS THE PLACE WHERE THE ENTIRE LEGION FACES ITS GREATEST TEST!
THIS BUILDING IS OF IMPERVIOUS METAL, BECAUSE THOSE DANGEROUS BEASTS OUTSIDE EAT ROCK AND STONE!
THEY'RE LIKE THE LIFE-FORMS OF YOUR HOME WORLD, MATTER-EATING LAD!
THEN, IN A GREAT ROOM OF THE SILENT, LABYRINTHINE BUILDING...
YOU'LL FIND ME UTTERLY RUTHLESS IN BRAIN-WASHING EACH OF YOU, FOR THE SAFETY OF MANY WORLDS DEPENDS ON THESE TESTS! ANY OF YOU WHO CRACK UP UNDER THE TEST WILL BE KEPT HERE, UNDER GUARD, IMPRISONED FOR LIFE!
6

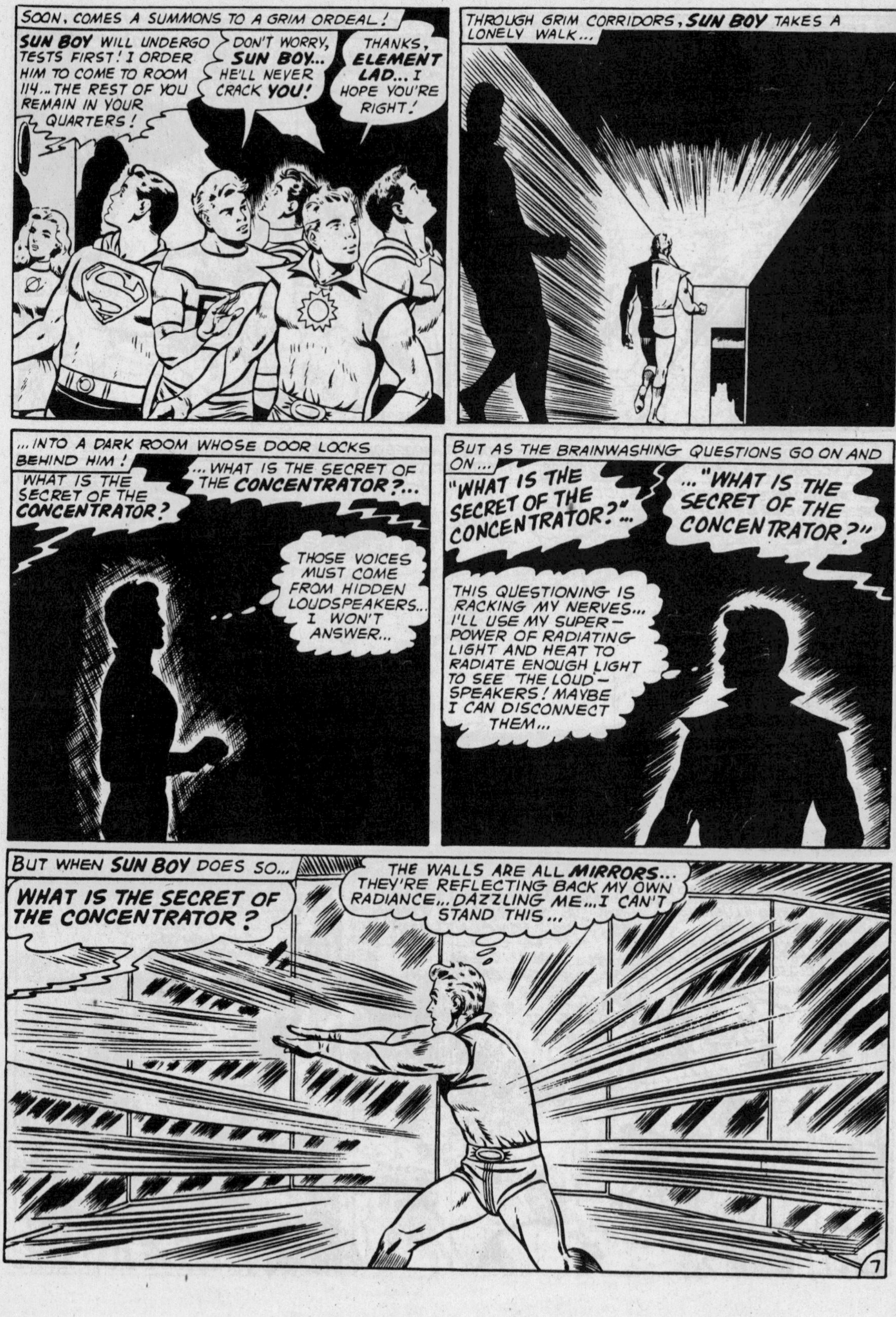
SOON, COMES A SUMMONS TO A GRIM ORDEAL!
SUN BOY WILL UNDERGO TESTS FIRST! I ORDER HIM TO COME TO ROOM 114... THE REST OF YOU REMAIN IN YOUR QUARTERS!
DON'T WORRY, SUN BOY... HE'LL NEVER CRACK YOU!
THANKS, ELEMENT LAD... I HOPE YOU'RE RIGHT!
THROUGH GRIM CORRIDORS, SUN BOY TAKES A LONELY WALK...
...INTO A DARK ROOM WHOSE DOOR LOCKS BEHIND HIM!
WHAT IS THE SECRET OF THE CONCENTRATOR?
...WHAT IS THE SECRET OF THE CONCENTRATOR?...
THOSE VOICES MUST COME FROM HIDDEN LOUDSPEAKERS... I WON'T ANSWER...
BUT AS THE BRAINWASHING QUESTIONS GO ON AND ON...
"WHAT IS THE SECRET OF THE CONCENTRATOR?"...
..."WHAT IS THE SECRET OF THE CONCENTRATOR?"
THIS QUESTIONING IS RACKING MY NERVES... I'LL USE MY SUPER-POWER OF RADIATING LIGHT AND HEAT TO RADIATE ENOUGH LIGHT TO SEE THE LOUD-SPEAKERS! MAYBE I CAN DISCONNECT THEM...
BUT WHEN SUN BOY DOES SO...
WHAT IS THE SECRET OF THE CONCENTRATOR?
THE WALLS ARE ALL MIRRORS... THEY'RE REFLECTING BACK MY OWN RADIANCE... DAZZLING ME... I CAN'T STAND THIS...
7

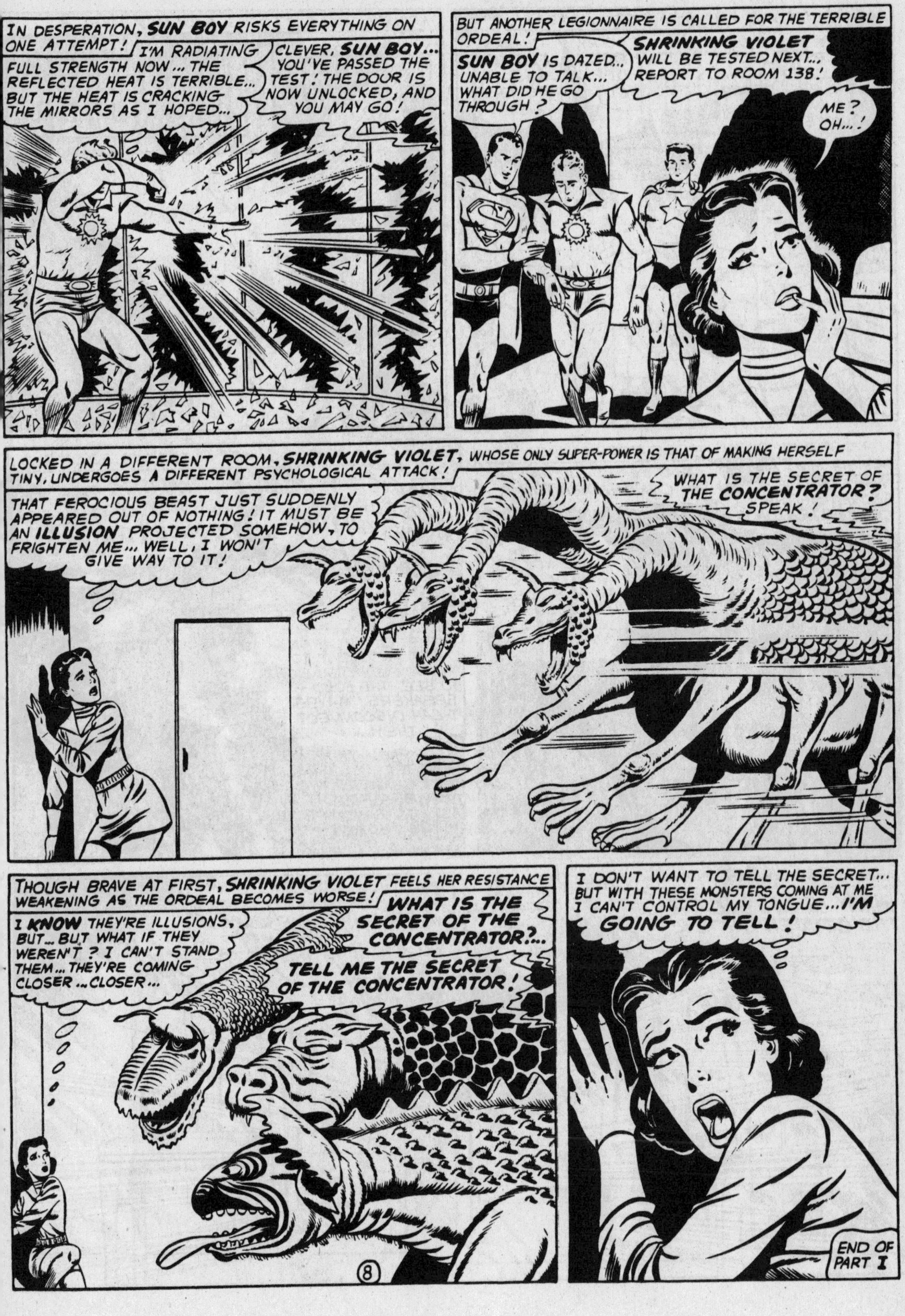
IN DESPERATION, SUN BOY RISKS EVERYTHING ON ONE ATTEMPT!
I'M RADIATING FULL STRENGTH NOW... THE REFLECTED HEAT IS TERRIBLE... BUT THE HEAT IS CRACKING THE MIRRORS AS I HOPED...
CLEVER, SUN BOY... YOU'VE PASSED THE TEST! THE DOOR IS NOW UNLOCKED, AND YOU MAY GO!
BUT ANOTHER LEGIONNAIRE IS CALLED FOR THE TERRIBLE ORDEAL!
SUN BOY IS DAZED... UNABLE TO TALK... WHAT DID HE GO THROUGH?
SHRINKING VIOLET WILL BE TESTED NEXT... REPORT TO ROOM 138!
ME? OH...!
LOCKED IN A DIFFERENT ROOM, SHRINKING VIOLET, WHOSE ONLY SUPER-POWER IS THAT OF MAKING HERSELF TINY, UNDERGOES A DIFFERENT PSYCHOLOGICAL ATTACK!
THAT FEROCIOUS BEAST JUST SUDDENLY APPEARED OUT OF NOTHING! IT MUST BE AN ILLUSION PROJECTED SOMEHOW, TO FRIGHTEN ME... WELL, I WON'T GIVE WAY TO IT!
WHAT IS THE SECRET OF THE CONCENTRATOR? SPEAK!
THOUGH BRAVE AT FIRST, SHRINKING VIOLET FEELS HER RESISTANCE WEAKENING AS THE ORDEAL BECOMES WORSE!
I KNOW THEY'RE ILLUSIONS, BUT... BUT WHAT IF THEY WEREN'T? I CAN'T STAND THEM... THEY'RE COMING CLOSER... CLOSER...
WHAT IS THE SECRET OF THE CONCENTRATOR?...
TELL ME THE SECRET OF THE CONCENTRATOR!
8
I DON'T WANT TO TELL THE SECRET... BUT WITH THESE MONSTERS COMING AT ME I CAN'T CONTROL MY TONGUE... I'M GOING TO TELL!
END OF PART I

TALES OF THE
LEGION of SUPER-HEROES

UNAWARE OF A DEADLY MENACE THAT THREATENS THEM, THE *LEGION OF SUPER-HEROES*, ONE BY ONE, ENDURE THE MOST TERRIFIC BRAINWASHING ORDEAL IN HISTORY! BUT THERE'S A STUNNING SURPRISE CLIMAX TO THIS STORY OF --

The WEAKEST LEGIONNAIRE

PART II

MUST KEEP FROM THINKING OF THE SECRET... I'LL THINK OF GREAT MENACES THE LEGIONNAIRES FOUGHT IN THE PAST, SO I WON'T GIVE AWAY THE SECRET!

SHRINKING VIOLET, FEELING HER RESISTANCE TO THE BRAINWASHING TEST CRACKING, RESORTS TO HER SUPER-POWER!

MY ONLY CHANCE... IS TO USE MY SUPER-POWER OF *SHRINKING...*

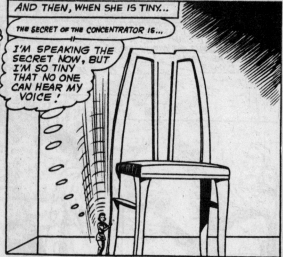

AND THEN, WHEN SHE IS TINY...

THE SECRET OF THE CONCENTRATOR IS...

I'M SPEAKING THE SECRET NOW, BUT I'M SO TINY THAT NO ONE CAN HEAR MY VOICE!

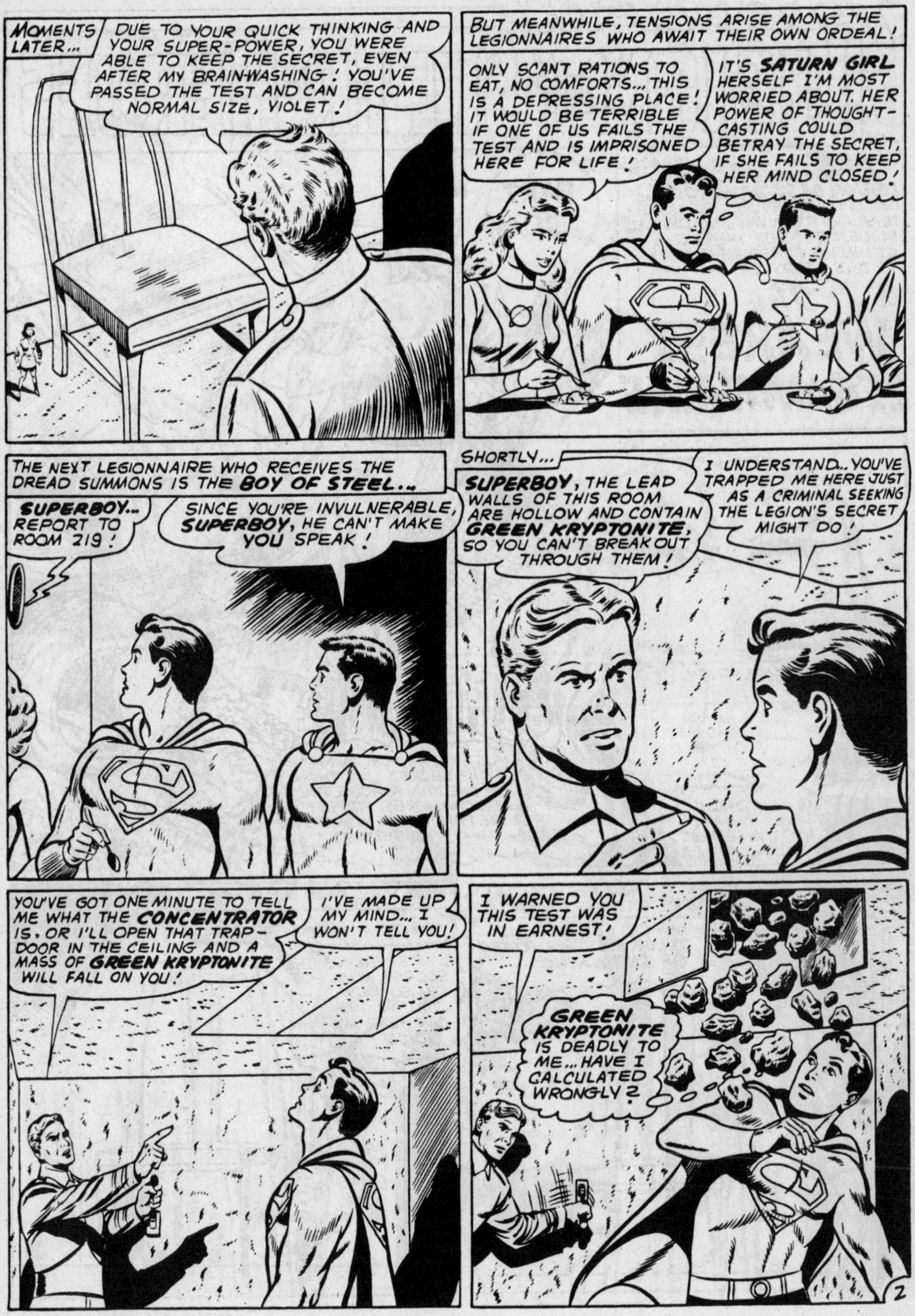
MOMENTS LATER...
DUE TO YOUR QUICK THINKING AND YOUR SUPER-POWER, YOU WERE ABLE TO KEEP THE SECRET, EVEN AFTER MY BRAIN-WASHING! YOU'VE PASSED THE TEST AND CAN BECOME NORMAL SIZE, VIOLET!
BUT MEANWHILE, TENSIONS ARISE AMONG THE LEGIONNAIRES WHO AWAIT THEIR OWN ORDEAL!
ONLY SCANT RATIONS TO EAT, NO COMFORTS... THIS IS A DEPRESSING PLACE! IT WOULD BE TERRIBLE IF ONE OF US FAILS THE TEST AND IS IMPRISONED HERE FOR LIFE!
IT'S SATURN GIRL HERSELF I'M MOST WORRIED ABOUT. HER POWER OF THOUGHT-CASTING COULD BETRAY THE SECRET, IF SHE FAILS TO KEEP HER MIND CLOSED!
THE NEXT LEGIONNAIRE WHO RECEIVES THE DREAD SUMMONS IS THE BOY OF STEEL..
SUPERBOY... REPORT TO ROOM 219!
SINCE YOU'RE INVULNERABLE, SUPERBOY, HE CAN'T MAKE YOU SPEAK!
SHORTLY...
SUPERBOY, THE LEAD WALLS OF THIS ROOM ARE HOLLOW AND CONTAIN GREEN KRYPTONITE, SO YOU CAN'T BREAK OUT THROUGH THEM!
I UNDERSTAND... YOU'VE TRAPPED ME HERE JUST AS A CRIMINAL SEEKING THE LEGION'S SECRET MIGHT DO!
YOU'VE GOT ONE MINUTE TO TELL ME WHAT THE CONCENTRATOR IS, OR I'LL OPEN THAT TRAP-DOOR IN THE CEILING AND A MASS OF GREEN KRYPTONITE WILL FALL ON YOU!
I'VE MADE UP MY MIND... I WON'T TELL YOU!
I WARNED YOU THIS TEST WAS IN EARNEST!
GREEN KRYPTONITE IS DEADLY TO ME... HAVE I CALCULATED WRONGLY?
2

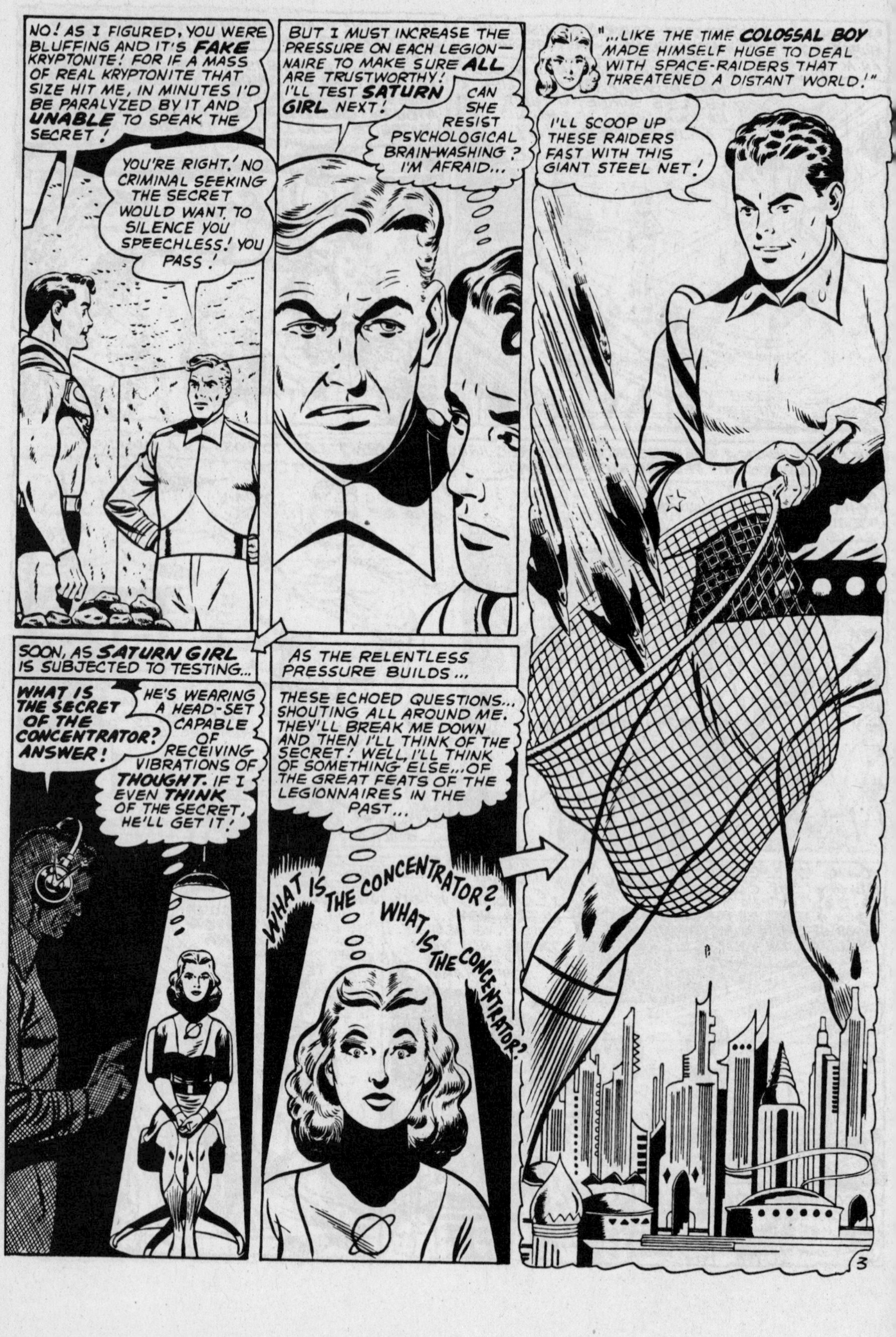
NO! AS I FIGURED, YOU WERE BLUFFING AND IT'S FAKE KRYPTONITE! FOR IF A MASS OF REAL KRYPTONITE THAT SIZE HIT ME, IN MINUTES I'D BE PARALYZED BY IT AND UNABLE TO SPEAK THE SECRET!
YOU'RE RIGHT! NO CRIMINAL SEEKING THE SECRET WOULD WANT TO SILENCE YOU SPEECHLESS! YOU PASS!
BUT I MUST INCREASE THE PRESSURE ON EACH LEGIONNAIRE TO MAKE SURE ALL ARE TRUSTWORTHY! I'LL TEST SATURN GIRL NEXT!
CAN SHE RESIST PSYCHOLOGICAL BRAIN-WASHING? I'M AFRAID...
"...LIKE THE TIME COLOSSAL BOY MADE HIMSELF HUGE TO DEAL WITH SPACE-RAIDERS THAT THREATENED A DISTANT WORLD!"
I'LL SCOOP UP THESE RAIDERS FAST WITH THIS GIANT STEEL NET!
SOON, AS SATURN GIRL IS SUBJECTED TO TESTING...
WHAT IS THE SECRET OF THE CONCENTRATOR? ANSWER!
HE'S WEARING A HEAD-SET CAPABLE OF RECEIVING VIBRATIONS OF THOUGHT. IF I EVEN THINK OF THE SECRET, HE'LL GET IT!
AS THE RELENTLESS PRESSURE BUILDS...
THESE ECHOED QUESTIONS... SHOUTING ALL AROUND ME. THEY'LL BREAK ME DOWN AND THEN I'LL THINK OF THE SECRET! WELL, I'LL THINK OF SOMETHING ELSE... OF THE GREAT FEATS OF THE LEGIONNAIRES IN THE PAST...
WHAT IS THE CONCENTRATOR?
WHAT IS THE CONCENTRATOR?
3

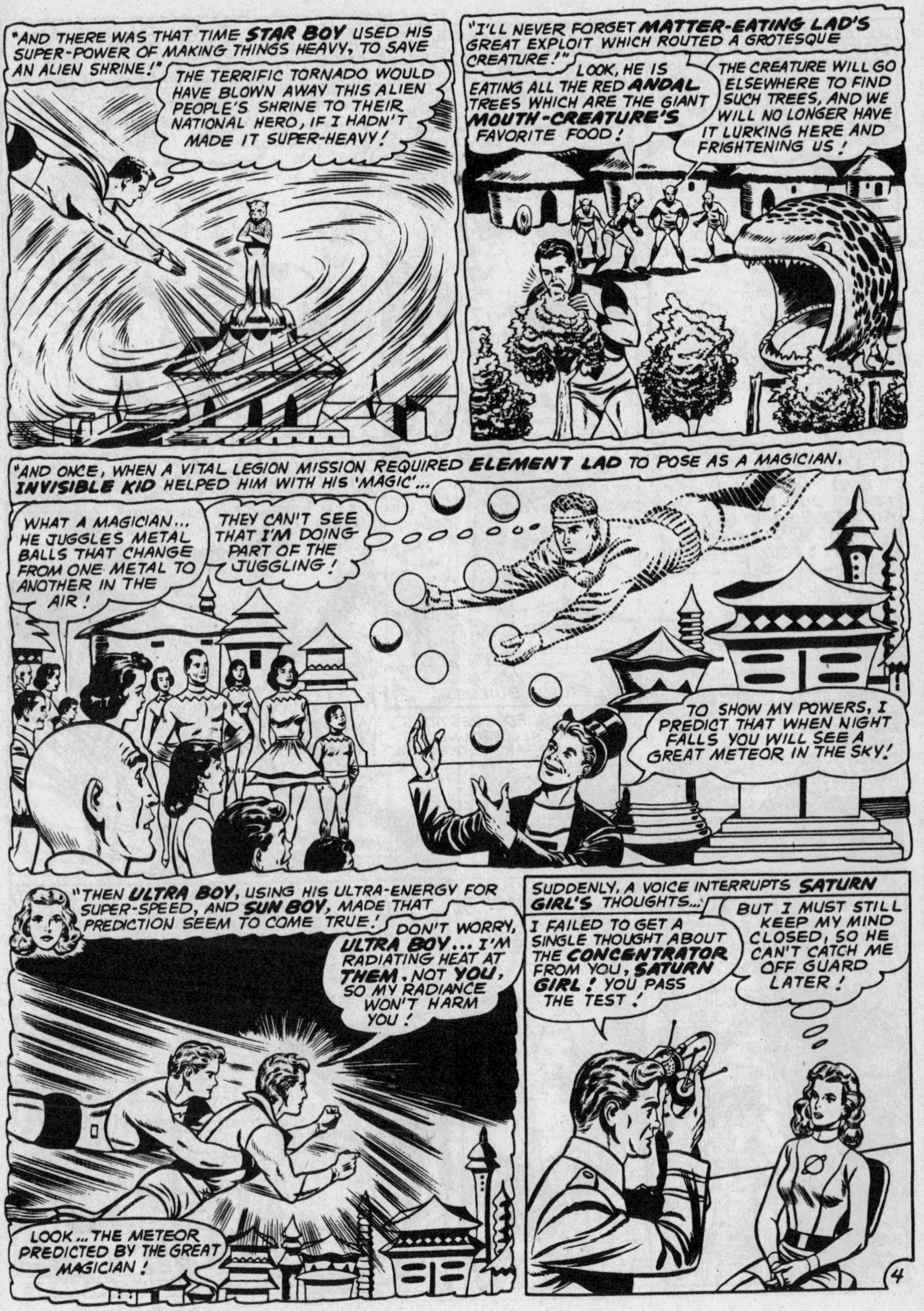
"AND THERE WAS THAT TIME STAR BOY USED HIS SUPER-POWER OF MAKING THINGS HEAVY, TO SAVE AN ALIEN SHRINE!"
THE TERRIFIC TORNADO WOULD HAVE BLOWN AWAY THIS ALIEN PEOPLE'S SHRINE TO THEIR NATIONAL HERO, IF I HADN'T MADE IT SUPER-HEAVY!
"I'LL NEVER FORGET MATTER-EATING LAD'S GREAT EXPLOIT WHICH ROUTED A GROTESQUE CREATURE!"
LOOK, HE IS EATING ALL THE RED ANDAL TREES WHICH ARE THE GIANT MOUTH-CREATURE'S FAVORITE FOOD!
THE CREATURE WILL GO ELSEWHERE TO FIND SUCH TREES, AND WE WILL NO LONGER HAVE IT LURKING HERE AND FRIGHTENING US!
"AND ONCE, WHEN A VITAL LEGION MISSION REQUIRED ELEMENT LAD TO POSE AS A MAGICIAN, INVISIBLE KID HELPED HIM WITH HIS 'MAGIC'...
WHAT A MAGICIAN... HE JUGGLES METAL BALLS THAT CHANGE FROM ONE METAL TO ANOTHER IN THE AIR!
THEY CAN'T SEE THAT I'M DOING PART OF THE JUGGLING!
TO SHOW MY POWERS, I PREDICT THAT WHEN NIGHT FALLS YOU WILL SEE A GREAT METEOR IN THE SKY!
"THEN ULTRA BOY, USING HIS ULTRA-ENERGY FOR SUPER-SPEED, AND SUN BOY, MADE THAT PREDICTION SEEM TO COME TRUE!"
DON'T WORRY, ULTRA BOY... I'M RADIATING HEAT AT THEM, NOT YOU, SO MY RADIANCE WON'T HARM YOU!
LOOK... THE METEOR PREDICTED BY THE GREAT MAGICIAN!
SUDDENLY, A VOICE INTERRUPTS SATURN GIRL'S THOUGHTS...
I FAILED TO GET A SINGLE THOUGHT ABOUT THE CONCENTRATOR FROM YOU, SATURN GIRL! YOU PASS THE TEST!
BUT I MUST STILL KEEP MY MIND CLOSED, SO HE CAN'T CATCH ME OFF GUARD LATER!
4

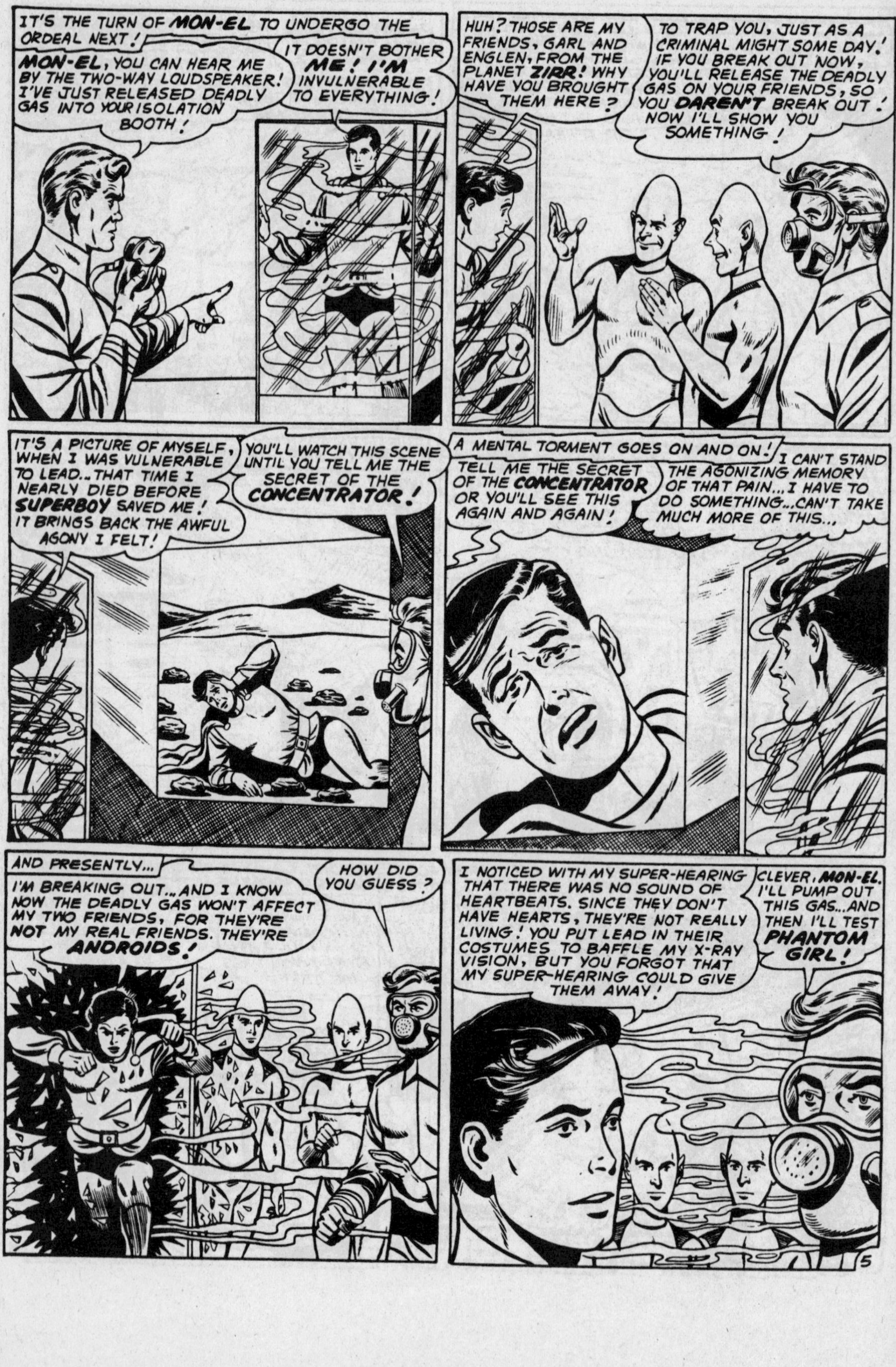
IT'S THE TURN OF MON-EL TO UNDERGO THE ORDEAL NEXT!
MON-EL, YOU CAN HEAR ME BY THE TWO-WAY LOUDSPEAKER! I'VE JUST RELEASED DEADLY GAS INTO YOUR ISOLATION BOOTH!
IT DOESN'T BOTHER ME! I'M INVULNERABLE TO EVERYTHING!
HUH? THOSE ARE MY FRIENDS, GARL AND ENGLEN, FROM THE PLANET ZIRR! WHY HAVE YOU BROUGHT THEM HERE?
TO TRAP YOU, JUST AS A CRIMINAL MIGHT SOME DAY! IF YOU BREAK OUT NOW, YOU'LL RELEASE THE DEADLY GAS ON YOUR FRIENDS, SO YOU DAREN'T BREAK OUT! NOW I'LL SHOW YOU SOMETHING!
IT'S A PICTURE OF MYSELF, WHEN I WAS VULNERABLE TO LEAD...THAT TIME I NEARLY DIED BEFORE SUPERBOY SAVED ME! IT BRINGS BACK THE AWFUL AGONY I FELT!
YOU'LL WATCH THIS SCENE UNTIL YOU TELL ME THE SECRET OF THE CONCENTRATOR!
A MENTAL TORMENT GOES ON AND ON!
TELL ME THE SECRET OF THE CONCENTRATOR OR YOU'LL SEE THIS AGAIN AND AGAIN!
THE AGONIZING MEMORY OF THAT PAIN...I HAVE TO DO SOMETHING...CAN'T TAKE MUCH MORE OF THIS...
I CAN'T STAND
AND PRESENTLY...
I'M BREAKING OUT...AND I KNOW NOW THE DEADLY GAS WON'T AFFECT MY TWO FRIENDS, FOR THEY'RE NOT MY REAL FRIENDS. THEY'RE ANDROIDS!
HOW DID YOU GUESS?
I NOTICED WITH MY SUPER-HEARING THAT THERE WAS NO SOUND OF HEARTBEATS. SINCE THEY DON'T HAVE HEARTS, THEY'RE NOT REALLY LIVING! YOU PUT LEAD IN THEIR COSTUMES TO BAFFLE MY X-RAY VISION, BUT YOU FORGOT THAT MY SUPER-HEARING COULD GIVE THEM AWAY!
CLEVER, MON-EL. I'LL PUMP OUT THIS GAS...AND THEN I'LL TEST PHANTOM GIRL!
5

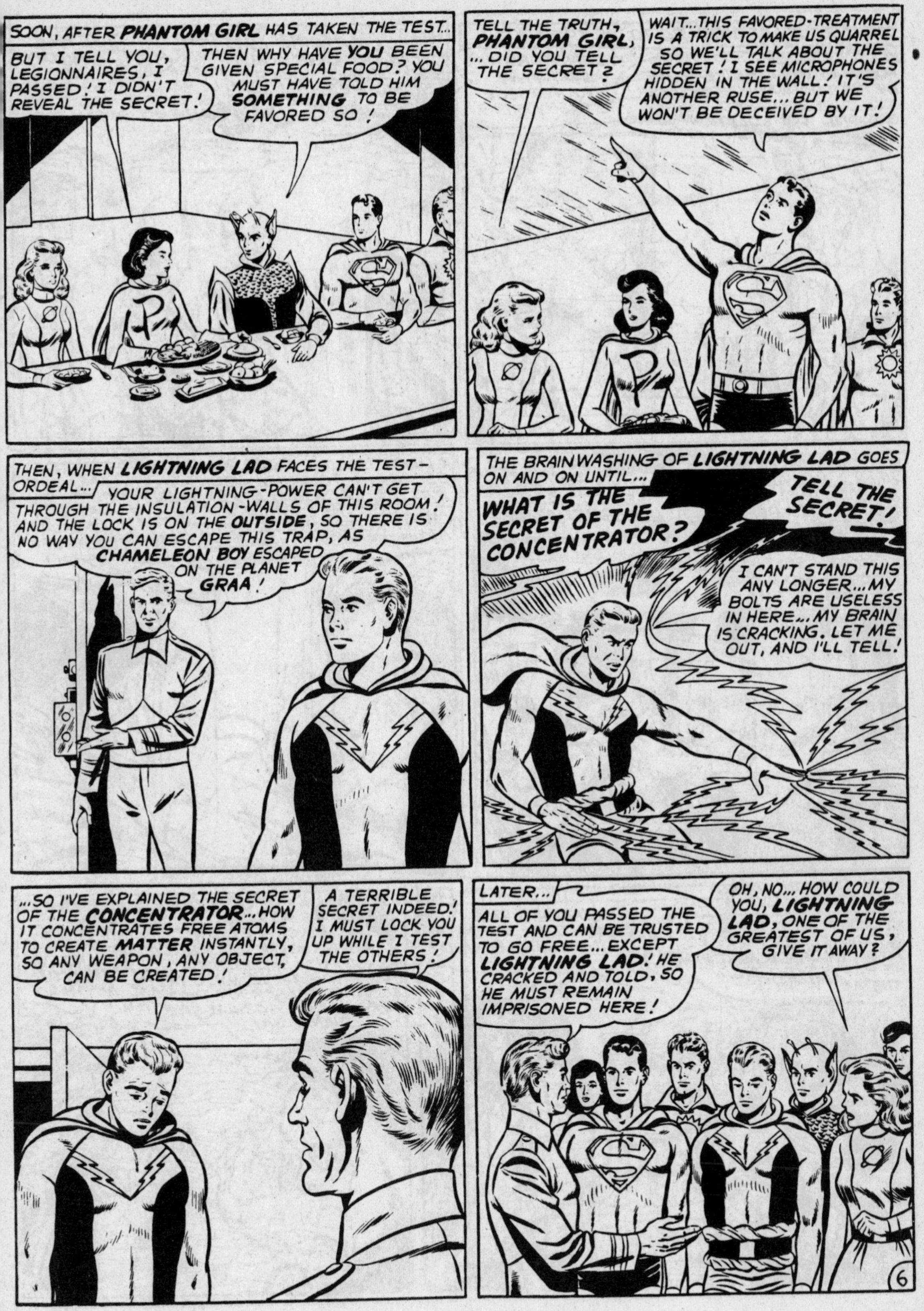
SOON, AFTER PHANTOM GIRL HAS TAKEN THE TEST...
BUT I TELL YOU, LEGIONNAIRES, I PASSED! I DIDN'T REVEAL THE SECRET!
THEN WHY HAVE YOU BEEN GIVEN SPECIAL FOOD? YOU MUST HAVE TOLD HIM SOMETHING TO BE FAVORED SO!
TELL THE TRUTH, PHANTOM GIRL, ...DID YOU TELL THE SECRET?
WAIT...THIS FAVORED-TREATMENT IS A TRICK TO MAKE US QUARREL SO WE'LL TALK ABOUT THE SECRET! I SEE MICROPHONES HIDDEN IN THE WALL! IT'S ANOTHER RUSE... BUT WE WON'T BE DECEIVED BY IT!
THEN, WHEN LIGHTNING LAD FACES THE TEST-ORDEAL...
YOUR LIGHTNING-POWER CAN'T GET THROUGH THE INSULATION-WALLS OF THIS ROOM! AND THE LOCK IS ON THE OUTSIDE, SO THERE IS NO WAY YOU CAN ESCAPE THIS TRAP, AS CHAMELEON BOY ESCAPED ON THE PLANET GRAA!
THE BRAINWASHING OF LIGHTNING LAD GOES ON AND ON UNTIL...
WHAT IS THE SECRET OF THE CONCENTRATOR?
TELL THE SECRET!
I CAN'T STAND THIS ANY LONGER...MY BOLTS ARE USELESS IN HERE...MY BRAIN IS CRACKING. LET ME OUT, AND I'LL TELL!
...SO I'VE EXPLAINED THE SECRET OF THE CONCENTRATOR...HOW IT CONCENTRATES FREE ATOMS TO CREATE MATTER INSTANTLY, SO ANY WEAPON, ANY OBJECT, CAN BE CREATED!
A TERRIBLE SECRET INDEED! I MUST LOCK YOU UP WHILE I TEST THE OTHERS!
LATER...
ALL OF YOU PASSED THE TEST AND CAN BE TRUSTED TO GO FREE...EXCEPT LIGHTNING LAD! HE CRACKED AND TOLD, SO HE MUST REMAIN IMPRISONED HERE!
OH, NO... HOW COULD YOU, LIGHTNING LAD, ONE OF THE GREATEST OF US, GIVE IT AWAY?
6

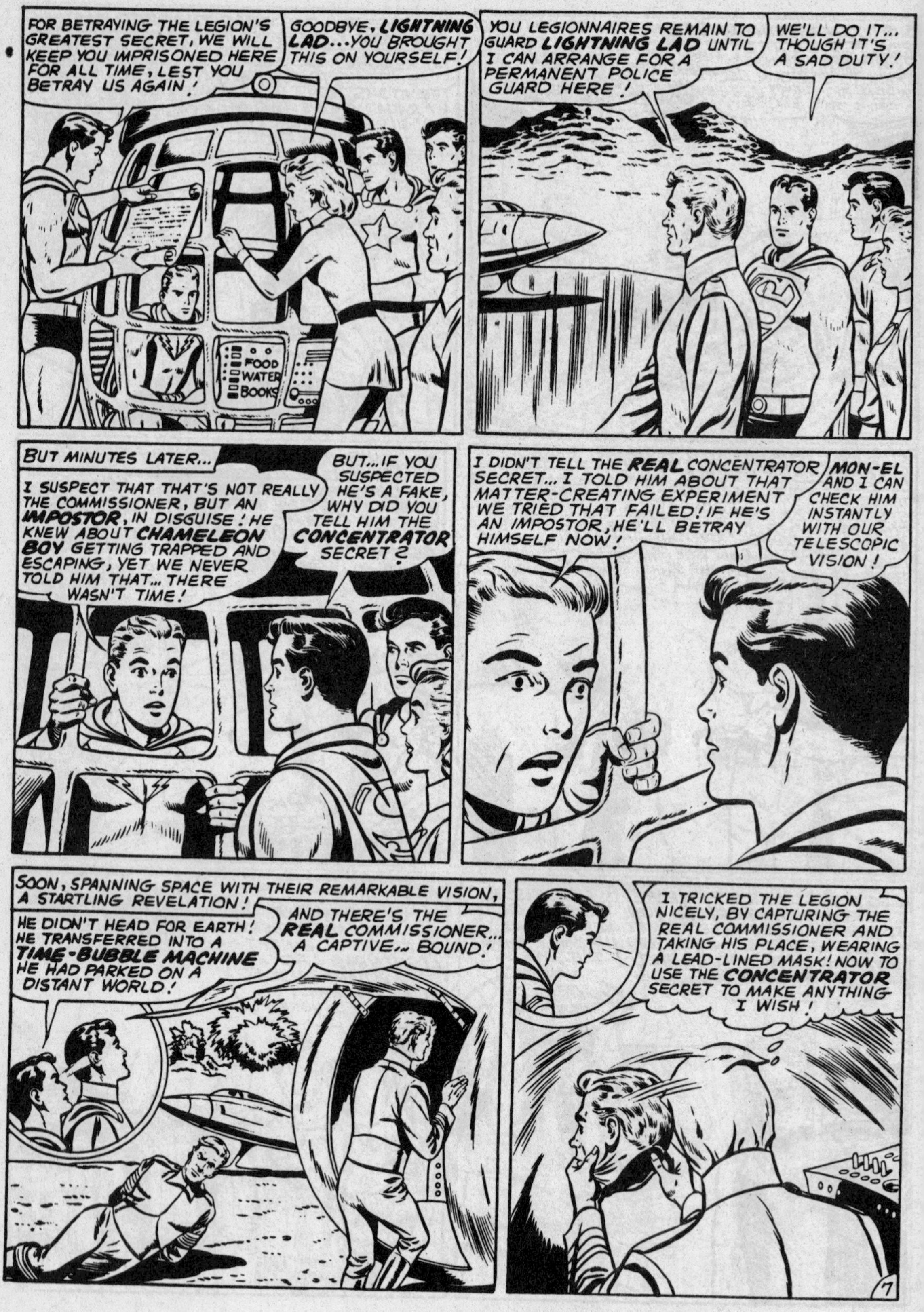
FOR BETRAYING THE LEGION'S GREATEST SECRET, WE WILL KEEP YOU IMPRISONED HERE FOR ALL TIME, LEST YOU BETRAY US AGAIN!
GOODBYE, LIGHTNING LAD...YOU BROUGHT THIS ON YOURSELF!
FOOD
WATER
BOOKS
YOU LEGIONNAIRES REMAIN TO GUARD LIGHTNING LAD UNTIL I CAN ARRANGE FOR A PERMANENT POLICE GUARD HERE!
WE'LL DO IT... THOUGH IT'S A SAD DUTY!
BUT MINUTES LATER...
I SUSPECT THAT THAT'S NOT REALLY THE COMMISSIONER, BUT AN IMPOSTOR, IN DISGUISE! HE KNEW ABOUT CHAMELEON BOY GETTING TRAPPED AND ESCAPING, YET WE NEVER TOLD HIM THAT... THERE WASN'T TIME!
BUT...IF YOU SUSPECTED HE'S A FAKE, WHY DID YOU TELL HIM THE CONCENTRATOR SECRET?
I DIDN'T TELL THE REAL CONCENTRATOR SECRET... I TOLD HIM ABOUT THAT MATTER-CREATING EXPERIMENT WE TRIED THAT FAILED! IF HE'S AN IMPOSTOR, HE'LL BETRAY HIMSELF NOW!
MON-EL AND I CAN CHECK HIM INSTANTLY WITH OUR TELESCOPIC VISION!
SOON, SPANNING SPACE WITH THEIR REMARKABLE VISION, A STARTLING REVELATION!
HE DIDN'T HEAD FOR EARTH! HE TRANSFERRED INTO A TIME-BUBBLE MACHINE HE HAD PARKED ON A DISTANT WORLD!
AND THERE'S THE REAL COMMISSIONER... A CAPTIVE... BOUND!
I TRICKED THE LEGION NICELY, BY CAPTURING THE REAL COMMISSIONER AND TAKING HIS PLACE, WEARING A LEAD-LINED MASK! NOW TO USE THE CONCENTRATOR SECRET TO MAKE ANYTHING I WISH!
7

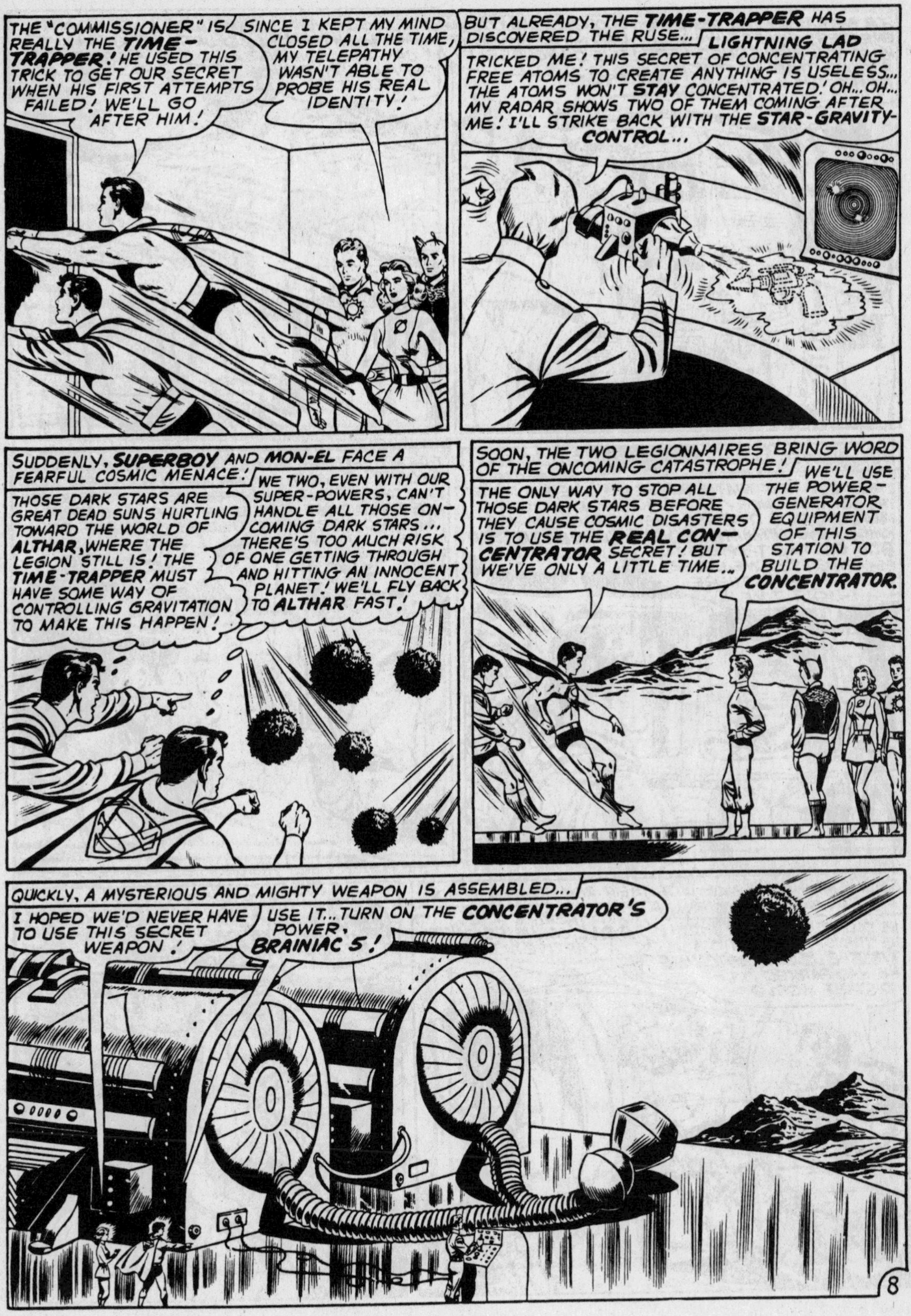
THE "COMMISSIONER" IS REALLY THE TIME-TRAPPER! HE USED THIS TRICK TO GET OUR SECRET WHEN HIS FIRST ATTEMPTS FAILED! WE'LL GO AFTER HIM!
SINCE I KEPT MY MIND CLOSED ALL THE TIME, MY TELEPATHY WASN'T ABLE TO PROBE HIS REAL IDENTITY!
BUT ALREADY, THE TIME-TRAPPER HAS DISCOVERED THE RUSE...
LIGHTNING LAD TRICKED ME! THIS SECRET OF CONCENTRATING FREE ATOMS TO CREATE ANYTHING IS USELESS... THE ATOMS WON'T STAY CONCENTRATED! OH...OH... MY RADAR SHOWS TWO OF THEM COMING AFTER ME! I'LL STRIKE BACK WITH THE STAR-GRAVITY-CONTROL...
SUDDENLY, SUPERBOY AND MON-EL FACE A FEARFUL COSMIC MENACE!
THOSE DARK STARS ARE GREAT DEAD SUNS HURTLING TOWARD THE WORLD OF ALTHAR, WHERE THE LEGION STILL IS! THE TIME-TRAPPER MUST HAVE SOME WAY OF CONTROLLING GRAVITATION TO MAKE THIS HAPPEN!
WE TWO, EVEN WITH OUR SUPER-POWERS, CAN'T HANDLE ALL THOSE ONCOMING DARK STARS... THERE'S TOO MUCH RISK OF ONE GETTING THROUGH AND HITTING AN INNOCENT PLANET! WE'LL FLY BACK TO ALTHAR FAST!
SOON, THE TWO LEGIONNAIRES BRING WORD OF THE ONCOMING CATASTROPHE!
THE ONLY WAY TO STOP ALL THOSE DARK STARS BEFORE THEY CAUSE COSMIC DISASTERS IS TO USE THE REAL CONCENTRATOR SECRET! BUT WE'VE ONLY A LITTLE TIME...
WE'LL USE THE POWER-GENERATOR EQUIPMENT OF THIS STATION TO BUILD THE CONCENTRATOR.
QUICKLY, A MYSTERIOUS AND MIGHTY WEAPON IS ASSEMBLED...
I HOPED WE'D NEVER HAVE TO USE THIS SECRET WEAPON!
USE IT...TURN ON THE CONCENTRATOR'S POWER, BRAINIAC 5!
8

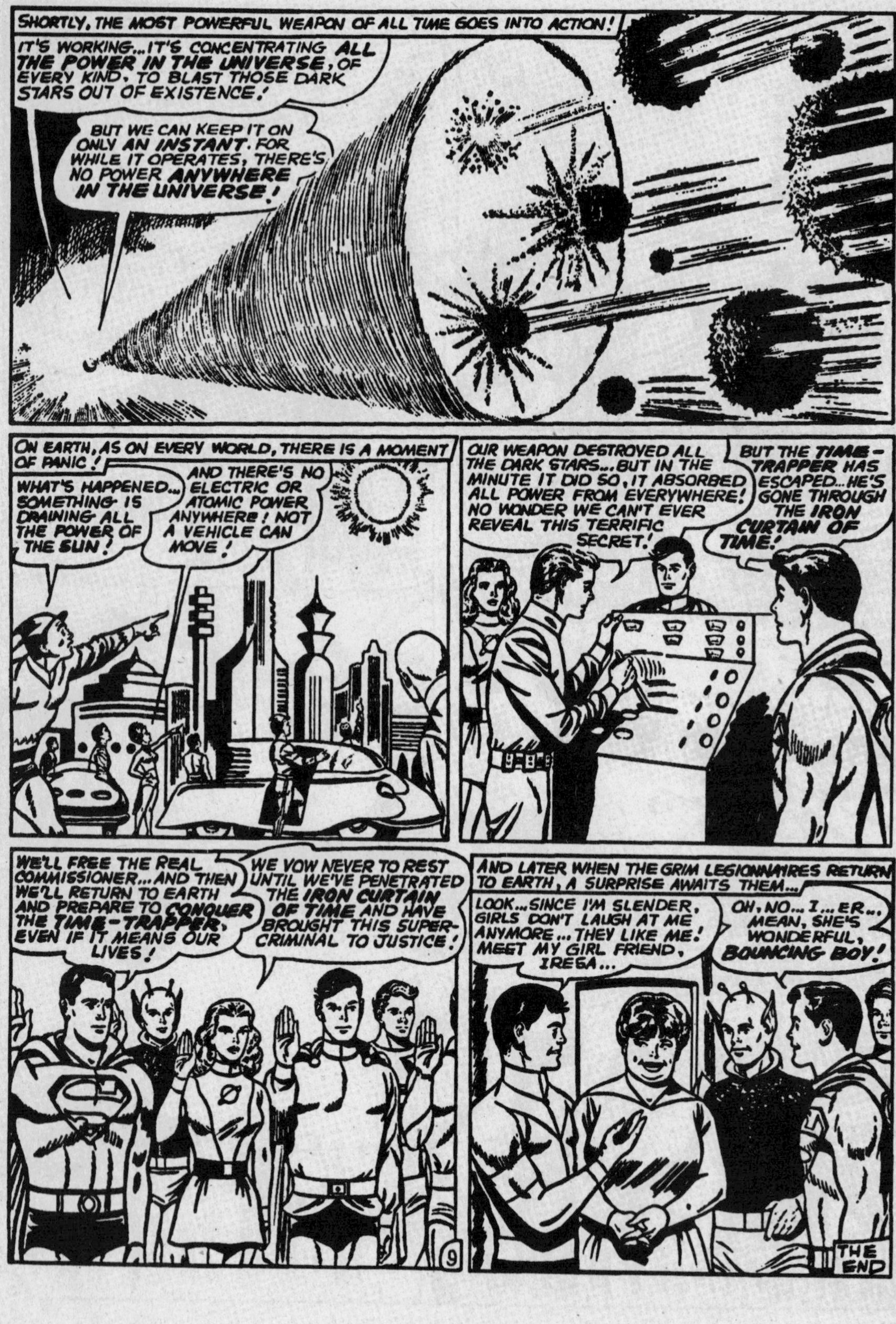
SHORTLY, THE MOST POWERFUL WEAPON OF ALL TIME GOES INTO ACTION!
IT'S WORKING...IT'S CONCENTRATING ALL THE POWER IN THE UNIVERSE, OF EVERY KIND, TO BLAST THOSE DARK STARS OUT OF EXISTENCE!
BUT WE CAN KEEP IT ON ONLY AN INSTANT. FOR WHILE IT OPERATES, THERE'S NO POWER ANYWHERE IN THE UNIVERSE!
ON EARTH, AS ON EVERY WORLD, THERE IS A MOMENT OF PANIC!
WHAT'S HAPPENED... SOMETHING IS DRAINING ALL THE POWER OF THE SUN!
AND THERE'S NO ELECTRIC OR ATOMIC POWER ANYWHERE! NOT A VEHICLE CAN MOVE!
OUR WEAPON DESTROYED ALL THE DARK STARS...BUT IN THE MINUTE IT DID SO, IT ABSORBED ALL POWER FROM EVERYWHERE! NO WONDER WE CAN'T EVER REVEAL THIS TERRIFIC SECRET!
BUT THE TIME-TRAPPER HAS ESCAPED...HE'S GONE THROUGH THE IRON CURTAIN OF TIME!
WE'LL FREE THE REAL COMMISSIONER...AND THEN WE'LL RETURN TO EARTH AND PREPARE TO CONQUER THE TIME-TRAPPER, EVEN IF IT MEANS OUR LIVES!
WE VOW NEVER TO REST UNTIL WE'VE PENETRATED THE IRON CURTAIN OF TIME AND HAVE BROUGHT THIS SUPER-CRIMINAL TO JUSTICE!
9
AND LATER WHEN THE GRIM LEGIONNAIRES RETURN TO EARTH, A SURPRISE AWAITS THEM...
LOOK...SINCE I'M SLENDER, GIRLS DON'T LAUGH AT ME ANYMORE...THEY LIKE ME! MEET MY GIRL FRIEND, IRESA...
OH, NO... I...ER... MEAN, SHE'S WONDERFUL, BOUNCING BOY!
THE END

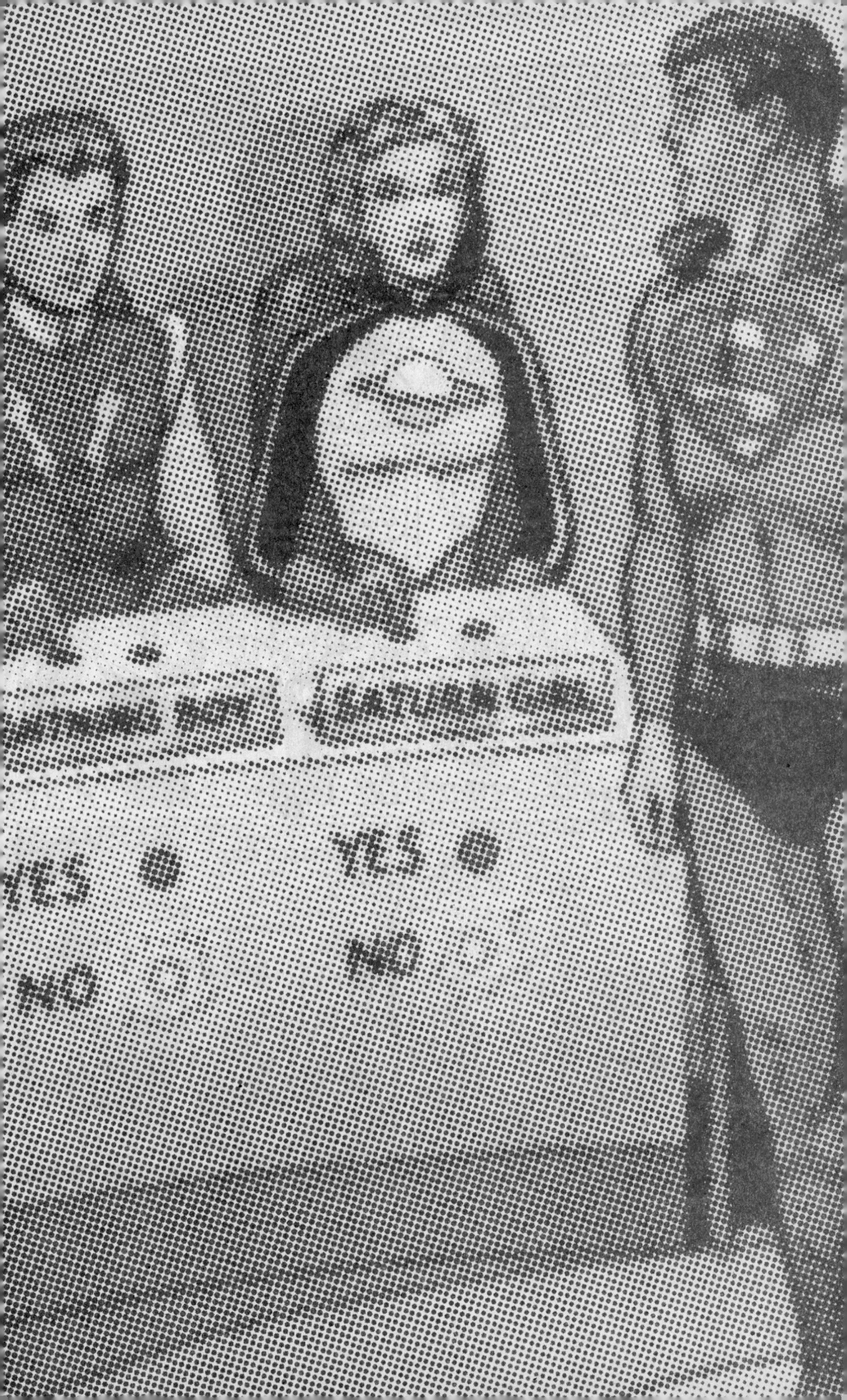
YES
NO

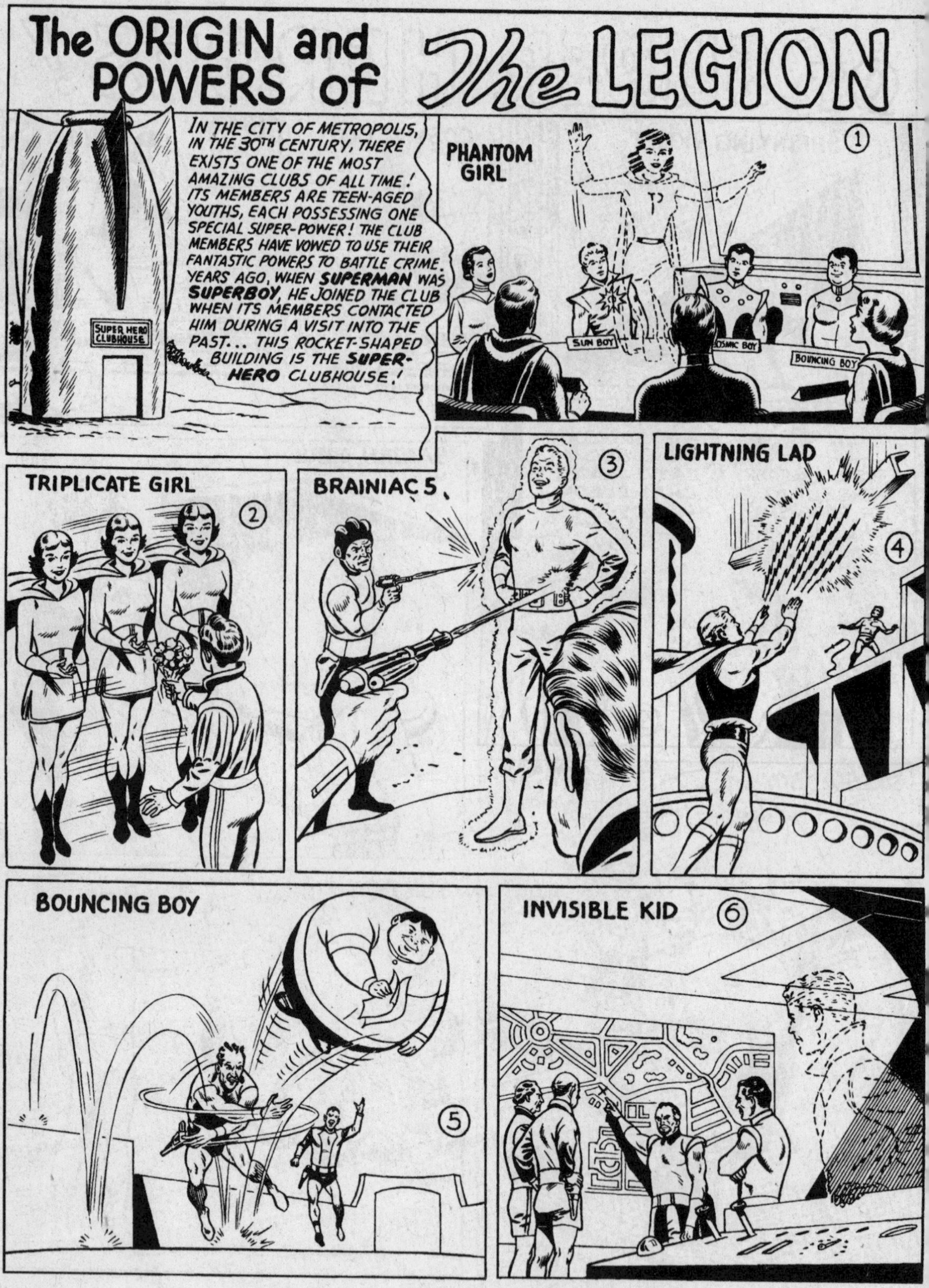
The ORIGIN and POWERS of The LEGION
IN THE CITY OF METROPOLIS, IN THE 30TH CENTURY, THERE EXISTS ONE OF THE MOST AMAZING CLUBS OF ALL TIME! ITS MEMBERS ARE TEEN-AGED YOUTHS, EACH POSSESSING ONE SPECIAL SUPER-POWER! THE CLUB MEMBERS HAVE VOWED TO USE THEIR FANTASTIC POWERS TO BATTLE CRIME. YEARS AGO, WHEN SUPERMAN WAS SUPERBOY, HE JOINED THE CLUB WHEN ITS MEMBERS CONTACTED HIM DURING A VISIT INTO THE PAST... THIS ROCKET-SHAPED BUILDING IS THE SUPER-HERO CLUBHOUSE!
SUPER HERO CLUBHOUSE
PHANTOM GIRL
SUN BOY
BOUNCING BOY
TRIPLICATE GIRL
BRAINIAC 5
LIGHTNING LAD
BOUNCING BOY
INVISIBLE KID

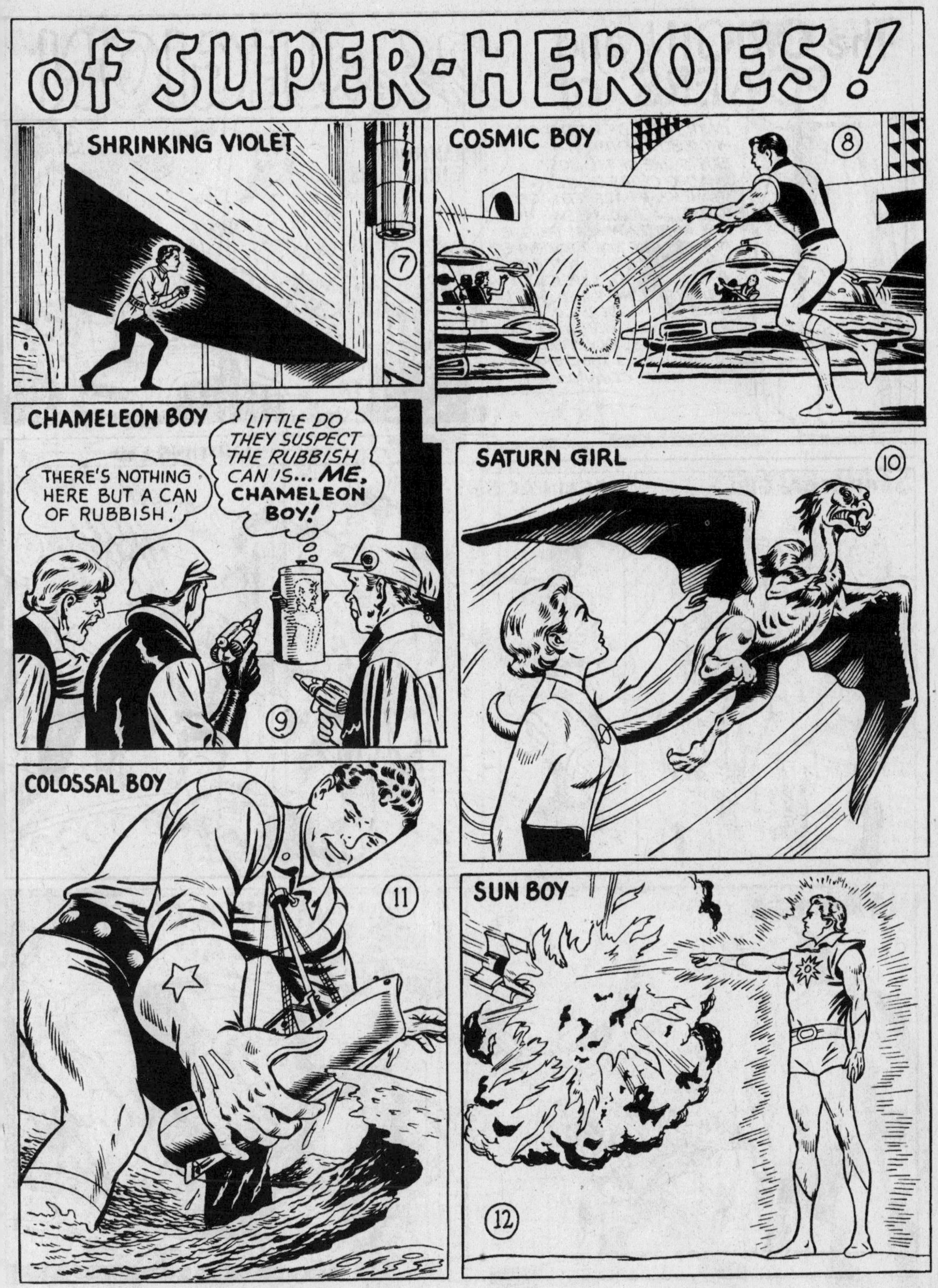
of SUPER-HEROES!
SHRINKING VIOLET
7
COSMIC BOY
8
CHAMELEON BOY
THERE'S NOTHING HERE BUT A CAN OF RUBBISH!
LITTLE DO THEY SUSPECT THE RUBBISH CAN IS... ME, CHAMELEON BOY!
9
SATURN GIRL
10
COLOSSAL BOY
11
SUN BOY
12

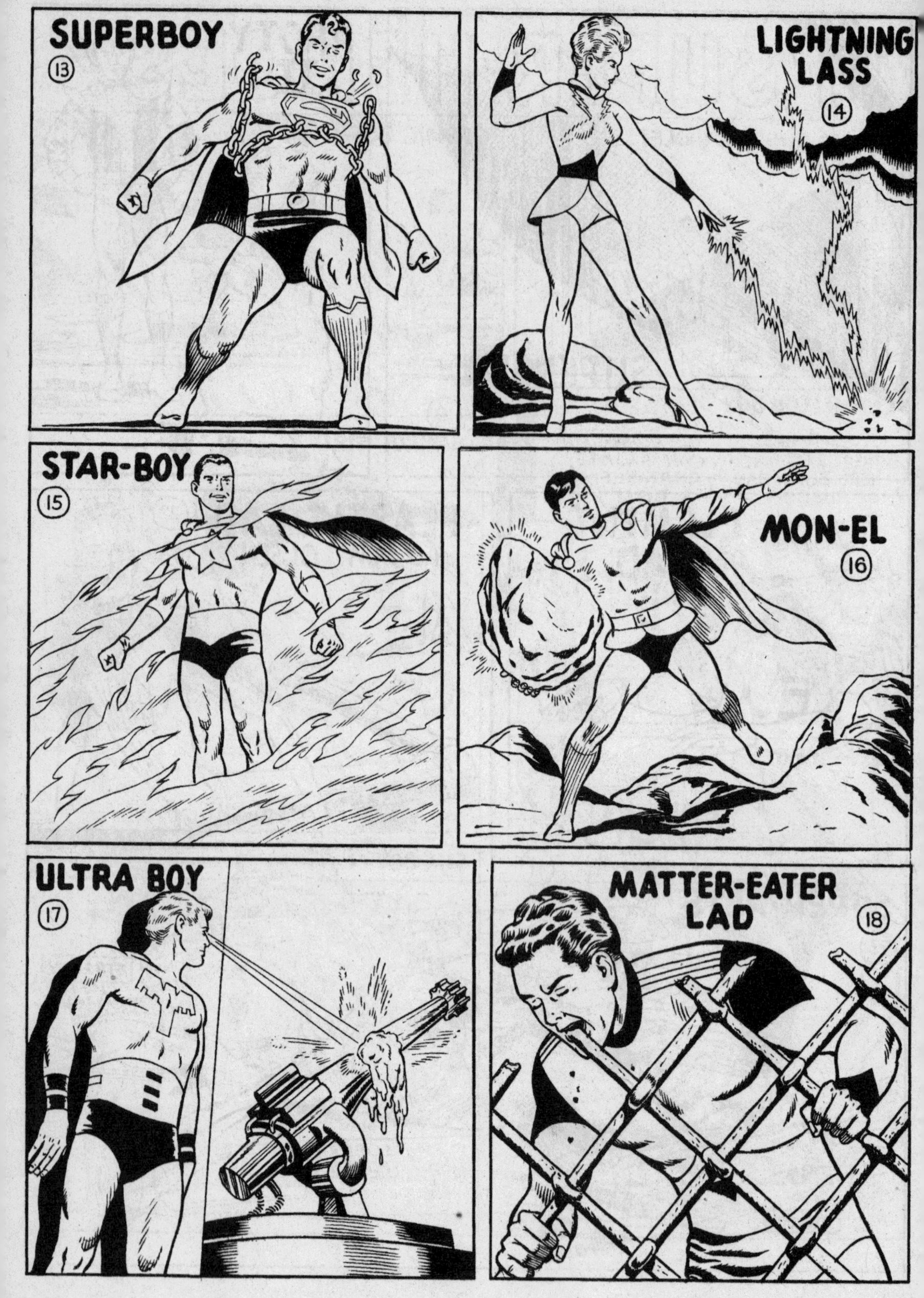
SUPERBOY
13
LIGHTNING LASS
14
STAR-BOY
15
MON-EL
16
ULTRA BOY
17
MATTER-EATER LAD
18

SUPERGIRL

(19)

PROTY II

(20)

ELEMENT LAD

(21)

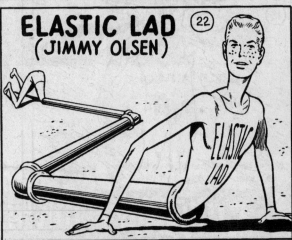

ELASTIC LAD
(JIMMY OLSEN)

(22)

SUPER-PETS

(23)

SUPER-MONKEY

STREAKY

SUPER-HORSE

KRYPTO

SHOWCASE PRESENTS

OVER 500 PAGES OF DC'S CLASSIC HEROES AND STORIES PRESENTED IN EACH VOLUME!

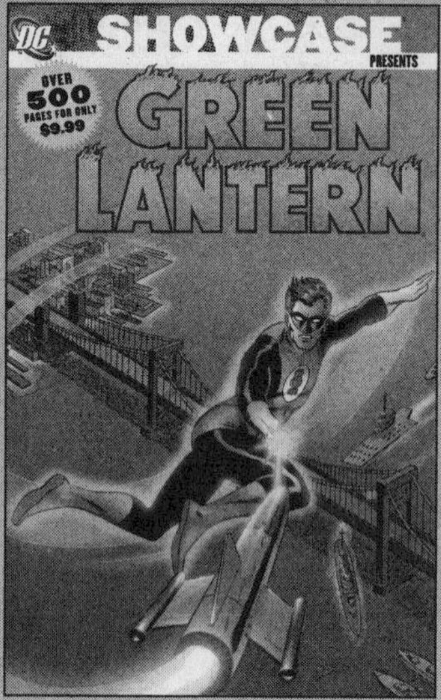
DC
SHOWCASE
PRESENTS
OVER 500 PAGES FOR ONLY $9.99
GREEN LANTERN

GREEN LANTERN
VOL. 1

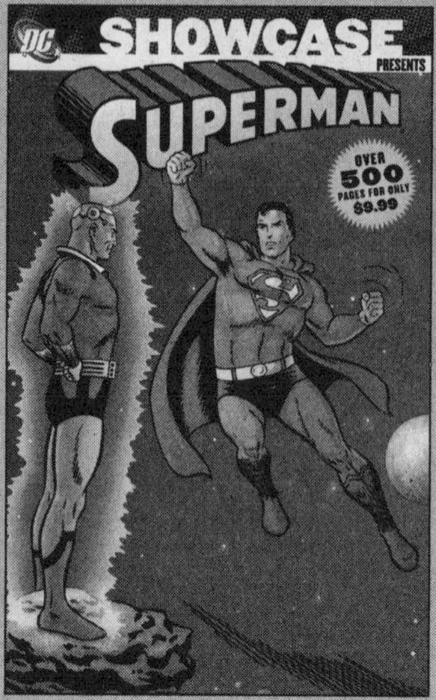
DC
SHOWCASE
PRESENTS
SUPERMAN
OVER 500 PAGES FOR ONLY $9.99

SUPERMAN
VOL. 1

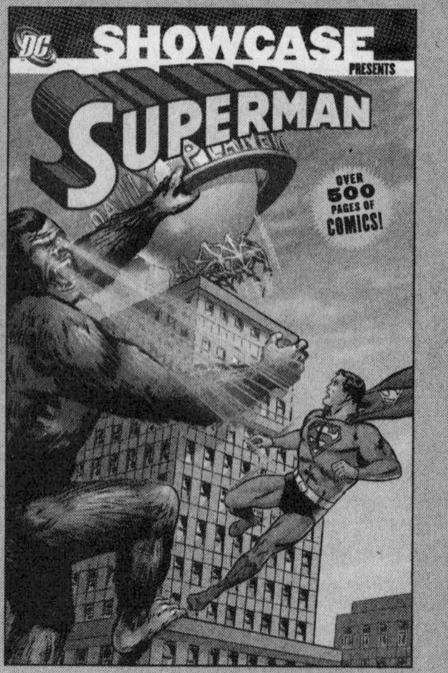
DC
SHOWCASE
PRESENTS
SUPERMAN
OVER 500 PAGES OF COMICS!

SUPERMAN
VOL. 2

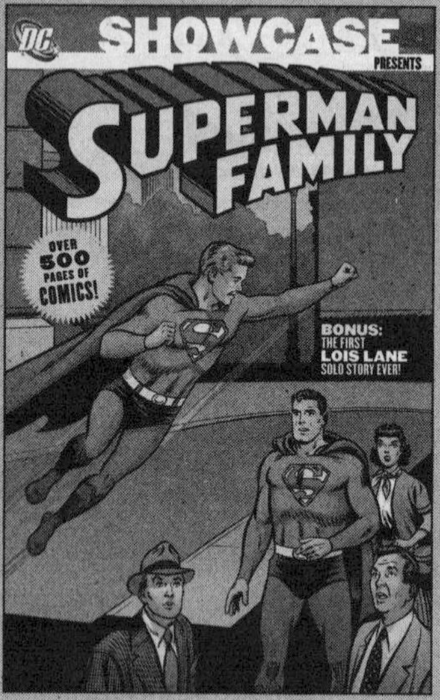
DC
SHOWCASE
PRESENTS
SUPERMAN FAMILY
OVER 500 PAGES OF COMICS!
BONUS: THE FIRST LOIS LANE SOLO STORY EVER!

SUPERMAN FAMILY
VOL. 1

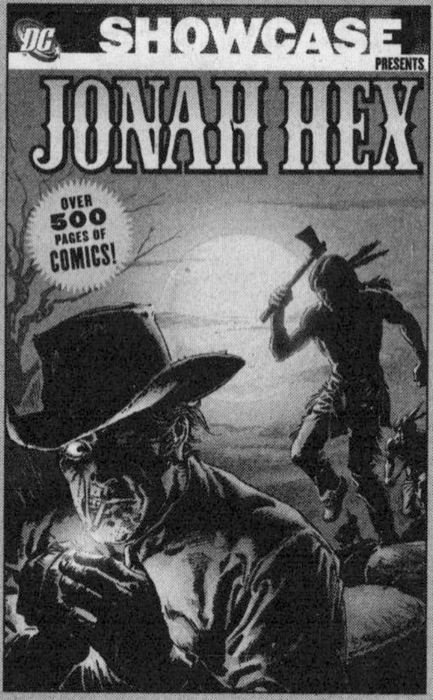
DC
SHOWCASE
PRESENTS
JONAH HEX
OVER 500 PAGES OF COMICS!

JONAH HEX
VOL. 1

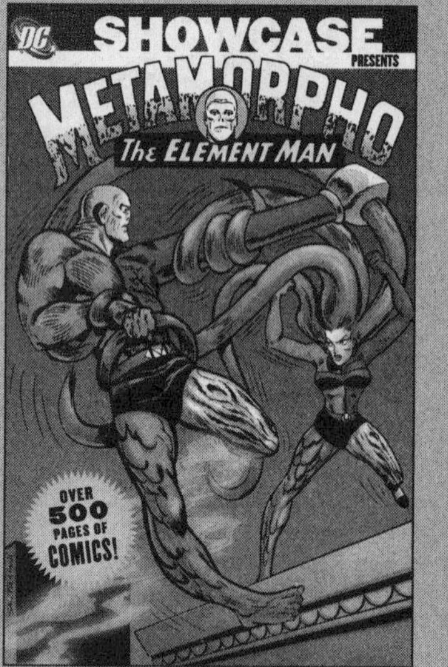
DC
SHOWCASE
PRESENTS
METAMORPHO
The ELEMENT MAN
OVER 500 PAGES OF COMICS!

METAMORPHO
VOL. 1

SEARCH THE GRAPHIC NOVELS SECTION OF
www.DCCOMICS.com
FOR ART AND INFORMATION ON ALL OF OUR BOOKS!

SHOWCASE

PRESENTS

SHOWCASE
PRESENTS